International Criminal Law

International Criminal Law

Cases and Materials

FIFTH EDITION

Ellen S. Podgor
Gary R. Trombley Family White-Collar Crime Research Professor
Professor of Law
Stetson University College of Law

Roger S. Clark
Board of Governors Professor of Law Emeritus
Rutgers, The State University of New Jersey
School of Law—Camden

Lucian E. Dervan
Professor of Law and Director of Criminal Justice Studies
Belmont University College of Law

Carolina Academic Press
Durham, North Carolina

ISBN 978-1-5310-2144-3
e-ISBN 978-1-5310-2145-0
LCCN 2022937120

Carolina Academic Press
700 Kent Street
Durham, NC 27701
Telephone (919) 489-7486
www.caplaw.com

Printed in the United States of America

To—
Cheryl L. Segal
&
Amelia H. Boss
&
Dalton and Adelaide

Contents

Table of Cases

Table of Statutes

United States Code—cont.

Tit:Sec.	Page
18 U.S.C. § 541	201
18 U.S.C. § 545	201
18 U.S.C. § 546	91, 95
18 U.S.C. § 641	80
18 U.S.C. § 666	522
18 U.S.C. § 78l	155, 165
18 U.S.C. § 844	292
18 U.S.C. § 921	712
18 U.S.C. § 922	710, 712, 714, 715
18 U.S.C. § 924	333, 712
18 U.S.C. § 956	292
18 U.S.C. § 1001	111, 112, 416
18 U.S.C. § 1029	75, 84, 95, 125
18 U.S.C. § 1030	75, 238, 239, 242, 243
18 U.S.C. § 1091	986, 987, 988
18 U.S.C. § 1092	986, 987
18 U.S.C. § 1093	986, 988
18 U.S.C. § 1111	543, 633, 820
18 U.S.C. § 1112	543
18 U.S.C. § 1116	98, 99, 100, 820
18 U.S.C. § 1117	98, 99
18 U.S.C. § 1119	439, 634
18 U.S.C. § 1203	87, 125, 126, 333, 334, 339
18 U.S.C. § 1341	82, 191, 196, 240, 249, 262, 632, 633
18 U.S.C. § 1343	82, 91, 92, 93, 94, 95, 96, 191, 243, 273, 599
18 U.S.C. § 1344	83
18 U.S.C. § 1361	292
18 U.S.C. § 1366	292
18 U.S.C. § 1385	143
18 U.S.C. § 1546	81, 416
18 U.S.C. § 1581	416, 420, 454, 522, 550
18 U.S.C. § 1583	55, 420, 454, 522, 550
18 U.S.C. § 1584	55, 416, 420, 454, 522, 550

United States Code—cont.

Tit:Sec.	Page
18 U.S.C. § 1585	55
18 U.S.C. § 1586	55
18 U.S.C. § 1589	416, 420, 424, 454, 522, 550
18 U.S.C. § 1590	416, 420, 454, 522, 550
18 U.S.C. § 1591	416, 420, 421
18 U.S.C. § 1592	416, 420
18 U.S.C. § 1593	422
18 U.S.C. § 1595	422
18 U.S.C. § 1596	262, 420, 423, 424
18 U.S.C. § 1621	75
18 U.S.C. § 1651	32, 279, 281, 282
18 U.S.C. § 1751	87, 292
18 U.S.C. § 1782	541, 542, 555, 556, 558, 560, 571, 572
18 U.S.C. § 1831	240, 241, 243
18 U.S.C. § 1832	240, 241
18 U.S.C. § 1839	241
18 U.S.C. § 1902	264
18 U.S.C. § 1956	95, 266, 267, 270, 271, 272, 274, 275, 276, 277
18 U.S.C. § 1957	87, 266, 277
18 U.S.C. § 1958	292
18 U.S.C. §§ 1961–1968	84
18 U.S.C. § 1961	87, 95, 289
18 U.S.C. § 1962	84, 85, 87, 88, 89, 90
18 U.S.C. § 1963	90
18 U.S.C. § 1964	84, 85, 89, 90, 190, 191
18 U.S.C. § 2152	292
18 U.S.C. § 2231	122
18 U.S.C. § 2241	994
18 U.S.C. § 2243	120, 121
18 U.S.C. § 2244	120, 121
18 U.S.C. § 2246	421, 826
18 U.S.C. § 2256	421
18 U.S.C. § 2280	294

United States Code—cont.

United States Code—cont.

United States Code—cont.

Other U.S. Statutory Provisions—cont.

Act of Sept. 24, 1789

American Servicemembers' Protection Act of 2002

Atomic Energy Act of 1954

Authorization for Use of Military Force

Clayton Act

Cloud Act

Criminal Justice Act 2003

Detainee Treatment Act

Other U.S. Statutory Provisions—cont.

Food, Conservation and Energy Act 2008

Sec.	Page
§ 8204	726

Foreign Assistance Act of 1961

Sec.	Page
§ 481	269
§ 489	269

Foreign Corrupt Practices Act

§ 12	155
§ 15	155, 159
§ 30A	159, 160

Immigration and Nationality Act

Sec.	Page
§ 101	155, 824, 987
§ 241	663, 664, 665, 666, 667
§ 243	668

Intelligence Reform and Terrorism Prevention Act of 2004

Sec.	Page
§ 7202	425

International Organizations Immunities Act

Sec.	Page
§ 1	157

Judiciary Act of 1789

Sec.	Page
§ 9	32

Military Commissions Act

Sec.	Page
§ 6	993, 994
§ 7	133, 134, 136, 137, 180

Other U.S. Statutory Provisions—cont.

Omnibus Diplomatic Security and Antiterrorism Act of 1986

Sec.	Page
§ 1202(a)	323

Securities and Exchange Commission Rules

Sec.	Page
Rule 10b-5	83, 195, 196, 373

Securities and Exchange Act 1924

Sec.	Page
§ 10(b)	82, 83, 85, 86, 192, 194, 195, 196, 197, 198

Torture Victim Protection Act of 1991

Sec.	Page
§ 2	35

Trade Act of 1974

Sec.	Page
§ 301	189

Trafficking Victims Protection Act

Sec.	Page
§ 103	429

United States Criminal Code, 40 Stat. 1015

Tit:Sec.	Page
c. 4, § 39	79
c. 4, § 42	79
c. 4, § 70	78
c. 194, § 35	77, 78, 79, 80
c. 194, § 36	79
c. 194, § 38	79
c. 194, § 72	79

Other U.S. Statutory Provisions—cont.

U.S.A. Patriot Act of 2001

Sec.	Page
§ 175	294
§ 201	289
§ 202, 289	
§ 206	289
§ 209–220	289
§ 215	303, 304
§ 229	294
§ 302	268
§ 314	268
§ 315	268
§ 320	268
§ 377	75
§ 802	289
§ 809	289
§ 810	289
§ 811	289, 352
§ 813	289

Violent Crime Control and Law Enforcement Act of 1994

Sec.	Page
§ 120002	121

Code of Federal Regulations

Title:Sec.	Page
8 C.F.R. § 208.16	358
8 C.F.R. § 208.18	358
15 C.F.R. § 730	205
15 C.F.R. § 730.3	205, 206
15 C.F.R. § 730.6	205, 207
15 C.F.R. § 736.2	205, 209
15 C.F.R. § 744.16	206
15 C.F.R. § 764.2	209
15 C.F.R. pt. 774	206, 209
17 C.F.R. § 240.10b-5	196
19 C.F.R. § 148.4	458
22 C.F.R. § 95	360
22 C.F.R. §§ 120.1–130.17	213
22 C.F.R. § 120.3	215

Other U.S. Statutory Provisions—cont.

Code of Federal Regulations–cont.

Title:Sec.	Page
22 C.F.R. § 121.1	213, 215
22 C.F.R. § 126.1	213
28 C.F.R. § 2.62	707
28 C.F.R. § 80.10	150
31 C.F.R. § 500.201	229
31 C.F.R. § 560.204	223, 224, 225
31 C.F.R. § 560.209	224
31 C.F.R. § 560.210	226
31 C.F.R. § 560.516	225, 226
31 C.F.R. pt. 560	223, 226

Federal Rules of Civil Procedure

Rule	Page
Rule 12	193
Rule 28	551

Federal Rules of Criminal Procedure

Rule	Page
Rule 15	551, 576, 577, 580, 581, 582
Rule 26.1	93

Federal Rules of Evidence

Rule	Page
Rule 902	549

U.S. State Materials

California

Sec.	Page
California Civil Code § 1714	426, 427
California Revenue and Taxation Code § 19547	427

Illinois

Sec.	Page
§ 103-1	789
§ 103-5	790
§ 109-1	789

Other U.S. Statutory Provisions—cont.

Model Penal Code

Oklahoma

Texas

Other U.S. Statutory Provisions and International Agreements

Other U.S. Statutory Provisions and International Agreements

Other U.S. Statutory Provisions and International Agreements

Other U.S. Statutory Provisions and International Agreements

Other U.S. Statutory Provisions and International Agreements

Other U.S. Statutory Provisions and International Agreements

Preface

This book contains a collection of cases, materials, notes, and questions concerning international criminal law. It is designed for use as a teaching tool, not as a reference work, although it does try to provide an overview of most of the topics that fall within the scope of international criminal law.

We have tried to keep the book short, as casebooks go, and to make it usable both by teachers who want to emphasize the increasingly important transnational dimension of U.S. criminal law and by those who want to explore the increasingly important use of criminal sanctions to enforce norms of international law. These two developments are interrelated and it is more and more difficult, in any event, to keep them separate.

The book is divided into four parts. The first part contains a brief introduction to the field of international criminal law, the question of what crimes are international crimes, and a chapter on the general jurisdictional principles, of both national and international law, that govern efforts to extend U.S. criminal law to foreign crimes and foreign criminals. The second part contains materials dealing with the specific application of those principles (especially in the United States) in cases involving the Foreign Corrupt Practices Act, antitrust and securities regulation, export controls, computer crimes, narcotics and money laundering, piracy and terrorism, human trafficking, and torture. In this fifth edition, a new chapter was added to this part to cover transnational organized crime. The third part deals with procedural aspects of trying such cases in the U.S. courts—and sometimes the courts of other countries. It covers the extraterritorial application of the U.S. Constitution, immunities from jurisdiction, mutual assistance in criminal cases, extradition, alternatives to extradition, prisoner transfer treaties, recognition of foreign criminal judgments and foreign laws, and the bearing of international human rights instruments on criminal procedure. The fourth and final part of the book deals with the prosecution of international crimes, including the Nuremberg and Tokyo precedents, the ad hoc tribunals for the former Yugoslavia and for Rwanda, the Rome Statute of the International Criminal Court, and the substantive law of the international crimes of aggression, genocide, crimes against humanity, and war crimes.

Our main focus in the first three parts is on relatively recent decisions of the United States courts and the effect of contemporary globalization on U.S. criminal law. We have tried, above all, to convey a sense of the "international flavor" that is developing in federal prosecutions.* As a result of this particular focus, some topics have been slighted that might figure more prominently in a longer, more comprehensive work on international criminal law. Nevertheless, we believe that the fourth part of the book provides the students an in-depth account of that other burgeoning area, the prosecution of grave crimes at the international level. In choosing material in this part, we have been particularly conscious of the value in directing students to international sources of material that are not always obvious to students and faculty in American law schools.

Our basic aim, in short, has been to construct a set of teaching materials that will provide students with a grounding in the transnational issues likely to arise in federal criminal cases and also in the law that has been produced as a consequence of international efforts to impose criminal responsibility on the perpetrators of human rights atrocities.

This book tries to provide a picture of the present state of a rapidly expanding and changing field. Events no doubt will quickly overtake much of what we present. We only hope that, in the meanwhile, teachers and students will be persuaded through using this book to regard international criminal law as an exciting field, worthy of their continuing attention as it grows and develops, as it inevitably will, in new directions.

We thank the American Law Institute for permission to reprint sections from the RESTATEMENT (THIRD & FOURTH) OF THE FOREIGN RELATIONS LAW OF THE UNITED STATES, 1987, The American Law Institute; and other copyright holders, including the VIRGINIA JOURNAL OF INTERNATIONAL LAW, Jack L. Goldsmith & Eric Posner (p. 30); the American Society of International Law (excerpt on p. 491 from 94 AJIL 535-36 (2000), © The American Society of International Law); the Academy of Political Science (excerpt on pp. 808–09 from the POLITICAL SCIENCE QUARTERLY, 1947); and Alfred P. Rubin (quotation on p. 956).

We also thank Professor Edward Wise, who was the lead author on the first edition of the book, but passed away thereafter. He noted the significant influence of Gerhard O.W. Mueller, who first introduced him to the problems of international criminal law, defined in the most comprehensive possible fashion, decades ago.**

In this fifth edition, the authors thank several very important people.

Professor Ellen S. Podgor thanks Stetson University College of Law, its terrific librarians, faculty support, and research assistants Ashley M. Adams, Sydnie P. Coraggio, Barrett E. Hand, as well as the many students throughout the years at

* For a preliminary sketch, see Ellen S. Podgor, Essay, *Globalization and the Federal Prosecution of White Collar Crime*, 34 AM. CRIM. L. REV. 325 (1997).

** *See* Edward M. Wise, *Gerhard O.W. Mueller and the Foundations of International Criminal Law*, in CRIMINAL SCIENCE IN A GLOBAL SOCIETY: ESSAYS IN HONOR OF GERHARD O.W. MUELLER 45 (Edward M. Wise ed., 1994).

Georgia State University College of Law, University of Georgia School of Law, and the students from the Temple Tel-Aviv and Rome Summer Abroad Programs.

Professor Roger S. Clark thanks the support of the Rutgers University School of Law, and David Batista, Hays Butler, Milosz Pierwola, Janelle Baptiste, Brian Johns, Michael Herdman, David Telson, Jacqueline Olsen and Jingwei Zhang for their research assistance over the years.

Professor Lucian E. Dervan thanks Belmont University College of Law, his research assistant Lacy Hansen, and the many other research assistants who have assisted him in the past. He also thanks Ellen Podgor and Roger Clark for their guidance and mentorship over the years.

We all owe large debts of intellectual gratitude to the late Professors Edward Wise and Gerhard Mueller, whose pioneering work introduced international criminal law in the United States. Cherif Bassiouni's writings on the subject are always a source of considerable inspiration.

Ellen S. Podgor
Roger S. Clark
Lucian E. Dervan

January 2022

International Criminal Law

Chapter 1

Introduction

§ 1.01 The Scope of International Criminal Law

What is meant by "international criminal law"? In a broad sense, the subject covers all of the problems lying in the area where criminal law and international law overlap and interact. It is a field that has undergone an enormous expansion in recent years. This expansion is a result both of (a) increasing "globalization" of criminal conduct and consequently of national criminal law, and (b) increasing reliance on criminal sanctions to enforce norms of international law, especially norms of international human rights law and of humanitarian law (the law of armed conflict).

International criminal law can be subdivided, in a rough and ready way, into three main sets of topics. These three topics are: [A] International Aspects of National Criminal Law, [B] Criminal Aspects of International Law: International Standards of Justice, and [C] Criminal Aspects of International Law: International Criminal Law *Stricto Sensu*. The term "international criminal law" sometimes has been used to refer to one or another of these three sets of topics standing alone. Thus, in an early essay on "International Criminal Law," Sir John Fischer Williams thought that only the third of these topics had "an interest for the international lawyer." SIR JOHN FISCHER WILLIAMS, CHAPTERS ON CURRENT INTERNATIONAL LAW AND THE LEAGUE OF NATIONS 232, 244 (1929). This book uses "international criminal law" in its broad sense to designate a field that includes all three. (The following discussion of these three subfields is based, in part, on Edward M. Wise, *Terrorism and the Problems of an International Criminal Law*, 19 CONN. L. REV. 799, 801–08 (1987)).

A. International Aspects of National Criminal Law

The first set of topics comprising international criminal law includes at its core questions concerning the extent to which national courts are permitted to assume jurisdiction over extraterritorial crime, the choice of the applicable law (usually the forum's) in cases involving such crimes, and the recognition of foreign penal judgments. These are all questions about how the courts of one country should act in criminal cases involving a foreign component. They are the counterpart on the criminal side of the questions dealt with in civil cases under the heading "conflict of laws" or "private international law." Taken together, they constitute international criminal law more or less in the original meaning of the term.

The term "international law" (indeed, the word "international") was coined by Jeremy Bentham in the 1780s to describe what older usage called the "law of nations"; the term "private international law" was invented by Joseph Story in 1834. An equivalent of the term "international criminal law" appeared in German in 1862. Similar cognates came into use in other European languages (but not English) during the 1870s, to designate the branch of law concerned with topics such as jurisdiction, choice of law, and the effect of foreign judgments in criminal cases.

In subsequent years, continental jurists debated the exact nature of the relationship between international criminal law, so defined, and private international law. Earlier writers, from the fourteenth century on, had treated questions arising in connection with divergent criminal laws as a problem of conflict of laws. Story devoted a chapter of his treatise on the conflict of laws to "penal laws and offenses," although it was only six pages in length and dealt mainly with whether foreign penal law could be "enforced" in the United States. (He thought not.) JOSEPH STORY, COMMENTARIES ON THE CONFLICT OF LAWS (1834). Yet he also thought of private international law as a "branch of public law." For nineteenth-century continental jurists preoccupied with the "scientific" or systematic arrangement of the law, private international law was a part of private law, criminal law was a part of public law, and the division between private and public law was too sharply drawn to permit anything connected with public law to be treated as part of private international law. Since international criminal law, as first conceived, was primarily a matter of national dispositions regarding the power and competence of a particular country's criminal courts, neither could it be classified as part of public international law. Assertions of power over events taking place abroad might ultimately be subject to limiting principles derived from international law; but the more immediate concern was with the antecedent question of what national law provided that judges should do in cases involving foreign crime. Since national rules regarding such questions did not seem to fit under any other legal rubric, they came, by a process of elimination, to be regarded as occupying a field of their own, which was designated "international criminal law." Some scholars rejected the view that this new field was wholly separate from private international law. Nonetheless, that it was separate came to be the commonly held view in Europe, and implicitly in the United States where, absent standard texts on the subject, international criminal law largely fell into a kind of legal limbo.

International criminal law in its original sense also can be regarded as including, by extension, on the one hand, exceptions from criminal jurisdiction, such as diplomatic immunity and asylum, and, on the other, forms of transnational cooperation, such as extradition, that enable states to circumvent the ordinary restrictions on their power to enforce criminal law outside their own borders. These subjects do not fit exactly within international criminal law as originally defined. Immunities from jurisdiction derive, in large part, from principles of public international law, whereas international criminal law was supposed to be primarily a matter of a state's own rules governing the exercise of its power to punish foreign crimes and crimes committed by foreigners. Extradition, likewise, is not so much a matter of national rules governing the exercise of penal powers, as it is a matter of international obligation, or at least an "international legal transaction" falling rather more clearly within the realm of public international law.

Yet it is hard, once one starts talking about a state's jurisdiction over foreigners and foreign crime, to avoid questions of immunity and extradition and other forms of international cooperation in criminal matters. These are connected topics that almost naturally have to be discussed together. There are other instances as well in which it seems inadequate to insist on a crisp distinction between national and international law; hence the tendency to attenuate the distinction and to speak instead about "transnational law." In dealing with problems of criminal law that cut across national boundaries, it is particularly difficult to keep questions of national and international law apart. As a result, international criminal law, practically from the beginning, has been treated as including virtually the whole gamut of problems connected with transnational aspects and applications of domestic systems of criminal law.

B. Criminal Aspects of Public International Law: International Standards of Criminal Justice

A second distinct group of topics that also has been designated as "international criminal law" concerns international standards of criminal justice, that is, principles or rules of public international law that impose obligations on states with respect to the content of their domestic criminal law and procedure. International standards may require states to respect the rights of persons accused or suspected of crime, or to prosecute and punish certain so-called "international offenses." Both kinds of standards appear in the older body of international law on state responsibility for injury to aliens. More recently, guarantees for persons accused of crime generally have been cast in the form of treaty provisions and other instruments (especially those adopted by the United Nations General Assembly) on human rights; indeed, a large part of contemporary law on the international protection of human rights is directed at setting standards of performance for domestic criminal procedure. A significant part of the United Nations program located in Vienna that deals with crime prevention and criminal justice, now known as the UN Office on Drugs and Crime (UNODC), has been devoted to standard-setting. *See* ROGER S. CLARK, THE UNITED NATIONS CRIME PREVENTION AND CRIMINAL JUSTICE PROGRAM: FORMULATION OF STANDARDS AND EFFORTS AT THEIR IMPLEMENTATION (1994). Current work in this area emphasizes the General Assembly's 2030 Sustainable Development Goals (SDGs). SDG 16 aims to '[p]romote Peaceful and Inclusive Societies for Sustainable Development, Provide Access to Justice for All and Build Effective, Accountable and Inclusive Institutions at All Levels." (*Available at* www.sdgs.un.org (2015). Likewise, obligations to prosecute specific types of offenders through the medium of local criminal law have tended to be imposed more and more by general conventions ("suppression conventions") — those dealing, for instance with the slave trade, traffic in narcotics, war crimes, genocide, torture, hijacking of aircraft, crimes against diplomats and other "internationally protected" persons, hostage-taking and other forms of terrorism, transnational organized crime, traffic in persons, and corruption. By virtue of these treaty obligations, states are required to cooperate in specified ways in suppressing certain kinds of conduct supposedly reprehended by the world at large. The conduct on the part of individuals which states are required to suppress is not necessarily itself a violation of international law; these variously-called "transnational crimes," "treaty crimes" or "offenses of international concern" generally are tried by national courts applying national law which has been enacted in order to implement a state's international obligations. But they are prosecuted in conformity with international rules stipulating that persons who commit these offenses should be tried and punished.

This second group of topics, unlike that in Subsection [A], falls largely within the domain of public international law. A part of it — the part concerned with holding states to observe certain basic procedural safeguards in administering criminal justice — usually is assigned to the separate subfield of international human rights law. The other part — the part concerned with international rules requiring states to cooperate in suppressing certain international offenses — sometimes is referred to simply as transnational criminal law. The effort to suppress such offenses may give rise, in turn, to questions of jurisdiction, extradition, and other forms of interstate cooperation. Indeed, contemporary treaties requiring states to suppress particular offenses typically contain provisions regarding mutual legal assistance, jurisdiction and extradition, and mandate that any state in whose territory an offender is found must itself exercise jurisdiction over the offense if it does not extradite to another state which is prepared to prosecute. In this respect, the topics comprising international criminal law, in the sense of a law of international offenses, have definite functional ties to, and more and more overlap with, the topics comprising international criminal law in its original sense of a body of rules concerned with the transnational applications of domestic criminal law. Nonetheless, these are two conceptually distinct sets of topics, or at least have different starting points: the one is concerned with what have been called the "criminal aspects of international law," the other with "international aspects of national criminal law."

C. Criminal Aspects of Public International Law: International Criminal Law *Stricto Sensu*

A third group of topics concerns questions of international criminal law in the "strict," "true," "proper," or "material" sense of the term. At one time it was possible to argue that international criminal law "in the material sense of the word" does not exist. *See* Georg Schwarzenberger, *The Problem of an International Criminal Law*, 3 Current Legal Probs. 263 (1950), *reprinted in* Gerhard O.W. Mueller & Edward M. Wise, International Criminal Law 3 (1965). That is a much less plausible argument today. Since the end of the Second World War, with the recognition that individuals can have both international rights and duties [*see* chap. 19], "there has been an increasing trend towards the expansion of individual responsibility directly established under international law." 1 OPPENHEIM'S INTERNATIONAL LAW 506 (Sir Robert Jennings & Sir Arthur Watts eds., 9th ed. 1992). But exactly what should be included under this heading remains controversial.

In its strictest possible sense, international criminal law would refer to the law applicable in an international criminal court having the power to impose specifically penal sanctions on offenders. Until recently, international criminal law in this sense seemed to be, for the most part, despite the Nuremberg and Tokyo precedents [*see* chap. 20], a purely hypothetical body of law, to be applied by an even more hypothetical court. However, with the creation of *ad hoc* tribunals for the trial of international offenses committed in the former Yugoslavia and in Rwanda [*see* chap. 21], and with the treaty establishing the permanent International Criminal Court in force since July 1, 2002 [*see* chap. 22], this body of law has begun to look much less hypothetical. It is now generally agreed that there are certain offenses—such as aggression, genocide, crimes against humanity, and war crimes—which are directly proscribed by international law; that international law itself imposes criminal responsibility on those who commit these crimes; and that individuals who commit them are potentially triable not only before national courts but also before an international tribunal having jurisdiction over these offenses.

For the most part, these so-called "crimes under international law" (for which rules of international law are said to impose criminal liability directly on individuals) also constitute what have been called "offenses of international concern" (as to which rules of international law impose an obligation on states to prosecute and punish those who commit such offenses). In this respect, the two categories overlap. But they are not coextensive. Not all "offenses of international concern" are "crimes under international law." Yet the categories are not set in stone and depend upon the development of state practice. Indeed, the whole distinction has been challenged, for example, in Kevin Jon Heller, *What Is an International Crime? (A Revisionist History)*, 58 HARV. INT'L L.J. 353 (2017). While states are bound, for instance, by a network of contemporary international treaties to cooperate in repressing certain forms of terrorism and narcotics trafficking, whether terrorism or narcotics trafficking are or should be offenses triable before an international criminal court is a question about which there has been considerable debate. A substantial minority of those participating in the 1998 Diplomatic Conference of Plenipotentiaries on the Establishment of an International Criminal Court wanted to include such crimes within the jurisdiction of the Court. Some of the argument turned on whether these were "really" "international crimes"; some was much more pragmatically cast, namely whether it was appropriate to have the International Criminal Court (ICC) take jurisdiction, or whether the current system of state prosecution was more effective. Consensus could not be obtained to include these crimes in the Statute of the Court. Resolution E adopted by the Conference nevertheless describes terrorist acts as "serious crimes of concern to the international community" and asserts that "international trafficking of illicit drugs is a very serious crime, sometimes destabilizing the political and economic order in States." Accordingly, the Resolution recommended that a Review Conference on the Statute should "consider the crimes of terrorism and drug crimes with a view to arriving at an acceptable definition and their inclusion in the list of crimes within the jurisdiction of the Court." Final Act of the United Nations Diplomatic Conference of Plenipotentiaries on the Establishment of an International Criminal Court, Annex, U.N. Doc. A/CONF. 183/13, Vol. I at 71–72. The first Review Conference took place in 2010 but there was no consensus about including drug and terrorism crimes in the agenda for the meeting. The issue remains in limbo at the ICC. On the other hand, the so-called "Malabo Protocol," adopted in 2014 but not yet in force, concerning the jurisdiction of the African Court of Justice and Human Rights, takes a radically different position. *See* Protocol on Amendments to the Protocol on the Statute of the African Court of Justice and Human Rights, *available at* www.au.int. In addition to conferring jurisdiction over aggression, genocide, crimes against humanity and war crimes, the Protocol would also confer jurisdiction over piracy, terrorism, mercenarism, corruption, money laundering, trafficking in persons, trafficking in drugs, trafficking in hazardous wastes and illicit exploitation of natural resources.

Much current writing on the scope and nature of international criminal law, indeed, tends to collapse the distinction between these two types of international crimes — those for which international law does and those for which it does not impose direct criminal liability on individuals. Both types of offenses are said to have a "common denominator," namely, "the preservation of certain interests which represent commonly shared values in the world community." M. Cherif Bassiouni, *Introduction to Symposium on the Teaching of International Criminal Law*, 1 Touro J. Transnat'l L. 129, 130 (1988). International criminal law is assumed to be ideally, although not entirely in practice, a more or less coherent system founded on a combination of some or all of the following premises: (1) Certain conduct is so reprehended by the world at large that it can be considered to amount to an international crime. (2) An authentic guide to the kind of conduct that amounts to an international crime is a multilateral treaty requiring its repression. (3) Conduct condemned in a widely ratified multilateral treaty also can be regarded as a violation of customary international law. (4) Individuals who engage in such conduct violate international law. (5) In prosecuting individuals who commit international crimes, states enforce international law as organs of the international community. (6) These crimes are the concern of all states. (7) All states therefore have "universal jurisdiction" to prosecute those who commit these crimes. (8) All states, indeed, are bound to prosecute or at least to assist in bringing to justice those who commit these crimes. *See* M. Cherif Bassiouni & Edward M. Wise, Aut Dedere aut Judicare: The Duty to Extradite or Prosecute in International Law 49–50 (1995). In this view, the existing body of international rules requiring states to prosecute various kinds of criminal conduct already constitutes a body of international criminal law properly so-called; whether it is enforced "directly" before an international tribunal or "indirectly" before national courts depends partly on questions of convenience, partly on contingent political factors.

Some writers use terms such as "transnational crime" and "transnational criminal law" to describe the crimes described here as "offenses of international concern" and the regimes developed, especially by the so-called suppression conventions, to deal with them. *See* Neil Boister, *"Transnational Criminal Law"?* 14 EUROP. J. INT'L L. 953 (2003); Roger S. Clark, *Countering Transnational and International Crime: Defining the Agenda*, in CRIME SANS FRONTIÈRES: INTERNATIONAL AND EUROPEAN LEGAL APPROACHES 20 (Peter J. Cullen & William C. Gilmore eds., 1998) (Hume Papers on Public Policy, Vol. 6, Nos. 1 & 2); ROUTLEDGE HANDBOOK OF TRANSNATIONAL CRIMINAL LAW (Neil Boister & Robert J. Currie eds., 2015).

§ 1.02 The Sources of International Criminal Law

International criminal law is an amalgam of rules and principles drawn from both national and international law. In national legal systems, legal rules and principles are identified and validated by reference to formal "sources of law" such as the constitution, statutes, case law, etc. What are the equivalent "sources" of international law rules?

The Restatement (Third) of the Foreign Relations Law of the United States (1987)

§ 102 Sources of International Law

(1) A rule of international law is one that has been accepted as such by the international community of states

(a) in the form of customary law;

(b) by international agreement; or

(c) by derivation from general principles common to the major legal systems of the world.

(2) Customary international law results from a general and consistent practice of states followed by them from a sense of legal obligation.

(3) International agreements create law for the states parties thereto and may lead to the creation of customary international law when such agreements are intended for adherence by states generally and are in fact widely accepted.

(4) General principles common to major legal systems, even if not incorporated or reflected in customary law or international agreement, may be invoked as supplementary rules of international law where appropriate.

See also Article 38 of the Statute of the International Court of Justice, reproduced in footnote 9 in *Filartiga v. Pena-Irala, infra*. In thinking about customary law, there is much food for thought in the current project of the International Law Commission (ILC) on "formation and evidence of customary international law." *See generally* documentation collected on the website of the ILC under this topic, *available at* http://www.legal.un.org.

The Case of the S.S. Lotus (France v. Turkey)

Permanent Court of International Justice P.C.I.J., Ser. A, No. 10 (1927)

. . . On August 2nd, 1926, just before midnight, a collision occurred between the French mail steamer *Lotus*, proceeding to Constantinople, and the Turkish collier *Boz-Kourt*, between five and six nautical miles to the north of Cape Sigri (Mitylene). The *Boz-Kourt*, which was cut in two, sank, and eight Turkish nationals who were on board perished. After having done everything possible to succour the shipwrecked persons, of whom ten were able to be saved, the *Lotus* continued on its course to Constantinople, where it arrived on August 3rd.

At the time of the collision, the officer of the watch on board the *Lotus* was Monsieur Demons, a French citizen, lieutenant in the merchant service and first officer of the ship, whilst the movements of the *Boz-Kourt* were directed by its captain, Hassan Bey, who was one of those saved from the wreck.

As early as August 3rd the Turkish police proceeded to hold an enquiry into the collision on board the *Lotus*; and on the following day, August 4th, the captain of the *Lotus* handed in his master's report at the French Consulate-General, transmitting a copy to the harbour master.

On August 5th, Lieutenant Demons was requested by the Turkish authorities to go ashore to give evidence. The examination, the length of which incidentally resulted in delaying the departure of the *Lotus*, led to the placing under arrest of Lieutenant Demons—without previous notice being given to the French Consul-General—and Hassan Bey, amongst others. This arrest, which has been characterized by the Turkish agent as arrest pending trial (*arrestation préventive*), was effected in order to ensure that the criminal prosecution instituted against the two officers, on a charge of manslaughter, by the Public Prosecutor of Stamboul, on the complaint of the families of the victims of the collision should follow its normal course.

The case was first heard by the Criminal Court of Stamboul on August 28th. On that occasion, Lieutenant Demons submitted that the Turkish Courts had no jurisdiction; the Court, however, overruled his objection. When the proceedings were resumed on September 11th, Lieutenant Demons demanded his release on bail; this request was complied with on September 13th, the bail being fixed at 6,000 Turkish pounds.

On September 15th, the Criminal Court delivered its judgment. . . . [I]t sentenced Lieutenant Demons to eighty days' imprisonment and a fine of twenty-two pounds, Hassan Bey being sentenced to a slightly more severe penalty. . . .

[The French government protested the action of the Turkish authorities in subjecting Lieutenant Demons to prosecution. It contended that only the state under whose flag a vessel sails has jurisdiction under international law to prosecute persons on board that vessel for actions leading to a collision on the high seas. France and Turkey were both parties to the Convention of Lausanne of July 24, 1923; under Article 15 of that Convention "all questions of jurisdiction shall, as between Turkey and other contracting Powers, be decided in accordance with the principles of international law." By a special agreement (a "*compromis*"), the French and Turkish governments submitted to the Permanent Court of International Justice two questions: (1) whether Turkey had, contrary to Article 15 of the Convention of Lausanne, acted in conflict with the principles of international law—and, if so, what principles—when it instituted criminal proceedings against M. Demons; and (2) should the reply to (1) be in the affirmative, what pecuniary reparation, if any, was due to M. Demons.]

I

. . . .

The prosecution was instituted in pursuance of Turkish legislation. The special agreement does not indicate what clause or clauses of that legislation apply. No document has been submitted to the Court indicating on what article of the Turkish Penal Code the prosecution was based; the French Government, however, declares that the Criminal Court claimed jurisdiction under Article 6 of the Turkish Penal Code, and far from denying this statement, Turkey, in submissions of her Counter-Case, contends that that article is in conformity with the principles of international law. It does not appear from the proceedings whether the prosecution was instituted solely on the basis of that article.

Article 6 of the Turkish Penal Code, Law No. 765 of March 1st, 1926 (Official Gazette No. 320 of March 13th, 1926), runs as follows:

> Any foreigner who, apart from the cases contemplated by Article 4, commits an offense abroad to the prejudice of Turkey or of a Turkish subject, for which offence Turkish law prescribes a penalty involving loss of freedom for a minimum period of not less than one year, shall be punished in accordance with the Turkish Penal Code provided that he is arrested in Turkey. The penalty shall however be reduced by one third and instead of the death penalty, twenty years of penal servitude shall be awarded.
>
> Nevertheless, in such cases, the prosecution will only be instituted at the request of the Minister of Justice or on the complaint of the injured Party. . . .

Even if the Court must hold that the Turkish authorities had seen fit to base the prosecution of Lieutenant Demons upon the above-mentioned Article 6, the question submitted to the Court is not whether that article is compatible with the principles of international law; it is more general. The Court is asked to state whether or not the principles of international law prevent Turkey from instituting criminal proceedings against Lieutenant Demons under Turkish law. Neither the conformity of Article 6 in itself with the principles of international law nor the application of that article by the Turkish authorities constitutes the point at issue; it is the very fact of the institution of proceedings which is held by France to be contrary to those principles. . . .

III

The Court, having to consider whether there are any rules of international law which may have been violated by the prosecution in pursuance of Turkish law of Lieutenant Demons, is confronted in the first place by a question of principle which, in the written and oral arguments of the two Parties, has proved to be a fundamental one. The French Government contends that the Turkish courts, in order to have jurisdiction, should be able to point to some title to jurisdiction recognized by international law in favour of Turkey. On the other hand, the Turkish Government takes the view that Article 15 allows Turkey jurisdiction whenever such jurisdiction does not come into conflict with a principle of international law.

The latter view seems to be conformity with the special agreement itself, No. 1 of which asks the Court to say whether Turkey has acted contrary to the principles of international law and, if so, what principles. According to the special agreement, therefore, it is not a question of stating principles which would permit Turkey to take criminal proceedings, but of formulating the principles, if any, which might have been violated by such proceedings.

This way of stating the question is also dictated by the very nature and existing conditions of international law. . . . International law governs relations between independent States. The rules of law binding upon States therefore emanate from their own free will as expressed in conventions or by usages generally accepted as expressing principles of law and established in order to regulate the relations between these co-existing independent communities or with a view to the achievement of commons aims. Restrictions upon the independence of States cannot therefore be presumed.

Now the first and foremost restriction imposed by international law upon a State is that — failing the existence of a permissive rule to the contrary — it may not exercise its power in any form in the territory of another state. In this sense jurisdiction is certainly territorial; it cannot be exercised by a State outside its territory except by virtue of a permissive rule derived from international custom or from a convention.

It does not, however, follow that international law prohibits a State from exercising jurisdiction in its own territory, in respect of any case which relates to acts which have taken place abroad, and in which it cannot rely on some permissive rule of international law. Such a view would only be tenable if international law contained a general prohibition to states to extend the application of their laws and the jurisdiction of their courts to persons, property and acts outside their territory, and if, as an exception to this general prohibition, it allowed States do so in certain specific cases. But this is certainly not the case under international law as it stands at present. Far from laying down a general prohibition to the effect that States may not extend the application of their laws and the jurisdiction of their courts to persons, property and acts outside their territory, it leaves them in this respect a wide measure of discretion which is only limited in certain cases by prohibitive rules; as regards other cases, every State remains free to adopt the principles which it regards as best and most suitable. . . .

In these circumstances, all that can be required of a State is that it should not overstep the limits which international law places upon its jurisdiction; within these limits, its title to exercise jurisdiction rests in its sovereignty.

It follows from the foregoing that the contention of the French Government to the effect that Turkey must in each case be able to cite a rule of international law authorizing her to exercise jurisdiction, is opposed to the generally accepted international law to which Article 15 of the Convention of Lausanne refers. Having regard to the terms of Article 15 and to the construction which the Court has just placed upon it, this contention would apply in regard to civil as well as to criminal cases, and would be applicable on conditions of absolute reciprocity as between Turkey and the other contracting Parties; in practice, it would therefore in many cases result in paralyzing the action of the courts, owing to the impossibility of citing a universally accepted rule on which to support the exercise of their jurisdiction.

Nevertheless, it has to be seen whether the foregoing considerations really apply as regards criminal jurisdiction or whether this jurisdiction is governed by a different principle; this might be the outcome of the close connection which for a long time existed between the conception of supreme criminal jurisdiction and that of a State, and also by the especial importance of criminal jurisdiction from the point of view of the individual.

Though it is true that in all systems of law the principle of the territorial character of criminal law is fundamental, it is equally true that all or nearly all these systems of law extend their action to offenses committed outside the territory of the State which adopts them, and they do so in ways which vary from State to State. The territoriality of criminal law, therefore, is not an absolute principle of international law and by no means coincides with territorial sovereignty. . . .

This situation may be considered from two different standpoints corresponding to the points of view respectively taken up by the Parties. According to one of these standpoints, the principle of freedom, in virtuè of which each State may regulate its legislation at its discretion, provided that in so doing it does not come in conflict with a restriction imposed by international law, would also apply as regards law governing the scope of jurisdiction in criminal cases. According to the other standpoint, the exclusively territorial character of law relating to this domain constitutes a principle which, except as otherwise expressly provided, would, *ipso facto*, prevent States from extending the criminal jurisdiction of their courts beyond their frontiers; the exceptions in question, which include for instance extraterritorial jurisdiction over nationals and over crimes directed against public safety, would therefore rest on special permissive rules forming part of international law.

Adopting, for the purposes of the argument, the standpoint of the latter of these two systems, it must be recognized that, in the absence of a treaty provision, its correctness depends upon whether there is a custom having the force of law establishing it. The same is true as regards the applicability of this system—assuming it to have been recognized as sound—in the particular case. It follows that, even from this point of view, before ascertaining whether there may be a rule of international law expressly allowing Turkey to prosecute a foreigner for an offense committed by him outside Turkey, it is necessary to begin by establishing both that the system is well-founded and that it is applicable in the particular case. Now, in order to establish the first of these points, one must, as has just been seen, prove the existence of a principle of international law restricting the discretion of States as regards criminal legislation.

Consequently, whichever of the two systems described above be adopted, the same result will be arrived at in this particular case; the necessity of ascertaining whether or not under international law there is a principle which would have prohibited Turkey, in the circumstances of the case before the Court, from prosecuting Lieutenant Demons. . . .

The Court therefore must, in any event, ascertain whether or not there exists a rule of international law limiting the freedom of States to extend the criminal jurisdiction of their courts to a situation uniting the circumstances of the present case. . . .

IV

. . . .

The arguments advanced by the French Government, other than those considered above, are, in substance, the three following:

(1) International law does not allow a state to take proceedings with regard to offenses committed by foreigners abroad, simply by reason of the nationality of the victim; and such is the situation in the present case because the offense must be regarded as having been committed on board the French vessel.

(2) International law recognizes the exclusive jurisdiction of the State whose flag is flown as regards everything which occurs on board a ship on the high seas.

(3) Lastly, this principle is especially applicable in a collision case. . . .

As has already been observed, the characteristic features of the situation of fact are as follows: there has been a collision on the high seas between two vessels flying different flags, on one of which was one of the persons alleged to be guilty of the offense, whilst the victims were on board the other.

This being so, the Court does not think it is necessary to consider the contention that a State cannot punish offenses committed abroad by a foreigner simply by reason of the nationality of the victim. For this contention only relates to the case where nationality of the victim is the only criterion on which the criminal jurisdiction of the state is based. Even if that argument were correct generally speaking—and in regard to this the Court reserves its opinion—it could only be used in the present case if international law forbade Turkey to take into consideration the fact that the offense produced its effects on the Turkish vessel and consequently in a place assimilated to Turkish territory in which the application of Turkish criminal law cannot be challenged, even in regard to offenses committed there by foreigners. But no such rule of international law exists. No argument has come to the knowledge of the Court from which it could be deduced that States recognize themselves to be under an obligation towards each other only to have regard to the place where the author of the offense happens to be at the time of the offense. On the contrary, it is certain that the courts of many countries, even of countries which have given their criminal legislation a strictly territorial character, interpret criminal law in the sense that offenses, the authors of which at the moment of commission are in the territory of another State, are nevertheless to be regarded as having been committed in the national territory, if one of the constituent elements of the offense, and more especially its effects, have taken place there. French courts have, in regard to a variety of situations, given decisions sanctioning this way of interpreting the territorial principle. Again, the Court does not know of any cases in which governments have protested against the fact that the criminal law of some country contained a rule to this effect or that the courts of a country construed their criminal law in this sense. Consequently, once it is admitted that the effects of the offense were produced on the Turkish vessel, it becomes impossible to hold that there is a rule of international law which prohibits Turkey from prosecuting Lieutenant Demons because of the fact that the author of the offense was on board the French ship. Since, as has already been observed, the special agreement does not deal with the provision of Turkish law under which the prosecution was instituted, but only with the question whether the prosecution should be regarded as contrary to the principles of international law, there is no reason preventing the Court from confining itself to observing that, in this case, a prosecution may also be justified from the point of view of the so-called territorial principle. . . .

The second argument put forward by the French Government is the principle that the State whose flag is flown has exclusive jurisdiction over everything which occurs on board a merchant ship on the high seas.

It is certainly true that—apart from special cases which are defined by international law—vessels on the high seas are subject to no authority except that of the State whose flag they fly. In virtue of the principle of the freedom of the seas, that is to say, the absence of any territorial sovereignty upon the high seas, no State may exercise any kind of jurisdiction over foreign vessels upon them. Thus, if a war vessel, happening to be at the spot where a collision occurs between a vessel flying its flag and a foreign vessel, were to send on board the latter an officer to make investigations or to take evidence, such an act would undoubtedly be contrary to international law.

But it by no means follows that a State can never in its own territory exercise jurisdiction over acts which have occurred on board a foreign ship on the high seas. A corollary of the principle of the freedom of the seas is that a ship on the high seas is assimilated to the territory of the State the flag of which it flies, for, just as in its own territory, that State exercises its authority upon it, and no other State may do so. All that can be said is that by virtue of the principle of the freedom of the seas, a ship is placed in the same position as national territory, but there is nothing to support the claim according to which the rights of the State under whose flag the vessel sails may go farther than the rights which it exercises within its territory properly so called. It follows that what occurs on board a vessel upon the high seas must be regarded as if it occurred on the territory of the State whose flag the ship flies. If, therefore, a guilty act committed on the high seas produces its effects on a vessel flying another flag or in foreign territory, the same principles must be applied as if the territories of two different States were concerned, and the conclusion must therefore be drawn that there is no rule of international law prohibiting the State to which the ship on which the effects of the offense have taken place belongs, from regarding the offense as having been committed in its territory and prosecuting, accordingly, the delinquent.

This conclusion could only be overcome if it were shown that there was a rule of customary international law which, going further than the principle stated above, established the exclusive jurisdiction of the State whose flag was flown. The French Government has endeavored to prove the existence of such a rule, having recourse for this purpose to the teachings of publicists, to decisions of municipal and international tribunals, and especially to conventions which, whilst creating exceptions to the principle of the freedom of the seas by permitting the war and police vessels of a State to exercise a more or less extensive control over the merchant vessels of another State, reserve jurisdiction to the courts of the country whose flag is flown by the vessel proceeded against.

In the Court's opinion the existence of such a rule has not been conclusively proved. . . . In the first place, as regards teachings of publicists, and apart from the question as to what their value may be from the point of view of establishing the existence of a rule of customary law, it is no doubt true that all or nearly all writers teach that ships on the high seas are subject exclusively to the jurisdiction of the State whose flag they fly. But the important point is the significance attached by them to this principle; now it does not appear that in general, writers bestow upon this principle a scope differing from or wider than that explained above and which is equivalent to saying that the jurisdiction of a State over vessels on the high seas is the same in extent as its jurisdiction in its own territory. On the other hand, there is no lack of writers who, upon a close study of the special question whether a State can prosecute for offenses committed on board a foreign ship on the high seas, definitely come to the conclusion that such offenses must be regarded as if they had been committed in the territory of the State whose flag the ship flies, and that consequently the general rules of each legal system in regard to offenses committed abroad are applicable.

In regard to precedents, it should first be observed that, leaving aside the collision cases which will be alluded to later, none of them relates to offenses affecting two ships flying the flags of different countries, and consequently they are not of much importance in the case before the Court. . . .

On the other hand, there is no lack of cases in which a State has claimed a right to prosecute for an offense, committed on board a foreign vessel, which it regarded as punishable under its legislation. . . .

The cases in which the exclusive jurisdiction of the State whose flag was flown has been recognized would seem rather to have been cases in which the foreign State was interested only by reason of the nationality of the victim, and in which, according to the legislation of that State itself or the practice of its courts, that ground was not regarded as sufficient to authorize prosecution for an offense committed abroad by a foreigner.

Finally, as regards conventions expressly reserving jurisdiction exclusively to the State whose flag is flown, it is not absolutely certain that this stipulation is to be regarded as expressing a general principle of law rather than as corresponding to the extraordinary jurisdiction which these conventions confer on the state-owned ships of a particular country in respect of ships of another country on the high seas. Apart from that, it should be observed that these conventions relate to matters of a particular kind, closely connected with the policing of the seas, such as the slave trade, damage to submarine cables,[a] fisheries, etc., and not to common-law offenses. Above all it should be pointed out that the offenses contemplated by the conventions in question only concern a single ship; it is impossible therefore to make any deduction from them in regard to matters which concern two ships and consequently the jurisdiction of two different States. . . . The Court therefore has arrived at the conclusion that the second argument put forward by the French Government does not, any more than the first, establish the existence of a rule of international law prohibiting Turkey from prosecuting Lieutenant Demons.

It only remains to examine the third argument advanced by the French Government and to ascertain whether a rule specially applying to collision cases has grown up, according to which criminal proceedings regarding such cases come exclusively within the jurisdiction of the State whose flag is flown. . . . In this connection, the Agent of the French Government has drawn the Court's attention to the fact that questions of jurisdiction in collision cases, which frequently arise before civil courts, are but rarely encountered in the practice of criminal courts. He deduces from this that, in practice, prosecutions only occur before the courts of the State whose flag is flown and that that circumstance is proof of a tacit consent on the part of States and, consequently, shows positive international law in collision cases.

In the Court's opinion, this conclusion is not warranted. Even if the rarity of the judicial decisions to be found among the reported cases were sufficient to prove in

---

a. *See* Roger S. Clark, *Some Aspects of the Concept of International Criminal Law: Suppression Conventions, Jurisdiction, Submarine Cables and* The Lotus, 22 CRIMINAL LAW FORUM 519 (2011).— Eds.

point of fact the circumstance alleged by the Agent for the French Government, it would merely show that States had often, in practice, abstained from instituting criminal proceedings, and not that they recognized themselves as being obliged to do so; for only if such abstention were based on their being conscious of having a duty to abstain would it be possible to speak of an international custom. The alleged fact does not allow one to infer that States have been conscious of having such a duty. On the other hand, as will presently be seen, there are other circumstances calculated to show that the contrary is true.

So far as the Court is aware there are no decisions of international tribunals in this matter; but some decisions of municipal courts have been cited. Without pausing to consider the value to be attributed to the judgments of municipal courts in connection with the establishment of the existence of a rule of international law, it will suffice to observe that the decisions sometimes support one view and sometimes the other. . . . [A]s municipal jurisprudence is thus divided, it is hardly possible to see in it an indication of the existence of the restrictive rule of international law which alone could serve as a basis for the contention of the French Government.

On the other hand, the Court feels called upon to lay stress upon the fact that it does not appear that the States concerned have objected to criminal proceedings in respect of collision cases before the courts of a country other than that the flag of which was flown, or that they have made protests: their conduct does not appear to have differed appreciably from that observed by them in all cases of concurrent jurisdiction. This fact is directly opposed to the existence of a tacit consent on the part of States to the exclusive jurisdiction of the State whose flag is flown. . . .

The conclusion at which the Court has therefore arrived is that there is no rule of international law in regard to collision cases to the effect that criminal proceedings are exclusively within the jurisdiction of the State whose flag is flown. . . .

The offense for which Lieutenant Demons appears to have been prosecuted was an act — of negligence or imprudence — having its origin on board the *Lotus*, whilst its effects made themselves felt on board the *Boz-Kourt*. These two elements are, legally, entirely inseparable so much so that their separation renders the offense non-existent. Neither the exclusive jurisdiction of either State, nor the limitations of the jurisdiction of each to the occurrences which took place on the respective ships would appear calculated to satisfy the requirements of justice and effectively to protect the interests of the two States. It is only natural that each should be able to exercise jurisdiction and to do so in respect of the incident as a whole. It is therefore a case of concurrent jurisdiction. . . .

. . . .

It must therefore be held that there is no principle of international law, within the meaning of Article 15 of the Convention of Lausanne of July 24th, 1923, which precludes the institution of the criminal proceedings under consideration. Consequently, Turkey, by instituting, in virtue of the discretion which international law leaves to every sovereign state, the criminal proceedings in question, has not, in the absence of such principles, acted in a manner contrary to the principles of international law within the meaning of the special agreement. . . .

V

Having thus answered the first question submitted by the special agreement in the negative, the Court need not consider the second question, regarding the pecuniary reparation which might have been due to Lieutenant Demons. . . .

Notes

(1) The *Lotus* court was evenly divided, 6-6; it was the president's double vote, in accordance with the Court's rule in the case of a tie, that resulted in judgment for Turkey. The judges who joined in the opinion of the court were the president, Max Huber (Switzerland), Bustamante (Cuba), Oda (Japan), Anzilotti (Italy), Pessôa (Brazil), and Feïzi-Daïm Bey, the Turkish national judge. Judges Loder (Netherlands), Lord Finlay (Great Britain), Weiss (France), Altamira (Spain), Nyholm (Denmark), and Moore (United States) all delivered separate dissenting opinions. Judge Moore evidently agreed with the six-person "majority" that the burden was on France and that it had not carried it in respect of the effects theory and the exclusivity of the flag state. He did, however, state that the criminal proceedings:

> so far as they rested on Article 6 of the Turkish Penal Code, were in conflict with the following principles of international law:
>
> (1) that the jurisdiction of a State over the national territory is exclusive;
>
> (2) that foreigners visiting a country are subject to the local law, and must look to the courts of that country for their judicial protection;
>
> (3) that a State cannot rightfully assume to punish foreigners for alleged infractions of laws to which they were not, at the time of the alleged offence, in any wise subject.

He also stated that his:

> dissent was based solely on the connection of the pending case with Article 6 of the Turkish Penal Code. In the judgment of the Court that there is no rule of international law by virtue of which the penal cognizance of a collision at sea, resulting in the loss of life, belongs exclusively to the country of the ship by or by means of which the wrong was done, I concur, thus making for the judgment on that question, as submitted by the *compromis*, a definitely ascertained majority of seven to five.

The other five judges, in varying degrees, disagreed with the basic premise that it was for France to establish why Turkey might not act, rather than for Turkey to show why it might. Lord Finlay stated:

> The question is put in the *compromis* with perfect fairness as between the two countries and the attempt to torture it into meaning that France must produce a rule forbidding what Turkey did arises from a misconception.

> The question is whether the principles of international law authorize what Turkey did in this matter.

(2) The *Lotus* case was decided by the Permanent Court of International Justice, which was created in 1921. It was the predecessor of the present International Court of Justice (ICJ), established in 1945 as "the principal judicial organ of the United Nations" (ICJ Statute, art. 1). Only states may be parties before this court in contentious proceedings. It has no jurisdiction over individuals and therefore no criminal jurisdiction. But, as in the *Lotus* case, disputes before the ICJ may raise questions of international criminal law involving the respective rights or obligations of the states which are parties to the dispute. In addition, the court can render advisory opinions at the request of the General Assembly, Security Council, and other authorized organs of the United Nations and its Specialized Agencies. These too may touch on questions of international criminal law. *See, e.g., Reservations to the Convention on the Prevention and Punishment of the Crime of Genocide*, 1951 I.C.J. 15. *See generally* K.J. Keith, *The International Court of Justice and Criminal Justice*, 59 INT'L & COMP. L. Q. 895 (2010).

(3) The judgment in the *Lotus* case is said to epitomize an "extreme positivism" in international law. "Positivism" has various meanings; in an international law context it usually refers to the proposition that international law depends on the consent of states and is to be determined by looking at what states have agreed to be the law. Is that an adequate and workable view of the nature of international law? What are the alternatives? What precisely is the "source" of the principle enunciated in the *Lotus* opinion that "restrictions on the independence of states cannot be presumed"? How far was this principle really determinative of the result in the *Lotus* case?

(4) How far is the *Lotus* decision good law today? Its specific result has been "reversed" by several multilateral treaties. For instance, Article 11(1) of the Convention on the High Seas, Apr. 29, 1958, 13 U.S.T 2312, 450 U.N.T.S. 82, provides:

> In the event of collision or of any other incident of navigation concerning a ship on the high seas, involving the penal or disciplinary responsibility of the master or of any other person in the service of the ship, no penal or disciplinary proceedings may be instituted against such persons except before the judicial or administrative authorities either of the flag State or of the State of which such person is a national.

Identical language appears in Article 97 of the Law of the Sea Convention, Dec. 10, 1982, U.N. Doc. A/CONF. 62/122, *reprinted in* 21 I.L.M. 1261 (1982). France is a party to both of these treaties, but Turkey is a party to neither. What if the exact facts in *Lotus* were to arise today? Does the fact that over 170 states are parties to one or both of the conventions mean that the treaty rules now also represent customary law, binding alike on parties and non-parties?

What about the "positivistic" premises of the judgment? How far do those have any residual validity today? This question is pervasive in modern international criminal law and is often an underlying factor in many of the later discussions in this book. In the Advisory Proceedings in the International Court of Justice on *The Legality of the Threat or Use of Nuclear Weapons*, 1996 I.C.J. Rep. 226, some of the nuclear powers, including France, relied on *The Lotus* for the proposition that they might use nuclear weapons since there was no specific rule against doing so. One of your authors chided the French during oral argument, suggesting that they had it right about the general issue in 1927; they should now be showing by what authorization of international law they invoked the potential power to destroy us all:

> Surely, speaking as we are today, about the alleged sovereign right to engage in actions that could destroy the planet, we might fairly ask whether it is "authorized" by international law. A moribund and controversial decision about two colliding vessels on the high seas is a very weak base on which to defend the raw power to destroy our Spaceship Earth.

Roger S. Clark & Madeleine Sann, The Case Against the Bomb: Marshall Islands, Samoa and Solomon Islands Before the International Court of Justice in Advisory Proceedings on the Legality of the Threat or Use of Nuclear Weapons 226 (Roger S. Clark, Counsel for Samoa) (1996). The Court ultimately finessed the *Lotus* issue by noting that:

> the nuclear-weapon States appearing before it either accepted, or did not dispute, that their independence to act was indeed restricted by the principles and rules of international law, more particularly humanitarian law. . . . Hence. . . . the questions of burden of proof . . . are without particular significance for the disposition of the issues before the Court.

1996 I.C.J. Rep. at 239.

(5) *Lotus* is about jurisdiction. International law has numerous "bases" of jurisdiction, such as territoriality and nationality. Some of the bases (like the "passive personality" theory contained in Article 6 of the Turkish Penal Code) are controversial but subject to development in state practice. Notwithstanding his disavowal of nationality of the victim of a crime such as manslaughter as a basis of jurisdiction, Judge Moore suggested in his dissent that there was "universal jurisdiction" which any state might claim in the case of pirates. We explore issues of jurisdiction more fully in Chapter 3 and at many other points throughout this casebook. For the moment, note that the Court had no problem with the possibility that both Turkey and France might exercise jurisdiction over the hapless M. Demons. Jurisdiction was, as the Court says, "concurrent." Turkey had (at least) its "effects" theory; France had nationality and flag state theories. The state in possession had, perforce in this instance, priority. While international law has never developed a general jurisdictional order, some specialized treaties set out priorities for prosecution. Consider, for example, *Wildenhus's Case*, 120 U.S. 1 (1887). Wildenhus was alleged to have murdered a fellow-Belgian on a Belgian ship moored at the docks in Jersey City, New Jersey. Responding to habeas corpus proceedings when the Jersey City authorities arrested Wildenhus and some material witnesses, the Court applied the priority provisions of a consular treaty with Belgium. The Court said, at 18:

> The principle which governs the whole matter is this: disorders which disturb only the peace of the ship or those on board are to be dealt with exclusively by the sovereignty of the home of the ship, but those which disturb the public peace may be suppressed, and, if need be, the offenders punished, by the proper authorities of the local jurisdiction. It may not be easy at all times to determine to which of the two jurisdictions a particular act of disorder belongs. Much will undoubtedly depend on the attending circumstances of the particular case, but all must concede that felonious homicide is a subject for the local jurisdiction, and that if the proper authorities are proceeding with the case in a regular way, the consul has no right to interfere to prevent it. That, according to the petition for the habeas corpus, is this case.

Article VII (3) of the 1951 North Atlantic Treaty Organization (NATO) Status of Forces Agreement, http://www.nato.int/cps/en/natohq/official_texts_17265.htm, provides:

> In cases where the right to exercise jurisdiction is concurrent the following rules shall apply:
>
> a. The military authorities of the sending State shall have the primary right to exercise jurisdiction over a member of a force or of a civilian component in relation to
>
> 1. offences solely against the property or security of that State, or offences solely against the person or property of another member of the force or civilian component of that State or of a dependent;
>
> 2. offences arising out of any act or omission done in the performance of official duty.
>
> b. In the case of any other offence the authorities of the receiving State shall have the primary right to exercise jurisdiction.
>
> c. If the State having the primary right decides not to exercise jurisdiction, it shall notify the authorities of the other State as soon as practicable. The authorities of the State having the primary right shall give sympathetic consideration to a request from the authorities of the other State for a waiver of its right in cases where that other state considers such waiver to be of particular importance.

A somewhat different "solution", a "process" one, is contained in a 2007 document agreed upon by the United Kingdom and the United States, entitled "Guidance for Handling Criminal Cases with Concurrent Jurisdiction between the United Kingdom and the United States."[1] The parties agree to share information and to consult closely in such cases. Similar regional agreements operate in Europe, and the

1. The instrument was signed by the U.S. and U.K Attorneys-General and the equivalent functionary in Scotland, Her Majesty's Advocate.

principle is beginning to find its way into multilateral treaties, such as the 2003 UN Convention against Corruption, Art. 42 (5), 2349 U.N.T.S. 41. (*See infra* § 4.01[A].)

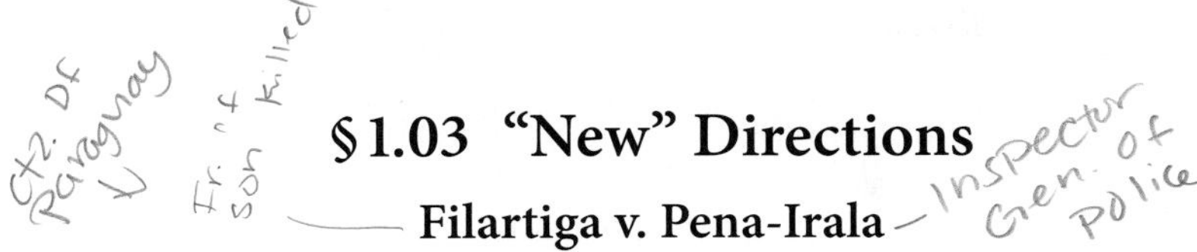

§ 1.03 "New" Directions

Filartiga v. Pena-Irala

United States Court of Appeals, Second Circuit
630 F.2d 876 (1980)

KAUFMAN, CIRCUIT JUDGE:

... Implementing the constitutional mandate for national control over foreign relations, the First Congress established original district court jurisdiction over "all causes where an alien sues for a tort only [committed] in violation of the law of nations." Judiciary Act of 1789, ch. 20, § 9(b), 1 Stat. 73, 77 (1789), codified at 28 U.S.C. § 1350. Construing this rarely-invoked provision, we hold that deliberate torture perpetrated under color of official authority violates universally accepted norms of the international law of human rights, regardless of the nationality of the parties. Thus, whenever an alleged torturer is found and served with process by an alien within our borders, § 1350 provides federal jurisdiction. Accordingly, we reverse the judgment of the district court dismissing the complaint for want of federal jurisdiction.

I

The appellants, plaintiffs below, are citizens of the Republic of Paraguay. Dr. Joel Filartiga, a physician, describes himself as a longstanding opponent of the government of President Alfredo Stroessner, which has held power in Paraguay since 1954. His daughter, Dolly Filartiga, arrived in the United States in 1978 under a visitor's visa, and has since applied for permanent political asylum. The Filartigas brought this action in the Eastern District of New York against Americo Norberto Pena-Irala (Pena), also a citizen of Paraguay, for wrongfully causing the death of Dr. Filartiga's seventeen-year old son, Joelito. Because the district court dismissed the action for want of subject matter jurisdiction, we must accept as true the allegations contained in the Filartigas' complaint and affidavits for purposes of this appeal.

The appellants contend that on March 29, 1976, Joelito Filartiga was kidnapped and tortured to death by Pena, who was then Inspector General of Police in Asuncion, Paraguay. Later that day, the police brought Dolly Filartiga to Pena's home where she was confronted with the body of her brother, which evidenced marks of severe torture. As she fled, horrified, from the house, Pena followed after her shouting, "Here you have what you have been looking for for so long and what you deserve. Now shut up." The Filartigas claim that Joelito was tortured and killed in retaliation for his father's political activities and beliefs.

Shortly thereafter, Dr. Filartiga commenced a criminal action in the Paraguayan courts against Pena and the police for the murder of his son. As a result,

Dr. Filartiga's attorney was arrested and brought to police headquarters where, shackled to a wall, Pena threatened him with death. This attorney, it is alleged, has since been disbarred without just cause.

During the course of the Paraguayan criminal proceeding, which is apparently still pending after four years, another man, Hugo Duarte, confessed to the murder. Duarte, who was a member of the Pena household, claimed that he had discovered his wife and Joelito in flagrante delicto, and that the crime was one of passion. The Filartigas have submitted a photograph of Joelito's corpse showing injuries they believe refute this claim. Dolly Filartiga, moreover, has stated that she will offer evidence of three independent autopsies demonstrating that her brother's death "was the result of professional methods of torture." Despite his confession, Duarte, we are told, has never been convicted or sentenced in connection with the crime.

In July of 1978, Pena sold his house in Paraguay and entered the United States under a visitor's visa. He was accompanied by Juana Bautista Fernandez Villalba, who had lived with him in Paraguay. The couple remained in the United States beyond the term of their visas, and were living in Brooklyn, New York, when Dolly Filartiga, who was then living in Washington, D. C., learned of their presence. Acting on information provided by Dolly the Immigration and Naturalization Service arrested Pena and his companion, both of whom were subsequently ordered deported on April 5, 1979 following a hearing. They had then resided in the United States for more than nine months.

Almost immediately, Dolly caused Pena to be served with a summons and civil complaint at the Brooklyn Navy Yard, where he was being held pending deportation. The complaint alleged that Pena had wrongfully caused Joelito's death by torture and sought compensatory and punitive damages of $10,000,000 . . . .

II

Appellants rest their principal argument in support of federal jurisdiction upon the Alien Tort Statute, 28 U.S.C. §1350, which provides: "The district courts shall have original jurisdiction of any civil action by an alien for a tort only, committed in violation of the law of nations or a treaty of the United States." Since appellants do not contend that their action arises directly under a treaty of the United States, a threshold question on the jurisdictional issue is whether the conduct alleged violates the law of nations. In light of the universal condemnation of torture in numerous international agreements, and the renunciation of torture as an instrument of official policy by virtually all of the nations of the world (in principle if not in practice), we find that an act of torture committed by a state official against one held in detention violates established norms of the international law of human rights, and hence the law of nations.

The Supreme Court has enumerated the appropriate sources of international law. The law of nations "may be ascertained by consulting the works of jurists, writing professedly on public law; or by the general usage and practice of nations; or by judicial decisions recognizing and enforcing that law." *United States v. Smith*,

18 U.S. (5 Wheat.) 153, 160–61(1820) .... In *Smith*, a statute proscribing "the crime of piracy (on the high seas) as defined by the law of nations," was held sufficiently determinate in meaning to afford the basis for a death sentence. The *Smith* Court discovered among the works of Lord Bacon, Grotius, Bouchard and other commentators a genuine consensus that rendered the crime "sufficiently and constitutionally defined."

The Paquete Habana, 175 U.S. 677 (1900), reaffirmed that

> where there is no treaty, and no controlling executive or legislative act or judicial decision, resort must be had to the customs and usages of civilized nations; and, as evidence of these, to the works of jurists and commentators, who by years of labor, research and experience, have made themselves peculiarly well acquainted with the subjects of which they treat. Such works are resorted to by judicial tribunals, not for the speculations of their authors concerning what the law ought to be, but for trustworthy evidence of what the law really is.

Id. at 700. Modern international sources confirm the propriety of this approach.[9]

Habana is particularly instructive for present purposes, for it held that the traditional prohibition against seizure of an enemy's coastal fishing vessels during wartime, a standard that began as one of comity only, had ripened over the preceding century into "a settled rule of international law" by "the general assent of civilized nations." Thus it is clear that courts must interpret international law not as it was in 1789, but as it has evolved and exists among the nations of the world today....

The requirement that a rule command the "general assent of civilized nations" to become binding upon them all is a stringent one. Were this not so, the courts of one nation might feel free to impose idiosyncratic legal rules upon others, in the name of applying international law.... [But] there are few, if any, issues in international law

---

9. The Statute of the International Court of Justice, Arts. 38 & 59, June 26, 1945, 59 Stat. 1055, 1060 (1945) provides:

> Art. 38
>
> 1. The Court, whose function is to decide in accordance with international law such disputes as are submitted to it, shall apply:
>
> (a) international conventions, whether general or particular, establishing rules expressly recognized by the contesting states;
>
> (b) international custom, as evidence of a general practice accepted as law;
>
> (c) the general principles of law recognized by civilized nations;
>
> (d) subject to the provisions of Article 59, judicial decisions and the teachings of the most highly qualified publicists of the various nations, as subsidiary means for the determination of the rules of law.
>
> 2. This provision shall not prejudice the power of the Court to decide a case *ex aequo et bono*, if the parties agree thereto.
>
> Art. 59.
>
> The decision of the Court has no binding force except between the parties and in respect of that particular case.

today on which opinion seems to be so united as the limitations on a state's power to torture persons held in its custody.

The United Nations Charter (a treaty of the United States, see 59 Stat. 1033 (1945)) makes it clear that in this modern age a state's treatment of its own citizens is a matter of international concern. It provides:

> With a view to the creation of conditions of stability and well-being which are necessary for peaceful and friendly relations among nations . . . the United Nations shall promote . . . universal respect for, and observance of, human rights and fundamental freedoms for all without distinctions as to race, sex, language or religion.

Id. Art. 55. And further:

> All members pledge themselves to take joint and separate action in cooperation with the Organization for the achievement of the purposes set forth in Article 55.

Id. Art. 56.

While this broad mandate has been held not to be wholly self-executing, this observation alone does not end our inquiry. For although there is no universal agreement as to the precise extent of the "human rights and fundamental freedoms" guaranteed to all by the Charter, there is at present no dissent from the view that the guaranties include, at a bare minimum, the right to be free from torture. This prohibition has become part of customary international law, as evidenced and defined by the Universal Declaration of Human Rights, General Assembly Resolution 217 (III)(A) (Dec. 10, 1948) which states, in the plainest of terms, "no one shall be subjected to torture." The General Assembly has declared that the Charter precepts embodied in this Universal Declaration "constitute basic principles of international law."

Particularly relevant is the Declaration on the Protection of All Persons from Being Subjected to Torture, General Assembly Resolution 3452 (1975). The Declaration expressly prohibits any state from permitting the dastardly and totally inhuman act of torture. Torture, in turn, is defined as "any act by which severe pain and suffering, whether physical or mental, is intentionally inflicted by or at the instigation of a public official on a person for such purposes as . . . intimidating him or other persons." The Declaration goes on to provide that "[w]here it is proved that an act of torture or other cruel, inhuman or degrading treatment or punishment has been committed by or at the instigation of a public official, the victim shall be afforded redress and compensation, in accordance with national law." This Declaration, like the Declaration of Human Rights before it, was adopted without dissent by the General Assembly.

These U.N. declarations are significant because they specify with great precision the obligations of member nations under the Charter. Since their adoption, "[m]embers can no longer contend that they do not know what human rights they promised in the Charter to promote." Moreover, a U.N. Declaration is, according to one authoritative definition, "a formal and solemn instrument, suitable for rare occasions when principles of great and lasting importance are being enunciated." Accordingly, it has been observed that the Universal Declaration of Human Rights "no longer fits into the dichotomy of 'binding treaty' against 'non-binding pronouncement,' but is rather an authoritative statement of the international community." Thus, a Declaration creates an expectation of adherence, and "insofar as the expectation is gradually justified by State practice, a declaration may by custom become recognized as laying down rules binding upon the States." Indeed, several commentators have concluded that the Universal Declaration has become, in toto, a part of binding, customary international law.

Turning to the act of torture, we have little difficulty discerning its universal renunciation in the modern usage and practice of nations. The international consensus surrounding torture has found expression in numerous international treaties and accords. *E.g.*, American Convention on Human Rights, Art. 5 ("No one shall be subjected to torture or to cruel, inhuman or degrading punishment or treatment"); International Covenant on Civil and Political Rights (Dec. 16, 1966) (identical language); European Convention for the Protection of Human Rights and Fundamental Freedoms, Art. 3 (semble). The substance of these international agreements is reflected in modern municipal, *i.e.* national law as well. Although torture was once a routine concomitant of criminal interrogations in many nations, during the modern and hopefully more enlightened era it has been universally renounced. According to one survey, torture is prohibited, expressly or implicitly, by the constitutions of over fifty-five nations, including both the United States and Paraguay. Our State Department reports a general recognition of this principle:

> There now exists an international consensus that recognizes basic human rights and obligations owed by all governments to their citizens.... There is no doubt that these rights are often violated; but virtually all governments acknowledge their validity.

We have been directed to no assertion by any contemporary state of a right to torture its own or another nation's citizens. Indeed, United States diplomatic contacts confirm the universal abhorrence with which torture is viewed:

> In exchanges between United States embassies and all foreign states with which the United States maintains relations, it has been the Department of State's general experience that no government has asserted a right to torture its own nationals. Where reports of torture elicit some credence, a state usually responds by denial or, less frequently, by asserting that the conduct was unauthorized or constituted rough treatment short of torture.

Having examined the sources from which customary international law is derived the usage of nations, judicial opinions and the works of jurists, we conclude that official torture is now prohibited by the law of nations. The prohibition is clear and unambiguous, and admits of no distinction between treatment of aliens and citizens. . . . The treaties and accords cited above, as well as the express foreign policy of our own government, all make it clear that international law confers fundamental rights upon all people vis-a-vis their own governments. While the ultimate scope of those rights will be a subject for continuing refinement and elaboration, we hold that the right to be free from torture is now among them. . . .

III

Appellee submits that even if the tort alleged is a violation of modern international law, federal jurisdiction may not be exercised consistent with the dictates of Article III of the Constitution. The claim is without merit. Common law courts of general jurisdiction regularly adjudicate transitory tort claims between individuals over whom they exercise personal jurisdiction, wherever the tort occurred. Moreover, as part of an articulated scheme of federal control over external affairs, Congress provided, in the first Judiciary Act, § 9(b), 1 Stat. 73, 77 (1789), for federal jurisdiction over suits by aliens where principles of international law are in issue. The constitutional basis for the Alien Tort Statute is the law of nations, which has always been part of the federal common law.

. . . .

A case properly "aris[es] under the . . . laws of the United States" for Article III purposes if grounded upon statutes enacted by Congress or upon the common law of the United States. . . . The law of nations forms an integral part of the common law, and a review of the history surrounding the adoption of the Constitution demonstrates that it became a part of the common law of the United States upon the adoption of the Constitution. Therefore, the enactment of the Alien Tort Statute was authorized by Article III.

During the eighteenth century, it was taken for granted on both sides of the Atlantic that the law of nations forms a part of the common law. 1 Blackstone, Commentaries 263–64 (1st ed. 1765–69); 4 *id.* at 67. Under the Articles of Confederation, the Pennsylvania Court of Oyer and Terminer at Philadelphia, per McKean, Chief Justice, applied the law of nations to the criminal prosecution of the Chevalier de Longchamps for his assault upon the person of the French Consul-General to the United States, noting that "[t]his law, in its full extent, is a part of the law of this state. . . ." *Respublica v. DeLongchamps*, 1 U.S. (1 Dall.) 113, 119 (1784). Thus, a leading commentator has written:

> It is an ancient and a salutary feature of the Anglo-American legal tradition that the Law of Nations is a part of the law of the land to be ascertained and administered, like any other, in the appropriate case. This doctrine was originally conceived and formulated in England in response to the demands of an expanding commerce and under the influence of theories widely accepted in the late sixteenth, the seventeenth and the eighteenth centuries. It was brought to America in the colonial years as part of the legal heritage

> from England. It was well understood by men of legal learning in America in the eighteenth century when the United Colonies broke away from England to unite effectively, a little later, in the United States of America.

Dickenson, *The Law of Nations as Part of the National Law of the United States*, 101 U. Pa. L. Rev. 26, 27 (1952).

Indeed, Dickenson goes on to demonstrate that one of the principal defects of the Confederation that our Constitution was intended to remedy was the central government's inability to "cause infractions of treaties or of the law of nations, to be punished." . . . .

As ratified, the judiciary article contained no express reference to cases arising under the law of nations. Indeed, the only express reference to that body of law is contained in Article I, sec. 8, cl. 10, which grants to the Congress the power to "define and punish . . . offenses against the law of nations." Appellees seize upon this circumstance and advance the proposition that the law of nations forms a part of the laws of the United States only to the extent that Congress has acted to define it. This extravagant claim is amply refuted by the numerous decisions applying rules of international law uncodified in any act of Congress. A similar argument was offered to and rejected by the Supreme Court in *United States v. Smith, supra*, and we reject it today. As John Jay wrote in The Federalist No. 3, "Under the national government, treaties and articles of treaties, as well as the laws of nations, will always be expounded in one sense and executed in the same manner, whereas adjudications on the same points and questions in the thirteen states will not always accord or be consistent." Federal jurisdiction over cases involving international law is clear.

Thus, it was hardly a radical initiative for Chief Justice Marshall to state in *The Nereide*, 13 U.S. (9 Cranch) 388 (1815), that in the absence of a congressional enactment, United States courts are "bound by the law of nations, which is a part of the law of the land." These words were echoed in *The Paquete Habana, supra*: "international law is part of our law, and must be ascertained and administered by the courts of justice of appropriate jurisdiction, as often as questions of right depending upon it are duly presented for their determination."

The Filartigas urge that 28 U.S.C. § 1350 be treated as an exercise of Congress's power to define offenses against the law of nations. While such a reading is possible, we believe it is sufficient here to construe the Alien Tort Statute, not as granting new rights to aliens, but simply as opening the federal courts for adjudication of the rights already recognized by international law. The statute nonetheless does inform our analysis of Article III, for we recognize that questions of jurisdiction "must be considered part of an organic growth part of an evolutionary process," and that the history of the judiciary article gives meaning to its pithy phrases. The Framers' overarching concern that control over international affairs be vested in the new national government to safeguard the standing of the United States among the nations of the world therefore reinforces the result we reach today. . . .

IV

. . . .

In the twentieth century the international community has come to recognize the common danger posed by the flagrant disregard of basic human rights and particularly the right to be free of torture. Spurred first by the Great War, and then the Second, civilized nations have banded together to prescribe acceptable norms of international behavior. From the ashes of the Second World War arose the United Nations Organization, amid hopes that an era of peace and cooperation had at last begun. Though many of these aspirations have remained elusive goals, that circumstance cannot diminish the true progress that has been made. In the modern age, humanitarian and practical considerations have combined to lead the nations of the world to recognize that respect for fundamental human rights is in their individual and collective interest. Among the rights universally proclaimed by all nations, as we have noted, is the right to be free of physical torture. Indeed, for purposes of civil liability, the torturer has become — like the pirate and slave trader before him — *hostis humani generis*, an enemy of all mankind. Our holding today, giving effect to a jurisdictional provision enacted by our First Congress, is a small but important step in the fulfillment of the ageless dream to free all people from brutal violence.

Notes

(1) Compare the decision in *Filartiga* with that in the *Lotus* case. To what extent do the two decisions rest on different understandings of the nature of customary international law? Consider the following statement:

> Every two hundred years, it seems, the jurisprudence of customary international law ("CIL") changes. Beginning in the seventeenth century, natural law was said to be the source of CIL. Beginning in the early nineteenth century, positivism was in the ascendency. The positivist view, according to which CIL results from the practice of nations acting out of a sense of legal obligation, was later endorsed by the United States Supreme Court in *The Paquete Habana*. Approximately two centuries after the rise of the positivist view, a new theory is beginning to take hold in some quarters. This theory derives norms of CIL in a loose way from treaties (ratified or not), U.N. General Assembly resolutions, international commissions, and academic commentary — but all colored by a moralism reminiscent of the natural law view. The Second Circuit's decision in *Filartiga v. Pena-Irala* is the most famous United States case to embrace this new understanding of CIL.

Jack L. Goldsmith & Eric A. Posner, *Understanding the Resemblance Between Modern and Traditional Customary International Law*, 40 Va. J. Int'l L. 639 (2000). Consider that John Jay, the first Chief Justice of the United States, and Associate Justice Joseph Story tended to have a strong natural law streak in their writing; the fourth Chief Justice, John Marshall, was much more of a positivist. "Loose theories" hardly began in the twentieth century. In argument before the Supreme Court in an 1825 slave-trade case, songwriter Francis Scott Key, who was also one of the leading Baltimore and Washington lawyers of his day, argued as follows:

> The documents laid before the court will show the present state of the world's opinion and practice upon this subject, and will prove that the time is at hand, if it has not already arrived, when the slave-trade is not only forbidden by the concurrent voice of most nations, but is denounced and punished as a crime of the deepest dye. This is shown by the declarations contained in the treaties of Paris and Ghent; by the acts and conferences at congresses of Vienna, London and Aix-la-Chapelle; by the treaties between Great Britain and Spain and Portugal; by the negotiations between the United States and Great Britain; and by the reports of the committees of the house of commons, and the house of representatives in congress. We contend, then, that whatever was once the fact, this trade is now condemned by the general consent of nations, who have publicly and solemnly declared it to be unjust, inhuman and illegal. We insist, that absolute unanimity on the subject is unnecessary; that, as it was introduced, so may it be abolished, by general concurrence.

The Antelope 23 U.S. 66, 76–7 (argument of Francis Scott Key). Marshall and Story seem to have been on opposite sides of an evenly divided Court in that case on whether this argument would pass muster. *See* Roger S. Clark, *Steven Spielberg's* Amistad *and Other Things I Have Thought About in the Past Forty Years: International (Criminal) Law, Conflict of Laws, Insurance and Slavery*, 30 RUTGERS. L. J. 371, 405 n.105 (1999). The "new" approach, in which principles deemed deserving of recognition as the positive law of the "international community" are assumed to have become the law, even in the face of inconclusive or contrary practice, has been quite influential, particularly in the development of human rights and international criminal law. *See, e.g.*, G. M. DANILENKO, LAW-MAKING IN THE INTERNATIONAL COMMUNITY (1993); J. SHAND WATSON, THEORY AND REALITY IN THE INTERNATIONAL PROTECTION OF HUMAN RIGHTS (1999); Beth Stephens, *The Law of Our Land: Customary International Law as Federal Law After Erie*, 66 FORDHAM. L. REV. 393 (1997). But consider the following:

> The notion that a law of nations, redefined to mean the consensus of states on *any* subject, can be used by a private citizen to control a sovereign's treatment of *its own citizens* within *its own territory* is a 20th century invention of internationalist law professors and human-rights advocates. See generally Bradley & Goldsmith, [Customary International Law as Federal Common Law: A] Critique of the Modern Position, 110 Harv. L. Rev., at 831–837. The Framers would, I am confident, be appalled at the proposition that, for example, the American peoples' democratic adoption of the death penalty, see, *e.g.*, Tex. Penal Code Ann. § 12.31 (2003), could be judicially nullified because of the disapproving views of foreigners.

Scalia J., joined by Thomas J. and Rehnquist, C.J., concurring in part and concurring in the judgment in *Sosa v. Alvarez-Machain*, 542 U.S. 692 (2004), at 749.

(2) What are the implications of the *Filartiga* decision, which was not a criminal case, for federal criminal law? Does it follow from Judge Kaufman's opinion that the federal courts could entertain *criminal* prosecutions for torture or other crimes in violation of international law, relying for jurisdiction on 18 U.S.C. § 3231, which provides: "The district courts of the United States shall have original jurisdiction, exclusive of the courts of the States, of all offenses against the laws of the United States"? Like the Alien Tort Statute (also known as the Alien Tort Claims Act), 18 U.S.C. § 3231 derives from Section 9 of the Judiciary Act of 1789. If international law is part of the law of the United States, and if torture is prohibited by international law, why should torture not be considered a federal common law offense? In this connection, consider the relevance of the holding in *United States v. Hudson & Goodwin*, 11 U.S. (7 Cranch) 32 (1812), that federal jurisdiction does not extend to common law crimes, there libel of President and Congress.

A similar question has arisen before the House of Lords in England. Just before hostilities began in the Second Gulf War in 2003, several activists entered military bases in the United Kingdom, committing damage in an endeavor to disrupt the preparations for the war. Charged with offences including criminal damage, conspiracy to cause criminal damage, aggravated trespass and attempted arson, they sought to justify their actions on the basis that the pending actions of the U.S. and U.K. Governments would amount to the crime of aggression. On appeal to the House of Lords, the appellants argued that they might therefore lawfully use force in an attempt to prevent that offence from taking place. The five judges were unanimous that, in the statutory framework in which the case arose, the defense could not be used. While they all agreed that aggression is a crime under international law, punishable in an international tribunal, they took the position that it had not been incorporated into English law. The common law, they agreed, is no longer a vehicle for creating (or incorporating) new domestic crimes. *R. v. Jones (Margaret)* [2006] U.K.H.L. 16.

Common law crimes (created or recognized by the courts) aside, does it follow from *Filartiga* that it would be "sufficient and constitutional" for *Congress* to give the federal courts blanket jurisdiction over any prosecution for "a crime committed in violation of the law of nations"? What about a statute giving the district courts jurisdiction over "the crime of torture committed in violation of international law"? How would such a statute differ from the piracy statute (codified at 18 U.S.C. § 1651) which, as *Filartiga* observes, was upheld in 1820 in *United States v. Smith*? In its entirety that statute now reads: "Whoever, on the high seas, commits the crime of piracy as defined by the law of nations, and is afterwards brought into or found in the United States, shall be imprisoned for life." Is the piracy statute significantly different because it specifies a particular penalty for the crime? Suppose Congress were to enact that "Whoever commits the crime of torture as defined by international law, and is afterwards found in the United States, shall be imprisoned not more than

20 years"? Would this be "sufficient and constitutional"? In *Smith*, Justice Story's opinion for the majority is balanced by a strong dissent from Justice Livingston. As he saw it, Congress got its power here from Article I, Section 8, Clause 10 of the Constitution which empowers it to "define and punish piracies and felonies committed on the high seas, and offenses against the law of nations." This it had not done. "[I]t is the duty of Congress to incorporate into their own statutes a definition *in terms*" (Livingston's emphasis) and not to refer the citizens to the laws of some foreign country or to the law of nations. One might imagine that the Founders conferred a power to "define" both so that the federal government might transform the international rules into rules of domestic law, and so that Congress could clarify (at least for the United States) what might be rather vague customary rules (even at some risk of getting out of line with other countries). Did Congress deliver on the first, but not the second? Consider the extent also to which the result in *Smith* may be undercut by the Supreme Court's later void for vagueness cases, such as *Papachristou v. City of Jacksonville*, 405 U.S. 156 (1972). This argument was essentially rejected in a Somali piracy case, discussed in chap. 9, *United States v. Dire*, 680 F.3d 446 (4th Cir. 2012). Consider also the discussion of Congressional power in Beth Stephens, *Federalism and Foreign Affairs: Congress's Power to "Define and Punish . . . Offenses Against the Law of Nations,"* 42 Wm & Mary L. Rev. 447 (2000). Stephens argues that "offenses" is used in a broad sense, permitting legislation not only of a criminal nature, but of a civil nature also. In *Filartiga*, Judge Kaufman was able to uphold the constitutionality of the statute without relying on this provision.

(3) *Filartiga* was decided in 1980, four years before the U.N. General Assembly adopted the 1984 Convention Against Torture and Other Cruel, Inhuman or Degrading Treatment or Punishment [*see* chap. 10]. The Convention entered into force in 1987 and was ratified by the United States in 1994. In 1994, Congress did make torture committed in other countries (although not in the U.S.) a federal offense, defining the crime in terms taken more or less from the Torture Convention as modified by U.S. treaty reservations. *See* 18 U.S.C. §§ 2340–2340B. Earlier, in 1992, Congress enacted the Torture Victim Protection Act (codified at 28 U.S.C. § 1350 note), which placed on a statutory basis the civil cause of action for torture (and for extrajudicial killing) perpetrated "under actual or apparent authority, or color of law, of any foreign nation," and extended it to plaintiffs who are U.S. citizens. We will come back to these statutes in chapter 10. Cases in which victims seek civil redress under the Alien Tort Claims Act or the Torture Victim Protection Act may serve as a proxy for criminal prosecution and, insofar as they involve determining what international law prohibits, also have an influence on the development of international criminal law. A notable example is *Kadic v. Karadzic*, 70 F.3d 232 (2d Cir. 1995), *cert. denied*, 518 U.S. 1005 (1996), a civil suit alleging "various atrocities, including brutal acts of rape, forced prostitution, forced impregnation, torture, and summary execution, carried out by Bosnian-Serb military forces as part of a genocidal campaign conducted in the course of the Bosnian civil war" (70 F.3d at 236–37); Judge Newman's opinion in the case opens with the words: "Many

Americans would probably be surprised to learn that victims of atrocities committed in Bosnia are suing the leader of the insurgent Bosnian-Serb forces in a United States District Court in Manhattan."

Sosa v. Alvarez-Machain

Supreme Court of the United States
542 U.S. 692 (2004)

Justice Souter delivered the opinion of the Court:

[Acting for the United States Drug Enforcement Agency, Sosa and other Mexicans kidnaped Alvarez from his house in Mexico, held him overnight in a motel, then brought him by private plane to El Paso, Texas, where he was arrested by federal officers. After his acquittal in the U.S. criminal case, Alvarez returned to Mexico and sued both the United States and his captors.[b] The Supreme Court held that a claim would not lie against the United States because of the exception to the Federal Tort Claims Act concerning "[a]ny claim arising in a foreign country." Alvarez had succeeded in the lower courts on an Alien Tort Statute [ATS] claim against Sosa and had been awarded $25,000 damages on summary judgment. The Court held unanimously that Sosa's claim for arbitrary arrest was not sufficiently established under international law for the purpose of the ATS. The Court discussed the history of the Statute and continued:]

[One] inference to be drawn from the history is that Congress intended the ATS to furnish jurisdiction for a relatively modest set of actions alleging violations of the law of nations. Uppermost in the legislative mind appears to have been offenses against ambassadors . . . ; violations of safe conduct were probably understood to be actionable, and individual actions arising out of prize captures and piracy may well have also been contemplated. But the common law appears to have understood only those three of the hybrid variety as definite and actionable, or at any rate, to have assumed only a very limited set of claims. As Blackstone had put it, "offences against this law [of nations] are principally incident to whole states or nations," and not individuals seeking relief in court. 4 Commentaries 68. [Justice Souter was using the term "hybrid" to refer to a "narrow set of violations of the law of nations, admitting of a judicial remedy and at the same time threatening serious consequences in international affairs."]

[The Court added, in a part of the judgment in which Justice Souter was joined only by Stevens, O'Connor, Kennedy, Ginsburg, and Breyer JJ.]

We must still, however, derive a standard or set of standards for assessing the particular claim Alvarez raises, and for this case it suffices to look to the historical antecedents. Whatever the ultimate criteria for accepting a cause of action

---

b. *See* chapter 17 for the earlier proceedings concerning the effect of his abduction on the jurisdiction of the courts. — Eds.

subject to jurisdiction under §1350 [ATS], we are persuaded that federal courts should not recognize private claims under federal common law for violations of any international law norm with less definite content and acceptance among civilized nations than the historical paradigms familiar when §1350 was enacted. See, *e.g., United States* v. *Smith*, 5 Wheat. 153, 163–180, *n.a* (1820) (illustrating the specificity with which the law of nations defined piracy). This limit upon judicial recognition is generally consistent with the reasoning of many of the courts and judges who faced the issue before it reached this Court. See *Filartiga, supra*, at 890 ("[F]or purposes of civil liability, the torturer has become—like the pirate and slave trader before him—*hostis humani generis*, an enemy of all mankind"); *Tel-Oren, supra*, at 781 (Edwards, J., concurring) (suggesting that the "limits of section 1350's reach" be defined by "a handful of heinous actions—each of which violates definable, universal and obligatory norms"); see also *In re Estate of Marcos Human Rights Litigation*, 25 F. 3d 1467, 1475 (CA9 1994) ("Actionable violations of international law must be of a norm that is specific, universal, and obligatory"). And the determination whether a norm is sufficiently definite to support a cause of action[11] should (and, indeed, inevitably must) involve an element of judgment about the practical consequences of making that cause available to litigants in the federal courts.[12] Thus, Alvarez's detention claim must be gauged against the

11. A related consideration is whether international law extends the scope of liability for a violation of a given norm to the perpetrator being sued, if the defendant is a private actor such as a corporation or individual. Compare *Tel-Oren* v. *Libyan Arab Republic*, 726 F. 2d 774, 791–795 (CADC 1984) (Edwards, J., concurring) (insufficient consensus in 1984 that torture by private actors violates international law), with *Kadic* v. *Karadzic*, 70 F. 3d 232, 239–241 (CA2 1995) (sufficient consensus in 1996 that genocide by private actors violates international law).

12. This requirement of clear definition is not meant to be the only principle limiting the availability of relief in the federal courts for violations of customary international law, though it disposes of this case. For example, the European Commission argues as amicus curiae that basic principles of international law require that before asserting a claim in a foreign forum, the claimant must have exhausted any remedies available in the domestic legal system, and perhaps in other fora such as international claims tribunals. See Brief for European Commission as Amicus Curiae 24, n.54 (citing I. Brownlie, Principles of Public International Law 472–481 (6th ed. 2003)); cf. Torture Victim Protection Act of 1991, §2(b), 106 Stat. 73 (exhaustion requirement). We would certainly consider this requirement in an appropriate case.

Another possible limitation that we need not apply here is a policy of case-specific deference to the political branches. For example, there are now pending in federal district court several class actions seeking damages from various corporations alleged to have participated in, or abetted, the regime of apartheid that formerly controlled South Africa. See In re South African Apartheid Litigation, 238 F. Supp. 2d 1379 (JPML 2002) (granting a motion to transfer the cases to the Southern District of New York). The Government of South Africa has said that these cases interfere with the policy embodied by its Truth and Reconciliation Commission, which "deliberately avoided a 'victors' justice' approach to the crimes of apartheid and chose instead one based on confession and absolution, informed by the principles of reconciliation, reconstruction, reparation and goodwill." Declaration of Penuell Mpapa Maduna, Minister of Justice and Constitutional Development, Republic of South Africa, reprinted in App. to Brief for Government of Commonwealth of Australia et al. as Amici Curiae 7a, ¶ 3.2.1 (emphasis deleted). The United States has agreed. See Letter of

current state of international law, looking to those sources we have long, albeit cautiously, recognized.

[After discussing various materials relied upon by Alvarez, the six members of the Court concluded:] It is enough to hold that a single illegal detention of less than a day, followed by the transfer of custody to lawful authorities and a prompt arraignment, violates no norm of customary international law so well defined as to support the creation of a federal remedy.

JUSTICE SCALIA, with whom THE CHIEF JUSTICE and JUSTICE THOMAS join, concurring in part and concurring in the judgment:

This Court seems incapable of admitting that some matters — *any* matters — are none of its business. . . . In today's latest victory for its Never Say Never Jurisprudence, the Court ignores its own conclusion that the ATS provides only jurisdiction, wags a finger at the lower courts for going too far and then — repeating the same formula the ambitious lower courts *themselves* have used — invites us to try again.

It would be bad enough if there were some assurance that future conversions of perceived international norms into American law would be approved by this Court itself. (Though we know ourselves to be eminently reasonable, self-awareness of eminent reasonableness is not really a substitute for democratic election.) But in this illegitimate lawmaking endeavor, the lower federal courts will be the principal actors; we review but a tiny fraction of their decisions. And no one thinks that all of them are eminently reasonable.

American law — the law made by the people's democratically elected representatives — does not recognize a category of activity that is so universally disapproved by other nations that it is automatically unlawful here, and automatically gives rise to a private action for money damages in federal court. That simple principle is what today's decision should have announced.

JUSTICE BREYER concurring in part and concurring in the judgment:

Today international law will sometimes similarly reflect not only substantive agreement as to certain universally condemned behavior but also procedural agreement that universal jurisdiction exists to prosecute a subset of that behavior. See Restatement § 404, and Comment *a*; International Law Association, Final Report on the Exercise of Universal Jurisdiction in Respect of Gross Human Rights Offences 2 (2000). That subset includes torture, genocide, crimes against humanity, and war crimes. See *id.*, at 5–8; see also, *e.g.*, *Prosecutor* v. *Furundzija*, Case No. IT-95-17/1-T,

---

William H. Taft IV, Legal Adviser, Dept. of State, to Shannen W. Coffin, Deputy Asst. Atty. Gen., Oct. 27, 2003, reprinted in id., at 2a. In such cases, there is a strong argument that federal courts should give serious weight to the Executive Branch's view of the case's impact on foreign policy. Cf. Republic of Austria v. Altmann, 541 U. S. 677, 701–2 (2004) (discussing the State Department's use of statements of interest in cases involving the Foreign Sovereign Immunities Act of 1976, 28 U. S. C. § 1602 et seq.).

¶¶ 155–156 (International Tribunal for Prosecution of Persons Responsible for Serious Violations of International Humanitarian Law Committed in Territory of Former Yugoslavia since 1991, Dec. 10, 1998); *Attorney Gen. of Israel* v. *Eichmann*, 36 I. L. R. 277 (Sup. Ct. Israel 1962).

The fact that this procedural consensus exists suggests that recognition of universal jurisdiction in respect to a limited set of norms is consistent with principles of international comity. That is, allowing every nation's courts to adjudicate foreign conduct involving foreign parties in such cases will not significantly threaten the practical harmony that comity principles seek to protect. That consensus concerns criminal jurisdiction, but consensus as to universal criminal jurisdiction itself suggests that universal tort jurisdiction would be no more threatening. Cf. Restatement §404, Comment *b*. That is because the criminal courts of many nations combine civil and criminal proceedings, allowing those injured by criminal conduct to be represented, and to recover damages, in the criminal proceeding itself. . . . Thus, universal criminal jurisdiction necessarily contemplates a significant degree of civil tort recovery as well.

Taking these matters into account, as I believe courts should, I can find no similar procedural consensus supporting the exercise of jurisdiction in this case. That lack of consensus provides additional support for the Court's conclusion that the ATS does not recognize the claim at issue here — where the underlying substantive claim concerns arbitrary arrest, outside the United States, of a citizen of one foreign country by another.

Notes

(1) *Sosa* cites to Section 702 of The Restatement (Third) of Foreign Relations Law of the United States in noting that a "state violates international law if, as a matter of state policy, it practices, encourages, or condones. . . . (e) prolonged arbitrary detention." Immunity problems aside, can someone picked up in Afghanistan, Iraq or elsewhere and held for months or years without being brought before a judge state a cause of action under the Alien Tort Statute?

(2) In footnote 21 of *Sosa* (reprinted above as footnote 12) there is a discussion of "deference to the political branches." How far can the executive go in asserting positions without upsetting the balance of power? *See* Beth Stephens, *Upsetting Checks and Balances: The Bush Administration's Efforts to Limit Human Rights Litigation*, 17 Harv. Hum. Rts. J. 169 (2004).

(3) For a discussion of *Filartiga* and its progeny from a wide spectrum of viewpoints, see Symposium Issue, 37 (3) Rutgers L. J. 623 (2006). Justice Breyer's *Sosa* concurrence underscores the conceptual connections here between crime and tort. For a more extended analysis of some of the connections, see Jaykumar A. Menon, *Blackstone and Criminal/Tort Law Hybridities*, 4 J. Int'l Crim. L. 372 (2006). For a comprehensive discussion of alien tort litigation, *see* Beth Stephens, et al., International Human Rights Litigation in US Courts (2d ed. 2008); Beth

Stephens, *The Curious History of the Alien Tort Statute*, 89 NOTRE DAME L. REV. 1467 (2014).

§ 1.04 Developments Post *Sosa*

Litigation under the Alien Tort Statute continued apace after *Sosa*, but it ran into another snag in *Kiobel v. Royal Dutch Petroleum Co.* decided in 2013. Plaintiffs found it was difficult to execute judgments against individual foreign defendants. Counsel began presenting cases against corporate entities that were not judgment-proof.

Kiobel v. Royal Dutch Petroleum Co.

Supreme Court of the United States
133 S. Ct. 1659 (2013)

ROBERTS, C.J., delivered the opinion of the Court, in which SCALIA, KENNEDY, THOMAS and ALITO, JJ., joined:

[Nigerian nationals residing in the United States sued under the ATS alleging that Dutch, British and Nigerian corporations aided and abetted the Nigerian Government in committing violations of international law in Nigeria. After the trial judge had dismissed some of the claims as too vague, the plaintiffs were left with allegations of arbitrary arrest and detention, crimes against humanity, and torture or cruel, inhuman or degrading treatment. The Second Circuit Court of Appeals dismissed the whole complaint on the basis that international law does not recognize corporate liability. The Supreme Court granted certiorari and ordered supplemental briefing on whether and under what circumstances courts may recognize a cause of action under the ATS for violations occurring within the territory of a sovereign other than the United States. The Court decided the case on this latter ground, leaving the corporate issue in limbo.]

The question here is not whether petitioners have stated a proper claim under the ATS, but whether a claim may reach conduct occurring in the territory of a foreign sovereign. Respondents contend that claims under the ATS do not, relying primarily on a canon of statutory interpretation known as the presumption against extraterritorial application. That canon provides that "[w]hen a statute gives no clear indication of an extraterritorial application, it has none," *Morrison v. National Australia Bank Ltd.*, 561 U. S. 247, 255 (2010) . . . , and reflects the "presumption that United States law governs domestically but does not rule the world," *Microsoft Corp. v. AT&T Corp.*, 550 U. S. 437, 454 (2007). . . .

Indeed, the danger of unwarranted judicial interference in the conduct of foreign policy is magnified in the context of the ATS, because the question is not what Congress has done but instead what courts may do. This Court in *Sosa* repeatedly stressed the need for judicial caution in considering which claims could be brought under the ATS, in light of foreign policy concerns. . . .

Nor does the historical background against which the ATS was enacted overcome the presumption against application to conduct in the territory of another sovereign. . . . [c]

Two notorious episodes involving violations of the law of nations occurred in the United States shortly before passage of the ATS. Each concerned the rights of ambassadors, and each involved conduct within the Union. In 1784, a French adventurer verbally and physically assaulted Francis Barbe Marbois — the Secretary of the French Legion [sic. Legation] — in Philadelphia. The assault led the French Minister Plenipotentiary to lodge a formal protest with the Continental Congress and threaten to leave the country unless an adequate remedy were provided. *Respublica v. De Longchamps*, 1 Dall. 111 (O. T. Phila. 1784); *Sosa*, *supra*, at 716–717, and n.11. And in 1787, a New York constable entered the Dutch Ambassador's house and arrested one of his domestic servants. See Casto, The Federal Courts' Protective Jurisdiction over Torts Committed in Violation of the Law of Nations, 18 Conn. L. Rev. 467, 494 (1986). At the request of Secretary of Foreign Affairs John Jay, the Mayor of New York City arrested the constable in turn, but cautioned that because "'neither Congress nor our [State] Legislature have yet passed any act respecting a breach of the privileges of Ambassadors,'" the extent of any available relief would depend on the common law. See Bradley, The Alien Tort Statute and Article III, 42 Va. J. Int'l L. 587, 641–642 (2002) (quoting 3 Dept. of State, The Diplomatic Correspondence of the United States of America 447 (1837)). The two cases in which the ATS was invoked shortly after its passage also concerned conduct within the territory of the United States. See *Bolchos*, 3 F. Cas. 810 (wrongful seizure of slaves from a vessel while in port in the United States); *Moxon*, 17 F. Cas. 942 (wrongful seizure in United States territorial waters). . . .

The third example of a violation of the law of nations familiar to the Congress that enacted the ATS was piracy. Piracy typically occurs on the high seas, beyond the territorial jurisdiction of the United States or any other country. See 4 Blackstone, *supra*, at 72 ("The offence of piracy, by common law, consists of committing those acts of robbery and depredation upon the high seas, which, if committed upon land, would have amounted to felony there"). This Court has generally treated the high seas the same as foreign soil for purposes of the presumption against extraterritorial application. See, *e.g.*, *Sale v. Haitian Centers Council, Inc.*, 509 U. S. 155–174 (1993) (declining to apply a provision of the Immigration and Nationality Act to conduct occurring on the high seas); *Argentine Republic v. Amerada Hess Shipping Corp.*, 488 U. S. 428, 440 (1989) (declining to apply a provision of the Foreign Sovereign Immunities Act of 1976 to the high seas). Petitioners contend that because Congress surely intended the ATS to provide jurisdiction for actions against pirates, it necessarily anticipated the statute would apply to conduct occurring abroad.

---

c. Notice how the Court's historical examples that follow underscore the connections between ATS claims and international criminal law. — Eds.

Applying U. S. law to pirates, however, does not typically impose the sovereign will of the United States onto conduct occurring within the territorial jurisdiction of another sovereign, and therefore carries less direct foreign policy consequences. Pirates were fair game wherever found, by any nation, because they generally did not operate within any jurisdiction. See 4 Blackstone, *supra*, at 71. We do not think that the existence of a cause of action against them is a sufficient basis for concluding that other causes of action under the ATS reach conduct that does occur within the territory of another sovereign; pirates may well be a category unto themselves. See *Morrison*, 130 S. Ct. at 2883 .... ("[W]hen a statute provides for some extraterritorial application, the presumption against extraterritoriality operates to limit that provision to its terms"); see also *Microsoft Corp.*, 550 U. S., at 455–456 ....

On these facts, all the relevant conduct took place outside the United States. And even where the claims touch and concern the territory of the United States, they must do so with sufficient force to displace the presumption against extraterritorial application. See *Morrison*, 130 S. Ct. at 2883–2888 .... Corporations are often present in many countries, and it would reach too far to say that mere corporate presence suffices. If Congress were to determine otherwise, a statute more specific than the ATS would be required.

The judgment of the Court of Appeals is affirmed.

Justice Breyer, with whom Justice Ginsburg, Justice Sotomayor and Justice Kagan join, concurring in the judgment.

I agree with the Court's conclusion but not with its reasoning....

Unlike the Court, I would not invoke the presumption against extraterritoriality. Rather, guided in part by principles and practices of foreign relations law, I would find jurisdiction under this statute where (1) the alleged tort occurs on American soil, (2) the defendant is an American national, or (3) the defendant's conduct substantially and adversely affects an important American national interest, and that includes a distinct interest in preventing the United States from becoming a safe harbor (free of civil as well as criminal liability) for a torturer or other common enemy of mankind. See *Sosa v. Alvarez-Machain*, 542 U. S. 692, 732 (2004) ("'[F]or purposes of civil liability, the torturer has become—like the pirate and slave trader before him—*hostis humani generis*, an enemy of all mankind.'" (quoting *Filartiga v. Pena-Irala*, 630 F. 2d 876,890 (CA2 1980) (alteration in original))). See also 1 Restatement (Third) of Foreign Relations Law of the United States §§ 402, 403, 404 (1986). In this case, however, the parties and relevant conduct lack sufficient ties to the United States for the ATS to provide jurisdiction.

[Referring to the majority's discussion of piracy, the opinion continues:] The majority cannot wish this piracy example away by emphasizing that piracy takes place on the high seas.... That is because the robbery and murder that make up piracy do not normally take place in the water; they take place on a ship. And a ship is like land, in that it falls within the jurisdiction of the nation whose flag it flies. See *McCulloch* v. *Sociedad Nacional de Marineros de Honduras*, 372 U. S. 10–21

(1963); 2 Restatement § 502, Comment *d* ("[F]lag state has jurisdiction to prescribe with respect to any activity aboard the ship"). Indeed, in the early 19th century Chief Justice Marshall described piracy as an "offenc[e] against the nation under whose flag the vessel sails, and within whose particular jurisdiction all on board the vessel are." *United States v. Palmer*, 3 Wheat. 610, 632 (1818). See *United States v. Furlong*, 5 Wheat. 184, 197 (1820) (a crime committed "within the jurisdiction" of a foreign state and a crime committed "in the vessel of another nation" are "the same thing").

The majority nonetheless tries to find a distinction between piracy at sea and similar cases on land. It writes, "Applying U. S. law to pirates . . . does not typically impose the sovereign will of the United States onto conduct occurring within the *territorial* jurisdiction of another sovereign and therefore carries less direct foreign policy consequences." *Ante*, at 10 (emphasis added). But, as I have just pointed out, "[a]pplying U. S. law to pirates" *does* typically involve applying our law to acts taking place within the jurisdiction of another sovereign. Nor can the majority's words "territorial jurisdiction" sensibly distinguish land from sea for purposes of isolating adverse foreign policy risks, as the Barbary Pirates, the War of 1812, the sinking of the *Lusitania*, and the Lockerbie bombing make all too clear.

The majority also writes, "Pirates were fair game wherever found, by any nation, because they generally did not operate within any jurisdiction." *Ibid.* I very much agree that pirates were fair game "wherever found." Indeed, that is the point. That is why we asked, in *Sosa*, who are today's pirates? Certainly today's pirates include torturers and perpetrators of genocide. And today, like the pirates of old, they are "fair game" where they are found. Like those pirates, they are "common enemies of all mankind and all nations have an equal interest in their apprehension and punishment." 1 Restatement § 404 Reporters' Note 1, p. 256 (quoting *In re Demjanjuk*, 612 F. Supp. 544, 556 (ND Ohio 1985) (internal quotation marks omitted)). See *Sosa*, *supra*, at 732. And just as a nation that harbored pirates provoked the concern of other nations in past centuries, . . . so harboring "common enemies of all mankind" provokes similar concerns today.

Thus the Court's reasoning, as applied to the narrow class of cases that *Sosa* described, fails to provide significant support for the use of any presumption against extraterritoriality; rather, it suggests the contrary. See also *ante*, at 10 (conceding and citing cases showing that this Court has "generally treated the high seas the same as foreign soil for purposes of the presumption against extraterritorial application").

In any event, as the Court uses its "presumption against extraterritorial application," it offers only limited help in deciding the question presented, namely "'under what circumstances the Alien Tort Statute . . . allows courts to recognize a cause of action for violations of the law of nations occurring within the territory of a sovereign other than the United States.'" 132 S. Ct. 472 (2012). The majority echoes in this jurisdictional context *Sosa*'s warning to use "caution" in shaping federal common-law causes of action. But it also makes clear that a statutory claim might sometimes "touch and concern the territory of the United States . . . with sufficient force to displace the presumption." It leaves for another day the determination of just when the presumption against extraterritoriality might be "overcome." . . . .

Under these circumstances, even if the New York office were a sufficient basis for asserting general jurisdiction, but see *Goodyear Dunlop Tires Operations, S. A. v. Brown*, 131 S. Ct. 2846 (2011), it would be farfetched to believe, based solely upon the defendants' minimal and indirect American presence, that this legal action helps to vindicate a distinct American interest, such as in not providing a safe harbor for an "enemy of all mankind." Thus I agree with the Court that here it would "reach too far to say" that such "mere corporate presence suffices."

Notes

(1) The incidents involving foreign diplomats mentioned early in the above extract from *Kiobel* had a significant impact on federal legislative power in the Constitution and on actions taken by the first Congress. Both took place under the Articles of Confederation when John Jay was Secretary of Foreign Affairs. The first involved two assaults on M. Marbois, who was the French Consul-General and Secretary of the French Legation in Philadelphia. The second involved an incursion into the Dutch Legation, residence of the Dutch Minister located in New York, and an arrest of the Minister's servant. (In early U.S. diplomatic practice, the U.S., like other republics, exchanged diplomatic representation at the level of "Minister" rather than Ambassador. The premises of the Minister were known as a Legation as opposed to an Embassy. The United States began changing this practice in the 1890s, with France and the U.K., but did not complete it for all countries until after the Second World War.) Jay, taking diplomatic heat from France and the Netherlands in the two incidents, had no federal criminal response and had to rely on the creativity of the Pennsylvania and New York courts. Pennsylvania came through with a common law crime under international law in the *De Longchamps* case. A federal solution was enshrined in Article I, Section 8, Clause 10, of the Constitution. The First Congress followed up with both the ATS and provisions in the Statutes at Large, Vol. 1, 1st Congress, 2nd Sess., Chapter 9 making it criminal to prosecute a writ or process against any ambassador or public minister or their domestic servants, to violate any safe conduct, or to "assault, strike, wound, imprison, or in any other manner infract the law of nations, by offering violence to the person of an ambassador or other public minister."

(2) A 5-4 majority of the Supreme Court narrowed further the impact of the ATS in *Jesner v. Arab Bank, PLC*, 138 S. Ct. 1386 (2018). It held that the statute did not extend to claims against foreign corporations, the question left open in *Kiobel*. Plaintiffs contended that a leading Jordanian bank with a branch in New York had contributed to breaches of the international law against terrorism financing by moving terrorist funds through the banking system. The majority insisted that international practice did not extend criminal, and thus tort, liability to corporations. For the dissent, Justice Sotomayor insisted that the majority was looking in the wrong place. The international obligation was for the U.S. to give effect to the

relevant international norms. How precisely it did so, including corporate liability, was a matter for the U.S. itself. She added that:

> Immunizing corporations that violate human rights from accountability undermines the system of accountability for law-of-nations violations that the First Congress endeavored to impose. It allows these entities to take advantage of the significant benefits of the corporate form and enjoy fundamental rights, see, e.g., *Citizens United v. Federal Election Comm'n*, 558 U.S. 310 (2010); *Burwell v. Hobby Lobby Stores, Inc.*, 134 S. Ct. 2751 (2014), without having to shoulder attendant fundamental responsibilities.

The saga continued in the consolidated cases of *Nestlé v. Doe I* and *Cargill Inc. v. Doe I*, 141 S, Ct. 1931 (2021). Here *domestic* U.S. corporations were charged with aiding and abetting child slavery, trafficking and forced labor in the chocolate industry in Côte D'Ivoire. The Supreme Court granted certiorari on the question whether domestic corporations are immune from liability under the Alien Tort Statute. However, eight members of the Court agreed with the relevant parts of an opinion by Justice Thomas that the extraterritoriality principle applied and that the case should be dismissed on that basis. The respondents argued that relevant decisions had been made at corporate offices in the U.S. Rejecting this, Justice Thomas insisted that "[nearly all the conduct that [respondents] say aided and abetted forced labor—providing training, fertilizer, tools and cash to overseas farms—occurred in Ivory Coast." He added that "allegations of general corporate activity—like decisionmaking—cannot alone establish domestic application of the ATS." In his lone dissent (there were several concurring opinions), Justice Alito insisted that he "would hold that if a particular claim may be brought under the ATS against a natural person who is a United Sates citizen, a similar claim may be brought against a domestic corporation." He thought that the extraterritoriality issue was not yet ready for decision. He would have remanded. Four others, Justices Gorsuch, Sotomayor, Breyer and Kagan, agreed with him on the domestic corporation point. Three Justices, Thomas, Gorsuch and Kavanaugh, would now confine ATS cases to the original three categories indicated by Blackstone and *Sosa*. Justice Sotomayor, joined by Breyer and Kagan, disagreed strongly with this position.

(3) The ATS cases involve civil actions for damages. Yet they have significant implications for much of the material that follows in this book. In the first place, they introduce the fundamental question of sources of international law, especially treaties and customary law, and the ways in which U.S. judges deal with such material. Secondly, the subject-matter of many of the torts alleged overlaps international criminal law norms (asserted or established) that will appear in later pages, such as: torture (still developing as an international crime when *Filartiga* was decided); cruel, inhuman and degrading treatment; genocide; crimes against humanity; kidnapping (or prolonged arbitrary detention); slavery and the slave trade; financing of terrorism; child labor; and trafficking in persons. Thirdly, the cases introduce us to the recurring themes of corporate responsibility and "secondary" liability such as that for aiding and abetting. (*See* Norman Farrell, *Attributing Criminal Liability to*

Corporate Actors: Some Lessons from the International Tribunals, 8 J. Int'l Crim. Just. 873 (2010).) Finally, they introduce the legislative presumption against extraterritoriality, a significant factor in international prosecutions, as later chapters will demonstrate.

(4) As the Supreme Court was limiting the extent to which the ATS could apply to corporate entities, international and transnational criminal law were inching in the other direction. *See, e.g.*, Carsten Stahn, *Liberals vs Romantics: Challenges of an Emerging Corporate International Criminal Law*, 50 Case W. Res. J. Int'l L. 91 (2018), and the many references therein (noting developments, inter alia, in the Special Tribunal for Lebanon, the African Union and the UN Convention on Transnational Organized Crime). Good accounts of the argument for the criminal responsibility of corporations in international and transnational law appear in Ronald Slye, *Corporations, Veils and International Criminal Liability*, 33 Brooklyn J. Int'l L. 955 (2008), and Mordechai Kremnitzer, *A Possible Case for Imposing Criminal Liability on Corporations in International Criminal Law*, 8 J. Int'l Crim. Just. 909 (2010).

Chapter 2

What Crimes Are International Crimes?

§ 2.01 The Concept of an International Crime and the Right and Duty to Suppress It

A. The Concept and Customary Obligations

Chapter One, in discussing the nature of "international criminal law," referenced phrases such as "international offenses," "international crimes," "crimes (or offenses) of international concern" (alias "transnational crimes") and "crimes (or offenses) under international law." Although there may be no totally agreed usage for many of these phrases, the term "international crime" is used here to encompass all of the above. The word "offenses" is used synonymously with the word "crimes," consistent with the understanding that the difference in words does not mean (as it does in some legal systems) that one is "more serious" than the other. The materials do distinguish between those crimes that are said to arise "under" international law and those which are "merely" of international concern or might better be described as "transnational."

It is, indeed, impossible to determine *a priori*, on the basis of its intrinsic characteristics, whether particular conduct constitutes an "international crime"—just as it is not possible in domestic law to distinguish criminal from non-criminal conduct on the basis of the intrinsic qualities of the conduct in question. In a domestic context, the only satisfactory definition of a crime, at least for legal purposes, is a formal definition to the effect that a crime is an act which the law prohibits and gives rise to certain consequences. Those consequences are roughly of two types. First, a criminal act triggers criminal proceedings, usually initiated and controlled by the state rather than by a private individual. Second, those proceedings involve punishment, as opposed to civil liability, as a possible outcome. In an international context as well, the only satisfactory definition of an "international crime" is one that focuses on whether the law, as revealed in state practice, prescribes that the conduct in question can or should give rise to criminal proceedings (whether national or international) and to penal consequences. "The practice of States is the conclusive determinant in the creation of international law (including international criminal law), and not the desirability of stamping out obnoxious patterns of human behaviour." Yoram Dinstein, *International Criminal Law*, 20 Israel L. Rev. 206, 221 (1985). That practice is often random on what it chooses to criminalize, reflecting the interests of major players at a particular time.

Under customary international law as it had developed before 1900, states were supposed to be responsible for treating foreigners admitted to their territory in accordance with international standards of justice. But similar rules did not apply to the treatment of a state's own citizens. As a result, a state might incur international liability not only for failing to accord an alien criminal defendant the minimal procedural guarantees discussed in chapter 19, but also for failing to use due diligence to prevent the commission of crimes of violence against aliens or for failing to take adequate steps to detect, prosecute, and punish the perpetrators of such crimes. Other customary international rules required states to repress crimes committed on their territory against foreign diplomats, and to suppress, by threatening criminal sanctions for, hostile expeditions launched from their territory against foreign governments with which they were not at war. Neutrality laws, for instance, represented an effort to implement these obligations. *See* Edward M. Wise, *Note on International Standards of Criminal Law and Administration, in* INTERNATIONAL CRIMINAL LAW 135, 152–59 (Gerhard O. W. Mueller & Edward M. Wise eds., 1965).

An example of a United States court acting consistently with such obligations was mentioned in *Filartiga v. Pena-Irala* and *Kiobel v. Royal Dutch Petroleum* [chap. 1]: the 1784 prosecution by Pennsylvania of an assault on M. Marbois, the French Consul-General to the United States and Secretary to the French Legation. The high-water mark in United States law in recognizing an obligation under international law to legislate and prosecute is perhaps the decision of the Supreme Court in *U.S. v. Arjona,* 120 U.S. 479 (1887). Arjona was charged with counterfeiting foreign currency and attacked the validity of the legislation making that an offense. The Court upheld the statute on the basis that it gave effect to the country's obligation, founded in international customary law, to criminalize. A fairly recent example of recognition of a duty of criminalization under customary law is the United Nations General Assembly resolution entitled Principles of International Co-operation in the Detection, Arrest, Extradition and Punishment of Persons Guilty of War Crimes and Crimes against Humanity, G.A. Res. 3074 (XXVIII), 28 U.N. GAOR, Supp. No. 30 at 78, U.N. Doc. A/9030 (1973). *See also* the fourth paragraph of the preamble to the Rome Statute of the International Criminal Court [chap. 22] which provides:

> *Affirming* that the most serious crimes of concern to the international community as a whole must not go unpunished and that their effective prosecution must be ensured by taking measures at the national level and by enhancing international cooperation.

Some of the customary law obligations have been converted into the treaty obligations of "suppression conventions," for example the obligations to suppress war crimes, in the Geneva Conventions of 1949 and the 1977 Protocols thereto, and the counterfeiting of currency, in the 1929 International Convention for the Suppression of the Counterfeiting of Currency, 112 L.N.T.S. 371. The customary law power to seize those who engaged in piracy on the high seas became part of a treaty obligation to co-operate to the fullest extent in their repression, in codifications of the law of the sea, culminating in Article 100 of the United Nations Convention on the Law of the Sea, U.N. Doc. A/CONF.62/122 (1982). Crimes against humanity, governed by customary law since the Nuremberg Trials, are now in effect subject to a suppression regime pursuant to the 1998 Rome Statute of the International Criminal Court [chap. 22]. The International Law Commission has drafted a Convention on Prevention and Punishment of Crimes against Humanity which awaits further diplomatic action in the General Assembly or a Diplomatic Conference. *See* Analytical Guide to the Work of the International Law Commission, Crimes against Humanity, *available at htttp://*www.legal.un.org. Custom has become a much less prominent source of suppression obligations.

B. The Suppression Conventions

In line with this trend, discussions of the circumstances under which states are obligated to enact municipal laws proscribing certain acts or omissions as "international crimes" have come to focus almost exclusively on obligations to criminalize that have their source in multilateral treaties, adopted usually under the auspices of global or regional international organizations. [*See, e.g.*, chaps. 4, 8, 9, 10, 11 & 12]. Early precedents of treaties with explicit requirements to criminalize were, in fact, bilateral rather than multilateral. *See, e.g.*, Treaty of Amity, Commerce and Navigation between Great Britain and the United States, signed at London, 19 November 1794, 52 Consol. T.S. 243 ("Jay's Treaty") article 20:

> [T]he Contracting Parties shall not only refuse to receive any Pirates into any of their Ports, Havens or Towns, or permit any of their Inhabitants to receive, protect, harbour, conceal or assist them in any manner, but will bring to condign punishment all such Inhabitants as shall be guilty of such acts or offences.

See also Additional Convention Between Great Britain and Portugal for the Prevention of the Slave Trade, signed at London, 28 July 1817, 67 Consol. T.S. 373, article III:

> His Most Faithful Majesty engages, within the space of two months of the ratifications of this present Convention, to promulgate in His Capital, and in other parts of His Dominions, as soon as possible, a Law, which shall prescribe the punishment of any of His subjects who may in the future participate in the illicit traffic of Slaves . . . and engages to assimilate, as much as possible, the Legislation of Portugal in this respect, to that of Great Britain.

See generally Jenny S. Martinez, The Slave Trade and the Origins of International Human Rights Law (2012); Roger S. Clark, *British Anti-Slave-Trade Treaties with African and Arab Leaders as Precursors of Modern Suppression Conventions, in* Histories of Transnational Criminal Law 129 (Neil Boister, Sabine Gless & Florian Jeβberger eds, 2021).

There were numerous other bilateral slave trade treaties throughout the first seventy years or so of the nineteenth century. They were followed by several multilateral ones. The bilateral treaties typically contained mutual rights for the parties to search vessels on the high seas flying the flag of the other and suspected of being engaged in the slave trade. Reality was that it was normally the British navy that did the searching. Slavery itself, as opposed to the trade, was an even tougher task to tackle. It was not until the 1926 League of Nations Convention to Suppress the Slave Trade and Slavery, 82 U.N.T.S. 51, that there was a general treaty suppression of the institution of slavery itself. Even then, the obligation followed the model set by many states in the nineteenth century—one of gradualism. The obligation was "[t]o bring about, progressively and as soon as possible, the complete abolition of slavery in all its forms." Underscoring the difficulties of securing actual enforcement of suppression obligations incurred by treaty or custom, research reported in 2020 suggests that many countries have not applied their criminal laws to the subject. *See* Katarina Schwarz, Jean Allain & Andrea Nicholson, *Slavery Is Not a Crime in Almost Half the Countries of the World—New Research*, The Conversation, 13 February 2020, *available at* https://theconversation.com/slavery-is-not-a-crime-in-almost-half-the-countries-of-the-world-new-research -115596.

Direct descendants of slave trade treaties are the bilateral agreements that the United States negotiated, beginning in 2004 with Liberia and Panama as part of the Proliferation Security Initiative. The Initiative is aimed at checking the flow of weapons of mass destruction, their delivery systems and related materials both from state and non-state actors. Just as the British started with Portugal and Spain, the largest flag-carriers of slaves, the proliferation agreements aim at the countries with the largest contemporary shipping registries. On these Proliferation treaties, see U.S. Department of State Fact Sheet, *The United States and Panama Proliferation Security Initiative Ship Boarding Agreement*, Fact Sheet No. 2004/525 of May 12, 2004. There are now such agreements with Liberia, Panama, the Marshall Islands, Croatia, Cyprus, Belize, Mongolia, Bahamas, St. Vincent and the Grenadines, and Antigua and Barbuda. Commenting on the treaty with Cyprus (which boasts the World's sixth largest ship registry by gross tonnage), the State Department noted that now "60 percent of the global commercial shipping fleet dead weight tonnage" was subject to the relevant procedures. Quoted in *Contemporary Practice of the United States, United States Concludes Additional Proliferation Security Initiative Ship Boarding Agreements*, 99 A.J.I.L. 919 (2005). An interesting jurisdictional feature of these treaties will be noted in Chapter 3. On the PSI in general, and some linkage to the nineteenth century slave trade treaties, see Michael Byers, *Policing the High Seas: The Proliferation Security Initiative*, 98 A.J.I.L. 526 (2004).

By one count, in 2008, there were at least 267 multilateral treaties that require states to treat certain conduct as criminal. The categories of crime covered by these treaties were said to include aggression, genocide, crimes against humanity, war crimes, crimes against U.N. and associated personnel, unlawful use of weapons, theft of nuclear materials, mercenarism, apartheid, slavery, torture, unlawful human experimentation, piracy, aircraft hijacking, unlawful acts against maritime navigation, unlawful acts against internationally protected persons, taking of civilian hostages, unlawful use of the mails, unlawful traffic in drugs, destruction or theft of national treasures, unlawful acts against the environment, international traffic in obscene materials, falsification and counterfeiting, unlawful interference with submarine cables, and bribery of foreign public officials. *See* M. Cherif Bassiouni, *International Crimes: The* Ratione Materiae *of International Criminal Law, in* 1 International Criminal Law 129 (M. Cherif Bassiouni ed., 3d ed. 2008). On such treaties in general, see M. Cherif Bassiouni, International Criminal Law Conventions with Excerpts of Relevant Penal Provisions (1997); Ethan Nadelmann, *Global Prohibition Regimes*, 44 Int'l Org. 479 (1990); Neil Boister, *Transnational Criminal Law?* 14 Europ. J. Int'l L. 953 (2003); Roger S. Clark, *Offenses of International Concern: Multilateral State Practice in the Forty Years Since Nuremberg*, 57 Nordic J. Int'l L. 49 (1988); Neil Boister, An Introduction to Transnational Criminal Law (2d ed. 2018); Robert J. Currie & Joseph Rikhof, International and Transnational Criminal Law (3d ed. 2020). Multilateral treaties of this ilk are useful both for generating a consensus on new areas that are ripe for international regulation and as a means of codifying/harmonizing areas where there is significant divergence in national approaches to the issues.

Multilateral suppression conventions continue to proliferate. Listing some of the significant current examples gives a good idea of the areas where States think it appropriate, at present, to develop principles of International Criminal Law. Among the relatively recent is the International Convention for the Suppression of Acts of Nuclear Terrorism, adopted by the United Nations General Assembly in G.A. Res. 59/290 of 13 April 2005 (in force July 7, 2007, ratified by the United States in 2015). (Work continues on a comprehensive terrorism suppression convention.) [*see* chap. 9]. The United Nations Convention against Transnational Organized Crime, adopted in 2000, G.A. Res. 55/25, U.N. GAOR, 55th Sess., Supp. No. 49, Vol. I, at 43, U.N. Doc. A/55/49 (2001), came into force in September 2003. Its Protocol to Prevent, Suppress and Punish Trafficking in Persons, Especially Women and Children, adopted at the same time, came into force in December 2003. Its contemporaneous Protocol against the Smuggling of Migrants by Land, Sea and Air came into force in January 2004. Its later Protocol against Illicit Manufacturing of and Trafficking in Firearms, Their Parts and Components and Ammunition, G.A. Res. 55/255, U.N. GAOR, 55th Sess., Supp. No. 49, Vol. III, at 12, U.N. Doc. A/55/49 (2001), came into force in July 2005. *See generally* Roger S. Clark, *The United Nations Convention against Transnational Organized Crime*, 50 Wayne L. Rev. 161 (2004). The 2003 United Nations Convention against Corruption, G.A. Res. 58/4, U.N. GAOR, 58th Sess., Supp. No. 49, U.N. Doc. A/58/49 (2004), came into force on December 14, 2005. It has resulted in a wide array of countries adopting legislation similar to the Foreign Corrupt Practices Act and instituting measures against domestic corruption. [*see* chap. 4]. In December 2006, the General Assembly adopted the International Convention for the Protection of All Persons from Enforced Disappearance, G.A. Res. 61/177, *available at* http://legal.un.org/avl/ha/icpped/icpped.html, in force 23 December 2010. This is the most recent multilateral suppression convention adopted under the auspices of the United Nations, although there are moves emanating from the International Law Commission to complete a Convention on the Prevention and Punishment of Crimes against Humanity. [chap. 23.] The Council of Europe Convention on Cybercrime [chap. 7], came into force on July 1, 2004. Note also, the Council of Europe's 2005 European Convention against Trafficking in Human Beings, EUROP. T. S., No. 196, and the Inter-American Convention against Terrorism of June 3, 2002, AG/RES.1840 (XXXII-0/02) (in force July 10, 2003).

The crimes that states are thereby obligated to repress can be classified in different ways. Perhaps the most useful scheme distinguishes between various types of international crime on the basis of the degree of official involvement in the conduct constituting the crime. Accordingly, international crime can be divided roughly into three general heads.

The first general heading includes violations of international norms directed toward restraining the conduct of state officials acting under color of law. (Offenses within this group are the ones that usually are singled out as well as constituting "crimes under international law" for which the individuals who commit them bear direct international responsibility.) The prototypical offenses under this heading are conventional war crimes such as violations of the Hague and Geneva Conventions. Also included are the two other categories of crime that were prosecuted at Nuremberg: crimes against peace (aggression) and crimes against humanity. These offenses comprise the "classical domain" of international criminal law. By extension, this heading also includes genocide, apartheid, disappearances and torture. With the possible exception of torture (as defined in the 1984 Convention on the subject [*see* chap. 10]) and aggression [*see* chap. 23], these crimes do not invariably require state action, nor do they always have to be connected to an armed conflict. But the underlying reason for international concern might be said to be that they all involve a misuse of power, of the monopoly of violence commanded by state or quasi-state officials.

The second heading includes the crimes associated with terrorist activities that have been the subject of the relatively recent conventions. [*see* chap. 9]. Unlike the first class of international crimes, the acts in question will not normally be committed directly by state or quasi-state officials. Nonetheless, a paramount reason for international concern has been the lax attitude, acquiescence sometimes seeming to amount to complicity, taken toward such offenses by states in which offenders have found refuge. The object of these conventions is to deny offenders "safe haven." Piracy is probably the prototypical offense under this heading.

The third heading covers other acts of private individuals that have been subjected to treaty prohibition because they involve either transnational traffic in illicit commodities (such as narcotics, persons, endangered species, weapons of mass destruction, small arms, and, at one time, obscene publications), or harm to a common or mutual interest of states requiring international cooperation for its effective suppression (for instance, money laundering, interference with submarine cables, unlawful use of the mails, or counterfeiting of currency). For a list of U.S. statutes implementing such treaties, see Edward M. Wise, *International Crimes and Domestic Criminal Law*, 38 DePaul L. Rev. 923, 956–66 (1989).

There is considerable variation in the language used in suppression treaties to impose an obligation to repress particular kinds of conduct. It can range from a statement by which the parties simply agree to cooperate in suppressing the conduct in question, to a more definite obligation to subject it to criminal sanctions and to prosecute and punish offenders. The preferred form of words in recent years has been the language first found in the 1970 Hague Convention on Unlawful Seizure of Aircraft, which requires states to make the offense defined in the convention a crime punishable by severe penalties under their own municipal law, to take steps to establish their jurisdiction over the offense, whether or not it was committed in their territory, and either to extradite an alleged offender who comes within their territory or else submit the case to the competent authorities for the purpose of prosecution. *See* M. Cherif Bassiouni & Edward M. Wise, Aut Dedere aut Judicare: The Duty to Extradite or Prosecute in International Law 8–9 (1995). In 2009 the International Law Commission began a project to analyze this practice under the rubric "Obligation to extradite or prosecute (*aut dedere aut judicare*)." The Commission gathered some useful material on state practice before abandoning the topic in 2014. *See* http://legal.un.org/ilc/texts/instruments/english/reports/7_6_2014.pdf; *see also Questions Relating to the Obligation to Prosecute or Extradite (Belgium v. Senegal)*, 2012 I.C.J. Rep. 422; Raphael van Steenberghe, *The Obligation to Extradite or Prosecute: Clarifying Its Nature*, 9 J. Int'l Crim. Just. 1089 (2011); Kriangsak Kittichaisaree, The Obligation to Extradite or Prosecute (2018).

United States practice in becoming party to suppression conventions is to first send the convention to the Senate to seek its advice and consent. Unless existing legislation suffices, such treaties typically require penal legislation to make them effective in U.S. law. Thus, if the advice and consent is forthcoming, they then go to the House and Senate for the enactment of the necessary legislation. Sometimes it takes a while for the process to play out. *See, e.g.*, Note, *United States Ratifies the International Convention for the Suppression of Acts of Nuclear Terrorism*, 109 Am J. Int'l L. 882 (2015). President George W. Bush had the Convention for the Suppression of Acts of Nuclear Terrorism signed on 15 September 2005, the day it was opened for signature. He submitted it to the Senate for its advice and consent nearly two years later. A little over another year later, 25 September 2008, the Senate gave its advice and consent. The Bush administration then proposed implementing legislation which contained two controversial (and strictly unnecessary) provisions on wiretapping and capital punishment. This held up enactment. The matter was carried over to the Obama administration, which was initially content to include the two controversial provisions. Ultimately, the legislation was adopted on 2 June 2015 as part of the USA Freedom Act 2015, without the two disputed provisions. The Obama administration deposited the instrument of ratification with the UN Secretary-General on 30 September 2015.

C. The Security Council as Suppressor

In addition to treaties, suppression obligations sometimes arise under customary international law or through the actions of international bodies, such as the UN Security Council. In Security Council Resolution 1373 of September 28, 2001, the Security Council responded dramatically to the September 11th attacks on the United States by adding itself to customary law and treaties as a source of suppression obligations. Notably, the Council, purporting to act under its powers dealing with the maintenance of peace in Chapter VII of the Charter:

> *Decides* that all States shall: . . . (b) Criminalize the wilful provision or collection, by any means, directly or indirectly, of funds by their nationals or in their territories with the intention that the funds should be used, or in the knowledge that they are to be used, in order to carry out terrorist acts. . . .

The obligation thus imposed is enforced vigorously through a monitoring Committee. The Resolution enacted, as Security Council law, the essence of a suppression convention that at the time had not garnered sufficient ratifications to come into force, the International Convention for the Suppression of Terrorist Financing, adopted by the General Assembly in 1999, G.A. Res. 54/109, U.N. GAOR, 54th Sess., Supp. No. 49, U.N. Doc. A/54/59 (2000). Even the main proponent of Resolution 1373, the United States, did not ratify the Convention until June of 2002. (The Convention is now overwhelmingly supported, having 189 parties.) Resolution 1373 presaged similar efforts to create obligations through the Council, thus bypassing the sometimes lengthy and arduous task of gleaning enough ratifications to bring suppression conventions into force, or the even harder task of achieving near universality for them. In 2004, for example, the Council adopted Resolution 1540, relating to the Proliferation Security Initiative which, also invoking Chapter VII of the Charter, requires all members of the United Nations to

> adopt and enforce appropriate effective laws which prohibit any non-State actor to manufacture, acquire, possess, develop, transport, transfer or use nuclear, chemical or biological weapons and their means of delivery, in particular for terrorist purposes, as well as attempts to engage in any of the foregoing activities, participate in them as an accomplice, assist or finance them.

Another example of the Security Council in law-making mode is S.C. Res. 1624 of 14 September 2005. It calls upon States to adopt such measures as may be necessary to prohibit by law incitement to terrorist acts, to prevent such conduct and to deny safe haven to any persons with respect to whom there is credible and relevant information giving serious reasons for considering that they have been guilty of such conduct.

On Resolution 1373 and the stringent efforts of the Committee and its bureaucratic arm, the Counter-Terrorism Executive Directorate, to enforce it, note the Committee's website at https://www.un.org/sc/ctc/about-us/. A striking feature of these enforcement efforts is preparation of detailed reports on individual countries' compliance records. *See also* Paul C. Szasz, *The Security Council Starts Legislating*, 96 A.J.I.L. 901 (2002); Eric Rosand, *Security Council Resolution 1373, the Counter-terrorism Committee, and the Fight Against Terrorism*, 97 A.J.I.L. 333 (2003); Ian Johnstone, *Legislation and Adjudication in the UN Security Council: Bringing Down the Deliberative Deficit*, 102 A.J.I.L. 275 (2008); *see also* Bruce Zagaris, *European Court of Human Rights Rules Against Switzerland and Enforcement of UN Security Council Sanctions*, 28 INT'L ENF. L. REP. 441 (2012).

Chapter VII of the United Nations Charter, which empowers the Security Council to act with respect to threats to the peace, breaches of the peace and acts of aggression, has generally been thought to be confined to dealing with specific concrete cases. Whether the power includes the general legislative power to affect all Members and require them to act, as these resolutions do, in their domestic legal order, is a matter of debate. Three especially perceptive discussions by participant diplomats in New York are Roberto Lavalle, *A Novel, if Awkward Exercise in International Law-Making: Security Council Resolution 1540*, 51 NETH. INT'L L. REV. 411 (2004); TAL BECKER, TERRORISM AND THE STATE: RETHINKING THE RULES OF STATE RESPONSIBILITY 121–31 (2006); Axel Marschik, *Legislative Powers of the Security Council, in* TOWARDS WORLD CONSTITUTIONALISM 457 (Ronald St. John MacDonald & Douglas M. Johnston eds., 2005). Marschik has some telling quotes from Member States which are not permanent members of the Security Council and which are less than enthusiastic about these developments. He also raises important points about the human rights dangers when the Council goes beyond norm creation to exercising quasi-judicial powers in individual cases. He notes, however, the substantial degree of practical acquiescence by States and explores the argument that, even if original moves by the Council were ultra vires, they might be "healed" by subsequent practice. On the human rights issues, and the difficulties of obtaining redress, see also Miša Zgonec-Rozej, Kadi v. Council of the EU and EC Commission: *European Court of Justice Quashes a Council of the EU Regulation Implementing UN Security Council Resolution*, 12 ASIL INSIGHT, *Issue 22* (2008). In Resolution 1617 of July 29, 2005, the Security Council asked the U.N. Secretary-General to cooperate with the International Criminal Police Organization (Interpol) "in developing effective tools to help a UN Security Council Al-Qaeda/Taliban committee to carry out its mandate concerning asset freezing, travel bans, and weapons embargos directed at groups and individuals associated with Al-Qaeda and the Taliban." Bruce Zagaris, *Interpol to Introduce New International Notice on Terrorist Financing and Travel*, 21 INT'L ENF. L. REP. 479 (2005). In agreeing to carry out this task, Interpol insisted that "the UN must ensure that persons who allege that their rights as contained in the Universal Declaration of Human Rights have been violated as a result of information duly processed by Interpol at the request of the Security Council through Interpol's channels pursuant to the present provisions will have recourse, whether direct or indirect, to a remedy pursuant to procedures as set forth in its 'Guidelines of the Committee for the Conduct of its Work'." *Id.*, at 480. The "1267 Committee", aimed at Al-Qaeda and Taliban, was the first of the Council's Committees to have power to make decisions involving specific individuals and groups. In 2009, the Security Council instituted the Office of Ombudsperson for its 1267 Committee. *See* http://www.un.org/en/sc/ombudsperson/. The Ombudsperson in an independent and impartial actor who reviews requests from individuals, groups, undertakings or entities seeking to be removed from the Council's Al-Qaida Sanctions Committee. The Human Rights Council has also appointed a Special Rapporteur on the promotion and protection of human rights and fundamental freedoms while countering terrorism. *See* the most recent Report by the Special Rapporteur, Fionnuala Ní Aoláin, U.N. Doc. A/HRC/46/36 (2021). The Special Rapporteur has been especially critical of the Council's discussion of the relationship between terrorism and organized crime, which fails to deal adequately with the human rights implications of this conflation. *See* Fionnuala Ní Aoláin, *A Post-Mortem on UN Security Council Resolution 2482 on Organized Crime and Counter-Terrorism*, Just Security, 12 August 2019, *available at* https://www.justsecurity.org/65777/a-post-mortem-on-un-security-council-resolution-2482-on-organized-crime-and-counter-terrorism/.

§ 2.02 Related Concepts

Some fundamental principles are of deep concern to the international community in general. For example, the Preamble to the Rome Statute of the International Criminal Court speaks of "the most serious crimes of concern to the international community as a whole." As such, many of the evils represented below will appear on a variety of lists related to international law.

A. Universal Jurisdiction

Universal jurisdiction, refers to the competence of any state which obtains custody of the offender to proscribe and punish an offense with which it has no connection based on territoriality or nationality and by which it has not been particularly affected. *See* Report of the Secretary-General prepared on the basis of comments and observations of Governments, The scope and application of the principle of universal jurisdiction, U.N. Doc. A/65/181 (2010). Universal jurisdiction authorizes states to apply their law to certain offenses. Whether they are obligated to do so as well is, in principle, a separate question. Some writers regard the question whether a particular offense is subject to universal jurisdiction as the determinative question of whether it is a "crime under international law."

The Restatement (Fourth) of The Foreign Relations Law of the United States § 413 (2018) indicates that the list of offenses subject to universal jurisdiction includes "genocide, crimes against humanity, war crimes, certain acts of terrorism, piracy, the slave trade, and torture, even if no specific connection exists between the state and the persons or conduct being regulated." *See also* Kenneth C. Randall, *Universal Jurisdiction under International Law*, 66 Tex. L. Rev. 785 (1988). The United States Congress has not always claimed universal jurisdiction in these cases. For example, it was not until the Genocide Accountability Act of 2007 that jurisdiction was extended to include the case where, after the conduct required for the offense occurs, the alleged offender is brought into or found in the United States, even if the conduct occurred outside the United States. In the Child Soldiers Accountability Act of 2008, universal jurisdiction was extended to the crime of recruitment or use of child soldiers.

While the United States now exercises universal jurisdiction over genocide, it does not criminalize crimes against humanity at all and, aside from the recent legislation on child soldiers, does not exercise universal jurisdiction over war crimes in its ordinary courts. Compare the potentially vast jurisdiction of a universal nature exercised by Military Commissions in Guantanamo *infra* § 9.03.

Most commentators agree that there is universal jurisdiction over pirates. The late Professor Alfred Rubin, however, fought a lonely rearguard action, arguing that the authorities and practice do not support even this. *See generally* ALFRED P. RUBIN, THE LAW OF PIRACY (2d ed. 1998). Some recent developments on prosecution of pirates will be noted in Chapter 9. The 1982 Convention on the Law of the Sea, *supra*, Article 105, contemplates universal jurisdiction over pirates. Any State may seize a pirate ship and decide upon the penalty to be imposed. On the other hand, while the Convention permits a state to "visit" a ship suspected of being engaged in the slave trade and some other lesser crimes (Article 110), and to free slaves, penal jurisdiction over slave traders seems to remain with the flag state (Article 99). Indeed, the RESTATEMENT view (made operative in some national legislation) that there is universal jurisdiction over slave traders rests mainly on the view of commentators. It is not supported by the specific language of any of the slave trade treaties, which speak to flag or nationality jurisdiction. *See* Roger S. Clark, *Steven Spielberg's Amistad and Other Things I Have Thought About in the Past Forty Years: International (Criminal) Law, Conflict of Laws, Insurance and Slavery*, 30 RUTGERS L.J. 371, 390 n.55 (1999). The United States, for example, exercises flag, territorial and nationality jurisdiction over the slave trade as such. *See* 18 U.S.C. § 1585 (seizure, detention, transportation or sale of slaves by citizens, residents or those on U.S.-flagged ships); § 1586 (citizens or residents serving on slave vessels). In 2008, however, a banner year in the U.S. for universal jurisdiction, Congress extended extraterritorial (and effectively universal) jurisdiction in 18 U.S.C. § 1583 (enticement into slavery) and § 1584 (sale into involuntary servitude).

The characterization of pirates as *hostes humani generis* — enemies of mankind — noted in *Filartiga* is often said to be the basis for the authority given to all states to capture and try pirates. In one view, the reason for universal jurisdiction over piracy is that pirates directly violate international law. In another view, international law simply authorizes states to subject piracy to their own municipal laws on the basis of universal jurisdiction. The prosecution takes place under municipal law. Universal jurisdiction serves to permit states with powerful navies to take action against pirate vessels without violating the principle that normally prohibits interference with foreign ships on the high seas.

The same difference of opinion has sometimes been expressed with regard to war crimes. In one view, the international rules regarding war crimes do no more than to create a basis for the exercise of an extraordinary jurisdiction on the part of belligerents to prosecute in their own courts enemy soldiers who commit violations of the laws of war. Insofar as criminal responsibility attaches for the commission of a war crime, it attaches only under national law. In another view, the punishment of war crimes always has proceeded on the assumption that the laws of war are binding not only on states but also on their individual nationals. In prosecuting violations of the laws of war, a state acts not merely to enforce its own law, but to enforce international law: "what is punished is the breach of international law; and the case is thus different from the punishment, under national law, of acts in respect of which international law gives a liberty to all states to punish, but does not itself declare criminal." IAN BROWNLIE, PRINCIPLES OF PUBLIC INTERNATIONAL LAW 303 (6th ed. 2003). Since the Nuremberg Trial, the view that they are crimes under international law has become the prevailing one with respect to crimes against humanity and genocide as well as violations of the laws of war.

The RESTATEMENT (FOURTH) includes "certain acts of terrorism" in its list of crimes over which there is universal jurisdiction. Today, in the wake of the *Pinochet* case [*see* chap. 14], the offense of torture has a prominent place on some lists. Whether this is always the same kind of "universal jurisdiction" as that over pirates is debated. The tendency in treaties modeled on the 1970 Hague Convention on Unlawful Seizure of Aircraft (including the Torture Convention) is to require a state to assert jurisdiction over an offender "present" in its territory ("found" there in some formulations) who has not been extradited to another state having closer jurisdictional ties to the offense. This is "secondary," "fallback," "subsidiary" or "last resort" jurisdiction, perhaps better characterized as "custodial" jurisdiction, rather than "true" universal jurisdiction.

Does the obligation to try a hijacker or torturer who happens to come within the jurisdiction extend to an obligation (or at least a right) to actively seek someone out in another state, for example by extradition, so that he or she might stand trial on the basis of universal jurisdiction? The underlying facts in such situations are described in recent literature, in what seems to be new usage of the words, as efforts at "universal jurisdiction *in absentia*." The accused was "absent" at the initiation of the proceedings, but he was expected to be "present" for the trial. Perhaps the problem does not arise only in respect of the line of treaties modeled on the Hague Convention. For example, the United Kingdom/United States Extradition Treaty of 1931, 47 Stat., includes in its list of extraditable offenses, "[p]iracy against the law of nations." The treaty is still in force between the U.S. and a number of former British colonies. Could a disinterested state whose shipping or nationals have not been victimized obtain extradition of a pirate in order to exercise universal jurisdiction? Does "pure" universal jurisdiction support an extradition request for one who is "absent" the jurisdiction? Consider the following case.

Case Concerning the Arrest Warrant of 11 April 2000 (D.R. Congo v. Belgium)

International Court of Justice
2002 I.C.J. Rep. 3

[A Belgian investigating magistrate issued an international arrest warrant against the incumbent Minister of Foreign Affairs of the Congo, Mr. Abdulaye Yerodia Ndombasi, alleging grave breaches of the Geneva Conventions of 1949 and the Additional Protocols thereto and crimes against humanity. Mr. Yerodia was not in Belgium when the warrant was issued. This resulted in the Belgian proceedings being described as an attempt at "universal jurisdiction *in absentia*." There was no indication that Belgium intended to try the Minister in his absence — they wanted his extradition. The Democratic Republic of the Congo (the Congo) instituted proceedings in the International Court of Justice against Belgium. In its initial Application, Congo contended that Belgium violated the "principle that a State may not exercise authority on the territory of another State," the "principle of sovereign equality among all Members of the United Nations," as well as the "diplomatic immunity of the Minister of Foreign Affairs. . . ." At argument, the Congo concentrated only on the immunity ground, on which it was successful [*see* chap. 14, excerpts on immunity]. The majority of the Court avoided the jurisdictional issue; but a minority dealt with this issue either in separate (concurring) or dissenting opinions.

The Court's Judgment described the legal and factual situation thus:]

15. In the arrest warrant, Mr. Yerodia is accused of having made speeches inciting racial hatred during the month of August 1998. The crimes with which Mr. Yerodia was charged were punishable in Belgium under the Law of 16 June 1993 "concerning the Punishment of Grave Breaches of the Geneva Conventions of 12 August 1949 and of Protocols I and II of 8 June 1977 Additional Thereto", as amended by the Law of 19 February 1999 "concerning the Punishment of Serious Violations of International Humanitarian Law" (hereinafter referred to as the "Belgian Law").

Article 7 of the Belgian Law provides that "The Belgian courts shall have jurisdiction in respect of the offences provided for in the present Law, wheresoever they may have been committed". In the present case, according to Belgium, the complaints that initiated the proceedings as a result of which the arrest warrant was issued emanated from 12 individuals all resident in Belgium, five of who were of Belgian nationality. It is not contested by Belgium, however, that the alleged acts to which the arrest warrant relates were committed outside Belgian territory, that Mr. Yerodia was not a Belgian national at the time of those acts, and that Mr. Yerodia was not in Belgian territory at the time that the arrest warrant was issued and circulated. That no Belgian nationals were victims of the violence that was said to have resulted from Mr. Yerodia's alleged offences was also uncontested.

Article 5, paragraph 3, of the Belgian law further provides that "[i]mmunity attaching to the official capacity of a person shall not prevent the application of the present Law."

16. At the hearings, Belgium further claimed that it offered "to entrust the case to the competent authorities [of the Congo] for enquiry and possible prosecution", and referred to a certain number of steps which it claimed to have taken in this regard from September 2000, that is, before the filing of the Application instituting proceedings. The Congo for its part stated the following: "We have scant information concerning the form [of these Belgian proposals]." It added that "these proposals . . . appear to have been made very belatedly, namely *after* an arrest warrant against Mr. Yerodia had been issued."

Joint Separate Opinion of Judges Higgins (United Kingdom), Kooijmans (the Netherlands) and Buergenthal (United States)

[The three Judges noted that Belgium, and many writers on the subject, "find support for the exercise of universal criminal jurisdiction *in absentia* in the *Lotus* case." They referred to the "famous dictum" that

. . . .

> Far from laying down a general prohibition to the effect that States may not extend the application of their laws and the jurisdiction of their courts to persons, property and acts outside their territory, it leaves them in this respect a wide measure of discretion which is only limited in certain cases by prohibitive rules; as regards other cases, every State remains free to adopt the principles which it regards as best and most suitable.

They continued:]

50. The application of this celebrated dictum would have clear attendant dangers in some fields of international law. (See, on this point, Judge Shahabudeen's dissenting opinion in the case concerning *Legality of the Threat or Use of Nuclear Weapons, Advisory Opinion, I.C.J. Reports 1996*, pp. 394–396.) Nevertheless, it represents a continuing potential in the context of jurisdiction over international crimes.

51. That being said, the dictum represents the high-water mark of *laissez-faire* in international relations, and an era that has been significantly overtaken by other tendencies. The underlying idea of universal jurisdiction properly so-called (as in the case of piracy, and possibly in the Geneva Conventions of 1949), as well as the *aut dedere aut prosequi* variation, is a common endeavour in the face of atrocities. The series of multilateral treaties with their special jurisdictional provisions reflect a determination by the international community that those engaged in war crimes, hijacking, hostage taking, torture should not go unpunished. Although crimes against humanity are not yet the object of a distinct convention, a comparable international indignation at such acts is not to be doubted. And those States and academic writers who claim the right to act unilaterally to assert a universal criminal jurisdiction over persons committing such acts, invoke the concept of acting

as "agents for the international community". This vertical notion of the authority of action is significantly different from the horizontal system of international law envisaged in the *"Lotus"* case.

At the same time, the international consensus that the perpetrators of international crimes should not go unpunished is being advanced by a flexible strategy, in which newly-established international criminal tribunals, treaty obligations and national courts all have their part to play. We reject the suggestion that the battle against impunity is "made over" to international treaties and tribunals, with national courts having no competence in such matters. Great care has been taken when formulating the relevant treaty provisions not to exclude other grounds of jurisdiction that may be exercised on a voluntary basis. (*See* Article 4 (3) Hague Convention for the Suppression of Unlawful Seizure of Aircraft, 1970; Article 5 (3) International Convention Against Taking of Hostages, 1979; Article 5 (3) Convention Against Torture; Article 9, Statute of the International Criminal Tribunal for the Former Yugoslavia and Article 19, Rome Statute of the International Criminal Court.)

52. We may thus agree with the authors of the Oppenheim, 9th Edition, at page 998, that:

> "While no general rule of positive international law can as yet be asserted which gives to states the right to punish foreign nationals for crimes against humanity in the same way as they are, for instance, entitled to punish acts of piracy, there are clear indications pointing to the gradual evolution of a significant principle of international law to that effect." . . .

53. This brings us once more to the particular point that divides the Parties in this case: is it a precondition of the assertion of universal jurisdiction that the accused be within the territory?

54. Considerable confusion surrounds this topic, not helped by the fact that legislators, courts and writers alike frequently fail to specify the precise temporal moment at which any such requirement is said to be in play. Is the presence of the accused within the jurisdiction said to be required at the time the offence was committed? At the time the arrest warrant is issued? Or at the time of the trial itself? An examination of national legislation, cases and writings reveals a wide variety of temporal linkages to the assertion of jurisdiction. This incoherent practice cannot be said to evidence a precondition to any exercise of universal criminal jurisdiction. The fact that in the past the only clear example of an agreed exercise of universal jurisdiction was in respect of piracy, *outside of any territorial jurisdiction*, is not determinative. The only prohibitive rule (repeated by the Permanent Court in the *"Lotus"* case) is that criminal jurisdiction should not be exercised, without permission, within the territory of another State. The Belgian arrest warrant envisaged the arrest of Mr. Yerodia in Belgium, or the possibility of his arrest in third States at the discretion of the States concerned. This would in principle seem to violate no existing prohibiting rule of international law.

55. In criminal law, in particular, it is said that evidence-gathering requires territorial presence. But this point goes to *any* extraterritoriality, including those that are well established and not just to universal jurisdiction.

56. Some jurisdictions provide for trial *in absentia*; others do not. If it is said that a person must be within the jurisdiction at the time of the trial itself, that may be a prudent guarantee for the right of fair trial but has little to do with bases of jurisdiction recognized under international law.

57. On what basis is it claimed, alternatively, that an arrest warrant may not be issued for non-nationals in respect of offences occurring outside the jurisdiction? The textual provisions themselves of the 1949 Geneva Convention and the First Additional Protocol give no support to this view. The great treaties on aerial offences, hijacking, narcotics and torture are built around the concept of *aut dedere aut prosequi. Definitionally, this envisages presence on the territory.* There cannot be an obligation to extradite someone you choose not to try unless that person is within your reach. National legislation, enacted to give effect to these treaties, quite naturally also may make mention of the necessity of the presence of the accused. These sensible realities are critical for the obligatory exercise of *aut dedere aut prosequi* jurisdiction, but cannot be interpreted *a contrario so as to exclude a* voluntary exercise of a universal jurisdiction.

58. If the underlying purpose of designating certain acts as international crimes is to authorize a wide jurisdiction to be asserted over persons committing them, there is no rule of international law (and certainly not the *aut dedere* principle) which makes illegal co-operative overt acts designed to secure their presence within a State wishing to exercise jurisdiction. . . .

59. If, as we believe to be the case, a State may choose to exercise a universal criminal jurisdiction *in absentia*, it must also ensure that certain safeguards are in place. They are absolutely essential to prevent abuse and to ensure that the rejection of impunity does not jeopardize stable relations between States.

No exercise of criminal jurisdiction may occur which fails to respect the inviolability or infringes the immunities of the person concerned. We return below to certain aspects of this facet, but will say at this juncture that commencing an investigation on the basis of which an arrest warrant may later be issued does not of itself violate those principles. The function served by the international law of immunities does not require that States fail to keep themselves informed.

A State contemplating bringing criminal charges based on universal jurisdiction must first offer to the national State of the prospective accused person the opportunity itself to act upon the charges concerned. The Court makes reference to these elements in the context of this case at paragraph 16 of its Judgment.

Further, such charges may only be laid by a prosecutor or *juge d'instruction* who acts in full independence, without links to or control by the government of that State. Moreover, the desired equilibrium between the battle against impunity and the promotion of good inter-State relations will only be maintained if there are some special circumstances that do require the exercise of an international criminal jurisdiction and if this has been brought to the attention of the prosecutor or *juge d'instruction*. For example, persons related to the victims of the case will have requested the commencement of legal proceedings.

Judge *Ad Hoc* Van den Wyngaert (appointed by Belgium), relying in part on the *Lotus* case, argued that universal jurisdiction was appropriate in the circumstances.

On the other hand, the President of the Court, Judge Guillaume of France, asserted forcefully that

> . . . [I]nternational law knows only one true case of universal jurisdiction: piracy. Further, a number of international conventions provide for the establishment of subsidiary universal jurisdiction for the purposes of trial of certain offenders arrested on national territory and not extradited to a foreign country. Universal jurisdiction *in absentia* as applied in the present case is unknown to international law.

In his view, times had changed since the *Lotus* case. Territoriality may today have even more force:

> The adoption of the United Nations Charter proclaiming the sovereign equality of States, and the appearance on the international scene of new States, born of decolonization, have strengthened the territorial principle. International criminal law has itself undergone considerable development and constitutes today an impressive legal *corpus*. It recognized in many situations the possibility, or indeed the obligation, for a State other than that on whose territory the offence was committed to confer jurisdiction on its courts to prosecute the authors of certain crimes where they are present on its territory. International criminal courts have been created. But at no time has it been envisaged that jurisdiction should be conferred upon the courts of every State in the world to prosecute such crimes, wherever their authors and victims and irrespective of the place where the offender is to be found. To do this would, moreover, risk creating total judicial chaos. It would also be to encourage the arbitrary for the benefit of the powerful, purportedly acting as agent for an ill-defined "international community". Contrary to what is advocated by certain publicists, such a development would represent not an advance in the law but a step backward.

Judges Rezak (Brazil) and Ranjeva (Madagascar) took much the same position as President Guillaume. (Judge Ranjeva was skeptical about applying the *Lotus* to support Belgium.) Judge *Ad Hoc* Bula-Bula (appointed by the Congo) emphasized the colonial history and was opposed to universal jurisdiction. Judge Oda (Japan), who believed that there was no genuine legal dispute between the parties and that the Court should not have decided anything, suggested in dissent that "the Court has shown wisdom in refraining from taking a definitive stance [on universal jurisdiction] as the law is not sufficiently developed and, in fact, the Court is not requested in the present case to take a decision on this point."

Notes

(1) Are the "certain safeguards" asserted in paragraph 59 of the Joint Separate Opinion useful? Do they render the exercise of universal jurisdiction more palatable? Is a national court exercising such jurisdiction acting as an agent of the international community? Is the requirement that the national State of the accused must first be given an opportunity to act a variation on the doctrine of "complementarity," enshrined in the Rome Statute of the International Criminal Court [chap. 22]? Does the Belgian offer to "entrust the case to the competent [Congolese] authorities" mentioned in paragraph 16 of the Court's Judgment amount to state practice supporting a complementarity requirement? In *A Full Stop to Amnesty in Argentina: The Simon Case*, 3 J. Int. Crim. Just. 1106 (2005), Christine A. E. Bakker discusses a decision of the Argentine Supreme Court holding that amnesty laws adopted in the 1980s to shield those responsible for human rights violations during the 1976–1983 "Dirty War" were unconstitutional and void. Bakker notes, at 1118, that some of the judges made reference to universal jurisdiction exercised by third states in respect of events in Argentina:

> They stated that the prosecution and trial of Argentineans by foreign courts based on universal jurisdiction resulted from non-compliance with Argentina's international obligations. This reality required urgent action. It was argued that the extradition requests presented by third states generate the legal option either to exercise the state's territorial jurisdiction, or to admit its incapacity to do so, and thus to renounce an attribution of national sovereignty, ceding jurisdiction over facts committed on Argentine territory by Argentine citizens. This factor may certainly have contributed to the perceived necessity to annul the amnesty laws. (Footnotes omitted.)

While welcoming the demise of the amnesty laws, Bakker adds that "the ability of third states to exercise universal jurisdiction will only end if the relevant crimes are effectively investigated and prosecuted by Argentine Courts *in practice*." *Id.* (Emphasis in original). She continues:

> Third states still have the duty to prosecute authors of international crimes — as confirmed in the Preamble of the Rome Statute — and the international rules on universal jurisdiction continue to apply. In accordance with the emerging customary rule that priority should be given to prosecution by the territorial state or the state of nationality of the accused, investigations or prosecutions launched before domestic courts will indeed bar the exercise of universal jurisdiction for the same acts. However, the decisive factor determining the competent forum is not the absence of amnesty laws, but

> rather the actual exercise of territorial jurisdiction by the Argentine courts. *Id.*

See generally Cedric Ryngaert, *Applying the Rome Statute's Complementarity Principle: Drawing Lessons from the Prosecution of Core Crimes by States Acting Under the Complementarity Principle*, 19 CRIM. L.F. 153 (2008).

(2) Comment e to § 413 of the RESTATEMENT (FOURTH) OF THE FOREIGN RELATIONS LAW OF THE UNITED STATES (2018) notes, at 212, that:

> Some states impose additional limits on exercises of universal jurisdiction, such as: (1) the territorial presence of the suspect before initiation of a criminal investigation or commencement of trial proceedings; (2) commission of the crime during a specified conflict or time period; (3) authorization or approval of the prosecution by an executive or judicial body; and (4) deference to the territorial state or the suspect's state of nationality if either state is willing and able to prosecute (i.e., complementarity). Considerations of international comity, rather than the obligations of international law, appear to motivate these limitations.

The RESTATEMENT proceeds on the basis of a distinction between jurisdiction to prescribe (i.e., to apply a state's own law to a topic), jurisdiction to enforce (typically through the executive branch), and jurisdiction to adjudicate (through the judiciary or administrative procedures). The "limits" in this Comment appear to be best characterized as "voluntary" curbs on adjudicative jurisdiction.

(3) Which way does the decolonization argument mentioned by President Guillaume and others cut? Belgium was the former colonial power of the Congo. Compare the relationship between Turkey and France as a result of the 1923 Convention of Lausanne (the "Convention respecting Conditions of Residence and Business and Jurisdiction"). Article 15 of that treaty was noted by the PCIJ in the context of relations between France and Turkey being governed by "international law." The Convention was a companion to the Treaty of Peace between Turkey on the one hand and the British Empire, France, Italy, Japan, Greece, Roumania and the Serb-Croat-Slovene State on the other. Essentially, it dealt with the ramifications of ending, in the Peace Treaty, the "capitulations" regime. Capitulation treaties meant that some of the Western Powers, France in particular, in addition to holding trade advantages, exercised extraterritorial jurisdiction within Turkey in respect of their own citizens and some religious minorities who were exempted from the application of Ottoman criminal law. Turkey, no doubt, regarded itself as partially colonized. Now relations between France and Turkey, including the fate of M. Demons, were to be "decided in accordance with the principles of international law."

(4) For useful information on state practice concerning universal jurisdiction, *see* AMNESTY INTERNATIONAL, UNIVERSAL JURISDICTION: A PRELIMINARY SURVEY OF LEGISLATION AROUND THE WORLD — 2012 UPDATE (2012), *available at* https://www.amnesty.org/en/documents/ior53/019/2012/en/. The Amnesty study is flawed in not including examples of assertions of universal jurisdiction over the crime of

aggression. *See also* the Reports of the Secretary-General of the United Nations prepared on the basis of information and observations received from Member States on the scope and application of the principle of universal jurisdiction, U.N. Doc. A/65/181 (2010), A/66/93 and Add.1 (2011) and A/67/116 (2012). The U.N. General Assembly has engaged in an inconclusive discussion of the subject.

(5) Universal jurisdiction is controversial. Many in the human rights community see it as an essential tool in preventing impunity for human rights violations. Officials on the receiving end of prosecutions see it as a basic attack on sovereignty. *See generally* LUC REYDAMS, UNIVERSAL JURISDICTION: INTERNATIONAL AND MUNICIPAL LEGAL PERSPECTIVES (2003); UNIVERSAL JURISDICTION: NATIONAL COURTS AND THE PROSECUTION OF SERIOUS CRIMES UNDER INTERNATIONAL LAW (Stephen Macedo ed., 2004) (pro); Henry Kissinger, *The Pitfalls of Universal Jurisdiction*, 80 FOR. AFF. 86 (2001) (con); Mohamed M. El Zeidy, *Universal Jurisdiction in Absentia: Is It a Legal Valid Option for Repressing Heinous Crimes?* 37 INT'L LAW. 835 (2003) (nuanced). The Macedo book contains the "Princeton Principles on Universal Jurisdiction," drafted by a group of academics and jurists meeting in Princeton in January 2000. The Principles embrace universal jurisdiction enthusiastically. Principle 3 of the Principles asserts that with respect to "serious crimes under international law" (including piracy, slavery, war crimes, crimes against peace, crimes against humanity, genocide and torture) "national judicial organs may rely on universal jurisdiction even if their national legislation does not specifically provide for it." Macedo ed., *supra* at 22. On the other hand, one practical effect of the decision of the British House of Lords in *R. v. Jones (Margaret)*, [2006] U.K.H.L. 16, [chap.1], is that, there being no common law crime of aggression under English law, aggression could not be prosecuted in England on a universal jurisdiction basis. For a very useful study of the politics of universal jurisdiction (and some doubts about it as a panacea for avoiding impunity), *see* Máximo Langer, *The Diplomacy of International Jurisdiction: The Political Branches and the Transnational Prosecution of International Crimes*, 105 AM. J. INT'L L. 1 (2011).

(6) In 2003, following a United States boycott of the main Belgian seaport and to threats to move the NATO headquarters from Belgium to Poland, the Belgian legislature abandoned universal jurisdiction. Now in respect of extraterritorial crime, the accused must be a Belgian citizen or normally resident in Belgium, or the victim must be a Belgian national or have resided in Belgium for at least three years. The legislation also incorporates immunity provisions derived from the *Yerodia* case. *See generally* Stefaan Smis & Kim Van Der Borght, *Introductory Note to Belgium's Amendment to the Law of June 16, 1993 (As Amended by the Law of February 10, 1999) Concerning the Punishment of Grave Breaches of Humanitarian Law*, 42 I.L.M. 740 (2003). Spain too, under pressure from the U.S., Israeli and Chinese Governments, modified its "pure" form of universal jurisdiction in 2009 to require that there needs to be a "connection to national interests," for example through the perpetrator being on Spanish territory or the victims being Spanish. *See* José Elías Esteve Moltó, *The "Great Leap Forward" to Impunity: Burying Universal Jurisdiction in Spain and*

Returning to the Paradigm of Human Rights as "domaine reserve" of States, 13 J. Int'l Crim. Just. 1121 (2015).

(7) Hays Butler notes that in legislation aimed at giving effect to the 1998 Rome Statute of the International Criminal Court, some states have endeavored to "complement" the Court by providing their courts with versions of universal (or at least extraterritorial) jurisdiction over the crimes contained in the Statute. Hays Butler, *The Growing Support for Universal Jurisdiction in National Legislation*, Chap. 3 *in* Macedo ed., *supra* p. 54 at 67. A number of them, however, require the accused to have some connection with the forum. For an example of a state taking universal jurisdiction regardless of any connection to the forum in legislating for the International Criminal Court, *see* Juliet Hay, *Implementing the ICC Statute in New Zealand*, 2 J. Int'l Crim. Just. 191 (2004). Note that, depending on the applicable extradition treaty, such universal jurisdiction may support an extradition request; jurisdiction based on the presence of the accused will almost certainly not.

(8) A sub-category of universal jurisdiction is the "extradite or prosecute" provision in many modern suppression conventions. *See* discussion of such provisions in § 2.01[B] *supra* and in paragraph 57 of the Joint Separate Opinion of Judges Higgins, Kooijmans and Burgenthal in the *Arrest Warrant Case, supra.*

(9) In his concurring opinion in *Sosa, supra* § 1.03, Justice Breyer, noting a Comment in the Restatement (Third) of the Foreign Relations Law of the United States (1987), suggested that the "consensus" that the exercise of universal criminal jurisdiction is appropriate in certain instances "suggests that tort jurisdiction would be no more threatening." The ATS cases can be viewed as a form of universal civil jurisdiction. The authors of the Restatement (Fourth) of the Foreign Relations Law of the United States (2018) are less enthusiastic. *See especially* Reporter's Note 4 to § 413, at 215-6. The Note references dissenting international cases and diplomatic complaints about ATS cases.

B. State Criminal Responsibility

States incur international responsibility if they violate international law. At one time it was fashionable to speak of any breach of international law as if it constituted an offense which subjected the offending state to penal sanctions "to be inflicted in open and solemn war by the injured party." 1 James Kent, Commentaries on American Law 169 (1826). There was always the difficult question of what sanction, other than conquest, could be imposed on a "criminal state." Dismemberment? Harsh reparation obligations? Enforced regime change? Banishment from the United Nations and other polite society? Since the middle of the nineteenth century, it has generally been recognized that the responsibility of states for acts in violation of international law more closely resembles civil, or more precisely, delictual liability. *See* Ian Brownlie, System of the Law of Nations: State Responsibility (Part I) 22–23 (1983). Even so, it has been urged from time to time that, at least for certain acts, states are or should be held criminally responsible. Since the Nuremberg Trial, the principle of individual rather than state responsibility for international crimes has occupied center stage in discussions of international criminal law. But the idea of state criminal responsibility still has its proponents. *See* Otto Triffterer, *Prosecution of States for Crimes of State*, *in* 3 INTERNATIONAL CRIMINAL LAW 99 (M. Cherif Bassiouni ed., 1987); John Dugard, *Criminal Responsibility of States*, *in* 1 INTERNATIONAL CRIMINAL LAW 239 (M. Cherif Bassiouni ed., 2d ed. 1999).

In 1976, the International Law Commission (ILC) provisionally adopted a draft article on state responsibility, a topic on which it began work in 1949, which incorporated the idea that there are certain "international crimes" which can give rise to a heightened form of state responsibility. According to Article 19 of the Commission's 1976 Draft Articles on State Responsibility:

1. An act of a State which constitutes a breach of an international obligation is an internationally wrongful act, regardless of the subject-matter of the obligation breached.

2. An internationally wrongful act which results from the breach by a State of an international obligation so essential for the protection of fundamental interests of the international community that its breach is recognized as a crime by that community as a whole, constitutes an international crime.

3. Subject to paragraph 2, and on the basis of the rules of international law in force, an international crime may result, *inter alia*, from:

   (a) a serious breach of an international obligation of essential importance for maintenance of international peace and security, such as that prohibiting aggression;

   (b) a serious breach of an international obligation of essential importance for safeguarding the right of self-determination of peoples, such as that prohibiting the establishment or maintenance by force of colonial domination;

   (c) a serious breach on a widespread scale of an international obligation of essential importance for safeguarding the human being, such as those prohibiting slavery, genocide and *apartheid*;

   (d) a serious breach of an international obligation of essential importance for the safeguarding and preservation of the human environment, such as those prohibiting massive pollution of the atmosphere or of the seas.

4. Any internationally wrongful act which is not an international crime in accordance with paragraph 2, constitutes an international delict.

Report of the International Law Commission, U.N. Doc. A/31/10 (1976), 170 at 175, *reprinted in* [1976] 2 Y.B. INT'L L. COMM'N pt. 2, U.N. Doc. A/CN.4/SER.A/Add 1 (pt. 2), 73, at 75.

The concept of an "international crime" enunciated by the ILC in 1976 came in for considerable criticism and no agreement could be reached on the sanctioning regime to go with it. When the Commission finally completed its work on state responsibility in 2001, Article 19 had gone into outer darkness. *Report of the International Law Commission*, U.N. Doc. A/56/10 at 29 (2001). Professor James Crawford, the ILC Rapporteur who encouraged deletion of article 19, writes:

> The deletion of article [19] itself and of the term "crime" is not just a terminological matter. Part One [of the Articles on State Responsibility] proceeds on the basis that internationally wrongful acts of a State form a single category and that the criteria for such acts (in particular the criteria for attribution and the circumstances precluding wrongfulness) apply to all, without reference to any distinction between "delictual" and "criminal" responsibility. A further consequence of this is that the old notion of "international crime" has been broken down into a number of distinct components, more closely related to the twin concepts of peremptory norms and obligations to the international community as a whole, which provided its legal (as distinct from rhetorical) underpinnings. Thus peremptory norms are referred to, expressly or implicitly, in situations involving non-derogability, while obligations to the international community as a whole are the vehicle for articulating the widest category of legal interests of States for the purposes of invoking responsibility.

James Crawford, The International Law Commission's Articles on State Responsibility 37 (2002) (footnotes omitted). We turn, in the next two subsections, to the two categories mentioned by Crawford.

C. Violations of *Jus Cogens* or Peremptory Norms

According to the Restatement (Third) of the Foreign Relations Law of the United States (1987), § 102, cmt. (k):

> Some rules of international law are accepted and recognized by the international community of states as peremptory, permitting no derogation, and prevailing over and invalidating international agreements and other rules of international law in conflict with them. Such a peremptory norm is subject to modification only by a subsequent norm of international law having the same character.

Much of the language of this section derives from Article 53 of the Vienna Convention on the Law of Treaties, May 23, 1969, 1155 U.N.T.S. 331, 344, which provides:

> A peremptory norm of general international law is a norm accepted and recognized by the international community of states as a whole as a norm from which no derogation is permitted and which can be modified only by a subsequent norm of general international law having the same character.

The concept of *jus cogens* depends on the idea that there is a hierarchy of international law norms, so that some "trump" others. This idea now seems to be widely accepted, at least in principle. *But see* Prosper Weil, *Towards Relative Normativity in International Law*?, 77 A.J.I.L. 413 (1983). There is less agreement, however, on what norms actually constitute rules of *jus cogens*. According to Reporters' Note 6 to Restatement (Third) § 102:

> There is general agreement that the principles of the United Nations Charter prohibiting the use of force are *jus cogens*.... It has been suggested that norms that create "international crimes" and obligate all states to proceed against violations are also peremptory.... Such norms might include rules prohibiting genocide, slave trade and slavery, apartheid and other gross violations of human rights, and perhaps attacks on diplomats.

There is a thorough discussion of the various candidates for inclusion in the category in Lauri Hannikainen, Peremptory Norms (Jus Cogens) in International Law: Historical Development, Criteria, Present Status (1988); Thomas Weatherall, Jus Cogens: International Law and Social Contract (2015); Robert A. Kolb, Peremptory International Law — Jus Cogens: A General Inventory (2015).

Although in its final report on state responsibility the ILC, *supra*, rejected the idea of crimes committed by states, it did include a chapter of provisions dealing with responsibility "which is entailed by a serious breach by a State of an obligation arising under a peremptory norm of general international law." (Article 40 (1)). A breach is "serious if it involves a gross or systematic failure by the responsible State to fulfil the obligation." (Article 40 (2)). After noting widespread agreement that Article 53 of the Vienna Convention extended at least to the prohibitions of aggression, slavery and the slave trade, genocide, racial discrimination and apartheid, the Commission's commentary continued, *supra* at 284 (footnotes omitted):

> Although not specifically listed in the Commission's commentary to article 53 of the Vienna Convention, the peremptory character of certain other norms seems to be generally accepted. This applies to the prohibition against torture as defined in article 1 of the Convention against Torture and Other Cruel, Inhuman or Degrading Treatment or Punishment of 10 December 1984. The peremptory character of this prohibition has been confirmed by decisions of international and national bodies. In the light of the International Court's description of the basic rules of international humanitarian law applicable in armed conflict as "intransgressible" in character, it would also seem justified to treat these as peremptory. Finally, the obligation to respect the right of self-determination deserves to be mentioned. As the International Court noted in the *East Timor* case, "[t]he principle of self-determination ... is one of the essential principles of contemporary international law," which gives rise to an obligation to the international community as a whole to permit and respect its exercise."
>
> It should be stressed that the examples given above may not be exhaustive. In addition, article 64 of the Vienna Convention contemplates that new peremptory norms of general international law may come into existence

> through the processes of acceptance and recognition by the international community of States as a whole, as referred to in article 53. The examples given here are thus without prejudice to existing or developing rules of international law which fulfil the criteria for peremptory norms under article 53.

The International Law Commission is currently undertaking a project entitled Peremptory Norms of General International Law (*Jus Cogens*), Dire Tladi, Special Rapporteur. *See* https://legal.un.org/ilc/guide/1_14.shtml.

D. Obligations *Erga Omnes* or Obligations to the International Community as a Whole

The classic statement about the nature of obligations *erga omnes* appears in a dictum contained in two paragraphs of the judgment of the International Court of Justice in the *Barcelona Traction* case. Those paragraphs read as follows:

> 33. When a State admits into its territory foreign investments or foreign nationals, whether natural or juristic persons, it is bound to extend to them the protection of the law and assumes obligations concerning the treatment to be afforded them. These obligations, however, are neither absolute nor unqualified. In particular, an essential distinction should be drawn between the obligations of a State towards the international community as a whole, and those arising vis-à-vis another State in the field of diplomatic protection. By their very nature the former are the concern of all States. In view of the importance of the rights involved, all States can be held to have a legal interest in their protection; they are obligations *erga omnes*.
>
> 34. Such obligations derive, for example in contemporary international law, from the outlawing of acts of aggression, and of genocide, as also from the principles and rules concerning the basic rights of the human person, including protection from slavery and racial discrimination. Some of the corresponding rights of protection have entered into the body of general international law; others are conferred by international instruments of a universal or quasi-universal character.

Case Concerning the Barcelona Traction, Light and Power Co., Ltd. (Belgium v. Spain), Second Phase, 1970 I.C.J. 3, 32 (Judgment of Feb. 5). On the concept generally, *see* MAURIZIO RAGAZZI, THE CONCEPT OF INTERNATIONAL OBLIGATIONS *ERGA OMNES* (1997).

In the Court's dictum, the concept of an obligation *erga omnes* is concerned with a state's standing to complain about a violation of international law by another state even though it was not particularly affected by the violation. If the other state has violated an obligation owing to "the international community as a whole," presumably any state has a correlative right to complain about the violation. This dictum is not immediately concerned with the criminal liability of individuals. Nonetheless, like the other concepts we are considering, the idea of an obligation *erga omnes* does assume that certain norms of international law have a special importance, a preferred position, because associated with the fundamental interests, or with the common good, of the entire "international community." It has been suggested that, insofar as the norms creating certain "international crimes" and requiring states to proceed against violations are peremptory (*jus cogens*) norms, the obligation to prosecute such crimes may itself be an obligation *erga omnes*. *See* Guy S. Goodwin-Gill, *Crime in International Law: Obligations* Erga Omnes *and the Duty to Prosecute*, *in* THE REALITY OF INTERNATIONAL LAW: ESSAYS IN HONOUR OF IAN BROWNLIE 199 (Guy S. Goodwin-Gill & Stefan Talmon eds., 1999). The ILC's Articles on State Responsibility avoid the term "erga omnes" but contemplate obligations owed to the international community as a whole. *See generally* CRAWFORD, *supra* at 276–80.

A significant application of the *erga omnes* principle occurred in *Questions Relating to the Obligation to Prosecute or Extradite (Belgium v. Senegal)*, 2012 I.C.J. REP. 422. Belgium claimed that Senegal was in breach of its obligation under the Convention against Torture (to which both States are parties) to investigate and prosecute the former president of Chad, Hissène Habré, who was present in its territory. Senegal disputed Belgium's standing to bring the claim on the basis that none of the alleged victims was a Belgian citizen at the time the acts were committed. Describing the situation between parties to the Convention as one of "*erga omnes partes*" the Court held that Belgium had standing to invoke the responsibility of Senegal. It also held that Senegal was under a duty to extradite or prosecute the former leader. Ultimately a successful trial resulting in a life sentence proceeded in Senegal, with financial assistance from Chad, Belgium, the United States and several others. *See* CELESTE HICKS, THE TRIAL OF HISSÈNE HABRÉ: HOW THE PEOPLE OF CHAD BROUGHT A TYRANT TO JUSTICE (2018).

E. Crimes Against the Peace and Security of Mankind

Following the Nuremberg Trial, the United Nations embarked on efforts to codify the law applied by the Nuremberg Tribunal. In 1946, the General Assembly affirmed the principles of international law recognized by the Charter and Judgment of the Nuremberg Tribunal. In 1947, it directed the ILC to "formulate" the principles which it had thus affirmed, and also to "prepare a draft code of offenses against the peace and security of mankind." The premise of the latter was that the "Nuremberg crimes" (crimes against peace, war crimes and crimes against humanity) were part of a broader category. The ILC submitted its formulation of the Nuremberg Principles to the General Assembly in 1950 [*see* chap. 20]. It also submitted a Draft Code of Offenses Against the Peace and Security of Mankind. A revised version was submitted in 1954. At the same time, the General Assembly had under consideration a Draft Statute for the Establishment of an International Criminal Court. A preliminary version of the statute was submitted in 1951, a revised version in 1953. In the end, however, the General Assembly decided to postpone further consideration of both the code and the statute until it had dealt with the question of defining the crime of aggression. It was not until 1974 that the Assembly agreed on an official definition of aggression [chap. 23]. In 1978, it asked the ILC to resume work on the draft code (but not the statute). Work proceeded slowly. In 1991, the ILC provisionally adopted a version of the draft code which included articles on the crimes of aggression, threat of aggression, intervention, colonial domination, genocide, apartheid, systematic or mass violations of human rights, exceptionally serious war crimes, recruitment, financing and training of mercenaries, international terrorism, illicit drug trafficking, and wilful and severe damage to the environment. The draft attracted considerable criticism and underwent further revision in which many of the crimes were gutted from it. In a version that covered a much narrower range of crimes — essentially the Nuremberg crimes expanded to include genocide and crimes against United Nations and associated personnel — it was finally adopted by the ILC in 1996, *Report of the International Law Commission*, U.N. GAOR, 51st Sess., Supp. No. 10, at 9, U.N. Doc. A/51/10 (1996). The 1996 draft Code espouses universal jurisdiction for all of its crimes except aggression. Article 8, headed "Establishment of jurisdiction," provides:

> Without prejudice to the jurisdiction of an international criminal court, each State Party shall take such measures as may be necessary to establish its jurisdiction over the crimes set out in articles 17, 18, 19 and 20 [genocide, crimes against humanity, crimes against United Nations and associated personnel, war crimes], irrespective of where those crimes were committed. Jurisdiction over the crime set out in article 16 [aggression] shall rest with an international criminal court. However, a State referred to in article 16 [one committing aggression] is not precluded from trying its nationals for the crime set out in that article.

Commentators often assume that the right to exert universal jurisdiction and the right to send something to an international tribunal are coterminous, but the choice made by the ILC here suggests that it thought the two could be separated.

Meanwhile, the question of establishing an international criminal court had resurfaced on the Commission's agenda. The ILC produced a draft statute in 1993 and a revised version in 1994. This served as a basis for the work which ultimately culminated in the 1998 Rome Statute for an International Criminal Court [chap. 22]. The substantive criminal law provisions of the Rome Statute ended up covering much of the same ground as the ILC's 1996 Draft Code but in far greater detail in both its general and its special part.

For a history of these developments, *see* Timothy L.H. McCormack & Gerry J. Simpson, *The International Law Commission's Draft Code of Crimes Against the Peace and Security of Mankind: An Appraisal of the Substantive Provisions*, 5 CRIM. L.F. 1 (1994); Rosemary Rayfuse, *The Draft Code of Crimes Against the Peace and Security of Mankind: Eating Disorders at the International Law Commission*, 8 CRIM. L.F. 43 (1997).

It should be noted that there is much substantive overlap in the concepts of state crimes, crimes *erga omnes*, crimes against the peace and security of mankind and matters that are *jus cogens*. Each of the concepts has, however, its own field of application and its own history.

F. *Ne Bis in Idem*

The term *"ne bis in idem"* is the international version of the concept of double jeopardy that prohibits repeated trials for the same crime. It is an important issue in international criminal law, as more than one State may choose to proceed with a prosecution. This can happen both in respect of "ordinary" crimes like transnational securities fraud, or in respect of crimes of international concern such as aircraft hijackings. Unfortunately, one cannot say with confidence that a previous conviction or acquittal in State A will preclude a subsequent prosecution in State B. State practice varies and many countries still follow some version of the dual sovereignty rule, a prominent feature of United States federal/state practice, which permits prosecution for the same conduct in separate "sovereignties". The main treaty provision dealing with rights in the criminal justice process, Article 17, paragraph 7 of the Covenant on Civil and Political Rights, is applicable only in the domestic sphere. It provides that "[n]o one shall be liable to be tried or punished again for an offense for which he has already been finally convicted or acquitted in accordance with the law and penal procedure of each country." International Covenant on Civil and Political Rights, Art. 14 (7) (1966), 999 U.N.T.S. 171. Note also, the U.S. "understanding" when ratifying the Covenant: "The United States understands the prohibition upon double jeopardy in paragraph 7 to apply only when the judgment of acquittal has been rendered by a court of the same governmental unit, whether the Federal Government or a constituent unit, as is seeking a new trial for the same cause." *See infra* chap. 19. The area is under development. Many extradition treaties contain various forms of *ne bis* provisions. The United Nations Model Treaty on Extradition, G.A. Res. 45/116 (1990) [chap. 16], provides, in Article 3 (d), that extradition "shall not be granted" where "there has been a final judgment rendered against the person in the requested State in respect of the offence for which the person's extradition is requested." Note also these optional grounds for refusing extradition in Article 4 of the Model Convention: "(b) If the competent authorities of the requested State have decided either not to institute or to terminate proceedings against the person for the offence in respect of which extradition has been requested," and "(c) if a prosecution in respect of the offence for which extradition is requested is pending in the requested State against the person whose extradition is requested." Article VII, paragraph 8 of the NATO Status of Forces Agreement, http://www.nato.int/cps/en/natolive/official_texts_17265.htm, provides that:

> Where an accused has been tried in accordance with the provisions of this Article by the authorities of one Contracting Party and has been acquitted, or has been convicted and is serving, or has served, his sentence or has been pardoned, he may not be tried again for the same offence within the same

> territory by the authorities of another Contracting Party. However, nothing in this paragraph shall prevent the military authorities of the sending State from trying a member of its force for any violation of rules of discipline arising from an act or omission which constituted an offence for which he was tried by the authorities of another Contracting Party.

Embodied within Article 20 of the Rome Statute for the International Criminal Court in 1998 is a sophisticated provision describing the concept of *ne bis in idem* in the context of potential international prosecution for genocide, crimes against humanity and war crimes. A 2010 amendment to the Statute, which came into force in 2018, extends the same rules to the crime of aggression. *See* ICC Res. RC/Res. 6 (Kampala, 11 June 2010) para. 7. Article 20 precludes a second trial in the ICC "with respect to conduct which formed the basis of crimes for which the person has been convicted or acquitted by the Court" (Paragraph 1). Moreover, "No person shall be tried by another court for a crime referred to in article 5 [genocide, crimes against humanity, war crimes, crime of aggression] for which that person has already been convicted or acquitted by the Court." (Paragraph 2). It adds, in respect of trials in domestic courts, in paragraph 3, that:

> No person who has been tried by another court for conduct also proscribed under article 6, 7 or 8 or 8 *bis* [genocide, crimes against humanity, war crimes and the crime of aggression] shall be tried by the Court with respect to the same conduct unless the proceedings in the other court:
>
> (a) Were for the purpose of shielding the persons concerned from criminal responsibility for crimes within the jurisdiction of the Court; or
>
> (b) Otherwise were not conducted independently or impartially in accordance with the norms of due process recognized by international law and were conducted in a manner which, in the circumstances, was inconsistent with an intent to bring the person concerned to justice.

It remains to be seen how these tentative steps will be worked out in national and international practice, as more states begin to exercise extraterritorial jurisdiction, especially on the basis of universal jurisdiction, and thus the opportunities for concurrent jurisdiction leading to issues of *ne bis in idem* become greater. In relation to the ICC, there are some early indications that all might not be well with defendants' rights under the Rome Statute structure. *See* Patryk I. Labuda, *The Flipside of Complementarity: Double Jeopardy in the International Criminal Court*, 17 J. Int'l Crim. Just. 369 (2019).

Chapter 3

General Principles of Jurisdiction

§ 3.01 Extraterritorial Application of United States Statutes

When does the United States have jurisdiction to prosecute criminal conduct that occurs outside its borders? The answer to this question depends on the examination of two further questions: (1) whether a statute should be read as having extraterritorial effect, and (2) whether international law permits (or at least does not forbid) the United States to apply its law to particular conduct?

In some instances, explicit Congressional language allows for an easy resolution in favor of extraterritorial application. For example, the Foreign Corrupt Practices Act focuses on bribery occurring outside the United States. [*see* chap. 4]. The Act's focus on international bribery offers a clear basis for finding jurisdiction to prosecute the illegal activity in the United States despite the fact that the actual bribery may have occurred outside the borders of the United States. Statutes also can have extraterritoriality provisions that explicitly allow for the prosecution of certain activities occurring outside the United States. For example, a key perjury statute provides that "[t]his section is applicable whether the statement or subscription is made within or without the United States." 18 U.S.C. § 1621.

Congress increased the extraterritorial application of some statutes in passing the "Uniting and Strengthening America by Providing Appropriate Tools Required to Intercept and Obstruct Terrorism Act of 2001" (USA Patriot Act). For example, § 377 of the Act permits extraterritorial jurisdiction in certain circumstances for 18 U.S.C. § 1029, a criminal statute concerning access devices. The Patriot Act also extended extraterritorial jurisdiction for "protected computers," under the computer fraud statute (18 U.S.C. § 1030).

In many situations courts are left to interpret whether the statute and conduct warrant extraterritorial application. Legislative intent may be difficult to discern in these instances. *See* Ellen S. Podgor, Essay, *Globalization and the Federal Prosecution of White Collar Crime*, 34 Am. Crim . L. Rev. 325 (1997). To assist in deciding issues of extraterritorial jurisdiction, courts often examine precedent, accepted jurisdiction bases [§ 3.03], language from the Restatement of the Foreign Relations Law of the United States [§§ 3.03 and 3.04], and also treaties [chap. 2].

Two doctrines of United States law are also relevant. The first is the famous dictum by Marshall, C.J. that "an act of Congress ought never to be construed to violate the law of nations if any other possible construction remains. . . ." *Murray v. Schooner Charming Betsy*, 6 U.S. (2 Cranch) 64, 118 (1804). The other is basic constitutional doctrine summarized in several sections of the following:

The Restatement (Fourth) of the Foreign Relations Law of the United States (2018)

§ 301 Treaties as Law of the United States

(1) Treaties made under the authority of the United States are part of the laws of the United States and are supreme over State and local law.

(2) Cases arising under treaties fall within the judicial power of the federal courts.

(3) Treaties create international legal obligations for the United States, and limitations on the domestic enforceability of treaties do not alter the United States' obligation under international law to comply with relevant treaty provisions.

§ 307 Relationship of Treaties to Individual Constitutional Rights

A treaty provision will not be given effect as law in the United States to the extent that giving it this effect would violate any individual constitutional rights.

§ 308 Conflicts Between Treaties and State or Local Law

Treaties are supreme over State and local law, and when there is a conflict between State or local law and a self-executing treaty provision, courts in the United States will apply the treaty provision.

United States v. Bowman

Supreme Court of the United States
260 U.S. 94 (1922)

MR. CHIEF JUSTICE TAFT Delivered the opinion of the Court:

This is a writ of error under the Criminal Appeals Act . . . to review the ruling of the District Court sustaining a demurrer of one of the defendants to an indictment for a conspiracy to defraud a corporation in which the United States was and is a stockholder. . . .

During the period covered by the indictment, i.e., between October, 1919, and January, 1920, the steamship Dio belonged to the United States. The United States owned all the stock in the United States Shipping Board Emergency Fleet Corporation. The National Shipping Corporation agreed to operate and manage the Dio for the Fleet Corporation, which under the contract was to pay for fuel, oil, labor and material used in the operation. The Dio was on a voyage to Rio de Janeiro under this management. Wry was her master, Bowman was her engineer, Hawkinson was the agent of the Standard Oil Company at Rio de Janeiro, and Millar was a merchant and ship repairer and engineer in Rio. Of these four, who were the defendants in the indictment, the first three were American citizens, and Millar was a British subject. Johnston & Company were the agents of the National Shipping Corporation at Rio. The indictment charged that the plot was hatched by Wry and Bowman on board the Dio before she reached Rio. Their plan was to order, through Johnston & Company, and receipt for, 1000 tons of fuel oil from the Standard Oil Company, but to take only 600 tons aboard, and to collect cash for a delivery of 1000 tons through Johnston & Company, from the Fleet Corporation, and then divide the money paid for the undelivered 400 tons among the four defendants. This plan was to be, and was, made possible through the guilty connivance of the Standard Oil agent Hawkinson and Millar the Rio merchant who was to, and did collect the money. Overt acts charged included a wireless telegram to the agents, Johnston & Company, from the Dio while on the high seas ordering the 1000 tons of oil. The Southern District of New York was the district into which the American defendants were first brought and were found, but Millar, the British defendant, has not been found.

The first count charged a conspiracy by the defendants to defraud the Fleet Corporation in which the United States was a stockholder, by obtaining and aiding to obtain the payment and allowance of a false and fraudulent claim against the Fleet Corporation. It laid the offense on the high seas, out of the jurisdiction of any particular State and out of the jurisdiction of any district of the United States, but within the admiralty and maritime jurisdiction of the United States. The second count laid the conspiracy on the Dio on the high seas and at the port of Rio de Janeiro as well as in the city. The third count laid it in the city of Rio de Janeiro. The fourth count was for making and causing to be made in the name of the Standard Oil Company, for payment and approval, a false and fraudulent claim against the Fleet Corporation in the form of an invoice for 1000 tons of fuel oil, of which 400 tons were not delivered. This count laid the same crime on board the Dio in the harbor of Rio de Janeiro. The fifth count laid it in the city and the sixth at the port and in the city.

No objection was made to the indictment or any count of it for lack of precision or fullness in describing all the elements of the crimes denounced in § 35 of the Criminal Code as amended. The sole objection was that the crime was committed without the jurisdiction of the United States or of any State thereof and on the high seas or within the jurisdiction of Brazil. The District Court considered only the first count, which charged the conspiracy to have been committed on the Dio on the high seas, and having held that bad for lack of jurisdiction, a fortiori it sustained the demurrer as to the others.

The court in its opinion conceded that under many authorities the United States as a sovereign may regulate the ships under its flag and the conduct of its citizens while on those ships.... The court said, however, that while private and public ships of the United States on the high seas were constructively a part of the territory of the United States, indeed peculiarly so as distinguished from that of the States, Congress had always expressly indicated it when it intended that its laws should be operative on the high seas. The court concluded that because jurisdiction of criminal offenses must be conferred upon United States courts and could not be inferred, and because § 35, like all the other sections of c. 4, contains no reference to the high seas as a part of the locus of the offenses defined by it, as the sections in cc. 11 and 12 of the Criminal Code do, § 35 must be construed not to extend to acts committed on the high seas. It confirmed its conclusion by the statement that § 35 had never been invoked to punish offenses denounced if committed on the high seas or in a foreign country.

We have in this case a question of statutory construction. The necessary locus, when not specially defined, depends upon the purpose of Congress as evidenced by the description and nature of the crime and upon the territorial limitations upon the power and jurisdiction of a government to punish crime under the law of nations. Crimes against private individuals or their property, like assaults, murder, burglary, larceny, robbery, arson, embezzlement and fraud of all kinds, which affect the peace and good order of the community, must of course be committed within the territorial jurisdiction of the government where it may properly exercise it. If punishment of them is to be extended to include those committed outside of the strict territorial jurisdiction, it is natural for Congress to say so in the statute, and failure to do so will negative the purpose of Congress in this regard. We have an example of this in the attempted application of the prohibitions of the Anti-Trust Law to acts done by citizens of the United States against other such citizens in a foreign country. *American Banana Co. v. United Fruit Co.*, 213 U.S. 347. That was a civil case, but as the statute is criminal as well as civil, it presents an analogy.

But the same rule of interpretation should not be applied to criminal statutes which are, as a class, not logically dependent on their locality for the Government's jurisdiction, but are enacted because of the right of the Government to defend itself against obstruction, or fraud wherever perpetrated, especially if committed by its own citizens, officers or agents. Some such offenses can only be committed within the territorial jurisdiction of the Government because of the local acts required to constitute them. Others are such that to limit their locus to the strictly territorial jurisdiction would be greatly to curtail the scope and usefulness of the statute and leave open a large immunity for frauds as easily committed by citizens on the high seas and in foreign countries as at home. In such cases, Congress has not thought it necessary to make specific provision in the law that the locus shall include the high seas and foreign countries, but allows it to be inferred from the nature of the offense. Many of these occur in c. 4, which bears the title "Offenses against the operations of the Government." Section 70 of that chapter punishes whoever as consul knowingly certifies a false invoice. Clearly the locus of this crime as intended by Congress is in a foreign country and certainly the foreign country in which he discharges his official duty could not object to the trial in a United States court of a United States consul for crime of this sort committed within its borders. Forging or altering ship's papers is made a crime by § 72 of c. 4. It would be going too far to say that because Congress does not fix any locus it intended to exclude the high seas in respect of this crime. The natural inference from the character of the offense is that the sea would be a probable place for its commission. Section 42 of c. 4 punishes enticing desertions from the naval service. Is it possible that Congress did not intend by this to include such enticing done aboard ship on the high seas or in a foreign port, where it would be most likely to be done? Section 39 punishes bribing a United States officer of the civil, military or naval service to violate his duty or to aid in committing a fraud on the United States. It is hardly reasonable to construe this not to include such offenses when the bribe is offered to a consul, ambassador, an army or a naval officer in a foreign country or on the high seas, whose duties are being performed there and when his connivance at such fraud must occur there. So, too, § 38 of c. 4 punishes the wilfully doing or aiding to do any act relating to the bringing in, custody, sale or other disposition of property captured as prize, with intent to defraud, delay or injure the United States or any captor or claimant of such property. This would naturally often occur at sea, and Congress could not have meant to confine it to the land of the United States. Again, in § 36 of c. 4, it is made a crime to steal, embezzle, or knowingly apply to his own use ordnance, arms, ammunition, clothing, subsistence, stores, money or other property of the United States furnished or to be used for military or naval service. It would hardly be reasonable to hold that if any one, certainly if a citizen of the United States, were to steal or embezzle such property which may properly and lawfully be in the custody of army or naval officers either in foreign countries, in foreign ports or on the high seas, it would not be in such places an offense which Congress intended to punish by this section.

What is true of these sections in this regard is true of § 35, under which this indictment was drawn. . . . It is directed generally against whoever presents a false claim against the United States, knowing it to be such, to any officer of the civil, military or naval service or to any department thereof, or any corporation in which the United States is a stockholder, or whoever connives at the same by the use of any cheating device, or whoever enters a conspiracy to do these things. The section was amended in 1918 to include a corporation in which the United States owns stock. This was evidently intended to protect the Emergency Fleet Corporation in which the United States was the sole stockholder, from fraud of this character. That Corporation was expected to engage in, and did engage in, a most extensive ocean transportation business and its ships were seen in every great port of the world open during the war. The same section of the statute protects the arms, ammunition, stores and property of the army and navy from fraudulent devices of a similar character. We can not suppose that when Congress enacted the statute or amended it, it did not have in mind that a wide field for such frauds upon the Government was in private and public vessels of the United States on the high seas and in foreign ports and beyond the land jurisdiction of the United States, and therefore intend to include them in the section.

Nor can the much quoted rule that criminal statutes are to be strictly construed avail. As said in *United States v. Lacher*, 134 U.S. 624, 629, quoting with approval from Sedgwick, Statutory and Constitutional Law, 2d ed., 282: "penal provisions, like all others, are to be fairly construed according to the legislative intent as expressed in the enactment." They are not to be strained either way. It needs no forced construction to interpret § 35 as we have done.

Section 41 of the Judicial Code provides that "the trial of all offenses committed upon the high seas, or elsewhere out of the jurisdiction of any particular State or district, shall be in the district where the offender is found, or into which he is first brought." The three defendants who were found in New York were citizens of the United States and were certainly subject to such laws as it might pass to protect itself and its property. Clearly it is no offense to the dignity or right of sovereignty of Brazil to hold them for this crime against the government to which they owe allegiance. The other defendant is a subject of Great Britain. He has never been apprehended, and it will be time enough to consider what, if any, jurisdiction the District Court below has to punish him when he is brought to trial.

The judgment of the District Court is reversed, with directions to overrule the demurrer and for further proceedings. . . .

Notes

(1) *Bowman* left open many questions. Is express language necessary to overcome the presumption, or is an implication, such as that in *Bowman*, enough? *See generally* Zachary D. Clopton, *Bowman Lives: The Extraterritorial Application of U.S. Criminal Law After* Morrison v. National Australia Bank, 67 N.Y.U. Ann. Surv. Am. L. 137 (2011). *See also* Ellen S. Podgor & Daniel M. Filler, *International Criminal Jurisdiction in the Twenty-first Century: Rediscovering* United States v. Bowman, 44 San Diego L. Rev. 585 (2007).

(2) Can the United States prosecute for theft of government property when the alleged criminal acts occur outside the United States? In *United States v. Cotton*, 471 F.2d 744, 749–50 (9th Cir. 1973), the court stated that "[t]his nation has a paramount interest in protecting its property, wherever located, by assertion of its penal laws." Applying *Bowman*, the court noted that "[i]t is inconceivable that Congress, in enacting Section 641, would proscribe only the theft of government property located within the territorial boundaries of the nation."

(3) How should *Bowman* be applied when the alleged criminal acts are not committed by United States citizens? In *United States v. Pizzarusso*, 388 F.2d 8 (2d Cir. 1968), Judge Medina stated:

> This case is of interest because it brings before this Court for the first time the question of the jurisdiction of the District Court to indict and convict a foreign citizen of the crime of knowingly making a false statement

under oath in a visa application to an American consular official located in a foreign country, in violation of 18 U.S.C. Section 1546. . . . The indictment charges that on March 4, 1965 Jean Philomena Pizzarusso wilfully made under oath a number of false statements in her "Application for Immigrant Visa And Alien Registration" at the American Consulate, Montreal, Canada. Each of these false statements was patently material to the matter in hand. For example: she falsely swore that since her sixteenth birthday her only places of residence for six months or more had been London, England and Montreal, Canada; she falsely swore that she had been in the United States only for short visits for pleasure; she falsely swore that she had never been arrested, and so on. Although at all times pertinent to this case she was a citizen of Canada, she was taken into custody in the Southern District of New York on April 18, 1966. . . .

18 U.S.C. Section 1546 is a significant and integral part of the pattern of immigration laws, including those affecting passports and visas. We think the Congress by the enactment of this law contemplated that it would be applied extraterritorially. Visas are documents issued to aliens permitting them to enter the country. In the ordinary course of events we would naturally expect false statements in visa applications to be made outside the territorial limits of the United States. This would seem to overcome the strong presumption that the Congress did not intend the statute to apply extraterritorially. . . . The utterance by an alien of a "false statement with respect to a material fact" in a visa application constitutes an affront to the very sovereignty of the United States. These false statements must be said to have a deleterious influence on valid governmental interests. Therefore, 18 U.S.C. Section 1546, as applied to an alien's perjurious statements before a United States consular officer in a foreign country, represents a law which is "necessary and proper for carrying into Execution," U.S. Const. Art. I, Section 8, the Congressional power over the conduct of foreign relations.

(4) In *Bowman*, the Court distinguishes between crimes against private individuals and property, and crimes that are "not logically dependent on their locality for the government's jurisdiction." Is this distinction valid in light of globalization? *See* Gary B. Born, *A Reappraisal of the Extraterritorial Reach of U.S. Law*, 24 LAW & POL'Y INT'L BUS. 1 (1992) ("the rationale for the territoriality presumption has become obsolete"). Is the United States increasing prosecution of acts occurring outside its borders? Is this indicated by an increase in the number of statutes in the United States calling for extraterritorial prosecution, or by an increase in existing statutes being interpreted to include extraterritoriality? *See, e.g.*, *Stegeman v. United States*, 425 F.2d 984 (9th Cir. 1970) (interpreting 18 U.S.C. § 152, a criminal bankruptcy statute, to have extraterritorial application); Michael J. Calhoun, Comment, *Tension on the High Seas of Transnational Securities Fraud: Broadening the*

Scope of United States Jurisdiction, 30 Loy. U. Chi. L.J. 679 (1999). Are there other ways to assess an increase in extraterritorial application, such as in the deployment of agents overseas? *See* David Johnston, *Strength Is Seen in a U.S. Export: Law Enforcement*, N.Y. Times, Apr. 17, 1995, at A1, A8 ("American law enforcement agencies are rapidly expanding overseas, deploying agents to dozens of countries in scores of joint investigations."); R. Jeffrey Smith & Thomas W. Lippman, *FBI Plans to Double Overseas Offices*, Atl. J. Const., Aug. 20, 1996, A1 ("The Federal Bureau of Investigation is planning to nearly double its presence overseas during the next four years, opening offices in 23 cities to cope with what officials say is a dramatic expansion of international terrorism, organized crime and narcotics trafficking affecting U.S. citizens."). On globalization of law enforcement, especially by Western Europe and the United States, see Peter Andreas & Ethan Nadelmann, Policing the Globe: Criminalization and Crime Control in International Relations (2006).

(5) What is the implication for extraterritorial effect when Congress uses the term "foreign commerce" in criminal statutes? In *United States v. Braverman*, 376 F.2d 249, 251 (2d Cir. 1967), the court stated, "There would seem to be no logical reason for holding that Congress intended to punish those who cause the violation of a law regulating and protecting foreign commerce only when they act within the borders of the United States or that Congress is powerless to protect foreign commerce and those who engage in foreign commerce from intentionally injurious acts, simply because those acts occur outside our borders." *See also United States v. Kaplan*, 171 F.3d 1351 (11th Cir. 1999) (transfer of funds from Panama to the United States for extortion found to be sufficient evidence of an effect on commerce for the Hobbs Act, a federal statute used to prosecute extortion conduct). *But see* Justice Scalia in *Morrison, supra*, who stated:

> First, they point to the definition of "interstate commerce," a term used in §10(b), which includes "trade, commerce, transportation, or communication . . . between any foreign country and any State." 15 U.S.C. §78c(a)(17). But "we have repeatedly held that even statutes that contain broad language in their definitions of 'commerce' that expressly refer to '*foreign* commerce' do not apply abroad." *Aramco*, 499 U.S., at 251 [*EEOC v. Arabian American Oil Co.*]; see *id.*, at 251–252 (discussing cases). The general reference to foreign commerce in the definition of "interstate commerce" does not defeat the presumption against extraterritoriality.

(6) The particular constitutional basis upon which the federal statute is premised may, nonetheless, influence a court's determination of whether there is a basis for federal criminal prosecution within the United States. In *United States v. Lewis*, 67 F.3d 225 (9th Cir. 1995), the Ninth Circuit reversed bank fraud convictions finding that, "[u]nlike §§1341 and 1343, federal jurisdiction is predicated not upon the use of the mails or wire communications in interstate commerce without regard to the victim bank's status, but upon the 'strong Federal interest' in the financial integrity of a 'federally controlled or insured institution,' defined as a 'federally chartered

or insured financial institution,' which is in turn defined as a bank 'operating under the laws of the United States.' Although the legislative history does not answer the ultimate question whether a non-federally insured, state-chartered branch of a foreign bank is 'federally controlled' for purposes of the bank fraud statute, the jurisdictional distinction between the mail and wire fraud statutes on the one hand and §1344 on the other suggests that the latter's reach is more limited than that of its sister statutes."

§ 3.02 Judicial Interpretation of Extraterritoriality

Three recent U.S. Supreme Court cases provide a more refined approach to determining when a statute should have an extraterritorial application, although all make strong statements for maintaining the presumption against extraterritoriality. Absent explicit congressional direction, extraterritoriality remains questionable. In *Morrison v. National Australia Bank Ltd.*, 561 U.S. 247 (2010), a civil case involving an action for damages under §§10(b) and 20(a) of the Securities and Exchange Act 1924 and SEC Rule 10b-5, Justice Scalia discussed a presumption against extraterritorial jurisdiction of statutes stating that "[i]t is a "longstanding principle of American law 'that legislation of Congress, unless a contrary intent appears, is meant to apply only within the territorial jurisdiction of the United States.'" He noted that "[t]his principle represents a canon of construction, or a presumption about a statute's meaning, rather than a limit upon Congress's power to legislate." He explained further that "[i]t rests on the perception that Congress ordinarily legislates with respect to domestic, not foreign matters." Setting forth a clear statement of when extraterritoriality applies, he said "unless there is the affirmative intention of the Congress clearly expressed" to give a statute extraterritorial effect, "we must presume it is primarily concerned with domestic conditions." As noted in the concurring opinion by Justice Stevens, and joined by Justice Ginsburg, "[T]he Court seeks to transform the presumption from a flexible rule of thumb into something more like a clear statement rule." (*See* §5.02, *infra.*)

In *Kiobel v. Royal Dutch Petroleum Co.,* 569 U.S. 108, 115 (2013), the Court considered the presumption against extraterritoriality applicable in a case involving the Alien Tort Statute, holding the presumption against extraterritoriality is founded in protection "against unintended clashes between" nations and assuring that there is no "international discord." Reaffirming the approach taken in *Morrison*, the Court stated that "even where the claims touch and concern the territory of the United States, they must do so with sufficient force to displace the presumption against extraterritorial application." (*See* §1.04, *supra.*)

In a third case, *RJR Nabisco,* also a civil action, the Court considers the extraterritoriality of the federal Racketeer Influenced and Corrupt Organization Act (RICO).

RJR Nabisco, Inc. v. European Community

Supreme Court of the United States
136 S. Ct. 2090 (2016)

Justice Alito delivered the opinion of the Court.

The Racketeer Influenced and Corrupt Organizations Act (RICO), 18 U.S.C. §§1961–1968, created four new criminal offenses involving the activities of organized criminal groups in relation to an enterprise. §§1962(a)-(d). RICO also created a new civil cause of action for "[a]ny person injured in his business or property by reason of a violation" of those prohibitions. §1964(c). We are asked to decide whether RICO applies extraterritorially—that is, to events occurring and injuries suffered outside the United States.

I

A

RICO is founded on the concept of racketeering activity. The statute defines "racketeering activity" to encompass dozens of state and federal offenses, known in RICO parlance as predicates. These predicates include any act "indictable" under specified federal statutes, as well as certain crimes "chargeable" under state law, and any offense involving bankruptcy or securities fraud or drug-related activity that is "punishable" under federal law. A predicate offense implicates RICO when it is part of a "pattern of racketeering activity"—a series of related predicates that together demonstrate the existence or threat of continued criminal activity....

This case arises from allegations that petitioners—RJR Nabisco and numerous related entities (collectively RJR)—participated in a global money-laundering scheme in association with various organized crime groups.... Greatly simplified, the complaint alleges a scheme in which Colombian and Russian drug traffickers smuggled narcotics into Europe and sold the drugs for euros that—through a series of transactions involving black-market money brokers, cigarette importers, and wholesalers—were used to pay for large shipments of RJR cigarettes into Europe. In other variations of this scheme, RJR allegedly dealt directly with drug traffickers and money launderers in South America and sold cigarettes to Iraq in violation of international sanctions. RJR is also said to have acquired Brown & Williamson Tobacco Corporation for the purpose of expanding these illegal activities....

Putting these pieces together, the complaint alleges that RJR violated each of RICO's prohibitions.... RJR moved to dismiss the complaint, arguing that RICO does not apply to racketeering activity occurring outside U.S. territory or to foreign enterprises. The District Court agreed and dismissed the RICO claims as impermissibly extraterritorial....

The Second Circuit reinstated the RICO claims.... RJR sought rehearing, arguing (among other things) that RICO's civil cause of action requires a plaintiff to allege a domestic injury, even if a domestic pattern of racketeering or a domestic enterprise is not necessary to make out a violation of RICO's substantive prohibitions. The panel denied rehearing and issued a supplemental opinion holding that RICO does not require a domestic injury. . . . The Second Circuit later denied rehearing en banc, with five judges dissenting.

[The Court notes the lower court jurisdictional split as the basis for accepting certiorari.]

II

The question of RICO's extraterritorial application really involves two questions. First, do RICO's substantive prohibitions, contained in § 1962, apply to conduct that occurs in foreign countries? Second, does RICO's private right of action, contained in § 1964(c), apply to injuries that are suffered in foreign countries? We consider each of these questions in turn. To guide our inquiry, we begin by reviewing the law of extraterritoriality.

It is a basic premise of our legal system that, in general, "United States law governs domestically but does not rule the world." *Microsoft Corp. v. AT & T Corp.*, 550 U.S. 437, 454 (2007). This principle finds expression in a canon of statutory construction known as the presumption against extraterritoriality: Absent clearly expressed congressional intent to the contrary, federal laws will be construed to have only domestic application. *Morrison v. National Australia Bank Ltd.*, 561 U.S. 247, 255 (2010). The question is not whether we think "Congress would have wanted" a statute to apply to foreign conduct "if it had thought of the situation before the court," but whether Congress has affirmatively and unmistakably instructed that the statute will do so. . . . "When a statute gives no clear indication of an extraterritorial application, it has none."

There are several reasons for this presumption. Most notably, it serves to avoid the international discord that can result when U.S. law is applied to conduct in foreign countries. See, e.g., *Kiobel v. Royal Dutch Petroleum Co.*, 133 S.Ct. 1659, 1663–1664; *EEOC v. Arabian American Oil Co.*, 499 U.S. 244, 248 (1991) (*Aramco*); *Benz v. Compania Naviera Hidalgo, S.A.*, 353 U.S. 138, 147 (1957). But it also reflects the more prosaic "commonsense notion that Congress generally legislates with domestic concerns in mind." *Smith v. United States*, 507 U.S. 197, 204, n. 5 (1993). We therefore apply the presumption across the board, "regardless of whether there is a risk of conflict between the American statute and a foreign law." . . .

Twice in the past six years we have considered whether a federal statute applies extraterritorially. In *Morrison*, we addressed the question whether § 10(b) of the Securities Exchange Act of 1934 applies to misrepresentations made in connection with the purchase or sale of securities traded only on foreign exchanges. We first examined whether § 10(b) gives any clear indication of extraterritorial effect, and found that it does not. . . . We then engaged in a separate inquiry to determine whether the complaint before us involved a permissible domestic application of § 10(b) because it alleged that some of the relevant misrepresentations were made in the United States. At this second step, we considered the "'focus' of congressional concern," asking whether § 10(b)'s focus is "the place where the deception originated" or rather "purchases and sale of securities in the United States." . . . We concluded that the statute's focus is on domestic securities transactions, and we therefore held that the statute does not apply to frauds in connection with foreign securities transactions, even if those frauds involve domestic misrepresentations.

In *Kiobel*, we considered whether the Alien Tort Statute (ATS) confers federal-court jurisdiction over causes of action alleging international-law violations committed overseas. We acknowledged that the presumption against extraterritoriality is "typically" applied to statutes "regulating conduct," but we concluded that the principles supporting the presumption should "similarly constrain courts considering causes of action that may be brought under the ATS." . . . We applied the presumption and held that the ATS lacks any clear indication that it extended to the foreign violations alleged in that case. . . . Because "all the relevant conduct" regarding those violations "took place outside the United States," . . . we did not need to determine, as we did in *Morrison*, the statute's "focus."

Morrison and *Kiobel* reflect a two-step framework for analyzing extraterritoriality issues. At the first step, we ask whether the presumption against extraterritoriality has been rebutted—that is, whether the statute gives a clear, affirmative indication that it applies extraterritorially. We must ask this question regardless of whether the statute in question regulates conduct, affords relief, or merely confers jurisdiction. If the statute is not extraterritorial, then at the second step we determine whether the case involves a domestic application of the statute, and we do this by looking to the statute's "focus." If the conduct relevant to the statute's focus occurred in the United States, then the case involves a permissible domestic application even if other conduct occurred abroad; but if the conduct relevant to the focus occurred in a foreign country, then the case involves an impermissible extraterritorial application regardless of any other conduct that occurred in U.S. territory.

What if we find at step one that a statute clearly does have extraterritorial effect? Neither *Morrison* nor *Kiobel* involved such a finding. But we addressed this issue in *Morrison*, explaining that it was necessary to consider § 10(b)'s "focus" only because we found that the statute does not apply extraterritorially: "If § 10(b) did apply abroad, we would not need to determine which transnational frauds it applied to; it would apply to all of them (barring some other limitation)." . . . The scope of an extraterritorial statute thus turns on the limits Congress has (or has not) imposed on the statute's foreign application, and not on the statute's "focus."

III

With these guiding principles in mind, we first consider whether RICO's substantive prohibitions in § 1962 may apply to foreign conduct. Unlike in *Morrison* and *Kiobel*, we find that the presumption against extraterritoriality has been rebutted—but only with respect to certain applications of the statute.

A

The most obvious textual clue is that RICO defines racketeering activity to include a number of predicates that plainly apply to at least some foreign conduct. These predicates include the prohibition against engaging in monetary transactions in criminally derived property, which expressly applies, when "the defendant is a United States person," to offenses that "tak[e] place outside the United States." 18 U.S.C. § 1957(d)(2). Other examples include the prohibitions against the assassination of Government officials, § 351(i) ("There is extraterritorial jurisdiction over the conduct prohibited by this section"); § 1751(k) (same), and the prohibition against hostage taking, which applies to conduct that "occurred outside the United States" if either the hostage or the offender is a U.S. national, if the offender is found in the United States, or if the hostage taking is done to compel action by the U.S. Government, § 1203(b). At least one predicate — the prohibition against "kill[ing] a national of the United States, while such national is outside the United States" — applies only to conduct occurring outside the United States. § 2332(a).

We agree with the Second Circuit that Congress's incorporation of these (and other) extraterritorial predicates into RICO gives a clear, affirmative indication that § 1962 applies to foreign racketeering activity — but only to the extent that the predicates alleged in a particular case themselves apply extraterritorially. Put another way, a pattern of racketeering activity may include or consist of offenses committed abroad in violation of a predicate statute for which the presumption against extraterritoriality has been overcome. To give a simple (albeit grim) example, a violation of § 1962 could be premised on a pattern of killings of Americans abroad in violation of § 2332(a) — a predicate that all agree applies extraterritorially — whether or not any domestic predicates are also alleged.

We emphasize the important limitation that foreign conduct must violate "a predicate statute that manifests an unmistakable congressional intent to apply extraterritorially." Although a number of RICO predicates have extraterritorial effect, many do not. The inclusion of some extraterritorial predicates does not mean that all RICO predicates extend to foreign conduct. This is apparent for two reasons. First, "when a statute provides for some extraterritorial application, the presumption against extraterritoriality operates to limit that provision to its terms." ... Second, RICO defines as racketeering activity only acts that are "indictable" (or, what amounts to the same thing, "chargeable" or "punishable") under one of the statutes identified in § 1961(1). If a particular statute does not apply extraterritorially, then conduct committed abroad is not "indictable" under that statute and so cannot qualify as a predicate under RICO's plain terms. . . .

We therefore conclude that RICO applies to some foreign racketeering activity. A violation of § 1962 may be based on a pattern of racketeering that includes predicate offenses committed abroad, provided that each of those offenses violates a predicate statute that is itself extraterritorial. This fact is determinative as to § 1962(b) and § 1962(c), both of which prohibit the employment of a pattern of racketeering.

Although they differ as to the end for which the pattern is employed—to acquire or maintain control of an enterprise under subsection (b), or to conduct an enterprise's affairs under subsection (c)—this difference is immaterial for extraterritoriality purposes.

Section 1962(a) presents a thornier question. Unlike subsections (b) and (c), subsection (a) targets certain uses of income derived from a pattern of racketeering, not the use of the pattern itself.... While we have no difficulty concluding that this prohibition applies to income derived from foreign patterns of racketeering (within the limits we have discussed), arguably § 1962(a) extends only to domestic uses of the income. The Second Circuit did not decide this question because it found that respondents have alleged "a domestic investment of racketeering proceeds in the form of RJR's merger in the United States with Brown & Williamson and investments in other U.S. operations." ... RJR does not dispute the basic soundness of the Second Circuit's reasoning, but it does contest the court's reading of the complaint.... Because the parties have not focused on this issue, and because it makes no difference to our resolution of this case, ... we assume without deciding that respondents have pleaded a domestic investment of racketeering income in violation of § 1962(a).

Finally, although respondents' complaint alleges a violation of RICO's conspiracy provision, § 1962(d), the parties' briefs do not address whether this provision should be treated differently from the provision (§ 1962(a), (b), or (c)) that a defendant allegedly conspired to violate. We therefore decline to reach this issue, and assume without deciding that § 1962(d)'s extraterritoriality tracks that of the provision underlying the alleged conspiracy.

B

RJR contends that, even if RICO may apply to foreign patterns of racketeering, the statute does not apply to foreign enterprises.... RICO—or at least §§ 1962(b) and (c)—applies abroad, and so we do not need to determine which transnational (or wholly foreign) patterns of racketeering it applies to; it applies to all of them, regardless of whether they are connected to a "foreign" or "domestic" enterprise. This rule is, of course, subject to the important limitation that RICO covers foreign predicate offenses only to the extent that the underlying predicate statutes are extraterritorial. But within those bounds, the location of the affected enterprise does not impose an independent constraint....

Although we find that RICO imposes no domestic enterprise requirement, this does not mean that every foreign enterprise will qualify. Each of RICO's substantive prohibitions requires proof of an enterprise that is "engaged in, or the activities of which affect, interstate or foreign commerce." §§ 1962(a), (b), (c). We do not take this reference to "foreign commerce" to mean literally all commerce occurring abroad. Rather, a RICO enterprise must engage in, or affect in some significant way, commerce directly involving the United States—e.g., commerce between the United States and a foreign country. Enterprises whose activities lack that anchor to U.S. commerce cannot sustain a RICO violation.

C

Applying these principles, we agree with the Second Circuit that the complaint does not allege impermissibly extraterritorial violations of §§ 1962(b) and (c).

The alleged pattern of racketeering activity consists of five basic predicates: (1) money laundering, (2) material support of foreign terrorist organizations, (3) mail fraud, (4) wire fraud, and (5) violations of the Travel Act. The Second Circuit observed that the relevant provisions of the money laundering and material support of terrorism statutes expressly provide for extraterritorial application in certain circumstances, and it concluded that those circumstances are alleged to be present here.... The court found that the fraud statutes and the Travel Act do not contain the clear indication needed to overcome the presumption against extraterritoriality. But it held that the complaint alleges domestic violations of those statutes because it "allege[s] conduct in the United States that satisfies every essential element of the mail fraud, wire fraud, and Travel Act claims." ...

IV

We now turn to RICO's private right of action, on which respondents' lawsuit rests. Section 1964(c) allows "[a]ny person injured in his business or property by reason of a violation of section 1962" to sue for treble damages, costs, and attorney's fees. Irrespective of any extraterritorial application of § 1962, we conclude that § 1964(c) does not overcome the presumption against extraterritoriality. A private RICO plaintiff therefore must allege and prove a domestic injury to its business or property....

The judgment of the United States Court of Appeals for the Second Circuit is reversed, and the case is remanded for further proceedings consistent with this opinion.

So ordered.

Justice Sotomayor took no part in the consideration or decision of this case.

Justice Ginsburg, with whom Justice Breyer and Justice Kagan join, concurring in Parts I, II, and III and dissenting from Part IV and from the judgment.

... Unsupported by RICO's text, inconsistent with its purposes, and unnecessary to protect the comity interests the Court emphasizes, the domestic-injury requirement for private suits replaces Congress' prescription with one of the Court's own invention. Because the Court has no authority so to amend RICO, I dissent....

Accordingly, the Court concludes, when the predicate crimes underlying invocation of § 1962 thrust extraterritorially, so too does § 1962. I agree with that conclusion.

I disagree, however, that the private right of action authorized by § 1964(c) requires a domestic injury to a person's business or property and does not allow recovery for foreign injuries. One cannot extract such a limitation from the text of § 1964(c), which affords a right of action to "[a]ny person injured in his business or property by reason of a violation of section 1962." Section 1962, at least subsections

(b) and (c), all agree, encompasses foreign injuries. How can §1964(c) exclude them when, by its express terms, §1964(c) is triggered by "a violation of section 1962"? To the extent RICO reaches injury abroad when the Government is the suitor pursuant to §1962 (specifying prohibited activities) and §1963 (criminal penalties) or §1964(b) (civil remedies), to that same extent, I would hold, RICO reaches extraterritorial injury when, pursuant to §1964(c), the suitor is a private plaintiff. . . .

JUSTICE BREYER, concurring in part, dissenting in part, and dissenting from the judgment.

I join Parts I through III of the Court's opinion. But I do not join Part IV. The Court there holds that the private right of action provision in the Racketeer Influenced and Corrupt Organizations Act (RICO), 18 U.S.C. §1964(c), has no extraterritorial application. Like JUSTICE GINSBURG, I believe that it does.

Unlike the Court, I cannot accept as controlling the Government's argument as amicus curiae that "[a]llowing recovery for foreign injuries in a civil RICO action . . . presents the . . . danger of international friction." . . . The Government does not provide examples, nor apparently has it consulted with foreign governments on the matter. . . . Consequently, I join JUSTICE GINSBURG's opinion.

Will the United States enforce the tax laws of another country, and when is conduct occurring within the United States implicating the Revenue Rule? Consider this question in the following case.

Pasquantino v. United States

Supreme Court of the United States
544 U.S. 349 (2005)

JUSTICE THOMAS delivered the opinion of the Court.

. . . Petitioners Carl J. Pasquantino, David B. Pasquantino, and Arthur Hilts were indicted for and convicted of federal wire fraud for carrying out a scheme to smuggle large quantities of liquor into Canada from the United States. According to the evidence presented at trial, the Pasquantinos, while in New York, ordered liquor over the telephone from discount package stores in Maryland. . . . They employed Hilts and others to drive the liquor over the Canadian border, without paying the required excise taxes. The drivers avoided paying taxes by hiding the liquor in their vehicles and failing to declare the goods to Canadian customs officials. During the time of petitioners' smuggling operation, between 1996 and 2000, Canada heavily taxed the importation of alcoholic beverages. . . . Uncontested evidence at trial showed that Canadian taxes then due on alcohol purchased in the United States and transported to Canada were approximately double the liquor's purchase price. . . .

Before trial, petitioners moved to dismiss the indictment on the ground that it stated no wire fraud offense. The wire fraud statute prohibits the use of interstate wires to effect "any scheme or artifice to defraud, or for obtaining money or property by means of false or fraudulent pretenses, representations, or promises." 18 U.S.C. § 1343. Petitioners contended that the Government lacked a sufficient interest in enforcing the revenue laws of Canada, and therefore that they had not committed wire fraud.... The District Court denied the motion and the case went to trial. The jury convicted petitioners of wire fraud.

Petitioners appealed their convictions to the United States Court of Appeals for the Fourth Circuit, again urging that the indictment failed to state a wire fraud offense.... Over Judge Hamilton's dissent, the panel agreed and reversed the convictions.... The Court of Appeals granted rehearing en banc, vacated the panel's decision, and affirmed petitioners' convictions....

We granted certiorari to resolve a conflict in the Courts of Appeals over whether a scheme to defraud a foreign government of tax revenue violates the wire fraud statute.... Compare *United States* v. *Boots*, 80 F.3d 580, 587 (1st Cir. 1996) (holding that a scheme to defraud a foreign nation of tax revenue does not violate the wire fraud statute), with *United States* v. *Trapilo*, 130 F.3d 547, 552–553 (2d Cir. 1997) (holding that a scheme to defraud a foreign nation of tax revenue violates the wire fraud statute). We agree with the Court of Appeals that it does and therefore affirm the judgment below.[1]

We first consider whether petitioners' conduct falls within the literal terms of the wire fraud statute.... Taking the latter element first, Canada's right to uncollected excise taxes on the liquor petitioners imported into Canada is "property" in its hands. This right is an entitlement to collect money from petitioners, the possession of which is "something of value" to the Government of Canada....

Turning to the second element at issue here, petitioners' plot was a "scheme or artifice to defraud" Canada of its valuable entitlement to tax revenue. The evidence showed that petitioners routinely concealed imported liquor from Canadian officials and failed to declare those goods on customs forms.... By this conduct, they represented to Canadian customs officials that their drivers had no goods to declare. This, then, was a scheme "designed to defraud by representations," ... and therefore a "scheme or artifice to defraud" Canada of taxes due on the smuggled goods.

Neither the antismuggling statute, 18 U.S.C. § 546, nor U.S. tax treaties, ..., convince us that petitioners' scheme falls outside the terms of the wire fraud statute. Unlike the treaties and the antismuggling statute, the wire fraud statute punishes fraudulent use of domestic wires, whether or not such conduct constitutes smuggling, occurs aboard a vessel, or evades foreign taxes....

---

1. We express no view on the related question whether a foreign government, based on wire or mail fraud predicate offenses, may bring a civil action under the Racketeer Influenced and Corrupt Organizations Act for a scheme to defraud it of taxes. See *Attorney General of Canada* v. *R. J. Reynolds Tobacco Holdings, Inc.*, 268 F.3d 103, 106 (2d Cir. 2001) (holding that the Government of Canada cannot bring a civil RICO suit to recover for a scheme to defraud it of taxes); *Republic of Honduras* v. *Philip Morris Cos.*, 341 F.3d 1253, 1255 (11th Cir. 2003) (same with respect to other foreign governments).

We next consider petitioners' revenue rule argument. Petitioners argue that, to avoid reading § 1343 to derogate from the common-law revenue rule, we should construe the otherwise-applicable language of the wire fraud statute to except frauds directed at evading foreign taxes. Their argument relies on the canon of construction that "statutes which invade the common law . . . are to be read with a presumption favoring the retention of long-established and familiar principles, except where a statutory purpose to the contrary is evident." *United States v. Texas,* 507 U.S. 529, 534 (1993) . . . . This presumption is, however, no bar to a construction that conflicts with a common-law rule if the statute "'speaks directly' to the question addressed by the common law." . . .

Whether the wire fraud statute derogates from the common-law revenue rule depends, in turn, on whether reading § 1343 to reach this prosecution conflicts with a well-established revenue rule principle.

The wire fraud statute derogates from no well-established revenue rule principle. We are aware of no common-law revenue rule case decided as of 1952 [when § 1343 was enacted by Congress] that held or clearly implied that the revenue rule barred the United States from prosecuting a fraudulent scheme to evade foreign taxes. The traditional rationales for the revenue rule, moreover, do not plainly suggest that it swept so broadly. . . .

Having concluded that revenue rule jurisprudence is no clear bar to this prosecution, we next turn to whether the purposes of the revenue rule, as articulated in the relevant authorities, suggest differently. They do not.

First, this prosecution poses little risk of causing the principal evil against which the revenue rule was traditionally thought to guard: judicial evaluation of the policy-laden enactments of other sovereigns. See, *e.g., Moore v. Mitchell,* 30 F.2d 600, 604 (2d Cir. 1929) (L. Hand, J., concurring). As Judge Hand put it, allowing courts to enforce another country's revenue laws was thought to be a delicate inquiry

> when it concerns the relations between the foreign state and its own citizens. . . . To pass upon the provisions for the public order of another state is, or at any rate should be, beyond the powers of a court; it involves the relations between the states themselves, with which courts are incompetent to deal, and which are intrusted to other authorities.

The present prosecution creates little risk of causing international friction through judicial evaluation of the policies of foreign sovereigns. This action was brought by the Executive to enforce a statute passed by Congress. . . . True, a prosecution like this one requires a court to recognize foreign law to determine whether the defendant violated U.S. law. But we may assume that by electing to bring this prosecution, the Executive has assessed this prosecution's impact on this Nation's relationship with Canada, and concluded that it poses little danger of causing international friction. We know of no common-law court that has applied the revenue rule to bar an action accompanied by such a safeguard, and neither petitioners nor the dissent directs us to any. The greater danger, in fact, would lie in our judging this prosecution barred based on the foreign policy concerns animating the revenue rule, concerns that we have "neither aptitude, facilities nor responsibility" to evaluate.

More broadly, petitioners argue that the revenue rule avoids giving domestic effect to politically sensitive and controversial policy decisions embodied in foreign revenue laws, regardless of whether courts need pass judgment on such laws. . . . This worries us little here. The present prosecution, if authorized by the wire fraud statute, embodies the policy choice of the two political branches of our Government — Congress and the Executive — to free the interstate wires from fraudulent use, irrespective of the object of the fraud. Such a reading of the wire fraud statute gives effect to that considered policy choice. It therefore poses no risk of advancing the policies of Canada illegitimately.

Still a final revenue rule rationale petitioners urge is the concern that courts lack the competence to examine the validity of unfamiliar foreign tax schemes. . . . Foreign law, of course, posed no unmanageable complexity in this case. The District Court had before it uncontroverted testimony of a Government witness that petitioners' scheme aimed at violating Canadian tax law. . . .

Nevertheless, Federal Rule of Criminal Procedure 26.1 addresses petitioners' concern by setting forth a procedure for interpreting foreign law that improves on those available at common law. Specifically, it permits a court, in deciding issues of foreign law, to consider "any relevant material or source — including testimony — without regard to the Federal Rules of Evidence." By contrast, common-law procedures for dealing with foreign law — those available to the courts that formulated the revenue rule — were more cumbersome. . . . Rule 26.1 gives federal courts sufficient means to resolve the incidental foreign law issues they may encounter in wire fraud prosecutions. . . .

Finally, our interpretation of the wire fraud statute does not give it "extraterritorial effect.[12]" . . . Petitioners used U.S. interstate wires to execute a scheme to defraud a foreign sovereign of tax revenue. Their offense was complete the moment they executed the scheme inside the United States; "the wire fraud statute punishes the scheme, not its success." . . . This domestic element of petitioners' conduct is what the Government is punishing in this prosecution, no less than when it prosecutes a scheme to defraud a foreign individual or corporation, or a foreign government acting as a market participant. . . . In any event, the wire fraud statute punishes frauds executed "in interstate or foreign commerce," 18 U.S.C. § 1343, so this is surely not a statute in which Congress had only "domestic concerns in mind." . . .

It may seem an odd use of the Federal Government's resources to prosecute a U.S. citizen for smuggling cheap liquor into Canada. But the broad language of the

12. As some indication of the novelty of the dissent's "extraterritoriality" argument, we note that this argument was not pressed or passed upon below and was raised only as an afterthought in petitioners' reply brief, depriving the Government of a chance to respond.

wire fraud statute authorizes it to do so and no canon of statutory construction permits us to read the statute more narrowly. The judgment of the Court of Appeals is affirmed. . . .

JUSTICE GINSBURG, with whom JUSTICE BREYER joins, and JUSTICE SCALIA and JUSTICE SOUTER join as to Parts II and III, dissenting.

. . . The Court today reads the wire fraud statute to draw into our courts, at the prosecutor's option, charges that another nation's revenue laws have been evaded. The common-law revenue rule does not stand in the way, the Court instructs, for that rule has no application to criminal prosecutions under the wire fraud statute.

As I see it, and as petitioners urged, the Court has ascribed an exorbitant scope to the wire fraud statute, in disregard of our repeated recognition that "Congress legislates against the backdrop of the presumption against extraterritoriality." See *EEOC v. Arabian American Oil Co.*, 499 U.S. 244, 248 (1991) *(ARAMCO)*; *Small* v. *United States* (The Court has "adopted the legal presumption that Congress ordinarily intends its statutes to have domestic, not extraterritorial, application."); . . .

Today's novel decision is all the more troubling for its failure to take account of Canada's primary interest in the matter at stake. United States citizens who have committed criminal violations of Canadian tax law can be extradited to stand trial in Canada. Canadian courts are best positioned to decide "whether, and to what extent, the defendants have defrauded the governments of Canada and Ontario out of tax revenues owed pursuant to their own, sovereign, excise laws." . . .

I

Construing §1343 to encompass violations of foreign revenue laws, the Court ignores the absence of anything signaling Congress' intent to give the statute such an extraordinary extraterritorial effect. "It is a longstanding principle of American law," that Congress, in most of its legislative endeavors, "is primarily concerned with domestic conditions." . . . Absent a clear statement of "the affirmative intention of the Congress," . . . this Court ordinarily does not read statutes to reach conduct that is "the primary concern of a foreign country," . . .

Section 1343, which contains no reference to foreign law as an element of the domestic crime of wire fraud, contrasts with federal criminal statutes that chart the courts' course in this regard. . . . These statutes indicate that Congress, which has the sole authority to determine the extraterritorial reach of domestic laws, is fully capable of conveying its policy choice to the Executive and the courts. I would not assume from legislative silence that Congress left the matter to Executive discretion.

The presumption against extraterritoriality, which guides courts in the absence of congressional direction, provides ample cause to conclude that §1343 does not extend to the instant scheme. Moreover, as to foreign customs and tax laws, there is scant room for doubt about Congress' general perspective: Congress has actively indicated, through both domestic legislation and treaties, that it intends "strictly [to] limit the parameters of any assistance given" to foreign nations. . . .

First, Congress has enacted a specific statute criminalizing offenses of the genre committed by the defendants here: 18 U.S.C. § 546 prohibits transporting goods "into the territory of any foreign government in violation of the laws there in force." Section 546's application, however, is expressly conditioned on the foreign government's enactment of reciprocal legislation prohibiting smuggling into the United States. . . . The reciprocity limitation reflects a legislative determination that this country should not provide other nations with greater enforcement assistance than they give to the United States. The limitation also cabins the Government's discretion as to which nation's customs laws to enforce, thereby avoiding the appearance of prosecutorial overreaching. . . . Significantly, Canada has no statute criminalizing smuggling into the United States, rendering § 546 inapplicable to schemes resembling the one at issue here.

Second, the United States and Canada have negotiated, and the Senate has ratified, a comprehensive tax treaty, in which both nations have committed to providing collection assistance with respect to each other's tax claims. . . . These provisions would preclude Canada from obtaining United States assistance in enforcing its claims against the Pasquantinos and Hilts. . . .

II

Complementing the principle that courts ordinarily should await congressional instruction before giving our laws extraterritorial thrust, the common-law revenue rule holds that one nation generally does not enforce another's tax laws. . . . The Government argues, and the Court accepts, that domestic wire fraud prosecutions premised on violations of foreign tax law do not implicate the revenue rule because the court, while it must "recognize foreign [revenue] law to determine whether the defendant violated U.S. law," . . . need only "enforce" foreign law "in an attenuated sense." . . . As discussed above, however, the defendants' conduct arguably fell within the scope of § 1343 only because of their purpose to evade Canadian customs and tax laws; shorn of that purpose, no other aspect of their conduct was criminal in this country. . . . It seems to me unavoidably obvious, therefore, that this prosecution directly implicates the revenue rule. It is equally plain that Congress did not endeavor, by enacting § 1343, to displace that rule.

III

Finally, the rule of lenity counsels against adopting the Court's interpretation of § 1343. It is a "close question" whether the wire fraud statute's prohibition of "any scheme . . . to defraud" includes schemes directed solely at defrauding foreign governments of tax revenues. . . . We have long held that, when confronted with "two rational readings of a criminal statute, one harsher than the other, we are to choose the harsher only when Congress has spoken in clear and definite language." . . . This interpretive guide is particularly appropriate here. Wire fraud is a predicate offense under the Racketeer Influenced and Corrupt Organizations Act (RICO), 18 U.S.C. § 1961(1), and the money laundering statute, § 1956(c)(7)(A). . . . A finding that particular conduct constitutes wire fraud therefore exposes certain defendants to the severe criminal penalties and forfeitures provided in both RICO, . . . and the money laundering statute. . . .

For the reasons stated, I would hold that § 1343 does not extend to schemes to evade foreign tax and customs laws. I would therefore reverse the judgment of the Court of Appeals.

§ 3.03 Jurisdictional Categories and Bases

A. Jurisdictional Categories

The Restatement (Fourth) of the Foreign Relations Law of the United States (2018)

§ 401 Categories of Jurisdiction

The foreign relations law of the United States divides jurisdiction into three categories:

(a) jurisdiction to prescribe, i.e., the authority of a state to make law applicable to persons, property, or conduct;

(b) jurisdiction to adjudicate, i.e., the authority of a state to apply law to persons or things, in particular through the processes of its courts or administrative tribunals; and

(c) jurisdiction to enforce, i.e., the authority of a state to exercise its power to compel compliance with law.

Note

In domestic practice, distinguishing between these three categories of jurisdiction is a matter of considering which branch of government exercises a particular function — legislative, judicial or executive. In international treaty practice, however, different sovereignties may be empowered to exercise different categories of jurisdiction. Take, for example, the 1884 Convention for the Protection of Submarine Cables, signed at Paris, March 14, 1884, French text in 163 Consol. T. S. 391. Article II of the Convention, a standard suppression provision, requires parties to make it "a punishable offense to break or injure a submarine cable, willfully or by culpable negligence, in such a manner as might interrupt or obstruct telegraphic communication." Jurisdiction to prescribe lies mainly with the flag state of the vessel where the offense is committed, with nationality jurisdiction in certain cases. Jurisdiction to enforce lies, however, with any state that is a party to the convention. Any state party may board vessels of other parties to obtain information and statements. But prosecution of thieves or careless sailors takes place only in the state of the flag or of nationality. *See* Roger S. Clark, *Some Aspects of the Concept of International Criminal Law: Suppression Conventions, Jurisdiction, Submarine Cables and*

The Lotus, 22 CRIM. L.F. 519 (2011). These principles have been carried forward into the twentieth century treaties on the law of the sea, Douglas Burnett, Tara Davenport & Robert Beckman, *Overview of the International Legal Regime Governing Submarine Cables in* SUBMARINE CABLES: THE HANDBOOK OF LAW AND POLICY 63 (Douglas R. Burnett, Robert C. Backman & Tara M. Davenport eds., 2014). There are other examples where one state (the "requested state") is exercising an enforcement jurisdiction in order that another state ("the requesting state") may exercise its prescriptive and adjudicative jurisdiction. *See* chap. 8 (Narcotics and Money Laundering); chap. 15 (Mutual Assistance); and chap. 16 (Extradition Treaties).

For a comprehensive discussion of jurisdiction in international practice, see THE OXFORD HANDBOOK OF JURISDICTION IN INTERNATIONAL LAW (Stephen Allen, Daniel Costello, Malgosia Fitzmaurice, Paul Grayl & Edward Guntrip eds., 2019).

B. Jurisdictional Bases

United States v. Layton

United States Court of Appeals for the Ninth Circuit
855 F.2d 1388 (1988)

ALARCON, CIRCUIT JUDGE:

... The Peoples Temple was a religious organization composed primarily of American citizens. In 1977, under the leadership of Jim Jones, the Peoples Temple established a settlement of more than 1,000 people in a remote jungle area of the Republic of Guyana. The settlement was known as Jonestown. Layton was a member of the Temple and resided at Jonestown.

On November 1, 1978, Congressman Leo J. Ryan, U.S. Representative from the 11th Congressional District of California, notified Jones that Ryan would be visiting Jonestown to investigate allegations of poor living conditions and mistreatment of residents. Jones opposed Ryan's visit and announced his opposition in several tape-recorded speeches delivered to the Jonestown community in the days preceding Ryan's arrival. In certain of the speeches, Jones intimated that Ryan would suffer physical harm if he insisted on entering Jonestown. Jones also prepared and circulated among the Jonestown residents a petition opposing Ryan's visit. Layton signed the petition.

On November 17, 1978, Ryan and his party, which included media representatives and concerned relatives of Jonestown residents, arrived in Jonestown. On November 17 and November 18, Ryan met with many of the residents. Some of them requested assistance in leaving Jonestown. In the afternoon of November 18, the members of Ryan's party and the departing residents boarded a truck to be transported to the Port Kaituma airstrip, approximately six miles from Jonestown....

Ryan had requested two planes to transport the departing group from Port Kaituma to Georgetown, Guyana. The two planes—a nineteen-seat Otter and a six-seat

Cessna—landed at the airstrip about 20 minutes after the arrival of the truck carrying the Ryan party. . . .

When boarding of the Cessna was completed, the airplane taxied down the runway in preparation for take-off. Boarding of the Otter was still in progress. A tractor-trailer carrying a group of Peoples Temple members drove in front of the Cessna and headed toward the Otter. The people on the tractor-trailer began shooting at the Otter. The bullets struck passengers seated inside the plane as well as those waiting to board. Ryan, who was standing outside the Otter, was killed in the attack. Richard Dwyer, United States Deputy Chief of Mission to Guyana, was wounded. . . .

In an indictment filed October 9, 1980, Layton was charged with conspiring to kill a member of Congress (Ryan), in violation of 18 U.S.C. § 351(d); aiding and abetting in the killing of a member of Congress, in violation of 18 U.S.C. §§ 2 and 351(a); conspiring to murder an internationally protected person (Dwyer), in violation of 18 U.S.C. § 1117; and aiding and abetting in the attempted murder of an internationally protected person, in violation of 18 U.S.C. § 1116(a). At the time the indictment was filed, Layton was being held in custody in Guyana, in connection with charges filed against him in that country. He returned to the United States, in the company of FBI agents, on or about November 20, 1980. . . . On December 1, 1986, the jury returned a verdict of guilty on all counts. On March 3, 1987, Layton was sentenced to fifteen years imprisonment on counts 1, 3, and 4, and to life in prison on count 2. . . .

Layton filed a motion in the district court for dismissal based on lack of subject matter jurisdiction. The district court concluded that it had jurisdiction over the charges contained in the indictment. *United States v. Layton*, 509 F. Supp. 212 (N.D. Cal. 1981). . . . For the following reasons, we hold that the district court properly exercised subject matter jurisdiction over each count in the indictment. . . .

Layton argues that § 351 cannot be applied in this case because the acts in question occurred outside the United States and Congress did not intend § 351 to be applied extraterritorially.

Where the language of a criminal statute does not indicate whether the statute is to be applied to extraterritorial conduct, resolution of the question "depends upon the purpose of Congress as evinced by the description and nature of the crime." *United States v. Bowman*, 260 U.S. 94, 97, 43 S. Ct. 39, 67 L. Ed. 149 (1922). When a statute describes a crime which is not logically dependent on its locality but which, instead, injures the government wherever the crime occurs, the statute will be applied to U.S. citizens who violate its provisions while outside United States territory. . . . The clearest statement of this principle appears in *Skiriotes v. Florida*, 313 U.S. 69, 61 S. Ct. 924, 85 L. Ed. 1193 (1941), where the Court declared: "[A] criminal statute dealing with acts that are directly injurious to the government, and are capable of perpetration without regard to particular locality, is to be construed as applicable to citizens of the United States upon the high seas or in a foreign country, though there be no express declaration to that effect." . . .

We have applied the foregoing principles to federal statutes prohibiting the theft of government property . . . and the concealment of assets in connection with a bankruptcy proceeding, *Stegeman v. United States*, 425 F.2d 984 (9th Cir.) (en banc), *cert. denied*, 400 U.S. 837, 91 S. Ct. 74, 27 L. Ed. 2d 70 (1970). Because the statutes at issue in each case were "enacted to serve important interests of government," . . . . and jurisdiction was "not logically dependent upon the locality of violation," . . . we held that Congress must have intended the statutes to apply regardless of where the proscribed acts occurred.

The act proscribed by § 351(a) — the killing of a member of Congress — is "directly injurious to the government, and [is] capable of perpetration without regard to particular locality." . . . The killing of a member of Congress obstructs the governing process, whether the act occurs within or without the United States. Like the statute prohibiting theft of government property, section 351(a) "prohibits conduct which is obstructive of the functions of government. The *locus* of the conduct is not relevant to the end sought by the enactment." . . .

As the district court noted, it would be a "perversion of logic" to infer extraterritorial jurisdiction under statutes governing theft of government property or concealment of assets in bankruptcy yet decline to infer such jurisdiction under a statute prohibiting the killing of a member of Congress. . . . Section 351(a), therefore, should be construed to apply extraterritorially. . . . Accordingly, we reject Layton's argument that § 351(d) applies only when the overt act required thereunder occurs within the United States. . . .

Count Three charged Layton with conspiracy to kill Deputy Chief of Mission Richard Dwyer, an internationally protected person, in violation of 18 U.S.C. § 1117. Count Four charged Layton with aiding and abetting the attempted murder of Dwyer, in violation of 18 U.S.C. §§ 2 and 1116. Section 1116(a) makes it a crime to "kill[] or attempt[] to kill a foreign official, official guest, or internationally protected person." Section 1116(c) provides: "If the victim of an offense under subsection (a) is an internationally protected person, the United States may exercise jurisdiction over the offense if the alleged offender is present within the United States, irrespective of the place where the offense was committed or the nationality of the victim or the alleged offender." Section 1117 forbids conspiracies to commit an act prohibited by § 1116.

Layton argues that § 1116(c) — which requires the offender's presence in the United States — identifies the *only* circumstance in which the courts may exercise jurisdiction over extraterritorial conduct violating § 1116(a). Since he was not present in the United States at the time he was indicted, Layton argues, subject matter jurisdiction is lacking under § 1116(a) and under § 1117, the corresponding conspiracy statute.

The legislative history of § 1116, however, "makes it abundantly clear that the intent of Congress was to pass the legislation necessary to fulfill the obligations of the United States under two treaties" concerning the prevention and punishment of terrorism and crimes against internationally protected persons. . . . "Congress, moreover, clearly intended to enforce the obligations of the United States under the treaties completely." . . . One of these instruments, a U.N. treaty, required signatory states to enact any legislation necessary to establish jurisdiction over specified crimes, including those with which Layton was charged "when the alleged offender is a national of that State" or "when the crime is committed against an internationally protected person . . . who enjoys his status as such by virtue of functions which he exercises on behalf of that State." . . . (quoting "Convention on the Prevention and Punishment of Crimes Against Internationally Protected Persons," Art. 3). Congress clearly intended that § 1116 be enforced in such circumstances. . . .

Moreover, it would have made no sense for Congress to enact a statute forbidding the murder or attempted murder of an internationally protected person representing the United States, which crime would likely occur outside the territory of the United States, yet not intend that the prohibition apply to extraterritorial acts.

In summary, we agree with the district court that the most reasonable reading of the statute, "in the context of its purpose and origins, is that Congress intended to meet its obligation to take jurisdiction under each of the circumstances delineated in" the U.N. treaty. . . . Since Layton is a national of the United States, and since Dwyer was an internationally protected person by virtue of the functions he exercised on behalf of the United States, the district court would have had jurisdiction to try Layton for the substantive offenses of murdering or attempting to murder Dwyer, even if those acts had occurred outside the territory of the United States. Layton was not charged with these substantive offenses but with conspiracy to murder and with aiding and abetting the attempted murder. . . . because jurisdiction would be proper over the underlying substantive offenses, it is also proper over the related offenses with which Layton was charged. . . . For the reasons set forth above, we AFFIRM the judgment. . . .

Notes

(1) Would there be a basis for jurisdiction if the defendant in *Layton* had been a foreign national? *See* Mark Peterson, Note, *The Extraterritorial Effect of Federal Criminal Statutes: Offenses Directed at Members of Congress*, 6 Hastings Int'l & Comp. L. Rev. 773 (1983) (arguing that a federal court would be justified in this scenario in asserting subject matter jurisdiction over a foreign defendant).

(2) The District Court in *Layton* looked at international law principles in deciding whether there was jurisdiction. The court stated:

> There are five principles under which the law of nations permits the exercise of criminal jurisdiction by a nation: territorial jurisdiction based on the location where the alleged crime was committed, and including "objective" territorial jurisdiction, which allows countries to reach acts committed outside territorial limits but intended to produce, and producing, detrimental effects within the nation; nationality jurisdiction based on the nationality of the offender; protective jurisdiction based on the protection of the interests

> and the integrity of the nation; universality jurisdiction for certain crimes where custody of the offender is sufficient; and passive personality jurisdiction based on the nationality of the victim. . . . [a] The fact that Congress in the past may have favored or disfavored any particular ground for asserting extra-territorial jurisdiction is irrelevant to the consideration of Congress's constitutional power to assert that jurisdiction. . . .
>
> The power of Congress to authorize extraterritorial jurisdiction over the alleged crimes in this matter can be located in at least four of these principles—protective, territorial, passive personality and nationality jurisdiction. The alleged crimes certainly had a potentially adverse effect upon the security or governmental functions of the nation, thereby providing the basis for jurisdiction under the protective principle. The charges also suggest that the alleged offenses were intended to produce and did produce harmful effects within this nation, allowing a claim of jurisdiction under the "objective" territorial principle. The nationality of the alleged victims would also support an assertion of jurisdiction under the passive personality principle. Finally, since Mr. Layton is a citizen of the United States, "American authority over (him) could be based upon the allegiance (he) owe(s) this country and its laws. . . ." . . . We therefore see no difficulty in upholding the authority of Congress, under the Constitution, to apply these statutes extraterritorially to the events charged in the indictment.

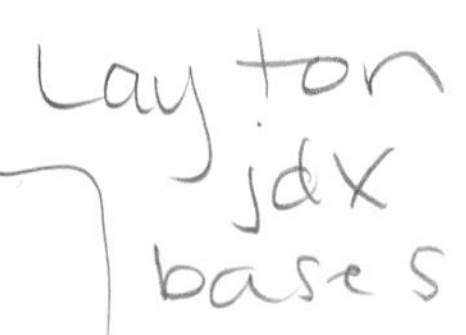

509 F. Supp. 212 (N.D. Cal. 1981).

(3) As indicated in the introductory note to this chapter, in deciding whether statutes have extraterritorial effect, courts often consider two questions: (1) whether it was the purpose of Congress to have the statute apply to acts occurring abroad; (2) whether international law permits the United States to exercise extraterritorial jurisdiction with respect to such acts. Which of these two questions should be considered first?

Courts have not followed a consistent approach. For example, in *United States v. Velasquez-Mercado*, 697 F. Supp. 292 (S.D. Texas 1988), the Southern District of Texas dismissed an indictment by examining first the extraterritorial application as intended by Congress. The court stated, "before exploring whether any theory of international law supports a congressional effort to apply our criminal laws extraterritorially, the initial question is whether the Congress even intended such an application. Criminal statutes are given extraterritorial application only if 'the nature of the law permits it and Congress intends it.'"

In *United States v. Felix-Gutierrez*, 940 F.2d 1200 (9th Cir. 1991), Circuit Judge Reinhardt considered international legal principles stating, "Prior to giving

---

a. *See also* Harvard Research in International Law, *Jurisdiction with Respect to Crime*, 29 A.J.I.L. 437 (Supp. 1935); The Restatement (Fourth) of the Foreign Relations Law of the United States (2018) § 402 (Bases of Jurisdiction to Prescribe).—Eds.

extraterritorial effect to any penal statute, we must consider whether extraterritorial application would violate international law. The law of nations permits the exercise of criminal jurisdiction by a nation under five general principles: territorial, national, protective, universality, and passive personality."

(4) In the district court opinion in *Layton*, as well as in other cases throughout this section, the courts do not always rely on a single basis of jurisdiction. Because the five jurisdictional bases overlap, more than one may be applicable in the same case. For example, in *United States v. Felix-Gutierrez*, *supra* note 3, the court stated:

> Here, three of the international law principles permitting extraterritorial jurisdiction have application: (i) territorial, (ii) protective, and (iii) passive personality. Under the first two of these, jurisdiction is based on the nature of the conduct or offense. Courts have defined the "territorial" principle to include not only acts occurring within the United States, but acts occurring outside the United States' borders that have effects within the national territory.... Under the "protective" principle, jurisdiction is based on whether the national interest or national security is threatened or injured by the conduct in question. Under the "passive personality" principle, courts may assert extraterritorial jurisdiction on the basis of the nationality of the victim.

(5) Consider the limitations to categorizing all jurisdictional questions in terms of five principles noted in Edward M. Wise, *Jurisdiction, Theories of Punishment, and the Idea of Community* (Paper presented at a Special Session organized by the Committee on Philosophy and Law, at the Annual Meeting of the American Philosophical Association, Eastern Division, Boston, December 30, 1999).

> There are difficulties with analyzing all jurisdictional questions in terms of these five categories. In the first place, these "principles" or categories originated as generalizations from a mass of national legislative provisions about the competence of criminal courts to act in certain kinds of cases. These empirical generalizations about state practice have been translated into permissive or limiting normative rules, on the assumption that international law is indeed what states in fact do. But state practice does not always come clearly labeled. As a result, these five categories overlap and interweave. Their contours are not entirely settled. For instance: does objective territoriality, based on the crime having had an effect within the territory, require intent to have such effect as well as an actual effect within the territory, or is one or the other sufficient? Who counts as a national? To what kinds of crimes does the protective principle extend? To what kinds of crimes does the universal principle extend? Moreover, there are cases in which states assert and are admitted to have jurisdiction that do not fit within the accepted contours of these five categories.

Consider also this question in the context of District Judge Weinstein's decision in *United States v. Georgescu*, 723 F. Supp. 912 (E.D.N.Y. 1989) (discussing what we would call "landing state" jurisdiction):

Over the mid-Atlantic on a Scandinavian Airlines flight from Copenhagen, Denmark to John F. Kennedy International Airport in Queens, the defendant, a Romanian national, allegedly accosted a nine year old girl who is a national of Norway by placing his hand on her genitals. He was indicted for committing a criminal sexual act while in the special aircraft jurisdiction of the United States. . . . In this case of first impression, he moves to dismiss, claiming lack of jurisdiction in United States courts. His motion must be denied for the reasons stated below. . . .

The special aircraft jurisdiction statute was originally created to comply with treaty obligations under the Tokyo Convention. While the Tokyo Convention was intended primarily to deal with the punishment of air piracy, it was also designed to cover any other criminal offense. . . . The Tokyo Convention's primary goal was to encourage nations to exercise jurisdiction over crimes committed aboard aircraft registered in that nation. Nevertheless, the Tokyo Convention explicitly provides for jurisdiction over crimes committed aboard aircraft of foreign registry. Article 3(3) provides, "This Convention does not exclude any criminal jurisdiction exercised in accordance with national law." . . .

Defendant contends that jurisdiction over foreign aircraft is limited by article 4 of the Tokyo Convention.[b] The limitations of article 4 apply to attempts to "interfere with an aircraft in flight to exercise . . . criminal jurisdiction." . . . Interference means forcing the aircraft to land, or unduly delaying the flight. . . .

The Tokyo Convention's concurrent jurisdiction provisions reflect the international legal community's acceptance of broad bases for jurisdiction over criminal offenses occurring on aircraft. *See generally Restatement,* [(THIRD) OF THE FOREIGN RELATIONS LAW OF THE UNITED STATES] § 402 Comment h, at 240–41, § 403 Reporters' Note 9, at 253–54 (suggesting that acts aboard aircraft be considered a basis of jurisdiction independent of traditional bases in international law, and approving the exercise of criminal jurisdiction over an offense committed on foreign aircraft, especially if the offense involved the use of force). . . . Numerous other signatories to the Tokyo Convention have passed statutes conferring jurisdiction over crimes committed aboard foreign aircraft. . . .

---

b. Article 4 of the Convention provides that a Contracting State which is not the State of registration may not interfere with an aircraft in flight in order to exercise its criminal jurisdiction over an offense committed on board except where (a) the offense has effect on the territory of such State; (b) the offense has been committed by or against a national or permanent resident of such State; (c) the offense is against the security of such State; (d) the offense consists of a breach of any rules or regulations relating to the flight or maneuver of aircraft in force in such State; or, (e) necessary to ensure the observance of any obligation of such State under a multilateral international agreement. (This article deals with enforcement not prescriptive jurisdiction.) — Eds.

Extension of jurisdiction to include criminal acts committed against foreign nationals aboard a foreign airliner bound for, and actually landing, at a United States airport makes good sense. The pilot can radio ahead for assistance, federal agents can be present to take the culprit into custody at once and the witnesses to the crime will be immediately available. If the United States did not exercise its jurisdiction, there is no guarantee that any other country would do so, since the Tokyo Convention does not oblige a state to prosecute alleged offenders. Mendelsohn, *In-Flight Crime: The International and Domestic Picture Under the Tokyo Convention*, 53 VA. L. REV. 509, 516 (1967). For would-be criminals, it may have an inhibiting effect to know that upon landing they may be immediately apprehended and prosecuted.

Even if Congress's criminalization of defendant's alleged acts and its exercise of jurisdiction were counter to international law, this fact does not lessen the validity of the statutes as superseding domestic legislation. International law is "subject to the Constitution, and is also subject to 'repeal' by other law of the United States." *Restatement, supra* ch. 2, Introductory Note, at 40; *id.* § 111 (2), at 42. While the courts must make a fair effort to interpret domestic law in a way consistent with international obligations . . . in the event of irreconcilable conflict, the courts are bound to apply domestic law if it was passed more recently. . . . The statutory provisions under which defendant is being prosecuted were passed subsequent to the development of the traditional notions of international law jurisdiction to which defendant argues this court is confined. They were also passed subsequent to the Tokyo Convention. The domestic statutes are controlling. . . .

Consistent with the Tokyo Convention, other interested countries could prosecute the defendant for his alleged acts. Since the defendant is Romanian and the victim is Norwegian, Romania and Norway would be the most likely countries to have an interest in this case. Both countries are party to the Tokyo Convention. . . .

It is unclear whether the domestic criminal statutes of Norway and Romania would apply to this case. This court's requests that the United States provide this information have been unavailing. It does appear, however, that the Norwegian Criminal Code makes punishable sexual molestation of a Norwegian national by a foreigner abroad. . . . Thus it is possible that defendant can be extradited to Norway to stand trial.

While extradition can be a complex process, prosecution in Norway may place less of a burden on the alleged victim, who has returned to Norway and must now be brought back to the United States for a trial, where she is likely to face further trauma on the witness stand.

In a case such as this one, the United States' initial exercise of jurisdiction may have been reasonable in order to detain the alleged criminal and gather evidence. Further prosecution in this country under these circumstances

> may create logistical problems involving the location of witnesses, and evidentiary obstacles involving the testimony of the alleged victim. Evidentiary issues in the taking of the child's testimony will be the subject of a subsequent memorandum....
>
> Despite this court's reservations about the wisdom of further prosecution in this country, it lacks the power to refuse jurisdiction on equitable grounds.... In this case, where jurisdiction exists, the indictment properly charges an offense, and the prosecution is timely, the court must allow the case to proceed. The decision on whether to prosecute or refrain and leave prosecution to another country is entirely one for the prosecutor, guided by the Departments of Justice and State....

(6) The Tokyo Convention on Offences and Certain Other Acts Committed on Board Aircraft, 704 U.N.T.S. 219 (1963) provides in Article 3:

1. The State of registration of the aircraft is competent to exercise jurisdiction over offences and acts committed on board.
2. Each Contracting State shall take such measures as may be necessary to establish its jurisdiction as the State of registration over offences committed on board aircraft registered in such State.
3. This Convention does not exclude any criminal jurisdiction exercised in accordance with national law.

When the Convention was being drafted, it was proposed to include a specific provision according jurisdiction to the "landing state" and, indeed, granting priority to that state, jurisdiction being concurrent with the state of registration (and probably other states as well). That proposal failed.

The Hague Convention on the Suppression of Unlawful Seizure of Aircraft (Hijacking), 860 U.N.T.S. 105 (1970) and the Montreal Convention for the Suppression of Unlawful Acts Against the Safety of Civil Aviation, 974 U.N.T.S 177 (1971) require the exercise of jurisdiction in a range of situations including "when the aircraft on which the offence is committed lands in its territory with the alleged offender still on board." Nevertheless, both Conventions (and most subsequent suppression conventions) contain the saving provision that they do "not exclude any criminal jurisdiction exercised in accordance with national law."

In 1963, the saving provision was apparently meant to protect existing examples of landing state jurisdiction. As used in later treaties does it mean that *any* jurisdiction exercised by a state is legitimated or must it be consistent with customary international law? Could it be used to justify passive personality or universal jurisdiction over treaty offences where the treaty itself does not provide for such jurisdiction? The saving provision continues to appear in 2010 updates of the Hague and Montreal Conventions (in force with limited parties since 2018) that already contain very broad bases of jurisdiction. *See* Roger S. Clark, *Jurisdiction over Transnational Crime*, *in* ROUTLEDGE HANDBOOK OF TRANSNATIONAL LAW 91, 96–100 (Neil Boister & Robert J. Currie eds., 2015).

The Convention for the Suppression of Unlawful Acts Against the Safety of Maritime Navigation, 28 I.L.M. 668 (1988), negotiated under the auspices of the International Maritime Organization, deals among other things with hijacking of and other violence on vessels. It does not contain an obligation on the landing state to exercise jurisdiction. (It does, however, "not exclude any criminal jurisdiction exercised in accordance with national law.")

(7) The New Zealand Crimes Act 1961, § 8(1) provides an example of landing state jurisdiction applying generally to crimes committed on ships and aircraft. *See* Roger S. Clark, *Criminal Code Reform in New Zealand? A Martian's View of the Erewhon Crimes Act 1961 with Some Footnotes to the 1989 Bill*, 21 VICT. U. OF WELLINGTON L. REV. 1 (1991). The New Zealand Act applies New Zealand law to the acts or omissions in question, but has a double criminality proviso:

> Provided that where any proceedings are taken by virtue of the jurisdiction conferred by this section it shall be a defence to prove that the act or omission would not have been an offence under the law of the country of which the person charged was a national or citizen at the time of the act or omission, if it had occurred in that country.

Consent of the Attorney-General is also required for the proceedings. The Attorney-General must certify that "it is expedient that the proceedings should be instituted" and may not give consent unless satisfied that "the Government of the country to which the ship or aircraft belongs has consented to the institution of the proceedings." New Zealand Crimes Act 1961, § 400 (1)(b).

(8) Which of the "categories" of jurisdiction in Restatement § 401, *supra* § 3.02[A] — to prescribe, to adjudicate, to enforce — is in play in *Layton* and these notes?

§ 3.04 Jurisdiction to Prescribe

The Restatement (Fourth) of the Foreign Relations Law of the United States (2018)

§ 402 United States Practice with Respect to Jurisdiction to Prescribe

(1) Subject to the constitutional limits set forth in § 403, the United States exercises jurisdiction to prescribe law with respect to:

(a) persons, property, and conduct within its territory;

(b) conduct that has a substantial effect within its territory;

(c) the conduct, interests, status, and relations of its nationals and residents outside its territory;

(d) certain conduct outside its territory that harms its nationals;

(e) certain conduct outside its territory by persons not its nationals or residents that is directed against the security of the United States or against a limited class of other fundamental U.S. interests; and

(f) certain offenses of universal concern, such as piracy, slavery, forced labor, trafficking in persons, recruitment of child soldiers, torture, extra-judicial killing, genocide, and certain acts of terrorism, even if no specific connection exists between the United States and the persons or conduct being regulated.

(2) In exercising jurisdiction to prescribe, the United States takes account of the legitimate interests of other nations as a matter of prescriptive comity.

(3) If the geographic scope of a federal law is not clear, federal courts apply the principles of interpretation set forth in §§ 404–406.

A. Territorial Principle

Chua Han Mow v. United States

United States Court of Appeals for the Ninth Circuit
730 F.2d 1308 (1984)

Hug, Circuit Judge:

On May 16, 1973, Chua Han Mow, a Malaysian citizen, was charged along with six others with violating United States laws against importation and distribution of controlled substances. Chua was in Malaysia at this time. Two of Chua's codefendants who were in the United States were arrested and eventually pled guilty to one count each. They each received a 10-year sentence, and they each served approximately three years before being deported.

On August 4, 1975, Chua was arrested by Malaysian authorities and incarcerated in Malaysia until October 1, 1977, pursuant to the Malaysian Emergency Ordinance of 1969. On November 2, 1977, a superseding indictment in the United States was returned against Chua and others. Chua was charged with violating 21 U.S.C. §§ 846 and 963 (Count I — conspiracy to import heroin) and 21 U.S.C. § 959 (Counts II and III — distribution of heroin). Chua was arrested by Malaysian authorities a second time on December 21, 1977. He remained incarcerated in Malaysia until he was extradited to the United States on November 28, 1979.

. . . .

On April 20, 1980, Chua withdrew his plea of not guilty and pled guilty to Counts I and III. Count II was dismissed along with a separate indictment from New York. Chua was sentenced to thirty years imprisonment — 15 years each on Counts I and III to run consecutively. . . . On August 30, 1982, Chua filed a petition for writ of habeas corpus in the District Court for the District of Kansas. He raised the same issues which are raised in the current motion. That court dismissed the habeas corpus action without prejudice on the grounds that the pro se motion pursuant to section 2255 filed with the sentencing court had not exhausted the section 2255 remedy. On November 22, 1982, Chua filed a second section 2255 motion in the sentencing court. The court denied the motion and this appeal followed. . . .

Chua argues that the United States lacked subject-matter jurisdiction to prosecute him because all the unlawful acts he committed were done in Malaysia. We disagree. There is no constitutional bar to the extraterritorial application of penal laws. *United States v. King*, 552 F.2d 833, 850 (9th Cir. 1976), *cert. denied*, 430 U.S. 966, 97 S. Ct. 1646, 52 L. Ed. 2d 357 (1977). Although courts have been reluctant to give extraterritorial effect to penal statutes, they have done so when congressional intent to give extraterritorial effect is clear. *United States v. Bowman*, [§ 3.01]. Section 959 specifically states that it is intended to reach prohibited acts committed outside the territorial jurisdiction of the United States. Sections 846 and 963, the statutory basis for the conspiracy count in this case, do not specifically provide for extraterritorial application. This court, however, has regularly inferred extraterritorial reach of conspiracy statutes on the basis of a finding that the underlying substantive statutes reach extraterritorial offenses. . . . Thus, the inference that Congress intended sections 846 and 963 to have extraterritorial application is readily made.

Before giving extraterritorial effect to penal statutes, courts have considered whether international law permits the exercise of jurisdiction. . . . International law recognizes five general principles whereby a sovereign may exercise this prescriptive jurisdiction: (1) territorial, wherein jurisdiction is based on the place where the offense is committed; (2) national, wherein jurisdiction is based on the nationality or national character of the offender; (3) protective, wherein jurisdiction is based on whether the national interest is injured; (4) universal, which amounts to physical custody of the offender; and (5) passive personal, wherein jurisdiction is based on the nationality or national character of the victim. . . . Many cases involve the prosecution of United States citizens for acts committed abroad, but extraterritorial authority is not limited to cases involving the nationality principle. Extraterritorial application of penal laws may be justified under any one of the five principles of extraterritorial authority. . . .

In *King*, this court upheld the authority of the United States to prosecute United States citizens for distribution of heroin in violation of section 959, the same statute involved in the present case. The distribution occurred in Japan, but the heroin was intended for importation into the United States. The court noted that the nationality principle applied because the appellants were United States citizens. However, the court stated that "appellants" prosecution for violating § 959 could also be justified under the territorial principle, since American courts have treated that as an 'objective' territorial principle." . . . Under the "objective" territorial principle,

> Acts done outside a jurisdiction, but intended to produce and producing detrimental effects within it, justify a State in punishing the cause of the harm as if he had been present at the effect, if the State should succeed in getting him within its power.

Strassheim v. Daily, 221 U.S. 280, 285, 31 S. Ct. 558, 55 L. Ed. 735 (1911). This rule applies to nations as well as states. *Rocha v. United States*, 288 F.2d 545, 549 (9th Cir. 1961). In the present case, Chua intended to create a detrimental effect in the United States and committed acts which resulted in such an effect when the heroin unlawfully entered the country. Chua's section 959 prosecution is therefore justified under the "objective" territorial principle. . . .

Other courts have relied on the protective principle to justify jurisdiction over extraterritorial crimes involving the unlawful importation of controlled substances. . . . Noting that drug smuggling compromises a sovereign's control of its own borders, the Seventh Circuit has suggested that it might uphold extraterritorial criminal jurisdiction over alien drug smugglers even if the territorial principle did not apply. . . . We are persuaded that the protective principle also justifies Chua's section 959 prosecution.

The objective territorial principle and the protective principle are equally applicable to the conspiracy count. Furthermore, the Supreme Court has held that extraterritorial jurisdiction over aliens exists when a conspiracy had for its object crime in the United States and overt acts were committed in the United States by co-conspirators. . . . In the present case, Chua's co-conspirators committed acts in furtherance of the conspiracy inside the United States. Co-conspirator Tang was arrested at the San Francisco Airport as he attempted to retrieve suitcases containing heroin. Therefore, the United States does have jurisdiction to prosecute Chua. . . .

Chua argues that the 1970 Drug Act under which he was convicted and sentenced incorporates the Single Convention on Narcotic Drugs, which limits the extraterritorial jurisdiction of the United States. Chua points to Article 36(a)(2)(iv) of the Single Convention which states:

> (iv) Serious offenses heretofore referred to committed either by nationals or by foreigners shall be prosecuted by the Party in whose territory the offense was committed, or by the Party in whose territory the offender is found *if extradition is not acceptable* in conformity with the law of the Party to which application is made, and if such offender has not already been prosecuted and judgment given.

18 U.S.T. 1407, 1425 (emphasis added).

Chua cites no authority supporting the proposition that the Single Convention limits the extraterritorial jurisdiction of the United States. The plain language of the cited provision does not limit the jurisdiction of the United States. The only effect of the provision is that Malaysia would have been required to prosecute Chua if extradition had not been acceptable to Malaysia. The provision is not applicable in this case because extradition was acceptable to Malaysia. . . . AFFIRMED.

Notes

(1) Does the territoriality principle require an act within the territorial jurisdiction of the United States? *See United States v. Noriega* [chap. 17]. Will the intent to

commit an act within the territorial jurisdiction of the United States, be sufficient in cases where a drug conspiracy is charged? In *United States v. Ricardo*, 619 F.2d 1124 (5th Cir. 1980), the Fifth Circuit affirmed a conviction stating:

> Appellants were convicted of two marijuana counts, stemming from the seizure of a shrimp boat, the SINCERE PROGRESS I, in the Gulf of Mexico, on the late evening and early morning of November 4–5, 1978.... The circumstances of the case reveal that the plan commenced outside the United States. Charts confiscated during the investigation indicate that the voyage originated in Colombia. According to the Americans, they left in their sailboat from Miami, Florida. Assuming their version is correct, the only nexus to the United States is indirect because they were not the masterminds behind the scheme. When the PROGRESS was intercepted, it was approximately 125–150 miles from the Texas Coast. From these facts alone, it is apparent that the Government failed to prove the existence of an overt act committed within the United States. The Government did prove, however, that the PROGRESS intended to rendezvous with another vessel off the coast of Texas, in order to unload their cargo. Given this proof, along with the proximity to the United States coast and the general heading of the ship, we are convinced that the object of appellants' plan had consequences within the United States. Under these circumstances, the question we now address is whether, pursuant to either conspiracy statute, a territorial act must be committed within the United States and in furtherance of the conspiracy before jurisdiction attaches.
>
> Under the conspiracy statutes in question, §§846 and 963, it is not incumbent upon the Government to allege or prove an overt act in order to obtain a conviction.... While it is now settled law that proof of an overt act is not required under the conspiracy statutes, the jurisdictional requisites are not settled. The United States and this Circuit have traditionally adhered to the objective principle of territorial jurisdictional [sic.], which attaches criminal consequences to extraterritorial acts that are intended to have effect in the sovereign territory, at least where overt acts within the territory can be proved.... Implicit in these statutes is the notion that the prescribed prohibitions apply extraterritorially.... It seems somewhat anomalous, however, that Congress intended these statutes to apply extraterritorially, but that jurisdiction attaches only after an act occurred within the sovereign boundaries. Thus, even though the statutes were designed to prevent one type of wrong ab initio, under the traditional approach, the courts were without power to act. This dichotomy directly contravenes the purpose of the enabling legislation.
>
> As a result, it is now settled in this Circuit that when the statute itself does not require proof of an overt act, jurisdiction attaches upon a mere showing of intended territorial effects.... The fact that appellants intended

the conspiracy to be consummated within the territorial boundaries satisfies jurisdictional requisites. . . .

(2) Can a statute grant "special territorial jurisdiction" in the United States? 18 U.S.C. § 7(3) provides that "special maritime and territorial jurisdiction of the United States" includes "(3) [a]ny lands reserved or acquired for the use of the United States, and under the exclusive or concurrent jurisdiction thereof, or any place purchased or otherwise acquired by the United States by consent of the legislature of the State in which the same shall be, for the erection of a fort, magazine, arsenal, dockyard, or other needful building." *See United States v. Erdos*, 474 F.2d 157 (4th Cir. 1973) (court found "special" territorial jurisdiction for a manslaughter prosecution of an American citizen who was an embassy employee in the Republic of Equatorial Guinea, for killing of another embassy employee who was also an American citizen, where the killing took place within a U.S. embassy in a foreign country).

B. Nationality Principle

United States v. Walczak

United States Court of Appeals for the Ninth Circuit
783 F.2d 852 (1986)

Per Curiam:

Following his conviction for making false statements on a Customs declaration form, Walczak appeals the denial of four pretrial motions. He argues that the district court did not have jurisdiction, that the Customs officials' search of his person and luggage violated the fourth amendment, that he should have been granted an evidentiary hearing on the suppression issue, and that he should have been permitted access to transcripts of the grand jury proceedings. We affirm the judgment of the district court. . . .

On October 10, 1984, Walczak, a United States citizen, was at the International Airport in Vancouver, British Columbia, Canada, about to board a non-stop flight to the United States. He completed Customs form 6059B, answering "no" to the statement "I am * * * carrying currency or monetary instruments over $5000 U.S. * * * ." U.S. Customs officials searched him and found over $52,000 in U.S. currency in his carry-on luggage. After questioning by U.S. Customs officials and by the Royal Canadian Mounted Police, he was released. Several days later, he voluntarily surrendered to U.S. Customs officials in Blaine, Washington.

A grand jury at Seattle, Washington indicted Walczak under 18 U.S.C. § 1001 (1982) (False Statements) and 18 U.S.C. § 3238 (1982) (Extraterritorial Jurisdiction). He pled not guilty, and moved to suppress the evidence of his false statement on the grounds that the search was not a valid border search and that the United States customs officials lacked authority to search him at the Vancouver airport in Canada. He requested an evidentiary hearing on the suppression issue. He also moved to discover transcripts of the grand jury proceedings, and to dismiss the indictment on the grounds that the district court lacked jurisdiction over the offense on foreign soil. The court denied all the motions. Walczak then entered a conditional plea of guilty, was fined $5000, given a three year sentence, which was suspended except for thirty days, and placed on probation.

The jurisdiction of the district court over an offense is a question of law to be reviewed *de novo*. . . . Walczak argues that a false statement made outside the borders is not punishable by a court of the United States. This argument fails for several reasons. First, section 1001 states that:

> Whoever, in any matter *within the jurisdiction of any department or agency of the United States* knowingly and wilfully falsifies, conceals or covers-up by any trick, scheme or device a material fact, or makes any false, fictitious or fraudulent statements or representations, or makes or uses any false writing or document knowing the same could contain any false, fictitious or fraudulent statement or entry, shall be fined not more than $10,000 or imprisoned not more than five years, or both.

(Emphasis added.) The preclearance procedure is within the jurisdiction of the United States Customs Service, Department of the Treasury. Since the Department of the Treasury is a "department * * * of the United States," the language of § 1001 literally applies to false statements made on Customs forms without regard to the place where the offense occurred.

Second, the rationale of the decision in *United States v. Bowman*, [§ 3. 01] extends the reach of certain laws such as § 1001 to cover acts committed outside the United States by United States citizens. *Bowman* stated that some offenses

> are such that to limit their *locus* to the strictly territorial jurisdiction would be greatly to curtail the scope and usefulness of the statute and leave open a large immunity for frauds as easily committed on the high seas and in foreign countries as at home. In such cases, Congress has not thought it necessary to make specific provisions in the law that the *locus* shall include the high seas and foreign countries, but allows it to be inferred from the nature of the offense.

. . . .

In the context of false statements on Customs declarations, § 1001 is such a law.

Third, at least as to Walczak, a United States citizen, the nationality principle of extraterritorial jurisdiction would apply: "American authority over [United States citizens] could be based upon the allegiance they owe this country and its laws if the statute concerned * * * evinces a legislative intent to control actions within and without the United States." *United States v. King*, 552 F.2d 833, 851 (9th Cir. 1976). Therefore the federal court system had jurisdiction to entertain the prosecution of Walczak for a violation of § 1001 committed in Canada.

Section 3238 states, "the trial of all offenses begun or committed upon the high seas, or elsewhere out of the jurisdiction of any particular state or district, shall be in the district where the offender * * * is arrested or first brought." Walczak surrendered to custom officials in the Western District of Washington, and therefore, that district court was the proper court in which to try him. Walczak's argument to the contrary therefore fails.... For the foregoing reasons, the district court's denial of appellant's motions is AFFIRMED.

Notes

What situations warrant use of the nationality principle? *See, e.g.*, 18 U.S.C. § 175 (prohibitions with respect to use of biological weapons "by or against a national of the United States"). How might diplomatic or other immunity play a factor in where a person may be prosecuted? Should a member of the United States armed forces, or a diplomat, or a dependent accompanying such an official, who commits a crime abroad be prosecuted in the United States? *See* Geoffrey R. Watson, *Offenders Abroad: The Case for Nationality-Based Criminal Jurisdiction*, 17 YALE J. INT'L L. 41 (1992).

C. Protective Principle

United States v. Gonzalez

United States Court of Appeals for the Eleventh Circuit
776 F.2d 931 (1985)

KRAVITCH, CIRCUIT JUDGE:

In this case, six defendants appeal the denial of their motion to dismiss an indictment charging them with knowingly and intentionally possessing, with intent to distribute, marijuana on board a vessel within the customs waters of the United States, 21 U.S.C. § 955a(c). They contend that the operation of section 955a(c), under which the United States may extend its customs waters to specific foreign vessels through arrangements with foreign nations violates their constitutional right to due process. They also claim that no "arrangement" within the meaning of the statute existed in this case.

This court already has held that by adopting the term "customs waters," Congress intended section 955a(c) to apply extra-territorially, and that Congress contemplated executive arrangements with foreign nations which would designate specific vessels as within "customs waters." *United States v. Romero-Galue*, 757 F.2d 1147 (11th Cir. 1985). We now hold that designating "customs waters" around a specific vessel on the high seas, thereby subjecting persons on board to United States prosecution, does not violate due process. We also hold that the arrangements regarding specific vessels may be informal, as long as there is a clear indication of consent by the foreign nation. Accordingly, we affirm the district court's refusal to dismiss the indictment....

The six defendants, all foreign nationals, were crew members aboard the ROSANGEL, a Honduran vessel. On May 24, 1984, the United States Coast Guard cutter V. LYPAN intercepted the ROSANGEL approximately 125 miles due east of Fort Lauderdale, Florida. A Coast Guard officer observed "bale type objects" on the main deck of the ROSANGEL. Coast Guard personnel boarded and searched the vessel, finding 114 bales of marijuana on the main deck and in the forward hold.

After a documentation check revealed that the vessel was of Honduran registry, the Coast Guard contacted the Honduran government by telephone and, with Captain Barrios' permission, waited on board the ROSANGEL for a response. When the Honduran government subsequently issued a statement of "no objection" to the boarding, search, seizure, and prosecution of the crew members of the ROSANGEL under United States law, the six defendants were arrested and transported to Miami for indictment and prosecution. . . .

The defendants were indicted under the Marijuana on the High Seas Act of 1980, 21 U.S.C. § 955a–955d. Congress adopted the Act in an effort "to prohibit all acts of illicit trafficking in controlled substances on the high seas which the United States can reach under international law." . . . . To achieve this goal, Congress created four different criminal offenses. Congress forbade possession with intent to distribute by any person on board United States vessels or vessels subject to United States jurisdiction, 21 U.S.C. § 955a(a), and on board any vessel by a citizen of the United States. 21 U.S.C. § 955a(b). Neither of these provisions require intent to distribute within the United States. Section 955a(d) proscribed possession with intent to distribute in the United States. These three provisions left a serious gap in Congress' effort to reach "all acts of illicit trafficking": possession with intent to distribute by foreign nationals on board foreign vessels, in cases where intent to distribute within the United States could not be shown. Congress filled the gap with section 955a(c), which states:

> It is unlawful for any person on board any vessel within the customs waters of the United States to knowingly or intentionally manufacture or distribute, or to possess with intent to manufacture or distribute, a controlled substance.

"Customs Waters" is defined in 19 U.S.C. § 1401(j):

> The term "customs waters" means, in the case of a foreign vessel subject to a treaty or other arrangement between a foreign government and the United States enabling or permitting the authorities of the United States to board, examine, search, seize, or otherwise to enforce upon such vessel upon the high seas the laws of the United States, *the waters within such distance of the coast of the United States as the said authorities are or may be so enabled or permitted by such treaty or arrangement* and, in the case of every other vessel, the waters within four leagues of the coast of the United States.

Id. (emphasis added).

The appellants' vessel was well beyond four leagues from the coast of the United States, and therefore we must consider whether a "treaty or other arrangement" had expanded this nation's "customs waters" to include those surrounding the vessel. . . . In enacting section 955a(c), Congress contemplated that the Coast Guard would seek permission from foreign governments to prosecute foreign nationals found on foreign vessels on the high seas. Obviously, Congress did not intend that the United States negotiate formal treaties with respect to each vessel; rather Congress contemplated the precise type of consent shown in the present case. . . .

Requiring execution of a formal agreement would defeat the purpose of the statute, which is to allow enforcement against particular vessels found hovering off the coast. Obviously, a vessel laden with marijuana would not leisurely lay at anchor just beyond four leagues from our shore while United States diplomats journeyed to Honduras, or other appropriate nation, negotiated an agreement, and awaited the approval of the proper bodies within the party nations. It is doubtful that the pride of our diplomats would be offended by this court's observation that during the course of obtaining such an agreement, convoys of vessels could journey back and forth laden with contraband. Once an agreement was in force, the smugglers could simply obtain a different vessel.

Nor would a formal agreement serve any useful purpose. All that the law contemplates is that the foreign nation give express consent to the enforcement of United States laws with respect to the particular vessel. The consenting nation's rights under international law or treaty remain unchanged, as the consent applies only to the particular vessel involved. Consent is a simple notion; it can be granted or refused, and no formal agreement is necessary to understand either option.

Finally, in the legislative history Congress noted that "the time required to obtain prior consent to board 'mother ships' on the high seas has apparently been significantly reduced," indicating that it intended to take advantage of such consent. . . . The record in this case demonstrates that such an arrangement existed. Honduras specifically consented to the United States asserting jurisdiction over the ROSANGEL.

The appellants also argue that even if the consent of Honduras satisfies the statutory requirement for an "arrangement," the statute only authorizes arrangements with "treaty nations." Accordingly, they argue that because no treaty between Honduras and the United States authorizes arrangements, no arrangement existed within the meaning of section 955a(c). . . . This contention also fails. First it runs contrary to the statutory language. The definition of "customs waters" refers to "treaty *or* other arrangement." 19 U.S.C. § 1401(j) (emphasis added). The appellants' argument would amend the definition to read "treaty or other arrangement executed pursuant to a treaty." We decline to rewrite the work of Congress. . . . Appellants advance no congressional purpose, and we can think of none that such a treaty requirement would serve; if the United States can achieve its goal of arrangements without a treaty, then why would Congress require one? Such a requirement would be directly contrary to the express statement of Congress that it intended to reach "all acts of illicit trafficking." . . . . Accordingly we hold that nothing in the Marijuana on the High Seas Act requires a treaty before the United States may seek an arrangement.

. . . .

Section 955a(c) requires consent by the foreign nation before enforcement of the United States law. Even absent consent, however, the United States could prosecute foreign nationals on foreign vessels under the "protective principle" of international law, . . . which permits a nation to assert jurisdiction over a person whose conduct outside the nation's territory threatens the nation's security or could potentially interfere with the operation of its governmental functions. *Id.* at 1154. Congress grounded section 955a(c) on this principle. . . .

Reliance on the protective principle is not a novel idea in American law. Indeed, the protective principle was the basis Congress cited for the Anti-Smuggling Act. S.Rep. No. 1036, 74th Cong. 1st Sess. 5 (1935). The Senate Report to that legislation noted that "there is no fixed rule among the customs and usages of nations which prescribes the limits of jurisdictional waters other than the rule of reasonableness, that a nation may exercise authority upon the high seas to such an extent and to so great a distance as is reasonable and necessary to protect itself and its citizens from injury." *Id.* The Senate Report also noted the opinion of Chief Justice Marshall in *Church v. Hubbart*, 6 U.S. (2 Cranch) 187, 2 L. Ed. 249 (1804), which observed that "if this right be extended too far it will be resisted." *Id.* at 235. The Chief Justice was discussing enforcement of a common type of law in the days of mercantilism, a colonial power's prohibition against trade with its colonies by other nations. He stated that:

> Thus in the channel, where a very great part of the commerce to and from all the north of Europe, passes through a very narrow sea, the seizure of vessels on suspicion of attempting an illicit trade, must necessarily be restricted to very narrow limits; but on the coast of South America, seldom frequented by vessels but for the purpose of illicit trade, the vigilance of the government may be extended somewhat further and foreign nations subject to such regulations as are reasonable in themselves and are really necessary. . . .

Id. at 235. Chief Justice Marshall's words are no less vital today. In the waters between certain areas of Latin America and our nation, nations judge what is reasonable in light of the massive drug trade in those waters. One need only glance at a map of the region and compare the vast length of United States coast to the narrow straits between Yucatan and Cuba . . . and the other narrow passages through the West Indies to understand the reasonableness of enforcing our drug laws outside of our territorial sea. Apparently, foreign nations such as Honduras recognize the reasonableness of current United States enforcement efforts, for consent has been given.

Congress' purpose in enacting section 955a was clearly stated. The Act was "designed to prohibit all acts of illicit trafficking in controlled substances on the high seas which the United States can reach under international law." . . . Congress adopted section 955a(c) and relied on the protective principle because it is often difficult to prove beyond a reasonable doubt that a vessel seized on the high seas carrying contraband was headed for the United States. . . . . The protective principle does not require that there be proof of an actual or intended effect inside the

United States. The conduct may be forbidden if it has a potentially adverse effect and is generally recognized as a crime by nations that have reasonably developed legal systems.... Congress has determined, therefore, that distribution of marijuana and other narcotics meets these criteria. Appellants do not contest the determination of Congress, nor do we believe there would be any basis to attack it. As noted above, that reasonable nations accept the authority advanced by Congress in section 955a(c) is demonstrated by the consent that has been given.

Congress faced a difficulty, however, in flexing fully its legal authority under the protective principle. Although Congress' planned extension of authority was reasonable, there was no need to risk unnecessary friction with foreign nations. Such friction would not stem from the extension of the United States' drug laws to foreign nationals on the high seas, but from the stopping and seizing of foreign vessels on the high seas. The legislative history reflects Congress' ambivalence between its respect for exclusive state flag jurisdiction on the one hand, and the long history of extra-territorial United States jurisdiction on the other. In light of the fact that nations already were giving consent before passage of the law, and considering the reasonableness of the law, Congress likely believed that obtaining consent would not unduly hinder enforcement efforts; it could achieve its enforcement goal and at the same time minimize any foreign objections. Accordingly, Congress borrowed the notion of "customs waters" and "customs enforcement areas" from the Anti-Smuggling Act; section 955a(c) would not be enforced without the consent of the foreign nation. The "customs waters" approach was adopted for these reasons and not because of any limitations on the authority of the United States in either international law or treaties. *It is misleading, therefore, to consider that consent an element of the offense*; rather, it is a diplomatic requisite illustrating the international partnership that ensures the rule of law on the high seas. The law will not be enforced on the high seas against a foreign nation's vessels without that nation's consent.

Our review of the basis and purpose of section 955a(c) convinces us that the appellants' due process contentions are illusory. There is nothing vague about the statute. Congress has provided clear notice of what conduct is forbidden: any possession of marijuana on the high seas with intent to distribute. The United States will enforce this law to the full extent of its ability under international law. Congress has afforded a legislative grace to our fellow nations by conditioning enforcement of the law upon their consent. This grace, however, does not create a notice problem. Both the offense and the intent of the United States are clear. Those embarking on voyages with holds laden with illicit narcotics, conduct which is contrary to laws of all reasonably developed legal systems, do so with the awareness of the risk that their government may consent to enforcement of the United States' laws against the vessel. Due process does not require that a person who violates the law of all reasonable nations be excused on the basis that his own nation *might* have requested that he not be prosecuted by a foreign sovereign. Accordingly we hold that appellants' challenge to the constitutionality of section 955a(c) is without merit.... On the basis of the foregoing discussion, the denial of the appellants' motion to dismiss the indictment is AFFIRMED.

HATCHETT, CIRCUIT JUDGE, specially concurring:

I specially concur in the majority opinion, rather than dissent, because *United States v. Romero-Galue* . . . is binding on this panel. Having considered the legislative history, I am of the opinion that Congress intended in enacting Title 19 U.S.C. § 1401 (j), defining customs waters, to require prior arrangement between the United States and other nations through treaty or other arrangement defining an area in which the United States would board vessels suspected of bearing controlled substances. The area described by treaty could include the whole world.

Notes

(1) In *Gonzalez* does the court use the protective principle exclusively? Is this also an illustration of what is variously referred to as "ceded" or "transferred" jurisdiction, or "vicarious administration of justice"? Did Honduras "transfer" its jurisdiction to prescribe, to enforce and to adjudicate to the United States? On this analysis, should there be proof of double criminality in both Honduras and the United States? The United Nations has drafted a Model Treaty on the Transfer of Proceedings in Criminal Matters, G. A. Res. 45/118, U.N. GAOR, 45th Sess., Supp. No. 49A, at 219 (1991). Professor Clark states:

> The Model Treaty . . . proceeds on the basis that when a person is suspected of having committed an offense under the law of a state which is party to the treaty, that state may, if the interests of the proper administration of justice so require, request another state which is a party to commence proceedings in respect of the offense. For the purposes of the Model Transfer of Proceedings treaty, a request provides the requested state with the necessary jurisdiction in respect of the offense if that state does not already maintain jurisdiction under its own law. Indeed, the Model . . . obligates the parties to take the necessary legislative measures to ensure that a request of the requesting state to take proceedings shall allow the requested state to exercise the necessary jurisdiction. . . . Dual criminality is required.

ROGER S. CLARK, THE UNITED NATIONS CRIME PREVENTION AND CRIMINAL JUSTICE PROGRAM: FORMULATION OF STANDARDS AND EFFORTS AT THEIR IMPLEMENTATION 220–21 (1994).

Should the New Zealand "landing state" jurisdiction, discussed in § 3.03, Note (7) *supra*, which requires the consent of the flag state, be regarded as an example of transferred jurisdiction applicable to ships and aircraft?

Article 5 of the "Proliferation Security Agreements" with Liberia and the Marshall Islands, § 2.01[B], provides:

> [In cases of boarding and search pursuant to the treaty] concerning the vessels of a Party located seaward of any State's territorial sea, that Party shall have the primary right to exercise jurisdiction over a detained vessel, cargo or other items on board (including seizure, forfeiture, arrest and prosecution), provided, however, that the Party with the right to exercise primary

> jurisdiction may, subject to its Constitution and laws, waive its primary right to exercise jurisdiction and authorize the enforcement of the other Party's law against the vessel, cargo and other item and persons aboard.

Is this an example of "transferred" (aka "ceded") jurisdiction? Or is it some kind of protective principle? Note the obvious premise that jurisdiction is concurrent.

The Restatement (Fourth) of the Foreign Relations Law of the United States §§ 151, 164 (2018) note that the U.S. may exercise jurisdiction to prescribe in the territory of another state when authorized by that state. It can be argued that the same principle must apply to jurisdiction to enforce and jurisdiction to adjudicate. Is there, in short, much more to be said about transferred jurisdiction in U.S. practice?

(2) Is it proper for a court to apply the protective principle in cases involving drugs aboard vessels on the high seas? In *United States v. Robinson*, 843 F.2d 1 (1st Cir. 1988), the defendant questioned "how can this principle justify prohibiting foreigners on foreign ships 500 miles offshore from possessing drugs that, as far as the statute (and clear proof here) are concerned, might be bound for Canada, South America, or Zanzibar?" The First Circuit rejected defendant's argument, noting that "appellants' arguments are beside the point, for there is another, different, but perfectly adequate basis in international law for the assertion of American jurisdiction. Panama agreed to permit the United States to apply its law on her ship." The court also stated, "[i]t is clear, under international law's 'territorial principle,' that a 'state has jurisdiction to prescribe and enforce a rule of law in the territory of another state to the extent provided by international agreement with the other state.'"

(3) What kinds of conduct are encompassed within the protective principle? In *United States v. Birch*, 470 F.2d 808 (4th Cir. 1972), the court stated: "[t]he basis found in international law for extraterritorial application of § 499 is the principle of protective jurisdiction. The protective principle determines jurisdiction 'by reference to the national interest injured by the offense.' It provides an appropriate jurisdictional base for prosecuting a person who, acting beyond the territorial boundaries of the United States, falsifies its official documents. Because the national interest is injured by the falsification of official documents no matter where the counterfeit is prepared, we conclude that Congress intended § 499 to apply to persons who commit its proscribed acts abroad." *See also* IAIN CAMERON, THE PROTECTIVE PRINCIPLE OF INTERNATIONAL CRIMINAL JURISDICTION (1994).

(4) After *Gonzalez* was decided, the following was included in the United Nations Convention against Illicit Traffic in Narcotic Drugs and Psychotropic Substances, U.N. Doc. E/CONF.15 (1988) (ratified by the United States in 1990):

Article 17 — ILLICIT TRAFFIC BY SEA

> 1. The Parties shall co-operate to the fullest extent possible to suppress illicit traffic by sea, in conformity with the international law of the sea.
>
> 2. A Party which has reasonable grounds to suspect that a vessel flying its flag or not displaying a flag or marks of registry is engaged in illicit traffic

> may request the assistance of other Parties in suppressing its use for that purpose. The Parties so requested shall render such assistance within the means available to them.
>
> 3. A Party which has reasonable grounds to suspect that a vessel exercising freedom of navigation in accordance with international law and flying the flag or displaying marks of registry of another Party is engaged in illicit traffic may so notify the flag State, request confirmation of registry and, if confirmed, request authorization from the flag State to take appropriate measures in regard to that vessel.
>
> 4. In accordance with paragraph 3 or in accordance with treaties in force between them or in accordance with any agreement or arrangement otherwise reached between those Parties, the flag State may authorize the requesting State to, *inter alia*:
>
> (a) Board the vessel;
>
> (b) Search the vessel;
>
> (c) If evidence of involvement in illicit traffic is found, take appropriate action with respect to the vessel, persons and cargo on board. . . .

This provision is devoted to jurisdiction to enforce. It is accompanied by Article 4, paragraph 1 (b) (ii) which empowers a Party to take "such measures as may be necessary to establish its jurisdiction over the offences [under the Convention] when [t]he offence is committed on board a vessel concerning which that Party has been authorized to take appropriate action pursuant to article 17. . . ." This is prescriptive jurisdiction.

Do these provisions support the United States Government's position? That is to say, action may be taken either under a general treaty that might cover the whole of the oceans, or pursuant to an arrangement involving a particular ship.

D. Passive Personality Principle

United States v. Roberts

United States District Court for the Eastern District of Louisiana
1 F. Supp. 2d 601 (1998)

VANCE, DISTRICT JUDGE:

. . . .

Defendant Roberts was indicted by a federal grand jury on December 11, 1997 and charged with one count of sexual abuse of a minor, 18 U.S.C. § 2243(a), and one count of abusive sexual contact with a minor, 18 U.S.C. § 2244(a). The crimes allegedly occurred on board a cruise ship, the Carnival Cruise Lines' vessel M/V CELEBRATION. Roberts is a national of St. Vincent & the Grenadines, and he was employed by the M/V CELEBRATION at the time the alleged incident took place. The victim is a United States citizen. The United States alleges that the crimes were committed "in an area within the special maritime and territorial jurisdiction of the United States" and that jurisdiction is proper under 18 U.S.C. §§7(1) or (8).

It is not disputed that the alleged incident occurred while the cruise ship was "in international waters approximately 63 miles off the coast of Puna Mols, Mexico." . . . The following facts are also uncontested: Carnival Corporation ("Carnival") owns the M/S CELEBRATION, and the company is incorporated under the laws of the Republic of Panama . . . The M/V CELEBRATION is registered in Liberia and flies a Liberian flag. Carnival is a public company, its stock is traded on the New York Stock Exchange, and some of its shareholders are United States citizens. . . . Further, the M/S CELEBRATION begins and ends its cruises in the United States, and the majority of its passengers are United States citizens. . . . It is also undisputed that neither Panama nor Liberia has taken any steps to prosecute the defendant.

The defendant moves this Court to dismiss the indictment on the grounds that the United States does not have jurisdiction over the alleged incident. Roberts contends that jurisdiction is not proper under §7(1) because the M/V CELEBRATION is not an American vessel. The defendant also states that jurisdiction under 18 U.S.C. §7(8) is limited "to the extent permitted by international law," and, in this case, jurisdiction is not proper under accepted principles of international law. The government argues that jurisdiction is proper because the M/V CELEBRATION is owned in part by American citizens, and international law permits this exercise of jurisdiction under the objective territorial and the passive personality theories. . . .

In this case, Congress intended for §2243 and 2244 to reach beyond the strict territorial jurisdiction of the United States because the statutes provide that the laws operate within the "special maritime and territorial jurisdiction of the United States." . . . . The question in this case is whether the alleged crimes occurred within the special maritime and territorial jurisdiction of the United States as set forth in 18 U.S.C. §§7(1) and 7(8). . . . Given the apparent conflict in Fifth Circuit authority over whether §7(1)'s special maritime jurisdiction covers prohibited acts committed on foreign flag vessels on the high seas, and the fact that the Court finds jurisdiction under 18 U.S.C. §7(8). . . . the Court finds it unnecessary to resolve whether jurisdiction likewise lies under §7(1). . . .

The Court concludes that jurisdiction over this case is proper pursuant to 18 U.S.C. §7(8). Section 7(8) was added to the United States' special maritime and territorial jurisdiction in 1994 as part of the Violent Crime Control and Law Enforcement Act of 1994, Pub. L. No. 103-322, §120002, 108 Stat. 2021 (Sept. 13, 1994). The statute expressly states that the special maritime jurisdiction of the United States is extended to include "to the extent permitted by international law, any foreign vessel during a voyage having a scheduled departure from or arrival in the United States with respect to an offense committed by or against a national of the United States." 18 U.S.C. §7(8).

Defendant Roberts argues that international treaties and principles of international law do not permit this Court to exercise jurisdiction over this matter. First,

Roberts contends that several international treaties prohibit the United States from asserting its jurisdiction because the treaties state that foreign vessels are subject to the exclusive jurisdiction of the country whose flag they fly under. Second, Roberts insists that this case does not fall under any of the recognized exceptions to the principle of the "law of the flag."

The treaties relied upon by the defendant do not prevent this Court from exercising jurisdiction over the offensive acts. Defendant has failed to show that any of the treaties are self-executing, and treaties "may act to deprive the United States, and hence its courts, of jurisdiction over property and individuals that would otherwise be subject to that jurisdiction" only if the treaties are self-executing. *United States v. Postal*, 589 F.2d 862, 875 (5th Cir. 1979). It is also well established that unless a treaty is self-executing, "that is, unless it expressly creates privately enforceable rights — an individual citizen does not have standing to protest when one nation does not follow the terms of such agreement." . . .

International law recognizes five theories of jurisdiction, under which a country is permitted to exercise extraterritorial criminal jurisdiction: . . . . In this case, the prosecution. . . . is a valid exercise of both passive personality jurisdiction and objective territorial jurisdiction. The principle of passive personality "asserts that a state may apply law — particularly criminal law — to an act committed outside its territory by a person not its national where the victim of the act was its national." Restatement § 402 cmt. g. Although courts are reluctant to embrace passive personality jurisdiction for ordinary torts or crimes . . . international law does not prohibit Congress from incorporating this principle into its legislation. Indeed, prior to the enactment of § 7(8), Congress applied the passive personality principle in the Omnibus Diplomatic Security and Antiterrorism Act of 1986, 18 U.S.C. § 2231 [codified as § 2332], which makes it a crime to kill, or attempt or conspire to kill, or to cause serious bodily injury, to a national of the United States outside the territory of the United States. Moreover, some courts have recently expressed approval of passive personality jurisdiction. . . . In addition, Congress is moving towards accepting passive personality jurisdiction outside the realm of terrorism, as evidence[d] by several pieces of legislation. . . .

This move towards accepting passive personality jurisdiction continued with the passage of § 7(8), which authorizes the United States to exercise its jurisdiction over "any foreign vessel during a voyage having a scheduled departure from or arrival in the United States with respect to an offense committed by or against a national of the United States." 18 U.S.C. § 7(8). Given the specific requirement that the vessel have a scheduled departure from or arrival in the United States, this statute expresses concern for United States nationals but limits jurisdiction to vessels that are most likely to have a connection to America. Indeed, in this case, the M/V CELEBRATION originates and terminates its voyage in the United States, and the majority of its passengers are American citizens. Further, Carnival Corporation has its corporate headquarters in this country and some of its shareholders are United States citizens. The Court must also add that the country whose flag the cruise ship flies under,

Liberia, has little to no interest in the alleged offense because neither the victim nor the defendant are Liberian, the vessel does not operate in or around Liberian territory, and the vessel's owners center their corporate operations in the United States. In short, the Court finds that jurisdiction is reasonable in this case pursuant to § 7(8), and it is permitted by international law because it does not intrude upon another sovereign's interest, and it serves to protect America's nationals abroad.

The objective territorial principle also supports jurisdiction over this matter. Jurisdiction under this principle is asserted over foreigners for an act committed outside the United States that produces substantial and detrimental effects within the United States. . . . IT IS ORDERED that defendant's motion to dismiss is DENIED.

Notes

(1) The use of the passive personality principle in the United States is relatively new. Is there a constitutional basis for this principle? Should the use of the passive personality principle be limited to situations where the defendant is not prosecuted by the state where the crime is alleged to have been committed? *See* Geoffrey R. Watson, *The Passive Personality Principle*, 28 TEX. INT'L L.J. 1 (1993).

(2) A striking example of the use of passive personality jurisdiction by a common law country is the Criminal Code Amendment (Offences Against Australians) Act 2002 which inserted the following provision into the Australian federal Criminal Code:

> *104.1 Murder of an Australian citizen or a resident of Australia*
>
> (1) A person is guilty of an offence if:
>
> (a) the person engages in conduct outside Australia; and
>
> (b) the conduct causes the death of another person; and
>
> (c) the other person is an Australian citizen or a resident of Australia; and
>
> (d) the first-mentioned person intends to cause, or is reckless as to causing, the death of an Australian citizen or resident of Australia or any other person by the conduct.
>
> Penalty: Imprisonment for life.
>
> (2) Absolute liability applies to paragraph (1) (c).

Similar provisions (imposing different penalties) apply to manslaughter, intentionally causing serious harm and recklessly causing serious harm to an Australian citizen or resident. Note that the jurisdictional hook here is that the victim is an Australian citizen or resident but that there is "absolute" (strict) liability as to this circumstance element of the crime. There is no need for the prosecution to prove that the defendant applied mind to the fact that this was an Aussie that he or she was messing with! A narrower application of passive personality (seasoned with a dash of protective theory) occurred in *United States v. Benitez*, 741 F.2d 1312

(11th Cir. 1984), *cert. den.*, 471 U.S. 1137 (1985). There, Benitez, operating entirely in Colombia, was convicted of various counts of conspiring to murder DEA agents, and assaulting and robbing them, even without proof that he knew they were DEA agents.

(3) Notice the reference in the last paragraph of *Roberts* to jurisdictional support from the objective territorial principle. The argument here must be that the (lasting) effects on the victim, especially psychological, would be felt in the United States *See also United States v. Neil*, 312 F. 3d 419 (9th Cir. 2002). If this is "effects" as understood in international law, it is significantly different from the effects in *The Lotus* [§ 1.02]. There, the effects, dead Turkish citizens, constituted one of the elements of the crime. In cases such as *Roberts*, the effect on the victim is not a specific element of the assault.

E. Universality Principle

United States v. Yunis

United States Court of Appeals for the District of Columbia Circuit
924 F.2d 1086 (1991)

MIKVA, CHIEF JUDGE:

Appellant Fawaz Yunis challenges his convictions on conspiracy, aircraft piracy, and hostage-taking charges stemming from the hijacking of a Jordanian passenger aircraft in Beirut, Lebanon. He appeals from orders of the district court denying his pretrial motions relating to jurisdiction, illegal arrest, alleged violations of the Posse Comitatus Act, and the government's withholding of classified documents during discovery. Yunis also challenges the district court's jury instructions as erroneous and prejudicial.

Although this appeal raises novel issues of domestic and international law, we reject Yunis' objections and affirm the convictions....

On June 11, 1985, appellant and four other men boarded Royal Jordanian Airlines Flight 402 ("Flight 402") shortly before its scheduled departure from Beirut, Lebanon. They wore civilian clothes and carried military assault rifles, ammunition bandoleers, and hand grenades. Appellant took control of the cockpit and forced the pilot to take off immediately. The remaining hijackers tied up Jordanian air marshals assigned to the flight and held the civilian passengers, including two American citizens, captive in their seats. The hijackers explained to the crew and passengers that they wanted the plane to fly to Tunis, where a conference of the Arab League was under way. The hijackers further explained that they wanted a meeting with delegates to the conference and that their ultimate goal was removal of all Palestinians from Lebanon.

After a refueling stop in Cyprus, the airplane headed for Tunis but turned away when authorities blocked the airport runway. Following a refueling stop at

Palermo, Sicily, another attempt to land in Tunis, and a second stop in Cyprus, the plane returned to Beirut, where more hijackers came aboard. These reinforcements included an official of Lebanon's Amal Militia, the group at whose direction Yunis claims he acted. The plane then took off for Syria, but was turned away and went back to Beirut. There, the hijackers released the passengers, held a press conference reiterating their demand that Palestinians leave Lebanon, blew up the plane, and fled from the airport.

An American investigation identified Yunis as the probable leader of the hijackers and prompted U.S. civilian and military agencies, led by the Federal Bureau of Investigation (FBI), to plan Yunis' arrest. After obtaining an arrest warrant, the FBI put "Operation Goldenrod" into effect in September 1987. Undercover FBI agents lured Yunis onto a yacht in the eastern Mediterranean Sea with promises of a drug deal, and arrested him once the vessel entered international waters. The agents transferred Yunis to a United States Navy munitions ship and interrogated him for several days as the vessel steamed toward a second rendezvous, this time with a Navy aircraft carrier. Yunis was flown to Andrews Air Force Base from the aircraft carrier, and taken from there to Washington, D.C. In Washington, Yunis was arraigned on an original indictment charging him with conspiracy, hostage taking, and aircraft damage. A grand jury subsequently returned a superseding indictment adding additional aircraft damage counts and a charge of air piracy.

Yunis filed several pretrial motions, among them a motion to suppress statements he made while aboard the munitions ship. In *United States v. Yunis (Yunis I)*, 859 F.2d 953 (D.C. Cir. 1988), this court reversed a district court order suppressing the statements, and authorized their introduction at trial. We revisited the case on a second interlocutory appeal relating to discovery of classified information, reversing the district court's disclosure order. *United States v. Yunis (Yunis II)*, 867 F.2d 617 (D.C. Cir. 1989).

Yunis admitted participation in the hijacking at trial but denied parts of the government's account and offered the affirmative defense of obedience to military orders, asserting that he acted on instructions given by his superiors in Lebanon's Amal Militia. The jury convicted Yunis of conspiracy, 18 U.S.C. § 371 (1988), hostage taking, 18 U.S.C. § 1203 (1988), and air piracy, 49 U.S.C. App. § 472(n) (1988). However, it acquitted him of three other charged offenses that went to trial: violence against people on board an aircraft, 18 U.S.C. § 32(b)(1) (1988), aircraft damage, 18 U.S.C. § 32(b)(2) (1988), and placing a destructive device aboard an aircraft, 18 U.S.C. § 32(b)(3) (1988). The district court imposed concurrent sentences of five years for conspiracy, thirty years for hostage taking, and twenty years for air piracy. Yunis appeals his conviction and seeks dismissal of the indictment. . . .

Yunis argues that the district court lacked subject matter and personal jurisdiction to try him on the charges of which he was convicted, that the indictment should have been dismissed because the government seized him in violation of the Posse Comitatus Act and withheld classified materials useful to his defense, and that the convictions should be reversed because of errors in the jury instructions. . . .

Yunis appeals first of all from the district court's denial of his motion to dismiss for lack of subject matter and personal jurisdiction. *See United States v. Yunis*, 681 F. Supp. 896 (D.D.C. 1988). Appellant's principal claim is that, as a matter of domestic law, the federal hostage taking and air piracy statutes do not authorize assertion of federal jurisdiction over him. Yunis also suggests that a contrary construction of these statutes would conflict with established principles of international law, and so should be avoided by this court. Finally, appellant claims that the district court lacked personal jurisdiction because he was seized in violation of American law....

The Hostage Taking Act provides, in relevant part:

> (a) Whoever, whether inside or outside the United States, seizes or detains and threatens to kill, to injure, or to continue to detain another person in order to compel a third person or a governmental organization to do or to abstain from any act ... shall be punished by imprisonment by any term of years or for life.
>
> (b)(1) It is not an offense under this section if the conduct required for the offense occurred outside the United States unless—
>
> (A) the offender or the person seized or detained is a national of the United States;
>
> (B) the offender is found in the United States; or
>
> (C) the governmental organization sought to be compelled is the Government of the United States.

18 U.S.C. § 1203. Yunis claims that this statute cannot apply to an individual who is brought to the United States by force, since those convicted under it must be "found in the United States." But this ignores the law's plain language. Subsections (A), (B), and (C) of section 1203(b)(1) offer independent bases for jurisdiction where "the offense occurred outside the United States." Since two of the passengers on Flight 402 were U.S. citizens, section 1203(b)(1)(A), authorizing assertion of U.S. jurisdiction where "the offender or the person seized or detained is a national of the United States," is satisfied. The statute's jurisdictional requirement has been met regardless of whether or not Yunis was "found" within the United States under section 1203(b)(1)(B).

Appellant's argument that we should read the Hostage Taking Act differently to avoid tension with international law falls flat. Yunis points to no treaty obligations of the United States that give us pause. Indeed, Congress intended through the Hostage Taking Act to execute the International Convention Against the Taking of Hostages, which authorizes any signatory state to exercise jurisdiction over persons who take its nationals hostage "if that State considers it appropriate." ...

Nor is jurisdiction precluded by norms of customary international law. The district court concluded that two jurisdictional theories of international law, the "universal principle" and the "passive personal principle," supported assertion of U.S. jurisdiction to prosecute Yunis on hijacking and hostage-taking charges.... Under the universal principle, states may prescribe and prosecute "certain offenses recognized by the community of nations as of universal concern, such as piracy, slave trade, attacks on or hijacking of aircraft, genocide, war crimes, and perhaps certain acts of terrorism," even absent any special connection between the state and the offense. *See* Restatement (Third) of the Foreign Relations Law of the United States §§ 404, 423 (1987). Under the passive personal principle, a state may punish non-nationals for crimes committed against its nationals outside of its territory, at least where the state has a particularly strong interest in the crime. . . .

Relying primarily on the Restatement, Yunis argues that hostage taking has not been recognized as a universal crime and that the passive personal principle authorizes assertion of jurisdiction over alleged hostage takers only where the victims were seized because they were nationals of the prosecuting state. Whatever merit appellant's claims may have as a matter of international law, they cannot prevail before this court. Yunis seeks to portray international law as a self-executing code that trumps domestic law whenever the two conflict. That effort misconceives the role of judges as appliers of international law and as participants in the federal system. Our duty is to enforce the Constitution, laws, and treaties of the United States, not to conform the law of the land to norms of customary international law. . . .

To be sure, courts should hesitate to give penal statutes extraterritorial effect absent a clear congressional directive. . . . Similarly, courts will not blind themselves to potential violations of international law where legislative intent is ambiguous. . . . But the statute in question reflects an unmistakable congressional intent, consistent with treaty obligations of the United States, to authorize prosecution of those who take Americans hostage abroad no matter where the offense occurs or where the offender is found. Our inquiry can go no further. . . .

The Antihijacking Act provides for criminal punishment of persons who hijack aircraft operating wholly outside the "special aircraft jurisdiction" of the United States, provided that the hijacker is later "found in the United States." 49 U.S.C. App. § 1472(n). Flight 402, a Jordanian aircraft operating outside of the United States, was not within this nation's special aircraft jurisdiction . . . Yunis urges this court to interpret the statutory requirement that persons prosecuted for air piracy must be "found" in the United States as precluding prosecution of alleged hijackers who are brought here to stand trial. But the issue before us is more fact-specific, since Yunis was indicted for air piracy while awaiting trial on hostage-taking and other charges; we must determine whether, once arrested and brought to this country on those other charges, Yunis was subject to prosecution under the Antihijacking Act as well.

The Antihijacking Act of 1974 was enacted to fulfill this nation's responsibilities under the Convention for the Suppression of Unlawful Seizure of Aircraft (the "Hague Convention"), which requires signatory nations to extradite or punish hijackers "present in" their territory. . . . This suggests that Congress intended the statutory term "found in the United States" to parallel the Hague Convention's "present in [a contracting state's] territory," a phrase which does not indicate the voluntariness limitation urged by Yunis. Moreover, Congress interpreted the Hague Convention as requiring the United States to extradite or prosecute "offenders in its custody," evidencing no concern as to how alleged hijackers came within U.S. territory. . . . From this legislative history we conclude that Yunis was properly indicted under section 1472(n) once in the United States and under arrest on other charges.

The district court correctly found that international law does not restrict this statutory jurisdiction to try Yunis on charges of air piracy. . . . Aircraft hijacking may well be one of the few crimes so clearly condemned under the law of nations that states may assert universal jurisdiction to bring offenders to justice, even when the state has no territorial connection to the hijacking and its citizens are not involved. . . . But in any event we are satisfied that the Antihijacking Act authorizes assertion of federal jurisdiction to try Yunis regardless of hijacking's status vel non as a universal crime. Thus, we affirm the district court on this issue. . . .

Notes

(1) Does Yunis really rely on the universality principle? Is there a proper basis in the United States Constitution to proceed against Yunis? *See* Andreas F. Lowenfeld, *U.S. Law Enforcement Abroad: The Constitution and International Law*, 83 A.J.I.L. 880 (1989). Was the method used by the FBI in arresting Yunis proper? *Id. See also* Abraham Abramovsky, *Extraterritorial Jurisdiction: The United States Unwarranted Attempt to Alter International Law in* United States v. Yunis, 15 YALE J. INT'L. L. 121 (1990).

(2) As to what crimes does international law permit the exercise of universal jurisdiction? [*see* chap. 2] To what extent should the United States rely on the universality principle to assert jurisdiction over war crimes and crimes against humanity committed by non-nationals abroad? *See* the RESTATEMENT, § 404, quoted at the end of this note, and Kenneth C. Randall, *Universal Jurisdiction Under International Law*, 66 TEX. L. REV. 785 (1988). *See also* the discussion of the *Demjanjuk* Case [chap. 20] and the discussion of the *Pinochet* Case [chap. 14]. The United States does not claim universal jurisdiction in all the cases mentioned in the Restatement, notably war crimes (except for the recruitment and use of child soldiers) and crimes against humanity.

The Restatement (Fourth) of the Foreign Relations Law of the United States (2018)

§ 404 Universal Jurisdiction

> International law recognizes a state's jurisdiction to prescribe law with respect to certain offenses of universal concern, such as genocide, crimes against humanity, war crimes, certain acts of terrorism, piracy, the slave trade, and torture, even if no specific connection exists between the state and the persons or conduct being regulated.

§ 3.05 Limitations on Jurisdiction to Prescribe

The Restatement (Fourth) of the Foreign Relations Law of the United States (2018)

§ 403 Federal Constitutional Limits

An exercise of prescriptive jurisdiction by the federal government, any State, or any component thereof may not exceed the limits set on the authority of those governments by the Constitution.

§ 404 Presumption Against Extraterritoriality

Courts in the United States interpret federal statutory provisions to apply only within the territorial jurisdiction of the United States unless there is a clear indication of congressional intent to the contrary.

§ 405 Reasonableness in Interpretation

As a matter of prescriptive comity, courts in the United States may interpret federal statutory provisions to include other limitations on their applicability.

Notes

(1) When might the exercise of jurisdiction be considered unreasonable? In *In re Grand Jury Proceedings (Marsoner)*, 40 F.3d 959 (9th Cir. 1994), the court stated:

> . . . In the past, courts have used section 40 of the Restatement (Second) of Foreign Relations Law (1965) to evaluate whether international comity precludes enforcement of an order compelling a witness to sign a consent authorizing disclosure of foreign bank records. . . . Section 40 of the Restatement has been revised and is now encompassed within section 403 of the Restatement (Third). Under the revised Restatement, reasonableness is "an essential element in determining whether, as a matter of international law, the state may exercise jurisdiction to prescribe." Restatement (Third) of Foreign Relations Law § 403 reporter's note 10 (1987).
>
> Applying these factors to the situation presented here, we hold that international comity does not preclude enforcement of the district court's order. Marsoner is suspected of using his Austrian bank accounts to evade taxes in the United States. The grand jury seeks Austrian bank information in an effort to link Marsoner to alleged illegal activities that occurred in the United States between 1989 and 1991. Although Marsoner is an Austrian citizen, he is a United States resident and his economic activity, which includes tax liabilities, involves the United States. The United States has a

> strong interest in collecting taxes, . . . and in prosecuting individuals for tax evasion, . . .

In *United States v. MacAllister*, 160 F.3d 1304 (11th Cir. 1998), the court stated:

> MacAllister asserts that extraterritorial application of § 963 is unreasonable based on the principles set forth in § 403(2) of the Restatement (Third) of the Foreign Relations Law of the United States. We conclude otherwise. "[D]rug smuggling is a serious and universally condemned offense," and therefore, "no conflict is likely to be created by extraterritorial regulation of drug traffickers."

(2) The *Restatement (Third) of the Foreign Relations Law of the United States* § 403 insisted that reasonableness had become a principle both of U.S. and of international law. The *Restatement (Fourth)* § 405 softens this to a matter of "prescriptive comity" rather than of "law."

§ 3.06 "New" Approaches

(1) Would a general statute assist in rationalizing the prosecution of extraterritorial crimes? Consider § 208 of the Final Report of the National Commission on Reform of Federal Criminal Laws:

> Except as otherwise expressly provided by statute or treaty, extraterritorial jurisdiction over an offense exists when:
>
> (a) one of the following is a victim or intended victim of a crime of violence: the President of the United States, the President-elect, the Vice-President, or, if there is no Vice-President, the officer next in the order of succession to the office of President of the United States, the Vice-President-elect, or any individual who is acting as President under the Constitution and laws of the United States, a candidate for President or Vice-President or any member or member designate of the President's cabinet, or a member of Congress, or a federal judge;
>
> (b) the offense is treason, or is espionage or sabotage by a national of the United States;
>
> (c) the offense consists of a forgery or counterfeiting, or an uttering of forged copies or counterfeits, of the seals, currency, instruments of credit, stamps, passports, or public documents issued by the United States; or perjury or a false statement in an official proceeding of the United States; or a false statement in a matter within the jurisdiction of the government of the United States; or other fraud against the United States, or a theft of property in which the United States has an interest, or, if committed by a national or resident of the United States, any other obstruction of or interference with United States government function;

> (d) the accused participates outside the United States in a federal offense committed in whole or in part within the United States, or the offense constitutes an attempt, solicitation, or conspiracy to commit a federal offense within the United States;
>
> (e) the offense is a federal offense involving entry of persons or property into the United States;
>
> (f) the offense is committed by a federal public servant who is outside the territory of the United States because of his official duties or by a member of his household residing abroad or by a person accompanying the military forces of the United States;
>
> (g) such jurisdiction is provided by treaty; or
>
> (h) the offense is committed by or against a national of the United States outside the jurisdiction of any nation.

FINAL REPORT OF THE NATIONAL COMMISSION ON REFORM OF FEDERAL CRIMINAL LAWS § 208 (1971); *see also* Kenneth R. Feinberg, *Extraterritorial Jurisdiction and the Proposed Federal Criminal Code*, 72 J. CRIM. L. & CRIMINOLOGY. 385 (1981). *See also* Julie Rose O'Sullivan, *The Extraterritorial Application of Federal Criminal Statutes: Analytical Roadmap, Normative Conclusions, and a Plea to Congress for Direction*, 106 GEO. L.J. 1021 (2018).

(2) Can jurisdiction be examined from other perspectives? Consider the approach to jurisdiction in terms of theories of punishment suggested in a report of the Committee on International Terrorism of the American Branch of the International Law Association:

> Debate in terms of the propriety of abstract "principles of jurisdiction" is likely to lead to a dead-end. THE RESTATEMENT (THIRD) OF FOREIGN RELATIONS LAW has tried to rephrase the debate in terms of whether it is unreasonable to exercise jurisdiction over a particular person or activity. But by what criteria should reasonableness be gauged? Prevailing fashion seeks to derive criteria of accommodation or priority from an analysis of relevant "state interests." Yet the usual mode of analysis tends to overlook "the criminological aspects of the problem"—the need to justify its extraterritorial applications in terms of the same purposes or "theories of punishment" (retribution, deterrence, etc.) that are used to justify criminal law generally. Patrick Fitzgerald, *The Territorial Principle in Penal Law: An Attempted Justification*, 1 GA. J. INT'L & COMP. L. 29 (1970).
>
> It may be fruitful to reexamine questions of extraterritorial jurisdiction in terms of criminal law theory and the "boundary assumptions" implicit in particular "theories of punishment." Lea Brilmayer has recently proposed generally considering all government coercion across borders in terms of the political theories that are supposed to justify a state's monopoly of

> legitimate violence within its borders. L. BRILMAYER, JUSTIFYING INTERNATIONAL ACTS (1989). "Theories of punishment" are, in a way, a special kind of political theory serving to justify and explain why it makes sense for government to use criminal law to exercise coercion against individuals. At least when extraterritorial coercion takes the form of prosecution in an ordinary domestic court, it seems obviously pertinent to ask whether it can be justified in terms of the purposes which criminal law generally is supposed to subserve.
>
> Suppose debate over the legitimacy of extraterritorial jurisdiction were recast in these terms. The idea of deterrence provides one superficially easy answer: punishing those who injure a state or its nationals will serve to discourage others from perpetrating like injuries in the future. But this ignores the "boundary assumptions" implicit in any well-developed theory of deterrence. An adequate theory of deterrence has to cope with the Kantian objection that we are never justified in using one individual solely as a means to influence the conduct of others. The individual has to have done something to invite punishment; and that something usually reduces to a breach of the ground rules tacitly accepted by members of a particular community. Where the offender is not a member of the community inflicting punishment, the ultimate basis for punishment is not the same as it is in a purely domestic context. . . .
>
> An alternate line of argument extends the relevant community to include all humanity. . . .
>
> This line of argument gives rise to a nest of questions. How far does it depend on recent treaties dealing with particular aspects of terrorism that permit a state to exercise jurisdiction over an offender found in its territory? What is the actual language in these treaties that is supposed to authorize the exercise of universal jurisdiction? Can such provisions confer jurisdiction over nationals of non-ratifying states? Does it make a difference if the offense occurred in the territory of a party? To what extent can such provisions be said to have created or to have become customary law? To what extent is the argument for universal jurisdiction independent of existing treaties? What precisely is there in state practice to support assertions of universal jurisdiction as a matter of customary law? How far does it really make sense to say that jurisdiction asserted by a self-appointed police force has been exercised on behalf of the international community? Does the international community sufficiently resemble a national community so as to permit enlarging the "boundary assumptions" implicit in particular "theories of punishment" to embrace the entire world?

Report of the Committee on International Terrorism, in PROCEEDINGS AND COMMITTEE REPORTS OF THE AMERICAN BRANCH OF THE INTERNATIONAL LAW ASSOCIATION 1989–1990, at 86, 92–94.

§ 3.07 Procedural Issues Related to Jurisdiction

Boumediene v. Bush

Supreme Court of the United States
553 U.S. 723 (2008)

Justice Kennedy delivered the opinion of the Court.

Petitioners are aliens designated as enemy combatants and detained at the United States Naval Station at Guantanamo Bay, Cuba. There are others detained there, also aliens, who are not parties to this suit.

Petitioners present a question not resolved by our earlier cases relating to the detention of aliens at Guantanamo: whether they have the constitutional privilege of habeas corpus, a privilege not to be withdrawn except in conformance with the Suspension Clause, Art. I, § 9, cl. 2. We hold these petitioners do have the habeas corpus privilege. Congress has enacted a statute, the Detainee Treatment Act of 2005 (DTA), 119 Stat. 2739, that provides certain procedures for review of the detainees' status. We hold that those procedures are not an adequate and effective substitute for habeas corpus. Therefore § 7 of the Military Commissions Act of 2006 (MCA), 28 U.S.C. A. § 2241(e) (Supp. 2007), operates as an unconstitutional suspension of the writ. We do not address whether the President has authority to detain these petitioners nor do we hold that the writ must issue. These and other questions regarding the legality of the detention are to be resolved in the first instance by the District Court. . . .

Under the Authorization for Use of Military Force (AUMF), § 2(a), ... the President is authorized "to use all necessary and appropriate force against those nations, organizations, or persons he determines planned, authorized, committed, or aided the terrorist attacks that occurred on September 11, 2001, or harbored such organizations or persons, in order to prevent any future acts of international terrorism against the United States by such nations, organizations or persons."

In *Hamdi v. Rumsfeld*, 542 U.S. 507 (2004), five Members of the Court recognized that detention of individuals who fought against the United States in Afghanistan "for the duration of the particular conflict in which they were captured, is so fundamental and accepted an incident to war as to be an exercise of the 'necessary and appropriate force' Congress has authorized the President to use." . . . After *Hamdi*, the Deputy Secretary of Defense established Combatant Status Review Tribunals (CSRTs) to determine whether individuals detained at Guantanamo were "enemy combatants," as the Department defines that term. . . . A later memorandum established procedures to implement the CSRTs. . . . The Government maintains these procedures were designed to comply with the due process requirements identified by the plurality in *Hamdi*. . . .

Interpreting the AUMF, the Department of Defense ordered the detention of these petitioners, and they were transferred to Guantanamo. Some of these individuals were apprehended on the battlefield in Afghanistan, others in places as far away from there as Bosnia and Gambia. All are foreign nationals, but none is a citizen of a nation now at war with the United States. Each denies he is a member of the al Qaeda terrorist network that carried out the September 11 attacks or of the Taliban regime that provided sanctuary for al Qaeda. Each petitioner appeared before a separate CSRT; was determined to be an enemy combatant; and has sought a writ of habeas corpus in the United States District Court for the District of Columbia.

The first actions commenced in February 2002. The District Court ordered the cases dismissed for lack of jurisdiction because the naval station is outside the sovereign territory of the United States.... The Court of Appeals for the District of Columbia Circuit affirmed.... We granted certiorari and reversed, holding that 28 U.S.C. § 2241 extended statutory habeas corpus jurisdiction to Guantanamo. See *Rasul v. Bush*, 542 U.S. 466, 473 (2004). The constitutional issue presented in the instant cases was not reached in *Rasul*....

After *Rasul*, petitioners' cases were consolidated and entertained in two separate proceedings. In the first set of cases, Judge Richard J. Leon granted the Government's motion to dismiss, holding that the detainees had no rights that could be vindicated in a habeas corpus action. In the second set of cases Judge Joyce Hens Green reached the opposite conclusion, holding the detainees had rights under the Due Process Clause of the Fifth Amendment....

While appeals were pending from the District Court decisions, Congress passed the DTA.... to provide that "no court, justice, or judge shall have jurisdiction to hear or consider ... an application for a writ of habeas corpus filed by or on behalf of an alien detained by the Department of Defense at Guantanamo Bay, Cuba." ... Section 1005 further provides that the Court of Appeals for the District of Columbia Circuit shall have "exclusive" jurisdiction to review decisions of the CSRTs....

In *Hamdan v. Rumsfeld*, 548 U.S. 557, 576–577 (2006), the Court held this provision did not apply to cases (like petitioners') pending when the DTA was enacted. Congress responded by passing the MCA, 10 U.S.C. A. § 948a *et seq.* (Supp. 2007), which again amended § 2241.... We granted certiorari....

As a threshold matter, we must decide whether MCA § 7 denies the federal courts jurisdiction to hear habeas corpus actions pending at the time of its enactment. We hold the statute does deny that jurisdiction, so that, if the statute is valid, petitioners' cases must be dismissed....

In deciding the constitutional questions now presented we must determine whether petitioners are barred from seeking the writ or invoking the protections of the Suspension Clause either because of their status, *i.e.*, petitioners' designation by the Executive Branch as enemy combatants, or their physical location, *i.e.*, their presence at Guantanamo Bay. The Government contends that noncitizens designated as enemy combatants and detained in territory located outside our Nation's borders have no constitutional rights and no privilege of habeas corpus. Petitioners contend they do have cognizable constitutional rights and that Congress, in seeking to eliminate recourse to habeas corpus as a means to assert those rights, acted in violation of the Suspension Clause. . . .

[The Court discusses the history and origins of the writ.]

Each side in the present matter argues that the very lack of a precedent on point supports its position. The Government points out there is no evidence that a court sitting in England granted habeas relief to an enemy alien detained abroad; petitioners respond there is no evidence that a court refused to do so for lack of jurisdiction.

Both arguments are premised, however, upon the assumption that the historical record is complete and that the common law, if properly understood, yields a definite answer to the questions before us. There are reasons to doubt both assumptions. Recent scholarship points to the inherent shortcomings in the historical record. . . . And given the unique status of Guantanamo Bay and the particular dangers of terrorism in the modern age, the common-law courts simply may not have confronted cases with close parallels to this one. We decline, therefore, to infer too much, one way or the other, from the lack of historical evidence on point. . . .

Drawing from its position that at common law the writ ran only to territories over which the Crown was sovereign, the Government says the Suspension Clause affords petitioners no rights because the United States does not claim sovereignty over the place of detention.

Guantanamo Bay is not formally part of the United States. . . . And under the terms of the lease between the United States and Cuba, Cuba retains "ultimate sovereignty" over the territory while the United States exercises "complete jurisdiction and control." . . . Under the terms of the 1934 Treaty, however, Cuba effectively has no rights as a sovereign until the parties agree to modification of the 1903 Lease Agreement or the United States abandons the base. . . .

The United States contends, nevertheless, that Guantanamo is not within its sovereign control. This was the Government's position well before the events of September 11, 2001. . . . And in other contexts the Court has held that questions of sovereignty are for the political branches to decide. . . . Even if this were a treaty interpretation case that did not involve a political question, the President's construction of the lease agreement would be entitled to great respect. . . .

We therefore do not question the Government's position that Cuba, not the United States, maintains sovereignty, in the legal and technical sense of the term, over Guantanamo Bay. But this does not end the analysis. Our cases do not hold it is improper for us to inquire into the objective degree of control the Nation asserts over foreign territory. As commentators have noted, "'[s]overeignty' is a term used in many senses and is much abused." . . . When we have stated that sovereignty is a political question, we have referred not to sovereignty in the general, colloquial sense, meaning the exercise of dominion or power, . . . but sovereignty in the narrow, legal sense of the term, meaning a claim of right, . . . Indeed, it is not altogether uncommon for a territory to be under the *de jure* sovereignty of one nation, while under the plenary control, or practical sovereignty, of another. Accordingly, for purposes of our analysis, we accept the Government's position that Cuba, and not the United States, retains *de jure* sovereignty over Guantanamo Bay. As we did in *Rasul*, however, we take notice of the obvious and uncontested fact that the United States, by virtue of its complete jurisdiction and control over the base, maintains *de facto* sovereignty over this territory. . . .

It is true that before today the Court has never held that noncitizens detained by our Government in territory over which another country maintains *de jure* sovereignty have any rights under our Constitution. But the cases before us lack any precise historical parallel. They involve individuals detained by executive order for the duration of a conflict that, if measured from September 11, 2001, to the present, is already among the longest wars in American history. . . . The detainees, moreover, are held in a territory that, while technically not part of the United States, is under the complete and total control of our Government. Under these circumstances the lack of a precedent on point is no barrier to our holding.

We hold that Art. I, § 9, cl. 2, of the Constitution has full effect at Guantanamo Bay. If the privilege of habeas corpus is to be denied to the detainees now before us, Congress must act in accordance with the requirements of the Suspension Clause. This Court may not impose a *de facto* suspension by abstaining from these controversies. The MCA does not purport to be a formal suspension of the writ; and the Government, in its submissions to us, has not argued that it is. Petitioners, therefore, are entitled to the privilege of habeas corpus to challenge the legality of their detention.

In light of this holding the question becomes whether the statute stripping jurisdiction to issue the writ avoids the Suspension Clause mandate because Congress has provided adequate substitute procedures for habeas corpus. The Government submits there has been compliance with the Suspension Clause because the DTA review process in the Court of Appeals . . . provides an adequate substitute. . . . Although we do not hold that an adequate substitute must duplicate § 2241 in all respects, it suffices that the Government has not established that the detainees' access to the statutory review provisions at issue is an adequate substitute for the writ of habeas corpus. MCA § 7 thus effects an unconstitutional suspension of the writ. In view of our holding we need not discuss the reach of the writ with respect to claims of unlawful conditions of treatment or confinement. . . .

In light of our conclusion that there is no jurisdictional bar to the District Court's entertaining petitioners' claims the question remains whether there are prudential barriers to habeas corpus review under these circumstances. . . . The Government argues petitioners must seek review of their CSRT determinations in the Court of Appeals before they can proceed with their habeas corpus actions in the District Court. . . .

The real risks, the real threats, of terrorist attacks are constant and not likely soon to abate. The ways to disrupt our life and laws are so many and unforeseen that the Court should not attempt even some general catalogue of crises that might occur. Certain principles are apparent, however. Practical considerations and exigent circumstances inform the definition and reach of the law's writs, including habeas corpus. The cases and our tradition reflect this precept.

In cases involving foreign citizens detained abroad by the Executive, it likely would be both an impractical and unprecedented extension of judicial power to assume that habeas corpus would be available at the moment the prisoner is taken into custody. If and when habeas corpus jurisdiction applies, as it does in these cases, then proper deference can be accorded to reasonable procedures for screening and initial detention under lawful and proper conditions of confinement and treatment for a reasonable period of time. Domestic exigencies, furthermore, might also impose such onerous burdens on the Government that here, too, the Judicial Branch would be required to devise sensible rules for staying habeas corpus proceedings until the Government can comply with its requirements in a responsible way. . . . Here, as is true with detainees apprehended abroad, a relevant consideration in determining the courts' role is whether there are suitable alternative processes in place to protect against the arbitrary exercise of governmental power.

The cases before us, however, do not involve detainees who have been held for a short period of time while awaiting their CSRT determinations. Were that the case, or were it probable that the Court of Appeals could complete a prompt review of their applications, the case for requiring temporary abstention or exhaustion of alternative remedies would be much stronger. These qualifications no longer pertain here. In some of these cases six years have elapsed without the judicial oversight that habeas corpus or an adequate substitute demands. And there has been no showing that the Executive faces such onerous burdens that it cannot respond to habeas corpus actions. To require these detainees to complete DTA review before proceeding with their habeas corpus actions would be to require additional months, if not years, of delay. . . .

Our decision today holds only that the petitioners before us are entitled to seek the writ; that the DTA review procedures are an inadequate substitute for habeas corpus; and that the petitioners in these cases need not exhaust the review procedures in the Court of Appeals before proceeding with their habeas actions in the District Court. The only law we identify as unconstitutional is MCA § 7, 28 U.S.C. A. § 2241(e) (Supp. 2007). Accordingly, both the DTA and the CSRT process remain intact. Our holding with regard to exhaustion should not be read to imply that a habeas court should intervene the moment an enemy combatant steps foot in a territory where the writ runs. The Executive is entitled to a reasonable period of time to determine a detainee's status before a court entertains that detainee's habeas corpus petition. The CSRT process is the mechanism Congress and the President set up to deal with these issues. Except in cases of undue delay, federal courts should refrain from entertaining an enemy combatant's habeas corpus petition at least until after the Department, acting via the CSRT, has had a chance to review his status. . . .

Although we hold that the DTA is not an adequate and effective substitute for habeas corpus, it does not follow that a habeas corpus court may disregard the dangers the detention in these cases was intended to prevent. . . . Certain accommodations can be made to reduce the burden habeas corpus proceedings will place on the military without impermissibly diluting the protections of the writ.

In the DTA Congress sought to consolidate review of petitioners' claims in the Court of Appeals. Channeling future cases to one district court would no doubt reduce administrative burdens on the Government. This is a legitimate objective that might be advanced even without an amendment to § 2241 . . . .

Another of Congress' reasons for vesting exclusive jurisdiction in the Court of Appeals, perhaps, was to avoid the widespread dissemination of classified information. The Government has raised similar concerns here and elsewhere. . . . We make no attempt to anticipate all of the evidentiary and access-to-counsel issues that will arise during the course of the detainees' habeas corpus proceedings. We recognize, however, that the Government has a legitimate interest in protecting sources and methods of intelligence gathering; and we expect that the District Court will use its discretion to accommodate this interest to the greatest extent possible. . . .

These and the other remaining questions are within the expertise and competence of the District Court to address in the first instance. . . . In considering both the procedural and substantive standards used to impose detention to prevent acts of terrorism, proper deference must be accorded to the political branches. See *United States v. Curtiss-Wright Export Corp.*, 299 U.S. 304, 320 (1936). Unlike the President and some designated Members of Congress, neither the Members of this Court nor most federal judges begin the day with briefings that may describe new and serious threats to our Nation and its people. The law must accord the Executive substantial authority to apprehend and detain those who pose a real danger to our security. . . .

Our opinion does not undermine the Executive's powers as Commander in Chief. On the contrary, the exercise of those powers is vindicated, not eroded, when confirmed by the Judicial Branch. Within the Constitution's separation-of-powers structure, few exercises of judicial power are as legitimate or as necessary as the responsibility to hear challenges to the authority of the Executive to imprison a person. Some of these petitioners have been in custody for six years with no definitive judicial determination as to the legality of their detention. Their access to the writ is a necessity to determine the lawfulness of their status, even if, in the end, they do not obtain the relief they seek. . . .

It bears repeating that our opinion does not address the content of the law that governs petitioners' detention. That is a matter yet to be determined. We hold that petitioners may invoke the fundamental procedural protections of habeas corpus. The laws and Constitution are designed to survive, and remain in force, in extraordinary times. Liberty and security can be reconciled; and in our system they are reconciled within the framework of the law. The Framers decided that habeas corpus, a right of first importance, must be a part of that framework, a part of that law.

The determination by the Court of Appeals that the Suspension Clause and its protections are inapplicable to petitioners was in error. The judgment of the Court of Appeals is reversed. The cases are remanded to the Court of Appeals with instructions that it remand the cases to the District Court for proceedings consistent with this opinion. . . . It is so ordered.

JUSTICE SOUTER, with whom JUSTICE GINSBURG and JUSTICE BREYER join, concurring.

I join the Court's opinion in its entirety and add this afterword only to emphasize two things one might overlook after reading the dissents. . . .

[Justice Souter discusses the *Rasul v. Bush* decision and the length of the imprisonments.]

After six years of sustained executive detentions in Guantanamo, subject to habeas jurisdiction but without any actual habeas scrutiny, today's decision is no judicial victory, but an act of perseverance in trying to make habeas review, and the obligation of the courts to provide it, mean something of value both to prisoners and to the Nation. . . .

CHIEF JUSTICE ROBERTS, with whom JUSTICE SCALIA, JUSTICE THOMAS, and JUSTICE ALITO join, dissenting.

Today the Court strikes down as inadequate the most generous set of procedural protections ever afforded aliens detained by this country as enemy combatants. The political branches crafted these procedures amidst an ongoing military conflict, after much careful investigation and thorough debate. The Court rejects them today out of hand, without bothering to say what due process rights the detainees possess, without explaining how the statute fails to vindicate those rights, and before a single petitioner has even attempted to avail himself of the law's operation. And to what effect? The majority merely replaces a review system designed by the people's representatives with a set of shapeless procedures to be defined by federal courts at some future date. One cannot help but think, after surveying the modest practical results of the majority's ambitious opinion, that this decision is not really about the detainees at all, but about control of federal policy regarding enemy combatants. . . .

The majority's overreaching is particularly egregious given the weakness of its objections to the DTA. Simply put, the Court's opinion fails on its own terms. The majority strikes down the statute because it is not an "adequate substitute" for habeas review . . . but fails to show what rights the detainees have that cannot be vindicated by the DTA system. . . . All told, the DTA provides the prisoners held at Guantanamo Bay adequate opportunity to contest the bases of their detentions, which is all habeas corpus need allow. The DTA provides more opportunity and more process, in fact, than that afforded prisoners of war or any other alleged enemy combatants in history. . . .

Despite these guarantees, the Court finds the DTA system an inadequate habeas substitute, for one central reason: Detainees are unable to introduce at the appeal stage exculpatory evidence discovered after the conclusion of their CSRT proceedings. . . . The Court hints darkly that the DTA may suffer from other infirmities, . . . but it does not bother to name them, making a response a bit difficult. . . . If this is the most the Court can muster, the ice beneath its feet is thin indeed. As noted, the CSRT procedures provide ample opportunity for detainees to introduce exculpatory evidence—whether documentary in nature or from live witnesses—before the military tribunals. . . . And if their ability to introduce such evidence is denied contrary to the Constitution or laws of the United States, the D. C. Circuit has the authority to say so on review. . . .

The Court's new method of constitutional adjudication only underscores its failure to follow our usual procedures and require petitioners to demonstrate that *they* have been harmed by the statute they challenge. In the absence of such a concrete showing, the Court is unable to imagine a plausible hypothetical in which the DTA is unconstitutional. . . .

For all its eloquence about the detainees' right to the writ, the Court makes no effort to elaborate how exactly the remedy it prescribes will differ from the procedural protections detainees enjoy under the DTA. The Court objects to the detainees' limited access to witnesses and classified material, but proposes no alternatives of its own. . . .

In sum, the DTA satisfies the majority's own criteria for assessing adequacy. This statutory scheme provides the combatants held at Guantanamo greater procedural protections than have ever been afforded alleged enemy detainees—whether citizens or aliens—in our national history. . . .

So who has won? Not the detainees. The Court's analysis leaves them with only the prospect of further litigation to determine the content of their new habeas right, followed by further litigation to resolve their particular cases, followed by further litigation before the D. C. Circuit—where they could have started had they invoked the DTA procedure. Not Congress, whose attempt to "determine—through democratic means—how best" to balance the security of the American people with the detainees' liberty interests . . . has been unceremoniously brushed aside. Not the Great Writ, whose majesty is hardly enhanced by its extension to a jurisdictionally quirky outpost, with no tangible benefit to anyone. Not the rule of law, unless by that is meant the rule of lawyers, who will now arguably have a greater role than military and intelligence officials in shaping policy for alien enemy combatants. And certainly not the American people, who today lose a bit more control over the conduct of this Nation's foreign policy to unelected, politically unaccountable judges. . . . I respectfully dissent.

Justice Scalia, with whom The Chief Justice, Justice Thomas, and Justice Alito join, dissenting.

Today, for the first time in our Nation's history, the Court confers a constitutional right to habeas corpus on alien enemies detained abroad by our military forces in the course of an ongoing war. The Chief Justice's dissent, which I join, shows that the procedures prescribed by Congress in the Detainee Treatment Act provide the essential protections that habeas corpus guarantees; there has thus been no suspension of the writ, and no basis exists for judicial intervention beyond what the Act allows. My problem with today's opinion is more fundamental still: The writ of habeas corpus does not, and never has, run in favor of aliens abroad; the Suspension Clause thus has no application, and the Court's intervention in this military matter is entirely ultra vires....

America is at war with radical Islamists. The enemy began by killing Americans and American allies abroad: 241 at the Marine barracks in Lebanon, 19 at the Khobar Towers in Dhahran, 224 at our embassies in Dar es Salaam and Nairobi, and 17 on the USS Cole in Yemen.... On September 11, 2001, the enemy brought the battle to American soil, killing 2,749 at the Twin Towers in New York City, 184 at the Pentagon in Washington, D. C., and 40 in Pennsylvania.... It has threatened further attacks against our homeland; one need only walk about buttressed and barricaded Washington, or board a plane anywhere in the country, to know that the threat is a serious one. Our Armed Forces are now in the field against the enemy, in Afghanistan and Iraq. Last week, 13 of our countrymen in arms were killed.

The game of bait-and-switch that today's opinion plays upon the Nation's Commander in Chief will make the war harder on us. It will almost certainly cause more Americans to be killed. That consequence would be tolerable if necessary to preserve a time-honored legal principle vital to our constitutional Republic. But it is this Court's blatant *abandonment* of such a principle that produces the decision today. The President relied on our settled precedent in *Johnson v. Eisentrager*, 339 U.S. 763 (1950), when he established the prison at Guantanamo Bay for enemy aliens. Citing that case, the President's Office of Legal Counsel advised him "that the great weight of legal authority indicates that a federal district court could not properly exercise habeas jurisdiction over an alien detained at [Guantanamo Bay]." Memorandum from Patrick F. Philbin and John C. Yoo, Deputy Assistant Attorneys General, Office of Legal Counsel, to William J. Haynes II, General Counsel, Dept. of Defense (Dec. 28, 2001). Had the law been otherwise, the military surely would not have transported prisoners there, but would have kept them in Afghanistan, transferred them to another of our foreign military bases, or turned them over to allies for detention. Those other facilities might well have been worse for the detainees themselves.

In the long term, then, the Court's decision today accomplishes little, except perhaps to reduce the well-being of enemy combatants that the Court ostensibly seeks to protect. In the short term, however, the decision is devastating. At least 30 of those prisoners hitherto released from Guantanamo Bay have returned to the battlefield.... Some have been captured or killed.... But others have succeeded in carrying on their atrocities against innocent civilians....

In sum, *all* available historical evidence points to the conclusion that the writ would not have been available at common law for aliens captured and held outside the sovereign territory of the Crown. Despite three opening briefs, three reply briefs, and support from a legion of *amici*, petitioners have failed to identify a single case in the history of Anglo-American law that supports their claim to jurisdiction. The Court finds it significant that there is no recorded case *denying* jurisdiction to such prisoners either.... But a case standing for the remarkable proposition that the writ could issue to a foreign land would surely have been reported, whereas a case denying such a writ for lack of jurisdiction would likely not. At a minimum, the absence of a reported case either way leaves unrefuted the voluminous commentary stating that habeas was confined to the dominions of the Crown. . . .

Today the Court warps our Constitution in a way that goes beyond the narrow issue of the reach of the Suspension Clause, invoking judicially brainstormed separation-of-powers principles to establish a manipulable "functional" test for the extraterritorial reach of habeas corpus (and, no doubt, for the extraterritorial reach of other constitutional protections as well). It blatantly misdescribes important precedents, most conspicuously Justice Jackson's opinion for the Court in *Johnson* v. *Eisentrager*. It breaks a chain of precedent as old as the common law that prohibits judicial inquiry into detentions of aliens abroad absent statutory authorization. And, most tragically, it sets our military commanders the impossible task of proving to a civilian court, under whatever standards this Court devises in the future, that evidence supports the confinement of each and every enemy prisoner.

The Nation will live to regret what the Court has done today. I dissent.

Note

There may be an interesting problem about (overlapping) enforcement jurisdiction. The Posse Comitatus Act of 1878 (PCA) was adopted against the backdrop both of the actions of British soldiers in pre-Revolutionary America and of the Northern occupation after the Civil War. In general, it prohibits the Executive from using the military for law enforcement. *See generally* Candidus Dougherty, *"Necessity Hath No Law": Executive Power and the* Posse Comitatus *Act*, 31 Campbell L. Rev. 1 (2008). But when exactly does military involvement in the prosecution or investigation violate the PCA? Consider this issue as it arises in the following case, bearing in mind the distinction made in § 3.02 *supra* between prescriptive, adjudicative and enforcement jurisdiction. Prescriptive jurisdiction in the case lies with Congress, adjudicative with federal district court; the issue is how far the military may participate in enforcement jurisdiction.

United States v. Hitchcock

United States Court of Appeals for the Ninth Circuit
286 F.3d 1064, amended on other grounds, 298 F.3d 1021 (2002)

B. Fletcher, Circuit Judge:

We must decide whether military participation in a civilian criminal investigation violated the Posse Comitatus Act or 10 U.S.C. § 375. Because we conclude that the military's participation falls under the "independent military purpose" exception, we affirm the district court's order denying Hitchcock's motion to dismiss the charges against him or to suppress all evidence because of a violation of the Posse Comitatus Act and § 375 . . . .

After the U.S. Army Criminal Investigation Division (CID) received information that Benjamin Lake, a U.S. Marine stationed in Hawai'i, was selling lysergic acid diethylamide (LSD) to other military personnel on his base, it began a joint investigation with the Naval Criminal Investigative Service (NCIS). Lake sold LSD to an undercover CID agent on October 31, 1998 and again on November 13, 1998. After the sale on November 13, NCIS agents arrested Lake. Lake agreed to cooperate with NCIS agents. He identified the defendant, Mark Hitchcock, as the source of the LSD. Because Hitchcock is a civilian, the lead NCIS agent on the case, Michael Moran, asked the Drug Enforcement Administration (DEA) to join the investigation. The DEA took control of the investigation, assigning Special Agent John Meade as the case agent. Two NCIS agents, Moran and Robert Rzepka, remained involved with the investigation. Under DEA Agent Meade's direction, Lake made two monitored calls to Hitchcock and discussed payment for LSD Lake had previously obtained. The calls were made from the DEA field office and were monitored using DEA equipment. NCIS Agent Rzepka brought Lake to and from the Naval brig so that Lake could make the calls....

....

Hitchcock filed another motion on May 10, 1999, seeking dismissal of all charges against him and suppression of all evidence on the grounds that NCIS [Naval Criminal Investigative Service] and CID [U.S. Army Criminal Investigation Division] participation in the investigation leading to Hitchcock's arrest violated the Posse Comitatus Act (PCA), 18 U.S.C. § 1385,[3] and 10 U.S.C. § 375,[4] both of which generally prohibit military involvement in civilian law enforcement. After hearing oral argument, the district court held that NCIS and CID involvement in the DEA's investigation of Hitchcock did not violate the PCA or § 375 because the military had only rendered "indirect assistance" to civilian law enforcement and such assistance is not prohibited by the acts.... Alternatively, the court held that the investigation did not violate the acts because the military's participation arose out of "legitimate military concerns." Hitchcock appeals from the district court's order denying his motion to dismiss or suppress all evidence because of a violation of the PCA and § 375.

---

3. The PCA states:

> Whoever, except in cases and under circumstances expressly authorized by the Constitution or Act of Congress, willfully uses any part of the Army or the Air Force as a posse comitatus or otherwise to execute the laws shall be fined under this title or imprisoned not more than two years, or both.

18 U.S.C. § 1385.

4. Section 375 states:

> The Secretary of Defense shall prescribe such regulations as may be necessary to ensure that any activity (including the provision of any equipment or facility or the assignment or detail of any personnel) under this chapter does not include or permit direct participation by a member of the Army, Navy, Air Force, or Marine Corps in a search, seizure, arrest, or other similar activity unless participation in such activity by such member is otherwise authorized by law.

... Hitchcock entered a conditional guilty plea to all five counts of the superseding indictment on September 17, 1999, reserving the right to appeal the district court's orders denying his motions to dismiss and suppress. . . .

Whether the Navy's involvement in Hitchcock's arrest violated the PCA is a mixed question of fact and law which is primarily legal. . . .

The PCA prohibits Army and Air Force personnel from participating in civilian law enforcement activities unless otherwise permitted by federal law. . . . Although the Navy and Marine Corps are not included by name in the PCA, Congress passed legislation requiring the Secretary of Defense to "prescribe such regulations as may be necessary" to prohibit members of all branches of the military from participating in civilian law enforcement activities as well. . . . Pursuant to this congressional directive, the Secretary of Defense promulgated a Department of Defense (DoD) Directive regulating the cooperation of military personnel with civilian law enforcement officials. . . . The Secretaries of the Navy and Army issued regulations implementing DoD Directive 5525.5 . . . .

These regulations generally prohibit "direct" military involvement in civilian law enforcement activities but permit "indirect" assistance such as the transfer of information obtained during the normal course of military operations or other actions that "do not subject civilians to the use [of] military power that is regulatory, prescriptive, or compulsory." . . . The regulations permit an exception to the general prohibition on direct involvement where the military participation is undertaken "for the primary purpose of furthering a military or foreign affairs function of the United States, regardless of incidental benefits to civilian authorities." . . .

In this case, the district court held that the participation of NCIS and CID agents in the investigation and arrest of Hitchcock and the search of Hitchcock's house and subsequent seizure of evidence did not violate the PCA or § 375 because the military agencies "merely provided indirect assistance to the DEA." . . . In reaching this conclusion, the district court relied on our opinion in *United States v. Kahn,* 35 F.3d 426 (9th Cir. 1994). Kahn set forth three tests for determining whether military involvement in civilian law enforcement constitutes permissible indirect assistance: "[1] The involvement must not constitute the exercise of regulatory, proscriptive, or compulsory military power, [2] must not amount to direct active involvement in the execution of the laws, and [3] must not pervade the activities of civilian authorities." . . . The district court held that NCIS and CID involvement constituted indirect assistance under Kahn because,

> although [NCIS] Agent Moran participated in the interrogation of Defendant, his involvement was extremely minimal, and was limited to questions pertaining to distribution of drugs on a military base. [In addition], while it is true that [NCIS] Agents Moran and Rzepka participated in the surveillance and that Agents Moran and Rzepka, along with two Army CID agents, were present during the search of Defendant's home, all evidence was recovered by the DEA, it was the DEA who was in command of both

> the surveillance and the search, and it was the DEA who instructed the other agents about the extent of their participation.

Hitchcock, 103 F. Supp. 2d at 1229–30.

The district court's conclusion that NCIS and CID involvement in Hitchcock's case did not constitute "direct assistance" under the regulations may have been erroneous. . . . However, we conclude that participation of military personnel in the DEA's investigation of Hitchcock did not violate the PCA, § 375, or the regulations implementing § 375, because the military's involvement in this case falls within the "independent military purpose" exception, as the district court held in the alternative . . . It is undisputed that Hitchcock sold LSD to Lake, a U.S. Marine, who was, in turn, selling LSD to other military personnel. NCIS Agent Rzepka specifically testified that NCIS agents were involved in Hitchcock's interrogation in order to determine whether Hitchcock had sold drugs to other military personnel besides Lake. Military participation in Hitchcock's investigation for the purpose of determining the extent to which his LSD was being used and distributed on the military base was justified. The regulations also permit direct assistance in "investigations and other actions related to the commander's inherent authority to maintain law and order on a military installation or facility." . . . Hitchcock's protestations notwithstanding, the proposition that the sale of LSD to persons who might use the drug on a military base or sell it to others on the base implicates the maintenance of law and order on a military installation is unassailable.

Because the participation of NCIS and CID agents in the investigation was permissible under the independent military purpose exception, the PCA and § 375 were not violated. Therefore, we affirm the district court's order denying Hitchcock's motion to dismiss the charges against him or to suppress all evidence. . . .

Chapter 4

Foreign Corrupt Practices Act

§ 4.01 Introduction

A. Overview of Act and Emerging International Framework

The Foreign Corrupt Practices Act (FCPA) was passed in 1977 with the purpose of criminalizing conduct relating to the bribing of foreign government officials. In 1988 there were amendments to the Act which "changed the focus of illegality from the status of the recipient to the purpose or nature of the payment. As a consequence, there is an exclusion for payments to secure routine governmental actions by any foreign official, regardless of the recipient's title, status, or responsibilities." DONALD R. CRUVER, COMPLYING WITH THE FOREIGN CORRUPT PRACTICES ACT 2016 (2d ed. 1999). The International Anti-Bribery and Fair Competition Act of 1998 again revisited this Act. Discussing the need for the initial legislation, as well as the modifications being made, House Report 105-802 states:

> Investigations by the Securities and Exchange Commission (SEC) in the mid-1970s revealed that over 400 U.S. companies admitted making questionable or illegal payments in excess of $300 million to foreign government officials, politicians, and political parties. Many public companies maintained cash "slush funds" from which illegal campaign contributions were being made in the United States and illegal bribes were being paid to foreign officials. Scandals involving payments by U.S. companies to public officials in Japan, Italy, and Mexico led to political repercussions within those countries and damaged the reputation of American companies throughout the world.
>
> In the wake of these disclosures, Congress enacted the Foreign Corrupt Practices Act of 1977 (the FCPA).... The FCPA amended the Securities Exchange Act of 1934, 15 U.S.C. § 78 et seq., to require issuers of publicly traded securities to institute adequate accounting controls and to maintain accurate books and records. Civil and criminal penalties were enacted for the failure to do so. In addition, the FCPA required both issuers and all other U.S. nationals or residents, as well as U.S. business entities and foreign entities with their primary place of business in the United States (defined as "domestic concerns") to refrain from making any unlawful payments to public officials, political parties, party officials, or candidates for public office, directly or through others, for the purpose of causing that person to

make a decision or take an action, or refrain from taking an action, for the purpose of obtaining or retaining business.

Since the passage of the FCPA, American businesses have operated at a disadvantage relative to foreign competitors who have continued to pay bribes without fear of penalty. . . . Such bribery is estimated to affect international contracts valued in the billions of dollars each year. Some of our trading partners have explicitly encouraged and subsidized such bribes by permitting businesses to claim them as tax-deductible business expenses.

Beginning in 1989, the U.S. government began an effort to convince our trading partners at the OECD to criminalize the bribery of foreign public officials. Achieving comparable prohibitions in other developed countries and combating corruption generally has been a major priority of the U.S. business community, the U.S. Congress, and successive Administrations since the late 1970s.

International bribery and corruption continue to be problems worldwide. They undermine the goals of fostering economic development, trade liberalization, and achieving a level playing field throughout the world for businesses. It is impossible to calculate with certainty the losses suffered by U.S. businesses due to bribery by foreign competitors. The Commerce Department has stated that it has learned of significant allegations of bribery by foreign firms in approximately 240 international commercial contracts since mid-1994 valued at nearly $108 billion. This legislation, coupled with implementation of the OECD Convention by our major trading partners, is designed to result in a substantial leveling of the playing field for U.S. businesses. . . .

Fortunately, in the 1990s the international community has made a concerted effort in the fight against corruption. Gradually, as awareness of the effects of transnational bribery became more apparent, progress was made in efforts to combat bribery overseas. After almost four years of substantial work in the OECD's Working Group on Bribery, on May 27, 1994, the OECD Council approved a Recommendation on Bribery in International Business Transactions (the Recommendation). The 29 OECD member states agreed that bribery distorts international competitive conditions; that all countries share a responsibility to combat bribery in international business transactions, however their nationals may be involved; and that further action is needed on the national and international level. Member states agreed to "take concrete and meaningful steps" to meet the goal of deterring, preventing, and combating bribery of foreign officials. However, the Recommendation did not require each member state to criminalize the bribery of officials of another country.

These efforts ultimately culminated in the signing of the Organization for Economic Cooperation and Development Convention on Combating

> Bribery of Foreign Public Officials in International Business Transactions (the OECD Convention). Thirty-three countries, composed of most of the world's largest trading nations, signed the OECD Convention on December 17, 1997. For twenty years after the passage of the Foreign Corrupt Practices Act, the United States was virtually alone in criminalizing foreign bribery. Now, thirty-four other countries have taken a step in this direction. Twenty-eight of the twenty-nine OECD member countries along with five other countries, Argentina, Bulgaria, Brazil, Chile, and the Slovak Republic, signed the OECD Convention....
>
> Under the OECD Convention: The U.S. and its trading partners agreed to criminalize bribery of foreign public officials, including officials in all branches of government, and to criminalize payments to officials of public agencies and public international organizations; The OECD Convention also calls for criminal penalties for those who bribe foreign public officials. If a nation's legal system lacks the concept of corporate criminal liability, the nation must provide for equivalent non-criminal sanctions, such as fines; Parties to the agreement pledged to work to provide legal assistance in investigations and proceedings within the scope of the OECD Convention and to make bribery of foreign public officials an extraditable offense; and The OECD Convention requires the Parties to cooperate in an OECD follow-up program to monitor and promote full implementation....

Notes

(1) Do bans on extraterritorial anti-bribery place United States corporations at a disadvantage in competing in the global market? Should the United States use "persuasion" or "coercion" in promoting anti-corruption laws? *See* Steven R. Salbu, Colloquy, *Are Extraterritorial Restrictions on Bribery a Viable and Desirable International Policy Goal Under the Global Conditions of the Late Twentieth Century?*, 24 Yale J. Int'l L. 223 (1999) ("global attitudes about what comprises bribery are so varied that extraterritorial application of anti-corruption laws creates two kinds of perils: a moral peril and a political peril").

(2) On November 18, 1998, President Clinton signed into law the International Anti-Bribery and Fair Competition Act of 1998. At the time of the signing, he stated that the Act "makes certain changes in existing law to implement the Convention on Combating Bribery of Foreign Public Officials in International Business Transactions which was negotiated under the auspices of the Organization for Economic Cooperation and Development (OECD)." The OECD's Convention (www.oecd.org/), which came into force on February 15, 1999, has been ratified by 38 OECD member States and 6 non-members (Argentina, Brazil, Bulgaria, Peru, Russia and South Africa). The organization has an active Working Group which monitors compliance with the Convention. In fact, the OECD Convention was preceded by the 1996 Inter-American Convention against Corruption, 35 I.L.M. 724 (1996) as the first international instrument to require that States make criminal the transnational bribery of

foreign public officials. It came into force on March 6, 1997. There are further Council of Europe, European Union and African Union treaties in the area. While the United States has not ratified the Council of Europe's 1999 Criminal Law Convention on Corruption, http://conventions.coe.int/Treaty/en/Treaties/Html/173.htm, it participates in the work of the Group of States against Corruption (GRECO), formed under the auspices of the Convention. It has submitted to evaluation by the Group. *See* http://www.coe.int/t/dghl/monitoring/greco/default_en.asp#Top. The World Bank also became involved. In 2007, its Board of Directors "endorsed a new Governance and Anti-Corruption (GAC) Strategy which is designed to increase the institution's focus on these areas as an integral part of its work to decrease poverty and promote economic growth." Bruce Zagaris, *World Bank Issues Corruption Report as Corruption Head Resigns*, 24 INT'L ENF. L. REP. 95 (2008). The United States continues to press parties to take action within their countries to implement the Conventions.

(3) The Department of Justice assists companies and nationals in complying with the FCPA through a *Resource Guide to the U.S. Foreign Corrupt Practices Act* (2d ed., July 2020). *See* https://www.justice.gov/criminal-fraud/file/1292051/download "Under this procedure, the Attorney General will issue an opinion within 30 days." *Id.* at 85. "To the extent that the opinion concludes that the proposed conduct would not violate the FCPA, a rebuttable presumption is created that the requestor's conduct that was the basis of the opinion is in compliance with the FCPA." *Id. See also* 28 C.F.R. § 80.10 (noting that DOJ can rebut this presumption by a preponderance of the evidence).

(4) The United Nations Convention against Transnational Organized Crime, G.A. Res. 55/25, U.N. GAOR, Supp. No. 49, Vol. I, at 43, U.N. Doc. A/55/49 (2001) came into force in September 2003. It contains criminalization provisions dealing with corruption of officials, in addition to the obligation to use criminal processes directly against transnational organized crime. Parties obligate themselves to establish as criminal in their domestic law both the promise, offering or giving to a public official and the solicitation or acceptance by such an official "of an undue advantage, for the official himself or another person or entity, in order that the official act or refrain from acting in the exercise of his or her official duties." (Article 8(1).) Parties are also required to "consider" criminalizing corruption involving a foreign public official or international civil servant. (Article 8(2).) States Parties must also take legislative, administrative and prosecutorial measures to promote integrity and to prevent, detect and punish the corruption of public officials. (Article 9(1).)

(5) On December 14, 2005, the 2003 United Nations Convention against Corruption ("CAC"), G.A. Res. 58/4, U.N. GAOR, 58th Sess., Supp. No. 49 (2004), came into force. It is much more specific in its focus than the Transnational Organized Crime Convention. We reproduce parts of the Convention here, both in view of its significance in the present context and as an example of a "state-of-the-art" multilateral suppression treaty. Notice that now, in Article 16(1), it is required that Parties make criminal the bribery of foreign officials. "Considering" is not enough!

The U.S. ratified the treaty on October 30, 2006, one of 189 states (along with the European Union) that had become parties by December 2021. Among the early parties to the U.N. Convention was China. Unlike the United Kingdom and the United States that endeavor to get their legislative structure in order before becoming a party to criminal law treaties, China (like many other parties) ratified and then began a study of how best to give effect to it. The Convention has generated much discussion in Government departments and among the Chinese academic community. See § 4.03 for further discussion of China's FCPA equivalent. *See generally* The United Nations Convention against Corruption: A Commentary (Cecily Rose, Michael Kubicial & Oliver Landwehr eds. 2019).

United Nations Convention Against Corruption (2003)

Chapter III Criminalization and law enforcement

Article 15 Bribery of national public officials

Each State Party shall adopt such legislative and other measures as may be necessary to establish as criminal offences, when committed intentionally:

(a) The promise, offering or giving, to a public official, directly or indirectly, of an undue advantage, for the official himself or herself or another person or entity, in order that the official act or refrain from acting in the exercise of his or her official duties;

(b) The solicitation or acceptance by a public official, directly or indirectly, of an undue advantage, for the official himself or herself or another person or entity, in order that the official act or refrain from acting in the exercise of his or her official duties.

Article 16 Bribery of foreign public officials and officials of public international organizations

1. Each State Party shall adopt such legislative and other measures as may be necessary to establish as a criminal offence, when committed intentionally, the promise, offering or giving to a foreign public official or an official of a public international organization, directly or indirectly, of an undue advantage, for the official himself or herself or another person or entity, in order that the official act or refrain from acting in the exercise of his or her official duties, in order to obtain or retain business or other undue advantage in relation to the conduct of international business.

2. Each State Party shall consider adopting such legislative and other measures as may be necessary to establish as a criminal offence, when committed intentionally, the solicitation or acceptance by a foreign public official or an official of a public international organization, directly or indirectly, of an undue advantage, for the official himself or herself or another person or entity, in order that the official act or refrain from acting in the exercise of his or her official duties.

Article 17 Embezzlement, misappropriation or other diversion of property by a public official

Each State Party shall adopt such legislative and other measures as may be necessary to establish as criminal offences, when committed intentionally, the embezzlement, misappropriation or other diversion by a public official for his or her benefit or for the benefit of another person or entity, of any property, public or private funds or securities or any other thing of value entrusted to the public official by virtue of his or her position.

Article 18 Trading in influence

Each State Party shall consider adopting such legislative and other measures as may be necessary to establish as criminal offences, when committed intentionally:

(a) The promise, offering or giving to a public official or any other person, directly or indirectly, of an undue advantage in order that the public official or the person abuse his or her real or supposed influence with a view to obtaining from an administration or public authority of the State Party an undue advantage for the original instigator of the act or for any other person;

(b) The solicitation or acceptance by a public official or any other person, directly or indirectly, of an undue advantage for himself or herself or for another person in order that the public official or the person abuse his or her real or supposed influence with a view to obtaining from an administration or public authority of the State Party an undue advantage.

Article 19 Abuse of functions

Each State Party shall consider adopting such legislative and other measures as may be necessary to establish as a criminal offence, when committed intentionally, the abuse of functions or position, that is, the performance of or failure to perform an act, in violation of laws, by a public official in the discharge of his or her functions, for the purpose of obtaining an undue advantage for himself or herself or for another person or entity.

Article 20 Illicit enrichment

Subject to its constitution and the fundamental principles of its legal system, each State Party shall consider adopting such legislative and other measures as may be necessary to establish as a criminal offence, when committed intentionally, illicit enrichment, that is, a significant increase in the assets of a public official that he or she cannot reasonably explain in relation to his or her lawful income.

Article 21 Bribery in the private sector

Each State Party shall consider adopting such legislative and other measures as may be necessary to establish as criminal offences, when committed intentionally in the course of economic, financial or commercial activities:

(a) The promise, offering or giving, directly or indirectly, of an undue advantage to any person who directs or works, in any capacity, for a private sector entity, for the person himself or herself or for another person, in order that he or she, in breach of his or her duties, act or refrain from acting;

(b) The solicitation or acceptance, directly or indirectly, of an undue advantage by any person who directs or works, in any capacity, for a private sector entity, for the person himself or herself or for another person, in order that he or she, in breach of his or her duties, act or refrain from acting.

Article 22 Embezzlement of property in the private sector

Each State Party shall consider adopting such legislative and other measures as may be necessary to establish as a criminal offence, when committed intentionally in the course of economic, financial or commercial activities, embezzlement by a person who directs or works, in any capacity, in a private sector entity of any property, private funds or securities or any other thing of value entrusted to him or her by virtue of his or her position.

Article 23 Laundering of proceeds of crime

1. Each State Party shall adopt, in accordance with fundamental principles of its domestic law, such legislative and other measures as may be necessary to establish as criminal offences, when committed intentionally:

(a) (i) The conversion or transfer of property, knowing that such property is the proceeds of crime, for the purpose of concealing or disguising the illicit origin of the property or of helping any person who is involved in the commission of the predicate offence to evade the legal consequences of his or her action; (ii) The concealment or disguise of the true nature, source, location, disposition, movement or ownership of or rights with respect to property, knowing that such property is the proceeds of crime;

(b) Subject to the basic concepts of its legal system: (i) The acquisition, possession or use of property, knowing, at the time of receipt, that such property is the proceeds of crime; (ii) Participation in, association with or conspiracy to commit, attempts to commit and aiding, abetting, facilitating and counselling the commission of any of the offences established in accordance with this article.

2. For purposes of implementing or applying paragraph 1 of this article:

(a) Each State Party shall seek to apply paragraph 1 of this article to the widest range of predicate offences;

(b) Each State Party shall include as predicate offences at a minimum a comprehensive range of criminal offences established in accordance with this Convention;

(c) For the purposes of subparagraph (b) above, predicate offences shall include offences committed both within and outside the jurisdiction of the State Party in question. However, offences committed outside the jurisdiction of a State Party shall constitute predicate offences only when the relevant conduct is a criminal offence under the domestic law of the State where it is committed and would be a criminal offence under the domestic law of the State Party implementing or applying this article had it been committed there;

(d) Each State Party shall furnish copies of its laws that give effect to this article and of any subsequent changes to such laws or a description thereof to the Secretary-General of the United Nations;

(e) If required by fundamental principles of the domestic law of a State Party, it may be provided that the offences set forth in paragraph 1 of this article do not apply to the persons who committed the predicate offence.

Article 42 Jurisdiction

1. Each State Party shall adopt such measures as may be necessary to establish its jurisdiction over the offences established in accordance with this Convention when:

(a) The offence is committed in the territory of that State Party; or

(b) The offence is committed on board a vessel that is flying the flag of that State Party or an aircraft that is registered under the laws of that State Party at the time that the offence is committed.

2. Subject to article 4 of this Convention, a State Party may also establish its jurisdiction over any such offence when:

(a) The offence is committed against a national of that State Party; or

(b) The offence is committed by a national of that State Party or a stateless person who has his or her habitual residence in its territory; or

(c) The offence is one of those established in accordance with article 23, paragraph 1 (b) (ii), of this Convention and is committed outside its territory with a view to the commission of an offence established in accordance with article 23, paragraph 1 (a) (i) or (ii) or (b) (i), of this Convention within its territory; or

(d) The offence is committed against the State Party.

3. For the purposes of article 44 of this Convention [extradition], each State Party shall take such measures as may be necessary to establish its jurisdiction over the offences established in accordance with this Convention when the alleged offender is present in its territory and it does not extradite such person solely on the ground that he or she is one of its nationals.

> 4. Each State Party may also take such measures as may be necessary to establish its jurisdiction over the offences established in accordance with this Convention when the alleged offender is present in its territory and it does not extradite him or her.
>
> 5. If a State Party exercising its jurisdiction under paragraph 1 or 2 of this article has been notified, or has otherwise learned, that any other States Parties are conducting an investigation, prosecution or judicial proceeding in respect of the same conduct, the competent authorities of those States Parties shall, as appropriate, consult one another with a view to coordinating their actions.
>
> 6. Without prejudice to norms of general international law, this Convention shall not exclude the exercise of any criminal jurisdiction established by a State Party in accordance with its domestic law.

(6) In the preamble to UNCAC, the parties express concern "about the seriousness of problems and threats posed by corruption to the stability and security of societies, undermining the institutions and values of democracy, ethical values and justice and jeopardizing sustainable development and the rule of law." For a comprehensive study of the relationship between corruption and human rights, see INTERNATIONAL COUNCIL OF HUMAN RIGHTS AND TRANSPARENCY INTERNATIONAL, CORRUPTION AND HUMAN RIGHTS: MAKING THE CONNECTION (2009).

B. Key Provisions of FCPA

§ 78dd-1 Prohibited foreign trade practices by issuers[a]

> (a) Prohibition. It shall be unlawful for any issuer which has a class of securities registered pursuant to section 12 of this title [15 U.S.C. § 78l] or which is required to file reports under section 15(d) of this title [15 U.S.C. § 78o(d)], or for any officer, director, employee, or agent of such issuer or

---

a. All of these provisions are in title 15 of the United States Code. The act also contains similar prohibitions with respect to domestic concerns (§ 78dd-2) and persons other than issuers or domestic concerns (§ 78dd-3). These sections also provide for affirmative defenses and exceptions that mirror the language seen in § 78dd-1. "Domestic concern" is defined in § 78dd-2 as "(A) any individual who is a citizen, national, or resident of the United States; and (B) any corporation, partnership, association, joint stock company, business trust, unincorporated association or sole proprietorship which has its principal place of business in the United States, or which is organized under the laws of a State of the United States or a territory, possession, or commonwealth of the United States." "Persons other than issuers or domestic concerns" (who can commit a FCPA offense only "while in the territory of the United States") are defined in § 78ff-3 as "any natural person other than a national of the United States (as defined in section 101 of the Immigration and Nationality Act (8 U.S.C. § 1101) or any corporation, partnership, association, joint-stock company, business trust, unincorporated, organization, or sole proprietorship organized under the law of a foreign national or political subdivision thereof." — Eds.

any stockholder thereof acting on behalf of such issuer, to make use of the mails or any means or instrumentality of interstate commerce corruptly in furtherance of an offer, payment, promise to pay, or authorization of the payment of any money, or offer, gift, promise to give, or authorization of the giving of anything of value to—

(1) any foreign official for purposes of—

(A)(i) influencing any act or decision of such foreign official in his official capacity, (ii) inducing such foreign official to do or omit to do any act in violation of the lawful duty of such official, or (iii) securing any improper advantage; or

(B) inducing such foreign official to use his influence with a foreign government or instrumentality thereof to affect or influence any act or decision of such government or instrumentality, in order to assist such issuer in obtaining or retaining business for or with, or directing business to, any person;

(2) any foreign political party or official thereof or any candidate for foreign political office for purposes of—

(A)(i) influencing any act or decision of such party, official, or candidate in its or his official capacity, (ii) inducing such party, official, or candidate to do or omit to do an act in violation of the lawful duty of such party, official, or candidate, or (iii) securing any improper advantage; or

(B) inducing such party, official, or candidate to use its or his influence with a foreign government or instrumentality thereof to affect or influence any act or decision of such government or instrumentality,

in order to assist such issuer in obtaining or retaining business for or with, or directing business to, any person; or

(3) any person, while knowing that all or a portion of such money or thing of value will be offered, given, or promised, directly or indirectly, to any foreign official, to any foreign political party or official thereof, or to any candidate for foreign political office, for purposes of—

(A)(i) influencing any act or decision of such foreign official, political party, party official, or candidate in his or its official capacity, (ii) inducing such foreign official, political party, party official, or candidate to do or omit to do any act in violation of the lawful duty of such foreign official, political party, party official, or candidate, or (iii) securing any improper advantage; or

(B) inducing such foreign official, political party, party official, or candidate to use his or its influence with a foreign government or instrumentality thereof to affect or influence any act or decision of such government or instrumentality,

in order to assist such issuer in obtaining or retaining business for or with, or directing business to, any person.

(b) Exception for routine governmental action. Subsections (a) and (g) shall not apply to any facilitating or expediting payment to a foreign official, political party, or party official the purpose of which is to expedite or to secure the performance of a routine governmental action by a foreign official, political party, or party official.

(c) Affirmative defenses. It shall be an affirmative defense to actions under subsection (a) or (g) that—

(1) the payment, gift, offer, or promise of anything of value that was made, was lawful under the written laws and regulations of the foreign official's, political party's, party official's, or candidate's country; or

(2) the payment, gift, offer, or promise of anything of value that was made, was a reasonable and bona fide expenditure, such as travel and lodging expenses, incurred by or on behalf of a foreign official, party, party official, or candidate and was directly related to—

(A) the promotion, demonstration, or explanation of products or services; or

(B) the execution or performance of a contract with a foreign government or agency thereof.

(d) Guidelines by the Attorney General. . . .

(e) Opinions of the Attorney General. . . .

(f) Definitions. For purposes of this section:

(1)

(A) The term "foreign official" means any officer or employee of a foreign government or any department, agency, or instrumentality thereof, or of a public international organization, or any person acting in an official capacity for or on behalf of any such government or department, agency, or instrumentality, or for or on behalf of any such public international organization.

(B) For purposes of subparagraph (A), the term "public international organization" means—

(i) an organization that is designated by Executive order pursuant to section 1 of the International Organizations Immunities Act (22 U.S.C. 288); or

(ii) any other international organization that is designated by the President by Executive order for the purposes of this section, effective as of the date of publication of such order in the Federal Register.

(2)

(A) A person's state of mind is "knowing" with respect to conduct, a circumstance, or a result if—

(i) such person is aware that such person is engaging in such conduct, that such circumstance exists, or that such result is substantially certain to occur; or

(ii) such person has a firm belief that such circumstance exists or that such result is substantially certain to occur.

(B) When knowledge of the existence of a particular circumstance is required for an offense, such knowledge is established if a person is aware of a high probability of the existence of such circumstance, unless the person actually believes that such circumstance does not exist.

(3)

(A) The term "routine governmental action" means only an action which is ordinarily and commonly performed by a foreign official in—

(i) obtaining permits, licenses, or other official documents to qualify a person to do business in a foreign country;

(ii) processing governmental papers, such as visas and work orders;

(iii) providing police protection, mail pick-up and delivery, or scheduling inspections associated with contract performance or inspections related to transit of goods across country;

(iv) providing phone service, power and water supply, loading and unloading cargo, or protecting perishable products or commodities from deterioration; or

(v) actions of a similar nature.

(B) The term "routine governmental action" does not include any decision by a foreign official whether, or on what terms, to award new business to or to continue business with a particular party, or any action taken by a foreign official involved in the decisionmaking process to encourage a decision to award new business to or continue business with a particular party.

(g) Alternative jurisdiction. . . .

§ 78ff. Penalties

(a) Willful violations; false and misleading statements. Any person who willfully violates any provision of this title (other than section 30A [15 U.S.C. § 78dd-1]), or any rule or regulation thereunder the violation of which is made unlawful or the observance of which is required under the terms of this title, or any person who willfully and knowingly makes, or causes to be made, any statement in any application, report, or document required to be filed under this title or any rule or regulation thereunder or any undertaking contained in a registration statement as provided in subsection (d) of section 15 of this title [15 U.S.C. § 78o(d)], or by any self-regulatory organization in connection with an application for membership or participation therein or to become associated with a member thereof, which statement was false or misleading with respect to any material fact, shall upon conviction be fined not more than $1,000,000, or imprisoned not more than 10 years, or both, except that when such person is a person other than a natural person, a fine not exceeding $2,500,000 may be imposed; but no person shall be subject to imprisonment under this section for the violation of any rule or regulation if he proves that he had no knowledge of such rule or regulation.

(b) Failure to file information, documents, or reports. Any issuer which fails to file information, documents, or reports required to be filed under subsection (d) of section 15 of this title [15 U.S.C. § 78o(d)] or any rule or regulation thereunder shall forfeit to the United States the sum of $100 for each and every day such failure to file shall continue. Such forfeiture, which shall be in lieu of any criminal penalty for such failure to file which might be deemed to arise under subsection (a) of this section, shall be payable to the Treasury of the United States and shall be recoverable in a civil suit in the name of the United States.

(c) Violations by issuers, officers, directors, stockholders, employees, or agents of issuers.

(1)

(A) Any issuer that violates subsection (a) or (g) of section 30A [15 U.S.C. § 78dd-1] shall be fined not more than $2,000,000.

(B) Any issuer that violates subsection (a) or (g) of section 30A [15 U.S.C. § 78dd-1] shall be subject to a civil penalty of not more than $10,000 imposed in an action brought by the Commission.

(2)

(A) Any officer, director, employee, or agent of an issuer, or stockholder acting on behalf of such issuer, who willfully violates subsection (a) or (g) of section 30A of this title [15 U.S.C. § 78dd-1] shall be fined not more than $100,000, or imprisoned not more than 5 years, or both.

(B) Any officer, director, employee, or agent of an issuer, or stockholder acting on behalf of such issuer, who violates subsection (a) or (g) of section 30A of this title [15 U.S.C. § 78dd-1] shall be subject to a civil penalty of not more than $10,000 imposed in an action brought by the Commission.

(3) Whenever a fine is imposed under paragraph (2) upon any officer, director, employee, agent, or stockholder of an issuer, such fine may not be paid, directly or indirectly, by such issuer.

Notes

(1) As noted above, the FCPA carries the potential for significant financial penalties. Below are some the most significant financial payments by corporations as part of FCPA settlements.

Alcoa	$384 million in 2014
Alstom	$772 million in 2014
Ericcsson	$1.06 billion in 2019
KBR/Halliburton	$579 million in 2009
Telia	$965 million in 2017
Airbus	$2.09 billion in 2020

For other examples, see FCPA Professor, *FCPA 101*, *available at* www.fcpaprofessor.com.

(2) As noted above, the Department of Justice targets companies both inside and outside the United States when enforcing the FCPA. Examples of foreign entities targeted by the DOJ for FCPA violations include Siemens (German), DaimlerChrysler AG (German), Alcatel Lucent (French), Magyar Telekom (Hungarian) and Ericsson (Sweden). Further, many individuals charged with FCPA violations have been individuals who are not United States citizens.

(3) Although the DOJ focus initially appeared to be on FCPA prosecutions against companies, with Deferred (DPA) or Non-Prosecution Agreements (NPA) used to resolve the cases, recently there has been an increase in the number of prosecutions against individuals. Stanford Law School's Foreign Corrupt Practices Act Clearinghouse, a collaboration with the law firm of Sullivan & Cromwell LLP, provides statistics on several areas from DOJ and SEC enforcement actions from 1977 through 2020. https://fcpa.stanford.edu/statistics-analytics.html. Deputy Attorney General Lisa Monaco, in a speech at a White Collar Crime American Bar Association program, noted the Department's intent to focus on individuals: "accountability starts with the individuals responsible for the criminal conduct." *Deputy Attorney General Lisa O. Monaco Gives Keynote Address at ABA's 36th National Institute on White Collar Crime*, Oct. 28, 2021, *available at* https://www.justice.gov/opa/speech/deputy-attorney-general-lisa-o-monaco-gives-keynote-address-abas-36th-national-institute.

§ 4.02 Scope of the FCPA

A. Individuals Liable

United States v. Castle

United States Court of Appeals for the Fifth Circuit
925 F.2d 831 (1991)

Per Curiam

In this case, we are called upon to consider the Foreign Corrupt Practices Act of 1977 (hereinafter "FCPA"), 15 U.S.C. §§ 78dd-1, 78dd-2, and determine whether "foreign officials," who are excluded from prosecution under the FCPA itself, may nevertheless be prosecuted under the general conspiracy statute, 18 U.S.C. § 371, for conspiring to violate the FCPA.

We hold that foreign officials may not be prosecuted under 18 U.S.C. § 371 for conspiring to violate the FCPA. The scope of our holding, as well as the rationale that undergirds it, is fully set out in Judge Sanders's memorandum opinion of June 4,1990, 741 F. Supp. 116, which we adopt and attach as an appendix hereto. . . .

Appendix

. . . .

Defendants Castle and Lowry have moved to dismiss the indictment against them on the grounds that as Canadian officials, they cannot be convicted of the offense charged against them. The two other defendants, Blondek and Tull, are U.S. private citizens, and they do not challenge their indictment on this ground. . . .

The indictment charges all four defendants with conspiring to bribe foreign officials in violation of the FCPA. Blondek and Tull were employees of Eagle Bus Company, a U.S. concern as defined in the FCPA. According to the indictment, they paid a $50,000 bribe to Defendants Castle and Lowry to ensure that their bid to provide buses to the Saskatchewan provincial government would be accepted.

There is no question that the payment of the bribe by Defendants Blondek and Tull is illegal under the FCPA, and that they may be prosecuted for conspiring to violate the Act. Nor is it disputed that Defendants Castle and Lowry could not be charged with violating the FCPA itself, since the Act does not criminalize the receipt of a bribe by a foreign official. The issue here is whether the Government may prosecute Castle and Lowry under the general conspiracy statute, 18 U.S.C. § 371, for conspiring to violate the FCPA. Put more simply, the question is whether foreign officials, whom the Government concedes it cannot prosecute under the FCPA itself, may be prosecuted under the general conspiracy statute for conspiring to violate the Act. . . .

The principle enunciated by the Supreme Court in *Gebardi [v. United States*, 287 U.S. 112, 53 S. Ct. 35, 77 L. Ed. 206 (1932)] squarely applies to the case before this

Court. Congress intended in both the FCPA and the Mann Act to deter and punish certain activities which necessarily involved the agreement of at least two people, but Congress chose in both statutes to punish only one party to the agreement. In Gebardi the Supreme Court refused to disregard Congress' intention to exempt one party by allowing the Executive to prosecute that party under the general conspiracy statute for precisely the same conduct. Congress made the same choice in drafting the FCPA, and by the same analysis, this Court may not allow the Executive to override the Congressional intent not to prosecute foreign officials for their participation in the prohibited acts.

. . . .

[T]he exclusive focus was on the U.S. companies and the effects of their conduct within and on the United States.

First, Congress was concerned about the domestic effects of such payments. In the early 1970's, the Watergate affair and resulting investigations revealed that the payment of bribes to foreign officials was a widespread practice among U.S. companies. In the House Report accompanying an earlier version of the Act, it was noted that more than 400 companies had admitted making such payments, distributing well over 300 million dollars in corporate funds to foreign officials. . . . Such massive payments had many negative domestic effects, not the least of which was the distortion of, and resulting lack of confidence in, the free market system within the United States.

> The payment of bribes to influence the acts or decision of foreign officials . . . is unethical. It is counter to the moral expectations and values of the American public. But not only is it unethical, it is bad business as well. It erodes public confidence in the integrity of the free market system. . . . In short, it rewards corruption instead of efficiency and puts pressure on ethical enterprises to lower their standards or risk losing business.

. . . .

The House Committee further noted that many of the payments were made not to compete with foreign companies, but rather to gain an edge over a competitor in the United States.

Congress' second motivation was the effect of such payments by U.S. companies on the United States' foreign relations. The legislative history repeatedly cited the negative effects the revelations of such bribes had wrought upon friendly foreign governments and officials. Yet the drafters acknowledged, and the final law reflects this, that some payments that would be unethical or even illegal within the United States might not be perceived similarly in foreign countries, and those payments should not be criminalized. For example, grease payments, those payments made "to assure or to speed the proper performance of a foreign official's duties," are not illegal under the Act since they were often a part of the custom of doing business in foreign countries. . . . Additionally, the Act was later amended to permit an affirmative defense on the grounds that the payment was legal in the country in which it was made. 15 U.S.C. § 78dd-2(c)(1). These exclusions reinforce the proposition that Congress had absolutely no intention of prosecuting the foreign officials involved, but was concerned solely with regulating the conduct of U.S. entities and citizens.[1]

[The Government argued that a statement in a House Report showed congressional intent to allow conspiracy prosecutions of foreign officials.] . . .

This language [in the House Report] does not refute the overwhelming evidence of a Congressional intent to exempt foreign officials from prosecution for receiving bribes, especially since Congress knew it had the power to reach foreign officials in many cases, and yet declined to exercise that power. . . . (United States has power to reach conduct of noncitizens under international law). Congress' awareness of the extent of its own power reveals the fallacy in the Government's position that only those classes of persons deemed by Congress to need protection are exempted from prosecution under the conspiracy statute. The question is not whether Congress could have included foreign officials within the Act's proscriptions, but rather whether Congress intended to do so, or more specifically, whether Congress intended the general conspiracy statute, passed many years before the FCPA, to reach foreign officials.

The drafters of the statute knew that they could, consistently with international law, reach foreign officials in certain circumstances. But they were equally well aware of, and actively considered, the "inherent jurisdictional, enforcement, and diplomatic difficulties" raised by the application of the bill to non-citizens of the United States. . . . In the conference report, the conferees indicated that the bill would reach as far as possible, and listed all the persons or entities who could be prosecuted. The list includes virtually every person or entity involved, including foreign nationals who participated in the payment of the bribe when the U.S. courts had jurisdiction over them. But foreign officials were not included.

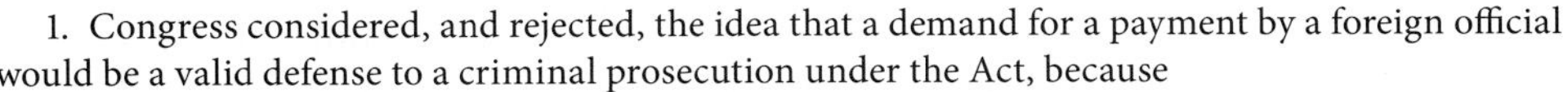

1. Congress considered, and rejected, the idea that a demand for a payment by a foreign official would be a valid defense to a criminal prosecution under the Act, because

> at some point the U.S. company would make a conscious decision whether or not to pay a bribe. That the payment may have been first proposed by the recipient rather than the U.S. company does not alter the corrupt purpose on the part of the person paying the bribe.

. . . .

The very fact that Congress considered this issue underscores Congress' exclusive focus on the U.S. companies in *making* the payment. If the drafters were concerned that a demand by a foreign official might be considered a defense to a prosecution, they clearly were expecting that only the payors of the bribes, and not the foreign officials demanding and/or receiving the bribes, would be prosecuted.

It is important to remember that Congress intended that these persons would be covered by the Act itself, without resort to the conspiracy statute. Yet the very individuals whose participation was required in every case — the foreign officials accepting the bribe — were excluded from prosecution for the substantive offense. Given that Congress included virtually every possible person connected to the payments except foreign officials, it is only logical to conclude that Congress affirmatively chose to exempt this small class of persons from prosecution.

Most likely Congress made this choice because U.S. businesses were perceived to be the aggressors, and the efforts expended in resolving the diplomatic, jurisdictional, and enforcement difficulties that would arise upon the prosecution of foreign officials was not worth the minimal deterrent value of such prosecutions. Further minimizing the deterrent value of a U.S. prosecution was the fact that many foreign nations already prohibited the receipt of a bribe by an official. . . . In fact, whenever a nation permitted such payments, Congress allowed them as well. See 15 U.S.C. § 78dd-2(c)(1).

Based upon the language of the statute and the legislative history, this Court finds in the FCPA what the Supreme Court in Gebardi found in the Mann Act: an affirmative legislative policy to leave unpunished a well-defined group of persons who were necessary parties to the acts constituting a violation of the substantive law. The Government has presented no reason why the prosecution of Defendants Castle and Lowry should go forward in the face of the congressional intent not to prosecute foreign officials. If anything, the facts of this case support Congress' decision to forego such prosecutions since foreign nations could and should prosecute their own officials for accepting bribes. . . .

Notes

(1) The DOJ guidance on the application of the FCPA's anti-bribery provisions to foreign persons notes:

> The FCPA also applies to certain foreign nationals or entities that are not issuers or domestic concerns. Since 1998, the FCPA's anti-bribery provisions have applied to foreign persons and foreign non-issuer entities that, either directly or through an agent, engage in any act in furtherance of a corrupt payment (or an offer, promise, or authorization to pay) while in the territory of the United States. Also, officers, directors, employees, agents, or stockholders acting on behalf of such persons or entities may be subject to the FCPA's anti-bribery provisions.

Resource Guide to the U.S. Foreign Corrupt Practices Act 10 (2d ed, July 2020), available at https://www.justice.gov/criminal-fraud/file/1292051/download.

(2) In *United States v. Hoskins*, 902 F.3d 69, 71–72 (2d Cir. 2018), the Second Circuit dismissed an FCPA case against a nonresident foreign national who was alleged to have participated in a bribery scheme. The court stated:

> The FCPA establishes three clear categories of persons who are covered by its provisions: (1) Issuers of securities registered pursuant to 15 U.S.C. § 78l or required to file reports under Section 78o(d), or any officer, director, employee, or agent of such issuer, or any stockholder acting on behalf of the issuer, using interstate commerce in connection with the payment of bribes, 15 U.S.C. § 78dd-1; (2) American companies and American persons using interstate commerce in connection with the payment of bribes, 15 U.S.C. § 78dd-2; and (3) foreign persons or businesses taking acts to further certain corrupt schemes, including ones causing the payment of bribes, while present in the United States, 15 U.S.C. § 78dd-3.
>
> Because we agree with the district court that the FCPA's carefully-drawn limitations do not comport with the government's use of the complicity or conspiracy statutes in this case, we AFFIRM the district court's ruling barring the government from bringing the charge in question.

(3) Article 16 of the U.N. Convention against Corruption requires States Parties to establish as a criminal offense the bribery of foreign public officials and officials of public international organizations. It also obligates States Parties to "consider adopting" measures to establish as a criminal offense the "solicitation or acceptance" by such officials of "an undue advantage." One can argue that this latter provision is meant to acknowledge that it would not be inappropriate under international law (at least between parties to the Convention) to exercise extraterritorial jurisdiction over the citizens of another State.

(4) Can private parties bring actions under the Foreign Corrupt Practices Act against companies who violate the statute? In *Lamb v. Phillip Morris, Inc.*, 915 F.2d 1024 (1990), the Sixth Circuit Court of Appeals, Circuit Judge Guy stated:

> . . . we find that the FCPA was primarily designed to protect the integrity of American foreign policy and domestic markets, rather than to prevent the use of foreign resources to reduce production costs. The plaintiffs, as competitors of foreign tobacco growers and suppliers of the defendants, cannot claim the status of intended beneficiaries of the congressional enactment under scrutiny. . . .[b]

---

b. Other courts have since ruled that there is no private cause of action under the FCPA. *See J.S.D. Service Center Corporation v. General Electric Technical Services Company, Inc.*, 937 F. Supp. 216, 226 (S.D. N.Y. 1996).—Eds.

B. Mens Rea

Stichting Ter Behartiging van de Belangen van Oudaandeelhouders in Het Kapitaal van Saybolt International B.V. (Foundation of the Shareholders' Committee Representing the Former Shareholders of Saybolt International B.V.) v. Schreiber

United States Court of Appeals for the Second Circuit
327 F.3d 173 (2003)

SACK, CIRCUIT JUDGE:

... This appeal is from the district court's grant of the defendants' motion for summary judgment. The facts we adduce here are undisputed except as otherwise noted....

Saybolt International's former shareholders assigned their legal malpractice causes of action to the plaintiff, which brought this diversity action in the United States District Court for the Southern District of New York on November 18, 1999. In its amended complaint, the plaintiff alleged that Schreiber, and through him Walter, Conston, Alexander & Green, P.C., defendant- third-party-plaintiff, a law firm with which Schreiber was affiliated, committed legal malpractice by failing to advise Saybolt North America that "the bribe payment as proposed to be paid by a Dutch company to Panamanian officials would violate the FCPA." ... Without Schreiber's malpractice, the amended complaint alleged, "the bribe payment would not have been made, even at the cost of the entire Panama deal." ... The plaintiff further alleged that by committing such malpractice, Schreiber also breached his lawyer's fiduciary duty to Saybolt North America and breached his contract to provide competent professional services. Finally, the plaintiff alleged that Schreiber's malpractice cost the former Saybolt International shareholders $4.2 million, mostly in criminal fines.

In a June 12, 2001, Memorandum Order, the district court granted the defendants' motion for summary judgment on all claims.... The court noted that the plaintiff alleged that Schreiber's erroneous advice led Saybolt North America to act without the knowledge that its conduct violated United States law.... The court then held that this allegation necessarily contradicts Saybolt North America's guilty plea to the charges that it violated the FCPA:

> To enter such a plea Saybolt [North America] had to affirm, as it did, that it undertook the misconduct in question with knowledge of the corruptness of its acts. Since, if it had in fact relied on Schreiber's allegedly erroneous and misleading advice, Saybolt [North America] would not have believed at the time that its misconduct was unlawful or corrupt, it could never have made this admission at its allocution or, indeed, entered its guilty plea at all.

....

On this basis, the district court concluded that under the doctrine of collateral estoppel, Saybolt North America's guilty plea forecloses the plaintiff's theory of causation. . . . The question, then, is whether there is a contradiction between the criminal convictions of Saybolt North America and the civil suit the plaintiff seeks to prosecute. We think not.

As the district court described it, the plaintiff's claim in its civil suit is that its lawyer, Schreiber, "advised Saybolt [North America] that a bribe payment by a foreign affiliate might be legal but also failed to advise Saybolt [North America] that any involvement by Saybolt [North America] or its officers in arranging the affiliate's payment could result in criminal liability." . . . "If Saybolt [North America] had in good faith relied on Schreiber's advice, Saybolt [North America] would have believed that its arranging the bribe through a foreign affiliate was permissible." . . .

By pleading guilty, Saybolt North America admitted the six elements of the FCPA crime: that (1) it was a domestic concern, (2) that it made use of a means or instrumentality of interstate commerce, (3) corruptly, (4) in furtherance of an offer or payment of something of value to a person, (5) while knowing that the money would be offered or given directly or indirectly to a foreign official, (6) for purposes of influencing an act or decision of that foreign official in his official capacity. But by pleading guilty, Saybolt North America did not admit that at the time of the criminal act it knew that the act of arranging, rather than paying, such a bribe was criminal. Knowledge by a defendant that it is violating the FCPA — that it is committing all the elements of an FCPA violation — is not itself an element of the FCPA crime. Federal statutes in which the defendant's knowledge that he or she is violating the statute is an element of the violation are rare; the FCPA is plainly not such a statute. Saybolt North America did not, therefore, by pleading guilty, preclude an assertion in a subsequent civil action — the case at bar — that it did not know it was violating the FCPA at the time of the violation. . . .

The plaintiff is thus not collaterally estopped by Saybolt North America's criminal plea from arguing in this civil suit that, even though Saybolt North America admittedly did commit a violation of the FCPA, it did not know that it was committing a violation the FCPA at the time; that it did not know it was committing such a violation because Schreiber negligently told it that it was not committing a violation by causing a foreign entity to pay the bribe; and that it suffered damages as a result of the negligent advice. . . .

To be sure, by pleading guilty, Saybolt North America admitted that it acted "corruptly" — the element of the crime that we numbered "3" in the discussion above — in its actions related to the Panamanian bribe. The defendants see in this admission a collateral bar to the plaintiff's assertion that Saybolt North America did not know that it was violating the FCPA at the relevant time and, indeed, was misled into believing that it was acting legally. The district court apparently agreed. . . . We do not. We conclude that an admission that an act was done "corruptly" in this context is not equivalent to an admission that the person committing it knew that it violated the particular law at the time the act was performed.

It is difficult to determine the meaning of the word "corruptly" simply by reading it in context. We therefore look outside the text of the statute to determine its intended meaning. . . . The Senate Report for the FCPA explains the statute's use of the term "corruptly" as follows:

> The word "corruptly" is used [in the FCPA] in order to make clear that the offer, payment, promise, or gift, must be intended to induce the recipient to misuse his official position in order to wrongfully direct business to the payor or his client, or to obtain preferential legislation or a favorable regulation. The word "corruptly" connotes an evil motive or purpose, an intent to wrongfully influence the recipient.

S. Rep. No. 95-114, at 10 (1977), reprinted in 1977 U.S.C.C.A.N. 4098, 4108. The 1977 House Report uses a similar description, adding that the word "corruptly" in the FCPA is intended to have the same meaning as in 18 U.S.C. § 201, the federal statute criminalizing the bribing of a federal official. . . .

The Senate's explanation of the term "corruptly" tracks closely our interpretation of that term in 18 U.S.C. § 201(b). We have repeatedly held in that context that "a fundamental component of a 'corrupt' act is a breach of some official duty owed to the government or the public at large." *United States v. Rooney*, 37 F.3d 847, 852 (2d Cir. 1994). . . . We have also, in the context of the federal statute criminalizing the bribing of agents of financial institutions, . . . approved jury instructions providing that a person acts "corruptly" if he or she acts with a "bad purpose." . . . Our case law defining the term "corruptly" in federal bribery statutes thus parallels the Senate Report's explanation of the term as denoting an evil motive or purpose and an intent to induce an official to misuse his position. . . .

We thus conclude that the word "corruptly" in the FCPA signifies, in addition to the element of "general intent" present in most criminal statutes, . . . a bad or wrongful purpose and an intent to influence a foreign official to misuse his official position. But there is nothing in that word or any thing else in the FCPA that indicates that the government must establish that the defendant in fact knew that his or her conduct violated the FCPA to be guilty of such a violation.

Finally in this connection, we note that had Saybolt North America gone to trial, it would have been allowed to present evidence that it relied on Schreiber's advice that the benefit sought from the Panamanian official would not require the official to misuse his position or breach his duties — i.e., that it did not act corruptly — precisely because "corruptly" is an element of the offense. Saybolt North America also would have been allowed a jury instruction on this allegation. . . . By pleading guilty, Saybolt North America effectively admitted that it could not factually support such a theory of reliance.

But Saybolt North America would not properly have been entitled to a jury instruction on an allegation that Schreiber led it to believe that its acts did not violate the FCPA. A defense of reliance on advice of counsel is available only to the extent that it might show that a defendant lacked the requisite specific intent, . . .

and specific intent to violate the FCPA is not an element of an FCPA violation. Thus, Saybolt North America's guilty plea does not constitute an admission that it could not factually support the theory of reliance on counsel that is the basis of the plaintiff's malpractice action....

We conclude that the question whether Saybolt North America acted with knowledge that its conduct violated the FCPA was not answered by its guilty plea, and thus that the plea does not collaterally estop the plaintiff from litigating the issue in its claim against Schreiber and the law firm with which he was affiliated....

For the foregoing reasons, the judgment of the district court is vacated, and the case remanded for further proceedings consistent with this opinion.

Notes

(1) Should payment of airline tickets for a foreign official's honeymoon be considered an act performed "corruptly"? *See United States v. Liebo*, 923 F.2d 1308 (8th Cir. 1990) (court reversed conviction based on newly discovered evidence).

(2) Is it necessary that the government prove a sufficient nexus between the bribe and the intended result? Should indirect payments, such as reductions in customs duties and sales tax liabilities fall within the scope of the Foreign Corrupt Practices Act? In *United States v. Kay*, 359 F.3d 738 (5th Cir. 2004), *appeal on remand*, 513 F.3d 432 (5th Cir. 2007), *denying reh. and reh. en banc*, 513 F.3d 461 (5th Cir. 2008), the court stated that the FCPA included "payments intended to assist the payor, either directly or indirectly, in obtaining or retaining business for some person." It is incumbent on the prosecution, however, to prove that "the bribery was intended to produce an effect."

(3) In an effort to deter bribery of foreign officials, Congress also included accounting provisions as part of the FCPA. These require record-keeping and internal controls. "Congress believed that almost all such bribery was covered up in the corporation's books, and that to require proper accounting methods and internal accounting controls would discourage corporations from engaging in illegal payments." *Lewis v. Sporck*, 612 F. Supp. 1316 (N.D. Cal. 1985). Like the anti-bribery provisions, the accounting provisions have been held not to provide a private cause of action. Enforcement is through "the SEC or the Department of Justice." *Id. See also Shields v. Erickson*, 710 F. Supp. 686, 688 (N.D. Ill. 1989) ("We find no convincing evidence in the legislative history to support plaintiff's contention that Congress intended this provision, which requires the corporation to use proper accounting methods and internal accounting controls, to create a private right of action.").

C. "Foreign Officials"

The vast majority of FCPA enforcement actions are resolved through a plea of guilty or a deferred (DPA) or non-prosecution (NPA) agreement. Therefore, there is limited case law examining the definition of key terms in the law or the theories under which the government has brought FCPA enforcement actions. *See* Mike Koehler, *A Snapshot of the Foreign Corrupt Practices Act*, 14 SANTA CLARA J. OF INT'L L. 143 (2016). In *United States v. Esquenazi*, 752 F.3d 912 (11th Cir. 2014), one of only a handful of FCPA appellate decisions, the court considered the definition of the term "foreign officials."

United States v. Esquinazi

United States Court of Appeals for the Eleventh Circuit
752 F.3d 912 (2014)

Joel Esquenazi and Carlos Rodriguez appeal their convictions and sentences imposed after a jury convicted them [in 2011] of conspiracy, violating the Foreign Corrupt Practices Act, and money-laundering. After careful review, and with the benefit of oral argument, we affirm.

[The defendants were former executives of Terra Telecommunications Corporation ("Terra"), a Florida based company that bought telephone time from foreign vendors and then sold the minutes to customers in the United States. According to the government, the defendants paid bribes to individuals at Telecommunications D'Haiti, S.A.M. ("Teleco") to reduce Terra's debts to Teleco. The government argued that Telecom was an "instrumentality" of the Haitian government and, therefore, the individuals receiving the bribes were "foreign officials" for purposes of the FCPA. The defendants challenged this application of the law.]

. . . .

The FCPA prohibits "any domestic concern" from "mak[ing] use of the mails or any means . . . of interstate commerce corruptly in furtherance of a bribe to "any foreign official," or to "any person, while knowing that all or a portion of such money or thing of value will be offered, given, or promised, directly or indirectly, to any foreign official," for the purpose of "influencing any act or decision of such foreign official . . . in order to assist such domestic concern in obtaining or retaining business for or with, or directing business to, any person." 15 U.S.C. §§ 78dd-2(a)(1), (3). A "foreign official" is "any officer or employee of a foreign government or any department, agency, or *instrumentality* thereof." Id. § 78dd-2(h)(2)(A) (emphasis added). The central question before us, and the principal source of disagreement between the parties, is what "instrumentality" means (and whether Teleco qualifies as one).

The FCPA does not define the term "instrumentality," and this Court has not either. For that matter, we know of no other court of appeals who has. The definition matters in this case, in light of the challenges to the district court's jury instructions on "instrumentality"; to the sufficiency of the evidence that Teleco qualified as an instrumentality of the Haitian government; and to Mr. Esquenazi's contention that the statute is unconstitutionally vague. Before we address these challenges, however, we must define "instrumentality" for purposes of the FCPA.

We begin, as we always do when construing statutory text, with the plain meaning of the word at issue. According to Black's Law Dictionary, an instrumentality is "[a] means or agency through which a function of another entity is accomplished, such as a branch of a governing body." Webster's Third New International Dictionary says the word means "something that serves as an intermediary or agent through which one or more functions of a controlling force are carried out: a part, organ, or subsidiary branch esp. of a governing body." These dictionary definitions foreclose Mr. Rodriguez's contention that only an actual part of the government would qualify as an instrumentality—that contention is too cramped and would impede the "wide net over foreign bribery" Congress sought to cast in enacting the FCPA. Beyond that argument, the parties do not quibble over the phrasing of these definitions, and they agree an instrumentality must perform a government function at the government's behest. The parties also agree, however, and we have noted in other cases interpreting similar provisions, that the dictionary definitions get us only part of the way there. Thus, we turn to other tools to decide what "instrumentality" means in the FCPA.

To interpret "instrumentality" as used in the Americans with Disabilities Act, we relied upon what the Supreme Court has called the "commonsense canon of noscitur a sociis," *United States v. Williams*, 553 U.S. 285, 294 (2008)—that is, "'a word is known by the company it keeps.'" In the FCPA, the company "instrumentality" keeps is "agency" and "department," entities through which the government performs its functions and that are controlled by the government. We therefore glean from that context that an entity must be under the control or dominion of the government to qualify as an "instrumentality" within the FCPA's meaning. And we can also surmise from the other words in the series along with "instrumentality" that an instrumentality must be doing the business of the government. What the defendants and the government disagree about, however, is what functions count as the government's business.

To answer that question, we examine the broader statutory context in which the word is used. In this respect, we find one other provision of the FCPA and Congress's relatively recent amendment of the statute particularly illustrative. First, the so-called "grease payment" provision establishes an "exception" to FCPA liability for "any facilitating or expediting payment to a foreign official . . . the purpose of which is to expedite or to secure the performance of a routine governmental action by a foreign official." 15 U.S.C. §78dd-2(b). "Routine governmental action" is defined as "an action . . . ordinarily and commonly performed by a foreign official in," among other things, "providing phone service." Id. §78dd-2(h)(4)(A). If an entity involved in providing phone service could never be a foreign official so as to fall under the FCPA's substantive prohibition, there would be no need to provide an express exclusion for payments to such an entity. In other words, if we read "instrumentality," as the defendants urge, to categorically exclude government-controlled entities that provide telephone service, like Teleco, then we would render meaningless a portion of the definition of "routine governmental action" in section 78dd-2(b). "It is a cardinal rule of statutory construction that significance and effect shall, if possible, be accorded to every word." Thus, that a government-controlled entity provides a commercial service does not automatically mean it is not an instrumentality. In fact, the statute expressly contemplates that in some instances it would.

Next, we turn to Congress's 1998 amendment of the FCPA, enacted to ensure the United States was in compliance with its treaty obligations. That year, the United States ratified the Organization for Economic Cooperation and Development's Convention on Combating Bribery of Foreign Public Officials in International Business Transactions (OECD Convention). In joining the OECD Convention, the United States agreed to "take such measures as may be necessary to establish that it is a criminal offence under [United States] law for any person intentionally to offer, promise or give . . . directly or through intermediaries, to a *foreign public official* . . . in order that the official act or refrain from acting in relation to the performance of official duties, in order to obtain or retain business or other improper advantage in the conduct of international business." "Foreign public official" is defined to include "any person exercising a public function for a foreign country, including for a . . . public enterprise." The commentaries to the OECD Convention explain that: "A 'public enterprise' is any enterprise, regardless of its legal form, over which a government, or governments, may, directly or indirectly, exercise a dominant influence." The commentary further explains: "An official of a public enterprise shall be deemed to perform a public function unless the enterprise operates on a normal commercial basis in the relevant market, i.e., on a basis which is substantially equivalent to that of a private enterprise, without preferential subsidies or other privileges." In addition to this, the OECD Convention also requires signatories make it a crime to pay bribes to agents of any "public international organisation."

To implement the Convention's mandates, Congress amended the FCPA in 1998. The only change to the definition of "foreign official" in the FCPA that Congress thought necessary was the addition of "public international organization." This seems to demonstrate that Congress considered its preexisting definition already to cover a "foreign public official" of an "enterprise . . . over which a government . . . exercise[s] a dominant influence" that performs a "public function" because it does not "operate[ ] on a normal commercial basis . . . substantially equivalent to that of . . . private enterprise[s]" in the relevant market "without preferential subsidies or other privileges." Although we generally are wary of relying too much on later legislative developments to decide a prior Congress' legislative intent, the circumstances in this case cause us less concern in that regard. This is not an instance in which Congress merely discussed previously enacted legislation and possible changes to it. Rather, Congress did make a change to the FCPA, and it did so specifically to ensure that the FCPA fulfilled the promise the United States made to other nations when it joined the Convention. The FCPA after those amendments is a different law, and we may consider Congress's intent in passing those amendments as strongly suggestive of the meaning of "instrumentality" as it exists today.

We are not alone in finding instruction from the obligations the United States undertook in the OECD Convention and Congress's resulting amendment of the FCPA made in order to comply with those obligations. The Fifth Circuit, in United

States v. Kay, concluded that, when Congress amended the FCPA to comply with the duties the United States assumed under the OECD Convention and left intact the FCPA's language outlawing bribery for the purpose of "obtaining or retaining business," the preexisting language should be construed to cover the Convention's mandate that signatories prohibit bribery "'to obtain or retain business or other improper advantage in the conduct of international business.'" "Indeed, given the United States's ratification and implementation of the Convention without any reservation, understandings or alterations specifically pertaining to its scope," the Fifth Circuit concluded the defendants' narrow construction of the FCPA "would likely create a conflict with our international treaty obligations, with which we presume Congress meant to fully comply."

Indeed, since the beginning of the republic, the Supreme Court has explained that construing federal statutes in such a way to ensure the United States is in compliance with the international obligations it voluntarily has undertaken is of paramount importance. "If the United States is to be able to gain the benefits of international accords and have a role as a trusted partner in multilateral endeavors, its courts should be most cautious before interpreting its domestic legislation in such manner as to violate international agreements." We are thus constrained to interpret "instrumentality" under the FCPA so as to reach the types of officials the United States agreed to stop domestic interests from bribing when it ratified the OECD Convention.

Based upon this reading, we must also reject the invitation from Messrs. Esquenazi and Rodriguez to limit the term only to entities that perform traditional, core government functions. Nothing in the statute imposes this limitation. And were we to limit "instrumentality" in the FCPA in that way, we would put the United States out of compliance with its international obligations.

The Supreme Court has cautioned that "the concept of a 'usual' or a 'proper' governmental function changes over time and varies from nation to nation." That principle guides our construction of the term "instrumentality." Specifically, to decide in a given case whether a foreign entity to which a domestic concern makes a payment is an instrumentality of that foreign government, we ought to look to whether that foreign government considers the entity to be performing a governmental function. And the most objective way to make that decision is to examine the foreign sovereign's actions, namely, whether it treats the function the foreign entity performs as its own. Presumably, governments that mutually agree to quell bribes flowing between nations intend to prevent distortion of the business they conduct on behalf of their people. We ought to respect a foreign sovereign's definition of what that business is. Thus, for the United States government to hold up its end of the bargain under the OECD Convention, we ought to follow the lead of the foreign government itself in terms of which functions it treats as its own.

Although we believe Teleco would qualify as a Haitian instrumentality under almost any definition we could craft, we are mindful of the needs of both corporations and the government for ex ante direction about what an instrumentality is. With this guidance, we define instrumentality as follows. An "instrumentality" under section 78dd-2(h)(2)(A) of the FCPA is an entity controlled by the government of a foreign country that performs a function the controlling government treats as its own. Certainly, what constitutes control and what constitutes a function the government treats as its own are fact-bound questions. It would be unwise and likely impossible to exhaustively answer them in the abstract. Because we only have this case before us, we do not purport to list all of the factors that might prove relevant to deciding whether an entity is an instrumentality of a foreign government. For today, we provide a list of some factors that may be relevant to deciding the issue.

To decide if the government "controls" an entity, courts and juries should look to the foreign government's formal designation of that entity; whether the government has a majority interest in the entity; the government's ability to hire and fire the entity's principals; the extent to which the entity's profits, if any, go directly into the governmental fisc, and, by the same token, the extent to which the government funds the entity if it fails to break even; and the length of time these indicia have existed. We do not cut these factors from whole cloth. Rather, they are informed by the commentary to the OECD Convention the United States ratified. They are also consistent with the approach the Supreme Court has taken to decide if an entity is an agent or instrumentality of the government in analogous contexts.

We then turn to the second element relevant to deciding if an entity is an instrumentality of a foreign government under the FCPA — deciding if the entity performs a function the government treats as its own. Courts and juries should examine whether the entity has a monopoly over the function it exists to carry out; whether the government subsidizes the costs associated with the entity providing services; whether the entity provides services to the public at large in the foreign country; and whether the public and the government of that foreign country generally perceive the entity to be performing a governmental function. Just as with the factors indicating control, we draw these in part from the OECD Convention. And we draw them from Supreme Court cases discussing what entities properly can be considered carrying out governmental functions.

§ 4.03 Foreign Equivalents to the FCPA

UK Bribery Act

The United States is not the only country to create and enforce anti-corruption measures with extraterritorial jurisdiction. As noted previously, 44 countries have ratified the OECD Convention on Combatting Bribery of Foreign Officials in International Business Transactions and there are currently 190 parties to the 2003 United Nations Convention against Corruption, including the European Union. In 2010, the United Kingdom passed the UK Bribery Act, which is arguably the most stringent anti-bribery statute in the world. It includes both broad prohibitions and significant compliance requirements.

General Bribery Offenses

1. Offences of Bribing Another Person

(1) A person ("P") is guilty of an offence if either of the following cases applies.

(2) Case 1 is where—

(a) P offers, promises or gives a financial or other advantage to another person, and

(b) P intends the advantage—

(i) to induce a person to perform improperly a relevant function or activity, or

(ii) to reward a person for the improper performance of such a function or activity.

(3) Case 2 is where—

(a) P offers, promises or gives a financial or other advantage to another person, and

(b) P knows or believes that the acceptance of the advantage would itself constitute the improper performance of a relevant function or activity.

(4) In case 1 it does not matter whether the person to whom the advantage is offered, promised or given is the same person as the person who is to perform, or has performed, the function or activity concerned.

(5) In cases 1 and 2 it does not matter whether the advantage is offered, promised or given by P directly or through a third party.

2. Offences Relating to Being Bribed

(1) A person ("R") is guilty of an offence if any of the following cases applies.

(2) Case 3 is where R requests, agrees to receive or accepts a financial or other advantage intending that, in consequence, a relevant function or activity should be performed improperly (whether by R or another person).

(3) Case 4 is where—

(a) R requests, agrees to receive or accepts a financial or other advantage, and

(b) the request, agreement or acceptance itself constitutes the improper performance by R of a relevant function or activity.

(4) Case 5 is where R requests, agrees to receive or accepts a financial or other advantage as a reward for the improper performance (whether by R or another person) of a relevant function or activity.

(5) Case 6 is where, in anticipation of or in consequence of R requesting, agreeing to receive or accepting a financial or other advantage, a relevant function or activity is performed improperly—

(a) by R, or

(b) by another person at R's request or with R's assent or acquiescence.

(6) In cases 3 to 6 it does not matter—

(a) whether R requests, agrees to receive or accepts (or is to request, agree to receive or accept) the advantage directly or through a third party,

(b) whether the advantage is (or is to be) for the benefit of R or another person.

(7) In cases 4 to 6 it does not matter whether R knows or believes that the performance of the function or activity is improper.

(8) In case 6, where a person other than R is performing the function or activity, it also does not matter whether that person knows or believes that the performance of the function or activity is improper.

3. Function or Activity to Which Bribe Relates

(1) For the purposes of this Act a function or activity is a relevant function or activity if—

(a) it falls within subsection (2), and

(b) meets one or more of conditions A to C.

(2) The following functions and activities fall within this subsection—

(a) any function of a public nature,

(b) any activity connected with a business,

(c) any activity performed in the course of a person's employment,

(d) any activity performed by or on behalf of a body of persons (whether corporate or unincorporate).

(3) Condition A is that a person performing the function or activity is expected to perform it in good faith.

(4) Condition B is that a person performing the function or activity is expected to perform it impartially.

(5) Condition C is that a person performing the function or activity is in a position of trust by virtue of performing it.

(6) A function or activity is a relevant function or activity even if it—

(a) has no connection with the United Kingdom, and

(b) is performed in a country or territory outside the United Kingdom.

(7) In this section "business" includes trade or profession.

4. Improper Performance to Which Bribe Relates

(1) For the purposes of this Act a relevant function or activity—

(a) is performed improperly if it is performed in breach of a relevant expectation, and

(b) is to be treated as being performed improperly if there is a failure to perform the function or activity and that failure is itself a breach of a relevant expectation.

(2) In subsection (1) "relevant expectation"—

(a) in relation to a function or activity which meets condition A or B, means the expectation mentioned in the condition concerned, and

(b) in relation to a function or activity which meets condition C, means any expectation as to the manner in which, or the reasons for which, the function or activity will be performed that arises from the position of trust mentioned in that condition.

(3) Anything that a person does (or omits to do) arising from or in connection with that person's past performance of a relevant function or activity is to be treated for the purposes of this Act as being done (or omitted) by that person in the performance of that function or activity.

5. Expectation Test

(1) For the purposes of sections 3 and 4, the test of what is expected is a test of what a reasonable person in the United Kingdom would expect in relation to the performance of the type of function or activity concerned.

(2) In deciding what such a person would expect in relation to the performance of a function or activity where the performance is not subject to the law of any part of the United Kingdom, any local custom or practice is to be disregarded unless it is permitted or required by the written law applicable to the country or territory concerned.

(3) In subsection (2) "written law" means law contained in—

(a) any written constitution, or provision made by or under legislation, applicable to the country or territory concerned, or

(b) any judicial decision which is so applicable and is evidenced in published written sources.

Bribery of Foreign Public Officials

6. Bribery of Foreign Public Officials

(1) A person ("P") who bribes a foreign public official ("F") is guilty of an offence if P's intention is to influence F in F's capacity as a foreign public official.

(2) P must also intend to obtain or retain—

(a) business, or

(b) an advantage in the conduct of business.

(3) P bribes F if, and only if—

(a) directly or through a third party, P offers, promises or gives any financial or other advantage—

(i) to F, or

(ii) to another person at F's request or with F's assent or acquiescence, and

(b) F is neither permitted nor required by the written law applicable to F to be influenced in F's capacity as a foreign public official by the offer, promise or gift.

(4) References in this section to influencing F in F's capacity as a foreign public official mean influencing F in the performance of F's functions as such an official, which includes—

(a) any omission to exercise those functions, and

(b) any use of F's position as such an official, even if not within F's authority.

(5) "Foreign public official" means an individual who—

(a) holds a legislative, administrative or judicial position of any kind, whether appointed or elected, of a country or territory outside the United Kingdom (or any subdivision of such a country or territory),

(b) exercises a public function—

(i) for or on behalf of a country or territory outside the United Kingdom (or any subdivision of such a country or territory), or

(ii) for any public agency or public enterprise of that country or territory (or subdivision), or

(c) is an official or agent of a public international organisation.

(6) "Public international organisation" means an organisation whose members are any of the following—

(a) countries or territories,

(b) governments of countries or territories,

(c) other public international organisations,

(d) a mixture of any of the above.

(7) For the purposes of subsection (3)(b), the written law applicable to F is—

(a) where the performance of the functions of F which P intends to influence would be subject to the law of any part of the United Kingdom, the law of that part of the United Kingdom,

(b) where paragraph (a) does not apply and F is an official or agent of a public international organisation, the applicable written rules of that organisation,

(c) where paragraphs (a) and (b) do not apply, the law of the country or territory in relation to which F is a foreign public official so far as that law is contained in—

(i) any written constitution, or provision made by or under legislation, applicable to the country or territory concerned, or

(ii) any judicial decision which is so applicable and is evidenced in published written sources.

(8) For the purposes of this section, a trade or profession is a business.

Failure of Commercial Organizations to Prevent Bribery

7. Failure of Commercial Organizations to Prevent Bribery

(1) A relevant commercial organisation ("C") is guilty of an offence under this section if a person ("A") associated with C bribes another person intending—

(a) to obtain or retain business for C, or

(b) to obtain or retain an advantage in the conduct of business for C.

(2) But it is a defence for C to prove that C had in place adequate procedures designed to prevent persons associated with C from undertaking such conduct.

(3) For the purposes of this section, A bribes another person if, and only if, A—

(a) is, or would be, guilty of an offence under section 1 or 6 (whether or not A has been prosecuted for such an offence), or

(b) would be guilty of such an offence if section 12(2)(c) and (4) were omitted.

. . . .

Prosecution and Penalties

. . . .

11. Penalties

(1) An individual guilty of an offence under section 1, 2 or 6 is liable—

(a) on summary conviction, to imprisonment for a term not exceeding 12 months, or to a fine not exceeding the statutory maximum, or to both,

(b) on conviction on indictment, to imprisonment for a term not exceeding 10 years, or to a fine, or to both.

(2) Any other person guilty of an offence under section 1, 2 or 6 is liable—

(a) on summary conviction, to a fine not exceeding the statutory maximum,

(b) on conviction on indictment, to a fine.

(3) A person guilty of an offence under section 7 is liable on conviction on indictment to a fine.

(4) The reference in subsection (1)(a) to 12 months is to be read—

(a) in its application to England and Wales in relation to an offence committed before the commencement of section 154(1) of the Criminal Justice Act 2003, and

(b) in its application to Northern Ireland,

as a reference to 6 months.

Notes

(1) In what ways is the UK Bribery Act distinct from the FCPA? Is the UK Bribery Act more or less stringent than the FCPA? How does the UK Bribery Act define "foreign public official"? *See* UK Ministry of Justice, *The Bribery Act 2010: Guidance*, *available at* http://www.justice.gov.uk/downloads/legislation/bribery-act-2010-guidance.pdf; Margaret Ryznar & Samer Korkor, *Anti-Bribery Legislation in the United States and United Kingdom: A Comparative Analysis of Scope and Sentencing*, 76 Mo. L. Rev. 415 (2010).

(2) In the United States, corporate criminal liability is established through the *respondeat superior* test. Under this test, corporate criminal liability may be established upon a mere showing that an employee's or agent's actions (a) were within the scope of his or her duties and (b) were intended, even if only in part, to benefit the corporation. There is no requirement that the offense involve high managerial agents. *See* Lucian E. Dervan, *Re-Evaluating Corporate Criminal Liability: The DOJ's Internal Moral Culpability Standard for Corporate Criminal Liability*, 41 Stetson L. Rev. 7 (2011).

In the UK, however, corporations are typically only held criminally liable for offenses involving a *mens rea* element, such as fraud, if the conduct is attributable to someone who was the "directing mind and will" of the company or "an embodiment of the company." In the context of the UK Bribery Act, however, the statute creates a strict liability offense for corporations in section 7. Why do you believe the UK departed from its traditional requirement of a corporate *mens rea* in this law? Should the United States increase its corporate *mens rea* requirements?

Note that in the same section containing the strict liability offense for corporations, the UK Bribery Act also contains an affirmative defense. The defense is available under section 7(2) and states, "but it is a defence for C to prove that C had in place adequate procedures designed to prevent persons associated with C from undertaking such conduct." How does this defense relate to the Act's departure from the traditional requirement of a corporate *mens rea* in the UK? Should the FCPA contain such a defense for entities?

(3) Examine the applicable penalties under both the FCPA and the UK Bribery Act. How do they compare to one another? Do the differences reflect fundamental disagreements regarding how to sentence offenders in the United State and the UK? Note that Thailand has a law that permits the death penalty for Thai officials and foreigners working for foreign governments or international organizations found guilty of bribery.

(4) On February 25, 2011, the Standing Committee of China's National People's Congress passed an amendment to Chinese law that created an anti-corruption statute similar to the FCPA and UK Bribery Act. Prior to this amendment, Chinese law already criminalized the "giving of money or property to any employee of a company or enterprise or other entity . . . for the purpose of seeking illegitimate benefits." The 2011 amendment added a new provision to expand the statute's reach to bribery of foreign government officials:

> Whoever, for purposes of seeking illegitimate commercial benefit, gives property to any foreign public official or official of an international public organization, shall be punished in accordance with the provisions of the preceding paragraph.

The penalties depend on the amount of the bribe. If the amount is large, the defendant shall be sentenced to a "fixed-term imprisonment of not more than three years." If the amount is very large, the defendant shall be sentenced to a "fixed-term imprisonment of not less than three years but not more than 10 years and shall, in addition, be fined." If the offense is committed by an entity, the entity shall be fined in addition to the individuals involved being held criminally liable.

(5) Given that so many countries have anti-corruption legislation, including statutes similar to the FCPA, it is possible that an individual might be prosecuted in several countries for the same underlying conduct. Should individuals be prosecuted in both jurisdictions for the same offense? Is this permissible? Is this an appropriate use of resources? In the 2010 case of *United States v. Gi-Hwan Jeong*, 624 F.3d 706 (5th Cir. 2010), the defendant was prosecuted both in South Korea and the United States for bribing an American official in relation to a lucrative telecommunications project. On appeal, the defendant argued that the OECD Bribery Convention prohibited double jeopardy when it stated, "When more than one Party has jurisdiction over an alleged offence described in this Convention, the Parties involved shall, at the request of one of them, consult with a view to determining the most appropriate jurisdiction for prosecution." S. TREATY DOC. NO. 105-43, ART. 4(3) (1998). The court, however, upheld the conviction and concluded that the treaty language was merely meant to encourage cooperation.

(6) The existing Anti-Corruption treaties are all Suppression Conventions with jurisdiction allocated among national jurisdictions. There are occasional suggestions that jurisdiction be granted to the International Criminal Court or more probably to a special Anti-Corruption Court. *See, e.g.*, Roundtable Discussion on the Proposal for an International Anti-Corruption Court at Columbia University, March 30, 2015, *available at* http://cgeg.sipa.columbia.edu/events-calendar/roundtable-discussion-proposal-international-anti-corruption-court.

Chapter 5

Antitrust and Securities Regulation

Should the United States be permitted to proceed against individuals and companies that violate securities and antitrust laws outside the United States? The Securities Exchange Commission (SEC) and the Antitrust Division of the Department of Justice pursue violations occurring extraterritorially. Congress has assisted by providing new legislation for international enforcement of securities and antitrust violations. What issues arise when enforcing these laws internationally?

§ 5.01 Antitrust

United States v. Nippon Paper Industries Co., Ltd.

United States Court of Appeals for the First Circuit
109 F.3d 1 (1997)

Selya, Circuit Judge:

This case raises an important, hitherto unanswered question. In it, the United States attempts to convict a foreign corporation under the Sherman Act, a federal antitrust statute, alleging that price-fixing activities which took place entirely in Japan are prosecutable because they were intended to have, and did in fact have, substantial effects in this country. The district court, declaring that a criminal antitrust prosecution could not be based on wholly extraterritorial conduct, dismissed the indictment . . . We reverse. . . .

In 1995, a federal grand jury handed up an indictment naming as a defendant Nippon Paper Industries Co., Ltd. (NPI), a Japanese manufacturer of facsimile paper. The indictment alleges that in 1990 NPI and certain unnamed coconspirators held a number of meetings in Japan which culminated in an agreement to fix the price of thermal fax paper throughout North America. NPI and other manufacturers who were privy to the scheme purportedly accomplished their objective by selling the paper in Japan to unaffiliated trading houses on condition that the latter charge specified (inflated) prices for the paper when they resold it in North America. The trading houses then shipped and sold the paper to their subsidiaries in the United States who in turn sold it to American consumers at swollen prices. The indictment further relates that, in 1990 alone, NPI sold thermal fax paper worth approximately $6,100,000 for eventual import into the United States; and that in order to ensure the success of the venture, NPI monitored the paper trail and confirmed that the prices charged to end users were those that it had arranged. These activities, the indictment posits, had a substantial adverse effect on commerce in the United States and unreasonably restrained trade in violation of Section One of the Sherman Act, 15 U.S.C. §1 (1994).

NPI moved to dismiss because, inter alia, if the conduct attributed to NPI occurred at all, it took place entirely in Japan, and, thus, the indictment failed to limn an offense under Section One of the Sherman Act. The government opposed this initiative on two grounds. First, it claimed that the law deserved a less grudging reading and that, properly read, Section One of the Sherman Act applied criminally to wholly foreign conduct as long as that conduct produced substantial and intended effects within the United States. Second, it claimed that the indictment, too, deserved a less grudging reading and that, properly read, the bill alleged a vertical conspiracy in restraint of trade that involved overt acts by certain coconspirators within the United States. Accepting a restrictive reading of both the statute and the indictment, the district court dismissed the case. . . .

Our law has long presumed that "legislation of Congress, unless a contrary intent appears, is meant to apply only within the territorial jurisdiction of the United States." *EEOC v. Arabian American Oil Co.*, 499 U.S. 244, 248, 111 S. Ct. 1227, 113 L. Ed. 2d 274 (1991). In this context, the Supreme Court has charged inquiring courts with determining whether Congress has clearly expressed an affirmative desire to apply particular laws to conduct that occurs beyond the borders of the United States. . . .

The earliest Supreme Court case which undertook a comparable task in respect to Section One of the Sherman Act determined that the presumption against extraterritoriality had not been overcome. In *American Banana Co. v. United Fruit Co.*, 213 U.S. 347, 29 S. Ct. 511, 53 L. Ed. 826 (1909), the Court considered the application of the Sherman Act in a civil action concerning conduct which occurred entirely in Central America and which had no discernible effect on imports to the United States. Starting with what Justice Holmes termed "the general and almost universal rule" holding "that the character of an act as lawful or unlawful must be determined wholly by the law of the country where the act is done," . . . and the ancillary proposition that, in cases of doubt, a statute should be "confined in its operation and effect to the territorial limits over which the lawmaker has general and legitimate power," . . . the Court held that the defendant's actions abroad were not proscribed by the Sherman Act.

Our jurisprudence is precedent-based, but it is not static. By 1945, a different court saw a very similar problem in a somewhat softer light. In *United States v. Aluminum Co. of Am.*, 148 F.2d 416 (2d Cir. 1945) (*Alcoa*), the Second Circuit, sitting as a court of last resort . . . mulled a civil action brought under Section One against a Canadian corporation for acts committed entirely abroad which, the government averred, had produced substantial anticompetitive effects within the United States. The *Alcoa* court read *American Banana* narrowly; that case, Judge Learned Hand wrote, stood only for the principle that "we should not impute to Congress an intent to punish all whom its courts can catch, for conduct which has no consequences within the United States." .... But a sovereign ordinarily can impose liability for conduct outside its borders that produces consequences within them, and while considerations of comity argue against applying Section One to situations in which no effect within the United States has been shown—the *American Banana* scenario—the statute, properly interpreted, does proscribe extraterritorial acts which were "intended to affect imports [to the United States] and did affect them." ... On the facts of *Alcoa*, therefore, the presumption against extraterritoriality had been overcome, and the Sherman Act had been violated....

Any perceived tension between *American Banana* and *Alcoa* was eased by the Supreme Court's most recent exploration of the Sherman Act's extraterritorial reach. In *Hartford Fire Ins. Co. v. California*, 509 U.S. 764, 113 S. Ct. 2891, 125 L. Ed. 2d 612 (1993), the Justices endorsed *Alcoa's* core holding, permitting civil antitrust claims under Section One to go forward despite the fact that the actions which allegedly violated Section One occurred entirely on British soil. While noting *American Banana's* initial disagreement with this proposition, the *Hartford Fire* Court deemed it "well established by now that the Sherman Act applies to foreign conduct that was meant to produce and did in fact produce some substantial effect in the United States." ... The conduct alleged, a London-based conspiracy to alter the American insurance market, met that benchmark....

To sum up, the case law now conclusively establishes that civil antitrust actions predicated on wholly foreign conduct which has an intended and substantial effect in the United States come within Section One's jurisdictional reach....

Were this a civil case, our journey would be complete. But here the United States essays a criminal prosecution for solely extraterritorial conduct rather than a civil action. This is largely uncharted terrain; we are aware of no authority directly on point, and the parties have cited none.

Be that as it may, one datum sticks out like a sore thumb: in both criminal and civil cases, the claim that Section One applies extraterritorially is based on the same language in the same section of the same statute: "Every contract, combination in the form of trust or otherwise, or conspiracy, in restraint of trade or commerce among the several States, or with foreign nations, is declared to be illegal." 15 U.S.C. §1. Words may sometimes be chameleons, possessing different shades of meaning in different contexts, ... but common sense suggests that courts should interpret the same language in the same section of the same statute uniformly, regardless of whether the impetus for interpretation is criminal or civil....

NPI and its amicus, the Government of Japan, urge that special reasons exist for measuring Section One's reach differently in a criminal context. We have reviewed their exhortations and found them hollow. We discuss the five most promising theses below. The rest do not require comment.

1. *Lack of Precedent.* NPI and its amicus make much of the fact that this appears to be the first criminal case in which the United States endeavors to extend Section

One to wholly foreign conduct. We are not impressed. There is a first time for everything, and the absence of earlier criminal actions is probably more a demonstration of the increasingly global nature of our economy than proof that Section One cannot cover wholly foreign conduct in the criminal milieu.

Moreover, this argument overstates the lack of precedent. There is, for example, solid authority for applying a state's criminal statute to conduct occurring entirely outside the state's borders. . . .

2. *Difference in Strength of Presumption*. The lower court and NPI both cite *United States v. Bowman*, [p. 66] for the proposition that the presumption against extraterritoriality operates with greater force in the criminal arena than in civil litigation. This misreads the opinion. To be sure, the *Bowman* Court, dealing with a charged conspiracy to defraud, warned that if the criminal law "is to be extended to include those [crimes] committed outside of the strict territorial jurisdiction, it is natural for Congress to say so in the statute, and failure to do so will negative the purpose of Congress in this regard." . . . But this pronouncement merely restated the presumption against extraterritoriality previously established in civil cases like *American Banana*. . . . The *Bowman* Court nowhere suggested that a different, more resilient presumption arises in criminal cases. . . .

3. *The Restatement.* NPI and the district court, . . . both sing the praises of the Restatement (Third) of Foreign Relations Law (1987), claiming that it supports a distinction between civil and criminal cases on the issue of extraterritoriality. The passage to which they pin their hopes states:

> In the case of regulatory statutes that may give rise to both civil and criminal liability, such as the United States antitrust and securities laws, the presence of substantial foreign elements will ordinarily weigh against application of criminal law. In such cases, legislative intent to subject conduct outside the state's territory to its criminal law should be found only on the basis of express statement or clear implication.

Id. at § 403 cmt. f. We believe that this statement merely reaffirms the classic presumption against extraterritoriality — no more, no less. After all, nothing in the text of the Restatement proper contradicts the government's interpretation of Section One. . . . What is more, other comments indicate that a country's decision to prosecute wholly foreign conduct is discretionary. . . .

4. *The Rule of Lenity.* The next arrow which NPI yanks from its quiver is the rule of lenity. The rule itself is venerable; it provides that, in the course of interpreting statutes in criminal cases, a reviewing court should resolve ambiguities affecting a statute's scope in the defendant's favor. . . . But the rule of lenity is inapposite unless a statutory ambiguity looms, and a statute is not ambiguous for this purpose simply because some courts or commentators have questioned its proper interpretation. . . . Put bluntly, the rule of lenity cannot be used to create ambiguity when the meaning of a law, even if not readily apparent, is, upon inquiry, reasonably clear. . . . .In view of the fact that the Supreme Court deems it "well established" that Section One of

the Sherman Act applies to wholly foreign conduct, *Hartford Fire*, 509 U.S. at 796, we effectively are foreclosed from trying to tease an ambiguity out of Section One relative to its extraterritorial application. Accordingly, the rule of lenity plays no part in the instant case.

5. *Comity.* International comity is a doctrine that counsels voluntary forbearance when a sovereign which has a legitimate claim to jurisdiction concludes that a second sovereign also has a legitimate claim to jurisdiction under principles of international law. . . . Comity is more an aspiration than a fixed rule, more a matter of grace than a matter of obligation. . . .

In this case the defendant's comity-based argument is even more attenuated. The conduct with which NPI is charged is illegal under both Japanese and American laws, thereby alleviating any founded concern about NPI being whipsawed between separate sovereigns. And, moreover, to the extent that comity is informed by general principles of reasonableness, *see* Restatement (Third) of Foreign Relations Law § 403, the indictment lodged against NPI is well within the pale. In it, the government charges that the defendant orchestrated a conspiracy with the object of rigging prices in the United States. If the government can prove these charges, we see no tenable reason why principles of comity should shield NPI from prosecution. We live in an age of international commerce, where decisions reached in one corner of the world can reverberate around the globe in less time than it takes to tell the tale. Thus, a ruling in NPI's favor would create perverse incentives for those who would use nefarious means to influence markets in the United States, rewarding them for erecting as many territorial firewalls as possible between cause and effect.

We need go no further. *Hartford Fire* definitively establishes that Section One of the Sherman Act applies to wholly foreign conduct which has an intended and substantial effect in the United States. We are bound to accept that holding. Under settled principles of statutory construction, we also are bound to apply it by interpreting Section One the same way in a criminal case. The combined force of these commitments requires that we accept the government's cardinal argument, reverse the order of the district court, reinstate the indictment, and remand for further proceedings.

Reversed and remanded.

LYNCH, CIRCUIT JUDGE (concurring).

. . . .

While courts, including this one, speak of determining congressional intent when interpreting statutes, the meaning of the antitrust laws has emerged through the relationship among all three branches of government. In this criminal case, it is our responsibility to ensure that the executive's interpretation of the Sherman Act does not conflict with other legal principles, including principles of international law.

That question requires examination beyond the language of Section One of the Sherman Act. It is, of course, generally true that, as a principle of statutory interpretation, the same language should be read the same way in all contexts to which the language applies. But this is not invariably true. New content is sometimes ascribed to statutory terms depending upon context. . . . Where Congress intends that our laws conform with international law, and where international law suggests that criminal enforcement and civil enforcement be viewed differently, it is at least conceivable that different content could be ascribed to the same language depending on whether the context is civil or criminal. . . .

Notes

(1) Would the United States have still been able to prosecute extraterritorial antitrust conduct if the First Circuit Court of Appeals had not reversed the district court decision? *See* John R. Wilke, *Appeals Court Says U.S. Antitrust Laws Cover Actions Abroad by Foreign Firms*, WALL ST. J. March 19, 1997, B7. ("Had the appeals court's decision gone the other way, 'executives could simply charter a cruise outside the territorial jurisdiction of the U.S. to fix and raise prices for American consumers without fear of prosecution,' said Gary Spratling, deputy assistant attorney general.").

(2) When does foreign conduct have "an intended and substantial effect in the United States?" Should the same standard be used in civil and criminal cases? What, if any, jurisdictional base is the court using in allowing an extraterritorial application? [*see* chap. 3].

(3) In 1994, Congress enacted the International Antitrust Enforcement Assistance Act. 15 U.S.C. §§ 6201–6212. The Act allows for mutual assistance in enforcing antitrust violations. Issued by the DOJ and Federal Trade Commission are *Antitrust Guidelines for International Enforcement and Cooperation* (Jan. 13, 2007), *available at* https://www.justice.gov/atr/internationalguidelines/download. "The International Guidelines provide updated guidance to businesses engaged in international activities on questions that concern the Agencies' international enforcement policy as well as the Agencies' related investigative tools and cooperation with foreign authorities." *Id.* at 1. The International Guidelines provide: 1) "a brief summary of the antitrust and related laws that are likely to have the greatest significance for businesses engaged in international activities"; 2) "describe[] what connections to the United States are sufficient for the Agencies to investigate or bring enforcement actions challenging conduct occurring abroad or involving or affecting foreign commerce"; 3) "describe[] the Agencies' consideration of international comity concerns and the role of foreign government involvement in determining whether to open an investigation or bring an enforcement action"; and 4) "provide[] guidance on the Agencies' pertinent investigatory tools and their enforcement cooperation with foreign authorities." "These International Guidelines also include a number of examples that are intended to illustrate how the principles and policies discussed may operate in certain contexts." *Id.* at 3. In examining international concerns, they cover the Federal Trade Commission Act, Clayton Antitrust Act, Hart-Scott-Rodino

Antitrust Improvements Act of 1976, Antitrust Criminal Penalty Enhancement and Reform Act of 2004, International Antitrust Enforcement Assistance Act, National Cooperative Research and Production Act, Webb-Pomerene Act, Export Trading Company Act of 1982, Wilson Tariff Act, Trade Act of 1974, Section 301, and the Tariff Act of 1930.

(4) In *F. Hoffmann-La Roche LTD v. Empagran*, 542 U.S. 155 (2004), the Supreme Court stated:

> . . . The Foreign Trade Antitrust Improvements Act of 1982 (FTAIA) excludes from the Sherman Act's reach much anticompetitive conduct that causes only foreign injury. It does so by setting forth a general rule stating that the Sherman Act "shall not apply to conduct involving trade or commerce . . . with foreign nations." . . . It then creates exceptions to the general rule, applicable where (roughly speaking) that conduct significantly harms imports, domestic commerce, or American exporters.
>
> We here focus upon anticompetitive price-fixing activity that is in significant part foreign, that causes some domestic antitrust injury, and that independently causes separate foreign injury. We ask two questions about the price-fixing conduct and the foreign injury that it causes. First, does that conduct fall within the FTAIA's general rule excluding the Sherman Act's application? That is to say, does the price-fixing activity constitute "conduct involving trade or commerce . . . with foreign nations"? We conclude that it does.
>
> Second, we ask whether the conduct nonetheless falls within a domestic-injury exception to the general rule, an exception that applies (and makes the Sherman Act nonetheless applicable) where the conduct (1) has a "direct, substantial, and reasonably foreseeable effect" on domestic commerce, and (2) "such effect gives rise to a [Sherman Act] claim." . . . We conclude that the exception does not apply where the plaintiff's claim rests solely on the independent foreign harm.
>
> To clarify: The issue before us concerns (1) significant foreign anticompetitive conduct with (2) an adverse domestic effect and (3) an independent foreign effect giving rise to the claim. In more concrete terms, this case involves vitamin sellers around the world that agreed to fix prices, leading to higher vitamin prices in the United States and independently leading to higher vitamin prices in other countries such as Ecuador. We conclude that, in this scenario, a purchaser in the United States could bring a Sherman Act claim under the FTAIA based on domestic injury, but a purchaser in Ecuador could not bring a Sherman Act claim based on foreign harm.

(5) In *RJR Nabisco, Inc. v. European Community*, 579 U.S. 325 (2016) (§ 3.02), the Supreme Court, in examining the extraterritoriality of the RICO statute, referenced

antitrust matters and distinguished the approach taken by the Court when examining extraterritoriality in the context of the Clayton Act. The Court stated:

> Respondents and Justice Ginsburg point out that RICO's private right of action was modeled after § 4 of the Clayton Act, 15 U.S.C. § 15; *see Holmes v. Securities Investor Protection Corporation*, 503 U.S. 258, 267–268 (1992), which we have held allows recovery for injuries suffered abroad as a result of antitrust violations, *see Pfizer Inc. v. Government of India*, 434 U.S. 308, 314–315 (1978). It follows, respondents and Justice Ginsburg contend, that § 1964(c) likewise allows plaintiffs to sue for injuries suffered in foreign countries. We disagree. Although we have often looked to the Clayton Act for guidance in construing § 1964(c), we have not treated the two statutes as interchangeable. We have declined to transplant features of the Clayton Act's cause of action into the RICO context where doing so would be inappropriate. * * *
>
> There is good reason not to interpret § 1964(c) to cover foreign injuries just because the Clayton Act does so. When we held in *Pfizer* that the Clayton Act allows recovery for foreign injuries, we relied first and foremost on the fact that the Clayton Act's definition of "person" — which in turn defines who may sue under that Act — "explicitly includes 'corporations and associations existing under or authorized by . . . the laws of any foreign country.'" . . . RICO lacks the language that the *Pfizer* Court found critical. . . . To the extent that the *Pfizer* Court cited other factors that might apply to § 1964(c), they were not sufficient in themselves to show that the provision has extraterritorial effect. For example, the *Pfizer* Court, writing before we honed our extraterritoriality jurisprudence in *Morrison* [*v. National Australia Bank Ltd.*, 561 U.S. 247 (2010),] and *Kiobel* [*v. Royal Dutch Petroleum Co.*, 569 U.S. 108, 115 (2013)], reasoned that Congress "[c]learly . . . did not intend to make the [Clayton Act's] treble-damages remedy available only to consumers in our own country" because "the antitrust laws extend to trade 'with foreign nations' as well as among the several States of the Union." . . . But we have emphatically rejected reliance on such language, holding that "'even statutes . . . that expressly refer to "foreign commerce" do not apply abroad.'" *Morrison*, 561 U.S., at 262–263. This reasoning also fails to distinguish between extending substantive antitrust law to foreign conduct and extending a private right of action to foreign injuries, two separate issues that, as we have explained, raise distinct extraterritoriality problems. . . . Finally, the *Pfizer* Court expressed concern that it would "defeat th[e] purposes" of the antitrust laws if a defendant could "escape full liability for his illegal actions." But this justification was merely an attempt to "divin[e] what Congress would have wanted" had it considered the question of extraterritoriality — an approach we eschewed in *Morrison*. Given all this, and in particular the fact that RICO lacks the language that *Pfizer* found integral

to its decision, we decline to extend this aspect of our Clayton Act jurisprudence to RICO's cause of action.

Underscoring our reluctance to read § 1964(c) as broadly as we have read the Clayton Act is Congress's more recent decision to define precisely the antitrust laws' extraterritorial effect and to exclude from their reach most conduct that "causes only foreign injury." [*F. Hoffmann-La Roche Ltd v.*] *Empagran*, 542 U.S., at 158 (describing Foreign Trade Antitrust Improvements Act of 1982) .... Although this later enactment obviously does not limit § 1964(c)'s scope by its own force, it does counsel against importing into RICO those Clayton Act principles that are at odds with our current extraterritoriality doctrine.

§ 5.02 Securities Regulation

Jurisdiction to prosecute securities violations is most commonly found in the Securities Act of 1933 and the Securities Exchange Act of 1934. "The preambles to both the 1933 and 1934 Acts provide that they are intended to apply to 'interstate and foreign commerce.'" Bruce Zagaras, *Avoiding Criminal Liability in the Conduct of International Business*, 21 Wm. Mitchell L. Rev. 749, 770 (1996). The International Securities Enforcement Cooperation Act of 1990, Pub. L. No. 101-550, 104 Stat. 2714, assists with these international prosecutions by providing mutual assistance among countries. The United States has also entered into specific agreements with countries to facilitate the process of acquiring information for utilization in these cases. In addition to relying on traditional securities laws, prosecutors have also used 18 U.S.C. § 1341 (mail fraud statute), 18 U.S.C. § 1343 (wire fraud statute), and 18 U.S.C. § 371 (conspiracy), in the prosecution of securities violations. The application of these generic statutes becomes questionable for extraterritorial conduct in light of *RJR Nabisco v. European Community*, 579 U.S. 325 (2016). And as noted below, *Morrison* places restraints on using an extraterritorial application with securities laws.

Extraterritorial securities prosecutions often include questions related to whether the United States has proper jurisdiction to proceed. Initially, courts used two jurisdictional tests in such matters, the "conduct test" and the "effect test," as described in *In re CP Ships LTD Securities Litigation*, 2009 U.S. App. Lexis 18290 (11th Cir., Aug. 13, 2009):

It is well recognized that the Securities Exchange Act is silent as to its extraterritorial application." ... Thus,

> [w]hen, as here, a court is confronted with transactions that on any view are predominantly foreign, it must seek to determine whether Congress would have wished the precious resources of United States courts and law enforcement agencies to be devoted to them rather than leave the problem to foreign countries.

> *Bersch v. Drexel Firestone, Inc.*, 519 F.2d 974, 985 (2d Cir. 1975). The provisions and purposes of the Securities Exchange Act serve as a guide.
>
> The courts have reached two broad conclusions with respect to transnational securities frauds. First, "it is consistent with the statutory scheme to infer that Congress would have wanted to redress harms perpetrated abroad which have a substantial impact on investors or markets within the United States." . . . . . Second, "Congress did not mean the United States to be used as a base for fraudulent securities schemes even when the victims are foreigners. . . ." *Bersch*, 519 F.2d at 987.
>
> These principles have been distilled into two jurisdictional tests: the "conduct test" and the "effects test." *S.E.C. v. Berger*, 322 F.3d 187, 193 (2d Cir. 2003). The court asks: "(1) whether the wrongful conduct occurred in the United States, and (2) whether the wrongful conduct had a substantial effect in the United States or upon United States citizens." . . . "Where appropriate, the two parts of the test are applied together becausee an admixture or combination of the two often gives a better picture of whether there is sufficient United States involvement to justify the exercise of jurisdiction by an American court." . . .

See also Kauthar SDN BHD v. Sternberg, 149 F.3d 659 (7th Cir. 1998).

In the 2010 case *Morrison v. Nat'l Australia Bank Ltd., infra*, the Supreme Court examined the extraterritorial application of securities laws and the existing criticisms of the above two tests.

Morrison v. National Australia Bank Ltd.

United States Supreme Court
561 U.S. 247 (2010)

Justice Scalia delivered the opinion of the Court.

We decide whether § 10(b) of the Securities Exchange Act of 1934 provides a cause of action to foreign plaintiffs suing foreign and American defendants for misconduct in connection with securities traded on foreign exchanges.

I

Respondent National Australia Bank Limited (National) was, during the relevant time, the largest bank in Australia. Its Ordinary Shares—what in America would be called "common stock"—are traded on the Australia Stock Exchange Limited and on other foreign securities exchanges, but not on any exchange in the United States. There are listed on the New York Stock Exchange, however, National's American Depositary Receipts (ADRs), which represent the right to receive a specified number of National's Ordinary Shares.

The complaint alleges the following facts, which we accept as true. In February 1998, National bought respondent HomeSide Lending, Inc., a mortgage servicing company headquartered in Florida. HomeSide's business was to receive fees for servicing mortgages (essentially the administrative tasks associated with collecting mortgage payments. The rights to receive those fees, so-called mortgage-servicing rights, can provide a valuable income stream. How valuable each of the rights is depends, in part, on the likelihood that the mortgage to which it applies will be fully repaid before it is due, terminating the need for servicing. HomeSide calculated the present value of its mortgage-servicing rights by using valuation models designed to take this likelihood into account. It recorded the value of its assets, and the numbers appeared in National's financial statements.

From 1998 until 2001, National's annual reports and other public documents touted the success of HomeSide's business, and respondents Frank Cicutto (National's managing director and chief executive officer), Kevin Race (HomeSide's chief operating officer), and Hugh Harris (HomeSide's chief executive officer) did the same in public statements. But on July 5, 2001, National announced that it was writing down the value of HomeSide's assets by $450 million; and then again on September 3, by another $1.75 billion. The prices of both Ordinary Shares and ADRs slumped. After downplaying the July write-down, National explained the September write-down as the result of a failure to anticipate the lowering of prevailing interest rates (lower interest rates lead to more refinancings, i.e., more early repayments of mortgages), other mistaken assumptions in the financial models, and the loss of goodwill. According to the complaint, however, HomeSide, Race, Harris, and another HomeSide senior executive who is also a respondent here had manipulated HomeSide's financial models to make the rates of early repayment unrealistically low in order to cause the mortgage-servicing rights to appear more valuable than they really were. The complaint also alleges that National and Cicutto were aware of this deception by July 2000, but did nothing about it. . . .

Respondents moved to dismiss for lack of subject-matter jurisdiction under Federal Rule of Civil Procedure 12(b)(1) and for failure to state a claim under Rule 12(b)(6). The District Court granted the motion on the former ground, finding no jurisdiction because the acts in this country were, "at most, a link in the chain of an alleged overall securities fraud scheme that culminated abroad." The Court of Appeals for the Second Circuit affirmed on similar grounds. The acts performed in the United States did not "compris[e] the heart of the alleged fraud." . . .

III

A

It is a "longstanding principle of American law 'that legislation of Congress, unless a contrary intent appears, is meant to apply only within the territorial jurisdiction of the United States.'" *EEOC v. Arabian American Oil Co.*, 499 U.S. 244, 248, 111 S.Ct. 1227, 113 L. Ed. 2d 274 (1991) (Aramco) (quoting *Foley Bros., Inc. v. Filardo*, 336 U.S. 281, 285, 69 S. Ct. 575, 93 L. Ed. 680 (1949)). This principle represents a canon of construction, or a presumption about a statute's meaning, rather than a limit upon Congress's power to legislate. It rests on the perception that Congress ordinarily legislates with respect to domestic, not foreign matters. Thus, "unless there is the affirmative intention of the Congress clearly expressed" to give a statute extraterritorial effect, "we must presume it is primarily concerned with domestic conditions." The canon or presumption applies regardless of whether there is a risk of conflict between the American statute and a foreign law. When a statute gives no clear indication of an extraterritorial application, it has none.

Despite this principle of interpretation, long and often recited in our opinions, the Second Circuit believed that, because the Exchange Act is silent as to the extraterritorial application of § 10(b), it was left to the court to "discern" whether Congress would have wanted the statute to apply. This disregard of the presumption against extraterritoriality did not originate with the Court of Appeals panel in this case. It has been repeated over many decades by various courts of appeals in determining the application of the Exchange Act, and § 10(b) in particular, to fraudulent schemes that involve conduct and effects abroad. That has produced a collection of tests for divining what Congress would have wanted, complex in formulation and unpredictable in application. . . .

As they developed, these tests were not easy to administer. The conduct test was held to apply differently depending on whether the harmed investors were Americans or foreigners: When the alleged damages consisted of losses to American investors abroad, it was enough that acts "of material importance" performed in the United States "significantly contributed" to that result; whereas those acts must have "directly caused" the result when losses to foreigners abroad were at issue. And "merely preparatory activities in the United States" did not suffice "to trigger application of the securities laws for injury to foreigners located abroad." This required the court to distinguish between mere preparation and using the United States as a "base" for fraudulent activities in other countries. But merely satisfying the conduct test was sometimes insufficient without "'some additional factor tipping the scales'" in favor of the application of American law. District courts have noted the difficulty of applying such vague formulations. There is no more damning indictment of the "conduct" and "effects" tests than the Second Circuit's own declaration that "the presence or absence of any single factor which was considered significant in other cases . . . is not necessarily dispositive in future cases." . . .

Commentators have criticized the unpredictable and inconsistent application of § 10(b) to transnational cases. Some have challenged the premise underlying the Courts of Appeals' approach, namely that Congress did not consider the extraterritorial application of § 10(b) (thereby leaving it open to the courts, supposedly, to determine what Congress would have wanted). Others, more fundamentally, have noted that using congressional silence as a justification for judge-made rules violates the traditional principle that silence means no extraterritorial application.

The criticisms seem to us justified. The results of judicial-speculation-made-law—divining what Congress would have wanted if it had thought of the situation before the court—demonstrate the wisdom of the presumption against extraterritoriality. Rather than guess anew in each case, we apply the presumption in all cases, preserving a stable background against which Congress can legislate with predictable effects.

B

Rule 10b-5, the regulation under which petitioners have brought suit, was promulgated under § 10(b), and "does not extend beyond conduct encompassed by § 10(b)'s prohibition." Therefore, if § 10(b) is not extraterritorial, neither is Rule 10b-5.

On its face, § 10(b) contains nothing to suggest it applies abroad:

> "It shall be unlawful for any person, directly or indirectly, by the use of any means or instrumentality of interstate commerce or of the mails, or of any facility of any national securities exchange . . . [t]o use or employ, in connection with the purchase or sale of any security registered on a national securities exchange or any security not so registered, . . . any manipulative or deceptive device or contrivance in contravention of such rules and regulations as the [Securities and Exchange] Commission may prescribe. . . . " 15 U.S.C. 78j(b).

[The Court then examined various arguments from the parties before concluding that "there is no affirmative indication in the Exchange Act that § 10(b) applies extraterritorially, and we therefore conclude that it does not."] . . .

Petitioners argue that the conclusion that § 10(b) does not apply extraterritorially does not resolve this case. They contend that they seek no more than domestic application anyway, since Florida is where HomeSide and its senior executives engaged in the deceptive conduct of manipulating HomeSide's financial models; their complaint also alleged that Race and Hughes made misleading public statements there. This is less an answer to the presumption against extraterritorial application than it is an assertion—a quite valid assertion—that that presumption here (as often) is not self-evidently dispositive, but its application requires further analysis. For it is a rare case of prohibited extraterritorial application that lacks all contact with the territory of the United States. But the presumption against extraterritorial application would be a craven watchdog indeed if it retreated to its kennel whenever some domestic activity is involved in the case. The concurrence seems to imagine just such a timid sentinel, but our cases are to the contrary. . . .

Applying the same mode of analysis here, we think that the focus of the Exchange Act is not upon the place where the deception originated, but upon purchases and sales of securities in the United States. Section 10(b) does not punish deceptive conduct, but only deceptive conduct "in connection with the purchase or sale of any security registered on a national securities exchange or any security not so registered." 15 U.S.C. § 78j(b). Those purchase-and-sale transactions are the objects of the statute's solicitude. It is those transactions that the statute seeks to "regulate" . . . ; it is parties or prospective parties to those transactions that the statute seeks to "protec[t]. . . ." And it is in our view only transactions in securities listed on domestic exchanges, and domestic transactions in other securities, to which § 10(b) applies. . . .

Section 10(b) reaches the use of a manipulative or deceptive device or contrivance only in connection with the purchase or sale of a security listed on an American stock exchange, and the purchase or sale of any other security in the United States. This case involves no securities listed on a domestic exchange, and all aspects of the purchases complained of by those petitioners who still have live claims occurred outside the United States. Petitioners have therefore failed to state a claim on which relief can be granted. We affirm the dismissal of petitioners' complaint on this ground.

It is so ordered.

JUSTICE BREYER, concurring in part and concurring in the judgment.

Section 10(b) of the Securities Exchange Act of 1934 applies to fraud "in connection with" two categories of transactions: (1) "the purchase or sale of any security registered on a national securities exchange" or (2) "the purchase or sale of . . . any security not so registered." 15 U.S.C. § 78j(b). In this case, the purchased securities are listed only on a few foreign exchanges, none of which has registered with the Securities and Exchange Commission as a "national securities exchange." See § 78f. The first category therefore does not apply. Further, the relevant purchases of these unregistered securities took place entirely in Australia and involved only Australian investors. And in accordance with the presumption against extraterritoriality, I do not read the second category to include such transactions. Thus, while state law or other federal fraud statutes, see, e.g., 18 U.S.C. § 1341 (mail fraud), § 1343 (wire fraud), may apply to the fraudulent activity alleged here to have occurred in the United States, I believe that § 10(b) does not. This case does not require us to consider other circumstances.

To the extent the Court's opinion is consistent with these views, I join it.

JUSTICE STEVENS, with whom JUSTICE GINSBURG joins, concurring in the judgment.

While I agree that petitioners have failed to state a claim on which relief can be granted, my reasoning differs from the Court's. I would adhere to the general approach that has been the law in the Second Circuit, and most of the rest of the country, for nearly four decades.

I

Today the Court announces a new "transactional test," for defining the reach of § 10(b) of the Securities Exchange Act of 1934 (Exchange Act), 15 U.S.C. § 78j(b), and SEC Rule 10b-5, 17 CFR § 240.10b-5(b) (2009): Henceforth, those provisions will extend only to "transactions in securities listed on domestic exchanges . . . and domestic transactions in other securities." If one confines one's gaze to the statutory text, the Court's conclusion is a plausible one. But the federal courts have been construing § 10(b) in a different manner for a long time, and the Court's textual analysis is not nearly so compelling, in my view, as to warrant the abandonment of their doctrine.

The text and history of § 10(b) are famously opaque on the question of when, exactly, transnational securities frauds fall within the statute's compass. As those types of frauds became more common in the latter half of the 20th century, the federal courts were increasingly called upon to wrestle with that question. The Court of Appeals for the Second Circuit, located in the Nation's financial center, led the effort. Beginning in earnest with *Schoenbaum v. Firstbrook*, 405 F.2d 200, rev'd on rehearing on other grounds, 405 F.2d 215 (1968) (en banc), that court strove, over an extended series of cases, to "discern" under what circumstances "Congress would have wished the precious resources of the United States courts and law enforcement agencies to be devoted to [transnational] transactions." Relying on opinions by Judge Henry Friendly, the Second Circuit eventually settled on a conduct-and-effects test. This test asks "(1) whether the wrongful conduct occurred in the Unites States, and (2) whether the wrongful conduct had a substantial effect in the United States or upon United States citizens." Numerous cases flesh out the proper application of each prong. . . .

III

In my judgment, if petitioners' allegations of fraudulent misconduct that took place in Florida are true, then respondents may have violated § 10(b), and could potentially be held accountable in an enforcement proceeding brought by the Commission. But it does not follow that shareholders who have failed to allege that the bulk or the heart of the fraud occurred in the United States, or that the fraud had an adverse impact on American investors or markets, may maintain a private action to recover damages they suffered abroad. Some cases involving foreign securities transactions have extensive links to, and ramifications for, this country; this case has Australia written all over it. Accordingly, for essentially the reasons stated in the Court of Appeals' opinion, I would affirm its judgment.

The Court instead elects to upend a significant area of securities law based on a plausible, but hardly decisive, construction of the statutory text. In so doing, it pays short shrift to the United States' interest in remedying frauds that transpire on American soil or harm American citizens, as well as to the accumulated wisdom and experience of the lower courts. I happen to agree with the result the Court reaches in this case. But "I respectfully dissent," once again, "from the Court's continuing campaign to render the private cause of action under § 10(b) toothless."

Notes

(1) Do you agree with the opinion by Justice Scalia or the concurrence by Justice Stevens? Should the "conduct test" and the "effects test" be retained? Should the approach be consistent in both civil and criminal cases? Do principles of comity suggest a preference for a particular approach? *See* Michael J. Calhoun, Comments, *Tension on the High Seas of Transnational Securities Fraud: Broadening the Scope of United States Jurisdiction*, 30 Loy. U. Chi. L.J. 679 (1999) ("Principles of international comity do not impose any absolute obligations on courts to deny jurisdiction since comity concerns are a matter of courtesy and good will.") Do the "effects" and "conduct" tests operate in the alternative, or does the existence of one prong permit extraterritoriality? Does the more recent decision in *RJR Nabisco, Inc. v. European Community*, 579 U.S. 325 (2016) (§ 3.02), make it even more difficult to have an extraterritorial application of securities law?

(2) In *Tamari v. Bache & Co. (Lebanon) S.A.L.*, 730 F.2d 1103, 1107–08 (7th Cir. 1984), the court considered issues of jurisdiction in the context of actions under the Commodity Exchange Act ("CEA"), 7 U.S.C. § § 6b and 6c, for damages resulting from alleged fraud and mismanagement of commodity futures trading accounts. Circuit Judge Swygert stated:

> Finding nothing in the Act or its legislative history to indicate that Congress did not intend the CEA to apply to foreign agents, but recognizing there also is no direct evidence that Congress intended such application, we believe it is appropriate to rely on the "conduct" and "effects" tests in discerning whether subject matter jurisdiction exists over this dispute. Both tests were developed in cases brought under the antifraud provisions of the federal securities laws and have recently been applied in similar cases arising under the Commodity Exchange Act.... When the conduct occurring in the United States is material to the successful completion of the alleged scheme, jurisdiction is asserted based on the theory that Congress would not have intended the United States to be used as a base for effectuating the fraudulent conduct of foreign companies.... Under the effects test, courts have looked to whether conduct occurring in foreign countries had caused foreseeable and substantial harm to interests in the United States.... The underlying theory is that Congress would have wished domestic markets and domestic investors to be protected from improper foreign transactions....

But see Mak v. Wocom Commodities Limited, 112 F.3d 287 (7th Cir. 1997) (declined to extend *Tamari* to "distant and uncertain circumstances"). How would the Court's decision in *Morrison* impact an application of the CEA today?

(3) Even before the *Morrison* decision, the Second Circuit Court of Appeals recognized there were limitations to extraterritorial application under the "effects" and "conduct" tests. In *Leasco Data Processing Equipment Corporation v. Maxwell*, 468 F.2d 1326 (2d Cir. 1972), Chief Judge Friendly stated:

> If all the misrepresentations here alleged had occurred in England, we would entertain most serious doubt whether, despite *United States v. Aluminum Co. of America,* 148 F.2d 416, 443–444 (2d Cir. 1954), and *Schoenbaum,* § 10(b) would be applicable simply because of the adverse effect of the fraudulently induced purchases in England of securities of an English corporation, not traded in an organized American securities market, upon an American corporation whose stock is listed on the New York Stock Exchange and its shareholders.... It is true, as Judge L. Hand pointed out in the *Aluminum* case ... that if Congress has expressly prescribed a rule with respect to conduct outside the United States, even one going beyond the scope recognized by foreign relations law, a United States court would be bound to follow the Congressional direction unless this would violate the due process clause of the Fifth Amendment. However, the language of § 10(b) of the Securities Exchange Act is much too inconclusive to lead us to

> believe that Congress meant to impose rules governing conduct throughout the world in every instance where an American company bought or sold a security. When no fraud has been practiced in this country and the purchase or sale has not been made here, we would be hard pressed to find justification for going beyond *Schoenbaum*....

(4) Are there policy reasons for permitting more expansive extraterritorial application of securities laws in cases involving allegations of fraud? Consider the following statement from *Securities and Exchange Commission v. Kasser*, 548 F.2d 109, 114–16 (3d Cir. 1977):

> ... In our view, the federal securities laws do grant jurisdiction in transnational securities cases where at least some activity designed to further a fraudulent scheme occurs within this country....
>
> From a policy perspective, ... we believe that there are sound rationales for asserting jurisdiction. First, to deny such jurisdiction may embolden those who wish to defraud foreign securities purchasers or sellers to use the United States as a base of operations. By sustaining the decision of the district court as to the lack of jurisdiction, we would, in effect, create a haven for such defrauders and manipulators. We are reluctant to conclude that Congress intended to allow the United States to become a "Barbary Coast," as it were, harboring international securities "pirates."
>
> We also are concerned that a holding of no jurisdiction might induce reciprocal responses on the part of other nations. Some countries might decline to act against individuals and corporations seeking to transport securities frauds to the United States. Such parties may well be outside the ambit of the power of our courts. For foreign nations to adopt the position that the defendants are urging this Court to take would enable defrauders beyond the reach of our courts to escape with impunity. By finding jurisdiction here, we may encourage other nations to take appropriate steps against parties who seek to perpetrate frauds in the United States. Accordingly, our inclination towards finding jurisdiction is bolstered by the prospect of reciprocal action against fraudulent schemes aimed at the United States from foreign sources.
>
> As a final policy justification for asserting jurisdiction here, we register the opinion that the antifraud provisions of the 1933 and 1934 Acts were designed to insure high standards of conduct in securities transactions within this country in addition to protecting domestic markets and investors from the effects of fraud....

There is precedent for the concept that fraud cases are different. Consider the following passage from *Europe and Overseas Commodity Traders v. Banque Paribas London*, 147 F.3d 118, 125 (2d Cir. 1998):

> [B]ecause it is well-settled in this Circuit that "the anti-fraud provisions of American securities laws have broader extraterritorial reach than American

> filing requirements," . . . the extent of conduct or effect in the United States needed to invoke U.S. jurisdiction over a claimed violation of the registration provisions must be greater than that which would trigger U.S. jurisdiction over a claim of fraud. To adapt the conduct and effects test for use in interpreting the registration provisions, we must take into account Congress's distinct purpose in drafting the registration laws.

See also Plessey Company PLC v. General Electric Company, 628 F. Supp. 477, 494 (D. Del. 1986) ("[a]lthough the Second Circuit has developed a substantial jurisprudence on the extraterritorial effect of the Exchange Act, its cases have focused largely on adjudicating acts of fraud. . . . As Judge Friendly has said, '[t]he problem of conflict between our laws and that of a foreign government is much less when the issue is the enforcement of the anti-fraud sections of the securities laws than with such provisions as those requiring registration of persons or securities.'" *ITT v. Cornfeld*, 619 F.2d at 921).

(5) Should parallel investigations, by the Securities Exchange Commission and a grand jury acting under the Department of Justice, be permitted to occur? *See Securities and Exchange Commission v. Dresser Industries, Inc.*, 628 F.2d 1368, 1377 (D.C. Cir. 1980) ("The SEC cannot always wait for Justice to complete the criminal proceedings if it is to obtain the necessary prompt civil remedy; neither can Justice always await the conclusion of the civil proceeding without endangering its criminal case. Thus, we should not block parallel investigations by these agencies in the absence of 'special circumstances' in which the nature of the proceedings demonstrably prejudices substantial rights of the investigated party or of the government."). *See also* Ellen S. Podgor & Jerold H. Israel, White Collar Crime in a Nutshell 6th 337 (2022).

(6) Are investigations of securities fraud always initially investigated by the Securities Exchange Commission? *See* R. Robin McDonald, *International Securities Fraud Probe Targets Marietta Woman*, Atl. J. Const., May 27, 1996, at D1 (describes U.S. Bureau of Alcohol, Tobacco & Firearms investigation of an individual being investigated for possible international securities fraud "for making 'straw purchases' of firearms for her fiancé, a convicted felon, to sell in South Africa.")

(7) The International Organization of Securities Commissions (http://www.iosco.org) is the "international body that brings together the world's securities regulators and is recognized as the global standard setter for the securities sector." It "develops, implements and promotes adherence to internationally recognized standards for securities regulation. It works intensively with the G20 and the Financial Stability Board (FSB) on the global regulatory reform agenda." The United States Securities and Exchange Commission is an active participant in the IOSCO. Established in 1983, its current membership includes 130 jurisdictions, and it regulates more than 95% of the world's securities markets. *Id.*

Chapter 6

Export Controls

§ 6.01 Generally

The United States government places restrictions on international trade through criminal statutes that control transfers on certain goods. There are statutes that control both imports and exports. Import controls address issues such as smuggling (18 U.S.C. § 545), the importation of narcotics (21 U.S.C. § 952), and the entry of improperly classified documents (18 U.S.C. § 541). Export controls restrict trade and the distribution of certain technologies to protect national security interests. Export controls are also relevant to foreign policy initiatives, such as where economic sanctions are imposed on a country, and may also be used to implement United States international obligations, such as economic measures required by the United Nations Security Council.

The U.S. Export Control System and the Export Control Reform Act of 2018

Congressional Research Services (Updated June 7, 2021)[1]

Balancing U.S. national security and export competitiveness in U.S. export control policy has been a complex and challenging issue for Congress and the executive branch for a number of decades. Through the Arms Export Control Act (AECA), the International Emergency Economic Powers Act (IEEPA), the Export Controls Reform Act (ECRA), and other authorities, the United States restricts the export of certain goods, including defense articles; dual-use goods and technology; nuclear materials and technology; and items that would assist in the proliferation of nuclear, chemical, and biological weapons or the missile technology used to deliver them. U.S. export controls are also used to restrict exports to certain countries on which the United States imposes economic sanctions. Additionally, the United States participates in several multilateral export control regimes.

The U.S. export control regime comprises several different licensing and enforcement agencies. Exports of dual-use goods and technologies — as well as some defense articles — are licensed by the Department of Commerce,

1. Available at https://crsreports.congress.gov/product/pdf/R/R46814.

munitions are licensed by the Department of State, and restrictions on exports based on U.S. sanctions are administered by the Department of the Treasury. In addition, the Department of Defense plays a key role in evaluating licenses referred to it by these agencies. Units of the Department of Homeland Security (DHS) and the Department of Justice issue criminal penalties for violations of export control regulations.

ECRA (, Subtitle B, Part I), enacted in 2018, provides broad legislative authority to the President to implement dual-use export controls. Unlike previous export control statutes, ECRA has no expiration date. Among its provisions, ECRA requires

- the President to establish an interagency process to establish new controls on emerging and foundational technologies;
- a review of license requirements for exports, reexports, or in-country transfers of items to countries subject to a comprehensive United States arms embargo, including China; and
- licensing procedures to
  - assess the impact of a proposed export on the U.S, defense industrial base;
  - examine foreign ownership interests of the consignee; and
  - review and evaluate the interagency export licensing referral, review, and escalation procedures.

ECRA reflects congressional concerns about dual-use technology trade and concurrent concerns about foreign investment in sensitive sectors resulting in simultaneous reforms of the U.S. foreign investment review process. The Trump Administration used the export control system primarily to counter China-related technology concerns. These actions included new restrictions on the telecommunications firm Huawei as part of a wider effort to block the adoption of Huawei technology in world-wide 5G networks; efforts to counter China's military-civilian fusion program (which seeks to apply commercial technologies toward military advances); termination of separate and differential treatment of Hong Kong in export control matters; and efforts to restrict U.S. technologies used in surveillance and repression.

Recently, some Members of Congress have expressed interest in thinking broadly about how congressional delegations of trade authority, including export controls, should be used as part of a coherent economic and national security policy. Additionally, although U.S. export controls may prevent certain U.S. technologies from ending up in certain countries, such controls may be both ineffective if they are available from foreign sources and also disadvantage U.S. firms. As such, Congress might also consider the role multilateral cooperation might play in any export control strategy.

§ 6.02 Export Control Reform Act of 2018 (ECRA)

50 U.S.C. § 4819(a)

(1) In General

It shall be unlawful for a person to violate, attempt to violate, conspire to violate, or cause a violation of this subchapter or of any regulation, order, license, or other authorization issued under this subchapter, including any of the unlawful acts described in paragraph (2).

(2) Specific Unlawful acts

The unlawful acts described in this paragraph are the following:

(A) No person may engage in any conduct prohibited by or contrary to, or refrain from engaging in any conduct required by this subchapter, the Export Administration Regulations, or any order, license or authorization issued thereunder.

(B) No person may cause or aid, abet, counsel, command, induce, procure, permit, or approve the doing of any act prohibited, or the omission of any act required by this subchapter, the Export Administration Regulations, or any order, license or authorization issued thereunder.

(C) No person may solicit or attempt a violation of this subchapter, the Export Administration Regulations, or any order, license or authorization issued thereunder.

(D) No person may conspire or act in concert with one or more other persons in any manner or for any purpose to bring about or to do any act that constitutes a violation of this subchapter, the Export Administration Regulations, or any order, license or authorization issued thereunder.

(E) No person may order, buy, remove, conceal, store, use, sell, loan, dispose of, transfer, transport, finance, forward, or otherwise service, in whole or in part, or conduct negotiations to facilitate such activities for, any item exported or to be exported from the United States, or that is otherwise subject to the Export Administration Regulations, with knowledge that a violation of this subchapter, the Export Administration Regulations, or any order, license or authorization issued thereunder, has occurred, is about to occur, or is intended to occur in connection with the item unless valid authorization is obtained therefor.

(F) No person may make any false or misleading representation, statement, or certification, or falsify or conceal any material fact, either directly to the Department of Commerce, or an official of any other United States agency, including the Department of Homeland Security and the Department of Justice, or indirectly through any other person —

(i) in the course of an investigation or other action subject to the Export Administration Regulations;

(ii) in connection with the preparation, submission, issuance, use, or maintenance of any export control document or any report filed or required to be filed pursuant to the Export Administration Regulations; or

(iii) for the purpose of or in connection with effecting any export, reexport, or in-country transfer of an item subject to the Export Administration Regulations or a service or other activity of a United States person described in section 4813 of this title.

(G) No person may engage in any transaction or take any other action with intent to evade the provisions of this subchapter, the Export Administration Regulations, or any order, license, or authorization issued thereunder.

(H) No person may fail or refuse to comply with any reporting or recordkeeping requirements of the Export Administration Regulations or of any order, license, or authorization issued thereunder.

(I) Except as specifically authorized in the Export Administration Regulations or in writing by the Department of Commerce, no person may alter any license, authorization, export control document, or order issued under the Export Administration Regulations.

(J) No person may take any action that is prohibited by a denial order or a temporary denial order issued by the Department of Commerce to prevent imminent violations of this subchapter, the Export Administration Regulations, or any order, license or authorization issued thereunder.

Though the below case is a civil suit, the discussion surrounding the need for export regulations and the deference afforded the executive branch in this area of law are equally significant for criminal prosecutions under the ECRA.

Federal Express Corp. v. U.S. Department of Commerce

United States District Court for the District of Columbia
486 F. Supp. 3d 69 (2020)

John Bates, United States District Judge:

Plaintiff Federal Express Corporation ("FedEx") is a global shipping company whose subsidiaries collectively ship millions of packages to over two hundred countries and territories daily. FedEx brings this suit against the U.S. Department of Commerce, Wilbur Ross in his official capacity as Secretary of Commerce, the Bureau of Industry and Security ("the Bureau"), and Nazak Nikakhtar in her official capacity as Assistant Secretary for Industry and Analysis (collectively, "the Department"), alleging that the Department's Export Administration Regulations ("the EAR"), see 15 C.F.R. § 730, violate the Due Process Clause of the Fifth Amendment and exceed the Department's delegated authority under the Export Control Reform Act of 2018, see 50 U.S.C. § 4801. Specifically, FedEx's amended complaint alleges that the EAR's export controls place such onerous restrictions on FedEx's shipping enterprise that it must either cease operations with certain foreign entities or risk imminent enforcement action. The Department moves for dismissal of both claims for lack of subject matter jurisdiction and failure to state a claim. For the reasons explained herein, the Court will grant the Department's motion and dismiss FedEx's amended complaint.

Background

I. The Export Controls Framework

The Department of Commerce, through the Bureau, oversees the nation's export control system. Historically, the Department's authority to promulgate and administer export control regulations, like the EAR, derived from the Export Administration Act of 1979 ("EAA"). *See* 50 U.S.C. § 4601. Over the years, the EAA lapsed several times, however, and during those periods, the EAR remained in force through a series of Executive Orders issued under the International Emergency Economic Powers Act ("IEEPA"), 50 U.S.C. § 1701.

In 2018, Congress overhauled the existing system with the Export Control and Reform Act ("ECRA"), which was passed as part of the National Defense Authorization Act for Fiscal Year 2019. *See* Pub. L. 115-232, 132 Stat. 1636 (2018). Under ECRA, the President, Secretary of Commerce, and various other officials are authorized to promulgate and administer the nation's export controls. *See* 50 U.S.C. § 4801. As relevant here, ECRA confers on the Secretary of Commerce the authority to "establish and maintain a list of items that are controlled" under the EAR, to "establish and maintain a list of foreign persons and end-uses that are determined to be a threat to the national security and foreign policy of the United States," and to "restrict exports, reexports, and in-country transfers of any controlled items to any foreign person or end-use" determined to threaten national security or foreign policy. *Id.* § 4813(a)(1)-(4).

The EAR are the Department's primary export control regulations and are "intended to serve the national security, foreign policy, nonproliferation of weapons of mass destruction, and other interests of the United States." 15 C.F.R. § 730.6. To that end, and with limited exceptions, the EAR regulate "any item warranting control that is not exclusively controlled for export, reexport, or transfer (in-country) by another [federal] agency." *Id.* § 730.3. If an item is subject to regulation, then the EAR prohibit its export, reexport, and in-country transfer unless the person attempting to do so acquires a license from the Bureau — or otherwise qualifies for an exemption not relevant to this case. *Id.* § 736.2(b).

The EAR's ambit is wide: "items subject to the EAR include purely civilian items, items with both civil and military, terrorism or potential [weapons-of-mass-destruction]-related applications, and items that are exclusively used for military applications." *Id.* § 730.3. For example, "the EAR regulate[] the export of commercial items which qualify as 'dual-use' items, meaning those that have 'both commercial and military or proliferation applications,' even if the item is purely commercial in its use." . . . Those items that qualify for regulation under the EAR are included on the Commerce Control List ("CCL"), which sets out the licensing requirements for exporting, re-exporting, or transferring such items. *See* 15 C.F.R. pt. 774, Supp. 1.

In addition to the CCL, the Bureau also oversees the Entity List, which "identifies persons reasonably believed to be involved, or to pose a significant risk of being or becoming involved, in activities contrary to the national security or foreign policy interests of the United States." *Id.* § 744.16. As a rule, the EAR prohibit the export, reexport, or transfer of items on the CCL to those listed on the Entity List without a license from the Bureau.

II. FedEx's Shipping Operations

FedEx is a private corporation that "provides a broad portfolio of transportation, e-commerce, and business services." . . . As relevant here, FedEx offers a range of shipping services that "receive approximately 15 million packages for shipment daily" and "span[] more than 220 countries and territories." . . .

FedEx has already been subject to administrative proceedings arising from alleged violations of the EAR — specifically, allegations by the Bureau that FedEx committed 53 violations of the EAR by shipping restricted items to France and Pakistan without the requisite Bureau licenses. . . . In April 2018, FedEx entered into a settlement agreement with the Bureau to pay a civil penalty of $500,000 and to audit its export controls compliance program in light of these alleged breaches. . . .

Analysis

I. Substantive Due Process Claim

The Department first challenges FedEx's Fifth Amendment Substantive Due Process claim. . . . FedEx alleges that the EAR, as currently formulated, "deprive FedEx of liberty and property by arbitrarily and irrationally precluding FedEx from carrying out the basic functions of its business as a common carrier." . . . Specifically, FedEx argues that the EAR require the company either "to cease all business operations that create a reasonable risk of violat[ing]" the EAR or to "proceed with its business operations and face a substantial risk that it will violate the EAR and suffer harm." . . .

"Unless legislation infringes a fundamental right, judicial scrutiny under the substantive due process doctrine is highly deferential." *Empresa Cubana Exportadora de Alimentos y Productos Varios v. U.S. Dep't of Treasury*, 638 F.3d 794, 800, 395 U.S. App. D.C. 19 (D.C. Cir. 2011). Under Supreme Court precedent, fundamental rights include the rights "to marry," "to have children," "to direct the education and upbringing of one's children," and "to bodily integrity." *Washington v. Glucksberg*, 521 U.S. 702, 720 (1997). This case, which turns on FedEx's putative right to continue its global shipping operations as currently practiced, concerns strictly economic burdens on FedEx's enterprise and involves no fundamental rights that the Supreme Court or the D.C. Circuit has ever identified. As FedEx acknowledges, . . . this Court must therefore "ask only whether the legislation is rationally related to a legitimate government interest," *Empresa Cubana*, 638 F.3d at 800.

"Rational basis review 'is not a license for courts to judge the wisdom, fairness, or logic of legislative choices.'" *Gordon v. Holder*, 721 F.3d 638, 656, 406 U.S. App. D.C. 6 (D.C. Cir. 2013) (quoting *FCC v. Beach Communications*, 508 U.S. 307, 315 (1993)). Under rational basis review, FedEx "has a claim only if [it] can show that there is no rational relationship between [the EAR regulations] and some legitimate governmental purpose." *Id.* (internal quotation marks omitted). Indeed, "[i]n the ordinary case, 'a law will be sustained if it can be said to advance a legitimate government interest, even if the law seems unwise or works to the disadvantage of a particular group, or if the rationale for it seems tenuous.'" *Id.* . . .

The EAR easily satisfy this forgiving standard. The regulations state that they advance "national security, foreign policy, nonproliferation of weapons of mass destruction, and other interests of the United States." 15 C.F.R. § 730.6 . . . . National security and foreign policy are core matters of legitimate federal concern, *see Holder v. Humanitarian Law Project*, 561 U.S. 1, 33–34 (2010), and the EAR rationally relate to those concerns by preventing hostile foreign actors from obtaining materials or technology that could harm U.S. interests. *See, e.g., Karn v. U.S. Dep't of State*, 925 F. Supp. 1, 13 (D.D.C. 1996) (concluding that "the regulation [under the Arms Export Control Act] of the export of . . . cryptographic software is a rational means of" promoting the government's "interest in preventing the proliferation of cryptographic software to foreign powers").

FedEx does not dispute that the EAR are intended "to promote national security and foreign policy interests," nor that such interests are legitimate. . . . Rather, FedEx contends that the rigid nature of the current regulations, "which hold FedEx strictly liable for EAR violations committed by others," is not rationally related to the government's legitimate interests. . . . In particular, FedEx challenges the rationality of imposing strict liability on common carriers, like FedEx, when they ship a package to a party on the Entity List, but holding customers liable only if they "knowingly" engage in a prohibited shipment. . . .

These arguments are unpersuasive. It is not irrational for the government to create a strict-liability regime to prevent companies from aiding or abetting export violations that would jeopardize the country's national security or foreign policy interests. *See Iran Air v. Kugelman*, 996 F.2d 1253, 1258, 302 U.S. App. D.C. 174 (D.C. Cir. 1993) ("It is not unusual for Congress . . . to permit the imposition of civil sanctions without proof of the violator's knowledge."). And it is not unreasonable for the Department to hold common carriers strictly liable for violations but to penalize customers only for knowing violations. Unlike potentially one-off consumers, common carriers are repeat players with the institutional knowledge and scale to navigate the EAR, thus it is reasonable that common carriers might be held to a higher standard. Even in the domestic realm, the D.C. Circuit has upheld under rational-basis review a ban on the shipment of tobacco products, noting that "Congress must be allowed leeway to approach a perceived problem incrementally" and that it is "entirely rational" to supplement such regulations—including implementing a total ban—if less rigorous measures prove ineffective. *Gordon*, 721 F.3d at 657 (internal quotation marks omitted).

Such reasoning applies with equal, if not greater, force in the context of national security and foreign policy, where Congress—and any agency to whom Congress delegates authority—is permitted to ban the shipping of certain products to a foreign country. *See, e.g., Freedom to Travel Campaign v. Newcomb*, 82 F.3d 1431, 1439 (9th Cir. 1996) (outlining "a history of judicial deference" to the political branches' foreign policy decisions, such as the Executive's decision to implement the Cuban embargo). That the EAR allow for some exports to persons designated on the Entity List, even if screening shipments for restricted items proves difficult, does not then make those regulations irrational or "substantially over-inclusive" .... And, indeed, "[e]ven if the classification involved here is to some extent both underinclusive and overinclusive, ... perfection is by no means required" under the Fifth Amendment when formulating an economic regulation. *Vance v. Bradley*, 440 U.S. 93, 108 (1979) (internal quotation marks omitted). For purposes of the Due Process Clause, all that is required is that the EAR be "rationally related to a legitimate government interest," *Empresa Cubana*, 638 F.3d at 801, which the Department has adequately demonstrated here....

II. Ultra Vires Claim Under Export Control Reform Act of 2018

....

C. Failure to State a Statutory Violation

Having addressed the Department's jurisdictional arguments, the Court turns to the merits of FedEx's ultra vires claim.... In essence, FedEx argues that the EAR as presently structured constitute an ultra vires assertion of authority by the Department because they impose strict liability on common carriers who, under ECRA itself, face liability only for violating the relevant regulations "with knowledge." ...

For this argument, FedEx focuses on the "Penalties" section of ECRA, 50 U.S.C. § 4819. There, FedEx highlights two provisions: subsection (B), which makes it unlawful for a person to "cause or aid, abet, counsel, command, induce, procure, permit, or approve the doing of any action prohibited" by the EAR (hereinafter, "aiding and abetting"); and subsection (E), which makes it unlawful—among other actions—to "transfer, transport, finance, forward, or otherwise service" an item subject to the EAR "with knowledge that a violation" of ECRA or the EAR will or is intended to arise (hereinafter, "transferring"). *Id.* 50 U.S.C. § 4819(a)(2)(B), (E). According to FedEx, the separation of aiding and abetting from transferring provides clear evidence that Congress intended for those two forms of action to be treated differently, with the latter form generating liability only when done knowingly.... Relying on this separation, FedEx posits that "ECRA ... commands that [transferring], which covers the core services provided by FedEx as a common carrier, only be punished if FedEx has knowledge that a violation of the EAR has occurred or will occur." . . .

FedEx contends that the Department's formulation of the EAR's "General prohibitions and determination of applicability" and "Violations" sections, *see* 15 C.F.R. §§736.2, 764.2, vitiates this statutory structure and, ultimately, eliminates this knowledge requirement for transferring violations. . . . Specifically, FedEx argues that, while the EAR prohibit transferring items subject to its regulations only "with knowledge," *see* 15 C.F.R. §§736.2(b)(10), 764.2(e), FedEx can still be held strictly liable for "aiding and abetting" transferring under 15 C.F.R. §764.2(b). . . . This regulatory scheme, FedEx concludes, "patently contravenes the plain language of ECRA" and renders subsection (E) "wholly superfluous." . . . In sum, the core of FedEx's revised ultra vires claim is that the Department acts beyond its authority under ECRA if it holds FedEx strictly liable for transferring regulated items, but does so under the guise of aiding and abetting liability. . . .

The scope of non-APA ultra vires review is "narrow." *Sears, Roebuck & Co. v. U.S. Postal Serv.*, 844 F.3d 260, 265, 427 U.S. App. D.C. 142 (D.C. Cir. 2016). "Courts will exercise their power to review alleged ultra vires agency action when an agency 'patently misconstrues a statute, disregards a specific and unambiguous statutory directive, or violates a specific command of a statute.'" *Hunter v. F.E.R.C.*, 569 F. Supp. 2d 12, 16 (D.D.C. 2008) (quoting *Griffith* [*v. Fed. Labor Rels. Auth.*], 842 F.2d at 493), *aff'd*, 348 F. App'x 592 (D.C. Cir. 2009) (per curiam).

FedEx's claim fails under this strict standard. FedEx alleges that the Department undermines the structure of ECRA's §4819 by crafting the EAR to make transferring strictly liable under the aiding and abetting provision. . . . But, as a textual matter, this argument is straightforwardly wrong. The language of subsections (b) and (e) of the EAR's §764.2 is almost identical to the language in subsection (B) and (E) of ECRA's §4918, with only minor adjustments to the lists of prohibited actions that are not relevant here. . . . It is thus the original structure of ECRA, rather than the Department's replication of that structure in §764.2, that raises the possibility that strict liability for aiding and abetting might swallow up any liability for transferring with knowledge and render §4819(a)(2)(E) superfluous.

Assuming, however, that FedEx's claim is not limited to the textual structure of §764.2, but rather concerns the Department's alleged practice of holding common carriers strictly liable for violations of the EAR, . . . the Court nevertheless concludes that FedEx's ultra vires claim must fail. To start, FedEx's argument that common carriers, like itself, can be liable only for transferring, and not for aiding and abetting, has no clear basis in the statutory language. *See* 50 U.S.C. §4819(a)(2)(B), (E). Although there is a strong argument to be made for interpreting §4819(a)(2)(E) to cover FedEx's core practices, the Department's potential interpretation of FedEx's behavior as aiding and abetting is hardly a patent misconstruction of ECRA or a violation of specific statutory commands. *See Hunter*, 569 F. Supp. 2d at 16. Moreover, FedEx's reading assumes that a particular action cannot lead to liability under multiple subparts of §4819(a)(2). . . . But an approach such as the one the

Department has taken is perfectly reasonable, and the Bureau structures its penalties to account for violators' "awareness of the conduct giving rise to the apparent violation." . . .

Conclusion

For all the foregoing reasons, FedEx's motion to dismiss will be granted. A separate order will be issued on this date.

ECRA Statement of Policy

50 U.S.C. § 4811

Statement of Policy

The following is the policy of the United States:

(1) To use export controls only after full consideration of the impact on the economy of the United States and only to the extent necessary—

(A) to restrict the export of items which would make a significant contribution to the military potential of any other country or combination of countries which would prove detrimental to the national security of the United States; and

(B) to restrict the export of items if necessary to further significantly the foreign policy of the United States or to fulfill its declared international obligations.

(2) The national security and foreign policy of the United States require that the export, reexport, and in-country transfer of items, and specific activities of United States persons, wherever located, be controlled for the following purposes:

(A) To control the release of items for use in—

(i) the proliferation of weapons of mass destruction or of conventional weapons;

(ii) the acquisition of destabilizing numbers or types of conventional weapons;

(iii) acts of terrorism;

(iv) military programs that could pose a threat to the security of the United States or its allies; or

(v) activities undertaken specifically to cause significant interference with or disruption of critical infrastructure.

(B) To preserve the qualitative military superiority of the United States.

(C) To strengthen the United States defense industrial base.

(D) To carry out the foreign policy of the United States, including the protection of human rights and the promotion of democracy.

(E) To carry out obligations and commitments under international agreements and arrangements, including multilateral export control regimes.

(F) To facilitate military interoperability between the United States and its North Atlantic Treaty Organization (NATO) and other close allies.

(G) To ensure national security controls are tailored to focus on those core technologies and other items that are capable of being used to pose a serious national security threat to the United States.

(3) The national security of the United States requires that the United States maintain its leadership in the science, technology, engineering, and manufacturing sectors, including foundational technology that is essential to innovation. Such leadership requires that United States persons are competitive in global markets. The impact of the implementation of this part on such leadership and competitiveness must be evaluated on an ongoing basis and applied in imposing controls under sections 1753 and 1754 [50 USCS §§ 4812, 4813] to avoid negatively affecting such leadership.

(4) The national security and foreign policy of the United States require that the United States participate in multilateral organizations and agreements regarding export controls on items that are consistent with the policy of the United States, and take all the necessary steps to secure the adoption and consistent enforcement, by the governments of such countries, of export controls on items that are consistent with such policy.

(5) Export controls should be coordinated with the multilateral export control regimes. Export controls that are multilateral are most effective, and should be tailored to focus on those core technologies and other items that are capable of being used to pose a serious national security threat to the United States and its allies.

(6) Export controls applied unilaterally to items widely available from foreign sources generally are less effective in preventing end-users from acquiring those items. Application of unilateral export controls should be limited for purposes of protecting specific United States national security and foreign policy interests.

(7) The effective administration of export controls requires a clear understanding both inside and outside the United States Government of which items are controlled and an efficient process should be created to regularly update the controls, such as by adding or removing such items.

(8) The export control system must ensure that it is transparent, predictable, and timely, has the flexibility to be adapted to address new threats in the future, and allows seamless access to and sharing of export control information among all relevant United States national security and foreign policy agencies.

(9) Implementation and enforcement of United States export controls require robust capabilities in monitoring, intelligence, and investigation, appropriate penalties for violations, and the ability to swiftly interdict unapproved transfers.

(10) Export controls complement and are a critical element of the national security policies underlying the laws and regulations governing foreign direct investment in the United States, including controlling the transfer of critical technologies to certain foreign persons. Thus, the President, in coordination with the Secretary, the Secretary of Defense, the Secretary of State, the Secretary of Energy, and the heads of other Federal agencies, as appropriate, should have a regular and robust process to identify the emerging and other types of critical technologies of concern and regulate their release to foreign persons as warranted regardless of the nature of the underlying transaction. Such identification efforts should draw upon the resources and expertise of all relevant parts of the United States Government, industry, and academia. These efforts should be in addition to traditional efforts to modernize and update the lists of controlled items under the multilateral export control regimes.

(11) The authority under this part may be exercised only in furtherance of all of the objectives set forth in paragraphs (1) through (10).

Note

The Export Control Reform Act of 2018 (ECRA) provides the President with broad powers related to dual-use export controls, items that have both commercial and military applications, and replaced the Export Administration Act of 1979 (EAA). The EAA had provided authority for dual-use export controls prior to its expiration in 2001, after which presidential declarations of a national emergency and the International Emergency Economic Powers Act (IEEPA) were used to continue export controls in this area until the enactment of the ECRA.

The ECRA states, "the President shall control—(1) the export, reexport, and in-country transfer of items subject to the jurisdiction of the United States, whether by United States persons or by foreign persons; and (2) the activities of United States persons, wherever located, relating to specific—(A) nuclear explosive devices; (B) missiles; (C) chemical or biological weapons; (D) whole plants for chemical weapons precursors; (E) foreign maritime nuclear projects; and (F) foreign military intelligence services." The Secretary of Commerce is charged with "establish[ing] and maintain[ing] a list" of controlled items and "a list of foreign persons and end-uses that are determined to be a threat to the national security and foreign policy of the United States." Public Law 115-232, Subtitle B, Part I (August 13, 2018). Unlike its predecessor, the ECRA has no expiration date.

Violation of the ECRA carries the potential for both civil and criminal sanctions. A willful violation of the ECRA carries a potential fine of up to $1,000,000, 20 years imprisonment, or both, per violation. In addition, the ECRA provides for civil penalties for each violation of up to $300,000 or an amount that is twice the value of the transaction that is the basis of the violation with respect to which the penalty is imposed, whichever is greater. The ECRA also contains criminal forfeiture provisions. 50 U.S.C. § 4819.

§ 6.03 Arms Export Control Act

United States v. Hsu

United States Court of Appeals for the Fourth Circuit
364 F.3d 192 (2004)

DIANA GRIBBON MOTZ, CIRCUIT JUDGE:

A jury convicted Eugene You-Tsai Hsu and David Tzuwei Yang of violations of the Arms Export Control Act and related offenses. On appeal, Hsu and Yang principally challenge their convictions on the ground that the Arms Export Control Act is unconstitutionally vague as applied to them....

The Arms Export Control Act ("AECA"), 22 U.S.C. § 2778 (2000), regulates the export of military products. The AECA authorizes the President to "designate those items which shall be considered as defense articles," and "promulgate regulations for the import and export of such articles...." § 2778(a)(1).

The President has delegated his rulemaking authority to the Secretary of State, *see* Exec. Order No. 11,958, who has promulgated the International Traffic in Arms Regulations ("ITAR"), 22 C.F.R. §§ 120.1–130.17 (2003). These regulations contain the United States Munitions List ("Munitions List"), a categorical list of "defense articles" that cannot be exported without first obtaining a license from the Department of State....

Of particular relevance here, the Munitions List includes military encryption devices, 22 C.F.R. § 121.1, Category XIII(b), such as the KIV-7HS ("KIV") encryption unit manufactured by Mykotronx, Inc. Because of the United States' arms embargo with the People's Republic of China, the State Department will not approve a license to export any Munitions List items, including KIV units, to that country. 22 C.F.R. § 126.1(a) (2003).

The AECA imposes both civil and criminal penalties for its violation. § 2778(c), (e). A criminal sanction requires that a person "willfully" violate the statute or its regulations....

On May 1, 2001, at the request of a business associate in China, Eugene You-Tsai Hsu telephoned Mykotronx seeking information on the company's KIV encryption device. A Mykotronx employee referred Hsu to "Daniel Stevenson," who was described to Hsu as a sales representative working for "Stellar International," a company purportedly selling Mykotronx products. Unbeknownst to Hsu, "Daniel

Stevenson" was in fact Dan Supnick, an undercover agent with the United States Customs Office, and "Stellar International" was an undercover company. It is undisputed that at the time Hsu made this initial call to Mykotronx, he did not know that exporting the encryption device without a license was illegal.

The following day, Hsu spoke with Agent Supnick (hereinafter "Stevenson") and requested information on the KIV unit; Hsu explained that he was planning on exporting it to a customer in China. (Stevenson recorded all of the conversations discussed herein, and the government played those tapes for the jury.) Stevenson immediately informed Hsu that the device was on the Munitions List; that it required a license for export; that no license would be approved if the end-user was in China; and that export of the device without the required license violated the law. After making these disclosures, Stevenson suggested "off the record," that he would still be willing to "make the sale" and "work with" Hsu if Hsu had "a way to get [the equipment] out" of the country. When Hsu stated that he did not want to do anything illegal, Stevenson responded, then "I don't think it's worth . . . sending you any information, 'cause it can't go legally to China." Nevertheless, Hsu insisted that Stevenson send him a brochure on the KIV unit, which Stevenson did.

More than two weeks passed without any interim contact between the parties. Hsu then telephoned Stevenson to discuss further the purchase and export of the encryption device. This phone call marked the beginning of a negotiation process spanning roughly the next three months. During this time, Stevenson repeatedly told Hsu that shipment of the KIV encryption device without a license violated the law and clarified that the shipment would still be illegal even if the devices were sent to Singapore or another country if the end-user remained in China. Hsu never stated that he did not want to go forward with the transaction.

A jury convicted Hsu and Yang (collectively "Defendants") of two criminal offenses: (1) conspiracy to export Munitions List articles without a license in violation of the AECA or to make materially false statements to the United States Customs Service in violation of 18 U.S.C. § 371 (2000), and (2) attempt to export items covered by the Munitions List without a license, in violation of the AECA. . . .

Defendants first contend that the AECA and its implementing regulations are unconstitutionally vague as applied to them. In particular, they argue that the regulations fail to provide sufficient clarity as to what encryption devices qualify as "military," and so are included on the Munitions List. We review challenges to the constitutionality of a statute or regulation *de novo*. *United States v. Sun*, 278 F.3d 302, 308–09 (4th Cir. 2002).

"Due process requires that a criminal statute provide adequate notice to a person of ordinary intelligence that his contemplated conduct is illegal, for no man shall be held criminally responsible for conduct which he could not reasonably understand to be proscribed." *Buckley v. Valeo*, 424 U.S. 1, 77, 96 S. Ct. 612, 46 L. Ed. 2d 659 (1976) (per curiam) . . . . But "where, as here, a criminal statute regulates economic activity, it generally is subject to a less strict vagueness test." . . .

The particular regulation upon which Defendants base their vagueness challenge states that the Munitions List includes "cryptographic devices . . . specifically designed or modified for military purposes." 22 C.F.R. § 121.1, Category XIII(b). To qualify as a "military" encryption device, a product must be "specifically designed, developed, configured, adapted, or modified for a military application," *and* (1) have no "predominant civil application" or "performance equivalent" used for civil applications, *or* (2) have "significant military or intelligence applicability such that control under this subchapter is necessary." 22 C.F.R. § 120.3. Defendants contend that these regulations "do not make clear what encryption products are covered by the Munitions List."

But the government charged, and the jury convicted, Defendants of "knowingly and willfully" violating the AECA when they acted to export the encryption devices. It is well-established that such a "scienter requirement may mitigate a law's vagueness, especially with respect to the adequacy of notice to the complainant that his conduct is proscribed." . . . After all, under the specific intent required as an element of this offense, the government must prove that a defendant intended to violate the law to obtain a conviction, thereby eliminating any genuine risk of holding a person "criminally responsible for conduct which he could not reasonably understand to be proscribed."

Not surprisingly, several courts have recognized the importance of the AECA's "knowing and willful" scienter requirement in denying as — applied vagueness challenges to the Act. . . . Nor do we find persuasive Defendants' argument that vagueness problems persist here because an undercover agent posing as a sales representative, rather than the government qua government, informed them of the illegality of the proposed exportation. Fair notice requirements are simply not implicated when a defendant engages in conduct *knowing* it is illegal, regardless of how he procured this information. . . . Accordingly, the AECA and its implementing regulations are not unconstitutionally vague as applied to Defendants.

Defendants next contend that the district court erred in refusing to instruct the jury on entrapment. [The court rejected defendant's argument on the district court's failure to give an entrapment instruction.]

. . . .

Defendants finally contend that we must vacate their attempt convictions because the State Department has not been delegated the authority to punish attempts, and any such delegation would be unconstitutional. These contentions are without merit.

The AECA broadly delegates authority to the President (which, in turn, he has delegated to the Secretary of State, . . . to issue regulations "to control the import and the export of defense articles," and authorizes a criminal penalty for violation of those regulations. . . . The regulation punishing the attempt to export these proscribed articles without a license . . . falls squarely within this delegated authority, and is fully consonant with Congress's "broad authority to [delegate to] the President in foreign affairs." *United States v. Gurrola-Garcia*, 547 F.2d 1075, 1079 (9th Cir.

1976); *cf. United States v. Mechanic*, 809 F.2d 1111, 1113–14 (5th Cir. 1987) (holding that the regulation punishing attempts under a similar statute, the Export Administration Act, was valid *prior* to a statutory amendment explicitly including attempt as a punishable offense).

In fact, "stopping smugglers as they approach an international border, to confiscate their munitions and to impose upon them criminal sanctions" is an especially "effective means of controlling the exportation of listed munitions." . . . It would be nonsensical to hold otherwise. . . . Thus, Defendants' final contention also fails. . . . For all of the foregoing reasons, the judgment of the district court is AFFIRMED.

Notes

(1) What elements must the government prove for showing a violation of the Arms Export Control Act? In *United States v. Murphy*, 852 F.2d 1 (1st Cir. 1988), the court stated:

> To sustain a conviction under sec. 2778, the government must prove that the defendant (1) willfully (2) engaged in the business of exporting (3) defense articles (4) that are on the United States Munitions List (5) without a license. *See United States v. Beck*, 615 F.2d 441, 450 (7th Cir. 1980). Murphy would like to escape conviction because the prosecution did not present evidence that Murphy knew he had to register with the United States government and that the arms were on the Munitions List before sending them to Ireland. While the act does require proof of specific intent, willfulness means that "defendant must know that his conduct in exporting from the United States articles proscribed by the statute is violative of the law." *United States v. Lizarraga-Lizarraga*, 541 F.2d 826, 828–29 (9th Cir. 1976) (requiring specific intent under 22 U.S.C. § 1934, the predecessor statute to sec. 2778). In other words, the "government must prove that the defendant voluntarily and intentionally violated a known legal duty not to export the proscribed articles." . . . Therefore, it is sufficient that the government prove that Murphy knew he had a legal duty not to export the weapons. . . .
>
> The prosecution proved beyond a reasonable doubt that Murphy knew it was illegal to send the weapons out of the country. Evidence of these year-long clandestine efforts, covert acts, and subterfuges to purchase weapons for shipment to Ireland for the IRA's use supports the jury's verdict that Murphy was aware of that duty. . . .
>
> The court's instruction incorporated all the elements of the offense and made clear that conviction would not require evidence that defendants knew of the licensing requirement or were aware of the munitions list. The instruction was as follows:
>
> > an act is done willfully if it is committed with the knowledge that it was prohibited by law and with the purpose of disobeying or disregarding the law. . . . Thus, while the government must show that a defendant

> knew that the exportation of firearms and munitions in this case was illegal, it is not necessary for the government to show that the defendants were aware of or had consulted the United States Munitions List or the licensing and registration provisions of the Arms Export Control Act and its regulations or the National Registration & Transfer Record or the Federal Firearms Law involved in count 2. . . . Ignorance of the law in this respect, in this case, is not an excuse. In this case, what is required is proof that the defendants acted knowingly and willfully with the specific intent to violate the law, and that's what I said to you.

The jury charge was proper under the statute and caselaw.

(2) "Willful" is a "word of many meanings" "often . . . influenced by its context." *Spies v. United States*, 317 U.S. 492, 497 (1943). Should willfulness under the Arms Export Control Act be redefined as a result of the Supreme Court decision in *Ratzlaf v. United States*, 510 U.S. 135 (1994), where the Court stated, "[w]e do not dishonor the venerable principle that ignorance of the law generally is no defense to a criminal charge. . . . In particular contexts, however, Congress may decree otherwise." *See also Cheek v. United States*, 498 U.S. 192 (1991) (complex tax statute). In *United States v. Muthana*, 60 F.3d 1217 (7th Cir. 1995), the court applied the *Ratzlaf* decision to a case of the defendant being convicted for "using an export control document which contained a false statement and omitted a material fact to export defense articles." The court, however, then went on to find sufficient evidence of the defendant "knowingly and willfully" lying on the waybill. The court stated:

> Muthana told Michalarias when Michalarias was preparing the waybill that the parcels contained only honey. Muthana knew that this was a lie and that the parcels instead contained thousands of rounds of ammunition.

See also United States v. Roth, 628 F.3d 827, 835 (6th Cir. 2011), where the Court held that "section 2778(c) does not require a defendant to know that the items being exported are on the Munitions List. Rather it only requires knowledge that the underlying action is unlawful."

(3) There is an exemption if the defense articles are "scrap." If the defendant claims that the item in question is "scrap," who bears the burden of proving its status for this exemption? In the case of *United States v. Sun*, 278 F.3d 302 (4th Cir. 2002), the court found the "scrap exemption" to be "an affirmative defense, not an element of a charge under the AECA." Does this shift the burden of persuasion or only the burden of going forward with the evidence?

(4) Do defendants have the right to contest whether an item is properly on the munitions list? In *United States v. Martinez*, 904 F.2d 601 (11th Cir. 1990), Senior Circuit Judge Roney stated:

> Relying principally upon the constitutional framework of the separation of powers between the coordinate branches of Government, the Supreme Court has recognized that some questions are so inherently political as to be excluded from judicial review. *Baker v. Carr*, 369 U.S. 186, 210, 82 S. Ct.

> 691, 706, 7 L. Ed. 2d 663 (1962). Where, as here, the controversy involves Presidential and Congressional handling of a foreign affairs matter, the political question doctrine routinely precludes judicial scrutiny. . . .
>
> The question whether a particular item should have been placed on the Munitions List possesses nearly every trait that the Supreme Court has enumerated traditionally renders a question "political." . . . No satisfactory or manageable standards exist for judicial determination of the issue, as defendants themselves acknowledge the disagreement among experts as to whether Videocipher II belongs on the List. . . . Neither the courts nor the parties are privy to reports of the intelligence services on which this decision, or decisions like it, may have been based. . . . The consequences of uninformed judicial action could be grave. Questions concerning what perils our nation might face at some future time and how best to guard against those perils are delicate, complex, and involve large elements of prophecy. They are and should be undertaken only by those directly responsible to the people whose welfare they advance or imperil. They are decisions of a kind for which the Judiciary has neither aptitude, facilities nor responsibility and which has long been held to belong in the domain of political power not subject to judicial intrusion or inquiry. . . .

On the other hand, see *United States v. Zhen Zhou Wu*, 711 F.3d 1 (1st Cir. 2013). There, the State Department's Directorate of Defense Trade Controls made a determination after the event that certain items were included within the definition of material on the Munitions List. The Court held that, in that situation, the Sixth Amendment required that the accused receive a jury trial on the issue of the propriety of the determination.

(5) The general regulation of exports may be modified for particular countries by treaty arrangements. On 30 September 2010, for example, the Office of the Spokesman, Department of State, announced the following in Press Release 2010/1378:

> On September 29, 2010, the United States Senate approved the U.S.-UK and the U.S.-Australia Defense Trade Cooperation Treaties. These treaties recognize and support the long-standing special relationship between the United States and two of its closest allies. The treaties allow for the export or transfer of certain defense articles and defense services controlled pursuant to the International Traffic in Arms Regulations (ITAR) between certain persons in the United States and the United Kingdom, pursuant to the U.S.-UK treaty, or between certain persons in the United States and Australia, pursuant to the U.S.-Australia treaty, without the need for export licenses or other ITAR approvals.
>
> In doing so, these treaties support U.S. national security interests by assisting our armed forces in obtaining the best technology possible in the most expeditious manner possible so that they may possess the critical

capability of interoperability, which is essential to our success in meeting shared security challenges.

(6) In 2021, the U.S. Department of State entered into a settlement agreement with Honeywell International, Inc. to resolve alleged violations of the Arms Export Control Act and the International Traffic in Arms Regulations.

> The Department of State and Honeywell have reached an agreement pursuant to ITAR §128.11 to address alleged unauthorized exports and retransfers of ITAR-controlled technical data that contained engineering prints showing dimensions, geometries, and layouts for manufacturing castings and finished parts for multiple aircraft, gas turbine engines, and military electronics to and/or within Canada, Ireland, Mexico, the People's Republic of China, and Taiwan.
>
> The settlement demonstrates the Department's role in strengthening U.S. industry by protecting U.S.-origin defense articles, including technical data, from unauthorized exports. The settlement also highlights the importance of obtaining appropriate authorization from the Department for exporting controlled articles.
>
> Under the terms of the 36-month Consent Agreement, Honeywell will pay a civil penalty of $13 million. The Department has agreed to suspend $5 million of this amount on the condition that the funds will be used for Department-approved Consent Agreement remedial compliance measures to strengthen Honeywell's compliance program. In addition, for an initial period of at least 18 months, an external Special Compliance Officer will be engaged by Honeywell to oversee the Consent Agreement, which will also require the company to conduct one external audit of its compliance program during the Agreement term as well as implement additional compliance measures.
>
> Honeywell voluntarily disclosed to the Department the alleged violations that are resolved under this settlement. Honeywell also acknowledged the serious nature of the alleged violations, cooperated with the Department's review, and instituted a number of compliance program improvements during the course of the Department's review. For these reasons, the Department has determined that it is not appropriate to administratively debar Honeywell at this time.

U.S. Department of State Concludes $13 Million Settlement of Alleged Export Violations by Honeywell International, Inc., Media Note, Office of the Spokesperson, U.S. Department of State (May 3, 2021).

(7) The Arms Export Control Act requires the President to provide notice to Congress of large arms sales, thus providing Congress a brief opportunity to object through passage of a resolution disapproving of the sale. The President, however, can veto such a resolution and can also utilize emergency powers to continue a sale

even when Congress has objected. During both the President Obama and President Trump terms in office, members of Congress attempted to intervene regarding arms sales to countries in the Middle East. In 2016, Senators Rand Paul, Mike Lee, Chris Murphy, and Al Franken introduced a measure that sought to block $1.15 billion in arms sales to Saudi Arabia. The measure failed to pass. *See* Patricia Zengerle, *Senators seek to black $1.15 billion U.S. arms sale to Saudi Arabia*, Reuters, available at https://www.reuters.com/article/us-usa-saudi-defense-congress-idUSKCN11E2OB (Sept. 8, 2016). In 2019, President Trump sought to bypass Congressional review of an $8 billion weapons sale to Saudi Arabia and the UAE by declaring an emergency under the Arms Export Control Act. Regardless, Congress passed a bipartisan resolution disapproving of the sale, but the measure was vetoed by the President. *See Trump uses veto to unblock $bn weapons sale to Saudi Arabia*, BBC, available at https://www.bbc.com/news/world-us-canada-49106989 (July 25, 2019). Each of these examples demonstrate the significant power and discretion that rests with the executive branch and the difficulty that exists for Congress to weigh in on arms sales in a meaningful way under the current laws.

§ 6.04 Executive Export Restrictions and Trade Embargoes

United States v. Banki

United States Court of Appeals for the Second Circuit
685 F.3d 99 (2012)

DENNY CHIN, CIRCUIT JUDGE:

Defendant-appellant Mahmoud Reza Banki ("Banki") appeals from a judgment of the United States District Court for the Southern District of New York convicting him, following a jury trial, of (1) conspiracy to violate the Iranian Transactions Regulations (the "ITR") and operate an unlicensed money-transmitting business; (2) violating the ITR; (3) operating an unlicensed money-transmitting business; and (4) two counts of making false statements in response to government subpoenas.

On appeal, Banki argues that the district court erred in several respects when instructing the jury on the conspiracy, ITR, and money-transmitting counts. . . .

We AFFIRM in part and VACATE and REMAND in part.

Statement of the Case

1. The Facts

Born in Tehran, Iran, Banki is a naturalized U.S. citizen who has lived in the United States since he was 18. After completing high school in Iran, Banki moved in 1994 to the United States to attend college. While Banki has lived in the United States, many of his family have continued to reside in Iran, including his father, mother, uncle, and cousin.

In Iran, Banki's family owned three power companies and a pharmaceutical company; his uncle was a director of all four companies, and his cousin was the CEO of one of the power companies.

Beginning in May 2006, Banki's family began to transfer large amounts of money—totaling some $3.4 million—from Iran to the United States. At trial, the defense argued these transfers were necessary to protect the family's assets. Banki's mother testified that the money was intended to be used to purchase an apartment in the United States for herself, Banki, and his brother.

The transfers were effectuated through an informal system called a "hawala." The hawala system is widely used in Middle Eastern and South Asian countries, and is primarily used to make international funds transfers. Though there are many forms of hawala, in the paradigmatic hawala system, funds are transferred from one country to another through a network of hawala brokers (i.e., "hawaladars"), with one hawaladar located in the transferor's country and one in the transferee's country. In this form, a hawala works as follows: If Person A in Country A wants to send $1,000 to Person B in Country B, Person A contacts Hawaladar A in Country A and pays him $1,000. Hawaladar A then contacts Hawaladar B in Country B and asks Hawaladar B to pay $1,000 in Country B currency, minus any fees, to Person B. The effect of this transaction is that Person A has remitted $1,000 (minus any fees) to Person B, although no money has actually crossed the border between Country A and Country B.

Eventually, Hawaladar B may need to send money to Country A on behalf of a customer in Country B; he will then contact Hawaladar A, with whom he now has a credit due to the previous transaction. Hawaladar A will remit the money in Country A to the designated person there, thus clearing the debt between the two hawaladars. Typically, Hawaladar A and Hawaladar B would engage in many parallel transactions moving in both directions. A number of transactions might be required before the books are balanced between the two hawaladars. If after some period of time their ledgers remain imbalanced, the hawaladars may "settle" via wire transfer or another, more formal method of money transmission. The hawala system operates in large part on trust, since, as in the example above, a hawaladar will remit money well before he receives full payment, and he does so without the benefit of a more formal legal structure to protect his investment.

To send money to Banki in the United States, Banki's family retained the services of Ali Bakhtiari, a Tehran-based hawaladar. In contrast to the paradigmatic, two-hawaladar system discussed above, Bakhtiari used a "matching" hawala system to facilitate the transfer of funds from Iran to the United States. Under the "matching" system, when Bakhtiari knew that Banki's family wanted to send a sum of money to the United States, he would search among his U.S.-based contacts for someone who wanted to send approximately the same amount to Iran. If he was unable to find a "match" among his U.S.-based contacts, which was often the case, he would reach out to his network of Iran-based brokers to see if any of them knew of a match. These brokers generally did not reveal the identity of their U.S.-based contact, for fear of being cut out of the transaction by Bakhtiari; instead, Bakhtiari would give the Iran-based broker Banki's account information, which the broker would relay to his U.S.-based contact. The U.S.-based contact would then transfer into Banki's account a sum comparable to the amount Banki's family wished to send. Once Bakhtiari confirmed that the U.S.-based contact had transferred the money into Banki's account, he would pay an equivalent amount to the U.S.-based contact's intended recipient or to the Iran-based broker who facilitated the match for the broker to distribute to the intended recipient. Bakhtiari and the broker would split the profits, which were derived from the difference in the "buy" and "sell" exchange rates, on any completed transaction.

Between May 2006 and September 2009, Banki received as many as 56 hawala-related deposits in his Bank of America account from at least 44 different individuals and companies. . . . In total, almost $3.4 million was deposited into Banki's account. Banki retained this $3.4 million for his personal use, including the purchase of a $2.4 million apartment in New York City.

. . . .

The transfers into Banki's account came to the attention of the government, and in 2008, the U.S. Treasury Department Office of Foreign Asset Control ("OFAC") served Banki with two administrative subpoenas. Both subpoenas requested information about transfers into Banki's account and advised Banki that "knowingly falsifying or concealing a material fact in [his] response . . . is a felony." The January 2008 subpoena requested information about a $100,000 transfer into Banki's account in January 2007. By letter dated January 16, 2008, Banki responded, identifying his cousin as the source of the transfer. Then, in a June 2008 subpoena, OFAC requested "details of all payments [Banki had] made, received, or facilitated in any manner involving Iran since July 1, 2003." In his response, Banki again identified his cousin as the source of the funds, and stated that Banki had "made no payments to anyone in Iran since [arriving] in the United States in 1994."

. . . .

Discussion

. . . .

A. ITR Instructions (Counts One and Two)

The International Emergency Economic Powers Act ("IEEPA") grants the President broad authority to issue regulations that restrict or prohibit international trade where he declares a "national emergency" with respect to an "unusual and extraordinary" foreign policy or national security threat. 50 U.S.C. §§ 1701–1702.

Though the President has exercised his authority under IEEPA to restrict trade with Iran since 1979, the trade restrictions at issue here date to 1995. That year, President Clinton issued Executive Order 12,957, which found that "the actions and policies of the Government of Iran constitute an unusual and extraordinary threat to the national security, foreign policy, and economy of the United States," and declared "a national emergency to deal with that threat." Exec. Order No. 12,957, 60 Fed.Reg. 14,615, 14,615 (Mar. 15, 1995). A subsequent 1995 executive order, Executive Order 12,959, imposed comprehensive trade and financial sanctions on Iran; it prohibited, *inter alia,* "the exportation from the United States to Iran, the Government of Iran, or to any entity owned or controlled by the Government of Iran, or the financing of such exportation, of any goods, technology, . . . or services." Exec. Order No. 12,959, 60 Fed.Reg. 24,757, 24,757 (May 6, 1995).

Pursuant to Executive Orders 12,957 and 12,959, the Secretary of the Treasury promulgated the ITR, 31 C.F.R. pt. 560. Like Executive Order 12,959, the ITR generally prohibit the exportation of goods, technology, or services to Iran:

> § 560.204 Prohibited exportation, reexportation, sale or supply of goods, technology, or services to Iran.
>
> Except as otherwise authorized pursuant to this part, . . . the exportation, reexportation, sale, or supply, directly or indirectly, from the United States, or by a United States person, wherever located, of any goods, technology, or services to Iran or the Government of Iran is prohibited. . . .

31 C.F.R. § 560.204. Thus, unless "otherwise authorized" in part 560 of title 31 of the Code of Federal Regulations, a United States person2 or person located in the United States may not export a service to Iran. Those who "willfully" violate the ITR are subject to criminal penalties. 50 U.S.C. § 1705(a), (c).

Banki raises two challenges to the district court's ITR instructions. First, he argues that the district court erred by failing to instruct the jury that executing money transfers to Iran on behalf of others qualified as "services" under the ITR only if undertaken *for a fee.* Second, he argues that the district court erred by failing to instruct the jury that non-commercial remittances to Iran, including family remittances, are exempt from the ITR's service-export ban.

1. The Requirement of a Fee

In *United States v. Homa International Trading Corp.,* this Court held that "the execution on behalf of others of money transfers from the United States to Iran is a 'service'" under the ITR. 387 F.3d 144, 146 (2d Cir. 2004) (per curiam). In so holding, the Court observed, "The term 'services' is unambiguous and refers to the performance of something useful *for a fee.*" *Id.* at 146 (emphasis added) . . . . Banki relies on this language, arguing that executing money transfers to Iran on behalf of others does not violate the ITR unless performed for a fee and that, accordingly, the district court erred by failing to so instruct the jury.

As a close reading of *Homa* reveals, however, the language in *Homa* suggesting that the receipt of a fee is a necessary element of a "service" is dicta. The defendant in *Homa,* in challenging the sufficiency of the evidence, did not argue that the receipt of a fee was required to be convicted of exporting a service to Iran in violation of the ITR. Rather, he argued: "It is simply unnatural to think of a transfer of funds as an 'exportation of services.' If anything is being exported, it is the funds themselves." . . . Thus, the Court was called upon to decide whether exporting funds on behalf of another constituted the exportation of a "service," not whether a "service" required receipt of a fee. Accordingly, the statement in *Homa* that "[t]he term 'services' is unambiguous and refers to the performance of something useful for a fee" is dicta, and we are not bound by it.

Our conclusion that the language on which Banki relies is dicta does not, however, end our inquiry. It merely clears the path for our analysis of whether the receipt of a fee is a necessary element of a service. . . .

For its definition of service, the *Homa* Court cited *United States v. All Funds on Deposit in United Bank of Switzerland*, [2003 U.S. Dist. LEXIS 101, 2003 WL 56999 (S.D.N.Y. Jan. 7, 2003),] which in turn quoted *Black's Law Dictionary*. . . . Although *Black's* defines "service" as having a fee component, other dictionaries do not. . . . We therefore look to the broader text and purpose of the ITR to aid our interpretation. . . . We have no difficulty concluding that the transfer of funds on behalf of another constitutes a "service" even if not performed for a fee.

The Iranian embargo is intended "to deal with the unusual and extraordinary threat to the national security, foreign policy, and economy of the United States" posed by "the actions and policies of the Government of Iran." Exec. Order No. 12,959, 60 Fed.Reg. 24,757, 24,757 (May 6, 1995); Exec. Order No. 12,957, 60 Fed.Reg. 14,615, 14,615 (Mar. 15, 1995). The embargo is primarily concerned with a few key actions and policies at the heart of the threat posed by the Iranian government — namely, the proliferation of weapons of mass destruction, state-sponsored terrorist activity, and efforts to frustrate Middle East diplomacy. . . .

By design, however, the embargo is deliberately overinclusive. Thus, for example, the ITR prohibit the exportation of not only advice on developing Iranian chemical weapons but also advice on developing Iranian petroleum resources, *see* § 560.209; not only services to the Iranian government but also services to Iranian businesses, *see* § 560.204; and not only bombs but also beer, *see* § 560.204. In other words, to reform the actions of the government of Iran, Executive Order 12,959 and the ITR adopt a blunt instrument: broad economic sanctions intended to isolate Iran. *See Homa,* 387 F.3d at 146 ("'[T]he obvious purpose of [Executive Order 12,959] is to isolate Iran from trade with the United States.'" (quoting *United States v. Ehsan,* 163 F.3d 855, 859 (4th Cir. 1998))).

Given that isolation of Iran is the tool that the embargo employs, there is no sound reason for the ITR to distinguish between (1) the exportation of a service to Iran for which the U.S. service provider *received a fee* and (2) the exportation of a service to Iran for which the U.S. service provider *did not receive a fee,* prohibiting only the former. After all, both exportations have the same impact *in Iran.*

Banki's argument that the term "services" has an inherent fee requirement also proves too much, for it would permit anomalies, such as permitting a U.S. entity to render uncompensated legal or consulting services to an Iranian corporation. We see no principled reason why the ITR would permit the exportation of consulting services to an Iranian corporation *gratis* but prohibit the exportation of the same consulting services for a fee.

Indeed, even without such broad economic sanctions intended to isolate Iran, Banki's argument that a fee is required fails because it would exempt from the ITR's service-export ban certain particularly high-risk transfers. Specifically, a fee requirement would provide a dangerous and unintended loophole for persons in the United States who are motivated to export services to Iran without regard to monetary compensation, including those seeking to foster the very actions and policies that prompted the establishment of the Iran embargo.

Thus, we conclude that the execution of money transfers from the United States to Iran on behalf of another, whether or not performed for a fee, constitutes the exportation of a service.

2. Non–Commercial Remittance Exception

Banki also argues that the district court erred by failing to instruct the jury that non-commercial remittances to Iran, including family remittances, are exempt from the ITR's service-export ban. He seeks a judgment of acquittal or, alternatively, a new trial on Count Two and a new trial on Count One.

As discussed above, the ITR generally prohibit the exportation of "services" to Iran. *See* 31 C.F.R. § 560.204. In arguing that the ITR exempt non-commercial remittances from the ITR's service-export ban, Banki relies on § 560.516, which reads as follows:

> § 560.516 Payment and United States dollar clearing transactions involving Iran.
>
> (a) United States depository institutions are authorized to process transfers of funds to or from Iran, or for the direct or indirect benefit of persons in Iran or the Government of Iran, if the transfer is covered in full by any of the following conditions and does not involve debiting or crediting an Iranian account:
>
> . . . .
>
> (2) The transfer arises from an underlying *transaction that is not prohibited by this part, such as a non-commercial remittance to or from Iran (e.g., a family remittance not related to a family-owned enterprise)*. . . .

31 C.F.R. § 560.516 (emphasis added).

The parties disagree as to the meaning of the regulation. Banki argues that, by its plain language, 560.516(a)(2) permits a "non-commercial remittance to or from Iran," including "a family remittance." The government argues, on the other hand, that § 560.516 permits non-commercial remittances between the United

States and Iran *only* if such remittances are processed through a U.S. depository institution.

. . . .

First, the plain wording of § 560.516 supports Banki's view that family remittances are not prohibited—at least not by 31 C.F.R. pt. 560. Indeed, the statute explicitly lists a "family remittance" as an example of a transaction that "is not prohibited" by Part 560. . . .

. . . .

Second, the government's contention that *only* U.S. depository institutions "are authorized" to process the permitted transfers is inconsistent—at least arguably—with the language of the regulation. A fair reading of § 560.516 is that it tells U.S. depository institutions (and securities brokers and dealers) that they are permitted to process non-commercial remittances, including family remittances, but the regulation does not provide that *only* U.S. depository institutions (and securities brokers and dealers) may do so. Indeed, nothing in section 560.516 specifically prohibits anyone from making a family remittance. . . .

We are not persuaded by the government that § 560.516 unambiguously grants U.S. depositary institutions exclusive authority to process non-commercial remittances between the United States and Iran. First, it is not at all clear that Banki's interpretation of the regulation would render the first clause a nullity. . . .

Second, the same principle of statutory construction can be applied to the government's interpretation of the regulation: If the first clause means that *only* U.S. banks (and U.S. securities brokers and dealers) are authorized by the first clause to process non-commercial remittances, arguably the language providing that such transactions are "not prohibited" likewise would be superfluous. The two clauses can both have meaning: non-commercial remittances are not prohibited, and U.S. banks are authorized to provide the service of processing them.

. . . .

The government also argues that its interpretation would further the purposes of the ITR. The ITR impose recordkeeping and reporting requirements on U.S. depository institutions when processing ITR-related transactions. . . . The government fairly argues that it seems unlikely that the ITR would impose such strict compliance procedures on U.S. depository institutions processing non-commercial remittances, but impose no such requirements on hawalas transmitting non-commercial remittances.

At the same time, the ITR were adopted to address the actions of the Iranian government while limiting the adverse impact of the sanctions on the Iranian people. *See* 31 C.F.R. § 560.210 (exempting from regulation certain personal communications, humanitarian donations, information and information materials, and travel); Exec. Order No. 12,957, 60 Fed.Reg. 14,615, 14,615 (Mar. 15, 1995) (finding "that the actions and policies of the *Government of Iran* constitute an unusual and extraordinary threat" (emphasis added)).

In light of the ambiguity in the regulation, Banki's conviction on Counts One and Two must be vacated and remanded for a new trial.

Notes

(1) The Trading with the Enemy Act (1917) ("TWEA") and the International Emergency Economic Powers Act (1977) ("IEEPA") are two of the most important pieces of legislation related to the imposition of sanctions. The TWEA was originally drafted to provide the President with powers related to "enemies," but was expanded during the Great Depression to provide powers during peacetime emergencies as well. The TWEA was utilized during much of the twentieth century to impose sanctions consistent with U.S. foreign policy during the Cold War. According to the Congressional Research Service, "Presidents used TWEA to block international financial transactions, seize U.S.-based assets held by foreign nationals, restrict exports, modify regulations to deter the hoarding of gold, limit foreign direct investment in U.S. companies, and impose tariffs on all imports into the United States." In 1977, Congress passed the IEEPA in an attempt to limit the powers the President had acquired under the TWEA. This was achieved by limiting the use of the TWEA to wartime and creating a new regime for peacetime emergency powers that included new oversight from Congress. According to the Congressional Research Service, "As of July 1, 2020, Presidents have declared 59 national emergencies invoking the IEEPA, 33 of which are still ongoing. . . . [T]he first state of emergency . . . was declared in response to the taking of the U.S. embassy staff as hostages by Iran in 1979 . . . ." The IEEPA may be used to impose sanctions on individuals, groups, or states. For example, in 2020, President Trump utilized the IEEPA to freeze the assets of and prevent the entry into the United States of officials of the International Criminal Court after the court opened an investigation regarding the actions of United States' military and intelligence personnel in Afghanistan. *See* Executive Order 13928 (June 11, 2020). That executive order was revoked by President Biden shortly after entering office in 2021. For a thorough discussion of the history of the TWEA and IEEPA, see *The International Emergency Economic Powers Act: Origins, Evolution, and Use*, Congressional Research Services (July 14, 2020).

(2) What level of intent is necessary for proving a violation of a trade embargo? Consider the court's discussion of this issue in *United States v. Macko*, 994 F.2d 1526, 1532–35 (11th Cir. 1993):

> Congress has authorized the President to declare and enforce comprehensive trade embargoes under certain circumstances. . . . The Cuban Assets Control Regulations (the "regulations"), promulgated in 1963, establish such an embargo. . . . Subject to narrow exceptions, the regulations prohibit all commercial transactions with Cuba or Cuban nationals. . . .

> At the time Macko and Van Ameringen engaged in the activities at issue here, an individual who willfully violated the TWEA or the regulations faced a possible fine of up to $50,000 and imprisonment for as long as ten years. . . . Because the regulations proscribe activity that is not generally perceived to be wrong, we have held that "willfulness" in this context requires a finding of specific intent to violate the trade provisions. . . . To establish that Macko and Van Ameringen acted with the requisite specific intent, the Government must prove that they actually knew of the prohibition against dealings with Cuba or Cuban nationals and deliberately violated it. . . .
>
> The facts and circumstances of this case, viewed in the light most favorable to the Government, show that Macko and Van Ameringen attempted to conceal the location of the cigarette factory. Macko actively misled his suppliers about the destination of equipment and goods, and he did not tell freight forwarders that Cuba was the final stop. He and Van Ameringen traveled to Cuba through Panama in a manner that left no reference to Cuba on their passports. Both were in possession of Department of the Treasury brochures that mention the Cuban embargo, albeit in relation to imports rather than exports. Macko initially lied to U.S. Customs agents about traveling and sending equipment to Cuba. Van Ameringen's correspondence about the project with other participants scrupulously avoided mentioning Cuba by name. Macko had experience in exporting machinery from the United States and Van Ameringen was involved in international sales of various goods. Also, their conduct occurred against the backdrop of a longstanding and widely publicized trade embargo against Cuba.
>
> Van Ameringen contends that his "secretive or covert behavior [falls] short of evidence of actual knowledge of the specific regulations at issue." . . . Such behavior may prove a general awareness of illegality but not specific intent, he says. In other contexts, however, we have acknowledged that juries may consider devious conduct along with other circumstantial evidence to infer specific intent. . . .
>
> After reviewing the record in this case, we conclude that the evidence was sufficient for a reasonable jury to find beyond a reasonable doubt that Macko and Van Ameringen knew about the Cuban trade embargo and deliberately violated it through their own conduct or by aiding and abetting other individuals. Consequently, the district court erred in granting Macko's and Van Ameringen's motions for a judgment of acquittal on the TWEA charges. . . .

(3) Can a state impose a trade restriction on companies doing business with a particular country? In *Crosby v. National Foreign Trade Council*, 530 U.S. 363 (2000), the Supreme Court found "the Burma law of the Commonwealth of Massachusetts, restricting the authority of its agencies to purchase goods or services from companies doing business with Burma, is invalid under the Supremacy Clause of the National Constitution owing to its threat of frustrating federal statutory objectives." The Court found "that the state law undermines the intended purpose and 'natural

effect' of at least three provisions of the federal Act, that is, its delegation of effective discretion to the President to control economic sanctions against Burma, its limitation of sanctions solely to United States persons and new investment, and its directive to the President to proceed diplomatically in developing a comprehensive, multilateral strategy towards Burma."

(4) To have a violation of the Trading with the Enemy Act, is it necessary for the government to prove that the defendant intended for the items shipped to arrive prior to the lifting of the embargo? Consider the court's discussion of the jury instructions in *United States v. Dien Duc Huynh*, 246 F.3d 734, 739–42 (5th Cir. 2001):

> The President lifted the embargo against Vietnam on February 3, 1994.... The lifting of the embargo did not apply retroactively.... Therefore, while we agree with Dien that upon the lifting of the embargo, the prohibitions contained in 31 C.F.R. § 500.201(b) and (c) as pertaining to Vietnam were eliminated, the essential element of that statement is that they were eliminated when the embargo was lifted and not before...
>
> We agree that the term exportation does not require that the merchandise actually arrive in the foreign country. Exportation occurs when the goods are shipped to another country with the intent that they will join the commerce of that country, not when they arrive in that country. The regulations that prohibit exporting goods to Vietnam remained in effect until the moment the embargo was lifted.... Dien argues that because the embargo was lifted, the government should have been required to prove that the goods were shipped from the United States with the intent that they arrive in Vietnam while the embargo was in effect. However, that is not the mental state required to prove a violation of the TWEA. For a conviction under the TWEA, "the government must prove that appellants 'had knowledge of [the restrictions] and acted with the specific intent to circumvent those requirements.'"...
>
> The jury was instructed that it had to find that the goods were exported to Vietnam without a license while the United States had an embargo against the country of Vietnam and that the defendant was acting "voluntarily and purposefully with a specific intent to do something the law forbids. That is to say, with bad purpose either to disobey or disregard the law." Furthermore, the jury was informed that the United States had an embargo against Vietnam between April 1975 and February 3, 1994. Dien was free to argue, and the jury was free to find, that although the goods were exported during the embargo, they were not exported with the intent to violate the embargo, but rather were exported to take advantage of the fact that the embargo was to be lifted.

(5) Since September 11, 2001, trade restrictions have also been tied to combating terrorism. On September 23, 2001, for example, President Bush issued Executive

Order 13224, titled, "Blocking Property and Prohibiting Transactions With Persons Who Commit, Threaten to Commit, or Support Terrorism." The Treasury Department, Office of Foreign Assets Control, maintains a list of individuals and companies that fall under such executive orders. They are called "Specially Designated Nationals" or "SDNs," and the list of such individuals and companies is publicly available at https://home.treasury.gov/policy-issues/financial-sanctions/specially-designated-nationals-and-blocked-persons-list-sdn-human-readable-lists.

(6) Export controls and related restrictions on the use of goods can also arise during domestic emergencies where needed resources are scarce. This occurred during the COVID-19 Pandemic when both President Trump and President Biden invoked the Defense Production Act of 1950 ("DPA") through executive order. As described by the Federal Emergency Management Agency,

> The Defense Production Act is the primary source of presidential authorities to expedite and expand the supply of materials and services from the U.S. industrial base needed to promote the national defense. DPA authorities are available to support: emergency preparedness activities conducted pursuant to title VI of the Stafford Act; protection or restoration of critical infrastructure; and efforts to prevent, reduce vulnerability to, minimize damage from, and recover from acts of terrorism within the United States. DPA authorities may be used to:
>
> - Require acceptance and preferential performance of contracts and orders under DPA Title I. . . .
> - Provide financial incentives and assistance (under DPA Title III) for U.S. industry to expand productive capacity and supply needed for national defense purposes;
> - Provide antitrust protection (through DPA voluntary agreements in DPA Title VII) for businesses to cooperate in planning and operations for national defense purposes, including homeland security.

Defense Production Act, FEMA Website, available at https://www.fema.gov/disasters/defense-production-act (last visited May 24, 2021). The DPA was used in April 2020 to restrict the exportation of personal protective equipment ("PPE"). The DPA was also used during the COVID-19 Pandemic to prioritize the manufacture of PPE, ventilators, syringes and vials and to assist companies manufacturing the COVID-19 vaccines to secure needed materials. Though not direct prohibitions on exportation, the later requirements often meant that there were few, if any, remaining resources for export after the needs of domestic entities were met.

(7) For an argument that the whole system is in need of drastic overhaul, see Ronald J. Sievert, *Urgent Message to Congress — Nuclear Triggers to Libya, Missile Guidance to China, Air Defense to Iraq, Arms Supplier to the World: Has the Time Finally Arrived to Overhaul the U.S. Export Control Regime? — The Case for Immediate Reform of Our Outdated, Ineffective, and Self-Defeating Export Control System*, 37 Tex. Int'l L.J. 89 (2002).

§ 6.05 The Protocol Against the Illicit Manufacturing of and Trafficking in Firearms, and the Arms Trade Treaty

Two significant multilateral treaties cover some of the ground occupied by the Arms Export Control Act, although the United States has not yet become a party to them.

The first is the Protocol against the Illicit Manufacturing of and Trafficking in Firearms, their Parts and Components and Ammunition, Supplementing the United Nations Convention against Transnational Organized Crime. It was adopted on 31 May 2001 by General Assembly Resolution 55/255 and came into force on 3 July 2005 and has 110 parties. As a Protocol to the Transnational Organized Crime Convention, it incorporates many of that treaty's basic provisions such as those on jurisdiction, extradition and mutual legal assistance. Article 3, paragraph (e) of the Convention defines "illicit trafficking" as "the import, export, acquisition, sale, delivery, movement or transfer of firearms, their parts and components and ammunition from or across the territory of one State Party to that of another State Party if any one of the States Parties concerned does not authorize it in accordance with the terms of this Protocol or if the firearms are not marked in accordance with article 8 of this Protocol." The key suppression provision in the Protocol is Article 5, which provides:

Article 5

Criminalization

1. Each State Party shall adopt such legislative and other measures as may be necessary to establish as criminal offences the following conduct, when committed intentionally:

(a) Illicit manufacturing of firearms, their parts and components and ammunition;

(b) Illicit trafficking in firearms, their parts and components and ammunition;

(c) Falsifying or illicitly obliterating, removing or altering the marking(s) on firearms required by article 8 of this Protocol.

2. Each State Party shall also adopt such legislative and other measures as may be necessary to establish as criminal offences the following conduct:

(a) Subject to the basic concepts of its legal system, attempting to commit or participating as an accomplice in an offence established in accordance with paragraph 1 of this article; and

(b) Organizing, directing, aiding, abetting, facilitating or counselling the commission of an offence established in accordance with paragraph 1 of this article.

Adopted by the United Nations General Assembly on 2 April 2013 by General Assembly Resolution 67/234B, the Arms Trade Treaty came into force on 24 December 2014. It was signed by the United States on 5 September 2013, but the Senate never gave its advice and consent to ratification. In 2019, President Trump "unsigned" the arms agreement, announcing that "the United States does not intend to become a party to the treaty. Accordingly, the United States has no legal obligations arising from its signature on April 2, 2013." (Letter received by U.N. Secretary-General on July 18, 2019.) The Biden Administration is reviewing its position. Several of the other major arms-exporting countries, France, the United Kingdom, Germany, Spain, Italy, the Netherlands, Sweden and Switzerland are already among the 123 parties to the treaty. China joined the treaty in 2020. Preambular paragraph 13 of the Treaty accommodates Second Amendment sensitivities which have been raised as an obstacle to United States ratification. It has the parties "[*m*]*indful of* the legitimate trade and lawful ownership, and use of certain conventional arms for recreational, cultural, historical, and sporting activities, where such trade, ownership and use are permitted or protected by law." The most significant parts of the treaty provide:

Article 1

Object and Purpose

The object of this Treaty is to:

- Establish the highest possible common international standards for regulating or improving the regulation of the international trade in conventional arms;

- Prevent and eradicate the illicit trade in conventional arms and prevent their diversion; for the purpose of:

- Contributing to international and regional peace, security and stability;

- Reducing human suffering;

- Promoting cooperation, transparency and responsible action by States Parties in the international trade in conventional arms, thereby building confidence among States Parties.

Article 2

Scope

1. This Treaty shall apply to all conventional arms within the following categories:

(a) Battle tanks;

(b) Armoured combat vehicles;

(c) Large-calibre artillery systems;

(d) Combat aircraft;

(e) Attack helicopters;

(f) Warships;

(g) Missiles and missile launchers; and

(h) Small arms and light weapons.

2. For the purposes of this Treaty, the activities of the international trade comprise export, import, transit, trans-shipment and brokering, hereafter referred to as "transfer".

3. This Treaty shall not apply to the international movement of conventional arms by, or on behalf of, a State Party for its use provided that the conventional arms remain under that State Party's ownership.

Article 3

Ammunition/Munitions

Each State Party shall establish and maintain a national control system to regulate the export of ammunition/munitions fired, launched or delivered by the conventional arms covered under Article 2 (1), and shall apply the provisions of Article 6 and Article 7 prior to authorizing the export of such ammunition/munitions.

Article 4

Parts and Components

Each State Party shall establish and maintain a national control system to regulate the export of parts and components where the export is in a form that provides the capability to assemble the conventional arms covered under Article 2(1) and shall apply the provisions of Article 6 and Article 7 prior to authorizing the export of such parts and components.

Article 5

General Implementation

1. Each State Party shall implement this Treaty in a consistent, objective and non-discriminatory manner, bearing in mind the principles referred to in this Treaty.

2. Each State Party shall establish and maintain a national control system, including a national control list, in order to implement the provisions of this Treaty.

3. Each State Party is encouraged to apply the provisions of this Treaty to the broadest range of conventional arms. National definitions of any of the categories covered under Article 2 (1) (a)–(g) shall not cover less than the descriptions used in the United Nations Register of Conventional Arms at the time of entry into force of this Treaty. For the category covered under

Article 2 (1) (h), national definitions shall not cover less than the descriptions used in relevant United Nations instruments at the time of entry into force of this Treaty.

4. Each State Party, pursuant to its national laws, shall provide its national control list to the Secretariat, which shall make it available to other States Parties. States Parties are encouraged to make their control lists publicly available.

5. Each State Party shall take measures necessary to implement the provisions of this Treaty and shall designate competent national authorities in order to have an effective and transparent national control system regulating the transfer of conventional arms covered under Article 2 (1) and of items covered under Article 3 and Article 4.

6. Each State Party shall designate one or more national points of contact to exchange information on matters related to the implementation of this Treaty. Each State Party shall notify the Secretariat, established under Article 18, of its national point(s) of contact and keep the information updated.

Article 6

Prohibitions

1. A State Party shall not authorize any transfer of conventional arms, covered under Article 2 (1) or of items covered under Article 3 or Article 4, if the transfer would violate its obligations under measures adopted by the United Nations Security Council acting under Chapter VII of the Charter of the United Nations, in particular arms embargoes.

2. A State Party shall not authorize any transfer of conventional arms covered under Article 2 (1) or of items covered under Article 3 or Article 4, if the transfer would violate its relevant international obligations under international agreements to which it is a Party, in particular those relating to the transfer of, or illicit trafficking in, conventional arms.

3. A State Party shall not authorize any transfer of conventional arms covered under Article 2 (1) or of items covered under Article 3 or Article 4, if it has knowledge at the time of authorization that the arms or items would be used in the commission of genocide, crimes against humanity, grave breaches of the Geneva Conventions of 1949, attacks directed against civilian objects or civilians protected as such, or other war crimes as defined by international agreements to which it is a Party.

Article 7

Export and Export Assessment

1. If the export is not prohibited under Article 6, each exporting State Party, prior to authorization of the export of conventional arms covered under Article 2 (1) or of items covered under Article 3 or Article 4, under its

jurisdiction and pursuant to its national control system, shall, in an objective and non-discriminatory manner, taking into account relevant factors, including information provided by the importing State in accordance with Article 8 (1), assess the potential that the conventional arms or items:

(a) would contribute to or undermine peace and security;

(b) could be used to:

(i) commit or facilitate a serious violation of international humanitarian law;

(ii) commit or facilitate a serious violation of international human rights law;

(iii) commit or facilitate an act constituting an offence under international conventions or protocols relating to terrorism to which the exporting State is a Party; or

(iv) commit or facilitate an act constituting an offence under international conventions or protocols relating to transnational organized crime to which the exporting State is a Party.

2. The exporting State Party shall also consider whether there are measures that could be undertaken to mitigate risks identified in (a) or (b) in paragraph 1, such as confidence-building measures or jointly developed and agreed programmes by the exporting and importing States.

3. If, after conducting this assessment and considering available mitigating measures, the exporting State Party determines that there is an overriding risk of any of the negative consequences in paragraph 1, the exporting State Party shall not authorize the export.

4. The exporting State Party, in making this assessment, shall take into account the risk of the conventional arms covered under Article 2 (1) or of the items covered under Article 3 or Article 4 being used to commit or facilitate serious acts of gender-based violence or serious acts of violence against women and children.

5. Each exporting State Party shall take measures to ensure that all authorizations for the export of conventional arms covered under Article 2 (1) or of items covered under Article 3 or Article 4 are detailed and issued prior to the export.

6. Each exporting State Party shall make available appropriate information about the authorization in question, upon request, to the importing State Party and to the transit or trans-shipment States Parties, subject to its national laws, practices or policies.

7. If, after an authorization has been granted, an exporting State Party becomes aware of new relevant information, it is encouraged to reassess the authorization after consultations, if appropriate, with the importing State.

Note

On preventing illicit transfers of arms, especially to non-state actors, see also S.C. Resolution 1540, discussed in § 2.01[C], and the Proliferation Security Initiative treaties, discussed in § 2.01[B].

There is a comprehensive analysis of the Arms Trade Treaty in THE ARMS TRADE TREATY: A COMMENTARY (Andrew Clapham et al. eds., 2016).

Chapter 7

Computer Crimes

§ 7.01 Generally

Computers provide increased accessibility and speed in communications. The abuse and misuse of this technology, however, can present unique issues in international criminal law. A report from the Twelfth United Nations Congress on Crime Prevention and Criminal Justice summarized the complexities of the computer age.

> In the discussion, many undeniable benefits of rapid technological development were recognized. At the same time, however, these developments made it possible to commit traditional forms of crime in new ways, including fraud and the dissemination of child pornography, and also to commit new forms of crime, such as hacking, spamming, "phishing" (using counterfeit websites — or messages directing users to them — for fraudulent purposes), digital piracy, the malicious spreading of viruses and other attacks on critical infrastructure. It was noted that terrorist organizations and organized criminal groups used rapidly evolving technologies to facilitate their criminal activities. There was agreement that cybercrime threatened economies, critical infrastructure, the credibility of institutions and social and cultural well-being.

Report of the Twelfth United Nations Congress on Crime Prevention and Criminal Justice, Salvador, Brazil, April 12–19, 2010, U.N. Doc. A/CONF.213/18, at 55 (para. 197).

Unlike the case with most criminal acts, the perpetrator of a computer crime can remain at home while the victims of the crime are in another country. As stated by Former Attorney General Janet Reno, "a hacker needs no passport and passes no checkpoints." Keynote Address by U.S. Attorney General Janet Reno on High-Tech and Computer Crime, Delivered at the Meeting of the P-8 Senior Experts' Group on Transnational Organized Crime, Jan. 21, 1997, *available at* http://www.usdoj.gov/criminal/cybercrime/agfranc.htm.

Questions can arise as to which country has jurisdiction to prosecute the crime. Differing criminal laws may offer different resolutions. In some instances, a jurisdiction may have no applicable criminal statute for the particular computer misuse. Should the alleged criminal activity in these instances be prosecuted in the jurisdiction with the strongest legal support? Should the location of the perpetrator, the computer, the victim, or the investigation be the proper place for prosecution? When more than one jurisdiction wants to prosecute the conduct, should this be allowed? These are some of the many questions that need to be resolved in international criminal law. *See also* Richard W. Aldrich, *Cyberterrorism and Computer Crimes: Issues Surrounding the Establishment of an International Regime*, Institute for National Securities Studies, Occasional Paper 32 (April 2000); Ellen S. Podgor, *International Computer Fraud: A Paradigm for Limiting National Jurisdiction*, 35 U.C. DAVIS L. REV. 267 (2002); Ellen S. Podgor, *Cybercrime: National, Transnational, or International?* 50 WAYNE L. REV. 97 (2004); RESEARCH HANDBOOK ON INTERNATIONAL LAW AND CYBERSPACE (N. Tsagourias & R. Buchan eds., 2d ed. 2021).

The speed with which technology develops can result in legal issues lagging behind scientific developments. As quickly as new laws are enacted to check an abuse of computers, new technology develops that can require changing the legal process. The breadth of computer crimes makes the possibility of a single criminal statute problematic. For example, computer crimes can entail theft of trade secrets, pornography, terrorism, and financial institution fraud.

Recent concerns with respect to cybercrime have elevated with the rise of cryptocurrency, identity theft, and ransomware. Issues of cybersecurity are faced by both businesses and the government, including concerns about political interference in government matters. In Special Counsel Robert S. Mueller, III, *Report on the Investigation into Russian Interference in the 2016 Presidential Election* (March 2019), it is noted that:

> The Russian government interfered in the 2016 presidential election in sweeping and systematic fashion. Evidence of Russian government operations began to surface in mid-2016. In June, the Democratic National Committee and its cyber response team publicly announced that Russian hackers had compromised its computer network. Releases of hacked materials—hacks that public reporting soon attributed to the Russian government—began that same month. Additional releases followed in July through the organization WikiLeaks, with further releases in October and November.

Id. at 1.

§ 7.02 National (United States) Approach

In the United States there are several statutes that are employed to prosecute computer misuses. A key piece of legislation is found in 18 U.S.C. § 1030, a statute initially passed as the Counterfeit Access Device and Computer Fraud and Abuse Act of 1984. Congress extended the reach of section 1030 as part of the "United and Strengthening America by Providing Appropriate Tools Required to Intercept and Obstruct Terrorism Act of 2001" (USA Patriot Act), allowing it to be used for the prosecution of extraterritorial conduct. As described in the 2014 case *United States v. Steele*, 595 Fed. Appx. 208 (4th Cir. Dec. 24, 2014), the complexities of computer crimes have led courts to struggle regarding the appropriate application of the Act.

The CFAA imposes criminal and civil penalties on individuals who unlawfully access computers. Specifically, § 1030(a)(2)(C), under which Steele was indicted, prohibits accessing a protected computer "without authorization" or in "exce[ss of] authorized access." Notably, the indictment itself charged Steele with violating only the first prong of this section.

Steele primarily relies on our opinion in *WEC Carolina Energy Solutions LLC v. Miller*, 687 F.3d 199 (4th Cir. 2012), to argue that because SRA did not change his access password when he resigned, Steele's post-employment access, though "ethically dubious" was not "without authorization" as contemplated by the statute. We cannot agree.

WEC Carolina contributes to a dialogue among the circuit courts on the reach of § 1030(a)(2). The broad view holds that when employees access computer information with the intent to harm their employer, their authorization to access that information terminates, and they are therefore acting "without authorization" under § 1030(a)(2). See *Int'l Airport Ctrs., L.L.C. v. Citrin*, 440 F.3d 418, 420–21 (7th Cir. 2006). The narrower construction, adopted by *WEC Carolina*, holds that § 1030(a)(2) applies to employees who unlawfully access a protected computer, but not to the improper use of information lawfully accessed. *See WEC Carolina*, 687 F.3d at 203–04 (citing *United States v. Nosal*, 676 F.3d 854, 863 (9th Cir. 2012) (en banc)).

Importantly, this split focuses on employees who are authorized to access their employer's computers but use the information they retrieve for an improper purpose. Steele's case is distinguishable for one obvious reason: he was not an employee of SRA at the time the indictment alleges he improperly accessed the company's server. In *WEC Carolina*, authorization did not hinge on employment status because that issue was not in dispute. Here, by contrast, the fact that Steele no longer worked for SRA when he accessed its server logically suggests that the authorization he enjoyed during his employment no longer existed. See, e.g., *LVRC Holdings LLC v. Brekka*, 581 F.3d 1127, 1136 (9th Cir. 2009) ("There is no dispute that if Brekka accessed LVRC's information . . . after he left the company . . . , Brekka would have accessed a protected computer 'without authorization' for purposes of the CFAA."); Restatement (Third) of Agency § 3.09 (2006) (Actual authority terminates "upon the occurrence of circumstances on the basis of which the agent should reasonably conclude" that authority is revoked.).

The Economic Espionage Act also provides for prosecution of computer crimes. The Economic Espionage Act (EEA), passed by Congress in 1996, focuses on misappropriation of trade secrets in both domestic and international related activity. *See* Kent B. Alexander & Kristen L. Wood, *The Economic Espionage Act: Setting the Stage for a New Commercial Code of Conduct*, 15 Ga. St. U. L. Rev. 907 (1999). In *United States v. Hsu*, 155 F.3d 189 (3rd Cir. 1998), Circuit Judge Rendell stated:

The EEA became law in October 1996 against a backdrop of increasing threats to corporate security and a rising tide of international and domestic economic espionage. The end of the Cold War sent government spies scurrying to the private sector to perform illicit work for businesses and corporations, . . . and by 1996, studies revealed that nearly $24 billion of corporate intellectual property was being stolen each year. . . .

The problem was augmented by the absence of any comprehensive federal remedy targeting the theft of trade secrets, compelling prosecutors to shoehorn economic espionage crimes into statutes directed at other offenses. . . . For example, the government often sought convictions under the National Stolen Property Act ("NSPA"), 18 U.S.C. § 2314, or the mail and wire fraud statutes, 18 U.S.C. § § 1341 and 1343. However, the NSPA "was drafted at a time when computers, biotechnology, and copy machines did not even exist,". . . . and industrial espionage often occurred without the use of mail or wire. Consequently, it soon became clear to legislators and commentators alike that a new federal strategy was needed to combat the increasing prevalence of espionage in corporate America. Congress recognized "the importance of developing a systematic approach to the problem of economic espionage," . . . and stressed that "only by adopting a national scheme to protect U.S. proprietary economic information can we hope to maintain our industrial and economic edge and thus safeguard our national security." . . . The House and Senate thus passed the Economic Espionage Act, and the President signed the bill into law on October 11, 1996.

The EEA consists of nine sections which protect proprietary information from misappropriation. Three sections are of particular import to our analysis: what acts are penalized by the statute, how the law defines a "trade secret," and when trade secrets are to remain confidential. . . .

The EEA criminalizes two principal categories of corporate espionage, including "Economic espionage" as defined by 18 U.S.C. § 1831, and the "Theft of trade secrets" as defined by § 1832. The former provision punishes those who knowingly misappropriate, or attempt or conspire to misappropriate, trade secrets with the intent or knowledge that their offense will benefit a foreign government, foreign instrumentality, or foreign agent. The legislative history indicates that § 1831 is designed to apply only when there is "evidence of foreign government sponsored or coordinated intelligence activity." . . . By contrast, § 1832, the section under which the defendants are charged, is a general criminal trade secrets provision. It applies to anyone who knowingly engages in the theft of trade secrets, or an attempt or conspiracy to do so, "with intent to convert a trade secret, that is related to or included in a product that is produced for or placed in interstate or foreign commerce, to the economic benefit of anyone other than the owner thereof, and intending or knowing that the offense will, injure any owner of that trade secret." Section 1832(a) makes clear that attempt and conspiracy are

> distinct offenses, and it lists them separately from those acts that constitute completed crimes under the statute.
>
> Section 1832 also contains at least three additional limitations not found in § 1831. First, a defendant charged under § 1832 must intend to convert a trade secret "to the economic benefit of anyone other than the owner thereof," including the defendant himself. This "economic benefit" requirement differs from § 1831, which states merely that the offense "benefit," in any manner, a foreign government, instrumentality, or agent. Therefore, prosecutions under § 1832 uniquely require that the defendant intend to confer an economic benefit on the defendant or another person or entity. Second, § 1832 states that the defendant must intend or know that the offense will injure an owner of the trade secret, a restriction not found in § 1831. The legislative history indicates that this requires "that the actor knew or was aware to a practical certainty that his conduct would cause such a result." . . . Finally, unlike § 1831, § 1832 also requires that the trade secret be "related to or included in a product that is produced for or placed in interstate or foreign commerce." . . .

As to what constitutes a "trade secret" for purposes of this statute, Circuit Judge Rendell looked to the statutory definition in stating:

> The EEA defines a "trade secret" to expressly extend protection to the misappropriation of intangible information for the first time under federal law. 18 U.S.C. § 1839(3) provides that a "trade secret" means:
>
> > all forms and types of financial, business, scientific, technical, economic, or engineering information, including patterns, plans, compilations, program devices, formulas, designs, prototypes, methods, techniques, processes, procedures, programs, or codes, whether tangible or intangible, and whether or how stored, compiled, or memorialized physically, electronically, graphically, photographically, or in writing if—
> >
> > (A) the owner thereof has taken reasonable measures to keep such information secret; and
> >
> > (B) the information derives independent economic value, actual or potential, from not being generally known to, and not being readily ascertainable through proper means by, the public.

Other federal statutes are also available to prosecute computer crimes, including the Electronic Communications Privacy Act (18 U.S.C. § 2510). Generic statutes may also be available to prosecute computer crimes, including the wire fraud and mail fraud statutes. When utilizing generic statutes, however, one must carefully consider whether the language of the particular statute covers present-day technology. For example, in *United States v. Aleynikov*, 676 F.3d 71 (2d Cir. 2012), the government brought a prosecution against a programmer at Goldman Sachs & Co. under the National Stolen Property Act (NSPA) (18 U.S.C. 2314–15). The programmer allegedly uploaded source code to a server in Germany prior to downloading it to his computer in New Jersey and later transferring it to Illinois. The court held that the programmer did not violate the NSPA because the statute did not cover "purely intangible property." When the individual printed out the stolen documents, however, it was held to have violated the NSPA because the documents were now in a tangible form. *See United States v. Agrawal*, 726 F.3d 235 (2d Cir. 2013).

Notes

(1) As noted above, the Computer Fraud and Abuse Act was amended by the USA PATRIOT ACT in 2001 to expand its extraterritorial reach. The statute now reads: "As used in this section . . . (2) the term 'protected computer' means a computer . . . (B) which is used in or affecting interstate or foreign commerce or communication, *including a computer located outside the United States that is used in a manner that affects interstate or foreign commerce or communication of the United States.*" 18 U.S.C. 1030(e)(2)(B). The language in italics reflects the 2001 amendments. What international criminal law scenarios does this amendment cover? Does the law apply where the individual engages in unauthorized access of a protected computer located outside the United States? *See* Charles Doyle, *Cybercrime: An Overview of the Federal Computer Fraud and Abuse Statute and Related Federal Criminal Laws*, Congressional Research Service (Oct. 15, 2014).

(2) In *United States v. Gasperini*, 729 Fed. Appx. 112 (2d Cir. 2018), the defendant challenged whether the term "protected computer" in the computer fraud statute allowed for an extraterritorial application. The Second Circuit held:

> Gasperini next argues that the prosecution fails because the Computer Fraud and Abuse Act of 1984 ("CFAA") does not apply extraterritorially, and that the crimes charged in the indictment were an extraterritorial application because the alleged "click fraud" scheme was directed at an Italian company. . . .
>
> There is a strong argument that § 1030(a)(2) applies extraterritorially. A 1996 amendment to the statute defines a "protected computer" to include any computer "used in interstate or *foreign* commerce or communication," 18 U.S.C. § 1030(e)(2) (emphasis added); see *United States v. Ivanov*, 175 F. Supp.2d 367, 374 75 (D. Conn. 2001) (adopting that argument). But we need not reach that argument here. The offense of which Gasperini was convicted requires no fraud victim, foreign or domestic. Rather, it prohibits unauthorized access to, and obtaining of information from, a computer. The jury had ample evidence to conclude beyond a reasonable doubt that Gasperini accessed, without authorization, nearly 2000 computers in the United States, including 200 within the Eastern District of New York. Whatever may have been true of crimes of which Gasperini was acquitted, the crime of which he was convicted was a domestic application of the statute, which was properly prosecuted even if the statute, or some portions of it, do not apply extraterritorially. The conviction is a domestic offense because the focus of the statute of conviction is gaining access to computers

> and obtaining information from them, and "[i]f the conduct relevant to the statute's focus occurred in the United States, then the case involves a permissible domestic application even if other conduct occurred abroad." *RJR Nabisco, Inc. v. European Cmty.* [§ 3.02].

(3) When the government uses the wire fraud statute, 18 U.S.C. § 1343, as opposed to computer fraud, 18 U.S.C. § 1030, as the basis for the prosecution, the court finds it necessary to use the "two-step framework" from *RJR Nabisco, Inc. v. European Cmty.* [§ 3.02]:

> At the first step, we ask whether the presumption against extraterritoriality has been rebutted — that is, whether the statute gives a clear, affirmative indication that it applies extraterritorially. . . . If the statute is not extraterritorial, then at the second step we determine whether the case involves a domestic application of the statute . . . by looking to the statute's "focus." If the conduct relevant to the statute's "focus" occurred in the United States, then the case involves a permissible domestic application even if other conduct relevant to the focus occurred in a foreign country; but if the conduct relevant to the focus occurred in a foreign country, then the case involves an impermissible extraterritorial application regardless of any other conduct that occurred in U.S. territory.

RJR Nabisco, 136 S. Ct. at 2101. This may prove a more difficult hurdle for the government when a domestic concern is lacking.

(4) Due to continued concerns regarding economic espionage, Congress passed the Foreign and Economic Espionage Penalty Enhancement Act of 2012. Pub. L. No. 112-269 (Jan. 14, 2013). The Act increased the applicable fine for violations under 18 U.S.C. § 1831 and requested that the United States Sentencing Commission review the applicable sentencing guidelines under the Economic Espionage Act to ensure the penalties "reflect the seriousness of these offenses, account for the potential and actual harm caused by these offenses, and provide adequate deterrence against such offenses." The Defend Trade Secrets Act of 2016 amended the Economic Espionage Act of 1996, allowing private parties to bring actions for trade secret misappropriation while also providing "increased penalties for corporations convicted of trade secret theft." Pub. L. No. 114-153 (May 11, 2016). The amendments also required a report to Congress "on the scope and breadth of trade secret theft affecting United States companies occurring outside the United States." Department of Justice Report to Congress Pursuant to the Defend Trade Secrets Act (2018), available at https://www.justice.gov/iptf/page/file/1101901/download.

§ 7.03 International Dimension

At the international level, there are several initiatives focusing on how best to curtail international computer crimes. In May 1998, the G-8 countries (United States, United Kingdom, France, Germany, Italy, Canada, Japan, and Russia) adopted a set of principles pertaining to computer crimes and they have continued to follow developments in the area. *See* http://www.cybercrimelaw.net/G8.html. The United Nations has also been concerned and developed a manual on the prevention and control of computer-related crime, although there is no United Nations convention in the area. *See* International Review of Criminal Policy, Nos 43 & 44, United Nations Manual on the Prevention and Control of Computer-Related Crime (1999); United Nations Office of Drugs and Crime (UNODC), Comprehensive Study on Cybercrime (2013). The International Telecommunications Union, the United Nations Specialized Agency that deals with information and communication technologies, issued an important study entitled Understanding Cybercrime: Phenomena, Challenges and Legal Response (2012). The consensus is that international cooperation is needed to combat international crimes involving computers. *See, e.g.,* David M. Cielusniak, *You Cannot Fight What You Cannot See: Securities Regulation on the Internet*, 22 Fordham L. Rev. 612 (1998). The FBI will often work with foreign agencies in prosecuting computer crimes. *See* Cassell Bryan-Low, *To Catch Crooks in Cyberspace, FBI Goes Global*, Wall St. Jrl., Nov. 26, 2006, *available at* http://online.wsj.com/article/SB116406726611228873.html ?mod=hps_us_pageone. Identity theft, often accomplished through computer access, has been a growing area of concern. *See* Michael J. Elston & Scott A. Stein, *International Cooperation in On-Line Identity Theft Investigations: A Hopeful Future but a Frustrating Present*, *available at* https://www.scribd.com/document/317963296/Elston-and-Stein. Following a recommendation from the 2010 Congress on Crime Prevention and Criminal Justice, an Open-Ended Intergovernmental Expert Group on Cybercrime has been meeting for several years in Vienna. *See, e.g.*, Report on the Meeting of the Expert Group to Conduct a Comprehensive Study on Cybercrime held in Vienna from April 6–8, 2021, UNODC/CCPCJ/EG.4/2021/2.

The Council of Europe ("COE") has been an advocate for international cooperation in combating computer crimes. The COE Convention on Cybercrime (known as the Budapest Convention), ETS No. 185, *available at* http://www.conventions.coe.int/Treaty/en/Treaties/Html/185.htm, is currently the only international agreement in the area. It is divided into five parts that provide the basics of who has jurisdiction and how to decide jurisdictional conflicts. It also covers procedural issues that can arise in combating computer criminality. The main objective of the Convention "is to pursue a common criminal policy aimed at the protection of society against cybercrime, especially by adopting appropriate legislation and fostering international co-operation." This Convention was opened for signature on November 23, 2001. It entered into force on July 1, 2004, having been ratified by five member states and, by December 2021, had a total of 66 ratifications. An Additional Protocol, "concerning the criminalisation of acts of a racist and xenophobic nature committed through computer systems" was opened for signature on January 28, 2003. *See* http://conventions.coe.int. As of December 2021, it had 33 ratifications. This did not include the United States, as the convention presents First Amendment concerns.

A Second Additional Protocol to the Convention on Cybercrime was adopted by the Committee of Ministers on November 17, 2021. It will be open for signature in May 2022. "The Protocol provides a legal basis for disclosure of domain name registration information and for direct co-operation with service providers for subscriber information, effective means to obtain subscriber information and traffic data, immediate co-operation in emergencies, mutual assistance tools, as well as personal data protection safeguards." *See Second Additional Protocol to the Cybercrime Convention adopted by the Committee of Ministers of the Council of Europe* (November 17, 2021), https://www.coe.int/en/web/cybercrime/-/second-additional-protocol-to-the-cybercrime-convention-adopted-by-the-committee-of-ministers-of-the-council-of-europe.

The NATO Cooperative Cyber Defence Centre of Excellence (CCDCOE) is a multinational and interdisciplinary cyber center that focuses on "research, training and exercises in four core areas: technology, strategy, operations and law." *See* https://ccdcoe.org/. The CCDCOE sponsors the *Tallinn Manuals* which have "served as an essential tool for policy and legal experts on how international law applies to cyber operations." Currently there is the "Tallinn Manual 3.0 project, which will revise and expand the 2017 edition, Tallinn Manual 2.0, in light of State practice and statements on the applicability of international law to cyber operations." *See* CCDCOE, The Tallinn Manual, available at https://ccdcoe.org/research/tallinn-manual/.

On May 10, 2006, the Bow Street Magistrates' Court in London held one Gary McKinnon, a legendary hacker, to be extraditable to the United States. Operating from the U.K., McKinnon is alleged to have accessed 92 computers at various U.S. military sites in 2001 and 2002. McKinnon claimed he was looking for information on UFOs. *See* Jed Borod, *U.K. Court Rules for U.S. Extradition Request in Military Hacker Case*, 22 INT'L ENF. L. REP. 261 (2006). Pink Floyd's David Gilmour issued a single "Chicago — Change the World" to publicize the case, which indeed became a British *cause célèbre*. What must have been the U.S. jurisdictional theory? If you were the British Home Secretary (who makes the final decisions on extradition), would you contemplate prosecuting him in England? Would it affect your answer that he could be liable to 70 years imprisonment in the U.S., but much less time in the U.K.? What does *The Lotus* [§ 1.02] have to say about all this? McKinnon, who suffers from Asperger's syndrome, was still fighting his extradition in the British courts and the European Court of Human Rights until 2012 when the Home Secretary announced that she had decided not to proceed with the extradition because McKinnon was seriously ill "and there was a real risk of him attempting suicide if he was sent to the US." See *Gary McKinnon's mother "overwhelmed" as extradition blocked*, http://www.bbc.com/news/uk-19968973. No English prosecution was mounted, apparently in view of the difficulty of obtaining evidence.

An area of increasing concern is "cyber warfare" in which electronic attacks are made by governmental or non-governmental actors against the computer systems of other countries. See. e.g., Kai Ambos, *International Criminal Responsibility in Cyberspace*, chapter 6, RESEARCH HANDBOOK ON INTERNATIONAL LAW AND

CYBERSPACE (N. TSAGOURIAS & R. BUCHAN eds., 2d ed. 2021); Lucian Dervan, *Information Warfare and Civilian Populations: How the Law of War Addresses a Fear of the Unknown*, 3 GOETTINGEN J. INT'L L. 373 (2011); Note: *Cyber Warfare and International Law: Unresolved Issues*, 11 N.Y.L. SCH. INT'L REV. 3 (2009). This type of "warfare" is often described as an "information operation" and, according to the United States Department of Defense, the term refers to operations that involve the use of "electronic means to gain access to or change information in a targeted information system without necessarily damaging its physical components." Department of Defense, Office of General Counsel, *Assessment of International Legal Issues in Information Operations* (May 1999). This is opposed to traditional kinetic military operations, such as using ground troops or aerial bombardment.

It is important to note that information operations are not always limited to purely military or governmental targets. For example, during the 2008 Russian intervention in South Ossetia, a separatist region of the former Soviet Republic of Georgia, kinetic operations occurred at the same time as computer network attacks against government, news, transportation, and banking websites. *See* Sean Watts, *Combatant Status and Computer Network Attack*, 50 VA. J. INT'L L. 391 (2010) (noting the precise source of the cyber attack remains unknown); *see also* Jonathan Clough, *The Council of Europe on Cybercrime: Defining "Crime" in a Digital World*, 23 CRIM. L.F. 363 (2012). Information operations can also extend beyond communication systems and websites to include vital infrastructure, including electric power grids and water supply stations. Many of these targets are "dual-use," which means they are both military and civilian in nature. For example, in 2009, United States intelligence officials disclosed that cyber attacks from China and Russia had infiltrated American electric power grid computer networks. *See* Siobham Gorman, *Electricity Grid in U.S. Penetrated by Spies*, WALL ST. JRL. (April 8, 2009).

While information operations grow in significance, concerns exist regarding the potential risks to civilians. First, because these operations often target infrastructure and dual-use objectives, it is likely that these operations will increasingly impact civilians. Second, there are various unpredictable collateral consequences of infiltrating and manipulating vital computer networks, including those controlling civilian infrastructure resources. As will be discussed further in Chap. 23 [The Substantive Law of International Crimes], conduct during war has been guided for centuries by the principles of *jus in bello*, which means justice in war. These principles have been codified into various international agreements, including the Geneva Conventions. *Jus in bello* requires that military operations satisfy three criteria. First, the operation must be militarily necessary. Second, a distinction must be made between military and civilian targets. Third, the attack must be proportional. Given the potential impact of information operations on civilian targets and dual-use targets, how should military forces weigh the risks when considering the three *jus in bello* principles above? Do information operations present a special difficulty given the full ramifications and collateral consequences of a cyber attack are often unpredictable? Consider, for example, that the Stuxnet computer virus, used against Iran's nuclear weapons program, is reported to have spread outside of Iran and infected industrial facilities across the globe. *See* Robert McMillan, *Siemens: Stuxnet Work Hit Industrial Systems*, PCWorld, available at http://www.pcworld.com/article/205420/article.html. For further discussion of these issues, including a detailed hypothetical, *see* Lucian Dervan, *Information Warfare and Civilian Populations: How the Law of War Addresses a Fear of the Unknown*, 3 GOETTINGEN J. INT'L L. 373 (2011), *see also* David P. Fidler, *Recent Development and Revelations Concerning Cybersecurity and Cyberspace: Implications for International Law*, 16 ASIL INSIGHTS, No. 22 (2012); Richard Brust, *Cyber Attacks: Computer Warfare Looms as the Next Big Conflict in International Law*, ABA J. May 2012, at 40.

Jus ad bellum is a distinct concept from *jus in bello*, but represents another historical approach to the regulation of war. *Jus ad bellum* refers to the conditions under which States are permitted to utilize war or armed force. An example is contained in the United Nations Charter, which requires that "[a]ll Members shall refrain in their international relations from the threat or use of force against the territorial integrity or political independence of any state, or in any other manner inconsistent with the Purposes of the United Nations," unless, for example, the Security Council has authorizes the use of force or the State is acting in self-defense. *See* UNITED NATIONS CHARTER, Articles 2, 39, 41–42, and 51. Are cyber attacks and information operations a "use of force?" If so, what types of cyber attacks or information operations would rise to a level significant enough to implicate the prohibitions and restrictions contained in the U.N. Charter? If a country suffered a cyber attack, would it be limited to defending itself through information operations or would it be permissible for the country to respond with a kinetic attack, such as launching air strikes or sending ground troops?

For extended discussion of the ways in which the crimes in the Rome Statute of the International Criminal Court—genocide, crimes against humanity, war crimes and the crime of aggression (a mixture of *jus ad bellum* and *jus in bello*)—can be committed by cyber attacks, see THE COUNCIL OF ADVISERS' REPORT ON THE APPLICATION OF THE ROME STATUTE OF THE INTERNATIONAL CRIMINAL COURT TO CYBERWARFARE (Prepared by the Government of Liechtenstein, August 2021).

Chapter 8

Narcotics and Money Laundering

§ 8.01 Jurisdiction for Narcotics Prosecutions

A. Statutory Interpretation

United States v. Larsen

United States Court of Appeals for the Ninth Circuit
952 F.2d 1099 (1991)

T.G. Nelson, Circuit Judge:

Charles Edward Larsen was convicted for his involvement in an international marijuana smuggling operation in violation of 18 U.S.C. §§ 2, 371, 1952(a)(3) and 21 U.S.C. §§ 841(a)(1), 846, 963, 952. Larsen challenges the legality of his conviction on numerous grounds, including the court's extraterritorial application of 21 U.S.C. § 841(a)(1). We affirm.

Larsen's conviction was based on evidence which established that he, along with codefendants and numerous other individuals, conspired to import shipments of Southeast Asian marijuana into the United States from 1985 to 1987, and to distribute the marijuana in the United States. The profits from these ventures were concealed by a fictitious partnership created by the defendant and others. This partnership was used to purchase the shipping vessel intended to transport the marijuana. During some of the smuggling operations, Larsen served as captain of the vessel.

Under Count Eight, Larsen was convicted of aiding and abetting codefendant Walter Ulrich in the crime of knowing and intentional possession with intent to distribute marijuana in violation of 21 U.S.C. § 841(a)(1). The marijuana was seized by customs inspectors from a ship on the high seas outside of Singapore. Larsen claims that the district court erred when it denied his motion to dismiss Count Eight because 21 U.S.C. § 841(a)(1) does not have extraterritorial jurisdiction. A district court's jurisdiction is a matter of law, and reviewed de novo. . . .

Congress is empowered to attach extraterritorial effect to its penal statutes so long as the statute does not violate the due process clause of the Fifth Amendment. . . . There is a presumption against extraterritorial application when a statute is silent on the matter. . . . However, this court has given extraterritorial effect to penal statutes when Congressional intent to do so is clear. . . . Since 21 U.S.C. § 841(a)(1) is silent about its extraterritorial application we are "faced with finding the construction that Congress intended." . . .

The Supreme Court has explained that to limit the *locus* of some offenses "to the strictly territorial jurisdiction would be greatly to curtail the scope and usefulness of the statute and leave open a large immunity for frauds as easily committed by citizens on the high seas and in foreign countries as at home." *United States v. Bowman*, [§ 3.01] Congressional intent to attach extraterritorial application "'may be inferred from the nature of the offenses and Congress' other legislative efforts to eliminate the type of crime involved.'" . . .

Until now, the Ninth Circuit has not applied this "intent of congress/nature of the offense test" to 21 U.S.C. § 841(a)(1); however, four other circuits have. They all held that Congress did intend the statute to have extraterritorial effect.

The Fifth Circuit held that Congress intended that 841(a)(1) have extraterritorial effect because it was a part of the Comprehensive Drug Abuse Prevention and Control Act of 1970, and the power to control illegal drug trafficking on the high seas was an essential incident to Congress' intent to halt drug abuse in the United States. . . .

The Third Circuit held that Congressional intent to apply 841(a)(1) extraterritorially could be implied because "Congress undoubtedly intended to prohibit conspiracies to [distribute] controlled substances into the United States . . . as part of its continuing effort to contain the evils caused on American soil by foreign as well as domestic suppliers of illegal narcotics. . . . To deny such use of the criminal provisions 'would be greatly to curtail the scope and usefulness of the statute[ ].'" . . .

The First Circuit concluded that the district court had jurisdiction over a crime committed on the high seas in violation of 841(a)(1) because "[a] sovereign may exercise jurisdiction over acts done outside its geographical jurisdiction which are intended to produce detrimental effects within it." . . .

The Second Circuit similarly held that "because section 841(a)(1) properly applies to schemes to distribute controlled substances within the United States," its extraterritorial application was proper. . . . .

Extraterritorial application of a drug possession/distribution statute comports with the reasoning behind the Supreme Court's *Bowman* decision, since such a statute is "not logically dependent on [its] locality for the Government's jurisdiction, but [was] enacted because of the right of the government to defend itself against obstruction, or fraud wherever perpetrated" and "it would be going too far to say that because Congress does not fix any locus it intended to exclude the high seas in respect of this crime." . . .

Defendant claims that Congress intended to limit section 841(a)(1) to only territorial crimes, as demonstrated by its later enactment of 21 U.S.C. § 955(a), recodified at 46 U.S.C. § 1903, which expressly confers jurisdiction over the high seas in cases dealing with controlled substance possession and distribution. Defendant implies that in providing a separate statute which expressly governs the high seas, Congress acknowledged that the former statute did not.

If the two statutes had precisely the same provisions, beyond the extraterritoriality issue, defendant's argument might have some merit. However, there are other differences between the statutes that can explain Congress' intent in enacting § 1903. For example, § 1903 does not require *intent* to distribute, as does § 841(a)(1). Recognizing this, the Second Circuit held that Congress did not enact § 1903 to fill a void left by the silence in § 841(a)(1) as to its extraterritorial effect but, rather, to extend drug possession/distribution laws to those cases where it was not possible to show intent to distribute....

Furthermore, as the Eleventh Circuit pointed out in a case dealing with a related matter, there is an enhanced penalty available for crimes charged under § 841(a)(1) which is not available under 1903....

Larsen cites to a passing reference in *Hayes* [653 F.2d 8, 15–16 (1st Cir. 1981)] which stated that Congress accepted the views of representatives from the Department of Justice and the DEA who testified that the Comprehensive Drug Abuse Prevention and Control Act of 1970 did not apply to American ships on the high seas. While the *Hayes* court acknowledged that some might conclude that § 841(a)(1) does not apply extraterritorially because of this Congressional testimony, the court nevertheless held that § 841(a)(1) did have extraterritorial application....

In affirming Larsen's conviction, we now join the First, Second, Third, and Fifth Circuit Courts in finding that 21 U.S.C. § 841(a)(1) has extraterritorial jurisdiction. We hold that Congress' intent can be implied because illegal drug trafficking, which the statute is designed to prevent, regularly involves importation of drugs from international sources.

AFFIRMED.

United States v. Lopez-Vanegas

United States Court of Appeals for the Eleventh Circuit
493 F.3d 1305 (2007)

WALTER, DISTRICT JUDGE:

Doris Mangeri Salazar ("Salazar") and Ivan Lopez-Vanegas ("Lopez") appeal their convictions on one count each of conspiracy to possess with the intent to distribute five kilograms or more of a mixture and substance containing cocaine, in violation of 21 U.S.C. §§ 841(a)(1) and (b)(1)(A)(ii), and 21 U.S.C. § 846. The Government alleged that Salazar and Lopez brokered a deal between a Colombian drug trafficking organization headed by Juan Gabriel Usuga ("Usuga") and a Saudi Arabian Prince, Nayef Al-Shaalan (the "Prince"), to transport cocaine on the Prince's airplane from Caracas, Venezuela to Paris, France, for distribution in Europe....

Appellants assert that the agreement to ship cocaine from Colombia to Venezuela to Saudi Arabia to France for distribution throughout Europe does not violate 21 U.S.C. § 846 because the object of the conspiracy-the possession and distribution of cocaine on foreign soil-is not a violation of 21 U.S.C. § 841(a)(1). Thus, the district court should have granted defendants' motion for acquittal at the close of the Government's case. The Government asserts that the defendants' conduct was encompassed by the prohibitions of 21 U.S.C. § 846 and § 841(a)(1), forbidding conspiracy to possess with intent to distribute cocaine. The issue of whether discussions occurring in the United States[a] related to possession of controlled substances outside of the United States with intent to distribute those substances outside of the United States is a crime in the United States is res nova in the Eleventh Circuit. We squarely address that issue now.

Title 21 U.S.C. § 841(a)(1), in conjunction with § 846, makes it unlawful for any person to conspire to possess with the intent to distribute a controlled substance, such as cocaine. Neither statute expressly requires that possession, distribution nor an act in furtherance of the conspiracy occur in the United States. A silent statute is presumed to apply only domestically. *Small v. United States*, 544 U.S. 385. Such statutes may be given extraterritorial application if the nature of the law permits it *and* Congress intends it. *United States v. Baker*, 609 F.2d 134, 136 (5th Cir. 1980). "Absent an express intention on the face of the statutes to do so, the exercise of that power may be inferred from the nature of the offenses and Congress' other legislative efforts to eliminate the type of crime involved." . . . The United States Supreme Court explained the issues involved with a statute silent as to its extraterritorial application: . . . *United States v. Bowman*, [§ 3.01].

Our case law, and that of our sister circuits, has applied § 841(a)(1) and § 846 extraterritorially in certain circumstances, even though Congress has not specifically expressed its intent on the matter. . . . However, in each of those cases some other nexus to the United States allowed for extraterritorial application of § 841(a)(1): defendants either possessed or conspired to possess controlled substances within the United States, or intended to distribute controlled substances within the United States. Our predecessor Court made clear in *Baker* that § 841(a)(1) does not apply to possession outside United States territory unless the possessor intends to distribute the contraband within the United States. . . . Furthermore, there can be no violation of § 846 if the object of the conspiracy is not a violation of the substantive offense. 21 U.S.C. § 846 . . . . Accordingly, where, as here, the object of the conspiracy was to possess controlled substances outside the United States with the intent to distribute outside the United States, there is no violation of § 841(a)(1) or § 846.

Further, Congress has shown it is capable of addressing acts involving controlled substances occurring outside of the United States, and has shown it thinks it necessary to make specific provisions in the law that allow the locus to include acts of manufacture or distribution of controlled substances on foreign soil when there is an intent to unlawfully import such substances or chemicals into the United States. *See e.g.*, 21 U.S.C. § 959. In 21 U.S.C. § 959, Congress specifically stated that the statute

a. The accused met in Miami, apparently to discuss the transaction. — Eds.

"is intended to reach acts of manufacture or distribution committed outside the territorial jurisdiction of the United States." 21 U.S.C. § 959. Under 21 U.S.C. §§ 841 and 846, Congress has not stated its intent to reach discussions held in the United States in furtherance of a conspiracy to *possess* controlled substances *outside* the territorial jurisdiction of the United States, with intent to *distribute* those controlled substances *outside* of the territorial jurisdiction of the United States.

Because the Court holds that 21 U.S.C. §§ 841 and 846 do not apply extraterritorially, the conduct of Lopez and Salazar does not violate those statutes. The judgments of conviction and sentences issued by the district court are vacated.

Notes

(1) Would the defendant's extraterritorial arguments in *Larsen* and *Lopez-Vanegas* be even stronger today in light of the Court's decisions in *Morrison* [§ 5.02] and *RJR Nabisco* [§ 3.02]? Consider *United States v. Sitzmann*, 893 F.3d 811, 822–23 (D.C. Cir. 2018), a case contesting the extraterritorial application of 21 U.S.C. §§ 841 and 846 that applies these Supreme Court decisions:

> Sitzmann first contends that the District Court "lacked jurisdiction" over evidence introduced at trial that he smuggled drugs into Europe between 2001 and 2004, including his 2004 arrest in France for illegal importation of narcotics. . . . He thus argues that the trial judge erred in permitting the Government to present evidence of his extraterritorial drug activities at trial. Sitzmann claims this was an error because the sole object of those foreign drug activities was to possess and distribute controlled substances outside of the United States. He further argues that there is no indication that 21 U.S.C. § 841(a)(1) and § 846, the statutes under which he was convicted, apply to conduct that occurred on foreign soil.
>
> "It is a longstanding principle of American law 'that legislation of Congress, unless a contrary intent appears, is meant to apply only within the territorial jurisdiction of the United States.'" *EEOC v. Arabian Am. Oil Co.*, 499 U.S. 244, 248 (1991) . . . . In *Morrison v. National Australia Bank Ltd.*, the Supreme Court established a two-step framework for determining issues involving the extraterritorial application of statutes. . . . The Court recently described the two-step inquiry as follows:
>
> > At the first step, we ask whether the presumption against extraterritoriality has been rebutted — that is, whether the statute gives a clear, affirmative indication that it applies extraterritorially. . . . If the statute is not extraterritorial, then at the second step we determine whether the case involves a domestic application of the statute, and we do this by looking to the statute's "focus." If the conduct relevant to the statute's focus occurred in the United States, then the case involves a permissible domestic application even if other conduct occurred abroad; but if the conduct relevant to the focus occurred in a foreign country, then the case

> involves an impermissible extraterritorial application regardless of any other conduct that occurred in U.S. territory.

RJR Nabisco, Inc. v. European Cmty., 136 S.Ct. 2090, 2101 (2016).

> Against this backdrop, we first consider whether 21 U.S.C. § 841(a)(1) and § 846 may apply to conduct that occurred outside of the United States. Read together, § 841(a)(1) and § 846 make it unlawful for "any person" to conspire to distribute or possess with the intent to distribute a controlled substance, such as cocaine. Neither § 841(a)(1) nor § 846 provides a "clear indication" of applying extraterritorially. . . . The presumption against extraterritoriality therefore applies.
>
> Our analysis, however, does not end there. At the second step, we find that "the conduct relevant to the statute[s'] focus occurred in the United States." *RJR Nabisco*, 136 S.Ct. at 2101. The evidence showed that Sitzmann entered the conspiratorial agreement in the United States, smuggled cocaine into and out of the United States, and engaged in other activity in the United States in furtherance of the conspiracy. Therefore, this "case involves a permissible domestic application" of § 841(a)(1) and § 846 "even if other conduct occurred abroad." Accordingly, we reject Sitzmann's claim.

(2) Statutes concerning drug offenses often receive extraterritorial application. For example, in *United States v. Valenzuela*, 849 F.3d 477 (1st Cir. 2017), the court considered extraterritoriality with a statute that did not expressly provide for an extraterritorial application. The court then looked to see whether there was a domestic base to allow the prosecution to proceed. Distinguishing *Lopez-Vanegas*, *supra*, the court stated, "there was sufficient evidence for a jury to find that this was not an entirely 'international' drug distribution scheme which, but for the meetings in the United States, would have had no connection to the country."

(3) In some cases, the statute may specifically include language of extraterritoriality. For example, 21 U.S.C. § 959 provides for extraterritoriality within the statute as follows:

> § 959. Possession, manufacture or distribution of controlled substance
>
> (a) Manufacture or distribution for purpose of unlawful importation
>
> It shall be unlawful for any person to manufacture or distribute a controlled substance in schedule I or II or flunitrazepam or a listed chemical intending, knowing, or having reasonable cause to believe that such substance or chemical will be unlawfully imported into the United States or into waters within a distance of 12 miles of the coast of the United States.
>
> (b) Manufacture or distribution of listed chemical for purpose of manufacture or unlawful importation of controlled substance
>
> It shall be unlawful for any person to manufacture or distribute a listed chemical—

(1) intending or knowing that the listed chemical will be used to manufacture a controlled substance; and

(2) intending, knowing, or having reasonable cause to believe that the controlled substance will be unlawfully imported into the United States.

(c) Possession, manufacture, or distribution by person on board aircraft

It shall be unlawful for any United States citizen on board any aircraft, or any person on board an aircraft owned by a United States citizen or registered in the United States, to—

(1) manufacture or distribute a controlled substance or listed chemical; or

(2) possess a controlled substance or listed chemical with intent to distribute.

(d) Acts committed outside territorial jurisdiction of United States

This section is intended to reach acts of manufacture or distribution committed outside the territorial jurisdiction of the United States.

(4) Who decides jurisdiction questions? Are these questions of law or fact? Compare § 1.13 of the Model Penal Code which includes jurisdiction and venue within the Code's definition of "element of an offense" with the following in the Maritime Drug Law Enforcement Act (MDLEA):

(a) Jurisdiction of the United States with respect to a vessel subject to this chapter is not an element of any offense. All jurisdictional issues arising under this chapter are preliminary questions of law to be determined solely by the trial judge.

46 U.S.C. § 70504.

B. Constitutional Issues

United States v. Bellaizac-Hurtado

United States Court of Appeals for the Eleventh Circuit
700 F.3d 1245 (2012)

PRYOR, CIRCUIT JUDGE:

This appeal presents a novel issue about the scope of congressional power to proscribe conduct abroad: whether the Maritime Drug Law Enforcement Act, 46 U.S.C. §§ 70503(a), 70506,[b] exceeds the power of Congress to "define and punish . . . Offences against the Law of Nations," U.S. Const. Art. I, § 8, cl. 10, as applied to the drug-trafficking activities of Yimmi Bellaizac-Hurtado, Pedro Felipe Angulo-Rodallega, Albeiro Gonzalez-Valois, and Luis Carlos Riascos-Hurtado in the territorial waters of Panama. Because we conclude that drug trafficking is not an "Offence[] against

b. The MDLEA provisions in question include within their ambit drug trafficking not only on the high seas, but also on "a vessel in the territorial waters of a foreign sovereign if the nation consents to the enforcement of United States law by the United States."—Eds.

the Law of Nations" and that Congress cannot constitutionally proscribe the defendants' conduct under the Offences Clause, we vacate their convictions.

I. Background

During a routine patrol of Panamanian waters in 2010, the United States Coast Guard observed a wooden fishing vessel operating without lights and without a flag. The Coast Guard informed the Panamanian National Aero-Naval Service of the vessel. The Panamanian Navy pursued the vessel until its occupants abandoned the vessel and fled into a jungle. When members of the Panamanian Navy searched the vessel the next morning, they discovered approximately 760 kilograms of cocaine. The Panamanian National Frontier Service searched on land for the occupants of the abandoned vessel and arrested Bellaizac-Hurtado, Angulo-Rodallega, Gonzalez-Valois, and Riascos-Hurtado in various locations on the beach and in the jungle. After an exchange of diplomatic notes, the Foreign Ministry of the Republic of Panama consented to the prosecution of the four suspects in the United States.

A federal grand jury indicted Bellaizac-Hurtado, Angulo-Rodallega, Gonzalez-Valois, and Riascos-Hurtado for conspiracy to possess with intent to distribute five kilograms or more of cocaine, and for actual possession with intent to distribute five kilograms or more of cocaine, on board a vessel subject to the jurisdiction of the United States. The defendants moved to dismiss the indictment "based upon the lack of jurisdiction and the unconstitutionality of the Maritime Drug Law Enforcement Act as applied to [their] conduct." A magistrate judge recommended that the motion be denied. The magistrate judge reasoned that the district court had jurisdiction because the defendants were operating a stateless vessel and that the Act was constitutional as applied because Congress and several courts had determined that drug trafficking was "universally condemned" by various nations with "reasonably developed" legal systems. The district court adopted the magistrate judge's report. The district court also explained that section 70505 of the Act "limits the actors that have standing to challenge the validity of an MDLEA prosecution on international law grounds."

The defendants conditionally pleaded guilty to the conspiracy charge. The district court sentenced Bellaizac-Hurtado to imprisonment for 90 months, supervised release for five years, and a $100 fine; Angulo-Rodallega to imprisonment for 36 months, supervised release for two years, and a $100 fine; Gonzalez-Valois to imprisonment for 36 months, supervised release for two years, and a $100 fine; and Riascos-Hurtado to imprisonment for 25 months, supervised release for two years, and a $100 fine. The defendants appealed their convictions on the ground that the Act, as applied, exceeded the power of Congress under Article I, Section 8, Clause 10. We consolidated their appeals....

III. Discussion

The United States argues that the Maritime Drug Law Enforcement Act, as applied to the defendants, is a constitutional exercise of the power granted to

Congress "[t]o define and punish Piracies and Felonies committed on the high Seas, and Offences against the Law of Nations." U.S. Const., Art. I, § 8, cl. 10. The Supreme Court has interpreted that Clause to contain three distinct grants of power: the power to define and punish piracies, the power to define and punish felonies committed on the high seas, and the power to define and punish offenses against the law of nations. *See United States v. Smith,* 18 U.S. (5 Wheat.) 153, 158–59, 5 L. Ed. 57 (1820). The first two grants of power are not implicated here: piracy is, by definition, robbery on the high seas, *United States v. Furlong,* 18 U.S. (5 Wheat.) 184, 198, 5 L. Ed. 64 (1820), and the Felonies Clause is textually limited to conduct on the high seas, *see* U.S. Const., Art. I, § 8, cl. 10. The United States relies instead on the third grant—the Offences Clause—as the source of congressional power to proscribe the defendants' drug trafficking in the territorial waters of Panama. The question whether Congress has the power under the Offences Clause to proscribe drug trafficking in the territorial waters of another nation is an issue of first impression in our Court.

A. Customary International Law Limits the Power of Congress to Define and Punish Crimes Under the Offences Clause.

The power granted to Congress in the Offences Clause is limited by customary international law for two reasons. First, the related Supreme Court precedent and the text, history, and structure of the Constitution confirm that the power to "define" is limited by the law of nations. Second, the phrase "Offences against the Law of Nations" is understood today to mean violations of customary international law....

B. Because Drug Trafficking Is Not a Violation of Customary International Law, Congress Lacks the Power to Proscribe Drug Trafficking Under the Offences Clause.

The text of the Offences Clause does not resolve the question whether it limits the power of Congress to define and punish only those violations of customary international law that were established at the Founding or whether the power granted under the Clause expands and contracts with changes in customary international law. The Supreme Court has not resolved the issue in either of the two cases in which it upheld federal statutes as a constitutional exercise of the power granted under the Offences Clause. *See Ex Parte Quirin,* 317 U.S. 1, 27–28. In both cases, the Court explained that the conduct at issue had been condemned as a violation of the law of nations since the time of the Founding. Scholars have long debated whether the Offences Clause is affected by the later development of customary international law....

We need not decide whether the power granted to Congress under the Offences Clause changes with the evolution of customary international law because, under either approach, the result is the same. Drug trafficking was not a violation of customary international law at the time of the Founding, and drug trafficking is not a violation of customary international law today.

1. Drug Trafficking Was Not a Violation of the Law of Nations During the Founding Period.

When the Constitution was ratified, the range of conduct that could be viewed as a violation of customary international law was even more limited than it is today.... Drug trafficking was not a matter of international concern in 1789, let alone a violation of customary international law. Vattel's *Law of Nations* contains no references to narcotics, opium, or drug trafficking. And the international community did not even begin its efforts to limit the drug trade until the turn of the twentieth century. As the United Nations Office on Drugs and Crime has observed, "[p]rior to the 1909 Shanghai Opium Commission, national governments and state-sponsored monopolies played an active role in peddling opium across borders. The profits to be made were enormous, generating as much as half of the national revenues of some island states serving as redistribution centres." United Nations Office on Drugs and Crime, *A Century of International Drug Control* 7 (2008). Because violations of customary international law during the Founding Period were so limited, and narcotics then were not even a subject of international concern, we cannot conclude that drug trafficking was an offense against the law of nations when the Constitution was ratified.

2. Drug Trafficking Is Not a Violation of Customary International Law Today.

Drug trafficking is also not a violation of contemporary customary international law. Although a number of specially affected States—States that benefit financially from the drug trade—have ratified treaties that address drug trafficking, they have failed to comply with the requirements of those treaties, and the international community has not treated drug trafficking as a violation of contemporary customary international law. Scholars also agree that drug trafficking is not a violation of contemporary customary international law.

The United States argues that the widespread ratification of the 1988 United Nations Convention Against Illicit Traffic in Narcotic Drugs and Psychotropic Substances establishes that drug trafficking violates a norm of customary international law, but we disagree. Treaties may constitute evidence of customary international law, but "will only constitute *sufficient proof* of a norm of customary international law if an overwhelming majority of States have ratified the treaty, *and* those States uniformly and consistently act in accordance with its principles." *Flores,* 414 F.3d at 256. "Of course, States need not be universally successful in implementing the principle in order for a rule of international law to arise.... But the principle must be more than merely professed or aspirational." *Id.* at 248. And as the International Court of Justice has explained, a customary international law norm will not form if specially affected States have not consented to its development through state practice consistent with the proposed norm. *North Sea Continental Shelf Cases* (Fed. Republic of Ger. v. Den.; Fed. Republic of Ger. v. Neth.), 1969 I.C.J. 3, 43 (Feb. 20).

The 1988 Convention was ratified by an overwhelming majority of States and currently has 188 States Parties, U.N. Treaty Collection Database, but the drug trade continues to flourish in many specially affected States despite their ratification of the Convention. In 2011, the President of the United States designated 21 of these States Parties as "major drug transit or major illicit drug producing countries." . . .

The practice of these specially affected States evidences that drug trafficking is not yet considered a violation of customary international law. Governments corrupted by the interests of drug traffickers are not simply unable to prosecute drug traffickers, but are often unwilling to do so because their economies are dependent upon the drug trade. . . . The persistent failure of these specially affected States to comply with their treaty obligations suggests that they view the curtailment of drug trafficking as an aspirational goal, not a matter of mutual legal obligation under customary international law.

The international community has also distinguished drug trafficking from established violations of customary international law in its efforts to combat drug trafficking. Comparing the 1988 Drug Convention with the Genocide Convention is instructive. Article 2 of the 1988 Drug Convention described drug trafficking as conduct "having an international dimension." Convention Against Illicit Traffic in Narcotic Drugs and Psychotropic Substances, art. 2(1), Dec. 19, 1988, 1582 U.N.T.S. 95, 28 I.L.M. 497. But Article 1 of the Genocide Convention defined genocide as a "crime under international law." Convention on the Prevention and Punishment of the Crime of Genocide, art. 1, Dec. 9, 1948, 78 U.N.T.S. 277, 280. And, unlike genocide, the international community has addressed drug trafficking at the domestic, instead of international, level. The 1988 Drug Convention, for example, relied on domestic enforcement mechanisms to combat drug trafficking and prohibited States Parties from interfering in the domestic enforcement efforts of other States Parties. Convention Against Illicit Traffic in Narcotic Drugs and Psychotropic Substances, art. 2, art. 3(1), Dec. 19, 1988, 1582 U.N.T.S. 95, 28 I.L.M. 497. By contrast, the Genocide Convention provided for trial by international tribunals, in addition to domestic tribunals, and permitted States Parties to appeal to the United Nations to take further action to prevent and suppress genocide. Convention on the Prevention and Punishment of the Crime of Genocide, art. 6, art. 8, Dec. 9, 1948, 78 U.N.T.S. 277, 280.

The drafters of the Rome Statute, which established the International Criminal Court, considered and rejected a proposal to make drug trafficking a crime within the jurisdiction of the court. Johan David Michels, *Keeping Dealers Off the Docket: The Perils of Prosecuting Serious Drug-Related Offences at the International Criminal Court,* 21 Fla. J. Int'l L. 449, 450 (2009). The negotiators of the Rome Statute repeatedly referred to drug crimes as "treaty crimes" only, in contrast to genocide, war crimes, and crimes against humanity, which are violations of customary international law. U.N. Diplomatic Conference of Plenipotentiaries on the Establishment of an International Criminal Court, A/CONF.183/2 at 172, 176–78, 278 (June 15–July 17, 1998).

Scholars who have considered the status of drug trafficking in international law agree too that it is not a violation of customary international law. Antonio Cassesse, a noted international criminal law scholar, has explained, for example, that drug trafficking is not an international crime because it is not a crime under customary international law and is not a matter of mutual concern.... "Uniform condemnation and criminalization does not make something an international crime. Murder and rape, and indeed, most malum in se offenses, are also universally condemned, and all fall outside of international law." Eugene Kontorovich, *Beyond the Article I Horizon: Congress's Enumerated Powers and Universal Jurisdiction over Drug Crimes,* 93 MINN. L. REV. 1191, 1226 (2009)....

The United States argues that this appeal is controlled by our decision in *United States v. Saac,* 632 F.3d 1203 (11th Cir. 2011), but we disagree. In *Saac,* we considered a constitutional challenge to the Drug Trafficking Vessel Interdiction Act, which provides for the punishment of any person who "knowingly operates ... or embarks in any submersible vessel or semi-submersible vessel that is without nationality" on the high seas "with the intent to evade detection." 18 U.S.C. § 2285(a). In *Saac,* we held that Congress had the authority, under the High Seas Clause, to prohibit this conduct. 632 F.3d at 1210–11. We did not hold that drug trafficking was an "Offence against the Law of Nations." Instead, we held that Congress had the authority under the High Seas Clause to punish the operation of these stateless vessels. *Saac* is inapposite.

Moreover, none of our earlier precedents about the extraterritorial application of our drug trafficking laws have answered the constitutional question presented in this appeal. Indeed, all of the appeals in which we have considered the constitutionality of those laws involved conduct on the high seas.... Congress possesses additional constitutional authority to restrict conduct on the high seas, including the Piracies Clause, U.S. Const., Art. I, § 8, cl. 10; the Felonies Clause, *id.*; and the admiralty power, *United States v. Flores,* 289 U.S. 137 (1933). And we have always upheld extraterritorial convictions under our drug trafficking laws as an exercise of power under the Felonies Clause. *See Estupinan,* 453 F.3d at 1339 ("[W]e readily hold that the district court committed no error in failing to *sua sponte* rule that Congress exceeded its authority under the Piracies and Felonies Clause in enacting the [Maritime Drug Law Enforcement Act]."). But we have never held that Congress has the power, under the Offences Clause, to apply our drug trafficking laws to conduct in the territorial waters of another State.

Judge Barkett argues in her special concurrence that we should decide this appeal on the ground that drug trafficking is not an offense of universal jurisdiction and, as a result, Congress may not punish the defendants' conduct under the Offences Clause, but that reasoning raises issues that we need not decide.... We need not decide whether the Constitution imposes any limit on the power of Congress to violate international law. *Cf. United States v. Pinto-Mejia,* 720 F.2d 248, 259 (2d Cir. 1983) ("[I]n enacting statutes, Congress is not bound by international law. If it chooses to do so, it may legislate with respect to conduct outside the United States, in excess of the limits posed by international law. As long as Congress has expressly indicated its intent to reach such conduct, a United States court would be bound to follow the Congressional direction unless this would violate the due process clause of the Fifth Amendment." . . . And we need not decide whether international law would permit the exercise of prescriptive jurisdiction by the United States over a stateless vessel in territorial waters when, as here, the sovereign of those waters has consented to that jurisdiction. . . .

Because drug trafficking is not a violation of customary international law, we hold that Congress exceeded its power, under the Offences Clause, when it proscribed the defendants' conduct in the territorial waters of Panama. And the United States has not offered us any alternative ground upon which the Act could be sustained as constitutional. As applied to these defendants, the Act is unconstitutional, and we must vacate their convictions.

Notes

(1) Notice the casual reference in the opinion to a "routine patrol of Panamanian waters." The patrol by the United States Coast Guard apparently took place pursuant to an Executive Agreement entitled *Supplementary Arrangement Between the Government of the United States of America and the Government of the Republic of Panama to the Arrangement Between the Government of the United States of America and the Government of Panama for Support and Assistance from the United States Coast Guard for the National Maritime Service of the Ministry of Government and Justice*, signed at Panama City, Panama, 5 February 2002, in force on the same date, *available at* https://www.state.gov/02-205-1. No reference is made to this agreement in the opinions in the Eleventh Circuit or in the arguments to the Court. The preamble to the 2002 Arrangement recalls all the major drug treaties and the 1982 United Nations Convention on the Law of the Sea. It refers in particular to Article 17 of the 1988 Convention Against Illicit Traffic in Narcotic Drugs and Psychotropic Substances, which is discussed in the Notes to § 3.04[C] *supra*. Article XI.2 of the Arrangement provides:

> In all cases arising in a Party's waters, or concerning vessels registered in or flying the flag of a Party seaward of any State's territorial sea, that Party ("the first party") shall have the right to exercise jurisdiction over a detained vessel, cargo and/or persons on board (including seizure, forfeiture, arrest and prosecution), provided, however, the first Party may, subject to its Constitution and laws, waive its right to exercise jurisdiction over and authorize the enforcement of the other Party's law against the vessel, cargo and/or persons on board. . . .

Is this a case of what we have called "transferred jurisdiction" in § 3.04[C]? Should the Government have argued that the legislation could be upheld under the treaty power and the "necessary and proper" power in the Constitution? The constitutional issue is of great significance, as the United States is a party to numerous other agreements containing almost identical language with countries in the Caribbean and Central America.

(2) Following the court's decision in *United States v. Bellaizac-Hurtado, supra*, the government then argued that the MDLEA as applied could be a valid exercise of Congress's authority under the Foreign Commerce Clause. Rejecting this position in *United States v. Davila-Mendoza*, 972 F.3d 1264 (11th Cir. 2020), the Eleventh Circuit stated:

> With this framework in mind, we turn to the question of whether the MDLEA as applied to the defendants' conduct in this case is a valid exercise of Congress's authority under the Foreign Commerce Clause to regulate those activities that have a "substantial effect" on the commerce of the United States "with foreign nations." U.S. Const. art. I, § 8, cl. 3. The government maintains the *Baston/Raich* framework requires us to conclude that the application of the MDLEA to the wholly foreign conduct in this case was a valid exercise of Congress's authority. *Baston*, however, is factually distinguishable. [*United States v. Baston*, 818 F.3d 651, 668 (11th Cir. 2016).]
>
> First, *Baston* involved statutory provisions enacted as part of the TVPA, "a comprehensive regulatory scheme" that included specific congressional findings "that trafficking of persons has an aggregate economic impact on interstate and foreign commerce." . . .
>
> Although the government argues that, similar to the TVPA, the MDLEA is a comprehensive regulatory scheme designed to combat a global problem (in this case, drug trafficking), the MDLEA does not contain any congressional findings regarding international drug trafficking's effect on United States commerce "with foreign nations." See 46 U.S.C. § 70501. The law mentions only that "trafficking in controlled substances aboard vessels is a serious international problem" and that it "presents a specific threat to the security and societal well-being of the United States[.]" 46 U.S.C. § 70501. It does not include any findings on the existence or extent of an economic impact, aggregate or otherwise, of the international drug trade on United States commerce with foreign nations. . . .
>
> Second, the statutes at issue in *Baston*, 18 U.S.C. §§ 1591(a) and 1596(a)(2) required both an effect on foreign commerce as an element of the offense and a physical connection to the United States. . . . The MDLEA does not contain a similar "in or affecting interstate or foreign commerce" element. See 46 U.S.C. §§ 70502(c), 70503.
>
> Additionally, and more importantly, although not a focal point of the analysis in *Baston* (but certainly a critical factual distinction when compared to the case at hand), under § 1596(a) the United States has jurisdiction over the extraterritorial sex-trafficking conduct only if the defendant is "a national of the United States," "an alien lawfully admitted for permanent residence," or otherwise "present in the United States, irrespective of the nationality of the alleged offender." See 18 U.S.C. § 1596(a). Thus, § 1596 provides a jurisdictional hook that precludes purely foreign activity

> with no nexus to the United States from being criminalized. In contrast, the MDLEA does not contain a similar jurisdictional hook or nexus to tie wholly foreign extraterritorial conduct to the United States.
>
> Furthermore, the facts in *Baston* demonstrated that the defendant's activities were so thoroughly intertwined with the United States's commerce with foreign nations that the issue was not a close call....
>
> Indeed, under the government's reasoning, nothing would prevent Congress from globally policing wholly foreign drug trafficking commerce, potentially intruding on the sovereignty of other Nations, and bringing foreign nationals into the United States for prosecution based solely on extraterritorial conduct when the United States was neither a party to, nor a target of, the commerce.... Accordingly, for the reasons set forth above, as applied to these defendants, the MDLEA is unconstitutional and exceeded Congress's authority under the Foreign Commerce Clause.

The court also rejected the government's argument that "the MDLEA's application to this case is a valid exercise of Congress's authority pursuant to Article I's Necessary and Proper Clause to enforce the 1989 Convention Against Illicit Traffic Treaty and the 1997 Jamaica Bilateral Agreement between the United States and Jamaica." The Court stated:

> But the MDLEA was enacted long before the Convention against Illicit Traffic Treaty or the Jamaica Bilateral Agreement; therefore, it was not *enacted* pursuant to the Necessary and Proper Clause *to effectuate* those international agreements. And the government has not provided us with any case in which legislation has been upheld as necessary and proper for carrying into execution a treaty which did not yet exist at the time the legislation was enacted. *Cf. United States v. Lara*, 541 U.S. 193, 201, (2004) ("The treaty power does not literally authorize Congress to act legislatively, for it is an Article II power authorizing the President, not Congress, 'to make Treaties.'" (quoting U.S. Const. art. II, § 2, cl. 2)). Moreover, "nothing in the legislative history of MDLEA mentions a treaty or intimates that the legislation is in compliance with treaty obligations." *United States v. Cardales-Luna*, 632 F.3d 731, 749 (1st Cir. 2011) (Torruella, J., dissenting). Similarly, "[n]o court decision dealing with [the] MDLEA refers to any treaty obligation as the source of Congress's Article I authority." *Id.* Accordingly, we do not find that, as applied to these defendants, the MDLEA was a valid exercise of Congress's authority under the Necessary and Proper Clause to effectuate the subsequently enacted Illicit Traffic Treaty or the Jamaica Bilateral Agreement.

What can Congress do now? Could it re-enact the jurisdictional statute, relying specifically on the international agreements and the treaty/necessary and proper powers?

(3) In *United States v. Suerte*, 291 F.3d 366 (5th Cir. 2002), the Court considered a question also addressed by several others: whether, for the extraterritorial

application of the MDLEA, the Fifth Amendment's Due Process Clause requires a nexus between a foreign citizen and the United States, where the flag nation for a vessel on the high seas (Malta in this case) has consented or waived objection to the enforcement of United States law. The Court concluded:

> Enforcement of the MDLEA in these circumstances is neither arbitrary nor fundamentally unfair (the due process standard agreed upon by Suerte and the Government). Those subject to its reach are on notice. In addition to finding "that trafficking in controlled substances aboard vessels . . . presents a specific threat to the security and societal well-being of the United States", Congress has also found that such activity "is a serious *international* problem and is *universally* condemned". 46 U.S.C. App. § 1902 (emphasis added). Along this line, the United Nations Convention Against Illicit Traffic in Narcotic Drugs and Psychotropic Substances, *opened for signature* 20 Dec. 1988, 28 I.L.M. 493, to which Malta and the United States are signatories, provides as its purpose: "to promote cooperation among the Parties so that they may address more effectively the various aspects of illicit traffic in narcotic drugs and psychotropic substances having an international dimension". *Id.* art. 2.

§ 8.02 International Narcotics Trafficking

In addition to statutes with extraterritorial jurisdiction like those discussed in § 8.01, there are also statutes specifically focused on international narcotics trafficking. The Foreign Narcotics Kingpin Designation Act which went into effect in the United States on December 3, 1999, "provide[s] authority for the identification of, and application of sanctions on a worldwide basis to, significant foreign narcotics traffickers, their organizations, and the foreign persons who provide support to those significant foreign narcotics traffickers and their organizations, whose activities threaten the national security, foreign policy, and economy of the United States." *See* 18 U.S.C. § 1902. By late 2021, many hundreds of persons and entities had been included on the list. *See* https://home.treasury.gov/system/files/126/narco_sanctions_kingpin.pdf.

There are also international initiatives focused on narcotics trafficking. The conventions that form the cornerstone of curbing international narcotics trafficking are the Single Convention on Narcotics Drugs, March 30, 1961; the Convention on Psychotropic Substances, 21 February, 1971; the Protocol Amending the Single Convention on Narcotics Drugs, March 25, 1972; and the United Nations [Vienna] Convention Against Illicit Traffic in Narcotic Drugs and Psychotropic Substances, December 20, 1988. *See* Neil Boister, Penal Aspects of the UN Drug Conventions (2001); United Nations, Commentary on the United Nations

CONVENTION AGAINST ILLICIT TRAFFIC IN NARCOTIC DRUGS AND PSYCHOTROPIC SUBSTANCES 1988 (1998). The newer treaties do not always completely supersede the older ones, so the earlier ones retain significance in some areas. These conventions make elaborate provision for international cooperation in suppressing the traffic in illicit drugs. They allow parties to exercise extraterritorial jurisdiction over offenders who are "found" within their territory and whose extradition is refused; but, unlike recent anti-terrorism conventions [*see* chap. 9], do not make it mandatory to do so with respect to non-nationals. *See* M. CHERIF BASSIOUNI & EDWARD M. WISE, AUT DEDERE AUT JUDICARE: THE DUTY TO EXTRADITE OR PROSECUTE IN INTERNATIONAL LAW 14 (1995).

The United States Department of State's Bureau of International Narcotics and Law Enforcement Affairs (INL) is responsible for managing well over a billion dollars a year for narcotics control and anti-crime assistance to foreign countries. Consider the following from the Bureau's 2021 *International Narcotics Control Strategy Report,* (Vol. I, at 2–4) *available at* https://www.state.gov/wp-content/uploads/2021/02/International-Narcotics-Control-Strategy-Report-Volume-I-FINAL-1.pdf:

> In 2020, America's ongoing illicit drug crisis was compounded by the worst public health crisis in 100 years — the COVID-19 pandemic. After a slight decline in 2018, drug overdose deaths in the United States increased to over 72,000 in 2019, according to preliminary data from the U.S. Centers for Disease Control and Prevention (CDC). In the 12 months ending in May 2020, the CDC recorded over 81,000 drug overdose deaths, the highest number ever in a 12-month period, with the largest increases occurring at the same time that U.S. cases of COVID-19 exploded in March, April, and May of 2020. The pandemic not only magnified the lethal effects of drug use, but also hampered counter drug efforts as governments diverted resources to other public health needs. Among the highest numbers of lives lost to the virus were those of law enforcement first responders. Social distancing, economic hardship, quarantine efforts, and delayed medical care due to overloaded health systems reduced access to treatment for drug users. The pandemic also initially hindered criminal activity. Border closures and travel restrictions disrupted trafficking routes and precursor chemical supply chains. However, traffickers quickly adopted alternative routes and methods, and drug availability in many regions reached new historic highs by year's end. In Europe, demand for cocaine from South America increased, as seizures and demand for treatment remained at record levels. Methamphetamine production, trafficking, and use set new record levels in many regions, especially in Southeast Asia and parts of Africa and North America. New psychoactive substances (NPS) expanded to new markets, the most lethal forms of which were synthetic opioids that enabled criminals to avoid international controls. The United States contributed approximately $95 million in 2020 to alleviate pandemic-related threats to law

enforcement. This included provision of personal protective equipment in over 35 countries and support for infrastructure improvements to enable social distancing and improve safety—for example, by reducing prison overcrowding.

§ 8.03 Money Laundering

Money laundering serves as an integral aspect of drug trafficking. In the United States, the two key money laundering statutes are 18 U.S.C. § 1956 and 18 U.S.C. § 1957. These money laundering statutes were initially enacted "to prevent organized crime from concealing the proceeds of drug trafficking by converting 'cash into manageable form.'" *Trujillo v. Banco Central Del Ecuador*, 35 F. Supp. 2d 908, 913 (S.D. Fla. 1998). Section 1956 of title 18 allows for prosecution when funds are going into or outside the United States. 18 U.S.C. § 1956(a)(2) provides:

> (2) Whoever transports, transmits, or transfers, or attempts to transport, transmit, or transfer a monetary instrument or funds from a place in the United States to or through a place outside the United States or to a place in the United States from or through a place outside the United States—
>
> (A) with the intent to promote the carrying on of specified unlawful activity; or
>
> (B) knowing that the monetary instrument or funds involved in the transportation, transmission or transfer represent the proceeds of some form of unlawful activity and knowing that such transportation, transmission, or transfer is designed in whole or in part—
>
> (i) to conceal or disguise the nature, the location, the source, the ownership, or the control of the proceeds of specified unlawful activity; or
>
> (ii) to avoid a transaction reporting requirement under State or Federal law, shall be sentenced to a fine of not more than $ 500,000 or twice the value of the monetary instrument or funds involved in the transportation, transmission, or transfer, whichever is greater, or imprisonment for not more than twenty years, or both. For the purpose of the offense described in subparagraph (B), the defendant's knowledge may be established by proof that a law enforcement officer represented the matter specified in subparagraph (B) as true, and the defendant's subsequent statements or actions indicate that the defendant believed such representations to be true.

Both sections 1956 and 1957 provide for extraterritorial jurisdiction in limited circumstances.

Department of Justice Guidelines restrict prosecutors from individually making the decision to bring international prosecutions under sections 1956 and 1957. The Justice Manual, 9-105.300 provides:

> There are four categories of money laundering prosecutions which require prior authorization from the Criminal or Tax Division:
>
> 1. Extraterritorial Jurisdiction. Criminal Division (Asset Forfeiture & Money Laundering Section) (AFMLS) approval is required before the commencement of any investigation where jurisdiction to prosecute is based solely on the extraterritorial jurisdiction provisions of §§1956 and 1957. Due to the potential international sensitivities, as well as proof problems, involved in using these extraterritorial provisions, no grand jury investigation may be commenced, no indictment may be returned, and no complaint may be filed without the prior approval of AFMLS, Criminal Division when jurisdiction to prosecute these offenses exists only because of these extraterritorial provisions. . . .

In recent years money laundering has been extended beyond drug trafficking. *See United States v. Piervinanzi*, 23 F.3d 670 (2nd Cir. 1994) (defendant charged with international money laundering in alleged bank fraud scheme). One now finds money laundering charges in many white collar offenses. *See United States v. Powers*, 168 F.3d 741 (5th Cir. 1999).

Enormous sums of money can be involved in money laundering schemes. *See* Larry Neumeister, *Couple Admit Laundering Russian Money*, Feb. 17, 2000, ATL. J. CONST., at A8 (discussing the laundering of seven billion dollars). The prosecution of international money laundering schemes raises issues not only with respect to which country should serve as the law enforcer, but there can also be issues of which agency within the United States should be responsible for a prosecution. *See* Timothy L. O'Brien & Lowell Bergman, *Law-Enforcement Rivalry in U.S. Slowed Inquiry on Russian Funds*, Sept. 29, 1999, N.Y. TIMES, at A1 (discussing rivalries between the Manhattan DA and FBI New York office).

Outside the United States, there have been cooperative efforts in the international sphere to combat money laundering. William M. Hannay & John A. Hedges, *International Trends in the Criminalization of Money Laundering*, INTERNATIONAL TRADE: AVOIDING RISKS 5-12 to 5-22 (W. M. Hannay ed. 1991). For example, "[t]he United Nations Convention against Illicit Traffic in Narcotic Drugs and Psychotropic Substances, adopted in 1988 in Vienna, includes significant money laundering control measures." *Id.* at 5–15.

Likewise, the Financial Action Task Force (FATF) is an inter-governmental body in which 36 states and two international entities, the European Commission and the Gulf Co-operation Council, participate. It has as its purpose "the development and promotion of policies to combat money laundering." Between 1990 and 2003, the FATF issued forty recommendations that include recommendations on how to strengthen international cooperation. *See* FATF Recommendations, as revised most recently in October 2021, *available at* https://www.fatf-gafi.org/media/fatf/documents/recommendations/pdfs/FATF%20Recommendations%202012.pdf. Additional recommendations deal with terrorist financing and the financing of proliferation of weapons of mass destruction. Provisions on money laundering are also a significant feature of the United Nations Convention Against Transnational Organized Crime, adopted by G.A. Res. 55/25 (2000) and the United Nations Convention Against Corruption adopted by G.A. Res. 58/4 (2003). *See generally* William C. Gilmore, Dirty Money: The Evolution of Money Laundering Countermeasures, (2d ed. 1999).

On May 16, 2005, the Council of Europe opened for signature and ratification its Convention on Laundering, Search, Seizure and Confiscation of the Proceeds from Crime and the Financing of Terrorism. The Convention came into force on May 1, 2008, when it had six ratifications. By late 2021, it had 31 parties. The United States, which is eligible to join the treaty, has not yet done so. Over time, the 2005 Convention will replace and expand upon the Council's 1990 Laundering Convention, applying a similar regime to the financing of terrorism.

Combating money laundering has not only been targeted by law enforcement, but private concerns also play a role in assisting the fight to curtail this illegal activity. For example, "[o]n October 30, 2000, a coalition of large international private banks announced a set of voluntary guidelines designed to reduce the incidence of anti-money laundering." Bruce Zagaris, *Multinational Banks Adopt Anti-Money Laundering Guidelines*, 16 Int'l Enforcement L. Rep. 1031 (Dec. 2000).

Modifications to money laundering provisions in the United States, as well as new provisions were added as a result of the passage of the "Uniting and Strengthening America by Providing Appropriate Tools Required to Intercept and Obstruct Terrorism Act of 2001" (USA Patriot Act). Title III of this Act is titled "International Money Laundering Abatement and Anti-Terrorist Financing Act of 2001." The Act commences with findings that include a statement that "money laundering, estimated by the International Monetary Fund amount to between 2 and 5 percent of global domestic product, which is at least $600,000,000,000 annually, provides the financial fuel that permits transnational criminal enterprises to conduct and expand their operations to the detriment of the safety and security of American citizens." § 302(a)(1).

The Patriot Act called for cooperation to deter money laundering. §§ 314, 328. It added new predicate offenses, such as "bribery of a public official, or the misappropriation, theft, or embezzlement of public funds by or for the benefit of a public official" and certain "smuggling and export control violations." § 315. It called for asset forfeiture for proceeds of certain foreign crimes. § 320. The Act also provided new currency transaction reporting requirements.

The U.S. Department of State's *International Narcotics Control Strategy Report*, 2021, Vol. II, at 13–4, *available at* https://www.state.gov/2021-incsr-volume-ii-money-laundering-as-submitted-to-congress/ asserts:

The 2021 volume on Money Laundering is a legislatively-mandated section of the annual International Narcotics Control Strategy Report (INCSR), in accordance with section 489 of the Foreign Assistance Act of 1961, as amended (the "FAA," 22 U.S.C. § 2291). The FAA requires the Department of State to produce a report on the extent to which each country or entity that received assistance under chapter 8 of Part I of the Foreign Assistance Act in the past two fiscal years has "met the goals and objectives of the United Nations Convention Against Illicit Traffic in Narcotic Drugs and Psychotropic Substances" ("1988 UN Drug Convention") (FAA § 489(a)(1)(A)). In addition to identifying countries in relation to illicit narcotics, the INCSR is mandated to identify "major money laundering countries" (FAA § 489(a)(3)(C)). The INCSR also is required to report findings on each country's adoption of laws and regulations to prevent narcotics-related money laundering (FAA § 489(a)(7)(C)). This volume is the section of the INCSR that reports on money laundering and country efforts to address it. The statute defines a "major money laundering country" as one "whose financial institutions engage in currency transactions involving significant amounts of proceeds from international narcotics trafficking" (FAA § 481(e)(7)). The determination is derived from the list of countries included in INCSR Volume I (which focuses on narcotics) and other countries proposed by U.S. government experts based on indicia of significant drug-related money laundering activities. Given money laundering activity trends, the activities of non-financial businesses and professions or other value transfer systems are given due consideration. Inclusion in Volume II is not an indication that a jurisdiction is not making strong efforts to combat money laundering or that it has not fully met relevant international standards. The INCSR is not a "black list" of jurisdictions, nor are there sanctions associated with it. The U.S. Department of State regularly reaches out to counterparts to request updates on money laundering and AML efforts, and it welcomes information. The following countries/jurisdictions have been identified this year:

Major Money Laundering Jurisdictions in 2020:

Afghanistan, Albania, Algeria, Antigua and Barbuda, Argentina, Armenia, Aruba, Bahamas, Barbados, Belgium, Belize, Benin, Bolivia, Brazil, British Virgin Islands, Burma, Cabo Verde, Canada, Cayman Islands, China, Colombia, Costa Rica, Cuba, Curacao, Cyprus, Dominica, Dominican Republic, Ecuador, El Salvador, Georgia, Ghana, Guatemala, Guyana, Haiti, Honduras, Hong Kong, India, Indonesia, Iran, Italy, Jamaica, Kazakhstan, Kenya, Kyrgyz Republic, Laos, Liberia, Macau, Malaysia, Mexico, Morocco, Mozambique, Netherlands, Nicaragua, Nigeria, Pakistan, Panama, Paraguay, Peru, Philippines, Russia, St. Kitts and Nevis, St. Lucia, St. Vincent and the Grenadines, Senegal, Sint Maarten, Spain, Suriname, Tajikistan, Tanzania, Thailand, Trinidad and Tobago, Turkey, Turkmenistan, Ukraine,

United Arab Emirates, United Kingdom, United States, Uzbekistan, Venezuela, and Vietnam.

United States v. Tarkoff

United States Court of Appeals for the Eleventh Circuit
242 F.3d 991 (2001)

Kravitch, Circuit Judge:

... This appeal presents an issue of first impression in this circuit: whether a defendant may be convicted for conspiring to violate and violating the money laundering statute, 18 U.S.C. § 1956(h) and (a)(1)(B)(i), where the indictment charged and the government proved that the two monetary transactions at issue occurred wholly outside the United States....

Michael Tarkoff appeals his conviction for conspiracy to commit money laundering, 18 U.S.C. § 1956(h), and two counts of money laundering, 18 U.S.C. § 1956(a)(1)(B)(i). In early 1995, Tarkoff, a criminal defense lawyer, represented Ismael Arnaiz, who was a target of a grand jury investigation of a scheme in which Arnaiz and his business partner, Akioshi Yamada, defrauded Medicare. Arnaiz and Yamada's scheme consisted of paying people to "recruit" sham patients to visit Arnaiz and Yamada's medical clinics and provide their Medicare numbers to the billing clerk. The clinics would then bill Medicare for medical services that either had not been provided to the sham patients, or if provided, were not necessary. During a two-and-one-half year period, the clinics fraudulently billed Medicare $ 120 million.

During negotiations in 1995 regarding a plea bargain for Arnaiz, Assistant United States Attorney ("AUSA") Marc Garber informed Tarkoff that Arnaiz's scheme resulted in losses to Medicare of approximately $20–$40 million. At that time, Tarkoff did not claim that Arnaiz was not guilty of Medicare fraud, but merely argued that the $20–$40 million dollar figure was too high and that Arnaiz caused losses to Medicare of only $ 6 million (the dollar amount was relevant to sentencing Arnaiz). In addition, Tarkoff did not indicate that Arnaiz had any legitimate sources of income, but repeatedly represented that Arnaiz had no significant assets. Moreover, Melissa Rockhill, Tarkoff's legal secretary at the time, testified that Tarkoff acknowledged to her that Arnaiz was involved in Medicare fraud.

Rockhill also testified that in late January or early February 1996, Tarkoff told her that he and another attorney who had dealings with Arnaiz, Joaquin "Jack" Fernandez, had discussed the need to move Arnaiz's money in order to hide it from the United States government. On February 2, 1996, Tarkoff met with FBI Agent Gramlich and the AUSA then responsible for the case, at which meeting Agent Gramlich told Tarkoff that all of the money in Arnaiz's possession came from Medicare fraud, was subject to seizure by the government, and was not to be moved.

Between February 5 and 8, 1996, there were three wire transfers totaling approximately $ 470,000 from two Smith Barney accounts in Miami that were controlled by Arnaiz, to an account in the name of Rockside Enterprises at a bank in Curacao.

The source of the funds in those accounts was Arnaiz's Medicare fraud. Tarkoff and Fernandez, using United States passports, traveled from the United States to Israel on February 10, 1996, and each opened a numbered account at the Bank Hapoalim in Tel Aviv on February 12, 1996. Rockhill and Cheryl Crane, Fernandez's girlfriend at the time, accompanied Tarkoff and Fernandez on this trip. On February 16, $ 400,000 was transferred from the Rockside Enterprises account in Curacao to Fernandez's Israeli account. Tarkoff told Rockhill that the $ 400,000 was Arnaiz's money, and that it was being routed from Curacao to Israel in order to hide it from the government. Fernandez gave power of attorney over his account to Sharon Gershoni, an Israeli attorney whom Tarkoff had recommended, and she directed that $ 50,000 of the $ 400,000 deposited in Fernandez's account be transferred to Tarkoff's account. On February 20, 1996, also at Gershoni's direction, two bank drafts of $ 50,000 each were made payable to Jack Fernandez from Fernandez's Israeli account. Those checks subsequently were deposited into two Miami accounts controlled by Fernandez. Some of this money was routed to Arnaiz.

Tarkoff gave Rockhill the documents relating to his Israeli bank account to store in a safe deposit box in her home town of Indianapolis, Indiana, in order to avoid their discovery in the event his home or office was searched. Tarkoff also instructed Rockhill to deny any knowledge of the bank transactions in Israel if she was questioned by the government. Tarkoff did not tell his accountant about the $ 50,000 in his Israeli account until after he learned that his accountant had received a grand jury subpoena for Tarkoff's financial records in 1997.

Tarkoff raises several issues on appeal: (1) whether his conviction for conspiring to violate and violating the money laundering statute can stand where the indictment charged and the government proved that the two transactions at issue occurred wholly outside the United States. . . . Applying the legal framework discussed below, we conclude that the record supports Tarkoff's conviction for conspiracy to commit money laundering, 18 U.S.C. § 1956(h), and two counts of money laundering, 18 U.S.C. § 1956(a)(1)(B)(i), and therefore affirm.

. . . .

Tarkoff contends that he was entitled to judgment of acquittal because the transactions in which he took part occurred wholly outside the United States, and therefore did not affect interstate or foreign commerce, which is a necessary component of an element of the money laundering statute under which he was convicted. Tarkoff's convictions are based on his participation in two transactions: (1) the wire transfer of $ 400,000 from Curacao to Fernandez's bank account in Israel, and (2) the transfer of $ 50,000 of those funds to Tarkoff's Israeli bank account. . . .

The statute defines "financial transaction" as "(A) a transaction which in any way or degree affects interstate or foreign commerce (i) involving the movement of funds by wire or other means or (ii) involving one or more monetary instruments . . . , or (B) a transaction involving the use of a financial institution which is engaged in, or the activities of which affect, interstate or foreign commerce in any way or degree." 18 U.S.C. § 1956(c)(4). Tarkoff argues that because the two transactions with the Israeli bank occurred wholly outside the United States, they were not "financial transactions" under 18 U.S.C. § 1956(c)(4). In support of this proposition, Tarkoff relies primarily on *United States v. Kramer,* 73 F.3d 1067 (11th Cir. 1996), in which this Court reversed a money laundering conviction under 18 U.S.C. § 1956(a)(2)(B)(i) because the defendant participated only in a transfer of money from Switzerland to Luxembourg, and not a transfer of money to or from the United States, as required to violate section 1956(a)(2)(B)(i).... *Kramer* does not control in this case, however, because Tarkoff was convicted under a different subsection of the money laundering statute (§ 1956(a)(1)(B)(i)) than the one at issue in *Kramer.* The difference between the two subsections is that violation of the subsection at issue in *Kramer* specifically requires a transfer of funds to or from the United States, ... whereas a violation of the subsection under which Tarkoff was convicted can occur so long as the defendant was involved in a "financial transaction." *See* 18 U.S.C. § 1956(a)(1)(B)(i).

There are two ways to establish that a defendant conducted a "financial transaction" under 18 U.S.C. § 1956(a)(1)(B)(i). To satisfy its burden, the government had to prove either (1) that Tarkoff participated in a transaction that *in any way or degree* affected interstate or foreign commerce and involved the transfer of funds or the use of one or more monetary instruments, *see* 18 U.S.C. § 1956(c)(4)(A), or (2) that Tarkoff participated in a transaction that involved the use of a financial institution that was engaged in, or the activities of which affected, interstate or foreign commerce *in any way or degree. See* 18 U.S.C. § 1956(c)(4)(B).

The government argues that it proved Tarkoff participated in a "financial transaction" as defined in section 1956(c)(4)(A) by virtue of the evidence that Tarkoff and Fernandez, two U.S. citizens, traveled from the United States to Israel to transact business with a bank there, and that the Israeli bank transactions required telephone communication between Israel and Miami, and between Miami and Curacao, to arrange for the funds transfer from Curacao to Israel. We agree that these facts support a finding that Tarkoff participated in a "financial transaction" as that term is defined in 18 U.S.C. § 1956(c)(4)(A) because the international travel and communication required to execute the wire transactions affected foreign commerce "in any way or degree." The evidence also supports a finding that Tarkoff participated in a "financial transaction" as that term is defined in 18 U.S.C. § 1956(c)(4)(B) because the transactions involved the use of the Israeli bank-a financial institution which, by communicating with parties in the United States and providing banking services to United States citizens, was a "financial institution that was engaged in, or the activities of which affected, foreign commerce in any way or degree." ...

Because Tarkoff knowingly participated in a financial transaction designed in whole or in part to conceal or disguise the nature, the location, the source, the ownership, or the control of the proceeds of specified unlawful activity, we affirm his conviction for violating and conspiring to violate 18 U.S.C. § 1956(a)(1)(B)(i).

AFFIRMED.

Notes

(1) The electronic transfer of funds, outside a money laundering context, can raise similar jurisdiction issues. Consider the court's resolution of this issue in *United States v. Gilboe*, 684 F.2d 235 (2d Cir. 1982):

> Defendant's massive fraud on the international shipping industry left victims on the continents of Asia, North America and Europe. The scheme involved several other apparently fraudulent transactions but the charges against defendant in this case stem from two shipments of grain arranged by defendant to the People's Republic of China, one from Argentina and the other from the United States. . . .
>
> Appellant argues that the district court did not have jurisdiction over the offenses charged because he was a nonresident alien whose acts occurred outside the United States and had no detrimental effect within the United States. In connection with the Argentina and New Orleans transactions, defendant was charged with both wire fraud under 18 U.S.C. § 1343 and transportation of funds obtained by fraud under 18 U.S.C. § 2314.
>
> Turning first to the former charges, defendant was convicted on four counts of wire fraud under § 1343 . . . . Defendant admitted that, in negotiating with the Manhattan shipowner for the shipment from Argentina, he had telephone and telex conversations with a ship broker in Bayshore, Long Island and that he caused other telex and telephone negotiations to occur between Manhattan and Hong Kong. These negotiations were to obtain ships to transport the grain, a key element of the fraud. The evidence was clearly sufficient to sustain jurisdiction on this offense, which forms the basis for count one. . . . With respect to the shipments from New Orleans, defendant also admitted that he caused the payments received from the Chinese corporation to be electronically transferred through Manhattan banks to accounts in the Bahamas, the basis for counts three, four and five. This evidence was sufficient to justify asserting jurisdiction over defendant. . . .
>
> With respect to the conviction on counts charging violations of § 2314, defendant's jurisdictional argument depends on his premise that the section applies only to the transportation of tangible items and does not cover "electronic crediting and debiting," the means by which the funds in defendant's scheme moved from one bank to another. However, if such transfers of money are covered by § 2314, defendant's attack on jurisdiction fails because the evidence clearly showed that defendant had aided and abetted the transportation in foreign commerce through banks in Manhattan of "securities or money . . . taken by fraud." The question whether the section covers electronic transfers of funds appears to be one of first impression, but we do not regard it as a difficult one. Electronic signals in this context are the means by which funds are transported. The beginning of the transaction is money in one account and the ending is money in another.

> The manner in which the funds were moved does not affect the ability to obtain tangible paper dollars or a bank check from the receiving account. Indeed, we suspect that actual dollars rarely move between banks, particularly in international transactions. If anything, the means of transfer here were essential to the success of the fraudulent scheme. Defendant depended heavily on his ability to move funds rapidly out of reach of disgruntled shipowners who were to receive payment within days of loading the grain. And it was not until the funds, through a series of bank transfers, came to rest in the Bahamas that defendant's scheme was complete. . . . The record amply shows that the direct transfers of precise amounts received through fraud were in a manner clearly indicating that the fraud and transfer were a single transaction. The primary element of this offense, transportation, "does not require proof that any specific means of transporting were used." . . . Therefore, since fraudulently obtained funds were transported within the meaning of the section and banks in Manhattan were utilized, there was sufficient evidence to support jurisdiction under § 2314.

(2) What happens when the government charges separate counts of domestic and international money laundering for the same financial transaction? In *United States v. Zvi*, 168 F.3d 49, 57 (2d Cir. 1999), the Second Circuit found it "multiplicitous" to charge both "domestic and international money laundering based on the same funds transfers."

(3) Are there limits to what is covered in the money laundering statutes? In *United States v. Santos*, 128 S. Ct. 2020 (2008), the Court in a plurality opinion used the rule of lenity to interpret the word "proceeds" in § 1956(a)(1), to mean "'profits,' as opposed to 'receipts.'" This case involved payments to "lottery operators" and employees' receipt of payments in an alleged gambling operation. But the holding was short-lived as Congress, as part of the Fraud Enforcement Recovery Act of 2009, added language to the money laundering statutes to provide that "proceeds" could include "gross receipts." A second Court decision was issued at the same time as *Santos*. Consider the limit provided in this case:

Cuellar v. United States

Supreme Court of the United States
553 U.S. 550 (2008)

Justice Thomas delivered the opinion of the Court.

. . . On July 14, 2004, petitioner Humberto Fidel Regalado Cuellar was stopped in southern Texas for driving erratically. Driving south toward the Mexican border, about 114 miles away, petitioner had just passed the town of Eldorado. In response to the officer's questions, petitioner, who spoke no English, handed the officer a stack of papers. Included were bus tickets showing travel from a Texas border town to San Antonio on July 13 and, in the other direction, from San Antonio to Big Spring, Texas, on July 14. A Spanish-speaking officer, Trooper Danny Nuñez, was called to the scene and began questioning petitioner. Trooper Nuñez soon became suspicious because petitioner was avoiding eye contact and seemed very nervous. Petitioner claimed to be on a 3-day business trip, but he had no luggage or extra clothing with him, and he gave conflicting accounts of his itinerary. When Trooper Nuñez asked petitioner about a bulge in his shirt pocket, petitioner produced a wad of cash that smelled of marijuana.

Petitioner consented to a search of the Volkswagen Beetle that he was driving. While the officers were searching the vehicle, Trooper Nuñez observed petitioner standing on the side of the road making the sign of the cross, which he interpreted to mean that petitioner knew he was in trouble. A drug detection dog alerted on the cash from petitioner's shirt pocket and on the rear area of the car. Further scrutiny uncovered a secret compartment under the rear floorboard, and inside the compartment the officers found approximately $81,000 in cash. The money was bundled in plastic bags and duct tape, and animal hair was spread in the rear of the vehicle. Petitioner claimed that he had previously transported goats in the vehicle, but Trooper Nuñez doubted that goats could fit in such a small space and suspected that the hair had been spread in an attempt to mask the smell of marijuana.

... Petitioner was charged with attempting to transport the proceeds of unlawful activity across the border, knowing that the transportation was designed "to conceal or disguise the nature, the location, the source, the ownership, or the control" of the money. 18 U.S.C. §1956(a)(2)(B)(i). After a 2-day trial, the jury found petitioner guilty. The District Court denied petitioner's motion for judgment of acquittal based on insufficient evidence and sentenced petitioner to 78 months in prison, followed by three years of supervised release.... On appeal, a divided panel of the Fifth Circuit reversed and rendered a judgment of acquittal.... The Fifth Circuit granted rehearing en banc and affirmed petitioner's conviction....

[P]etitioner was convicted under §1956(a)(2)(B)(i), which, in relevant part, makes it a crime to attempt to transport "funds from a place in the United States to ... a place outside the United States ... knowing that the ... funds involved in the transportation ... represent the proceeds of some form of unlawful activity and knowing that such transportation ... is designed in whole or in part ... to conceal or disguise the nature, the location, the source, the ownership, or the control of the proceeds of specified unlawful activity." Accordingly, the Government was required in this case to prove that petitioner (1) attempted to transport funds from the United States to Mexico, (2) knew that these funds "represent[ed] the proceeds of some form of unlawful activity," *e.g.*, drug trafficking, and (3) knew that "such transportation" was designed to "conceal or disguise the nature, the location, the source, the ownership, or the control" of the funds.

It is the last of these that is at issue before us, viz., whether petitioner knew that "such transportation" was designed to conceal or disguise the specified attributes of the illegally obtained funds. In this connection, it is important to keep in mind that the critical transportation was not the transportation of the funds within this country on the way to the border. Instead, the term "such transportation" means transportation "from a place in the United States to . . . a place outside the United States"—here, from the United States to Mexico. Therefore, what the Government had to prove was that petitioner knew that taking the funds to Mexico was "designed," at least in part, to conceal or disguise their "nature," "location," "source," "ownership," or "control" . . . .

We agree with petitioner that merely hiding funds during transportation is not sufficient to violate the statute, even if substantial efforts have been expended to conceal the money. Our conclusion turns on the text of § 1956(a)(2)(B)(i), and particularly on the term "design." In this context, "design" means purpose or plan; *i.e.*, the intended aim of the transportation. . . . Congress wrote "knowing that such transportation is designed . . . to conceal or disguise" a listed attribute of the funds, § 1956(a)(2)(B)(i), and when an act is "designed to" do something, the most natural reading is that it has that something as its purpose. The Fifth Circuit employed this meaning of design when it referred to the "transportation design or plan to get the funds out of this country." . . .

But the Fifth Circuit went on to discuss the "design" of the transportation in a different sense. It described the packaging of the money, its placement in the hidden compartment, and the use of animal hair to mask its scent as "*aspects* of the transportation" that "were designed to conceal or disguise" the nature and location of the cash. . . . (emphasis added). Because the Fifth Circuit used "design" to refer not to the purpose of the transportation but to the manner in which it was carried out, its use of the term in this context was consistent with the alternate meaning of "design" as structure or arrangement. . . . The Government at times also appears to adopt this meaning of "design." . . . If the statutory term had this meaning, it would apply whenever a person transported illicit funds in a secretive manner. Judge Smith supplied an example of this construction: A petty thief who hides money in his shoe and then walks across the border to spend the money in local bars, . . . has engaged in transportation designed to conceal the location of the money because he has hidden it in an unlikely place.

We think it implausible, however, that Congress intended this meaning of "design." If it had, it could have expressed its intention simply by writing "knowing that such transportation conceals or disguises," rather than the more complex formulation "knowing that such transportation . . . is designed . . . to conceal or disguise." § 1956(a)(2)(B)(i). It seems far more likely that Congress intended courts to apply the familiar criminal law concepts of purpose and intent than to focus exclusively on how a defendant "structured" the transportation. In addition, the structural meaning of "design" is both overinclusive and underinclusive: It would capture individuals who structured transportation in a secretive way but lacked any criminal intent (such as a person who hid illicit funds *en route* to turn them over to law enforcement); yet it would exclude individuals who fully intended to move the funds in order to impede detection by law enforcement but failed to hide them during the transportation. . . .

Although transporting money in a conventional manner may suggest no particular purpose other than simply to move it from one place to another, secretively transporting it suggests, at least, that the defendant did not want the money to be detected during transport. In this case, evidence of the methods petitioner used to transport the nearly $81,000 in cash—bundled in plastic bags and hidden in a secret compartment covered with animal hair—was plainly probative of an underlying goal to prevent the funds from being detected while he drove them from the United States to Mexico. The same secretive aspects of the transportation also may be circumstantial evidence that the transportation itself was intended to avoid detection of the funds, because, for example, they may suggest that the transportation is only one step in a larger plan to facilitate the cross-border transport of the funds.... But its probative force, in that context, is weak. "There is a difference between concealing something to transport it, and transporting something to conceal it," ...; that is, *how* one moves the money is distinct from *why* one moves the money. Evidence of the former, standing alone, is not sufficient to prove the latter....

In sum, we conclude that the evidence introduced by the Government was not sufficient to permit a reasonable jury to conclude beyond a reasonable doubt that petitioner's transportation was "designed in whole or in part... to conceal or disguise the nature, the location, the source, the ownership, or the control of the proceeds." §1956(a)(2)(B)(i).

The provision of the money laundering statute under which petitioner was convicted requires proof that the transportation was "designed in whole or in part to conceal or disguise the nature, the location, the source, the ownership, or the control" of the funds. §1956(a)(2)(B)(i). Although this element does not require proof that the defendant attempted to create the appearance of legitimate wealth, neither can it be satisfied solely by evidence that a defendant concealed the funds during their transport. In this case, the only evidence introduced to prove this element showed that petitioner engaged in extensive efforts to conceal the funds *en route* to Mexico, and thus his conviction cannot stand. We reverse the judgment of the Fifth Circuit. It is so ordered.

[A concurring opinion was authored by JUSTICE ALITO, with whom The CHIEF JUSTICE and JUSTICE KENNEDY joined.]

§8.04 Currency Transaction Reports

There are other statutes besides 18 U.S.C. §1956 and §1957 that can be attributed to efforts to decrease national and international drug activity. For example, the array of reporting statutes that are directed at curtailing money laundering include the Bank Secrecy Act which requires banks to file currency transactions reports with the Internal Revenue Service for certain monetary transactions. In certain circumstances individuals transporting money into and out of the United

States are required to report the currency on a customs form. Businesses have also been subject to Internal Revenue reporting requirements for certain monetary transactions.

In *United States v. Bajakajian*, 524 U.S. 321 (1998) the accused "attempted to leave the United States without reporting, as required by federal law, that he was transporting more than $10,000 in currency." The Supreme Court held that "forfeiture of the entire $357,144 that respondent failed to declare would violate the Excessive Fines Clause of the Eighth Amendment" as "grossly disproportional to the gravity of his offense." Congress, however, responded to this decision by adding a new provision in the Patriot Act that created new penalties for bulk cash smuggling into and out of the United States. Section 371 states as its purposes "to make the act of smuggling bulk cash itself a criminal offense," "to authorize forfeiture of any cash or instruments of the smuggling offense," and "to emphasize the seriousness of the act of bulk cash smuggling."

Chapter 9

Piracy and Terrorism

§ 9.01 Piracy

Pirates of a bygone age were the terrorists of their day. Interest in an age-old problem had a dramatic revival in 2008–9 in response to numerous pirate attacks on the high seas beyond the territorial limits of Somalia. The Security Council, the European Union and several naval forces became involved. *See* Eugene Kontorovich, *International Legal Responses to Piracy Off the Coast of Somalia*, 13 ASIL INSIGHT, No. 2 (2009); Michael Plachta, *Somalia Piracy: Responses of the United Nations and International Community*, 25 INT'L ENF. L. REP. 114 (2009). These events highlighted the difficulties of gathering evidence and witnesses to bring such cases to trial as well as the absence of appropriate legislation in many countries. In recent years, in addition to the waters off the coast of Somalia, the Gulf of Guinea and the South China Seas are areas experiencing active piracy.

Crimes committed on board a ship generally come under the jurisdiction of the state whose flag the ship flies, as was noted in Chapter 1. This is regarded as an aspect of "territorial jurisdiction"; the ship is considered, in effect, a "floating part" of that state's territory. The U.S. Code catalogues jurisdiction over crimes committed on board U.S. ships (and also certain aircraft and space flights) as a part of the "special maritime and territorial jurisdiction of the United States." *See* 18 U.S.C. § 7(1).

The policing of attacks by pirate ships poses a special problem in that pirate ships tend not to have a "flag state." This has been dealt with by making piracy subject to the "universal jurisdiction" of all states (although for questions about how "universal" this jurisdiction really has been, see ALFRED P. RUBIN, THE LAW OF PIRACY (2d ed. 1998)). Not all countries have legislated for universal jurisdiction over piracy. U.S. law provides, however: "Whoever on the high seas, commits the crime of piracy as defined by the law of nations, and is afterwards brought into or found in the United States, shall be imprisoned for life." 18 U.S.C. § 1651. Many of the persons captured as pirates on the high seas off the coast of Somalia were delivered by European and U.S. naval vessels to the authorities in Kenya which claims universal jurisdiction similar to that of the U.S. Kenya received support from the European Union and the UN Office of Drugs and Crime (UNODC) in these endeavors. *See* JOINT EUROPEAN COMMISSION/UNODC PROGRAMME, EU SUPPORT TO THE TRIAL AND RELATED TREATMENT OF PIRACY SUSPECTS (May 2009). The U.S. brought a few accused for trial in the United States. In one such case, a federal appeals court examined whether the piracy statute's mandatory life imprisonment violated the Eighth

Amendment. The court concluded that the defendant was unable to make out an Eighth Amendment claim and stated, the "mandatory life sentence 'reflects a rational legislative judgment, entitled to deference,' that piracy in international waters is a crime deserving of one of the harshest of penalties. . . . [F]or centuries, pirates have been universally condemned as *hostis humani generis*—enemies of all mankind—because they attack vessels on the high seas, and thus outside of any nation's territorial jurisdiction, with devastating effect to global commerce and navigation." *United States v. Said*, 798 F.3d 182 (4th Cir. 2015).

What are the elements of "the crime of piracy as defined by the law of nations" in modern usage? These are set out in Article 15 of the Geneva Convention on the High Seas, Apr. 28, 1958, 13 U.S.T. 2312, T.I.A.S. No. 5200, 450 U.N.T.S. 82:

> Piracy consists of any of the following acts:
>
> (1) Any illegal acts of violence, detention or any act of depredation, committed for private ends by the crew or the passengers of a private ship or a private aircraft, and directed:
>
> > (a) On the high seas, against another ship or aircraft, or against persons or property on board such ship or aircraft;
> >
> > (b) Against a ship, aircraft, persons or property in a place outside the jurisdiction of any State;
>
> (2) Any act of voluntary participation in the operation of a ship or of an aircraft with knowledge of facts making it a pirate ship or aircraft;
>
> (3) Any act of inciting or of intentionally facilitating an act described in sub-paragraph (1) or sub-paragraph (2) of this article.

Practically identical language appears in Article 101 of the 1982 Convention on the Law of the Sea ("UNCLOS"), Dec. 10, 1982, 516 U.N.T.S. 205, 21 I.L.M. 1216. Other articles in the two conventions authorize all states to seize pirate ships and to arrest and try the persons on board. Article 14 of the High Seas Convention and Article 100 of the Law of the Sea Convention both provide: "All States shall co-operate to the fullest extent in the repression of piracy on the high seas or in any other place outside the jurisdiction of any State." The United States is a party to the 1958 Convention but not to UNCLOS.

The definition of piracy contained in Article 15 of the 1958 Convention on the High Seas was supposed, more or less, to reflect customary international law at the time—although the inclusion of aircraft, at least, was a clear innovation. Under this definition, piracy must be committed for private ends. It cannot be committed by warships or other government vessels.

Would the hijacking of an aircraft over the high seas constitute "piracy as defined by the law of nations"? That would depend, in part, on whether the hijackers can be said to have acted for "private ends." In any event, there is the question of whether an "internal seizure" by those already on board a ship or aircraft constitutes piracy. This was a matter of controversy before 1958. The Convention on the High Seas sought to resolve the controversy by requiring that piracy must be directed "against another ship or aircraft."

The difficulties involved in applying the law of piracy to terrorism on board a ship on the high seas were vividly illustrated by the seizure of the Italian cruise ship, the *Achille Lauro*, in the Mediterranean in October 1985. The terrorists threatened to kill the passengers unless Israel released fifty Palestinian prisoners; before surrendering, they did kill Leon Klinghoffer, a Jewish passenger of U.S. nationality. No other ship was involved. This incident led to adoption of the 1988 Convention for the Suppression of Unlawful Acts Against the Safety of Maritime Navigation. *See* Malvina Halberstam, *Terrorism on the High Seas: The Achille Lauro, Piracy and the IMO Convention on Maritime Safety*, 82 A.J.I.L. 269 (1988). Such actions also typically involve hostage taking within the scope of the 1979 International Convention against the Taking of Hostages, discussed in § 9.06. Indeed, the piracy suspects brought to the U.S. have typically been indicted for piracy, unlawful acts against shipping and hostage taking (along with associated conspiracies and weapons offenses).

Consider the treatment of "piracy as defined by the law of nations" in the following case.

United States v. Dire

Court of Appeals for the Fourth Circuit
680 F.3d 446 (2012)

King, Circuit Judge, joined by Judges Davis and Keenan:

In the early morning hours of April 1, 2010, on the high seas between Somalia and the Seychelles (in the Indian Ocean off the east coast of Africa), the defendants—Abdi Wali Dire, Gabul Abdullahi Ali, Abdi Mohammed Umar, Abdi Mohammed Gurewardher, and Mohammed Modin Hasan—imprudently launched an attack on the USS Nicholas, having confused that mighty Navy frigate for a vulnerable merchant ship. The defendants, all Somalis, were swiftly apprehended and then transported to the Eastern District of Virginia, where they were convicted of the crime of piracy, as proscribed by 18 U.S.C. § 1651, plus myriad other criminal offenses. In this appeal, the defendants challenge their convictions and life-plus-eighty-year sentences on several grounds, including that their fleeting and fruitless strike on the Nicholas did not, as a matter of law, amount to a § 1651 piracy offense. As explained below, we reject their contentions and affirm....

According to the trial evidence, the USS Nicholas was on a counter-piracy mission in the Indian Ocean when, lit to disguise itself as a merchant vessel, it encountered the defendants shortly after midnight on April 1, 2010. The Nicholas was approached by an attack skiff operated by defendant Hasan and also carrying defendants Dire and Ali, while defendants Umar and Gurewardher remained with a larger mothership some distance away. From their posts on the Nicholas, crew members could see by way of night-vision devices that Hasan was armed with a loaded rocket-propelled grenade launcher (commonly referred to as an "RPG"), and that Dire and Ali carried AK-47 assault rifles. . . .

According to the defendants, the crime of piracy has been narrowly defined for purposes of § 1651 as robbery at sea, i.e., seizing or otherwise robbing a vessel. Because they boarded the Nicholas only as captives and indisputably took no property, the defendants contest their convictions on Count One, as well as the affixed life sentences.

. . . .

The crux of the defendants' position is now, as it was in the district court, that the definition of general piracy was fixed in the early Nineteenth Century, when Congress passed the Act of 1819 first authorizing the exercise of universal jurisdiction by United States courts to adjudicate charges of "piracy as defined by the law of nations." Most notably, the defendants assert that the "law of nations," as understood in 1819, is not conterminous with the "customary international law" of today. The defendants rely on Chief Justice Marshall's observation that "[t]he law of nations is a law founded on the great and immutable principles of equity and natural justice," The Venus, 12 U.S. (8 Cranch) 253, 297 (1814) (Marshall, C.J., dissenting), to support their theory that "[t]he Congress that enacted the [Act of 1819] did not view the universal law of nations as an evolving body of law." Br. of Appellants 12; see also Br. of Amicus Curiae 11 (arguing that, in 1819, "'the law of nations' was well understood to refer to an immutable set of obligations — not evolving practices of nations or future pronouncements of international organizations that did not yet exist").

The defendants' view is thoroughly refuted, however, by a bevy of precedent, including the Supreme Court's 2004 decision in *Sosa v. Alvarez-Machain*. The Sosa Court was called upon to determine whether Alvarez could recover under the Alien Tort Statute, 28 U.S.C. § 1350 (the "ATS"), for the U.S. Drug Enforcement Administration's instigation of his abduction from Mexico for criminal trial in the United States. See 542 U.S. at 697. The ATS provides, in full, that "[t]he district courts shall have original jurisdiction of any civil action by an alien for a tort only, committed in violation of the law of nations or a treaty of the United States." 28 U.S.C. § 1350. Significantly, the ATS predates the criminalization of general piracy, in that it was passed by "[t]he first Congress . . . as part of the Judiciary Act of 1789." See Sosa, 542 U.S. at 712–13 (citing Act of Sept. 24, 1789, ch. 20, § 9, 1 Stat. 77 (authorizing federal district court jurisdiction over "all causes where an alien sues for a tort only in violation of the law of nations or a treaty of the United States")). Yet the Sosa Court did not regard the ATS as incorporating some stagnant notion of the law of nations. Rather, the Court concluded that, while the first Congress probably understood the ATS to confer jurisdiction over only the three paradigmatic law-of-nations torts of the time — including piracy — the door was open to ATS jurisdiction over additional "claim[s] based on the present-day law of nations," albeit in narrow circumstances. See id. at 724–25. Those circumstances were lacking in the case of Alvarez, whose ATS claim could not withstand being "gauged against the current state of international law." See id. at 733.

Although, as the defendants point out, the ATS involves civil claims and the general piracy statute entails criminal prosecutions, there is no reason to believe that the "law of nations" evolves in the civil context but stands immobile in the criminal context. Moreover, if the Congress of 1819 had believed either the law of nations generally or its piracy definition specifically to be inflexible, the Act of 1819 could easily have been drafted to specify that piracy consisted of "piracy as defined on March 3, 1819 [the date of enactment], by the law of nations," or solely of, as the defendants would have it, "robbery upon the sea." The government helpfully identifies numerous criminal statutes "that incorporate a definition of an offense supplied by some other body of law that may change or develop over time," see Br. of Appellee 18 (citing, inter alia, 16 U.S.C. § 3372(a)(2)(A) (the Lacey Act, prohibiting commercial activities involving "any fish or wildlife taken, possessed, transported, or sold in violation of any law or any regulation of any State or in violation of any foreign law")) . . . .

. . . .

We also agree with the district court that the definition of piracy under the law of nations, at the time of the defendants' attack on the USS Nicholas and continuing today, had for decades encompassed their violent conduct. That definition, spelled out in the UNCLOS, as well as the High Seas Convention before it, has only been reaffirmed in recent years as nations around the world have banded together to combat the escalating scourge of piracy. For example, in November 2011, the United Nations Security Council adopted Resolution 2020, recalling a series of prior resolutions approved between 2008 and 2011 "concerning the situation in Somalia"; expressing "grave[ ] concern[ ] [about] the ongoing threat that piracy and armed robbery at sea against vessels pose"; and emphasizing "the need for a comprehensive response by the international community to repress piracy and armed robbery at sea and tackle its underlying causes." Of the utmost significance, Resolution 2020 reaffirmed "that international law, as reflected in the [UNCLOS], sets out the legal framework applicable to combating piracy and armed robbery at sea." Because the district court correctly applied the UNCLOS definition of piracy as customary international law, we reject the defendants' challenge to their Count One piracy convictions, as well as their mandatory life sentences.

Notes

(1) John Jay, whose eponymous treaty sought "condign punishment" for those who "receive, protect, harbour, conceal or assist" pirates (*see* § 2.01[B] *supra*), would no doubt have applauded the conviction in *United States v. Shibin*, 722 F.3d 233 (4th Cir. 2013). Shibin was a negotiator for Somali pirates, convicted for his activities in relation to two seized vessels. His activities took place in Somali waters and on land in Somalia, where he was captured. In one case he remained on board a captured vessel in Somali waters for some seven months (apart from his summer vacation of 10 to 12 days) until the ransom was delivered from the air. In the other case he was designated as negotiator but the vessel was ultimately recaptured by

the United States navy before it entered Somali waters. Shibin argued that he could be guilty of piracy only if he acted on the high seas. The Court quoted UNCLOS, Article 101, *supra*, and stated:

> . . . [A]s relevant here, Article 101(a) defines piracy to include specified acts "directed on the high seas against another ship or against persons or property on board such ship," and Article 101(c) defines piracy to include any act that "intentionally facilitat[es]" any act described in Article 101(a). The parties agree that the facilitating conduct of Article 101(c) is "functionally equivalent" to aiding and abetting criminal conduct, as proscribed in 18 U.S.C. § 2.
>
> While Shibin's conduct unquestionably amounted to acts that intentionally facilitated Article 101(a) piracies on the high seas, he claims that in order for his facilitating conduct to amount to piracy, his conduct must also have been carried out on the high seas. The text, however, hardly provides support for this argument. To the contrary, the better reading suggests that Articles 101(a) and 101(c) address distinct acts that are defined in their respective sections.
>
> Article 101(a), which covers piracies on the high seas, explicitly requires that the specified acts be directed at ships on the high seas. But Article 101(c), which defines different piratical acts, independent of the acts described in Article 101(a), is linked to Article 101(a) only to the extent that the acts must facilitate Article 101(a) acts. Article 101(c) does not limit the facilitating acts to conduct on the high seas. Moreover, there is no conceptual reason why acts facilitating high-seas acts must themselves be carried out on the high seas. The text of Article 101 describes one class of acts involving violence, detention, and depredation of ships on the high seas and another class of acts that facilitate those acts. In this way, Article 101 reaches all the piratical conduct, wherever carried out, so long as the acts specified in Article 101(a) are carried out on the high seas.
>
> We thus hold that conduct violating Article 101(c) does not have to be carried out on the high seas, but it must incite or intentionally facilitate acts committed against ships, persons, and property on the high seas.

(2) The real-life Somali pirate from the Tom Hanks movie *Captain Phillips* (2013) was Abdulwali Abdukhadir Muse. He was indicted in 2009 in the Southern District of New York in relation to the hijacking of the *Maersk Alabama* container ship. The charges included piracy under the law of nations, seizing a ship by force, hostage taking, and kidnapping. *See Somalian Pirate Indicted for Hijacking the Maersk Alabama and Holding the Ship's Captain Hostage*, Press Release, S.D.N.Y U.S. Attorney's Office (May 19, 2009). In 2010, a superseding indictment was filed against Muse charging him with involvement in two additional hijackings. *See Manhattan U.S. Attorney Files Superseding Indictment Against Alleged Somali Piracy Charging Involvement in Two Additional Hijackings*, Press Release, S.D.N.Y U.S. Attorney's

Office (January 12, 2010). In announcing the charges, the U.S. Attorney stated, "Piracy on the high seas is a threat against the community of nations. . . . Modern-day pirates who wreak havoc off faraway coasts will be met with modern-day justice in the United States." Muse later pled guilty to two counts of hijacking maritime vessels, two counts of kidnapping, and two counts of hostage taking. He was not required to plead guilty to the piracy charges, which carried a mandatory term of life in prison. *See Somali Pirate Pleads Guilty in Manhattan Federal Court to Maritime Hijacking, Kidnapping, and Hostage Taking*, S.D.N.Y U.S. Attorney's Office (January 12, 2010). Muse was sentenced to over 33 years in prison for his offenses. *See Somalian Pirate Sentenced in Manhattan Federal Court to 405 Months in Prison for Hijacking Three Ships and for Hostage Taking*, FBI Press Release (February 16, 2011).

(3) What type of court is best suited to prosecute piracy cases has garnered much debate. Some argue piracy should be prosecuted, as at present, primarily in national court systems. Others believe these types of international offenses are better prosecuted by special tribunals with international components or even, perhaps, by the International Criminal Court in The Hague or the Law of the Sea Tribunal in Hamburg. *See* Chapters 21 and 22 for discussion of international tribunals and court structures. What at the advantages and disadvantages of these differing venues for piracy prosecutions?

§ 9.02 Terrorism in General

Fighting terrorism is a priority of the United States Department of Justice. This includes both domestic and international terrorism. Terrorism is not, however, an easily defined term. *See* CHRISTOPHER L. BLAKESLEY, TERRORISM, DRUGS, INTERNATIONAL LAW, AND THE PROTECTION OF HUMAN LIBERTY (1992). The United Nations has been very active in the area. In September 2006, for example, the General Assembly adopted a comprehensive United Nations Global Counter-Terrorism Strategy, U.N. Doc. A/RES.60/288, but without specifically defining the phenomenon.

A. In International Law

Absent agreement on a comprehensive international anti-terrorism treaty, numerous multilateral conventions have been concerned with specific forms of terrorism. The Tokyo Convention on Offenses and Certain Other Acts Committed on Board Aircraft, Sept. 14, 1963, 20 U.S.T. 2941, T.I.A.S. No. 6768, 704 U.N.T.S. 219, dealt generally with jurisdiction over crimes committed on aircraft, although it actually antedates the first big wave of aircraft hijacking that began around 1968. International concern specifically with hijacking then led to adoption of the Hague Convention for the Suppression of Unlawful Seizure of Aircraft, Dec. 16, 1970, 22 U.S.T. 1641, T.I.A.S. No. 7192, 860 U.N.T.S. 105.

In addition to the Hague Convention, the list of anti-terrorism treaties includes (in chronological order) the OAS Convention to Prevent and Punish the Acts of

Terrorism Taking the Form of Crimes Against Persons and Related Extortion that are of International Significance, Feb. 2, 1971, 27 U.S.T. 3949, T.I.A.S. No. 8413; Montreal Convention for the Suppression of Unlawful Acts Against the Safety of Civil Aviation, Sept. 23, 1971, 24 U.S.T. 564, T.I.A.S. No. 7570, 974 U.N.T.S. 177; New York Convention on the Prevention and Punishment of Crimes Against Internationally Protected Persons, Including Diplomatic Agents, Dec. 14, 1973, 28 U.S.T. 1975, T.I.A.S. No. 8532, 1035 U.N.T.S. 167; International Convention Against the Taking of Hostages, Dec. 17, 1979, T.I.A.S. No. 11081, 18 I.L.M. 1456 (1979); Convention on the Physical Protection of Nuclear Materials, Mar. 3, 1980, I.A.E.A. Legal Series No. 12 (1982), 18 I.L.M. 1419 (1979); Protocol [to the 1971 Montreal Convention] for the Suppression of Unlawful Acts of Violence at Airports Serving Civil Aviation, Feb. 24, 1988, 27 I.L.M. 627 (1988); I.M.O. Rome Convention for the Suppression of Unlawful Acts Against the Safety of Maritime Navigation, Mar. 10, 1988, 27 I.L.M. 668 (1988), together with a Protocol for the Suppression of Unlawful Acts Against the Safety of Fixed Platforms Located on the Continental Shelf, Mar. 10, 1988, 27 I.L.M. 685 (1988); Convention on the Safety of United Nations and Associated Personnel, Dec. 9, 1994, U.N. Doc. A/49/742 (1994), 34 I.L.M. 482 (1995); International Convention for the Suppression of Terrorist Bombings, Jan. 9, 1998, 37 I.L.M. 249 (1998); and International Convention for the Suppression of Financing of Terrorism, December 9, 1999, 39 I.L.M. 270 (1999); Inter-American Convention Against Terrorism, June 3, 2002, AG/RES. 1840 (XXXII-0/02); International Convention for the Suppression of Acts of Nuclear Terrorism, April 13, 2005, G. A. Res. 59/290.

The provisions of these treaties generally are modeled on those contained in the 1970 Hague Convention. The same pattern appears in the Torture Convention [*see* chap. 10]. The principal object of the Hague Convention was to deny "safe haven" to offenders. Accordingly, the convention stipulates that certain conduct shall be considered an "offense." Each party to the convention is obligated to make the offense punishable by severe penalties. Parties also are obligated to treat the offense as one for which they will grant extradition. Any state in whose territory an alleged offender is present is bound, if it does not extradite the offender, to "submit the case to its competent authorities for the purpose of prosecution." So that states will be in a position to prosecute in default of extradition, the convention requires each party to make provision for exercising extraterritorial "jurisdiction over the offense in the case where the alleged offender is present in its territory and it does not extradite him. . . ."

There has been some debate about whether the residual, fallback, jurisdiction which these conventions require a state to exercise when it does not extradite an offender can properly be characterized as "universal jurisdiction." Recall the questions following *United States v. Yunis* [§ 3.03[E]]. Could such jurisdiction be exercised, for instance, over nationals of a state that had not ratified the pertinent convention?

There are many reasons why it might be useful to "define" terrorism: for rhetorical purposes as a pejorative term to label "them"; for social science purposes (in order to describe a phenomenon and try to find a solution); or for functional legal purposes (such as devising a suppression regime and an obligation to extradite or prosecute). For a comprehensive examination of many attempts at definition in various contexts, see Alex Schmid, *Terrorism—The Definitional Problem*, 36 CASE W. RES. J. INT'L L. 375 (2004).

In 2011, the Special Tribunal for Lebanon insisted that a customary rule of international law regarding the crime of terrorism had emerged and offered a definition of the term.

> [A] number of treaties, UN resolutions, and the legislative and judicial practice of States evince the formation of a general *opinio juris* in the international community, accompanied by practice consistent with such *opinio*, to the effect that a customary rule of international law regarding the crime of terrorism, at least *in time of peace*, has emerged. This customary rule requires the following three key elements: (i) the perpetration of a criminal act (such as murder, kidnapping, hostage-taking, arson, and so on), or threatening such an act; (ii) the intent to spread fear among the population (which would generally entail the creation of public danger) or directly or indirectly coerce a national or international authority to take some action, or to refrain from taking it; (iii) when the act involved a transnational element.

Interlocutory Decision on the Applicable Law: Terrorism, Conspiracy, Homicide, Perpetration, Cumulative Charging, STL-11-01/I/A/A/R176bis, 16 Feb. 2011, para. 85.

Efforts to negotiate a general terrorism suppression convention, including an obligation to extradite or prosecute, continue at the U.N. *See* TAL BECKER, TERRORISM AND THE STATE: RETHINKING THE RULES OF STATE RESPONSIBILITY 83–116 (2006); Bruce Broomhall, *State Actors in an International Definition of Terrorism from a Human Rights Perspective*, 36 CASE W. RES. J. INT'L L. 421 (2004).

The twin sticking points involve the inclusion or exclusion, as the case may be, of violent acts committed by Governments and those committed by Liberation Movements. The instinct of many Governments is to cover within a convention definition only the acts of non-State actors, but this is controversial. No one argues against including non-State actors as a general matter; issue is however joined on whether some exceptions should be made and whether those engaged in comparable acts on behalf of a government should also be included. Bear in mind that in the case of the Torture Convention it is precisely the work of Government agents that is criminalized. The General Assembly adopted the International Convention for the Protection of all Persons from Enforced Disappearance in December 2006, U.N. Doc. A/RES. 61/177. Disappearances are quintessential examples of state terrorism. *See* Maureen R. Berman & Roger S. Clark, *State Terrorism: Disappearances*, 13 RUTGERS L.J. 531 (1982). Article 2 of the Convention defines "enforced disappearance" as follows:

> For the purposes of this Convention, "enforced disappearance" is considered to be the arrest, detention, abduction or any other form of deprivation

> of liberty by agents of the State or by persons or groups of persons acting with the authorization, support or acquiescence of the State, followed by a refusal to acknowledge the deprivation of liberty or by concealment of the fate or whereabouts of the disappeared person, which place such a person outside the protection of the law.

The Security Council did take partial action regarding the crime of terrorism in 2001, when it adopted a resolution requiring states to take action to criminalize the provision or collection of funds for terrorist entities. *See* S.C. Res. 1373 (2001). Monitoring Committees have been established to enforce the Council's mandate. In December 2016, the General Assembly recommended the establishment of a working group to finalize a comprehensive convention on terrorism. Work towards that end continues glacially.

An area of growing concern in the modern age is the use of the internet by terrorist organizations. These concerns focus on at least two aspects of modern technology's impact on terrorist actors and organizations. First, the internet and social media platforms associated with internet-based communications have become a tool for recruitment, fundraising, and radicalization. Second, the vulnerabilities of an interconnected global internet have increased the incentives and abilities of terrorist organizations to engage in cyber attacks. *See* David P. Fidler, *Cyberspace, Terrorism and International Law*, 21 J. Conflict & Sec. L. 475 (2016).

B. Terrorism Laws in the U.S.

So far as U.S. law is concerned, an array of federal statutes proscribes terrorist activity. Many of these statutes implement international obligations under the relatively recent treaties mentioned above. Some are older. *United States v. Rahman*, 189 F.3d 88 (2d Cir. 1999), *cert. denied,* 120 S. Ct. 830 (2000), upheld the convictions of 10 defendants charged with "offenses arising out of a wide-ranging plot to conduct a campaign of urban terrorism"; they were convicted after a nine-month trial which included evidence of the defendants "rendering assistance to those who bombed the World Trade Center, planning to bomb bridges and tunnels in New York City, murdering Rabbi Meir Kahane, and planning to murder the President of Egypt." The principal charge against them was "seditious conspiracy" under a statute (18 U.S.C. § 2384) that dates back to the Civil War.

The term "international terrorism" as defined in 18 U.S.C. § 2331(1) for purposes of various offenses under 18 U.S.C. Chapter 113B, means activities that:

> (A) involve violent acts or acts dangerous to human life that are a violation of the criminal laws of the United States or of any State, or that would be a criminal violation if committed within the jurisdiction of the United States or of any State;
>
> (B) appear to be intended—
>
> (i) to intimidate or coerce a civilian population;

(ii) to influence the policy of a government by intimidation or coercion; or

(iii) to affect the conduct of a government by mass destruction, assassination, or kidnapping; and

(C) occur primarily outside the territorial jurisdiction of the United States, or transcend national boundaries in terms of the means by which they are accomplished, the persons they appear intended to intimidate or coerce, or the locale in which their perpetrators operate or seek asylum. . . .

September 11th has increased the United States' awareness of terrorism and many legal developments have resulted from this devastating tragedy. At the forefront of the legal changes was the passage of the "Uniting and Strengthening America by Providing Appropriate Tools Required to Intercept and Obstruct Terrorism (USA PATRIOT ACT) Act of 2001." (P.L. 107-56). This Act is divided as follows: Title I—Enhancing Domestic Security Against Terrorism, Title II—Enhanced Surveillance Procedures, Title III—International Money Laundering Abatement and Anti-Terrorist Financing Act of 2001, Title IV—Protecting the Border, Title V—Removing Obstacles to Investigating Terrorism, Title VI—Providing for Victims of Terrorism, Public Safety Officers, and Their Families, Title VII—Increased Information Sharing for Critical Infrastructure Protection, Title VIII—Strengthening the Criminal Laws Against Terrorism, Title IX—Improved Intelligence, and Title X—Miscellaneous.

The USA Patriot Act provided a definition for domestic terrorism (Sec. 802), expanding what was included within 18 U.S.C. § 2332b, thus allowing additional offenses to serve as a basis for terrorism, and included acts of terrorism as predicate offenses for a Racketeering (RICO) charge under 18 U.S.C. § 1961 (Sec. 813). As now found in 18 U.S.C. § 2331(5), the term "domestic terrorism" tracks the above definition of "international terrorism" found in the same Code provision, except the conduct "occur[s] primarily within the territorial jurisdiction of the United States." 18 U.S.C. § 2331(5)(C). As a result of the Patriot Act, the statute of limitations for the prosecution of some terrorism offenses was extended beyond the usual limits imposed for criminal activity (Sec. 809). Penalties for terrorism offenses were increased (Sec. 810 & 811).

As a result of this Act, terrorism crimes were also added to the list of offenses that could be used to intercept wire, oral, and electronic communications (Sec. 201 & 202). Roving wiretap surveillance was also permitted for foreign surveillance (Sec. 206). As a result of the USA Patriot Act, there were also fewer restrictions placed on some searches (Sec. 209–220). As discussed more fully in the Notes below, several of the more controversial provisions of the Patriot Act have now expired, but the law's impact on the legal landscape of terrorism investigations and prosecutions remains significant.

In addition to statutes defining substantive offenses, there also are specific procedural provisions applicable when the offense involves terrorism. For example, some terrorism offenses have an extended statute of limitations. *See* 18 U.S.C. § 3286.

Matters involving overseas terrorism require that prosecutors obtain authorization from the Assistant Attorney General in charge of the Criminal Division prior to starting a criminal investigation, filing an information, or seeking an indictment.

Statutes implementing the treaties mentioned above generally provide for extraterritorial jurisdiction over the specific forms of terrorism dealt with in those treaties. A fairly sweeping provision of the Omnibus Diplomatic Security and Antiterrorism Act of 1986 established federal "long-arm" jurisdiction over all terrorist attacks on U.S. nationals abroad (*see* 18 U.S.C. § 2332). An equally sweeping provision contained in the Antiterrorism and Effective Death Penalty Act of 1996 concerns acts of terrorism transcending national boundaries that affect the United States.

Key among the terrorism statutes in the United States is the following, found in title 18:

§ 2332b Acts of terrorism transcending national boundaries

(a) Prohibited acts.—

(1) Offenses.—Whoever, involving conduct transcending national boundaries and in a circumstance described in subsection (b)—

(A) kills, kidnaps, maims, commits an assault resulting in serious bodily injury, or assaults with a dangerous weapon any person within the United States; or

(B) creates a substantial risk of serious bodily injury to any other person by destroying or damaging any structure, conveyance, or other real or personal property within the United States or by attempting or conspiring to destroy or damage any structure, conveyance, or other real or personal property within the United States;

in violation of the laws of any State, or the United States, shall be punished as prescribed in subsection (c).

(2) Treatment of threats, attempts and conspiracies.—Whoever threatens to commit an offense under paragraph (1), or attempts or conspires to do so, shall be punished under subsection (c).

(b) Jurisdictional bases.—

(1) Circumstances.—The circumstances referred to in subsection (a) are—

(A) the mail or any facility of interstate or foreign commerce is used in furtherance of the offense;

(B) the offense obstructs, delays, or affects interstate or foreign commerce, or would have so obstructed, delayed, or affected interstate or foreign commerce if the offense had been consummated;

(C) the victim, or intended victim, is the United States Government, a member of the uniformed services, or any official, officer, employee, or agent of the legislative, executive, or judicial branches, or of any department or agency, of the United States;

(D) the structure, conveyance, or other real or personal property is, in whole or in part, owned, possessed, or leased to the United States, or any department or agency of the United States;

(E) the offense is committed in the territorial sea (including the airspace above and the seabed and subsoil below, and artificial islands and fixed structures erected thereon) of the United States; or

(F) the offense is committed within the special maritime and territorial jurisdiction of the United States.

(2) Co-conspirators and accessories after the fact.—Jurisdiction shall exist over all principals and co-conspirators of an offense under this section, and accessories after the fact to any offense under this section, if at least one of the circumstances described in subparagraphs (A) through (F) of paragraph (1) is applicable to at least one offender.

(c) Penalties.—

(1) Penalties.—Whoever violates this section shall be punished—

(A) for a killing, or if death results to any person from any other conduct prohibited by this section, by death, or by imprisonment for any term of years or for life;

(B) for kidnapping, by imprisonment for any term of years or for life;

(C) for maiming, by imprisonment for not more than 35 years;

(D) for assault with a dangerous weapon or assault resulting in serious bodily injury, by imprisonment for not more than 30 years;

(E) for destroying or damaging any structure, conveyance, or other real or personal property, by imprisonment for not more than 25 years;

(F) for attempting or conspiring to commit an offense, for any term of years up to the maximum punishment that would have applied had the offense been completed; and

(G) for threatening to commit an offense under this section, by imprisonment for not more than 10 years.

(2) Consecutive sentence.—Notwithstanding any other provision of law, the court shall not place on probation any person convicted of a violation of this section; nor shall the term of imprisonment imposed under this section run concurrently with any other term of imprisonment.

(d) Proof requirements.—The following shall apply to prosecutions under this section:

(1) Knowledge.—The prosecution is not required to prove knowledge by any defendant of a jurisdictional base alleged in the indictment.

(2) State law.—In a prosecution under this section that is based upon the adoption of State law, only the elements of the offense under State law, and not any provisions pertaining to criminal procedure or evidence, are adopted.

(e) Extraterritorial jurisdiction.—There is extraterritorial Federal jurisdiction—

(1) over any offense under subsection (a), including any threat, attempt, or conspiracy to commit such offense; and

(2) over conduct which, under section 3, renders any person an accessory after the fact to an offense under subsection (a).

(f) Investigative authority.—In addition to any other investigative authority with respect to violations of this title, the Attorney General shall have primary investigative responsibility for all Federal crimes of terrorism, and any violation of section 351(e), 844(e), 844(f)(1), 956(b), 1361, 1366(b), 1366(c), 1751(e), 2152, or 2156 of this title, and the Secretary of the Treasury shall assist the Attorney General at the request of the Attorney General. Nothing in this section shall be construed to interfere with the authority of the United States Secret Service under section 3056.

(g) Definitions.—As used in this section—

(1) the term "conduct transcending national boundaries" means conduct occurring outside of the United States in addition to the conduct occurring in the United States;

(2) the term "facility of interstate or foreign commerce" has the meaning given that term in section 1958(b)(2);

(3) the term "serious bodily injury" has the meaning given that term in section 1365(g)(3);

(4) the term "territorial sea of the United States" means all waters extending seaward to 12 nautical miles from the baselines of the United States, determined in accordance with international law; and

(5) the term "Federal crime of terrorism" means an offense that—

(A) is calculated to influence or affect the conduct of government by intimidation or coercion, or to retaliate against government conduct; and

(B) is a violation of—

(i) section 32 (relating to destruction of aircraft or aircraft facilities), 37 (relating to violence at international airports), 81 (relating to arson within special maritime and territorial jurisdiction), 175 or 175b (relating to biological weapons), 175c (relating to variola virus), 229 (relating to chemical weapons), subsection (a), (b), (c), or

(d) of section 351 (relating to congressional, cabinet, and Supreme Court assassination and kidnaping), 831 (relating to nuclear materials), 832 (relating to participation in nuclear and weapons of mass destruction threats to the United States)1 842(m) or (n) (relating to plastic explosives), 844(f)(2) or (3) (relating to arson and bombing of Government property risking or causing death), 844(i) (relating to arson and bombing of property used in interstate commerce), 930(c) (relating to killing or attempted killing during an attack on a Federal facility with a dangerous weapon), 956(a)(1) (relating to conspiracy to murder, kidnap, or maim persons abroad), 1030(a)(1) (relating to protection of computers), 1030(a)(5)(A) resulting in damage as defined in 1030(c)(4)(A)(i)(II) through (VI) (relating to protection of computers), 1114 (relating to killing or attempted killing of officers and employees of the United States), 1116 (relating to murder or manslaughter of foreign officials, official guests, or internationally protected persons), 1203 (relating to hostage taking), 1361 (relating to government property or contracts), 1362 (relating to destruction of communication lines, stations, or systems), 1363 (relating to injury to buildings or property within special maritime and territorial jurisdiction of the United States), 1366(a) (relating to destruction of an energy facility), 1751(a), (b), (c), or (d) (relating to Presidential and Presidential staff assassination and kidnaping), 1992 (relating to terrorist attacks and other acts of violence against railroad carriers and against mass transportation systems on land, on water, or through the air), 2155 (relating to destruction of national defense materials, premises, or utilities), 2156 (relating to national defense material, premises, or utilities), 2280 (relating to violence against maritime navigation), 2280a (relating to maritime safety), 2281 through 2281a (relating to violence against maritime fixed platforms), 2332 (relating to certain homicides and other violence against United States nationals occurring outside of the United States), 2332a (relating to use of weapons of mass destruction), 2332b (relating to acts of terrorism transcending national boundaries), 2332f (relating to bombing of public places and facilities), 2332g (relating to missile systems designed to destroy aircraft), 2332h (relating to radiological dispersal devices), 2332i (relating to acts of nuclear terrorism), 2339 (relating to harboring terrorists), 2339A (relating to providing material support to terrorists), 2339B (relating to providing material support to terrorist organizations), 2339C (relating to financing of terrorism), 2339D (relating to military-type training from a foreign terrorist organization), or 2340A (relating to torture) of this title;

(ii) sections 92 (relating to prohibitions governing atomic weapons) or 236 (relating to sabotage of nuclear facilities or fuel) of the Atomic Energy Act of 1954 (42 U.S.C. 2122 or 2284);

(iii) section 46502 (relating to aircraft piracy), the second sentence of section 46504 (relating to assault on a flight crew with a dangerous weapon), section 46505(b)(3) or (c) (relating to explosive or incendiary devices, or endangerment of human life by means of weapons, on aircraft), section 46506 if homicide or attempted homicide is involved (relating to application of certain criminal laws to acts on aircraft), or section 60123(b) (relating to destruction of interstate gas or hazardous liquid pipeline facility) of title 49; or

(iv) section 1010A of the Controlled Substances Import and Export Act (relating to narco-terrorism).

Notes

(1) In section 803 of the USA Patriot Act, section 2339 was added to title 18. It states:

§ 2339. Harboring or concealing terrorists

(a) Whoever harbors or conceals any person who he knows, or has reasonable grounds to believe, has committed, or is about to commit, an offense under section 32 (relating to destruction of aircraft or aircraft facilities), section 175 (relating to biological weapons), section 229 (relating to chemical weapons), section 831 (relating to nuclear materials), paragraph (2) or (3) of section 844(f) (relating to arson and bombing of government property risking or causing injury or death), section 1366(a) (relating to the destruction of an energy facility), section 2280 (relating to violence against maritime navigation), section 2332a (relating to weapons of mass destruction), or section 2332b (relating to acts of terrorism transcending national boundaries) of this title, section 236(a) (relating to sabotage of nuclear facilities or fuel) of the Atomic Energy Act of 1954 (42 U.S.C. 2284(a)), or section 46502 (relating to aircraft piracy) of title 49, shall be fined under this title or imprisoned not more than ten years, or both.

(b) A violation of this section may be prosecuted in any Federal judicial district in which the underlying offense was committed, or in any other Federal judicial district as provided by law. . . .

(2) Section 805 of the Patriot Act expanded the jurisdictional scope for crimes related to providing material support for terrorists. By removing the words "within the United States" from the material support provision adopted in 1994 as 18 U.S.C. § 2339A, the 2001 amendment made it extraterritorial in impact. What constitutes material support? Osama Bin Laden's chauffeur and publicist were later prosecuted before military commissions for providing material support, on the basis of the services they supplied (although their convictions were reversed on constitutional

grounds). Can a lawyer representing a client accused of terrorist acts, be considered part of the client's criminal acts? *See* Steve Fainaru & Brooke A. Masters, WASH. POST, Apr. 10, 2002, at A01 (discussing the indictment of "a prominent New York defense attorney and three others" "on charges of helping to pass unlawful messages between an Egyptian terrorist organization and an imprisoned Muslim cleric convicted in 1995 of plotting to blow up New York landmarks."); *see also Holder v. Humanitarian Law Project*, 561 U.S. 1 (2010) (upholding constitutionality of 18 U.S.C. § 2339B [Providing material support or resources to designated foreign terrorism organizations] as applied to plaintiffs seeking to "facilitate only the lawful, non-violent purposes" of two specified organizations). For an overview of the various sections of the U.S. Code applying to terrorism offenses, see ELLEN S. PODGOR, ROGER S. CLARK, AND LUCIAN E. DERVAN, UNDERSTANDING INTERNATIONAL CRIMINAL LAW 95–97 (4th ed. 2022).

(3) Domestic terrorism continues to be an area of growing concern in the United States. In 2021 testimony before the United States Congress, FBI Director Christopher Wray stated, "[t]he problem of domestic terrorism has been metastasizing across the country for a long time now and it's not going away anytime soon. . . . At the FBI, we've been sounding the alarm on it for a number of years now." *See* Eric Tucker & Mary Clare Jalonick, *FBI Chief Warns Violent "Domestic Terrorism" Growing in US*, AP NEWS (March 2, 2021). Further, according to a 2015 report from the Southern Poverty Law Center, many domestic terrorist acts are committed by "lone wolf" attackers (those operating on their own) and, therefore, are harder to identify in advance and thwart. In the SPLC study, 74% of the terrorist incidents identified between 2009 and 2015 were perpetrated by lone wolf attackers, while 90% of the incidents were carried out by one or two people. *See* Southern Poverty Law Center, *Lone Wolf Report* (February 12, 2015).

C. How Does Terrorism Affect Investigative Techniques?

The Foreign Intelligence Surveillance Act 1978 was amended as a result of the USA Patriot Act. Consider the following interpretation provided in this landmark decision:

In re Sealed Case

United States Foreign Intelligence Surveillance Court of Review
310 F.3d 717 (2002)

PER CURIAM: This is the first appeal from the Foreign Intelligence Surveillance Court to the Court of Review since the passage of the Foreign Intelligence Surveillance Act (FISA), 50 U.S.C. §§ 1801–1862 . . . in 1978. This appeal is brought by the United States from a FISA court surveillance order which imposed certain restrictions on the government. Since the government is the only party to FISA proceedings, we have accepted briefs filed by the American Civil Liberties Union (ACLU) and the National Association of Criminal Defense Lawyers (NACDL) as amici curiae.

The court's decision from which the government appeals imposed certain requirements and limitations accompanying an order authorizing electronic surveillance of an "agent of a foreign power" as defined in FISA. There is no disagreement between the government and the FISA court as to the propriety of the electronic surveillance; the court found that the government had shown probable cause to believe that the target is an agent of a foreign power and otherwise met the basic requirements of FISA. The government's application for a surveillance order contains detailed information to support its contention that the target, who is a United States person, is aiding, abetting, or conspiring with others in international terrorism. The FISA court authorized the surveillance, but imposed certain restrictions, which the government contends are neither mandated nor authorized by FISA. . . .

To ensure the Justice Department followed these strictures the court also fashioned what the government refers to as a "chaperone requirement"; that a unit of the Justice Department, the Office of Intelligence Policy and Review (OIPR) (composed of 31 lawyers and 25 support staff), "be invited" to all meetings between the FBI and the Criminal Division involving consultations for the purpose of coordinating efforts "to investigate or protect against foreign attack or other grave hostile acts, sabotage, international terrorism, or clandestine intelligence activities by foreign powers or their agents." If representatives of OIPR are unable to attend such meetings, "OIPR shall be apprized of the substance of the meetings forthwith in writing so that the Court may be notified at the earliest opportunity."

These restrictions are not original to the order appealed. They are actually set forth in an opinion written by the former Presiding Judge of the FISA court on May 17 of this year. But since that opinion did not accompany an order conditioning an approval of an electronic surveillance application it was not appealed. It is, however, the basic decision before us and it is its rationale that the government challenges. The opinion was issued after an oral argument before all of the then-serving FISA district judges and clearly represents the views of all those judges.

We think it fair to say, however, that the May 17 opinion of the FISA court does not clearly set forth the basis for its decision. It appears to proceed from the assumption that FISA constructed a barrier between counterintelligence/intelligence officials and law enforcement officers in the Executive Branch—indeed, it uses the word "wall" popularized by certain commentators (and journalists) to describe that supposed barrier. Yet the opinion does not support that assumption with any relevant language from the statute.

The "wall" emerges from the court's implicit interpretation of FISA. The court apparently believes it can approve applications for electronic surveillance only if the government's objective is not primarily directed toward criminal prosecution of the foreign agents for their foreign intelligence activity. . . .

Instead the court relied for its imposition of the disputed restrictions on its statutory authority to approve "minimization procedures" designed to prevent the acquisition, retention, and dissemination within the government of material gathered in an electronic surveillance that is unnecessary to the government's need for foreign intelligence information. 50 U.S.C. § 1801(h).... [The court discussed its authority to review.]

The government makes two main arguments. The first, it must be noted, was not presented to the FISA court; indeed, insofar as we can determine it has never previously been advanced either before a court or Congress. That argument is that the supposed pre-Patriot Act limitation in FISA that restricts the government's intention to use foreign intelligence information in criminal prosecutions is an illusion; it finds no support in either the language of FISA or its legislative history. The government does recognize that several courts of appeals, while upholding the use of FISA surveillances, have opined that FISA may be used only if the government's primary purpose in pursuing foreign intelligence information is not criminal prosecution, but the government argues that those decisions, which did not carefully analyze the statute, were incorrect in their statements, if not incorrect in their holdings.

Alternatively, the government contends that even if the primary purpose test was a legitimate construction of FISA prior to the passage of the Patriot Act, that Act's amendments to FISA eliminate that concept. And as a corollary, the government insists the FISA court's construction of the minimization procedures is far off the mark both because it is a misconstruction of those provisions per se, as well as an end run around the specific amendments in the Patriot Act designed to deal with the real issue underlying this case. The government, moreover, contends that the FISA court's restrictions, which the court described as minimization procedures, are so intrusive into the operation of the Department of Justice as to exceed the constitutional authority of Article III judges.

The government's brief, and its supplementary brief requested by this court, also set forth its view that the primary purpose test is not required by the Fourth Amendment. The ACLU and NACDL argue, inter alia, the contrary; that the statutes are unconstitutional unless they are construed as prohibiting the government from obtaining approval of an application under FISA if its "primary purpose" is criminal prosecution....

....

The government argues persuasively that arresting and prosecuting terrorist agents of, or spies for, a foreign power may well be the best technique to prevent them from successfully continuing their terrorist or espionage activity. The government might wish to surveil the agent for some period of time to discover other participants in a conspiracy or to uncover a foreign power's plans, but typically at some point the government would wish to apprehend the agent and it might be that only a prosecution would provide sufficient incentives for the agent to cooperate with the government.... Congress was concerned about the government's use of FISA surveillance to obtain information not truly intertwined with the government's efforts to protect against threats from foreign powers.... But Congress did not impose any restrictions on the government's use of the foreign intelligence information to prosecute agents of foreign powers for foreign intelligence crimes....

In sum, we think that the FISA as passed by Congress in 1978 clearly did not preclude or limit the government's use or proposed use of foreign intelligence information, which included evidence of certain kinds of criminal activity, in a criminal prosecution....

Apparently to avoid running afoul of the primary purpose test used by some courts, the 1995 Procedures limited contacts between the FBI and the Criminal Division in cases where FISA surveillance or searches were being conducted by the FBI for foreign intelligence (FI) or foreign counterintelligence (FCI) purposes.... The Department's attitude changed somewhat after the May 2000 report by the Attorney General and a July 2001 Report by the General Accounting Office both concluded that the Department's concern over how the FISA court or other federal courts might interpret the primary purpose test has inhibited necessary coordination between intelligence and law enforcement officials.... But it does not appear that the Department thought of these internal procedures as "minimization procedures" required under FISA. Nevertheless, the FISA court was aware that the procedures were being followed by the Department and apparently adopted elements of them in certain cases....

The passage of the Patriot Act altered and to some degree muddied the landscape.... Although the Patriot Act amendments to FISA expressly sanctioned consultation and coordination between intelligence and law enforcement officials, in response to the first applications filed by OIPR under those amendments, in November 2001, the FISA court for the first time adopted the 1995 Procedures, as augmented by the January 2000 and August 2001 Procedures, as "minimization procedures" to apply in all cases before the court.

The Attorney General interpreted the Patriot Act quite differently. On March 6, 2002, the Attorney General approved new "Intelligence Sharing Procedures" to implement the Act's amendments to FISA. The 2002 Procedures supersede prior procedures and were designed to permit the complete exchange of information and advice between intelligence and law enforcement officials.... Undeterred, the government submitted the application at issue in this appeal on July 19, 2002, and expressly proposed using the 2002 Procedures without modification....

The FISA court's decision and order not only misinterpreted and misapplied minimization procedures it was entitled to impose, but as the government argues persuasively, the FISA court may well have exceeded the constitutional bounds that restrict an Article III court. The FISA court asserted authority to govern the internal organization and investigative procedures of the Department of Justice which are the province of the Executive Branch (Article II) and the Congress (Article I)....

But in today's world things are not so simple. In many cases, surveillance will have two key goals—the gathering of foreign intelligence, and the gathering of evidence for a criminal prosecution. Determining which purpose is the "primary" purpose of the investigation can be difficult, and will only become more so as we coordinate our intelligence and law enforcement efforts in the war against terror.

Rather than forcing law enforcement to decide which purpose is primary—law enforcement or foreign intelligence gathering, this bill strikes a new balance. It will now require that a "significant" purpose of the investigation must be foreign intelligence gathering to proceed with surveillance under FISA. The effect of this provision will be to make it easier for law enforcement to obtain a FISA search or surveillance warrant for those cases where the subject of the surveillance is both a potential source of valuable intelligence and the potential target of a criminal prosecution. Many of the individuals involved in supporting the September 11 attacks may well fall into both of these categories....

In sum, there can be no doubt as to Congress' intent in amending section 1804(a)(7)(B). Indeed, it went further to emphasize its purpose in breaking down barriers between criminal law enforcement and intelligence (or counterintelligence) gathering by adding section 1806(k).... The FISA court noted this amendment but thought that Congress' approval of consultations was not equivalent to authorizing law enforcement officers to give advice to officers who were conducting electronic surveillance nor did it sanction law enforcement officers "directing or controlling" surveillances.... Beyond that, when Congress explicitly authorizes consultation and coordination between different offices in the government, without even suggesting a limitation on who is to direct and control, it necessarily implies that either could be taking the lead.

Neither amicus brief defends the reasoning of the FISA court. NACDL's brief makes no attempt to interpret FISA or the Patriot Act amendments but rather argues the primary purpose test is constitutionally compelled.... The ACLU insists that the significant purpose amendment only "clarified" the law permitting FISA surveillance orders "even if foreign intelligence is not its exclusive purpose" (emphasis added).

Accordingly, the Patriot Act amendments clearly disapprove the primary purpose test. And as a matter of straightforward logic, if a FISA application can be granted even if "foreign intelligence" is only a significant—not a primary—purpose, another purpose can be primary. One other legitimate purpose that could exist is to prosecute a target for a foreign intelligence crime. We therefore believe the Patriot Act amply supports the government's alternative argument but, paradoxically, the Patriot Act would seem to conflict with the government's first argument because by using the term "significant purpose," the Act now implies that another purpose is to be distinguished from a foreign intelligence purpose....

That leaves us with something of an analytic conundrum. On the one hand, Congress did not amend the definition of foreign intelligence information which, we have explained, includes evidence of foreign intelligence crimes. On the other hand, Congress accepted the dichotomy between foreign intelligence and law enforcement by adopting the significant purpose test. Nevertheless, it is our task to do our best to read the statute to honor congressional intent. The better reading, it seems to us, excludes from the purpose of gaining foreign intelligence information a sole objective of criminal prosecution. We therefore reject the government's argument to the contrary. Yet this may not make much practical difference. Because, as the government points out, when it commences an electronic surveillance of a foreign agent, typically it will not have decided whether to prosecute the agent (whatever may be the subjective intent of the investigators or lawyers who initiate an investigation). So long as the government entertains a realistic option of dealing with the agent other than through criminal prosecution, it satisfies the significant purpose test.

The important point is — and here we agree with the government — the Patriot Act amendment, by using the word "significant," eliminated any justification for the FISA court to balance the relative weight the government places on criminal prosecution as compared to other counterintelligence responses. If the certification of the application's purpose articulates a broader objective than criminal prosecution — such as stopping an ongoing conspiracy — and includes other potential non-prosecutorial responses, the government meets the statutory test. Of course, if the court concluded that the government's sole objective was merely to gain evidence of past criminal conduct — even foreign intelligence crimes — to punish the agent rather than halt ongoing espionage or terrorist activity, the application should be denied.

The government claims that even prosecutions of non-foreign intelligence crimes are consistent with a purpose of gaining foreign intelligence information so long as the government's objective is to stop espionage or terrorism by putting an agent of a foreign power in prison. That interpretation transgresses the original FISA. It will be recalled that Congress intended section 1804(a)(7)(B) to prevent the government from targeting a foreign agent when its "true purpose" was to gain non-foreign intelligence information — such as evidence of ordinary crimes or scandals.... It can be argued, however, that by providing that an application is to be granted if the government has only a "significant purpose" of gaining foreign intelligence information, the Patriot Act allows the government to have a primary objective of prosecuting an agent for a non-foreign intelligence crime. Yet we think that would be an anomalous reading of the amendment. For we see not the slightest indication that Congress meant to give that power to the Executive Branch. Accordingly, the manifestation of such a purpose, it seems to us, would continue to disqualify an application. That is not to deny that ordinary crimes might be inextricably intertwined with foreign intelligence crimes. For example, if a group of international terrorists were to engage in bank robberies in order to finance the manufacture of a bomb, evidence of the bank robbery should be treated just as evidence of the terrorist act itself. But the FISA process cannot be used as a device to investigate wholly unrelated ordinary crimes.

One final point; we think the government's purpose as set forth in a section 1804(a)(7)(B) certification is to be judged by the national security official's articulation and not by a FISA court inquiry into the origins of an investigation nor an examination of the personnel involved. It is up to the Director of the FBI, who typically certifies, to determine the government's national security purpose, as approved by the Attorney General or Deputy Attorney General. This is not a standard whose application the FISA court legitimately reviews by seeking to inquire into which Justice Department officials were instigators of an investigation. All Justice Department officers — including those in the FBI — are under the control of the Attorney General. If he wishes a particular investigation to be run by an officer of any division, that is his prerogative. There is nothing in FISA or the Patriot Act that suggests otherwise. That means, perforce, if the FISA court has reason to doubt that the government has any real non-prosecutorial purpose in seeking foreign intelligence information it can demand further inquiry into the certifying officer's purpose — or perhaps even the Attorney General's or Deputy Attorney General's reasons for approval. The important point is that the relevant purpose is that of those senior officials in the Executive Branch who have the responsibility of appraising the government's national security needs. . . .

Having determined that FISA, as amended, does not oblige the government to demonstrate to the FISA court that its primary purpose in conducting electronic surveillance is not criminal prosecution, we are obliged to consider whether the statute as amended is consistent with the Fourth Amendment. . . . [The court then discusses Title III's relationship and Fourth Amendment concerns].

FISA's general programmatic purpose, to protect the nation against terrorists and espionage threats directed by foreign powers, has from its outset been distinguishable from "ordinary crime control." After the events of September 11, 2001, though, it is hard to imagine greater emergencies facing Americans than those experienced on that date.

We acknowledge, however, that the constitutional question presented by this case — whether Congress's disapproval of the primary purpose test is consistent with the Fourth Amendment — has no definitive jurisprudential answer. The Supreme Court's special needs cases involve random stops (seizures) not electronic searches. In one sense, they can be thought of as a greater encroachment into personal privacy because they are not based on any particular suspicion. On the other hand, wiretapping is a good deal more intrusive than an automobile stop accompanied by questioning.

Although the Court in City of Indianapolis cautioned that the threat to society is not dispositive in determining whether a search or seizure is reasonable, it certainly remains a crucial factor. Our case may well involve the most serious threat our country faces. Even without taking into account the President's inherent constitutional authority to conduct warrantless foreign intelligence surveillance, we think the procedures and government showings required under FISA, if they do not meet the minimum Fourth Amendment warrant standards, certainly come close. We, therefore, believe firmly, applying the balancing test drawn from Keith, that FISA as amended is constitutional because the surveillances it authorizes are reasonable.

Accordingly, we reverse the FISA court's orders in this case to the extent they imposed conditions on the grant of the government's applications, vacate the FISA court's Rule 11, and remand with instructions to grant the applications as submitted and proceed henceforth in accordance with this opinion.

Notes

(1) The Patriot Act and counter-terrorism operations after 9/11 raised many questions about how the government was collecting and using data as part of its investigations. Large data collection programs targeting telephone records, for example, date back at least to the 1980s when the DEA began collecting "toll records" as part of drug cartel investigations. By the 1990s, the DEA had expanded the operation to collect data on all telephone calls from the United States to countries linked to the narcotics trade, not just particular suspects. Initially, the data was used in limited investigations involving large narcotics or terrorism investigations. Over time, however, the use of the data expanded and is reported to have included up to 116 countries. In 2013, then Attorney General Eric Holder suspended the program, and the data that had been collected was eventually purged. *See* Brad Heath, *U.S. Secretly Tracked Billions of Calls for Decades*, USA Today (April 7, 2015).

(2) Soon after September 11, 2001, the Executive instituted a warrantless electronic surveillance program ("Terrorist Surveillance Program" or "TSP") outside the aegis of FISA. It permitted surveillance of communications between an overseas person and someone in the United States where one person was suspected of being associated with Al Qaeda. The constitutionality of TSP was litigated in *ACLU v. NSA*. The District Court held that the program violated "the APA; the Separation of Powers doctrine; the First and Fourth Amendments of the United States Constitution; and the statutory law." 438 F. Supp. 2d 754 (E.D. Mich. 2006). On appeal, a two-judge majority of the Court of Appeals held that the plaintiffs lacked standing. The dissent contended that the attorney-plaintiffs had standing because of the chilling effects the program could have on their international practice. He would have held that the program ran counter to the clear language of FISA. 493 F.3d 644 (6th Cir. 2007). The Supreme Court denied certiorari without comment. 552 U.S. 1179 (2008). The dissent also dealt with the Government's argument of mootness, based on its January 2007 announcement that it reached a secret agreement with the FISA Court that the TSP would comply with FISA. Nonetheless, the Government maintained its position that the TSP did not violate the Constitution or any statute and that the President has authority to "opt out" of the FISA framework.

(3) In August 2007, soon after the Court of Appeals decision in Note (2), Congress adopted the Protect America Act, Public Law No: 110-55, which re-defined electronic surveillance under FISA so as not to include "surveillance directed at a person reasonably believed to be located outside the United States." The Attorney-General or the Director of National Intelligence was empowered to authorize the acquisition of foreign intelligence information with the assistance of a communications service provider (such as phone companies, AOL, Gmail, Skype, internet services). The

FISA Court had only a limited role. The legislation was subject to a sunset clause expiring in February 2008. Congress and the President tussled over a renewal Bill that included immunity for providers who had cooperated with the Government between 2001 and January 2007. Ultimately the Foreign Intelligence Surveillance Act of 1978 Amendments Act of 2008, Public Law No. 110-261, renewed the Executive's power. The FISA Court was empowered only to review and approve, or order modifications to, the procedures required by the Act to ensure compliance with the Fourth Amendment. The Act includes a complex procedure for determining immunity for past cooperation with the Government. The FISA Amendments Act Reauthorization Act of 2012, Public Law No. 112-238, extended the Protect America Act for another five years. In 2018, the FISA Amendments Reauthorization Act of 2017 reauthorized section 702 for six years and included additional privacy safeguards under FISA. According to a 2019 FISA court decision, the FBI has been regularly committing "widespread violations" of the FISA court's rules when analysts are querying the data set. *See* Charlie Savage, *Court Approves Warrantless Surveillance Rules While Scolding F.B.I.*, New York Times (September 5, 2020).

(4) In *In re: Directives [redacted text] pursuant to Section 105B of the Foreign Surveillance Act*, 551 F.3d 1004 (2008) the Foreign Intelligence Surveillance Court of Review upheld the constitutionality of directives made to a service provider under the Protect America Act. Recapitulating its discussion, the Court said:

> After assessing the prophylactic procedures available here, including the provisions of the PAA, the affidavits supporting the certifications, section 2.5 of Executive order 12333, and the declaration mentioned above, we conclude that they are very much in tune with the considerations discussed in the *Sealed Case*. Collectively, these procedures require a showing of particularity, a meaningful probable cause determination, and a showing of necessity. They also require a durational limit not to exceed 90 days — an interval that we previously found reasonable. *See In re Sealed Case, supra.* Finally, the risks of error and abuse are within acceptable limits and effective minimization procedures are in place.
>
> Balancing these findings against the vital nature of the government's national security interest and the manner of the intrusion, we hold that the surveillances at issue satisfy the Fourth Amendment's reasonableness requirement.

(5) Section 215 of the Patriot Act, which sunset in 2020, amended FISA to provide:

> The Director of the Federal Bureau of Investigation or a designee of the Director (whose rank shall be no lower than Assistant Special Agent in Charge) may make an application [to the Foreign Intelligence Surveillance Court] for an order requiring the production of any tangible things (including books, records, papers, documents, and other items) for an investigation to protect against international terrorism or clandestine intelligence activities, provided that such investigation of a United States person is not

> conducted solely upon the basis of activities protected by the first amendment to the Constitution.

Such an application was required to include "a statement of facts showing that there are reasonable grounds to believe that the tangible things sought are *relevant to an authorized investigation* (*other than a threat assessment*) conducted . . . to obtain foreign intelligence information not concerning a United States person or to protect against international terrorism or clandestine intelligence activities. . . ." (Emphasis added.).

A document leaked by Edward Snowden in 2013 revealed that, since at least 2006, the National Security Agency ("NSA") had obtained secret authority from FISA courts, purportedly on the basis of section 215, to collect "telephone metadata." This involved the collection in bulk on a daily and ongoing basis of the metadata associated with all telephone calls made by and to Americans, aggregated into a repository or data bank that could later be queried. In *American Civil Liberties Union v. Clapper*, 785 F.3d 787 (2d Cir. 2015) the Court, focusing particularly on the language emphasized above, held that the program was not authorized by the statute. It thus found no need to address the substantial Fourth and First Amendment issues that were raised. It is believed that section 215 never provided information that prevented a terrorist attack. According to reports, the program's only achievement throughout its many years was to lead the government to reopen an investigation that led to the prosecution of several men for sending money to a Somali terrorist group. *See* Charlie Savage, *Court Approves Warrantless Surveillance Rules While Scolding F.B.I.*, New York Times (September 5, 2020). The defendants in that case appealed their convictions based on the government's use of the data collection program. In an opinion only released after section 215 had sunset in 2020, the Ninth Circuit Court of Appeals affirmed those convictions, but found that the "government may have violated the Fourth Amendment and did violate the Foreign Intelligence Surveillance Act ("FISA") when it collected the telephony metadata of millions of Americans, including at least one of the defendants. . . ." *See United States v. Ahmed Nasir Taalil*, 973 F.3d 977 (9th Cir. 2020).

§ 9.03 Enemy Combatants and Military Commissions

The appropriate forum for prosecuting terrorists has been the subject of significant controversy in the United States. There have been questions concerning the propriety of military tribunals and the holding of individuals without legal recourse. Key questions have been whether individuals being held by the military, should be considered terrorists, prisoners of war, enemy combatants, or another status; and what, if any, rights do these individuals have? *See* Gail Gibson, *Secret Anti-Terror Court at Issue*, The Sun, Nov. 19, 2001, at 1; William Glaberson, *Critics' Attack on Tribunals Turn to Law Among Nations*, N.Y. Times, Dec. 26, 2001, at B1. *But see* Ruth

Wedgewood, Commentary, *The Case for Military Tribunals*, WALL ST. J., Dec. 3, 2001 (advocating for military tribunals).

The following case considers the role of courts relating to cases of individuals held at Guantanamo Bay Naval Base in Cuba:

Hamdan v. Rumsfeld

Supreme Court of the United States
548 U.S. 557 (2006)

JUSTICE STEVENS announced the judgment of the Court and delivered the opinion of the Court with respect to Parts I through IV, Parts VI through VI-D-iii, Part VI-D-v, and Part VII, and an opinion with respect to Parts V and VI-D-iv, in which JUSTICE SOUTER, JUSTICE GINSBURG, and JUSTICE BREYER join.

Petitioner Salim Ahmed Hamdan, a Yemeni national, is in custody at an American prison in Guantanamo Bay, Cuba. In November 2001, during hostilities between the United States and the Taliban (which then governed Afghanistan), Hamdan was captured by militia forces and turned over to the U.S. military. In June 2002, he was transported to Guantanamo Bay. Over a year later, the President deemed him eligible for trial by military commission for then-unspecified crimes. After another year had passed, Hamdan was charged with one count of conspiracy "to commit ... offenses triable by military commission." ...

Hamdan filed petitions for writs of habeas corpus and mandamus to challenge the Executive Branch's intended means of prosecuting this charge. He concedes that a court-martial constituted in accordance with the Uniform Code of Military Justice.... would have authority to try him. His objection is that the military commission the President has convened lacks such authority, for two principal reasons: First, neither congressional Act nor the common law of war supports trial by this commission for the crime of conspiracy—an offense that, Hamdan says, is not a violation of the law of war. Second, Hamdan contends, the procedures that the President has adopted to try him violate the most basic tenets of military and international law, including the principle that a defendant must be permitted to see and hear the evidence against him....

For the reasons that follow, we conclude that the military commission convened to try Hamdan lacks power to proceed because its structure and procedures violate both the UCMJ and the Geneva Conventions. Four of us also conclude, see Part V, *infra*, that the offense with which Hamdan has been charged is not an "offense that by ... the law of war may be tried by military commissions."

I

On September 11, 2001, agents of the al Qaeda terrorist organization hijacked commercial airplanes and attacked the World Trade Center in New York City and the national headquarters of the Department of Defense in Arlington, Virginia. Americans will never forget the devastation wrought by these acts. Nearly 3,000 civilians were killed.

Congress responded by adopting a Joint Resolution authorizing the President to "use all necessary and appropriate force against those nations, organizations, or persons he determines planned, authorized, committed, or aided the terrorist attacks . . . in order to prevent any future acts of international terrorism against the United States by such nations, organizations or persons." Authorization for Use of Military Force (AUMF) . . . . Acting pursuant to the AUMF, and having determined that the Taliban regime had supported al Qaeda, the President ordered the Armed Forces of the United States to invade Afghanistan. In the ensuing hostilities, hundreds of individuals, Hamdan among them, were captured and eventually detained at Guantanamo Bay.

On November 13, 2001, while the United States was still engaged in active combat with the Taliban, the President issued a comprehensive military order intended to govern the "Detention, Treatment, and Trial of Certain Non-Citizens in the War Against Terrorism," . . . (hereinafter November 13 Order or Order). Those subject to the November 13 Order include any noncitizen for whom the President determines "there is reason to believe" that he or she (1) "is or was" a member of al Qaeda or (2) has engaged or participated in terrorist activities aimed at or harmful to the United States. . . . Any such individual "shall, when tried, be tried by military commission for any and all offenses triable by military commission that such individual is alleged to have committed, and may be punished in accordance with the penalties provided under applicable law, including imprisonment or death." The November 13 Order vested in the Secretary of Defense the power to appoint military commissions to try individuals subject to the Order, but that power has since been delegated to John D. Altenberg, Jr., a retired Army major general and longtime military lawyer who has been designated "Appointing Authority for Military Commissions."

On July 3, 2003, the President announced his determination that Hamdan and five other detainees at Guantanamo Bay were subject to the November 13 Order and thus triable by military commission. . . . The charging document, which is unsigned, contains 13 numbered paragraphs. The first two paragraphs recite the asserted bases for the military commission's jurisdiction — namely, the November 13 Order and the President's July 3, 2003, declaration that Hamdan is eligible for trial by military commission. The next nine paragraphs, collectively entitled "General Allegations," describe al Qaeda's activities from its inception in 1989 through 2001 and identify Osama bin Laden as the group's leader. Hamdan is not mentioned in these paragraphs.

Only the final two paragraphs, entitled "Charge: Conspiracy," contain allegations against Hamdan. Paragraph 12 charges that "from on or about February 1996 to on or about November 24, 2001," Hamdan "willfully and knowingly joined an enterprise of persons who shared a common criminal purpose and conspired and agreed with [named members of al Qaeda] to commit the following offenses triable by military commission: attacking civilians; attacking civilian objects; murder by an unprivileged belligerent; and terrorism." . . . There is no allegation that Hamdan had any command responsibilities, played a leadership role, or participated in the planning of any activity.

Paragraph 13 lists four "overt acts" that Hamdan is alleged to have committed sometime between 1996 and November 2001 in furtherance of the "enterprise and conspiracy": (1) he acted as Osama bin Laden's "bodyguard and personal driver," "believing" all the while that bin Laden "and his associates were involved in" terrorist acts prior to and including the attacks of September 11, 2001; (2) he arranged for transportation of, and actually transported, weapons used by al Qaeda members and by bin Laden's bodyguards (Hamdan among them); (3) he "drove or accompanied Osama bin Laden to various al Qaida-sponsored training camps, press conferences, or lectures," at which bin Laden encouraged attacks against Americans; and (4) he received weapons training at al Qaeda-sponsored camps....

After this formal charge was filed, the United States District Court for the Western District of Washington transferred Hamdan's habeas and mandamus petitions to the United States District Court for the District of Columbia. Meanwhile, a Combatant Status Review Tribunal (CSRT) convened pursuant to a military order issued on July 7, 2004, decided that Hamdan's continued detention at Guantanamo Bay was warranted because he was an "enemy combatant."[1] Separately, proceedings before the military commission commenced.

On November 8, 2004, however, the District Court granted Hamdan's petition for habeas corpus and stayed the commission's proceedings.... The Court of Appeals for the District of Columbia Circuit reversed.... On November 7, 2005, we granted certiorari to decide whether the military commission convened to try Hamdan has authority to do so, and whether Hamdan may rely on the Geneva Conventions in these proceedings.

II

On February 13, 2006, the Government filed a motion to dismiss the writ of certiorari. The ground cited for dismissal was the recently enacted Detainee Treatment Act of 2005 (DTA), Pub. L. 109-148, 119 Stat. 2739. We postponed our ruling on that motion pending argument on the merits, ... and now deny it.

III

Relying on our decision in [*Schlesinger v.*] *Councilman,* 420 U.S. 738, the Government argues that, even if we have statutory jurisdiction, we should apply the "judge-made rule that civilian courts should await the final outcome of on-going military proceedings before entertaining an attack on those proceedings." ... Like the District Court and the Court of Appeals before us, we reject this argument.

1. An "enemy combatant" is defined by the military order as "an individual who was part of or supporting Taliban or al Qaeda forces, or associated forces that are engaged in hostilities against the United States or its coalition partners." ...

In *Councilman*, an army officer on active duty was referred to a court-martial for trial on charges that he violated the UCMJ by selling, transferring, and possessing marijuana. . . . Objecting that the alleged offenses were not "'service connected,'" . . . the officer filed suit in Federal District Court to enjoin the proceedings. He neither questioned the lawfulness of courts-martial or their procedures nor disputed that, as a serviceman, he was subject to court-martial jurisdiction. His sole argument was that the subject matter of his case did not fall within the scope of court-martial authority. . . . The District Court granted his request for injunctive relief, and the Court of Appeals affirmed.

We granted certiorari and reversed. . . . We did not reach the merits of whether the marijuana charges were sufficiently "service connected" to place them within the subject-matter jurisdiction of a court-martial. Instead, we concluded that, as a matter of comity, federal courts should normally abstain from intervening in pending court-martial proceedings against members of the Armed Forces, and further that there was nothing in the particular circumstances of the officer's case to displace that general rule. . . . *Councilman* identifies two considerations of comity that together favor abstention pending completion of ongoing court-martial proceedings against service personnel. . . . First, military discipline and, therefore, the efficient operation of the Armed Forces are best served if the military justice system acts without regular interference from civilian courts. . . . Second, federal courts should respect the balance that Congress struck between military preparedness and fairness to individual service members when it created "an integrated system of military courts and review procedures, a critical element of which is the Court of Military Appeals, consisting of civilian judges 'completely removed from all military influence or persuasion. . . .'" Just as abstention in the face of ongoing state criminal proceedings is justified by our expectation that state courts will enforce federal rights, so abstention in the face of ongoing court-martial proceedings is justified by our expectation that the military court system established by Congress — with its substantial procedural protections and provision for appellate review by independent civilian judges — "will vindicate servicemen's constitutional rights," . . . .

The same cannot be said here; indeed, neither of the comity considerations identified in *Councilman* weighs in favor of abstention in this case. First, Hamdan is not a member of our Nation's Armed Forces, so concerns about military discipline do not apply. Second, the tribunal convened to try Hamdan is not part of the integrated system of military courts, complete with independent review panels that Congress has established. Unlike the officer in *Councilman*, Hamdan has no right to appeal any conviction to the civilian judges of the Court of Military Appeals (now called the United States Court of Appeals for the Armed Forces, see Pub. L. 103-337, 108 Stat. 2831). Instead, under Dept. of Defense Military Commission Order No. 1 (Commission Order No. 1), which was issued by the President on March 21, 2002, and amended most recently on August 31, 2005, and which governs the procedures for Hamdan's commission, any conviction would be reviewed by a panel consisting of three military officers designated by the Secretary of Defense.... Commission Order No. 1 provides that appeal of a review panel's decision may be had only to the Secretary of Defense himself, § 6(H)(5), and then, finally, to the President, § 6(H)(6).

We have no doubt that the various individuals assigned review power under Commission Order No. 1 would strive to act impartially and ensure that Hamdan receive all protections to which he is entitled. Nonetheless, these review bodies clearly lack the structural insulation from military influence that characterizes the Court of Appeals for the Armed Forces, and thus bear insufficient conceptual similarity to state courts to warrant invocation of abstention principles.

In sum, neither of the two comity considerations underlying our decision to abstain in *Councilman* applies to the circumstances of this case. Instead, this Court's decision in *Quirin* is the most relevant precedent. [*Ex parte Quirin*, 317 U.S. 1 (1942).] In *Quirin*, seven German saboteurs were captured upon arrival by submarine in New York and Florida.... The President convened a military commission to try the saboteurs, who then filed habeas corpus petitions in the United States District Court for the District of Columbia challenging their trial by commission. We granted the saboteurs' petition for certiorari to the Court of Appeals before judgment.... Far from abstaining pending the conclusion of military proceedings, which were ongoing, we convened a special Term to hear the case and expedited our review. That course of action was warranted, we explained, "in view of the public importance of the questions raised by [the cases] and of the duty which rests on the courts, in time of war as well as in time of peace, to preserve unimpaired the constitutional safeguards of civil liberty, and because in our opinion the public interest required that we consider and decide those questions without any avoidable delay."...

As the Court of Appeals here recognized, *Quirin* "provides a compelling historical precedent for the power of civilian courts to entertain challenges that seek to interrupt the processes of military commissions."... The circumstances of this case, like those in *Quirin*, simply do not implicate the "obligations of comity" that, under appropriate circumstances, justify abstention....

Finally, the Government has identified no other "important countervailing interest" that would permit federal courts to depart from their general "duty to exercise the jurisdiction that is conferred upon them by Congress."... To the contrary, Hamdan and the Government both have a compelling interest in knowing in advance whether Hamdan may be tried by a military commission that arguably is without any basis in law and operates free from many of the procedural rules prescribed by Congress for courts-martial—rules intended to safeguard the accused and ensure the reliability of any conviction. While we certainly do not foreclose the possibility that abstention may be appropriate in some cases seeking review of ongoing military commission proceedings (such as military commissions convened on the battlefield), the foregoing discussion makes clear that, under our precedent, abstention is not justified here. We therefore proceed to consider the merits of Hamdan's challenge.

IV

The military commission, a tribunal neither mentioned in the Constitution nor created by statute, was born of military necessity.... Exigency alone, of course, will not justify the establishment and use of penal tribunals not contemplated by Article I, §8 and Article III, §1 of the Constitution unless some other part of that document authorizes a response to the felt need.... And that authority, if it exists, can derive only from the powers granted jointly to the President and Congress in time of war....

V

The common law governing military commissions may be gleaned from past practice and what sparse legal precedent exists. Commissions historically have been used in three situations.... First, they have substituted for civilian courts at times and in places where martial law has been declared.... Second, commissions have been established to try civilians "as part of a temporary military government over occupied enemy territory or territory regained from an enemy where civilian government cannot and does not function."... Illustrative of this second kind of commission is the one that was established, with jurisdiction to apply the German Criminal Code, in occupied Germany following the end of World War II....

The third type of commission, convened as an "incident to the conduct of war" when there is a need "to seize and subject to disciplinary measures those enemies who in their attempt to thwart or impede our military effort have violated the law of war,"..., has been described as "utterly different" from the other two.... Not only is its jurisdiction limited to offenses cognizable during time of war, but its role is primarily a factfinding one — to determine, typically on the battlefield itself, whether the defendant has violated the law of war. The last time the U.S. Armed Forces used the law-of-war military commission was during World War II. In *Quirin*, this Court sanctioned President Roosevelt's use of such a tribunal to try Nazi saboteurs captured on American soil during the *War*.... And in *Yamashita*, we held that a military commission had jurisdiction to try a Japanese commander for failing to prevent troops under his command from committing atrocities in the *Philippines*. [*In re Yamashita*,] 327 U.S. 1....

Quirin is the model the Government invokes most frequently to defend the commission convened to try Hamdan. That is both appropriate and unsurprising. Since Guantanamo Bay is neither enemy-occupied territory nor under martial law, the law-of-war commission is the only model available. At the same time, no more robust model of executive power exists; *Quirin* represents the high-water mark of military power to try enemy combatants for war crimes....

The charge against Hamdan,... alleges a conspiracy extending over a number of years, from 1996 to November 2001. All but two months of that more than 5-year-long period preceded the attacks of September 11, 2001, and the enactment of the AUMF — the Act of Congress on which the Government relies for exercise of its war powers and thus for its authority to convene military commissions. Neither the purported agreement with Osama bin Laden and others to commit war crimes, nor a single overt act, is alleged to have occurred in a theater of war or on any specified date after September 11, 2001. None of the overt acts that Hamdan is alleged to have committed violates the law of war....

There is no suggestion that Congress has, in exercise of its constitutional authority to "define and punish ... Offences against the Law of Nations," U.S. Const., Art. I, § 8, cl. 10, positively identified "conspiracy" as a war crime. As we explained in *Quirin*, that is not necessarily fatal to the Government's claim of authority to try the alleged offense by military commission; Congress, through Article 21 of the UCMJ, has "incorporated by reference" the common law of war, which may render triable by military commission certain offenses not defined by statute.... When, however, neither the elements of the offense nor the range of permissible punishments is defined by statute or treaty, the precedent must be plain and unambiguous. To demand any less would be to risk concentrating in military hands a degree of adjudicative and punitive power in excess of that contemplated either by statute or by the Constitution....

This high standard was met in *Quirin;* the violation there alleged was, by "universal agreement and practice" both in this country and internationally, recognized as an offense against the law of war.... At a minimum, the Government must make a substantial showing that the crime for which it seeks to try a defendant by military commission is acknowledged to be an offense against the law of war. That burden is far from satisfied here. The crime of "conspiracy" has rarely if ever been tried as such in this country by any law-of-war military commission not exercising some other form of jurisdiction, and does not appear in either the Geneva Conventions or the Hague Conventions—the major treaties on the law of war....

The Government cites three sources that it says show otherwise. First, it points out that the Nazi saboteurs in *Quirin* were charged with conspiracy.... Second, it observes that Winthrop at one point in his treatise identifies conspiracy as an offense "prosecuted by military commissions."..... Finally, it notes that another military historian, Charles Roscoe Howland, lists conspiracy "'to violate the laws of war by destroying life or property in aid of the enemy'" as an offense that was tried as a violation of the law of war during the Civil War.... On close analysis, however, these sources at best lend little support to the Government's position and at worst undermine it. By any measure, they fail to satisfy the high standard of clarity required to justify the use of a military commission....

Finally, international sources confirm that the crime charged here is not a recognized violation of the law of war.... [N]one of the major treaties governing the law of war identifies conspiracy as a violation thereof. And the only "conspiracy" crimes that have been recognized by international war crimes tribunals (whose jurisdiction often extends beyond war crimes proper to crimes against humanity and crimes against the peace) are conspiracy to commit genocide and common plan to wage aggressive war, which is a crime against the peace and requires for its commission actual participation in a "concrete plan to wage war."...

In sum, the sources that the Government and JUSTICE THOMAS rely upon to show that conspiracy to violate the law of war is itself a violation of the law of war in fact demonstrate quite the opposite. Far from making the requisite substantial showing, the Government has failed even to offer a "merely colorable" case for inclusion of conspiracy among those offenses cognizable by law-of-war military commission. . . . Because the charge does not support the commission's jurisdiction, the commission lacks authority to try Hamdan.

The charge's shortcomings are not merely formal, but are indicative of a broader inability on the Executive's part here to satisfy the most basic precondition — at least in the absence of specific congressional authorization — for establishment of military commissions: military necessity. Hamdan's tribunal was appointed not by a military commander in the field of battle, but by a retired major general stationed away from any active hostilities. . . . Hamdan is charged not with an overt act for which he was caught redhanded in a theater of war and which military efficiency demands be tried expeditiously, but with an *agreement* the inception of which long predated the attacks of September 11, 2001 and the AUMF. That may well be a crime, but it is not an offense that "by the law of war may be tried by military commission." None of the overt acts alleged to have been committed in furtherance of the agreement is itself a war crime, or even necessarily occurred during time of, or in a theater of, war. Any urgent need for imposition or execution of judgment is utterly belied by the record; Hamdan was arrested in November 2001 and he was not charged until mid-2004. These simply are not the circumstances in which, by any stretch of the historical evidence or this Court's precedents, a military commission established by Executive Order under the authority of Article 21 of the UCMJ may lawfully try a person and subject him to punishment.

VI

Whether or not the Government has charged Hamdan with an offense against the law of war cognizable by military commission, the commission lacks power to proceed. The UCMJ conditions the President's use of military commissions on compliance not only with the American common law of war, but also with the rest of the UCMJ itself, insofar as applicable, and with the "rules and precepts of the law of nations," . . . . the four Geneva Conventions signed in 1949. . . . The procedures that the Government has decreed will govern Hamdan's trial by commission violate these laws.

A

The commission's procedures are set forth in Commission Order No. 1, which was amended most recently on August 31, 2005 — after Hamdan's trial had already begun. Every commission established pursuant to Commission Order No. 1 must have a presiding officer and at least three other members, all of whom must be commissioned officers. § 4(A)(1). The presiding officer's job is to rule on questions of law and other evidentiary and interlocutory issues; the other members make findings and, if applicable, sentencing decisions. § 4(A)(5). The accused is entitled to appointed military counsel and may hire civilian counsel at his own expense so long as such counsel is a U.S. citizen with security clearance "at the level SECRET or higher." §§ 4(C)(2)–(3). The accused also is entitled to a copy of the charge(s) against him, both in English and his own language (if different), to a presumption of innocence, and to certain other rights typically afforded criminal defendants in civilian courts and courts-martial. See §§ 5(A)–(P). These rights are subject, however, to one glaring condition: The accused and his civilian counsel may be excluded from, and precluded from ever learning what evidence was presented during, any part of the proceeding that either the Appointing Authority or the presiding officer decides to "close." Grounds for such closure "include the protection of information classified or classifiable . . . ; information protected by law or rule from unauthorized disclosure; the physical safety of participants in Commission proceedings, including prospective witnesses; intelligence and law enforcement sources, methods, or activities; and other national security interests." § 6(B)(3). Appointed military defense counsel must be privy to these closed sessions, but may, at the presiding officer's discretion, be forbidden to reveal to his or her client what took place therein.

Another striking feature of the rules governing Hamdan's commission is that they permit the admission of *any* evidence that, in the opinion of the presiding officer, "would have probative value to a reasonable person." § 6(D)(1). Under this test, not only is testimonial hearsay and evidence obtained through coercion fully admissible, but neither live testimony nor witnesses' written statements need be sworn. See §§ 6(D)(2)(b), (3). Moreover, the accused and his civilian counsel may be denied access to evidence in the form of "protected information" (which includes classified information as well as "information protected by law or rule from unauthorized disclosure" and "information concerning other national security interests," §§ 6(B)(3), 6(D)(5)(a)(v)), so long as the presiding officer concludes that the evidence is "probative" under § 6(D)(1) and that its admission without the accused's knowledge would not "result in the denial of a full and fair trial." § 6(D)(5)(b). Finally, a presiding officer's determination that evidence "would not have probative value to a reasonable person" may be overridden by a majority of the other commission members. § 6(D)(1).

Once all the evidence is in, the commission members (not including the presiding officer) must vote on the accused's guilt. A two-thirds vote will suffice for both a verdict of guilty and for imposition of any sentence not including death (the imposition of which requires a unanimous vote). § 6(F). Any appeal is taken to a three-member review panel composed of military officers and designated by the Secretary of Defense, only one member of which need have experience as a judge. § 6(H)(4). The review panel is directed to "disregard any variance from procedures specified in this Order or elsewhere that would not materially have affected the outcome of the trial before the Commission." Once the panel makes its recommendation to the Secretary of Defense, the Secretary can either remand for further proceedings or forward the record to the President with his recommendation as to final disposition.

§6(H)(5). The President then, unless he has delegated the task to the Secretary, makes the "final decision." §6(H)(6). He may change the commission's findings or sentence only in a manner favorable to the accused. . . .

B

Hamdan raises both general and particular objections to the procedures set forth in Commission Order No. 1. His general objection is that the procedures' admitted deviation from those governing courts-martial itself renders the commission illegal. Chief among his particular objections are that he may, under the Commission Order, be convicted based on evidence he has not seen or heard, and that any evidence admitted against him need not comply with the admissibility or relevance rules typically applicable in criminal trials and court-martial proceedings. . . .

C

. . . The uniformity principle is not an inflexible one; it does not preclude all departures from the procedures dictated for use by courts-martial. But any departure must be tailored to the exigency that necessitates it. . . . Without reaching the question whether any provision of Commission Order No. 1 is strictly "contrary to or inconsistent with" other provisions of the UCMJ, we conclude that the "practicability" determination the President has made is insufficient to justify variances from the procedures governing courts-martial. . . .

D

The procedures adopted to try Hamdan also violate the Geneva Conventions. The Court of Appeals dismissed Hamdan's Geneva Convention challenge on three independent grounds: (1) the Geneva Conventions are not judicially enforceable; (2) Hamdan in any event is not entitled to their protections; and (3) even if he is entitled to their protections, *Councilman* abstention is appropriate. . . .

i

The Court of Appeals relied on *Johnson v. Eisentrager*, 339 U.S. 763 (1950), to hold that Hamdan could not invoke the Geneva Conventions to challenge the Government's plan to prosecute him in accordance with Commission Order No. 1. *Eisentrager* involved a challenge by 21 German nationals to their 1945 convictions for war crimes by a military tribunal convened in Nanking, China, and to their subsequent imprisonment in occupied Germany. The petitioners argued, *inter alia*, that the 1929 Geneva Convention rendered illegal some of the procedures employed during their trials, which they said deviated impermissibly from the procedures used by courts-martial to try American soldiers. . . . We rejected that claim on the merits because the petitioners (unlike Hamdan here) had failed to identify any prejudicial disparity "between the Commission that tried [them] and those that would try an offending soldier of the American forces of like rank," and in any event could claim no protection, under the 1929 Convention, during trials for crimes that occurred before their confinement as prisoners of war. . . .

Buried in a footnote of the opinion, however, is this curious statement suggesting that the Court lacked power even to consider the merits of the Geneva Convention argument.... The Court of Appeals, on the strength of this footnote, held that "the 1949 Geneva Convention does not confer upon Hamdan a right to enforce its provisions in court."...

Whatever else might be said about the *Eisentrager* footnote, it does not control this case. We may assume that "the obvious scheme" of the 1949 Conventions is identical in all relevant respects to that of the 1929 Convention, and even that that scheme would, absent some other provision of law, preclude Hamdan's invocation of the Convention's provisions as an independent source of law binding the Government's actions and furnishing petitioner with any enforceable right. For, regardless of the nature of the rights conferred on Hamdan, ... they are, as the Government does not dispute, part of the law of war.... And compliance with the law of war is the condition upon which the authority set forth in Article 21 is granted.

ii

For the Court of Appeals, acknowledgment of that condition was no bar to Hamdan's trial by commission. As an alternative to its holding that Hamdan could not invoke the Geneva Conventions at all, the Court of Appeals concluded that the Conventions did not in any event apply to the armed conflict during which Hamdan was captured. The court accepted the Executive's assertions that Hamdan was captured in connection with the United States' war with al Qaeda and that that war is distinct from the war with the Taliban in Afghanistan. It further reasoned that the war with al Qaeda evades the reach of the Geneva Conventions....

We need not decide the merits of this argument because there is at least one provision of the Geneva Conventions that applies here even if the relevant conflict is not one between signatories ... Article 3, often referred to as Common Article 3 because, like Article 2, it appears in all four Geneva Conventions, provides that in a "conflict not of an international character occurring in the territory of one of the High Contracting Parties, each Party to the conflict shall be bound to apply, as a minimum," certain provisions protecting "persons taking no active part in the hostilities, including members of armed forces who have laid down their arms and those placed *hors de combat* by ... detention." ... One such provision prohibits "the passing of sentences and the carrying out of executions without previous judgment pronounced by a regularly constituted court affording all the judicial guarantees which are recognized as indispensable by civilized peoples." ...

The Court of Appeals thought, and the Government asserts, that Common Article 3 does not apply to Hamdan because the conflict with al Qaeda, being "'international in scope,'" does not qualify as a "'conflict not of an international character.'" ... That reasoning is erroneous. The term "conflict not of an international character" is used here in contradistinction to a conflict between nations.... Common Article 2 provides that "the present Convention shall apply to all cases of declared war or of any other armed conflict which may arise between two or more of the High Contracting Parties." . . .

Although the official commentaries accompanying Common Article 3 indicate that an important purpose of the provision was to furnish minimal protection to rebels involved in one kind of "conflict not of an international character," *i.e.*, a civil war, . . . the commentaries also make clear "that the scope of the Article must be as wide as possible," . . . . In fact, limiting language that would have rendered Common Article 3 applicable "especially [to] cases of civil war, colonial conflicts, or wars of religion," was omitted from the final version of the Article, which coupled broader scope of application with a narrower range of rights than did earlier proposed iterations. . . .

iii

Common Article 3, then, is applicable here and, as indicated above, requires that Hamdan be tried by a "regularly constituted court affording all the judicial guarantees which are recognized as indispensable by civilized peoples." . . . . While the term "regularly constituted court" is not specifically defined in either Common Article 3 or its accompanying commentary, other sources disclose its core meaning. The commentary accompanying a provision of the Fourth Geneva Convention, for example, defines "'regularly constituted'" tribunals to include "ordinary military courts" and "definitely exclude all special tribunals." . . . .

iv

Inextricably intertwined with the question of regular constitution is the evaluation of the procedures governing the tribunal and whether they afford "all the judicial guarantees which are recognized as indispensable by civilized peoples." . . . Like the phrase "regularly constituted court," this phrase is not defined in the text of the Geneva Conventions. But it must be understood to incorporate at least the barest of those trial protections that have been recognized by customary international law. . . . That the Government has a compelling interest in denying Hamdan access to certain sensitive information is not doubted. . . . But, at least absent express statutory provision to the contrary, information used to convict a person of a crime must be disclosed to him.

v

Common Article 3 obviously tolerates a great degree of flexibility in trying individuals captured during armed conflict; its requirements are general ones, crafted to accommodate a wide variety of legal systems. But *requirements* they are nonetheless. The commission that the President has convened to try Hamdan does not meet those requirements.

VII

We have assumed, as we must, that the allegations made in the Government's charge against Hamdan are true. We have assumed, moreover, the truth of the message implicit in that charge—viz., that Hamdan is a dangerous individual whose beliefs, if acted upon, would cause great harm and even death to innocent civilians, and who would act upon those beliefs if given the opportunity. It bears emphasizing that Hamdan does not challenge, and we do not today address, the Government's power to detain him for the duration of active hostilities in order to prevent such harm. But in undertaking to try Hamdan and subject him to criminal punishment, the Executive is bound to comply with the Rule of Law that prevails in this jurisdiction.

The judgment of the Court of Appeals is reversed, and the case is remanded for further proceedings.

It is so ordered.

THE CHIEF JUSTICE took no part in the consideration or decision of this case.[a]

JUSTICE BREYER, with whom JUSTICE KENNEDY, JUSTICE SOUTER, and JUSTICE GINSBURG join, concurring.

The dissenters say that today's decision would "sorely hamper the President's ability to confront and defeat a new and deadly enemy." . . . They suggest that it undermines our Nation's ability to "prevent future attacks" of the grievous sort that we have already suffered. . . . That claim leads me to state briefly what I believe the majority sets forth both explicitly and implicitly at greater length. The Court's conclusion ultimately rests upon a single ground: Congress has not issued the Executive a "blank check." . . . Indeed, Congress has denied the President the legislative authority to create military commissions of the kind at issue here. Nothing prevents the President from returning to Congress to seek the authority he believes necessary.

Where, as here, no emergency prevents consultation with Congress, judicial insistence upon that consultation does not weaken our Nation's ability to deal with danger. To the contrary, that insistence strengthens the Nation's ability to determine — through democratic means — how best to do so. The Constitution places its faith in those democratic means. Our Court today simply does the same.

JUSTICE KENNEDY, with whom JUSTICE SOUTER, JUSTICE GINSBURG, and JUSTICE BREYER join as to Parts I and II, concurring in part.

Military Commission Order No. 1, which governs the military commission established to try petitioner Salim Hamdan for war crimes, exceeds limits that certain statutes, duly enacted by Congress, have placed on the President's authority to convene military courts. This is not a case, then, where the Executive can assert some unilateral authority to fill a void left by congressional inaction. It is a case where Congress, in the proper exercise of its powers as an independent branch of government, and as part of a long tradition of legislative involvement in matters of military justice, has considered the subject of military tribunals and set limits on the President's authority. Where a statute provides the conditions for the exercise of governmental power, its requirements are the result of a deliberative and reflective

a. The Chief Justice had been a member of the Court whose judgment was under appeal. — Eds.

process engaging both of the political branches. Respect for laws derived from the customary operation of the Executive and Legislative Branches gives some assurance of stability in time of crisis. The Constitution is best preserved by reliance on standards tested over time and insulated from the pressures of the moment. . . .

I join the Court's opinion, save Parts V and VI-D-iv. To state my reasons for this reservation, and to show my agreement with the remainder of the Court's analysis by identifying particular deficiencies in the military commissions at issue, this separate opinion seems appropriate.

I

Trial by military commission raises separation-of-powers concerns of the highest order. Located within a single branch, these courts carry the risk that offenses will be defined, prosecuted, and adjudicated by executive officials without independent review. . . . Concentration of power puts personal liberty in peril of arbitrary action by officials, an incursion the Constitution's three-part system is designed to avoid. It is imperative, then, that when military tribunals are established, full and proper authority exists for the Presidential directive. . . .

II

In sum, as presently structured, Hamdan's military commission exceeds the bounds Congress has placed on the President's authority in §§ 836 and 821 of the UCMJ. Because Congress has prescribed these limits, Congress can change them, requiring a new analysis consistent with the Constitution and other governing laws. At this time, however, we must apply the standards Congress has provided. By those standards the military commission is deficient.

III

In light of the conclusion that the military commission here is unauthorized under the UCMJ, I see no need to consider several further issues addressed in the plurality opinion by Justice Stevens and the dissent by Justice Thomas. . . .

There should be reluctance, furthermore, to reach unnecessarily the question whether, as the plurality seems to conclude, . . . Article 75 of Protocol I to the Geneva Conventions is binding law notwithstanding the earlier decision by our Government not to accede to the Protocol. For all these reasons, and without detracting from the importance of the right of presence, I would rely on other deficiencies noted here and in the opinion by the Court — deficiencies that relate to the structure and procedure of the commission and that inevitably will affect the proceedings — as the basis for finding the military commissions lack authorization under 10 U.S.C. § 836 and fail to be regularly constituted under Common Article 3 and § 821.

I likewise see no need to address the validity of the conspiracy charge against Hamdan. . . . In light of the conclusion that the military commissions at issue are unauthorized Congress may choose to provide further guidance in this area. Congress, not the Court, is the branch in the better position to undertake the "sensitive task of establishing a principle not inconsistent with the national interest or international justice." *Banco Nacional de Cuba v. Sabbatino,* 376 U.S. 398, 428 (1964). . . .

With these observations I join the Court's opinion with the exception of Parts V and VI-D-iv.

JUSTICE SCALIA, with whom JUSTICE THOMAS and JUSTICE ALITO join, dissenting.

On December 30, 2005, Congress enacted the Detainee Treatment Act (DTA). It unambiguously provides that, as of that date, "no court, justice, or judge" shall have jurisdiction to consider the habeas application of a Guantanamo Bay detainee. Notwithstanding this plain directive, the Court today concludes that, on what it calls the statute's *most natural* reading, *every* "court, justice, or judge" before whom such a habeas application was pending on December 30 has jurisdiction to hear, consider, and render judgment on it. This conclusion is patently erroneous. And even if it were not, the jurisdiction supposedly retained should, in an exercise of sound equitable discretion, not be exercised. . . .

In the face of such concerns, the Court relies heavily on *Ex parte Quirin,* 317 U.S. 1 (1942): "Far from abstaining pending the conclusion of military proceedings, which were ongoing, [in *Quirin*] we convened a special Term to hear the case and expedited our review." . . . It is likely that the Government in *Quirin*, unlike here, preferred a hasty resolution of the case in this Court, so that it could swiftly execute the sentences imposed, . . . But the Court's reliance on *Quirin* suffers from a more fundamental defect: Once again, it ignores the DTA, which creates an avenue for the consideration of petitioner's claims that did not exist at the time of *Quirin*. Collateral application for habeas review was the *only* vehicle available. And there was no compelling reason to postpone consideration of the *Quirin* application until the termination of military proceedings, because the only cognizable claims presented were general challenges to the authority of the commissions that would not be affected by the specific proceedings. . . . In the DTA, by contrast, Congress has expanded the scope of Article III review and has channeled it exclusively through a single, post-verdict appeal to Article III courts. Because Congress has created a novel unitary scheme of Article III review of military commissions that was absent in 1942, *Quirin* is no longer governing precedent. . . . For the foregoing reasons, I dissent.

JUSTICE THOMAS, with whom JUSTICE SCALIA joins, and with whom JUSTICE ALITO joins in all but Parts I, II-C-1, and III-B-2, dissenting.

For the reasons set forth in JUSTICE SCALIA's dissent, it is clear that this Court lacks jurisdiction to entertain petitioner's claims, ... The Court having concluded otherwise, it is appropriate to respond to the Court's resolution of the merits of petitioner's claims because its opinion openly flouts our well-established duty to respect the Executive's judgment in matters of military operations and foreign affairs. The Court's evident belief that *it* is qualified to pass on the "military necessity," . . . , of the Commander in Chief's decision to employ a particular form of force against our enemies is so antithetical to our constitutional structure that it simply cannot go unanswered. I respectfully dissent. . . .

JUSTICE ALITO, with whom JUSTICES SCALIA and THOMAS join in Parts I-III, dissenting.

For the reasons set out in JUSTICE SCALIA's dissent, which I join, I would hold that we lack jurisdiction. On the merits, I join JUSTICE THOMAS' dissent with the exception of Parts I, II-C-1, and III-B-2, which concern matters that I find unnecessary to reach. I add the following comments to provide a further explanation of my reasons for disagreeing with the holding of the Court....

II

....

A

I see no basis for the Court's holding that a military commission cannot be regarded as "a regularly constituted court" unless it is similar in structure and composition to a regular military court or unless there is an "evident practical need" for the divergence. There is no reason why a court that differs in structure or composition from an ordinary military court must be viewed as having been improperly constituted. Tribunals that vary significantly in structure, composition, and procedures may all be "regularly" or "properly" constituted. Consider, for example, a municipal court, a state trial court of general jurisdiction, an Article I federal trial court, a federal district court, and an international court, such as the International Criminal Tribunal for the Former Yugoslavia. Although these courts are "differently constituted" and differ substantially in many other respects, they are all "regularly constituted."

If Common Article 3 had been meant to require trial before a country's military courts or courts that are similar in structure and composition, the drafters almost certainly would have used language that expresses that thought more directly....

Insofar as respondents propose to conduct the tribunals according to the procedures of Military Commission Order No. 1 and orders promulgated thereunder—and nobody has suggested respondents intend otherwise—then it seems that petitioner's tribunal, like the hundreds of others respondents propose to conduct, is very much regular and not at all special.

B

I also disagree with the Court's conclusion that petitioner's military commission is "illegal," ... because its procedures allegedly do not comply with 10 U.S.C. § 836. Even if § 836(b), unlike Common Article 3, does impose at least a limited uniformity requirement amongst the tribunals contemplated by the UCMJ, ..., and even if it is assumed for the sake of argument that some of the procedures specified in Military Commission Order No. 1 impermissibly deviate from court-martial procedures, it does not follow that the military commissions created by that order are not "regularly constituted" or that trying petitioner before such a commission would be inconsistent with the law of war. If Congress enacted a statute requiring the federal district courts to follow a procedure that is unconstitutional, the statute would be invalid, but the district courts would not. Likewise, if some of the procedures that may be used in military commission proceedings are improper, the appropriate remedy is to proscribe the use of those particular procedures, not to outlaw the commissions. I see no justification for striking down the entire commission structure simply because it is possible that petitioner's trial might involve the use of some procedure that is improper.

III

Returning to the three elements of Common Article 3—(1) a court, (2) that is appointed, set up, and established in compliance with domestic law, and (3) that respects universally recognized fundamental rights—I conclude that all of these elements are satisfied in this case.

A

First, the commissions qualify as courts.

Second, the commissions were appointed, set up, and established pursuant to an order of the President, just like the commission in *Ex parte Quirin,* 317 U.S. 1 (1942), and the Court acknowledges that *Quirin* recognized that the statutory predecessor of 10 U.S.C. § 821 "preserved" the President's power "to convene military commissions," . . . . Although JUSTICE KENNEDY concludes that "an acceptable degree of independence from the Executive is necessary to render a commission 'regularly constituted' by the standards of our Nation's system of justice," . . . . he offers no support for this proposition (which in any event seems to be more about fairness or integrity than regularity). The commission in *Quirin* was certainly no more independent from the Executive than the commissions at issue here, and 10 U.S.C. §§ 821 and 836 do not speak to this issue.

Finally, the commission procedures, taken as a whole, and including the availability of review by a United States Court of Appeals and by this Court, do not provide a basis for deeming the commissions to be illegitimate. The Court questions the following two procedural rules: the rule allowing the Secretary of Defense to change the governing rules "'from time to time'" (which does not rule out mid-trial changes), ..., and the rule that permits the admission of any evidence that would have "'probative value to a reasonable person'" (which departs from our legal system's usual rules of evidence), ... Neither of these two rules undermines the legitimacy of the commissions.

Surely the entire commission structure cannot be stricken merely because it is possible that the governing rules might be changed during the course of one or more proceedings. *If* a change is made and applied during the course of an ongoing proceeding and *if* the accused is found guilty, the validity of that procedure can be considered in the review proceeding for that case. After all, not every midtrial change will be prejudicial. A midtrial change might amend the governing rules in a way that is inconsequential or actually favorable to the accused.

As for the standard for the admission of evidence at commission proceedings, the Court does not suggest that this rule violates the international standard incorporated into Common Article 3 .... Rules of evidence differ from country to country, and much of the world does not follow aspects of our evidence rules, such as the general prohibition against the admission of hearsay.... If a particular accused claims to have been unfairly prejudiced by the admission of particular evidence, that claim can be reviewed in the review proceeding for that case. It makes no sense to strike down the entire commission structure based on speculation that some evidence might be improperly admitted in some future case.

In sum, I believe that Common Article 3 is satisfied here because the military commissions (1) qualify as courts, (2) that were appointed and established in accordance with domestic law, and (3) any procedural improprieties that might occur in particular cases can be reviewed in those cases.

B

The commentary on Common Article 3 supports this interpretation.... Whatever else may be said about the system that was created by Military Commission Order No. 1 and augmented by the Detainee Treatment Act, §1005(e)(1), 119 Stat. 2742, this system—which features formal trial procedures, multiple levels of administrative review, and the opportunity for review by a United States Court of Appeals and by this Court—does not dispense "summary justice." ... For these reasons, I respectfully dissent.

Notes

(1) Congress responded to *Hamdan* with a very complex piece of legislation, the Military Commissions Act of 2006, which was revised in 2009. It provided a statutory basis for jurisdiction of Commissions over essentially the same crimes as the President's 2001 Order, but with procedures more favorable to the accused. The crimes included not only conspiracy to commit war crimes, but also offenses for which there were even weaker grounds for arguing that they had traditionally been prosecuted before military commissions, such as terrorism, airplane hijacking, material support for terrorism and solicitation to commit offenses contained in the legislation. Hamdan was eventually charged before such a Commission. Tried late in 2008, he was acquitted of a conspiracy count but convicted of providing material support to al Qaeda. He was sentenced to five and a half years of imprisonment. Given an allowance for time served in Guantanamo, he was transferred to Yemen in November 2008 to serve out the last month of his sentence. He was released in January 2009. *See Yemen Releases Former bin Laden Driver from Jail, available at* http://www.nytimes.com/2009/01/12/world/middleeast/12yemen.html (Jan. 11, 2009). Meanwhile his appeal was progressing through the military appeal system and, as the 2006 legislation provided, into the Court of Appeals for the District of Columbia Circuit. In 2012, a panel of that Court held that the 2006 MCA "does not authorize retroactive prosecution for conduct committed before enactment of that Act unless the conduct was already prohibited under existing U.S. law as a war crime triable by military commission." *Hamdan v. United States*, 696 F.3d 1238, 1248 (D.C. Cir. 2012). The Court held that providing material support for terrorism

was not a pre-existing crime triable by military commission and, accordingly, vacated Hamdan's conviction. In a later case, *Al Bahlul v. United States*, 767 F.3d 1 (D.C. Cir. 2014), the Circuit Court, *en banc*, took a different approach, although the end result did not upset the vacation of Hamdan's conviction. Al Bahlul, a personal assistant and media person for Osama Bin Laden, was convicted in Guantanamo of conspiracy to commit war crimes, providing material support for terrorism and solicitation of others to commit war crimes. He was sentenced to life imprisonment. The *en banc* panel addressed the issue of whether his convictions violated the *ex post facto* clause of the Constitution. Because Al Bahlul had essentially refused to participate in the commission proceedings, the majority of the Court held that he had forfeited the right to make his constitutional arguments. Thus, the appropriate standard of review on the *ex post facto* issue was "plain error." The Court concluded that the 2006 Act was unambiguous in its intent to authorize retroactive prosecution for the crimes enumerated in the statute and thus over-ruled the panel's 2012 decision in *Hamdan*. Nevertheless, it held that the *ex post facto* clause of the Constitution meant that the convictions for material support of terrorism and solicitation of others to commit war crimes could not stand. In a complex piece of reasoning, however, it upheld the conspiracy conviction against the *ex post facto* attack. The basic argument was that, although four members of the plurality of the Supreme Court had held in its *Hamdan* decision that conspiracy to commit war crimes was not triable by military commission, three dissenting judges had held to the contrary and the fourth had not expressed an opinion. Accordingly, it could not be said that any error was "plain." Moreover, the majority of the Circuit Court believed that the conduct for which he was convicted was already criminalized under 18 U.S.C. § 2332(b). The Court stated:

> Although the 2006 MCA post-dates Bahlul's conduct, section 2332(b) has long been on the books, making it a crime to, "outside the United States," "engage[] in a conspiracy to kill[] a national of the United States." 18 U.S.C. § 2332(b); see Omnibus Diplomatic Security and Antiterrorism Act of 1986, Pub. L. No. 99-399, § 1202(a), 100 Stat. 853, 896. Section 2332(b) is not an offense triable by military commission but, the Government argues, "[t]he fact that the MCA provides a different forum for adjudicating such conduct does not implicate *ex post facto* concerns." E.B. Br. of United States 67. We agree.

Bahlul had raised four other challenges that the Court had not addressed at this stage, (1) that Congress exceeded its Article I, § 8 authority by defining crimes triable by military commission that are not offenses under the international law of war; (2) that Congress violated Article III by vesting military commissions with jurisdiction to try crimes that are not offenses under the international law of war; (3) his convictions violate the First Amendment; and (4) that the 2006 MCA discriminates against aliens in violation of the equal protection component of the Due Process Clause. These issues were remanded to the original panel that had decided his earlier appeal. In *Bahlul v. United States*, decided in mid-June 2015, a 2-1 majority of the panel concluded that the objection under Article III was a "structural" objection that could not be forfeited. Accordingly, the appropriate standard of review on this issue was *de novo*. It held that "Bahlul's conviction for inchoate conspiracy by a law of war military commission violated the separation of powers enshrined in Article III § 1 and must be vacated. We need not and do not address Bahlul's other contentions." The dissent would have shown more deference to the political branches acting together. 767 F.3d at 51.

(2) On January 22, 2009, President Barak Obama issued Executive Order 13492 that called for the prompt closure of detention facilities at Guantanamo Bay Naval Base. The Order provided in part that:

> The detention facilities at Guantánamo for individuals covered by this order shall be closed as soon as practicable, and no later than 1 year from the date of this order. If any individuals covered by this order remain in detention at Guantánamo at the time of closure of those detention facilities, they shall be returned to their home country, released, transferred to a third country, or transferred to another United States detention facility in a manner consistent with law and the national security and foreign policy interests of the United States.

The Order also provided a process to review participants presently detained at Guantanamo. See Executive Order — Review and Disposition of Individuals Detained at the Guantánamo Bay Naval Base and Closure of Detention Facilities, available at https://www.whitehouse.gov/the_press_office/ClosureOfGuantanamoDetentionFacilities.

A combination of Congressional intransigence and the difficulty of re-locating some of the prisoners caused the failure of this initiative. *See* Charlie Savage, *New Envoy for Prison Transfers*, N.Y. TIMES, June 30, 2015. In the ensuing years, policy regarding the facility has shifted back and forth. On January 30, 2018, President Donald Trump signed an executive order to keep the detention facility at Guantanamo Bay open. Upon entering office, President Joseph Biden announced plans to close the facility by the end of his term. One detainee was released to Morocco in July 2021, leaving 39 individuals detained in the facility as of December 2021.

Meanwhile, few convictions have been obtained in the Commissions, or upheld on review. According to the *New York Times*, as of December 2021, there have been a total of 780 individuals detained at GTMO since 2002. At the end of 2021, there were 39 remaining. Of those remaining at Guantanamo Bay, two individuals have been convicted of war crimes before the military commission and ten are awaiting trial on war crimes charges. The remaining individuals at GTMO are not facing criminal charges before the military commission but are instead being held pursuant to the laws of war. Of this number, thirteen have been recommended for transfer to other countries. *See The Guantanamo Docket*, NEW YORK TIMES (Last Updated December 9, 2021).

§ 9.04 Aircraft Hijacking and Sabotage

United States v. Rezaq

United States Court of Appeals, District of Columbia
134 F.3d 1121 (1998)

WALD, CIRCUIT JUDGE:

Omar Mohammed Ali Rezaq appeals his conviction on one count of aircraft piracy under 49 U.S.C. app. § 1472(n) (1994). In 1985, Rezaq hijacked an Air Egypt flight shortly after takeoff from Athens, and ordered it to fly to Malta. On arrival, Rezaq shot a number of passengers, killing two of them, before he was apprehended. Rezaq pleaded guilty to murder charges in Malta, served seven years in prison, and was released in February 1993. Shortly afterwards, he was taken into custody in Nigeria by United States authorities and brought to the United States for trial. . . .

The jury did not credit Rezaq's defenses, and found him guilty of the one count with which he was charged, ... [T]he district court sentenced Rezaq to life imprisonment. (The United States had not sought the death sentence.) The district court also ordered Rezaq to pay a total of $254,000 in restitution, an amount which it found to represent the financial cost to the victims of his crime.

Rezaq's first group of arguments on this appeal all derive from the international nature of the crime of air piracy. He argues, first, that the international treaty barring air piracy prohibits sequential prosecutions for the same offense, and that it was therefore impermissible for the United States to try him anew for crimes for which he had already been prosecuted in Malta. Second, he asserts that the United States manufactured jurisdiction over him by bringing him into its territory, and that section 1472(n)'s statement that it applies to those "found in the United States" bars the application of section 1472(n) to those forcibly brought to the United States specifically for trial on air piracy charges. Third, Rezaq avers that it was improper for the district court to apply section 1472(n)'s "death results" provision (that is, its provision requiring the imposition of the death sentence or of life imprisonment in cases in which death results), as that provision was only intended to apply if certain jurisdictional criteria were met. Rezaq's next group of arguments relates to the conduct of his trial. . . .

We begin with Rezaq's argument that it was impermissible for the United States to try him a second time, as he had already been tried in Malta. Rezaq cannot base this argument on the Constitution's Double Jeopardy Clause, for two reasons. First, that clause does not prohibit sequential trials by different sovereigns. . . . Second, Rezaq was prosecuted in Malta for murder, attempted murder, and hostage-taking, but the United States prosecution was for air piracy. The offense of air piracy contains elements — related to the control of an airplane — that the crimes for which Rezaq was tried in Malta do not. This means, under the usual double jeopardy analysis, that the first prosecution does not bar the second. . . .

Rezaq asserts, however, that this case is subject to a more exacting standard than the traditional double-jeopardy one. Section 1472(n), 49 U.S.C. app. § 1472(n) (1994), was enacted to implement the Convention for the Suppression of Unlawful Seizure of Aircraft (also called the "Hague Convention"), Dec. 16, 1970, 22 U.S.T. 1643, a multilateral treaty directed at preventing and punishing air piracy. . . . Rezaq claims that both the Hague Convention and section 1472(n) incorporate a special ban on sequential prosecution that is more restrictive than the Double Jeopardy Clause, and argues that his prosecution on air piracy charges violates that ban.

It is certainly possible that a treaty could contain a double jeopardy provision more restrictive — that is, barring more prosecutions — than the Constitution's Double Jeopardy Clause. . . . But Rezaq has not shown that the Hague Convention falls in this category. . . . Rezaq points to the provisions of the Hague Convention that require states to either extradite or prosecute offenders, and argues that they imply that a more restrictive double jeopardy rule applies. For instance, he cites Article 4(2), which provides: "Each Contracting State shall likewise take such measures as may be necessary to establish its jurisdiction over the offence in the case where the alleged offender is present in its territory and it does not extradite him pursuant to Article 8. . . ." Rezaq argues that this provision implies that extradition and prosecution are mutually exclusive options: a Contracting Party may not both extradite an offender and prosecute him. This rule, he asserts, in turn implies that the Hague Convention intended to bar all sequential prosecutions, whether they occur after extradition or not.

The first step in Rezaq's argument is flawed: the Hague Convention's requirement that a state either prosecute offenders or extradite them does not imply a bar on (at different times) doing both. In general, a requirement to "do A or B" does not necessarily imply a bar on doing both A and B; one must look at the context and the purpose of the requirement to decide whether such a bar is meant. For example, if a religious organization requires that its members either do volunteer work or make cash contributions to charity, the organization clearly does not mean to foreclose them from doing both. The purpose of this hypothetical religious mandate is to ensure that believers try to do good deeds, and this purpose is served if a believer chooses to both do volunteer work and make charitable contributions. . . .

Here, the context makes clear that the statute's injunction to extradite or prosecute is not meant to state mutually exclusive alternatives. The extradite-or-prosecute requirement is intended to ensure that states make some effort to bring hijackers to justice, either through prosecution or extradition. There is no indication that Article 4 is intended to go beyond setting a minimum, and limit the options of states; indeed, Article 4(3) specifically provides that "this Convention does not exclude any jurisdiction exercised in accordance with national law." A reading of Article 4 that focuses on bringing hijackers to justice is also consistent with the Convention's (short) preamble, one clause of which states that "for the purpose of deterring [acts of air piracy], there is an urgent need to provide appropriate measures for punishment of offenders." Thus, the extradite-or-prosecute requirement is like the hypothetical donate-or-volunteer requirement described above; it is intended to ensure a minimum level of effort, and does not necessarily preclude the recipient of the mandate from doing more.

A reading under which the options of prosecution and extradition are mutually exclusive could also undermine the Convention's goal of ensuring "punishment of offenders." For instance, if a person is extradited from state A to state B, and B then discovers that a technical obstacle prevents it from prosecuting her, B should be able to return her to A for prosecution; any other reading of the treaty might allow a suspect to escape prosecution altogether. Or, to choose an example closer to the facts of this case, if state A tries and convicts a defendant for certain crimes associated with a hijacking (as Malta tried Rezaq for murder, attempted murder, and hostage-taking), there is no indication that A is barred from then extraditing her to B once she has served her sentence, so that B may try the defendant for different crimes associated with the same hijacking (as the United States tried Rezaq for air piracy).

The travaux preparatoires for the Hague Convention reinforce our conclusion that the treaty does not incorporate a special bar on sequential prosecution. They show that the treaty's negotiators considered and rejected the possibility of expressly barring sequential prosecutions through a ne bis in idem provision (a term for double-jeopardy provisions in international instruments; another term is *non bis in idem*). The states opposed to this idea, whose views carried the day, argued that "the principle was not applied in exactly the same manner in all States," and that "in taking a decision whether to prosecute, and, similarly, a decision whether to extradite, the State concerned will, in each case, apply its own rule on the subject of *ne bis in idem*." . . . This is, of course, exactly what the United States has done in applying its own double jeopardy rules.

Nor is there any indication that Congress, in enacting section 1472(n), read the Hague Convention differently, or intended to subject prosecutions under section 1472(n) to a heightened double jeopardy standard. The text and legislative history of section 1472(n) are both devoid of evidence pointing to such a conclusion. In the absence of any sign that either section 1472(n) or the Hague Convention undertook to impose a more stringent than usual double-jeopardy rule, we conclude that Rezaq's prosecution in Malta was not an obstacle to his subsequent prosecution, in this proceeding, on air piracy charges. . . .

Rezaq's next argument is that section 1472(n) only applies to defendants that are "afterward found in the United States," and that he was not "afterward found in the United States," but involuntarily brought here for the express purpose of prosecution.

Under a rule known as the *Ker-Frisbie* doctrine, "the power of a court to try a person for crime is not impaired by the fact that he had been brought within the court's jurisdiction by reason of a 'forcible abduction'." *Frisbie v. Collins*, 342 U.S. 519, 522, 72 S. Ct. 509, 96 L. Ed. 541 (1952) (quoting *Ker v. Illinois*, 119 U.S. 436, 7 S. Ct. 225, 30 L. Ed. 421 (1886)). This general rule does admit of some exceptions; for instance, an extradition treaty may provide that it is "the only way by which one country may gain custody of a national of the other country for the purposes of prosecution," *United States v. Alvarez-Machain*, [§ 17.03], and we have also suggested that there may be a "very limited" exception for certain cases of "'torture, brutality, and similar outrageous conduct.'" . . .

Rezaq's argument is, in effect, that the phrase "afterward found in the United States" appearing in section 1472(n) creates a statutory exception to the *Ker-Frisbie* rule, and prevents the government from bringing a defendant into the United States for the express purpose of prosecution. Although we agree that Congress has the power to create statutory exceptions to the *Ker-Frisbie* doctrine, we do not think that section 1472(n) creates such an exception.

We first consider the United States's contention that *Yunis* [§ 3.03[E]] controls this case. . . . Rezaq, unlike Yunis, was brought to the United States for the specific purpose of prosecution on hijacking charges. . . . [T]here are no strong policies underlying section 1472(n) that render it inappropriate for the government to bring a defendant to the United States against his will for the specific purpose of prosecution. Neither the Hague Convention nor section 1472(n) appears to have been intended to establish a firm allocation of prosecutorial authority between nations. It is possible to imagine a treaty that would do so; for instance, in adopting a treaty to criminalize mislabeling of products, nations might decide that it was best for each country's consumer protection authorities to have the sole power to decide when and how mislabeling should lead to criminal charges, and draft the treaty accordingly. It might then be inappropriate for United States authorities to bring a foreign offender to the United States for trial under a criminal law enacted to implement this hypothetical treaty.

Here, however, we have already concluded that Article 4 of the Hague Convention, which addresses the assertion of national jurisdiction, is intended to establish a minimum set of circumstances in which states must assert jurisdiction, rather than to limit the circumstances in which they may do so. It follows that the Hague Convention was not intended to establish a compartmentalized scheme of national jurisdiction (like that in our hypothetical product-labeling treaty). Nor does section 1472(n) enact such a scheme. The Senate Report on the implementing legislation explained that section 1472(n) was included to implement Article 4(2) of the Convention, and therefore

> includes a special provision establishing jurisdiction over the offense of hijacking wherever it occurs anywhere outside the special aircraft jurisdiction of the United States but the alleged offender is later found in the United States. This is the so-called universal jurisdiction provision which makes hijackers outlaws wherever they are found.

S. Rep. No. 93-13 at 3–4 (1973). This passage — particularly its statement that the provision "makes hijackers outlaws wherever they are found" — indicates that Congress saw section 1472(n) as permitting broad assertion of jurisdiction over hijackers. It shows no signs that Congress envisioned the provision as allocating jurisdiction between the United States and other nations.

The question remains, then: what does the phrase "afterward found in the United States" mean? As we observed in *Yunis*, this phrase appears to have been intended to implement the Hague Convention's requirement that the United States either extradite or prosecute all hijackers "present in" its territory. . . . Thus, the word "found" means only that the hijacker must be physically located in the United States, not that he must be first detected here. Rezaq notes that the fact that a defendant is present before a United States court necessarily implies that he is "found in the United States," so that the latter requirement will always be satisfied. But this does not mean that this language is empty of meaning; at a minimum, it confirms the rule, issuing from the Confrontation Clause of the Sixth Amendment and from the Due Process Clause, that a defendant ordinarily may not be tried in absentia. *See United States v. Gagnon*, 470 U.S. 522, 526, 105 S. Ct. 1482, 84 L. Ed. 2d 486 (1985) (per curiam).[2]

Rezaq avers that it was improper for the district court to apply section 1472(n)'s "death results" provision (that is, its provision requiring the imposition of the death sentence or of life imprisonment in cases in which death results), as the Hague Convention only permits states to punish additional crimes associated with a hijacking if certain jurisdictional prerequisites are met. . . . But Article 4(3) expressly provides that the Convention "does not exclude any criminal jurisdiction exercised in accordance with national law." Thus, if Congress wished to reach "other acts of violence," the Hague Convention allowed it to do so. . . . It is abundantly clear that Congress intended for the "death results" provision of section 1472(n) to apply irrespective of whether the additional jurisdictional elements of Article 4(1) are present. . . .

Rezaq also argues that applying the "death results" provision to this case would violate the normal jurisdictional rules of international law. International law

2. Rezaq also points out that Congress revised section 1472(n) in 1996, and asserts that our reading of the "afterward found" language would render much of the revised statute surplusage. The revised statute, which now appears at 49 U.S.C. § 46502(b), provides in relevant part:

(2) There is jurisdiction over the offense in paragraph (1) if

(A) a national of the United States was aboard the aircraft;

(B) an offender is a national of the United States; or

(C) an offender is afterwards found in the United States.

49 U.S.C. § 46502(b). Rezaq argues that, under our reading of "afterward found," every case will always be within section 46501(2)(C), as a defendant who is before a United States court will always be present in the United States; thus, he argues, under this reading sections (A) and (B) of the statute become unnecessary. Congress may well have had good reasons to include the three alternative bases of jurisdiction in section 46501(2). For example, some of the United States's extradition treaties require that, in order to obtain custody over a fugitive, the United States present an arrest warrant to the other state. *See, e.g.*, Agreement for the Surrender of Fugitive Offenders, Dec. 6, 1996, U.S.-Hong Kong, Art. 8, 36 I.L.M. 847, 852. Although we do not decide this question, we note that the United States might find it difficult to obtain an arrest warrant for a fugitive in Hong Kong under a statute that provides that the offender be "found in the United States"; the alternative bases of jurisdiction may thus serve as long-arm provisions.

imposes limits on a state's "jurisdiction to prescribe," that is, its ability to render its law applicable to persons or activities outside its borders; states may only exercise jurisdiction to prescribe under a limited number of theories. *See* RESTATEMENT (THIRD) OF FOREIGN RELATIONS LAW § 401 (1987). [p. 96] This case, however, clearly falls within at least one such theory, the so-called "passive personality principle." That principle "asserts that a state may apply law—particularly criminal law—to an act committed outside its territory by a person not its national where the victim of the act was its national." RESTATEMENT (THIRD) OF FOREIGN RELATIONS LAW § 402 cmt. g (1987). "The principle has not been generally accepted for ordinary torts or crimes, but it is increasingly accepted as applied to terrorist and other organized attacks on a state's nationals by reason of their nationality. . . ." Scarlett Rogenkamp was a United States citizen,[b] and there was abundant evidence that she was chosen as a victim because of her nationality. . . . This suffices to support jurisdiction on the passive personality theory. . . .

[The court found all of Rezaq's arguments to be without merit.]

Notes

(1) "The offense of aircraft piracy has four elements: (1) seizure or exercise of control of an aircraft; (2) by force, violence, or intimidation, or the threat thereof; (3) with wrongful intent; and (4) within the special aircraft jurisdiction of the United States." *United States v. Calloway*, 116 F.3d 1129 (6th Cir. 1997). In examining the "wrongful intent" element the court in Calloway stated:

> In the context of an "attempt" crime, specific intent means that the defendant consciously intends the completion of acts comprising the choate offense. In other words, the completion of such acts is the defendant's purpose. Where nothing more than general criminal intent is required, in contrast, the requirement may typically be satisfied by a showing that the defendant knew his actions would produce the prohibited result, or recklessly disregarded a known risk that they would do so. . . .
>
> We shall assume for purposes of analysis that the instruction did not require the jury to find specific intent. This brings us to the question whether the statute requires such an intent.
>
> Two of our sister circuits have held that it does not. *See United States v. Compton*, 5 F.3d 358, 360 (9th Cir. 1993); *United States v. Castaneda-Reyes*, 703 F.2d 522, 525 (11th Cir.), *cert. denied*, 464 U.S. 856, 104 S. Ct. 174, 78 L. Ed. 2d 157 (1983). Aircraft piracy is defined as "any seizure or exercise of control, by force or violence or threat of force or violence, or by any other form of intimidation, and with wrongful intent, of an aircraft within the special aircraft jurisdiction of the United States." 49 U.S.C. § 1472(i)(2) (now codified at 49 U.S.C. § 46502(a)(1)(A)) (emphasis supplied). The Compton

b. She was a passenger on the plane and an employee of the United States Air Force.—Eds.

> and Castaneda-Reyes courts concluded that the "wrongful intent" required by this section is only a general criminal intent, and that this general criminal intent applies to the inchoate offense as well as the choate offense.
>
> The issue is an open one in our circuit, as we believe it is in every circuit except the Ninth and the Eleventh. The general rule, however, is that attempt crimes require proof of a specific intent to complete the acts constituting the substantive offense. . . . The intent to finish the crime, coupled with affirmative acts toward that end, is a sine qua non of a punishable attempt. . . .
>
> We find it difficult to see why the specific intent requirement should not apply to attempted aircraft piracy. It is true that the definition of aircraft piracy in former 49 U.S.C. § 1472(i)(2) requires only a general criminal intent, but the relevance of this datum is not immediately apparent to us — for many attempt crimes require a specific intent even though the completed offense does not. . . . If we had to decide the issue — which, for reasons to be explained shortly, we do not — we should be inclined to hold that the offense of attempted aircraft piracy requires proof of a specific intent to complete the acts constituting aircraft piracy.[c]

(2) On December 21, 1987, the explosion of a bomb on board Pan Am Flight 103 killed 259 passengers and crew and 11 residents of Lockerbie, Scotland, where the plane crashed. On November 14, 1991, criminal charges were brought in both the U.S. and the U.K. against two Libyan nationals accused of causing the explosion. The U.N. Security Council adopted a series of resolutions imposing sanctions on Libya for not complying with requests to surrender the two defendants for trial. Libya meanwhile instituted proceedings against the U.S. and U.K. in the International Court of Justice, arguing that its obligations under the Montreal Convention were met by its own willingness to prosecute the defendants if the evidence against them were supplied to the Libyan authorities, and that the U.S. and the U.K. had breached their obligations under the convention by trying to coerce Libya into surrendering suspects whom it was entitled to try itself.

The Court's decisions regarding Provisional Measures and Preliminary Objections in the two Cases Concerning Questions of Interpretation and Application of the 1971 Montreal Convention Arising from the Aerial Incident at Lockerbie appear in 1992 I.C.J. Rep. 3, 114, & 1998 I.C.J. Rep. 9, 115. In 1999, arrangements were made to try the two defendants for multiple counts of murder ("unlawful homicide with malice aforethought") in the air and on the ground, before a Scottish court sitting in the Netherlands. *See* Anthony Aust, *Lockerbie: The Other Case*, 49 Int'l & Comp.

---

c. "The evidence of Mr. Calloway's guilt was overwhelming, and in no way did the jury instructions seriously affect the fairness or integrity of Mr. Calloway's trial. No reasonable jury could have found that Mr. Calloway did *not* have the specific intent to seize control of the plane." *Id.* at 1136. — Eds.

L. Q. (2000); Special Section on Trial of Lockerbie Suspects in the Netherlands, 38 I.L.M. 926 (1999).

In January 2001, the Scottish court convicted one individual and acquitted another. Anthony Deutsch, *A Conviction, Acquittal in Lockerbie Bombing*, ATL. J. CONST., Jan. 31, 2001, at 1. "The verdict was the climax of an $80 million trial and nearly nine months of hearings at a special court in the Netherlands." On appeal the court found "none of the grounds of appeal. . . . [ ]well founded." http://www.scotcourts.gov.uk/docs/default-source/sc---lockerbie/lockerbieappealjudgement.pdf?sfvrsn=2

The primary source material on the Lockerbie trial is very usefully collected in JOHN P. GRANT, THE LOCKERBIE TRIAL: A DOCUMENTARY HISTORY (2004). Other useful discussions include David R. Andrews, *A Thorn on the Tulip—A Scottish Trial in the Netherlands: The Story Behind the Lockerbie Trial*, 36 CASE W. RES. J. INT'L L. 307 (2004) and Julian B. Knowles, *The Lockerbie Judgments: A Short Analysis*, *id.*, at 473. Mr. Andrews, as Legal Adviser at the U.S. State Department, played a leading role in the negotiations that resulted in the trial in the Netherlands; Mr. Knowles assisted the defense. Edinburgh Law Professor Robert Black argues that the evidence for conviction was inadequate as was the representation of the defense both at trial and on appeal. He concludes that "a shameful miscarriage of justice has been perpetrated and that the Scottish criminal justice system has been gravely sullied." Robert Black, *Lockerbie: A Satisfactory Process but a Flawed Result*, 36 CASE W. RES. J. INT'L L. 443 (2004). In 2007, a second appeal was ordered by the Scottish Criminal Cases Review Commission. There were discussions in mid-2009 about transferring the convicted person, Abdelbaset al-Megrahi, from Scotland to Libya either under the terms of a U.K.-Libya Prisoner Transfer Treaty or as a compassionate gesture since he was apparently suffering from terminal cancer. He was sent home in August of 2009 by the Scottish Government, amid considerable outcry. The second appeal was discontinued. He died in May 2012. *See* Professor Black's ongoing blog of the case: http://lockerbiecase.blogspot.com/.

(3) In September 2010, members of the International Civil Aviation Organization adopted a Protocol Supplementary to the Convention for the Suppression of Unlawful Seizure of Aircraft and a new Convention on the Suppression of Unlawful Acts relating to International Civil Aviation. *See* texts, with introductory note in 50 INT'L LEG. MAT. 141 (2011). These instruments supersede earlier obligations in the situations where both States are party to the revisions and went into effect on July 1, 2018. The instruments contain new provisions, including new rules regarding mutual legal assistance and extradition. The new instruments also contain conspiracy type elements, though that terminology is not used. The new Unlawful Acts Convention contains an expanded definition of the proscribed acts to include not only direct sabotage of aircraft, but also various acts with radioactive and similar weapons. The new Convention also contains language pertaining to the use of an aircraft in service "for the purpose of causing death, serious bodily injury, or serious damage to property or the environment," as occurred on September 11th.

§ 9.05 Hostage Taking

United States v. Lue

United States Court of Appeals, Second Circuit
134 F.3d 79 (1998)

WALKER, CIRCUIT JUDGE:

Defendant, Chen De Yian,[d] appeals from a judgment of conviction entered by the United States District Court for the Southern District of New York (Denise L. Cote, Judge), following a conditional plea of guilty arising from defendant's attempt to abduct and hold a person hostage until the hostage's relatives paid a sum of money to secure the victim's release. The defendant pled guilty to (1) violating 18 U.S.C. § 1203, the Act for the Prevention and Punishment of the Crime of Hostage-Taking ("Hostage Taking Act"), Pub. L. No. 98-473, Title II, § 2002(a), 98 Stat. 2186 (1984), and (2) carrying a firearm in relation to the hostage taking in violation of 18 U.S.C. § 924(c). The district court sentenced the defendant to imprisonment for 147 months followed by supervised release for five years and a special assessment of $100. . . .

The counts to which defendant pled guilty arose from his unsuccessful efforts to abduct Chan Fung Chung in order to force the victim's family to pay ransom to obtain his release. The indictment alleges that in or about May 1991 Chen and his co-conspirators met in New York City to discuss and plan the seizure of Chan Fung Chung. On April 24, 1992, Chen and his co-conspirators attempted to force Chan Fung Chung into an automobile on East 13th Street in Manhattan. The defendants' attempt to abduct the victim was thwarted by a firefighter and an off-duty police officer who heard the victim's cries. Although his co-conspirators escaped, Chen was arrested by New York City police officers with a .30 caliber handgun in his possession. Following the arrest, Chen pled guilty in state court to weapons-use charges and served 18 months in state prison. Subsequently, Chen was indicted on federal charges relating to the attempted abduction as well as two homicides in Virginia which were part of an alleged murder-for-hire scheme.

After the district court denied the defendant's motion to dismiss the hostage taking counts on constitutional grounds, the defendant entered into a plea agreement with the government. On November 22, 1995, Chen entered a plea of guilty to two counts of the multi-count indictment, including the only count at issue in this appeal: the violation of the Hostage Taking Act, 18 U.S.C. § 1203. Under the plea agreement, Chen preserved his right to appellate review of the district court's decision that 18 U.S.C. § 1203 was constitutional. . . .

On April 26, 1984, President Reagan proposed legislation to Congress to combat international terrorism. See Message from the President of the United States Transmitting Four Drafts of Proposed Legislation to Attack the Pressing and

---

d. The court appears to assume that Mr. Chen is not an American national — Eds.

Urgent Problem of International Terrorism, H.R. Doc. No. 98-211, 98th Cong., 2d Sess. (1984) ("Presidential Message"). This proposal included a predecessor version of the Hostage Taking Act. . . . The legislation was designed to implement the International Convention Against the Taking of Hostages, . . . ratified by the Executive in 1981, ... The Convention binds the signatories to take specific steps to adopt "effective measures for the prevention, prosecution and punishment of all acts of taking of hostages as manifestations of international terrorism." In particular, the signatories agreed that

> any person who seizes or detains and threatens to kill, to injure or to continue to detain another person (hereinafter referred to as the "hostage") in order to compel a third party, namely, a State, an international intergovernmental organization, a natural or juridical person, or a group of persons, to do or abstain from doing any act as an explicit or implicit condition for the release of the hostage commits the offense of taking of hostages . . . within the meaning of this Convention.

Id. art. 1. The signatories also agreed to make hostage taking punishable in accordance with the deep gravity of the offense. Presumably to accommodate jurisdictional concerns, the terms of the Convention are inapplicable if a covered offense was committed within a single nation, the hostage and the alleged offender are nationals of that nation, and the alleged offender is found within the territory of that nation. . . .

Pursuant to its obligation under the Convention, in late 1984, Congress passed, and the President signed, the Hostage Taking Act, which provides in pertinent part:

> (a) Except as provided in subsection (b) of this section, whoever, whether inside or outside the United States, seizes or detains and threatens to kill, to injure, or to continue to detain another person in order to compel a third person or a governmental organization to do or abstain from doing any act as an explicit or implicit condition for the release of the person detained, or attempts or conspires to do so, shall be punished by imprisonment for any term of years or for life and, if the death of any person results, shall be punished by death or life imprisonment.
>
> . . . .
>
> (b)(2) It is not an offense under this section if the conduct required for the offense occurred inside the United States, each alleged offender and each person seized or detained are nationals of the United States, and each alleged offender is found in the United States, unless the governmental organization sought to be compelled is the Government of the United States.

18 U.S.C. § 1203. This statute is the focus of defendant's constitutional challenge. . . .

Defendant first argues that the district court erred in holding that Congress has the authority to pass the Hostage Taking Act under the Necessary and Proper

Clause of Article I, as an adjunct to the Executive's acknowledged authority under Article II to enter into treaties, with the advice and consent of the Senate. Chen contends that (1) the Hostage Taking Act is unconstitutional because the Hostage Taking Convention upon which it is based exceeds the Executive's authority under the Treaty Clause and (2) even if entry into the Convention is in accord with the treaty-making authority, the Hostage Taking Act is not a "plainly adapted" means of effectuating the Convention's ends and thus exceeds Congress's authority under the Necessary and Proper clause.

At the outset we note that Congress's authority under the Necessary and Proper Clause extends beyond those powers specifically enumerated in Article I, section 8. As the clause specifically states, "Congress shall have Power. . . . to make all Laws which shall be necessary and proper for carrying into Execution the foregoing powers, and all other Powers vested by this Constitution in the Government of the United States, or in any Department or Officer thereof." U.S. Const. art. I, § 8, cl. 18. Accordingly, Congress may enact laws necessary to effectuate the treaty power, enumerated in Article II of the Constitution. . . .

We need not pause long over defendant's contention that entry into the Hostage Taking Convention was beyond the Executive's authority under Article II to sign (and Congress to assent to) treaties. As defendant himself acknowledges, "to hold that the Treaty Power has been exceeded. . . . would of course be a drastic step." . . . His argument rests on the fundamental, but somewhat ambiguous, proposition in *Asakura v. City of Seattle* that the Executive's treaty power "extends to all proper subjects of negotiation between our government and other nations." . . . But, defendant argues that the Hostage Taking Convention regulates matters of purely domestic concern not touching on relations with other nations. Accordingly, he concludes that entry into the Convention was beyond the constitutional authority of the executive. Defendant is in error on two counts: (1) his overly restrictive view of the federal treaty power and (2) his evaluation of the Convention as addressing purely domestic interests. . . .

The defendant relies far too heavily on a dichotomy between matters of purely domestic concern and those of international concern, a dichotomy appropriately criticized by commentators in the field. . . .

> Contrary to what was once suggested, the Constitution does not require that an international agreement deal only with "matters of international concern." The references in the Constitution presumably incorporate the concept of treaty and of other agreements in international law. International law knows no limitations on the purpose or subject matter of international agreements, other than that they may not conflict with a peremptory norm of international law. States may enter into an agreement on any matter of concern to them, and international law does not look behind their motives or purposes in doing so. Thus, the United States may make an agreement on any subject suggested by its national interests in relations with other nations.

Restatement (Third) of the Foreign Relations Law of the United States § 302, cmt. c (1986)(citation omitted). . . .

Whatever the potential outer limit on the treaty power of the Executive, the Hostage Taking Convention does not transgress it. At the most general level, the Convention addresses — at least in part — the treatment of foreign nationals while they are on local soil, a matter of central concern among nations. More specifically, the Convention addresses a matter of grave concern to the international community: hostage taking as a vehicle for terrorism. In fact, the preamble of the Convention explicitly so states:

> the taking of hostages is an offence of grave concern to the international community and . . . in accordance with the provisions of this Convention, any person committing an act of hostage taking shall either be prosecuted or extradited . . . [I]t is urgently necessary to develop international cooperation between States in devising and adopting effective measures for the prevention, prosecution and punishment of all acts of taking of hostages as manifestations of international terrorism.

Hostage Taking Convention, preamble, T.I.A.S. No. 11,081. In short, the Hostage Taking Convention is well within the boundaries of the Constitution's treaty power. . . .

The defendant next challenges the means by which Congress effectuated the terms of the Convention: the enactment of the Hostage Taking Act. Defendant contends that the Act sweeps too broadly and, thus, exceeds Congress's authority to pass laws "necessary and proper" to the effectuation of the Convention. U.S. Const. Art. 1, § 8, cl. 18. More precisely, defendant argues that because the Hostage Taking Convention targets a specific aspect of international terrorism — hostage taking — the statute effectuating the Convention must deal narrowly with international terrorism or risk invalidity under the Necessary and Proper Clause. However, defendant's view of the congressional authority under the Necessary and Proper Clause is too cramped.

If the Hostage Taking Convention is a valid exercise of the Executive's treaty power, there is little room to dispute that the legislation passed to effectuate the treaty is valid under the Necessary and Proper Clause. . . . The Act here plainly bears a rational relationship to the Convention; indeed, it tracks the language of the Convention in all material respects. . . . The defendant contends that, even if the Hostage Taking Act passes muster under the Necessary and Proper Clause as an adjunct to the Executive's authority under the Treaty Clause, the Act nonetheless must be struck down because it impermissibly invades the authority of the states in violation of the Tenth Amendment. Specifically, defendant contends that because the Hostage Taking Act potentially criminalizes "domestic, non-political abductions," . . . . and because such abductions "are not in any meaningful way a uniquely international (or national) problem," . . . . the Act violates the principles of federalism embodied in the Tenth Amendment. We reject this argument.

The Tenth Amendment provides, in full: "The powers not delegated to the United States by the Constitution, nor prohibited by it to the States, are reserved to the States respectively, or to the people." U.S. Const. amend. X. The Constitution expressly vests the power to enter into treaties in the Executive, U.S. Const. art II, §2, cl. 2; accordingly, the power wielded by the Executive (with the advice and consent of the Senate) is "delegated" to the federal government and not "reserved" to the states. As one distinguished commentator has noted:

> Since the Treaty Power was delegated to the federal government, whatever is within its scope is not reserved to the states: the Tenth Amendment is not material. Many matters, then, may appear to be "reserved to the States" as regards domestic legislation if Congress does not have power to regulate them; but they are not reserved to the states so as to exclude their regulation by international agreement.

Louis Henkin, Foreign Affairs and the United States Constitution 191 (2d ed. 1996).... Thus, the treaty power is not subject to meaningful limitation under the terms of the Tenth Amendment....

Defendant's primary Tenth Amendment challenge to the Hostage Taking Act rests on his contention that hostage taking is a local concern and that, under Holland [Missouri v. Holland, 252 U.S. 416 (1920)], a legislative enactment effectuating a treaty will not pass muster under the Tenth Amendment unless such an enactment addresses a uniquely national or international matter. Such a reading finds some support in the language of the Court's opinion.... However, we need not decide the question, because in this case there is a sufficient national (indeed, international) interest supporting Congress's passage of the Hostage Taking Act....

Finally, defendant contends that the Hostage Taking Act violates the equal protection principles embodied in the Fifth Amendment's Due Process Clause. *See Bolling v. Sharpe*, 347 U.S. 497, 499, 74 S. Ct. 693, 98 L. Ed. 884 (1954). In particular, the defendant contends that the Act runs afoul of these principles because it criminalizes conduct undertaken by foreign nationals which would not be criminal if undertaken by United States' nationals and because such a classification is not supported by a substantial governmental interest.

There is little doubt, despite government protestations to the contrary, that the Hostage Taking Act discriminates against offenders on the basis of alienage. If the hostage-taking victim is a national, the Act criminalizes conduct by an alien that would not be sanctionable if undertaken by a United States citizen (except where the purpose of the crime is to compel the United States to act or refrain from acting)....

The principle [sic] area in dispute in defendant's equal protection challenge is, then, the appropriate level of judicial scrutiny to which the Act must be subjected. Defendant argues that the Hostage Taking Act is subject to heightened judicial scrutiny because it discriminates on the basis of alienage, an inherently suspect classification. Although defendant is correct that alienage has been treated as a suspect classification requiring heightened scrutiny, . . . he fails to properly acknowledge the context in which the Court has so ruled. The Court has recognized alienage as a suspect classification only when a state or local government has sought to employ the classification to disadvantage foreign nationals. . . .

The situation is different when it is the federal government that is drawing the distinction between citizens of the United States and those of foreign countries. Generally, the federal government is not held to the same searching scrutiny when it draws lines on the basis of alienage. The Court has recognized that the federal government has national interests when dealing with aliens that are different from those of the individual states. . . . In light of the federal government's primary authority in these areas, and because "it is the business of the political branches of the Federal Government, rather than that of either the States or the Federal Judiciary, to regulate the conditions of entry and residence of aliens," . . . state or local laws that disadvantage aliens are presumptively invalid while federal laws doing the same are accorded substantial deference.

This is not to say that foreign nationals on our soil are without any protection from federal governmental action under the equal protection component of the Fifth Amendment. They do enjoy such protection; however, it is constrained in light of the responsibility of the political branches to regulate the relationship between the United States and noncitizens. . . . [A]n array of constitutional and statutory provisions rests on the assumption that there are legitimate distinctions between citizens and aliens that "may justify attributes and benefits for one class not accorded the other." . . . In short, "the fact that an Act of Congress treats aliens differently from citizens does not in itself imply that such disparate treatment is 'invidious.'" . . .

As long as the Hostage Taking Act is rationally related to a legitimate government interest it satisfies principles of equal protection in this context. . . . In our view, the Act clears this constitutional hurdle.

The classification drawn by the Hostage Taking Act covers all aliens involved in hostage-taking incidents. The asserted purpose of the statute, along with the antecedent Convention, is to address a matter of grave concern to the international community: hostage taking as a manifestation of international terrorism. . . . We recognize that in the Hostage Taking Act Congress employs the classification of alienage to proscribe conduct which may not always bear a direct relationship to the Act's principal object of stemming acts of terrorism, and that at some point a classification of this sort may have a "relationship to [the] asserted goal [which] is so attenuated as to render the distinction arbitrary or irrational." . . . However, in this instance, Congress rationally concluded that a hostage taking within our jurisdiction involving a noncitizen is sufficiently likely to involve matters implicating foreign policy or immigration concerns as to warrant a federal criminal proscription. The connection between the act and its purpose is not so attenuated as to fail to meet the rational-basis standard. . . . For the foregoing reasons, we affirm the judgment of the district court.

Notes

(1) Other circuits have also found that the Hostage Taking Act does not violate equal protection. *See United States v. Ferreira*, 275 F.3d 1020 (11th Cir. 2001); *United States v. Montenegro*, 231 F.3d 389 (7th Cir. 2000).

(2) One suspects that the other parties to the Hostage Convention, who typically regard it as a "terrorism" instrument, would not have objected if the United States implementing legislation had not caught (or had not been interpreted to catch) the exact facts in *Lue*. Nor have any of them objected to the ultimate result in the unusual case of *Bond v. United States* 134 S. Ct. 2077 (2014). *Bond* involved the implementing legislation for the 1993 International Convention on the Prohibition of the Development, Production, Stockpiling and Use of Chemical Weapons and on Their Destruction. The legislation, 18 U.S.C. § 229(a)(1), forbids, inter alia, any person knowingly to "possess[] or use . . . any chemical weapon." A "chemical weapon" is a "toxic chemical and it precursors, except where intended for a purpose not prohibited under this chapter." A "toxic chemical" is "any chemical which through its chemical action on life processes can cause death, temporary incapacitation or permanent harm to humans or animals." When Carol Anne Bond's friend Myrlinda became pregnant by Bond's husband, Bond visited her home on at least 24 occasions and spread chemicals on her car door, mail box and door knob. It was agreed that she had no intent to kill. Apart from a minor burn on her thumb, Myrlinda was easily able to avoid the chemicals. Bond argued that extending the crime to her was an unconstitutional incursion by the federal government into an area traditionally reserved to the States and that it could not be supported by the treaty and necessary and proper powers. Writing for a six-judge majority, Chief Justice Roberts avoided the constitutional issue by interpreting the legislation as not applying in this situation, it being far from that contemplated by the Convention and the statute. Justices Scalia, Thomas and Alito thought that the legislation plainly applied to Bond. As so applied, they would have held it unconstitutional.

(3) In *United States v. Noel*, the defendant was charged with kidnapping in violation of 18 U.S.C. § 1203. The events giving rise to the charges occurred entirely in Haiti, where the defendant, a Haitian citizen, was alleged to have kidnapped an American citizen and held her for $150,000 in ransom. In appealing his conviction, the defendant raised three issues. First, the defendant argued that the prosecution was required to demonstrate that he knew his victim was an American citizen. Second, he argued that § 1203 was not intended to apply to a "street crime like his when committed by a foreign national in a foreign country." Rather, he argued, Congress intended the statute only to apply to acts of terrorism. Third, the defendant argued that the statute was unconstitutional in both its creation and application to a Haitian citizen who committed his crime entirely in Haiti. In rejecting all of the arguments, the court of appeals found first that there was no requirement that the defendant know his victim was an American citizen because this was "purely jurisdictional." The court found, second, that while the statute focuses on terrorism offenses, the statute is not limited to only these types of ransom offenses.

Rather, the court concluded, "[section] 1203 includes acts of hostage taking for ransom between private parties and not involving governmental organizations. . . ." Finally, the court concluded that the defendant's constitutional arguments were without merit and that the statute appropriately applied extraterritoriality. Noel was sentenced to 235 months imprisonment. *See United States v. Noel*, 893 F.3d 1294 (11th Cir. 2018).

Chapter 10

Torture

§ 10.01 The Torture Convention

Convention Against Torture and Other Cruel, Inhuman or Degrading Treatment or Punishment

General Assembly Resolution 39/46, Dec. 10, 1984, 39 U.N. GAOR, Supp. No. 51, at 197, U.N. Doc. A/39/51 (1985), in force June 26, 1987

Article 1

1. For the purposes of this Convention, the term "torture" means any act by which severe pain or suffering, whether physical or mental, is intentionally inflicted on a person for such purposes as obtaining from him or a third person information or a confession, punishing him for an act he or a third person has committed or is suspected of having committed, or intimidating or coercing him or a third person, or for any reason based on discrimination of any kind, when such pain or suffering is inflicted by or at the instigation of or with the consent or acquiescence of a public official or other person acting in an official capacity. It does not include pain or suffering arising only from, inherent in or incidental to lawful sanctions.

2. This article is without prejudice to any international instrument or national legislation which does or may contain provisions of wider application.

Article 2

1. Each State Party shall take effective legislative, administrative, judicial or other measures to prevent acts of torture in any territory under its jurisdiction.

2. No exceptional circumstances whatsoever, whether a state of war or a threat of war, internal political instability or any other public emergency, may be invoked as a justification of torture.

3. An order from a superior officer or a public authority may not be invoked as a justification of torture.

Article 3

1. No State Party shall expel, return ("*refouler*") or extradite a person to another State where there are substantial grounds for believing that he would be in danger of being subjected to torture.

2. For the purpose of determining whether there are such grounds, the competent authorities shall take into account all relevant considerations including, where applicable, the existence in the State concerned of a consistent pattern of gross, flagrant or mass violations of human rights.

Article 4

1. Each State Party shall ensure that all acts of torture are offences under its criminal law. The same shall apply to an attempt to commit torture and to an act by any person which constitutes complicity or participation in torture.
2. Each State Party shall make these offences punishable by appropriate penalties which take into account their grave nature.

Article 5

1. Each State Party shall take such measures as may be necessary to establish its jurisdiction over the offences referred to in article 4 in the following cases:
   (a) When the offences are committed in any territory under its jurisdiction or on board a ship or aircraft registered in that State;
   (b) When the alleged offender is a national of that State;
   (c) When the victim is a national of that State if that State considers it appropriate.
2. Each State Party shall likewise take such measures as may be necessary to establish its jurisdiction over such offences in cases where the alleged offender is present in any territory under its jurisdiction and it does not extradite him pursuant to article 8 to any of the States mentioned in paragraph 1 of this article.
3. This Convention does not exclude any criminal jurisdiction exercised in accordance with internal law.

Article 6

1. Upon being satisfied, after an examination of information available to it, that the circumstances so warrant, any State Party in whose territory a person alleged to have committed any offence referred to in article 4 is present shall take him into custody or take other legal measures to ensure his presence. The custody and other legal measures shall be as provided in the law of that State but may be continued only for such time as is necessary to enable any criminal or extradition proceedings to be instituted.
2. Such State shall immediately make a preliminary inquiry into the facts.
3. Any person in custody pursuant to paragraph 1 of this article shall be assisted in communicating immediately with the nearest appropriate representative of the State of which he is a national, or, if he is a stateless person, with the representative of the State where he usually resides.
4. When a State, pursuant to this article, has taken a person into custody, it shall immediately notify the States referred to in article 5, paragraph 1, of the fact

that such person is in custody and of the circumstances which warrant his detention. The State which makes the preliminary inquiry contemplated in paragraph 2 of this article shall promptly report its findings to the said States and shall indicate whether it intends to exercise jurisdiction.

Article 7

1. The State Party in the territory under whose jurisdiction a person alleged to have committed any offence referred to in article 4 is found shall in the cases contemplated in article 5, if it does not extradite him, submit the case to its competent authorities for the purpose of prosecution.
2. These authorities shall take their decision in the same manner as in the case of any ordinary offence of a serious nature under the law of that State. In the cases referred to in article 5, paragraph 2, the standards of evidence required for prosecution and conviction shall in no way be less stringent than those which apply in the cases referred to in article 5, paragraph 1.
3. Any person regarding whom proceedings are brought in connection with any of the offences referred to in article 4 shall be guaranteed fair treatment at all stages of the proceedings.

Article 8

1. The offences referred to in article 4 shall be deemed to be included as extraditable offences in any extradition treaty existing between States Parties. States Parties undertake to include such offences as extraditable offences in every extradition treaty to be concluded between them.
2. If a State Party which makes extradition conditional on the existence of a treaty receives a request for extradition from another State Party with which it has no extradition treaty, it may consider this Convention as the legal basis for extradition in respect of such offences. Extradition shall be subject to the other conditions provided by the law of the requested State.
3. States Parties which do not make extradition conditional on the existence of a treaty shall recognize such offences as extraditable offences between themselves subject to the conditions provided by the law of the requested State.
4. Such offences shall be treated, for the purpose of extradition between States Parties, as if they had been committed not only in the place in which they occurred but also in the territories of the States required to establish their jurisdiction in accordance with article 5, paragraph 1.

Article 9

1. States Parties shall afford one another the greatest measure of assistance in connection with criminal proceedings brought in respect of any of the offences referred to in article 4, including the supply of all evidence at their disposal necessary for the proceedings.

2. States Parties shall carry out their obligations under paragraph 1 of this article in conformity with any treaties on mutual judicial assistance that may exist between them.

Article 10

1. Each State Party shall ensure that education and information regarding the prohibition against torture are fully included in the training of law enforcement personnel, civil or military, medical personnel, public officials and other persons who may be involved in the custody, interrogation or treatment of any individual subjected to any form of arrest, detention or imprisonment.
2. Each State Party shall include this prohibition in the rules or instructions issued in regard to the duties and functions of any such person.

Article 11

Each State Party shall keep under systematic review interrogation rules, instructions, methods and practices as well as arrangements for the custody and treatment of persons subjected to any form of arrest, detention or imprisonment in any territory under its jurisdiction, with a view to preventing any cases of torture.

Article 12

Each State Party shall ensure that its competent authorities proceed to a prompt and impartial investigation, wherever there is reasonable ground to believe that an act of torture has been committed in any territory under its jurisdiction.

Article 13

Each State Party shall ensure that any individual who alleges he has been subjected to torture in any territory under its jurisdiction has the right to complain to, and to have his case promptly and impartially examined by, its competent authorities. Steps shall be taken to ensure that the complainant and witnesses are protected against all ill-treatment or intimidation as a consequence of his complaint or any evidence given.

Article 14

1. Each State Party shall ensure in its legal system that the victim of an act of torture obtains redress and has an enforceable right to fair and adequate compensation, including the means for as full rehabilitation as possible. In the event of the death of the victim as a result of an act of torture, his dependents shall be entitled to compensation.
2. Nothing in this article shall affect any right of the victim or other persons to compensation which may exist under national law.

Article 15

Each State Party shall ensure that any statement which is established to have been made as a result of torture shall not be invoked as evidence in any proceedings, except against a person accused of torture as evidence that the statement was made.

Article 16

1. Each State Party shall undertake to prevent in any territory under its jurisdiction other acts of cruel, inhuman or degrading treatment or punishment which do not amount to torture as defined in article 1, when such acts are committed by or at the instigation of or with the consent or acquiescence of a public official or other person acting in an official capacity. In particular, the obligations contained in articles 10, 11, 12 and 13 shall apply with the substitution for references to torture of references to other forms of cruel, inhuman or degrading treatment or punishment.
2. The provisions of this Convention are without prejudice to the provisions of any other international instrument or national law which prohibits cruel, inhuman or degrading treatment or punishment or which relates to extradition or expulsion.

Notes

(1) Articles 1–16 comprise Part I of the Torture Convention. Part II (composed of Articles 17–24) establishes a 10-member Committee Against Torture, to monitor compliance on the basis of reports submitted by the parties, its own confidential inquiries, and (if a state chooses to allow them) complaints by other states and by aggrieved individuals. Part III (composed of Articles 25–33) contains "final clauses" pertaining to signature, ratification, amendment, etc. The Convention entered into force on June 26, 1987.

(2) The *Filartiga* case [§ 1.03], decided in 1980, already had concluded that torture violates customary international law, relying in significant part on General Assembly Resolution 3452 (XXX) (1975). What did the Convention add to this prohibition? Consider the following observation. What are the "supportive measures" to which this statement refers:

> Many people assume that the Convention's principal aim is to *outlaw* torture and other cruel, inhuman or degrading treatment or punishment. This assumption is not correct insofar as it would imply that the prohibition of these practices is established under international law by the Convention only and that this prohibition will be binding as a rule of international law only for those States which have become parties to the Convention. On the contrary, the Convention is based upon the recognition that the above-mentioned practices are already outlawed under international law. The principal aim of the Convention is to *strengthen* the existing prohibition of such practices by a number of supportive measures.

J. Herman Burgers & Hans Danelius, The United Nations Convention Against Torture: A Handbook on the Convention Against Torture and Other Cruel, Inhuman or Degrading Treatment or Punishment 1 (1988).

The Council of Europe has instituted even more stringent "supportive measures" within its sphere of influence. *See* Protecting Prisoners: The Standards of the European Committee for the Prevention of Torture in Context (Rod Morgan & Malcolm D. Evans eds., 1999). The United Nations also has one of its "theme mechanisms" devoted to the struggle against torture, the Special Rapporteur on Torture, who reports to the Human Rights Council. *See* Peter K. Kooijmans, *The Role and Action of the UN Special Rapporteur on Torture in* The International Fight Against Torture 56 (Antonio Cassese ed., 1991).

(3) Article 1 of the Convention, in defining torture for the purposes of the Convention, required the action or inaction of "a public official or other person acting in an official capacity." In its General Comment No. 2 which discusses its understanding of the suppression obligation in Article 2 of the Convention, the Committee against Torture opined that:

> 18. The Committee has made clear that where State authorities or others acting in official capacity or under colour of law, know or have reasonable grounds to believe that acts of torture or ill-treatment are being committed by non-State officials or private actors and they fail to exercise due diligence to prevent, investigate, prosecute and punish such non-State officials or private actors consistently with the Convention, the State bears responsibility and its officials should be considered as authors, complicit or otherwise responsible under the Convention for consenting to or acquiescing in such impermissible acts. Since the failure of the State to exercise due diligence to intervene to stop, sanction and provide remedies to victims of torture facilitates and enables non-State actors to commit acts impermissible under the Convention with impunity, the State's indifference or inaction provides a form of encouragement and/or de facto permission. The Committee has applied this principle to States parties' failure to prevent and protect victims from gender-based violence, such as rape, domestic violence, female genital mutilation, and trafficking.

Is this a reasonable interpretation of the Convention, or does it stretch the obligations beyond those fairly stated in its plain language? How heavy a burden is this on States to curb non-State actors as opposed to the officials with which the Convention is primarily concerned?

(4) The United States ratified the Torture Convention in 1994. The Senate's advice and consent to ratification was accompanied by two reservations, five understandings, two declarations, and a proviso. These read:

> I. The Senate's advice and consent is subject to the following reservations:
>
> (1) That the United States considers itself bound by the obligation under Article 16 to prevent "cruel, inhuman or degrading treatment or punishment," only insofar as the term "cruel, inhuman or degrading treatment or punishment" means the cruel, unusual and inhumane treatment or

punishment prohibited by the Fifth, Eighth, and/or Fourteenth Amendments to the Constitution of the United States.

(2) That pursuant to Article 30(2) the United States declares that it does not consider itself bound by Article 30(1) [which provides that disputes between parties concerning the interpretation or application of the convention shall be settled by arbitration or else by submission to the ICJ], but reserves the right specifically to agree to follow this or any other procedure for arbitration in a particular case.

II. The Senate's advice and consent is subject to the following understandings, which shall apply to the obligations of the United States under this Convention:

(1)(a) That with reference to Article 1, the United States understands that, in order to constitute torture, an act must be specifically intended to inflict severe physical or mental pain or suffering and that mental pain or suffering refers to prolonged mental harm caused by or resulting from: (1) the intentional infliction or threatened infliction of severe physical pain or suffering; (2) the administration or application, or threatened administration or application, of mind altering substances or other procedures calculated to disrupt profoundly the senses or the personality; (3) the threat of imminent death; or (4) the threat that another person will imminently be subjected to death, severe physical pain or suffering, or the administration or application of mind altering substances or other procedures calculated to disrupt profoundly the senses or personality.

(b) That the United States understands that the definition of torture in Article 1 is intended to apply only to acts directed against persons in the offender's custody or physical control.

(c) That with reference to Article 1 of the Convention, the United States understands that "sanctions" includes judicially-imposed sanctions and other enforcement actions authorized by United States law or by judicial interpretation of such law. Nonetheless, the United States understands that a State Party could not through its domestic sanctions defeat the object and purpose of the Convention to prohibit torture.

(d) That with reference to Article 1 of the Convention, the United States understands that the term "acquiescence" requires that the public official, prior to the activity constituting torture, have awareness of such activity and thereafter breach his legal responsibility to intervene to prevent such activity.

(e) That with reference to Article 1 of the Convention, the United States understands that noncompliance with applicable legal procedural standards does not per se constitute torture.

(2) That the United States understands the phrase, "where there are substantial grounds for believing that he would be in danger of being subjected to torture," as used in Article 3 of the Convention, to mean "if it is more likely than not that he would be tortured."

(3) That it is the understanding of the United States that Article 14 requires a State Party to provide a private right of action for damages only for acts of torture committed in territory under the jurisdiction of that State Party.

(4) That the United States understands that international law does not prohibit the death penalty, and does not consider this Convention to restrict or prohibit the United States from applying the death penalty consistent with the Fifth, Eighth and/or Fourteenth Amendments to the Constitution of the United States, including any constitutional period of confinement prior to the imposition of the death penalty.

(5) That the United States understands that this Convention shall be implemented by the United States Government to the extent that it exercises legislative and judicial jurisdiction over the matters covered by the Convention and otherwise by the state and local governments. Accordingly, in implementing Articles 10–14 and 16, the United States Government shall take measures appropriate to the Federal system to the end that the competent authorities of the constituent units of the United States of America may take appropriate measures for the fulfillment of the Convention.

III. The Senate's advice and consent is subject to the following declarations:

(1) That the United States declares that the provisions of Articles 1 through 16 of the Convention are not self-executing.

(2) That the United States declares, pursuant to Article 21, paragraph 1, of the Convention, that it recognizes the competence of the Committee against Torture to receive and consider communications to the effect that a State Party claims that another State Party is not fulfilling its obligations under the Convention. It is the understanding of the United States that, pursuant to the above mentioned article, such communications shall be accepted and processed only if they come from a State Party which has made a similar declaration.

IV. The Senate's advice and consent is subject to the following proviso, which shall not be included in the instrument of ratification to be deposited by the President:

The President of the United States shall not deposit the instrument of ratification until such time as he has notified all present and prospective ratifying parties to this Convention that nothing in this Convention requires or authorizes legislation, or other action, by the United States of America prohibited by the Constitution of the United States as interpreted by the United States.

See also David P. Stewart, *The Torture Convention and the Reception of International Criminal Law Within the United States*, 15 NOVA L. REV. 449 (1991); *but see* Louis Henkin, *U.S. Ratification of Human Rights Conventions: The Ghost of Senator Bricker*, 89 A.J.I.L. 341 (1995).

(5) Article 2 of the 1969 Vienna Convention on the Law of Treaties, widely regarded as codifying customary law, defines "reservation" as "a unilateral statement, however phrased or named, made by a State when signing, ratifying, accepting, approving or acceding to a treaty, whereby it purports to exclude or to modify the legal effect of certain provisions in the treaty in their application to that State." The "reservations" (so named) in the Senate's advice and consent plainly fit this definition. Some of the "understandings" may simply be efforts at clarification; others (such as Understanding 1(a), with its apparently narrowing and exclusive set of examples, and Understanding (2) which affects the burden and standard of proof) may be functionally reservations. Each of these is carried forward into implementing legislation and Regulations. The "non-self-executing" declaration, much criticized in the human rights community, is probably just an assertion on the way the convention will be given effect in domestic law. It has no import internationally, except to the extent that it may prevent the courts from picking up the slack when the other branches fail to implement the treaty obligations, thus leaving the U.S. in breach of those obligations.

Reservation (1) limits the effect of Article 16 of the Convention ("cruel, inhuman or degrading treatment or punishment") to "the cruel, unusual and inhumane treatment or punishment prohibited by the Fifth, Eighth, and/or Fourteenth Amendments to the Constitution of the United States." It is plainly meant to narrow the scope of that article. Finland, the Netherlands and Sweden objected to the reservation to Article 16 as "incompatible with the object and purpose" of the Convention. (*See* Vienna Convention on the Law of Treaties, Article 19.)

(6) Article 2 (2) of the Convention says that no exceptional circumstances may be invoked as a justification of *torture*. Might it be argued, that in time of emergency (the "war on terrorism", for example) it would nonetheless be lawful to engage in cruel, etc. treatment or punishment? (In the case of the United States this would be subject to the Constitution, in places where it applies. Indeed, should the Constitution itself bend in such circumstances?) *See generally,* John T. Parry, *Escalation and Necessity: Defining Torture at Home and Abroad, in* TORTURE: A COLLECTION 145 (Sanford Levinson ed., 2004). Other international instruments, such as the International Covenant on Civil and Political Rights, Articles 4 and 7, do not distinguish, for purposes of derogability, between the two classes of violation of rights.

Giving Effect to the Convention in U.S. Law

President Ronald Reagan had the Torture Convention signed on behalf of the U.S. in April 1988 and sent it to the Senate, which gave its advice and consent on 27 October 1990, during the term of President George H.W. Bush. President Bush then asked Congress to adopt the necessary legislation to criminalize torture and provide for appropriate jurisdiction. The legislation stalled in Congress. Meanwhile Congress completed its unrelated work on the Torture Victim Protection Act (TVPA) (introduced as H.R. 2092) and sent it to the President. The TVPA builds on *Filartiga v. Pena-Irala* [chap. 1] and allows suits against persons who, acting "under actual or apparent authority, or color of law, of any foreign nation" engage in torture or extrajudicial killing. Claimants under this Act may be either aliens or US citizens. Only natural persons, not corporations, may be defendants. In a 12 March 1992 signing statement accompanying his signature of the TVPA, the President said, in part:

> I regret that the legislation proposed by the Administration to implement the United Nations Convention Against Torture and Other Cruel, Inhuman or Degrading Treatment or Punishment has not yet been enacted. This proposed implementing legislation would provide a tougher and more effective response to the problem, putting in place for torturers the same international "extradite or prosecute" regime we have for terrorists. The Senate gave its advice and consent to the Torture Convention on October 27, 1990, but the United States cannot proceed to become a party until the necessary implementing legislation is in place. I again call upon the Congress to take prompt action to approve the Torture Convention implementing legislation.
>
> I note that H.R. 2092 does not help to implement the Torture Convention and does present a number of potential problems about which the Administration has expressed concern in the past. This legislation concerns acts of torture and extrajudicial killing committed overseas by foreign individuals. With rare exceptions, the victims of these acts will be foreign citizens. There is thus a danger that U.S. courts may become embroiled in difficult and sensitive disputes in other countries, and possibly ill-founded or politically motivated suits, which have nothing to do with the United States and which offer little prospect of successful recovery.
>
> Such potential abuse of this statute undoubtedly would give rise to serious frictions in international relations and would also be a waste of our own limited and already overburdened judicial resources. As I have noted in connection with my own Civil Justice Reform Initiative, there is too much litigation at present even by Americans against Americans. The expansion of litigation by aliens against aliens is a matter that must be approached with prudence and restraint. It is to be hoped that U.S. courts will be able to avoid these dangers by sound construction of the statute and the wise application of relevant legal procedures and principles.
>
> These potential dangers, however, do not concern the fundamental goals that this legislation seeks to advance. In this new era, in which countries throughout the world are turning to democratic institutions and the rule of law, we must maintain and strengthen our commitment to ensuring that human rights are respected everywhere. I again call upon the Congress to make a real contribution to the fight against torture by enacting the

implementing legislation for the Torture Convention so that we can finally ratify that important treaty.

Finally, I must note that I am signing the bill based on my understanding that the Act does not permit suits for alleged human rights violations in the context of United States military operations abroad or law enforcement actions. Because the Act permits suits based only on actions "under actual or apparent authority, or color of law, of any foreign nation," I do not believe it is the Congress' intent that H.R. 2092 should apply to United States Armed Forces or law enforcement operations, which are always carried out under the authority of United States law.

Congress did not oblige during the remainder of the Bush term, and it was left to President Clinton to sign the legislation and to deposit the U.S. instrument of ratification in October 1994. The initial federal statute implementing the criminalization obligations of the Convention, effective April 30, 1994, codified at 18 U.S.C. §§ 2340–2340B, reads:

18 U.S.C. § 2340. Definitions.

As used in this chapter

(1) "torture" means an act committed by a person acting under the color of law specifically intended to inflict severe physical or mental pain or suffering (other than pain or suffering incidental to lawful sanctions) upon another person within his custody or physical control;

(2) "severe mental pain or suffering" means the prolonged mental harm caused by or resulting from—

(A) the intentional infliction or threatened infliction of severe physical pain or suffering;

(B) the administration or application, or threatened administration or application, of mind-altering substances or other procedures calculated to disrupt profoundly the senses or the personality;

(C) the threat of imminent death; or

(D) the threat that another person will imminently be subjected to death, severe physical pain or suffering, or the administration or application of mind-altering substances or other procedures calculated to disrupt profoundly the senses or personality; and

(3) "United States" means the several States of the United States, the District of Columbia, and the commonwealths, territories, and possessions of the United States.[a]

---

a. Subsection (3) was amended in this form in 2004. The previous definition was worded in such a way that Guantanamo was apparently in the U.S.—a position different from that argued by the Government in habeas cases. Perversely, this meant that, since the torture offense was punishable

18 U.S.C. § 2340A. Torture.

(a) Offense. Whoever outside the United States commits or attempts to commit torture shall be fined under this title or imprisoned not more than 20 years, or both, and if death results to any person from conduct prohibited by this subsection, shall be punished by death or imprisoned for any term of years or for life.

(b) Jurisdiction. There is jurisdiction over the activity prohibited in subsection (a) if—

(1) the alleged offender is a national of the United States; or

(2) the alleged offender is present in the United States, irrespective of the nationality of the victim or alleged offender.

(c) [Added by § 811(g) of the U.S.A. Patriot Act of 2001] CONSPIRACY—A person who conspires to commit an offense under this section shall be subject to the same penalties (other than the penalty of death) as the penalties prescribed for the offense, the commission of which was the object of the conspiracy. [Added by 811(g) of the U.S.A. Patriot Act of 2001.]

18 U.S.C. § 2340B. Exclusive remedies.

Nothing in this chapter shall be construed as precluding the application of State or local laws on the same subject, nor shall anything in this chapter be construed as creating any substantive or procedural right enforceable by law by any party in any civil proceeding.

Notes

(1) Do the provisions in 18 U.S.C. §§ 2340–2340B fully implement the obligation to make torture, as defined in the Convention, a punishable offense? Do they do so at least with respect to torture perpetrated outside the United States by a United States national or by an offender who is later present in the United States? What about torture perpetrated within the United States? Is that not fully covered, in any event, by other state and federal laws dealing with various kinds of assaults? Or does the Torture Convention require that parties create a specific, separate (federal?) offense corresponding to torture as defined in Article 1? Consider this and other questions raised in the Committee against Torture's Concluding observations on

only "outside the United States" under 18 U.S.C. § 2340A, it was not punishable in respect of Guantanamo, since Guantanamo was by definition within the U.S. Now torture in Guantanamo is, in theory, punishable, since Guantanamo is not on the list of places defined as the United States, although no one has been punished for torture there, or, for that matter, anywhere else in the "war on terror."—Eds.

the third to fifth periodic reports[1] submitted by the United States about its efforts to comply with the Convention (CAT/C/USA/CO/3-5 (November 20, 2014):

A. Introduction

2. The Committee expresses its appreciation to the State party for accepting the optional reporting procedure as this improves the dialogue between the State party and the Committee and helps the State party to prepare a more focused report. It notes, however, that the report was submitted with a two-year delay.

3. The Committee appreciates the quality of its dialogue with the State party's high-level delegation and of the responses provided orally to the questions and concerns raised during the consideration of the report.

B. Positive aspects

4. The Committee welcomes the changes in the State party's legislation and jurisprudence in areas of relevance to the Convention, including:

(a) Recognition by the Supreme Court in Boumediene v. Bush, 553 U.S. 723 (2008), of the extraterritorial application of constitutional habeas corpus rights to aliens detained by the military as enemy combatants at Guantanamo Bay;

(b) Presidential Executive Orders 13491-Ensuring Lawful Interrogations, 13492-Review and Disposition of Individuals Detained at the Guantanamo Bay Naval Base and Closure of Detention Facilities, and 13493-Review of Detention Policy Options, issued on 22 January 2009;

(c) Presidential Executive Order 13567 establishing a periodic review of detainees at the Guantanamo Bay detention facility who have not been charged, convicted or designated for transfer, issued on 7 March 2011;

(d) Supreme Court's rulings in Graham v. Florida (2010), prohibiting sentences of life imprisonment without parole for children convicted of non-homicide offences, and Miller v. Alabama (2012), barring sentences of mandatory life imprisonment without parole for children convicted of homicide offences.

5. The Committee also welcomes the efforts of the State party to amend its policies, programmes and administrative measures to give effect to the Convention, including:

1. The U.S., like many states, is slow in furnishing its reports. The Torture Committee has a backlog exacerbated by Covid. The U.S.'s Sixth Report, due in 2018, was sent to the U.N. in September 2021 and will be considered by the Committee in 2022 or 2023.

(a) Adoption of the Directive on the appropriate use of segregation in Immigration and Customs Enforcement (ICE) detention facilities, in 2013; and, ICE revised Performance-Based National Detention Standards, in 2011;

(b) Promulgation of the National Standards to Prevent, Detect, and Respond to Sexual Abuse in Confinement Facilities, in accordance with the Prison Rape Elimination Act of 2003 (PREA), in 2012; and, the efforts undertaken by the State party to ensure the respect of the act in federal, state and local facilities and to collect data on the extent of sexual violence in detention.

6. The Committee welcomes the firm and principled position adopted by the State party with regard to the applicability of the Convention during armed conflict, stating that a time of war does not suspend the operation of the Convention, which continues to apply even when the State is engaged in an armed conflict.

7. It also welcomes the State party's long standing commitment to the United Nations Voluntary Funds for Victims of Torture and its mission.

8. Finally the Committee notes with appreciation President Obama's public statement of 1 August 2014 in which he qualified some of the so-called "enhanced interrogation-techniques" as acts of torture. [The President specifically referenced waterboarding.]

C. Principal subjects of concern and recommendations

Definition and criminalization of torture

9. Notwithstanding the State party's statement that under U.S. law, acts of torture are prohibited by various statutes and may be prosecuted in a variety of ways, the Committee regrets that a specific offence of torture has not been introduced yet at the federal level. The Committee is of the view that the introduction of such offence, in full conformity with article 1 of the Convention, would strengthen the human rights protection framework in the State party. The Committee also regrets that the State party maintains a restrictive interpretation of the provisions of the Convention and does not intend to withdraw any of its interpretative understandings lodged at the time of ratification. In particular, the concept of "prolonged mental harm" introduces a subjective non-measurable element which undermines the application of the treaty. While noting the delegation's explanations on this matter, especially with regard to articles 1 and 16 of the Convention, the Committee recalls that, under international law, reservations that are contrary to the object and purpose of a treaty are impermissible (arts. 1, 2, paragraph 1 and 4). The Committee reiterates its previous recommendation (A/55/44, para. 180 (a) and CAT/C/USA/CO/2, para. 13) that the State party should criminalize torture at the federal level, in full conformity with article 1 of the Convention, and ensure that penalties for torture

are commensurate with the gravity of this crime. It recommends the re-introduction of the Law Enforcement Torture Prevention Act, a bill which contains a definition of torture and specifically criminalizes acts of torture by law enforcement personnel and others under the color of law. The State party should give further consideration to withdrawing its interpretative understandings and reservations. In particular, it should ensure that acts of psychological torture are not qualified as "prolonged mental harm". In this regard, the Committee draws the attention to its General Comment No. 2 (2007), on the implementation of article 2 of the Convention by State parties, which states that serious discrepancies between the Convention's definition and that incorporated into domestic law create actual or potential loopholes for impunity (CAT/C/GC/2, para. 9).

Extraterritoriality

10. The Committee welcomes the State party's unequivocal commitment to abide by the universal prohibition of torture and ill-treatment everywhere, including Bagram and Guantanamo Bay detention facilities, as well as the assurances that U.S. personnel are legally prohibited under international and domestic law from engaging in torture or cruel, inhuman, or degrading treatment or punishment at all times, and in all places. The Committee notes that the State party has reviewed its position concerning the extraterritorial application of the Convention, and stated that it applies to "certain areas beyond" its sovereign territory, and more specifically to "all places that the State party controls as a governmental authority", noting that it currently exercises such control at "the U.S. Naval Station at Guantanamo Bay, Cuba, and over all proceedings conducted there, and with respect to U.S. — registered ships and aircraft". The Committee also values the statement made by the State party's delegation that the reservation to article 16 of the Convention, whose intended purpose is to ensure that existing U.S. constitutional standards satisfy the State party's obligations under article 16, "does not introduce any limitation to the geographic applicability of article 16", and that "the obligations in article 16 apply beyond the sovereign territory of the United States to any territory under its jurisdiction" under the terms mentioned above. However, the Committee is dismayed that the State party's reservation to article 16 of the Convention features in various declassified memoranda containing legal interpretations on the extraterritorial applicability of U.S. obligations under the Convention issued by the Department of Justice's Office of Legal Counsel (OLC) between 2001 and 2009, as part of deeply flawed legal arguments used to advise that interrogation techniques, which amounted to torture, could be authorized and used lawfully. While noting that these memoranda were revoked by Presidential Executive Order 13491 to the extent of their inconsistency with that order, the Committee remains concerned that the State party has not withdrawn yet its reservation to article 16 which could permit interpretations

incompatible with the absolute prohibition of torture and ill-treatment. The Committee reiterates its view (CAT/C/USA/CO/2, para. 15) that the State party should take effective measures to prevent acts of torture not only in its sovereign territory but also "in any territory under its jurisdiction". In this respect, the Committee recalls, as stated in its General Comment No. 2, that 'any territory' includes "all areas where the State party exercises, directly or indirectly, in whole or in part, de jure or de facto effective control, in accordance with international law. The reference to 'any territory' in article 2, like that in articles 5, 11, 12, 13 and 16 [of the Convention], refers to prohibited acts committed not only on board a ship or aircraft registered by a State party, but also during military occupation or peacekeeping operations and in such places as embassies, military bases, detention facilities, or other areas which a State party exercises factual or effective control" (para. 16). The State party should amend the relevant laws and regulations accordingly, and withdraw its reservation to article 16 as a means to avoid wrongful interpretations.

Counter-terrorism measures

11. The Committee expresses its grave concern over the extraordinary rendition, secret detention and interrogation programme operated by the U.S. Central Intelligence Agency (CIA) between 2001 and 2008, which involved numerous human rights violations, including torture, ill-treatment and enforced disappearance of persons suspected of involvement in terrorism-related crimes. While noting the content and scope of Presidential E.O. 13491, the Committee regrets the scant information provided by the State party with regard to the now shuttered network of secret detention facilities, which formed part of the high-value detainee programme publicly referred to by President Bush on 6 September 2006. It also regrets the lack of information provided on the practices of extraordinary rendition and enforced disappearance; and, on the extent of the CIA's abusive interrogation techniques used on suspected terrorists, such as water-boarding. In this regard, the Committee is closely following the declassification process of the U.S. Senate Select Committee on Intelligence's report on the CIA's detention and interrogation programme (art. 2, 11 and 16). The Committee recalls the absolute prohibition of torture reflected in article 2, paragraph 2, of the Convention, stating that "no exceptional circumstances whatsoever, whether a state of war or a threat of war, internal political instability or any other public emergency, may be invoked as a justification of torture". In this regard, the Committee draws the attention to paragraph 5 of its General Comment No. 2 (2007), in which it states that those 'exceptional circumstances' include "any threat of terrorist acts or violent crime as well as armed conflict, international or non-international". The Committee urges the State party to:

(a) Ensure that no one is held in secret detention under its de facto effective control. The Committee reiterates that detaining individuals in such conditions constitutes per se a violation of the Convention;

(b) Take all necessary measures to ensure that its legislative, administrative and other anti-terrorism measures are compatible with the provisions of the Convention, especially with article 2;

(c) Adopt effective measures to ensure, in law and in practice, that all detainees are afforded all legal safeguards from the very outset of their deprivation of liberty, including those mentioned in paragraphs 13 and 14 of the Committee's General Comment No. 2. The Committee calls for the declassification and prompt public release of the Senate Select Committee on Intelligence's report on the CIA's secret detention and interrogation programme with minimal redactions. [A lengthy, but still redacted version of that Report was subsequently released. *See* § 10.02.]

The Committee also encourages the State party to ratify the International Convention for the Protection of All Persons from Enforced Disappearance. [The U.S. had not ratified this Convention by late 2021.]

(2) Article 3 of the Convention (on not expelling, returning or extraditing a person where there are substantial grounds for believing that a person would be in danger of being subjected to torture) was implemented later, some time after ratification, in 1998 and 1999, by statute and regulation. Non-governmental organizations had drawn attention to the difficulty of enforcing it, given that the Senate had declared the Convention to be non-self-executing. Article 3 has given rise to numerous applications for relief from removal from the United States, some of them successful. *See, e.g., Al-Saher v. INS*, 268 F.3d 1143 (9th Cir. 2001); *Zheng v. Ashcroft*, 332 F.3d 1186 (2003); *Azanor v. Ashcroft*, 364 F.3d 1013 (9th Cir. 2004); *In re G- A-*, 23 I. & N. Dec. 366 (Bd. of Immigration Appeals, 2002). Consider, however, the following, more typical, case:

Julmiste v. Ashcroft

United States District Court for New Jersey
212 F. Supp. 2d 341 (2002)

Irenas, District Judge:

Presently before the Court is the pro se application for a writ of habeas corpus, pursuant to 28 U.S.C. § 2241, of petitioner Paul R. Julmiste ("Julmiste" or "Petitioner"). The Petitioner challenges an order of removal, entered by an Immigration Judge and affirmed by the Board of Immigration Appeals, claiming that removal will violate his rights under the U.S. Constitution, federal statutes and international human rights law. For the reasons set forth below, Petitioner's application for habeas corpus relief will be denied. . . .

The Convention Against Torture Treaty (CAT)

Petitioner brings this claim under Article III of the United Nations Convention Against Torture and Other Cruel, Inhuman or Degrading Treatment or Punishment[1] Petitioner asserts that he will be tortured upon return to Haiti, and the U.S. is therefore obligated by the CAT to not remove him.

Torture is defined as "any act by which severe pain or suffering, whether physical or mental, is intentionally inflicted on a person for such purposes as obtaining . . . information or a confession, punishing him or her for an act he or she or a third person has committed or is suspected of having committed or intimidating or coercing him or her or a third person, or for any reason based on discrimination of any kind, when such pain or suffering is inflicted by or at the instigation of or with consent or acquiescence of a public official or other person acting in an official capacity." 8 C.F.R. § 208.18(a)(1). Furthermore, torture "is an extreme form of cruel and inhuman treatment and does not include lesser forms of cruel, inhuman or degrading treatment." 8 C.F.R. § 208.18(a)(2). "[P]ain and suffering" stemming from lawful sanctions will not be considered torture. 8 C.F.R. § 208.18(a)(3). When invoking the protections of this treaty, a petitioner has the burden of proof to show that it is "more likely than not" that he will be tortured, as defined above, upon removal to the said country. 8 C.F.R. § 208.16(c)(2) (Burden of proof is on the applicant to "establish that it is more likely than not that he or she would be tortured . . ."). . . .

The evidence put forth in support of Petitioner's claim under CAT regarding potential torture in Haiti is comprised of findings of fact that this court should review under the deferential substantial evidence standard. Because this Court finds the INS' holding was supported by substantial evidence, Petitioner's application for a writ of habeas corpus will be denied.

At his removal hearing and appeal to the BIA, Petitioner put forth evidence from the U.S. Department of State, Amnesty International, media sources and personal contacts. While these articles do show that Haiti is a poor, unstable, war torn country, they do not suggest that the Petitioner, himself, will personally suffer torture upon return to Haiti. Mr. Julmiste has cited no evidence showing has been active in any of the political, economic or social happenings in Haiti. It is possible that Mr. Julmiste will serve a lengthy prison term in Haiti, as a consequence of his criminal offenses in the U.S., but that possibility alone does not fall within the definition

1. On December 10, 1984, the U.N. General Assembly adopted the Convention Against Torture and Other Cruel, Inhuman or Degrading Treatment or Punishment. 24 I L.M. 535, 535 (1985). The treaty was ratified by the United States . . . on October 21, 1994, and became effective [for the U.S.] one month later. 35 I.L.M. 590, 591 (1995). [Article III] was later implemented into legislation by Congress as part of the Foreign Affairs Reform and Restructuring Act of 1998 ("FARRA") which is incorporated as a note to 8 U.S.C.A. § 1231. *See* § 2242 of the Foreign Affairs Reform and Restructuring Act of 1998 ("FARRA"), Pub.L. No. 105-277, Div. G. 112 Stat. 2681-821 (Oct. 21, 1998) ("CAT" or "Convention"). Regulations were passed in 1999 to harmonize the immigration rules with the provisions of CAT. *See* Regulations Concerning the Convention Against Torture, 64 Fed Reg 8478 (1999), codified at 8 C.F.R. § 298. 16–18.

of torture. While the CAT can protect an individual from removal to a country when he has shown it is more likely than not he will be tortured, the CAT does not provide protection from general ills, such as corruption, poverty and dilapidated prison conditions. *See e.g. Sevoian v. Ashcroft*, 290 F.3d 166, 175–176 (3d Cir. 2002) (State Department Report showing that prisoners are routinely abused and certain political defendants have been tortured in the past did not "suggest whether much or any of the 'beating and abuse' . . . [would match] the extreme level that violates the Convention Against Torture.").

Petitioner has provided letters from his family and a political refugee named Alerte Noel which contend that Mr. Julmiste is in danger because his parents have offered support to Ms. Noel. Mr. Julmiste's arguments that by name association alone he will be tortured in retribution for his parents involvements with Ms. Noel are unpersuasive and do not satisfy his burden of proof. *See e.g., Sevoian*, 290 F.3d at 176 (Second hand testimony regarding abuses against similarly situated third parties is not sufficient, "in light of other evidence, to outweigh the deference" accorded to the BIA.); *Merisier*, 2000 U.S. Dist. LEXIS 13813, at *12 (S.D.N.Y. Sept 12, 2000) ("Haiti's violent past, and even [Petitioner's] relatives' alleged participation in it, is not, without more, substantial grounds for believing that removing [Petitioner] to Haiti would likely result in his being tortured.")

While the BIA recognized the dangers and hardships associated with living in Haiti, it properly concluded that the Petitioner failed to produce sufficient evidence to suggest a likelihood that he, himself, would be subjected to torture. In spite of the unfortunate consequences that may befall the Petitioner, living without his family in a war torn, politically unstable and poor country, neither the federal immigration laws nor the treaty obligations under CAT provide relief for him.

Notes

(1) The question of how much the Government should rely on diplomatic assurances against torture has been much-discussed. Consider the following extracts from *Khouzam v. Attorney General*, 549 F.3d 235 (3rd Cir. 2008):

> Sameh Sami S. Khouzam, a citizen of Egypt and a Coptic Christian, challenges the legality of his detention and imminent removal based on diplomatic assurances by Egypt that he would not be tortured if he was returned. In 1998, Khouzam was denied admission to the United States and taken into custody upon arriving without proper documentation. After years of proceedings, Khouzam was granted relief from removal because it was more likely than not that he would be tortured if returned to Egypt. His removal was deferred, rather than withheld, because there were serious reasons to believe that he committed a murder prior to departing Egypt. Khouzam was released from custody in 2006. In 2007, without notice or a hearing, the Department of Homeland Security ("DHS") again detained Khouzam, and prepared to remove him based on diplomatic assurances by Egypt that he would not be tortured. Khouzam filed an emergency habeas petition in

> the District Court for the Middle District of Pennsylvania, and a petition for review in this Court, arguing that the DHS's actions were unlawful. The District Court granted Khouzam's habeas petition after concluding, in a comprehensive, thoughtful opinion, that Khouzam was denied due process. The Government appeals that ruling.
>
> The arguments before us may be summarized as follows: Khouzam argues that (1) the Government violated certain statutes and the Due Process Clause by failing to provide him a hearing to test the reliability of the diplomatic assurances; (2) diplomatic assurances from Egypt are categorically unreliable; and (3) the Government failed to comply with relevant regulations. The Government argues, in the alternative, that (1) federal courts lack jurisdiction to consider Khouzam's claims; (2) Khouzam's claims are non-justiciable; (3) Khouzam received all of the process to which he was entitled; and (4) the Government complied with all relevant regulations.
>
> We will find for Khouzam for the reasons discussed at length below. We will reverse the District Court's order granting the habeas petition because we disagree with the Court's conclusion that habeas relief was available. However, we will grant Khouzam's petition for review because we agree with the District Court that he was denied due process. We will accordingly remand the matter to the Board of Immigration Appeals ("BIA") for further proceedings consistent with this opinion.

(2) In addition to the regulations in the immigration area, discussed in the preceding case, there are also regulations pursuant to the Foreign Affairs Reform and Restructuring Act of 1998 dealing with denying extradition where torture is likely. *See* 22 C.F.R. §95 (2004). Power to give effect to the Convention rests here with the Secretary of State. Human rights groups are not comfortable with the way this works. In *Mironescu v. Costner*, 480 F.3d 664 (4th Cir. 2007), *cert denied*, 128 S. Ct. 976 (2006), the court held that there is no judicial power of review over the Secretary of State's determination in such cases.

For a nuanced discussion of the diplomatic assurances issue from a Canadian governmental official's perspective, *see* Jeffrey G. Johnston, *The Risk of Torture as a Basis for Refusing Extradition and the Use of Diplomatic Assurances to Protect against Torture after 9/11*, 11 J. INT'L CRIM. L. REV. 1 (2011) (accepting that extraditing with assurances is not forbidden by international law, but that each case requires careful consideration and follow up with the requesting state if the suspect has been returned).

(3) Article 3 of the European Convention for the Protection of Human Rights and Fundamental Freedoms (1950) states that "No one shall be subjected to torture or to inhuman or degrading treatment or punishment." In grappling with giving concrete content to this very general provision, the organs of the Council of Europe have paid significant attention to the United Nations material as they try both to

determine what is forbidden and what fits which category — "torture" as opposed to "inhuman or degrading treatment or punishment." In *Ireland v. United Kingdom*, 2 E.H.R.R. 25 (1977), the European Court of Human Rights was faced with "five techniques" used by the British in Northern Ireland:

> 96. Twelve persons arrested on 9 August 1971 and two persons arrested in October 1971 were singled out and taken to one or more unidentified centres. There, between 11 to 17 August and 11 to 18 October respectively, they were submitted to a form of "interrogation in depth" which involved the combined application of five particular techniques.
>
> These methods, sometimes termed "disorientation" or "sensory deprivation" techniques, . . . consisted of:
>
> (a) *wall-standing*: forcing the detainees to remain for periods of some hours in a "stress position," described by those who underwent it as being "spreadeagled against the wall, with their fingers put high above the head against the wall, the legs spread apart and the feet back, causing them to stand on their toes with the weight of the body mainly on the fingers";
>
> (b) *hooding*: putting a black or navy coloured bag over the detainees' heads and, at least initially, keeping it there all the time except during interrogation;
>
> (c) *subjection to noise*: pending their interrogations, holding the detainees in a room where there was a continuous loud and hissing noise;
>
> (d) *deprivation of sleep*: pending their interrogations, depriving the detainees of sleep;
>
> (e) *deprivation of food and drink*: subjecting the detainees to a reduced diet during their stay at the centre and pending interrogations. . . .
>
> 97. From the start, it has been conceded by the respondent Government that the use of the five techniques was authorised at "high level." Although never committed to writing or authorised in any official document, the techniques had been orally taught to members of the RUC by the English Intelligence Centre at a seminar held in April 1971.
>
> 98. The two operations of interrogation in depth by means of the five techniques led to the obtaining of a considerable quantity of intelligence information, including the identification of 700 members of both IRA factions and the discovery of individual responsibility for about 85 previously unexplained criminal incidents. . . .
>
> [In the course of the proceedings, the British Government, speaking through the Attorney-General, gave an "unqualified undertaking" that the "five techniques" would not be reintroduced. It did not contest the characterization of "torture" that had been made by the other organ of the treaty,

the Commission. Nevertheless, the Court undertook its own analysis and concluded:]

167. . . . In order to determine whether the five techniques should also be qualified as torture, the Court must have regard to the distinction, embodied in Article 3, between this notion and that of inhuman or degrading treatment.

In the Court's view, this distinction derives principally from a difference in the intensity of the suffering inflicted.

The Court considers in fact that, whilst there exists on the one hand violence which is to be condemned both on moral grounds and also in most cases under the domestic law of the Contracting States but which does not fall within Article 3 of the Convention, it appears on the other hand that it was the intention that the Convention, with its distinction between "torture" and "inhuman or degrading treatment," should by the first of these terms attach a special stigma to deliberate inhuman treatment causing very serious and cruel suffering.

Moreover, this seems to be the thinking lying behind Article 1 in fine of Resolution 3452 (XXX) adopted by the General Assembly of the United Nations on 9 December 1975, which declares; "Torture constitutes an aggravated and deliberate form of cruel, inhuman or degrading treatment or punishment."

Although the five techniques, as applied in combination, undoubtedly amounted to inhuman and degrading treatment, although their object was the extraction of confessions, the naming of others and/or information and although they were used systematically, they did not occasion suffering of the particular intensity and cruelty implied by the word torture as so understood.

168. The court concludes that recourse to the five techniques amounted to a practice of inhuman and degrading treatment, which practice was in breach of Article 3 . . . .

(4) More recently, in *Selmouni v. France*, 29 E.H.R.R. 403 (2000), the European Court commented:

94. [France] contended in the light of both the Court's case-law . . . and the circumstances of the case that the ill-treatment allegedly inflicted by the police officers did not amount to "torture" within the meaning of Article 3 of the Convention.

95. The Court reiterates that Article 3 enshrines one of the most fundamental values of democratic societies. Even in the most difficult circumstances, such as the fight against terrorism and organized crime, the Convention prohibits in absolute terms torture or inhuman or degrading treatment or punishment. Unlike most of the substantive clauses of the Convention and

of Protocols Nos. 1 and 4, Article 3 makes no provision for exceptions and no derogation from it is permissible under Article 15(2) even in the event of a public emergency threatening the life of the nation. . . .

96. In order to determine whether a particular form of ill-treatment should be qualified as torture, the Court must have regard to the distinction, embodied in Article 3, between this notion and that of inhuman or degrading treatment. As the European Court has previously found, it appears that it was the intention that the Convention should, by means of this distinction, attach a special stigma to deliberate inhuman treatment causing very serious and cruel suffering (see the Ireland v United Kingdom judgment . . . para. 167).

97. The United Nations Convention against Torture and Other Cruel, Inhuman or Degrading Treatment or Punishment, which came into force on 26 June 1987, also makes such a distinction, as can be seen from Articles 1 and 16 . . . .

98. The Court finds that all the injuries recorded in the various medical certificates . . . (see paras. 11–15 and 17–20 above) and the applicant's statements regarding the ill-treatment to which he had been subjected while in police custody (see paras. 18 and 24 above) . . . establish the existence of physical and — undoubtedly (notwithstanding the regrettable failure to order a psychological report on Mr. Selmouni after the events complained of) — mental pain and suffering. The course of the events also shows that pain and suffering were inflicted on the applicant intentionally for the purpose of, inter alia, making him confess to the offence which he was suspected of having committed. Lastly, the medical certificates annexed to the case file show clearly that the numerous acts of violence were directly inflicted by police officers in the performance of their duties.

99. The acts complained of were such as to arouse in the applicant feelings of fear, anguish and inferiority capable of humiliating and debasing him and possibly breaking his physical and moral resistance. The court therefore finds elements which are sufficiently serious to render such treatment inhuman and degrading. . . . In any event, the Court reiterates that, in respect of a person deprived of his liberty, recourse to physical force which has not been made strictly necessary by his own conduct diminishes human dignity and is in principle an infringement of the right set forth in Article 3 (see the Ribtsch v Austria judgment of 4 December 1995, Series A no. 336, p. 26, para. 38, and the Tekin v Turkey judgment of 9 June 1998, Reports 1998-IV, pp. 1517–8, para. 53) . . . .

100. In other words, it remains to establish in the instant case whether the "pain or suffering" inflicted on Mr. Selmouni can be defined as "severe" within the meaning of Article 1 of the United Nations Convention. The court considers that this "severity" is, like the "minimum severity" required

for the application of Article 3, in the nature of things, relative; it depends on all the circumstances of the case, such as the duration of the treatment, its physical or mental effects and, in some cases, the sex, age and state of health of the victim, etc.

101. The Court has previously examined cases in which it concluded that there had been treatment which could only be described as torture.... However, having regard to the fact that the Convention is a "living instrument which must be interpreted in the light of present-day conditions" (see, among other authorities, the following judgments: Tyrer v United Kingdom, 25 April 1978, Series A no. 26, p. 15, para. 31; Soering v United Kingdom [See Chap. 19] p. 40, para. 102; and Loizidou v Turkey, 23 March 1995, Series A no. 310, p. 26, para. 71) . . . , the Court considers that certain acts which were classified in the past as "inhuman and degrading treatment" as opposed to "torture" could be classified differently in future. It takes the view that the increasingly high standard being required in the area of the protection of human rights and fundamental liberties correspondingly and inevitably requires greater firmness in assessing breaches of the fundamental values of democratic societies.

102. The Court is satisfied that a large number of blows were inflicted on Mr. Selmouni. Whatever a person's state of health, it can be presumed that such intensity of blows will cause substantial pain. Moreover, a blow does not automatically leave a visible mark on the body. However, it can be seen from Dr. Garnier's medical of 7 December 1991 that the marks of the violence Mr. Selmouni had endured covered almost all of his body.

103. The Court also notes that the applicant was dragged along by his hair; that he was made to run along a corridor with police officers positioned on either side to trip him up; that he was made to kneel down in front of a young woman to whom someone said "Look, you're going to hear somebody sing"; that one police officer then showed him his penis, saying "Look, suck this", before urinating over him; and that he was threatened with a blowlamp and then a syringe. Besides the violent nature of the above acts, the Court is bound to observe that they would be heinous and humiliating for anyone, irrespective of their condition.

104. The Court notes, lastly, that the above events were not confined to any one period of police custody during which—without this in any way justifying them—heightened tension and emotions might have led to such excesses. It has been clearly established that Mr. Selmouni endured repeated and sustained assaults over a number of days of questions.

105. Under these circumstances, the Court is satisfied that the physical and mental violence, considered as a whole, committed against the applicant's person caused "severe" pain and suffering and was particularly serious and

cruel. Such conduct must be regarded as acts of torture for the purposes of Article 3 of the Convention.

§ 10.02 Torture Post 9-11

"All I want to say was that there was 'before' 9/11 and 'after' 9/11. After 9/11 the gloves come off." These are the words of Cofer Black, former Director of the CIA's Counterterrorist Center from 1999 until May of 2002. He was testifying on September 26, 2002, to a Joint Congressional Investigation into September 11th. *See* https://fas.org/irp/congress/2002_hr/092602black.html. This sentiment was widely shared in the Bush Administration and beyond. In May 2004, however, the media was replete with stories about ill-treatment by United States personnel (including intelligence agents and contractors) of prisoners in Abu Ghraib Prison in Iraq. And there were the pictures. The general point was not new. As early as 2002, several human rights organizations had been reporting on abuses in Guantanamo Bay, Cuba, at Bagram Base in Afghanistan, and at "undisclosed locations." A leaked report from the International Committee of the Red Cross (ICRC) (which normally operates very discreetly) indicated that it had been expressing its concerns also. *See generally* Diane Marie Amann, *Abu Ghraib*, 153 U. Pa. L. Rev. 2085 (2005); *see also* The Torture Papers: The Road to Abu Ghraib (Karen J. Goldberg & Joshua L. Dratel eds., 2005).

Among the "stress and duress" methods used, allegedly in an effort to obtain information, were beatings, hooding, sleep deprivation, noise, being stripped naked (sometimes in extremes of hot and cold), sexual humiliation of various kinds (including abuse by female soldiers and sexual assaults with light sticks), smearing in feces, attack dogs, deprivation of food, medication and water, sodomizing a male detainee with a broomstick, binding or forcing prisoners to stand in uncomfortable positions for a long time, handing prisoners over to countries with worse human rights records than the United States.

How would you characterize the professional responsibility of a government lawyer who is asked to advise on the legality of such issues? What about the responsibility of a doctor who is asked to participate on the fringes of such actions? *See* Jesselyn Raduck, *Tortured Legal Ethics: The Role of the Government Adviser in the War on Terrorism*, 77 Colorado L. Rev. 1 (2006); M. Gregg Bloche, *When Doctors First Do Harm*, New York Times, 23 November 2016, at A25 (op. ed) ("Buried in a trove of documents released last summer is the revelation that the C.I.A. physicians played a central role in designing the agency's post-Sept. 11 torture program. The documents, declassified in response to an American Civil Liberties Union lawsuit, show in chilling detail how C.I.A. medicine lost its moral moorings. It's long been known that doctors attended torture as monitors. What's new is their role as its engineers."). *See also* Larry Siems, *CIA torture: lawsuit settled against psychologists who designed techniques*, THE GUARDIAN, 17 August 2017. Siems records the settlement in the case of Drs. James Mitchell and John "Bruce" Jessen who devised abusive interrogation methods and billed the CIA between $75m and $81m. The suit accused them of aiding and abetting torture, non-consensual human experimentation and war crimes in Afghanistan. The settlement, which does not disclose whether money changed hands, records that the plaintiffs were subjected to abuses which resulted in pain and suffering.

Notes

(1) Calls for an end to impunity carried over into the Obama Administration. On August 24, 2009, Attorney-General Holder issued the following statement:*

> The Office of Professional Responsibility has now submitted to me its report regarding the Office of Legal Counsel memoranda related to so-called enhanced interrogation techniques. I hope to be able to make as much of that report available as possible after it undergoes a declassification review and other steps. Among other findings, the report recommends that the Department reexamine previous decisions to decline prosecution in several cases related to the interrogation of certain detainees.
>
> I have reviewed the OPR report in depth. Moreover, I have closely examined the full, still-classified version of the 2004 CIA Inspector General's report, as well as other relevant information available to the Department. As a result of my analysis of all of this material, I have concluded that the information known to me warrants opening a preliminary review into whether federal laws were violated in connection with the interrogation of specific detainees at overseas locations. The Department regularly uses preliminary reviews to gather information to determine whether there is sufficient predication to warrant a full investigation of a matter. I want to emphasize that neither the opening of a preliminary review nor, if evidence warrants it, the commencement of a full investigation, means that charges will necessarily follow.
>
> Assistant United States Attorney John Durham was appointed in 2008 by then-Attorney General Michael Mukasey to investigate the destruction of CIA videotapes of detainee interrogations. During the course of that investigation, Mr. Durham has gained great familiarity with much of the information that is relevant to the matter at hand. Accordingly, I have decided to expand his mandate to encompass this related review. Mr. Durham, who is a career prosecutor with the Department of Justice and who has assembled a strong investigative team of experienced professionals, will

* *Statement of Attorney General Eric Holder Regarding a Preliminary Review into the Interrogation of Certain Detainees*, Aug. 24, 2009, *available at* http://www.usdoj.gov/ag/speeches/2009/ag-speech-0908241.html.

recommend to me whether there is sufficient predication for a full investigation into whether the law was violated in connection with the interrogation of certain detainees.

There are those who will use my decision to open a preliminary review as a means of broadly criticizing the work of our nation's intelligence community. I could not disagree more with that view. The men and women in our intelligence community perform an incredibly important service to our nation, and they often do so under difficult and dangerous circumstances. They deserve our respect and gratitude for the work they do. Further, they need to be protected from legal jeopardy when they act in good faith and within the scope of legal guidance. That is why I have made it clear in the past that the Department of Justice will not prosecute anyone who acted in good faith and within the scope of the legal guidance given by the Office of Legal Counsel regarding the interrogation of detainees. I want to reiterate that point today, and to underscore the fact that this preliminary review will not focus on those individuals.

I share the President's conviction that as a nation, we must, to the extent possible, look forward and not backward when it comes to issues such as these. While this Department will follow its obligation to take this preliminary step to examine possible violations of law, we will not allow our important work of keeping the American people safe to be sidetracked.

I fully realize that my decision to commence this preliminary review will be controversial. As Attorney General, my duty is to examine the facts and to follow the law. In this case, given all of the information currently available, it is clear to me that this review is the only responsible course of action for me to take.

On August 30, 2012, Attorney-General Holder announced the closure of the investigation.[2] The Statement included this:

In June of last year, the Attorney General announced that Mr. Durham recommended opening full criminal investigations regarding the death of two individuals while in United States custody at overseas locations, and closing the remaining matters. The Attorney General accepted that recommendation. Today, the Attorney General announced that those two investigations conducted over the past year have now been closed.

AUSA John Durham has now completed his investigations, and the Department has decided not to initiate criminal charges in these matters. In reaching this determination, Mr. Durham considered all potentially

2. *Statement of Attorney General Holder on the Closure of Investigation into the Interrogation of Certain Detainees*, Aug. 30, 2012, *available at* http://www.justice.gov/opa/pr/statement-attorney-general-eric-holder-closure-investigation-interrogation-certain-detainees.

applicable substantive criminal statutes as well as the statutes of limitations and jurisdictional provisions that govern prosecutions under those statutes. Mr. Durham and his team reviewed a tremendous volume of information pertaining to the detainees. That review included both information and matters that were not examined during the Department's prior reviews. Based on the fully developed factual record concerning the two deaths, the Department has declined prosecution because the admissible evidence would not be sufficient to obtain and sustain a conviction beyond a reasonable doubt.

During the course of his preliminary review and subsequent investigations, Mr. Durham examined any possible CIA involvement with the interrogation and detention of 101 detainees who were alleged to have been in United States custody subsequent to the terrorist attacks of September 11, 2001. He determined that a number of the detainees were never in CIA custody. Mr. Durham identified the matters to include within his review by examining various sources including the Office of Professional Responsibility's report regarding the Office of Legal Counsel memoranda related to enhanced interrogation techniques, the 2004 CIA Inspector General's report on enhanced interrogations, additional matters investigated by the CIA Office of Inspector General, the February 2007 International Committee of the Red Cross Report on the Treatment of Fourteen 'High Value Detainees' in CIA Custody, and public source information.

Mr. Durham and his team of agents and prosecutors have worked tirelessly to conduct extraordinarily thorough and complete preliminary reviews and investigations. I am grateful to his team and to him for their commitment to ensuring that the preliminary review and the subsequent investigations fully examined a broad universe of allegations from multiple sources. I continue to believe that our Nation will be better for it.

I also appreciate and respect the work of and sacrifices made by the men and women in our intelligence community on behalf of this country. They perform an incredibly important service to our nation, and they often do so under difficult and dangerous circumstances. They deserve our respect and gratitude for the work they do. I asked Mr. Durham to conduct this review based on existing information as well as new information and matters presented to me that I believed warranted a thorough examination of the detainee treatment issue.

I am confident that Mr. Durham's thorough reviews and determination that the filing of criminal charges would not be appropriate have satisfied that need. Our inquiry was limited to a determination of whether prosecutable offenses were committed and was not intended to, and does not resolve, broader questions regarding the propriety of the examined conduct.

(2) The Committee against Torture commented in its 2014 Observations, *supra*:

Inquiries into allegations of torture overseas

12. The Committee expresses concern over the ongoing failure to fully investigate allegations of torture and ill-treatment of suspects held in U.S. custody abroad, evidenced by the limited number of criminal prosecutions and convictions. In this respect, the Committee notes that during the period under review, the Department of Justice (DoJ) successfully prosecuted two instances of extrajudicial killings of detainees by Department of Defense and CIA contractors in Afghanistan. It also notes the additional information provided by the State party's delegation regarding the criminal investigation undertaken by Assistant U.S. Attorney John Durham into allegations of detainee mistreatment while in U.S. custody at overseas locations. The Committee regrets, however, that the delegation was not in a position to describe the investigative methods employed by Mr. Durham or the identities of any witnesses his team may have interviewed. Thus, the Committee remains concerned about information before it that some former CIA detainees, who had been held in U.S. custody abroad, were never interviewed during the investigations, casting doubts as to whether this high-profile inquiry was properly conducted. The Committee also notes that the DoJ announced on 30 June 2011 the opening of a full investigation into the deaths of two individuals while in U.S. custody at overseas locations. However, Mr. Durham's review concluded that the admissible evidence would not be sufficient to obtain and sustain convictions beyond a reasonable doubt. The Committee shares the concerns expressed at the time by the UN Special Rapporteur on Torture over the decision not to prosecute and punish the alleged authors of these deaths. It further expresses concern about the absence of criminal prosecutions for the alleged destruction of torture evidence by CIA personnel, such as the destruction of the 92 videotapes of interrogations of Abu Zubaydah and Abd al-Nashiri that triggered Mr. Durham's initial mandate. The Committee notes that in November 2011 the DoJ determined, based on the Mr. Durham's review, not to initiate prosecutions of those cases (arts. 2, 12, 13 and 16). The Committee urges the State party to:

(a) Carry out prompt, impartial and effective investigations wherever there is reasonable ground to believe that an act of torture and ill-treatment has been committed in any territory under its jurisdiction, especially in those cases resulting in death in custody;

(b) Ensure that alleged perpetrators and accomplices are duly prosecuted, including persons in positions of command and those who provided legal cover to torture, and, if found guilty, handed down penalties commensurate with the grave nature of their acts;

In this connection, the Committee draws the attention to paragraphs 9 and 26 of its General Comment No. 2;

(c) Provide effective remedies and redress to victims, including fair and adequate compensation, and as full rehabilitation as possible, in accordance with the Committee's General Comment No. 3 (2012) on the implementation of article 14 of the Convention by State parties (CAT/C/GC/3);

(d) Undertake a full review into the way the CIA's responsibilities were discharged in relation to the allegations of torture and ill-treatment against suspects during U.S. custody abroad. In the event of a re-opening of investigations, the State party should ensure that any such inquiries are designed to address the alleged shortcomings in the thoroughness of the previous reviews and investigations.

Military accountability for abuses

13. The information provided by the State party's delegation indicates that the U.S. Department of Defense (DoD) has conducted "thousands of investigations since 2001 and prosecuted or disciplined hundreds of service members for mistreatment of detainees and other misconduct". However, the Committee regrets that in the course of the dialogue, the delegation provided minimal statistics on the number of investigations, prosecutions, disciplinary proceedings and corresponding reparations. It has also received insufficient information about the sentences and criminal or disciplinary sanctions imposed on offenders, or on whether the alleged perpetrators of these acts were suspended or expelled from the U.S. military pending the outcome of the investigation of the abuses. In the absence of this information, the Committee finds itself unable to assess whether the State party's actions are in conformity with the provisions of article 12 of the Convention (arts. 2, 12, 13, 14 and 16). The Committee urges the State party to:

(a) Ensure the prompt and impartial investigation of all instances of torture and ill-treatment by military personnel, that alleged perpetrators are prosecuted, and, if found guilty, punished appropriately, and that effective reparation, including adequate compensation, is granted to every victim;

(b) Ensure that alleged perpetrators of torture or ill-treatment are suspended from duty immediately for the duration of the investigation, particularly when there is a risk that they might otherwise be in a position to repeat the alleged act or to obstruct the investigation.

Guantanamo Bay detention facilities

14. The Committee expresses its deep concern about the fact that the State party continues to hold a number of individuals without charge at Guantanamo Bay detention facilities. Notwithstanding the State party's position that these individuals have been captured and detained as "enemy belligerents" and that under the law of war is permitted "to hold them until the end of the hostilities", the Committee reiterates that indefinite detention

constitutes per se a violation of the Convention. According to the figures provided by the delegation, to date, out of the 148 men still held at the facility, only 33 have been designated for potential prosecution, either in federal court or by military commissions—a system that fails to meet international fair trial standards. The Committee notes with concern that 36 others have been designated for "continued law of war detention". While noting that detainees held in Guantanamo have the constitutional privilege of the writ of habeas corpus, the Committee is concerned at reports that indicate that federal courts have rejected a significant number of habeas corpus petitions. While noting the explanations provided by the State party concerning the conditions of detention at Guantanamo, the Committee remains concerned about the secrecy surrounding conditions of confinement, especially in Camp 7 where high-value detainees are housed. It also notes the studies received on the cumulative effect that the conditions of detention and treatment in Guantanamo have had on the psychological health of detainees. There have been nine deaths in Guantanamo during the period under review, including seven suicides. In this respect, another cause of concern is the repeated suicide attempts and recurrent mass hunger strike protests by detainees over indefinite detention and conditions of detention. In this connection, the Committee considers that force-feeding of prisoners on hunger strike constitutes ill-treatment in violation of the Convention. Furthermore, it notes that detainees' lawyers have argued in court that force feedings are allegedly administered in an unnecessarily brutal and painful manner (arts. 2, 11, 12, 13, 14, 15 and 16). The Committee calls upon the State party to take immediate and effective measures to:

(a) Cease the use of indefinite detention without charge or trial for individuals suspected of terrorism-related activities;

(b) Ensure that detainees held at Guantanamo who are designated for potential prosecution be charged and tried in ordinary federal civilian courts. Any other detainees who are not to be charged or tried should be immediately released. Detainees and their counsels must have access to all evidence used to justify the detention;

(c) Investigate allegations of detainee abuse, including torture and ill-treatment, appropriately prosecute those responsible, and ensure effective redress for victims;

(d) Improve the detainees' situation so as to persuade them to cease the hunger strike;

(e) Put an end to force-feeding of detainees in hunger strike as long as they are able to take informed decisions;

(f) Invite the UN Special Rapporteur on torture to visit Guantanamo Bay detention facilities, with full access to the detainees, including private meetings with them, in conformity with the terms of reference for fact-finding missions by Special Procedures of the UN Human Rights Council. The Committee reiterates its earlier recommendation (CAT/C/USA/CO/2, para 22) that the State party should close the detention facilities at Guantanamo Bay, as instructed in section 3 of Executive Order 13492 of 22 January 2009.

Abuse of State secrecy provisions and mutual judicial assistance

15. The Committee expresses its serious concern at the use of State secrecy provisions and immunities to evade liability. While noting the delegation's statement that the State party abides by its obligations under article 15 of the Convention in the administrative procedures established to review the status of law of war detainees in Guantanamo, the Committee is particularly disturbed at reports describing a draconian system of secrecy surrounding high-value detainees that keeps their torture claims out of the public domain. Furthermore, the regime applied to these detainees prevents access to an effective remedy and reparations, and hinders investigations into human rights violations by other States (arts. 9, 12, 13, 14 and 16). The Committee calls for the declassification of torture evidence, in particular Guantanamo detainees' accounts of torture. The State party should ensure that all victims of torture are able to access a remedy and obtain redress, wherever acts of torture occurred and regardless of the nationality of the perpetrator or the victim. The State party should take effective steps to ensure the provision of mutual judicial assistance in all matters of criminal procedure regarding the offence of torture and related crimes of attempting to commit, complicity and participation in torture. The Committee recalls that article 9 of the Convention requests States parties to "afford one another the greatest measure of assistance" in connection with criminal proceedings related to violations of the Convention.

Transfer of detainees from Guantanamo Bay and reliance on diplomatic assurances

16. The Committee takes note of the explanations provided by the delegation concerning the processes involved in transferring the remaining detainees from Guantanamo Bay detention facilities, and the lifting of the detainee transfer moratorium to Yemen. However, it expresses its concern at the fact that most of the 79 detainees who are currently designated for transfer had already been cleared for transfer five years ago by the Review Task Force. While noting the information provided by the State party on the practice of obtaining torture-related diplomatic assurances, the Committee remains disturbed by reports from non-governmental sources which indicate that some former Guantanamo Bay detainees have experienced abuse during treatment post release (art. 3). The Committee calls on the State party to ensure that no individual, including persons suspected of terrorism, who are expelled, returned, extradited or deported, is exposed to the danger of torture or other cruel, inhuman or degrading treatment or punishment.

It urges the State party to refrain from seeking and relying on diplomatic assurances "where there are substantial grounds for believing that [the person] would be in danger of being subjected to torture" (art. 3). The principle of non-réfoulement should always have precedence over any other protection measure.

Interrogation techniques

17. The Committee appreciates the initiatives of the State party to eliminate interrogation methods which constitute torture or ill-treatment. Nevertheless, the Committee is concerned about certain aspects of Appendix M of the Army Field Manual Human Intelligence Collector Operations, FM 2-22.3 of September 2006, in particular the description of some "authorized methods of interrogation," such as the interrogation techniques of "physical separation" and "field expedient separation". While noting the information by the delegation to the effect that such practices are consistent with the State party's obligations under the Convention, the Committee remains concerned over the possibilities for abuse such techniques may entail (arts. 1, 2, 11 and 16). The State party should ensure that interrogation methods contrary to the Convention are not used under any circumstances. The Committee urges the State party to review Appendix M of the Army Field Manual in light of its obligations under the Convention. In particular, the State party should abolish the provision contained in the "physical separation technique" which establishes that "use of separation must not preclude the detainee getting four hours of continued sleep every 24 hours". Such provision, applicable over an initial period of 30 days, which is renewable, amounts to authorizing sleep deprivation—a form of ill-treatment—and is unrelated to the aim of the "physical separation technique" which is to preventing communication among detainees. The State party should ensure detainee's needs in terms of sleep time and that sleeping accommodation provided for the use of prisoners is in conformity with the requirements of Rule 10 of the Standard Minimum Rules for the Treatment of Prisoners. Equally, the State party should abolish sensory deprivation in the "field expedient separation technique" aimed at prolonging the shock of capture by applying goggles or blindfolds and earmuffs to generate a perception of separation, which based on recent scientific findings with high probability will create a state of psychosis with the detainee (Daniel C., Lovatt A., Manson OJ. Psychotic-like experiences and their cognitive appraisal under short-term sensory deprivation. Frontiers in Psychiatry; Vol. 5, Art 106:1), raising concerns of torture and ill-treatment.

(3) The Senate Select Committee on Intelligence produced a Committee Study of the Central Intelligence Agency's Detention and Interrogation Program, an edited (and somewhat redacted) report of over 500 pages based on still-classified material of some 6000 pages. The Study is *available at* https://fas.org/irp/congress/2014_rpt/ssci-rdi.pdf.

Its summary contained 20 major findings:

1. The CIA's use of its enhanced interrogation techniques was not an effective means of acquiring intelligence or gaining cooperation from detainees.
2. The CIA's justification for the use of its enhanced interrogation techniques rested on inaccurate claims of their effectiveness.
3. The interrogations of CIA detainees were brutal and far worse than the CIA represented to policymakers and others.
4. The conditions of confinement for CIA detainees were harsher than the CIA had represented to policymakers and others.
5. The CIA repeatedly provided inaccurate information to the Department of Justice (DOJ), impeding a proper legal analysis of the CIA's Detention and Interrogation Program.
6. The CIA has actively avoided or impeded congressional oversight of the program.
7. The CIA impeded effective White House oversight and decision-making.
8. The CIA's operation and management of the program complicated, and in some cases impeded, the national security missions of other Executive Branch agencies.
9. The CIA impeded oversight by the CIA's office of the Inspector-General.
10. The CIA coordinated the release of classified information to the media, including inaccurate information concerning the effectiveness of the CIA's enhanced interrogation techniques.
11. The CIA was unprepared as it began operating its Detention and Interrogation Program more than six months after being granted detention authorities.
12. The CIA's management and operation of its Detention and Interrogation Program was deeply flawed throughout the program's duration, particularly so in 2002 and early 2003.
13. Two contract psychologists devised the CIA's enhanced interrogation techniques and played a central role in the operation, assessments, and management of the CIA's Detention and Interrogation Program. By 2005, the CIA had overwhelmingly outsourced operations related to the program.
14. CIA detainees were subjected to coercive interrogation techniques that had not been approved by the Department of Justice or had not been authorized by CIA Headquarters.
15. The CIA did not conduct a comprehensive or accurate accounting of the number of individuals it detained, and held individuals who did not meet the legal standard for detention. The CIA's claims about the number of detainees held and subjected to its enhanced interrogation techniques were inaccurate.

16. The CIA failed to adequately evaluate the effectiveness of its enhanced interrogation techniques.
17. The CIA rarely reprimanded or held personnel accountable for serious or significant violations, inappropriate activities, and systematic and individual management failures.
18. The CIA marginalized and ignored numerous internal critiques, criticisms, and objections concerning the operation and management of the CIA's Detention and Interrogation Program.
19. The CIA's Detention and Interrogation Program was inherently unsustainable and had effectively ended by 2006 due to unauthorized press disclosures, reduced cooperation from other nations, and legal and oversight concerns.
20. The CIA's Detention and Interrogation Program damaged the United States' standing in the world, and resulted in other significant monetary and non-monetary costs.

(4) A feature of the CIA program was rendition to "Black Sites." Perhaps the circumstances of rendition were torture in themselves; certainly, they facilitated ill-treatment. Many CIA rendition flights between 2001 and 2004 operated through North Carolina, using state facilities, connecting to sites in Afghanistan, Algeria, Egypt, Guantanamo, Iraq, Jordan, Libya, Morocco, Poland, Romania and Thailand. The flights were operated by Aero Contractors (Ltd), incorporated in North Carolina, which flew planes owned by CIA shell companies. *See* the report of the (non-governmental) North Carolina Commission of Inquiry on Torture, *Torture Flights: North Carolina's Role in the CIA Rendition and Torture Program* (2018), *available at* https://www.nctorturereport.org/pdfs/NC_Torture_Report.pdf. In May 2018, the European Court of Human Rights held that Romania and Lithuania had committed several violations of the European Convention on Human Rights through their complicity in hosting "black sites" in their territory. European Court of Human Rights, *Case of Al Nashiri v. Romania*, Application no. 33434/12, Judgment, 31 May 2018; *Case of Abu Zubaydah v. Lithuania*, Application no. 46454/11, Judgment, 31 May 2018. The Court was very critical of the performance of the U.S. *Al Nashiri* and *Zubaydah* were two cases of abuse dropped by Mr. Durham. Both are awaiting trial in Guantanamo.

(5) Is it appropriate to use some "physical means" of interrogation when under continual terrorist attacks? When will this violate the Torture Convention and are there any exceptions for extreme situations? According to the Supreme Court of Israel, the State of Israel "has been engaged in an unceasing struggle for both its existence and its security, from the day of its founding." *Judgment Concerning the Legality of the General Security Service's Interrogation Methods*, 38 I.L.M. 1471, 1472 (Sup. Ct. Israel, 1999). The Executive had issued "directives" authorizing investigators to apply certain "physical means" against those suspected of committing crimes against Israel's security. These means were shaking, placing in the "shabach" position (a very uncomfortable position on a low chair with hands tied and a sack over

the head), the "frog crouch" (periodic crouches on tiptoe, lasting for five minute intervals), excessive tightening of handcuffs, and sleep deprivation. In a judgment of the Supreme Court of Israel, the Court suggests that in appropriate cases of extreme emergency, investigators might be able to avail themselves of a necessity defense.

Nevertheless, the Israeli Supreme Court concluded (38 I.L.M. 1488) that "... neither the government nor the heads of security services possess the authority to establish directives and bestow authorization regarding the use of liberty infringing physical means during the interrogation of suspects suspected of hostile terrorist activities, beyond the general directives which can be inferred from the very concept of an interrogation." The methods were thus illegal in the current state of the law, although the legislature might decree otherwise:

> If it will nonetheless be decided that it is appropriate for Israel, in light of its security difficulties to sanction physical means in interrogations (and the scope of these means which deviate from the ordinary investigation rules), this is an issue that must be decided by the legislative branch which represents the people. We do not take any stand on this matter at this time. It is there that various considerations must be weighed. The pointed debate must occur there. It is there that the required legislation may be passed, provided, of course, that a law infringing upon a suspect's liberty "befitting the values of the State of Israel," is enacted for a proper purpose and to an extent no greater than is required. (Article 8 to the Basic Law: Human Dignity and Liberty.)

Should a democratic legislature of a country that is party to the Torture Convention ignore the Convention and empower the courts to issue warrants to torture? If we know that the executive will in extreme situations authorize torture, should we not empower it up front to do so and subject its work to judicial scrutiny? *See generally* Alan M. Dershowitz, Why Terrorism Works: Understanding the Threat, Responding to the Challenge, 141, 156–60, 247–48 n.6 (2002). If so, should its use be limited to the situation where there is a ticking time-bomb set to explode, or should it be more generally available?

The British and the Israelis apparently believed that the information they gained through extreme measures was useful, although the value of information given under torture is debated. *See* Marcy Strauss, *Torture*, 48 N.Y.L. Sch. L. Rev. 201, 261–65 (2003–4). Should it matter if it can be shown empirically that torture is a valuable tool for gaining information from terrorists? Is the argument about permitting torture a utilitarian one? Or are we in an area where moral imperatives are the bedrock of the debate? For nuanced discussions, see generally Strauss, *supra* and Alan M. Dershowitz, *The Torture Warrant: A Response to Professor Strauss*, 48 N.Y.L. Sch. L. Rev. 275 (2003–4).

(6) The Torture Convention prohibits only practices which are officially sanctioned or in some way involve the participation of public officials or those acting in an official capacity. (The latter is probably broad enough to encompass

revolutionaries and those purporting to exercise state or quasi-state power, as in *Kadic v. Karadzic*, 70 F.3d 232 (1995), which involved the leader of the unrecognized Serb entity in Bosnia Herzegovina, "Republica Srpska.") In prosecuting public officials, especially high ranking officials, there is a possible problem of official immunity under national law. Does the Convention speak to this problem? Can it be read tacitly to require that immunity not be allowed as a defense? What about the immunity of a foreign official under international law?

Consider, in this connection, the decision of the House of Lords denying Augusto Pinochet, as a *former* head of state, immunity from extradition on charges of torture, and other cases involving official and diplomatic immunity [*see* chap. 14].

(7) How successful was the US legal system in dealing with these crimes? No one has been convicted concerning the events in Guantanamo or any of the so-called "Black Sites." Eleven enlisted soldiers, but ultimately no officers, were convicted under the Uniform Code of Military Justice of crimes relating to Abu Ghraib. War crimes as such are not prosecuted under the UCMJ which contains crimes essentially like those found in domestic penal codes. Typical charges were conspiracy, dereliction of duty, assault and committing an indecent act. *See* CNN Editorial Research, *Iraq Prison Abuse Scandal Fast Facts*, updated March 22, 2020, *available at* https://www.cnn.com/2013/10/30/world/meast/iraq-prison-abuse-scandal-fast-facts/index.html. No-one involved, military or civilian, has been convicted for torture arising out of Guantanamo and Abu Ghraib. *See* Hina Shamsi, Rita Siemion, Ron Stief, Terry Rockefeller, Scott Roehm & Katherine Gallagher, *Toward a New Approach to National and Human Security: Uphold the Prohibition on Torture*, JUST SECURITY, Sept. 11, 2020, *available at* https://www.justsecurity.org/72373/toward-a-new-approach-to-national-and-human-security-uphold-the-prohibition-on-torture/.

§ 10.03 Sexual Violence as Torture

Commentators have written of "an international movement to force recognition of women's rights as human rights, and to include protections against violence against women within the international human rights framework." Beth Stephens & Jennifer Green, *Suing for Genocide in the United States: The Case of Jane Doe v. Radovan Karadzic*, *in* WAR CRIMES: THE LEGACY OF NUREMBERG 265, 268 (Belinda Cooper ed., 1999). One product of this movement has been the recognition that rape can constitute a form of torture or inhuman treatment. Since 1986, reports of the Special Rapporteur on Torture of the U.N. Commission on Human Rights have defined the rape of female prisoners while in detention or under interrogation as an act of torture. The characterization of rape and other gender-based violence as torture triggers a number of international legal consequences. An aspect of this is the effort to define rape as a war crime. *See* Theodor Meron, *Rape as a Crime Under International Humanitarian Law*, 87 A.J.I.L. 424 (1993). Rape by soldiers has long been prohibited, at least in principle, by the laws of war. Although the Geneva Conventions of 1949 and the two Additional Protocols of 1977 prohibit rape during the course of armed conflict, it is not listed specifically as one of the "grave breaches" of those conventions over which states have "universal jurisdiction." However, "grave breaches" do include "wilful killing, torture or inhuman treatment" and "wilfully causing great suffering or serious injury to body or health." Thus, recognition of rape as a form of torture or inhuman treatment buttresses the conclusion, now widely accepted, that it also can be treated as a "grave breach" of the Geneva Conventions.

Rape figured prominently in the "ethnic cleansing" in Bosnia and in the genocide in Rwanda that led the U.N. Security Council to establish ad hoc international criminal tribunals for the former Yugoslavia and for Rwanda in 1993 and 1994 respectively. (Mass rape also figured in the campaign against supporters of President Aristide in Haiti; in 1995, the Inter-American Commission on Human Rights characterized these rapes as torture.) Rape and other forms of sexual violence have figured prominently as well in the jurisprudence of the two *ad hoc* tribunals. *See* Kelly D. Askin, *Sexual Violence in Decisions and Indictments of the Yugoslav and Rwandan Tribunals: Current Status*, 93 A.J.I.L. 97 (1999). Cases decided by these tribunals hold that rape, under the requisite circumstances, may constitute a "grave breach" of the Geneva Conventions, a violation of the laws or customs of war, an act of genocide, or a "crime against humanity."

The statute establishing the International Criminal Tribunal for the former Yugoslavia (ICTY) gave it jurisdiction over genocide, crimes against humanity, and two categories of war crime: "grave breaches" of the Geneva Conventions of 1949 and "violations of the laws or customs of war." The statute establishing the International Criminal Tribunal for Rwanda (ICTR) gave it jurisdiction over genocide, crimes against humanity, and "serious violations" of either common Article 3 of the Geneva Conventions or Additional Protocol II, both of which set out rules applicable in "armed conflicts not of an international character."[3] In both statutes, rape was included among the enumerated acts that can constitute crimes against humanity.

---

3. While Common Article 3 of the 1949 Geneva Conventions applies specifically to non-international conflict, it is widely regarded as a minimum standard in any armed conflict, international or non-international. It provides:

> (1) Persons taking no active part in the hostilities, including members of armed forces who have laid down their arms and those placed hors de combat by sickness, wounds, detention, or any other cause, shall in all circumstances be treated humanely, without any adverse distinction founded on race, colour, religion or faith, sex, birth or wealth, or any other similar criteria.
>
> To this end, the following acts are and shall remain prohibited at any time and in any place whatsoever with respect to the above-mentioned persons:
>
> (a) violence to life and person, in particular murder of all kinds, mutilation, cruel treatment and torture;
> (b) taking of hostages;
> (c) outrages upon personal dignity, in particular humiliating and degrading treatment;
> (d) the passing of sentences and the carrying out of executions without previous judgement pronounced by a regularly constituted court, affording all the judicial guarantees which are recognized as indispensable by civilized peoples.

Otherwise, the ICTY statute does not mention rape. The International Criminal Tribunal for Rwanda (ICTR) statute, in specifying the kind of conduct that violates common Article 3 of the Geneva Conventions or Additional Protocol II, includes "outrages upon personal dignity, in particular humiliating and degrading treatment, *rape, enforced prostitution and any form of indecent assault.*" (This language tracks Article 4(e) of Additional Protocol II; compare the language of common Article 3 of the 1949 Conventions which does not include the words in italics.)

In *Prosecutor v. Delalic*, Case No. IT-96-21-T, Judgement (Nov. 16, 1998), three of the four defendants were convicted by the Yugoslav tribunal on various counts alleging the mistreatment of civilian detainees at the Celebici prison camp in central Bosnia in 1992. The convictions were upheld on appeal, Appeals Chamber, Judgement (Feb. 20, 2001). One defendant in particular, Hazim Delic, the deputy commander, was found to be a brutal sadist who, in addition to his other crimes, raped women in order to exert his power and instill absolute fear in them. In holding that rape could be torture and therefore a "grave breach" of the Geneva Conventions and a violation of the laws or customs of war, the Trial Chamber observed (paras. 476, 495–96):

> There can be no doubt that rape and other forms of sexual assault are expressly prohibited under international humanitarian law. The terms of article 27 of the Fourth Geneva Convention specifically prohibit rape, any form of indecent assault and the enforced prostitution of women. A prohibition on rape, enforced prostitution and any form of indecent assault is further found in article 4(2) of Additional Protocol II, concerning internal armed conflicts. This Protocol also implicitly prohibits rape and sexual assault in article 4(1) which states that all persons are entitled to respect for their person and honour. Moreover, article 76(1) of Additional Protocol I expressly requires that women be protected from rape, forced prostitution and any other form of indecent assault. An implicit prohibition on rape and sexual assault can also be found in article 46 of the 1907 Hague Convention (IV) that provides for the protection of family honour and rights. Finally, rape is prohibited as a crime against humanity under article 6(c) of the Nürnberg Charter and expressed as such in Article 5 of the [ICTY] Statute. . . .
>
> The Trial Chamber considers the rape of any person to be a despicable act which strikes at the very core of human dignity and physical integrity. The condemnation and punishment of rape becomes all the more urgent where it is committed by, or at the instigation of, a public official, or with the consent or acquiescence of such an official. Rape causes severe pain and suffering, both physical and psychological. The psychological suffering of persons upon whom rape is inflicted may be exacerbated by social and cultural conditions and can be particularly acute and long lasting. Furthermore, it is difficult to envisage circumstances in which rape, by, or at the instigation of a public official, or with the consent or acquiescence of an official, could

> be considered as occurring for a purpose that does not, in some way, involve punishment, coercion, discrimination or intimidation. In the view of this Trial Chamber this is inherent in situations of armed conflict.

Accordingly, whenever rape and other forms of sexual violence meet the aforementioned criteria, then they shall constitute torture, in the same manner as any other acts that meet these criteria.

Prosecutor v. Furundzija

International Criminal Tribunal for the former Yugoslavia
Case No. IT-95-17/1-T, Trial Chamber II, Judgement, Dec. 10, 1998

1. The International Tribunal is governed by its Statute, adopted by the Security Council of the United Nations on 25 May 1993, and by the Rules of Procedure and Evidence of the International Tribunal, adopted by the Judges of the International Tribunal on 11 February 1994, as amended. Under the Statute, the International Tribunal has the power to prosecute persons responsible for serious violations of international humanitarian law committed in the territory of the former Yugoslavia since 1991. Articles 2 through 5 of the Statute further confer upon the International Tribunal jurisdiction over grave breaches of the Geneva Conventions of 12 August 1949 (Article 2); violations of the laws or customs of war (Article 3); genocide (Article 4); and crimes against humanity (Article 5). . . .

[The Trial Chamber found that the defendant, Anton Furundzija, was the commander of a special military police unit, "the Jokers," within the armed forces of the Croatian Community in Bosnia, which had declared itself an independent political entity. In May 1993, "Witness A," a Bosnian Moslem woman, was arrested by the Jokers and taken to their headquarters for interrogation. She was forced to undress and remain naked before a large number of soldiers while she was interrogated by the defendant. During the interrogation, another soldier (who was the commander of another unit) rubbed his knife against her thigh and lower stomach and threatened to put his knife inside her vagina if she did not tell the truth. The defendant then left her in the custody of this other soldier, who proceeded to rape her. Afterwards, the defendant continued to interrogate "Witness A" in another room, once more before an audience of soldiers. She was naked but covered by a small blanket. A friend of her family's, a Croatian male, was brought into the room and interrogated as well. The other soldier beat both of them on their feet with a baton. He repeatedly raped "Witness A," by the mouth, vagina, and anus, and forced her to lick his penis; the friend was made to watch in an effort to induce him to admit the allegations against her. The defendant was present or nearby throughout and did nothing to stop these acts. In fact, the tribunal found, they were performed in pursuance of the defendant's interrogation of the witnesses: as the interrogation intensified, so did the sexual assaults and rape.

The defendant was found guilty on two counts, one charging torture, the other charging "outrages on personal dignity including rape," both alleged to be in violation of the laws or customs of war referred to in Article 3 of the Tribunal's Statute. The defendant was sentenced to ten years' imprisonment—or, more precisely, to concurrent sentences of ten years on the first count and to eight years on the second count. His conviction and sentence subsequently were affirmed by the Tribunal's Appeals Chamber. *See Prosecutor v. Furundzija*, Case No. IT-95-17/1-A, Judgement (July 21, 2000).

The Trial Chamber's judgment contains the following observations on the law applicable to the charges of torture and rape with which the Appeals Chamber agreed.]

A. Article 3 of the Statute (Violations of the Laws or Customs of War)

131. Article 3 of the Statute of the International Tribunal provides as follows:

> The International Tribunal shall have the power to prosecute persons violating the laws or customs of war. Such violations shall include, but not be limited to:
>
> (a) employment of poisonous weapons or other weapons calculated to cause unnecessary suffering;
>
> (b) wanton destruction of cities, towns or villages, or devastation not justified by military necessity;
>
> (c) attack, or bombardment, by whatever means, of undefended towns, villages, dwellings, or buildings;
>
> (d) seizure of, destruction or wilful damage done to institutions dedicated to religion, charity and education, the arts and sciences, historic monuments and works of art and science;
>
> (e) plunder of public or private property.

132. As interpreted by the Appeals Chamber in the *Tadic Jurisdiction Decision*, Article 3 has a very broad scope. It covers any serious violation of a rule of customary international humanitarian law entailing, under international customary or conventional law, the individual criminal responsibility of the person breaching the rule. It is immaterial whether the breach occurs within the context of an international or internal armed conflict.

133. It follows that the list of offences contained in Article 3 is merely illustrative; according to the interpretation propounded by the Appeals Chamber, and as is clear from the text of Article 3, this provision also covers serious violations of international rules of humanitarian law not included in that list.

B. Torture in International Law

1. International Humanitarian Law

134. Torture in times of armed conflict is specifically prohibited by international treaty law, in particular by the Geneva Conventions of 1949 and the two Additional Protocols of 1977.

135. Under the Statute of the International Tribunal, as interpreted by the Appeals Chamber in the *Tadic Jurisdiction Decision*, these treaty provisions may be applied as such by the International Tribunal if it is proved that at the relevant time all the parties to the conflict were bound by them. *In casu*, Bosnia and Herzegovina ratified the Geneva Conventions of 1949 and both Additional Protocols of 1977 on 31 December 1992. Accordingly, at least common article 3 of the Geneva Conventions of 1949 and article 4 of Additional Protocol II, both of which explicitly prohibit torture, were applicable as minimum fundamental guarantees of treaty law in the territory of Bosnia and Herzegovina at the time relevant to the Indictment. In addition, in 1992, the parties to the conflict in Bosnia and Herzegovina undertook to observe the most important provisions of the Geneva Conventions, including those prohibiting torture. Thus undoubtedly the provisions concerning torture applied *qua* treaty law in the territory of Bosnia and Herzegovina as between the parties to the conflict.

136. The Trial Chamber also notes that torture was prohibited as a war crime under article 142 of the Penal Code of the Socialist Federal Republic of Yugoslavia (hereafter "SFRY"), and that the same violation has been made punishable in the Republic of Bosnia and Herzegovina by virtue of the decree-law of 11 April 1992.

137. The Trial Chamber does not need to determine whether the Geneva Conventions and the Additional Protocols passed into customary law in their entirety, as was recently held by the Constitutional Court of Colombia, or whether, as seems more plausible, only the most important provisions of these treaties have acquired the status of general international law. In any case, the proposition is warranted that a general prohibition against torture has evolved in customary international law. . . . Torture was not specifically mentioned in the London Agreement of 8 August 1945 establishing the International Military Tribunal at Nuremberg, but it was one of the acts expressly classified as a crime against humanity under article II(1)(c) of Allied Control Council Law No. 10. As stated above, the Geneva Conventions of 1949 and the Protocols of 1977 prohibit torture in terms.

138. That these treaty provisions have ripened into customary rules is evinced by various factors. First, these treaties and in particular the Geneva Conventions have been ratified by practically all States of the world. Admittedly those treaty provisions remain as such and any contracting party is formally entitled to relieve itself of its obligations by denouncing the treaty (an occurrence that seems extremely unlikely in reality); nevertheless the practically universal participation in these treaties shows that all States accept among other things the prohibition of torture. In other words, this participation is highly indicative of the attitude of States to the prohibition of torture. Secondly, no State has ever claimed that it was authorised to practice torture in time of armed conflict, nor has any State shown or manifested opposition to the implementation of treaty provisions against torture. When a State has been taken to task because its officials allegedly resorted to torture, it has normally responded that the allegation was unfounded, thus expressly or implicitly upholding the prohibition of this odious practice. Thirdly, the International Court

of Justice has authoritatively, albeit not with express reference to torture, confirmed this custom-creating process: in the *Nicaragua* case it held that common article 3 of the 1949 Geneva Conventions, which *inter alia* prohibits torture against persons taking no active part in hostilities, is now well-established as belonging to the corpus of customary international law and is applicable both to international and internal armed conflicts.

139. It therefore seems incontrovertible that torture in time of armed conflict is prohibited by a general rule of international law. In armed conflicts this rule may be applied both as part of international customary law and — if the requisite conditions are met — *qua* treaty law, the content of the prohibition being the same.

140. The treaty and customary rules referred to above impose obligations upon States and other entities in an armed conflict, but first and foremost address themselves to the acts of individuals, in particular to State officials or more generally, to officials of a party to the conflict or else to individuals acting at the instigation or with the consent or acquiescence of a party to the conflict. Both customary rules and treaty provisions applicable in times of armed conflict prohibit any act of torture. Those who engage in torture are personally accountable at the criminal level for such acts. As the International Military Tribunal at Nuremberg put it in general terms: "Crimes against international law are committed by men, not by abstract entities, and only by punishing individuals who commit such crimes can the provisions of international law be enforced." Individuals are personally responsible, whatever their official position, even if they are heads of State or government ministers. . . .

141. It should be stressed that in international humanitarian law, depending upon the specific circumstances of each case, torture may be prosecuted as a category of such broad international crimes as serious violations of humanitarian law, grave breaches of the Geneva Conventions, crimes against humanity or genocide. . . .

2. International Human Rights Law

143. The prohibition of torture laid down in international humanitarian law with regard to situations of armed conflict is reinforced by the body of international treaty rules on human rights: these rules ban torture both in armed conflict and in time of peace. In addition, treaties as well as resolutions of international organizations set up mechanisms designed to ensure that the prohibition is implemented and to prevent resort to torture as much as possible.

144. It should be noted that the prohibition of torture laid down in human rights treaties enshrines an absolute right, which can never be derogated from, not even in time of emergency (on this ground the prohibition also applies to situations of armed conflicts). This is linked to the fact, discussed below, that the prohibition on torture is a peremptory norm or *jus cogens*. This prohibition is so extensive that States are even barred by international law from expelling, returning or extraditing a person to another State where there are substantial grounds for believing that the person would be in danger of being subjected to torture.

145. These treaty provisions impose upon States the obligation to prohibit and punish torture, as well as to refrain from engaging in torture through their officials. In international human rights law, which deals with State responsibility rather than individual criminal responsibility, torture is prohibited as a criminal offence to be punished under national law; in addition, all States parties to the relevant treaties have been granted, and are obliged to exercise, jurisdiction to investigate, prosecute and punish offenders. Thus, in human rights law too, the prohibition of torture extends to and has a direct bearing on the criminal liability of individuals. . . .

3. Main Features of the Prohibition Against Torture in International Law

147. There exists today universal revulsion against torture: as a USA Court put it in *Filartiga v. Pena-Irala*, "the torturer has become, like the pirate and the slave trader before him, *hostis humani generis*, an enemy of all mankind." This revulsion, as well as the importance States attach to the eradication of torture, has led to the cluster of treaty and customary rules on torture acquiring a particularly high status in the international normative system, a status similar to that of principles such as those prohibiting genocide, slavery, racial discrimination, aggression, the acquisition of territory by force and the forcible suppression of the right of peoples to self-determination. The prohibition against torture exhibits three important features, which are probably held in common with the other general principles protecting fundamental human rights.

(a) The Prohibition Even Covers Potential Breaches

148. Firstly, given the importance that the international community attaches to the protection of individuals from torture, the prohibition against torture is particularly stringent and sweeping. . . . As was authoritatively held by the European Court of Human Rights in *Soering* [*see* chap. 17], international law intends to bar not only actual breaches but also potential breaches of the prohibition against torture (as well as any inhuman and degrading treatment). It follows that international rules prohibit not only torture but also (i) the failure to adopt the national measures necessary for implementing the prohibition and (ii) the maintenance in force or passage of laws which are contrary to the prohibition. . . .

(b) The Prohibition Imposes Obligations Erga Omnes

151. Furthermore, the prohibition of torture imposes upon States obligations *erga omnes*, that is, obligations owed towards all the other members of the international community, each of which then has a correlative right. In addition, the violation of such an obligation simultaneously constitutes a breach of the correlative right of all members of the international community and gives rise to a claim for compliance accruing to each and every member, which then has the right to insist on fulfilment of the obligation or in any case to call for the breach to be discontinued.

152. Where there exist international bodies charged with impartially monitoring compliance with treaty provisions on torture, these bodies enjoy priority over individual States in establishing whether a certain State has taken all the necessary

measures to prevent and punish torture and, if they have not, in calling upon that State to fulfil its international obligations. The existence of such international mechanisms makes it possible for compliance with international law to be ensured in a neutral and impartial manner.

(c) The Prohibition Has Acquired the Status of Jus Cogens

153. While the *erga omnes* nature just mentioned appertains to the area of international enforcement (*lato sensu*), the other major feature of the principle proscribing torture relates to the hierarchy of rules in the international normative order. Because of the importance of the values it protects, this principle has evolved into a peremptory norm or *jus cogens*, that is, a norm that enjoys a higher rank in the international hierarchy than treaty law and even "ordinary" customary rules. The most conspicuous consequence of this higher rank is that the principle at issue cannot be derogated from by States through international treaties or local or special customs or even general customary rules not endowed with the same normative force.

154. Clearly, the *jus cogens* nature of the prohibition against torture articulates the notion that the prohibition has now become one of the most fundamental standards of the international community. Furthermore, this prohibition is designed to produce a deterrent effect, in that it signals to all members of the international community and the individuals over whom they wield authority that the prohibition of torture is an absolute value from which nobody must deviate.

155. The fact that torture is prohibited by a peremptory norm of international law has other effects at the inter-state and individual levels. At the inter-state level, it serves to internationally de-legitimise any legislative, administrative or judicial act authorising torture. It would be senseless to argue, on the one hand, that on account of the *jus cogens* value of the prohibition against torture, treaties or customary rules providing for torture would be null and void *ab initio*, and then be unmindful of a State say, taking national measures authorising or condoning torture or absolving its perpetrators through an amnesty law.... If such a situation were to arise, the national measures, violating the general principle and any relevant treaty provision, would produce the legal effects discussed above and in addition would not be accorded international legal recognition. Proceedings could be instituted by potential victims if they had locus standi before a competent international or national judicial body with a view to asking it to hold the national measure to be internationally unlawful; or the victim could bring a civil suit for damage in a foreign court, which would therefore be asked inter alia to disregard the legal value of the national authorising act. What is even more important is that perpetrators of torture acting upon or benefitting from those national measures may nevertheless be held criminally responsible for torture, whether in a foreign State, or in their own State under a subsequent regime. In short, in spite of possible national authorisation by legislative or judicial bodies to violate the principle banning torture, individuals remain bound to comply with that principle. As the International Military Tribunal at Nuremberg put it:

"individuals have international duties which transcend the national obligations of obedience imposed by the individual State."

156. Furthermore, at the individual level, that is, that of criminal liability, it would seem that one of the consequences of the *jus cogens* character bestowed by the international community upon the prohibition of torture is that every State is entitled to investigate, prosecute and punish or extradite individuals accused of torture, who are present in a territory under its jurisdiction. Indeed, it would be inconsistent on the one hand to prohibit torture to such an extent as to restrict the normally unfettered treaty-making power of sovereign States, and on the other hand bar States from prosecuting and punishing those torturers who have engaged in this odious practice abroad. This legal basis for States' universal jurisdiction over torture bears out and strengthens the legal foundation for such jurisdiction found by other courts in the inherently universal character of the crime. It has been held that international crimes being universally condemned wherever they occur, every State has the right to prosecute and punish the authors of such crimes. As stated in general terms by the Supreme Court of Israel in *Eichmann*, and echoed by a USA court in *Demjanjuk* [*see* chap. 20], "it is the universal character of the crimes in question *i.e.* international crimes which vests in every State the authority to try and punish those who participated in their commission."

157. It would seem that other consequences include the fact that torture may not be covered by a statute of limitations, and must not be excluded from extradition under any political offence exemption.

4. Torture Under Article 3 of the Statute

158. Torture is not specifically prohibited under Article 3 of the Statute. As noted in paragraph 133 of this Judgement, Article 3 constitutes an 'umbrella rule,' which makes an open-ended reference to all international rules of humanitarian law. In its "Decision On The Defendant's Motion To Dismiss Counts 13 and 14 of The Indictment (Lack Of Subject Matter Jurisdiction)" issued on 29 May 1998, the Trial Chamber held that Article 3 of the Statute covers torture and outrages upon personal dignity including rape, and that the Trial Chamber has jurisdiction over alleged violations of Article 3 of the Statute.

5. The Definition of Torture

159. International humanitarian law, while outlawing torture in armed conflict, does not provide a definition of the prohibition. Such a definition can instead be found in article 1(1) of the 1984 Torture Convention [*supra*] . . . .

160. This definition was regarded by Trial Chamber I of ICTR, in *Prosecutor v. Jean-Paul Akayesu*, as *sic et simpliciter* applying to any rule of international law on torture, including the relevant provisions of the ICTR Statute. However, attention should be drawn to the fact that article 1 of the Convention explicitly provides that the definition contained therein is "for the purposes of this Convention." It thus seems to limit the purport and contents of that definition to the Convention solely. An extra-conventional effect may however be produced to the extent that the

definition at issue codifies, or contributes to developing or crystallising customary international law. Trial Chamber II of the International Tribunal has rightly noted in *Delalic* that indeed the definition of torture contained in the 1984 Torture Convention is broader than, and includes, that laid down in the 1975 Declaration of the United Nations General Assembly and in the 1985 Inter-American Convention, and has hence concluded that that definition "thus reflects a consensus which the Trial Chamber considers to be representative of customary international law." This Trial Chamber shares such conclusion, although on legal grounds that it shall briefly set out. First of all, there is no gainsaying that the definition laid down in the Torture Convention, although deliberately limited to the Convention, must be regarded as authoritative, *inter alia*, because it spells out all the necessary elements implicit in international rules on the matter. Secondly, this definition to a very large extent coincides with that contained in the United Nations Declaration on Torture of 9 December 1975. It should be noted that this Declaration was adopted by the General Assembly by consensus. This fact shows that no member State of the United Nations had any objection to such definition. In other words, all the members of the United Nations concurred in and supported that definition. Thirdly, a substantially similar definition can be found in the Inter-American Convention. Fourthly, the same definition has been applied by the United Nations Special Rapporteur and is in line with the definition suggested or acted upon by such international bodies as the European Court of Human Rights and the Human Rights Committee.

161. The broad convergence of the aforementioned international instruments and international jurisprudence demonstrates that there is now general acceptance of the main elements contained in the definition set out in article 1 of the Torture Convention.

162. The Trial Chamber considers however that while the definition referred to above applies to any instance of torture, whether in time of peace or of armed conflict, it is appropriate to identify or spell out some specific elements that pertain to torture as considered from the specific viewpoint of international criminal law relating to armed conflicts. The Trial Chamber considers that the elements of torture in an armed conflict require that torture:

(i) consists of the infliction, by act or omission, of severe pain or suffering, whether physical or mental; in addition

(ii) this act or omission must be intentional;

(iii) it must aim at obtaining information or a confession, or at punishing, intimidating, humiliating or coercing the victim or a third person, or at discriminating, on any ground, against the victim or a third person;

(iv) it must be linked to an armed conflict;

(v) at least one of the persons involved in the torture process must be a public official or must at any rate act in a non-private capacity, *e.g.* as a de facto organ of a State or any other authority-wielding entity.

As is apparent from this enumeration of criteria, the Trial Chamber considers that among the possible purposes of torture one must also include that of humiliating the victim. This proposition is warranted by the general spirit of international humanitarian law: the primary purpose of this body of law is to safeguard human dignity. The proposition is also supported by some general provisions of such important international treaties as the Geneva Conventions and Additional Protocols, which consistently aim at protecting persons not taking part, or no longer taking part, in the hostilities from "outrages upon personal dignity." The notion of humiliation is, in any event close to the notion of intimidation, which is explicitly referred to in the Torture Convention's definition of torture.

163. As evidenced by international case law, the reports of the United Nations Human Rights Committee and the United Nations Committee Against Torture, those of the Special Rapporteur, and the public statements of the European Committee for the Prevention of Torture, this vicious and ignominious practice can take on various forms. International case law, and the reports of the United Nations Special Rapporteur evince a momentum towards addressing, through legal process, the use of rape in the course of detention and interrogation as a means of torture and, therefore, as a violation of international law. Rape is resorted to either by the interrogator himself or by other persons associated with the interrogation of a detainee, as a means of punishing, intimidating, coercing or humiliating the victim, or obtaining information, or a confession, from the victim or a third person. In human rights law, in such situations the rape may amount to torture, as demonstrated by the finding of the European Court of Human Rights in *Aydin* and the Inter-American Court of Human Rights in *Meijia*.

164. Depending upon the circumstances, under international criminal law rape may acquire the status of a crime distinct from torture; this will be covered in the following section of the Judgement.

C. Rape and Other Serious Sexual Assaults in International Law

1. International Humanitarian Law

165. Rape in time of war is specifically prohibited by treaty law: the Geneva Conventions of 1949, Additional Protocol I of 1977 and Additional Protocol II of 1977. Other serious sexual assaults are expressly or implicitly prohibited in various provisions of the same treaties.

166. At least common article 3 to the Geneva Conventions of 1949, which implicitly refers to rape, and article 4 of Additional Protocol II, which explicitly mentions rape, apply *qua* treaty law in the case in hand because Bosnia and Herzegovina ratified the Geneva Conventions and both Additional Protocols on 31 December 1992. Furthermore, as stated in paragraph 135 above, on 22 May 1992, the parties to the conflict undertook to observe the most important provisions of the Geneva Conventions and to grant the protections afforded therein.

167. In addition, the Trial Chamber notes that rape and inhuman treatment were prohibited as war crimes by article 142 of the Penal Code of the SFRY and that

Bosnia and Herzegovina, as a former Republic of that federal State, continues to apply an analogous provision.

168. The prohibition of rape and serious sexual assault in armed conflict has also evolved in customary international law. . . . While rape and sexual assaults were not specifically prosecuted by the Nuremberg Tribunal, rape was expressly classified as a crime against humanity under article II(1)(c) of Control Council Law No. 10. The Tokyo International Military Tribunal convicted Generals Toyoda and Matsui of command responsibility for violations of the laws or customs of war committed by their soldiers in Nanking, which included widespread rapes and sexual assaults. The former Foreign Minister of Japan, Hirota, was also convicted for these atrocities. This decision and that of the United States Military Commission in *Yamashita*, along with the ripening of the fundamental prohibition of "outrages upon personal dignity" laid down in common article 3 into customary international law, has contributed to the evolution of universally accepted norms of international law prohibiting rape as well as serious sexual assault. These norms are applicable in any armed conflict.

169. It is indisputable that rape and other serious sexual assaults in armed conflict entail the criminal liability of the perpetrators.

2. International Human Rights Law

170. No international human rights instrument specifically prohibits rape or other serious sexual assaults. Nevertheless, these offences are implicitly prohibited by the provisions safeguarding physical integrity, which are contained in all of the relevant international treaties. The right to physical integrity is a fundamental one, and is undeniably part of customary international law.

171. In certain circumstances, however, rape can amount to torture and has been found by international judicial bodies to constitute a violation of the norm prohibiting torture, as stated above in paragraph 163.

3. Rape Under the Statute

172. The prosecution of rape is explicitly provided for in Article 5 of the Statute of the International Tribunal as a crime against humanity. Rape may also amount to a grave breach of the Geneva Conventions, a violation of the laws or customs of war or an act of genocide, if the requisite elements are met, and may be prosecuted accordingly.

173. The all-embracing nature of Article 3 of the Statute has already been discussed in paragraph 133 of this Judgement. In its "Decision on the Defendant's Motion to Dismiss Counts 13 and 14 of the Indictment (Lack of Subject-Matter Jurisdiction)" of 29 May 1998, the Trial Chamber held that Article 3 of the Statute covers outrages upon personal dignity including rape.

4. The Definition of Rape

174. The Trial Chamber notes the unchallenged submission of the Prosecution in its Pre-trial Brief that rape is a forcible act: this means that the act is "accomplished

by force or threats of force against the victim or a third person, such threats being express or implied and must place the victim in reasonable fear that he, she or a third person will be subjected to violence, detention, duress or psychological oppression." This act is the penetration of the vagina, the anus or mouth by the penis, or of the vagina or anus by other object. In this context, it includes penetration, however slight, of the vulva, anus or oral cavity, by the penis and sexual penetration of the vulva or anus is not limited to the penis.

175. No definition of rape can be found in international law. However, some general indications can be discerned from the provisions of international treaties. In particular, attention must be drawn to the fact that there is prohibition of both rape and "any form of indecent assault" on women in article 27 of Geneva Convention IV, article 76(1) of Additional Protocol I and article 4(2)(e) of Additional Protocol II. The inference is warranted that international law, by specifically prohibiting rape as well as, in general terms, other forms of sexual abuse, regards rape as the most serious manifestation of sexual assault. This is, *inter alia*, confirmed by Article 5 of the International Tribunal's Statute, which explicitly provides for the prosecution of rape while it implicitly covers other less grave forms of serious sexual assault through Article 5(i) as "other inhuman acts."

176. Trial Chamber I of the ICTR has held in *Akayesu* that to formulate a definition of rape in international law one should start from the assumption that "the central elements of the crime of rape cannot be captured in a mechanical description of objects or body parts." According to that Trial Chamber, in international law it is more useful to focus "on the conceptual framework of State sanctioned violence." It then went on to state the following:

> Like torture, rape is used for such purposes as intimidation, degradation, humiliation, discrimination, punishment, control or destruction of a person. Like torture, rape is a violation of personal dignity, and rape in fact constitutes torture when inflicted by or at the instigation of or with the consent or acquiescence of a public official or others person acting in an official capacity. The Chamber defines rape as a physical invasion of a sexual nature, committed on a person under circumstances which are coercive.

This definition has been upheld by Trial Chamber II *quarter* of the International Tribunal in *Delalic*.

177. This Trial Chamber notes that no elements other than those emphasised may be drawn from international treaty or customary law, nor is resort to general principles of international criminal law or to general principles of international law of any avail. The Trial Chamber therefore considers that, to arrive at an accurate definition of rape based on the criminal law principle of specificity (*Bestimmtheitgrundsatz*, also referred to by the maxim *nullum crimen sine lege stricta*), it is necessary to look for principles of criminal law common to the major legal systems of the world. These principles may be derived, with all due caution, from national laws.

178. Whenever international criminal rules do not define a notion of criminal law, reliance upon national legislation is justified, subject to the following conditions: (i) unless indicated by an international rule, reference should not be made to one national legal system only, say that of common-law or that of civil-law States. Rather, international courts must draw upon the general concepts and legal institutions common to all the major legal systems of the world. This presupposes a process of identification of the common denominators in these legal systems so as to pinpoint the basic notions they share; (ii) since "international trials exhibit a number of features that differentiate them from national criminal proceedings," account must be taken of the specificity of international criminal proceedings when utilising national law notions. In this way a mechanical importation or transposition from national law into international criminal proceedings is avoided, as well as the attendant distortions of the unique traits of such proceedings.

179. The Trial Chamber would emphasise at the outset, that a trend can be discerned in the national legislation of a number of States of broadening the definition of rape so that it now embraces acts that were previously classified as comparatively less serious offences, that is sexual or indecent assault. This trend shows that at the national level States tend to take a stricter attitude towards serious forms of sexual assault: the stigma of rape now attaches to a growing category of sexual offences, provided of course they meet certain requirements, chiefly that of forced physical penetration.

180. In its examination of national laws on rape, the Trial Chamber has found that although the laws of many countries specify that rape can only be committed against a woman, others provide that rape can be committed against a victim of either sex. The laws of several jurisdictions state that the *actus reus* of rape consists of the penetration, however slight, of the female sexual organ by the male sexual organ. There are also jurisdictions which interpret the *actus reus* of rape broadly. The provisions of civil law jurisdictions often use wording open for interpretation by the courts. Furthermore, all jurisdictions surveyed by the Trial Chamber require an element of force, coercion, threat, or acting without the consent of the victim: force is given a broad interpretation and includes rendering the victim helpless. Some jurisdictions indicate that the force or intimidation can be directed at a third person. Aggravating factors commonly include causing the death of the victim, the fact that there were multiple perpetrators, the young age of the victim, and the fact that the victim suffers a condition, which renders him/her especially vulnerable such as mental illness. Rape is almost always punishable with a maximum of life imprisonment, but the terms that are imposed by various jurisdictions vary widely.

181. It is apparent from our survey of national legislation that, in spite of inevitable discrepancies, most legal systems in the common and civil law worlds consider rape to be the forcible sexual penetration of the human body by the penis or the forcible insertion of any other object into either the vagina or the anus.

182. A major discrepancy may, however, be discerned in the criminalisation of forced oral penetration: some States treat it as sexual assault, while it is categorised as rape in other States. Faced with this lack of uniformity, it falls to the Trial Chamber to establish whether an appropriate solution can be reached by resorting to the general principles of international criminal law or, if such principles are of no avail, to the general principles of international law.

183. The Trial Chamber holds that the forced penetration of the mouth by the male sexual organ constitutes a most humiliating and degrading attack upon human dignity. The essence of the whole corpus of international humanitarian law as well as human rights law lies in the protection of the human dignity of every person, whatever his or her gender. The general principle of respect for human dignity is the basic underpinning and indeed the very *raison d'être* of international humanitarian law and human rights law; indeed in modern times it has become of such paramount importance as to permeate the whole body of international law. This principle is intended to shield human beings from outrages upon their personal dignity, whether such outrages are carried out by unlawfully attacking the body or by humiliating and debasing the honour, the self-respect or the mental well-being of a person. It is consonant with this principle that such an extremely serious sexual outrage as forced oral penetration should be classified as rape.

184. Moreover, the Trial Chamber is of the opinion that it is not contrary to the general principle of *nullum crimen sine lege* to charge an accused with forcible oral sex as rape when in some national jurisdictions, including his own, he could only be charged with sexual assault in respect of the same acts. It is not a question of criminalising acts which were not criminal when they were committed by the accused, since forcible oral sex is in any event a crime, and indeed an extremely serious crime. Indeed, due to the nature of the International Tribunal's subject-matter jurisdiction, in prosecutions before the Tribunal forced oral sex is invariably an aggravated sexual assault as it is committed in time of armed conflict on defenceless civilians; hence it is not simple sexual assault but sexual assault as a war crime or crime against humanity. Therefore so long as an accused, who is convicted of rape for acts of forcible oral penetration, is sentenced on the factual basis of coercive oral sex — and sentenced in accordance with the sentencing practice in the former Yugoslavia for such crimes, pursuant to Article 24 of the Statute and Rule 101 of the Rules — then he is not adversely affected by the categorisation of forced oral sex as rape rather than as sexual assault. His only complaint can be that a greater stigma attaches to being a convicted rapist rather than a convicted sexual assailant. However, one should bear in mind the remarks above to the effect that forced oral sex can be just as humiliating and traumatic for a victim as vaginal or anal penetration. Thus the notion that a greater stigma attaches to a conviction for forcible vaginal or anal penetration than to a conviction for forcible oral penetration is a product of questionable attitudes. Moreover any such concern is amply outweighed by the fundamental principle of protecting human dignity, a principle which favours broadening the definition of rape.

185. Thus, the Trial Chamber finds that the following may be accepted as the objective elements of rape:

> (i) the sexual penetration, however slight:
>
> (a) of the vagina or anus of the victim by the penis of the perpetrator or any other object used by the perpetrator; or
>
> (b) of the mouth of the victim by the penis of the perpetrator;
>
> (ii) by coercion or force or threat of force against the victim or a third person.

186. As pointed out above, international criminal rules punish not only rape but also any serious sexual assault falling short of actual penetration. It would seem that the prohibition embraces all serious abuses of a sexual nature inflicted upon the physical and moral integrity of a person by means of coercion, threat of force or intimidation in a way that is degrading and humiliating for the victim's dignity. As both these categories of acts are criminalised in international law, the distinction between them is one that is primarily material for the purposes of sentencing.

Notes

(1) On July 21, 2000, the Appeals Chamber rejected each ground of appeal in the Furundzija case and affirmed the conviction (IT-96-17/1).

(2) How should rape be defined in international law? In *Prosecutor v. Kunarac*, Case No. IT-96-23, Appeals Chamber, June 12, 2002, the Appeals Chamber for the ICTY discussed rape as torture and also discussed the definition of rape. The Tribunal stated:

> 125. The Appellants challenge the Trial Chamber's definition of rape. With negligible differences in diction, they propose instead definitions requiring, in addition to penetration, a showing of additional elements: force or threat of force and the victim's "continuous" or "genuine" resistance. . . .
>
> 128. The Appeals Chamber concurs with the Trial Chamber's definition of rape. Nonetheless, the Appeals Chamber believes that it is worth emphasizing two points. First, it rejects the Appellants' "resistance" requirement, an addition for which there is no basis in customary international law. The Appellants' bald assertion that nothing short of continuous resistance provides adequate notice to the perpetrator that his attentions are unwanted is wrong on the law and absurd on the facts.
>
> 129. Secondly, with regard to the role of force in the definition of rape, the Appeals Chamber notes that the Trial Chamber appeared to depart from the Tribunal's prior definitions of rape. However, in explaining its focus on the absence of consent as the *conditio sine qua non* of rape, the Trial Chamber did not disavow the Tribunal's earlier jurisprudence, but instead sought to explain the relationship between force and consent. Force or threat of force provides clear evidence of non-consent, but force is not an element *per*

> *se* of rape. In particular, the Trial Chamber wished to explain that there are "factors [other than force] which would render an act of sexual penetration *non-consensual or non-voluntary* on the part of the victim". A narrow focus on force or threat of force could permit perpetrators to evade liability for sexual activity to which the other party had not consented by taking advantage of coercive circumstances without relying on physical force. . . .
>
> 132. For the most part, Appellants in this case were convicted of raping women held in *de facto* military headquarters, detention centres and apartments maintained as soldiers' residences. As the most egregious aspect of the conditions, the victims were considered the legitimate sexual prey of their captors. Typically, the women were raped by more than one perpetrator and with a regularity that is nearly inconceivable. (Those who initially sought help or resisted were treated to an extra level of brutality.) Such detentions amount to circumstances that were so coercive as to negate any possibility of consent.

(3) For thorough discussions of the case-law and practice, *see* the publication by the British NGO, "Redress": REDRESS FOR RAPE: USING INTERNATIONAL JURISPRUDENCE ON RAPE AS A FORM OF TORTURE OR OTHER ILL-TREATMENT (2013), and PROSECUTING CONFLICT-RELATED SEXUAL VIOLENCE AT THE ICTY (Serge Brammertz & Michelle Jarvis eds., 2016) (Brammertz and Jarvis were respectively ICTY Prosecutor and Deputy to the Prosecutor).

Chapter 11

United Nations Convention on Transnational Organized Crime

§ 11.01 Generally

We have seen in earlier chapters how the term "transnational criminal law" is used to describe suppression obligations that arise from treaty proscriptions rather than from customary law obligations. The material that follows engages a subtly different usage of the term "transnational" to describe organizational structures ("transnational organized crime") for carrying out certain kinds of cross-border crime. These structures have earned their own suppression convention (and three protocols to it). The late Gerhard Mueller, a long-time member of the faculty of the Rutgers School of Criminal Justice in Newark, is credited with coining the term "transnational crime," as a "criminological" rather than a "juridical" term, in his capacity as Executive Secretary of the 1975 Fifth United Nations Congress on the Prevention of Crime and the Treatment of Offenders. *See* Mangai Natarajan, *Gerhard Mueller's Role in Developing the Concept of Transnational Crime for the United Nations, in* Histories of Transnational Criminal Law 71 (Neil Boister, Sabine Gless & Florian Jeβberger eds., 2021). The criminological variety of the concept consolidated a substantial place on the international criminal justice agenda from then on. And the notion slowly gained steam as one that should be a basis for a suppression convention. That convention would act as a "framework convention" for some of the Criminal Justice work of the UN Office in Vienna, just as the 1988 Convention on Narcotic Drugs and Psychotropic Substances provided a focal point for the "Drugs" part of that UN outpost. ("Crime" and the rather larger "Drugs" bureaucracy were combined in Vienna in 2002 to form the United Nations Office on Drugs and Crime, or UNDOC.) By the mid-1990s, Italy—with Sicily the birthplace of the Mafia—and the United States were supporting the idea of a convention in the area, although it was Poland which first presented a draft convention to the UN General Assembly in 1996. (We suspect that the draft was largely the work of the UN Secretariat.)

Now, as a "juridical concept," transnational organized crime found its way into the title (and definition) of the 2000 UN Convention against Transnational Organized Crime, adopted by G.A Res. 55/25 of Nov. 15, 2000, Annex I, *available at* https://www.unodc.org/documents/treaties/UNTOC/Publications/TOC%20Convention/TOCebook-e.pdf. The Convention is often known as the "Palermo Convention" after the city in Sicily where it was opened for signature. The Convention itself is free of references to specific criminal law subject-matter for organized crime, but it was accompanied by three Protocols which each delved into a particular subject-area, the "Protocol on Trafficking in Persons, Especially Women and Children," the "Protocol on Smuggling Migrants by Land, Sea and Air," and the "Protocol on Illicit Manufacturing and Trafficking in Firearms." The first two Protocols were adopted in the same resolution as the main Convention (as Annexes II and III of the resolution); the third was adopted by G.A. Res. 55/255 of May 31, 2001. (All are reproduced in the UNODOC document referenced earlier in this paragraph.) The most widely-ratified Protocol, that on Trafficking in Persons, will be discussed in the next Chapter. Other areas of criminality than those in the Protocols which appear often in discussions of organized crime include drug trafficking, trafficking in cultural property, environmental degradation, hunting and trading endangered species, trade and export of fragments of coral reefs, illegal logging, distribution of child pornography, terrorism, organ trafficking, cigarette smuggling and the distribution of fraudulent medicine—even maritime piracy. Notably, the crimes covered generically in the 2000 Convention overlap sectoral treaties such as those on drug trafficking (and, a few years later, corruption). The innovations of the 2000 Convention are not in highlighting these particular activities but in creating a new international obligation to criminalize group activities, pushing for wider acceptance of criminalizing ancillary activities like laundering (a matter taken further three years later in the UN Convention against Corruption [chap. 4]) and obstruction of justice. The Convention also aimed at fostering enforcement tools like extradition, mutual legal assistance and confiscation, as well as techniques such as "controlled delivery." Including corporate responsibility was another big breakthrough in the 2000 instrument.

On the history and the Convention in general, *see* COMBATING TRANSNATIONAL CRIME (Phil Williams & Dmitri Vlassis eds., 2001); JOHN D. MCCLEAN, TRANSNATIONAL ORGANISED CRIME: A COMMENTARY ON THE UN CONVENTION AND ITS PROTOCOLS (2007); TOM OBOKATA, TRANSNATIONAL ORGANISED CRIME IN INTERNATIONAL LAW (2010); INTERNATIONAL LAW AND TRANSNATIONAL ORGANISED CRIME (Pierre Hauck and Sven Peterke eds., 2016); IAN TENNANT, THE PROMISE OF PALERMO: A POLITICAL HISTORY OF THE UN CONVENTION AGAINST TRANSNATIONAL ORGANISED CRIME (for Global Initiative against Transnational Organised Crime, 2020); UNODC, TRAVAUX PRÉPARATOIRES OF THE NEGOTIATIONS FOR THE ELABORATION OF THE UNITED NATIONS CONVENTION AGAINST TRANSNATIONAL ORGANIZED CRIME AND THE PROTOCOLS THERETO (2006).

In the United States, this was, like the Convention against Corruption [chap. 4], an unusual suppression convention which could be ratified without new legislation. The Racketeer Influenced and Corrupt Organizations Act (RICO), with a boost from crimes like wire and mail fraud—and money laundering—provided ample scope for prosecution. Not to be underestimated in the organized crime context was that old staple of the Anglo-American common law, inchoate or preparatory conspiracy, and its American offshoot, conspiracy as an alternative theory of complicity that spreads the net wider than theories like aiding and abetting. *See* Edward M. Wise, *RICO and its Analogues: Some Comparative Considerations,* 27 SYRACUSE J. INT'L L. & COM. 303 (2000); Roger S. Clark, *The United Nations Convention against Transnational Organized Crime*, 50 WAYNE L. REV. 161 (2004). For the United States, as in the case of the Corruption Convention, the main agenda was to sell the ideas in the Convention to the rest of the world.

If success is measured in ratifications and accessions, the TOC Convention has done very well. It has 190 of them, including the Holy See and the European Union. (EU Members have delegated some of their criminal law power to the Union, so it is necessary for the Union to be a party in order to achieve maximum application of its provisions.) Ian Tennant (THE PROMISE OF PALERMO *supra* at 4) argues that it has been disappointing in its legislative and other implementation. He places significant hopes on the Implementation Review Mechanism, adopted by the Conference of the Parties, which States Parties are laboriously making operational as we write. (How enthusiastically they are working is a matter of debate.) On the Review Mechanism, which sets out to do a peer review of the performance of all parties to the Convention over the next few years, *see Mechanism for the Review of the Implementation of the United Nations Convention against Transnational Organised Crime and the Protocols thereto, available at* https://www.unodc.org/unodc/en/organized-crime/intro/revew-mechanism-untoc.html. Another leading commentator of the topic, Professor Neil Boister, also observes a disinclination to adopt the Convention's basic tools, especially its obligation to criminalize along the lines of the treaty. *See* Neil Boister, *The UN Convention against Transnational Organised Crime 2000, in* INTERNATIONAL LAW AND TRANSNATIONAL ORGANISED CRIME 126 (Pierre Hauck & Sven Peterke eds., 2016).

§ 11.02 The Convention

United Nations Convention on Transnational Organized Crime

General Assembly Resolution 55/25, Nov. 15, 2000

Article 1 Statement of purpose

The purpose of this Convention is to promote cooperation to prevent and combat transnational organized crime more effectively.

Article 2 Use of terms

For the purposes of this Convention:

(a) "Organized criminal group" shall mean a structured group of three or more persons, existing for a period of time and acting in concert with the aim of committing one or more serious crimes or offences established in accordance with this Convention, in order to obtain, directly or indirectly, a financial or other material benefit;

(b) "Serious crime" shall mean conduct constituting an offence punishable by a maximum deprivation of liberty of at least four years or a more serious penalty;

(c) "Structured group" shall mean a group that is not randomly formed for the immediate commission of an offence and that does not need to have formally defined roles for its members, continuity of its membership or a developed structure;

(d) "Property" shall mean assets of every kind, whether corporeal or incorporeal, movable or immovable, tangible or intangible, and legal documents or instruments evidencing title to, or interest in, such assets;

(e) "Proceeds of crime" shall mean any property derived from or obtained, directly or indirectly, through the commission of an offence;

(f) "Freezing" or "seizure" shall mean temporarily prohibiting the transfer, conversion, disposition or movement of property or temporarily assuming custody or control of property on the basis of an order issued by a court or other competent authority;

(g) "Confiscation", which includes forfeiture where applicable, shall mean the permanent deprivation of property by order of a court or other competent authority;

(h) "Predicate offence" shall mean any offence as a result of which proceeds have been generated that may become the subject of an offence as defined in article 6 of this Convention;

(i) "Controlled delivery" shall mean the technique of allowing illicit or suspect consignments to pass out of, through or into the territory of one or more States, with the knowledge and under the supervision of their competent authorities, with a view to the investigation of an offence and the identification of persons involved in the commission of the offence;

(j) "Regional economic integration organization" shall mean an organization constituted by sovereign States of a given region, to which its member States have transferred competence in respect of matters governed by this Convention and which has been duly authorized, in accordance with its internal procedures, to sign, ratify, accept, approve or accede to it; references to "States Parties" under this Convention shall apply to such organizations within the limits of their competence.

Article 3 Scope of application

1. This Convention shall apply, except as otherwise stated herein, to the prevention, investigation and prosecution of:

   (a) The offences established in accordance with articles 5, 6, 8 and 23 of this Convention; and

   (b) Serious crime as defined in article 2 of this Convention;

where the offence is transnational in nature and involves an organized criminal group.

2. For the purpose of paragraph 1 of this article, an offence is transnational in nature if:

(a) It is committed in more than one State;

(b) It is committed in one State but a substantial part of its preparation, planning, direction or control takes place in another State;

(c) It is committed in one State but involves an organized criminal group that engages in criminal activities in more than one State; or

(d) It is committed in one State but has substantial effects in another State.

Article 4 Protection of sovereignty

1. States Parties shall carry out their obligations under this Convention in a manner consistent with the principles of sovereign equality and territorial integrity of States and that of non-intervention in the domestic affairs of other States.

2. Nothing in this Convention entitles a State Party to undertake in the territory of another State the exercise of jurisdiction and performance of functions that are reserved exclusively for the authorities of that other State by its domestic law.

Article 5 Criminalization of participation in an organized criminal group

1. Each State Party shall adopt such legislative and other measures as may be necessary to establish as criminal offences, when committed intentionally:

(a) Either or both of the following as criminal offences distinct from those involving the attempt or completion of the criminal activity:

(i) Agreeing with one or more other persons to commit a serious crime for a purpose relating directly or indirectly to the obtaining of a financial or other material benefit and, where required by domestic law, involving an act undertaken by one of the participants in furtherance of the agreement or involving an organized criminal group;

(ii) Conduct by a person who, with knowledge of either the aim and general criminal activity of an organized criminal group or its intention to commit the crimes in question, takes an active part in:

a. Criminal activities of the organized criminal group;

b. Other activities of the organized criminal group in the knowledge that his or her participation will contribute to the achievement of the above-described criminal aim;

(b) Organizing, directing, aiding, abetting, facilitating or counselling the commission of serious crime involving an organized criminal group.

2. The knowledge, intent, aim, purpose or agreement referred to in paragraph 1 of this article may be inferred from objective factual circumstances.

3. States Parties whose domestic law requires involvement of an organized criminal group for purposes of the offences established in accordance with paragraph 1 (a) (i) of this article shall ensure that their domestic law covers all serious crimes involving organized criminal groups. Such States Parties, as well as States Parties whose domestic law requires an act in furtherance of the agreement for purposes of the offences established in accordance with paragraph 1 (a) (i) of this article, shall so inform the Secretary-General of the United Nations at the time of their signature or of deposit of their instrument of ratification, acceptance or approval of or accession to this Convention.

Article 6 Criminalization of the laundering of proceeds of crime

1. Each State Party shall adopt, in accordance with fundamental principles of its domestic law, such legislative and other measures as may be necessary to establish as criminal offences, when committed intentionally:

(a)(i) The conversion or transfer of property, knowing that such property is the proceeds of crime, for the purpose of concealing or disguising the illicit origin of the property or of helping any person who is involved in the commission of the predicate offence to evade the legal consequences of his or her action;

(ii) The concealment or disguise of the true nature, source, location, disposition, movement or ownership of or rights with respect to property, knowing that such property is the proceeds of crime;

(b)Subject to the basic concepts of its legal system:

(i) The acquisition, possession or use of property, knowing, at the time of receipt, that such property is the proceeds of crime;

(ii) Participation in, association with or conspiracy to commit, attempts to commit and aiding, abetting, facilitating and counselling the commission of any of the offences established in accordance with this article.

2. For purposes of implementing or applying paragraph 1 of this article:

(a) Each State Party shall seek to apply paragraph 1 of this article to the widest range of predicate offences;

(b) Each State Party shall include as predicate offences all serious crime as defined in article 2 of this Convention and the offences established in accordance with articles 5, 8 and 23 of this Convention. In the case of States Parties whose legislation sets out a list of specific predicate offences, they shall, at a minimum, include in such list a comprehensive range of offences associated with organized criminal groups;

(c) For the purposes of subparagraph (b), predicate offences shall include offences committed both within and outside the jurisdiction of the State Party in question. However, offences committed outside the jurisdiction of a State Party shall constitute predicate offences only when the relevant conduct is a criminal offence under the domestic law of the State where it is committed and would be a criminal offence under the domestic law of the State Party implementing or applying this article had it been committed there;

(d) Each State Party shall furnish copies of its laws that give effect to this article and of any subsequent changes to such laws or a description thereof to the Secretary-General of the United Nations;

(e) If required by fundamental principles of the domestic law of a State Party, it may be provided that the offences set forth in paragraph 1 of this article do not apply to the persons who committed the predicate offence;

(f) Knowledge, intent or purpose required as an element of an offence set forth in paragraph 1 of this article may be inferred from objective factual circumstances.

Article 7 Measures to combat money-laundering

1. Each State Party:

(a) Shall institute a comprehensive domestic regulatory and supervisory regime for banks and non-bank financial institutions and, where appropriate, other bodies particularly susceptible to money-laundering, within its competence, in order to deter and detect all forms of money-laundering, which regime shall emphasize requirements for customer identification, record-keeping and the reporting of suspicious transactions;(b)Shall, without prejudice to articles 18 and 27 of this Convention, ensure that administrative, regulatory, law enforcement and other authorities dedicated to combating money-laundering (including, where appropriate under domestic law, judicial authorities) have the ability to cooperate and exchange information at the national and international levels within the conditions prescribed by its domestic law and, to that end, shall consider the establishment of a financial intelligence unit to serve as a national centre for the collection, analysis and dissemination of information regarding potential money-laundering.

2. States Parties shall consider implementing feasible measures to detect and monitor the movement of cash and appropriate negotiable instruments across their borders, subject to safeguards to ensure proper use of information and without impeding in any way the movement of legitimate capital. Such measures may include a requirement that individuals and businesses report the cross-border transfer of substantial quantities of cash and appropriate negotiable instruments. . . . .

Article 8 Criminalization of corruption

1. Each State Party shall adopt such legislative and other measures as may be necessary to establish as criminal offences, when committed intentionally:

(a) The promise, offering or giving to a public official, directly or indirectly, of an undue advantage, for the official himself or herself or another person or entity, in order that the official act or refrain from acting in the exercise of his or her official duties;

(b) The solicitation or acceptance by a public official, directly or indirectly, of an undue advantage, for the official himself or herself or another person or entity, in order that the official act or refrain from acting in the exercise of his or her official duties.

2. Each State Party shall consider adopting such legislative and other measures as may be necessary to establish as criminal offences conduct referred to in paragraph 1 of this article involving a foreign public official or inter-national civil servant. Likewise, each State Party shall consider establishing as criminal offences other forms of corruption.

3. Each State Party shall also adopt such measures as may be necessary to establish as a criminal offence participation as an accomplice in an offence established in accordance with this article.

4. For the purposes of paragraph 1 of this article and article 9 of this Convention, "public official" shall mean a public official or a person who provides a public service as defined in the domestic law and as applied in the criminal law of the State Party in which the person in question performs that function. . . . .

Article 10 Liability of legal persons

1. Each State Party shall adopt such measures as may be necessary, consistent with its legal principles, to establish the liability of legal persons for participation in serious crimes involving an organized criminal group and for the offences established in accordance with articles 5, 6, 8 and 23 of this Convention.

2. Subject to the legal principles of the State Party, the liability of legal persons may be criminal, civil or administrative.

3. Such liability shall be without prejudice to the criminal liability of the natural persons who have committed the offences.

4. Each State Party shall, in particular, ensure that legal persons held liable in accordance with this article are subject to effective, proportionate and dissuasive criminal or non-criminal sanctions, including monetary sanctions.

Article 11 Prosecution, adjudication and sanctions

1. Each State Party shall make the commission of an offence established in accordance with articles 5, 6, 8 and 23 of this Convention liable to sanctions that take into account the gravity of that offence. . . . .

6. Nothing contained in this Convention shall affect the principle that the description of the offences established in accordance with this Convention and of the applicable legal defences or other legal principles controlling the lawfulness of conduct is reserved to the domestic law of a State Party and that such offences shall be prosecuted and punished in accordance with that law.

Article 12 Confiscation and seizure

1. States Parties shall adopt, to the greatest extent possible within their domestic legal systems, such measures as may be necessary to enable confiscation of:

(a) Proceeds of crime derived from offences covered by this Convention or property the value of which corresponds to that of such proceeds;

(b) Property, equipment or other instrumentalities used in or destined for use in offences covered by this Convention.

2. States Parties shall adopt such measures as may be necessary to enable the identification, tracing, freezing or seizure of any item referred to in paragraph 1 of this article for the purpose of eventual confiscation.

3. If proceeds of crime have been transformed or converted, in part or in full, into other property, such property shall be liable to the measures referred to in this article instead of the proceeds.

4. If proceeds of crime have been intermingled with property acquired from legitimate sources, such property shall, without prejudice to any powers relating to freezing or seizure, be liable to confiscation up to the assessed value of the intermingled proceeds. . . . .

Article 13 International cooperation for purposes of confiscation

1. A State Party that has received a request from another State Party having jurisdiction over an offence covered by this Convention for confiscation of proceeds of crime, property, equipment or other instrumentalities referred to in article 12, paragraph 1, of this Convention situated in its territory shall, to the greatest extent possible within its domestic legal system:

(a) Submit the request to its competent authorities for the purpose of obtaining an order of confiscation and, if such an order is granted, give effect to it; or

(b) Submit to its competent authorities, with a view to giving effect to it to the extent requested, an order of confiscation issued by a court in the territory of the requesting State Party in accordance with article 12, paragraph 1, of this Convention insofar as it relates to proceeds of crime, property, equipment or other instrumentalities referred to in article 12, paragraph 1, situated in the territory of the requested State Party. . . . .

6. If a State Party elects to make the taking of the measures referred to in paragraphs 1 and 2 of this article conditional on the existence of a relevant treaty, that State Party shall consider this Convention the necessary and sufficient treaty basis. . . . .

9. States Parties shall consider concluding bilateral or multilateral treaties, agreements or arrangements to enhance the effectiveness of inter-national cooperation undertaken pursuant to this article. . . . .

Article 15 Jurisdiction

1. Each State Party shall adopt such measures as may be necessary to establish its jurisdiction over the offences established in accordance with articles 5, 6, 8 and 23 of this Convention when:

(a) The offence is committed in the territory of that State Party; or

(b) The offence is committed on board a vessel that is flying the flag of that State Party or an aircraft that is registered under the laws of that State Party at the time that the offence is committed.

2. Subject to article 4 of this Convention, a State Party may also establish its jurisdiction over any such offence when:

(a) The offence is committed against a national of that State Party;

(b) The offence is committed by a national of that State Party or a stateless person who has his or her habitual residence in its territory; or

(c) The offence is:

(i) One of those established in accordance with article 5, paragraph 1, of this Convention and is committed outside its territory with a view to the commission of a serious crime within its territory;

(ii) One of those established in accordance with article 6, paragraph 1 (b) (ii), of this Convention and is committed outside its territory with a view to the commission of an offence established in accordance with article 6, paragraph 1 (a) (i) or (ii) or (b) (i),of this Convention within its territory.

3. For the purposes of article 16, paragraph 10, of this Convention, each State Party shall adopt such measures as may be necessary to establish its jurisdiction over the offences covered by this Convention when the alleged offender is present in its territory and it does not extradite such person solely on the ground that he or she is one of its nationals.

4. Each State Party may also adopt such measures as may be necessary to establish its jurisdiction over the offences covered by this Convention when the alleged offender is present in its territory and it does not extradite him or her.

5. If a State Party exercising its jurisdiction under paragraph 1 or 2 of this article has been notified, or has otherwise learned, that one or more other States Parties are conducting an investigation, prosecution or judicial proceeding in respect of the same conduct, the competent authorities of those States Parties shall, as appropriate, consult one another with a view to coordinating their actions.

6. Without prejudice to norms of general international law, this Convention does not exclude the exercise of any criminal jurisdiction established by a State Party in accordance with its domestic law.

Article 16 Extradition

1. This article shall apply to the offences covered by this Convention or in cases where an offence referred to in article 3, paragraph 1 (a) or (b), involves an organized criminal group and the person who is the subject of the request for extradition is located in the territory of the requested State Party, provided that the offence

for which extradition is sought is punishable under the domestic law of both the requesting State Party and the requested State Party.

2. If the request for extradition includes several separate serious crimes, some of which are not covered by this article, the requested State Party may apply this article also in respect of the latter offences.

3. Each of the offences to which this article applies shall be deemed to be included as an extraditable offence in any extradition treaty existing between States Parties. States Parties undertake to include such offences as extraditable offences in every extradition treaty to be concluded between them.

4. If a State Party that makes extradition conditional on the existence of a treaty receives a request for extradition from another State Party with which it has no extradition treaty, it may consider this Convention the legal basis for extradition in respect of any offence to which this article applies.

5. States Parties that make extradition conditional on the existence of a treaty shall:

(a) At the time of deposit of their instrument of ratification, acceptance, approval of or accession to this Convention, inform the Secretary-General of the United Nations they will take this Convention as the legal basis for cooperation on extradition with other States Parties to this Convention; and

(b) If they do not take this Convention as the legal basis for cooperation on extradition, seek, where appropriate, to conclude treaties on extradition with other States Parties to this Convention in order to implement this article.

6. States Parties that do not make extradition conditional on the existence of a treaty shall recognize offences to which this article applies as extraditable offences between themselves.

7. Extradition shall be subject to the conditions provided for by the domestic law of the requested State Party or by applicable extradition treaties, including, inter alia, conditions in relation to the minimum penalty requirement for extradition and the grounds upon which the requested State Party may refuse extradition.

8. States Parties shall, subject to their domestic law, endeavour to expedite extradition procedures and to simplify evidentiary requirements relating thereto in respect of any offence to which this article applies.

9. Subject to the provisions of its domestic law and its extradition treaties, the requested State Party may, upon being satisfied that the circumstances so warrant and are urgent and at the request of the requesting State Party, take a person whose extradition is sought and who is present in its territory into custody or take other appropriate measures to ensure his or her presence at extradition proceedings.

10. A State Party in whose territory an alleged offender is found, if it does not extradite such person in respect of an offence to which this article applies solely on the ground that he or she is one of its nationals, shall, at the request of the State

Party seeking extradition, be obliged to submit the case without undue delay to its competent authorities for the purpose of prosecution. Those authorities shall take their decision and conduct their proceedings in the same manner as in the case of any other offence of a grave nature under the domestic law of that State Party. The States Parties concerned shall cooperate with each other, in particular on procedural and evidentiary aspects, to ensure the efficiency of such prosecution.

11. Whenever a State Party is permitted under its domestic law to extradite or otherwise surrender one of its nationals only upon the condition that the person will be returned to that State Party to serve the sentence imposed as a result of the trial or proceedings for which the extradition or surrender of the person was sought and that State Party and the State Party seeking the extradition of the person agree with this option and other terms that they may deem appropriate, such conditional extradition or surrender shall be sufficient to discharge the obligation set forth in paragraph 10 of this article.

12. If extradition, sought for purposes of enforcing a sentence, is refused because the person sought is a national of the requested State Party, the requested Party shall, if its domestic law so permits and in conformity with the requirements of such law, upon application of the requesting Party, consider the enforcement of the sentence that has been imposed under the domestic law of the requesting Party or the remainder thereof.

13. Any person regarding whom proceedings are being carried out in connection with any of the offences to which this article applies shall be guaranteed fair treatment at all stages of the proceedings, including enjoyment of all the rights and guarantees provided by the domestic law of the State Party in the territory of which that person is present.

14. Nothing in this Convention shall be interpreted as imposing an obligation to extradite if the requested State Party has substantial grounds for believing that the request has been made for the purpose of prosecuting or punishing a person on account of that person's sex, race, religion, nationality, ethnic origin or political opinions or that compliance with the request would cause prejudice to that person's position for any one of these reasons.

15. States Parties may not refuse a request for extradition on the sole ground that the offence is also considered to involve fiscal matters.

16. Before refusing extradition, the requested State Party shall, where appropriate, consult with the requesting State Party to provide it with ample opportunity to present its opinions and to provide information relevant to its allegation.

17. States Parties shall seek to conclude bilateral and multilateral agreements or arrangements to carry out or to enhance the effectiveness of extradition.

Article 17 Transfer of sentenced persons

States Parties may consider entering into bilateral or multilateral agreements or arrangements on the transfer to their territory of persons sentenced to imprisonment or other forms of deprivation of liberty for offences covered by this Convention, in order that they may complete their sentences there.

Article 18 Mutual legal assistance

1. States Parties shall afford one another the widest measure of mutual legal assistance in investigations, prosecutions and judicial proceedings in relation to the offences covered by this Convention as provided for in article 3 and shall reciprocally extend to one another similar assistance where the requesting State Party has reasonable grounds to suspect that the offence referred to in article 3, paragraph 1 (a) or (b), is transnational in nature, including that victims, witnesses, proceeds, instrumentalities or evidence of such offences are located in the requested State Party and that the offence involves an organized criminal group. . . . .

Article 19 Joint investigations

States Parties shall consider concluding bilateral or multilateral agreements or arrangements whereby, in relation to matters that are the subject of investigations, prosecutions or judicial proceedings in one or more States, the competent authorities concerned may establish joint investigative bodies. In the absence of such agreements or arrangements, joint investigations may be undertaken by agreement on a case-by-case basis. The States Parties involved shall ensure that the sovereignty of the State Party in whose territory such investigation is to take place is fully respected.

Article 20 Special investigative techniques

1. If permitted by the basic principles of its domestic legal system, each State Party shall, within its possibilities and under the conditions prescribed by its domestic law, take the necessary measures to allow for the appropriate use of controlled delivery and, where it deems appropriate, for the use of other special investigative techniques, such as electronic or other forms of surveillance and undercover operations, by its competent authorities in its territory for the purpose of effectively combating organized crime. . . . .

Article 21 Transfer of criminal proceedings

States Parties shall consider the possibility of transferring to one another proceedings for the prosecution of an offence covered by this Convention in cases where such transfer is considered to be in the interests of the proper administration of justice, in particular in cases where several jurisdictions are involved, with a view to concentrating the prosecution.

Article 22 Establishment of criminal record

Each State Party may adopt such legislative or other measures as may be necessary to take into consideration, under such terms as and for the purpose that it deems appropriate, any previous conviction in another State of an alleged offender for the purpose of using such information in criminal to an offence covered by this Convention. . . . .

Article 23 Criminalization of obstruction of justice

Each State Party shall adopt such legislative and other measures as may be necessary to establish as criminal offences, when committed intentionally

(a) The use of physical force, threats or intimidation or the promise, offering or giving of an undue advantage to induce false testimony or to interfere in the giving of testimony or the production of evidence in a proceeding in relation to the commission of offences covered by this Convention;(

(b) The use of physical force, threats or intimidation to interfere with the exercise of official duties by a justice or law enforcement official in relation to the commission of offences covered by this Convention. Nothing in this subparagraph shall prejudice the right of States Parties to have legislation that protects other categories of public officials.

Article 25 Assistance to and protection of victims

1. Each State Party shall take appropriate measures within its means to provide assistance and protection to victims of offences covered by this Convention, in particular in cases of threat of retaliation or intimidation.

2. Each State Party shall establish appropriate procedures to provide access to compensation and restitution for victims of offences covered by this Convention.

3. Each State Party shall, subject to its domestic law, enable views and concerns of victims to be presented and considered at appropriate stages of criminal proceedings against offenders in a manner not prejudicial to the rights of the defence. . . . .

Article 32 Conference of the Parties to the Convention

1. A Conference of the Parties to the Convention is hereby established to improve the capacity of States Parties to combat transnational organized crime and to promote and review the implementation of this Convention.

2. The Secretary-General of the United Nations shall convene the Conference of the Parties not later than one year following the entry into force of this Convention. The Conference of the Parties shall adopt rules of procedure and rules governing the activities set forth in paragraphs 3 and 4 of this article (including rules concerning payment of expenses incurred in carrying out those activities).

3. The Conference of the Parties shall agree upon mechanisms for achieving the objectives mentioned in paragraph 1 of this article, including:

(a) Facilitating activities by States Parties under articles 29, 30 and 31 of this Convention, including by encouraging the mobilization of voluntary contributions;

(b) Facilitating the exchange of information among States Parties on patterns and trends in transnational organized crime and on successful practices for combating it;

(c) Cooperating with relevant international and regional organizations and non-governmental organizations;

(d) Reviewing periodically the implementation of this Convention;

(e) Making recommendations to improve this Convention and its implementation.

4. For the purpose of paragraphs 3 (d) and (e) of this article, the Conference of the Parties shall acquire the necessary knowledge of the measures taken by States Parties in implementing this Convention and the difficulties encountered by them in doing so through information provided by them and through such supplemental review mechanisms as may be established by the Conference of the Parties.

5. Each State Party shall provide the Conference of the Parties with information on its programmes, plans and practices, as well as legislative and administrative measures to implement this Convention, as required by the Conference of the Parties. . . . .

Article 34 Implementation of the Convention

1. Each State Party shall take the necessary measures, including legislative and administrative measures, in accordance with fundamental principles of its domestic law, to ensure the implementation of its obligations under this Convention.

2. The offences established in accordance with articles 5, 6, 8 and 23 of this Convention shall be established in the domestic law of each State Party independently of the transnational nature or the involvement of an organized criminal group as described in article 3, paragraph 1, of this Convention, except to the extent that article 5 of this Convention would require the involvement of an organized criminal group.

3. Each State Party may adopt more strict or severe measures than those provided for by this Convention for preventing and combating transnational organized crime.

Notes

(1) The United States ratified with three reservations:

Reservation:

(1) The United States of America reserves the right to assume obligations under the Convention in a manner consistent with its fundamental principles of federalism, pursuant to which both federal and state criminal laws must be considered in relation to the conduct addressed in the Convention. U.S. federal criminal law, which regulates conduct based on its effect on interstate or foreign commerce, or another federal interest, serves as the

principal legal regime within the United States for combating organized crime, and is broadly effective for this purpose. Federal criminal law does not apply in the rare case where such criminal conduct does not so involve interstate or foreign commerce, or another federal interest. There are a small number of conceivable situations involving such rare offenses of a purely local character where U.S. federal and state criminal law may not be entirely adequate to satisfy an obligation under the Convention. The United States of America therefore reserves to the obligations set forth in the Convention to the extent they address conduct which would fall within this narrow category of highly localized activity. This reservation does not affect in any respect the ability of the United States to provide international cooperation to other Parties as contemplated in the Convention.

(2) The United States of America reserves the right not to apply in part the obligation set forth in Article 15, paragraph 1 (b) with respect to the offenses established in the Convention. The United States does not provide for plenary jurisdiction over offenses that are committed on board ships flying its flag or aircraft registered under its laws. However, in a number of circumstances, U.S. law provides for jurisdiction over such offenses committed on board U.S. -flagged ships or aircraft registered under U.S. law. Accordingly, the United States will implement paragraph 1 (b) to the extent provided for under its federal law.

(3) In accordance with Article 35, paragraph 3 [obligation to refer disputes to the ICJ], the United States of America declares that it does not consider itself bound by the obligation set forth in Article 35, paragraph 2.

The first reservation is an acknowledgment of federalism. But what it means may be questioned. Could *Missouri v. Holland*, 252 U.S. 416 (1920), have been invoked to justify any necessary federal legislation? The second reservation relates back to the *Lotus* issue in Chapter 1. Customary international law, to say nothing of Article 15 of the present Convention, permits (requires?) U.S. jurisdiction over what happens aboard its ships and aircraft. And, as a matter of domestic law, federal power could be asserted via the commerce, treaty, and necessary and proper clauses of the Constitution. But the reservation suggests that the U.S. does not want to legislate to the full extent permitted by international law. Can this be explained, and if so, what explanations would be provided? Surprisingly perhaps, no other States Parties to the Convention objected to these two reservations. (The third reservation is standard in multilateral treaty practice, although such reservations sometimes generate objections by other parties.)

(2) This Convention, like many legal instruments, makes sense only upon a careful reading of its definition provisions. Note in particular in Article 2 ("use of terms"), the definitions of "organized criminal group," "serious crime" and "structured group." Then, in Article 3 ("scope of application"), note the definition of "transnational in nature." Notice how the possibility of four years imprisonment,

rather than any specific subject-matter content, supplies the threshold for what crimes are included.

(3) In 2012, UNODC, in cooperation with the Governments of Colombia and Italy, and of INTERPOL, published a very useful study of then-existing domestic case-law and experience with the Convention. *See* UNODC, DIGEST OF ORGANISED CRIME CASES: A COMPILATION OF CASES WITH COMMENTARIES AND LESSONS LEARNED (2012). The study comments, at 21 (footnotes omitted), that:

> The core aim of the Palermo Convention's criminal policy is "dismantling organized criminal groups" and it is reflected in every sector, including prevention, investigation and prosecution. The offence of participation in an organized criminal group as foreseen in article 5 of the Convention can be considered a reflection of the same policy applied to criminalization. Criminal offences such as conspiracy and criminal association existed in many legal systems long before that policy was affirmed at the international level but they took on primary importance when the underlying criminal structure was declared one of the main targets of law enforcement.... In addition, the expanded criminal liability targets not only the heads of a criminal organization, who plan, coordinate and manage, but do not always participate in, the material commission of the "final offences," but also persons participating in non-criminal activities that nevertheless contribute to the criminal capacity of a group.

(4) The Convention has some language that provides deference to state sovereignty and fundamental principles of domestic criminal law. *See, e.g.*, Article 4(1), Article 5(1)(i), Article 6(1), Article 11(6), Article 12(1), Article 19 and Article 34(1). Article 4(2) is a reiteration of the fundamental point made in *The Lotus* [chap. 1] that "[t]he first and foremost restriction imposed by international law upon a State is that—failing the existence of a permissive rule to the contrary—it may not exercise its power in any form in the territory of another State." Some may argue that several provisions in the Convention (dealing for example with extradition and mutual legal assistance) could be seen as intrusive, but the Convention itself creates a "permissive rule." And if considered "permissive," there are limits that can also be asserted. International and transnational criminal law always have the issue of balancing with domestic criminal law.

(5) Article 5(1) is the core suppression obligation to criminalize group activities. It is obligatory to criminalize one of two suppression crimes (or both). (There does not appear to be a situation where a State adopted both options.) It provides an example of drafting which takes account of different legal traditions but aims at a functional end which all parties can live with. The first (Article 5 (a)(i)), while it studiously avoids the word, can be claimed to be aimed at the Anglo-American doctrine of conspiracy as an inchoate offense. With a few exceptions (such as the Genocide Convention), conspiracy is not a common doctrine in international or transnational suppression treaties. As the example of Article 5 indicates, it may be gaining more

traction. Article 5(a)(ii), on the other hand, is more attractive to civil law systems where conspiracy has not found favor. It penalizes those who associate themselves with a criminal group.

(6) We have seen, for example, in dealing with the drug trade [chap. 8] that ancillary offenses like money laundering have become increasingly important in modern suppression conventions. This Convention added corruption to the mix, a proscription taken further in the Convention against Corruption [chap. 4].

(7) Article 10 on liability of legal persons can be regarded as a significant breakthrough in negotiation. Some legal systems still have conceptual problems with an acceptance of corporate responsibility (especially of a criminal nature). Only two years earlier when the Statute of the International Criminal Court was being finalized in Rome, proponents of criminality of corporate entities for the international crimes therein (genocide, crimes against humanity war crimes and the crime of aggression) were unable to negotiate adequate language to include in the Rome Statute. [chap. 22.] One can look at Article 10 and see how "criminal" the obligation is and the extent to which it also preserves individual criminal responsibility. Shell corporations and even partially legitimate operations may, for example, be deeply involved in the laundering of money gained by organized crime. Art galleries and museums may be involved knowingly with organized crime in the illicit trade in cultural property. Otherwise legitimate trucking companies may be engaged in transporting drugs or smuggling arms or migrants. For a comprehensive discussion of corporate criminal responsibility with many useful references, *see* Carsten Stahn, *Liberals vs Romantics: Challenges of an Emerging Corporate International Criminal Law*, 50 Case West. Res. J. Int'l L. 91 (2018).

(8) Article 15 is the key jurisdictional provision. Note the (now typical) mix of obligatory and permissive jurisdictional bases aimed at diminishing the scope for safe havens. Is it as far-reaching as some of the other treaties encountered in this area of law?

(9) Extradition (Article 16), transfer of sentenced prisoners (Article 17), mutual legal assistance (Article 18) and transfer of proceedings (Article 21) are all important issues in bilateral and regional practice which are discussed in other chapters. Here, detailed multilateral provisions are available to fill the gaps in bilateral or regional treaty obligations. They do not appear to have been used all that much. They require domestic legislation, bureaucratic domestication and a culture of cooperation which is still lacking in some quarters.

(10) Article 22 addresses the age-old problem of the relevance of "foreign" convictions for evidentiary, sentencing or other recidivism purposes. [*See also* § 18.02.] Is the result here obligatory or permissive?

(11) In 1985, the UN General Assembly adopted its Declaration of Basic Principles of Justice for Victims of Crime and Abuse of Power, G.A. Res. 40/34. The sentiments of that Declaration are carried forward here in Article 25 of the Organized Crime

Convention which promises assistance and protection for victims. Paragraph 2 and 3 of Article 25 echo specific language from the 1985 Declaration, and similar material appears in Article 6 of the Trafficking Protocol [§12.02]. *See also* Article 68 of the Rome Statute of the International Criminal Court [chap. 22].

(12) The Convention did not provide directly for any international implementation devices. But it did empower the Assembly of the Parties to "agree upon mechanisms," *inter alia*, for "[r]eviewing periodically the implementation of this Convention." (Article 32(3)(d).) It is pursuant to this provision that the parties have created an Implementation Review Mechanism, aimed at encouraging legislative and administrative compliance with the obligations of the Convention. A feature of many human rights and some international criminal law treaties is the establishment of regular meeting of those who have ratified or acceded to the relevant treaty to examine developments. This is one such Assembly of the Parties at work, using the notion of a living instrument and creating a further entity to take matters further.

Chapter 12

Human Trafficking

§ 12.01 Domestic Legislation

Human trafficking is considered a "form of modern-day slavery," and its victims can be "subjected to force, fraud, or coercion for the purpose of commercial sex or forced labor." National Human Trafficking Hotline, available at https://humantraffickinghotline.org/; *see also* U.S. Department of Health & Human Services, Office on Trafficking in Persons, What Is Human Trafficking, *available at* https://www.acf.hhs.gov/otip/about/what-human-trafficking. The importance of combatting human trafficking in the United States is emphasized by the May 2015 statute that calls for the Attorney General to "implement and maintain" a national strategy to combat human trafficking. 34 U.S.C. § 20701; *see also* 22 U.S.C. § 7103(d) (establishing an interagency task force to monitor and combat trafficking). The strategy is to ensure "[i]ntegrated Federal, State, local, and tribal efforts to investigate and prosecute trafficking cases."

A. The Trafficking Victims Protection Act

In 2000, the United States passed the Trafficking Victims Protection Act ("TVPA"). The stated purpose of the TVPA was to "combat trafficking in persons, especially into the sex trade, slavery, and involuntary servitude, to reauthorize certain Federal programs to prevent violence against women, and for other purposes." *See* Trafficking Victims Protection Act (P.L. 106-386) (Oct. 28, 2000); *see also* 22 U.S.C. § 7101(b) (congressional findings regarding human trafficking). To further this purpose, the TVPA called for the creation of a President's Interagency Task Force to Monitor and Combat Trafficking to coordinate efforts amongst various agencies. *See* 22 U.S.C. § 7103. The main federal agencies involved in this effort are the Department of Health and Human Services, Department of Justice, Department of Labor, Department of State, and Department of Homeland Security.

The TVPA also created new federal criminal provisions addressing human trafficking, many of which have been amended over the years. *See* Trafficking Victims Protection Reauthorization Act of 2003 (H.R. 2620); Trafficking Victims Protection Reauthorization Act of 2005 (H.R. 972); Trafficking Victims Protection Reauthorization Act of 2008 (H.R. 7311); Trafficking Victims Protection Reauthorization Act of 2013 (H.R. 898); Trafficking Victims Protection Act of 2017 (S. 1312). The laws added in 2000 supplemented existing federal laws regarding slavery, peonage, and involuntary servitude.

Current statutes provide penalties for "[w]hoever holds or returns any person to a condition of peonage, or arrests any person with the intent of placing him in or returning him to a condition of peonage." The statute provides for a 20-year penalty that can be increased for certain aggravating factors such as when death results. Obstructing or attempting to obstruct the enforcement of this activity is also penalized. (*See* 18 U.S.C. §1581—Peonage; obstructing enforcement). Likewise, there are statutes for Sale into involuntary servitude (18 U.S.C. §1584); Forced labor (18 U.S.C. §1589); Trafficking with respect to peonage, slavery, involuntary servitude, or forced labor (18 U.S.C. §1590); and Sex trafficking of children or by force, fraud, or coercion (18 U.S.C. §1591). Consider the following case:

United States v. Farrell

United States Court of Appeals for the Eighth Circuit
563 F.3d 364 (2009)

MELLOY, CIRCUIT JUDGE.

A jury convicted Robert John Farrell and Angelita Magat Farrell of four counts of peonage in violation of 18 U.S.C. §1581, one count of conspiracy to commit peonage in violation of 18 U.S.C. §371, two counts of making false statements in violation of 18 U.S.C. §1001, one count of visa fraud in violation of 18 U.S.C. §1546, and one count of document servitude in violation of 18 U.S.C. §1592. The Farrells appeal, arguing that the evidence was insufficient to support the jury's verdict as to the charges of peonage, conspiracy to commit peonage, and document servitude. The Farrells further argue that the district court erred in admitting certain expert testimony....

The Farrells own and operate the Comfort Inn & Suites in Oacoma, South Dakota. In both 2005 and 2006, the Farrells contracted to bring nine non-immigrant workers from the Philippines to the United States under temporary visas for the stated purpose of working as housekeepers in their hotel. The Government charged the Farrells with committing crimes against four of the nine. The Farrells assert that the Government presented insufficient evidence at trial to allow a reasonable jury to convict them of peonage, conspiracy to commit peonage, and document servitude....

While visiting family in the Philippines in 2005, the Farrells began actively recruiting Filipino workers to come and work for them in the United States. After soliciting several individuals, the Farrells submitted an I-129 Petition for a Nonimmigrant Worker ("Petition") to the Department of Homeland Security on August 17, 2005. The Petition stated that they were seeking housekeepers from October 1, 2005, until January 31, 2006, at a salary of $300 per week. The Farrells were required to pay the government a one-time processing fee of $1,200 with the submission of the Petition.

In addition to the Petition, the Farrells drafted employment contracts for each of the nine workers they had solicited. As with the Petition, these contracts stated that the Farrells would employ the workers as housekeepers and that the workers would work six days per week for eight hours each day. The contracts set compensation at $6.05 per hour and also provided for holiday and overtime pay. In addition to these provisions, the contracts stated that the Farrells were responsible for housing the workers and that each worker would reimburse the Farrells $150 per month for this expense. The contracts also provided that the Farrells were responsible for the cost of transportation to and from the United States, as required by law. After the Farrells submitted the Petition and drafted the employment contracts, the workers filed their applications for non-immigrant visas with the U.S. Embassy in Manila, Philippines. The applications reflected the terms of the employment contracts as recounted above, including the promise that the Farrells would pay for the workers' transportation to and from the United States.

Prior to the consular officers' adjudication of the workers' visa applications, the workers met with the Farrells in a Manila hotel. During this meeting, the Farrells prepped the workers for the visa interviews at the Embassy. The Farrells also revealed additional details about the job, including the fact that despite the provisions in the employment contracts and the requirements of U.S. law, the Farrells would not reimburse the workers for transportation to and from the United States. The Farrells stressed, however, that the workers' visas would be denied if the workers told this information to the consular officers and that they should refrain from mentioning it. The Farrells further stated that despite the contractual provisions, the workers would not receive holiday or overtime pay. Finally, the Farrells informed the workers that the $1,200 Petition-processing fee would be divided equally among them. . . .

When the workers arrived in South Dakota in November 2005, the employment situation was not as they had anticipated. [Immediately they were required] to surrender their passports, visas, and immigration documents. Many of the workers were reluctant to do so but obeyed out of the "honor and respect" Filipino culture demanded they show their employers. Upon starting their jobs, the Farrells informed the workers that instead of an hourly wage they would be paid $3 per room. . . . The Farrells further informed the workers that each of the nine would be individually responsible for the entire amount of the $1,200 processing fee, despite the fact that the Farrells only paid the fee once.

In addition to the processing fee, the Farrells began charging the workers for transportation to and from work (which had not been agreed to in the employment contract) and began charging them for personal items that the workers neither requested nor desired. Thus, once in the United States, the workers' debt increased dramatically while the income with which they anticipated being able to pay down that debt had decreased by at least one-half. Recognizing that the workers would not be able to pay their increasing debt from their hotel paychecks, the Farrells required that the workers obtain outside employment. The Farrells facilitated the workers' interviews at local fast-food restaurants and other service-industry establishments. Many of the locations where the workers interviewed eventually employed the workers, in direct violation of their visas.

Other than when at their non-hotel employment, the workers spent little time away from the hotel. This was, in part, because of the manner in which the Farrells controlled the workers' free time. The workers were not permitted to leave their shared apartment, even to visit the drug store, without asking permission from either the Farrells or the hotel manager.... Frequently, the Farrells told the workers that they were not to speak with anyone outside of the hotel and that they were prohibited from socializing with Americans. The prohibition against speaking to other people went so far as to preclude the workers from speaking to the non-Filipino workers who were employed at the same hotel....

Peonage is "compulsory service in payment of a debt." ... "[C]ompulsory service" is the equivalent of "involuntary servitude," ... which the Supreme Court has defined as "a condition of servitude in which the victim is forced to work for the defendant by the use or threat of physical restraint or physical injury, or by the use or threat of coercion through law or the legal process." ... Thus, in order to prove peonage, the government must show that the defendant intentionally held a person against his or her will and coerced that person to work in order to satisfy a debt by (1) physical restraint or force, (2) legal coercion, or (3) threats of legal coercion or physical force.... In determining whether "physical or legal coercion or threats thereof could plausibly have compelled the victim to serve," the jury is entitled to consider "evidence of other means of coercion, or of poor working conditions, or of the victim's special vulnerabilities."

In this case, a reasonable jury could have found that the Government proved the elements of peonage beyond a reasonable doubt.... [T]he workers testified extensively about their treatment while in the Farrells' employment. They testified that Robert threatened them with physical force; namely, that if they attempted to "run away" he would find them, "put them in a balikbayan box," and ship them back to the Philippines....

In addition to showing the Farrells threatened the workers with physical force, arrest, and imprisonment, the evidence further supports the jury's finding that these threats actually compelled the workers to serve in order to satisfy their debt when viewed in conjunction with the workers' working and living conditions, as well as their particular vulnerabilities.... The evidence is clear that the workers subjectively feared the Farrells.... There was also sufficient evidence to show that the workers reasonably believed that their employers were "powerful people" and could indeed "hunt them down" if the workers left....

The Farrells continually isolated the workers from others in the community by refusing to allow them to speak or socialize with non-Filipino co-workers, by channeling all mail through the hotel where it had to be opened in the presence of the hotel manager, by refusing to allow them to leave the apartment to perform even the most mundane tasks without asking for permission, and by refusing to allow the workers to travel or otherwise spend their free time outside the hotel or apartment.... In addition to this social isolation, the Farrells attempted to control every other aspect of the workers' lives. They dictated the amount of money the workers were able to send back to the Philippines and for what purpose; required the workers to post-date checks that the workers knew they would not be able to cover unless they continued working at the hotel; and kept a key to the workers' residence so that they could conduct random inspections of the premises while refusing to allow the workers a key of their own

Furthermore, the coercive nature of the threats is amplified by the workers' "special vulnerabilities," . . . which include the fact that the workers were in the United States under temporary-work visas sponsored by the Farrells. Many of the workers arrived in the United States with very little money and were entirely dependent upon the Farrells for their housing and transportation. . . .

The Farrells argue that the possibility of deportation alone was insufficient to provide the requisite compulsion for peonage because being deported to the Philippines was not the equivalent of "imprisonment or worse," . . . Even assuming, as the Farrells' argument requires, that the only thing that kept the workers laboring was a fear of being deported, we are not persuaded. Here, the threat of deportation was more than a threat of removal from the United States or a threat to legitimately use the legal process to ensure that the workers abided by the terms of their visas. The Farrells had made it clear during various meetings that they would seek to collect the money the workers owed no matter where the workers went. It would have been extremely difficult, if not impossible, for the workers to meet their debt obligations on salaries in the Philippines. Based on Robert's threats that he would hunt the workers down and harm them if they failed to pay their debts, it was not unreasonable for the workers to believe that failure to pay their debt, even when back in the Philippines, would result in physical harm. As a consequence, here the threat of deportation was, in essence, a threat of force. . . .

The Farrells repeatedly claim that the workers' employment was voluntary and because voluntariness is a defense to the peonage charge, it is impossible for the workers' employment to have constituted involuntary servitude. As evidence of the voluntary nature of the employment, they cite the workers' return to the United States in the spring of 2006 for a second contractual term and to the fact that they allowed one worker to return to the Philippines to care for her ailing mother. Despite their argument, however, based on the evidence recounted above, a reasonable trier of fact could have concluded that the workers were not, in fact, free to leave and that it was the Farrells' coercive acts that compelled the workers to stay in the United States and return on a second work visa in order to satisfy their debts. . . .

The jury's conviction of the Farrells of conspiracy to commit peonage was sufficiently supported by the Government's evidence. The jury could infer from the Farrells' joint and extensive involvement in the visa application procedure, in the running of the hotel, and in the administration of the housing that the Farrells knowingly entered into an agreement to hold the workers in a condition of peonage. . . .

The Farrells also contest the sufficiency of the evidence with regard to their conviction for document servitude. In order to prove that the Farrells committed document servitude, the Government must show that the Farrells (1) concealed, removed, confiscated, or possessed the workers' passports, visas, or other immigration documents; (2) did these acts in the course of violating the peonage statute with the intent to violate the statute; and (3) acted knowingly and intentionally. 18 U.S.C. § 1592(a).

The evidence at trial was sufficient for a reasonable jury to convict the Farrells of document servitude. The Farrells do not contest that Angelita [Farrell] confiscated the workers' passports, visas, and entry cards upon their arrival in the United States in both 2005 and 2006. The Farrells also do not contest that they knowingly retained possession of these documents throughout the workers' entire stay.... The chief of police further indicated that even after he specifically requested that Robert turn the workers' immigration documents over to the workers, Robert still refused. It was only after the chief of police threatened to arrest him for theft that Robert complied.

In addition to having confiscated and knowingly possessed the passports, as outlined extensively above, there was sufficient evidence that the Farrells had the intent to commit peonage and retained the documents while committing peonage. Because the evidence was such that a reasonable jury could have concluded that the Farrells committed document servitude, we affirm the conviction....

For the foregoing reasons, we affirm the convictions.

Notes

(1) 18 U.S.C. § 1596 (Additional Jurisdiction in Certain Trafficking Offenses), added as part of the William Wilberforce Victims Protection Reauthorization Act of 2008 (P.L.) (Dec. 23, 2008), permits extraterritorial jurisdiction in cases involving offenses under 18 U.S.C. §§ 1581, 1583, 1584, 1589, 1590, and 1591 if "an alleged offender is a national of the United States or an alien lawfully admitted for permanent residence" or "an alleged offender is present in the United States, irrespective of the nationality of the alleged offender." What principles form the basis for these assertions of jurisdiction?

(2) In addition to 18 U.S.C. § 1591 (Sex trafficking in children or by force, fraud, or coercion), the PROTECT Act of 2003 created criminal liability under 18 U.S.C. § 2423 for U.S. citizens and permanent residents who travel abroad to engage in any "illicit sexual conduct" with a minor.

> (b) Travel With Intent To Engage in Illicit Sexual Conduct.—A person who travels in interstate commerce or travels into the United States, or a United States citizen or an alien admitted for permanent residence in the United States who travels in foreign commerce, with a motivating purpose of engaging in any illicit sexual conduct with another person shall be fined under this title or imprisoned not more than 30 years, or both.
>
> (c) Engaging in Illicit Sexual Conduct in Foreign Places.—Any United States citizen or alien admitted for permanent residence who

> travels in foreign commerce or resides, either temporarily or permanently, in a foreign country, and engages in any illicit sexual conduct with another person shall be fined under this title or imprisoned not more than 30 years, or both.
>
> . . . .
>
> (f) DEFINITION.—As used in this section, the term "illicit sexual conduct" means—
>
> > (1) a sexual act (as defined in section 2246) with a person under 18 years of age that would be in violation of chapter 109A if the sexual act occurred in the special maritime and territorial jurisdiction of the United States;
> >
> > (2) any commercial sex act (as defined in section 1591) with a person under 18 years of age; or
> >
> > (3) production of child pornography (as defined in section 2256(8)).
>
> (g) DEFENSE.—In a prosecution under this section based on illicit sexual conduct as defined in subsection (f)(2), it is a defense, which the defendant must establish by clear and convincing evidence, that the defendant reasonably believed that the person with whom the defendant engaged in the commercial sex act had attained the age of 18 years.

(3) The United States has provided for special protections to victims of this illicit activity. This includes the creation of special immigration provisions for victims of human trafficking in the United States.

T Nonimmigrant Eligibility

You may be eligible for a T visa if you:

- Are or were a victim of a severe form of trafficking in persons as defined above;
- Are physically present in the United States, American Samoa, the Commonwealth of the Northern Mariana Islands, or at a port of entry due to trafficking;
- Have complied with any reasonable request from a law enforcement agency for assistance in the investigation or prosecution of human trafficking (unless you were under the age of 18 at the time at least one of the acts of trafficking occurred or you are unable to cooperate due to physical or psychological trauma; if either case applies, you may not need to show that you complied with reasonable requests from law enforcement);
- Demonstrate that you would suffer extreme hardship involving unusual and severe harm if you were removed from the United States; and
- Are admissible to the United States. (If you are not admissible, you may be eligible for a waiver of certain grounds of inadmissibility. You may apply for a waiver using a Form I-192, Application for Advance Permission to Enter as a Nonimmigrant, *available at* https://www.uscis.gov/i-192).

Victims of Human Trafficking: T Nonimmigrant Status, U.S. Citizenship and Immigration Services, U.S. Department of Homeland Security, *available at* http://www.uscis.gov/humanitarian/victims-human-trafficking-other-crimes/victims-human-trafficking-t-nonimmigrant-status. Additional immigration options available to victims of human trafficking include U visas (for victims of serious crimes) and asylum. For an extensive discussion of the various options available, see BRIDGETTE CARR, ANNE MILGRAM, KATHLEEN KIM, & STEPHEN WARNATH, HUMAN TRAFFICKING LAW AND POLICY Ch. 12 (2014).

(4) In addition to creating criminal liability, U.S. law requires mandatory restitution for violations of human trafficking laws and also provides victims the opportunity to bring civil actions against the perpetrator. *See* 18 U.S.C. § 1593 (Mandatory Restitution) and 18 U.S.C. § 1595 (Civil Remedy).

(5) Today, the U.S. Department of Defense contracts out many of its functions to private organizations. In *Adhikari, et al. v. Daoud & Partners, et al.*, the United States District Court for the Southern District of Texas considered a civil suit against various corporations by a group of Nepali citizens who alleged the entities engaged in human trafficking.

> Plaintiffs allege that KBR and Defendant Daoud & Partners ("Daoud") engaged in a scheme to traffic the Plaintiffs from Nepal to Iraq, where one KBR subsidiary served as a contractor with the United States government to perform specific duties at United States military facilities. According to Plaintiffs, Defendants "established, engaged and/or contracted with a network of suppliers, agents, and/or partners in order to procure laborers from third world countries."
>
> The Deceased Plaintiffs, whose ages ranged from 18 to 27, were recruited from their places of residence by Moonlight Consultant Pvt., Ltd., a recruiting company based in Nepal. Most of the men were told that they would be employed by a luxury hotel in Amman, Jordan. Some were told that that they would be working in an American camp.... All of the men were led to believe that they would not be placed in a dangerous location, and that, if they found themselves in a dangerous area, they would be sent home at the employer's expense....
>
> After they were recruited, the Deceased Plaintiffs were then transferred to the custody of ... Daoud. The men were held in Jordan by agents of Daoud, and were required to turn over their passports to Daoud. It was there that the Deceased Plaintiffs first discovered that they were actually being sent to work at Al Asad, north of Ramadi, Iraq.... At least one of the Deceased Plaintiffs informed his family that he and the other men were being kept in a dark room and were unable to see. In Jordan, the men were also informed for the first time that they would be paid only three quarters of what they were initially promised. Although they wanted to return

home to Nepal, rather than proceed into the Iraqi war zone, the men were compelled to proceed to Iraq because of the debts that their families had assumed to pay the brokers.

Daoud transported the Deceased Plaintiffs into Iraq on or about August 19, 2004, via an unprotected automobile caravan of seventeen vehicles. . . . As they were nearing Al Asad, the two lead cars in which the Deceased Plaintiffs were being transported were stopped by a group of men who later revealed themselves to be members of the Ansar al-Sunna Army, an insurgent group in Iraq. . . .

On or about August 31, 2004, international media outlets broadcasted video of the Ansar al-Sunna Army executing the Deceased Plaintiffs. The group beheaded one of the men, and shot the other eleven men, one by one, in the back of their heads . . .

. . . .

B. Plaintiffs' TVPRA Claim

1. Retroactivity of Section 1596

Extraterritoriality principles have also foreclosed Plaintiffs' TVPRA claim. As discussed in the Court's most recent summary judgment ruling, the TVPRA had no extraterritorial application at the time of the tragic events recounted above. Although Congress amended the TVPRA in 2008 to provide for extraterritorial application, the Court found that the relevant provision — 18 U.S.C. § 1596 — could not be applied retroactively to KBR's pre-2008 conduct. . . .

. . . [Plaintiffs] offer several arguments as to how the Court's most recent summary judgment ruling gets the retroactivity analysis wrong. With the utmost respect to Plaintiffs' counsel, however, these are not new arguments. . . .

The Court clarifies, however, the role that *Morrison v. National Australia Bank Ltd.*, 561 U.S. 247, 130 S. Ct. 2869, 177 L. Ed. 2d 535 (2010), played in its most recent decision. Plaintiffs forcefully argue that the case sheds no light on whether Section 1596 can be retroactively applied. The Court cannot agree. Although its most recent decision not to apply Section 1596 to this pending case was governed by the standards articulated in *Landgraf*, *Hughes Aircraft*, and *Republic of Austria*, the Court drew upon *Morrison* for guidance as to how Section 1596 should be classified under those standards. As previously explained, "a nominally jurisdictional statute" which "necessarily affects the substantive rights of the parties" cannot be categorized as "mere procedure"; rather, it represents a substantive change in operative law, thereby "trigger[ing]" the presumption against retroactivity.

This decision comports with the Supreme Court's acknowledgment in Morrison that whether a federal conduct-regulating statute is intended to govern extraterritorial conduct is inherently a merits question.... Congress may express that intent through a statute phrased in jurisdictional terms, as it has in Section 1596. But because Section 1596 "adheres to the [TVPRA] cause of action in this fashion," it is "essentially substantive." *Republic of Austria v. Altmann*, 541 U.S. 677, 695 n.15, 124 S. Ct. 2240, 159 L. Ed. 2d 1 (2004).

....

2. Applicability of MEJA

a. As to the TVPRA

Plaintiffs argue, alternatively, that the Military Extraterritorial Jurisdiction Act ("MEJA") provides a jurisdictional basis for Plaintiffs' TVPRA claim. MEJA has long been at the periphery of this case, primarily as an alternative justification for finding that Plaintiffs' RICO claims could be applied extraterritorially. Plaintiffs only recently began to argue that MEJA also provides an alternative jurisdictional basis for their TVPRA claims. The Court rejected the argument; not simply because MEJA is a "murky" area of law, but because the Court disagreed that MEJA has any implication for the availability and extraterritoriality of Plaintiffs' civil TVPRA claim....

Plaintiffs have provided no cause for the Court to retreat from its position. MEJA is not part of the TVPRA. It provides for criminal prosecution of certain felonies committed abroad "while employed by or accompanying the Armed Forces" or "while a member of the Armed Forces." 18 U.S.C. § 3261(a). It appears to be undisputed that Sections 1589 and 1590 of the TVPRA — the provisions KBR is alleged to have violated — would qualify for prosecution under MEJA. Plaintiffs argue that MEJA's limited extraterritorial extension of a host of federal offenses — including Sections 1589 and 1590 of the TVPRA — can be married with the TVPRA's civil remedy provision to provide an alternative "jurisdictional" basis for Plaintiffs' claim.

Plaintiffs' argument loses sight of the central inquiry before the Court — whether Congress, when it enacted the civil remedy provision of the TVPRA, intended it to have extraterritorial effect.... Plaintiffs would have this Court find that Congress affirmatively and clearly expressed its intent to give (limited) extraterritorial effect to the TVPRA's civil remedy provision *first* by reference to the TVPRA's conduct-regulating provisions and *then* by reference to an unrelated criminal statute which is not part of the TVPRA and is nowhere referenced in the TVPRA. To the extent this was Congress's intent, it was neither affirmative nor clear. MEJA does not provide the answer that Plaintiffs seek.

Adhikari, et al. v. Daoud & Partners, et al., 95 F. Supp. 3d 1013 (2015). The court denied the plaintiff's motion for rehearing. In its concluding paragraph, that court wrote:

> The Court again notes its profound regret at the outcome of this action. The crimes that are at the core of this litigation are more vile than anything the Court has previously confronted. Moreover, the herculean efforts of Plaintiffs' counsel have been in the highest traditions of the bar. No lawyer or group of lawyers could have done more or done better. But, the perpetrators of the subject crimes are not before the Court, and the relief that Plaintiffs seek is not appropriate as to those who are before the Court.

The lower court was affirmed on appeal to the United States Court of Appeals for the Fifth Circuit. *See Adhikari v. Kellogg Brown & Root, Inc.*, 845 F.3d 184 (5th Cir. 2017).

(6) The *Intelligence Reform and Terrorism Prevention Act of 2004* ("IRTPA") established the Human Smuggling and Trafficking Center ("HSTC"). *See* Intelligence Reform and Terrorism Prevention Act of 2004, Publ. Law 108-458 (Dec. 17, 2004), Section 7202(a). According to a 2017 Fact Sheet from the U.S. Department of State:

> The HSTC is an interagency fusion center and information clearinghouse that has three main mission areas: human smuggling, human trafficking, and criminal facilitation of clandestine terrorist travel. Human smuggling and terrorist travel facilitation threaten U.S. national security; human trafficking is a serious human rights issue not only globally, but also in the United States. The HSTC is unique among U.S. organizations in that it concentrates on illicit travel globally.
>
> The HSTC brings together experienced law enforcement, intelligence, and diplomacy specialists from U.S. agencies to work together full time to convert intelligence into effective law enforcement, policy, and diplomatic actions.

Human Smuggling and Trafficking Center Background Fact Sheet, U.S. Department of State Human Smuggling and Trafficking Center (April 16, 2014).

Various governmental entities are involved in the fight against human trafficking. For example, in October 2020, the U.S. Department of Homeland Security announced the opening of the DHS Center for Countering Human Trafficking, which DHS described as the "government's first-ever integrated law enforcement operations center directly supporting federal criminal investigations, victim assistance efforts, intelligence analysis, and outreach and training activities related to human trafficking and forced labor."

> The center, which has been operational since early September [2020], is based in Washington and led by U.S. Immigration and Customs Enforcement (ICE), a global leader of criminal investigations into human trafficking and sexual exploitation. The center will be staffed with law enforcement officials from Homeland Security Investigations (HSI) and across DHS, as

> well as subject matter experts and support staff from 16 DHS components—all focused on the "4 Ps" of the center's mission: prevention, protection, prosecution and partnerships.

DHS Launches New Center for Countering Human Trafficking, DHS News Release (October 20, 2020).

In addition to governmental entities, there are also many non-profit organizations conducting work related to human trafficking. For example, the National Center for Victims of Crime has a Human Trafficking Capacity Building Center. The Center "helps organizations and tribes start, sustain, or grow their anti-trafficking services by providing no-cost customized coaching, material development, and strategic planning support." More information is available at https://victimsofcrime.org/human-trafficking-capacity-building-center/.

There is also increased focus on research related to human trafficking. For example, the United States Office of Justice Programs has also created a Human Trafficking Division within the Office for Victims of Crime. In the Office of Victims of Crime *Vision 21: Transforming Victim Services* final report, the importance of research in this area was discussed.

> Once hidden in the shadows, human trafficking is becoming more and more visible in cities, towns, and rural areas. We need data about the origins and immigration status of trafficking victims and perpetrators, as well as the factors that contribute to the sex trafficking of children in the United States and the interventions that are most effective in rescuing them. We need to know what percentage of victims participate in the criminal investigations that are essential to bringing traffickers to justice, and the reasons they are willing and able to take part in these investigations.

Vision 21: Transforming Victim Services (Final Report), Office for Victims of Crime, United States Office of Justice Programs, p.3 (May 2014). In 2015, an academic journal, entitled the *Journal on Human Trafficking*, was established to support "the greater understanding of human trafficking by publishing diverse scholarship on all forms of contemporary slavery." *Journal of Human Trafficking*, available at https://www.tandfonline.com/toc/uhmt20/current.

B. Transparency in Supply Chains

Corporations are seldom charged with trafficking offenses. *See* Jennifer M. Chacon, *Misery and Myopia: Understanding the Failures of U.S. Efforts to Stop Human Trafficking*, 74 FORDHAM L. REV. 2977, 3033–36 (2006). Corporations have, however, been handed responsibility for assisting in the detection and prevention of human trafficking. For example, in 2010, California adopted a law entitled the "Transparency in Supply Chains Act." *See* California Civil Code Section 1714.43 (2015). The law went into effect on January 1, 2012, and applies to any retail seller or manufacturer doing business in California and having annual worldwide gross receipts of $100 million or more.

Senate Bill No. 657

CHAPTER 556

An act to add Section 1714.43 to the Civil Code, and to add Section 19547.5 to the Revenue and Taxation Code, relating to human trafficking.

[Approved by Governor September 30, 2010.
Filed with Secretary of State September 30, 2010.]

SB 657, Steinberg. Human trafficking.

The federal Victims of Trafficking and Violence Protection Act of 2000 establishes an Interagency Task Force to Monitor and Combat Trafficking, as specified.

Existing state law makes human trafficking a crime. Existing state law also allows a victim of human trafficking to bring a civil action for actual damages, compensatory damages, punitive damages, injunctive relief, any combination of those, or any other appropriate relief.

Existing law generally regulates various business activities and practices, including those of retail sellers and manufacturers of products.

This bill would enact the California Transparency in Supply Chains Act of 2010, and would, beginning January 1, 2012, require retail sellers and manufacturers doing business in the state to disclose their efforts to eradicate slavery and human trafficking from their direct supply chains for tangible goods offered for sale, as specified. That provision would not apply to a retail seller or manufacturer having less than $100,000,000 in annual worldwide gross receipts. The bill would also make a specified statement of legislative intent regarding slavery and human trafficking. The bill would also require the Franchise Tax Board to make available to the Attorney General a list of retail sellers and manufacturers required to disclose efforts to eradicate slavery and human trafficking pursuant to that provision, as specified. . . .

Notes

(1) The California Department of Justice assists in implementing the California Transparency in Supply Chains Act by, among other things, providing guidance to businesses. The guidance includes this discussion of the importance of transparency in the supply chain.

> An estimated 21 million people — 11.4 million women and girls and 9.5 million men and boys — are victims of forced labor around the globe. These victims work in virtually every industry and across sectors, including manufacturing, agriculture, construction, entertainment and domestic service. California, which boasts the world's seventh-largest economy and the country's largest consumer base, is unique in its ability to address this issue, and as a result, to help eradicate human trafficking and slavery worldwide.

In recent years, California consumers have demanded that producers provide greater transparency about goods brought to market. Consumers utilize this additional information to drive their purchasing decisions, and various indicators suggest that Californians are not alone. A recent survey of western consumers revealed that people would be willing to pay extra for products they could identify as being made under good working conditions.

A recent law in California is poised to help California consumers make better and more informed purchasing choices. The California Transparency in Supply Chains Act (Steinberg, 2010) (the "Act") provides consumers with critical information about the efforts that companies are undertaking to prevent and root out human trafficking and slavery in their product supply chains — whether here or overseas.

This Act requires large retailers and manufacturers doing business in California to disclose on their websites their "efforts to eradicate slavery and human trafficking from [their] direct supply chain for tangible goods offered for sale." The law applies to any company doing business in California that has annual worldwide gross receipts of more than $100 million and that identifies itself as a retail seller or manufacturer on its California tax return. Companies subject to the Act must post disclosures on their Internet websites related to five specific areas: verification, audits, certification, internal accountability, and training.

The California Transparency in Supply Chains Act does not mandate that businesses implement new measures to ensure that their product supply chains are free from human trafficking and slavery. Instead, the law only requires that covered businesses make the required disclosures — even if they do little or nothing at all to safeguard their supply chains. Companies subject to the Act must therefore disclose particular information within each disclosure category, and the Act offers companies discretion in how to do so.

The California Transparency in Supply Chains Act: A Resource Guide, California Department of Justice (2015), *available at* https://oag.ca.gov/sites/all/files/agweb/pdfs/sb657/resource-guide.pdf; *see also Compliance is Not Enough: Best Practices in Responding to the California Transparency in Supply Chains Act*, Verite White Paper (Nov. 2011), *available at* http://www.verite.org/sites/default/files/VTE_WhitePaper_California_Bill657FINAL5.pdf. Along with Verite.org, another website containing significant information for consumers about supply chains is KnowTheChain.org. In 2015, KnowTheChain published a report regarding the first five years of the California Transparency in Supply Chains Act. *See Five Years of the California Transparency in Supply Chains Act*, KnowTheChain (September 30, 2015), *available at* https://www.knowthechain.org/wp-content/uploads/2015/10/KnowTheChain_InsightsBrief_093015.pdf.

(2) In 2012, just as corporations were beginning to implement the California law, President Barack Obama signed an executive order regarding human trafficking and federal contracting. The language of the order sought to strengthen protections against human trafficking and included certification requirements, prevention efforts, detailed compliance programs, and self-reporting obligations. The order applies to federal contractors and subcontractors. The executive order states:

> Section 1. Policy. More than 20 million men, women, and children throughout the world are victims of severe forms of trafficking in persons ("trafficking" or "trafficking in persons")—defined in section 103 of the TVPA, 22 U.S.C. 7102(8), to include sex trafficking in which a commercial sex act is induced by force, fraud, or coercion, or in which the person induced to perform such act has not attained 18 years of age, or the recruitment, harboring, transportation, provision, or obtaining of a person for labor or services, through the use of force, fraud, or coercion, for the purpose of subjection to involuntary servitude, peonage, debt bondage, or slavery.
>
> The United States has long had a zero-tolerance policy regarding Government employees and contractor personnel engaging in any form of this criminal behavior. As the largest single purchaser of goods and services in the world, the United States Government bears a responsibility to ensure that taxpayer dollars do not contribute to trafficking in persons. By providing our Government workforce with additional tools and training to apply and enforce existing policy, and by providing additional clarity to Government contractors and subcontractors on the steps necessary to fully comply with that policy, this order will help to protect vulnerable individuals as contractors and subcontractors perform vital services and manufacture the goods procured by the United States.
>
> In addition, the improved safeguards provided by this order to strengthen compliance with anti-trafficking laws will promote economy and efficiency in Government procurement. These safeguards, which have been largely modeled on successful practices in the private sector, will increase stability, productivity, and certainty in Federal contracting by avoiding the disruption and disarray caused by the use of trafficked labor and resulting investigative and enforcement actions.

See Executive Order 13627, Strengthening Protections Against Trafficking In Persons In Federal Contracts (Sept. 25, 2012).

(3) In 2011, the United Nations Human Rights Office of the High Commissioner issued a report entitled, *Guiding Principles on Business and Human Rights*. Though the document is non-binding and does not create any new legal obligations, it represents the establishment of guiding principles to begin addressing the role of private enterprises in human rights efforts.

> Human rights due diligence

17. In order to identify, prevent, mitigate and account for how they address their adverse human rights impacts, business enterprises should carry out human rights due diligence. The process should include assessing actual and potential human rights impacts, integrating and acting upon the findings, tracking responses, and communicating how impacts are addressed. Human rights due diligence:

(a) Should cover adverse human rights impacts that the business enterprise may cause or contribute to through its own activities, or which may be directly linked to its operations, products or services by its business relationships;

(b) Will vary in complexity with the size of the business enterprise, the risk of severe human rights impacts, and the nature and context of its operations;

(c) Should be ongoing, recognizing that the human rights risks may change over time as the business enterprise's operations and operating context evolve.

Commentary

This Principle defines the parameters for human rights due diligence, while Principles 18 through 21 elaborate its essential components.

Human rights risks are understood to be the business enterprise's potential adverse human rights impacts. Potential impacts should be addressed through prevention or mitigation, while actual impacts — those that have already occurred — should be a subject for remediation (Principle 22).

Human rights due diligence can be included within broader enterprise risk-management systems, provided that it goes beyond simply identifying and managing material risks to the company itself, to include risks to rights-holders.

Human rights due diligence should be initiated as early as possible in the development of a new activity or relationship, given that human rights risks can be increased or mitigated already at the stage of structuring contracts or other agreements, and may be inherited through mergers or acquisitions.

Where business enterprises have large numbers of entities in their value chains it may be unreasonably difficult to conduct due diligence for adverse human rights impacts across them all. If so, business enterprises should identify general areas where the risk of adverse human rights impacts is most significant, whether due to certain suppliers' or clients' operating context, the particular operations, products or services involved, or other relevant considerations, and prioritize these for human rights due diligence.

Questions of complicity may arise when a business enterprise contributes to, or is seen as contributing to, adverse human rights impacts caused by other parties. Complicity has both non-legal and legal meanings. As a non-legal matter, business enterprises may be perceived as being "complicit" in

> the acts of another party where, for example, they are seen to benefit from an abuse committed by that party.
>
> As a legal matter, most national jurisdictions prohibit complicity in the commission of a crime, and a number allow for criminal liability of business enterprises in such cases. Typically, civil actions can also be based on an enterprise's alleged contribution to a harm, although these may not be framed in human rights terms. The weight of international criminal law jurisprudence indicates that the relevant standard for aiding and abetting is knowingly providing practical assistance or encouragement that has a substantial effect on the commission of a crime.
>
> Conducting appropriate human rights due diligence should help business enterprises address the risk of legal claims against them by showing that they took every reasonable step to avoid involvement with an alleged human rights abuse. However, business enterprises conducting such due diligence should not assume that, by itself, this will automatically and fully absolve them from liability for causing or contributing to human rights abuses.

Guiding Principles on Business and Human Rights, United Nations Human Rights Office of the High Commissioner, p. 17–19 (2011); *see also* Rose Ireland, *Rights and Modern Slavery: The Obligations of States and Corporations in Relation to Forced Labour in Global Supply Chains*, 6 UCLJLJ 100 (2017) (examining the three pillars of the United Nations Guiding Principles of Business and Human Rights as they apply to corporate supply chains).

(4) In 2015, the United Kingdom Parliament passed the Modern Slavery Act. *See* Modern Slavery Act of 2015, *available at* http://www.legislation.gov.uk/ukpga/2015/30/contents/enacted. The Act addresses anti-slavery and anti-trafficking initiatives through criminal enforcement, preventive measures, and support systems. Included among the many provisions in the Act is a transparency in supply chains section. *See* Modern Slavery Act of 2015, Part 6 (Transparency in Supply Chains etc.), *available at* http://www.legislation.gov.uk/ukpga/2015/30/part/6/enacted.

(5) In addition to policy and legislative efforts to create incentives or obligations for corporations to better monitor their supply chains, consumers have also begun attempting to bring corporate accountability for human rights violations in the supply chain through litigation. Such efforts, however, often encounter great difficulty in the courts. In *Tomasella v. Nestle USA*, for example, a consumer brought a class action suit alleging that the defendant's failure to "disclose on the packaging of their chocolate products that the worst forms of child labor exist in their cocoa supply chains violates the Massachusetts Consumer Protection Act." In affirming the lower court's dismissal of the suit, the United States Court of Appeals for the First Circuit said:

> The exploitation of children in the supply chain from which U.S. confectionary corporations continue to source the cocoa beans that they turn into chocolate is a humanitarian tragedy. This case thus serves as a haunting

> reminder that eradicating the evil of slavery in all its forms is a job far from finished. Before us, however, is the very narrow question of whether Defendants' failure to include on the packing of their chocolate products information regarding upstream labor abuses in their cocoa bean supply chains constitutes an unfair or deceptive business practice within the meaning of Chapter 93A. Because we agree with the district court that Tomasella has not plausibly stated a claim for relief under Chapter 93A based on the alleged packaging omissions, and that Tomasella's unjust enrichment claim is foreclosed by the availability of a remedy at law, we affirm the dismissal of her complaints against Defendants.

Tomasella v. Nestle USA, Inc., 962 F.3d 60 (1st Cir. 2020).

§ 12.02 International Law

Human trafficking is specifically prohibited under international law by the Protocol to Prevent, Suppress and Punish Trafficking in Persons, Especially Women and Children, known as the "Palermo Protocol." Along with defining the term "human trafficking," the so-called Palermo Protocol calls on parties to "adopt such legislative and other measures" to "establish as criminal offences the conduct set forth [in this definition] when committed intentionally." *See* Protocol to Prevent, Suppress and Punish Trafficking in Persons, Especially Women and Children, supplementing the United Nations Convention against Transnational Organized Crime, G.A. Res. 55/25 Annex II (2000), *available at* https://www.unodc.org/unodc/treaties/CTOC/.

Protocol to Prevent, Suppress and Punish Trafficking in Persons Especially Women and Children, supplementing the United Nations Convention Against Transnational Organized Crime

Adopted and opened for signature, ratification and accession by General Assembly resolution 55/25 of 15 November 2000

Preamble

The States Parties to this Protocol,

Declaring that effective action to prevent and combat trafficking in persons, especially women and children, requires a comprehensive international approach in the countries of origin, transit and destination that includes measures to prevent such trafficking, to punish the traffickers and to protect the victims of such trafficking, including by protecting their internationally recognized human rights,

Taking into account the fact that, despite the existence of a variety of international instruments containing rules and practical measures to combat the exploitation of persons, especially women and children, there is no universal instrument that addresses all aspects of trafficking in persons,

Concerned that, in the absence of such an instrument, persons who are vulnerable to trafficking will not be sufficiently protected,

Recalling General Assembly resolution 53/111 of 9 December 1998, in which the Assembly decided to establish an open-ended intergovernmental ad hoc committee for the purpose of elaborating a comprehensive international convention against transnational organized crime and of discussing the elaboration of, inter alia, an international instrument addressing trafficking in women and children,

Convinced that supplementing the United Nations Convention against Transnational Organized Crime with an international instrument for the prevention, suppression and punishment of trafficking in persons, especially women and children, will be useful in preventing and combating that crime,

Have agreed as follows: . . .

I. General provisions

Article 2

Statement of purpose

The purposes of this Protocol are:

(a) To prevent and combat trafficking in persons, paying particular attention to women and children;

(b) To protect and assist the victims of such trafficking, with full respect for their human rights; and

(c) To promote cooperation among States Parties in order to meet those objectives.

Article 3

Use of terms

For the purposes of this Protocol:

(a) "Trafficking in persons" shall mean the recruitment, transportation, transfer, harbouring or receipt of persons, by means of the threat or use of force or other forms of coercion, of abduction, of fraud, of deception, of the abuse of power or of a position of vulnerability or of the giving or receiving of payments or benefits to achieve the consent of a person having control over another person, for the purpose of exploitation. Exploitation shall include, at a minimum, the exploitation of the prostitution of others or other forms of sexual exploitation, forced labour or services, slavery or practices similar to slavery, servitude or the removal of organs;

(b) The consent of a victim of trafficking in persons to the intended exploitation set forth in subparagraph (a) of this article shall be irrelevant where any of the means set forth in subparagraph (a) have been used;

(c) The recruitment, transportation, transfer, harbouring or receipt of a child for the purpose of exploitation shall be considered "trafficking in persons" even if this does not involve any of the means set forth in subparagraph (a) of this article; . . .

Article 5

Criminalization

1. Each State Party shall adopt such legislative and other measures as may be necessary to establish as criminal offences the conduct set forth in article 3 of this Protocol, when committed intentionally.

2. Each State Party shall also adopt such legislative and other measures as may be necessary to establish as criminal offences:

(a) Subject to the basic concepts of its legal system, attempting to commit an offence established in accordance with paragraph 1 of this article;

(b) Participating as an accomplice in an offence established in accordance with paragraph 1 of this article; and

(c) Organizing or directing other persons to commit an offence established in accordance with paragraph 1 of this article.

II. Protection of victims of trafficking in persons

Article 6

Assistance to and protection of victims of trafficking in persons

1. In appropriate cases and to the extent possible under its domestic law, each State Party shall protect the privacy and identity of victims of trafficking in persons, including, inter alia, by making legal proceedings relating to such trafficking confidential.

2. Each State Party shall ensure that its domestic legal or administrative system contains measures that provide to victims of trafficking in persons, in appropriate cases:

(a) Information on relevant court and administrative proceedings;

(b) Assistance to enable their views and concerns to be presented and considered at appropriate stages of criminal proceedings against offenders, in a manner not prejudicial to the rights of the defence.

3. Each State Party shall consider implementing measures to provide for the physical, psychological and social recovery of victims of trafficking in persons, including, in appropriate cases, in cooperation with non-governmental organizations, other relevant organizations and other elements of civil society, and, in particular, the provision of:

(a) Appropriate housing;

(b) Counselling and information, in particular as regards their legal rights, in a language that the victims of trafficking in persons can understand;

(c) Medical, psychological and material assistance; and

(d) Employment, educational and training opportunities.

4. Each State Party shall take into account, in applying the provisions of this article, the age, gender and special needs of victims of trafficking in persons, in particular the special needs of children, including appropriate housing, education and care.

5. Each State Party shall endeavour to provide for the physical safety of victims of trafficking in persons while they are within its territory.

6. Each State Party shall ensure that its domestic legal system contains measures that offer victims of trafficking in persons the possibility of obtaining compensation for damage suffered. . . .

III. Prevention, cooperation and other measures

Article 9

Prevention of trafficking in persons

1. States Parties shall establish comprehensive policies, programmes and other measures:

(a) To prevent and combat trafficking in persons; and

(b) To protect victims of trafficking in persons, especially women and children, from revictimization. . . .

Notes

(1) There are currently 178 parties to the Palermo Protocol. The United States ratified the Protocol in 2005. In ratifying, the United States made three reservations, including the following:

> The United States of America reserves the right to assume obligations under this Protocol in a manner consistent with its fundamental principles of federalism, pursuant to which both federal and state criminal laws must be considered in relation to conduct addressed in the Protocol. U.S. federal criminal law, which regulates conduct based on its effect on interstate or foreign commerce, or another federal interest, such as the Thirteenth Amendment's prohibition of "slavery" and "involuntary servitude," serves as the principal legal regime within the United States for combating the conduct addressed in this Protocol, and is broadly effective for this purpose. Federal criminal law does not apply in the rare case where such criminal conduct does not so involve interstate or foreign commerce, or otherwise implicate another federal interest, such as the Thirteenth Amendment. There are a small number of conceivable situations involving such rare offenses of a purely local character where U.S. federal and state criminal law may not be entirely adequate to satisfy an obligation under the Protocol. The United States of America therefore reserves to the obligations set forth in

> the Protocol to the extent they address conduct which would fall within this narrow category of highly localized activity. This reservation does not affect in any respect the ability of the United States to provide international cooperation to other Parties as contemplated in the Protocol.

For further reading regarding human trafficking and slavery, *see* BRIDGETTE CARR, ANNE MILGRAM, KATHLEEN KIM, & STEPHEN WARNATH, HUMAN TRAFFICKING LAW AND POLICY (2014); U.N. Human Rights Council, *Report of the Special Rapporteur on Contemporary Forms of Slavery, Including Its Causes and Consequences*, U.N. Doc A/HRC/9/20 (2008); Tobias Barrington Wolff, *The Thirteenth Amendment and Slavery in the Global Economy*, 102 COLUM. L. REV. 973 (2002); A. Yasmine Rassam, *Contemporary Forms of Slavery and the Evolution of the Prohibition of Slavery and the Slave Trade Under Customary International Law*, 39 VA. J. INT'L L. 303 (1999). Criminal law is important, but it is not on its own the complete solution to the trafficking problem. For some other perspectives, *see* Alexis A. Aranowitz & Annette Koning, *Understanding Human Trafficking as a Market System: Addressing the Demand Side of Trafficking for Sexual Exploitation*, 85 R.I.D.P. 669 (2014).

(2) Article 1 of the Palermo Protocol states, "This Protocol supplements the United Nations Convention against Transnational Organized Crime. It shall be interpreted together with the Convention." The United Nations Convention against Transnational Organized Crime was opened for signature in December 2000 and is considered one of the most important international instruments in the fight against international organized crime. *See* United Nations Convention against Transnational Organized Crime, G.A. Res. 55/25 Annex I (2000), *available at* https://www.unodc.org/unodc/treaties/CTOC/. The Convention is supplemented by three protocols—(a) The Protocol to Prevent, Suppress and Punish Trafficking in Persons, especially Women and Children ("Palermo Protocol"), (b) the Protocol against the Smuggling of Migrants by Land, Sea and Air, and (c) The Protocol against the Illicit Manufacturing of and Trafficking in Firearms, Their Parts and Components and Ammunition. States must become a party to the Convention before becoming party to any of the Protocols. There are currently 190 parties to the Convention. The United States ratified the Convention in 2005. The Protocols each incorporate by reference the basic provisions of the Convention on such issues as jurisdiction, extradition, mutual legal assistance, transfer of proceedings and other forms of cooperation. *See generally* Roger S. Clark, *The United Nations Convention Against Transnational Organized Crime*, 50 WAYNE L. REV. 161 (2004).

(3) In addition to the Convention against Transnational Organized Crime and the Palermo Protocol, there are now many additional initiatives throughout the world to address human trafficking. As an example, on February 1, 2008, the Council of Europe Convention on Action against Trafficking in Human Beings went into force. The Convention seeks to build upon the framework created by the Convention against Transnational Organized Crime and the Palermo Protocol. One of its aims is "to promote international cooperation on action against trafficking in human beings." Council of Europe Convention on Action against Trafficking in

Human Beings (Feb. 1, 2008), *available at* https://www.coe.int/t/dghl/monitoring/trafficking/Docs/Convntn/CETS197_en.asp; *see also Rantsev v. Cyprus and Russia*, No. 25965/04, Eur. Ct.H.R. (2010) (examining the obligations of countries regarding the issues of human trafficking and human rights); Roza Pati, *States' Positive Obligations with Respect to Human Trafficking: The European Court of Human Rights Breaks New Ground in* Rantsev v. Cyprus and Russia, 29 B.U. Int'l L.J. 79 (2011).

In the 2021 case of *V.C.L. and A.N. v. The United Kingdom*, the European Court of Human Rights examined a case in which two trafficked juveniles were prosecuted by authorities in England after being discovered working as gardeners in cannabis grow operations. This was the first time the court had examined the appropriateness of prosecuting victims of human trafficking under Article 4 of the European Convention on Human Rights, which prohibits slavery and forced labor. In determining that authorities had failed to meet their obligations to protect the victims of trafficking in this case, the court made several findings. First, the court noted that "It is clear that no general prohibition on the prosecution of victims of trafficking can be construed from the Anti-Trafficking Convention or any other international instrument." *V.C.L. and A.N.* at 51. However, the court went on to note:

> Nevertheless, the Court considers that the prosecution of victims, or potential victims, of trafficking may, in certain circumstances, be at odds with the State's duty to take operational measures to protect them where they are aware, or ought to be aware, of circumstances giving rise to a credible suspicion that an individual has been trafficked. . . .
>
> . . . .
>
> In order for the prosecution of a victim or potential victim of trafficking to demonstrate respect for the freedoms guaranteed by Article 4, his or her early identification is of paramount importance. It follows that, as soon as the authorities are aware, or ought to be aware, of circumstances giving rise to a credible suspicion that an individual suspected of having committed a criminal offence may have been trafficked or exploited, he or she should be assessed promptly by individuals trained and qualified to deal with victims of trafficking. . . .
>
> . . . .
>
> Moreover, given that an individual's status as a victim of trafficking may affect whether there is sufficient evidence to prosecute and whether it is in the public interest to do so, any decision on whether or not to prosecute a potential victim of trafficking should — insofar as possible — only be taken once a trafficking assessment has been made by a qualified person. This is particularly important where children are concerned. . . .
>
> . . . .
>
> Once a trafficking assessment has been made by a qualified person, any subsequent prosecutorial decision would have to take that assessment into

> account. While the prosecutor might not be bound by the findings made in the course of such a trafficking assessment, the prosecutor would need to have clear reasons which are consistent with the definition of trafficking contained in the Palermo Protocol and the Anti-Trafficking Convention for disagreeing with it.

V.C.L. and A.N. v. The United Kingdom, European Court of Human Rights, 51–52 (Feb. 16, 2021).

(4) Each year, the U.S. Department of State issues a *Trafficking in Persons Report. See 2021 Trafficking in Persons Report*, U.S. Department of States (2021), *available at* http://www.state.gov/j/tip/rls/tiprpt/. According to the State Department's 2015 report, "The Trafficking in Persons (TIP) Report is the U.S. Government's principal diplomatic tool to engage foreign governments on human trafficking. It is also the world's most comprehensive resource of governmental anti-human trafficking efforts and reflects the U.S. Government's commitment to global leadership on this key human rights and law enforcement issue. It represents an updated, global look at the nature and scope of trafficking in persons and the broad range of government actions to confront and eliminate it." *2015 Trafficking in Persons Report*, U.S. Department of State (2015), *available at* http://www.state.gov/j/tip/rls/tiprpt/.

Chapter 13

Extraterritorial Application of U.S. Constitution

§ 13.01 Introduction

With increased globalization, questions arise as to whether the U.S. Constitution applies extraterritorially. Does it apply to criminal investigations being conducted outside the United States? Does it apply when other countries seek United States assistance with their investigations? Does the U.S. Constitution only afford rights to citizens of the United States? What happens when the laws of another country conflict with U.S. law? These, and other questions, serve as the focus of this chapter. First, it is necessary to say a little about United States exercise (or non-exercise) of jurisdiction in certain extraterritorial contexts. These examples offer a backdrop to some of the Constitutional issues, by suggesting contexts in which they might arise.

In years past, the United States maintained consular courts in certain countries that were thought to have sub-standard legal systems. *See* Geoffrey R. Watson, *Offenders Abroad: The Case for Nationality-Based Criminal Jurisdiction*, 17 Yale J. Int'l L. 41, 49–52 (1992). These courts exercised criminal jurisdiction over U.S. citizens accused of committing crimes in those countries. These courts did not provide a right to a grand jury indictment or jury trial, but did offer the right to confrontation and right to counsel. *See* Michael Abbell & Mark Andrew Sherman, *The Bill of Rights in Transnational Criminal Litigation*, 41 The Champion 22 (Sept./Oct. 1992). Consular courts do not exist today. Often considered to be "a form of legal imperialism," "consular jurisdiction died slowly." *See* Watson, *supra* at 91 and 101.

Following World War II, with large numbers of U.S. military personnel stationed abroad, the question of jurisdiction over their criminal activities became acute. A series of U.S. Supreme Court decisions held that U.S. military courts could not constitutionally try civilian dependents accompanying the armed forces overseas because those courts do not offer trial by jury and other procedures guaranteed by the Bill of Rights. *See, e.g.*, *Reid v. Covert*, 354 U.S. 1 (1957). Since the U.S. has not established general nationality-based jurisdiction, this left them to be tried by foreign courts for crimes committed abroad, if to be tried at all. Congress dealt ultimately with the specific scenario in *Reid v. Covert* (alleged murder of soldier husband by accompanying wife), and indeed all murder and manslaughter of Americans by Americans abroad (and attempts thereat), in 1994 by adding § 1119 ("foreign murder of United States nationals") to Title 18 of the United States Code.

Status of Forces Agreements negotiated with NATO and other countries where U.S. troops are stationed allocate criminal jurisdiction as between the United States and the host country. *See* Joseph M. Snee & A. Kenneth Pye, Status of Forces Agreements: Criminal Jurisdiction (1957). Article VII(9) of the NATO Status of Forces Agreement provides:

> Whenever a member of a force or civilian component or a dependent is prosecuted under the jurisdiction of a receiving State he shall be entitled:
>
> a. to a prompt and speedy trial;
>
> b. to be informed, in advance of trial, of the specific charge or charges made against him;
>
> c. to be confronted with the witnesses against him;
>
> d. to have compulsory process for obtaining witnesses in his favour, if they are within the jurisdiction of the receiving State;
>
> e. to have legal representation of his own choice for his defence or to have free or assisted legal representation under the conditions prevailing for the time being in the receiving State;
>
> f. if he considers it necessary, to have the services of a competent interpreter; and
>
> g. to communicate with a representative of the Government of the sending State and when the rules of the court permit, to have such a representative present at his trial.

NATO Basic Documents: SOFA, London, 19 June 1951 (http://nato.int/docu/basictxt/b510619a.htm). There is an obvious effort here to assure certain minimal procedural guarantees when individuals face charges in foreign courts.

In *United States v. Gatlin*, 216 F.3d 207 (2d Cir. 2000), the court noted a jurisdictional gap, there being no authority for federal district courts to try civilians who accompany military overseas and commit crimes on a military installation. (Gatlin, a non-military spouse, was alleged to have molested his step-daughter on a base in Germany). Congress responded with the Military Extraterritorial Jurisdiction Act of 2000. It extended federal jurisdiction "over offenses committed outside the United States by persons employed by or accompanying the Armed Forces, or by members of the Armed Forces who are released or separated from active duty prior to being identified and prosecuted for the commission of such offenses." It is not limited to offenses on military installations. The category "employed" encompassed a Department of Defense contractor or subcontractor whose contract "relates to supporting the mission of the Department of Defense overseas." Some private contractors abroad, especially those providing security, are contracted to the State Department and may not come within the ambit of the statute. They may also be immune from local prosecution. [*see infra* § 14.04]

Questions regarding the extraterritorial application of the Bill of Rights have been presented in several different contexts. *See generally* Bruce Zagaris, *U.S.*

International Cooperation Against Transnational Organized Crime, 44 WAYNE L. REV. 1401, 1447–63 (1998). Questions about whether the U.S. government could agree to trial of U.S. citizens before an international court that does not provide all the procedural protections guaranteed by the Bill of Rights have been offered as an objection to U.S. participation in the International Criminal Court [*see* chap. 22].

§ 13.02 Fourth Amendment

United States v. Verdugo-Urquidez

Supreme Court of the United States
494 U.S. 259 (1990)

CHIEF JUSTICE REHNQUIST delivered the opinion of the Court.

The question presented by this case is whether the Fourth Amendment applies to the search and seizure by United States agents of property that is owned by a nonresident alien and located in a foreign country. We hold that it does not.

Respondent Rene Martin Verdugo-Urquidez is a citizen and resident of Mexico. He is believed by the United States Drug Enforcement Agency (DEA) to be one of the leaders of a large and violent organization in Mexico that smuggles narcotics into the United States. Based on a complaint charging respondent with various narcotics-related offenses, the Government obtained a warrant for his arrest on August 3, 1985. In January 1986, Mexican police officers, after discussions with United States marshals, apprehended Verdugo-Urquidez in Mexico and transported him to the United States Border Patrol station in Calexico, California. There, United States marshals arrested respondent and eventually moved him to a correctional center in San Diego, California, where he remains incarcerated pending trial.

Following respondent's arrest, Terry Bowen, a DEA agent assigned to the Calexico DEA office, decided to arrange for searches of Verdugo-Urquidez's Mexican residences located in Mexicali and San Felipe. Bowen believed that the searches would reveal evidence related to respondent's alleged narcotics trafficking activities and his involvement in the kidnaping and torture-murder of DEA Special Agent Enrique Camarena Salazar (for which respondent subsequently has been convicted in a separate prosecution. . . . Bowen telephoned Walter White, the Assistant Special Agent in charge of the DEA office in Mexico City, and asked him to seek authorization for the search from the Director General of the Mexican Federal Judicial Police (MFJP). After several attempts to reach high ranking Mexican officials, White eventually contacted the Director General, who authorized the searches and promised the cooperation of Mexican authorities. Thereafter, DEA agents working in concert with officers of the MFJP searched respondent's properties in Mexicali and San Felipe and seized certain documents. In particular, the search of the Mexicali residence uncovered a tally sheet, which the Government believes reflects the quantities of marijuana smuggled by Verdugo-Urquidez into the United States.

The District Court granted respondent's motion to suppress evidence seized during the searches, concluding that the Fourth Amendment applied to the searches and that the DEA agents had failed to justify searching respondent's premises without a warrant. A divided panel of the Court of Appeals for the Ninth Circuit affirmed. 856 F.2d 1214 (1988). It cited this Court's decision in *Reid v. Covert*, 354 U.S. 1 (1957), which held that American citizens tried by United States military authorities in a foreign country were entitled to the protections of the Fifth and Sixth Amendments, and concluded that "The Constitution imposes substantive constraints on the federal government, even when it operates abroad." . . . Relying on our decision in *INS v. Lopez-Mendoza*, 468 U.S. 1032 (1984), where a majority of Justices assumed that illegal aliens in the United States have Fourth Amendment rights, the Ninth Circuit majority found it "difficult to conclude that Verdugo-Urquidez lacks these same protections." . . . It also observed that persons in respondent's position enjoy certain trial-related rights, and reasoned that "it would be odd indeed to acknowledge that Verdugo-Urquidez is entitled to due process under the fifth amendment, and to a fair trial under the sixth amendment, . . . and deny him the protection from unreasonable searches and seizures afforded under the fourth amendment." . . . Having concluded that the Fourth Amendment applied to the searches of respondent's properties, the court went on to decide that the searches violated the Constitution because the DEA agents failed to procure a search warrant. Although recognizing that "an American search warrant would be of no legal validity in Mexico," the majority deemed it sufficient that a warrant would have "substantial constitutional value in this country," because it would reflect a magistrate's determination that there existed probable cause to search and would define the scope of the search. . . .

The dissenting judge argued that this Court's statement in *United States v. Curtiss-Wright Export Corp.*, 299 U.S. 304, 318 (1936), that "neither the Constitution nor the laws passed in pursuance of it have any force in foreign territory unless in respect of our own citizens," foreclosed any claim by respondent to Fourth Amendment rights. More broadly, he viewed the Constitution as a "compact" among the people of the United States, and the protections of the Fourth Amendment were expressly limited to "the people." We granted certiorari. . . .

Before analyzing the scope of the Fourth Amendment, we think it significant to note that it operates in a different manner than the Fifth Amendment, which is not at issue in this case. The privilege against self-incrimination guaranteed by the Fifth Amendment is a fundamental trial right of criminal defendants. . . . Although conduct by law enforcement officials prior to trial may ultimately impair that right, a constitutional violation occurs only at trial. . . . The Fourth Amendment functions differently. It prohibits "unreasonable searches and seizures" whether or not the evidence is sought to be used in a criminal trial, and a violation of the Amendment is "fully accomplished" at the time of an unreasonable governmental intrusion. . . . For purposes of this case, therefore, if there were a constitutional violation, it occurred solely in Mexico. Whether evidence obtained from respondent's Mexican residences should be excluded at trial in the United States is a remedial question separate from the existence *vel non* of the constitutional violation....

The Fourth Amendment provides:

> "The right of the people to be secure in their persons, houses, papers, and effects, against unreasonable searches and seizures, shall not be violated, and no Warrants shall issue, but upon probable cause, supported by Oath or affirmation, and particularly describing the place to be searched, and the persons or things to be seized."

That text, by contrast with the Fifth and Sixth Amendments, extends its reach only to "the people." Contrary to the suggestion of *amici curiae* that the Framers used this phrase "simply to avoid [an] awkward rhetorical redundancy, ..."the people" seems to have been a term of art employed in select parts of the Constitution. The Preamble declares that the Constitution is ordained and established by "the People of the United States." The Second Amendment protects "the right of the people to keep and bear Arms," and the Ninth and Tenth Amendments provide that certain rights and powers are retained by and reserved to "the people." *See also* U.S. Const., Amdt. 1 ("Congress shall make no law ... abridging ... *the right of the people* peaceably to assemble") (emphasis added); Art. I, § 2, cl. 1 ("The House of Representatives shall be composed of Members chosen every second Year *by the People of the several States*") (emphasis added). While this textual exegesis is by no means conclusive, it suggests that "the people" protected by the Fourth Amendment, and by the First and Second Amendments, and to whom rights and powers are reserved in the Ninth and Tenth Amendments, refers to a class of persons who are part of a national community or who have otherwise developed sufficient connection with this country to be considered part of that community.... The language of these Amendments contrasts with the words "person" and "accused" used in the Fifth and Sixth Amendments regulating procedure in criminal cases.

What we know of the history of the drafting of the Fourth Amendment also suggests that its purpose was to restrict searches and seizures which might be conducted by the United States in domestic matters. The Framers originally decided not to include a provision like the Fourth Amendment, because they believed the National Government lacked power to conduct searches and seizures.... Many disputed the original view that the Federal Government possessed only narrow delegated powers over domestic affairs, however, and ultimately felt an Amendment prohibiting unreasonable searches and seizures was necessary. Madison, for example, argued that "there is a clause granting to Congress the power to make all laws which shall be necessary and proper for carrying into execution all of the powers vested in the Government of the United States," and that general warrants might be considered "necessary" for the purpose of collecting revenue.... The driving force behind the adoption of the Amendment, as suggested by Madison's advocacy, was widespread hostility among the former colonists to the issuance of writs of assistance empowering revenue officers to search suspected places for smuggled goods, and general search warrants permitting the search of private houses, often to uncover papers that might be used to convict persons of libel. . . . The available historical data show, therefore, that the purpose of the Fourth Amendment was to protect the people of the United States against arbitrary action by their own Government; it was never suggested that the provision was intended to restrain the actions of the Federal Government against aliens outside of the United States territory.

There is likewise no indication that the Fourth Amendment was understood by contemporaries of the Framers to apply to activities of the United States directed against aliens in foreign territory or in international waters. . . . The global view taken by the Court of Appeals of the application of the Constitution is also contrary to this Court's decisions in the *Insular Cases*, which held that not every constitutional provision applies to governmental activity even where the United States has sovereign power. . . . Indeed, we have rejected the claim that aliens are entitled to Fifth Amendment rights outside the sovereign territory of the United States. . . .

To support his all-encompassing view of the Fourth Amendment, respondent points to language from the plurality opinion in *Reid v. Covert*, 354 U.S. 1 (1957). *Reid* involved an attempt by Congress to subject the wives of American servicemen to trial by military tribunals without the protection of the Fifth and Sixth Amendments. The Court held that it was unconstitutional to apply the Uniform Code of Military Justice to the trials of the American women for capital crimes. Four Justices "rejected the idea that when the United States acts *against citizens* abroad it can do so free of the Bill of Rights." . . . (emphasis added). The plurality went on to say:

> "The United States is entirely a creature of the Constitution. Its power and authority have no other source. It can only act in accordance with all the limitations imposed by the Constitution. When the Government reaches out to punish *a citizen* who is abroad, the shield which the Bill of Rights and other parts of the Constitution provide to protect his life and liberty should not be stripped away just because he happens to be in another land." . . .

Respondent urges that we interpret this discussion to mean that federal officials are constrained by the Fourth Amendment wherever and against whomever they act. But the holding of *Reid* stands for no such sweeping proposition: it decided that United States citizens stationed abroad could invoke the protection of the Fifth and Sixth Amendments. The concurring opinions by Justices Frankfurter and Harlan in *Reid* resolved the case on much narrower grounds than the plurality and declined even to hold that United States citizens were entitled to the full range of constitutional protections in all overseas criminal prosecutions. . . . Since respondent is not a United States citizen, he can derive no comfort from the *Reid* holding.

Verdugo-Urquidez also relies on a series of cases in which we have held that aliens enjoy certain constitutional rights. . . . These cases, however, establish only that aliens receive constitutional protections when they have come within the territory of the United States and developed substantial connections with the country. . . .

Respondent is an alien who has had no previous significant voluntary connection with the United States, so these cases avail him not.

Justice Stevens' concurrence in the judgment takes the view that even though the search took place in Mexico, it is nonetheless governed by the requirements of the Fourth Amendment because respondent was "lawfully present in the United States . . . even though he was brought and held here against his will." . . . But this sort of presence—lawful but involuntary—is not of the sort to indicate any substantial connection with our country. The extent to which respondent might claim the protection of the Fourth Amendment if the duration of his stay in the United States were to be prolonged—by a prison sentence, for example—we need not decide. When the search of his house in Mexico took place, he had been present in the United States for only a matter of days. We do not think the applicability of the Fourth Amendment to the search of premises in Mexico should turn on the fortuitous circumstance of whether the custodian of its nonresident alien owner had or had not transported him to the United States at the time the search was made.

The Court of Appeals found some support for its holding in our decision in *INS v. Lopez-Mendoza*, 468 U.S. 1032 (1984), where a majority of Justices assumed that the Fourth Amendment applied to illegal aliens in the United States. We cannot fault the Court of Appeals for placing some reliance on the case, but our decision did not expressly address the proposition gleaned by the court below. The question presented for decision in *Lopez-Mendoza* was limited to whether the Fourth Amendment's exclusionary rule should be extended to civil deportation proceedings; it did not encompass whether the protections of the Fourth Amendment extend to illegal aliens in this country. . . .

Respondent also contends that to treat aliens differently from citizens with respect to the Fourth Amendment somehow violates the equal protection component of the Fifth Amendment to the United States Constitution. . . . Not only are history and case law against respondent, but as pointed out in *Johnson v. Eisentrager*, 339 U.S. 763 (1950), the result of accepting his claim would have significant and deleterious consequences for the United States in conducting activities beyond its boundaries. The rule adopted by the Court of Appeals would apply not only to law enforcement operations abroad, but also to other foreign policy operations which might result in "searches or seizures." The United States frequently employs armed forces outside this country—over 200 times in our history—for the protection of American citizens or national security. . . . Application of the Fourth Amendment to those circumstances could significantly disrupt the ability of the political branches to respond to foreign situations involving our national interest. Were respondent to prevail, aliens with no attachment to this country might well bring actions for damages to remedy claimed violations of the Fourth Amendment in foreign countries or in international waters. . . .

We think that the text of the Fourth Amendment, its history, and our cases discussing the application of the Constitution to aliens and extraterritorially require rejection of respondent's claim. At the time of the search, he was a citizen and resident of Mexico with no voluntary attachment to the United States, and the place searched was located in Mexico. Under these circumstances, the Fourth Amendment has no application.

For better or for worse, we live in a world of nation-states in which our Government must be able to "function effectively in the company of sovereign nations." . . . Some who violate our laws may live outside our borders under a regime quite different from that which obtains in this country. Situations threatening to important American interests may arise halfway around the globe, situations which in the view of the political branches of our Government require an American response with armed force. If there are to be restrictions on searches and seizures which occur incident to such American action, they must be imposed by the political branches through diplomatic understanding, treaty, or legislation.

The judgment of the Court of Appeals is accordingly Reversed.

JUSTICE KENNEDY, concurring.

I agree that no violation of the Fourth Amendment has occurred and that we must reverse the judgment of the Court of Appeals. Although some explanation of my views is appropriate given the difficulties of this case, I do not believe they depart in fundamental respects from the opinion of the Court, which I join.

In cases involving the extraterritorial application of the Constitution, we have taken care to state whether the person claiming its protection is a citizen, . . . or an alien. . . . The distinction between citizens and aliens follows from the undoubted proposition that the Constitution does not create, nor do general principles of law create, any juridical relation between our country and some undefined, limitless class of noncitizens who are beyond our territory. We should note, however, that the absence of this relation does not depend on the idea that only a limited class of persons ratified the instrument that formed our Government. Though it must be beyond dispute that persons outside the United States did not and could not assent to the Constitution, that is quite irrelevant to any construction of the powers conferred or the limitations imposed by it. . . .

For somewhat similar reasons, I cannot place any weight on the reference to "the people" in the Fourth Amendment as a source of restricting its protections. With respect, I submit these words do not detract from its force or its reach. Given the history of our Nation's concern over warrantless and unreasonable searches, explicit recognition of "the right of the people" to Fourth Amendment protection may be interpreted to underscore the importance of the right, rather than to restrict the category of persons who may assert it. The restrictions that the United States must observe with reference to aliens beyond its territory or jurisdiction depend, as a consequence, on general principles of interpretation, not on an inquiry as to who formed the Constitution or a construction that some rights are mentioned as being those of "the people."

I take it to be correct, as the plurality opinion in *Reid v. Covert* sets forth, that the Government may act only as the Constitution authorizes, whether the actions in question are foreign or domestic. . . . But this principle is only a first step in resolving this case. The question before us then becomes what constitutional standards apply when the Government acts, in reference to an alien, within its sphere of foreign operations. . . .

The conditions and considerations of this case would make adherence to the Fourth Amendment's warrant requirement impracticable and anomalous. Just as the Constitution in the *Insular Cases* did not require Congress to implement all constitutional guarantees in its territories because of their "wholly dissimilar traditions and institutions," the Constitution does not require United States agents to obtain a warrant when searching the foreign home of a nonresident alien. If the search had occurred in a residence within the United States, I have little doubt that the full protections of the Fourth Amendment would apply. But that is not this case. The absence of local judges or magistrates available to issue warrants, the differing and perhaps unascertainable conceptions of reasonableness and privacy that prevail abroad, and the need to cooperate with foreign officials all indicate that the Fourth Amendment's warrant requirement should not apply in Mexico as it does in this country. For this reason, in addition to the other persuasive justifications stated by the Court, I agree that no violation of the Fourth Amendment has occurred in the case before us. The rights of a citizen, as to whom the United States has continuing obligations, are not presented by this case.

I do not mean to imply, and the Court has not decided, that persons in the position of the respondent have no constitutional protection. The United States is prosecuting a foreign national in a court established under Article III, and all of the trial proceedings are governed by the Constitution. All would agree, for instance, that the dictates of the Due Process Clause of the Fifth Amendment protect the defendant. . . . Nothing approaching a violation of due process has occurred in this case.

Justice Stevens, concurring in the judgment.

In my opinion aliens who are lawfully present in the United States are among those "people" who are entitled to the protection of the Bill of Rights, including the Fourth Amendment. Respondent is surely such a person even though he was brought and held here against his will. I therefore cannot join the Court's sweeping opinion. I do agree, however, with the Government's submission that the search conducted by the United States agents with the approval and cooperation of the Mexican authorities was not "unreasonable" as that term is used in the first Clause of the Amendment. I do not believe the Warrant Clause has any application to searches of noncitizens' homes in foreign jurisdictions because American magistrates have no power to authorize such searches. I therefore concur in the Court's judgment. . . .

Justice Brennan, with whom Justice Marshall joins, dissenting.

Today the Court holds that although foreign nationals must abide by our laws even when in their own countries, our Government need not abide by the Fourth Amendment when it investigates them for violations of our laws. I respectfully dissent. . . .

Particularly in the past decade, our Government has sought, successfully, to hold foreign nationals criminally liable under federal laws for conduct committed entirely beyond the territorial limits of the United States that nevertheless has effects in this country. Foreign nationals must now take care not to violate our drug laws, our antitrust laws, our securities laws, and a host of other federal criminal statutes. The enormous expansion of federal criminal jurisdiction outside our Nation's boundaries has led one commentator to suggest that our country's three largest exports are now "rock music, blue jeans, and United States law." . . .

The Constitution is the source of Congress' authority to criminalize conduct, whether here or abroad, and of the Executive's authority to investigate and prosecute such conduct. But the same Constitution also prescribes limits on our Government's authority to investigate, prosecute, and punish criminal conduct, whether foreign or domestic. . . .

What the majority ignores, however, is the most obvious connection between Verdugo-Urquidez and the United States: he was investigated and is being prosecuted for violations of United States law and may well spend the rest of his life in a United States prison. The "sufficient connection" is supplied not by Verdugo-Urquidez, but by the Government. Respondent is entitled to the protections of the Fourth Amendment because our Government, by investigating him and attempting to hold him accountable under United States criminal laws, has treated him as a member of our community for purposes of enforcing our laws. He has become, quite literally, one of the governed. Fundamental fairness and the ideals underlying our Bill of Rights compel the conclusion that when we impose "societal obligations," . . . such as the obligation to comply with our criminal laws, on foreign nationals, we in turn are obliged to respect certain correlative rights, among them the Fourth Amendment.

By concluding that respondent is not one of "the people" protected by the Fourth Amendment, the majority disregards basic notions of mutuality. If we expect aliens to obey our laws, aliens should be able to expect that we will obey our Constitution when we investigate, prosecute, and punish them. We have recognized this fundamental principle of mutuality since the time of the Framers. . . .

Mutuality also serves to inculcate the values of law and order. By respecting the rights of foreign nationals, we encourage other nations to respect the rights of our citizens. Moreover, as our Nation becomes increasingly concerned about the domestic effects of international crime, we cannot forget that the behavior of our law enforcement agents abroad sends a powerful message about the rule of law to individuals everywhere. . . . This principle is no different when the United States applies its rules of conduct to foreign nationals. If we seek respect for law and order, we must observe these principles ourselves. Lawlessness breeds lawlessness.

Finally, when United States agents conduct unreasonable searches, whether at home or abroad, they disregard our Nation's values. For over 200 years, our country has considered itself the world's foremost protector of liberties. The privacy and sanctity of the home have been primary tenets of our moral, philosophical, and judicial beliefs. Our national interest is defined by those values and by the need to preserve our own just institutions. We take pride in our commitment to a Government that cannot, on mere whim, break down doors and invade the most personal of places. We exhort other nations to follow our example. How can we explain to others—and to ourselves—that these long cherished ideals are suddenly of no consequence when the door being broken belongs to a foreigner? . . .

The majority's rejection of respondent's claim to Fourth Amendment protection is apparently motivated by its fear that application of the Amendment to law enforcement searches against foreign nationals overseas "could significantly disrupt the ability of the political branches to respond to foreign situations involving our national interest." . . . The majority's doomsday scenario-that American Armed Forces conducting a mission to protect our national security with no law enforcement objective "would have to articulate specific facts giving them probable cause to undertake a search or seizure" . . . is fanciful. Verdugo-Urquidez is protected by the Fourth Amendment because our Government, by investigating and prosecuting him, has made him one of "the governed." . . . Accepting respondent as one of "the governed," however, hardly requires the Court to accept enemy aliens in wartime as among "the governed" entitled to invoke the protection of the Fourth Amendment. . . .

Moreover, with respect to non-law-enforcement activities not directed against enemy aliens in wartime but nevertheless implicating national security, doctrinal exceptions to the general requirements of a warrant and probable cause likely would be applicable more frequently abroad, thus lessening the purported tension between the Fourth Amendment's strictures and the Executive's foreign affairs power. Many situations involving sensitive operations abroad likely would involve exigent circumstances such that the warrant requirement would be excused. . . . Therefore, the Government's conduct would be assessed only under the reasonableness standard, the application of which depends on context. . . .

Because the Fourth Amendment governs the search of respondent's Mexican residences, the District Court suppressed the evidence found in that search because the officers conducting the search did not obtain a warrant. . . . The Warrant Clause would serve the same primary functions abroad as it does domestically, and I see no reason to distinguish between foreign and domestic searches. . . .

The Warrant Clause cannot be ignored simply because Congress has not given any United States magistrate authority to issue search warrants for foreign searches. . . . Congress cannot define the contours of the Constitution. If the Warrant Clause applies, Congress cannot excise the Clause from the Constitution by failing to provide a means for United States agents to obtain a warrant. . . .

Nor is the Warrant Clause inapplicable merely because a warrant from a United States magistrate could not "authorize" a search in a foreign country. Although this may be true as a matter of international law, it is irrelevant to our interpretation of the Fourth Amendment. As a matter of United States constitutional law, a warrant serves the same primary function overseas as it does domestically; it assures that a neutral magistrate has authorized the search and limited its scope. The need to protect those suspected of criminal activity from the unbridled discretion of investigation officers is no less important abroad than at home. . . .

When we tell the world that we expect all people, wherever they may be, to abide by our laws, we cannot in the same breath tell the world that our law enforcement officers need not do the same. Because we cannot expect others to respect our laws until we respect our Constitution, I respectfully dissent.

Justice Blackmun, dissenting.

I cannot accept the Court of Appeals' conclusion, echoed in some portions of Justice Brennan's dissent, that the Fourth Amendment governs every action by an American official that can be characterized as a search or seizure. American agents acting abroad generally do not purport to exercise *sovereign* authority over the foreign nationals with whom they come in contact. The relationship between these agents and foreign nationals is therefore fundamentally different from the relationship between United States officials and individuals residing within this country. . . .

I am inclined to agree with Justice Brennan, however, that when a foreign national is held accountable for purported violations of United States criminal laws, he has effectively been treated as one of "the governed" and therefore us entitled to Fourth Amendment protections. Although the Government's exercise of power abroad does not ordinarily implicate the Fourth Amendment, the enforcement of domestic criminal law seems to me to be the paradigmatic exercise of sovereignty over those who are compelled to obey. . . . Under these circumstances I believe that respondent is entitled to invoke protections of the Fourth Amendment. I agree with the Government, however, that an American magistrate's lack of power to authorize a search abroad renders the Warrant Clause inapplicable to the search of a noncitizen's residence outside this country.

The Fourth Amendment nevertheless requires that the search be "reasonable." And when the purpose of a search is the procurement of evidence for a criminal prosecution, we have consistently held that the search, to be reasonable, must be based upon probable cause. Neither the District Court nor the Court of Appeals addressed the issue of probable cause, and I do not believe that a reliable determination could be made on the basis of the record before us. I therefore would vacate the judgment of the Court of Appeals and remand the case for further proceedings.

Notes

(1) Does the *Verdugo* case still apply after the Court's decision in *Boumediene* [§ 3.07]? *See* Gerald L. Neuman, *The Extraterritorial Constitution After* Boumediene v. Bush, 82 S. Cal. L. Rev. 259 (2009) ("The decision [in *Boumediene*] repudiates the stance of the plurality in *United States v. Verdugo-Urquidez* which sought to deny all constitutional rights to foreign nationals involuntarily subjected to U.S. action abroad."); A. Hays Butler, *The Supreme Court's Decision in* Boumediene v. Bush: *The*

Military Commissions Act of 2006 and Habeas Corpus Jurisdiction, 6 Rutgers J. L. & Pub. Pol'y 149 (2008) (discussing how *Boumediene* recognizes "that when the U.S. exercises sovereign power over aliens, those aliens have fundamental constitutional rights.") Justice Scalia in his dissent in *Boumediene* states that *Verdugo* "could not be clearer that the privilege of habeas corpus does not extend to aliens abroad." 128 S. Ct. 2229, 2302 (2008) (Scalia, dissenting). Consider *Hernandez v. United States*, 757 F.3d 249 (5th Cir. 2014). In 2010, Sergio Hernandez was one of a group of Mexican teenagers playing a game in Ciudad Juarez that included running up to the El Paso, Texas, border. He was shot by a United States Border Patrol Agent from the El Paso side. His survivors made claims based on the Fourth Amendment and on a substantive due process Fifth Amendment argument. The Fifth Circuit, en banc, dismissed the action. Relying on *Verdugo*, the Court held that "Hernandez, a Mexican citizen who had no 'significant voluntary connection' to the United States . . . and who was on Mexican soil at the time he was shot, cannot assert a claim under the Fourth Amendment." As to the Fifth Amendment claim, the Court acknowledged that "the strongest authority for the plaintiff may be *Boumediene*." The Court saw *Boumediene* as a special case applying only to habeas corpus. It concluded that "[a]lthough the en banc court is somewhat divided on the question of whether Agent Mesa's conduct violated the Fifth Amendment, the court . . . is unanimous in concluding that any properly asserted right was not clearly established to the extent the law requires." Thus, qualified immunity applied to the Fifth Amendment claim.

(2) What does *Verdugo-Urquidez* imply about Fourth Amendment rights of U.S. citizens abroad? Does the case apply to foreign nationals within the United States? To what extent do excludable foreign nationals in the United States have Fourth Amendment rights? Even if the Fourth Amendment is found to apply outside the United States, would the warrant requirements of the United States be applicable? In *United States v. Stokes*, 726 F.3d 880 (7th Cir. 2013), the Seventh Circuit examined the requirements of the Fourth Amendment in the context of evidence gathered during a search abroad. The search was conducted as part of a joint operation by U.S. and Thai law enforcement and targeted the home of a U.S. citizen living in Thailand. Based on the evidence discovered during the search, Stokes was extradited to the United States and convicted of traveling in foreign commerce for the purpose of engaging in a sex act with a minor (a violation of 18 U.S.C. § 2423(b)). Regarding the warrant issue, the court stated:

> Evidence obtained in a search of an American citizen by foreign authorities operating within their own country is generally admissible in the courts of the United States even if the search does not otherwise comply with our law, including the law of the Fourth Amendment. But if U.S. agents substantially participate in an extraterritorial search of a U.S. citizen and the foreign officials were essentially acting as agents for their American counterparts or the search amounted to a joint operation between American and foreign authorities, the Fourth Amendment generally applies.
>
> . . . .

Stokes argues that the Thai warrant violated the Warrant Clause because it did not describe the items to be seized with particularity and the search exceeded the scope of the warrant. There is no question that the warrant used very general language. Stokes's argument thus requires us to decide whether an extraterritorial search by U.S. agents is subject to the Warrant Clause.

The Warrant Clause is phrased as a limitation on the power to issue warrants and is distinct from the Fourth Amendment's "warrant requirement," which though not expressed in the text of the Amendment is implied as a matter of long-standing Supreme Court doctrine. The Supreme Court has never addressed whether the Warrant Clause or the doctrinal requirement of a warrant applies extraterritorially. Nor have we.

The Supreme Court's reasoning in *United States v. Verdugo-Urquidez*, 494 U.S. 259, 110 S. Ct. 1056, 108 L. Ed. 2d 222 (1990), sheds some light on the question. In *Verdugo-Urquidez* the Court held that the Fourth Amendment has no application to a warrantless search by U.S. agents of a nonresident alien's property located in a foreign country—there, Mexico. . . . Because the Amendment did not apply at all, the Court had no need to separately address whether the warrant requirement and the Warrant Clause applied to foreign searches by American agents. But the Court noted in passing that any warrant issued by a judicial officer in this country "would be a dead letter outside the United States." Justice Kennedy's concurring opinion was more direct:

> The absence of local judges or magistrates available to issue warrants, the differing and perhaps unascertainable conceptions of reasonableness and privacy that prevail abroad, and the need to cooperate with foreign officials all indicate that the Fourth Amendment's warrant requirement should not apply in Mexico as it does in this country.

Justice Stevens echoed the point in his concurrence, as did Justice Blackmun in dissent.

Among the circuit courts of appeals, only the Second has addressed whether the Fourth Amendment's warrant requirement applies to searches conducted by U.S. agents overseas, concluding that it does not. *See In re Terrorist Bombings*, [552 F.3d 157 (2nd Cir. 2008)]. The Second Circuit took its cues from *Verdugo-Urquidez*, in which no fewer than "seven justices of the Supreme Court endorsed the view that U.S. courts are not empowered to issue warrants for foreign searches."

Beyond reading the clear signals from the Supreme Court in *Verdugo-Urquidez*, the Second Circuit noted the absence of any historical support for the argument that the Fourth Amendment's warrant requirement applies to searches carried out by U.S. agents overseas. The court also considered the foreign-policy implications of extending the warrant requirement to extraterritorial searches, noting that "nothing in the history of the foreign relations of the United States would require that U.S. officials obtain warrants from foreign magistrates . . . or, indeed, to suppose that all other states have search and investigation rules akin to our own."

Finally, the court returned to the basic difficulty that "if U.S. judicial officers were to issue search warrants intended to have extraterritorial effect, such warrants would have dubious legal significance, if any, in a foreign nation." And "it is by no means clear that U.S. judicial officers could be authorized to issue warrants for overseas searches." For these reasons, the court concluded that "the Fourth Amendment's Warrant Clause has no extraterritorial application," and "foreign searches of U.S. citizens conducted by U.S. agents are subject only to the Fourth Amendment's requirement of reasonableness."

. . . .

We agree with the Second Circuit's reasoning and now hold that the Fourth Amendment's warrant requirement, and by extension the strictures of the Warrant Clause, do not apply to extraterritorial searches by U.S. agents. The search of Stokes's home in Thailand is governed by the Amendment's basic requirement of reasonableness, to which we now turn.

2. Reasonableness of the Search

Whether a search is reasonable under the Fourth Amendment depends on the totality of the circumstances and requires the court to weigh the intrusion on individual privacy against the government's need for information and evidence. On the individual side of the ledger, the privacy of the home is central to the Fourth Amendment right. Against that core individual right is the government's strong interest in preventing the sexual exploitation of children.

. . . Because the search of Stokes's home was reasonable, the district court properly denied suppression of the evidence recovered there.

See also In Re Terrorist Bombings of U.S. Embassies in East Africa, 552 F.3d 157 (2d Cir. 2008) (holding that "the Fourth Amendment's warrant requirement does not govern searches conducted abroad by U.S. agents; such searches of U.S. citizens need only satisfy the Fourth Amendment's requirement of reasonableness.").

(3) How would the Fourth Amendment apply to a search outside the United States by foreign officials acting alone? "[T]he Fourth Amendment does not restrict actions of foreign law enforcement officers acting outside the United States." Thus, "[e]vidence independently secured by a foreign officer, therefore, if turned over to an American court, may be admitted against the victim of the search." Joshua Dressler, Understanding Criminal Procedure Vol. 1 § 4.04(F) (8th ed. 2021). Two exceptions have developed to this general premise. One exception applies where the search is related to a joint operation between U.S. and foreign law enforcement officials, as

previously discussed above in *United States v. Stokes* [note 2]. The second exception involves situations where the search "shocks" the judicial conscience. In *United States v. Barona*, 56 F.3d 1087 (9th Cir. 1995), the court discussed both exceptions.

> ... When determining the validity of a foreign wiretap, we start with two general and undisputed propositions. The first is that Title III of the Omnibus Crime Control and Safe Streets Act of 1968, 18 U.S.C. § § 2510–21, "has no extraterritorial force." ... Our analysis, then, is guided only by the applicable principles of constitutional law. The second proposition is that "neither our Fourth Amendment nor the judicially created exclusionary rule applies to acts of foreign officials." ...
>
> Two "very limited exceptions" apply.... One exception, clearly inapplicable here, occurs "if the circumstances of the foreign search and seizure are so extreme that they 'shock the [judicial] conscience,' [so that] a federal appellate court in the exercise of its supervisory powers can require exclusion of the evidence." ... This type of exclusion is not based on our Fourth Amendment jurisprudence, but rather on the recognition that we may employ our supervisory powers when absolutely necessary to preserve the integrity of the criminal justice system....
>
> The second exception to the inapplicability of the exclusionary rule applies when "United States agents' participation in the investigation is so substantial that the action is a joint venture between United States and foreign officials." ... If a joint venture is found to have existed, "the law of the foreign country must be consulted at the outset as part of the determination whether or not the search was reasonable." If foreign law was not complied with, "the good faith exception to the exclusionary rule becomes part of the analysis." "The good faith exception is grounded in the realization that the exclusionary rule does not function as a deterrent in cases in which the law enforcement officers acted on a reasonable belief that their conduct was legal." ...

Id. at 1090–93. In *United States v. Emmanuel*, 565 F.3d 1324 (11th Cir. 2009), the Eleventh Circuit held that a Bahamian wiretap did not shock the judicial conscience and that the "standard is meant to protect against conduct that violates fundamental international norms of decency." In *United States v. Maturo*, 982 F.2d 57, 61 (2nd Cir. 1992), the court noted that,

> [w]ithin the second category for excluding evidence, constitutional requirements may attach in two situations: (1) where the conduct of foreign law enforcement officials' rendered them agents, or virtual agents, of United States law enforcement officials ...; or (2) where the cooperation between the United States and foreign law enforcement agencies is designed to evade constitutional requirements applicable to American officials.

"[P]roviding information to foreign authorities does not transform a subsequent search by foreign officials into a joint venture." *United States v. Baboolal*, 2010 WL

2730984 (E.D. Wisc. 2006); *see also United States v. Getto*, 729 F.3d 221, 224 (2d Cir. 2012) (holding that "ongoing collaboration between an American law enforcement agency and its foreign counterpart in the course of parallel investigations does not— without American control, direction, or an intent to evade the Constitution—give rise to a relationship sufficient to apply the exclusionary rule to evidence obtained abroad by foreign law enforcement.").

(4) The court in *Verdugo-Urquidez* stated "that aliens receive constitutional protections when they have come within the territory of the United States and developed substantial connections with this country." When has one "developed substantial connections with this country"? Should courts interpret "substantial connections" as it "has been used in the minimum-contacts test in personal jurisdiction questions"? David Haug, Recent Developments, *United States: Extraterritorial Application of the Fourth Amendment— United States v. Verdugo-Urquidez*, 110 S. Ct. 1056 (1990), 32 Harv. Int'l L.J. 295, 301 n.39 (1991).

(5) In *Wang v. Reno*, 81 F.3d 808 (9th Cir. 1996), the court distinguished the Verdugo decision when placed in the context of the Fifth Amendment. In addition to noting that the Fifth Amendment "provides protection to the 'person' rather than 'the people,'" the court stated that "unlike *Verdugo-Urquidez*, this case does not concern an isolated, extraterritorial violation of the Constitution. . . . Rather, the two-year American prosecutorial effort violated Wang's due process rights on American soil, where he as forced in an American courtroom, to choose between committing the crime of perjury or telling the truth and facing torture and possible execution. Thus, we conclude that Wang is guaranteed due process under the Fifth Amendment."

(6) What role does the Fourth Amendment have with regard to searches at U.S. borders? Does it make a difference if a person is exiting or entering the United States? In *United States v. Beras*, 183 F.3d 22 (1st Cir. 1999), the court stated:

> It is well established that "the Fourth Amendment's balance of reasonableness is qualitatively different at the international border than in the interior." . . . Under the border search exception, "routine searches of the persons and effects of entrants are not subject to any requirement of reasonable suspicion, probable cause, or warrant." . . . The Supreme Court, however, has not yet addressed the issue of whether the border search exception applies to outgoing as well as incoming travelers. Nor has this circuit ruled on the issue. . . . Every other circuit to consider the issue, to our knowledge, has held that the border search exception applies to outgoing as well as incoming travelers. *See United States v. Ezeiruaku*, 936 F.2d 136, 143 (3d Cir. 1991); *United States v. Berisha*, 925 F.2d 791, 795 (5th Cir. 1991); *United States v. Udofot*, 711 F.2d 831, 839–40 (8th Cir. 1983); *United States v. Ajlouny*, 629 F.2d 830, 834–35 (2d Cir. 1980); *United States v. Stanley*, 545 F.2d 661, 667 (9th Cir. 1976); *cf. United States v. Hernandez-Salazar*, 813 F.2d 1126, 1138 (11th Cir. 1987) (without deciding whether the border search exception "applies equally in all respects to incoming and outgoing searches," holding

that the Fourth Amendment "permits warrantless searches of persons and property departing the United States on the basis of reasonable suspicion that a currency reporting violation is occurring"). These cases have drawn support from dicta in *California Bankers Ass'n v. Shultz*, 416 U.S. 21, 63, 94 S. Ct. 1494, 39 L. Ed. 2d 812 (1974), where the Supreme Court stated: "Those entering and leaving the country may be examined as to their belongings and effects, all without violating the Fourth Amendment."

We join our sister circuits and conclude that the border search exception to the Fourth Amendment applies to outgoing travelers. In our view, there is a convincing policy justification for extending the exception. The border search exception arises from the "longstanding concern for the protection of the integrity of the border[, . . . a] concern [that] is, if anything, heightened by the veritable national crisis in law enforcement caused by smuggling of illicit narcotics." . . . As the Third Circuit has recognized, this concern also arises with respect to outgoing travelers:

> National interests in the flow of currency justify the diminished recognition of privacy inherent in crossing into and out of the borders of the United States. . . . Although there is not the slightest suggestion that the appellee here was implicated in drug trafficking, in an environment that sees a massive importation of drugs across our borders, we are cognizant that there must be a concomitant outflow of cash to pay for this nefarious traffic.

U.S. v. Ezeiruaku, 936 F.2d 136 at 143.

(7) When travel is via airplane, is there an extension of where the search may be conducted? Can international agreements foreclose Fourth Amendment arguments? In *United States v. Walczak*, [§ 3.04[B]] the Ninth Circuit Court of Appeals held:

. . . Walczak argues that the search violated the fourth amendment's proscription against unreasonable searches. Searches at the border are reasonable as an essential prerogative of a sovereign to protect its border. Therefore persons and vehicles crossing the border into this country may be searched without probable cause or a warrant. . . . The Supreme Court has held that searches may take place at the border or at its "functional equivalent." *Almeida-Sanchez v. United States*, 413 U.S. 266, 272, 93 S. Ct. 2535, 37 L. Ed. 2d 596 (1973). This is because modern air travel renders it "unreasonable to expect that persons can [always] be searched at the exact moment they cross an international border." . . .

Modern advances in air transportation call for even more responsive protective procedures. Accordingly, in 1974, the United States and Canada entered into an executive agreement authorizing United States Customs "preclearance" operations at various Canadian airports, including Vancouver Airport. . . .

International agreements other than treaties may fall into any of three categories: congressional-executive agreements, executed by the President upon specific authorizing legislation from Congress; executive agreements pursuant to treaty, executed by the President in accord with specific instructions in a prior, formal treaty; and executive agreements executed pursuant to the President's own constitutional authority. . . . Congress has not specifically authorized the President to conclude executive agreements such as this in the realm of civil aviation, but clearly did contemplate that the executive branch would negotiate "agreement[s] with foreign governments for the establishment or development of air navigation, including air routes and services." . . . The agreement is not specifically of the second category, because while there is some relationship to the Convention on International Civil Aviation, Dec. 7, 1944, . . . the Convention does not literally authorize the President to enter into agreements implementing it.

The Supreme Court has recognized that of necessity the President may enter into certain binding agreements with foreign nations not strictly congruent with the formalities required by the Constitution's Treaty Clause [Art. II, § 2] . . . The authority to enter into executive agreements derives from the power over foreign relations accorded to the President by the Constitution. . . .

If an agreement is within the President's power over foreign concords and relations, there seem to be no formal requirements as to how it must be made. It can be signed by the President or by his authority; it may be by delegation by him to his Secretaries of State, Ambassadors, or lesser authorized government officials. . . . The Supreme Court has never held an executive agreement *ultra vires* for lack of Senate consent. . . . Since the 1974 Agreement was designed to implement the goals of the Convention, which itself is an Article II treaty, and since Congress contemplated that agreements having to do with civil aviation would be negotiated by the executive branch, the agreement in question is among those which the President may conclude on his own authority.

Because constitutionally valid executive agreements are to be applied by the courts as the law of the land, . . . the Agreement on Air Transport Preclearance has the full force of law, and it governs in this case.

The agreement provides that

> the inspecting party may extend the application of any of its customs, immigration, agriculture and public health laws and regulations to aircraft, passengers, aircraft crew, baggage, cargo and aircraft stores in the territory of the other Party which are subject to preclearance to the extent consistent with the law of the country in which the inspection takes place.

Art. VII, at 767.

> Various regulations define the activities which are to take place at preclearance facilities. "Preclearance is the tentative examination and inspection of air travelers and their baggage at foreign places where U.S. Customs personnel are stationed for that purpose." ... "Articles in baggage ... shall be considered as accompanying a passenger if examined at an established preclearance station and the baggage is hand-carried. . . ." 19 C.F.R. § 148.4(c) (1985). By allowing preclearance at Vancouver, the agreement authorizes U.S. Customs officials stationed at a preclearance facility to search persons bound for the United States as thoroughly as though the search were taking place at the border. Therefore the search of Walczak at the preclearance station did not violate the fourth amendment. . . .

(8) What is the role of the Fourth Amendment when outside the United States, but on the high seas? In *United States v. Hayes*, 653 F.2d 8 (5th Cir. 1981) the court stated:

> We address next appellants' claim that the CHARLES M was seized and boarded in violation of the fourth amendment and, therefore, the district court erred in not suppressing the fruits of the search. In *United States v. Hilton*, 619 F.2d 127 (1st Cir.), *cert. denied*, 449 U.S. 887, 101 S. Ct. 243, 66 L. Ed. 2d 113 (1980), this court sustained the Coast Guard's authority pursuant to 14 U.S.C. § 89(a)[3] to conduct safety and document investigations on American flag vessels located in international waters. We conclude that "the limited intrusion presented by a document and safety inspection on the high seas even in the absence of a warrant or suspicion of wrongdoing, is reasonable under the fourth amendment." ... The search here was within the scope of Coast Guard authority. Once on board and in the routine course of inspection, a member of the boarding party found marijuana in plain view. The Coast Guard did not proceed beyond the bounds of its inspection authority. . . .

---

3. 14 U.S.C. § 89(a) provides:

(a) The Coast Guard may make inquiries, examinations, inspections, searches, seizures, and arrests upon the high seas and waters over which the United States has jurisdiction, for the prevention, detection, and suppression of violations of laws of the United States. For such purposes, commissioned, warrant, and petty officers may at any time go on board of any vessel subject to the jurisdiction, or to the operation of any law, of the United States, address inquiries to those on board, examine the ship's documents and papers, and examine, inspect, and search the vessel and use all necessary force to compel compliance. When from such inquires, examination, inspection or search it appears that a breach of the laws of the United States rendering a person liable to arrest is being, or had been committed, by any person, such person shall be arrested or, if escaping to shore, shall be immediately pursued and arrested on shore, or other lawful and appropriate action shall be taken; or if it shall appear that a breach of the laws of the United States has been committed so as to render such vessel, or the merchandise, or any part thereof, on board of, or brought into the United States by, such vessel, liable to forfeiture, or so as to render such vessel liable to a fine or penalty and if necessary to secure such fine or penalty, such vessel or such merchandise, or both, shall be seized.

See also Note, Megan Jaye Kight, *Constitutional Barriers to Smooth Sailing: 14 U.S.C. § 89(a) and the Fourth Amendment*, 72 Ind. L.J. 571 (1997). Additionally consider 19 U.S.C.A. § 1581 which provides:

> (a) Customs officers. Any officer of the customs may at any time go on board of any vessel or vehicle at any place in the United States or within the customs waters or, as he may be authorized, within a customs-enforcement area established under the Anti-Smuggling Act, or at any other authorized place without as well as within his district, and examine the manifest and other documents and papers and examine, inspect, and search the vessel or vehicle and every part thereof and any person, trunk, package, or cargo on board, and to this end may hail and stop such vessel or vehicle, and use all necessary force to compel compliance....
>
> (h) Application of section to treaties of United States. The provisions of this section shall not be construed to authorize or require any officer of the United States to enforce any law of the United States upon the high seas upon a foreign vessel in contravention of any treaty with a foreign government enabling or permitting the authorities of the United States to board, examine, search, seize, or otherwise to enforce upon said vessel upon the high seas the laws of the United States except as such authorities are or may otherwise be enabled or permitted under special arrangement with such foreign government.

(9) Even if the Fourth Amendment is found applicable to a citizen who is abroad, are there exceptions to the Fourth Amendment that might come into play in these situations? You may want to consider this issue as raised in the case below:

United States v. Bin Laden

United States District Court for the Southern District of New York
126 F. Supp. 2d 264 (2000)

Sand, District Judge:

The Defendants are charged with numerous offenses arising out of their alleged participation in an international terrorist organization led by Defendant Usama Bin Laden and that organization's alleged involvement in the August 1998 bombings of the United States Embassies in Nairobi, Kenya and Dar es Salaam, Tanzania. Presently before the Court are Defendant El-Hage's motions which seek the following: suppression of evidence seized from the search of his residence in Nairobi, Kenya in August 1997 and suppression of evidence obtained from electronic surveillance, conducted from August 1996 to August 1997, of four telephone lines in Nairobi, Kenya....

The charges currently pending against each of the Defendants in this case arise from their alleged involvement with an international terrorist organization known as "al Qaeda" or "the Base." ... Since its emergence in 1989, al Qaeda is alleged to have planned and financed (both independently and in association with other terrorist groups) numerous violent attacks against United States personnel and property abroad.... The United States Attorney's Office in the Southern District of New York has been investigating al Qaeda since at least 1996.... In the spring of 1996, Bin Laden, the founder and leader of al Qaeda ... was identified by the United States Government as "a serious threat to national security" ...

Among other things, the Government alleges that al Qaeda coordinates the activities of its global membership, sends its members to camps for military and intelligence training, obtains and transports weapons and explosives, and explicitly provides Muslims with religious authority for acts of terrorism against American citizens.... In August 1996, Bin Laden "effectively declared a war of terrorism against all members of the United States military worldwide." ... In February of 1998, this declaration was expanded to include attacks on American civilians....

The Defendant seeks suppression of the evidence which was seized during the warrantless search of his home in Kenya and the fruits thereof. In addition, he seeks the suppression of evidence derived from electronic surveillance of several telephone lines over which his conversations were recorded, including the telephone for his Nairobi residence and his cellular phone....

El-Hage bases his challenge to the evidence on the Fourth Amendment and asserts that the search and the electronic surveillance were unlawful because they were not conducted pursuant to a valid warrant. If the Court accepts the Government's argument that no warrant was required, El-Hage argues, in the alternative, that the searches were unreasonable. In its response to the Defendant's motion, the Government asserts that the searches were primarily conducted for the purpose of foreign intelligence collection and are, therefore, not subject to the Warrant Clause of the Fourth Amendment. As a result, it is the Government's position that the aforementioned evidence should not be suppressed....

El-Hage's suppression motion raises significant issues of first impression concerning the applicability of the full panoply of the Fourth Amendment to searches conducted abroad by the United States for foreign intelligence purposes and which are directed at an American citizen believed to be an agent of a foreign power. Although numerous courts and Congress have dealt with searches in the United States for foreign intelligence purposes and other courts have dealt with searches of foreigners abroad, we believe this to be the first case to raise the question whether an American citizen acting abroad on behalf of a foreign power may invoke the Fourth Amendment, and especially its warrant provision, to suppress evidence obtained by the United States in connection with intelligence gathering operations....

Before proceeding to that Fourth Amendment analysis, it is necessary to ascertain whether the Amendment applies in this situation. El-Hage is an American citizen and the searches at issue were conducted in Kenya. The Defendant argues that the protection of the Fourth Amendment "does not dissolve once a United States citizen leaves the borders of the United States." ... The Government seems to concede the general applicability of the Fourth Amendment to American citizens abroad, but asserts that the particular searches contested in this case (which were conducted overseas to collect foreign intelligence) call for a more limited application of the Amendment.

The Supreme Court cases on point suggest that the Fourth Amendment applies to United States citizens abroad.... Thus, this Court finds that even though the searches at issue in this case occurred in Kenya, El-Hage can bring a Fourth Amendment challenge. However, the extent of the Fourth Amendment protection, in particular the applicability of the Warrant Clause, is unclear....

The Government urges that the searches at issue in this case fall within an established exception to the warrant requirement. According to the Government, searches conducted for the purpose of foreign intelligence collection which target persons who are agents of a foreign power do not require a warrant. The Defendant asserts that such an exception does not exist and should not be recognized by this Court.

The Supreme Court has acknowledged but has not resolved this issue.... No court has considered the contours of such an exception when the searches at issue targeted an American citizen overseas.

The question, for this Court, is twofold. First, it is necessary to evaluate whether there is an exception to the warrant requirement for searches conducted abroad for purposes of foreign intelligence collection. Second, if such an exception exists, the Court must evaluate whether the searches conducted in this case properly fall within the parameters of that exception....

In all of the cases finding an exception to the warrant requirement for foreign intelligence collection, a determinative basis for the decision was the constitutional grant to the Executive Branch of power over foreign affairs. On numerous occasions, the Supreme Court has addressed the constitutional competence of the President in the field of foreign affairs.... It is also generally recognized that this authority includes power over foreign intelligence collection....

At the same time, in these cases and others, the Supreme Court has established that even in the exercise of his foreign affairs power, the President is constrained by other provisions of the Constitution.... Thus, even if this Court deems it necessary to establish an exception to the warrant requirement for foreign intelligence collection, these cases require vigilant protection of the Fourth Amendment interests which are at stake.

Warrantless foreign intelligence collection has been an established practice of the Executive Branch for decades.... Congress has legislated with respect to domestic incidents of foreign intelligence collection, ... but has not addressed the issue of foreign intelligence collection which occurs abroad. The Supreme Court has remained, in the three decades since *Keith*, [407 U.S. 297 (1972)] essentially, silent on both aspects of the issue.... While the fact of this silence is not dispositive of the question before this Court, it is by no means insignificant....

It is generally the case that imposition of a warrant requirement better safeguards the Fourth Amendment rights of citizens in the Defendant's position. But several cases direct that when the imposition of a warrant requirement proves to be a disproportionate and perhaps even disabling burden on the Executive, a warrant should not be required.... For several reasons, it is clear that imposition of a warrant requirement in the context of foreign intelligence searches conducted abroad would be a significant and undue burden on the Executive.

It has been asserted that the judicial branch is ill-suited to the task of overseeing foreign intelligence collection. Foreign affairs decisions, it has been said, are often particularly complex.... These arguments have, to some extent, been undercut by both the Supreme Court, in *Keith*, and Congress.... The Government makes several persuasive points about the intricacies of foreign intelligence collection conducted abroad. First, the Government cautions that a court would have greater difficulty (than in the domestic context) predicting "the international consequences flowing from a decision on the merits' regarding Executive Branch foreign policy decisions." Often these decisions have significant impacts on the essential cooperative relationships between United States officials and foreign intelligence services.... In addition, when some members of the government of the country in which the searches are sought to be conducted are perceived as hostile to the United States or sympathetic to the targets of the search, a procedure requiring notification to that government could be self-defeating. The Government also explains that too much involvement could place American courts in an "institutionally untenable position" when the operations which are authorized are violative of foreign law....

These concerns about the complexity of foreign intelligence decisions should not be taken to mean that the judiciary is not capable of making these judgments. Judges will, of course, be called on to assess the constitutionality of these searches ex post. Requiring judicial approval in advance, however, would inevitably mean costly increases in the response time of the Executive Branch. Although the Defendant asserts that such concerns are accommodated by existing allowances for exigent circumstances, the Court is not persuaded that the exigent circumstances doctrine provides enough protection for the interests at stake....

In addition to concerns about the impact of a warrant requirement on the speed of the executive response, there is an increased possibility of breaches of security when the Executive is required to take the Judiciary into its confidence. The Government emphasizes the detrimental impact that the existence of a warrant requirement for foreign intelligence searches might have on the cooperative relationships which are integral to overseas foreign intelligence collection efforts. As the Government explains, "the mere *perception* that inadvertent disclosure is more likely is sufficient to obstruct the intelligence collection imperative." ... The United States' heightened dependence on foreign governments for assistance in overseas foreign intelligence collection is a concern that was not addressed by the circuit courts that considered an exception to the warrant requirement for foreign intelligence collection within this country....

The final consideration which persuades the Court of the need for an exception to the warrant requirement for foreign intelligence collection conducted overseas is that there is presently no statutory basis for the issuance of a warrant to conduct searches abroad.... In addition, existing warrant procedures and standards are simply not suitable for foreign intelligence searches. The Defendant, nevertheless, argues strenuously that "if the government insists on exercising jurisdiction over conduct occurring extra-territorially, it must also abide by constitutional limitations on *its own* conduct in pursuing criminality in those same foreign locales." ...

Thus, although this Court does not accept as settled the Government's proposition that it is impossible to secure a warrant for overseas searches or surveillance, it is clear that the acquisition would certainly have been impracticable given the absence of any statutory provisions empowering a magistrate to issue a warrant and the unsuitability of traditional warrant procedures to foreign intelligence collection. As an additional point, the people and agencies upon whom the Executive relies in the foreign intelligence context for information and cooperation would undoubtedly be wary of any warrant procedures that did not adequately protect sensitive foreign intelligence information....

In light of the concerns outlined here, the Court finds that the power of the Executive to conduct foreign intelligence collection would be significantly frustrated by the imposition of a warrant requirement in this context. Therefore, this Court adopts the foreign intelligence exception to the warrant requirement for searches targeting foreign powers (or their agents) which are conducted abroad....

Before the Court can find that the exception applies to this case, it is necessary to show, first, that Mr. El-Hage was an agent of a foreign power; second, that the searches in question were conducted "primarily" for foreign intelligence purposes; and finally, that the searches were authorized by the President or the Attorney General.... [The court found that the three tests were met here.] [The court then discussed issues that were not premised upon the foreign intelligence exception and concluded by denying El Hage's motion to suppress the evidence obtained from the search "of his Kenya residence and electronic surveillance."]

Note

After a three-month trial, the four defendants, "followers of international terrorist Osama bin Laden were sentenced ... to life in prison without parole for the 1998 simultaneous bombings of the U.S. embassies in Kenya and Tanzania...." Jerry Seper, *4 Sentenced to Life in '98 Bombings in Africa*, Washington Times, Oct. 19, 2001, at A3. Although sentencing was initially vacated and remanded for resentencing, the rulings on the Fourth Amendment challenges were affirmed. In *In re Terrorist Bombings of U.S. Embassies in East Africa*, the Second Circuit held:

> (1) The evidence obtained from the search of El-Hage's Kenyan residence and the surveillance of his Kenyan telephone lines was properly admitted at trial because (a) the Fourth Amendment's requirement of reasonableness—but

> not the Warrant Clause — applies to extraterritorial searches and seizures of U.S. citizens, and (b) the searches of El-Hage's Kenyan home and the surveillance of his telephone lines were reasonable under the circumstances presented here; and
>
> (2) The District Court's ex parte, in camera evaluation of evidence submitted by the government in opposition to El-Hage's suppression motion was appropriate in light of national security considerations that militated in favor of maintaining the confidentiality of that evidence.

552 F.3d 157 (2d Cir. 2008).

§ 13.03 Fifth Amendment

United States v. Balsys

Supreme Court of the United States
524 U.S. 666 (1998)

JUSTICE SOUTER delivered the opinion of the Court.*

I

Respondent Aloyzas Balsys is a resident alien living in Woodhaven, New York, having obtained admission to this country in 1961 under the Immigration and Nationality Act, 8 U.S.C. § 1201, on an immigrant visa and alien registration issued at the American Consulate in Liverpool. In his application, he said that he had served in the Lithuanian army between 1934 and 1940, and had lived in hiding in Plateliai, Lithuania, between 1940 and 1944. Balsys swore that the information was true, and signed a statement of understanding that if his application contained any false information or materially misleading statements, or concealed any material fact, he would be subject to criminal prosecution and deportation.

OSI, [Office of Special Investigations of the Criminal Division of the United States Department of Justice] which was created to institute denaturalization and deportation proceedings against suspected Nazi war criminals, is now investigating whether, contrary to his representations, Balsys participated in Nazi persecution during World War II. Such activity would subject him to deportation for persecuting persons because of their race, religion, national origin, or political opinion under §§ 1182(a)(3)(E), 1251(a)(4)(D) as well as for lying on his visa application under §§ 1182(a)(6)(C)(i), 1251(a)(1)(A).

When OSI issued a subpoena requiring Balsys to testify at a deposition, he appeared and gave his name and address, but he refused to answer any other questions, such as those directed to his wartime activities in Europe between 1940–1945 and his immigration to the United States in 1961. In response to all such questions,

* JUSTICE SCALIA and JUSTICE THOMAS join only Parts I, II, and III of this opinion.

Balsys invoked the Fifth Amendment privilege against compelled self-incrimination, claiming that his answers could subject him to criminal prosecution. He did not contend that he would incriminate himself under domestic law, but claimed the privilege because his responses could subject him to criminal prosecution by Lithuania, Israel, and Germany.

OSI responded with a petition in Federal District Court to enforce the subpoena under § 1225(a). Although the District Court found that if Balsys were to provide the information requested, he would face a real and substantial danger of prosecution by Lithuania and Israel (but not by Germany), it granted OSI's enforcement petition and ordered Balsys to testify, treating the Fifth Amendment as inapplicable to a claim of incrimination solely under foreign law. 918 F. Supp. 588 (EDNY 1996). Balsys appealed, and the Court of Appeals for the Second Circuit vacated the District Court's order, holding that a witness with a real and substantial fear of prosecution by a foreign country may assert the Fifth Amendment privilege to avoid giving testimony in a domestic proceeding, even if the witness has no valid fear of a criminal prosecution in this country. 119 F.3d 122 (1997). We granted certiorari to resolve a conflict among the Circuits on this issue and now reverse....

II

....

The Self-Incrimination Clause of the Fifth Amendment provides that "no person ... shall be compelled in any criminal case to be a witness against himself." U.S. Const., Amdt. 5. Resident aliens such as Balsys are considered "persons" for purposes of the Fifth Amendment and are entitled to the same protections under the Clause as citizens.... The parties do not dispute that the Government seeks to "compel" testimony from Balsys that would make him "a witness against himself." The question is whether there is a risk that Balsys's testimony will be used in a proceeding that is a "criminal case."

Balsys agrees that the risk that his testimony might subject him to deportation is not a sufficient ground for asserting the privilege, given the civil character of a deportation proceeding. *See INS v. Lopez-Mendoza*, 468 U.S. 1032, 1038–1039, 104 S. Ct. 3479, 82 L. Ed. 2d 778 (1984). If, however, Balsys could demonstrate that any testimony he might give in the deportation investigation could be used in a criminal proceeding against him brought by the Government of either the United States or one of the States, he would be entitled to invoke the privilege. It "can be asserted in any proceeding, civil or criminal, administrative or judicial, investigatory or adjudicatory," in which the witness reasonably believes that the information sought, or discoverable as a result of his testimony, could be used in a subsequent state or federal criminal proceeding.... But Balsys makes no such claim, contending rather that his entitlement to invoke the privilege arises because of a real and substantial fear that his testimony could be used against him by Lithuania or Israel in a criminal prosecution. The reasonableness of his fear is not challenged by the Government, and we thus squarely face the question whether a criminal prosecution by a foreign government not subject to our constitutional guarantees presents a "criminal case" for purposes of the privilege against self-incrimination.

III

Balsys relies in the first instance on the textual contrast between the Sixth Amendment, which clearly applies only to domestic criminal proceedings, and the compelled self-incrimination Clause, with its facially broader reference to "any criminal case." The same point is developed by Balsys's *amici*, who argue that "any criminal case" means exactly that, regardless of the prosecuting authority. According to the argument, the Framers' use of the adjective "any" precludes recognition of the distinction raised by the Government, between prosecution by a jurisdiction that is itself bound to recognize the privilege and prosecution by a foreign jurisdiction that is not.... In the Fifth Amendment context, the Clause in question occurs in the company of guarantees of grand jury proceedings, defense against double jeopardy, due process, and compensation for property taking. Because none of these provisions is implicated except by action of the government that it binds, it would have been strange to choose such associates for a Clause meant to take a broader view, and it would be strange to find such a sweep in the Clause now.... The oddity of such a reading would be especially stark if the expansive language in question is open to another reasonable interpretation, as we think it is. Because the Fifth Amendment opens by requiring a grand jury indictment or presentment "for a capital, or otherwise infamous crime," the phrase beginning with "any" in the subsequent Self-Incrimination Clause may sensibly be read as making it clear that the privilege it provides is not so categorically limited. It is plausible to suppose the adjective was inserted only for that purpose, not as taking the further step of defining the relevant prosecutorial jurisdiction internationally. We therefore take this to be the fair reading of the adjective "any," and we read the Clause contextually as apparently providing a witness with the right against compelled self-incrimination when reasonably fearing prosecution by the government whose power the Clause limits, but not otherwise. Since there is no helpful legislative history, and because there was no different common law practice at the time of the Framing, ... there is no reason to disregard the contextual reading. This Court's precedent has indeed adopted that so-called same-sovereign interpretation.

In 1964 our precedent took a turn away from the unqualified proposition that fear of prosecution outside the jurisdiction seeking to compel testimony did not implicate a Fifth or Fourteenth Amendment privilege, as the case might be. In *Murphy v. Waterfront Comm'n of N.Y. Harbor*, 378 U.S. 52, 84 S. Ct. 1594, 12 L. Ed. 2d 678 (1964), we reconsidered the converse of the situation in *Murdock*, whether a witness in a state proceeding who had been granted immunity from state prosecution could invoke the privilege based on fear of prosecution on federal charges. In the course of enquiring into a work stoppage at several New Jersey piers, the Waterfront Commission of New York Harbor subpoenaed the defendants, who were given immunity from prosecution under the laws of New Jersey and New York.... This Court held the defendants could be forced to testify not because fear of federal prosecution was irrelevant but because the Self-Incrimination Clause barred the National Government from using their state testimony or its fruits to obtain a federal conviction. We explained "that the constitutional privilege against self-incrimination protects a state witness against incrimination under federal as well as state law and a federal witness against incrimination under state as well as federal law." . . .

Murphy is a case invested with two alternative rationales. Under the first, the result reached in *Murphy* was undoubtedly correct, given the decision rendered that very same day in *Malloy v. Hogan*, 378 U.S. 1, 84 S. Ct. 1489, 12 L. Ed. 2d 653 (1964), which applied the doctrine of Fourteenth Amendment due process incorporation to the Self-Incrimination Clause, so as to bind the States as well as the National Government to recognize the privilege. . . . Prior to *Malloy*, the Court had refused to impose the privilege against self-incrimination against the States through the Fourteenth Amendment, . . . thus leaving state-court witnesses seeking exemption from compulsion to testify to their rights under state law, as supplemented by the Fourteenth Amendment's limitations on coerced confessions. *Malloy*, however, established that "the Fourteenth Amendment secures against state invasion the same privilege that the Fifth Amendment guarantees against federal infringement — the right of a person to remain silent unless he chooses to speak in the unfettered exercise of his own will, and to suffer no penalty . . . for such silence." . . .

As the Court immediately thereafter said in *Murphy*, *Malloy* "necessitated a reconsideration" of the unqualified *Murdock* rule that a witness subject to testimonial compulsion in one jurisdiction, state or federal, could not plead fear of prosecution in the other. . . . After *Malloy*, the Fifth Amendment limitation could no longer be seen as framed for one jurisdiction alone, each jurisdiction having instead become subject to the same claim of privilege flowing from the one limitation. Since fear of prosecution in the one jurisdiction bound by the Clause now implicated the very privilege binding upon the other, the *Murphy* opinion sensibly recognized that if a witness could not assert the privilege in such circumstances, the witness could be "whipsawed into incriminating himself under both state and federal law even though the constitutional privilege against self-incrimination is applicable to each." . . . *Murphy* accordingly held that a federal court could not receive testimony compelled by a State in the absence of a statute effectively providing for federal immunity, and it did this by imposing an exclusionary rule prohibiting the National Government "from making any such use of compelled testimony and its fruits" . . . After *Murphy*, the immunity option open to the Executive Branch could only be exercised on the understanding that the state and federal jurisdictions were as one, with a federally mandated exclusionary rule filling the space between the limits of state immunity statutes and the scope of the privilege. As so understood, *Murphy* stands at odds with Balsys's claim.

There is, however, a competing rationale in *Murphy*, investing the Clause with a more expansive promise. The *Murphy* majority opened the door to this view by rejecting this Court's previous understanding of the English common-law evidentiary privilege against compelled self-incrimination, which could have informed the

Framers' understanding of the Fifth Amendment privilege. . . . In sum, to the extent that the *Murphy* majority went beyond its response to *Malloy* and undercut *Murdock*'s rationale on historical grounds, its reasoning cannot be accepted now. Long before today, indeed, *Murphy*'s history was shown to be fatally flawed. . . .

Murphy's policy catalog would provide support, at a rather more concrete level, for Balsys's argument that application of the privilege in situations like his would promote the purpose of preventing government overreaching, which on anyone's view lies at the core of the Clause's purposes. This argument begins with the premise that "cooperative internationalism" creates new incentives for the Government to facilitate foreign criminal prosecutions. Because crime, like legitimate trade, is increasingly international, a corresponding degree of international cooperation is coming to characterize the enterprise of criminal prosecution. The mission of the OSI as shown in this case exemplifies the international cooperation that is said to undermine the legitimacy of treating separate governmental authorities as separate for purposes of liberty protection in domestic courts. Because the Government now has a significant interest in seeing individuals convicted abroad for their crimes, it is subject to the same incentive to overreach that has required application of the privilege in the domestic context. Balsys says that this argument is nothing more than the reasoning of the *Murphy* Court when it justified its recognition of a fear of state prosecution by looking to the significance of "'cooperative federalism,'" the teamwork of state and national officials to fight interstate crime.

But Balsys invests *Murphy*'s "cooperative federalism" with a significance unsupported by that opinion. . . . Since in this case there is no analog of *Malloy*, imposing the Fifth Amendment beyond the National Government, there is no premise in *Murphy* for appealing to "cooperative internationalism" by analogy to "cooperative federalism." Any analogy must, instead, be to the pre-*Murphy* era when the States were not bound by the privilege. Then, testimony compelled in a federal proceeding was admissible in a state prosecution, despite the fact that shared values and similar criminal statutes of the state and national jurisdictions presumably furnished incentive for overreaching by the Government to facilitate criminal prosecutions in the States.

But even if *Murphy* were authority for considering "cooperative federalism" and "cooperative internationalism" as reasons supporting expansion of the scope of the privilege, any extension would depend ultimately on an analysis of the likely costs and benefits of extending the privilege as Balsys requests. If such analysis were dispositive for us, we would conclude that Balsys has not shown that extension of the protection would produce a benefit justifying the rule he seeks.

The Court of Appeals directed careful attention to an evaluation of what would be gained and lost on Balsys's view. It concluded, for example, that few domestic cases would be adversely affected by recognizing the privilege based upon fear of foreign prosecution, . . . that American contempt sanctions for refusal to testify are so lenient in comparison to the likely consequences of foreign prosecution that a witness would probably refuse to testify even if the privilege were unavailable to him, that by statute and treaty the United States could limit the occasions on which a reasonable fear of foreign prosecution could be shown, as by modifying extradition and deportation standards in cases involving the privilege, and that because a witness's refusal to testify may be used as evidence in a civil proceeding, deportation of people in Balsys's position would not necessarily be thwarted by recognizing the privilege as he claims it.

The Court of Appeals accordingly thought the net burden of the expanded privilege too negligible to justify denying its expansion. We remain skeptical, however. While we will not attempt to comment on every element of the Court of Appeals's calculation, two of the points just noted would present difficulty. First, there is a question about the standard that should govern any decision to justify a truly discretionary ruling by making the assumption that it will induce the Government to adopt legislation with international implications or to seek international agreements, in order to mitigate the burdens that the ruling would otherwise impose. Because foreign relations are specifically committed by the Constitution to the political branches, U.S. Const., Art II, § 2, cl. 2, we would not make a discretionary judgment premised on inducing them to adopt policies in relation to other nations without squarely confronting the propriety of grounding judicial action on such a premise.

Second, the very assumption that a witness's silence may be used against him in a deportation or extradition proceeding due to its civil nature, . . . raises serious questions about the likely gain from recognizing fear of foreign prosecution. For if a witness claiming the privilege ended up in a foreign jurisdiction that, for whatever reason, recognized no privilege under its criminal law, the recognition of the privilege in the American courts would have gained nothing for the witness. This possibility, of course, presents a sharp contrast with the consequences of recognizing the privilege based on fear of domestic prosecution. If testimony is compelled, *Murphy* itself illustrates that domestic courts are not even wholly dependent on immunity statutes to see that no use will be made against the witness; the exclusionary principle will guarantee that. . . . Whatever the cost to the Government may be, the benefit to the individual is not in doubt in a domestic proceeding.

Since the likely gain to the witness fearing foreign prosecution is thus uncertain, the countervailing uncertainty about the loss of testimony to the United States cannot be dismissed as comparatively unimportant. That some testimony will be lost is highly probable, since the United States will not be able to guarantee immunity if testimony is compelled (absent some sort of cooperative international arrangement that we cannot assume will occur). While the Court of Appeals is doubtless correct that the expected consequences of some foreign prosecutions may be so severe that a witness will refuse to testify no matter what, not every foreign prosecution may measure up so harshly as against the expectable domestic consequences of contempt for refusing to testify. We therefore must suppose that on Balsys's view some evidence will in fact be lost to the domestic courts, and we are accordingly unable to dismiss the position of the United States in this case, that domestic law enforcement would suffer serious consequences if fear of foreign prosecution were recognized as sufficient to invoke the privilege.

In sum, the most we would feel able to conclude about the net result of the benefits and burdens that would follow from Balsys's view would be a Scotch verdict. If, then, precedent for the traditional view of the scope of the Clause were not dispositive of the issue before us, if extending the scope of the privilege were open to consideration, we still would not find that Balsys had shown that recognizing his claim would be a sound resolution of the competing interests involved.

V

This is not to say that cooperative conduct between the United States and foreign nations could not develop to a point at which a claim could be made for recognizing fear of foreign prosecution under the Self-Incrimination Clause as traditionally understood. If it could be said that the United States and its allies had enacted substantially similar criminal codes aimed at prosecuting offenses of international character, and if it could be shown that the United States was granting immunity from domestic prosecution for the purpose of obtaining evidence to be delivered to other nations as prosecutors of a crime common to both countries, then an argument could be made that the Fifth Amendment should apply based on fear of foreign prosecution simply because that prosecution was not fairly characterized as distinctly "foreign." The point would be that the prosecution was as much on behalf of the United States as of the prosecuting nation, so that the division of labor between evidence-gatherer and prosecutor made one nation the agent of the other, rendering fear of foreign prosecution tantamount to fear of a criminal case brought by the Government itself.

Whether such an argument should be sustained may be left at the least for another day, since its premises do not fit this case. It is true that Balsys has shown that the United States has assumed an interest in foreign prosecution, as demonstrated by OSI's mandate and American treaty agreements requiring the Government to give to Lithuania and Israel any evidence provided by Balsys. But this interest does not rise to the level of cooperative prosecution. There is no system of complementary substantive offenses at issue here, and the mere support of one nation for the prosecutorial efforts of another does not transform the prosecution of the one into the prosecution of the other.... In this case there is no basis for concluding that the privilege will lose its meaning without a rule precluding compelled testimony when there is a real and substantial risk that such testimony will be used in a criminal prosecution abroad.... Accordingly, the judgment of the Court of Appeals is reversed, and the case is remanded for further proceedings consistent with this opinion.... It is so ordered.

Justice Stevens, concurring.

While I join the Court's opinion without reservation, I write separately to emphasize these points.

The clause that protects every person from being "compelled in any criminal case to be a witness against himself" is a part of the broader protection afforded by the

Fifth Amendment to the Constitution. That Amendment constrains the power of the Federal Government to deprive any person "of life, liberty, or property, without due process of law," just as the Fourteenth Amendment imposes comparable constraints on the power of the States. The primary office of the clause at issue in this case is to afford protection to persons whose liberty has been placed in jeopardy in an American tribunal. The Court's holding today will not have any adverse impact on the fairness of American criminal trials.

The fact that the issue in this case has been undecided for such a long period of time suggests that our ruling will have little, if any, impact on the fairness of trials conducted in other countries. Whether or not that suggestion is accurate, I do not believe our Bill of Rights was intended to have any effect on the conduct of foreign proceedings. If, however, we were to accept respondent's interpretation of the clause, we would confer power on foreign governments to impair the administration of justice in this country.... A law enacted by a foreign power making it a crime for one of its citizens to testify in an American proceeding against another citizen of that country would immunize those citizens from being compelled to testify in our courts. Variants of such a hypothetical law are already in existence. Of course, the Court might craft exceptions for such foreign criminal laws, but it seems far wiser to adhere to a clear limitation on the coverage of the Fifth Amendment, including its privilege against self-incrimination. That Amendment prescribes rules of conduct that must attend any deprivation of life, liberty, or property in our Nation's courts.

JUSTICE GINSBURG, dissenting.

The privilege against self-incrimination, "closely linked historically with the abolition of torture," is properly regarded as a "landmark in man's struggle to make himself civilized." E. GRISWOLD, THE FIFTH AMENDMENT TODAY 7 (1955).... In my view, the Fifth Amendment privilege against self-incrimination prescribes a rule of conduct generally to be followed by our Nation's officialdom. It counsels officers of the United States (and of any State of the United States) against extracting testimony when the person examined reasonably fears that his words would be used against him in a later criminal prosecution. As a restraint on compelling a person to bear witness against himself, the Amendment ordinarily should command the respect of United States interrogators, whether the prosecution reasonably feared by the examinee is domestic or foreign.... On this understanding of the "fundamental decency" the Fifth Amendment embodies, "its expression of our view of civilized governmental conduct," ... I join JUSTICE BREYER's dissenting opinion.

JUSTICE BREYER, with whom JUSTICE GINSBURG joins, dissenting.

Were Aloyzas Balsys to face even a theoretical possibility that his testimony could lead a State to prosecute him for murder, the Fifth Amendment would prohibit the Federal Government from compelling that testimony. The Court concludes, however, that the Fifth Amendment does not prohibit compulsion here because Balsys faces a real and substantial danger of prosecution not, say, by California, but by a foreign nation. The Fifth Amendment, however, provides that "no person ... shall be compelled in *any* criminal case to be a witness against himself." ... That precedent, as well as the basic principles underlying the privilege, convince me that the Fifth Amendment's privilege against self-incrimination should encompass, not only feared domestic prosecutions, but also feared foreign prosecutions where the danger of an actual foreign prosecution is substantial....

In sum, I see no reason why the Court should resurrect the pale shadow of *Murdock*'s "same sovereign" rule, a rule that *Murphy* demonstrated was without strong historical foundation and that would serve no more valid a purpose in today's world than it did during *Murphy*'s time. *Murphy* supports recognizing the privilege where there is a real and substantial threat of prosecution by a foreign government. Balsys is among the few to have satisfied this threshold. The basic values which this Court has said underlie the Fifth Amendment's protections are each diminished if the privilege may not be claimed here. And surmountable practical concerns should not stand in the way of constitutional principle.

For these and related reasons elaborated by the Second Circuit, I respectfully dissent.

Notes

(1) As a result of the Court's ruling in this case, Balsys left the United States "rather than testify about his World War II activities in Lithuania." As part of a settlement with the Department of Justice, Balsys agreed to leave the United States permanently and "conceded that he misrepresented and concealed his true wartime activities when he entered the United States." William C. Mann, *War Criminal Suspect Won't Testify, Quits U.S.*, Atl. J. Const., May 31, 1999, at B9.

(2) Can a court order a defendant or witness to sign a directive authorizing a foreign financial institution to release documents? Does such an order violate the defendant or witnesses' rights against self-incrimination? In *In re Grand Jury Subpoena (Two Grand Jury Contemnors v. United States)*, 826 F.2d 1166 (2nd Cir. 1987), Circuit Judge Altimari stated:

> Appellants, two witnesses before the grand jury, appeal from orders of the United States District Court for the Southern District of New York (Vincent L. Broderick, *Judge*), which held them in civil contempt for refusing to sign directives authorizing foreign financial institutions to release documents and information to the government, and ordered them confined until they signed the directives. 28 U.S.C. § 1826(a). Appellants contend *inter alia* that compelled execution of the directives, as written, would violate their fifth amendment privilege against self-incrimination and right to due process of law....
>
> To establish a fifth amendment violation, appellants must therefore demonstrate the existence of three elements: 1) compulsion, 2) a testimonial communication, and 3) the incriminating nature of that communication.... The compulsion element is clearly present here.... More troublesome,

though, is the question of whether ordering appellants to sign the directives—and thus requiring them to authorize disclosure of records and information if any exist—constitutes testimonial self-incrimination. We conclude, however, that it does not.

At the outset, we emphasize that appellants do not contend, nor could they argue, that their fifth amendment privilege extends to preclude the financial institutions from producing records or information regarding appellants' transactions.... Thus, since the directives are the only communications which appellants were compelled to make, they are the only possible source of a fifth amendment violation....

In this regard, we have twice approved of the compelled execution of a directive in the face of fifth amendment self-incrimination challenges.... [w]e adopted the Eleventh Circuit's approach toward resolving these questions as set forth in *United States v. Ghidoni*, [732 F.2d 814 (11th Cir. 1984)]. In *Ghidoni*, the Eleventh Circuit was confronted with the same question presented in the instant appeal. The directive at issue there differed from the ones here in only minor respects. For example, it was entitled "consent directive," rather than "directive," and, in addition to using language indicating that it was directed to any bank where appellant had an account, it also named a specific bank, whereas the directives at issue here do not name any specific bank or financial institution.

After first setting out general fifth amendment principles, the *Ghidoni* court then reviewed the directive in light of those Supreme Court decisions addressing the testimonial and incriminating aspects of the compelled production of documents, *i.e.*, *United States v. Doe*, 465 U.S. 605, 104 S. Ct. 1237, 79 L. Ed. 2d 552 (1984), and *Fisher v. United States*, 425 U.S. 391, 96 S. Ct. 1569, 48 L. Ed. 2d 39 (1976). Thus, the *Ghidoni* court likened the situation before it—where an individual was being compelled to authorize and direct a third party, *i.e.*, the banks, to produce documents—to the situations presented in *Doe* and *Fisher*, where an individual was compelled to produce the documents himself.

The *Ghidoni* court, accordingly, examined the directive to determine whether it contained any testimonial assertion regarding the documents sought from the banks. The court concluded that the directive was "devoid of any testimonial aspects," ... after it found that "nothing in the directive implie[d] that [bank] accounts exist," that it contained no statements regarding possession or control over such accounts, and that it could not be used to authenticate any records obtained.... The court thus concluded that compelled execution of the directive would not violate the privilege against self-incrimination because the directive itself was not testimonial in nature.... In upholding the compelled execution of the directive, the court further observed that the defendant was only being compelled to "waive a barrier [i.e., foreign states' confidentiality laws] to permit the bank to produce documents" — an *act* which it concluded provided no testimonial assertions. . . .

The *Ghidoni* decision is not without criticism. Its approach to these questions was recently rejected by the First Circuit in *In Re Grand Jury Proceedings (Ranauro)*, 814 F.2d 791 (1st Cir. 1987). *In Ranauro*, the First Circuit agreed with the *Ghidoni* court's conclusion that the directive itself does not assert that any records exist, that the appellant has control over such accounts, or that any records obtained would be authentic. . . . The court observed, however, that the directive did "admit and assert [the appellant's] consent," . . . and thus it concluded that his assertion of consent could be potentially incriminating, because it might later be used "to prove the ultimate facts that accounts in [appellant's] name existed or that [appellant] controlled those accounts." . . . The court, accordingly, concluded that compelled execution of the directive would violate the fifth amendment. . . .

While we see some merit in the First Circuit's approach, we are constrained here to apply our precedent in *N.D.N.Y. Grand Jury Subpoena*, and follow the analysis set forth in *Ghidoni*. We therefore hold that because the directives here contain no testimonial assertions, the district court orders compelling appellants to sign the directives provide no basis for a fifth amendment violation. The directives here, as in *Ghidoni*, do not contain any assertions by appellant regarding the existence of, or control over, foreign bank accounts. They authorize disclosure of records and information only if such accounts exist. We also agree with the *Ghidoni* court's conclusion that the directives could not be used to authenticate any bank records obtained.

. . . .

In light of our holding today, it is clear that the fifth amendment would not stand as a bar to admission of the directives into evidence at trial because the directives contain no testimonial assertions that are incriminating, and thus do not implicate fifth amendment questions. . . . We also note, however, that since the directives contain no statements regarding existence of, or control over, any accounts, they should be excluded from evidence because they lack any probative value. . . .

Appellants argue that when the district court entered its order excluding the directives from evidence, it accordingly created a de facto use immunity for statements made in the directives. We disagree. When the district court entered its orders precluding admission of the directives into evidence, it was merely ruling on evidentiary questions relating to materiality, relevance, prejudice, etc., all of which could be and were resolved in the sound discretion of the district court. We conclude here that, because the directives lack any probative testimonial value on the issue of existence or control, . . . the district court properly excluded them from evidence. . . .

(3) Will a grand jury subpoena duces tecum be enforced, where producing the records will subject a bank to a violation of another country's criminal laws? In *In re Grand Jury Proceedings (United States v. Bank of Nova Scotia)*, 691 F.2d 1384, 1391 (11th Cir. 1982), the court stated:

> Absent direction from the Legislative and Executive branches of our federal government, we are not willing to emasculate the grand jury process whenever a foreign nation attempts to block our criminal justice process. It is unfortunate the Bank of Nova Scotia suffers from differing legal commands of separate sovereigns, but as we stated in *Field*:
>
> > In a world where commercial transactions are international in scope, conflicts are inevitable. Courts and legislatures should take every reasonable precaution to avoid placing individuals in the situation [the Bank] finds itself. Yet, this court simply cannot acquiesce in the proposition that United States criminal investigations must be thwarted whenever there is conflict with the interest of other states.
>
> *In re Grand Jury Proceedings, United States v. Field*, 532 F.2d at 410.

Some courts use a balancing test to determine whether an Internal Revenue summons, that would subject individuals to criminal liability in another country, should be enforced. *See United States v. First National Bank of Chicago*, 699 F.2d 341 (7th Cir. 1983) (using a balancing test, court said compelling disclosure would be improper); *United States v. Chase Manhattan Bank*, 584 F. Supp. 1080 (S.D. N.Y. 1984) (balancing of national interests required order enforcing the summons). Will the *Balsys* decision affect how future courts resolve these issues?

(4) Can compelled testimony in violation of the Fifth Amendment be used against a defendant at trial, when the testimony was compelled by a foreign government? This question was considered in the following case:

United States v. Allen

United States Court of Appeals for the Second Circuit
864 F.3d 63 (2d Cir. 2017)

José A. Cabranes, Circuit Judge:

This case—the first criminal appeal related to the London Interbank Offered Rate ("LIBOR") to reach this (or any) Court of Appeals—presents the question, among others, whether testimony given by an individual involuntarily under the legal compulsion of a foreign power may be used against that individual in a criminal case in an American court. As employees in the London office of Coöperatieve Centrale Raiffeisen-Boerenleenbank B.A. ("Rabobank") in the 2000s, defendants-appellants Anthony Allen and Anthony Conti ("Defendants") played roles in that bank's LIBOR submission process during the now-well-documented heyday of the rate's manipulation.... The U.K. enforcement agency, the Financial Conduct Authority ("FCA"), interviewed Allen and Conti (each a U.K. citizen and resident) that year, along with several of their coworkers. At these interviews, Allen and Conti were compelled to testify and given "direct use" — but not "derivative use" — immunity. In accordance with U.K. law, refusal to testify could result in imprisonment.... Ultimately, Robson was the sole source of certain material information supplied to the grand jury that indicted Allen and Conti and, after being called as a trial witness by the Government, Robson provided significant testimony to the petit jury that convicted Defendants.... We address only their Fifth Amendment challenge....

... Defendants contend that the Government violated their Fifth Amendment rights when it used — in the form of tainted evidence from Robson — their own compelled testimony against them.

The Government takes a different view. It submits, as a threshold argument, that testimony compelled by a foreign sovereign and used in a U.S. criminal prosecution "do[es] not implicate the Fifth Amendment." In the event that the Fifth Amendment does apply, the Government argues that the District Court employed the correct legal standard to determine, properly, that evidence provided by Robson was untainted. In the alternative, the Government argues that any use of tainted evidence was harmless.

For the reasons that follow, we conclude that Defendants prevail on each point....

In arguing that Fifth Amendment protections apply in this case, Defendants rely on our cases pertaining to foreign and cross-border law enforcement, which have consistently held that "in order to be admitted in our courts, inculpatory statements obtained overseas by foreign officials must have been made voluntarily." In so holding, we joined our sister circuits that have considered the issue. Defendants contend that these cases are sufficient to resolve the present dispute regarding whether compulsion by a foreign power implicates the Fifth Amendment. We agree.

The Supreme Court has "recognized two constitutional bases for the requirement that a confession be voluntary to be admitted into evidence: the Fifth Amendment right against self-incrimination and the Due Process Clause of the Fourteenth Amendment." Of these two potential "constitutional bases," our precedents applying such a requirement to confessions procured by foreign law enforcement have been grounded in the Self-Incrimination Clause.... This constitutional footing is significant.

The freedom from self-incrimination guaranteed by the Fifth Amendment is a personal trial right of the accused in any American "criminal case." To that end, "a violation of the Fifth Amendment's right against self-incrimination occurs only when a compelled statement is offered at trial against the defendant." Whatever may occur prior to trial, the right not to testify against oneself at trial is "absolute." Even a negative comment by a judge or prosecutor on a defendant's silence violates that defendant's constitutional right.

These features of the Self-Incrimination Clause distinguish it from the exclusionary rules attached to unreasonable searches and seizures and to otherwise-valid confessions given without *Miranda* warnings. As the Supreme Court has explained, the Fourth Amendment's exclusionary rule "is a judicially created remedy designed to safeguard Fourth Amendment rights generally through its deterrent effect, rather than a personal constitutional right of the party aggrieved." So too with the exclusionary rule buttressing *Miranda* warnings, which "were primarily designed to prevent United States police officers from relying upon improper interrogation techniques." Such exclusionary rules "have little, if any, deterrent effect upon foreign police officers." Accordingly, we do not apply the strictures of our Fourth Amendment and *Miranda* jurisprudence to foreign authorities. . . .

The Supreme Court has taken care, however, to distinguish extraterritorial applications of the Fourth Amendment from those of the Self-Incrimination Clause of the Fifth Amendment. The Fourth Amendment "prohibits unreasonable searches and seizures whether or not the evidence is sought to be used in a criminal trial," such that "a violation of the Amendment is fully accomplished at the time of an unreasonable governmental intrusion." By contrast, in the case of the Fifth Amendment's Self-Incrimination Clause, "a constitutional violation occurs only at trial," even if "conduct by law enforcement officials prior to trial may ultimately impair that right." In light of that distinction, "it naturally follows that, regardless of the origin — i.e., domestic or foreign — of a statement, it cannot be admitted at trial in the United States if the statement was 'compelled.'" . . .

Thus, the Self-Incrimination Clause's prohibition of the use of compelled testimony arises from the text of the Constitution itself, and directly addresses what happens in American courtrooms, in contrast to the exclusionary rules that are crafted as remedies to deter unconstitutional actions by officers in the field. Its protections therefore apply in American courtrooms even when the defendant's testimony was compelled by foreign officials. . . .

Moreover, for much the same reasons, the Clause applies in American courtrooms even where, as here, the defendant's testimony was compelled by foreign officials lawfully — that is, pursuant to foreign legal process — in a manner that does not shock the conscience or violate fundamental fairness. The Clause flatly prohibits the use of compelled testimony and is not based on any matter of misconduct or illegality on the part of the agency applying the compulsion.

In short, compelled testimony cannot be used to secure a conviction in an American court. This is so even when the testimony was compelled by a foreign government in full accordance with its own law.

It is true that, with respect to statements taken abroad by foreign agents, we have often referred to the Fifth Amendment's prohibition against illicit use as encompassing "involuntary," rather than "compelled," statements. But this semantic distinction does not bear significant, much less dispositive, weight. Accordingly, we agree with Defendants that our cases applying a voluntariness test in the context of physical coercion extend to the present context of lawful compulsion. . . .

The Government's three principal counterarguments are unpersuasive. The Government first questions the validity of our precedents on the basis of *Colorado v.*

Connelly [479 U.S. 157 (1986),] and subsequent cases involving foreign and cross-border law enforcement that have relied on *Connelly*. That case concerned a mentally ill defendant who sought out police and confessed to a murder. Despite the absence of any law enforcement misconduct, the Colorado Supreme Court affirmed the suppression from evidence of Connelly's statements because they were "'involuntary'"—that is, not "'the product of a rational intellect and a free will.'" In reversing, the Supreme Court held "that coercive police activity is a necessary predicate to the finding that a confession is not 'voluntary' within the meaning of the Due Process Clause of the Fourteenth Amendment."

We are not persuaded that *Connelly* requires reconsideration of our precedents. For one thing, *Connelly* is explicitly a Due Process Clause case, whereas the precedents we rely on today were grounded in the Self-Incrimination Clause—which, by its terms, is an exclusionary rule grounded in the very text of the Constitution and designed to protect a defendant at trial. For another, *Connelly* did not concern cross-border investigations or foreign government conduct. . . . And the final reason we do not believe Connelly renders our precedents invalid stems from an important acknowledgment the Government makes on appeal. . . .

The Government's second counterargument extends from the premise that foreign governments are on the same footing as private employers when it comes to compelled testimony. In particular, the Government points to the fact that private employers may question an employee under threat of discharge without Fifth Amendment consequence, whereas in certain circumstances courts have found that the same threat by an American government employer rendered an employee's testimony "compelled" and excludable under the Fifth Amendment. "For purposes of the Fifth Amendment," the Government submits, "the British government is on the same footing as a private entity such as the New York Stock Exchange." We disagree.

Only sovereign power exposes "'those suspected of crime to the cruel trilemma of self-accusation, perjury or contempt.'" Only the U.K. government could have immunized Defendants (neither of whom were employed by Rabobank at the time), compelling them to testify or go to jail. To the extent there may be an "official/private action spectrum," when foreign authorities compel testimony they are acting in the quintessence of their sovereign authority, not in their capacity as a mere employer, and thus their compulsion is cognizable by the Fifth Amendment (when testimony so compelled is used in a U.S. trial). . . . If our Constitution is to prohibit the use in American trials of confessions coerced or compelled by a foreign sovereign under some circumstances, as the Government suggests "may be" the case, it cannot be the case that compulsion by a foreign authority ipso facto ends the constitutional inquiry.

Finally, the Government's third counterargument is that testimony is only "compelled" for purposes of the Self-Incrimination Clause if the compelling sovereign is bound by the Fifth Amendment. Here, too, we disagree. . . . This "same-sovereign" principle has never been fully abandoned; it still applies, for example, where the prosecuting sovereign is not bound by the Fifth Amendment (i.e., where the prosecuting authority is a foreign government). But where, as here, the prosecuting sovereign is bound by the Fifth Amendment, the "same-sovereign" principle no longer has force. As already explained, it is now clear that the Fifth Amendment is a personal trial right—one violated only at the time of "use" rather than at the time of "compulsion." Accordingly, the Government's reliance on the "same-sovereign" principle in the circumstances of this case is unavailing. . . .

The Government also asserts that a prohibition on its use in U.S. courts of testimony compelled by a foreign authority "could seriously hamper the prosecution of criminal conduct that crosses international borders." . . . As to the Government's concerns that a hostile foreign government might hypothetically endeavor to sabotage U.S. prosecutions by immunizing a suspect and publicizing his or her testimony—that, of course, is not this case. This case raises no questions regarding the legitimacy or regularity of the procedures employed by the U.K. government or the U.K. government's investigation more generally. We thus need only say here that should U.S. prosecutors or judges face the situation suggested by the Government, our holding today would not necessarily prevent prosecution in the United States. . . . In short, the situation hypothesized by the Government is not before us today, and our resolution of this case on the facts that are before us leaves open the issue of foreign efforts to sabotage a U.S. prosecution. . . .

We do not presume to know exactly what this brave new world of international criminal enforcement will entail. Yet we are certain that these developments abroad need not affect the fairness of our trials at home. If as a consequence of joint investigations with foreign nations we are to hale foreign men and women into the courts of the United States to fend for their liberty we should not do so while denying them the full protection of a "trial right" we regard as "fundamental" and "absolute."

Accordingly, we adhere to our precedent in assessing the voluntariness of inculpatory testimony compelled abroad by foreign governments. In the instant appeal, there is no question that the Defendants' testimony was compelled and, thus, involuntary. We therefore conclude in this case that the Fifth Amendment prohibited the Government from using Defendants' compelled testimony against them. . . .

To summarize:

(1) The Fifth Amendment's prohibition on the use of compelled testimony in American criminal proceedings applies even when a foreign sovereign has compelled the testimony. To be clear, we do not purport to prescribe what the U.K. authorities (or any foreign authority) may do in their witness interviews or their criminal trials. We merely hold that the Self-Incrimination Clause prohibits the use and derivative use of compelled testimony in an American criminal case against the defendant who provided that testimony.

(2) When the government uses a witness who has been substantially exposed to a defendant's compelled testimony, it is required under *Kastigar v. United States*, 406 U.S. 441 (1972), to prove, at a minimum, that the witness's review

of the compelled testimony did not shape, alter, or affect the evidence used by the government.

(3) Where, as here, the witness's account of events before exposure was significantly different, and less incriminating, than the testimony ultimately used against the defendants, the witness's bare, generalized denial of taint—here, the witness's conclusory responses to the Government's leading questions during the *Kastigar* hearing—is insufficient as a matter of law to sustain the prosecution's burden of proof.

(4) In this prosecution, Defendants' compelled testimony was "used" against them through evidence provided by a tainted witness, a key cooperator and prominent witness both at trial and (via a hearsay presentation) before the grand jury. This tainted testimony was significant both at trial and in the grand jury, because it provided the only first-hand eyewitness account that refuted the Defendants' central argument for acquittal, and was therefore not harmless beyond a reasonable doubt.

For the foregoing reasons, we REVERSE the judgments of conviction and hereby DISMISS the indictment.

§ 13.04 Sixth Amendment

United States v. Kole

United States Court of Appeals for the Third Circuit
164 F.3d 164 (1998)

McKee, Circuit Judge:

... In the instant case, Kole and a coconspirator were apprehended in New Jersey and charged with attempting to import heroin. Kole subsequently pled guilty to one count of conspiring to import 3.5 kilograms of heroin into the United States in violation of 21 U.S.C. § 942(a). Following the change of plea proceeding, the government filed an information under 21 U.S.C. § 851(a) in an effort to enhance Kole's sentence to a term of imprisonment of at least 20 years based upon her drug conviction in the Philippines.

Kole argued that 21 U.S.C. § 851(c)(2) precluded the court from using the Philippine conviction to enhance her sentence because she had been denied a jury trial in the Philippines, and because her defense counsel there labored under a conflict of interest that caused her to be denied effective assistance of counsel. Since § 851(c)(2) expressly bars consideration of any prior conviction that "was obtained in violation of the Constitution of the United States," Kole asserted that the sentencing court could not apply the mandatory minimum for repeat felony drug offenders contained in 21 U.S.C. § 960(b)(1)(A).... [T]he court ruled that the Philippine conviction was a prior drug felony for purposes of sentencing, and sentenced Kole to the mandatory minimum period of incarceration (20 years) under 21 U.S.C. § 960(b)(1). This appeal followed. . . .

Here, we must decide whether the Constitution applies Ex Proprio vigore to the Philippines. . . . We conclude that Congress did not intend a contrary result when it enacted 21 U.S.C. § 851. Rather, as the district court concluded, Congress intended only to ensure fundamental fairness by excluding any conviction that was obtained in a manner inconsistent with concepts of fundamental fairness and liberty endemic in the Due Process Clause of the Fifth Amendment of the United States Constitution. . . .

Kole's argument is bottomed upon an assumption that Congress could not have intended to allow a conviction that was obtained in violation of such a fundamental right to enhance a subsequent sentence in a court of the United States. However, this position overlooks the purpose behind § 960 as well as the fact that jury trials, though fundamental to the system of justice established under the United States Constitution, are nevertheless relatively unique to that system. . . . Although the Court answered that question in the affirmative as applied to the American legal system, it left no doubt that other societies may well be able to fashion a system with no juries that is fundamentally fair to the accused, thus comporting with our concept of due process. . . .

. . . .

We do not think that Congress enacted a law that was intended to reach persons involved in international drug trafficking and then limited enhanced penalties to those persons who had previously been convicted in a court in the United States. That is inconsistent with Congress' attempt to reach those involved in importing or exporting controlled substances. Yet, since the United States Constitution does not apply to any foreign sovereign, that would be the result of adopting Ms. Kole's argument. . . .

Kole also argues that use of the Philippine conviction violated her Sixth Amendment right to counsel because her trial attorney labored under an irreconcilable conflict of interest that prevented him from effectively representing her. In *Strickland v. Washington*, 466 U.S. 668, 687, 104 S. Ct. 2052, 80 L. Ed. 2d 674 (1984), the Court established a two-part test for evaluating a claim of ineffective assistance of counsel and we apply it here. Under *Strickland*, a defendant must show that "counsel's representation fell below an objective standard of reasonableness." . . . If defendant is able to make that showing, he or she must then establish that counsel's dereliction prejudiced the defendant. Where the claim rests upon an alleged conflict of interest, defendant "must identify something that counsel chose to do or not do, as to which he had conflicting duties, and must show that the course taken was influenced by that conflict." In other words, the defendant must "show some actual conflict of interest that adversely affected his counsel's performance in order to prevail." . . .

Here, Kole alleges that the joint representation created a simultaneous duty to represent Ike that prevented her defense attorney from distinguishing between her involvement and his. . . . Her argument suggests that her attorney could have attempted to equate Kole's role with that of the codefendants who were acquitted rather than being lumped with her fiance. However, "hindsight rationalization alone cannot support a claim of ineffective assistance of counsel." . . . Kole's attorney mounted a vigorous attack on the credibility of the police, and informant Williams. As noted above, he was able to raise serious questions as to the credibility of the prosecutor's witnesses. In fact, the trial judge did not credit substantial portions of the prosecution's case.

Moreover, the appendix filed in this court contains a "Demurrer to Evidence" that defense counsel filed following trial, and prior to Judge Felix issuing his opinion. . . . In that demurrer Kole's attorney argues that all of the physical evidence must be suppressed based upon the warrantless search, the lack of credibility of the prosecution witnesses including the police, the chemist's expertise and bias, Jacqueline Williams' open case with the police, and the likelihood of her bias based upon asserted promises that the case would be dismissed if she cooperated against Kole. . . .

There is no irreconcilable tension in defense counsel's strategy. Indeed, Kole's attorney would have been hard pressed to draw distinctions between her involvement and Ike's while arguing that the police and Williams were lying about finding evidence inside of their apartment. As noted above, "an actual conflict of interest occurs when counsel cannot use his best efforts to exonerate one defendant for fear of implicating the other." . . .

Although Kole asserts her Philippine attorney could have used a different strategy had he not also represented Ike, she has not met her burden of proving that she was prejudiced by the joint representation. Moreover, we do not think that the strategy actually adopted compromised her defense. Since Kole and Ike occupied the apartment and had equal access to the suitcase with the heroin, a coordinated attack on the prosecution's cooperating witness, and upon the police was strategically sound. . . . It is the particular circumstances of a joint prosecution of husband and wife, rather than the fact of the relationship, that creates any conflict of interest between spouses in a joint prosecution. Although the circumstances could be such that a conflict of interest would flow from the relationship of husband and wife, this is not such a case. Kole has not established such circumstances existed when she was convicted in the Philippines. Judge Felix did conclude that Kole and Ike had joint control over the apartment, and joint access to the heroin inside of it, but the conflict of interest Kole complains of is more a creature of hindsight than of record. . . . For the reasons set forth above, we affirm the district court's imposition on Kole of an enhanced sentence of twenty years under 21 U.S.C. § 960(b)(1)(A).*

* For further discussion of the use of foreign convictions, see chap. 18. — Eds.

Notes

(1) Defendants are accorded compulsory process under the Sixth Amendment. May the government deport a person from the United States that may be a witness the defendant may wish to call at his or her trial in the United States? Consider the following statements from Justice Rehnquist's majority opinion in *United States v. Valenzuela-Bernal*, 458 U.S. 858 (1982):

> The power to regulate immigration — an attribute of sovereignty essential to the preservation of any nation — has been entrusted by the Constitution to the political branches of the Federal Government.... In exercising this power, Congress has adopted a policy of apprehending illegal aliens at or near the border and deporting them promptly....
>
> The only recent decision of this Court dealing with the right to compulsory process guaranteed by the Sixth Amendment suggests that more than the mere absence of testimony is necessary to establish a violation of the right. See *Washington v. Texas*, 388 U.S. 14 (1967). Indeed, the Sixth Amendment does not by its terms grant to a criminal defendant the right to secure the attendance and testimony of any and all witnesses: it guarantees him "compulsory process for obtaining witnesses in his favor." U.S. Const., Amdt. 6 (emphasis added).... Such an absence of fairness is not made out by the Government's deportation of the witnesses in this case unless there is some explanation of how their testimony would have been favorable and material....

Justice Brennan, with whom Justice Marshall joins, dissenting.

> Today's holding flaunts a transparent contradiction. On the one hand, the Court recognizes respondent's constitutional right, under the Compulsory Process Clause of the Sixth Amendment, to the production of all witnesses whose testimony would be relevant and material to his defense.... But on the other hand, the Court holds that the Government may deport illegal-alien eyewitnesses to respondent's alleged crime immediately upon their apprehension, before respondent or his attorney have had any opportunity to interview them — thus depriving respondent of the surest and most obvious means by which he could establish the materiality and relevance of such witnesses' testimony.... Truly, the Court giveth, and the Court taketh away. But surely a criminal defendant has a constitutional right to interview eyewitnesses to his alleged crime before they are whisked out of the country by his prosecutor. The Court's decision today makes a mockery of that right....

(2) The Sixth Amendment also provides defendants with the right "to be confronted with the witnesses against him." In *United States v. Davis*, 767 F.2d 1025, 1032 (2d Cir. 1985), the court admitted Swiss bank records despite defendant not being present at the hearing at which the records were authenticated. Finding no

violation of the confrontation clause, the court noted that "the Swiss bank records bore the best possible indication of reliability—Davis' admission of their authenticity." The court stated, "[i]n light of the rigorous procedures used to authenticate the documents and Davis' concession, it is highly unlikely that Davis' presence at the hearing (or the authenticating witnesses' presence at the trial) would have weakened the reliability of the records."

(3) Do defendants have Confrontation Rights when witnesses are outside the jurisdiction of the United States? This issue has arisen in several cases. *See, e.g., United States v. McKeeve*, 131 F.3d 1 (1st Cir. 1997). Can emails and foreign depositions be admitted absent the defendant's consent? *See United States v. Siddiqui*, 235 F.3d 1318 (11th Cir. 2000). The Supreme Court decision in *Crawford v. Washington*, 541 U.S. 36 (2004) may also change this landscape in that reliability of the statement is no longer the decisive factor. Under *Crawford*, testimonial out of court statements by a witness cannot be used unless the witness is unavailable and the defendant had the opportunity to cross-examine. The later decision of *Melendez-Diaz v. Massachusetts*, 557 U.S. 305 (2009), took a step further in saying that an analyst's affidavit on a chemical test result was covered by the confrontation clause. *See also Bullcoming v. New Mexico*, 131 S. Ct. 2705 (2011), *but see Williams v. Illinois*, 567 U.S. 50 (2012) (allowing experts to rely on their reports).

Chapter 14

Immunities from Jurisdiction

§ 14.01 Diplomatic and Consular Immunities

Salazar v. Burresch

United States District Court for the Central District of California
47 F. Supp. 2d 1105 (1999)

MATZ, DISTRICT JUDGE:

In 1997, Plaintiff Rafael Salazar was the Consul General of the Republic of Guatemala in Los Angeles, California. On April 4, 1997, at approximately 1:00 p.m., Plaintiff was involved in a car accident on the Pomona Freeway. Defendant California Highway Patrol ("CHP") Officer J. Burresch arrived on the scene shortly after the accident. According to Burresch, Plaintiff appeared intoxicated. Plaintiff informed Burresch that he was consul general and entitled to immunity. After Plaintiff allegedly became unruly, Burresch handcuffed Plaintiff and caused him to be transported to the police station. At the station, Plaintiff's handcuffs were removed and Burresch completed his investigation by issuing Plaintiff a citation. Plaintiff then submitted to a breath test which showed a blood alcohol level of .20%, well above the .08% level of presumed intoxication under California law. He is currently awaiting trial in Los Angeles Municipal Court on drunk driving charges.

[Salazar filed a civil rights action against various defendants, including Officer Burresch and Officer Myhre who had administered the breath test. Among other claims, the complaint alleged] "violation of federal treaty rights," i.e., Article 41 of the 1963 Vienna Convention on Consular Relations ("VCCR") . . . . This matter is currently before the Court on these Defendants' motion for summary judgment. . . .

For purposes of this order, it is unnecessary for the Court to resolve the question of whether there is a private right of action under the VCCR. The Court will assume (without in any way finding) that there is such a cause of action. . . . As set forth in detail below, the Court concludes that even if a private right of action under the VCCR does exist, no material issue of fact exists on the question of whether the CHP Officer Defendants violated Plaintiff's rights under the VCCR; they did not. . . .

Article 41 of the 1963 Vienna Convention on Consular Relations ("VCCR") provides that "Consular officers shall not be liable to arrest or detention pending trial, except in the case of a grave crime and pursuant to a decision by a competent judicial authority." "A 'grave crime' has been interpreted by the Department of State to mean a felony." *U.S. v. Cole*, 717 F. Supp. 309, 323 n.5 (E.D. Pa. 1989) (holding that Yugoslavian consul-general was not entitled to consular immunity from money laundering charges because money-laundering constituted a "grave offense"). "Article 41 does not provide consular officers with immunity for non-grave crimes; rather, it has been interpreted as requiring only that consular officers not be imprisoned until convicted." *Id.* at 323 n.5 . . . .

The United States Department of State has published guidelines interpreting the VCCR and thereby providing guidance to law enforcement officers on how the VCCR applies to their duties. That publication, titled "Guidance for Law Enforcement Officers — Personal Rights and Immunities of Foreign Diplomatic and Consular Personnel," provides in pertinent part as follows:

> General
>
> The vast majority of the persons entitled to privileges and immunities in the United States are judicious in their actions and keenly aware of the significance attached to their actions as representatives of their sending country. On rare occasions, however, a member of this class or of his or her family may be involved in a criminal law violation. The more common violations involve traffic offenses, such as . . . driving while intoxicated. . . .
>
> When, in the course of responding to or investigating an apparent violation of criminal law, a police officer is confronted with a person claiming immunity, official Department of State identification should immediately be requested in order to verify the person's status and immunity. . . .
>
> When proper identification is available, the individual's immunity should be fully respected to the degree to which the particular individual is entitled. If it is established that the individual is entitled to the full inviolability and immunity of a diplomatic agent, he or she may not be arrested and should not, except in extraordinary circumstances (see Personal Inviolability vs. Public Safety below), be handcuffed or detained in any way. . . .
>
> Personal Inviolability vs. Public Safety
>
> . . . All such personal inviolability is, however, qualified by the understanding, well established in international law, that the host country does not give up its right to protect the safety and welfare of its populace and retains the right, in extraordinary circumstances, to prevent the commission of a crime. Thus, in circumstances where public safety is in imminent danger or it is apparent that a serious crime may otherwise be committed, police authorities may intervene to the extent necessary to halt such activity. This naturally includes the power of the police to defend themselves from personal harm.
>
> Traffic Enforcement
>
> . . . [A] police officer should never hesitate to follow normal procedures to intervene in a traffic violation which he or she has observed — even if immunity ultimately bars any further action at the scene, the officer should

> always stop persons committing moving violations, issue a citation if appropriate, and report the incident in accordance with usual procedures. Sobriety tests may be offered in accordance with local procedures but may not be required or compelled. If the police officer judges the individual to be intoxicated, the officer should not (even in the case of diplomatic agents) permit the individual to continue to drive. The officer's primary concern in this connection should be the safety of the community and of the intoxicated individual. Depending on the circumstances, the following options are available. The officer may, with the individual's permission, take the individual to the police station or other location where he or she may recover sufficiently to drive. The officer may summon, or allow the individual to summon, a friend or relative to drive; or the police officer may call a taxi for the individual. If appropriate, the police may choose to provide the individual with transportation.

Plaintiff contends that Burresch violated his rights under the VCCR by handcuffing Plaintiff and by taking him to the station (essentially "arresting" him). Plaintiff contends Defendant Myhre violated his rights under the VCCR by administering the breath test. The Court deals with each of these allegations separately.

A. Handcuffing Plaintiff.

The undisputed facts demonstrate that only after Plaintiff became "extremely agitated and began shouting and flailing his arms about wildly . . . [and] due to plaintiff's obvious intoxication and combative behavior," did Burresch handcuff Plaintiff. Moreover, Burresch did so out of concern for his own safety. . . . Although Plaintiff disputes Burresch's description of Plaintiff's behavior as "combative" and denies that he was ever a threat to Burresch's safety, Plaintiff does not dispute that he was shouting or flailing his arms about wildly. . . .

The provision in the Department of State manual that permits officers to "intervene to the extent necessary" to halt activity that places public safety in "imminent danger" includes (but is not limited to) defending themselves from personal harm. Under these facts, this Court concludes that there is no triable issue on whether Burresch's initial handcuffing of Plaintiff violated the VCCR; it did not. . . .

Moreover, even assuming that Plaintiff remained handcuffed for an hour and a half, this Court concludes that, under the circumstances, that length of time was permissible under the VCCR. . . .

C. Breath Test.

Plaintiff's next argument is that the CHP Officer Defendants violated his rights by giving him a breath test. Plaintiff has submitted no evidence, however, that Burresch had anything to do with a breath test. Instead, the undisputed evidence is that Officer Gutierrez offered Plaintiff the test and that Defendant Myhre administered it.

As to Myhre, moreover, the Court must grant the motion because the evidence is undisputed that Gutierrez asked Plaintiff whether he would agree to take the test and that he agreed to do so.... To be sure, his counsel claimed at the hearing that Salazar had no choice, but there is no evidence that Salazar was threatened, beaten, tricked or coerced. He was asked and he agreed.

The undisputed evidence demonstrates that the conduct of Burresch and Myhre was in compliance with the VCCR, as interpreted by the Department of State Guidelines. Accordingly, this Court grants these Defendants' motion for summary judgment as to Plaintiff's claim under the VCCR.

Notes

(1) For an overview of the whole field of immunities, *see* RESEARCH HANDBOOK ON JURISDICTION AND IMMUNITIES IN INTERNATIONAL LAW (Alexander Orakhelashvili ed. 2015). Consuls, like diplomats, represent their country abroad, but ordinarily are concerned with matters such as commercial relations, attending to the interests of their nationals and passport and visa matters, rather than with political relations. The multilateral Vienna Convention on Consular Relations, April 24, 1963, 21 U.S.T. 77, T.I.A.S. No. 6820, 596 U.N.T.S. 261, brought the status of career consuls (as opposed to honorary consuls) closer to that of diplomats. Nonetheless, even under the Convention, as the foregoing case indicates, consuls, unlike diplomats, have limited immunity from criminal prosecution, and have immunity from arrest only for non-grave crimes. Under Article 43 (1) of the Convention, they "shall not be amenable to the jurisdiction of the judicial or administrative authorities of the receiving State in respect of acts performed in the exercise of consular functions." Much consular business, like diplomatic business, is transacted at official receptions. What if Consul-General Salazar was driving home (drunk) after an official function he had hosted when he was stopped? Is he immune from prosecution?

(2) The modern law on diplomatic immunity is codified in the Vienna Convention on Diplomatic Relations, April 18, 1961, 23 U.S.T. 3227, T.I.A.S. No. 7502, 500 U.N.T.S. 95. Article 29 of that Convention provides: "The person of a diplomatic agent [defined in Article 1 of the Convention as 'the head of mission or a member of the diplomatic staff of the mission'] shall be inviolable. He shall not be liable to any form of arrest or detention...." Article 31(1) provides, without qualification: "A diplomatic agent shall enjoy immunity from the criminal jurisdiction of the receiving State." With limited exceptions, Article 31(1) confers on a diplomatic agent immunity from the civil and administrative jurisdiction of the receiving State. Article 37(1) of the Convention confers similar immunities on "members of the family of a diplomatic agent forming part of his household." Article 37(2) introduces a cast of characters described as "members of the administrative and technical staff of the mission" (not all that helpfully defined in Article 1 of the Convention as "members of the staff of the mission employed in the administrative and technical service of the mission)." They have absolute criminal immunity but no civil immunity for "acts performed outside the course of their duties." As we shall see, *infra* Note (7) and § 14.05, this appears to have become an expansive class in U.S. practice. The United

States became a party to the Convention in 1972. It was generally regarded as self-executing, without the need for further legislation. The Diplomatic Relations Act of 1978 (codified at 22 U.S.C. §§254a–254e) describes itself as an act "[t]o complement the Vienna Convention," and it deals with some practical issues on the edges of the Convention. It provides, for example, that: "Any action or proceeding brought against an individual who is entitled to immunity with respect to such action or proceeding under the Vienna Convention on Diplomatic Relations . . . shall be dismissed" (22 U.S.C. §254d). It also deals with requiring diplomats and missions to obtain automobile insurance and enables direct actions against insurers as an end-run around immunity.

(3) Suppose Salazar, the plaintiff in the foregoing case, had been a diplomat rather than a consul. Would the case have come out differently? Note that, with respect to traffic violations, the State Department guidelines, on which the court relies, do not distinguish between diplomats and consuls. Is this in keeping with the words "inviolable" and "not be liable to any form of arrest or detention?" There must be situations in the real world where even a diplomatic agent may be "detained"—although not prosecuted. What of the police officer who sees someone he knows to be a diplomat strangling the diplomat's wife? Does he tell himself "Whoops, diplomatic immunity"? Diplomatic premises are inviolate; should the local police, aware that a murder is taking place, break down the door? Does the Fire Brigade watch the Embassy burn (perhaps along with those inside) if no one answers their knocking? It can be argued that the silence of the text concerning such issues reflects the drafters' insistence on the policy that immunity means what it says and allows no room for exceptions that could blend into subterfuge.

(4) Does immunity from arrest and prosecution exempt the diplomat from observance of local law? On the contrary, diplomats are said to be immune from the receiving state's efforts to *enforce* its rules, but not (except perhaps with respect to official acts) from its jurisdiction to *prescribe* rules of proper conduct for all persons within its territory. Article 41(1) of the 1961 Vienna Convention expressly stipulates that "it is the duty of all persons enjoying [diplomatic] privileges and immunities to respect the laws and regulations of the receiving State." In principle, then, the diplomat can commit a crime and is exempt only from prosecution. Thus, a person who conspires with a diplomat to engage in criminal activity can be found guilty of conspiracy or complicity, even though the diplomat is immune from prosecution. *See Farnsworth v. Zerbst*, 98 F.2d 541, 544 (5th Cir. 1938). And, if the sending state waives this immunity, the diplomat can be prosecuted as well. Likewise, since the immunity is only from prosecution, not from observing substantive law, a diplomat who remains in the receiving state after diplomatic status terminates can be arrested and tried for crimes committed, at least in a private capacity, while still a diplomat. *See* Restatement (Third) of Foreign Relations Law §464, Reporters' Note 10 (1986). Moreover, Article 31 (4) of the Convention says that "[t]he immunity of a diplomatic agent from the jurisdiction of the receiving State does not exempt him from the jurisdiction of the sending State." There is an expectation that the sending State

will prosecute its own in egregious cases. Some common law states that do not normally exercise nationality jurisdiction have legislation in place enabling jurisdiction specifically over their diplomats and sometimes other governmental personnel such as civilian police who are sent abroad, for example in peacekeeping missions. *See, e.g.*, Crimes Act 1961 (NZ), § 8A (person with diplomatic or consular immunity); Policing Act 2008 (NZ) §§ 86–95 (police and civilian employees). In 2018, a court in the Vatican sentenced Mgr. Carlo Alberto Capella to prison and a fine for possessing and distributing child pornography. He was charged under a 2013 Vatican law on pornography that has extraterritorial effect to crimes committed by "internationally protected" Vatican citizens. The events behind the charge occurred when he was a Vatican diplomat in Washington, D.C. A request by the United States to waive immunity so that he might be tried in the U.S. was apparently declined. He was also sought in Canada in connection with similar charges. *See Vatican Court Sentences Cleric to 5 Years on Child Pornography Charges,* New York Times, June 23, 2018, *available at* https://www.nytimes.com/2018/06/23/world/europe/vatican-child-pornography-carlo-alberto-capella.html.

The US does not appear to have any legislation dealing specifically with diplomats in such situations. But the Military Extraterritorial Jurisdiction Act of 2000, 18 U.S.C. § 3261, provides for jurisdiction over former military no longer subject to trial by court-martial and by those accompanying the military, including family and contractors.

(5) Are there any circumstances in which diplomats who abuse their position for criminal purposes can be said to have forfeited their immunity? Is the nature and seriousness of a crime relevant to whether immunity should be recognized or denied? It has been suggested from time to time that a state may be justified in refusing to allow diplomatic immunity in cases of serious crimes, such as espionage, directed against the receiving state itself. In 1916, Secretary of State Lansing indicated that, in part because of the seriousness of the offense, the United States would not recognize the immunity of a German military attaché accused of conspiracy to violate the neutrality laws. *See* 4 Green Hackworth, Digest of International Law 517 (1942). Most commentators, however, have criticized this statement as a departure from generally accepted principles of international law. The receiving state is not entirely without options in the case of serious offenses. In the first instance it may request a waiver:

> There is no legal obligation on the sending state to waive immunity, but receiving states often request waiver in the case of serious offenses. If the sending state does not waive immunity, it may recall the individual, or the receiving state may declare him *persona non grata*.

1 Restatement of the Foreign Relations Law of the United States (Third) § 464, comm. j at 462 (1987).

(6) Does diplomatic immunity necessarily bar prosecution for war crimes or other international offenses? Former diplomats were convicted in war crimes trials

held after World War II [*see* chap. 20]. But they did not enjoy diplomatic status at the time of trial. They therefore had no immunity from prosecution, only immunity from having their official acts questioned in foreign courts, and the latter is trumped by the rule that, in prosecutions for crimes under international law, the fact that the defendant acted as a head of state or responsible government official cannot exempt the defendant from criminal responsibility. (How far this rule applies to crimes other than war crimes, and in national as well as in international criminal courts, was a central issue in the *Pinochet* case, *see* § 14.02).

It has been suggested in the wake of the *Pinochet* decision that, for the sake of "normative coherence," *active* as well as *former* heads of state should be denied immunity from prosecution in other countries for crimes under international law. *See* Andrea Bianchi, *Immunity Versus Human Rights: The Pinochet Case*, 10 Eur. J. Int'l L. 237 (1999). On the same grounds, one might argue, so should *active* diplomats. Consider, however, the following episode, as more indicative, perhaps, of actual state practice:

> In early April 1997, a Peruvian army-intelligence officer, Leonor La Rosa, stated publicly that fellow intelligence officers had committed acts of torture against her in early 1997. On April 8, Peruvian authorities acted on those accusations by relieving Major Tomás Ricardo Anderson Kohatsu and three other officers of their duties, and by arresting and charging them, under Peru's military code, with abuse of authority. On May 9, a Peruvian military court convicted the four officers of negligence and abuse of authority. In addition to imposing fines, the court sentenced them to eight years in prison. In February 1998, however, Major Anderson and another officer were quietly released from prison.
>
> In March 2000, Major Anderson traveled to Washington, D.C., to take part in a hearing on wiretapping before the Inter-American Commission on Human Rights. On March 9, the Federal Bureau of Investigation (FBI) detained Major Anderson at an airport in Houston, Texas, for possible arrest and prosecution for acts of torture. When the Justice Department consulted the U.S. Department of State, however, Under Secretary of State Thomas R. Pickering decided that Major Anderson was entitled to immunity from prosecution as a diplomatic representative of his government present in the United States for an official appearance before an international organization. The FBI therefore allowed Major Anderson to depart the United States on March 10.

Sean D. Murphy, *Contemporary Practice of the United States Relating to International Law*, 94 A.J.I.L. 516, 535–36 (2000). Pursuant to 22 U.S.C.A. §§ 288 and 288a (the International Organizations Immunities Act) and the Executive Order made thereunder, *permanent* representatives of members of the OAS located in Washington appear to be entitled to immunity only in respect of acts performed in their official capacity ("functional" immunity). Why should someone coming temporarily, like Major Anderson, receive greater protection?

Compare Anderson's position and that of Radovan Karadzic in *Kadic v. Karadzic*, 70 F.3d 232 (2nd Cir. 1995), *cert. denied*, 518 U.S. 1005 (1996). Karadzic was the president of the "Republic of Srpska" a Serbian entity within Bosnia Herzegovina, not recognized by either the United States or the United Nations. He came to New York for negotiations on the issue of Former Yugoslavia. He was held not to have immunity from service of process either on the basis of the U.N. Headquarters Agreement between the United States and the United Nations, or on federal common law grounds.

(7) In Note (2) we encountered the category of administrative and technical staff. Consider the following incident as a taste of the problems such status, interpreted expansively, may create:

> In early 2011, the United States and Pakistan grappled with a potentially serious disagreement involving the status of U.S. official Ray Davis, who shot and killed two Pakistanis in Lahore, Pakistan, in late January 2011 and was then arrested and detained. The controversy intensified following reports that Davis was employed as a security officer by the U.S. Central Intelligence Agency. In Mid-March 2011, the dead men's families agreed to accept monetary compensation in accordance with Pakistani law, and Davis was released from custody and left Pakistan. The issue of his legal status in Pakistan was not resolved.

Note, *Controversy Regarding Status of U.S. Official Involved in Shootings in Lahore*, 105 Am. J. Int'l L. 336 (2011) (footnotes omitted). The U.S. regarded him as part of the administrative and technical staff of the Embassy. According to the U.S. Ambassador at the time, "[w]e decide who a diplomat is. Raymond Davis did not look like a diplomat. He had tattoos, he had big muscles . . . he had an unregistered weapon in his car." Nicholas Schmidle, *After Pakistan*, The New Yorker 23 (Nov. 26, 2012). Davis was released after a couple of months. According to the BBC, "[t]he Pakistan media has reported that the families received 200 million rupees ($2.34m . . .) but U.S. Secretary of State Hillary Clinton denied the US government had paid any blood money." BBC News, March 18, 2011, *CIA contractor Ray Davis freed over Pakistan killings, available at* http://www.bbc.com/news/world-south-asia-12757244.

Another example of the expansive nature of "administrative and technical staff" in U.S. usage is the case of Anne Sacoolas, a cause celèbre between the U.S. and the UK. Ms. Sacoolas is the wife of Jonathan Sacoolas, a State Department employee sent by the U.S. to work at "RAF Croughton," a communications and listening post about sixty miles from London. In spite of the "RAF" title, the base seems currently to be operated entirely by the U.S. After some negotiation, and an apparently unpublished exchange of letters between the Governments, Mr. Sacoolas and his cohorts were classified as members of the administrative and technical staff of the Embassy in London. (Compare the sophisticated negotiations here and the insistence in Pakistan that "We decide"). Ms. Sacoolas drove out of Croughton on the wrong side of the road and killed a local lad on a motorbike, who was in his correct lane. Ms. Sacoolas left the UK shortly afterwards, before any criminal proceedings;

her husband left a bit later. Subsequently, the British authorities began extradition proceedings on a charge of death by dangerous driving. In a case brought by the parents of the deceased, the Divisional Court in London held that, as the spouse of a diplomat, Ms. Sacoolas was entitled to diplomatic immunity at the relevant time. *See The Queen (on the application of Charlotte James and Tim Dunn) v. Secretary of State for Foreign and Commonwealth Affairs and Chief Constable of Northamptonshire Police*, decided 24 November 2020, *available at* https://www.judiciary.uk/wp-content/uploads/2020/11/R-Dunn-v-SOS-for-Foreign-and-Commonwealth-Affairs.pdf. Some interesting questions remain (aside from issues of what is "diplomatic"). Should the U.S. waive immunity in such cases, more or less as a matter of course? Given that Ms. Sacoolas is no longer "on mission," presumably she now has only functional immunity in respect of her official acts. There appears nothing official about her trip off base. If she were to return to the UK as a tourist to visit the Tower of London, she could be arrested. Should the U.S. extradite her on the basis she now has only functional immunity? Or does her immunity at the time of the fatal event apply to the extradition request? *See also* § 14.05, *infra*, on Immunities and the International Criminal Court for more on "administrative and technical" personnel.

§ 14.02 Head of State and Act of State Immunities

Regina v. Bow Street Metropolitan Stipendiary Magistrate and Others, Ex Parte Pinochet Ugarte (No. 3)

House of Lords [2000] 1 App. Cas. 147, [1999] 2 All E. R. 97

[Augusto Pinochet Ugarte was the former president of Chile. While he was visiting England for medical treatment, the Spanish authorities requested his extradition. On October 16, 1998, he was served with a provisional arrest warrant, issued by a metropolitan stipendiary magistrate in London, alleging that, during the decade between September 1973 and December 1983, he participated in the murder of Spanish citizens living in Chile. A second provisional arrest warrant, issued on October 22, 1998, alleged his participation in torture, conspiracy to torture, detention of hostages, conspiracy to detain hostages, and in a conspiracy to commit murder which extended to Spain and other European countries. Pinochet applied for judicial review and habeas corpus. On October 28, 1998, both warrants were quashed by the Queen's Bench Divisional Court. The first warrant was found not to allege an extraditable offense because it involved the assertion of extraterritorial jurisdiction by Spain under circumstances where a British court would not have extraterritorial jurisdiction in the analogous situation of British citizens murdered abroad. Both warrants were found to be invalid, in any event, because Pinochet, as a former head of state, was held to have immunity from arrest and extradition proceedings in the United Kingdom for acts committed when he was head of state. [1998] All E.R. 509.

The Crown Prosecution Service, representing the Spanish government, was granted leave to appeal to the House of Lords on the ground that a point of law of general public importance was involved, "namely, the proper interpretation and scope of the immunity enjoyed by a former head of state from arrest and extradition proceedings in the United Kingdom in respect of acts committed while head of state." Before the appeal was heard, the list of charges against Pinochet was expanded to include numerous other acts perpetrated between 1972 and 1989. On November 25, 1998, by a 3-2 decision, the appeal was allowed and Pinochet was held not to enjoy immunity with respect to international crimes such as torture and hostage-taking committed when he was head of state. [1998] 4 All E.R. 897. However, on January 15, 1999, the House of Lords set aside this decision and ordered the matter reheard because Lord Hoffman, one of the Law Lords participating in the decision, had undisclosed ties to Amnesty International, an intervenor in the proceedings. [1999] 1 All E.R. 577. The panel that reheard the case was composed of seven members: Lord Browne-Wilkinson, Lord Goff of Chieveley, Lord Hope of Craighead, Lord Hutton, Lord Saville of Newdigate, Lord Millett, and Lord Phillips of Worth Matravers. Each delivered a separate opinion, the vote being 6-1 in favor of extradition (Lord Goff dissenting).]

Lord Browne-Wilkinson:

My Lords, as is well known, this case concerns an attempt by the government of Spain to extradite Senator Pinochet from this country to stand trial in Spain for crimes committed (primarily in Chile) during the period when Senator Pinochet was head of state in Chile. . . . The power to extradite from the United Kingdom for an 'extradition crime' is now contained in the Extradition Act 1989. That Act defines what constitutes an 'extradition crime.' For the purposes of the present case, the most important requirement is that the conduct complained of must constitute a crime under the law both of Spain and of the United Kingdom. This is known as the double criminality rule.

Since the Nazi atrocities and the Nuremberg trials, international law has recognised a number of offences as being international crimes. Individual states have taken jurisdiction to try some international crimes even in cases where such crimes were not committed within the geographical boundaries of such states. The most important of such international crimes for present purposes is torture which is regulated by the Convention against Torture and Other Cruel, Inhuman or Degrading Treatment or Punishment, 1984 [*see* chap. 10]. The obligations placed on the United Kingdom by that convention (and on the other 110 or more signatory states who have adopted the Convention) were incorporated into the law of the United Kingdom by section 134 of the Criminal Justice Act 1988. That Act came into force on 29 September 1988. Section 134 created a new crime under United Kingdom law, the crime of torture. As required by the Torture Convention 'all' torture wherever committed worldwide was made criminal under United Kingdom law and triable in the United Kingdom. No one has suggested that before section 134 came into effect torture committed outside the United Kingdom was a crime under United

Kingdom law. Nor is it suggested that section 134 was retrospective so as to make torture committed outside the United Kingdom before 29 September 1988 a United Kingdom crime. Since torture outside the United Kingdom was not a crime under U.K. law until 29 September 1988, the principle of double criminality which requires an act to be a crime under both the law of Spain and of the United Kingdom cannot be satisfied in relation to conduct before that date if the principle of double criminality requires the conduct to be criminal under United Kingdom law *at the date it was committed*. If, on the other hand, the double criminality rule only requires the conduct to be criminal under UK law *at the date of extradition* the rule was satisfied in relation to all torture alleged against Senator Pinochet whether it took place before or after 1988. . . .

On 11 September 1973 a right-wing coup evicted the left-wing regime of President Allende. The coup was led by a military junta, of whom Senator (then General) Pinochet was the leader. At some stage he became head of state. The Pinochet regime remained in power until 11 March 1990 when Senator Pinochet resigned.

There is no real dispute that during the period of the Senator Pinochet regime appalling acts of barbarism were committed in Chile and elsewhere in the world: torture, murder and the unexplained disappearance of individuals, all on a large scale. Although it is not alleged that Senator Pinochet himself committed any of those acts, it is alleged that they were done in pursuance of a conspiracy to which he was a party, at his instigation and with his knowledge. He denies these allegations. None of the conduct alleged was committed by or against citizens of the United Kingdom or in the United Kingdom.

In 1998 Senator Pinochet came to the United Kingdom for medical treatment. The judicial authorities in Spain sought to extradite him in order to stand trial in Spain on a large number of charges. Some of those charges had links with Spain. But most of the charges had no connection with Spain. . . .

[Because the expanded list of charges included conduct occurring before Pinochet became head of state, counsel for Pinochet argued at the second hearing before the House of Lords] that certain of the charges, in particular those relating to torture and conspiracy to torture, were not 'extradition crimes' because *at the time the acts were done* the acts were not criminal under the law of the United Kingdom. Once raised, this point could not be confined simply to the period (if any) before Senator Pinochet became head of state. If the double criminality rule requires it to be shown that at the date of the conduct such conduct would have been criminal under the law of the United Kingdom, any charge based on torture or conspiracy to torture occurring before 29 September 1988 (when section 134 of the 1988 Act came into force) could not be an 'extradition crime' and therefore could not in any event found an extradition order against Senator Pinochet. . . .

[Lord Browne-Wilkinson found that the wording and history of the definition of an "extradition crime" in section 2 of the Extradition Act 1989 indicated that] the conduct must be criminal under the law of the United Kingdom at the conduct date and not only at the request date.... The consequences of requiring torture to be a crime under U.K. law at the date the torture was committed are considered in Lord Hope's speech. As he demonstrates, the charges of torture and conspiracy to torture relating to conduct before 29 September 1988 (the date on which section 134 came into effect) are not extraditable, i.e. only those parts . . . which relate to the period after that date . . . are extradition crimes relating to torture. . . .

Lord Hope also considers, and I agree, that the only charge relating to hostage-taking does not disclose any offence under the Taking of Hostages Act, 1982 [since there was no allegation that hostages were taken in order to compel a third party to do or abstain from doing some action]. I must therefore consider whether, in relation to the two surviving categories of charge, Senator Pinochet enjoys sovereign immunity. But first it is necessary to consider the modern law of torture.

Apart from the law of piracy, the concept of personal liability under international law for international crimes is of comparatively modern growth. The traditional subjects of international law are states not human beings. But consequent upon the war crime trials after the 1939–45 World War, the international community came to recognise that there could be criminal liability under international law for a class of crimes such as war crimes and crimes against humanity. Although there may be legitimate doubts as to the legality of the Charter of the [Nuremberg Tribunal], in my judgment those doubts were stilled by the Affirmation of the Principles of International Law recognised by the Charter of Nuremberg Tribunal adopted by the United Nations General Assembly on 11 December 1946 [*see* chap. 19]. . . . At least from that date onwards the concept of personal liability for a crime in international law must have been part of international law. In the early years state torture was one of the elements of a war crime. In consequence torture, and various other crimes against humanity, were linked to war or at least to hostilities of some kind. But in the course of time this linkage with war fell away and torture, divorced from war or hostilities, became an international crime on its own. *See Prosecutor v. Furundzija* [chap. 10, *supra*]. Ever since 1945, torture on a large scale has featured as one of the crimes against humanity.

Moreover, the Republic of Chile accepted before your Lordships that the international law prohibiting torture has the character of *jus cogens* or a peremptory norm, i.e. one of those rules of international law which have a peculiar status. . . . The *jus cogens* nature of the international crime of torture justifies states in taking universal jurisdiction over torture wherever committed. International law provides that offences *jus cogens* may be punished by any state because the offenders are 'common enemies of all mankind and all nations have an equal interest in their apprehension and prosecution': *Demjanjuk v Petrovsky*, 776 F.2d 571 (6th Cir. 1985) [*see* chap. 20].

It was suggested by Miss Montgomery Q.C., for Senator Pinochet, that although torture was contrary to international law it was not strictly an international crime in the highest sense. In the light of the authorities . . . I have no doubt that long before the Torture Convention state torture was an international crime in the highest sense. The Torture Convention was agreed not in order to create an international crime which had not previously existed but to provide an international system under which the international criminal — the torturer — could find no safe haven....

The first question on the Convention is to decide whether acts done by a head of state are done by 'a public official or a person acting in an official capacity' within the meaning of Article 1. The same question arises under section 134 of the 1988 Act. The answer to both questions must be the same.... It became clear during the argument that both the Republic of Chile and Senator Pinochet accepted that the acts alleged against Senator Pinochet, if proved, were acts done by a public official or person acting in an official capacity within the meaning of Article 1. In my judgment these concessions were correctly made. Unless a head of state authorising or promoting torture is an official or acting in an official capacity within Article 1, then he would not be guilty of the international crime of torture even within his own state. That plainly cannot have been the intention. In my judgment it would run completely contrary to the intention of the Convention if there was anybody who could be exempt from guilt. The crucial question is not whether Senator Pinochet falls within the definition in Article 1: he plainly does. The question is whether, even so, he is procedurally immune from process. To my mind the fact that a head of state can be guilty of the crime casts little, if any, light on the question whether he is immune from prosecution for that crime in a foreign state....

[I]f Senator Pinochet is not entitled to immunity in relation to the acts of torture alleged to have occurred after 29 September 1988 it will be the first time, so far as counsel have discovered, when a local domestic court has refused to afford immunity to a head of state or former head of state on the grounds that there can be no immunity against prosecution for certain international crimes.... Given the importance of the point, it is surprising how narrow is the area of dispute.... The issue is whether international law grants state immunity in relation to the international crime of torture and, if so, whether the Republic of Chile is entitled to claim such immunity even though Chile, Spain and the United Kingdom are all parties to the Torture Convention and therefore 'contractually' bound to give effect to its provisions from 8 December 1988 at the latest.[a]

It is a basic principle of international law that one sovereign state (the forum state) does not adjudicate on the conduct of a foreign state. The foreign state is entitled to procedural immunity from the processes of the forum state. This immunity extends to both criminal and civil liability. State immunity probably grew from the historical immunity of the person of the monarch. In any event, such personal immunity of the head of state persists to the present day: the head of state is entitled to the same immunity as the state itself. The diplomatic representative of the foreign state in the forum state is also afforded the same immunity in recognition of the dignity of the state which he represents. This immunity enjoyed by a head of state in power

a. Spain had ratified the Convention on October 21, 1987. Chile ratified effective October 30, 1988; the United Kingdom effective December 8, 1988. — Eds.

and an ambassador in post is a complete immunity attaching to the person of the head of state or ambassador and rendering him immune from all actions or prosecutions whether or not they relate to matters done for the benefit of the state. Such immunity is said to be granted *ratione personae.*

What then when the ambassador leaves his post or the head of state is deposed? The position of the ambassador is covered by the Vienna Convention on Diplomatic Relations, 1961. After providing for immunity from arrest (art. 29) and from criminal and civil jurisdiction (art. 31), Article 39(1) provides that the ambassador's privileges shall be enjoyed from the moment he takes up post; and subsection 2(2) provides:

> When the functions of a person enjoying privileges and immunities have come to an end, such privileges and immunities shall normally cease at the moment when he leaves the country, or on expiry of a reasonable period in which to do so, but shall subsist until that time, even in case of armed conflict. However, with respect to acts performed by such a person in the exercise of his functions as a member of the mission immunity shall continue to subsist.

The continuing partial immunity of the ambassador after leaving post is of a different kind from that enjoyed *ratione personae* while he was in post. Since he is no longer the representative of the foreign state he merits no particular privileges or immunities as a person. However in order to preserve the integrity of the activities of the foreign state during the period when he was ambassador, it is necessary to provide that immunity is afforded to his *official* acts during his tenure in post. If this were not done the sovereign immunity of the state could be evaded by calling in question acts done during the previous ambassador's time. Accordingly under Article 39(2) the ambassador, like any other official of the state, enjoys immunity in relation to his official acts done while he was an official. This limited immunity, *ratione materiae*, is to be contrasted with the former immunity *ratione personae* which gave complete immunity to all activities whether public or private.

In my judgment at common law a former head of state enjoys similar immunities, *ratione materiae*, once he ceases to be head of state. He too loses immunity *ratione personae* on ceasing to be head of state. As ex-head of state he cannot be sued in respect of acts performed whilst head of state in his public capacity. Thus, at common law, the position of the former ambassador and the former head of state appears to be much the same: both enjoy immunity for acts done in performance of their respective functions whilst in office. . . . Accordingly, in my judgment, Senator Pinochet as former head of state enjoys immunity *ratione materiae* in relation to acts done by him as head of state as part of his official functions as head of state.

The question then which has to be answered is whether the alleged organisation of state torture by Senator Pinochet (if proved) would constitute an act committed by Senator Pinochet as part of his official functions as head of state. It is not enough to say that it cannot be part of the functions of the head of state to commit a crime.

Actions which are criminal under the local law can still have been done officially and therefore give rise to immunity *ratione materiae*. The case needs to be analysed more closely.

Can it be said that the commission of a crime which is an international crime against humanity and *jus cogens* is an act done in an official capacity on behalf of the state? I believe there to be strong ground for saying that the implementation of torture as defined by the Torture Convention cannot be a state function. . . .

I have doubts whether, before the coming into force of the Torture Convention, the existence of the international crime of torture as *jus cogens* was enough to justify the conclusion that the organisation of state torture could not rank for immunity purposes as performance of an official function. At that stage there was no international tribunal to punish torture and no general jurisdiction to permit or require its punishment in domestic courts. Not until there was some form of universal jurisdiction for the punishment of the crime of torture could it really be talked about as a fully constituted international crime. But in my judgment the Torture Convention did provide what was missing: a worldwide universal jurisdiction. Further, it required all member states to ban and outlaw torture. How can it be for international law purposes an official function to do something which international law itself prohibits and criminalises? Thirdly, an essential feature of the international crime of torture is that it must be committed 'by or with the acquiescence of a public official or other person acting in an official capacity.' As a result all defendants in torture cases will be state officials. Yet, if the former head of state has immunity, the man most responsible will escape liability while his inferiors (the chiefs of police, junior army officers) who carried out his orders will be liable. I find it impossible to accept that this was the intention.

Finally, and to my mind decisively, if the implementation of a torture regime is a public function giving rise to immunity *ratione materiae*, this produces bizarre results. Immunity *ratione materiae* applies not only to ex-heads of state and ex-ambassadors but to all state officials who have been involved in carrying out the functions of the state. . . . [I]f the implementation of the torture regime is to be treated as official business sufficient to found an immunity for the former head of state, it must also be official business sufficient to justify immunity for his inferiors who actually did the torturing. . . . Therefore the whole elaborate structure of universal jurisdiction over torture committed by officials is rendered abortive and one of the main objectives of the Torture Convention — to provide a system under which there is no safe haven for torturers — will have been frustrated. In my judgment all these factors together demonstrate that the notion of continued immunity for ex-heads of state is inconsistent with the provisions of the Torture Convention.

For these reasons in my judgment if, as alleged, Senator Pinochet organised and authorised torture after 8 December 1988 he was not acting in any capacity which gives rise to immunity *ratione materiae* because such actions were contrary to international law, Chile had agreed to outlaw such conduct and Chile had agreed with the other parties to the Torture Convention that all signatory states should have jurisdiction to try official torture (as defined in the Convention) even if such torture were committed in Chile. . . .

As to the charges of murder and conspiracy to murder, no one has advanced any reason why the ordinary rules of immunity should not apply and Senator Pinochet is entitled to such immunity.

For these reasons, I would allow the appeal so as to permit the extradition proceedings to proceed on the allegation that torture in pursuance of a conspiracy to commit torture . . . was being committed by Senator Pinochet after 8 December 1988 when he lost his immunity. . . .

Lord Goff of Chieveley:

The central question in the appeal is whether Senator Pinochet is entitled as former head of state to the benefit of state immunity *ratione materiae* in respect of the charges advanced against him. . . . Before the Divisional Court, and again before the first Appellate Committee, it was argued on behalf of the government of Spain that Senator Pinochet was not entitled to the benefit of state immunity basically on two grounds, *viz.* first, that the crimes alleged against Senator Pinochet are so horrific that an exception must be made to the international law principle of state immunity; and second, that the crimes with which he is charged are crimes against international law, in respect of which state immunity is not available. Both arguments were rejected by the Divisional Court, but a majority of the first Appellate Committee accepted the second argument. . . . Lord Slynn of Hadley and Lord Lloyd of Berwick, however, delivered substantial dissenting opinions. In particular, Lord Slynn considered in detail 'the developments in international law relating to what are called international crimes.' On the basis of the material so reviewed by him, he concluded:

> It does not seem to me that it has been shown that there is any state practice or general consensus let alone a widely supported convention that all crimes against international law should be justiciable in national courts on the basis of the universality of jurisdiction. Nor is there any *jus cogens* in respect of such breaches of international law which require that a claim of state or head of state immunity, itself a well-established principle of international law, should be overridden.

He went on to consider whether international law now recognises that some crimes, and in particular crimes against humanity, are outwith the protection of head of state immunity. He referred to the relevant material, and observed:

> . . . except in regard to crimes in particular situations before international tribunals these measures did not in general deal with the question as to whether otherwise existing immunities were taken away. Nor did they always specifically recognise the jurisdiction of, or confer jurisdiction on, national courts to try such crimes.

He then proceeded to examine the Torture Convention (1984), the Genocide Convention (1948), and the Taking of Hostages Convention (1983), and concluded that none of them had removed the long established immunity of former heads of state. . . . I wish to record my respectful agreement with the analysis, and conclusions, of Lord Slynn set out in the passages from his opinion to which I have referred. . . .

The principle of state immunity is expressed in the Latin maxim *par in parem non habet imperium*, the effect of which is that one sovereign state does not adjudicate on the conduct of another. This principle applies as between states, and the head of a state is entitled to the same immunity as the state itself, as are the diplomatic representatives of the state. That . . . principle applies in criminal proceedings. . . . [T]he mere fact that the conduct is criminal does not of itself exclude the immunity, otherwise there would be little point in the immunity from criminal process; and this is so even where the crime is of a serious character. It follows, in my opinion, that the mere fact that the crime in question is torture does not exclude state immunity. It has however been stated by Sir Arthur Watts [*The Legal Position in International Law of Heads of States, Heads of Government and Foreign Ministers*, 247 HAGUE RECUEIL DES COURS (1994-III)] that a head of state may be personally responsible "for acts of such seriousness that they constitute not merely international wrongs (in the broad sense of a civil wrong) but rather international crimes which offend against the public order of the international community." . . .

So far as torture is concerned, however, there are two points to be made. The first is that it is evident . . . that Sir Arthur is referring not just to a specific crime as such, but to a crime which offends against the public order of the international community, for which a head of state may be *internationally* (his emphasis) accountable. The instruments cited by him show that he is concerned here with crimes against peace, war crimes and crimes against humanity. Originally these were limited to crimes committed in the context of armed conflict, as in the case of the Nuremberg and Tokyo Charters, and still in the case of the Statute of the Tribunal for the Former Yugoslavia, though there it is provided that the conflict can be international or internal in character. Subsequently, the context has been widened to include (*inter alia*) torture "when committed as part of a widespread or systematic attack against a civilian population" on specified grounds. A provision to this effect appeared in the International Law Commission's Draft Code of Crimes of 1996 (which was, I understand, provisionally adopted in 1988), and also appeared in the Statute of the Tribunal for Rwanda (1994), and in the Rome Statute of the International Criminal Court (1998). . . . I should add that these developments were foreshadowed in the International Law Commission's Draft Code of Crimes of 1954; but this was not adopted, and there followed a long gap of about 35 years before the developments in the 1990s to which I have referred. It follows that these provisions are not capable of evidencing any settled practice in respect of torture outside the context of armed conflict until well after 1989 which is the latest date with which we are concerned in the present case. The second point is that these instruments are all concerned with international responsibility before international tribunals, and not with the exclusion of state immunity in criminal proceedings before national courts. This supports the conclusion of Lord Slynn that "except in regard to crimes in particular situations before international tribunals these measures did not in general deal with the question whether otherwise existing immunities were taken away," with which I have already expressed my respectful agreement.

It follows that, if state immunity in respect of crimes of torture has been excluded at all in the present case, this can only have been done by the Torture Convention itself. . . . It is to be observed that no mention is made of state immunity in the Convention. Had it been intended to exclude state immunity, it is reasonable to assume that this would have been the subject either of a separate article, or of a separate paragraph in Article 7. . . . Since therefore exclusion of immunity is said to result from the Torture Convention and there is no express term of the Convention to this effect, the argument has, in my opinion, to be formulated as dependent upon an implied term in the Convention. . . .

On behalf of the government of Chile Dr Collins [submitted] that a state's waiver of its immunity by treaty must always be express. With that submission, I agree. . . . [I]t appears to me to be clear that, in accordance both with international law, and with the law of this country which on this point reflects international law, a state's waiver of its immunity by treaty must, as Dr Collins submitted, always be express. Indeed, if this was not so, there could well be international chaos as the courts of different state parties to a treaty reach different conclusions on the question whether a waiver of immunity was to be implied.

However it is, as I understand it, suggested that this well-established principle can be circumvented in the present case on the basis that it is not proposed that state parties to the Torture Convention have agreed to waive their state immunity in proceedings brought in the states of other parties in respect of allegations of torture within the Convention. It is rather that, for the purposes of the Convention, such torture does not form part of the functions of public officials or others acting in an official capacity including, in particular, a head of state. Moreover since state immunity *ratione materiae* can only be claimed in respect of acts done by an official in the exercise of his functions as such, it would follow, for example, that the effect is that a former head of state does not enjoy the benefit of immunity *ratione materiae* in respect of such torture after he has ceased to hold office.

In my opinion, the principle which I have described cannot be circumvented in this way. I observe first that the meaning of the word 'functions' as used in this context is well established. The functions of, for example, a head of state are governmental functions, as opposed to private acts; and the fact that the head of state performs an act, other than a private act, which is criminal does not deprive it of its governmental character. This is as true of a serious crime, such as murder or torture, as it is of a lesser crime. As Lord Bingham of Cornhill C.J. said in the Divisional Court:

> . . . a former head of state is clearly entitled to immunity in relation to criminal acts performed in the course of exercising public functions. One cannot therefore hold that any deviation from good democratic practice is outside

> the pale of immunity. If the former sovereign is immune from process in respect of some crimes, where does one draw the line?

It was in answer to that question that the appellants advanced the theory that one draws the line at crimes which may be called 'international crimes.' If, however, a limit is to be placed on governmental functions so as to exclude from them acts of torture within the Torture Convention, this can only be done by means of an implication arising from the Convention itself. Moreover, as I understand it, the only purpose of the proposed implied limitation upon the functions of public officials is to deprive them, or as in the present case a former head of state, of the benefit of state immunity; and in my opinion the policy which requires that such a result can only be achieved in a treaty by express agreement, with the effect that it cannot be so achieved by implication, renders it equally unacceptable that it should be achieved indirectly by means of an implication such as that now proposed. . . .

[T]he assumption underlying the argument that the continued availability of state immunity is inconsistent with the obligations of state parties to the Convention is in my opinion not justified. . . . First of all, in the majority of cases which may arise under the Convention, no question of state immunity will arise at all, because the public official concerned is likely to be present in his own country. Even when such a question does arise, there is no reason to assume that state immunity will be asserted by the state of which the alleged torturer is a public official; on the contrary, it is only in unusual cases, such as the present, that this is likely to be done. In any event, however, not only is there no mention of state immunity in the Convention, but in my opinion it is not inconsistent with its express provisions that, if steps are taken to extradite him or to submit his case to the authorities for the purpose of prosecution, the appropriate state should be entitled to assert state immunity. In this connection, I comment that it is not suggested that it is inconsistent with the Convention that immunity *ratione personae* should be asserted; if so, I find it difficult to see why it should be inconsistent to assert immunity *ratione materiae*.

. . . .

[N]othing in the negotiating history of the Torture Convention throws any light on the proposed implied term. Certainly the *travaux preparatoires* shown to your Lordships reveal no trace of any consideration being given to waiver of state immunity. . . . It is surely most unlikely that during the years in which the draft was under consideration no thought was given to the possibility of the state parties to the Convention waiving state immunity. Furthermore, if agreement had been reached that there should be such a waiver, express provision would inevitably have been made in the Convention to that effect. Plainly, however, no such agreement was reached. . . . In this connection it must not be overlooked that there are many reasons why states, although recognising that in certain circumstances jurisdiction should be vested in another national court in respect of acts of torture committed by public officials within their own jurisdiction, may nevertheless have considered it imperative that they should be able, if necessary, to assert state immunity. The Torture Convention applies not only to a series of acts of systematic torture, but to the commission of, even acquiescence in, a single act of physical or mental torture. Extradition can nowadays be sought, in some parts of the world, on the basis of a simple allegation unsupported by prima facie evidence. In certain circumstances torture may, for compelling political reasons, be the subject of an amnesty, or some other form of settlement, in the state where it has been, or is alleged to have been, committed.

Furthermore, if immunity *ratione materiae* was excluded, former heads of state and senior public officials would have to think twice about travelling abroad, for fear of being the subject of unfounded allegations emanating from states of a different political persuasion. In this connection, it is a mistake to assume that state parties to the Convention would only wish to preserve state immunity in cases of torture in order to shield public officials guilty of torture from prosecution elsewhere in the world. Such an assumption is based on a misunderstanding of the nature and function of state immunity, which is a rule of international law restraining one sovereign state from sitting in judgment on the sovereign behaviour of another. . . . State immunity *ratione materiae* operates therefore to protect former heads of state, and (where immunity is asserted) public officials, even minor public officials, from legal process in foreign countries in respect of acts done in the exercise of their functions as such, including accusation and arrest in respect of alleged crimes. It can therefore be effective to preclude any such process in respect of alleged crimes, including allegations which are misguided or even malicious — a matter which can be of great significance where, for example, a former head of state is concerned and political passions are aroused. Preservation of state immunity is therefore a matter of particular importance to powerful countries whose heads of state perform an executive role, and who may therefore be regarded as possible targets by governments of states which, for deeply felt political reasons, deplore their actions while in office. But, to bring the matter nearer home, we must not overlook the fact that it is not only in the United States of America that a substantial body of opinion supports the campaign of the IRA to overthrow the democratic government of Northern Ireland. It is not beyond the bounds of possibility that a state whose government is imbued with this opinion might seek to extradite from a third country, where he or she happens to be, a responsible Minister of the Crown, or even a more humble public official such as a police inspector, on the ground that he or she has acquiesced in a single act of physical or mental torture in Northern Ireland. . . .

For the above reasons, I am of the opinion that by far the greater part of the charges against Senator Pinochet must be excluded as offending against the double criminality rule; and that, in respect of the surviving charges . . . Senator Pinochet is entitled to the benefit of state immunity *ratione materiae* as a former head of state. I would therefore dismiss the appeal of the government of Spain from the decision of the Divisional Court.

Lord Millett:

. . . .

In my opinion, crimes prohibited by international law attract universal jurisdiction under customary international law if two criteria are satisfied. First, they must be contrary to a peremptory norm of international law so as to infringe a jus cogens. Secondly, they must be so serious and on such a scale that they can justly be regarded as an attack on the international legal order. Isolated offences, even if committed by public officials, would not satisfy these criteria.... Every state has jurisdiction under customary international law to exercise extraterritorial jurisdiction in respect of international crimes which satisfy the relevant criteria. Whether its courts have extraterritorial jurisdiction under its internal domestic law depends, of course, on its constitutional arrangements and the relationship between customary international law and the jurisdiction of its criminal courts. The jurisdiction of the English criminal courts is usually statutory, but it is supplemented by the common law. Customary international law is part of the common law, and accordingly I consider that the English courts have and always have had extraterritorial criminal jurisdiction in respect of crimes of universal jurisdiction under customary international law.

In my opinion, the systematic use of torture on a large scale and as an instrument of state policy had joined piracy, war crimes and crimes against peace as an international crime of universal jurisdiction well before 1984. I consider that it had done so by 1973. For my own part, therefore, I would hold that the courts of this country already possessed extraterritorial jurisdiction in respect of torture and conspiracy to torture on the scale of the charges in the present case and did not require the authority of statute to exercise it....

I turn finally to the plea of immunity *ratione materiae* in relation to the ... allegations of torture, conspiracy to torture and murder. I can deal with the charges of conspiracy to murder quite shortly. The offences are alleged to have taken place in the requesting state. The plea of immunity *ratione materiae* is not available in respect of an offence committed in the forum state, whether this be England or Spain....

[As to torture:] ... The international community had created an offence for which immunity *ratione materiae* cannot possibly be available. International law cannot be supposed to have established a crime having the character of a *jus cogens* and at the same time to have provided an immunity which is coextensive with the obligation it seeks to impose....

For my own part, I would allow the appeal in respect of the charges relating to the offences in Spain and to torture and conspiracy to torture, wherever and whenever carried out....

Notes

(1) In presenting the Report of the Appellate Committee to the full House of Lords on March 24, 1999, Lord Browne-Wilkinson provided the following summary of the result of the rehearing:

> . . . In today's judgment, six members of the Committee hold that, under the ordinary law of extradition, Senator Pinochet cannot be extradited to face charges in relation to torture occurring before 29th September 1988 because until that date the double criminality principle was not satisfied.
>
> The result of this decision is to eliminate the majority of the charges levelled against Senator Pinochet. . . . Most of the allegations against Senator Pinochet relate to the period of the coup in Chile in 1973 and the years immediately thereafter. The only charges left which are extradition crimes comprise one isolated charge of torture after 29th September 1988, certain conspiracies to torture relating to the period from 29th September 1988 to January 1990 and certain charges of conspiracy in Spain to commit murder in Spain. As to these very limited charges the question of immunity remains relevant. . . .
>
> Although six members of the Appellate Committee hold that he is not entitled to immunity on torture charges, our reasons vary somewhat. Three of us (my noble and learned friends Lord Hope of Craighead, Lord Saville of Newdigate and myself) consider that Senator Pinochet only lost his immunity when the Torture Convention became binding on Spain, United Kingdom and Chile. This occurred on 8th December 1988 when the United Kingdom ratified the Convention. Lord Hutton holds that Senator Pinochet's immunity ended on 29th September 1988 (when the Criminal Justice Act 1988, section 134, came into force). Lord Millett and Lord Phillips of Worth Matravers hold that Senator Pinochet was never at any stage entitled to immunity. Although the reasoning varies in detail, the basic proposition common to all, save Lord Goff of Chieveley, is that torture is an international crime over which international law and the parties to the Torture Convention have given universal jurisdiction to all courts wherever the torture occurs. A former head of state cannot show that to commit an international crime is to perform a function which international law protects by giving immunity. Lord Goff is of the view that neither in international law nor by virtue of the Torture Convention has Senator Pinochet been deprived of the benefit of immunity as a former head of state.
>
> The majority therefore considers that Senator Pinochet can be extradited only for the extradition crimes of torture and conspiracy to torture alleged to have been committed after 8th December 1988.

Reproduced in Reed Brody & Michael Ratner eds., The Pinochet Papers: The Case of Augusto Pinochet in Spain and Britain 251 (2000) (a very useful collection of the original documents in the case).

Speaking of the charges of murder and conspiracy to murder *in Spain*, Lord Browne-Wilkinson says in his judgment that "no one has advanced any reason why the ordinary rules of immunity should not apply and Senator Pinochet is entitled to such immunity." In fact, Lord Millett advanced arguments to exactly that effect, but could apparently get only one other vote, that of Lord Phillips. The law grows in strange ways, does it not? If one tortures, but does not kill, in a land other than the requesting state, there is no immunity; if one kills, even in the requesting state, there is immunity.

(2) Why should the date on which the Torture Convention was ratified be treated as a decisive consideration? What does it mean to say (in Lord Browne-Wilkinson's words) that torture was an "international crime in the highest sense" before 1984, but not a "fully constituted international crime"? If official torture already violated a norm of *jus cogens*, why should a treaty be required to confer universal jurisdiction?

Assuming that universal jurisdiction over a particular crime is permitted by international law, can it be exercised as a matter of national law in the absence of statute? In any event, does universal jurisdiction necessarily license the courts of one state to pronounce unilaterally on the conduct of officials of another state? Is there a possible difference, in this regard, between torture, which by definition requires "state action," and other international crimes? What are the implications of the decision for immunity with respect to international crimes other than torture?

Is universal jurisdiction over torture necessarily incompatible with retention of immunity for former heads of state? What does this case imply, moreover, with respect to the immunity of *current* heads of state? Would a current head of state be immune from prosecution before an international tribunal? If not, why should there be immunity before a national tribunal? Does the majority in *Pinochet* "weaken the moral force of its ruling" on immunity by limiting it to former heads of state? *See* Hazel Fox, *The Pinochet Case No. 3*, 48 INT'L & COMP. L.Q. 687, 702 (1999). Or does the immunity of a current head of state, like that of the state itself, at least for official acts, have to be taken as a given in the present international system?

In his opinion (not reproduced here) Lord Hope refers to "[t]he *jus cogens* character of the immunity enjoyed by serving heads of state *ratione personae*." However, article 27 of the Rome Statute for an International Criminal Court [*see* chap. 22] provides that no immunities under either national or international law "shall bar the court from exercising its jurisdiction." Insofar as Article 27 seems to subject current heads of state to the court's jurisdiction, does it impermissibly derogate from a rule of *jus cogens*?

(3) The *Pinochet* proceedings are said to have "posed, in the most direct terms, a choice between two competing visions of international legal order." Michael Byers, *The Law and Politics of the Pinochet Case*, 10 DUKE J. COMP. & INT'L L. 415, 421 (2000). One is the "classical theory" which in the past obligated states to abstain from interfering in the internal affairs of other states. The other is the picture of an emerging world order in which protection of human rights against egregious violations, if need be by imposing criminal sanctions on the responsible officials, is regarded as a universal imperative. *See also* William J. Aceves, *Liberalism and International Legal Scholarship: The Pinochet Case and the Move Toward a Universal System of Transnational Law Litigation*, 41 HARV. INT'L L.J. 129 (2000). Which of

these "visions" more nearly describes present-day international law? Do they have to be treated as mutually exclusive? In thinking about this question, consider the relevance of Faulkner's dictum: "The past is never dead. It's not even past." WILLIAM FAULKNER, REQUIEM FOR A NUN 92 (1951).

(4) According to one observer, "the second panel of judges, with the exception of Lord Millett — and possibly Lord Hutton — clearly desired that Pinochet be allowed to leave for Chile." Michael Byers, *supra* Note (3), at 436. But "[t]o overrule the decision of the initial panel would have been to suggest that justice was only luck of the draw," which was "the last thing the Law Lords wanted to suggest." *Id.* at 434. Eliminating all but a few relatively insignificant charges offered a way out of this dilemma, since it would give the Home Secretary (whose "authority to proceed" is required for extradition proceedings to continue) grounds for reconsidering his earlier decision to authorize proceedings against Pinochet, and so might serve to release Pinochet without explicitly overruling the first panel. *See also* THE ECONOMIST, Mar. 27, 1999, at 57, 58.

The Home Secretary reconsidered his decision, but on April 15, 1999, again gave authority for extradition to proceed. Meanwhile, the Spanish added further allegations of torture taking place after 1988 to the extradition request. Extradition between Spain and Britain is governed by the European Convention on Extradition, Dec. 13, 1957, E.T.S. No. 24, 359 U.N.T.S. 273, which does not require a requesting state to produce even *prima facie* evidence of the charges against the accused. The only question is whether the offense for which extradition is requested is one for which the accused properly can be extradited. Thus, on the basis of the Spanish allegations, the magistrates' court committed Pinochet for extradition on thirty-four charges of torture and one of conspiracy to commit torture. *Kingdom of Spain v. Augusto Pinochet Ugarte, Judgment* (Bow Street Magistrates' Court, Oct. 8, 1999), *available at* http://www.elclarin.cl/fpa/pdf/p_081099_en.pdf and in REED BRODY & MICHAEL RATNER eds., THE PINOCHET PAPERS: THE CASE OF AUGUSTO PINOCHET IN SPAIN AND BRITAIN 397 (2000).

Normally, in extradition law, the principle of specialty precludes trying a defendant for any offenses other than those for which he was extradited [*see* chap. 16]. Had Pinochet ultimately been extradited, would the trial in Spain have been limited to proof of incidents of torture after 1988, with evidence of the worst part of the repression in Chile in the 1970s excluded? Not necessarily. *See* Edward M. Wise, *Pinochet, Speciality, and Jus Cogens, in* PROCEEDINGS OF THE AMERICAN BRANCH OF THE INTERNATIONAL LAW ASSOCIATION 1999–2000, at 359 (2000). Crimes committed before December 8, 1988, could still be used as evidence of participation in a conspiracy which extended beyond that date. For a U.S. case in point, *see United States v. Flores*, 538 F.2d 939 (2d Cir. 1976).

In the end, the Home Secretary announced on January 11, 2000, that he was "minded" to deny extradition on the ground that Pinochet was medically unfit to stand trial. Despite efforts to challenge this finding, the Home Secretary affirmed his decision on March 2, 2000. Pinochet left for Chile the same day. *See* Parl. Deb., H.C. (Hansard), Mar. 2, 2000, cols. 571–75.

Since the United Kingdom declined to extradite Pinochet, was it obligated under Article 7 of the Torture Convention [chap. 10] to "submit the case to its competent authorities for the purpose of prosecution"? Look carefully at the language of Article 7 and of Article 5 to which it refers. Is this one of the "cases contemplated in Article 5"? In fact, before releasing Pinochet, the British government did submit the case to the Director of Public Prosecutions, who decided that there was no realistic prospect of trying him in England. *See* Parl. Deb., H.C. (Hansard), Mar. 2, 2000, cols. 589–92.

(5) In Chile, an amnesty decreed by the Pinochet regime on March 10, 1978, covered official crimes committed between the 1973 coup and the date of the amnesty. (At the insistence of the United States, an exception was made for the assassins of former foreign minister Orlando Letelier, who was killed by Chilean agents in Washington, D.C., in 1976.) The amnesty was upheld by the Chilean Supreme Court in 1990. However, after Pinochet's arrest in London, criminal proceedings were initiated in Chile involving crimes committed by his regime both before and after 1978. *See* N.Y. Times, Oct. 3, 1999, § 1, at 1, 6. In July 1999, the Supreme Court endorsed the doctrine that the amnesty does not cover cases involving the disappearances of victims whose bodies have never been accounted for: in such cases, the crime is ongoing and extends beyond the amnesty. As a senator-for-life, Pinochet himself had personal immunity from prosecution. Pinochet returned to Chile after he was found "medically unfit to stand trial." On August 8, 2000, the Supreme Court upheld a ruling stripping him of this immunity. *See* N.Y. Times, Aug. 9, 2000, at A3. While he never actually faced trial, he spent the remainder of his life dealing with proceedings aimed at removing any immunities that he might have and disputing his fitness to stand trial. The Chilean court system tried valiantly to come to terms with the past. In a triumph of poetic justice, he died on Human Rights Day, 10 December 2006, at the age of 91, *See* N.Y. Times, Dec. 11, 2006 (front page).

(6) When Pinochet was detained in England, the argument was made that outsiders had no business upsetting the delicate compromise by which democracy in Chile had been restored. If anything, the proceedings against him seem to have strengthened democracy in Chile. Even so, the questions of how far a successor regime is obligated to punish human rights violations committed by a despotic predecessor, how far it is bound to respect an amnesty insisted on by the prior regime as a condition of relinquishing power, how far "truth commissions" represent an acceptable substitute for criminal prosecution in the effort to come to terms with the past, and similar questions of "transitional justice," remain controversial. Amnesty laws, such as the Chilean decree-law of March 10, 1978, have been found to be incompatible with international obligations to respect human rights by both the Inter-American Commission on Human Rights and the U.N. Human Rights Committee. *See Chanfeau Orayce v. Chile*, Case 11.505 et al., Report No. 25/98, Inter-Am. C.H.R.

512, OEA/ser. L/V/II.98, doc. 7 rev. (1997); *Rodriguez v. Uruguay*, U.N. Doc. CCPR/C/51/D/322/1988 (1994); Diane Orentlicher, *Settling Accounts: The Duty to Prosecute Human Rights Violations of a Prior Regime*, 100 YALE L.J. 2537 (1991).

(7) Would U.S. law allow criminal proceedings against a current or former foreign head of state or head of government? *See United States v. Noriega*, 117 F.3d 1206 (11th Cir. 1997) [chap. 17]. As *Noriega* indicates, and as *Samantar v. Yousuf*, 560 U.S. 305 (2010), holds, head-of-state immunity is not covered by the Foreign Sovereign Immunities Act of 1976; and U.S. courts are apt to defer to the executive branch in deciding this (common/customary law) question. In June 2004, Pavel Lazarenko, former Ukrainian Prime Minister (and holder of several official posts before that), was convicted by a federal jury in San Francisco of money laundering, wire fraud, transportation of stolen property and conspiracy. "Federal prosecutors said Lazarenko, in his subordinate posts and then as prime minister demanded a share of the profits from government license-holders and amassed wealth that he deposited abroad. They said he hid the money in overseas bank accounts, including $114 million that allegedly flowed through U.S. banks." Bob Elko, *Former Ukraine Prime Minister Convicted in S.F.*, SAN FRANCISCO CHRON., June 4, 2004, p. A3. Lazarenko had unsuccessfully sought political asylum in the U.S. and had been stripped of immunity in Ukraine. His convictions for conspiracy and money laundering were upheld on appeal, but the appellate court held that there was a failure of proof in respect of the wire fraud and transportation of stolen property counts. *U.S. v. Lazarenko*, 564 F.3d 1026 (9th Cir. 2009). He completed his sentence in 2012.

(8) The case against Pinochet inspired efforts to bring proceedings in Senegal on charges of torture against the former president of Chad, Hissène Habré, who had been living in Senegal since he was toppled from power in 1990. *See* N.Y. TIMES, Feb. 4, 2000, at A3. Later in 2000 and early 2001, charges against Habré were filed in Belgium, notably by a Belgian citizen of Chadian origin. Chad lifted Habré's immunity in 2003. Belgium insisted that Senegal either prosecute Habré on a universal jurisdiction basis or extradite him to Belgium which planned to prosecute him on a passive personality theory. Senegal, which had not complied with its obligation under the Torture Convention to criminalize torture, amended its legislation to make a trial possible, but claimed that the cost would be prohibitive. On 19 February 2009, Belgium instituted proceedings in the International Court of Justice alleging that Senegal was in breach of its treaty and customary law obligations. The Court found that it did not have jurisdiction over the customary law claims but held that Senegal was in breach of its extradite-or-prosecute obligation under the Torture Convention. *Questions Relating to the Obligation to Prosecute or Extradite (Belgium v. Senegal)*, 2012 I.C.J. REP. 422. Extradition to Belgium was not the only way for Senegal to fulfil its obligations. A trial was then held under a specially-created body, the Extraordinary African Chambers in the Senegal court system. Funding for the trial came from the international community. Chad, no doubt happy not to have Habré back, was the largest donor; other contributors included the European Union, The Netherlands, the African Union, the United States, Belgium, Germany,

France, and Luxembourg. Habré was convicted and sentenced to life imprisonment. *See* CELESTE HICKS, THE TRIAL OF HISSÈNE HABRÉ: HOW THE PEOPLE OF CHAD BROUGHT A TYRANT TO JUSTICE (2018). He died in 2021 while being treated for a coronavirus infection, BBC, Aug. 24, 2021, available at https://www.bbc.com/news/world-africa-58316923. Does the criminalization of torture in Senegalese law after the events had taken place, and the even later creation of a special tribunal, contravene the principle against ex post facto laws? *See also* § 20.01 Nuremberg Trial.

(9) On June 4, 2003, the Special Court for Sierra Leone announced that it had "indicted Liberian President Charles Taylor for war crimes and issued an international warrant for his arrest." Taylor and Slobodan Milosevic were, at the time, the only two sitting heads of state ever to be indicted by an international tribunal. (President Al-Bashir of Sudan was later indicted by the ICC.) *See* Douglas Farah, *Tribunal Indicts Liberia's Leader; Taylor Charged with War Crimes During Long Conflict in Sierra Leone*, WASH. POST, June 5, 2003, at A22. The Special Court, established by agreement between the United Nations and the Government of Sierra Leone, held that it was an international court and that, even as a sitting head of state, Taylor had no immunity from its jurisdiction. *Decision on Immunity*, May 31, 2004, Special Court for Sierra Leone, Case No. SCSL-2003-01, *available at* www.rscsl.org. On the Sierra Leone Special Court, see chap. 21.03. Taylor was taken into custody in Nigeria in March 2006. His trial ended in September 2013 with the Appeals Chamber of the Special Court upholding his conviction on 11 counts of aiding and abetting war crimes, crimes against humanity and serious violations of humanitarian law. He was sentenced to 50 years imprisonment which he is serving in the United Kingdom. In addition to the Court's website, there is very useful information on the trial at http://www.ijmonitor.org/category/charles-taylor/.

(10) Immunity is also likely to arise in litigation under the Alien Tort Statute and the Torture Victim Protection Act. *See* Beth Stephens, *The Modern Common Law of Foreign Official Immunity*, 79 FORDHAM L. REV. 2669 (2011).

Case Concerning the Arrest Warrant of 11 April 2000 (D.R. Congo v. Belgium)

I.C.J. REP. 2002

THE COURT:

. . . 1. On 17 October 2000 the Democratic Republic of the Congo (hereinafter referred to as "the Congo") filed in the Registry of the Court an Application instituting proceedings against the Kingdom of Belgium (hereinafter referred to as "Belgium") in respect of a dispute concerning an "international arrest warrant issued on 11 April 2000 by a Belgian investigating judge . . . against the Minister for Foreign Affairs in office of the Democratic Republic of the Congo, Mr. Abdulaye Yerodia Ndombasi".

In that Application the Congo contended that Belgium had violated the "principle that a State may not exercise its authority on the territory of another State", the "principle of sovereign equality among all Members of the United Nations, as laid down in Article 2, paragraph 1, of the Charter of the United Nations", as well as "the diplomatic immunity of the Minister for Foreign Affairs of a sovereign State, as recognized by the jurisprudence of the Court and following from Article 41, paragraph 2, of the Vienna Convention of 18 April 1961 on Diplomatic Relations". . . .

[The issue of Belgium's jurisdiction, which the majority of the Court did not reach, is addressed in chap. 2.]

15. In the arrest warrant, Mr. Yerodia is accused of having made various speeches inciting racial hatred during the month of August 1998. The crimes with which Mr. Yerodia was charged were punishable in Belgium under the Law of 16 June 1993 "concerning the Punishment of Grave Breaches of the International Geneva Conventions of 12 August 1949 and of Protocols I and II of 8 June 1977 Additional Thereto", as amended by the Law of 19 February 1999 "concerning the Punishment of Serious Violations of International Humanitarian Law" (hereinafter referred to as the "Belgian Law").

Article 7 of the Belgian Law provides that "The Belgian courts shall have jurisdiction in respect of the offences provided for in the present Law, wheresoever they may have been committed". . . .

Article 5, paragraph 3, of the Belgian Law further provides that "[i]mmunity attaching to the official capacity of a person shall not prevent the application of the present Law". . . .

[The Court disposed of preliminary objections made by Belgium and continued:]

45. As indicated above . . . in its Application instituting these proceedings, the Congo originally challenged the legality of the arrest warrant of 11 April 2000 on two separate grounds: on the one hand, Belgium's claim to exercise a universal jurisdiction and, on the other, the alleged violation of the immunities of the Minister for Foreign Affairs of the Congo then in office. However, in its submissions in its Memorial, and in its final submissions at the close of the oral proceedings, the Congo invokes only the latter ground.

46. As a matter of logic, the second ground should be addressed only once there has been a determination in respect of the first, since it is only where a State has jurisdiction under international law in relation to a particular matter that there can be any question of immunities in regard to the exercise of that jurisdiction. However, in the present case, and in view of the final form of the Congo's submissions, the Court will address first the question whether, assuming that it had jurisdiction under international law to issue and circulate the arrest warrant of 11 April 2000, Belgium in so doing violated the immunities of the then Minister for Foreign Affairs of the Congo. . . .

51. The Court would observe at the outset that in international law it is firmly established that, as also diplomatic and consular agents, certain holders of high-ranking office in a State, such as the Head of State, Head of Government and

Minister for Foreign Affairs, enjoy immunities from jurisdiction in other States, both civil and criminal. For the purposes of the present case, it is only the immunity from criminal jurisdiction and the inviolability of an incumbent Minister for Foreign Affairs that fall for the Court to consider. . . .

53. In customary international law, the immunities accorded to Ministers for Foreign Affairs are not granted for their personal benefit, but to ensure the effective performance of their functions on behalf of their respective States. In order to determine the extent of these immunities, the Court must therefore first consider the nature of the functions exercised by a Minister for Foreign Affairs. He or she is in charge of his or her Government's diplomatic activities and generally acts as its representative in international negotiations and intergovernmental meetings. Ambassadors and other diplomatic agents carry out their duties under his or her authority. His or her acts may bind the State represented, and there is a presumption that a Minister for Foreign Affairs, simply by virtue of that office, has full powers to act on behalf of the State (*see, e.g.*, Art. 7, para. 2 (a), of the 1969 Vienna Convention on the Law of Treaties). In the performance of these functions, he or she is frequently required to travel internationally, and thus must be in a position freely to do so whenever the need should arise. He or she must also be in constant communication with the Government, and with its diplomatic missions around the world, and be capable at any time of communicating with representatives of other States. The Court further observes that a Minister for Foreign Affairs, responsible for the conduct of his or her State's relations with all other States, occupies a position such that, like the Head of State or the Head of Government, he or she is recognized under international law as representative of the State solely by virtue of his or her office. He or she does not have to present letters of credence: to the contrary, it is generally the Minister who determines the authority to be conferred upon diplomatic agents and countersigns their letters of credence. Finally, it is to the Minister for Foreign Affairs that *chargés d'affaires* are accredited.

54. The Court accordingly concludes that the functions of a Minister for Foreign Affairs are such that, throughout the duration of his or her office, he or she when abroad enjoys full immunity from criminal jurisdiction and inviolability. That immunity and that inviolability protect the individual concerned against any act of authority of another State which would hinder him or her in the performance of his or her duties.

55. In this respect, no distinction can be drawn between acts performed by a Minister for Foreign Affairs in an "official" capacity, and those claimed to have been performed in a "private capacity", or, for that matter, between acts performed before the person concerned assumed office as Minister for Foreign Affairs and acts committed during the period of office. . . .

58. The Court has carefully examined State practice, including national legislation and those few decisions of national higher courts, such as the House of Lords or the French Court of Cassation. It has been unable to deduce from this practice that there exists under customary international law any form of exception to the

rule according immunity from criminal jurisdiction and inviolability to incumbent Ministers for Foreign Affairs, where they are suspected of having committed war crimes or crimes against humanity.

The Court has also examined the rules concerning the immunity or criminal responsibility of persons having an official capacity contained in the legal instruments creating international criminal tribunals, ... It finds that these rules likewise do not enable it to conclude that any such an exception exists in customary international law in regard to national courts.

Finally, none of the decisions of the Nuremberg and Tokyo international military tribunals, or of the International Criminal Tribunal for the former Yugoslavia, cited by Belgium deal with the question of the immunities of incumbent Ministers for Foreign Affairs before national courts where they are accused of having committed war crimes or crimes against humanity. The Court accordingly notes that those decisions are in no way at variance with the findings it has reached above.

In view of the foregoing, the Court accordingly cannot accept Belgium's argument in this regard.

59. It should further be noted that the rules governing the jurisdiction of national courts must be carefully distinguished from those governing jurisdictional immunities: jurisdiction does not imply absence of immunity, while absence of immunity does not imply jurisdiction. Thus, although various international conventions on the prevention and punishment of certain serious crimes impose on States obligations of prosecution or extradition, thereby requiring them to extend their criminal jurisdiction, such extension of jurisdiction in no way affects immunities under customary international law, including those of Ministers for Foreign Affairs. These remain opposable before the courts of a foreign State, even where those courts exercise such a jurisdiction under these conventions.

60. The Court emphasizes, however, that the *immunity* from jurisdiction enjoyed by incumbent Ministers for Foreign Affairs does not mean that they enjoy *impunity* in respect of any crimes they might have committed, irrespective of their gravity. Immunity from criminal jurisdiction and individual criminal responsibility are quite separate concepts. While jurisdictional immunity is procedural in nature, criminal responsibility is a question of substantive law. Jurisdictional immunity may well bar prosecution for a certain period or for certain offences; it cannot exonerate the person to whom it applies from all criminal responsibility.

61. Accordingly, the immunities enjoyed under international law by an incumbent or FORMER Minister for Foreign Affairs do not represent a bar to criminal prosecution in certain circumstances.

First, such persons enjoy no criminal immunity under international law in their own countries, and may thus be tried by those countries' courts in accordance with the relevant rules of domestic law.

Secondly, they will cease to enjoy immunity from foreign jurisdiction if the State which they represent or have represented decides to waive that immunity.

Thirdly, after a person ceases to hold the office of Minister for Foreign Affairs, he or she will no longer enjoy all of the immunities accorded by international law in other States. Provided that it has jurisdiction under international law, a court of one State may try a former Minister for Foreign Affairs of another State in respect of acts committed prior or subsequent to his or her period of office, as well as in respect of acts committed during that period of office in a private capacity.

Fourthly, an incumbent or former Minister for Foreign Affairs may be subject to criminal proceedings before certain international criminal courts, where they have jurisdiction. . . .

78. For these reasons,

THE COURT,

(2) By thirteen votes to three,

Finds that the issue . . . of the arrest warrant of 11 April 2000 and its international circulation, constituted violations of a legal obligation of the Kingdom of Belgium towards the Democratic Republic of the Congo, in that they failed to respect the immunity from criminal jurisdiction and the inviolability which the incumbent Minister for Foreign Affairs of the Democratic Republic of the Congo enjoyed under international law;

> IN FAVOUR: *President* Guillaume; *Vice-President* Shi; *Judges* Ranjeva, Herczegh, Fleischhauer, Koroma, Vereshchetin, Higgins, Parra-Aranguren, Kooijmans, Rezek, Buergenthal; *Judge* ad hoc Bula-Bula; AGAINST: Judges Oda, Al-Khasawneh, *Judge* ad hoc Van den Wynegaert;

(3) By ten votes to six,

Finds that the Kingdom of Belgium must, by means of its own choosing, cancel the arrest warrant of 11 April 2000 and so inform the authorities to whom the warrant was circulated;

[The six no votes on this point were *Judges* Oda, Higgins, Kooijmans, Al-Khasawneh, Buergenthal; and *Judge* ad hoc Van den Wyngaert.]

Dissenting Opinion of JUDGE ODA:

. . . .

1. I voted against all provisions of the operative part of the Judgment. My objections are not directed individually at the various provisions since I am unable to support any aspect of the position the Court has taken in dealing with the presentation of this case by the Congo. . . .

16. In conclusion, I find the present case to be not only unripe for adjudication at this time but also fundamentally inappropriate for the Court's consideration. There is not even agreement between the Congo and Belgium concerning the issues in dispute in the present case. The potentially significant questions (the validity of universal jurisdiction, the general scope of diplomatic immunity) were transmuted into a simple question of the issuance and international circulation of an arrest warrant

as they relate to diplomatic immunity. It is indeed unfortunate that the Court chose to treat this matter as a contentious case suitable for judicial resolution. . . .

Separate Opinion of JUDGE KOROMA:

. . . .

1. The Court in paragraph 46 of the Judgment acknowledged that, as a matter of legal logic, the question of the alleged violation of the immunities of the Minister for Foreign Affairs of the Democratic Republic of the Congo should be addressed only once there has been a determination in respect of the legality of the purported exercise of universal jurisdiction by Belgium. However, in the context of the present case and given the main legal issues in contention, the Court chose another technique, another method, of exercising its discretion in arranging the order in which it will respond when more than one issue has been submitted for determination. This technique is not only consistent with the jurisprudence of the Court, but the Court is also entitled to such an approach, given the position taken by the Parties. . . .

Joint Separate Opinion of JUDGES HIGGINS, KOOIJMANS and BUERGENTHAL:

. . . .

1. We generally agree with what the Court has to say on the issues of jurisdiction and admissibility and also with the conclusions it reaches. There are, however, reservations that we find it necessary to make, both on what the Court has said and what it has chosen not to say when it deals with the merits. Moreover, we consider that the Court erred in ordering Belgium to cancel the outstanding arrest warrant. . . .

3. In our opinion it was not only desirable, but indeed necessary, that the Court should have stated its position on this issue of jurisdiction. The reasons are various. "Immunity" is the common shorthand phrase for "immunity from jurisdiction". If there is no jurisdiction *en principe*, then the question of an immunity from a jurisdiction which would otherwise exist simply does not arise. The Court, in passing over the question of jurisdiction, has given the impression that "immunity" is a free-standing topic of international law. It is not. "Immunity" and "jurisdiction" are inextricably linked. Whether there is "immunity" in any given instance will depend not only upon the status of Mr. Yerodia but also upon what type of jurisdiction, and on what basis, the Belgian authorities were seeking to assert it. . . .

76. . . . Belgium claims that under international law it is permitted to initiate criminal proceedings against a State official who is under suspicion of having committed crimes which are generally condemned by the international community; and it contends that because of the nature of these crimes the individual in question is no longer shielded by personal immunity. The Congo does not deny that a Foreign Minister is responsible in international law for all of his acts. It asserts instead that he has absolute personal immunity from criminal jurisdiction as long as he is in office and that his status must be assimilated in this respect to that of a Head of State. . . .

77. Each of the Parties, therefore, gives particular emphasis in its argument to one set of interests referred to above: Belgium to that of the prevention of impunity, the Congo to that of the prevention of unwarranted outside interference as the result of an excessive curtailment of immunities and an excessive extension of jurisdiction.

78. In the Judgment, the Court diminishes somewhat the significance of Belgium's arguments. . . . We feel less than sanguine about examples given by the Court of such circumstances.

The chance that a Minister for Foreign Affairs will be tried in his own country in accordance with the relevant rules of domestic law or that his immunity will be waived by his own State is not high as long as there has been no change of power, whereas the existence of a competent international criminal court to initiate criminal proceedings is rare; moreover, it is quite risky to expect too much of a future international criminal court in this respect. The only credible alternative therefore seems to be the possibility of starting proceedings in a foreign court after the suspected person ceases to hold the office of Foreign Minister. This alternative, however, can also be easily forestalled by an uncooperative government that keeps the Minister in office for an as yet indeterminate period.

79. We wish to point out, however, that the frequently expressed conviction of the international community that perpetrators of grave and inhuman international crimes should not go unpunished does not *ipso facto* mean that immunities are unavailable whenever impunity would be the outcome. . . . International law seeks the accommodation of this value with the fight against impunity, and not the triumph of one norm over the other. A State may exercise the criminal jurisdiction which it has under international law, but in doing so it is subject to other legal obligations, whether they pertain to the non-exercise of power in the territory of another State or to the required respect for the law of diplomatic relations or, as in the present case, to the procedural immunities of State officials. In view of the worldwide aversion to these crimes, such immunities have to be recognized with restraint, in particular when there is reason to believe that crimes have been committed which have been universally condemned in international conventions. It is, therefore, necessary to analyse carefully the immunities which under customary international law are due to high State officials and, in particular, to Ministers for Foreign Affairs. . . .

83. We agree, therefore, with the Court that the purpose of the immunities attaching to Ministers for Foreign Affairs under customary international law is to ensure the free performance of their functions on behalf of their respective States (Judgment, para. 53). During their term of office, they must therefore be able to travel freely whenever the need to do so arises. There is broad agreement in the literature that a Minister for Foreign Affairs is entitled to full immunity during official visits in the exercise of his function. This was also recognized by the Belgian investigating judge in the arrest warrant of 11 April 2000. The Foreign Minister must also be immune whenever and wherever engaged in the functions required by his office and when in transit therefor.

84. Whether he is also entitled to immunities during private travels and what is the scope of any such immunities, is far less clear. Certainly, he or she may not be subjected to measures which would prevent effective performance of the functions of a Foreign Minister. Detention or arrest would constitute such a measure and must therefore be considered an infringement of the inviolability and immunity from criminal process to which a Foreign Minister is entitled. The arrest warrant of 11 April 2000 was directly enforceable in Belgium and would have obliged the police authorities to arrest Mr. Yerodia had he visited that country for non-official reasons. The very issuance of the warrant therefore must be considered to constitute an infringement on the inviolability to which Mr. Yerodia was entitled as long as he held the office of Minister for Foreign Affairs of the Congo. . . .

86. We have voted against paragraph (3) of the *dispositif* for several reasons.

87. . . . Having previously found that the issuance and circulation of the warrant by Belgium was illegal under international law, the Court concludes that it must be withdrawn because "the warrant is still extant, and remains unlawful, notwithstanding the fact that Mr. Yerodia has ceased to be Minister for Foreign Affairs". . . .

89. . . . However, the Court's finding in the instant case that the issuance and circulation of the warrant was illegal, a conclusion which we share, was based on the fact that these acts took place at a time when Mr. Yerodia was Minister for Foreign Affairs. As soon as he ceased to be Minister for Foreign Affairs, the illegal consequences attaching to the warrant also ceased. The mere fact that the warrant continues to identify Mr. Yerodia as Minister for Foreign Affairs changes nothing in this regard as a matter of international law, although it may well be that a misnamed arrest warrant, which is all it now is, may be deemed to be defective as a matter of Belgian domestic law; but that is not and cannot be of concern to this Court. Accordingly, we consider that the Court erred in its finding on this point. . . .

Dissenting Opinion of Judge Al-Khasawneh:

. . . .

8. In conclusion, this Judgment is predicated on two faulty premises.

(a) That a Foreign Minister enjoys absolute immunity from both jurisdiction and enforcement of foreign States as opposed to only functional immunity from enforcement when on official mission, a proposition which is neither supported by precedent, *opinio juris*, legal logic or the writings of publicists.

(b) That as international law stands today, there are no exceptions to the immunity of high-ranking State officials even when they are accused of grave crimes. While, admittedly, the readiness of States and municipal courts to admit of exceptions is still at a very nebulous stage of development, the situation is much more fluid than the Judgment suggests. I believe that the move towards greater personal accountability represents a higher norm than the rules on immunity and should prevail over the latter. In consequence, I am unable to join the majority view.

Dissenting Opinion of Judge Ad Hoc Van Den Wyngaert:

. . . .

1. I have voted against paragraphs (2) and (3) of the *dispositif* of this Judgment. International law grants no immunity from criminal process to incumbent Foreign Ministers suspected of war crimes and crimes against humanity. There is no evidence for the proposition that a State is under an obligation to grant immunity from criminal process to an incumbent Foreign Minister under customary international law. By issuing and circulating the warrant, Belgium may have acted contrary to international comity. It has not, however, acted in violation of an international legal obligation. . . .

Surely, the warrant based on charges of war crimes and crimes against humanity cannot infringe rules on immunity *today*, given the fact that Mr. Yerodia has now ceased to be a Foreign Minister and has become an ordinary citizen. Therefore, the Court is wrong when it finds, in the last part of its *dispositif*, that Belgium must cancel the arrest warrant and so inform the authorities to which the warrant was circulated. . . .

85. For the reasons set out in this opinion, I think the International Court of Justice has erred in finding that there is a rule of customary international law protecting incumbent Foreign Ministers suspected of war crimes and crimes against humanity from the criminal process in other States. No such rule of customary international law exists. The Court has not engaged in the balancing exercise that was crucial for the present dispute. Adopting a minimalist and formalistic approach, the Court has *de facto* balanced in favour of the interests of States in conducting international relations, not the international community's interest in asserting international accountability of State officials suspected of war crimes and crimes against humanity. . . .

86. . . . the question that was before the Court was not whether Belgium is naive or has acted in a politically wise manner or whether international comity would command a stricter application of universal jurisdiction or a greater respect for foreign dignitaries. The question was whether Belgium had violated an obligation under international law to refrain from issuing and circulating an arrest warrant on charges of war crimes and crimes against humanity against an incumbent Foreign Minister.

. . . .

87. An implicit consideration behind this Judgment may have been a concern for abuse and chaos, arising from the risk of States asserting unbridled universal jurisdiction and engaging in abusive prosecutions against incumbent Foreign Ministers of other States and thus paralysing the functioning of these States. . . . The argument can be summarized as follows: if a State would prosecute members of foreign governments without respecting their immunities, chaos will be the result; likewise, if

States exercise unbridled universal jurisdiction without any point of linkage to the domestic legal order, there is a danger for political tensions between States. In the present dispute, there was no allegation of abuse of process on the part of Belgium. Criminal proceedings against Mr. Yerodia were not frivolous or abusive. The warrant was issued after two years of criminal investigations and there were no allegations that the investigating judge who issued it acted on false factual evidence. The accusation that Belgium applied its War Crimes Statute in an offensive and discriminatory manner against a Congolese Foreign Minister was manifestly ill founded. Belgium, rightly or wrongly, wishes to act as an agent of the world community by allowing complaints brought by foreign victims of serious human rights abuses committed abroad. . . .

In the abstract, the chaos argument may be pertinent. This risk may exist, and the Court could have legitimately warned against this risk in its Judgment without necessarily reaching the conclusion that a rule of customary international law exists to the effect of granting immunity to Foreign Ministers. However, granting immunities to incumbent Foreign Ministers may open the door to other sorts of abuse. It dramatically increases the number of persons that enjoy international immunity from jurisdiction. Recognizing immunities for other members of government is just one step further: in present-day society, all Cabinet members represent their countries in various meetings. If Foreign Ministers need immunities to perform their functions, why not grant immunities to other Cabinet members as well? The International Court of Justice does not state this, but doesn't this flow from its reasoning leading to the conclusion that Foreign Ministers are immune? The rationale for assimilating Foreign Ministers with diplomatic agents and Heads of State, which is at the centre of the Court's reasoning, also exists for other Ministers who represent the State officially, for example, Ministers of Education who have to attend Unesco conferences in New York or other Ministers receiving honorary doctorates abroad. *Male fide* Governments may appoint persons to Cabinet posts in order to shelter them from prosecutions on charges of international crimes. Perhaps the International Court of Justice, in its effort to close one box of Pandora for fear of chaos and abuse, has opened another one: that of granting immunity and thus *de facto* impunity to an increasing number of government officials.

Notes

(1) Belgium's universal jurisdiction law has proved extremely controversial. In June 2003, Belgium limited its scope. [*See* chap. 2]

(2) It appears that the crimes with which Mr. Yerodia was charged occurred before his time in office, while he was a private citizen. At the time of the International Court's decision, he no longer held any office in the Congo. Putting aside the jurisdictional issues, would there be any immunity problem if the Belgian magistrate had decided the day after the decision to issue a new warrant, something he did not do, for Citizen Yerodia?

(3) Consider the propositions in paragraph 61 of the Court's judgment, especially the material beginning with "[t]hirdly, after a person ceases to hold the office of Minister for Foreign Affairs. . . ." and assume that the rules for former heads of state are the same as those for former ministers of foreign affairs. How would Pinochet fare if the Court's proposition was applied to Spain's exercise of jurisdiction?

(4) The International Law Commission has, since 2006, been engaged in a project on *Immunity of State officials from foreign criminal jurisdiction. See* summary of its work *available at* http://legal.un.org/docs/?path=../ilc/reports/2015/english/chp10.pdf&lang=EFSRAC. Like the judges in the *Pinochet* and *Yerodia*, the Commission has been wrestling with the differences between immunity *ratione personae* (absolute personal immunity) and *ratione materiae* (functional immunity). In 2013, "the Commission provisionally adopted three draft articles and commentaries identifying three categories of senior governmental officials — heads of state, heads of government, and foreign ministers — as entitled to immunity *ratione personae* from jurisdiction for their public or private acts, an immunity that ceases once they leave office." Sean D. Murphy, *Immunity Ratione Personae of Foreign Government Officials and Other Topics: The Sixty-Fifth Session of the International Law Commission*, 108 A.J.I.L. 41 (2014). Should the list have included other Ministers, such as those dealing with Trade, Health, or Education? The Commission has since been exploring *ratione materiae* immunities. In 2017, U.N. Doc. A/CN.4/L.803, it arrived at a tentative list of crimes under international law in respect of which it believed that such immunity should not apply: genocide, crimes against humanity, war crimes, crimes of *apartheid*, torture, and enforced disappearance. A controversial omission from this list is the crime of aggression.

§ 14.03 Persons Associated with International Organizations

Members of the United Nations Secretariat, experts on missions for the United Nations and peacekeepers lent to the organization by Member States are entitled to various immunities from local jurisdiction. *See generally Difference Relating to Immunity from Legal Process of a Special Rapporteur of the Commission on Human Rights*, Advisory Opinion of 29 April, 1999, 1999 I.C.J. REP. 62. Some immunities are functional; some are absolute. The United Nations, while it can take contractual disciplinary action over those in its employ, has no powers of criminal enforcement. Under the 1945 Convention on Privileges and Immunities of the United Nations, § 20, immunities are said to be "granted to officials in the interests of the United Nations, and not for the personal benefit of the individuals themselves" and thus may be waived by the Secretary-General. Such was the case in *United States v. Bahel*, 662 F.3d 610 (2nd Cir. 2011), where the court upheld the conviction of a corrupt United Nations procurement official on four counts that he used the mail or wires in furtherance of a fraud that deprived his employer of its right to honest services in violation of 18 U.S.C. §§ 1341, 1343, and 1346; one count of corrupt receipt of things of value with intent to be rewarded with respect to official business in violation of 18 U.S.C. § 666; and one count of conspiracy in violation of 18 U.S.C. § 371. The court also held that the United Nations had expressly waived Bahel's immunity, and even if it had not, he had waived any claim by failing to raise the issue until the trial was complete. Since the United Nations Headquarters are in New York, there will typically be territorial jurisdiction in the United States (in the federal or state courts) over such fraudulent activities aimed at the organization itself, so long as there is an appropriate substantive statute.

Matters are more difficult in the field, which is where sexual assaults and human trafficking by officials of the organization are more likely to occur. See generally Roison Burke, Sexual Exploitation and Abuse by UN Military Contingents (2014), and the classic report on the subject by HRH Prince Zeid Ra'ad Zeid Al-Hussein, *A comprehensive strategy to eliminate future sexual exploitation and abuse in United Nations peacekeeping operations*, UN Doc. A/59/710 (2005). In order to deal more adequately with immunity issues and with other gaps in national jurisdiction over crime, especially crimes against the person, and to implement the organization's "zero tolerance" approach to the ongoing problem of sexual exploitation, the General Assembly has been engaged in a project entitled "Criminal Accountability of United Nations officials and experts on mission." Under consideration is a draft convention that would try to close jurisdictional gaps. Discussions continue on whether such a treaty should be concluded and, if so, what its scope should be. Some would stop short of including military personnel in such a regime. Criminal jurisdiction would have to be allocated between the Host State, the Sending State (or perhaps the State of nationality or residence in the case of employees of international organizations) and any universal jurisdiction regime that might be negotiated. *See* U.N. Doc. A/60/980 (Report of Group of Legal Experts) (2005), U.N. Doc. A/62/54 (Report of Ad Hoc Committee) (2007), G.A. Res. 69/114 (2014). The discussion is carried forward from year to year with no consensus in sight.

Representatives of states who are accredited to the U.N. will, depending on their status, be entitled either to absolute or functional immunity. It is possible for their sending States to waive immunity; and sometimes there is no immunity in any event when charges are brought in New York. For example, in 2015, charges of bribery were made against a former President of the U.N. General Assembly who had been the Permanent Representative to the U.N. of Antigua and Barbuda. He was no longer in the employ of that country when the charges were filed, but had managed to obtain U.S. residence. Among those also charged with him was the Deputy Permanent Representative of the Dominican Republic to the U.N. He was a dual U.S. and Dominican citizen who was not entitled to personal immunity. He pled guilty. *See* Dulcie Leimbach, *John Ashe, Ex-UN Diplomat Facing Criminal Charges, Goes Begging*, Pass Blue, 14 March 2016, *available at* https://www.passblue.com/2016/03/14/former-head-of-un-general-assembly-facing-criminal-charges-goes-begging

/. Ambassador Ashe, soliciting his friends to pay for his defense, died before trial when he dropped a barbell on himself while exercising at his home in Dobbs Ferry.

§14.04 Visiting Forces

In *The Schooner Exchange v. McFaddon*, 11 U.S. (7 Cranch) 116 (1812), a landmark case involving a claim to title of a French warship docked in Philadelphia, Marshall C.J. discussed cases in which there is immunity. One "case in which a sovereign is understood to cede a portion of his territorial jurisdiction," he said, "is, where he allows the troops of a foreign prince to pass through his dominions." *Id.* at 139. In both World Wars, the United States insisted on absolute immunity not only for troops "passing through," but also for those stationed on another's territory. *See generally* G.P. Barton, *Foreign Armed Forces: Immunity from Criminal Jurisdiction*, 27 Brit Y.B. Int'l Law 186 (1950); Rain Liivoja, Criminal Jurisdiction over Armed Forces Abroad (2017). Modern practice on "visiting forces" is typically governed by agreement or sometimes by fiat of the United Nations Security Council or an occupying force. *See generally* The Handbook of the Law of Visiting Forces (Dieter Fleck ed. 2d ed. 2018); Roger S. Clark, *Peacekeeping Forces, Jurisdiction and Immunity: A Tribute to George Barton*, 43 VUWLR 77 (2012).

Broadly-speaking, the arrangements follow one of two models. One model, essentially that contemplated by Marshall C. J., confers immunity in the Host State along with an expectation of prosecution, where appropriate, by the Sending State. The United Nations Model status-of-forces agreement for peacekeeping operations, U.N. Doc. A/45/594 (1990), is of this ilk. Some agreements authorize the Sending State to set up military tribunals in the Host State. In the second model, typified originally by the 1951 NATO Status of Forces Agreement, http://www.nato.int/cps/en/natohq/official_texts_17265.htm?, discussed in §1.02, there is no immunity but an acceptance of concurrent jurisdiction which is allocated between the two states by giving one or the other priority in specific situations. Compare the way in which the matters were dealt with in Iraq in the two instruments that follow—by the Coalition Provisional Authority in 2004 and later by agreement between the United States and Iraq.

Coalition Provisional Authority Order No. 17*

Section 2—Iraqi Legal Process

1) Unless provided otherwise herein, the MNF [Multinational Force], the CPA [Coalition Provisional Authority], Foreign Liaison Missions, their Personnel,

* http://www.iraqcoalition.org/regulations/20040627_CPAORD_17_Status_of_Coalition__Rev__with_Annex_A.pdf. The Coalition Provisional Authority, or CPA, was set up by the "Coalition of the Willing."

property, funds and assets, and all International Consultants shall be immune from Iraqi legal process.

2) All MNF, CPA and Foreign Liaison Mission Personnel and International Consultants shall respect the Iraqi laws relevant to those Personnel, and Consultants in Iraq including the Regulations, Orders, Memoranda and Public Notices issued by the Administrator of the CPA.

3) All MNF, CPA and Foreign Liaison Mission Personnel and International Consultants shall be subject to the exclusive jurisdiction of their Sending States. They shall be immune from any form of arrest or detention other than by persons acting on behalf of their Sending States, except that nothing in this provision shall prohibit MNF Personnel from preventing acts of serious misconduct by the above-mentioned Personnel or Consultants, or otherwise temporarily detaining any such Personnel or Consultants who pose a risk of injury to themselves or others, pending expeditious turnover to the appropriate authorities of the Sending State. In all such circumstances, the appropriate senior representative of the detained person's Sending State in Iraq shall be notified immediately.

4) The Sending States of MNF Personnel shall have the right to exercise within Iraq any criminal and disciplinary jurisdiction conferred on them by the law of that Sending State over all persons subject to the military law of that Sending State.

5) The immunities set forth in this Section for Foreign Liaison Missions, their Personnel, property, funds and assets shall operate only with respect to acts or omissions by them during the period of authority of the CPA ending on June 30, 2004.

Agreement Between the United States of America and the Republic of Iraq on the Withdrawal of United States Forces from Iraq and the Organization of Their Activities During Their Temporary Presence in Iraq, Nov. 17, 2008*

Article 12 Jurisdiction

Recognizing Iraq's sovereign right to determine and enforce the rules of criminal and civil law in its territory, in light of Iraq's request for temporary assistance from the United States Forces set forth in Article 4, and consistent with the duty of the members of the United States Forces and the civilian component to respect Iraqi laws, customs, traditions, and conventions, the Parties have agreed as follows:

1. Iraq shall have the primary right to exercise jurisdiction over members of the United States Forces and of the civilian component for the grave premeditated felonies enumerated pursuant to paragraph 8, when such crimes are committed outside agreed facilities and areas and outside duty status.

2. Iraq shall have the primary right to exercise jurisdiction over United States contractors and United States contractor employees.

---

* http://www.globalsecurity.org/military/library/policy/dod/iraq-sofa.htm.

3. The United States shall have the primary right to exercise jurisdiction over members of the United States Forces and of the civilian component for matters arising inside agreed facilities and areas; during duty status outside agreed facilities and areas; and in circumstances not covered by paragraph 1.

4. At the request of either Party, the Parties shall assist each other in the investigation of incidents and the collection and exchange of evidence to ensure the due course of justice.

5. Members of the United States Forces and of the civilian component arrested or detained by Iraqi authorities shall be notified immediately to United States Forces authorities and handed over to them within 24 hours from the time of detention or arrest. Where Iraq exercises jurisdiction pursuant to paragraph 1 of this Article, custody of an accused member of the United States Forces or of the civilian component shall reside with United States Forces authorities. United States Forces authorities shall make such accused persons available to the Iraqi authorities for purposes of investigation and trial.

6. The authorities of either Party may request the authorities of the other Party to waive its primary right to jurisdiction in a particular case. The Government of Iraq agrees to exercise jurisdiction under paragraph 1 above, only after it has determined and notifies the United States in writing within 21 days of the discovery of an alleged offense, that it is of particular importance that such jurisdiction be exercised.

7. Where the United States exercises jurisdiction pursuant to paragraph 3 of this Article, members of the United States Forces and of the civilian component shall be entitled to due process standards and protections pursuant to the Constitution and laws of the United States. Where the offense arising under paragraph 3 of this Article may involve a victim who is not a member of the United States Forces or of the civilian component, the Parties shall establish procedures through the Joint Committee to keep such persons informed as appropriate of. the status of the investigation of the crime; the bringing of charges against a suspected offender; the scheduling of court proceedings and the results of plea negotiations; opportunity to be heard at public sentencing proceedings, and to confer with the attorney for the prosecution in the case; and, assistance with filing a claim under Article 21 of this Agreement. As mutually agreed by the Parties, United States Forces authorities shall seek to hold the trials of such cases inside Iraq. If the trial of such cases is to be conducted in the United States, efforts will be undertaken to facilitate the personal attendance of the victim at the trial.

8. Where Iraq exercises jurisdiction pursuant to paragraph 1 of this Article, members of the United States Forces and of the civilian component shall be entitled to due process standards and protections consistent with those available under United States and Iraqi law. The Joint Committee shall establish procedures and mechanisms for implementing this Article, including an enumeration of the grave premeditated felonies that are subject to paragraph 1 and procedures that meet such due process standards and protections. Any exercise of jurisdiction pursuant to

paragraph 1 of this Article may proceed only in accordance with these procedures and mechanisms.

9. Pursuant to paragraphs I and 3 of this Article, United States Forces authorities shall certify whether an alleged offense arose during duty status. In those cases where Iraqi authorities believe the circumstances require a review of this determination, the Parties shall consult immediately through the Joint Committee, and United States Forces authorities shall take full account of the facts and circumstances and any information Iraqi authorities may present bearing on the determination by United States Forces authorities.

10. The Parties shall review the provisions of this Article every 6 months including by considering any proposed amendments to this Article taking into account the security situation in Iraq, the extent to which the United States Forces in Iraq are engaged in military operations, the growth and development of the Iraqi judicial system, and changes in United States and Iraqi law.[b]

§ 14.05 Immunities and the International Criminal Court

The United States is not a party to the Rome Statute of the International Criminal Court (I.C.C.) and is less than enthusiastic about the possibility that its nationals might come before the Court. The most likely scenario in which a United States citizen could become a defendant in the I.C.C. is where he or she is alleged to have committed a crime within the jurisdiction of the Court on the territory of a state which is a party to the Statute of the Court or which accepts the exercise of the jurisdiction of the Court specifically with respect to the crime in question. *See* Rome Statute Article 12, paragraphs (2) and (3). Consent of either the territorial state or the state of nationality is a sufficient "precondition" for the Court to exercise its jurisdiction. The United States has argued that this is contrary to international law. Its basic objection is that "by purporting to confer upon the Court jurisdiction over the nationals of non-consenting non-party states, the Treaty would bind non-parties in contravention of the law of treaties." Madeline Morris, *High Crimes and Misconceptions: The ICC and Non-Party States, in* International Crimes, Peace, and Human Rights: The Role of the International Criminal Court 219, 220 (Dinah Shelton, ed., 2000). Supporters of the Court argue that the consent of the territorial state, which after all has jurisdiction itself—territorial jurisdiction being a bedrock position of the *Lotus* case—is sufficient. Its jurisdiction may be delegated to an international tribunal. *See generally* Dapo Akande, *The Jurisdiction of the International Criminal Court over Nationals of Non-Parties: Legal Basis and Limits* 1 J. Int'l Crim. Just. 618 (2003). The United States argues also that, by taking

b. This Agreement expired on 31 December 2011.—Eds.

jurisdiction over its nationals in situations where official acts are at stake, jurisdiction is, in effect, being improperly exercised over the state itself. Proponents of the I.C.C. view this as an unwarranted assertion of immunity in respect of crimes under international law, *id.*, at 637–40.

The United States has adopted several strategies to discourage surrender of its nationals to the Court by other states. Congress set out a number of them in the "American Servicemembers' Protection Act of 2002," 116 Stat. 820. Section 2005 prohibits U.S. participation in any peacekeeping operation under chapter VI of the United Nations Charter, or peace enforcement operation under chapter VII, unless members of the Armed Forces are able to participate without risk of prosecution by the I.C.C. Section 2007 prohibits military assistance to governments of a country that is a party to the Rome Statute. There are exceptions for NATO members and other "major non-NATO" allies. There is a further exception for any other country when the President certifies that country "has entered into an agreement with the United States pursuant to Article 98 of the Rome Statute preventing the International Criminal Court from proceeding against United States personnel present in such country." Section 2008 of the Act "authorizes" the President "to use all means necessary and appropriate" to bring about the release of certain United States and allied "persons" held by the Court. (European humorists call the Act the "Hague Invasion Act.")

Article 27 of the Rome Statute of the International Criminal Court [chap. 22] asserts that "official capacity as a Head of State or Government, a member of a Government or parliament, an elected representative or a government official shall in no case exempt a person from criminal responsibility under this Statute. . . ." There is no immunity of any kind before the Court. On the other hand, Article 98 of the treaty, which deals with surrender of persons to the Court, has two paragraphs which, in different but potentially overlapping ways, make immunity issues a distinct possibility when surrender is requested.

Article 98, paragraph 1 of the Rome Statute prevents the Court from proceeding with a request for surrender or assistance "which would require the requested State to act inconsistently with its obligations under international law with respect to the State or diplomatic immunity of a person or property of a third State [i.e., a State which is not a party to the Statute], unless the Court can first obtain the cooperation of that third State for the waiver of immunity." Consider the case of a diplomat or an official like Mr. Yerodia [*see D.R. Congo v. Belgium, supra* § 14. 02] from State A (a non-party) who is found in State B. If the I.C.C. seeks surrender of that person from B, State A can successfully prevent the surrender unless it agrees to waive the relevant immunity.

The United States has entered into some bilateral status of forces treaties, with for example Timor-Leste (formerly known as East Timor), South Africa, Niger and Colombia, in which its military personnel (and accompanying civilian component, including contractors) in country are treated as equivalent to administrative and technical staff of the local Embassy, bringing Article 98 (1) potentially into play. *See*, e.g., Defense, Status of Forces, Agreement Between the United States of America ad Niger, effected by an Exchange of Notes at Niamey July 6, 2012 and January 28, 2013, T.I.A.S. 13-128. The practice is not altogether new. The U.S. had comparable arrangements with the Shah's Iran. The Ayatollah Khomeini, then in opposition, found considerable propaganda value in what he saw as an undermining of Iranian sovereignty, comparable to the capitulations regimes of yore. *See* Richard Pfau, *The Legal Status of American Forces in Iran*, 28 Middle East J. 141 (1974).

"Administrative and technical staff" of an Embassy are entitled, pursuant to Articles 37(2), 29 and 31 of the Vienna Convention on Diplomatic Relations, *supra*, to be "inviolable." They are not "liable to any form of arrest or detention" and "enjoy immunity from the criminal jurisdiction of the receiving State." *See* § 14.01, Note (7). Treating military personnel as diplomats probably makes sense, as in Timor-Leste, where it is just a question of a few people engaged in humanitarian projects. But what if there are hundreds or even thousands of them? In Colombia, the number of personnel involved in the "war on drugs" and potentially possessing diplomatic immunity has at several times been at least in the hundreds; 800 U.S. troops were in Niger at one point. Was this what the Vienna Convention had in mind? Should law enforcement officials stationed in a host country have similar diplomatic status?

Paragraph 2 of Article 98 is where the United States has, however, directed most of its efforts. It provides:

> The Court may not proceed with a request for surrender which would require the requested State to act inconsistently with its obligations under international agreements pursuant to which the consent of a sending State is required to surrender a person of that State to the Court, unless the Court can first obtain the cooperation of the sending State for the giving of consent for the surrender.

The United States has negotiated numerous agreements claiming reliance on paragraph 2. Typical in title and content is a second agreement with Timor-Leste, the Agreement regarding the surrender of persons to the International Criminal Court, of August 23, 2002. Its relevant articles are:

> 1. For purposes of this agreement, "persons" are current or former government officials, employees (including contractors), or military personnel or nationals of one Party.
>
> 2. Persons of one Party present in the territory of the other shall not, absent the expressed consent of the first Party,
>
> > (a) be surrendered or transferred by any means to the International Criminal Court for any purpose, or
> >
> > (b) be surrendered or transferred by any means to any other entity or third country, or expelled to a third country for the purpose of surrender to or transfer to the International Criminal Court.

Timor-Leste, like other countries entering into such agreements, has been rewarded by a "presidential determination" made pursuant to Section 2007 of the Servicemembers' Protection Act, and is thus eligible for military assistance. The Coalition for the International Criminal Court, a non-governmental group deeply involved in the creation and support of the Court, lists 102 concluded "Bilateral Immunity Agreements (BIAs)" relying on Article 98(2) as of December 11, 2006. That included 46 States Parties. According to its calculations, 54 States have publicly refused to sign and 24 have not signed despite loss of U.S. aid. *See* the Coalition's web-site http://iccnow.org/documents/USandICC/BIA.html. There do not appear to be more recent agreements.

Notes

(1) Is the agreement with Timor-Leste (and similarly worded ones — many have exactly the same language) limited to military personnel? What is the effect of the words "or nationals" at the end of the definition of "persons"? Is the earlier part of the definition surplusage concealing that the agreement really applies to *all* Americans, and for good measure to members of the forces or civilian contractors who may be foreigners?

(2) Critics of the Article 98 Agreements suggest that, when entered into by states which are party to the Rome Statute, the Agreements are incompatible with the totality of the Statute. *See, e.g.*, Amnesty International, International Criminal Court: US Efforts to Obtain Impunity for Genocide, Crimes Against Humanity and War Crimes, AI Index: IOR 40/25/2002. Can the basic structure of the non-surrender treaties be justified by Article 98(2)? Note in particular the reference to a "sending State." The term "sending State" could be a term of art taken from practice involving status of forces agreements, where it refers to the State which sends its forces to another. That, at least, seems to have been the understanding of Ambassador David Scheffer, the United States chief negotiator on the Rome Statute. David Scheffer, *Commentary, Original Intent at the Global Criminal Court*, Wall St. J, Sept. 20, 2002. Is the scope of Article 98(2) limited to agreements that involve those who can legitimately be regarded as "forces" and as having been "sent?" The term "sending State" is also used in the 1961 Vienna Convention on Diplomatic Relations, *supra*, and in the 1963 Vienna Convention on Consular Relations, *supra*. In context in those treaties, the reference is clearly to the officials who are "sent" — not to the whole citizenry of the sending State whom those officials represent. Is the same true here, that military are sent, but other persons are merely "there?" *See also* Dieter Fleck, *Are Foreign Military Personnel Exempt from International Criminal Jurisdiction Under Status of Forces Agreements?* 1 J. Int'l Crim. Just. 651 (2003) (arguing, controversially, that foreign servicemembers enjoy functional immunity under general principles of international law and that Article 98(1) is thus sufficient to protect them from being handed over, so that Article 98(2) Agreements are unnecessary for them). The United States has also concluded a few extradition treaties, for example with South Africa and Sri Lanka in which the parties agree that any American transferred to the

other party will not be re-extradited to the I.C.C. without American consent. "Sending state" is not a term of art in extradition treaties, the usage there being "requesting state" and "requested state." Are these agreements compatible with Article 98(2)?

(3) In modern multilateral treaty practice, treaties are open to signature for a period after their conclusion (sometimes indefinitely). Signature signals that a State is contemplating whether to become a party. Becoming a party entails "ratification" or, if a State did not sign in time, "accession." Late in the Clinton Administration, on the last day the treaty was open for signature, the United States signed the Rome Statute. Article 18 of the Vienna Convention on the Law of Treaties says that a State which has signed a treaty is "obliged to refrain from acts which would defeat the object and purpose of a treaty . . . until it shall have made its intention clear not to become a party to the treaty." When the United States first began looking for ways to avoid any possible application of the Statute to its personnel, critics drew attention to this principle. Shortly before the Statute came into force on July 1, 2002 John Bolton, Under Secretary of State for Arms Control and International Security, on behalf of the United States, notified the United Nations Secretary-General, as depositary of the treaty, that:

> This is to inform you, in connection with the Rome Statute of the International Criminal Court adopted on July 17, 1998, that the United States does not intend to become a party to the treaty. Accordingly, the United States has no legal obligations arising from its signature on December 31, 2000. The United States requests that its intention not to become a party, as expressed in this letter, be reflected in the depositary's status lists relating to this treaty.

Quoted in *U.S. Notification of Intent Not to Become a Party to the Rome Statute*, 96 A.J.I.L. 706, 724 (2002). Such an "un-signing" (as its critics derided it) or "notification" was previously unprecedented. It was followed by letters to the same effect from Israel, Sudan and, most recently, the Russian Federation.

(4) Not being party to the Rome Statute, and having disavowed its signature, the United States is not bound *by the Statute* to bring to justice those who commit treaty crimes. It may, however, be bound by other treaty obligations such as the Geneva Conventions, the Torture Convention and the Genocide Convention, to say nothing of customary law, to punish those of its citizenry and camp followers who commit such crimes. Reference is made to investigation and prosecution in the preamble to the Agreement with Timor-Leste in these words:

> Considering that the United States of America has expressed its intention to investigate and to prosecute where appropriate acts within the jurisdiction of the International Criminal Court alleged to have been committed by its officials, employees, military personnel or other nationals.

The extent to which the United States has statutory jurisdiction enabling it to deliver fully on such a promise is debated. Suffice it to say, not all war crimes in the Statute are within the Uniform Code of Military Justice or the War Crimes Act, 18 U.S. C. § 2441, as amended by the Military Commissions Act of 2006 (giving federal district court jurisdiction in certain cases); not all contractors are subject to the UCMJ or to other legislation with extraterritorial effect (a potentially huge issue in Iraq); crimes against humanity are not criminalized, as such, in US law, whether committed at home or abroad — although there may be domestic crimes that "fit" them. *See generally* Douglass Cassel, *Empowering United States Courts to Hear Crimes Within the Jurisdiction of the International Criminal Court*, 35 NEW ENG. L. REV. 421 (2001); Michael P. Hatchell, *Closing the Gaps in United States Law and Implementing the Rome Statute: A Comparative Approach*, 12 ILSA J. INT'L & COMP. L. 183 (2005). *See also* Military Extraterritorial Jurisdiction Act of 2000, 18 U.S.C. § 3261 (affording some federal jurisdiction over former military, those accompanying military and military contractors).

(5) In 2010, parties to the Rome Statute, meeting as a Review Conference in Kampala, adopted amendments to the Statute designed to enable the Court to exercise its dormant jurisdiction over the crime of aggression. Resolution RC/Res.6 (2010). The amendments came into force in July 2018. Several parties have adopted criminal legislation consistent with the amendments enabling domestic prosecution on a territorial, nationality and even in some cases a universal jurisdiction basis. *See* Annegret Hartig, *The Early Implementers of the Crime of Aggression*, 17 INT'L CRIM. JUST. 485 (2019). The definition of the crime includes the element that a perpetrator must be "a person in a position effectively to exercise control over or to direct the political or military affairs of a State." Under Article 27 of the Statute, there is no immunity for such persons before the Court itself. But given decisions like *Yerodia*, life is more complicated at the domestic level. Some such persons will be entitled to immunity if prosecuted, for example, in the victim-State or on a universal basis — Heads of State, Heads of Government and Foreign Ministers at least. But what of the Minister of Defense or the head of the military?

(6) Invoking § 2005 of the American Servicemembers' Protection Act, the United States has, on occasion, insisted that immunity from local jurisdiction be enshrined in a Security Council resolution, at least where there is some possibility of ICC jurisdiction. Thus, in resolution 1497 (2003), which created a Multinational Force for Liberia, the Security Council:

> 7. *Decides* that current or former officials or personnel from a contributing State, which is not a party to the Rome Statute of the International Criminal Court, shall be subject to the exclusive jurisdiction of that contributing State for all alleged acts or omissions arising out of or related to the Multinational Force or United Nations stabilization force in Liberia, unless such exclusive jurisdiction is waived by that contributing State.

The United States is, in fact, a small contributor to UN peacekeeping forces, supplying about 50 of the 100,000 or so currently deployed.

(7) The Liberian resolution was not the first encounter with the issue in the Security Council. In 2002, the United States persuaded the Security Council to adopt Resolution 1422 in which the Council:

> 1. Requests, consistent with the provisions of Article 16 of the Rome Statute, that the ICC, if a case arises involving current or former officials or personnel from a contributing State not a Party to the Rome Statute over acts or omissions relating to a United Nations established or authorized operation, shall for a twelve-month period starting 1 July 2002 not commence or proceed with investigation or prosecution of any such case, unless the Security Council decides otherwise.

A year later the Council renewed its "request" for another twelve-month period, in Security Council Resolution 1487 (2003), although three States (France, Germany and Syria) now abstained, whereas the vote had been unanimous the year before. In June of 2004 the question of renewal came up at a time when the mistreatment of prisoners at Abu Ghraib prison in Iraq and elsewhere was in the forefront of the news. Sufficient members of the Council were prepared to abstain so that the United States could not achieve the necessary nine positive votes that it needed. *See* Frederic L. Kirgis, *U.S. Drops Plan to Exempt G.I.'s from U.N. Court,* ASIL Insight, July 2004, *available at* https://www.asil.org/insights/volume/8/issue/15/us-drops-plan-exempt-gis-un-court.

Does Article 16 of the Rome Statute support a blanket request like that in Security Council resolution 1422? Or does it refer only to deferrals in particular cases? *See generally* Roberto Lavalle, *A Vicious Storm in a Teacup: The Action by the United Nations Security Council to Narrow the Jurisdiction of the International Criminal Court*, 14 CRIM. L.F. 195 (2003); Axel Marschik, *Legislative Powers of the Security Council, in* TOWARDS WORLD CONSTITUTIONALISM 457 (Ronald St. John MacDonald & Douglas M. Johnston eds., 2005).

(8) As *D.R. Congo v. Belgium* [chap. 2 and *supra* § 14.02] indicates, questions of jurisdiction and immunity are closely related. To what extent are the U.S. arguments and strategies jurisdictional ones? On the close connections between jurisdictional and immunity issues *see* Dapo Akande, *International Immunities and the International Criminal Court*, 98 A.J.I.L. 407 (2004). *See also* Kenneth S. Gallant, *Jurisdiction to Adjudicate and Jurisdiction to Prescribe in International Criminal Courts*, 48 VILLANOVA L. REV. 763 (2003).

(9) In Resolution 1593 of 31 March 2005, the Security Council referred the situation in Darfur, Sudan, to the ICC. Although Sudan is not a party to the Rome Statute, and has in fact disavowed an early signature to it, the Council was acting under it powers pursuant to Chapter VII of the UN Charter and the Statute. In 2009 and 2010, a Pre-Trial Chamber of the Court issued arrest warrants for, among others, the President of Sudan, Omar Hassan Ahmad Al-Bashir, on charges of genocide, crimes against humanity and war crimes. Mr. Bashir, before his ultimate overthrow and arrest in Sudan, visited the territory of several State Parties to the Rome Statute, such as Chad, Djibouti, Kenya, Nigeria, the Democratic Republic of Congo and the Republic of South Africa. These visits purported to be either on bilateral business or to meetings of regional organizations. Bashir (and those failing to arrest him) claimed reliance on his head-of-state immunity under customary law or on

the particular immunity arrangements made for the regional meetings. Parties to the Statute have an obligation, particularly under Articles 89 and 91 of the Rome Statute, to execute warrants of arrest. To the extent that parties have justified their failure to act, they have invoked Article 98(1) of the Statute and argued that they are bound by the "State immunity . . . of a third State."

Various panels of the Court came to the same conclusion that Bashir should have been arrested as a matter of law, but there were various rationales for their decisions. Some argued that Article 27(2) carried the day. Others believed that the key was in S.C Resolution 1593 which impliedly stripped any immunity arguments that might otherwise have been open to Sudan. Others insisted that there was a principle of customary law that denied immunity in the context of a request for transfer to the Court. Jordan, generally a strong supporter of the Court, but apparently conflicted about its obligations, forced the issue into the Appellate Chamber of the Court which unanimously accepted all three rationales. But it placed emphasis on the customary law argument in the decision which follows.

Judgment in the Jordan Referral re Al-Bashir Appeal

International Criminal Court, Appeals Chamber
No. ICC-02-05-01/09 OA2, 6 May 2019

97. The central issue in this appeal is whether Mr. Bashir, in his capacity as Head of State of Sudan, enjoyed immunity before this Court which Jordan was obligated to respect in the absence of a waiver from Sudan. In the circumstances of this Court, it is possible to follow different structures of judicial reasoning that may yield reasonable answers to that question. Nothing thus turns ultimately on the complaint that different compositions of the Pre-Trial Chamber may have used varied paths of judicial reasoning to answer that question. For present purposes, the issues in the appeal are adequately resolved along the same general framework of reasoning that the Pre-Trial Chamber had adopted in this case, with the exception of a strain of reasoning concerning customary international law. Following that approach, in keeping with article 21(1)(a) of the Statute, which stipulates that the Court shall apply '[i]n the first place, [the] Statute', the Appeals Chamber is satisfied that the issues in this appeal ultimately rest on a proper construction of provisions of the Rome Statute, in particular articles 27(2), 86, 89 and 98 of the Statute. It will address the impact of article 27(2) of the Statute on requests for cooperation relating to Heads of State of States Parties [below, section (b)]. It will then address the legal situation of Sudan in light of the UN Security Council referral of the Darfur situation [below, section (c)]. [Sections (b) and (c) are not reproduced in this excerpt. — Eds.]

98. In the context of construing the provisions of the Statute, the Appeals Chamber considers it convenient to address whether customary international law actually provides for immunity of a Head of State if arrest and surrender are sought by the Court [below, section (a)], especially given the importance generated by that question in the context of this appeal. While the Appeals Chamber notes that Jordan submits that the question of whether Head of State immunity vis-à-vis the Court

exists is not on appeal, this is a question that is intrinsically linked to the issues in relation to which leave to appeal was granted and the Appeals Chamber cannot disregard it.

. . . .

(a) Article 27(2) of the Statute and customary international law

100. Article 27(2) of the Statute provides as follows:

> Immunities or special procedural rules which may attach to the official capacity of a person, whether under national or international law, shall not bar the Court from exercising its jurisdiction over such a person.

101. The Appeals Chamber notes that Head of State immunity, which has been asserted in the case at hand, is a manner of immunity that is, as such, accepted under customary international law. That immunity prevents one State from exercising its criminal jurisdiction over the Head of State of another State. It is important to stress that immunity of that kind operates in the context of relations between States.

102. The most direct effect of article 27(2) of the Statute is that a Head of State cannot claim Head of State immunity when he or she appears before the ICC for prosecution in accordance with the provisions on the exercise of jurisdiction under articles 12 et seq. of the Statute. Nor does Head of State immunity present a bar to the Court opening an investigation in relation to or issuing a warrant of arrest against a Head of State. This was specifically recognised by the ICJ in the *Arrest Warrant Case* [para.61].

103. It is of note that article 27(2) of the Statute is a clear provision in conventional law; but it also reflects the status of customary international law. In this regard, the Appeals Chamber notes, first, article 7 of the Nuremberg Charter of the International Military Tribunal at Nuremberg, which provides as follows:

> The official position of defendants, whether as Heads of State or responsible officials in Government Departments, shall not be considered as freeing them from responsibility or mitigating punishment.

104. On 11 December 1946, the UN General Assembly expressly affirmed the 'principles of international law recognized by the Charter of the Nürnberg Tribunal and the judgment of the Tribunal' and directed the newly established International Law Commission to 'treat as a matter of primary importance plans for the formulation [. . .] of the principles recognized' therein. The International Law Commission subsequently [in 1950] formulated the Nuremberg Principles, Principle III of which reads as follows:

> The fact that a person who committed an act which constitutes a crime under international law acted as Head of State or responsible Government official does not relieve him from responsibility under international law.

105. The same principle was included in article 3 of the International Law Commission's draft Code of Offences against the Peace and Security of Mankind [in 1951].

The Convention against Genocide contains a similar provision, providing in its article IV:

> Persons committing genocide or any of the other acts enumerated in article III shall be punished, *whether they are constitutionally responsible rulers, public officials or private individuals.* [Emphasis added]

106. There is no suggestion in any of these instruments that immunity of Heads of State could stand in the way of their prosecution before an international court for international crimes.

107. Further milestones in this regard were the Statutes of the international criminal tribunals — the International Criminal Tribunal for the former Yugoslavia and the International Criminal Tribunal for Rwanda [the 'ICTY' and the 'ICTR'] — which the UN Security Council adopted in 1993 and 1994, respectively. Both Statutes include provisions similar to Principle III of the Nuremberg Principles. In his reports on the draft Statutes of the ICTY and ICTR, the UN Secretary General indicated that they should contain provisions 'which specify that a plea of head of State immunity [. . .] will not constitute a defence, nor will it mitigate punishment'. It is of note that the ICTY issued an indictment against President Slobodan Milošević on 22 May 1999, while he was still President of Serbia

108. The Statute of the Special Court for Sierra Leone [the 'SCSL'], a court established pursuant to a UN Security Council resolution by an agreement between the Government of Sierra Leone and the UN Secretary-General, also contains a provision rejecting the suggestion that Head of State immunity could be invoked against the SCSL's exercise of jurisdiction. Article 6(2) of the SCSL Statute stipulates:

> The official position of any accused persons, whether as Head of State or Government or as a responsible government official, shall not relieve such person of criminal responsibility nor mitigate punishment.

109. The SCSL confirmed an indictment against Mr. Charles Taylor on 7 March 2003 and issued a warrant for his arrest, while he was still President of Liberia. Mr. Taylor filed an application before the SCSL, requesting that the court quash the indictment and set aside the arrest warrant on the ground that he was immune from the SCSL's jurisdiction. A panel of the SCSL's Appeals Chamber heard this application, noting that it was called upon to decide 'whether it was lawful for the Special Court to issue an indictment and to circulate an arrest warrant in respect of a serving Head of State'. It answered this question in the affirmative, noting, first, that the SCSL was an international court, and, second, relying, inter alia, on the ICJ's finding in the *Arrest Warrant Case*, that Head of State immunity did not find application before international courts. It found that 'the principle seems now established that the sovereign equality of states does not prevent a Head of State from being prosecuted before an international criminal tribunal or state [sic., "state" reads "court" in the decision of the Special Court]'.

110. Turning to the jurisprudence of the ICC, the Appeals Chamber recalls that Pre-Trial Chamber I, in the 'Corrigendum to the Decision Pursuant to Article 87(7)

of the Rome Statute on the Failure by the Republic of Malawi to Comply with the Cooperation Requests Issued by the Court with Respect to the Arrest and Surrender of Omar Hassan Ahmad Al Bashir' [the 'Malawi Decision'], reached the same conclusion in a situation that was identical to the case at hand: a State Party to the Rome Statute having failed to execute a request for the arrest and surrender of Mr. Al- Bashir. Pre-Trial Chamber I, having recalled the irrelevance of Head of State immunity in respect of international courts since the end of the First World War, distinguished the case before it from that decided by the ICJ in the *Arrest Warrant Case*, noting that the latter was 'concerned solely with immunity across national jurisdictions' and therefore 'distinct from the present circumstances, as here an international court is seeking arrest for international crimes'. Pre-Trial Chamber I also recalled the passage of the judgment in the *Arrest Warrant Case* that recognises that Head of State immunity does not find application before international courts.

111. Pre-Trial Chamber I found that:

> T]he principle in international law is that immunity of either former or sitting Heads of State can not be invoked to oppose a prosecution by an international court. This is equally applicable to former or sitting Heads of States not Parties to the Statute whenever the Court may exercise jurisdiction. In this particular case, the Chamber notes that it is exercising jurisdiction following a referral by the United Nations Security Council made under Chapter VII of the United Nations Charter, in accordance with article 13(b) of the Statute.

112. Pre-Trial Chamber I considered that 'Malawi, and by extension the African Union, are not entitled to rely on article 98(1) of the Statute to justify refusing to comply with the Cooperation Requests', noting, inter alia, 'an increase in Head of State prosecutions by international courts in the last decade', which shows 'that initiating international prosecutions against Heads of State have gained widespread recognition as accepted practice'. It also noted the number of States Parties to the Rome Statute and the fact that States not parties to the Statute allowed twice for situations to be referred to the Court by the UN Security Council. Pre-Trial Chamber I concluded that the 'international community's commitment to rejecting immunity in circumstances where international courts seek arrest for international crimes has reached a critical mass' and that '[t]here is no conflict between Malawi's obligations towards the Court and its obligations under customary international law; therefore, article 98(1) of the Statute does not apply'.

113. The Appeals Chamber fully agrees with Pre-Trial Chamber I's conclusions in the Malawi Decision as well as that of the SCSL's Appeals Chamber in the Taylor case and notes that there is neither State practice nor *opinio juris* that would support the existence of Head of State immunity under customary international law vis-à-vis an international court. To the contrary, as shown in more detail in the Joint Concurring Opinion of Judges Eboe-Osuji, Morrison, Hofmański and Bossa, such immunity has never been recognised in international law as a bar to the jurisdiction of

an international court. To be noted in that regard is the role of judicial pronouncements in confirming whether or not a rule of customary international law has as such 'crystallized'. The Appeals Chamber is satisfied that the pronouncements of both the Pre-Trial Chamber in the Malawi Decision and of the Appeals Chamber of the Special Court for Sierra Leone have adequately and correctly confirmed the absence of a rule of customary international law recognising Head of State immunity before international courts in the exercise of jurisdiction. The Appeals Chamber accordingly rejects any contrary suggestion of the Pre-Trial Chamber in that regard, in both this case and in the case concerning South Africa.

114. The absence of a rule of customary international law recognising Head of State immunity vis-à-vis international courts is relevant not only to the question of whether an international court may issue a warrant for the arrest of a Head of State and conduct proceedings against him or her, but also for the horizontal relationship between States when a State is requested by an international court to arrest and surrender the Head of State of another State. As further explained in the Joint Concurring Opinion of Judges Eboe-Osuji, Morrison, Hofmański and Bossa and correctly found by the Pre-Trial Chamber in the Malawi Decision, no immunities under customary international law operate in such a situation to bar an international court in its exercise of its own jurisdiction.

115. The Appeals Chamber considers that the absence of a rule of customary international law recognising Head of State immunity vis-à-vis an international court is also explained by the different character of international courts when compared with domestic jurisdictions. While the latter are essentially an expression of a State's sovereign power, which is necessarily limited by the sovereign power of the other States, the former, when adjudicating international crimes, do not act on behalf of a particular State or States. Rather, international courts act on behalf of the international community as a whole. Accordingly, the principle of *par in parem non habet imperium*, which is based on the sovereign equality of States, or justice finds no application in relation to an international court such as the International Criminal Court.

116. The Appeals Chamber notes further that, given the fundamentally different nature of an international court as opposed to a domestic court exercising jurisdiction over a Head of State, it would be wrong to assume that an exception to the customary international law rule on Head of State immunity applicable in the relationship between States has to be established; rather, the onus is on those who claim that there is such immunity in relation to international courts to establish sufficient State practice and *opinio juris*. As further explained in the Joint Concurring Opinion of Judges Eboe-Osuji, Morrison, Hofmański and Bossa, there is no such practice or *opinio juris*.

117. In sum, the Appeals Chamber finds that there was no rule of customary international law that would have given Mr. Al-Bashir immunity from arrest and surrender by Jordan on the basis of the request for arrest and surrender issued by the Court. It follows that there was no ground for Jordan not to execute the request for arrest and

surrender and that therefore it did not comply with its obligation to cooperate with the Court pursuant to articles 86 et seq. of the Statute.

118. As recalled above, the Pre-Trial Chamber in the decision under review took a different approach to the one it adopted in the Malawi Decision. Contrary to that decision and the Appeals Chamber's above finding, it found that it was unable to identify 'a rule in customary international law that would exclude immunity for Heads of State when their arrest is sought for international crimes by another State, even when the arrest is sought on behalf of an international court, including, specifically, this Court'. Nevertheless, it concluded that Head of State immunity did not stand in the way of Mr. Al-Bashir's arrest by Jordan, based on the interplay between the relevant provisions of the Statute and Sudan's obligation to 'cooperate fully' with the Court pursuant to paragraph 2 of Resolution 1593.

119. While the Appeals Chamber, for the reasons set out above, rejects the Pre-Trial Chamber's finding that there is immunity under customary international law for Heads of State when their arrest is sought for international crimes by this Court, the Appeals Chamber notes that the Pre-Trial Chamber nevertheless reached the same conclusion as the Appeals Chamber, namely that Jordan should have arrested and surrendered Mr. Al-Bashir. The Pre-Trial Chamber did so based on its interpretation of the Statute and bearing in mind Sudan's position under Resolution 1593. The Appeals Chamber considers that this interpretation of the Statute was, as such, correct, as will be demonstrated in the subsequent sections

Notes

(1) Consider the analysis in *The Lotus* in §1.02 in light of the above. Is the rule applied here about which side carries the burden of persuasion on whether there is a customary rule of immunity the same as in *The Lotus*?

(2) The Pre-Trial-Chamber in Jordan's case had taken the position that Jordan's failure to arrest Bashir merited referral, under Article 86(7) of the Rome Statute, of Jordan's situation to the Court's Assembly of States Parties and, since the case began with the actions of the Security Council, to the Council. (It is not clear what action those bodies might take, except shaming.) A 3-2 majority of the Appeals Chamber decided that, given Jordan's efforts to consult under Article 97 of the Statute, the Pre-Trial Chamber had improperly exercised its discretion under Article 86(7).

Chapter 15

Mutual Assistance and Obtaining Evidence from Abroad

§ 15.01 Letters Rogatory

28 U.S.C. § 1781. Transmittal of letter rogatory or request

(a) The Department of State has power, directly, or through suitable channels—

(1) to receive a letter rogatory issued, or request made, by a foreign or international tribunal, to transmit it to the tribunal, officer, or agency in the United States to whom it is addressed, and to receive and return it after execution; and

(2) to receive a letter rogatory issued, or request made, by a tribunal in the United States, to transmit it to the foreign or international tribunal, officer, or agency to whom it is addressed, and to receive and return it after execution.

(b) This section does not preclude—

(1) the transmittal of a letter rogatory or request directly from a foreign or international tribunal to the tribunal, officer, or agency in the United States to whom it is addressed and its return in the same manner; or

(2) the transmittal of a letter rogatory or request directly from a tribunal in the United States to the foreign or international tribunal, officer, or agency to whom it is addressed and its return in the same manner.

28 U.S.C. § 1782. Assistance to foreign and international tribunals and to litigants before such tribunals

(a) The district court of the district in which a person resides or is found may order him to give his testimony or statement or to produce a document or other thing for use in a proceeding in a foreign or international tribunal, including criminal investigations conducted before formal accusation. The order may be made pursuant to a letter rogatory issued, or request made, by a foreign or international tribunal or upon the application of any interested person and may direct that the testimony or statement be given, or the document or other thing be produced, before a person appointed by the court. By virtue of his appointment, the person appointed has power

> to administer any necessary oath and take the testimony or statement. The order may prescribe the practice and procedure, which may be in whole or part the practice and procedure of the foreign country or the international tribunal, for taking the testimony or statement or producing the document or other thing. To the extent that the order does not prescribe otherwise, the testimony or statement shall be taken, and the document or other thing produced, in accordance with the Federal Rules of Civil Procedure.
>
> A person may not be compelled to give his testimony or statement or to produce a document or other thing in violation of any legally applicable privilege.
>
> (b) This chapter [28 USCS §§1781 et seq.] does not preclude a person within the United States from voluntarily giving his testimony or statement, or producing a document or other thing, for use in a proceeding in a foreign or international tribunal before any person and in any manner acceptable to him.

In re: Letter Rogatory from the Justice Court, District of Montreal, Canada. — John Fecarotta

United States Court of Appeals for the Sixth Circuit
523 F.2d 562 (1975)

MILLER, CIRCUIT JUDGE:

Appellant, John Fecarotta, a resident of Detroit, challenges the district court's refusal to quash a subpoena duces tecum it had directed to the appellant's bank in Detroit. The subpoena was in response to a request by a Canadian tribunal for judicial assistance in a pending criminal prosecution against appellant.

On August 19, 1974, the Justice Court of Sessions of the Peace, District of Montreal, Canada, ordered that a letter rogatory[1] be sent to the appropriate United States authorities requesting the production of all bank account records listed in the names of John Fecarotta and/or Juanita Fecarotta held by the Detroit Bank and Trust Company. John Fecarotta had been charged with a violation of the Narcotic Control Act of Canada, and the prosecution sought access to his bank records in connection with the prosecution of the alleged offense. The Justice Court requested the assistance of our country's federal courts only after it had been satisfied that the bank account information was necessary to the prosecution's case. Upon receipt of

1. Letters rogatory are defined in *The Signe*, 37 F. Supp. 819, 820 (E.D. La. 1941):

> Letters rogatory are the medium, in effect, whereby one country, speaking through one of its courts, requests another country, acting through its own courts and by methods of court procedure peculiar thereto and entirely within the latter's control, to assist the administration of justice in the former country; such request being made, and being usually granted, by reason of the comity existing between nations in ordinary peaceful times.

the letter rogatory, the Department of Justice made application to the District Court for the Eastern District of Michigan for an order to compel the bank to produce the documents sought by the foreign tribunal. On September 5, 1974, the district court accepted the letter rogatory and, under the authority of 28 U.S.C. §1782, issued a subpoena duces tecum to officers of the Detroit Bank and Trust Company. The subpoena commanded the bank's officials to appear with the records in question to be deposed concerning their contents. Fecarotta was notified of the date of the taking of the deposition and he immediately sought to quash the subpoena on the grounds that §1782 is not applicable to criminal prosecutions, or in the alternative,[a] that the court in its discretion could and should refuse to grant the subpoena because of the danger that the information might be used improperly in the Canadian trial. This motion was overruled and the subpoena was ordered to be issued. Pending appeal to this Court, the production order has been stayed.

. . . .

While it has been held that federal courts have inherent power to issue and respond to letters rogatory, . . . such jurisdiction has largely been regulated by congressional legislation. Where Congress has intervened, the scope of the congressional authorization necessarily limits and defines the judicial power to render and seek such assistance. Thus, a party against whom the requested information is to be used has standing to challenge the validity of such a subpoena on the ground that it is in excess of the terms of the applicable statute, here 28 U.S.C. §1782. We hold that Fecarotta has standing to challenge the validity of the subpoena on the theory that it is not authorized by §1782, the governing statute.

We turn to the appellant's contention that §1782 does not authorize or permit the compulsory production of evidence for use in a foreign *criminal* proceeding. Traditionally, the United States has enacted statutes to provide judicial assistance for courts in other countries. . . . The original enactment authorizing federal courts to assist foreign tribunals was the Act of March 2, 1855. This statute granted broad powers to the United States courts to compel the testimony of witnesses to assist foreign courts. . . . Primarily because of misindexing, the Act passed into obscurity and later was crippled by a subsequent statute. . . .

This country's early begrudging attitude in granting assistance to foreign courts was evidenced by the Act of March 3, 1863, a law that largely undercut the 1855 legislation. The 1863 Act permitted the federal courts to take testimony [only in suits] "for the recovery of money or property depending in any court in any foreign country with which the United States are at peace, and in which the government of such foreign country shall be a party or shall have an interest. . . ." It was not until

---

a. In 1996 Congress amended 28 U.S.C. §1782 inserting "including criminal investigations conducted before formal accusations," after "proceedings in a foreign or international tribunal." Pub.L. 104-106 §1342(b). — Eds.

1948 that the requirement that the foreign government be a party or have an interest was deleted. The 1948 amendment also expanded the statute to encompass "*any civil action* pending in any court in a foreign country." [emphasis added]. One year later the restrictive phrase "civil action" was changed to read "*any judicial proceeding* pending in any court in a foreign country." [emphasis added].

The narrow scope of these statutes was underscored and reinforced by the decisions of federal courts. For instance, in *Janssen v. Belding-Corticelli, Ltd.*, 84 F.2d 577 (3d Cir. 1936), the court declared that the only power it had regarding letters rogatory was that granted to it by the Constitution or by statute. Under the statutes then in force, the district court could neither issue a subpoena duces tecum to secure documentary evidence nor could it conduct a "roving oral examination" of the witnesses in the absence of interrogatories. . . . Additionally, the courts have not favored the use of letters rogatory to secure evidence for introduction in criminal cases or investigations. . . .

The 1964 amendments, however, were a significant departure by Congress from its cautious approach to international judicial assistance over the past century. The revisions were the result of proposals submitted by the Commission on International Rules of Judicial Procedure. Congress created the Commission in 1958 and authorized it to study and evaluate all the federal code provisions and rules, both civil and criminal, relating to international judicial assistance. The goal of the Commission was to revise the law in order to provide "wide judicial assistance . . . on a wholly unilateral basis." . . . As the legislative history reveals, the purpose behind the proposals was to prod other nations into following the lead of the United States in expanding procedures for the assistance of foreign litigants. . . . The current § 1782 represents in part the changes made by the 1964 amendments.

The crucial issue on this appeal is whether § 1782 applies to documentary evidence sought for use in a foreign *criminal* proceeding. Noting that the statute's predecessors were not thought to cover criminal cases, the appellant argues that § 1782 neither expressly nor impliedly applies to the instant situation. We are convinced, however, that Congress clearly intended for the provision to extend this nation's assistance to the *criminal* processes of a foreign country. . . .

In his remaining argument, Fecarotta maintains that any testimony taken under § 1782 and later introduced against him at trial would contravene his right of confrontation under the sixth amendment. The letter rogatory from the Canadian court specifically provides that Fecarotta is to be represented by his counsel at the deposition. . . . Since the appellant's claim is based upon nothing more than the bald assertion of potential harm, we find his argument to be without merit. . . .

Under § 1782 "the grant of power is unrestricted, but entirely within the discretion of the Court." . . . There is no showing that the district court abused its discretion either in applying the provision to a pending criminal case or in permitting the evidence to be taken in compliance with Canadian practice and procedure.

AFFIRMED. . . .

United States v. Reagan

United States Court of Appeals for the Sixth Circuit
453 F.2d 165 (1971)

William E. Miller, Circuit Judge:

This is an appeal from a conviction for voluntary manslaughter. 18 U.S.C. § 1111 provides that murder in the first degree is the unlawful killing of a human being with malice aforethought or if committed in perpetration of any robbery or burglary within "the special maritime * * * jurisdiction of the United States."

....

The appellant was charged with three counts under 18 U.S.C. § 1111: first, with intentional and premeditated murder of Joseph Speidell, a fellow seaman; second, with murder in perpetration of a robbery; and third, with murder in perpetration of burglary. After a five week trial beginning in October 1970, the district court dismissed the third count of the indictment and submitted the case to the jury on the first two counts, also charging the jury that it could consider whether the appellant was guilty of the lesser included offense of voluntary manslaughter made a federal offense by 18 U.S.C. § 1112 if committed within the special maritime jurisdiction of the United States. The jury found the appellant guilty of the lesser included offense of voluntary manslaughter and not guilty of all other charges. Following denial of his motion for a new trial appellant perfected his appeal to this Court.

The events out of which the charges against appellant arose occurred on an American vessel, the SS Thunderbird, in the harbor of Bremerhaven, Germany, close to the noon hour on December 16, 1966. The harbor is located on the east bank of the Weser River which flows north past Bremen and Bremerhaven into the North Sea. Bremerhaven is approximately sixty kilometers inland from the boundary which separates German inland waters and the international waters of the North Sea. As a result of extreme tides, the harbor is separated from the Weser River by locks. These are opened to permit vessels to enter and depart the harbor only at certain stages of the tide....

The German authorities were called and Reagan was taken into custody. On December 17, 1966, the day after the slaying, he was judicially committed to a State mental institution in Bremen. The *SS Thunderbird* departed Bremerhaven about 1:00 p.m. on this date. Reagan remained in the German institution till after the ship returned to Bremerhaven about April 1, 1967. On April 5, 1967 a Judge of the appropriate German County Court refused to issue a Warrant of Arrest for the crime of murder sought by the German Prosecutor, finding no probable cause for an arrest.

After his release in Bremen, Reagan returned to the Kennedy Airport where, though no charges were pending against him, he was met by agents of the Coast Guard and F.B.I. and told to return to his home in Cleveland and not to sail on foreign voyages. Thereafter, the U.S. Coast Guard in Bremen, acting for the F.B.I., requested the appropriate German authorities to release to them the records pertaining to the Reagan matter. This request was denied on the ground that under German law such records may not be released without the consent of the accused, a consent which Reagan refused to give. On November 3, 1967 Judge James C. Connell of the United States District Court for the Northern District of Ohio, Eastern Division, requested from the "appropriate judicial authorities in Land Bremen, Federal Republic of Germany" the records sought by the F.B.I. and the Coast Guard. The request in the form but not in the words of a "letter rogatory" is set forth below.[2] Pursuant to this request, the German file was sent to the district court and made available to the office of the U. S. Attorney in early 1968.

On September 12, 1969 a grand jury indictment was returned. On September 15, 1969 it was opened, docketed and a warrant for the appellant's arrest was issued. He was then taken into custody. The trial and appellant's conviction followed. From this conviction appellant perfected his appeal.

Appellant makes numerous contentions. He asserts: the district court was without subject matter jurisdiction; the indictment was deficient in that it failed to allege an essential element of jurisdiction; the delay in prosecuting him constituted a denial of his due process rights . . . ; the request for international judicial assistance was without the jurisdiction of the district court at the time issued and constituted an abuse of discretion; the failure of the district court to suppress evidence which was the fruit of the request was reversible error; the admission of the testimony of a German police official who was brought to this country by the government was reversible error in light of the court's failure to provide for the bringing of defense witnesses to this country from Germany; he was placed in double jeopardy because of the German proceeding; the failure to declare a mistrial upon his emotional outburst at trial constituted a reversible error; and finally appellant says that the evidence was insufficient to support a conviction for voluntary manslaughter. We have carefully considered each of these contentions on the basis of the record and pertinent authorities. We find it necessary to discuss only the issues concerning jurisdiction and the issuance of a letter rogatory.

. . . .

2. . . . There is currently pending within the jurisdiction of this Court an investigation into an alleged homicide committed on December 16, 1966, by Howard Reagan, an American National, on Joseph J. Speidell, at Bremerhaven, Germany. It is this Court's understanding that the Prosecutor in Bremerhaven, Federal Republic of Germany conducted an investigation of the alleged offense beginning in the month of December, 1966.

The United States authorities in this district are currently conducting an investigation of the same incident. It would be most helpful, and in the furtherance of justice, if the investigative files of the German authorities in Bremerhaven, including, but not limited to, oral or written statements of all witnesses, reports of investigative officers, reports of any autopsy or post-mortem medical examination of the deceased, medical or psychiatric reports from any examination of the suspect (Reagan), any photographs, and any oral or written statements of the suspect (Reagan), could be made available to the United States investigative authorities. To that end, a request is hereby made that the pertinent files and exhibits, currently in the possession or in the custody of the German authorities in Bremerhaven, be made available to this Court. . . .

It is our view that there was no "assertion of jurisdiction" by Germany and, therefore, that the district court was not without jurisdiction.... A different case would be presented if Reagan had been brought to trial in Germany or perhaps even if he had been indicted in Germany. We hold that the district court did have proper subject matter jurisdiction.

Letters Rogatory

The appellant argues that the district court exceeded its jurisdiction in requesting international judicial assistance through the medium of a "letter rogatory" since there was no "case or controversy" before it, and that it therefore erred in not suppressing the fruits of this request. We must disagree although concededly the contention is not without some support.

28 U.S.C. §1781 recognizes, impliedly at least, the power of federal courts to transmit letters rogatory to foreign tribunals.... In *United States v. Staples*, 256 F.2d 290 (1958), the Ninth Circuit pointed correctly to the source of a court's power to issue letters rogatory:

> This Court, like all courts of the United States, has *inherent* power to issue Letters Rogatory. The manner of taking proof is left to our discretion.... (Emphasis added.)

We find no definitive authority, however, as to precisely when this power attaches in a given case.

The opinion of the Court of Appeals in *In re Pacific Ry. Comm'n*, 32 F. 241, 12 SAWY. 559 (Cir. Ct. N.D. Cal., 1887), is suggestive though not squarely in point. There the Court held that the Pacific Railway Commission created by Act of Congress did not have the power to issue letters rogatory. Speaking of this instrument, the Court stated:

> There are certain powers inherent in all courts. The power to preserve order in their proceedings, and to punish for contempt of their authority, are instances of this kind. And by jurists and text writers the power of the courts of record of one country, as a matter of comity, to furnish assistance, so far as is consistent with their own jurisdiction, to the courts of another country, by taking the testimony of witnesses to be used in the foreign country, or by ordering it to be taken before a magistrate or commissioner, has also been classed among their inherent powers. "For by the law of nations," says Greenleaf, "courts of justice of different countries are bound mutually to aid and assist each other, for the furtherance of justice; and hence, when the testimony of a foreign witness is necessary, the court before which the action is pending may send to the court within whose jurisdiction the witness resides a writ, either patent or close, usually termed a letter rogatory, or a commission *sub mutuae vicissitudinis obtentu ac in juris subsidium*, from those words contained in it. By this instrument the court abroad is informed of the pendency of the cause, and the names of the foreign witnesses, and is requested to cause their depositions to be taken in

> due course of law, for the furtherance of justice, *with an offer on the part of the tribunal making the request to do the like for the other in a similar case.*" Treatise on Evidence, vol. 1, § 320. The comity in behalf of which this power is exercised cannot, of course, be invoked by any mere investigating commission.... (Emphasis added.)

....

Proceedings to perpetuate testimony, where litigation is expected or apprehended, are within the ordinary jurisdiction of courts of equity, and come under the designation of "cases in equity" in the constitution....

Similarly, it would seem that preliminary steps taken by a federal court to obtain evidence from a foreign power, in aid of its jurisdiction in criminal cases, would be within its Article III power over cases and controversies.

Absent substantial and controlling authority, we are unwilling to hold here that a court may only issue a letter rogatory after an indictment is returned in a criminal case. We are not persuaded that the issuance of such an ex parte instrument is incompatible with the fair operation of our system of justice.

It should be pointed out that the German record was used not as the principal part of the prosecution's case, but for purposes which appear to have been limited in nature.... Ample testimony was presented to the jury, apart from the foreign record, concerning Reagan's appearance and actions immediately following the stabbing and his own incriminating statements made in the presence of shipmates. Such evidence appears to us to have been decisive in linking the appellant with the murder on shipboard....

Appellant's further contentions enumerated above have been carefully considered and we find them to be without merit.

The judgment of the district court is therefore Affirmed.

Notes

(1) There are some serious drawbacks to using the letters rogatory process. Consider the comments of Lisa Cacheris, a member of the Office of International Affairs, Criminal Division of the U.S. Department of Justice:

> The obvious pitfall of the letter rogatory process is that it can be extremely time consuming, and when a prosecutor wants a particular piece of evidence for use at a trial that is set for a date certain chances are the prosecutor may not get it in time.

Remarks of Lisa Cacheris, Proceedings, *Annual Meeting of the American Society of International Law,* 85 AM. SOC'Y INT'L L. PROC. 383, 392 (1991). The Justice Manual echoes these sentiments by noting that prosecutors should "[c]ontact the Office of International Affairs as soon as it appears that assistance from overseas will be needed." *Time Required,* Justice Manual, Section 9–13.514, U.S. Department of Justice. In a prior version of the Justice Manual, called the U.S. Attorney's Manual, the

U.S. Department of Justice stated, "Prosecutors should assume that the process will take a year or more. Letters rogatory are customarily transmitted via the diplomatic channel, a time-consuming means of transmission." *Letters Rogatory*, Section 275, Justice Manual, U.S. Department of Justice.

(2) *United States v. Reagan*, 453 F.2d 165 (6th Cir. 1971), above discusses the use of letters rogatory by U.S. authorities to gather evidence from abroad prior to an indictment. What about a case where a foreign government requests information from a U.S. court prior to indictment in the foreign country? Should such assistance be permitted? In 1996, Congress clarified its view on this issue by amending 28 U.S.C. § 1782 to include the italicized language below.

> (a) The district court of the district in which a person resides or is found may order him to give his testimony or statement or to produce a document or other thing for use in a proceeding in a foreign or international tribunal, *including criminal investigations conducted before formal accusation*. The order may be made pursuant to a letter rogatory issued, or request made, by a foreign or international tribunal or upon the application of any interested person and may direct that the testimony or statement be given, or the document or other thing be produced, before a person appointed by the court. By virtue of his appointment, the person appointed has power to administer any necessary oath and take the testimony or statement. The order may prescribe the practice and procedure, which may be in whole or part the practice and procedure of the foreign country or the international tribunal, for taking the testimony or statement or producing the document or other thing. To the extent that the order does not prescribe otherwise, the testimony or statement shall be taken, and the document or other thing produced, in accordance with the Federal Rules of Civil Procedure.
>
> A person may not be compelled to give his testimony or statement or to produce a document or other thing in violation of any legally applicable privilege.

28 U.S.C. section 1782 (emphasis added); Pub.L. 104-106, Div. A, Title XIII, § 1342(b), Feb. 10, 1996, 110 Stat. 486.

(3) The government, however, can have the statute of limitations suspended when requesting information from a foreign country. Will this suspension apply to letters rogatory? How long can the statute of limitations be extended? Consider this issue as presented in *Bischel v. United States*, 61 F.3d 1429 (9th Cir. 1995):

> This appeal requires us to decide when there has been "final action" on an official request for evidence in a foreign country, where the court has suspended the running of the statute of limitations pursuant to 18 U.S.C. § 3292.[3]

---

3. 18 U.S.C. § 3292 provides:

(a)(1) Upon application of the United States, filed before return of an indictment, indicating that evidence of an offense is in a foreign country, the district court before which a

Stephen Bischel was convicted of numerous offenses arising out of "broker's crosses" on investments sold by La Jolla Trading Group, which he owned. Because these transactions involved British commodity brokers, the government requested assistance of United Kingdom authorities through letters rogatory and obtained a court order under § 3292(a)(1) to suspend the running of the statute of limitations pending "final action" on the request.

Records were received pursuant to the official request at a time when the statute of limitations would normally have run on many of the offenses charged in the indictment; a Certificate of Authenticity that was also requested had not yet been received when the indictment was returned. We hold that "final action on the request" for purposes of § 3292 includes all of the items requested in the letters rogatory. Since the certification had been requested but had not yet been received, the district court did not clearly err in finding that "final action" had not been taken. The statute of limitations, therefore, continued to be suspended so that none of the counts now at issue was time barred. We also conclude that a § 3292 order suspending the running of the statute of limitations speaks as of the date the official request is made, not when the order suspending the statute is entered, and that to begin the period of suspension when the letters rogatory are issued does not run afoul either of the Ex Post Facto Clause or of Bischel's rights to due process. . . .

"Final action" is not defined in the text of the statute. However, construing the concept of "final action" to include a dispositive response to each item set out in the official request, including a request for certification, is consistent with the statutory structure and legislative history. It also makes practical sense.

Section 3292(b) hinges the end of the period of suspension on final action by foreign authorities on "the request." The "request" referred to is the official request for "evidence of an offense" that is in a foreign country. 18

grand jury is impaneled to investigate the offense shall suspend the running of the statute of limitations for the offense if the court finds by a preponderance of the evidence that an official request has been made for such evidence and that it reasonably appears, or reasonably appeared at the time the request was made, that such evidence is, or was, in such foreign country. . . .

(b) Except as provided in subsection (c) of this section, a period of suspension under this section shall begin on the date on which the official request is made and end on the date on which the foreign court or authority takes final action on the request.

(c) The total of all periods of suspension under this section with respect to an offense—

(1) shall not exceed three years; and

(2) shall not extend a period within which a criminal case must be initiated for more than six months if all foreign authorities take final action before such period would expire without regard to this section.

U.S.C. § 3292(a)(1). "Evidence of an offense" is essentially worthless unless admissible. Admissibility turns in part on authenticity. Fed. R. Evid. 902(3). Thus, certifying that primary evidence is what it purports to be is inevitably part of the "evidence of an offense" within the meaning of § 3292(a)(1). We also look at legislative history here because the statutory words "final action" do not unambiguously resolve the interpretational task we face. Our construction comports with the legislative history indicating that § 3292, which was passed as part of the Comprehensive Crime Control Act of 1984, P.L. 98-473, was prompted by concern both for the difficulty of obtaining records in other countries, and of admitting them into evidence.... Finally, the interests of certainty counsel against the construction Bischel suggests. He would have us hold that "final action" takes place when the last of the records requested has been received. However, there is no ready way of knowing when the last of anything has happened. Instead, pegging "final action" to disposition, up or down, of each of the items in the official request provides a more certain benchmark by which to measure whether the action that has been taken is "final" or not.

We therefore conclude that "final action" for purposes of § 3292 means a dispositive response by the foreign sovereign to both the request for records and for a certificate of authenticity of those records, as both were identified in the "official request." ...

Bischel maintains that § 3292 violates the Due Process Clause as applied to him because it takes away his right to a fixed statute of limitations and removes the predictability of a specific time limit beyond which he could not be prosecuted. Yet Bischel fails to locate the source of any right to a fixed period of limitations. In any event, § 3292(c) sets a clear point beyond which the limitations period may not be extended: either three years if there is no "final action" at all, or no more than six months if there is "final action" within the period.

Bischel also argues that § 3292 is constitutionally infirm because it lacks any requirement that the government diligently seek evidence located in a foreign country.... [W]e decline to read a diligence requirement into § 3292.... AFFIRMED.

See also United States v. Meador, 138 F.3d 986 (5th Cir. 1998) ("[W]hen the foreign government believes it has completed its engagement and communicates that belief to our government, that foreign government has taken a 'final action' for the purposes of § 3292(b).").

(4) When will a defendant be permitted to use letters rogatory to obtain evidence from a foreign country? Consider District Judge Scheindlin's "Opinion and Order" concerning a defense request for letters rogatory in the case of *United States v. Korogodsky*, 4 F. Supp. 2d 262 (S.D. N.Y. 1998):

On March 16, 1998, Defendant Alex Korogodsky ("Korogodsky") requested the issuance of a letter rogatory to Russian authorities. Korogodsky also moves to dismiss the Indictment, arguing that his inability to subpoena foreign witnesses will (1) deprive him of his Sixth Amendment right to compulsory process, and (2) violate the confrontation clause of the Sixth Amendment....

Korogodsky is charged, inter alia, with conspiracy to commit wire fraud and wire fraud, in violation of 18 U.S.C. §§ 371 and 1343. The charges arise out of an alleged scheme by Korogodsky and others ("the conspirators") to defraud 30 Russian firms (the "victim firms") of over $ 10 million and to transport the funds to the United States....

The Government has represented that it expects to call witnesses from only five of the 30 victim firms. The Government will apparently prove that the conspirators attempted to defraud the remaining 25 victim firms by offering (1) accomplice testimony, (2) the purported contracts between the conspirators and the victim firms, and (3) bank documents allegedly reflecting money transfers from the victim firms to Newtel. These contracts and bank records will be offered pursuant to 18 U.S.C. § 3505.[4]

....

Korogodsky's letter rogatory seeks sworn statements from 32 persons who fall into three categories: (1) representatives of victim firms; (2) representatives of banks and other businesses that provided the victim firms with financing to make payments to Newtel; and (3) representatives of companies that agreed to insure the victim firms' performance under the contracts. The Government does not intend to call any of these individuals at trial.

Korogodsky's letter rogatory would require these persons to provide written information about the following: their educational background and employment history; background information about the formation,

---

4. Section 3505 provides, in pertinent part, that:

(a)(1) In a criminal proceeding in a court of the United States, a foreign record of regularly conducted activity, or a copy of such record, shall not be excluded by the hearsay rule if a foreign certification attests that—

(A) such record was made at, or near the time of the occurrence of the matters set forth, by (or from information transmitted by) a person with knowledge of those matters;

(B) such record was kept in the course of a regularly conducted business activity;

(C) the business activity made such a record as a regular practice; and

(D) if such record is not the original, such record is a duplicate of the original;

unless the source of the information or the method or circumstances of its preparation indicate lack of trustworthiness.

(2) A foreign certification under this section shall authenticate such record or duplicate.

ownership, capitalization and bank accounts of their firm; their dealings, if any, with Newtel, Korogodsky or (regarding the banks and insurers) Newtel's contract partners; any criminal record of the witness, his company, or their status as a target or subject of a criminal or civil investigation; any physical or mental disability or emotional disturbance or drug or alcohol addiction of the witness; and any payments, leniency promises or immun ity grants from law enforcement officials.

Korogodsky contends that he should be permitted to pursue the letter rogatory because it: (1) might generate evidence of the victim firms' own misconduct; and (2) would allow him to test the reliability of the § 3505 foreign certifications. The Government opposes the letter rogatory request, in part, because it believes that obtaining responses to the request may take months or even years. . . .

The use of depositions in criminal cases is governed by Fed. R. Crim. P. 15, which permits a party in "exceptional circumstances" to depose its own witness in order to preserve the witness' testimony. Rule 15(d) directs that depositions are to be taken in the manner provided in civil actions, and Fed. R. Civ. P. 28(b)(3) authorizes the taking of depositions in foreign countries "pursuant to a letter rogatory." Thus, a court has discretion to issue letters rogatory on behalf of a party in a criminal action pursuant to Rule 15. . . .

Courts have interpreted the "exceptional circumstances" standard of Rule 15 to require (1) that the witness will be unavailable at trial; and (2) that the information sought is material to the party's case. . . . The burden is on the party seeking the foreign deposition to prove such exceptional circumstances. Thus, to obtain a letter rogatory, the moving party must prove both the materiality of the information sought and the witness' unavailability.

. . . .

Korogodsky's first asserted purpose for questioning the officers of the victim firms is to establish that these firms were themselves engaged in criminal misconduct when they allegedly contracted with Newtel. Thus, as an initial matter, Korogodsky must show that evidence of the victim firms' alleged wrongdoing would be material to his defense.

To convict Korogodsky of the wire fraud charges, the Government must prove that the conspirators contracted to sell goods to the victim firms with the intent to defraud them. It is no defense that the victims of the fraud may have been engaged in some misconduct. Moreover, the Government does not intend to call any of the individuals whom Korogodsky seeks to depose. Thus, the credibility of the victim firms' officers will not be an issue at trial. Accordingly, Korogodsky's letter rogatory questions concerning the possible misconduct of the victim firms are not relevant, much less material, to the wire fraud counts with which he is charged....

Korogodsky has also failed to show that the prospective deponents would be unavailable at trial.... Here, the defendant has made no representation whatsoever that the potential deponents would be unavailable at trial. In fact, at oral argument defense counsel suggested that the deponents could well be available to testify at trial....

Korogodsky argues that under the confrontation clause of the Sixth Amendment, he has a right to the letter rogatory as a means of determining the reliability of the Government's § 3505 certifications. The confrontation clause does not bar the statement of a hearsay declarant who is unavailable to testify at trial, so long as his statement "bears sufficient indicia of reliability to assure an adequate basis for evaluating the truth of the declaration." ... Several courts have addressed the question whether the admissibility of evidence pursuant to § 3505 violates the confrontation clause because the records custodian is unavailable for cross-examination. These courts have uniformly held that so long as the documents bear sufficient indicia of reliability, the confrontation clause is not violated....

However, none of these decisions directly addresses the issue presented here: Under what circumstances should a court grant a defendant's pre-trial request to depose a company's officers, via letter rogatory, in order to determine the reliability of the company's records.... A defendant is entitled to a letter rogatory which questions a foreign witness who has submitted a § 3505 certification, but only with respect to the reliability of the relevant document. This approach affords a defendant the opportunity to challenge the testimony that the government intends to use against him at trial. The question, then, is whether the questions propounded by Korogodsky concern the reliability of either the Newtel contracts obtained from the files of the victim firms or money transfer records obtained from the Russian banks.... Finally, because it appears that the Government does not intend to introduce documents obtained from Russian insurance companies, there is no basis for questioning officers of these companies....

With respect to the questions directed at the officers of the alleged victim firms, the Defendant has failed to show either (1) that any misconduct on the part of the victim firms is material to his defense; or (2) that his questions relate to the reliability of the Newtel contracts obtained from their files. Nor do the questions directed at the banks challenge the reliability of the banks' money transfer records. Finally, Korogodsky's questions for the insurance companies have no apparent bearing on his defense in general or on the Government's § 3505 evidence in particular. Accordingly, Korogodsky's letter rogatory request is denied in its entirety.

....

> Defendant contends that because the Court cannot subpoena Russian citizens to testify at his trial, the Indictment should be dismissed as violative of his Sixth Amendment right to compulsory process. This argument fails for two reasons. First, the right to compulsory process exists only where a defendant "make[s] some plausible showing of how [the desired witness'] testimony would have been both material and favorable to his defense." ...
>
> Second, the Sixth Amendment provides a right to compulsory process only if the desired witness is within the court's subpoena power.... A court's inability to subpoena a foreign witness does not implicate the compulsory process clause, even if that witness could provide testimony that is material and favorable to the defendant.... Thus, Korogodsky's right to compulsory process is not violated though the court cannot compel the testimony of the Russian citizens whom Korogodsky may wish to call at trial.
>
> ....
>
> Defendant has cited to no authority in support of his assertion that the confrontation clause of the Sixth Amendment requires the dismissal of the Indictment. If the admission of any of the Government's proposed evidence would violate Korogodsky's rights under the confrontation clause, then the Court will exclude the proposed evidence, not dismiss the Indictment.
>
> It appears that the Government's § 3505 certifications contain the only testimony that Korogodsky will not have an opportunity to challenge through cross-examination. The admissibility of this evidence will be determined at a hearing to be held....
>
> For the reasons stated above, Defendant's letter rogatory request and his motion to dismiss the Indictment based on the confrontation clause and the right to compulsory process and are denied. A hearing to determine the admissibility of the Government's § 3505 evidence will be held....

See also United States v. Liner, 435 F.3d 920 (8th Cir. 2006) (holding that defendant was not entitled to have letters rogatory issued where there was no showing that the testimony would be material).

(5) Note that letters rogatory are available in both criminal and civil cases. Note also that many criminal cases have parallel civil proceedings, whether brought by the government or private parties. What complications might arise during the use of letters rogatory in these parallel proceedings? Consider *Societe Nationale Industrielle Aerospatiale v. U.S. District Court for the Southern District of Iowa*, 482 U.S. 522 (1987), in which the Court examined whether a U.S. court could order a party to produce materials in violation of a French blocking statute. *See also Strauss v. Credit Lyonnais, S.A.*, 249 F.R.D. 429 (E.D.N.Y. 2008) (in suit under 18 U.S.C. § 2333(a) against bank for injuries sustained in an international terrorist attack, court analyses whether to require disclosure despite existence of French blocking statute).

§ 15.02 Mutual Legal Assistance Treaties & Executive Agreements

A. Legal Principles

In re: Commissioner's Subpoenas

United States Court of Appeals for the Eleventh Circuit
325 F.3d 1287 (2003)

ANDERSON, CIRCUIT JUDGE:

This case involves a request made by Canadian law enforcement authorities, pursuant to a mutual legal assistance treaty between Canada and the United States, for the legal assistance of the United States government in subpoenaing seven individuals residing in the Southern District of Florida. The Canadian authorities sought to interview these individuals in connection with an ongoing investigation into possible criminal activities. The subpoenas were initially issued, but upon a motion filed by the subpoenaed witnesses, the district judge quashed the subpoenas. The United States, on behalf of the Canadian authorities, appeals the district court's order quashing the subpoenas.

This case presents an issue of first impression for the federal appellate courts. We must ascertain whether this mutual legal assistance treaty between the two countries obligates the United States, at the request of Canada, to issue subpoenas to compel the testimony of witnesses in a criminal investigation prior to the filing of formal charges. Because we construe this Treaty to obligate both countries to execute requests for the issuance of subpoenas for purposes of compelling testimony in criminal investigations and to arrange for the taking of such testimony even prior to the actual initiation of formal charges, we hold that the Canadian request for assistance should have been granted and the subpoenas should not have been quashed by the district court....

The Treaty Between the United States and Canada on Mutual Legal Assistance in Criminal Matters, Mar. 18, 1985, U.S.-Can., 24 I.L.M. 1092 ("MLAT" or "Treaty"), was signed at Quebec City, Canada on March 18, 1985, the advice and consent of the United States Senate was received on October 24, 1989, and the Treaty was entered into force on January 24, 1990. The Treaty obligates the two governments to provide "mutual legal assistance in all matters relating to the investigation, prosecution and suppression of offences." ... The MLAT with Canada is "one of a series of modern mutual legal assistance treaties being negotiated by the United States in order to counter more effectively criminal activities." ...

Traditionally, evidence sought by a foreign government had to be obtained through a process whereby a written request known as a "letter rogatory" was sent from the court of one country to the court of another asking the receiving court to provide the assistance. A federal statute authorizes federal district courts in this country to entertain such requests and provides that "[t]he district court of the district in which a person resides or is found may order him to give his testimony or statement or to produce a document or other thing for use in a proceeding in a foreign or international tribunal, including criminal investigations conducted before formal accusation." 28 U.S.C. § 1782. Not only can a foreign tribunal bring a request in the form of a "letter rogatory," but section 1782 has been amended to also allow similar requests for assistance to be brought by "interested persons" including foreign governments in foreign investigations or proceedings and private litigants of a foreign proceeding. . . . Requests for assistance initiated directly by an interested person rather than a foreign court are often referred to as "letters of request." Despite the apparent versatility of 28 U.S.C. § 1782, law enforcement authorities found the statute to be an unattractive option in practice because it provided wide discretion in the district court to refuse the request and did not obligate other nations to return the favor that it grants. MLATs, on the other hand, have the desired quality of compulsion as they contractually obligate the two countries to provide to each other evidence and other forms of assistance needed in criminal cases while streamlining and enhancing the effectiveness of the process for obtaining needed evidence. This MLAT between the United States and Canada provides for a broad range of cooperation in criminal matters.

Under this Treaty, Canada makes a request for assistance by contacting the United States' "Central Authority" under the Treaty, which is "the Attorney General or officials designed by him." . . . If the particular type of assistance requested requires action of a federal district court, the Attorney General and his officials utilize existing statutory authority including 28 U.S.C. § 1782 to bring an action seeking the requested evidence or information. Because the Attorney General simply utilizes the preexisting statutory authority provided under 28 U.S.C. § 1782 when satisfying treaty obligations under the MLAT, the Treaty itself is self-executing obviating the need for implementing legislation. . . . Upon its entry into force on January 24, 1990, the MLAT became a law of this land on par with a federal statute. . . .

For the past several years, Canadian law enforcement authorities have been investigating an alleged smuggling operation. According to Canadian authorities, goods have been legally exported to the United States and then smuggled back into Canada without payment of the Canadian duty, resulting in a revenue loss for the Canadian government. The smuggling activities allegedly began in 1989. The United States began its own investigation. During the investigations, the two governments shared information and resources. Appellees in this case are seven individuals allegedly involved. After unsuccessfully attempting to conduct voluntary interviews with the seven appellees, the Canadian authorities turned to formal legal process. . . .

In 2000, Canadian authorities asked the United States for assistance. On February 22, 2001, the United States filed a petition in the United States District Court for the Southern District of Florida seeking an order appointing an assistant United States attorney as a "commissioner" to assist the Canadian government in obtaining the requested evidence. This request was made pursuant to the MLAT and 28 U.S.C. § 1782. On March 2, 2001, the district court entered an order appointing an assistant

United States attorney from the Southern District of Florida, as the "commissioner" and authorizing him to "take such steps as are necessary, including issuance of commissioner's subpoenas to be served on persons within the jurisdiction of this Court, to collect the evidence requested." On April 30, 2001, he issued subpoenas to each of the appellees commanding their appearance at the federal courthouse in Miami on a given date and time, to give testimony to Canadian authorities concerning the Canadian smuggling investigation. Prior to the scheduled testimony, however, the appellees moved in the district court to quash the subpoenas and for a protective order.

On August 23, 2001, a magistrate judge ordered that the subpoenas be quashed. First, the magistrate judge held that by its own terms, the MLAT fully incorporates the existing substantive law of the United States as the "Requested State," including 28 U.S.C. § 1782. According to this Circuit, section 1782 contains an implicit foreign discoverability requirement. This rule requires that the information sought in the United States be discoverable under the laws of the foreign jurisdiction. The magistrate judge reasoned that since Canadian authorities are not allowed to compel witness testimony in domestic criminal investigations at the pre-charge stage, such testimony cannot be compelled in this case by virtue of this circuit's construction of 28 U.S.C. § 1782. Second, the magistrate judge focused on the second paragraph of section 1782(a) which explicitly states that "a person may not be compelled to give his testimony . . . in violation of any legally applicable privilege." The magistrate judge held that the inability under Canadian law to compel witness testimony in a criminal investigation prior to the filing of formal charges amounted to a "legally applicable privilege" and therefore, for this additional reason, the appellees could not be compelled to provide the testimony. On behalf of the Canadian authorities, the appointed commissioner and the United States sought reconsideration of the magistrate judge's ruling in the district court. After further briefing by the parties, the district court affirmed the magistrate judge's order quashing the subpoenas, finding the magistrate judge's order not "clearly erroneous or contrary to law." The district court entered a final order quashing the subpoenas. . . . This Court reviews de novo the district court's interpretation of a treaty or federal statute. . . .

We must decide whether the magistrate judge correctly interpreted the MLAT between the United States and Canada. That question turns on the intended role of 28 U.S.C. § 1782 in requests for assistance under the MLAT. The precise issue facing this court is whether the MLAT permits, at the request of Canada, the issuance of subpoenas and the taking of compelled testimony in a pre-charge Canadian criminal investigation of seven witnesses who reside in the Southern District of Florida. . . .

To decide the question presented, we turn to fundamental principles of treaty construction and interpretation. The goal of treaty interpretation is to determine the actual intention of the parties "because it is our responsibility to give the specific words of the treaty a meaning consistent with the shared expectations of the contracting parties." *Air France v. Saks*, 470 U.S. 392, 399, 105 S. Ct. 1338, 1342, 84 L. Ed.

2d 289 (1985). The analysis of the parties' intentions "begin[s] with the text of the treaty and the context in which the written words are used." . . . The clear import of treaty language controls unless application of the words of the treaty according to their obvious meaning effects a result inconsistent with the intent or expectations of its signatories." *Sumitomo Shoji America, Inc. v. Avagliano*, 457 U.S. 176, 180, 102 S. Ct. 2374, 2377, 72 L. Ed. 2d 765 (1982). . . .

Upon our reading of the text of this Treaty, we conclude that the magistrate judge erred in construing the MLAT to express a clear and unambiguous intent to make requests under the Treaty subject to the limitations of all other substantive law of the United States including 28 U.S.C. § 1782. Undeniably, the magistrate judge's interpretation finds some support in the treaty text. As the magistrate judge points out, Article VII, P 2 states that "[a] request shall be executed in accordance with the law of the Requested State and, to the extent not prohibited by the law of the Requested State." While not mentioned by the magistrate judge, Article XII, P 1 also contains a similar reference to the "law of the Requested State." Those two sentences, if read in isolation, arguably incorporate the substantive limitations of 28 U.S.C. § 1782 as a law of the United States. And as discussed above, that statute has been held to implicitly require a showing of foreign discoverability, at least in the traditional case involving a letter rogatory or letter of request. Given the fact acknowledged by all parties that Canada lacks the power to compel the taking of testimony in a pre-charge setting, the application of a foreign discoverability requirement to MLAT requests by Canada would deny the court the power to grant Canada the type of assistance sought in this case. But when the entire Treaty is read in context, we conclude that other language in its text, apparently overlooked in the lower court, suggests an alternate, reasonable, construction of the "law of the Requested State" phrases contained in Articles VII and XII of the MLAT. . . .

[W]e conclude that the treaty text is ambiguous with respect to the propriety of Canadian requests under the Treaty for assistance regarding pre-charge compelled testimony in a criminal investigation. We are presented with two reasonable alternative interpretations: on the one hand, the "law of the Requested State" might incorporate all the laws of the Requested State, including laws that provide standards for granting or denying requests made by way of a letter rogatory or letter of request; on the other hand, the "law of the Requested State" might only refer to the laws providing the ways and means for executing valid MLAT requests for assistance. "Where the text — read in the context of its structure and purpose — is ambiguous, we may resort to extraneous tools of interpretation." . . . "Treaties are construed more liberally than private agreements, and to ascertain their meaning we may look beyond the written words to the history of the treaty, the negotiations, and the practical construction adopted by the parties." . . .

While the foregoing reasoning has led us to conclude that the text of the Treaty is ambiguous with respect to the instant issue, affording two reasonable interpretations, we conclude that our ultimate construction is decidedly the more plausible of the two. We conclude that the most logical construction of the phrase "law of the

Requested State" in the MLAT is that the Treaty partners intended to utilize the established procedures set forth in the existing laws of the Requested State to execute the treaty requests, rather than to subject each and every treaty request to any and all limitations of existing law of the Requested State. That is, the Treaty utilizes § 1782 as a procedure for executing requests, but not as a means for deciding whether or not to grant or deny a request so made. This construction is more plausible primarily because of Article V, which delineates only narrowly confined circumstances in which the Requested State "may deny assistance." ...

The treaty negotiations and ratification history, fundamental canons of treaty construction, and analogous cases construing similar language in the text of other treaties also point strongly to our ultimate construction.... [The court describes two basis of support for its interpretation].... Another provision of the Treaty lends additional support to this interpretation. Article II of the MLAT, entitled "Scope of Application," contains a provision rejecting the rule of "dual criminality." "Dual criminality" is the rule that the offense for which the foreign state seeks assistance must also constitute a crime in the requested state. Article II, P 3 explicitly provides that "[a]ssistance shall be provided without regard to whether the conduct under investigation or prosecution in the Requesting State constitutes an offence or may be prosecuted by the Requested State." The negotiators state in the Technical Analysis that "[b]y avoiding a dual criminality provision in this Treaty, the United States expects to receive assistance for such important crimes as, for instance, money laundering, even though Canada has yet to enact similar legislation." ... This provision makes clear an intent that requests for assistance not be routinely impeded or denied by virtue of the Requested State's own laws.... Therefore, if Article VII, P 2 is read as the appellees contend, dual criminality provision will be brought into the Treaty through the back door. On the other hand, construing Article VII, P 2 as we do to refer only to the procedures and methods of executing a request and taking evidence pursuant to such a request is completely consistent with and in no way undermines Article II's rejection of the dual criminality rule....

Interpreting the MLAT to subject each and every request to the existing substantive law of the requested state runs contrary to another fundamental principle of treaty interpretation. "Treaties that lay down rules to be enforced by the parties through their internal courts or administrative agencies should be construed so as to achieve uniformity of result despite differences between national legal systems." Restatement (Third) of Foreign Relations § 325 cmt. d; *United States v. Lombera-Camorlinga*, 206 F.3d 882, 888 (9th Cir. 2000). Obviously, the United States and Canada have their own domestic substantive law. Consequently, under the appellees' construction of the MLAT, the viability of requests under the Treaty would often turn on which country is entertaining the request, even if the information requested is identical.

We find no statements anywhere in the text of the Treaty or its negotiation and ratification history to suggest that the parties did not intend the obligations to be reciprocal and uniform. In fact, a desire for uniform treatment of similar requests made by the two countries underlies the decision to enter into the MLAT in the first place. The Treaty's ratification history reveals that in conjunction with signing the Treaty, Canada enacted implementing legislation to give its courts the authority to execute requests from the United States for assistance in criminal investigations prior to the filing of formal charges....

Prior to the MLAT, because Canada's domestic law prohibited compelled testimony from witnesses prior to charges being filed, assistance was denied to authorities from the United States. The MLACMA was enacted along with the MLAT "to remove the legal barrier and permit (indeed, obligate) Canada to provide assistance prior to indictment... [and make] assistance available at the investigative stage." That legislation was intended to make sure that there would be no remaining legal impediments to MLAT requests made back-and-forth between the two countries.

If the circumstances were reversed in this case and the United States sought this type of assistance from the Canadian courts, such assistance would seemingly be available under the MLAT by virtue of the Canadian implementing legislation. This treaty negotiation and ratification history makes clear that uniformity and reciprocity regarding requests for assistance in criminal matters were a vital concern of the two countries in entering into the MLAT. That is precisely what the United States was seeking to accomplish in requiring Canada to enact the implementing legislation along with the MLAT.... Nevertheless, the appellees urge us to construe this Treaty in a way that destroys the uniformity and reciprocity that the treaty drafters intended to create by requiring Canada to adopt this implementing legislation concurrent with the Treaty. We cannot faithfully construe the Treaty in such a manner....

The purposes and objectives stated in the Treaty's preamble supports an interpretation of the MLAT that allows the issuance of subpoenas at the request of Canada to compel testimony of witnesses pursuant to a criminal investigation occurring prior to the filing of formal charges. The Preamble of the MLAT states that it was created out of a desire "to improve the effectiveness of both countries in the investigation, prosecution and suppression of crime through cooperation and mutual assistance in law enforcement matters." MLAT, Preamble. We agree with the appellant that if the MLAT is read to only allow assistance that is already obtainable through the letter rogatory process, it would have accomplished very little. While such a reading would at least allow the Treaty to serve to make assistance between the two countries part of a binding agreement, the scope of assistance would be unchanged, rendering the Treaty of little practical significance and no great improvement would have been achieved in the area of international criminal investigation and prosecution....

Appellees' also argue in their brief that they enjoy a privilege under Canadian domestic law to remain silent and refuse to give compelled testimony as a witness in a pre-charge criminal investigation. This argument is based upon the second paragraph of 28 U.S.C. § 1782(a) which provides that "[a] person may not be compelled to give his testimony or statement or to produce a document or other thing in violation of any legally applicable privilege." The appellees correctly note that the legislative history makes clear that this language embraces privileges recognized by foreign law." S. Rep. 1580, 88th Cong., 2d Sess. (1964), reprinted in U.S.C.C.A.N. 3782, 3790. Therefore, if this case involved a letter of request brought under 28 U.S.C. § 1782, then this court would have to ascertain whether the inability of a Canadian court in a domestic criminal pre-charge investigation to compel witness testimony amounts to a "legally applicable privilege" under Canadian law.

But we need not determine whether appellees had a "legally applicable privilege" under Canadian law. The Canadian request in this case was made pursuant to an MLAT rather than a letter of request under 28 U.S.C. § 1782. And for all the reasons already discussed in this opinion, we do not read the MLAT to incorporate and subject itself to the substantive law of the Requested State including 28 U.S.C. § 1782(a) and its "legally applicable privilege" limitation. Like the foreign discoverability requirement which, according to this Circuit, is an implicit part of 28 U.S.C. § 1782 at least with respect to letters of request and letter rogatory cases, the "legally applicable privilege" is an explicit part of section 1782 but does not control the resolution of this case for the reasons above discussed.

Our conclusion in this particular case is supported by the ratification history which provides that "[t]he parties agreed that questions concerning the applicability of privileges provided by the law of the Requesting State would be preserved for consideration by the courts of that State." . . .

In closing, we must emphasize that we have not abandoned this circuit's holding in *Trinidad and Tobago*, 848 F.2d 1151, 1156 (11th Cir. 1988). We in no way alter or amend its holding that letters of request made pursuant to 28 U.S.C. § 1782 in a criminal investigation require a showing that the information sought is discoverable in the foreign country. Nor could we as a panel do that in any event. . . . This case is simply distinguishable as it involves an MLAT request rather than a letter of request under 28 U.S.C. § 1782. Because the MLAT obligates both countries to provide the assistance in this case regardless of whether the information sought would actually be discoverable in the requesting state, we find *Trinidad and Tobago* inapplicable. . . .

For the foregoing reasons, we hold that the information sought by Canada in this case, subpoena-compelled testimony pursuant to a Canadian criminal investigation occurring prior to the filing of formal charges, was within the scope of the two countries' obligations under the MLAT. Consequently, the subpoenas should not have been quashed. Accordingly, we VACATE the order of the district court quashing the commissioner's subpoenas. On receipt of our mandate, the district court shall enter an appropriate order enforcing the subpoenas. . . .

Notes

(1) A U.S. Department of State list of treaties in force as of January 1, 2020, contains reference to 75 mutual legal assistance treaties. *See* Treaties in Force, U.S. Department of State (January 1, 2020), available at https://www.state.gov/wp-content/uploads/2020/08/TIF-2020-Full-website-view.pdf On their history, see *In re 840 140th Ave, NE*, 634 F.3d 557, 563–64 (9th Cir. 2011).

(2) In *Commissioner's Subpoenas*, the court comments that "Despite the apparent versatility of 28 U.S.C. § 1782, law enforcement authorities found the statute to be an unattractive option in practice because it provided wide discretion in the district court to refuse the request and did not obligate other nations to return the favor that it grants." In respect both of "versatility" and the discretion of the district court, *see Intel Corp. v. Advanced Micro Devices, Inc.*, 542 U.S. 241 (2004). Speaking for the Court, Justice Ginsburg said:

> This case concerns the authority of federal district courts to assist in the production of evidence for use in a foreign or international tribunal. In the matter before us, respondent Advanced Micro Devices, Inc. (AMD) filed an antitrust complaint against petitioner Intel Corporation (Intel) with the Directorate-General for Competition of the Commission of the European Communities (European Commission or Commission). In pursuit of that complaint, AMD applied to the United States District Court for the Northern District of California, invoking 28 U. S. C. § 1782(a), for an order requiring Intel to produce potentially relevant documents. Section 1782(a) provides that a federal district court "may order" a person "resid[ing]" or "found" in the district to give testimony or produce documents "for use in a proceeding in a foreign or international tribunal . . . upon the application of any interested person."
>
> Concluding that § 1782(a) did not authorize the requested discovery, the District Court denied AMD's application. The Court of Appeals for the Ninth Circuit reversed that determination and remanded the case, instructing the District Court to rule on the merits of AMD's application. In accord with the Court of Appeals, we hold that the District Court had authority under § 1782(a) to entertain AMD's discovery request. The statute, we rule, does not categorically bar the assistance AMD seeks: (1) A complainant before the European Commission, such as AMD, qualifies as an "interested person" within § 1782(a)'s compass; (2) the Commission is a § 1782(a) "tribunal" when it acts as a first-instance decisionmaker; (3) the "proceeding" for which discovery is sought under § 1782(a) must be in reasonable contemplation, but need not be "pending" or "imminent"; and (4) § 1782(a) contains no threshold requirement that evidence sought from a federal district court would be discoverable under the law governing the foreign proceeding. We caution, however, that § 1782(a) authorizes, but does not require, a federal district court to provide judicial assistance to foreign or international tribunals or to "interested person[s]" in proceedings abroad. Whether such assistance is appropriate in this case is a question yet unresolved. To guide the District Court on remand, we suggest considerations relevant to the disposition of that question.

(3) Law enforcement investigations have grown increasingly complex in the digital age, where information is stored around the world in different electronic mediums. While MLATs offer a mechanism for United States law enforcement to access this

diverse and disseminated information, the complexities regarding accessing such data, including data privacy concerns, have created much confusion and many complications. *See* Jonah F. Hill, *Problematic Alternatives: MLAT Reform for the Digital Age*, Harvard Law School National Security Journal Online (Jan. 28, 2015). The government's concerns that MLATs are no longer efficient enough for the digital age is demonstrated in the "Microsoft-Ireland" case. In this case, the government sought data from a Microsoft Outlook email account based in Ireland as part of a narcotics investigation. Rather than using an MLAT, the government issued Microsoft a warrant for the materials. The company challenged the warrant, arguing that the materials were located in Ireland and that the warrant constituted an unauthorized extraterritorial application of the Electronic Communications Privacy Act of 1986's warrant provision (18 U.S.C. § 2703(a)). Instead of issuing a warrant, argued Microsoft, the government must utilize its existing treaties to secure the materials. The district court rejected Microsoft's arguments and held the company in contempt when it continued to refuse to produce the data. The case was then appealed to the United States Court of Appeals for the Second Circuit. In its brief to the Second Circuit, the government wrote:

> Microsoft and amici principally argue that the government should be required to rely on mutual legal assistance treaties ("MLATs"), rather than the compelled disclosure provisions of the SCA [Stored Communications Act], when seeking records stored abroad. There are at least four flaws in this argument. First, there is nothing in international law that requires the government to use an MLAT to obtain evidence located in a foreign country when other lawful means of obtaining the evidence are available. *See In re Grand Jury Subpoena*, 646 F.3d 159, 165 (4th Cir. 2011) (finding that MLAT was "not the exclusive means for the government to obtain documents from a party located in [a foreign] country"); *United States v. Rommy*, 506 F.3d 108, 129 (2d Cir. 2007) (finding that MLAT had "no application to evidence obtained outside the MLAT process"); *cf. United States v. Alvarez-Machain*, 504 U.S. 655, 664–67 (1992) (holding that a treaty does not prohibit actions "outside of its terms" where it "does not purport to specify the only way" in which the United States may accomplish a task); *Societe Nationale Industrielle Aerospatiale*, 482 U.S. at 542–43 ("A rule of first resort in all cases would therefore be inconsistent with the overriding interest in the just, speedy, and inexpensive determination of litigation in our courts." (internal quotation marks omitted)). Microsoft's view would upend these precedents and effectively require the Government to use an MLAT even though the SCA provides a far more efficient means of obtaining the relevant evidence.
>
> Second, most countries in the world do not have MLATs with the United States, and some MLATs are topic-restricted. A U.S. provider could easily choose to locate its user data in such a country either for legitimate business reasons or for the specific purpose of evading the reach of U.S. law enforcement. Such data would remain largely outside the court's power and the

prosecutor's reach even if the emails were sent by U.S. citizens within the United States and there was probable cause to believe that criminal activity was afoot. There is no reason to believe that Congress intended to exclude such plainly relevant evidence from the comprehensive disclosure framework established by the SCA.

Third, even when MLATs are available, they may be entirely ineffective if the records do not reside in any single country for very long. For example, a provider might move a particular user's data between servers in multiple countries for any number of reasons, including network maintenance or load-balancing reasons, a practice that is becoming increasingly common with the growth of cloud computing. In this case, for example, a Microsoft engineer described how "[s]everal times each day, Microsoft's backend software runs an automatic scan to determine whether newly-created accounts should be migrated to the Dublin datacenter." In light of this ease of mobility, the government would find itself unable to anticipate where data might reside at the time an MLAT could be served, and therefore unable to use an MLAT to compel the production of records. SCA warrants do not suffer from that limitation. They require providers, who know and control the location of the records, to disclose them upon receipt of a subpoena, order, or warrant.

Fourth, resort to an MLAT will hardly ever result in as prompt a disclosure of records as is available with an SCA warrant. In contrast to an SCA warrant, which can be served upon a provider immediately upon issuance by a judge, an MLAT request typically takes months to process, with the turnaround time varying widely based on the foreign country's willingness to cooperate, the law enforcement resources it has to spare for outside requests for assistance, and the procedural idiosyncrasies of the country's legal system. It is no accident that federal law specifically provides for an exclusion of time under the Speedy Trial Act (for up to a year), as well as the suspension of a criminal statute of limitations (for up to three years), while the government is waiting to receive foreign evidence in response to an MLAT request.

While Microsoft faults the District Court for giving undue weight to the negative effects Microsoft's construction of the SCA would have on the investigation and prosecution of criminals, that very real concern is fully entitled to the weight it received below. Email and other electronic communications are used extensively by criminals of all types in the United States and abroad, from fraudsters to hackers to drug dealers, in furtherance of violations of U.S. law. The ability to obtain electronically stored information from domestic service providers — pursuant to judicial authorization as required by the SCA — is a fundamental component of effective modern law enforcement. Yet such information, like the data sought by the Warrant here, can be maintained in any location and moved around the world easily,

> at any time and for any reason. Were Microsoft's position adopted, the government's ability to obtain such information from a provider would turn entirely on whether it happens to be stored here or abroad, even though the provider, based in the United States, maintains continuing control over the data wherever it may be stored at any given time. Such a regime would be rife with potential for arbitrary outcomes and criminal abuse.

Brief for the United States at 48–53, *Microsoft Corp. v. United States*, No. 14-2985 (2d Cir. March 9, 2015). Microsoft's brief stated:

> Law enforcement agents have been using MLATs and informal processes for decades to pursue all manner of evidence strewn all across the globe. If the Government needs to obtain any private papers from Ireland—mail in an envelope, documents in a safe deposit box, and the like—it relies on the MLAT or other bilateral arrangements to do so. When an international crime syndicate leaves such evidence behind in multiple countries, as they often do, agents engage with multiple governments. There is no reason why digital letters should be treated differently from physical letters or why Ireland's sovereign interests are diminished when letters are not written in ink.
>
> Any complaints the Government has about the MLAT process should be addressed by reforming the MLAT process, rather than distorting § 2703(a)'s text. But the evidence refutes the district court's concerns. Ireland has implemented its MLAT obligations with "highly effective" legislation that is "efficient and well-functioning." . . .
>
> The district court's ruling will encourage foreign governments to sidestep their own MLAT commitments and unilaterally seek data stored in the United States from providers that operate in their jurisdictions. Indeed, Brazil has recently enacted legislation expressly imposing its privacy rules on all internet companies with at least one Brazilian user. As foreign countries increasingly assert unilateral jurisdiction over data stored in the United States, the primary objective of ECPA—protecting U.S. citizens' most private electronic information—will be thwarted.
>
> The Government's unilateral exercise of law enforcement powers in Ireland also puts at risk the U.S. information technology sector's continued ability to operate and compete globally. Foreign leaders have expressed concern about the district court's expansive interpretation of ECPA, and noted that compliance with extraterritorial U.S. search warrants may cause providers to be "caught in the middle" of a "conflict" between U.S. criminal law and the data protection laws of the countries where the targeted data is stored.
>
> Microsoft has also encountered rising concerns among both current and potential customers overseas about the Government's extraterritorial access to their information. In some instances, potential customers—specifically referencing the decision below—have decided not to purchase

> services from Microsoft and have opted instead for a provider based outside the United States. The opinion below threatens to undermine the U.S. technology sector's competitive edge.

Brief for Appellant at 57–60, *Microsoft Corp. v. United States*, No. 14-2985 (2d Cir. Dec. 8, 2014). Eventually, the Second Circuit "reversed the denial of the motion to quash and vacated the civil contempt finding, holding that requiring Microsoft to disclose the electronic communications in question would be an unauthorized extraterritorial application of § 2703." *United States v. Microsoft Corp.*, 584 U.S. __, 138 S. Ct. 1186 (2018). The case was then appealed to the Supreme Court. Before the Court could rule, however, Congress intervened. From the Supreme Court decision dismissing the action.

> The parties now advise us that on March 23, 2018, Congress enacted and the President signed into law the Clarifying Lawful Overseas Use of Data Act (CLOUD Act), as part of the Consolidated Appropriations Act, 2018, Pub. L. 11-141. The CLOUD Act amends the Stored Communications Act, 18 U.S.C. § 2701 et seq., by adding the following provision: "A [service provider] shall comply with the obligations of this chapter to preserve, backup, or disclose the contents of a wire or electronic communication and any record or other information pertaining to a customer or subscriber within such provider's possession, custody, or control, regardless of whether such communication, record, or other information is located within or outside of the United States." CLOUD Act § 103(a)(1). Soon thereafter, the Government obtained, pursuant to the new law, a new § 2703 warrant covering the information requested in the § 2703 warrant at issue in this case.

United States v. Microsoft Corp., 138 S. Ct. 1187–88.

The CLOUD Act did more than simply address the specific issue raised in the Microsoft-Ireland case. The Act also addressed larger issues regarding the global importance of electronic evidence, the growing difficulty of responding to large volumes of MLAT requests for such information, and the need for data privacy considerations. The U.S. Department of Justice describes the significance of the Act as follows:

> The United States enacted the Clarifying Lawful Overseas Use of Data (CLOUD) Act in March 2018 to speed access to electronic information held by U.S.-based global providers that is critical to our foreign partners' investigations of serious crime, ranging from terrorism and violent crime to sexual exploitation of children and cybercrime.
>
> In recent years, the number of mutual legal assistance requests seeking electronic evidence from the United States has increased dramatically, straining resources and slowing response times. Foreign authorities have relatedly expressed a need for increased speed in obtaining this evidence. In addition, many of the assistance requests the United States receives seek electronic information related to individuals or entities located in other

> countries, and the only connection of the investigation to the United States is that the evidence happens to be held by a U.S.-based global provider. The CLOUD Act is designed to permit our foreign partners that have robust protections for privacy and civil liberties to enter into bilateral agreements with the United States to obtain direct access to this electronic evidence, wherever it happens to be located, in order to fight serious crime and terrorism.
>
> The CLOUD Act thus represents a new paradigm: an efficient, privacy and civil liberties-protective approach to ensure effective access to electronic data that lies beyond a requesting country's reach due to the revolution in electronic communications, recent innovations in the way global technology companies configure their systems, and the legacy of 20th century legal frameworks. The CLOUD Act authorizes bilateral agreements between the United States and trusted foreign partners that will make both nations' citizens safer, while at the same time ensuring a high level of protection of those citizens' rights.

Cloud Act Resources, U.S. Department of Justice (last updated August 20, 2021), available at https://www.justice.gov/dag/cloudact. The CLOUD Act's authorization of executive agreements between the United States and foreign governments to more quickly share data signals a new shift in evidence gathering procedures. Where once the MLAT was considered the faster alternative to the Letters Rogatory, the MLAT is now viewed as a slower and more cumbersome option when compared to an executive agreement. Such executive agreements also offer the possibility of addressing the complexities sometimes experienced by companies seeking to respond to U.S. requests for information held in countries with strict data privacy laws that may limit such dissemination outside the bounds of an executive agreement of this kind. The U.S. and U.K. entered into the first such executive agreement on October 3, 2019. The U.S. and Australia entered into such an agreement on December 15, 2021. Of the U.S.-Australia agreement, the DOJ stated:

> The CLOUD Act Agreement will help ensure Australian and U.S. law enforcement agencies are able to timely access electronic data to prevent, detect, investigate and prosecute serious crime, including child sexual abuse, ransomware attacks, terrorism and the sabotage of critical infrastructure over the internet.
>
> The CLOUD Act Agreement enables authorities in each country to obtain certain electronic data more efficiently from communications service providers operating in the other's jurisdiction, thereby significantly reducing the time taken to obtain information relevant to ongoing investigations. The agreement also includes strong protections for the rule of law, privacy and civil liberties.

United States and Australia Enter CLOUD Act Agreement to Facilitate Investigations of Serious Crime, Department of Justice News Release (Dec. 15, 2021). It is likely that the use of such executive agreements will continue to grow in the coming years in this and other areas of evidence collection.

(4) The 2015 International Narcotics Control Strategy Report comments that the United States has also entered into numerous executive agreements on forfeiture cooperation. The Report notes:

> From Fiscal Year (FY) 1989 through FY 2014, the international asset sharing program administered by the Department of Justice shared $249,543,192 with 46 countries. In FY 2014, DOJ shared a total of $9,446,826 with ten countries and shared with the Czech Republic, Italy, Sweden, and Turks and Caicos Islands for the first time. Prior recipients of shared assets include: Anguilla, Antigua and Barbuda, Argentina, Bahamas, Barbados, Belgium, Bermuda, British Virgin Islands, Canada, Cayman Islands, Colombia, Costa Rica, Dominican Republic, Ecuador, Egypt, Germany, Greece, Guatemala, Guernsey, Honduras, Hong Kong, Hungary, Indonesia, Ireland, Isle of Man, Israel, Jersey, Jordan, Liechtenstein, Luxembourg, Mexico, Netherlands Antilles, Panama, Paraguay, Peru, Romania, South Africa, Switzerland, Thailand, Turkey, the United Kingdom, Uruguay, and Venezuela.
>
> Treasury's Financial Crimes Enforcement Network (FinCEN) is part of a global network of more than 100 FIUs [Financial Intelligence Units], known as the Egmont Group. Through this network, FinCEN can facilitate information exchange on law enforcement investigations that have an international component.

- These FIUs were created to collect information on suspicious or unusual financial activity, to analyze that data, and to make it available to appropriate authorities.
- Law Enforcement agencies can submit requests to FinCEN for information from its global partners that can significantly expand their knowledge of financial activities and reduce delays often associated with international investigative efforts.
- FinCEN's staff has developed in-depth knowledge of FIU partner countries, and established relationships with FIU personnel that can be shared/utilized to enhance investigative efforts.

See https://2009-2017.state.gov/j/inl/rls/nrcrpt/2015/index.htm.

(5) While the first three MLATS entered into by the United States (Switzerland, Turkey, and the Netherlands) included provisions for defendants to utilize the MLAT process to collect evidence, this practice quickly disappeared, and the Department of Justice has opposed the use of MLATs by criminal defendants. *See* T. Markus Funk, *Mutual Legal Assistance Treaties and Letters Rogatory: A Guide for Judges*, Federal Judicial Center (2014); Michael Abbell, *DOJ Renews Assault on Defendants' Right to Use Treaties to Obtain Evidence from Abroad*, 21 CHAMPION 20

(1997). Defendants have also failed in raising issues regarding purported treaty violations. In *United States v. Davis*, 767 F.2d 1025 (2d Cir. 1985), Senior District Judge Palmieri stated:

> That Davis has no standing to raise a purported violation of Article 18, Paragraph 5 of the Treaty in this context is made absolutely clear by both the interpretative letters signed by the United States and Switzerland and by the Technical Analysis of the Treaty. The interpretative letters signed on May 25, 1973 provide that it is the understanding of the United States and Swiss governments that a person alleging a violation of Article 5 of the Treaty (which deals with limitations on the use of information obtained pursuant to the Treaty) "has no standing to have such allegations considered in any proceeding in the United States.... His recourse would be for him to inform the Central Authority of Switzerland for consideration only as a matter between governments." ... The Technical Analysis provides that "restrictions in the Treaty shall not give rise to a right of any person to take action to suppress or exclude evidence or to obtain judicial relief." *Technical Analysis of the Treaty Between the United States and Switzerland on Mutual Assistance in Criminal Matters* (reprinted in *Message from the President Transmitting the Treaty with the Swiss Confederation on Mutual Assistance in Criminal Matters*, 94th Cong., 2d Sess. at 63–64 (1976)). *See Cardenas v. Smith*, 733 F.2d 909, 918 (D.C. Cir. 1984). More generally, this Court has written that "even where a treaty provides certain benefits for nationals of a particular state—such as fishing rights—it is traditionally held that 'any rights arising from such provisions are, under international law, those of states and ... individual rights are only derivative through the states.'" *United States Ex Rel. Lujan v. Gengler*, 510 F.2d 62, 67 (2d Cir.), *cert. denied*, 421 U.S. 1001, 95 S. Ct. 2400, 44 L. Ed. 2d 668 (1975), quoting *Restatement (Second) of the Foreign Relations Law of the United States* §115, comment e (1965) (criminal defendant abducted in Bolivia and brought to the United States for trial had no standing to raise violation of the charters of the United Nations and the Organization of American States in the absence of protest by a signatory state). *See also United States v. Reed*, 639 F.2d 896, 902 (2d Cir. 1981) (criminal defendant abducted in Bahamas in violation of extradition treaty had no standing to raise its violation in absence of protest by the Bahamas).

Id. at 1029–30. There, however, may be standing to raise a deprivation of a constitutional right when there is a violation of a mutual assistance treaty. *See United States v. Sturman*, 951 F.2d 1466 (6th Cir. 1992) (court found that since defendants had not been deprived of their constitutional rights, there was no need to consider whether they had standing to raise these claims).

(6) There has also been a growing use of "mini-MLATS." These are mutual legal assistance treaties that "have specialized issues relating to the specific substantive areas concerned," such as drugs. Bruce Zagaris, *Uncle Sam Extends Rearch for Evidence Worldwide*, 15 CRIM. JUST. 5 (Winter 2001).

(7) On 4 June 2008, the International Court of Justice issued its Judgment in the *Case Concerning Certain Questions of Mutual Assistance in Criminal Matters* (Djibouti v. France), 2008 I.C.J. 177 available at https://www.icj-cij.org/en/case/136.

The decision contains an interesting discussion of various aspects of a 1986 Convention on Mutual Assistance in Criminal Matters between the parties. In particular, the Court considers the power of a Requested State to refuse assistance on the ground, commonly found in such treaties, that it considers that "execution of the request is likely to prejudice its sovereignty, its *ordre public* or others of its essential interests." Can a reviewing court go beyond the State's assertions to this effect? How does the general treaty obligation to act in "good faith" play out here? In a concurring Declaration, Judge Keith noted that:

> And counsel for France accepted that the principles of abuse of rights and misuse of power (*abus de droit* and *détournment de pouvoir*) may be relevant to the exercise of the power in issue in this case. The Agent added that, while the requested State retains for itself a wide discretion, this in no way means that States indiscriminately invoke these derogation clauses; it is moreover obvious, she said, that the notion of essential interests remains very narrow, as the words themselves indicate.

The Court also considers the parameters of the treaty obligation to give reasons for a refusal of assistance and, indeed, finds France in breach of that obligation. There is also some useful, but ultimately inconclusive, discussion of the nature of immunities of the Head of State and other officials when it comes to requesting their appearance to give testimony in domestic proceedings.

B. MLAT Issues: Boston College, the IRA, and the British

Efforts by the British authorities to gain access to oral history material concerning the IRA have given rise to a series of decisions in the First Circuit Court of Appeals. Fundamental questions about research privilege, the confidentiality of scholarly data and the First Amendment were raised in addition to significant MLAT issues. Below are some extracts of MLAT issues that have been raised:

United States v. Moloney, In re Dolours Price

United States Court of Appeals for the First Circuit
685 F.3d 1 (2012), cert den., 2013 U.S. LEXIS 2757 (Apr. 15, 2013)

These consolidated appeals are from the denial, in two cases, of the efforts of two academic researchers to prevent the execution of two sets of subpoenas issued in May and August of 2011. The subpoenas were issued to Boston College ("BC") by a commissioner appointed pursuant to 18 U.S.C. § 3512 and the "US-UK MLAT," the mutual legal assistance treaty between the United States and the United Kingdom. The subpoenas are part of an investigation by United Kingdom authorities into the 1972 abduction and death of Jean McConville, who was thought to have acted as an informer for the British authorities on the activities of republicans in Northern Ireland. This appears to be the first court of appeals decision to deal with an MLAT and § 3512.

The May 2011 subpoenas sought oral history recordings and associated documentation from interviews BC researchers had conducted with two former members of the Irish Republican Army ("IRA"): Dolours Price and Brendan Hughes. BC turned over the Hughes materials because he had died and so he had no confidentiality interests at stake. BC moved to quash or modify the Price subpoenas. The second set of subpoenas issued in August 2011 sought any information related to the death or abduction of McConville contained in any of the other interview materials held by BC. BC moved to quash these subpoenas as well. . . .

The appellants here, Ed Moloney and Anthony McIntyre, who unsuccessfully sought to intervene in BC's case on both sets of subpoenas, pursue in the first appeal a challenge to the district court's denial of their motions to intervene as of right and for permissive intervention. Their intervention complaint largely repeated the claims made by BC and sought declarations that the Attorney General's compliance with the United Kingdom's request violates the US-UK MLAT and injunctive relief or mandamus compelling him to comply with the terms of that treaty. The effect of the relief sought would be to impede the execution of the subpoenas.

. . . .

The United States has entered into a number of mutual legal assistance treaties ("MLATs") which typically provide for bilateral, mutual assistance in the gathering of legal evidence for use by the requesting state in criminal investigations and proceedings. A description of the history and evolution of such MLATs may be found in the Ninth Circuit's decision in *In re 840 140th Ave. NE*, 634 F.3d 557, 563–64 (9th Cir. 2011).

The MLAT between the United States and the United Kingdom was signed on January 6, 1994, and entered into force on December 2, 1996. *See* Treaty Between the Government of the United States and the Government of the United Kingdom of Great Britain and Northern Ireland on Mutual Legal Assistance in Criminal Matters, U.S.-U.K., Dec. 2, 1996, S. Treaty Doc. No. 104-2. In 2003, the United States signed a mutual legal assistance treaty with the European Union ("US-EU MLAT") that made additions and amendments to the US-UK MLAT; the latter is in turn included as an annex to the US-EU MLAT. *See* Agreement on Mutual Legal Assistance Between the United States of America and the European Union, U.S.-E.U., June 25, 2003, S. Treaty Doc. No. 109–13. Both MLATs are self-executing treaties. S. Treaty Doc. No. 109–13, at vii ("The U.S.-EU Mutual Legal Assistance Agreement and bilateral instruments [including the annexed US-UK MLAT] are regarded as self-executing treaties under U.S. law . . .").

Article 1 of the US-UK MLAT provides that the parties to the agreement shall assist one another in taking testimony of persons; providing documents, records, and evidence; serving documents; locating or identifying persons; transferring persons in custody for testimony or other purposes; executing requests for searches and seizures; identifying, tracing, freezing, seizing, and forfeiting the proceeds and instrumentalities of crime; and providing other assistance the parties' representatives may agree upon. *See* US-UK MLAT, art. 1, 2.

Importantly, article 1 further states: "This treaty is intended solely for mutual legal assistance between the Parties. The provisions of this Treaty shall not give rise to a right on the part of any private person to obtain, suppress, or exclude any evidence, or to impede the execution of a request." US-UK MLAT, art. 1, 3. This treaty expressly prohibits the creation of private rights of action.

Article 2 concerns Central Authorities: each party's representative responsible for making and receiving requests under the US-UK MLAT. US-UK MLAT, art. 2, 3. The treaty states that the Central Authority for the United States is "the Attorney General or a person or agency designated by him." US-UK MLAT, art. 2, 2. Article 3 sets forth certain conditions under which the Central Authority of the Requested Party may refuse assistance.[7] Before the Central Authority of a Requested Party denies assistance for any of the listed reasons, the treaty states that he or she "shall consult with the Central Authority of the Requesting Party to consider whether assistance can be given subject to such conditions as it deems necessary." US-UK MLAT, art. 3, 2.

In article 18, entitled "Consultation," the treaty states that [t]he Parties, or Central Authorities, shall consult promptly, at the request of either, concerning the implementation of this Treaty either generally or in relation to a particular case. Such consultation may in particular take place if . . . either Party has rights or obligations under another bilateral or multilateral agreement relating to the subject matter of this Treaty. US-UK MLAT, art. 18, 1. The requests from the United Kingdom in this case were executed under 18 U.S.C. § 3512, which was enacted as part of the Foreign Evidence Request Efficiency Act of 2009, Pub. L. No. 111-79, 123 Stat. 2086. When the US-UK MLAT was entered into, requests for assistance were to be executed under a different statute, 28 U.S.C. § 1782. *See* S. Exec. Rep. No. 104–23, at 13 (1996) (report of the Senate Committee on Foreign Relations accompanying the US-UK MLAT). Among other differences, § 3512 provides for a more streamlined process than under § 1782 for executing requests from foreign governments related to the prosecution of

---

7. Article 3, paragraph one states that [t]he Central Authority of the Requested Party may refuse assistance if: (a) the Requested Party is of the opinion that the request, if granted, would impair its sovereignty, security, or other essential interests or would be contrary to important public policy; (b) the request relates to an offender who, if proceeded against in the Requested Party for the offense for which assistance is requested, would be entitled to be discharged on the grounds of previous acquittal or conviction; or (c) the request relates to an offense that is regarded by the Requested Party as: (i) an offense of a political character; or (ii) an offense under military law of the Requested Party which is not also an offense under the ordinary civilian law of the Requested Party. US-UK MLAT, art. 3.

criminal offenses.[8] Enforcement of similar MLATs under the provisions of § 1782 was the subject of consideration in *In re 840 140th Ave. NE*, 634 F.3d 557 (9th Cir. 2011); *In re Commissioner's Subpoenas*, 325 F.3d 1287 (11th Cir. 2003), *abrogated in part by Intel Corp. v. Advanced Micro Devices, Inc.*, 542 U.S. 241 (2004); and *In re Erato*, 2 F.3d 11 (2d Cir. 1993) . . .

Interpretation of the treaty takes place against "the background presumption . . . that '[i]nternational agreements, even those directly benefitting private persons, generally do not create rights or provide for a private cause of action in domestic courts.'" *Medellín v. Texas*, 552 U.S. 491, 128 S.Ct. 1346, 1357 n.3 (2008) (alteration in original) (quoting 2 Restatement (Third) of Foreign Relations Law of the United States § 907 cmt. a, at 395 (1986)). The First Circuit and other courts of appeals have held that "treaties do not generally create rights that are privately enforceable in the federal courts." *United States v. Li*, 206 F.3d 56, 60 (1st Cir. 2000) (en banc); *see also Mora v. New York*, 524 F.3d 183, 201 & n.25 (2d Cir. 2008) (collecting cases from ten circuits holding that there is a presumption that treaties do not create privately enforceable rights in the absence of express language to the contrary). Express language in a treaty creating private rights can overcome this presumption. *See Mora*, 524 F.3d at 188.

The US-UK MLAT contains no express language creating private rights. To the contrary, the treaty expressly states that it does not give rise to any private rights. Article 1, paragraph 3 of the treaty states, in full: "This treaty is intended solely for mutual legal assistance between the Parties. The provisions of this Treaty shall not give rise to a right on the part of any private person to obtain, suppress, or exclude any evidence, or to impede the execution of a request." US-UK MLAT, art. 1, 3. The language of the treaty is clear: a "private person," such as Moloney or McIntyre here, does not have any right under the treaty to "suppress . . . any evidence, or to impede the execution of a request."

If there were any doubt, and there is none, the report of the Senate Committee on Foreign Relations that accompanied the US-UK MLAT confirms this reading of the treaty's text:

> [T]he Treaty is not intended to create any rights to impede execution of requests or to suppress or exclude evidence obtained thereunder. Thus, a person from whom records are sought may not oppose the execution of

8. Section 1782 effectively requires the Attorney General as Central Authority to respond to requests for evidence from foreign governments by filing requests with the district court in every district in which evidence or a witness may be found. *See* 155 Cong. Rec. S6810 (daily ed. June 18, 2009) (letter from Acting Assistant Att'y Gen. Burton to Sen. Whitehouse). In practice this requires involving multiple U.S. Attorneys' Offices and district courts in a single case. *Id.* Section 3512, on the other hand, permits a single Assistant United States Attorney to pursue requests in multiple judicial districts, *see* 18 U.S.C. § 3512(a)(1); 155 Cong. Rec. S6809 (daily ed. June 18, 2009) (statement of Sen. Whitehouse), and allows individual district court judges to oversee and approve subpoenas and other orders (but not search warrants) in districts other than their own, see 18 U.S.C. § 3512(f).

the request by claiming that it does not comply with the Treaty's formal requirements set out in article 3. S. Exec. Rep. No. 104-23, at 14.

Other courts considering MLATs containing terms similar to the US-UK MLAT here have uniformly ruled that no such private right exists. . . . Moloney and McIntyre attempt to get around the prohibition on the creation of private causes of action with three arguments based on the treaty language. Appellants appear to argue that the text of the US-UK MLAT only covers requests for documents in the possession of the Requested Party but not for documents held by third persons who are merely under the jurisdiction of the government which is the Requested Party. This is clearly wrong. Article 1, paragraph 2 of the treaty states that a form of assistance provided for under the treaty includes "providing documents, records, and evidence." US-UK MLAT, art. 1, 2(b). As the Senate report explains, the treaty "permits a State to compel a person in the Requested State to testify and produce documents there." S. Exec. Rep. No. 104-23, at 7.

Appellants' second argument is that article 1, paragraph 3 applies only to criminal defendants who try to block enforcement. This argument has no support in the text of the treaty. The US–UK MLAT plainly states that the treaty does not "give rise to a right on the part of *any private person* . . . to impede the execution of a request." US-UK MLAT, art. 1, 3 (emphasis added). This prohibition by its terms encompasses all private persons, not just criminal defendants.

Appellants finally contend that they do not seek to "obtain, suppress, or exclude any evidence, or to impede the execution of a request," but instead merely to enforce the treaty requirements before there can be compliance with a subpoena. Their own requests for relief make it clear they are attempting to do exactly what they say they are not. Because the US-UK MLAT expressly disclaims the existence of any private rights under the treaty, appellants cannot state a claim under the treaty upon which relief can be granted.

In re: Request from the United Kingdom Pursuant to the Treaty Between the Government of the United States of America and the Government of the United Kingdom on Mutual Assistance

United States Court of Appeals for the First Circuit
718 F.3d 13 (2013)

[In another round of the litigation, the First Circuit addressed federal court discretion to quash MLAT-issued subpoenas]:

[I]n *In re Dolours Price*, we explicitly declined to pass judgment upon the question of federal court discretion to review motions to quash subpoenas under the US-UK MLAT. We now address this question directly. Pursuant to Article 3 of the US-UK MLAT, it is the Attorney General who decides whether to accede to a request from the UK, to narrow compliance to a certain aspect of said request or to decline to cooperate altogether. *See* Art. 3, US-UK MLAT. The government, however, erroneously concludes that the Attorney General's exclusive prerogative in initiating proceedings translates into a general bar on judicial oversight of the subpoena enforcement process. The treaty is silent as to the role of federal courts in the process of enforcing subpoenas issued in furtherance of a request by the UK. This silence, of course, does not mean that the actions taken by the Executive once the Attorney General decides to comply with a request are totally insulated and beyond the purview of oversight by the courts. In fact, courts play a prominent role in aiding the Executive's administration of its obligations under the treaty. *See* 18 U.S.C. § 3512.[9] In most cases, as here, the Attorney General will request that a federal judge issue an order appointing a commissioner to carry out specific actions in furtherance of the request, and will ask a court to enforce subpoenas when the recipients refuse to comply. See § 3512(a)(2) and (b). Hence, even if a court is not free to decline, delay or narrow a request by the UK because that power to initiate the process lies with the Attorney General under the treaty, federal courts play an indispensable role in the process of executing a request. Nevertheless, Section 3512, does not, on its face, provide us with an answer to the inquiry at hand: whether federal courts have discretion to quash a subpoena in this context. In the context of the issues raised by this appeal, judicial enforcement of the August 2011 subpoena implicates structural principles of the separation of powers which are "concerned with the allocation of official power among the three co-equal branches of our Government." . . . Of course, it goes without saying that the separation of powers does not forbid cooperation and interdependence between branches . . . But there are certain core boundaries that need to be respected and observed. *See In re 840 140th Ave. NE*, 634 F.3d at 571–72 (9th Cir. 2011). . . . In deciding the role of federal courts in enforcing subpoenas issued pursuant to the treaty, we must that our decision does not offend basic separation of powers principles by allowing (1) "encroachment or aggrandizement of one branch at the expense of the other," . . . ; or (2) "a branch . . . [to] impair another in the performance of its constitutional duties," . . . If we were to accede to the government's position and hold that courts must always enforce a commissioner's subpoenas, we would be (1) allowing the executive branch to virtually exercise judicial powers by issuing subpoenas that are automatically enforced by the courts; and (2) impairing our powers by acceding to act as rubber stamps for commissioners appointed pursuant to the. Such subservience is constitutionally prohibited and, ergo, we must forcefully conclude that preserving the judicial power to supervise the enforcement of subpoenas in the context of the present case, guarantees the

9. 18 U.S.C. § 3512(a)(1) states:

> Upon application, duly authorized by an appropriate official of the Department of Justice, of an attorney for the Government, a Federal judge may issue such orders as may be necessary to execute a request from a foreign authority for assistance in the investigation or prosecution of criminal offenses, or in proceedings related to the prosecution of criminal offenses, including proceedings regarding forfeiture, sentencing, and restitution.

Although not decisive in the present appeal, we note that in enacting this provision Congress used the term "may," which usually denotes a modicum of discretion, rather than the mandatory "shall. . . .

preservation of a balance of powers. Precisely because we recognize the importance here of "the governmental and public interest in not impeding criminal investigations," we must necessarily recognize the importance of judicially checking and balancing these interests in order to control excesses and preserve the balance in the symbiotic relationship between the commissioner conducting the investigation on behalf of the UK, and the courts before which the commissioner seeks the enforcement of the subpoenas. *In re Dolours Price*, 685 F.3d at 18. In substance, we rule that the enforcement of subpoenas is an inherent judicial function which, by virtue of the doctrine of separation of powers, cannot be constitutionally divested from the courts of the United States. Nothing in the text of the US-UK MLAT, or its legislative history, has been cited by the government to lead us to conclude that the courts of the United States have been divested of an inherent judicial role that is basic to our function as judges. . . .

§ 15.03 Depositions and Grand Jury Subpoenas

United States v. Drogoul

United States Court of Appeals for the Eleventh Circuit
1 F.3d 1546 (1993)

KRAVITCH, CIRCUIT JUDGE:

This interlocutory appeal stems from a pretrial dispute in the government's prosecution of appellee Christopher Drogoul. The sole question before us is whether the district court abused its discretion in denying the government's motion to take the depositions of several foreign nationals in Italy. We hold that it did and, accordingly, reverse. . . .

Drogoul was manager of the Atlanta branch of Banca Nazionale del Lavoro (BNL), a bank headquartered in Rome, Italy and owned largely by the Italian government. He is charged in a multicount indictment with, inter alia, wire fraud, conspiracy, and making false statements to government agencies. The crux of the government's allegations is that Drogoul defrauded BNL by making and concealing unauthorized loans and credit extensions totalling several billion dollars to agencies and instrumentalities of the Republic of Iraq.

Drogoul pled guilty in June 1992 to sixty counts of a 347-count original indictment. . . . In April 1993, the government moved the district court for an order authorizing it to take the video and audiotaped depositions of thirteen Italian nationals before an Italian judicial officer in Rome, for potential use at trial in the United States. The government averred that the prospective deponents' testimony is material to the prosecution, that the deponents are unwilling to testify in the United States, and that they cannot be compelled to do so. In a written order entered on April 30, 1993, the district court denied the government's request. The court found that the government had shown neither that the witnesses are unavailable to testify in the United States nor that the procedures for taking the depositions would comport with due process. The court noted in particular that "the government has failed to procure the affidavits of any of the witnesses themselves indicating that they are unwilling to travel to the United States for Drogoul's trial." Accordingly, the court concluded that the government failed to demonstrate exceptional circumstances justifying the taking of foreign depositions. In addition, the court expressed concern that the government had approached Italian authorities as early as February 1993 to arrange for the possible taking of the depositions, but did not inform either the court or the defendant about its intentions until April 1993 when it filed its original motion to take the depositions.

In response to the district court's concerns regarding the prospective deponents' availability, the government enlisted the assistance of the Government of Italy to ascertain more conclusively the witnesses' willingness to testify in the United States. Pursuant to a treaty request lodged with the Italian government, an Italian judicial officer interviewed the thirteen potential witnesses as to whether they would travel to the United States to testify at Drogoul's trial. Six of the witnesses declared they would be willing to testify in the United States; seven declared they would not.

Based on the witnesses' declarations — particularly those of the seven who indicated they would not testify in this country — the government moved for reconsideration of the order denying its motion to take foreign depositions. Supporting this motion was a letter from the Italian magistrate who had interviewed the thirteen witnesses. The letter certified that the seven witnesses had announced they would not testify at Drogoul's trial. Despite this new information, in an oral ruling rendered June 10, 1993, the district court refused to reconsider its earlier decision, apparently because the government's request was untimely under local court rules. . . .

The government appealed, and we reversed. Because the government's "Motion for Reconsideration" was based in part on significant new information not contained in its original motion — the letter from the Italian magistrate reporting the witnesses' in-court declarations — we held that the district court should have construed the motion as a timely renewed motion to take foreign depositions. . . . Accordingly, we remanded the case to the district court to consider the merits of the government's motion.

On remand, the district court denied the government's motion once more. This time the court did not focus on the availability of the witnesses or the materiality of their testimony: It "assumed that the government has finally shown unavailability and materiality as required by Rule 15 [of the Federal Rules of Criminal Procedure]." Rather the court held that the government "has not shown that the procedures surrounding the taking of the deposition testimony will meet constitutional standards." In particular, the court had misgivings about the potential accuracy of the translation of the Italian testimony and about the provisions for Drogoul to engage in meaningful cross-examination. The court also reiterated its earlier displeasure with the government's delay in notifying both the court and Drogoul of its intention to take the foreign depositions.

The government's appeal from this order of the district court is what is at issue.... We now reverse.

Depositions generally are disfavored in criminal cases.... Their "only authorized purpose is to preserve evidence, not to afford discovery." ... In particular, because of the absence of procedural protections afforded parties in the United States, foreign depositions are suspect and, consequently, not favored.... Nevertheless, the Federal Rules of Criminal Procedure expressly authorize parties to take depositions and use them at trial, when doing so is necessary to achieve justice and may be done consistent with the defendant's constitutional rights.

Whenever due to exceptional circumstances of the case it is in the interest of justice that the testimony of a prospective witness of a party be taken and preserved for use at trial, the court may upon motion of such party and notice to the parties order that testimony of such witness be taken by deposition ... Fed. R. Crim. P. 15(a)....

The burden is on the moving party to establish exceptional circumstances justifying the taking of depositions.... Whether to authorize depositions is a decision committed to the discretion of the district court which will be disturbed only for an abuse of discretion.... For purposes of analysis, we divide the prospective deponents into two groups: the seven who have declared they will not testify at Drogoul's trial and the six who have declared they would....

The primary reasons for the law's normal antipathy toward depositions in criminal cases are the factfinder's usual inability to observe the demeanor of deposition witnesses, and the threat that poses to the defendant's Sixth Amendment confrontation rights.... On the other hand, it is well established that when a witness is unavailable to testify at trial, former testimony given by that witness may be introduced consistent with the defendant's constitutional rights.... Thus, ordinarily, exceptional circumstances exist within the meaning of Rule 15(a) when the prospective deponent is unavailable for trial and the absence of his or her testimony would result in an injustice.... The principal consideration guiding whether the absence of a particular witness's testimony would produce injustice is the materiality of that testimony to the case.... When a prospective witness is unlikely to appear at trial and his or her testimony is critical to the case, simple fairness requires permitting the moving party to preserve that testimony—by deposing the witness—absent significant countervailing factors which would render the taking of the deposition unjust.

In denying the government's motion to take foreign depositions the district court assumed that the government established the unavailability of the prospective deponents and the materiality of their expected testimony. The court held nonetheless that those factors were outweighed by countervailing considerations: the lack of guaranteed procedures protecting the defendant's due process rights and the government's supposed dilatory conduct in providing notice of its intent to seek the depositions. To determine whether these factors offset the unavailability of the witnesses and the materiality of their testimony, we must review the evidence regarding the prospective deponents' willingness to testify at trial and the importance of the deponents' testimony to the case. Accordingly, notwithstanding the district court's assumption that they were minimally satisfied, we elaborate on these two paramount considerations. . . .

The moving party may demonstrate the probable unavailability of a prospective deponent "through affidavits or otherwise." . . . Significantly, that showing need not be conclusive before a deposition can be taken. . . . "It would be unreasonable and undesirable to require the government to assert with certainty that a witness will be unavailable for trial months ahead of time, simply to obtain authorization to take his deposition." . . . A more concrete showing of unavailability, of course, may be required at the time of trial before a deposition will be admitted in evidence. . . . A potential witness is unavailable for purposes of Rule 15(a), however, whenever a substantial likelihood exists that the proposed deponent will not testify at trial. In that situation, justice usually will be served by allowing the moving party to take the deposition, thereby preserving the party's ability to utilize the testimony at trial, if necessary. . . .

The government has made a strong showing that seven of the thirteen potential deponents are substantially unlikely to be available to testify at Drogoul's trial. Because the witnesses are foreign nationals located outside the United States, they are beyond the subpoena power of the district court. . . . Under a treaty between the United States and Italy, potential witnesses may be ordered by the Italian government to testify in the United States, but one who refuses to do so may not be removed to this country. Treaty on Mutual Assistance in Criminal Matters, Nov. 9, 1985, U.S.-Italy, art. 15, 24 I.L.M. 1539, 1541.[10] Thus, the prospective deponents cannot be compelled to testify at Drogoul's trial. The government has proffered a letter from an Italian judicial officer (the authenticity of which Drogoul has not challenged) certifying that the seven witnesses have declared in open court their unwillingness to testify in the United States. This evidence is potent proof of unavailability for purposes of Rule 15(a). . . .

---

10. The treaty provides, in pertinent part:

> 1. The Requested State, upon request that a person in that State appear and testify in connection with a criminal investigation or proceeding in the Requesting State, shall compel that person to appear and testify in the Requesting State by means of the procedures for compelling the appearance and testimony of witnesses in the Requested State if:
>
> a. the Requested State has no reasonable basis to deny the request;
>
> b. the person could be compelled to appear and testify in similar circumstances in the Requested State; and
>
> c. the Central Authority of the Requesting State certifies that the person's testimony is relevant and material.
>
> 2. A person who fails to appear as directed shall be subject to sanctions under the laws of the Requested State as if that person had failed to appear in similar circumstances in that State. Such sanctions shall not include removal of the person to the Requesting State.

Treaty on Mutual Assistance in Criminal Matters, art. 15., 24 I.L.M. at 1541. . . .

The government also has made a strong showing of materiality. Indeed, the expected testimony of all thirteen prospective deponents is highly material to this case. . . . Perhaps Drogoul expressed it best when he acknowledged in his brief to this court: "The testimony of these thirteen witnesses lies at the very core of the charges in the indictment, and its refutation the heart of the defense." . . . We can hardly imagine testimony more critical to this case.

Because the government established the key factors of probable unavailability and materiality (in this case, substantial materiality), the question becomes whether the district court acted within its discretion when it held that these considerations were, in this case, outweighed by certain countervailing factors. . . .

Of "primary concern" to the district court were the potential accuracy of the translation from Italian of the deposition testimony and the availability (or unavailability) to Drogoul of meaningful cross-examination. We believe these concerns to be largely premature and speculative. To the extent they are valid, they are insufficient to counterbalance the government's need to preserve for possible use at trial testimony which Drogoul concedes goes to the very core of this case.

Nothing in the record suggests that a correct translation cannot be obtained in this case, or that Drogoul even will object to the translation. Translations are an established part of practice in the federal courts. . . . Moreover, the depositions in this case are to be both audio and videotaped. If any question does arise with respect to the translation, an appropriate translator may be appointed to review the tapes and help resolve the dispute. Until the depositions are taken and translated, and an objection lodged, it is sheer speculation that the translation will pose a problem in this case.

Similarly, the district court's concerns regarding Drogoul's right of cross-examination are premature. To be sure, the defendant's right to confront witnesses is "the most important factor to be taken into account in determining whether to allow the use of a deposition at a criminal trial." . . . We fail to see, however, how the mere taking of depositions threatens that right. Only when deposition testimony is sought to be introduced in evidence are the defendant's confrontation rights truly implicated. Before then the process is simply one of preserving testimony for possible subsequent use. At trial, if admission of the deposition would violate the Sixth Amendment, the court could — indeed should — exclude the deposition. . . . At the time, the district court will be in a superior position to analyze the confrontation issue, because it will be able to review the actual deposition transcripts, audiotapes, and/or videotapes to determine whether in fact introducing the depositions would be inconsistent with the defendant's constitutional rights. . . .

It might have been within the district court's discretion to deny the government's deposition request — notwithstanding the unavailability of the prospective deponents and the crucial nature of their testimony — were it abundantly clear that the depositions could not possibly be admitted at trial. The court need not, at the cost of time and money, engage in an act of futility by authorizing depositions that clearly will be inadmissible at trial. But such is not the case here. Although oral questioning by counsel generally is not permitted in Italian courts, the government apparently has received assurances that oral examination will be allowed. Even if it is not, defense counsel will be able to submit questions for the Italian court to ask. In addition, the depositions will be videotaped, enabling a jury to observe the demeanor of the witnesses.... Both Drogoul and his counsel may travel to the depositions at the government's expense. Fed. R. Crim. P. 15(c). Several courts of appeals have affirmed the use at trial of deposition testimony obtained pursuant to procedures akin to those proposed in this case.... Thus, the likelihood that the Confrontation Clause would preclude admission of the highly material deposition testimony in this case is not so absolute as to warrant forbidding the government from at least preserving that testimony.

Likewise, the possibility that irremediable problems will develop with respect to translation of the depositions is too remote for one to conclude that taking the depositions would be a mere exercise in futility. If irreconcilable differences arise after the depositions have been taken and the translations made, then the depositions might properly be excluded from evidence at that time....

In refusing to allow the government to depose the Italian witnesses, the district court failed to recognize the crucial distinction that exists between the propriety of taking depositions versus the propriety of using the depositions at trial.... The court's concerns about the procedures surrounding the depositions are best addressed if and when the government seeks to introduce the depositions in evidence....

The district court's second main reason for denying the request for foreign depositions was the government's purported delay in seeking the depositions and in notifying both Drogoul and the court as to its intentions.... We hold that the district court erred to the extent that it denied the request for depositions solely on the ground that taking the depositions would delay the trial. As Drogoul has conceded, the expected deposition testimony goes to the heart of the issues in this case. Setting forth a per se rule against delay in the face of this crucial testimony is an abuse of discretion....

Furthermore, the district court grossly overweighed the government's dilatoriness in informing both it and Drogoul regarding the plan to depose the Italian witnesses. Rule 15(b) provides merely that the party taking the deposition "shall give to every party reasonable written notice of the time and place for taking the deposition." The reasonableness of the notice is a function of the time necessary for the opposing party to prepare for the deposition and thereby protect his rights. Here, the government filed its original motion on April 21, 1993. The motion requested that the depositions be taken May 25–28, 1993, more than a month later. This would have afforded Drogoul ample time to prepare. Rule 15 does not require a moving party to consult with the opposing party in advance regarding the scheduling of a deposition.

We do have some concerns about the fact that the government, which apparently was in contact with the Italian authorities as early as February 1993, did not move to take the depositions until late April 1993. We are also aware that allowing the depositions at this point might necessitate delaying the trial, and that Drogoul already has been in jail for sixteen months. Nevertheless, when the government filed its original motion the rescheduled trial was almost five months away. The government then acted diligently in responding to the district court's original concerns regarding the unavailability of the witnesses, working with the Italian judiciary to obtain the in-court declarations of the prospective deponents regarding their willingness to testify in the United States. Immediately upon receiving the letter from the Italian magistrate, on June 4, 1993 — still more than three months before trial — the government filed its renewed request to take depositions. The district court erred in holding that the government's lack of due diligence outweighed the strong showing of unavailability and materiality in this case. Accordingly, the district court should have allowed the government to depose the seven prospective witnesses who declared they would not testify in the United States.

. . . .

Exceptional circumstances and the interests of justice also warrant allowing the government to take the depositions of the six prospective witnesses who announced they would be willing to testify at Drogoul's trial. Whether to allow the depositions of these witnesses is, admittedly, a more difficult question than whether to allow the depositions of the other seven, because the government's showing as to the unavailability of these witnesses is obviously not as strong. We must remember, however, that unavailability is not the focus per se of Rule 15(a). Unavailability is required for use of the depositions at trial. Fed. R. Crim. P. 15(e). All that is necessary to take depositions is a showing that "exceptional circumstances" exist and that justice would be served by preserving the deposition testimony. . . .

. . . .

Far from being a substantial waste of time and resources, therefore, allowing the depositions of the six additional witnesses would involve the expenditure of only marginally more time, money, and effort. Furthermore, although the six prospective deponents stated in May 1993 that they were willing to come to the United States, they too are beyond the subpoena power of the United States courts. The possibility remains that they could change their minds, in which case it would be impossible for the government to present their testimony. . . .

Of course, before the depositions of the six could be used at trial the government would have to establish the deponents' unavailability. . . . This might be a difficult task in view of the witnesses' previous declarations. Nevertheless, we believe that three factors together — the significance to the case of the deponents' expected testimony; the fact that the deponents are beyond the reach of any American subpoena; and, critically, the fact that the parties already must take depositions in

Italy—provide sufficiently exceptional circumstances to satisfy Rule 15(a).... The district court should have allowed the depositions of these prospective witnesses as well.... The August 4, 1993 order of the district court denying the government's renewed motion to take the depositions of thirteen Italian witnesses in Italy is REVERSED. The case is REMANDED to the district court for further proceedings consistent with this opinion.

Notes

(1) In *Marc Rich & Co. v. United States*, 707 F.2d 663 (2d Cir. 1983), the Second Circuit affirmed a lower court decision involving a grand jury subpoena duces tecum for production of records. The appellant had moved to "quash the subpoena on the grounds that appellant was not subject to the in personam jurisdiction of the court and that Swiss law prohibited the production of the materials demanded." The district court "denied the motion to quash, finding that personal jurisdiction existed and that the operation of Swiss law was no bar to the production of the documents." When the appellant continued to refuse, the district judge issued a civil contempt. Appellant argued on appeal that the district court did not have personal jurisdiction over him to enforce the grand jury subpoena. The Second Circuit held that "[w]e agree with counsel for both sides that Judge Sand should not have looked to New York State's long-arm statutes in answering this question." The court stated, "[t]he subject of the grand jury's investigation is the possible violation of federal revenue statutes, and its right to inquire of appellant depends upon appellant's contacts with the entire United States, not simply the state of New York. Immediately prior to leaving the presidency, President Clinton pardoned Marc Rich. This pardon proved to be controversial, receiving significant press. *See Begging Pardons*, WALL ST. JRL., Jan. 29, 2001, at 1; William Jefferson Clinton, *My Reasons for the Pardons*, N.Y. TIMES, Feb. 18, 2001, at WK13.

(2) On the history of United States practice in negotiating MLATs, *see* ETHAN A. NADELMANN, COPS ACROSS BORDERS: THE INTERNATIONALIZATION OF U.S. CRIMINAL LAW ENFORCEMENT, Chapter 6 ("International Evidence-Gathering") (1993). In general, *see* DAVID MCCLEAN, INTERNATIONAL CO-OPERATION IN CIVIL AND CRIMINAL MATTERS (3rd ed. 2012).

(3) The United Nations has developed a Model Treaty on Mutual Assistance in Criminal Matters that states may find helpful in negotiating such treaties, G.A. Res. 45/117, 45 U.N. GAOR, Supp. No. 49A, at 215, U.N. Doc. A/45/49 (1991). *See* ROGER S. CLARK, THE UNITED NATIONS CRIME PREVENTION AND CRIMINAL JUSTICE PROGRAM: FORMULATION OF STANDARDS AND EFFORTS AT THEIR IMPLEMENTATION, 216–19 (1994); UNITED NATIONS OFFICE ON DRUGS AND CRIME, MANUAL ON MUTUAL LEGAL ASSISTANCE AND EXTRADITION (2012). "Mini-treaties" on mutual legal assistance also appear in specialized multilateral treaties such as the 1988 United Nations Convention Against Illicit Traffic in Narcotic Drugs and Psychotropic Substances, articles 5 and 7, U.N. Doc. E/CONF.82/15 (1988), and the 2000 United Nations Convention Against Transnational Organized Crime, article

18, G.A. Res. 55/25, 55 U.N. GAOR, Supp. No. 49, at 43, U.N. Doc. A/55/49 (Vol. I) (20001), the United Nations Convention against Corruption, G.A. Res. 58/4, U.N. GAOR, 58th Sess., Supp. No. 49 (2004) (in force December 14, 2005) and the Convention against Nuclear Terrorism, G.A. Res. 59/290 of 13 April 2005 (in force July 7, 2007).

(4) In 2005, the United Nations Economic and Social Council approved the terms of a Model Bilateral Agreement on the Sharing of Confiscated Proceeds of Crime or Property covered by the United Nations Convention against Transnational Organized Crime and the United Nations Convention against Illicit Traffic in Narcotic Drugs, ECOSOC Res. 2005/14. The Model Agreement was developed by an intergovernmental expert group held in Vienna under the auspices of the Commission on Crime Prevention and Criminal Justice and funded through extra-budgetary resources provided by the United States. *See* the Secretary-General's Report on the meeting of the expert group in U.N. Doc. E/CN.15/2005/7. The Model Agreement notes the importance of giving "priority consideration to returning the confiscated proceeds of crime or property to the requesting State party so that it can give compensation to the victims of the crime or return such proceeds of crime or property to their legitimate owners." It also notes the possibility that such a model of sharing may be useful for the Convention against Corruption, the International Convention for the Suppression of the Financing of Terrorism and the Recommendations of the Financial Action Task Force against Money Laundering.

(5) Most treaties on mutual legal assistance (and extradition — to be discussed in the next chapter) are bilateral. An important project for a *multilateral* treaty with both mutual legal assistance and extradition provisions is the "MLA Initiative." This project, led by Argentina, Belgium, Mongolia, the Netherlands, Senegal and Slovenia, envisages the adoption of a Convention on International Cooperation in the Investigation and Prosecution of the Crime of Genocide, Crimes against Humanity and War Crimes. While the current draft (note its title) limits the scope of the proposed Convention to three of the four core crimes contained in the Rome Statute of the International Criminal Court, excluding the crime of aggression, the draft contemplates potential expansion to other crimes such as aggression, torture and disappearances. A Diplomatic Conference aimed at completing the project in June of 2020 was a casualty of Covid and no new date has yet been set. The best account of the Initiative, including various drafts and comments, is on the Slovenian Government's website: https://www.gov.si/en/registries/projects/mla-initiative/.

Chapter 16

Extradition

§ 16.01 A Brief History of Extradition

Extradition, the return of fugitives from criminal justice from one sovereignty to another, is probably the oldest topic in International Criminal Law. Around 1259 B.C.E., Hattusilis, King of the Hittites (in what is now modern Turkey) and Ramses II, Pharoah of Egypt, entered into a Treaty of Alliance which contained provisions on extradition. *See* S. Langdon & Alan H. Gardner, *Treaty of Alliance Between Hattisili and Ramesses II*, 6 J. Egyptian Archaeology 181 (1920). The meaning of the two surviving versions of the treaty, in cuneiform and hieroglyphics, may not be identical. What was understood by the rules about extradition was not quite the same as in modern law. Nevertheless, the concept seems to have been alive and well that early. From at least the eleventh century, English monarchs entered into extradition treaties, especially with Scotland and France. *See* Paul O'Higgins, *The History of Extradition in British Practice*, 13 Indian Y.B. Int'l Aff. 78 (1964). Until England lost its continental holdings, France and Scotland were both countries with whom England shared land borders; it is typically with neighbors, tourist destinations and trading partners that extradition arrangements are essential.

Many countries render fugitives between them without treaty relations governing the matter. Members of the Commonwealth (Great Britain and most of its former colonies plus Mozambique and Rwanda) function among themselves on the basis of a "Scheme for the Rendition of Fugitive Offenders within the Commonwealth," adopted at a meeting of Commonwealth Law Ministers in 1966 and amended from time to time. It does not amount to a treaty but operates through parallel legislation which members have adopted. The United States, however, usually takes the position that, in addition to the statutory framework, a treaty relationship is a necessary basis for extradition. Whether that is constitutionally required is, as we shall see, debated. The United States has over 100 extradition treaties (including one with the European Union), but is well short of having a relationship with all the 193 United Nations members. *See* M. Cherif Bassiouni, International Extradition: United States Law and Practice (6th ed. 2014); Extradition Laws and Treaties, United States (loose-leaf, I.I. Kavass & A. Sprudzs comp. 1980); Michael Abbell, Extradition to and from the United States (2010). On extradition and rendition in general, see Geoff Gilbert, Transnational Fugitive Offenders in International Law (1998); United Nations Office on Drugs and Crime, Manual on Mutual Legal Assistance and Extradition

(2012); Neil Boister, *Global Simplification of Extradition: Interviews with Selected Extradition Experts in New Zealand, Canada, the United States and the European Union,* 29 CRIM. L.F. 327 (2018).

The first United States extradition arrangement* was in the Treaty of Amity, Commerce and Navigation between Great Britain and the United States, signed at London, 19 November 1794, 52 CONSOL. T.S. 243 ("Jay Treaty"). Article 27 of the Jay Treaty obligated the parties to "deliver up to justice all persons who, being charged with murder or forgery, committed within the jurisdiction of either, shall seek asylum within any of the countries of the other. . . ." The Treaty of 1794 provided the setting for the "Robbins Affair," in which President John Adams and the federal district court, acting without clear federal legislation implementing the treaty, handed over a fugitive who claimed to be an American. The British promptly tried and executed him. The extradition provisions of the Jay Treaty expired in 1806 and no further extraditions were made by the U.S. for over forty years. It was not until 1842, in Article 10 of the Webster-Ashburton Treaty, 8 Stat. 572, 576, T.S. 119, that provision was again made for extradition between Great Britain (including Canada) and the United States. *See generally* John T. Parry, *The Lost History of International Extradition Litigation*, 43 VA. J. INT'L L. 93 (2002).

A good starting-place for understanding modern extradition law is the United Nations Model Treaty on Extradition which tried to capture the state of play in the area late in the twentieth century. The United Nations thought it would be helpful to states whose extradition arrangements were limited to have a model to use when they began negotiating with others. Scores of developing countries, in particular, had not entered into new arrangements after independence. To the extent they had extradition relationships, they relied on treaty succession to treaties of their former colonial power. A significant number of the United States arrangements with former British colonies, for example, are still based on the British treaty of 1931 which is no longer applicable between the U.S. and the U.K., but applies to several of the former colonies by succession. Most modern treaties are similar in essentials to the Model Treaty. The Model Treaty is reinforced by a U.N. MANUAL ON THE MODEL TREATY ON EXTRADITION, *in* 45 and 46 INT'L REV. CRIM. POL'Y 1 (1995). Basic extradition arrangements (usually done by bilateral treaty, although there is an increasing number of significant multilateral treaties in the area) are not only essential for dealing with thieves and murderers. They are also crucial to sophisticated multilateral efforts in such areas as terrorism, the drug traffic and organized crime.

The Jay Treaty, with its reference to murder and forgery, was standard for older Treaties in defining what was extraditable in terms of a list of offenses. (The typical list gradually expanded through the nineteenth and the first part of the twentieth centuries when this approach held sway.) More modern treaties adopt a minimum

* A 1788 consular convention between France and the U.S. obligated the parties to surrender deserting sailors. Such arrangements are quite common, even in relatively modern usage, and are not usually regarded as "extradition" although they are obviously analogous. — Eds.

penalty approach, subject to a flexible requirement of criminality in both places ("double criminality"). *See* Article 2 of the Model Treaty.

Extradition relationships may be affected by considerations of the death penalty and other human rights issues such as torture and the increasing prohibition of life without parole. *See* the *Soering* case and the Notes following it in Chap. 19.

Model Treaty on Extradition

General Assembly Resolution 45/116, 45 U.N. GAOR, Supp. No. 49A, at 211, U.N. Doc. A/45/49A (1991), as amended by General Assembly Resolution 52/88, 52 U.N. GAOR, Supp. No. 49, at 213, U.N. Doc. A/52/49 (Vol. I) (1998) (amendments incorporated in text)

The ____________________ and the ____________________

Desirous of making more effective the co-operation of the two countries in the control of crime by concluding a treaty on extradition,

Have agreed as follows:

Article 1

Obligation to extradite

Each Party agrees to extradite to the other, upon request and subject to the provisions of the present Treaty, any person who is wanted in the requesting State for prosecution for an extraditable offence or for the imposition or enforcement of a sentence in respect of such an offence.[1]

Article 2

Extraditable offences

1. For the purposes for the present Treaty, extraditable offences are offences that are punishable under the laws of both Parties by imprisonment or other deprivation of liberty for a maximum period of at least [one/two] year(s), or by a more severe penalty. Where the request for extradition relates to a person who is wanted for the enforcement of a sentence of imprisonment or other deprivation of liberty imposed for such an offence, extradition shall be granted only if a period of at least [four/six] months of such sentence remains to be served.

2. In determining whether an offence is an offence punishable under the laws of both Parties, it shall not matter whether:

(a) The laws of the Parties place the acts or omissions constituting the offence within the same category of offence or denominate the offence by the same terminology;

1. Reference to the imposition of a sentence may not be necessary for all countries.

(b) Under the laws of the Parties the constituent elements of the offence differ, it being understood that the totality of the acts or omissions as presented by the requesting State shall be taken into account.

3. Where extradition of a person is sought for an offence against a law relating to taxation, customs, duties, exchange control or other revenue matters, extradition may not be refused on the ground that the law of the requested State does not impose the same kind of tax or duty or does not contain a tax, customs duty or exchange regulation of the same kind as the law of the requesting State.[2]

4. If the request for extradition includes several separate offences each of which is punishable under the laws of both Parties, but some of which do not fulfil the other conditions set out in paragraph 1 of the present article, the requested Party may grant extradition for the latter offences provided that the person is to be extradited for at least one extraditable offence.

Article 3

Mandatory grounds for refusal

Extradition shall not be granted in any of the following circumstances:

(a) If the offence for which extradition is requested is regarded by the requested state as an offence of a political nature. Reference to an offence of a political nature shall not include any offence in respect of which the Parties have assumed an obligation, pursuant to any multilateral convention, to take prosecutorial action where they do not extradite, or any other offence that the Parties have agreed is not an offence of a political character for the purposes of extradition;[3]

(b) If the requested State has substantial grounds for believing that the request for extradition has been made for the purpose of prosecuting or punishing a person on account of that person's race, religion, nationality, ethnic origin, political opinions, sex or status, or that that person's position may be prejudiced for any of those reasons;

(c) If the offence for which extradition is requested is an offence under military law, which is not also an offence under ordinary criminal law;

(d) If there has been a final judgment rendered against the person in the requested State in respect of the offence for which the person's extradition is requested;

(e) If the person whose extradition is requested has, under the law of either party, become immune from prosecution or punishment for any reason, including lapse of time or amnesty;[4]

---

2. Some countries may wish to omit this paragraph or provide an optional ground for refusal under article 4.

3. Countries may wish to exclude certain conduct, e.g., acts of violence, such as serious offences involving an act of violence against the life, physical integrity or liberty of a person, from the concept of political offence.

4. Some countries may wish to make this an optional ground for refusal under article 4. Countries may also wish to restrict consideration of the issue of lapse of time to the law of the requesting

(f) If the person whose extradition is requested has been or would be subjected in the requesting state to torture or cruel, inhuman or degrading treatment or punishment or if that person has not received or would not receive the minimum guarantees in criminal proceedings, as contained in the International Covenant on Civil and Political Rights, article 14;

(g) If the judgement of the requesting State has been rendered *in absentia*, the convicted person has not had sufficient notice of the trial or the opportunity to arrange for his or her defense and he has not had or will not have the opportunity to have the case retried in his or her presence.[5]

Article 4

Optional grounds for refusal

Extradition may be refused in any of the following circumstances;

(a) If the person whose extradition is requested is a national of the requested State. Where extradition is refused on this ground, the requested State shall, if the other State so requests, submit the case to its competent authorities with a view to taking appropriate action against the person in respect of the offence for which extradition had been requested,[6]

(b) If the competent authorities of the requested State have decided either not to institute or to terminate proceedings against the person for the offence in respect of which extradition had been requested;

(c) If a prosecution in respect of the offence for which extradition is requested is pending in the requested State against the person whose extradition is requested;

(d) If the offence for which extradition is requested carries the death penalty under the law of the requesting State, unless that State gives such assurance as the requested State considers sufficient that the death penalty will not be imposed or, if imposed, will not be carried out. Where extradition is refused on this ground, the requested State shall, if the other State so requests, submit the case to its competent authorities with a view to taking appropriate action against the person for the offence for which extradition had been requested;[7]

State only or to provide that acts of interruption in the requesting State should be recognized in the requested State.

5. Some countries may wish to add to article 3 the following ground for refusal: "If there is insufficient proof, according to the evidentiary standards of the requested State, that the person whose extradition is requested is a party to the offence" (see also footnote 10).

6. Some countries may also wish to consider, within the framework of national legal systems, other means to ensure that those responsible for crimes do not escape punishment on the basis of nationality, such as, *inter alia*, provisions that would permit surrender for serious offences or permit temporary transfer of the person for the trial and return of the person to the requested State for service of sentence.

7. Some countries may wish to apply the same restriction to the imposition of a life, or indeterminate, sentence.

(e) If the offence for which extradition is requested has been committed outside the territory of either Party and the law of the requested State does not provide for jurisdiction over such an offence committed outside its territory in comparable circumstances;

(f) If the offence for which extradition is requested is regarded under the law of the requested State as having been committed in whole or in part within that State.[8] Where extradition is refused on this ground, the requested State shall, if the other State so requests, submit the case to its competent authorities with a view to taking appropriate action against the person for the offence for which extradition had been requested;

(g) If the person whose extradition is requested has been sentenced or would be liable to be tried or sentenced in the requesting state by an extraordinary or *ad hoc* court or tribunal;

(h) If the requested State, while also taking into account the nature of the offence and the interests of the requesting State, considers that, in the circumstances of the case, the extradition of that person would be incompatible with humanitarian considerations in view of age, health or other personal circumstances of that person.

Article 5

Channels of communication and required documents[9]

1. A request for extradition shall be made in writing. The request, supporting documents and subsequent communications shall be transmitted through the diplomatic channel, directly between the ministries of justice or any other authorities designated by the Parties.

2. A request for extradition shall be accompanied by the following:

(a) In all cases,

(i) As accurate a description as possible of the person sought, together with any other information that may help to establish that person's identity, nationality and location;

(ii) The text of the relevant provision of the law creating the offence or, where necessary, a statement of the law relevant to the offence and a statement of the penalty that can be imposed for the offence;

(b) If the person is accused of an offence, by a warrant issued by a court or other competent judicial authority for the arrest of the person or a certified copy of that warrant, a statement of the offence for which

---

8. Some countries may wish to make specific reference to a vessel under its flag or an aircraft registered under its laws at the time of the commission of the offence.

9. Countries may wish to consider including the most advanced techniques for the communication of requests and means which could establish the authenticity of documents emanating from the requesting State.

extradition is requested and a description of the acts or omissions constituting the alleged offence, including an indication of the time and place of its commission.[10]

(c) If the person has been convicted of an offence, by a statement of the offence for which extradition is requested and a description of the acts or omissions constituting the offence and by the original or certified copy of the judgment or any other document setting out the conviction and the sentence imposed, the fact that the sentence is enforceable, and the extent to which the sentence remains to be served;

(d) If the person has been convicted of an offence in his or her absence, in addition to the documents set out in paragraph 2(c) of the present article, by a statement as to the legal means available to the person to prepare his or her defence or to have the case retried in his or her presence;

(e) If the person has been convicted of an offence but no sentence has been imposed, by a statement of the offence for which extradition is requested and a description of the acts or omissions constituting the offence and by a document setting out the conviction and a statement affirming that here is an intention to impose a sentence.

3. The documents submitted in support of a request for extradition shall be accompanied by a translation into the language of the requested State or in another language acceptable to that State.

Article 6

Simplified extradition procedure[11]

The requested State, if not precluded by its law, may grant extradition after receipt of a request for provisional arrest, provided that the person sought explicitly consents before a competent authority.

Article 7

Certification and authentication

Except as provided by the present treaty, a request for extradition and the documents in support thereof, as well as documents or other material supplied in response to such a request, shall not require certification or authentication.[12]

10. Countries requiring evidence in support of a request for extradition may wish to define the evidentiary requirements necessary to satisfy the test for extradition and in doing so should take into account the need to facilitate effective international cooperation.

11. Countries may wish to provide for the waiver of speciality in the case of simplified extradition.

12. The laws of some countries require authentication before documents transmitted from other countries can be admitted in their courts and, therefore, would require a clause setting out the authentication required.

Article 8

Additional Information

If the requested State considers that the information provided in support of a request for extradition is not sufficient, it may request that additional information be furnished within such reasonable time as it specifies.

Article 9

Provisional arrest

1. In case of urgency the requesting State may apply for the provisional arrest of the person sought pending the presentation of the request for extradition. The application shall be transmitted by means of the facilities of the International Criminal Police Organization, by post or telegraph or by any other means affording a record in writing.

2. The application shall contain a description of the person sought, a statement that extradition is to be requested, a statement of the existence of one of the documents mentioned in paragraph 2 of article 5 of the present Treaty, authorizing the apprehension of the person, a statement of the punishment that can be or has been imposed for the offence, including the time left to be served and a concise statement of the facts of the case, and statement of location, where known, of the person.

3. The requested State shall decide on the application in accordance with its law and communicate its decision to the requesting State without delay.

4. The person arrested upon such an application shall be set at liberty upon expiration of [40] days from the date of arrest if a request for extradition, supported by the relevant documents specified in paragraph 2 of article 5 of the present Treaty, has not been received. The present paragraph does not preclude the possibility of conditional release of the person prior to the expiration of the [40] days.

5. The release of the person pursuant to paragraph 4 of the present article shall not prevent rearrest and institution of proceedings with a view to extraditing the person sought if the request and supporting documents are subsequently received.

Article 10

Decision on the request

1. The requested State shall deal with the request for extradition pursuant to procedures provided by its own law, and shall promptly communicate its decision to the requesting State.

2. Reasons shall be given for any complete or partial refusal of the request.

Article 11

Surrender of the person

1. Upon being informed that extradition has been granted, the Parties shall, without undue delay, arrange for the surrender of the person sought and the requested State

shall inform the requesting State of the length of time for which the person sought was detained with a view to surrender.

2. The person shall be removed from the territory of the requested State within such reasonable period as the requested State specifies and, if the person is not removed within that period, the requested State may release the person and may refuse to extradite that person for the same offence.

3. If circumstances beyond its control prevent a Party from surrendering or removing the person to be extradited, it shall notify the other Party. The two Parties shall mutually decide upon a new date of surrender, and the provisions of paragraph 2 of the present article shall apply.

Article 12

Postponed or conditional surrender

1. The requested State may, after making its decision on the request for extradition, postpone the surrender of a person sought, in order to proceed against that person, or, if that person has already been convicted, in order to enforce a sentence imposed for an offence other than that for which extradition is sought. In such a case the requested State shall advise the requesting State accordingly.

2. The requested State may, instead of postponing surrender, temporarily surrender the person sought to the requesting State in accordance with conditions to be determined between the Parties.

Article 13

Surrender of property

1. To the extent permitted under the law of the requested State and subject to the rights of third parties, which shall be duly respected, all property found in the requested State that has been acquired as a result of the offence or that may be required as evidence shall, if the requesting State so requests, be surrendered if extradition is granted.

2. The said property may, if the requesting State so requests, be surrendered to the requesting State even if the extradition agreed to cannot be carried out.

3. When the said property is liable to seizure or confiscation in the requested State, it may retain it or temporarily hand it over.

4. Where the law of the requested State or the protection of the rights of third parties so require, any property so surrendered shall be returned to the requested State free of charge after the completion of the proceedings, if that State so requests.

Article 14

Rule of Speciality

1. A person extradited under the present Treaty shall not be proceeded against, sentenced, detained, re-extradited to a third State, or subjected to any other restriction

of personal liberty in the territory of the requesting State for any offence committed before surrender other than:

(a) An offence for which extradition was granted;[13]

(b) Any other offence in respect of which the requested State consents. Consent shall be given if the offence for which it is requested is itself subject to extradition in accordance with the present Treaty.[14]

2. A request for the consent of the requested State under the present article shall be accompanied by the documents mentioned in paragraph 2 of article 5 of the present Treaty and a legal record of any statement made by the extradited person with respect to the offence.[15]

3. Paragraph 1 of the present article shall not apply if the person has had an opportunity to leave the requesting State and has not done so within [30/45] days of final discharge in respect of the offence for which that person was extradited or if the person has voluntarily returned to the territory of the requesting State after leaving it.

Article 15

Transit

1. Where a person is to be extradited to a Party from a third State through the territory of the other Party, the Party to which the person is to be extradited shall request the other Party to permit the transit of that person through its territory. This does not apply where air transport is used and no landing in the territory of the other Party is scheduled.

2. Upon receipt of such a request, which shall contain relevant information, the requested State shall deal with this request pursuant to procedures provided by its own law. The requested State shall grant the request expeditiously unless its essential interests would be prejudiced thereby.[16]

3. The State of transit shall ensure that legal provisions exist that would enable detaining the person in custody during transit.

4. In the event of an unscheduled landing, the Party to be requested to permit transit may, at the request of the escorting officer, hold the person in custody for [48] hours, pending receipt of the transit request to be made in accordance with paragraph 1 of the present article.

---

13. Countries may also wish to provide that the rule of speciality is not applicable to extraditable offences provable on the same facts and carrying the same or a lesser penalty as the original offence for which extradition was requested.

14. Some countries may not wish to assume that obligation and may wish to include other grounds in determining whether or not to grant consent.

15. Countries may wish to waive the requirement for the provision of some or all of these documents.

16. Some countries may wish to agree on other grounds for refusal, which may also warrant refusal for extradition, such as those related to the nature of the offence (e.g. political, fiscal, military) or to the status of the person (e.g. their own nationals). However, countries may wish to provide that transit should not be denied on the basis of nationality.

Article 16

Concurrent Requests

If a Party receives requests for extradition for the same person from both the other Party and a third State it shall, at its discretion, determine to which of those States the person is to be extradited.

Article 17

Costs

1. The requested State shall meet the cost of any proceedings in its jurisdiction arising out of a request for extradition.

2. The requested State shall also bear the costs incurred in its territory in connection with the seizure and handing over of property, or the arrest and detention of the person whose extradition is sought.[17]

3. The requesting State shall bear the costs incurred in conveying the person from the territory of the requested State, including transit costs.

Article 18

Final Provisions

1. The present Treaty is subject to [ratification, acceptance, or approval]. The instruments of [ratification, acceptance or approval] shall be exchanged as soon as possible.

2. The present Treaty shall enter into force on the thirtieth day after the day on which the instruments of [ratification, acceptance or approval] are exchanged.

3. The present Treaty shall apply to requests made after its entry into force, even if the relevant acts or omissions occurred prior to that date.

4. Either Contracting Party may denounce the present Treaty by giving notice in writing to the other Party. Such denunciation shall take effect six months following the date on which such notice is received by the other Party.

IN WITNESS WHEREOF the undersigned, being duly authorized thereto by their respective Governments, have signed the present Treaty.

DONE at ______________________________

on ____________________________________ in

the __________________________________ and

________________________ languages, [both/all]

texts being equally authentic.

17. Some countries may wish to consider reimbursement of costs incurred as a result of withdrawal of a request for extradition or provisional arrest. There may also be cases for consultation between the requesting and requested States for the payment by the requesting State of extraordinary costs, particularly in complex cases where there is a significant disparity in the resources available to the two States.

Note

The political offense exception to extradition, see Article 3(a) of the Model Treaty, is increasingly subject to exceptions like those in the model. This has been occurring both in bilateral and in multilateral treaty practice.

Article VII of the Genocide Convention, for example, provided that "Genocide and the other acts enumerated in article III [the basic definition provision] shall not be considered as political crimes for the purpose of extradition." This provision was aimed at modifying any existing bilateral or multilateral treaties among States that were also parties to the Genocide Convention by ensuring that genocide does not come within the scope of a political offense exception contained in such treaties, thus denying safe haven.

The "exception-to-the-exception" technique of dealing with the safe haven problem did not find favor in the early global treaties on terrorism such as those listed in § 9.02[A], *supra*. In a departure from the genocide precedent, those treaties addressed the safe haven problem through their "extradite or prosecute" provisions. A State might grant "asylum" to an airplane hijacker, for example, by not extraditing him or her, but would then be required to prosecute on a "fallback" or "secondary" universal jurisdiction basis. The Council of Europe's 1977 European Convention for the Suppression of Terrorism, Europ. T. S., No. 90, took a different tack. It went back to the genocide model and sought to modify various European extradition arrangements by defining various violent acts and offenses against some multilateral terrorism treaties as exceptions to political offence exceptions. So far as treaties like those on hijacking or offenses against aircraft were concerned, the obligation of parties to the European Terrorism Convention became one where the primary duty appears to be to extradite rather than to prosecute. The Council's Protocol amending the European Convention for the Suppression of Terrorism, of 15 May 2003, continued this technique and included a long list of multilateral terrorism treaties, through the 1999 U.N. Convention for the Suppression of the Financing of Terrorism, as exceptions for political offense purposes. The U.N.'s Model Treaty on Extradition (see Article 3(a) and its footnote 3, *supra*), contemplated that States might wish to include such exclusions for crimes of violence from the political offense exception in treaties negotiated using the Model Treaty as a basis. A number of bilateral treaties did just that, an example being the now superseded United States/United Kingdom Supplementary Extradition Treaty of 1985, noted in the Casebook. Most such treaties that cut back on the political offense exception also (like the U.S./U.K. treaty) contain some variation of the "persecution" or "human rights" ground for the mandatory refusal of extradition contained in Article 3(b) of the Model Treaty, *supra*. (That clause seems to have originated in the 1977 European Terrorism Convention and then found its way into bilateral usage.) This trend towards providing exceptions to the political offense exception in what might generally be described as terrorism cases continues, as noted in the following paragraphs.

The 2002 Inter-American Convention Against Terrorism, AG/RES.1840 (XXXII-0/02) obligates parties to endeavor to become parties to the basic U.N. terrorism treaties (which are listed in Article 2 of the 2002 Convention). Article 11 provides:

> For the purposes of extradition or mutual legal assistance, none of the offenses established in the international instruments listed in Article 2 shall be regarded as a political offense or an offense connected with a political offense or an offense inspired by political motives. Accordingly, a request for extradition or mutual legal assistance may not be refused on the sole ground that it concerns a political offense or an offense connected with a political offense or an offense inspired by political motives.

Article 12 of the Inter-American Convention goes further than previous instruments. It requires parties to "take appropriate measures, consistent with the relevant provisions of national and international law, for the purpose of ensuring that refugee status is not granted to any person in respect of whom there are serious reasons for considering that he or she has committed an offense established in the [U.N. instruments]." Article 13, moreover, makes a similar requirement to ensure that "asylum is not granted to any person in respect of whom there are reasonable grounds to believe that he or she has committed an offense established in the [U.N. instruments]." It is not clear whether the disparity between "serious reasons for considering" in Article 12 and "reasonable grounds to believe" in Article 13 is a quirk of the negotiating process or an inconsistency in translation. Article 14, headed "Non-discrimination", is a human rights exception to the obligation to extradite similar to that in the Model Treaty. Indeed, Article 15 makes further reference to the obligation of States Parties to carry out measures under the Convention "with full respect for the rule of law, human rights and fundamental freedoms." There are some tensions here among the various objectives!

A number of more recent U.N. treaties, the International Convention for the Suppression of the Financing of Terrorism of 9 December 1999, G.A. Res. 54/109, the Convention against Nuclear Terrorism of 13 April 2005, G.A. Res. 59/290, and the International Convention for the Protection of all Persons from Enforced Disappearance of December 20, 2006, G.A. Res. 61/177, return to the model of the Genocide Convention. They provide that none of the offenses created by the Convention shall be regarded as a political offense or as an activity connected with a political offense or inspired by political motives and that extradition requests may not be refused on this ground alone. They still have extradite-or-prosecute requirements. On the principle "extradite or prosecute," *see* § 2.01[B] (discussing its role in suppression conventions generally), and *Questions relating to the Obligation to Prosecute or Extradite (Belgium v. Senegal)*, 2012 I.C.J. Rep. 422 (discussing specific provision in Torture Convention).

In bilateral practice, the newest United States/United Kingdom Extradition Treaty is a dramatic example of the trend towards carving out exceptions to the political offense exception:

ARTICLE 4 — Political and Military Offenses

1. Extradition shall not be granted if the offense for which extradition is requested is a political offense.

2. For the purposes of this Treaty, the following offenses shall not be considered political offenses:

(a) an offense for which both Parties have the obligation pursuant to a multilateral international agreement to extradite the person sought or to submit the case to their competent authorities for decision as to prosecution;

(b) a murder or other violent crime against the person of a Head of State of one of the Parties, or of a member of the Head of State's family;

(c) murder, manslaughter, malicious wounding, or inflicting grievous bodily harm;

(d) an offense involving kidnaping, abduction, or any form of unlawful detention, including the taking of a hostage;

(e) placing or using, or threatening the placement or use of, an explosive, incendiary, or destructive device or firearm capable of endangering life, of causing grievous bodily harm, or of causing substantial property damage;

(f) possession of an explosive, incendiary, or destructive device capable of endangering life, of causing grievous bodily harm, or of causing substantial property damage;

(g) an attempt or a conspiracy to commit, participation in the commission of, aiding or abetting, counseling or procuring the commission of, or being an accessory before or after the fact to any of the foregoing offenses.

3. Notwithstanding the terms of paragraph 2 of this Article, extradition shall not be granted if the competent authority of the Requested State determines that the request was politically motivated. In the United States, the executive branch is the competent authority for the purposes of this Article.

4. The competent authority of the Requested State may refuse extradition for offenses under military law that are not offenses under ordinary criminal law. In the United States, the executive branch is the competent authority for the purposes of this Article.[18]

---

18. Extradition Treaty between the Government of the United Kingdom of Great Britain and Northern Ireland and the Government of the United States of America, Washington, 31 March, 2003, Instruments of Ratification exchanged 26 April, 2007, *available at* http://www.fco.gov.uk/resources/en/pdf/pdf8/fco_pdf_usextraditiontreaty.

§ 16.02 Extradition to the United States

United States v. Van Cauwenberghe

United States Court of Appeals for the Ninth Circuit
827 F.2d 424 (1987)

NELSON, CIRCUIT JUDGE:

Wilfried Van Cauwenberghe, a citizen of Belgium, appeals from a criminal conviction on one count of wire fraud under 18 U.S.C. § 1343 (1982) and one count of interstate transportation of a victim of fraud under 18 U.S.C. § 2314 (1982). Following a jury trial, Van Cauwenberghe was convicted of participating with two Americans in a scheme to defraud a Belgian investment broker and a family-owned Belgian corporation of 3.6 million dollars relating to the purchase and development of a condominium tract near Kansas City. Van Cauwenberghe argues that numerous errors were made requiring reversal of his extradition from Switzerland, his indictment, and his trial. In addition, Van Cauwenberghe argues that the district court should have returned certain property to him because it was seized illegally, and that his sentence was improper. . . .

Between 1979 and 1981, Van Cauwenberghe participated with two Americans, Alan H. Blair and Gerald L. Bilton, in a scheme to defraud Roger Biard, a Belgian investment broker, and a Belgian corporation owned by members of the Vanden Stock family, of 3.6 million dollars relating to the purchase and development of Concorde Bridge Townhouses, an apartment complex near Kansas City, Missouri. Van Cauwenberghe, Blair, and Bilton were indicted on seven counts, including three counts of wire fraud (18 U.S.C. § 1343), three counts of interstate transportation of a victim of fraud (18 U.S.C. § 2314), and one count of conspiracy to commit fraud (18 U.S.C. § 371), in October 1984. The government learned that Van Cauwenberghe, a Belgian citizen, would be traveling from Brussels to Geneva on a brief business trip and, on November 20, 1984, filed a provisional arrest request with Swiss authorities pursuant to Article VI of the Treaty on Extradition, May 14, 1900, United States-Switzerland, 31 Stat. 1928, T.S. No. 354 ("Treaty").[19] Van Cauwenberghe was arrested by Swiss authorities as he stepped off his plane in Geneva on January 14, 1985. . . . The government subsequently filed a formal extradition request on March 12, 1985.

Van Cauwenberghe challenged his extradition before the Swiss courts including the Swiss Federal Tribunal, Switzerland's highest court, which, on September 25, 1985, held that Van Cauwenberghe was extraditable under the Treaty for all of the offenses charged except conspiracy. Accordingly, Van Cauwenberghe was extradited to the United States on September 26, 1985.

. . . .

19. The government could not proceed against Van Cauwenberghe in Belgium because Belgium does not extradite its nationals.

The theory of Van Cauwenberghe's defense at trial was that he was merely an innocent pawn in the fraudulent scheme, not a culpable participant. . . . The jury found all three defendants guilty on both counts. . . .

The right "to demand and obtain extradition of an accused criminal is created by treaty." . . . The offense complained of must ordinarily, therefore, be listed as an extraditable crime in the treaty. . . . In addition, "under the doctrine of 'dual criminality,' an accused person can be extradited only if the conduct complained of is considered criminal by the jurisprudence or under the laws of both the requesting and requested nations." . . . This dual criminality requirement has been expressly incorporated into the Treaty. . . . To satisfy this "dual criminality" requirement,

> "the law does not require that the name by which the crime is described in the two countries shall be the same; nor that the scope of liability shall be coextensive, or, in other respects, the same in the two countries. It is enough if the particular act charged is criminal in both jurisdictions."

. . . .

As a matter of international comity, "the doctrine of 'specialty' prohibits the requesting nation from prosecuting the extradited individual for any offense other than that for which the surrendering state agreed to extradite." . . . However, since the doctrine is based on comity, its "protection exists only to the extent that the surrendering country wishes." . . . Therefore, the "'extradited party may be tried for a crime other than that for which he was surrendered *if the asylum country consents*.'" . . .

Van Cauwenberghe argues that his extradition was improper because the Treaty does not identify wire fraud and interstate transportation of a victim of fraud as extraditable offenses. The Treaty does not expressly name these specific offenses but includes "obtaining money or other property by false pretenses [and] receiving money . . . knowing the same to have been . . . fraudulently obtained." . . . Moreover, the government insists that Van Cauwenberghe's argument is foreclosed by the Swiss Federal Tribunal's decision because "determination of whether a crime is within the provisions of an extradition treaty is within the sole purview of the requested state," . . . We agree.

Johnson [*v. Browne*, 205 U.S. 309 (1907)] involved an extradition request by the United States to Canada. The Canadian government determined that one of the offenses for which extradition was sought, conspiring to defraud the government, was not a form of fraud provided for in the subdivision of the article of the treaty listing extraditable fraud offenses. . . . The Supreme Court held that "whether the crime came within the provision of the treaty was a matter for the decision of the Dominion authorities, and such decision was final by the express terms of the treaty itself." . . . Article II of the treaty in *Johnson* dealt only with offenses of a political character and expressly stated that "if any question shall arise as to whether a case comes within the provisions of this article, the decision of the authorities of the government in whose jurisdiction the fugitive shall be at the time shall be final." . . .

Because of this language in the *Johnson* treaty, Van Cauwenberghe argues that the holding in *Johnson* should be read narrowly. We believe, however, that the *Johnson* holding need not be read narrowly and that the first half of the sentence makes a broader statement regarding the proper deference to be accorded a surrendering country's decision on extraditability. The Canadian government's decision was not that the offense was non-extraditable because it was of a political character, a position that might have justified a narrower reading of *Johnson*. Instead, it maintained that the offense did not fall within the treaty's category of extraditable fraud offenses.... Thus, we believe that the first half of the sentence addressed the proper deference to be accorded a surrendering country's decision as to whether a particular offense comes within a treaty's extradition provision.

In *McGann*, [*v. U.S. Bd. of Parole*, 488 F.2d 39 (3rd Cir. 1973)] the Third Circuit also construed *Johnson* broadly. *McGann* involved the propriety of an extradition from Jamaica in which the Jamaican court held a parole violator extraditable under its treaty with the United States. The *McGann* court found the *Johnson* language controlling: "The holding of *Johnson v. Browne*... precludes any review of the Jamaican court's decision as to the extraditable nature of the offense...." We agree with the Third Circuit's reading of *Johnson*. According deference to the surrendering country's decision as to extraditability already underlies the related "doctrine of specialty." It would render that doctrine practically meaningless to hold that courts cannot try an extradited party for offenses other than those for which the surrendering government agreed to extradite, but need not defer to the surrendering government's threshold decision as to whether an offense is extraditable.

We therefore defer to the Swiss Federal Tribunal's decision as to Van Cauwenberghe's extraditability under the Treaty and hold that Van Cauwenberghe was properly extradited....

Notes

(1) Do the underlying policies behind the principle of dual criminality and the rule of specialty suggest that these two principles are closely aligned? Consider the discussion of these concepts as presented in *United States v. Saccoccia*, 58 F.3d 754 (1st Cir. 1995):

> Although the principles of dual criminality and specialty are closely allied, they are not coterminous....
>
> The principle of dual criminality dictates that, as a general rule, an extraditable offense must be a serious crime (rather than a mere peccadillo) punishable under the criminal laws of both the surrendering and the requesting state.... The current extradition treaty between the United States and Switzerland embodies this concept. *See* Treaty of Extradition, May 14, 1900, U.S.-Switz., Art. II, 31 Stat. 1928, 1929–30 (Treaty).
>
> The principle of dual criminality does not demand that the laws of the surrendering and requesting states be carbon copies of one another. Thus,

dual criminality will not be defeated by differences in the instrumentalities or in the stated purposes of the two nations' laws. . . . By the same token, the counterpart crimes need not have identical elements. *See Matter of Extradition of Russell*, 789 F.2d 801, 803 (9th Cir. 1986). Instead, dual criminality is deemed to be satisfied when the two countries' laws are substantially analogous. . . . Moreover, in mulling dual criminality concerns, courts are duty bound to defer to a surrendering sovereign's reasonable determination that the offense in question is extraditable. . . .

Mechanically, then, the inquiry into dual criminality requires courts to compare the law of the surrendering state that purports to criminalize the charged conduct with the law of the requesting state that purports to accomplish the same result. If the same conduct is subject to criminal sanctions in both jurisdictions, no more is exigible. . . .

The principle of specialty—a corollary to the principle of dual criminality, ... generally requires that an extradited defendant be tried for the crimes on which extradition has been granted, and none other. . . . The extradition treaty in force between the United States and Switzerland embodies this concept, providing that an individual may not be "prosecuted or punished for any offense committed before the demand for extradition, other than that for which the extradition is granted. . . ." Treaty, Art. IX.

Enforcement of the principle of specialty is founded primarily on international comity. . . . The requesting state must "live up to whatever promises it made in order to obtain extradition" because preservation of the institution of extradition requires the continuing cooperation of the surrendering state. . . . Since the doctrine is grounded in international comity rather than in some right of the defendant, the principle of specialty may be waived by the asylum state. . . .

Specialty, like dual criminality, is not a hidebound dogma, but must be applied in a practical, commonsense fashion. Thus, obeisance to the principle of specialty does not require that a defendant be prosecuted only under the precise indictment that prompted his extradition, . . . or that the prosecution always be limited to specific offenses enumerated in the surrendering state's extradition order. . . . In the same vein, the principle of specialty does not impose any limitation on the particulars of the charges lodged by the requesting nation, nor does it demand departure from the forum's existing rules of practice.

In the last analysis, then, the inquiry into specialty boils down to whether, under the totality of the circumstances, the court in the requesting state reasonably believes that prosecuting the defendant on particular charges contradicts the surrendering state's manifested intentions, or, phrased another way, whether the surrendering state would deem the conduct for which the

> requesting state actually prosecutes the defendant as interconnected with (as opposed to independent from) the acts for which he was extradited. . . .

(2) What is the procedure to be followed by a United States Attorney in trying to extradite someone to the United States? What documents are necessary to process the extradition? Consider the following procedure outlined in the Department of Justice's Justice Manual.[20]

> 9-15.240 — Documents Required in Support of Request for Extradition
>
> The request for extradition is made by diplomatic note prepared by the Department of State and transmitted to the foreign government through diplomatic channels. The documents specified in the treaty must accompany the extradition request. The Office of International Affairs (OIA) attorney will advise the prosecutor of the documentary requirements and provide exemplars, but it is the responsibility of the prosecutor to prepare and assemble the documents. The OIA attorney will review and approve the draft documents. Once the documents are finalized, following consultation with OIA, the prosecutor forwards the original and an OIA-specified number of copies to OIA in time for the documents to be translated, assembled, authenticated, and sent through the Department of State to the foreign government within any specified deadline.
>
> Although variations exist, extradition requests generally are composed of:
>
> - An affidavit from the prosecutor explaining the facts of the case and the charged offenses.
> - Copies of the statutes alleged to have been violated and the statute of limitations.
> - If the fugitive has not been prosecuted, certified copies of the arrest warrant and complaint or indictment.
> - Evidence, which may need to be in the form of witness affidavits, reports or documentary evidence, or summaries thereof, establishing that the crime was committed, including sufficient evidence (i.e., photograph, fingerprints, and affidavit of identifying witness) to establish the defendant's identity.
> - If the fugitive has been convicted, a certified copy of the order of judgment and committal establishing the conviction, and an affidavit (i) stating that the sentence was not served or was only partially served, (ii) specifying the amount of time remaining to be served, and (iii) providing evidence concerning identity.

---

20. http://www.justice.gov/usam/usam-9-15000-international-extradition-and-related-matters#9-15.240.

> Prosecutors should be aware that while there are few workable defenses to extradition, appeals and delays are common. Fugitives may be able to contest extradition on the basis of minor inconsistencies resulting from clerical or typographical errors. Although it may be possible to remedy these alleged defects, that process takes time. Therefore, pay careful attention to detail in preparing the documents.

18 U.S.C. § 3187 sets out the procedure for obtaining provisional arrest and detention pending formal documentation.

(3) What steps should be taken by a United States Attorney when he or she is unable to extradite an individual to the United States?[21] Consider section 9-15.600 of the DOJ Justice Manual:

> A fugitive may not be subject to extradition for any number of reasons, if he or she is a national of the country of refuge and that country does not extradite its nationals, the crime is not an extraditable offense, the statute of limitations has run in the foreign country, or the fugitive has been prosecuted in the country of refuge or in another country for the same conduct for which extradition is requested.
>
> There may be alternative methods available to secure the return of the fugitive or to limit his or her ability to live or travel overseas. OIA will advise the prosecutor concerning the availability of these methods. These alternative methods are discussed in JM 9-15.610-650.

(4) Where extradition is not possible in one country, can the government lure the individual into another country in order to proceed with an extradition? Consider section 9-15.630 of the DOJ Justice Manual.

> A lure involves using a subterfuge to entice a criminal defendant to leave a foreign country so that he or she can be arrested in the United States, in international waters or airspace, or in a third country for subsequent extradition, expulsion, or deportation to the United States. Lures can be complicated schemes or they can be as simple as inviting a fugitive by telephone to a party in the United States.
>
> Some countries will not extradite a person to the United States if the person's presence in that country was obtained through the use of a lure or other ruse. In addition, some countries may view a lure of a person from its territory as an infringement on its sovereignty or criminal law. Consequently, a prosecutor must consult with the Office of International Affairs (OIA) and secure approval from the Criminal Division before undertaking a lure. Prosecutors contemplating a lure should consult with OIA as early as possible. If OIA concurs with the lure proposal, OIA will recommend

21. Another (illegal) possibility is abduction which is discussed in chap. 16.

that a Deputy Assistant Attorney General (DAAG) in the Criminal Division approve the lure. Lure approval authority resides with the DAAG.

(5) The DOJ Justice Manual provides the government policy on the rule of specialty:

> § 9-15.500 Post Extradition Considerations: Limitations on Further Prosecution
>
> Every extradition treaty limits extradition to certain offenses. As a corollary, all extradition treaties restrict prosecution or punishment of the fugitive to the offense for which extradition was granted unless (1) an offense was committed after the fugitive's extradition or (2) the fugitive remains in the jurisdiction that requested extradition after expiration of a reasonable time (generally specified in the extradition treaty itself) following acquittal or completion of his or her punishment. This limitation is referred to as the Rule of Specialty. Federal prosecutors who wish to proceed against an extradited person on charges other than those for which extradition was granted must contact the Office of International Affairs (OIA) for guidance regarding the availability of a waiver of the Rule by the sending State.
>
> Frequently, defendants who have been extradited to the United States attempt to dismiss or limit the government's case against them by invoking the Rule of Specialty. There is a split in the courts on whether the defendant has standing to raise specialty: some courts hold that only a party to the Treaty (i.e., the sending State) may complain about an alleged violation of the specialty provision, other courts allow the defendant to raise the issue on his or her own behalf, and still other courts take a middle position and allow the defendant to raise the issue if it is likely that the sending State would complain as well. Whenever a defendant raises a specialty claim, the prosecutor should contact OIA for assistance in responding.
>
> OIA attorneys are subject-matter experts on extradition, and OIA is responsible for ensuring that the government's position in such cases remains consistent. Federal prosecutors should consult with OIA regarding issues raised by a fugitive after return to the United States regarding his or her extradition.

(6) Do prosecutors have to strictly adhere to the rule of specialty? Although many courts in the U.S. allow prosecutors leeway in adding charges following an extradition, there are some courts that adhere to a strict application of the doctrine of specialty. *See generally* Hugh Chadwick Thatcher, Note, *The Doctrine of Specialty: An Argument for a More Restrictive Rauscher Interpretation After State v. Pang*, 31 VAND. J. TRANSNAT'L L. 1321 (1998).

Does it make a difference in applying the doctrine of specialty how many counts are charged against the defendant? In *United States v. LeBaron*, 156 F.3d 621(5th Cir. 1998), Circuit Judge Emilio M. Garza stated:

> [T]he doctrine of specialty is concerned primarily with prosecution for different substantive offenses than those for which consent has been given, and not prosecution for additional or separate counts of the same offense. The appropriate test for a violation of specialty "is 'whether the extraditing country would consider the acts for which the defendant was prosecuted as independent from those for which he was extradited.'"

See also United States v. Saccoccia, 58 F.3d 757, 784 (1st Cir. 1995) ("forfeiture is neither a free-standing criminal offense nor an element of a racketeering offense under RICO, but is simply an incremental punishment for that prescribed conduct. Consequently, a defendant may be subjected to a forfeiture order even if extradition was not specifically granted in respect to the forfeiture allegations.").

In some cases the court can avoid resolving this issue by applying specialty strictly to the charges of the accused. In *United States v. Nosov*, 153 F. Supp.2d 477, 479–80 (S.D. N.Y. 2001), the prosecution added new charges against two of Noxov's co-defendants. He argued that the rule of specialty precluded this. The court stated:

> Nosov's argument fails for two reasons. As a preliminary matter, it appears that he lacks standing to make this petition. Nosov is correct that the circuit courts are split as to whether a defendant, as opposed to the country from which he was extradited, may invoke the specialty doctrine. Compare *United States v. Kaufman*, 874 F.2d 242, 243 (5th Cir. 1989) (holding that "only an offended nation can complain about the purported violation of an extradition. . . . Decisions from the Second Circuit — the binding authority for this court — suggest that a defendant would not have standing to invoke the rule of specialty. See *United States v. Reed*, 639 F.2d 896, 902 (2d Cir. 1981) (holding that "absent protest or objection by the offended sovereign, [a defendant] has no standing to raise violation of [an extradition treaty] as an issue") . . .
>
> The court, however, need not consider this issue in great detail, because even if Nosov had standing, his argument would fail. The rule of specialty is only violated if a superseding indictment charges new "separate offenses" against the defendant. . . . The two new counts contained in the S2 Indictment implicate only Ermichine and Gozman. In other words, Nosov does not face any charges of which the German government was not aware when it agreed to his extradition.

(7) What is the reasoning used by circuits that maintain that a defendant does not have standing to invoke the rule of specialty? In *United States v. Valencia-Trujillo*, 573 F.3d 1171 (11th Cir. 2009), the court stated:

> "Panama Express" sounds like the name of a train running through Central America, and in a sense it was. It is the code name of a joint operation in which the Coast Guard and a virtual alphabet soup of federal law

enforcement agencies (FBI, DEA, ICE, IRS), assisted by state and local agencies, investigated and infiltrated an international drug smuggling and distribution ring in South and Central America. The criminal enterprise was huge, and the Panama Express had a successful run. In its first seven years it hauled in over 600 tons of cocaine, worth about $8 billion, along with more than 1,200 convictions. This appeal involves one of those convictions.

Joaquin Mario Valencia-Trujillo, a Colombian citizen, organized and led the criminal enterprise. After Colombia extradited him to this country, Valencia-Trujillo was convicted by a jury of several drug and money laundering crimes. He was sentenced to 480 months imprisonment and ordered to forfeit $110 million. His appeal brings us issues involving the rule of specialty in international extradition, . . .

Valencia-Trujillo first contends that the district court violated the rule of specialty by prosecuting him for offenses beyond those Colombia authorized in his extradition papers. The rule of specialty "stands for the proposition that the requesting state, which secures the surrender of a person, can prosecute that person only for the offense for which he or she was surrendered by the requested state or else must allow that person an opportunity to leave the prosecuting state to which he or she had been surrendered." . . . The rule is grounded in concerns of international comity. As we have explained, "[b]ecause the surrender of the defendant requires the cooperation of the surrendering state, preservation of the institution of extradition requires that the petitioning state live up to whatever promises it made in order to obtain extradition." . . .

. . . [N]ot all treaties give defendants rights that can be asserted in the courts of this country.[a] As the Supreme Court recently explained:

A treaty is, of course, primarily a compact between independent nations. It ordinarily depends for the enforcement of its provisions on the interest and the honor of the governments which are parties to it. If these interests fail, its infraction becomes the subject of international negotiations and reclamations. It is obvious that with all this the judicial courts have nothing to do and can give no redress. Only if the treaty contains stipulations which are self-executing, that is, require no legislation to make them operative, will they have the force and effect of a legislative enactment.

Medellin v. Texas, 128 S. Ct. 1346, 1357 (2008) . . . . Unless extradition conditions or restrictions are grounded in self-executing provisions of a treaty, they do not have "the force and effect of a legislative enactment" that

a. The court interpreted the U.S. government's request for extradition as being based on Colombian law rather than on the existing Extradition treaty between the two countries. — Eds.

> the defendant has standing to assert in the courts of this country. Because Colombia's extradition of Valencia-Trujillo to the United States was not based on an extradition treaty between the two countries Valencia-Trujillo lacks standing to assert the rule of specialty.

By comparison, the district court in *In re Extradition of Handanovic*, 829 F. Supp. 2d 979 (D. Or. 2011), noted that the Ninth Circuit had allowed an individual "to raise whatever objections the extraditing country would have been entitled to raise." However, the district court went on to state that since Handanovic had not yet been extradited, "she ha[d] no standing to raise the issue now."

(8) Do many countries refuse to extradite their nationals? Are countries following a recognized principle of international law when they refuse to extradite their nationals? *See generally* Michael Plachta, *(Non-) Extradition of Nationals: A Never-ending Story?*, 13 Emory Int'l L. Rev. 77 (1999); Joshua H. Warmund, Comment, *Removing Drug Lords and Street Pushers: The Extradition of Nationals in Colombia and the Dominican Republic*, 22 Fordham Int'l L.J. 2373 (1999). Consider the case of Samuel Sheinbein, who was born in the United States, and fled to Israel fighting extradition under the Israeli nationality law. His eventual plea to committing a homicide in the United States was criticized when he received a sentence that was considered to be lenient in comparison to what he might have received in the United States. *See Teen's Plea Deal in Israel Angers U.S. Prosecutor*, Atl. J. Const., Aug. 26, 1999, at A8; Jack Katzenell, *Israel Convicts U.S. Teen of Murder*, Atl. J. Const, Sept. 3, 1999, at C4. *See also* Abraham Abramovsky & Jonathan I. Edelstein, *The Sheinbein Case and the Israeli-American Extradition Experience: A Need for Compromise*, 32 Vand. J. Transat'l L. 305 (1999).

(9) Do some countries face internal repercussions if they extradite individuals to the United States? *See* Barry Meier, *Pledges of Extradition Accompany Colombian Drug Arrests*, N.Y. Times, Oct. 14, 1999, at A3 (in the past Colombia did not extradite individuals to the U.S. arguing that they faced "terrorists [sic] acts by drug traffickers opposed to facing trial in the United States."). In 1997 Colombia changed its Constitution, permitting extradition. *Id.*

(10) Do countries refuse to extradite individuals to the United States if they oppose the proceedings that may occur within the United States? France initially refused to extradite one Ira Einhorn to the United States in that a Philadelphia court convicted him of murder in absentia, sentenced him to life, and there was no opportunity for a retrial. After the decision refusing extradition to the United States, Pennsylvania passed a law that would provide a possible retrial. A French court ruled that Einhorn could now be extradited to the United States. See Martha Moore & Vivian Walt, France Sends Fugitive Back to USA, USA Today, July 20, 2001, at 3A. Einhorn was tried again and convicted again. He argued that the legislation allowing for his re-trial was unconstitutional under the Pennsylvania Constitution, essentially on separation of powers grounds. *See* Dave Lindorf, *For Ira Einhorn a Fate Worse Than Death*, http://www.Salon.com, Oct. 18, 2002. In denying his appeal, the Superior Court of Pennsylvania stated:

> We need not address the constitutionality of that section, however, as this Court cannot deem Einhorn's extradition unlawful. France's decision to extradite Einhorn was predicated upon, inter alia, his receiving a new trial. At Einhorn's request, he received a new trial. Accordingly, we must defer to France's decision to extradite Einhorn, as we have no authority to rule that the action of La Cour Administrative d'Appel de Bordeaux was unlawful. *See United States v. Campbell*, 300 F.3d 202, 209 (2d Cir. 2002), cert. denied, 538 U.S. 1049 (2003) ("[O]ur courts cannot second-guess another country's grant of extradition to the United States."); *United States v. Medina*, 985 F. Supp. 397, 401 (S.D.N.Y. 1997) ("[A] foreign government's decision to extradite an individual in response to a request from the United States is not subject to review by United States courts."). Therefore, we do not reach the constitutional issue because we do not have the authority to grant the relief requested by Einhorn.

Commonwealth v. Einhorn, 911 A. 2d 960, 2006 PA Super 322 (2006).

(11) Do countries refuse to extradite individuals for reasons other than nationality and procedural unfairness? Spain refused to extradite a former auto-industry executive charged with giving confidential documents to a rival company. The court found that there was not "sufficient cause for his extradition" and "also cited his poor health and the fact that the U.S. took seven years to formulate the extradition request." Spain did welcome the United States to proceed in their courts "as the extradition treaty between the two countries allows." *Madrid Court Rejects Extradition in GM Case*, Wall St. J., June 20, 2001, at A15.

On March 14, 2002, the United States issued an indictment charging Ahmad Omar Saeed Sheikh with: Count 1—Conspiracy to commit hostage taking resulting in the death of Daniel Pearl, Count 2—Hostage taking resulting in the death of Daniel Pearl. Daniel Pearl was a United States national who, prior to his death, worked for the Wall Street Journal. Pakistan refused to extradite the accused to the United States. Pervez Musharraf, President of Pakistan's reasoning was "so that their punishment at home could serve as an example to those defying his crackdown on terrorism." *Pakistan Resists U.S. Extradition*, Wall St. J., May 6, 2002, at A18. He was sentenced to death in July of 2002 and—shades of the United States—his appeal is apparently still pending.

Can extradition be contingent upon the extradited individual being exempt from receiving a death sentence? See Chapter 19 for further discussion.

(12) Can individuals who are extradited to the United States successfully raise claims of procedural violations in the extradition process? In *United States v. Antonakeas*, 255 F.3d 714 (9th Cir. 2001), the court held that "unlike the substantive right of specialty, procedural violations do not give rise to individually enforceable rights."

(13) Can the accused claim a right to a speedy trial when he or she is not extradited to face trial after charges are brought? In *United States v. Fernandes*, 618 F. Supp. 2d 62 (D.D.C. 2009), the court stated:

> In cases such as this one—where a defendant is located abroad for much of the delay—the hallmark of government diligence is extradition. When the United States has a valid extradition treaty in place with a foreign country and prosecutors formally seek extradition pursuant to that treaty, courts routinely hold that the government has satisfied its diligence obligation.... On the other hand, if the government presents "substantial evidence" that extradition would be futile, then an extradition request normally is not necessary. For example, in *United States v. Corona-Verbera*, 509 F.3d 1105, 1114–15 (9th Cir. 2007), the court held that a representation from an Assistant U.S. Attorney that Mexico would not surrender its own citizens wanted on drug charges, bolstered by expert testimony, a U.S. State Department report, and statistical evidence, constituted "substantial evidence" that seeking extradition of a Mexican national wanted on drug charges during the 1990s would be futile.... Similarly, the government usually satisfies its diligence obligation if it shows that it attempted extradition informally....
>
> Here, the government has not sought extradition formally or informally, nor has it presented substantial evidence that extradition would have been futile. The government does not dispute that the United States and India have a functioning extradition treaty in place.... But the only conversation government investigators and prosecutors had about the possibility of extradition occurred in mid-November 2007—more than sixteen months after defendant was indicted.... This is meager evidence that extradition would have been futile; it does not approach the definitive, multi-source evidence other courts have found sufficient to excuse a failure to request extradition....

(14) Many countries do not accept either the inchoate or the complicity (Pinkerton) doctrines of conspiracy that are a feature of United States law. Can the government circumvent the speciality rule by not charging conspiracy but requesting at trial a Pinkerton instruction that permits a conviction of a substantive offense that is in furtherance of the conspiracy? In *Gallo-Chamorro v. United States*, 233 F.3d 1298 (11th Cir. 2000), the court stated:

> Gallo asserts that the Pinkerton instruction violated the doctrine of specialty because the Colombian government failed to authorize a Pinkerton charge in Resolution 235. Gallo also points to Diplomatic Note E-1518, expressly stating that Colombian courts do not recognize *Pinkerton* because it is "vicarious" in nature.
>
> Our ruling in Gallo's direct appeal is controlling herein. Gallo was prosecuted only for the crimes for which Colombia granted extradition; there was no specialty violation. Rather than mandating exact uniformity between the charges set forth in the extradition request and the actual indictment, "what the doctrine of specialty requires is that the prosecution be 'based on the same facts as those set forth in the request for extradition.'" The district

court tried Gallo on the facts included in the request for extradition, and gave jury instructions in accordance therewith.

We view such reasoning as persuasive, as we did on direct appeal, and conclude that the Pinkerton instruction did not violate the specialty doctrine.

(15) What evidence will be allowed in an extradition hearing? In *In the Matter of the Extradition of Ben-Dak*, 2008 U.S. Dist. Lexis 29460 (S.D.N.Y. 2008), the court stated:

While the evidence in support of extradition must be "competent and adequate," *Bingham v. Bradley*, 241 U.S. 511, 517, (1916), neither the Federal Rules of Criminal Procedure nor the Federal Rules of Evidence apply, . . . Instead, the admissibility of evidence is governed by 18 U.S.C. § 3190, which provides that:

> [d]epositions, warrants, or other papers or copies thereof offered in evidence upon the hearing of any extradition case shall be received and admitted as evidence on such hearing for all the purposes of such hearing if they shall be properly and legally authenticated so as to entitle them to be received for similar purposes by the tribunals of the foreign country from which the accused party shall have escaped, and the certificate of the principal diplomatic or consular officer of the United States resident in such foreign country shall be proof that the same, so offered, are authenticated in the manner required.

18 U.S.C. § 3190.

Accordingly, hearsay evidence is admissible. . . . The court may even rely on "unsworn statements of absent witnesses." . . . . However, this does not mean that the hearing court should act as a "rubber stamp." . . . . Rather, "a court must conduct an independent assessment of the evidence and closely examine the requesting country's submissions to ensure that any hearsay bears sufficient indicia of reliability to establish probable cause." . . .

See also Mike Scarcella, *DOJ Extradition Hearings are not Mini Trials*, The BLT Blog, Sept. 17, 2009, *available at* http://legaltimes.typepad.com/blt/2009/09/doj-extradition-hearings-are-not-mini-trials.html.

(16) What level of evidence in necessary to establish "identity" for the purposes of an extradition? In *Joseph v. Hoover*, 254 F. Supp.2d 595 (D. V.I. 2003), the court stated:

Joseph's final argument in his effort to avoid extradition is that there was insufficient evidence regarding his identity as the person committing the offenses or that the offenses even occurred. As noted by the Third Circuit Court of Appeals,

> the probable cause standard applicable in extradition proceedings is identical to that used by courts in federal preliminary hearings. The burden

of the government is to offer evidence that "would support a reasonable belief that [the defendant] was guilty of the crime charged." The probable cause standard applicable in extradition proceedings has been described as "evidence sufficient to cause a person of ordinary prudence and caution to conscientiously entertain a reasonable belief of the accused's guilt."

Sidali, 107 F.3d at 199 . . . . Thus, in an extradition proceeding, the magistrate judge's role is "to determine whether there is competent evidence to justify holding the accused to await trial, and not to determine whether the evidence is sufficient to justify a conviction." *Id*. . . . Accordingly, the magistrate judge need only determine that a reasonable belief exists that the defendant committed the charged offense, and not that he is guilty beyond a reasonable doubt. . . .

(17) Traditional Anglo-American extradition practice required the requesting state to establish a "prima facie case" in support of an extradition request. Countries like the United Kingdom, Canada, and Australia are increasingly dispensing with that requirement in their treaty relations. Consider the following provision in Article 8 of the most recent extradition treaty between the U.K. and the U.S.:

2. All requests for extradition shall be supported by:

(a) as accurate a description as possible of the person sought, together with any other information that would help to establish identity and probable location;

(b) a statement of the facts of the offense(s);

(c) the relevant text of the law(s) describing the essential elements of the offense for which extradition is requested;

(d) the relevant text of the law(s) prescribing punishment for the offense for which extradition is requested; and

(e) documents, statements, or other types of information specified in paragraphs 3 or 4 of this Article, as applicable.

3. In addition to the requirements in paragraph 2 of this Article, a request for extradition of a person who is sought for prosecution shall be supported by:

(a) a copy of the warrant or order of arrest issued by a judge or other competent authority

(b) a copy of the charging document, if any; and

(c) for requests to the United States, such information as would provide a reasonable basis to believe that the person sought committed the offense for which extradition is requested.**

** Extradition Treaty between the Government of the United Kingdom of Great Britain and Northern Ireland and the Government of the United States of America, Washington, 31 March,

§ 16.03 Extradition from the United States

United States v. Lui Kin-Hong

United States Court of Appeals for the First Circuit
110 F.3d 103 (1997); stay denied 520 U.S. 1206 (1997)
*reh. en banc denied 1997 U.S. App. LEXIS 7587**

Lynch, Circuit Judge:

The United States District Court granted a writ of habeas corpus to Lui Kin-Hong ("Lui"), who sought the writ after a magistrate judge certified to the Secretary of State that she may, in her discretion, surrender Lui for extradition to the Crown Colony of Hong Kong. The United Kingdom, on behalf of Hong Kong, had sought Lui's extradition on a warrant for his arrest for the crime of bribery. Lui's petition for habeas corpus was premised on the fact that the reversion of Hong Kong to the People's Republic of China will take place on July 1, 1997, and it will be impossible for the Crown Colony to try and to punish Lui before that date. The United States appeals. We reverse the order of the district court granting the writ of habeas corpus.

The United States argues that Lui is within the literal terms of the extradition treaties between the United States and the United Kingdom, that the courts may not vary from the language of the treaties, and that the certification must issue. Lui argues that the language of the treaties does not permit extradition, an argument which is surely wrong. Lui's more serious argument is that the Senate, in approving the treaties, did not mean to permit extradition of someone to be tried and punished by a government different from the government which has given its assurances in the treaties.

Lui does not claim that he faces prosecution in Hong Kong on account of his race, religion, nationality, or political opinion. He does not claim to be charged with a political offense.[b] The treaties give the courts a greater role when such considerations are present. Here, Lui's posture is that of one charged with an ordinary crime. His claim is that to surrender him now to Hong Kong is, in effect, to send him to trial and punishment in the People's Republic of China. The Senate, in approving the treaties, could not have intended such a result, he argues, and so the court should interpret the treaties as being inapplicable to his case. Absent a treaty permitting extradition, he argues, he may not be extradited.

2003, Instruments of Ratification exchanged 26 April, 2007, *available at* http://www.fco.gov.uk/resources/en/pdf/pdf8/fco_pdf_usextraditiontreaty.

* Although the en banc vote was to deny a rehearing, Circuit Judge Stahl wrote a dissenting opinion stating that, "the district court correctly concluded that Lui cannot be certified for extradition because the United Kingdom fails to 'live up to the terms of its extradition agreement with the United States.'" — Eds.

b. *See supra* § 16.01 and *infra* § 16.03 on the political offense exception. — Eds.

While Lui's argument is not frivolous, neither is it persuasive. The Senate was well aware of the reversion when it approved a supplementary treaty with the United Kingdom in 1986. The Senate could easily have sought language to address the reversion of Hong Kong if it were concerned, but did not do so. The President has recently executed a new treaty with the incoming government of Hong Kong, containing the same guarantees that Lui points to in the earlier treaties, and that treaty has been submitted to the Senate.[c] In addition, governments of our treaty partners often change, sometimes by ballot, sometimes by revolution or other means, and the possibility or even certainty of such change does not itself excuse compliance with the terms of the agreement embodied in the treaties between the countries. Treaties contain reciprocal benefits and obligations. The United States benefits from the treaties at issue and, under their terms, may seek extradition to the date of reversion of those it wants for criminal offenses.

Fundamental principles in our American democracy limit the role of courts in certain matters, out of deference to the powers allocated by the Constitution to the President and to the Senate, particularly in the conduct of foreign relations. Those separation of powers principles, well rehearsed in extradition law, preclude us from rewriting the treaties which the President and the Senate have approved. The plain language of the treaties does not support Lui. Under the treaties as written, the courts may not, on the basis of the reversion, avoid certifying to the Secretary of State that Lui may be extradited. The decision whether to surrender Lui, in light of his arguments, is for the Secretary of State to make.

This is not to say American courts acting under the writ of habeas corpus, itself guaranteed in the Constitution, have no independent role. There is the ultimate safeguard that extradition proceedings before United States courts comport with the Due Process Clause of the Constitution. On the facts of this case, there is nothing presenting a serious constitutional issue of denial of due process. Some future case may, on facts amounting to a violation of constitutional guarantees, warrant judicial intervention. This case does not.

. . . .

Lui is charged in Hong Kong with conspiring to receive and receiving over US $3 million in bribes from Giant Island Ltd. ("GIL") or GIL's subsidiary, Wing Wah Company ("WWC"). Lui, formerly a senior officer of the Brown & Williamson Co., was "seconded" in 1990 to its affiliated company, the British American Tobacco Co. (Hong Kong) Ltd. ("BAT-HK"), where he became Director of Exports in 1992. The charges result from an investigation by the Hong Kong Independent Commission Against Corruption ("ICAC"). The Hong Kong authorities charge that GIL and WWC, to which BAT-HK distributed cigarettes, paid bribes in excess of HK $100 million (approximately US $14 to $15 million) to a series of BAT-HK executives, including Lui. The bribes were allegedly given in exchange for a virtual monopoly on

c. The U.S./Hong Kong treaty entered into force Jan. 21, 1998. — Eds.

the export of certain brands of cigarettes to the People's Republic of China ("PRC") and to Taiwan. Among the cigarettes distributed were the popular Brown & Williamson brands of Kent, Viceroy, and Lucky Strike. GIL purchased three-quarters of a billion dollars in cigarettes from 1991 to 1994, mostly from BAT-HK.

A former GIL shareholder, Chui To-Yan ("Chui"), cooperated with the authorities and, it is said, would have provided evidence of Lui's acceptance of bribes. Some of Lui's alleged co-conspirators attempted to dissuade Chui from cooperating. Chui was later abducted, tortured, and murdered. The ICAC claims that the murder was committed to stop Chui from testifying. Lui is not charged in the murder conspiracy. Lui was in the Philippines (which has no extradition treaty with Hong Kong) on a business trip when the Hong Kong authorities unsuccessfully sought to question him in April 1994. Lui has not returned to Hong Kong since then.

At the request of the United Kingdom ("UK"), acting on behalf of Hong Kong, United States marshals arrested Lui as he got off a plane at Boston's Logan Airport on December 20, 1995. The arrest was for the purpose of extraditing Lui to Hong Kong.... The magistrate judge commenced extradition hearings on May 28, 1996.... The magistrate judge found that there was probable cause to believe that Lui had violated Hong Kong law on all but one of the charges in the warrant. Magistrate Judge Karol, pursuant to 18 U.S.C. § 3184,[d] issued a careful decision certifying Lui's extraditability on August 29, 1996. *In re Extradition of Lui Kin-Hong ("Lui Extradition")*, 939 F. Supp. 934 (D. Mass. 1996). On September 3, 1996, Lui filed an amended petition for a writ of habeas corpus, the only avenue by which a fugitive

---

d. 18 U.S.C. § 3184 provides:

> Whenever there is a treaty or convention for extradition between the United States and any foreign government, or in cases arising under section 3181(b), any justice or judge of the United States, or any magistrate [United States magistrate judge] authorized so to do by a court of the United States, or any judge of a court of record of general jurisdiction of any State, may, upon complaint made under oath, charging any person found within his jurisdiction, with having committed within the jurisdiction of any such foreign government any of the crimes provided for by such treaty or convention, or provided for under section 3181(b), issue his warrant for the apprehension of the person so charged, that he may be brought before such justice, judge, or magistrate [United States magistrate judge], to the end that the evidence of criminality may be heard and considered. Such complaint may be filed before and such warrant may be issued by a judge or magistrate [United States magistrate judge] of the United States District Court for the District of Columbia if the whereabouts within the United States of the person charged are not known or, if there is reason to believe the person will shortly enter the United States. If, on such hearing, he deems the evidence sufficient to sustain the charge under the provisions of the proper treaty or convention, or under section 3181(b), he shall certify the same, together with a copy of all the testimony taken before him, to the Secretary of State, that a warrant may issue upon the requisition of the proper authorities of such foreign government, for the surrender of such person, according to the stipulations of the treaty or convention; and he shall issue his warrant for the commitment of the person so charged to the proper jail, there to remain until such surrender shall be made.

Id. — Eds.

sought for extradition (a "relator") may attack the magistrate judge's decision, with the district court. . . .

After a hearing, the district court issued a memorandum and order granting the writ on January 7, 1997. Lui Kin-Hong v. United States ("Lui Habeas"), 957 F. Supp. 1280 (D. Mass. Jan. 7, 1997). The district court reasoned that, because the Crown Colony could not try Lui and punish him before the reversion date, the extradition treaty between the United States and the UK, which is applicable to Hong Kong, prohibited extradition. . . . Because no extradition treaty between the United States and the new government of Hong Kong has been confirmed by the United States Senate, the district court reasoned, the magistrate judge lacked jurisdiction to certify extraditability. . . . The district court denied the government's motion for reconsideration on January 13, 1997. This court then stayed the district court's order and expedited the present appeal. At the time Lui was arrested in Boston in December 1995, more than eighteen months remained before the reversion of Hong Kong to the PRC on July 1, 1997.

. . . .

The extradition request was made pursuant to the Extradition Treaty Between the Government of the United States of America and the Government of the United Kingdom of Great Britain and Northern Ireland, June 8, 1972, 28 U.S.T. 227 (the "Treaty"), as amended by the Supplementary Treaty Between the Government of the United States of America and the Government of the United Kingdom of Great Britain and Northern Ireland, June 25, 1985, T.I.A.S. No. 12050 (the "Supplementary Treaty"). The original Treaty was made applicable to Hong Kong, among other British territories, . . . The Supplementary Treaty is applicable to Hong Kong by its terms. . . .

Hong Kong's status as a Crown Colony is coming to an end on July 1, 1997, when Hong Kong is to be restored to the PRC. The impending reversion, at the expiration of the UK's ninety-nine year leasehold, was formally agreed upon by the UK and the PRC in 1984; the United States was not a party to this agreement. . . . United States Senate ratification of the Supplementary Treaty occurred on July 17, 1986, well after the widely publicized signing of the Joint Declaration. . . . Clearly, the Senate was aware of the planned reversion when it approved the applicability to Hong Kong of the Supplementary Treaty. The Supplementary Treaty does not contain an exception for relators who can show that their trial or punishment will occur after the date of reversion. Indeed, the Supplementary Treaty is entirely silent on the question of reversion.

The United States does not have an extradition treaty with the PRC. However, on December 20, 1996, the United States signed an extradition treaty with the government of the nascent HKSAR, which provides for reciprocal post-reversion extradition. . . . The New Treaty will not enter into force until the Senate gives its advice and consent. . . .

In the United States, the procedures for extradition are governed by statute. . . . The statute establishes a two-step procedure which divides responsibility for extradition between a judicial officer and the Secretary of State. The judicial officer's duties are set out in 18 U.S.C. § 3184. In brief, the judicial officer, upon complaint, issues an arrest warrant for an individual sought for extradition, provided that there is an extradition treaty between the United States and the relevant foreign government and that the crime charged is covered by the treaty. . . . If a warrant issues, the judicial officer then conducts a hearing to determine if "he deems the evidence sufficient to sustain the charge under the provisions of the proper treaty." . . . If the judicial officer makes such a determination, he "shall certify" to the Secretary of State that a warrant for the surrender of the relator "may issue." . . . The judicial officer is also directed to provide the Secretary of State with a copy of the testimony and evidence from the extradition hearing. . . .

It is then within the Secretary of State's sole discretion to determine whether or not the relator should actually be extradited. . . . Additionally, the Secretary may attach conditions to the surrender of the relator. . . . The State Department alone, and not the judiciary, has the power to attach conditions to an order of extradition. . . . Of course, the Secretary may also elect to use diplomatic methods to obtain fair treatment for the relator. . . .

Thus, under 18 U.S.C. § 3184, the judicial officer's inquiry is limited to a narrow set of issues concerning the existence of a treaty, the offense charged, and the quantum of evidence offered. The larger assessment of extradition and its consequences is committed to the Secretary of State. This bifurcated procedure reflects the fact that extradition proceedings contain legal issues peculiarly suited for judicial resolution, such as questions of the standard of proof, competence of evidence, and treaty construction, yet simultaneously implicate questions of foreign policy, which are better answered by the executive branch. Both institutional competence rationales and our constitutional structure, which places primary responsibility for foreign affairs in the executive branch, ... support this division of labor.

In implementing this system of split responsibilities for extradition, courts have developed principles which ensure, among other things, that the judicial inquiry does not unnecessarily impinge upon executive prerogative and expertise. . . . These principles of construction require courts to:

> interpret extradition treaties to produce reciprocity between, and expanded rights on behalf of, the signatories: "[Treaties] should be liberally construed so as to effect the apparent intention of the parties to secure equality and reciprocity between them. For that reason, if a treaty fairly admits of two constructions, one restricting the rights which may be claimed under it, and the other enlarging it, the more liberal construction is to be preferred."

. . . .

Another principle that guides courts in matters concerning extradition is the rule of non-inquiry. More than just a principle of treaty construction, the rule of non-inquiry tightly limits the appropriate scope of judicial analysis in an extradition proceeding. Under the rule of non-inquiry, courts refrain from "investigating the fairness of a requesting nation's justice system," . . . and from inquiring "into the procedures or treatment which await a surrendered fugitive in the requesting country." . . . The rule of non-inquiry, like extradition procedures generally, is shaped by concerns about institutional competence and by notions of separation of powers. . . . It is not that questions about what awaits the relator in the requesting country are irrelevant to extradition; it is that there is another branch of government, which has both final say and greater discretion in these proceedings, to whom these questions are more properly addressed.

Lui contends that, on July 1, 1997, the reversion of Hong Kong to the PRC will result in his being subjected to trial and punishment by a regime with which the United States has no extradition treaty. This future event, Lui argues, operates retroactively to render his extradition illegal, as of today, because, he says, extradition is only legitimate where trial and punishment will be administered by the regime with which the United States has a treaty.

Although Lui is correct that the government has conceded that he will not be tried before reversion, it is also quite possible that the scenario he depicts will not arise. The new extradition treaty with the HKSAR may be approved by the United States Senate [it was — eds.], establishing a continuity of treaties through and beyond July 1, 1997. The United States government may choose to extend the current Treaty by executive agreement. To the extent that Lui's argument depends on the fairness of the procedures he will be subjected to, he asks this court to decide that the PRC will not adhere to the Joint Declaration with the UK, in which it declared its intention to maintain Hong Kong's legal system for fifty years.

All of these questions involve an evaluation of contingent political events. The Supreme Court has said that the indicia of a non-justiciable political question include:

> a textually demonstrable constitutional commitment of the issue to a coordinate political department; or a lack of judicially discoverable and manageable standards for resolving it; or the impossibility of deciding without an initial policy determination of a kind clearly for nonjudicial discretion; or the impossibility of a court's undertaking independent resolution without expressing lack of respect due coordinate branches of government; or an unusual need for unquestioning adherence to a political decision already made; or the potentiality of embarrassment from multifarious pronouncements by various departments on one question.

Baker v. Carr, 369 U.S. 186, 217, 82 S. Ct. 691, 7 L. Ed. 2d 663 (1962). While not all of these ingredients are present here, several are. Moreover, unlike many "political questions," whose resolution, absent judicial determination, must await the vagaries of the political process, here there is a statutory scheme which provides for the resolution of these questions by an identified member of the executive branch. The case for judicial resolution is thus weaker than with many such questions.

The principles of reciprocity and liberal construction also counsel against construing the Treaties so as to prohibit Lui's extradition. Hong Kong, through the United Kingdom, has entered bilateral treaties with the United States. The United States has sought extradition of criminals from Hong Kong in the past, and may wish to continue to do so up until July 1, 1997. If the executive chooses to modify or abrogate the terms of the Treaties that it negotiated, it has ample discretion to do so. However, if this court were to read a cut-off date vis-a-vis extraditions to Hong Kong into the Treaties, it would risk depriving both parties of the benefit of their bargain.

None of these principles, including non-inquiry, may be regarded as an absolute. We, like the Second Circuit, "can imagine situations where the relator, upon extradition, would be subject to procedures or punishment so antipathetic to a federal court's sense of decency as to require reexamination of the principles" discussed above.... This is not such a case. Lui is wanted for economic, not political, activities whose criminality is fully recognized in the United States. His extradition is sought by the current Hong Kong regime, a colony of Great Britain, which, as Lui himself points out, is one of this country's most trusted treaty partners. Moreover, Lui has been a fugitive from Hong Kong since 1994. He has been subject to extradition since entering the United States in December 1995. That now only a few months remain before the reversion of Hong Kong is partly attributable to strategic choices made by Lui himself. There is nothing here which shocks the conscience of this court....

There is no dispute that the Treaty, as supplemented by the Supplementary Treaty, is currently in effect and is applicable to Hong Kong. The district court, in granting Lui's habeas petition, reasoned that "the Treaty, by its own terms, does not allow the extradition of a person to Hong Kong if the Crown Colony of Hong Kong is unable to try and to punish that person." ... The government counters that the terms of the Treaty clearly allow Lui's extradition. There is nothing in the plain language of the Treaties that would permit the construction made by the district court. The principles discussed above argue persuasively against reading judicially created limitations into the Treaties' unambiguous text....

We begin our analysis of the Treaties with a brief overview of the Treaties' operative provisions. Article I of the Treaty states the basic reciprocal compact, providing that:

> Each Contracting Party undertakes to extradite to the other, in the circumstances and subject to the conditions specified in this Treaty, any person found in its territory who has been accused or convicted of any offense within Article III, committed within the jurisdiction of the other Party.

Treaty, art. I.

Article III contains the "dual criminality" requirement, a requirement that is "central to extradition law and [one that] has been embodied either explicitly or implicitly in all prior extradition treaties between the United States and Great Britain." ... Article III, in relevant part, provides that:

> Extradition shall be granted for an act or omission the facts of which disclose an offense within any of the descriptions listed in the Schedule annexed to this Treaty . . . or any other offense, if: (a) the offense is punishable under the laws of both Parties by imprisonment or other form of detention for more than one year or by the death penalty. . . .

Treaty, art. III(1). The annexed Schedule lists twenty-nine general crimes, including bribery, the crime of which Lui is accused. . . .

Article V contains various affirmative defenses, including the "political offense" exception. As a general matter, the political offense exception "is now a standard clause in almost all extradition treaties of the world." . . . The political offense exception in the Treaty prohibits extradition where "(i) the offense for which extradition is requested is regarded by the requested Party as one of a political character; or (ii) the person sought proves that the request for his extradition has in fact been made with a view to try or punish him for an offense of a political character." . . .

The Supplementary Treaty narrows the availability of this political offense exception. It lists a range of crimes—all crimes of violence—that may not be regarded as political offenses for the purpose of raising the political offense exception. . . . The Supplementary Treaty also offers an affirmative defense to fugitives sought for crimes of violence who, by virtue of its article 1, are unable to raise the political offense exception. . . . Such a fugitive may block extradition by establishing:

> by a preponderance of the evidence that the request for extradition has in fact been made with a view to try or punish him on account of his race, religion, nationality, or political opinions, or that he would, if surrendered, be prejudiced at his trial or punished, detained or restricted in his personal liberty by reason of his race, religion, nationality or political opinions.

Id. art. 3(a).

The procedural requisites of an extradition request are specified in article VII of the Treaty. The request must be accompanied by, inter alia, a description of the fugitive, a statement of facts of the offense, and the text of the law under which he is charged. . . . For accused (as opposed to already convicted) fugitives, the request must also include a valid arrest warrant and "such evidence as, according to the law of the requested Party, would justify his committal for trial if the offense had been committed in the territory of the requested Party, including evidence that the person requested is the person to whom the warrant of arrest refers." . . .

Article XII contains the "specialty" requirement, a common feature of extradition treaties. Specialty has two basic components. First, the requesting state may not try the fugitive for any crimes other than the specific crime for which extradition was sought and granted. Second, the requesting state may not re-extradite the fugitive to a third state. . . .

Both the district court and Lui focus on four Treaty provisions in concluding that the Treaty is inapplicable to Lui. . . . We address these provisions in turn, concluding that the obligation of the United States to extradite Lui, specified in article I of the Treaty, is not undermined by any of these provisions. . . .

The district court understood the warrant requirement of article VII(3) to serve the purpose of permitting "the requested sovereign to know that the relator has been accused . . . pursuant to the laws of the requesting sovereign, and that he will be tried and punished in accordance with that sovereign's laws." . . . In this case, the district court reasoned, since Lui would not be tried in accordance with the present Hong Kong regime's laws, the warrant requirement was not met. . . .

There is nothing in the language of article VII(3), or the rest of article VII, which indicates that the warrant requirement serves the greater function attributed to it by the district court. Indeed, the warrant requirement appears to do nothing more than to help the judicial officer in the requested country to confirm that there are in fact charges properly pending against the relator in the requested country, and that the relator is actually the person sought. It does not authorize the investigation which the district court envisioned, and indeed such an investigation is foreclosed by the rule of non-inquiry. A warrant was provided by the Hong Kong authorities here, and Lui does not attack its validity or authenticity. The warrant requirement was plainly satisfied. . . .

The district court understood the purpose of the dual criminality requirement, as stated in article III of the Treaty, to be "to provide the requested sovereign with the opportunity to examine the substantive law of the requesting sovereign in the context of the Treaty." . . . The court stated that the requirement serves to "underscore[] the expectation running through the Treaty that [Lui] is to be tried, judged, and punished in accordance with the laws of the requesting sovereign." . . .

There is nothing in the text of article III of the Treaty that supports this sweeping conclusion. The dual criminality requirement, by its plain terms, is satisfied if the crime of which the relator is accused appears on the annexed Schedule or is punishable in both countries by at least one year's imprisonment. Bribery, as noted above, appears on the annexed Schedule.

The purpose of the dual criminality requirement is simply to ensure that extradition is granted only for crimes that are regarded as serious in both countries. . . . The dual criminality requirement is satisfied here. . . .

The district court also relied on article 3(a) of the Supplementary Treaty, which, it stated, requires the judicial officer "to examine the reasons for the requesting sovereign's desire to try and to punish the relator." . . . In this case, stated the district court, article 3(a) "underscores again the Treaty's requirement and expectation that extradition . . . may not take place if the requesting sovereign . . . is unable to try and punish Lui in the relatively few days left before its reversion to China." . . .

The Supplementary Treaty article 3(a) defense is simply inapplicable here. Supplementary Treaty article 3(a) describes a defense which is available only to fugitives charged with one of the crimes specified in article 1 of the Supplementary Treaty, all of which are crimes of violence. Lui's alleged crime — bribery — is not among the crimes enumerated in the Supplementary Treaty's article 1.

Indeed, the very purpose of the Supplementary Treaty was to cabin the political offense exception so that perpetrators of certain violent offenses would be precluded from avoiding extradition simply because their criminal activity was inspired by political motivation.... Lui properly does not claim that he is entitled to the article V(1)(c) political offense exception.... Moreover, article 3(a) allows the judicial officer to make only a narrowly circumscribed inquiry. "An extradition target must establish by a preponderance of the evidence that, if he were surrendered, the legal system of the requesting country would treat him differently from other similarly situated individuals because of his race, religion, nationality, or political opinions." ... Lui made no such showing of discrimination, and the district court, in making its own predictions about the post-reversion justice system in Hong Kong, exceeded the narrow inquiry permitted by article 3(a)....

The district court understood the Treaty's specialty provision to signify that "the Treaty allows only for extradition for offenses that can be tried and punished by the requesting sovereign." ... Because the specialty obligation cannot be enforced by the United States after reversion, reasoned the district court, article XII is violated ab initio, and Lui cannot be extradited.... The rule of specialty literally has no application here. The rule has two basic requirements: that the relator be tried for the crimes charged in the extradition warrant and that the relator not be re-extradited to another country. There is no claim that either of these is violated....

If Lui's position were correct, the enforceability of many extradition treaties to which the United States is a party would be thrown into grave doubt. Regimes come and go, as, indeed, do states. Moreover, 18 U.S.C. § 3184, which defines the role of the courts in the extradition process, gives no discretion to the judicial officer to refuse to certify extraditability on the ground that a treaty partner cannot assure the requested country that rights under a treaty will be enforced or protected....

Of course, Lui may express his concerns about the post-reversion enforceability of specialty to the Secretary of State, who, in her discretion, may choose not to surrender him. We note that the newly signed, as yet unratified, extradition treaty between the United States and the HKSAR provides that specialty protection "shall apply to fugitive offenders who have been surrendered between the parties prior to the entry into force" of the new treaty.... It is not the role of the judiciary to speculate about the future ability of the United States to enforce treaty obligations....

Lui also challenges the determination of the magistrate judge that there was probable cause to believe that Lui had violated Hong Kong law on eight of the nine charges in the warrant.... Lui argued that the government's evidence was insufficient to support an inference of bribery and that there was, in any event, an innocent explanation. The government argued that the undisputed facts were sufficient to establish probable cause, and that the explanation was inherently implausible. In addition, the government argued, it had two "smoking gun" statements directly saying the payments were bribes. [The court found the statements reliable.]

For these reasons we reverse the grant of habeas corpus by the district court. . . .

Notes

(1) Does extradition from the U.S. require a treaty? In *Ntakirutimana v. Reno*, 184 F.3d 419 (5th Cir. 1999), *cert. denied*, 528 U.S. 1135 (2000), Circuit Judge Garza stated:

> . . . Ntakirutimana alleges that Article II of the Constitution of the United States requires that an extradition occur pursuant to a treaty. It is unconstitutional, he claims, to extradite him to the ICTR [International Criminal Tribunal of Rwanda][e] pursuant to a statute in the absence of a treaty. Accordingly, he claims it is unconstitutional to extradite him on the basis of the Agreement and Pub. Law 104–106 (the "Congressional-Executive Agreement"). The district court concluded that it is constitutional to surrender Ntakirutimana in the absence of an "extradition treaty," because a statute authorized extradition. . . .
>
> To determine whether a treaty is required to extradite Ntakirutimana, we turn to the text of the Constitution. Ntakirutimana contends that Article II, Section 2, Clause 2 of the Constitution requires a treaty to extradite. This Clause, which enumerates the President's foreign relations power, provides in part that "[the President] shall have Power, by and with the Advice and Consent of the Senate, to make Treaties, provided two thirds of the Senators present concur; and he shall nominate, and by and with the Advice and Consent of the Senate, shall appoint Ambassadors, other public Ministers and Consuls. . . ." U.S. Const. art. II, § 2, cl. 2. This provision does not refer either to extradition or to the necessity of a treaty to extradite. The Supreme Court has explained, however, that "the power to surrender is clearly included within the treaty-making power and the corresponding power of appointing and receiving ambassadors and other public ministers." *Terlinden v. Ames*, 184 U.S. 270, 289, 22 S. Ct. 484, 492, 46 L. Ed. 534 (1902) (citation omitted).
>
> Yet, the Court has found that the Executive's power to surrender fugitives is not unlimited. In *Valentine v. United States*, 299 U.S. 5, 57 S. Ct. 100, 81 L. Ed. 5 (1936), the Supreme Court considered whether an exception clause in the United States's extradition treaty with France implicitly granted to the Executive the discretionary power to surrender citizens. The Court first stated that the power to provide for extradition is a national power that "is not confided to the Executive in the absence of treaty or legislative provision." . . .

---

e. See Chapter 21 for additional discussion of International Criminal Tribunal for Rwanda. — Eds.

The Court then considered whether any statute authorized the Executive's discretion to extradite. The Court commented that:

> Whatever may be the power of the Congress to provide for extradition independent of treaty, that power has not been exercised save in relation to a foreign country or territory "occupied by or under the control of the United States." Aside from that limited provision, the Act of Congress relating to extradition simply defines the procedure to carry out an existing extradition treaty or convention.

Id. at 9, 57 S. Ct. at 102–03 (citations omitted). The Court concluded that no statutory basis conferred the power on the Executive to surrender a citizen to the foreign government. . . . The Court subsequently addressed whether the treaty conferred the power to surrender, and found that it did not. . . . The Court concluded that, "we are constrained to hold that [the President's] power, in the absence of statute conferring an independent power, must be found in the terms of the treaty and that, as the treaty with France fails to grant the necessary authority, the President is without the power to surrender the respondents." . . . The Court added that the remedy for this lack of power "lies with the Congress, or with the treaty-making power wherever the parties are willing to provide for the surrender of citizens." . . .

Valentine indicates that a court should look to whether a treaty *or statute* grants executive discretion to extradite. Hence, *Valentine* supports the constitutionality of using the Congressional-Executive Agreement to extradite Ntakirutimana. Ntakirutimana attempts to distinguish *Valentine* on the ground that the case dealt with a *treaty* between France and the United States. Yet, *Valentine* indicates that a statute suffices to confer authority on the President to surrender a fugitive. . . . Ntakirutimana suggests also that *Valentine* expressly challenged the power of Congress, independent of treaty, to provide for extradition. *Valentine*, however, did not place a limit on Congress's power to provide for extradition. . . . Thus, although some authorization by law is necessary for the Executive to extradite, neither the Constitution's text nor *Valentine* require that the authorization come in the form of a treaty.

Notwithstanding the Constitution's text or *Valentine*, Ntakirutimana argues that the intent of the drafters of the Constitution supports his interpretation. He alleges that the delegates to the Constitutional Convention intentionally placed the Treaty power exclusively in the President and the Senate. The delegates designed this arrangement because they wanted a single executive agent to negotiate agreements with foreign powers, and they wanted the senior House of Congress — the Senate — to review the agreements to serve as a check on the executive branch. Ntakirutimana also claims that the rejection of alternative proposals suggests that the framers

> believed that a treaty is the only means by which the United States can enter into a binding agreement with a foreign nation.
>
> We are unpersuaded by Ntakirutimana's extended discussion of the Constitution's history. Ntakirutimana does not cite to any provision in the Constitution or any aspect of its history that requires a treaty to extradite. Ntakirutimana's argument, which is not specific to extradition, is premised on the assumption that a treaty is required for an international agreement. To the contrary, "the Constitution, while expounding procedural requirements for treaties alone, apparently contemplates alternate modes of international agreements." . . .
>
> Ntakirutimana next argues that historical practice establishes that a treaty is required to extradite. According to Ntakirutimana, the United States has never surrendered a person except pursuant to an Article II treaty, and the only involuntary transfers without an extradition treaty have been to "a foreign country or territory 'occupied by or under the control of the United States.'" . . . This argument fails for numerous reasons. First, *Valentine* did not suggest that this "historical practice" limited Congress's power. . . . Second, the Supreme Court's statements that a statute may confer the power to extradite also reflect a historical understanding of the Constitution. . . . Even if Congress has rarely exercised the power to extradite by statute, a historical understanding exists nonetheless that it may do so. Third, in some instances in which a fugitive would not have been extraditable under a treaty, a fugitive has been extradited pursuant to a statute that "filled the gap" in the treaty. . . . Thus, we are unconvinced that the President's practice of usually submitting a negotiated treaty to the Senate reflects a historical understanding that a treaty is required to extradite. . . .

Circuit Judge DeMoss, dissenting in this case stated:

> The executive and legislative branches of government erroneously disregarded their obligation to respect the structure provided by the Constitution when they purported to enter this extradition agreement. We should issue a writ of habeas corpus, and Ntakirutimana should not be surrendered. The extradition agreement in place between the United States and the Tribunal is unenforceable, as it has not been properly ratified. The agreement's implementing legislation is unconstitutional insofar as it purports to ratify the Surrender Agreement by a means other than that prescribed by the Treaty Clause. The two acts seek impermissibly to evade the mandatory constitutional route for implementing such an agreement. I therefore respectfully dissent.

(2) What constitutional rights will be afforded individuals that the United States government is considering for extradition? In the absence of probable cause, does a provisional arrest in anticipation of an extradition meet constitutional standards? If

this individual flees the United States prior to a resolution of whether the government can extradite, will the unauthorized departure foreclose raising constitutional issues? Consider the majority and dissenting opinion in the case of *Parretti v. United States*, 143 F.3d 508 (9th Cir. 1998):

Pregerson, Circuit Judge:

> . . . We took this case en banc to consider whether the arrest of Giancarlo Parretti pursuant to an Extradition Treaty with France violated the Fourth Amendment and whether his detention without bail prior to France's decision to request his extradition violated the Due Process Clause of the Fifth Amendment, or, whether this appeal should be dismissed under the fugitive disentitlement doctrine because Parretti fled the United States while his appeal was pending before a panel of this court. Because Parretti is a fugitive from justice, we exercise our discretion under the disentitlement doctrine and dismiss his appeal. Therefore, we find it unnecessary to address his constitutional claims. . . . The Supreme Court has "consistently and unequivocally approved dismissal as an appropriate sanction when a prisoner is a fugitive during the ongoing appellate process." . . . The fugitive disentitlement doctrine empowers us to dismiss the appeal of a defendant who flees the jurisdiction of the United States after timely appealing. An appellate court's power to disentitle a fugitive from access to the appellate process is grounded in equity. . . . Our court has exercised its discretion and dismissed the appeal of a criminal defendant who became a fugitive from justice while his appeal was pending. . . .
>
> Several rationales that underlie the fugitive disentitlement doctrine apply to this appeal. First, although Parretti's status as a fugitive does not "strip the case of its character as an adjudicable case or controversy," it does disentitle him from calling upon the resources of the court to resolve his claims. . . . By fleeing the jurisdiction of the United States, Parretti forfeited his right to appellate review under the fugitive disentitlement doctrine. . . .
>
> Second, Parretti has fled the United States. He remains a fugitive beyond the reach of this court's jurisdiction. If we were to reach the merits of Parretti's constitutional claims and affirm the district court, such a decision could not secure Parretti's presence before the district court, nor could it assure that any "judgment . . . issued would prove enforceable." . . .
>
> Third, "dismissal by an appellate court after a defendant has fled its jurisdiction serves an important deterrent function and advances an interest in efficient, dignified appellate practice." . . .
>
> Fourth, the adversary character of criminal litigation may be compromised when the defendant is a fugitive. . . . A defendant's flight threatens the effective operation of the appellate process because the fugitive's counsel may have little or no incentive to represent his client should further proceedings be necessary. . . .

APPEAL DISMISSED

REINHARDT, CIRCUIT JUDGE dissenting:

In this case, the court faces two extremely important issues that warrant our most thorough consideration. The positions advanced by the government on both constitutional questions are remarkable and should be examined with the greatest of care. In doing so, we should bear in mind that what the government tells us it can do to a foreign citizen in this case, it can just as easily do to a United States citizen in the next....

First, the government maintains that when a foreign country simply suggests that it is considering requesting extradition, the United States government can arrest the person without a showing of probable cause and keep him locked up for months without bail. This position is at odds with one of our most basic constitutional principles—that the government cannot seize a person off the streets (or from a lawyer's office) and deny him his liberty without first showing probable cause to believe he has engaged in criminal activity. The government's contention that probable cause in the context of a provisional arrest is merely probable cause to believe that a foreign country has issued an arrest warrant is plainly incorrect. Such a showing would never, in any other circumstances, suffice to support the arrest of a person in this country, and there is no reason why it should suffice in the case of provisional arrests.

As to the bail issue, the government relies on cryptic language in an ambiguous case written by the Supreme Court almost 100 years ago for its argument that an almost irrebuttable presumption against bail exists in extradition cases.... By failing to address the government's argument, we leave this circuit's law on the bail issue exactly where it was before this case—in total disarray....

The fallacy in the government's positions is amply demonstrated in the panel's majority opinions, which I adopt in full; they still accurately set forth the law. Notwithstanding the compelling nature of the constitutional issues, however, the majority has avoided deciding them by invoking the fugitive disentitlement doctrine under the most unusual of circumstances. Because the doctrine is inapplicable to the circumstances presented here, it is this court's duty to reach the merits of the case. Accordingly, I dissent.

I briefly review the procedural history of this case in order to demonstrate why applying the fugitive disentitlement doctrine in this case is unusual and serves no purpose. On October 18, 1995, Giancarlo Parretti was arrested by federal agents, pursuant to a warrant issued by a United States Magistrate Judge on the basis of allegations that an international warrant had been issued against him in France. On the basis of a letter from the government of France indicating that it would seek Parretti's extradition, the magistrate judge denied bail and ordered that he be detained pending the extradition hearing. Parretti filed a petition for habeas corpus in the district court, arguing that his prolonged detention was unconstitutional. On November 9, the district court denied the petition.

Soon thereafter, Parretti filed an emergency motion with this court. On November 21, after Parretti had been incarcerated for 33 days, a panel of this court heard oral argument and ordered his immediate release on two independent grounds. First, the panel found that Parretti's arrest violated the Fourth Amendment because it was effected without a showing of probable cause to believe that he had committed an extraditable offense. Second, the panel concluded that Parretti's continued detention violated his Fifth Amendment right to due process because the district court specifically found that he presented neither a risk of flight nor a danger to the community. In a published opinion issued subsequently, the panel elaborated fully on its reasons for granting Parretti's emergency motion.

After the panel issued its order, but prior to the time the panel issued its full opinion, the district court implemented the order and Parretti was released on bail. Eight days after his release, the government, at the behest of France, filed a formal request for Parretti's extradition, at which time the district court made the requisite probable cause finding. The government did not, however, seek to have Parretti taken into federal custody again. Instead, sometime afterwards, jurisdiction over Parretti was assumed by the state of Delaware. He was then tried and convicted on criminal charges in a Delaware state court. Pending sentencing on these offenses, Parretti fled the Delaware court's jurisdiction. Thereafter, the panel's full opinion was released, and the government sought and we granted, at its suggestion, rehearing en banc because of the government's objections to the content of the panel's decision on the constitutional questions. Parretti has, of course, obtained all the relief he ever desired from the court and seeks nothing further.

In light of these procedural and factual circumstances, it is clear that the fugitive disentitlement doctrine has no applicability. Indeed, neither party has urged the court to invoke the doctrine and both parties agree that the doctrine has no relevance to the case. The purpose of the doctrine is to deny to those who have fled the court's jurisdiction any benefits of the court system. Here, Parretti received all the relief he could possibly obtain prior to fleeing and he seeks no further benefit from the court. Our dismissal of the case will deny Parretti nothing—it is only the government that seeks relief now, and it seeks relief not from the order we issued, but from the precedential effect of our opinion on the serious constitutional questions that arise in many extradition cases. The fugitive disentitlement doctrine makes sense *only* when we deny the *fugitive* some form of relief

> from the court, not when we frustrate our own ability to resolve critical constitutional questions. In the words of the Supreme Court, as quoted by the majority, . . . the doctrine makes sense only as a "sanction" against the defendant.
>
> As the majority's opinion amply demonstrates, the fugitive disentitlement doctrine is properly invoked only in cases in which the defendant seeks to benefit from the use of our limited judicial resources. That is not the case here. I therefore dissent.

(3) In 1985, a District of Columbia District Court held the federal extradition statute, 18 U.S.C. § 3184, unconstitutional. The court agreed with plaintiffs "that the extradition statute purports to confer upon the Secretary of State the power to review and set aside the legal conclusions of federal extradition judges and is therefore unconstitutional." *Lobue v. Christopher*, 893 F. Supp. 65, 67 (D.D.C. 1995). Although the plaintiffs were provided relief, the Circuit Court vacated the order. *Lobue v. Christopher*, 82 F.3d 1081 (D.C. Cir. 1996). Other courts have, likewise, found that the statute is constitutional. *See, e.g., Manrique Carreno v. Johnson*, 899 F. Supp. 624 (S.D. Fl. 1995), *Extradition of Sutton*, 905 F. Supp. 631 (E.D. Mo. 1995). Does the extradition statute raise concerns with regard to separation of powers? *See generally* Allison Marston, Comment, *Innocents Abroad: An Analysis of the Constitutionality of the International Extradition Statute*, 33 STAN. J. INT'L L. 343 (1997) (suggesting reforms to extradition statute).

(4) In *Skaftouros v. United States*, 667 F.3d 144 (2d Cir. 2011), the court stated:

> At an extradition hearing, the "judicial officer's inquiry is confined to the following: whether a valid treaty exists; whether the crime charged is covered by the relevant treaty; and whether the evidence marshaled in support of the complaint for extradition is sufficient under the applicable standard of proof." *Cheung v. United States*, 213 F.3d 82, 88 (2d Cir. 2000). An extradition hearing is "not to be regarded as in the nature of a final trial by which the prisoner could be convicted or acquitted of the crime charged against him," *Benson v. McMahon*, 127 U.S. 457, 463 (1888), and is "not the occasion for an adjudication of guilt or innocence," *Melia v. United States*, 667 F.2d 300, 302 (2d Cir. 1981). Rather, "it is 'essentially a preliminary examination to determine whether a case is made out which will justify the holding of the accused and his surrender to the demanding nation.'" . . . . In this way, the judicial officer's function is much the same as his "accustomed task of determining if there is probable cause to hold a defendant to answer for the commission of an offense." As we have stressed in the past, "[w]hat is at issue in the proceeding . . . is not punishability but prosecutability."

(5) If an extradition treaty includes a statute of limitations, can an individual be extradited after the applicable time period? Consider this issue as raised in the case below.

Ross v. United States Marshal for the Eastern District of Oklahoma

United States Court of Appeals for the Tenth Circuit
168 F.3d 1190 (1999)

Brorby Circuit Judge:

The Government of Northern Ireland, United Kingdom issued warrants for the arrest of Appellant, George Finbar Ross, for forty-one charged offenses stemming from Mr. Ross' alleged involvement in a fraudulent investment scheme. The United States subsequently arrested Mr. Ross pursuant to an extradition treaty existing between the United States and the United Kingdom. After a magistrate judge certified his extradition, Mr. Ross filed a petition for writ of habeas corpus pursuant to 28 U.S.C. § 2241 challenging his extradition. The district court denied the petition and Mr. Ross filed this appeal. We exercise jurisdiction pursuant to 28 U.S.C. § 2253 and we affirm. . . .

The scope of review of a magistrate judge's extradition order under a treaty with a foreign country is limited to "determining whether the magistrate had jurisdiction, whether the offense charged is within the treaty and, by a somewhat liberal construction, whether there was any evidence warranting the finding that there was reasonable ground to believe the accused guilty." . . . In this case, Mr. Ross does not contest the magistrate's jurisdiction nor challenge the evidence of his guilt. Rather, he argues the offenses charged are not within the treaty because: (1) the charges are time-barred under the relevant statute of limitations, and (2) the warrants charging Mr. Ross with "false accounting" do not meet the dual criminality requirement. . . .

Article V of the Extradition Treaty provides extradition shall not be granted if the prosecution has become time-barred according to the law of either the requesting or requested country. . . No Northern Ireland statute of limitations applies to Mr. Ross' charges. The applicable United States law provides for a five-year statute of limitations. 18 U.S.C. § 3282. The statute may be tolled, however, if the accused is a fugitive "fleeing from justice." 18 U.S.C. § 3290.

In this case, Northern Ireland seeks extradition based on charges brought approximately twelve years after Mr. Ross committed the alleged offenses — well beyond the statutory limit. However, the district court concluded the statute tolled because Mr. Ross was fleeing from justice when he moved to the United States in October 1983. . . .

As a preliminary matter, we must first determine what constitutes "fleeing from justice" under the statute. The circuit courts are currently split on the issue. A small minority of circuits have held mere absence from the jurisdiction in which the crime was committed is enough to toll the statute . . . *In re Assarsson*, 687 F.2d 1157, 1162 (8th Cir. 1982); McGowen v. United States, 105 F.2d 791, 792, 70 App. D.C. 268 (D.C. Cir. 1939). The district court, on the other hand, adopted the majority view, which requires the prosecution to prove the accused had an intent to avoid arrest or prosecution. See Greever, 134 F.3d at 780; United States v. Rivera-Ventura, 72 F.3d 277, 283 (2d Cir. 1995); United States v. Fonseca-Machado, 53 F.3d 1242, 1244 (11th Cir.), cert. denied, 516 U.S. 925 (1995); United States v. Marshall, 856 F.2d 896, 900 (7th Cir. 1988); United States v. Gonsalves, 675 F.2d 1050, 1052 (9th Cir.), cert. denied, 459 U.S. 837, 103 S. Ct. 83, 74 L. Ed. 2d 78 (1982); Donnell v. United States, 229 F.2d 560, 565 (5th Cir. 1956); Brouse v. United States, 68 F.2d 294, 295 (1st Cir. 1933). The Supreme Court has not squarely addressed the issue. However, in considering the predecessor to 18 U.S.C. § 3290, the Court in *Streep v. United States*, 160 U.S. 128, 16 S. Ct. 244, 40 L. Ed. 365 (1895) implicitly recognized intent as an element of fleeing from justice, ... Consistent with *Streep*, we conclude "fleeing from justice" requires the government to prove, by a preponderance of the evidence, the accused acted with the intent to avoid arrest or prosecution.

Having thus determined the appropriate standard of proof, we must decide whether the district court committed clear error in finding Mr. Ross had the requisite intent to flee arrest or prosecution when he moved to the United States. We believe the record supports the district court's conclusion. By October 1983, the investigatory record indicates Mr. Ross was aware of the International Investment's ongoing fraudulent scheme—he knew International Investment used investors' money to make multiple unsecured loans for his benefit and to pay interest to previous investors. Mr. Ross also likely knew International Investment was insolvent or rapidly approaching insolvency, and that International Investment would soon have to submit to a full audit to maintain its Gibraltar banking license, thereby revealing the fraudulent scheme. Based on this evidence, it was not clearly erroneous for the district court to infer Mr. Ross' intent to flee arrest or prosecution.

The fact that Northern Ireland had not yet initiated its investigation does not change this conclusion. An accused may form the requisite intent even though prosecution has not actually begun.... In other words, an intent to avoid an *anticipated* arrest or prosecution is sufficient to toll the statute.

We likewise reject Mr. Ross' argument that he did not have the intent to avoid prosecution because the charged conduct occurred after he moved. A prosecutor's decision as to which charges to file is a matter of discretion and involves consideration of many factors.... We fail to see how this decision-making process limited or restricted Mr. Ross' intent to flee prosecution in October 1983. More important, the record indicates Mr. Ross was aware of the potential criminality of his conduct and its imminent discovery in October 1983. Because this evidence forms a sufficient basis from which to infer Mr. Ross' intent to avoid an anticipated prosecution, we conclude the district court's determination was not clearly erroneous....

Under Article III of the Extradition Treaty, an offense must meet the dual criminality requirement in order to be extraditable.... The doctrine of dual criminality requires the offense with which the accused is charged to be "punishable as a serious crime in both the requesting and requested states." ... To satisfy the dual criminality requirement, the requesting and requested countries' statutes must be substantially analogous or "punish conduct falling within the broad scope of the same generally recognized crime." . . .

The magistrate concluded the offenses listed in Mr. Ross' extradition request met the dual criminality requirement. Specifically, the magistrate determined Mr. Ross' alleged conduct is criminal under the United States statutes prohibiting mail and wire fraud, 18 U.S.C. §§1341 and 1343, and the Oklahoma false pretenses statute; Okla. Stat. tit. 21, §1541.2. Mr. Ross argues the warrants charging him with "false accounting" do not meet the duality requirement. . . .

Warrants six through forty-one charge Mr. Ross with violating §17(1)(b) of the Theft Act (Northern Ireland) of 1969 which makes it a crime for one to produce or make use of a misleading, false or deceptive account or other document made for accounting purposes, "with a view to gain for himself or another or with intent to cause loss to another." Mr. Ross argues this section of the Theft Act is not substantially analogous to the federal mail and wire fraud statutes because those statutes, unlike the Theft Act, require proof the defendant carried out a fraudulent scheme through use of the mails or wire transmissions. We disagree. The Theft Act and the mail and wire fraud statutes proscribe the same basic conduct-use of false representations to defraud or obtain property. . . . The element requiring use of the mails or interstate wire transmission is merely a jurisdictional requirement which makes the underlying crime federal in nature. . . . The criminal conduct each statute proscribes remains substantially analogous, thus satisfying the dual criminality requirement. . . .

The judgment of the district court is AFFIRMED.

Notes

(1) Statutes of limitation were also an issue of contention in the extradition of Avelino Cruz Martinez to Mexico for a homicide committed in 2006. In affirming the district court's denial of Martinez's claims, the Sixth Circuit Court of Appeals engaged in a detailed discussion of extradition and statutes of limitation.

> After people commit violent crimes, they sometimes flee, leaving the city of the crime in some instances, even leaving the country in others. If a fugitive leaves the country, that complicates law enforcement efforts. One trait of sovereignty is that countries have no legal, as opposed to moral, obligation to turn criminal suspects over to another country for prosecution. The point of extradition treaties is to prevent such crimes from going unpunished by imposing a golden rule obligation on each party to the treaty—an agreement by each country to return haven-seeking fugitives to the other.
>
> The golden rule is not the first thing that came to anyone's mind after two murders occurred at a New Year's Eve party gone awry in a small Mexican village in 2006. Avelino Cruz Martinez, now a citizen of the United States, attended the party and admits that there is probable cause to believe he was

the assailant. After the murders, Cruz Martinez returned to his home in the United States.

Invoking a 1978 extradition treaty, Mexico asked its northern neighbor to return Cruz Martinez to Mexico to be tried for murder. Cruz Martinez filed a habeas corpus petition, claiming that his extradition would violate Article 7 of the treaty, which prohibits extradition when "prosecution" or "enforcement of the penalty" for the charged offense "has become barred by lapse of time according to the laws of the requesting or requested Party." Extradition Treaty, U.S.-Mex., art. 7, May 4, 1978, 31 U.S.T. 5059, 5064–65. In particular, he argued that his extradition would violate (1) the relevant statute of limitations and (2) his Sixth Amendment right to a speedy trial. The district court rejected his arguments and denied his petition for habeas corpus. So do we.

. . . .

"Extradition shall not be granted," Article 7 of the United States-Mexico Extradition Treaty says, "when the prosecution or the enforcement of the penalty" for the charged offense "has become barred by lapse of time according to the laws of the requesting or requested Party." Extradition Treaty, U.S.-Mex., *supra*, art. 7, 31 U.S.T. at 5064–65. Cruz Martinez argues that his prosecution has become barred by (1) the relevant American statute of limitations. . . .

Cruz Martinez argues that the charged offense is analogous to second-degree murder under American federal law, which means a five-year limitations period applies to the charge. 18 U.S.C. §§ 1111(a)–(b), 3282(a). The government disagrees, comparing the offense to first-degree murder, which comes with no limitations period. *Id.* §§ 1111(a)–(b), 3281, 3591(a)(2). We need not take sides on this dispute because, for the reasons forcefully expressed in the panel majority's opinion, the statute of limitations did not expire even if the five-year period applies. *Cruz Martinez v. United States*, 793 F.3d 533, 542–44 (6th Cir. 2015).

"[N]o person shall be prosecuted, tried, or punished for any [non-capital] offense," the five-year limitations statute provides, "unless the indictment is found or the information is instituted within five years next after such offense shall have been committed." 18 U.S.C. § 3282(a). Because statutes of limitations protect defendants from excessive delay between the time of the offense and the time of prosecution, they stop running when the prosecution begins — which means, in American federal courts, when an indictment or information is returned. *United States v. Marion*, 404 U.S. 307, 320–23, 92 S.Ct. 455, 30 L.Ed.2d 468 (1971). But Mexico, which models its legal system not on Blackstone's common law but on Napoleon's civil law, lacks the sort of indictment and information procedures that exist in the United States. Miguel Sarré & Jan Perlin, "Mexico," in *Criminal Procedure:*

> *A Worldwide Study* 351, 372 (Craig M. Bradley ed., 2d ed. 2007). Does that mean there is nothing Mexico can do under § 3282 to prevent a "lapse of time" from occurring? No: Because the issuance of an arrest warrant marks the end of the preliminary investigation and the beginning of the prosecution in Mexico, that event stops the American statute of limitations from running. And because a Mexican court issued an arrest warrant within two months of Cruz Martinez's alleged offense, the five-year limitations period does not bar his prosecution.
>
> The only other circuit to consider this question agrees. It held that "a Mexican arrest warrant is the equivalent of a United States indictment and may toll the United States statute of limitations" for purposes of an extradition treaty. *Sainez v. Venables*, 588 F.3d 713, 717 (9th Cir. 2009). The *Third Restatement of Foreign Relations Law* echoes the point. "For purposes of applying statutes of limitation to requests for extradition," it notes, courts generally calculate the limitations period "from the time of the alleged commission of the offense to the time of the warrant, arrest, indictment, or similar step in the requesting state, or of the filing of the request for extradition, whichever occurs first." *Restatement (Third) of the Foreign Relations Law of the United States* § 476 cmt. e (1987).

Martinez v. United States, 828 F.3d 451 (6th Cir. 2016).

(2) Does the existence of an extradition treaty raise due process concerns when the United States decides to prosecute an individual as opposed to extraditing him or her to another country? Consider this issue as raised in *United States v. Wharton*, 320 F.3d 526, 532–34 (5th Cir. 2003):

> Defendant . . . argues that the foreign murder statute, 18 U.S.C. § 1119, is unconstitutional as applied to him. Subsection (c)(2) of 18 U.S.C. § 1119 provides that:
>
> > No prosecution shall be approved under this section unless the Attorney General, in consultation with the Secretary of State, determines that the conduct took place in a country in which the person is no longer present, and the country lacks the ability to lawfully secure the person's return. A determination by the Attorney General under this paragraph is not subject to judicial review.
>
> Defendant argues that because the United States and Haiti have a valid extradition treaty, the statute is inapplicable to him.
>
> The statute, however, clearly states that the Attorney General's determination on this issue is not subject to review. Defendant argues that the prohibition against judicial review violates his Fifth Amendment due process rights here because the Attorney General's determination was erroneous. Defendant contends that the Attorney General should not be permitted to make a determination that a person is beyond the reach of the foreign country when facts establish that the country could secure his return. The

Government responds that the Attorney General's determination is not an element of the crime and, therefore, does not raise Fifth Amendment due process concerns. We agree....

In *United States v. White*, 51 F. Supp. 2d 1008, 1012 (E.D. Cal. 1997), the court faced a similar question. There, the defendant was also charged under the foreign murder statute and argued that, because Japan had the ability to secure the defendant's return under an extradition treaty, the Attorney General's determination was unreasonable. The court refused to review that determination, upholding the statute's prohibition against judicial review....

While not binding, we find *White* persuasive. We conclude that the statutory structure suggests that Congress intentionally separated the Attorney General's prosecutorial decisions from the elements of the crime.

§ 16.04 Political Offense Exception

Quinn v. Robinson

United States Court of Appeals for the Ninth Circuit
783 F.2d 776 (1986)

Reinhardt, Circuit Judge:

Pursuant to 18 U.S.C. § 3184 (1982) and the governing treaty between the United States and the United Kingdom of Great Britain and Northern Ireland ("United Kingdom"), Extradition Treaty of June 8, 1972, United States — United Kingdom, 28 U.S.T. 227, T.I.A.S. No. 8468 [hereinafter cited as Treaty], the United Kingdom seeks the extradition of William Joseph Quinn, a member of the Irish Republican Army ("IRA"), in order to try him for the commission of a murder in 1975 and for conspiring to cause explosions in London in 1974 and 1975. After a United States magistrate found Quinn extraditable, Quinn filed a petition for a writ of habeas corpus. The district court determined that Quinn cannot be extradited because a long-standing principle of international law which has been incorporated in the extradition treaty at issue — the political offense exception — bars extradition for the charged offenses. The United States government, on behalf of the United Kingdom, appeals.

This case requires us to examine the parameters of a foreign sovereign's right to bring about the extradition of an accused who maintains that the offenses with which he is charged are of a political character. Ultimately we must determine whether the political offense exception is applicable to the type of violent offenses Quinn is alleged to have committed. We undertake this task with the aid of very little helpful precedent. The United States Supreme Court has discussed the political offense exception only once, and then during the nineteenth century. *See Ornelas v. Ruiz*, 161 U.S. 502, 16 S. Ct. 689, 40 L. Ed. 787 (1896).... The only time we considered the subject, *see Karadzole v. Artukovic*, 247 F.2d 198 (9th Cir. 1957), the Supreme

Court vacated our opinion, *see Karadzole v. Artukovic*, 355 U.S. 393, 78 S. Ct. 381, 2 L. Ed. 2d 356 (1958) (mem.), an opinion which, in any event, has subsequently been roundly and uniformly criticized. . . . Only one circuit has previously considered in any detail how or whether the exception applies when the accused person or persons have engaged in conduct involving the use of some of the more violent techniques or tactics that have come to mark the activities of contemporary insurgent or revolutionary movements. *Eain v. Wilkes*, 641 F.2d 504 (7th Cir.), *cert. denied*, 454 U.S. 894, 102 S. Ct. 390, 70 L. Ed. 2d 208 (1981). The few opinions of other circuits that have considered the exception shed no light on the difficult questions we must resolve here. Therefore, we must carefully examine the historic origins of the political offense exception, analyze the various underpinnings of the doctrine, trace its development in the lower courts and elsewhere, and seek to apply whatever principles emerge to the realities of today's political struggles. . . .

A. The Extradition Treaty

The right of a foreign sovereign to demand and obtain extradition of an accused criminal is created by treaty. . . . In the absence of a treaty there is no duty to extradite, . . . and no branch of the United States government has any authority to surrender an accused to a foreign government except as provided for by statute or treaty. . . .

The extradition treaty between the United States and the United Kingdom provides for the reciprocal extradition of persons found within the territory of one of the nations who have been accused or convicted of certain criminal offenses committed within the jurisdiction of the other nation. . . . Murder and conspiracy to cause explosions, the offenses with which Quinn has been charged, are extraditable offenses under the Treaty. . . . United States citizenship does not bar extradition by the United States. . . . However, under the doctrine of "dual criminality," an accused person can be extradited only if the conduct complained of is considered criminal by the jurisprudence or under the laws of both the requesting and requested nations. . . . In addition, there must be evidence that would justify committing the accused for trial under the law of the nation from whom extradition is requested if the offense had been committed within the territory of that nation. . . . The doctrine of "specialty" prohibits the requesting nation from prosecuting the extradited individual for any offense other than that for which the surrendering state agreed to extradite. . . .

The treaty between the United States and the United Kingdom provides certain exceptions to extradition, notwithstanding the existence of probable cause to believe that the accused has committed the charged offense. In particular, the treaty specifies that "extradition shall not be granted if . . . the offense for which extradition is requested is regarded by the requested party as one of a political character. . . ."

As it has in other recent extradition cases, . . . the government contends that both the magistrate and the district court lacked jurisdiction to determine whether the political offense exception bars extradition. According to the government, the language of both the jurisdictional statute and the treaty precludes a judicial determination of whether the exception applies. Moreover, the government contends, such a determination involves political questions that only the executive branch of the government can resolve. Like every court before us that has considered these arguments, . . . and like those that have not explicitly considered them but have proceeded to determine whether the exception applies, . . . we believe the government's contentions to be meritless. . . .

The government next argues that because three of the factors enumerated in *Baker v. Carr*, 369 U.S. 186, 217, 82 S. Ct. 691, 7 L. Ed. 2d 663 (1962), are present in this case, the judiciary should abstain, under the political question doctrine, from determining whether the political offense exception applies. The government contends that determining whether the exception applies requires a policy determination of a kind clearly inappropriate for the exercise of judicial discretion, that different pronouncements from the executive and judiciary on matters necessary to a determination of the applicability of the exception could embarrass the government, and that the issue does not lend itself to resolution through judicially discoverable manageable standards. . . . In identifying the specific *Baker v. Carr* factors that it claims are present in this case, the government begins by noting that in order to consider whether the political offense exception applies, a court must determine whether a political uprising was in progress in the foreign land when the offense occurred. . . . The government contends that such a factual finding requires a policy determination. We disagree. We need not determine whether the uprising was "justified" or was motivated by political forces of which we approve. Rather, we must determine simply whether an uprising was in progress. . . .

The government also contends that the presence of a second factor enumerated in *Baker v. Carr* counsels judicial abstention. The government argues that a judicial determination that Quinn's extradition is precluded by the political offense exception would "recognize" political terrorists and would thus constitute a potentially embarrassing pronouncement different than the pronouncements of the executive branch. . . . [W]e do not believe the executive branch has refused to recognize the existence of terrorists. Rather, in some cases, it may have refused to recognize the *legitimacy* of these groups. We fail to see why a judicial acknowledgment that terrorist groups exist would constitute a "recognition" of those groups in the sense of legitimizing their actions. . . .

Far from embarrassing the executive branch, assigning to the judiciary the responsibility for determining when the exception applies actually affords a degree of protection to the executive branch. As a political branch, the executive could face undue pressure when public and international opposition to the activities of an unpopular group create conflicts with the treaty obligation created by the political offense exception. . . . By assigning the initial determination of when the exception applies to the impartial judiciary — particularly life-tenured Article III judges — Congress has substantially lessened the risk that majoritarian consensus of favor due or not due to the country seeking extradition will interfere with individual liberty. . . . The treaty's assignment to the judiciary of the task of determining the applicability of the political offense exception "reflects a congressional judgment that that decision not be made on the basis of what may be the current view of any one political administration." *In re Doherty*, 599 F. Supp. 270, 277 n.6 (S.D.N.Y. 1984).

Nor does the assignment to the judiciary of the initial determination of the applicability of the political offense exception deprive the executive branch of all discretion to determine that a person claiming the protection of that exception should not be extradited. The executive branch has the ultimate authority to decide whether to extradite the accused after a judicial determination that the individual is, in fact, extraditable. . . . Although the Secretary of State's authority to refuse extradition is presumably constrained by our treaty obligations, the contours of executive branch discretion in this area have never been expressly delineated. . . .

Finally, the government points out the difficulty of defining which offenses are of a political character. It suggests that this difficulty demonstrates an absence of judicially discoverable manageable standards, another factor that, according to *Baker v. Carr*, counsels for judicial abstention. As in many areas of the law, and as we discuss further in the remainder of this opinion, there has always been debate about the precise contours of the political offense exception. But the absence of perfect predictive ability in discerning whether a given act falls within the exception is not synonymous with an absence of manageable standards. Rather, as with other complex legal problems, the basic standards that guide us in deciding whether the exception applies are refined on a case-by-case basis as new situations arise. The determination whether there was a violent political disturbance in the requesting country at the time of the alleged acts and whether the acts were incidental to the disturbance, ... are mixed questions of law and fact, that do not require a political judgment. . . . We fail to see how the judicial construction of 18 U.S.C. § 3184 and the applicable treaty, and the application of these laws to the facts of a given case, differs from all other judicial decisionmaking. . . .

The scope of the district court's review of a magistrate's extradition order on a petition for writ of habeas corpus is limited to "whether the magistrate had jurisdiction, whether the offense [sic] charged is within the treaty and, by a somewhat liberal extension, whether there was any evidence warranting the finding that there was reasonable ground to believe the accused guilty." . . .

It would make little sense for us to ignore the factual findings of the judicial tribunal that made the initial factual determinations and defer, instead, to the differing factual findings made by a similar tribunal that merely reviewed the record of the earlier proceedings and held no evidentiary hearing of its own. Rather, we must determine whether the habeas court erred, as a matter of law, in overruling the magistrate's factual findings. Accordingly, we will defer to the extradition tribunal's factual findings unless we agree with the district court that they are clearly erroneous. . . .

IV. The Development of the Political Offense Exception

A. Origin of the Exception

The first-known extradition treaty was negotiated between an Egyptian Pharaoh and a Hittite King in the Thirteenth Century B.C.... However, the concept of political offenses as an exception to extradition is a rather recent development. In the centuries after the first known extradition treaty, and throughout the Middle Ages, extradition treaties were used primarily to return political offenders, rather than the perpetrators of common crimes, to the nations seeking to try them for criminal acts.... It was not until the early nineteenth century that the political offense exception, now almost universally accepted in extradition law, was incorporated into treaties....

The political offense exception is premised on a number of justifications. First, its historical development suggests that it is grounded in a brief that individuals have a "right to resort to political activism to foster political change." ... Second, the exception reflects a concern that individuals—particularly unsuccessful rebels—should not be returned to countries where they may be subjected to unfair trials and punishments because of their political opinions.... Third, the exception comports with the notion that governments—and certainly their nonpolitical branches—should not intervene in the internal political struggles of other nations....

B. Comparative Legal Standards

None of the political offense provisions in treaties includes a definition of the word "political." ... Thus, the term "political offense" has received various interpretations by courts since the mid-nineteenth century.... Not every offense that is politically motivated falls within the exception. Instead, courts have devised various tests to identify those offenses that comport with the justifications for the exception and that, accordingly, are not extraditable.

Within the confusion about definitions it is fairly well accepted that there are two distinct categories of political offenses: "pure political offenses" and "relative political offenses." ... Pure political offenses are acts aimed directly at the government, ... and have none of the elements of ordinary crimes, ... These offenses, which include treason, sedition, and espionage, ... do not violate the private rights of individuals.... Because they are frequently specifically excluded from the list of extraditable crimes given in a treaty, ... courts seldom deal with whether these offenses are extraditable, ... and it is generally agreed that they are not....

The definitional problems focus around the second category of political offenses—the relative political offenses. These include "otherwise common crimes committed in connection with a political act," ... or "common crimes ... committed for political motives or in a political context." ... Courts have developed various tests for ascertaining whether "the nexus between the crime and the political act is sufficiently close ... [for the crime to be deemed] not extraditable." ... The judicial approaches can be grouped into three distinct categories: (1) the French "objective" test; (2) the Swiss "proportionality" or "predominance" test; and (3) the Anglo-American "incidence" test.... More recent developments allow for further distinctions between the British test and the test employed in the United States....

The early French test, most clearly represented in *In re Giovanni Gatti*, [1947] Ann. Dig. 145 (No. 70) (France, Ct. App. of Grenoble), considered an offense non-extraditable only if it directly injured the rights of the state.... Applying this rigid formula, French courts refused to consider the motives of the accused.... The test primarily protects only pure political offenses,... and is useless in attempts to define whether an otherwise common crime should not be extraditable because it is connected with a political act, motive, or context.... Because politically motivated and directed acts may injure private as well as state rights, the objective test fails to satisfy the various purposes of the political offense exception.... Nevertheless, this test has one benefit: because it is so limited, it is not subject to abuse; perpetrators of common crimes will not be protected because of alleged political motivations....

In contrast to the traditional French test, Swiss courts apply a test that protects both pure and relative political offenses. The Swiss test examines political motivation of the offender, ... but also requires (a) a consideration of the circumstances surrounding the commission of the crime,... and (b) either a proportionality between the means and the political ends, or a predominance of the political elements, over the common criminal elements....

At least one commentator has suggested that the first condition of the Swiss test is a requirement of a direct connection between the crime and the political goal—a condition that essentially requires the presence of a political movement.... Others point out that the early Swiss requirement that a crime be incident to a political movement has been explicitly rejected in later cases.... More recent Swiss cases concentrate less on the accused's motive, relying instead almost entirely on an ends-means test under which potentially motivated conduct is protected by the exception only if the danger created by the conduct is proportionate to the objectives, *i.e.*, if the means employed are the only means of accomplishing the end and the interests at stake are sufficiently important to justify the danger and harm to others....

The comprehensiveness and flexibility of the "predominance" or "proportionality" test allows it to be conformed to changing realities of a modern world.... But because the relative value of the ends and the necessity of using the chosen means must be considered, the criteria applied by Swiss courts incorporate highly subjective and partisan political considerations within the balancing test.... The test explicitly requires an evaluation of the importance of the interests at stake, the desirability of political change, and the acceptability of the means used to achieve the ends. The infusion of ideological factors in the determination which offenses are non-extraditable threatens both the humanitarian objectives underlying the exception and the concern about foreign non-intervention in domestic political struggles. Moreover, it severely undermines the notion that such determinations can be made by an apolitical, unbiased judiciary concerned primarily with individual liberty....

The "incidence" test that is used to define a non-extraditable political offense in the United States and Great Britain was first set forth by the Divisional Court in *In re Castioni*, [1891] 1 Q.B. 149 (1890). In that case, the Swiss government requested that Great Britain extradite a Swiss citizen who, with a group of other angry citizens, had stormed the palace gates and killed a government official in the process. . . . The court denied extradition, finding that Castioni's actions were "incidental to and formed a part of political disturbances, ... and holding that common crimes committed "in the course" and "in the furtherance" of a political disturbance would be treated as political offenses. . . .

Although both the United States and Great Britain rely explicitly on *Castioni*, each has developed its own version of the incidence test. . . .

C. Original Formulation of the United States Incidence Test

The United States, in contrast to Great Britain, has adhered more closely to the *Castioni* test in determining whether conduct is protected by the political offense exception. The seminal United States case in this area is *In re Ezeta*, 62 F. 972 (N.D. Cal. 1894), in which the Salvadoran government requested the extradition of a number of individuals accused of murder and robbery. The fugitives maintained that the crimes had been committed while they unsuccessfully attempted to thwart a revolution. . . . Extradition was denied because the acts were "committed during the progress of actual hostilities between contending forces," . . . and were "closely identified" with the uprising "in an unsuccessful effort to suppress it." . . . However, an alleged act that occurred four months prior to the start of armed violence was held not to be protected by the incidence test despite the accused's contention that El Salvador's extradition request was politically motivated. . . .

As we noted at the outset, the Supreme Court has addressed the political offense issue only once. In *Ornelas v. Ruiz*, [161 U.S. 502 (1896)], . . . Mexico sought the extradition of an individual for murder, arson, robbery and kidnapping committed in a Mexican border town, at or about the time revolutionary activity was in progress. The Court allowed extradition on the basis that the habeas court had applied an improper, non-deferential standard of review to the extradition court's findings. . . . It continued by listing four factors pertinent to the political offense inquiry in the case: (1) the character of the foray; (2) the mode of attack; (3) the persons killed or captured; and (4) the kind of property taken or destroyed. . . . It found that although the raid (in December 1892) may have been contemporaneous with a revolutionary movement (in 1891), it was not of a political character because it was essentially unrelated to the uprising. The Court noted that the purported political aspects of the crimes were negated "by the fact that immediately after this occurrence, though no superior armed force of the Mexican government was in the vicinity to hinder their advance into the country, the bandits withdrew with their booty across the river into Texas." . . .

Since *Ornelas*, lower American courts have continued to apply the incidence test set forth in *Castioni* and *Ezeta* with its two-fold requirement: (1) the occurrence of an uprising or other violent political disturbance at the time of the charged offense, . . . and (2) a charged offense that is "incidental to," "in the course of," or "in furtherance of" the uprising. . . . While the American view that an uprising must exist is more restrictive than the modern British view and while we, unlike the British, remain hesitant to consider the motives of the accused or the requesting state. . . . American courts have been rather liberal in their construction of the requirement that the act be "incidental to" an uprising. . . .

The American approach has been criticized as being "both underinclusive and overinclusive," . . . and as "yield[ing] anomalous . . . results." . . . Although these criticisms have some merit, neither flaw in the American incidence test is serious. Some commentators have suggested that the test is underinclusive because it exempts from judicially guaranteed protection all offenses that are not contemporaneous with an uprising even though the acts may represent legitimate political resistance. . . .

A number of commentators suggest, on the other hand, that the American test is overbroad because it makes non-extraditable some offenses that are not of a political character merely because the crimes took place contemporaneously with an uprising. . . .

[W]e do not consider the "underinclusiveness" and "overinclusiveness" problems of the incidence test to have been as severe as has been suggested by some of the commentators. Rather, we believe that the incidence test, when properly applied, has served the purposes and objectives of the political offense exception well. More recently, a number of courts have begun to question whether, in light of changing political practices and realities, properly applied, has served the purposes and objectives of the political offense exception well. More recently, a number of courts have begun to question whether, in light of changing political practices and realities, we should continue to use the traditional American version of that test. They have suggested that basic modifications may be required and, specifically, that certain types of conduct engaged in by some contemporary insurgent groups, conduct that we in our society find unacceptable, should be excluded from coverage. For the reasons we explain below, we believe that the American test in its present form remains not only workable but desirable; that the most significant problems that concern those advocating changes in the test can be dealt with without making the changes they propose; and that efforts to modify the test along the lines suggested would plunge our judiciary into a political morass and require the type of subjective judgments we have so wisely avoided until now.

D. The Recent Political Offense Cases

Recently, the American judiciary has split almost evenly over whether the traditional American incidence test should be applied to new methods of political violence in two categories — domestic revolutionary violence and international terrorism — or whether fundamental new restrictions should be imposed on the use of the political offense exception. . . .

V. The Political Offense Exception and the Realities of Contemporary Political Struggles

A. The Political Reality: The Contours of Contemporary Revolutionary Activity

The recent lack of consensus among United States courts confronted with requests for the extradition of those accused of violent political acts committed outside the context of an organized military conflict reflects some confusion about the purposes underlying the political offense exception.... The premise of the analysis performed by modern courts favoring the adoption of new restrictions on the use of the exception is either that the objectives of revolutionary violence undertaken by dispersed forces and directed at civilians are by definition, not political, ... or that, regardless of the actors' objectives, the conduct is not politically legitimate because it "is inconsistent with intentional standards of civilized conduct." ...

A number of courts appear tacitly to accept a suggestion by some commentators that begins with the observation that the political offense exception can be traced to the rise of democratic governments.... Because of this origin, these commentators argue, the exception was only designed to protect the right to rebel against tyrannical governments, ... and should not be applied in an ideologically neutral fashion.... These courts then proceed to apply the exception in a non-neutral fashion but, in doing so, focus on and explicitly reject only the *tactics*, rather than the true object of their concern, the political *objectives*.... The courts that are narrowing the applicability of the exception in this manner appear to be moving beyond the role of an impartial judiciary by determining tacitly that particular political objectives are not "legitimate."

We strongly believe that courts should not undertake such a task. The political offense test traditionally articulated by American courts, as well as the text of the treaty provisions, ... is ideologically neutral. We do not believe it appropriate to make qualitative judgments regarding a foreign government or a struggle designed to alter that government....

A second premise may underlie the analyses of courts that appear to favor narrowing the exception, namely, that modern revolutionary *tactics* which include violence directed at civilians are not politically "legitimate." This assumption, which may well constitute an understandable response to the recent rise of international terrorism, skews any political offense analysis because of an inherent conceptual shortcoming. In deciding what tactics are acceptable, we seek to impose on other nations and cultures our own traditional notions of how internal political struggles should be conducted.

The structure of societies and governments, the relationships between nations and their citizens, and the modes of altering political structures have changed dramatically since our courts first adopted the *Castioni* test. Neither wars nor revolutions are conducted in as clear-cut or mannerly a fashion as they once were. Both the nature of the acts committed in struggles for self-determination.... and the geographic location of those struggles have changed considerably since the time of the French and American revolutions. Now challenges by insurgent movements to the existing order take place most frequently in Third World countries rather than in Europe or North America. In contrast to the organized, clearly identifiable, armed forces of past revolutions, today's struggles are often carried out by networks of individuals joined only by a common interest in opposing those in power.

It is understandable that Americans are offended by the tactics used by many of those seeking to change their governments. Often these tactics are employed by persons who do not share our cultural and social values or mores. Sometimes they are employed by those whose views of the nature, importance, or relevance of individual human life differ radically from ours. Nevertheless, it is not our place to impose our notions of civilized strife on people who are seeking to overthrow the regimes in control of their countries in contexts and circumstances that we have not experienced, and with which we can identify only with the greatest difficulty. It is the fact that the insurgents are seeking to change their governments that makes the political offense exception applicable, not their reasons for wishing to do so or the nature of the acts by which they hope to accomplish that goal.

Politically motivated violence, carried out by dispersed forces and directed at private sector institutions, structures, or civilians, is often undertaken—like the more organized, better disciplined violence of preceding revolutions—as part of an effort to gain the right to self-government. . . . We believe the tactics that are used in such internal political struggles are simply irrelevant to the question whether the political offense exception is applicable.

B. Relationship Between the Justifications for the Exception, the Incidence Test, and Contemporary Political Realities

One of the principal reasons our courts have had difficulty with the concept of affording certain contemporary revolutionary tactics the protection of the political offense exception is our fear and loathing of international terrorism. . . . The desire to exclude international terrorists from the coverage of the political offense exception is a legitimate one; the United States unequivocally condemns all international terrorism. However, the restrictions that some courts have adopted in order to remove terrorist activities from coverage under the political offense exception are overbroad. As we have noted, not all politically-motivated violence undertaken by dispersed forces and directed at civilians is international terrorism and not all such activity should be exempted from the protection afforded by the exception. . . .

There is no need to create a new mechanism for defining "political offenses" in order to ensure that the two important objectives we have been considering are met: (a) that international terrorists will be subject to extradition, and (b) that the exception will continue to cover the type of domestic revolutionary conduct that inspired its creation in the first place. While the precedent that guides us is limited, the applicable principles of law are clear. The incidence test has served us well and requires no significant modification. The growing problem of international terrorism, serious as it is, does not compel us to reconsider or redefine that test. The test we have used since the 1800's simply does not cover acts of international terrorism.

1. The "Incidence" Test

As all of the various tests for determining whether an offense is extraditable make clear, not every offense of a political character is non-extraditable. In the United States, an offense must meet the incidence test which is intended, like the tests designed by other nations, to comport with the justifications for the exception. We now explain the reasons for our conclusion that the traditional United States incidence test by its terms (a) protects acts of domestic violence in connection with a struggle for political self-determination, but (b) was not intended to and does not protect acts of international terrorism.

2. The "Uprising" Component

The incidence test has two components—the "uprising" requirement and the "incidental to" requirement. The first component, the requirement that there be an "uprising," "rebellion," or "revolution," has not been the subject of much discussion in the literature, although it is firmly established in the case law. . . . Most analyses of whether the exception applies have focused on whether the act in question was in furtherance of or incidental to a given uprising. Nevertheless, it is the "uprising" component that plays the key role in ensuring that the incidence test protects only those activities that the political offense doctrine was designed to protect. . . .

The uprising component serves to limit the exception to its historic purposes. It makes the exception applicable only when a certain level of violence exists and when those engaged in that violence are seeking to accomplish a particular objective. The exception does not apply to political acts that involve less fundamental efforts to accomplish change or that do not attract sufficient adherents to create the requisite amount of turmoil. . . . Equally important, the uprising component serves to exclude from coverage under the exception criminal conduct that occurs outside the country or territory in which the uprising is taking place. The term "uprising" refers to a revolt by indigenous people against their own government or an occupying power. That revolt can occur only within the country or territory in which those rising up reside. By definition acts occurring in other lands are not part of the uprising. The political offense exception was designed to protect those engaged in internal or domestic struggles over the form or composition of their own government, including, of course, struggles to displace an occupying power. It was not designed to protect international political coercion or blackmail, or the exportation of violence and strife to other locations—even to the homeland of an oppressor nation. Thus, an uprising is not only limited temporally, it is limited spatially. . . .

While determining the proper geographic boundaries of an "uprising" involves a legal issue that ordinarily will be fairly simple to resolve, there may be some circumstances under which it will be more difficult to do so. We need not formulate a general rule that will be applicable to all situations. It is sufficient in this case to state that for purposes of the political offense exception an "uprising" cannot extend beyond the borders of the country or territory in which a group of citizens or residents is seeking to change their particular government or governmental structure.

It follows from what we have said that an "uprising" can exist only when the turmoil that warrants that characterization is created by nationals of the land in which the disturbances are occurring. . . .

3. The "Incidental to" Component

When describing the second requirement of the incidence test, the "incidental to" component, American courts have used the phrases "in the course of," "connected to," and "in furtherance of" interchangeably. We have applied a rather liberal standard when determining whether this part of the test has been met and have been willing to examine all of the circumstances surrounding the commission of the crime. . . . We believe the traditional liberal construction of the requirement that there be a nexus between the act and the uprising, ... is appropriate. There are various types of acts that, when committed in the course of an uprising, are likely to have been politically motivated. There is little reason, under such circumstances, to impose a strict nexus standard. Moreover, the application of a strict test would in some instances jeopardize the rights of the accused. . . .

VI. The Incidence Test Applied to the Charged Offenses

. . . .

Quinn is accused of having been a member of a conspiracy involving the Balcombe Street Four and he does not challenge the probable cause finding on this charge; his fingerprints were found on the bombs and within the flats where bombs were constructed. Quinn has already been convicted of and has served a prison sentence for his membership in the IRA. There is no evidence that he was involved in the conspiracy for other than political reasons, and his alleged co-conspirators, the Balcombe Street Four, were convicted of politically motivated bombings. Moreover, the PIRA's use of bombing campaigns as a political tactic is well-documented. Accepting the magistrate's factual findings, which are not clearly erroneous, and applying the legal standards we have explained above, we think it quite clear that if an uprising, as that term is defined for purposes of the political offense exception, existed at the time the offenses were committed, the bombings were incidental to that uprising.

Furthermore, because various disparate acts may be incidental to an uprising, we agree with the district court's conclusion that the Tibble murder would be incidental to the uprising, although we believe the analysis performed by both the magistrate and the district court is in error with respect to this incident. It does not matter if the killer's motivation in killing Officer Tibble was to conceal a bomb factory or to avoid capture. A murder of a police officer is related to an uprising whether the reason for the act is to avoid discovery of munitions or to avoid reduction of "forces" by capture. Regardless which of these goals motivated the killer, if an uprising existed at the time, this offense as well was incidental to it. . . .

With regard to the uprising prong of the incidence test, we must again review the magistrate's factual findings under the clearly erroneous standard and his legal conclusions *de novo*. The district court failed to do this, construing the magistrate's conclusion that there was an uprising throughout the United Kingdom solely as a finding of fact. The district court summarized the magistrate's factual findings as to the levels of violence that existed in Northern Ireland and elsewhere in the United Kingdom at the time Quinn allegedly committed the charged offenses, and properly adopted them. However, the district court failed to analyze the magistrate's legal conclusion that because the requisite level of violence existed in Northern Ireland and because Northern Ireland is "in a constitutional sense" a part of the United Kingdom, an uprising existed in the United Kingdom as a whole. . . . It is clear from the record that the magistrate correctly concluded that the level of violence outside Northern Ireland was insufficient in itself to constitute an "uprising."

There is a second and even more significant reason why the "uprising" prong is not met in this case. As the magistrate found, what violence there was not being generated by citizens or residents of England. In fact, the magistrate determined that a large percentage of the bombing incidents in England were attributable to the Balcombe Street Four. The critical factor is that nationals of Northern Ireland, seeking to alter the government in that territorial entity, exported their struggle for political change across the seas to a separate geographical entity—and conducted that struggle in a country in which the nationals and residents were not attempting to alter their own political structure.

. . . .

We do not question whether the PIRA sought to coerce the appropriate sovereign. Nor do we pass judgment on the use of violence as a form of political coercion or the efficacy of the violent attacks in England. But, as we have already said, ... the word "uprising" means exactly that: it refers to a people *rising up*, in their own land, against the government of that land. It does not cover terrorism or other criminal conduct exported to other locations. Nor can the existence of an uprising be based on violence committed by persons who do not reside in the country or territory in which the violence occurs.

In light of the justifications for the political offense exception, the formulation of the incidence test as it has traditionally been articulated, and the cases in which the exception has historically been applied, we do not believe it would be proper to stretch the term "uprising" to include acts that took place in England as a part of a struggle by nationals of Northern Ireland to change the form of government in their own land. Accordingly, we need not decide whether had an uprising occurred, the protection afforded by the exception would have been extended to one who, like Quinn, is a citizen of a different and uninvolved nation. . . . Because the incidence test is not met, neither the bombing conspiracy nor the murder of Police Constable Tibble is a non-extraditable offense under the political offense exception to the extradition treaty between the United States and the United Kingdom. . . .

VIII. Conclusion

For extradition to be denied for an otherwise extraditable crime on the basis that it falls within the protective ambit of the political offense exception, the incidence test must ordinarily be met. (We reserve the question whether offenses committed by government officials or in connection with wars between nations are covered by the exception and, if so, whether a different test would be appropriate.) The incidence test has two components, designed so that the exception comports with its original justifications and protects acts of the kind that inspired its inclusion in extradition treaties. First, there must be an uprising—a political disturbance related to the struggle of individuals to alter or abolish the existing government in their country. An uprising is both temporarily and spatially limited. Second, the charged offense must have been committed in furtherance of the uprising; it must be related to the political struggle or be consequent to the uprising activity. Neither the objectives of the uprising nor the means employed to achieve those objectives are subject to judicial scrutiny. And while the nature of the uprising group and any evidence of the accused's motivations may be relevant, proof on these elements is not required or necessarily determinative. Acts of international terrorism do not meet the incidence test and are thus not covered by the political offense exception. Crimes against humanity also are beyond the scope of the exception.

The conspiracy to cause explosions and the murder with which Quinn is charged do not fall within the political offense exception. Although an uprising existed in Northern Ireland at the time the charged offenses were committed, there was no uprising in England. The crimes did not take place within a territorial entity in which a group of nationals were seeking to change the form of the government under which they live; rather the offenses took place in a different geographical location. We do not decide whether Quinn's status as a citizen of an uninvolved nation would also preclude him from receiving the protection of the exception. . . . We vacate the writ of habeas corpus and remand to the district court. We hold that Quinn may be extradited on the murder charge but that the district court must consider whether the conspiracy charge is time-barred before extradition is permitted for that offense.

VACATED AND REMANDED

DUNIWAY, CIRCUIT JUDGE . . . :

I concur in the judgment, but I cannot concur in the lengthy opinion of Judge Reinhardt and the very extensive dicta that it expounds.

I agree that the magistrate had jurisdiction, including jurisdiction to determine whether the offenses with which Quinn is charged were of a political character. I agree that the district court had jurisdiction on habeas corpus to decide that question and that we have jurisdiction on appeal to consider it. I have no doubt that the evidence is sufficient to enable, indeed, to require, the magistrate, the district court, and this court to say that the offenses charged against Quinn are extraditable offenses, and that the only basis upon which extradition could be denied is the treaty provision that "extradition shall not be granted if . . . the offense . . . is regarded by the requested party, [the United States], as one of a political character."

My principal difficulty is with part V of Judge Reinhardt's thoughtful and careful opinion, and especially with part V, B, 2, and the geographical limitation announced there. . . . The limitation may be useful to us in this case, but I doubt that it is a valid one. . . . Particularly today, with the airplane, the helicopter the high speed motor vehicle, the railroad, the speedboat and submarine genuinely revolutionary activities can take place outside the geographic boundaries of the requesting state. I fear that if we adopt the geographic limitation propounded in the opinion today, we will find ourselves trying to work our way around it tomorrow. . . .

FLETCHER, CIRCUIT JUDGE, concurring and dissenting:

I respectfully dissent from my colleagues' conclusion that Quinn may now be extradited on the murder charge. The decision facing this court is excruciatingly difficult. Quinn is accused of hideous crimes — violent and cruel and some of them cowardly. Innocent victims were targeted for receipt of letter bombs mailed anonymously. A decision that the full force of the law should not be invoked to punish persons found guilty of such acts seems inconceivable. However, the political offense exception to the treaty of extradition has a long history of protecting persons rebelling against their governments.

This longstanding tradition among western nations is an acknowledgment of the right of the governed to oppose unjust governments. Although the nations, ours included, have acknowledged the heinous nature of violent political crimes, they have nonetheless, under treaties and statutes, denied extradition when an individual's conduct falls within the narrow exception for the "political offense." . . . Judge Reinhardt is rightly concerned that "uprising" not encompass "terrorism or other criminal conduct exported to other locations." I share his concern. But in my view, the acts of Irish nationalists against the British in London are not international "terrorism or other criminal conduct exported to other locations." The longstanding ties between England and Northern Ireland, which Judge Reinhardt acknowledges are "well established," cannot be avoided or ignored. Although Northern Ireland may have been "separated" from Great Britain by treaty when the Irish Free State was created, it remained a part of the United Kingdom with representation in the British Parliament and it has been occupied by British troops lo these many years. The acts of terrorism in England by members of the PIRA can hardly be termed acts of international terrorism. . . .

Given my conclusion that the offenses of which Quinn is accused are protected under the political offense exception, I must address whether this protection extends to one who, like Quinn, is a citizen of a different nation from that in which the uprising is occurring. I do not believe that mercenaries or volunteers in a foreign conflict can claim protection under the political offense exception. I deduce from Judge Reinhardt's views on international terrorism that he would agree. To be entitled to protection, an individual would have to demonstrate tangible and substantial connections with the country in which an uprising occurs. It could be short of citizenship, but there must be a showing of substantial connection — for example, that he or she had lived in the country or territory and planned to continue to live there under a changed regime.

In Quinn's case, we lack sufficient information with which to make any such evaluation. We know that Quinn is a United States citizen, and that he resided in San Francisco during the years immediately preceding his arrest.... Because we do not know the extent of Quinn's ties to Northern Ireland, I would remand the case for an initial determination by the district court as to whether Quinn should be treated as an Irish national and afforded the protection of the political offense exception. Accordingly, I dissent from the holding that Quinn may now be extradited on the murder charge.

I agree with my colleagues that Quinn may not be extradited on the conspiracy charge at least until after the district court considers the question of the statute of limitations. However, I believe that the district court should not be required to reach that question unless it first concludes that Quinn's ties to Northern Ireland were insufficient to invoke the protection of the political offense exception. For the reasons I have explained, I concur in the holding remanding the conspiracy count.

Notes

(1) How much evidence needs to be produced to support a refusal to extradite under the exception to the political offense exception? *In The Matter of the Extradition of Smyth*, 61 F.3d 711 (9th Cir. 1995), the Ninth Circuit Court of Appeals examined a district court denial of certification of extradition. In reversing the lower court decision, Circuit Judge Schroeder stated:

> This is a proceeding brought by the United States on behalf of the United Kingdom to extradite James J. Smyth to Northern Ireland. Smyth was convicted of the attempted murder of a prison officer in Belfast, Northern Ireland in 1978 and sentenced to 20 years' imprisonment. He escaped from the Maze Prison in Northern Ireland in September of 1983 and arrived in San Francisco several months later. The United States, at the request of the United Kingdom, seeks Smyth's extradition to Northern Ireland to serve the remainder of his prison term. Extradition is sought pursuant to the United States-United Kingdom Extradition Treaty, June 8, 1972, U.S-U.K., 28 U.S.T. 227, and the Supplementary Extradition Treaty, June 25, 1985, U.S.-U.K., art. 3(a), reprinted in S. Exec. Rep. No. 17, 99th Cong., 2nd Sess. 15–17 (1986) (Supplementary Treaty).... The Supplementary Treaty followed in the wake of a series of decisions by United States courts refusing to extradite to Northern Ireland individuals who had been charged with or convicted of acts of political violence. The treaty provisions, negotiated by President Reagan and Prime Minister Thatcher, and modified by the United States Senate, represent a difficult compromise between outrage and compassion: the outrage of the British government over the refusal of the

United States to extradite persons whom the United Kingdom considered terrorists, and the compassion of the United States for individuals who, if extradited, might suffer unfair treatment and incarceration on account of their religious or political associations, not because of their criminal acts.

The Supplementary Treaty's key substantive provision, Article 3(a), creates a defense to extradition. It provides:

> Notwithstanding any other provision of this Supplementary Treaty, extradition shall not occur if the person sought establishes to the satisfaction of the competent judicial authority by a preponderance of the evidence that the request for extradition has in fact been made with a view to try or punish him on account of his race, religion, nationality or political opinions, or that he would, if surrendered, be prejudiced at his trial or punished, detained or restricted in his personal liberty by reason of his race, religion, nationality or political opinions.

Supplementary Treaty, art. 3(a). . . .

Beginning in 1979, a series of United States court decisions denied extradition of IRA members because the underlying offenses constituted "political acts." . . . These decisions angered the British Government, which viewed them as condoning violent terrorist conduct. . . . The Reagan Administration in 1981 proposed legislation for a new treaty that would have entirely eliminated judicial application of the political offense exception to extraditions to the United Kingdom. The Departments of Justice and State, both of whom assisted in drafting the original bill, expressed concern that continued judicial application of the political offense exception to extradition would turn the United States into a haven for terrorists and adversely affect foreign relations. *See* Barbara Ann Banoff & Christopher H. Pyle, "To Surrender Political Offenders": The Political Offense Exception to Extradition in United States Law, 16 N.Y.U. J. Int'l L. & Pol. 169, 170 (1984).

The Senate, however, was not comfortable with the wholesale elimination of the political offense exception from U.S.-U.K. extradition proceedings. It therefore limited the abrogation of the political offense exception in Article 1 of the Supplementary Treaty to enumerated violent offenses and added Article 3(a) as a means by which fugitives sought for extradition on such offenses could nonetheless challenge their extradition.

The Senate Report described the Supplementary Treaty as "one of the most divisive and contentious issues the Committee [on Foreign Relations] has faced this Congress. The Committee has worked long and hard to develop a compromise that can win broad, bipartisan support." . . . The Report further characterized the compromise as "an effort to balance antiterrorism concerns and the right of due process for individuals." . . . As such, Article 3(a) is not a mere reformulation of the political offense exception; the provision invites an altogether new inquiry in the extradition context. Rather than focusing on the motivations of the accused (which the political offense exception encourages), the Article 3(a) defense to extradition focuses on the treatment the accused will likely receive at the hands of the requesting country's criminal justice system. . . .

Article 3(a) clearly places the burden upon the person sought for extradition to establish "by a preponderance of the evidence" that the exception applies. Supplementary Treaty, art. 3(a). To establish a defense under the second clause of Article 3(a), the extraditee must establish that if surrendered, he would be "prejudiced at his trial or punished, detained or restricted in his personal liberty by reason of his race, religion, nationality, or political opinions." Id. . . .

This is the first case in which a person challenging extradition to Northern Ireland has raised a defense under Article 3(a) of the Supplementary Treaty. Because of the lack of precedent, the district court held several preliminary hearings to decide the scope of the evidence that would be discoverable and admissible to support the Article 3(a) defense. On May 6, 1993, the district court issued its first written order in the case, *In re Extradition of Smyth*, 820 F. Supp. 498 (N.D. Cal. 1993). The court ruled that Article 3(a) created an exception to, but did not nullify, the traditional rule of non-inquiry in extradition matters and that it permitted an individual asserting the defense to establish that the individual would be prejudiced as a result of discriminatory treatment within the requesting country's criminal justice system. . . . The court went on to define the scope of permissible inquiry along lines which set the course of the litigation and shaped the nature of its ultimate findings. The court held that Article 3(a) authorized inquiry regarding three categories of evidence:

> (1) evidence of Smyth's treatment by security forces prior to his 1977 arrest, admissible as "background [that could] tend to show a pattern of discriminatory treatment aimed specifically at . . ."
>
> (2) evidence of the conditions of confinement in Northern Ireland that Smyth would face, provided the evidence showed "that any poor treatment suffered is a result of discrimination on the basis of race, religion, nationality or political view," . . . . and
>
> (3) evidence related to likely post-incarceration "restraints on . . . liberty" motivated by the grounds listed in Article 3(a), admissible only if such evidence showed that the government "explicitly tolerated or has been materially involved in any plots to restrain [Smyth's] liberty or assassinate him" or if it showed a "pattern of [such] conduct involving a government entity," . . .

We believe that had Smyth demonstrated by a preponderance of the evidence that, after he served the approximately two to five years of his remaining prison time, he likely would be a target of similar conduct by persons within Northern Ireland's justice system, then he would have qualified for the defense to extradition contained in Article 3(a). There was, however, little such evidence. Nearly all of the testimony of harassment of Republican ex-prisoners concerned conduct that occurred in the past. Some of it related to conduct of security forces in the Republic of Ireland rather than in Northern Ireland. There was conflicting evidence as to whether in the future Smyth would be barred from travel outside Northern Ireland after his release....

Here, we conclude the district court erred in at least two respects. In the first place, resort to the withholding of deportation regulation that presumes a present danger of persecution from past experience of persecution cannot validate the district court's presumption of a risk of persecution two to five years in the future. Second, the district court erred in relying extensively upon evidence of the general discriminatory effects of the Diplock system upon Catholics and suspected Republican sympathizers. That evidence does not relate to the treatment Smyth is likely to receive as a consequence of extradition, as required under Article 3(a)....

Considered in this context, the language of Article 3(a) must mean that a federal court in an extradition proceeding may look to the treatment that likely will be accorded the extraditee upon the charge for which extradition is sought. This inquiry need not necessarily be limited to the prosecution and formal term of imprisonment, but Article 3(a) does not permit denial of extradition on the basis of an inquiry into the general political conditions extant in Northern Ireland. The history of the provision shows that it requires an individualized inquiry.

Accordingly, in order to defeat extradition on the basis of his prospective treatment at the hands of the justice system extending beyond the duration of his formal imprisonment term, Smyth would have to demonstrate by a preponderance of the evidence that the criminal justice system in Northern Ireland likely would exact additional retribution for his crime beyond the remaining term of imprisonment, and that such additional punishment would be inflicted on account of Smyth's political or religious beliefs, and not on account of his having attempted to murder a prison guard. This is a difficult burden and one which Smyth did not shoulder successfully. The evidence did not establish, independent of the presumptions discussed below, that Smyth would suffer religiously or politically motivated punishment after serving his prison term....

(2) How would the analysis of the situation in *Quinn* differ if it arose under the U.N. Model Treaty or the 2003 U.S./U.K. Treaty, *supra* § 16.01?

(3) Interpol red notices are an international mechanism to assist governmental enforcement bodies in securing the arrest of those who may be outside of their jurisdiction. The Department of Justice's Justice Manual discusses red notices as follows:

> An Interpol Red Notice is an international "lookout" and is the closest instrument to an international arrest warrant in use today. Please be aware that if a fugitive is arrested pursuant to a Red Notice, the prosecutor's office is obligated to do whatever work is required to produce the necessary extradition documents within the time limits prescribed by the controlling extradition treaty or, in the absence of a treaty, the arresting country's domestic law, whenever and wherever the fugitive is arrested. Further, the prosecutor's office is obliged to pay the expenses pursuant to the controlling treaty.
>
> Interpol Red Notices are useful when the fugitive's location or countries to which he or she may travel, are unknown. Red Notices may be broadly distributed or tailored specifically to countries to which it is believed the fugitive will travel. For additional information about Interpol Red Notices, see www.interpol.int//INTERPOL-expertise/Notices.
>
> Because many countries will arrest a fugitive based solely on a Red Notice, it is the responsibility of the prosecutor to inform Interpol if a Red Notice should be withdrawn.

Interpol Red Notices, section 9-15.635, Justice Manual, U.S. Department of Justice. In recent years, red notices have come under much criticism because of their vulnerability to abuse. In particular, allegations have been made that some countries use red notices to abuse political dissidents and opponents. According to a report published in 2012, "In the public Red Notice database, published reports, court documents and interviews with lawyers and other experts in Interpol's process found at least 17 countries in the last five years have used the agency to go after dissidents or political opponents, economic targets or environmental activists." Libby Lewis, *Interpol's Red Notices used by some to pursue political dissenters, opponents*, International Consortium of Investigative Journalists (March 12, 2012). A 2013 report from Fair Trial stated,

> 'Red Notices', international wanted person alerts published by INTERPOL at national authorities' request, come with considerable human impact: arrest, detention, frozen freedom of movement, employment problems, and reputational and financial harm. These interferences with basic rights can, of course, be justified when INTERPOL acts to combat international crime. However, our casework suggests that countries are, in fact, using INTERPOL's systems against exiled political opponents, usually refugees, and based on corrupt criminal proceedings, pointing to a structural problem.

Strengthening respect for human rights, strengthening INTERPOL, Fair Trial International (November 2013).

(4) Does an extradition ruling, under the political offense exception, have any effect on the "serious nonpolitical crime" assessment in a deportation determination? In *Barapind v. Reno*, 2000 U.S. App. Lexis 21760 (9th Cir. 2000), the court stated:

> In a parallel, but converse, provision to the "political offense" exception to extradition, the INA excludes from withholding of deportation aliens for whom "there are serious reasons for considering that the alien has committed a serious nonpolitical crime." 8 U.S.C. § 1253(h)(2)(C); *see also* 8 U.S.C. §§ 1101(a)(42)(A) and 1253(h)(2)(A). However, the "political offense" determination in extradition proceedings and the "serious nonpolitical crime" assessment in immigration proceedings are separate and distinct inquiries. . . . A determination that an alien's acts are "political offenses" for purposes of denying extradition should have no effect on the BIA's determination of whether an asylum applicant has committed a serious nonpolitical offense because "extradition determinations have no *res judicata* effect in subsequent judicial proceedings." . . .

Can the Board of Immigration Appeals (BIA) hold in abeyance an asylum application, pending a resolution of an extradition proceeding? *See id.* (holding that BIA may hold asylum adjudication in abeyance pending extradition proceeding) (*see also* chap. 17).

United States v. Pitawanakwat

United States District Court for the District of Oregon
120 F. Supp. 2d 921 (D. Or. 2000)

STEWART, MAGISTRATE JUDGE:

. . . Defendant was arrested in Oregon on June 20, 2000, pursuant to a complaint and warrant of arrest seeking defendant's extradition to Canada. The Canadian government wants defendant extradited to serve the remaining 702 days of his three-year sentence of imprisonment imposed in 1997 for his convictions for one count of mischief causing actual danger to life and one count of possession of a weapon for a purpose dangerous to the public peace. Defendant's convictions stem from his participation in a 1995 incident referred to as the "Lake Gustafsen incident." Defendant and other native people, known as the Ts'peten Defenders, occupied private property in British Columbia near Lake Gustafsen which encompasses a contested parcel of sacred ground. When the Ts'peten Defenders refused to leave, an armed standoff ensued with the Royal Canadian Mounted Police ("RCMP"). During the standoff, defendant discharged a rifle in the air at a police helicopter and rode in a vehicle which contained an AK-47 assault rifle. The Ts'peten Defenders eventually surrendered. . . .

Given the close political and legal similarities between Canada and the United States, it seems antithetical to ever deny extradition to Canada based on the political offense exception. Unlike some other countries, Canada can hardly be characterized as an unjust or oppressive nation where defendants may be subjected to unfair trials and punishments because of their political opinions. Nevertheless, the Extradition Treaty contains the political offense exception, and defendant is entitled to seek its protection.

Assuming that the Lake Gustafsen incident was an "uprising or violent political disturbance," then the "incidental to" requirement is easily satisfied in this case. Defendant is not only accused, but convicted, of two offenses which occurred during the Lake Gustafsen incident and which are directly related to the armed confrontation with the RCMP. He also proudly admits that he was a member of the insurgent group which defended the encampment to achieve a political end, namely sovereignty of native people over sacred tribal land. His later parole violation for which Canada seeks extradition is based upon his earlier convictions and therefore also is "incidental to" the Lake Gustafsen incident. . . .

The crime for which Canada seeks extradition is a parole violation based on defendant's change of residence to the United States without permission. That crime clearly was not committed as part of any "uprising or other violent political disturbance." However, defendant's move to the United States constitutes a crime only because he was previously convicted and sentenced for crimes committed during the Lake Gustafsen incident. Therefore, the parole violation is inextricably intertwined with the previous crimes. The fact that defendant came to the United States after his convictions and partial service of his sentence places him in substantially the same position as if he had fled Canada before his convictions or after escaping from prison.

From defendant's viewpoint, the Lake Gustafsen incident was not only an attempt to displace an occupying power from sacred tribal burial ground, but also was part of a larger uprising in the summer of 1995 in Canada seeking sovereignty by indigenous peoples over their unceded lands. Whereas Canada and the provincial governments desired to continue negotiations with the tribal chiefs to resolve the issue of unceded lands, the Ts'peten Defenders viewed the tribal chiefs as government collaborators and desired to move the land claims and other issues to an international arena with a third-party resolution process. . . .

Harking back to the language in *Quinn*, the political offense exception protects "a people *rising up*, in their own land, against the government of that land." . . . The uprising must be "both temporally and spatially limited" and involve "a certain level of violence" by those "seeking to accomplish a particular objective." . . . The Lake Gustafsen incident easily satisfies many of these criteria.

The Lake Gustafsen incident involved indigenous people rising up in their own land against the government of that land. Although the crimes were committed while trespassing and occupying private property, the type of property occupied makes this case unique. James acquired title to the land through the Canadian government, but his land included tribal land over which native people believed they had a valid legal claim. Thus, the protest by the Ts'peten Defenders was directed largely against the Canadian government which had granted title to James, not against James. In addition, the violence was aimed not at James, but at the Canadian government and its military forces.

Furthermore, the Lake Gustafsen incident was temporally and spatially limited and sought to accomplish a particular objective. The actions by defendant and other activists in 1995 clearly played a role in prompting Canada and British Columbia in 1996 to begin intensive negotiations with more than 40 Indian councils and nations. As a result of the negotiations, the Nisga'a tribe received fishing and forestry rights as well as the ability to set up its own government, policing, and courts. Those treaty negotiations may not have occurred or been successful without the impetus provided by the Lake Gustafsen incident and other incidents by native people during the summer of 1995.

However, the level of violence must be sufficient to invoke the political offense exception. Arguing that the level of violence is not sufficient, the government first points to the fact that the encampment did not begin as a violent event. Nevertheless, what began as a non-violent occupation escalated into a violent confrontation because the Ts'peten Defenders were heavily armed and used those arms to fend off a military siege to accomplish their particular objective. Whether the insurgents or the government initiated the violence is not critical to application of the political offense exception. . . .

Although Canada seeks defendant's return only for a parole violation, this court concludes that defendant's crimes for which he was convicted and later paroled were "of a political character" and therefore may not provide the basis for extradition of defendant to Canada. Extradition Treaty, Art. IV(1)(iii).

For the foregoing reasons, the government's request for extradition is denied and the Complaint is dismissed.

Chapter 17

Abduction and Other Alternatives to Extradition

§ 17.01 Generally

Depending on the circumstances, various devices apart from extradition may be used to obtain the return of a fugitive for trial. *See* Ethan A. Nadelmann, Cops Across Borders: The Internationalization of U.S. Criminal Law Enforcement 436–57 (1993). These alternative methods sometimes are referred to as "disguised," "informal," or "irregular" extradition or rendition. Not all of them are unlawful. Three kinds of alternatives to extradition can be distinguished. *See* Alona E. Evans, *Acquisition of Custody over the International Fugitive Offender—Alternatives to Extradition: A Survey of United States Practice*, 40 Brit. Y.B. Int'l L. 77 (1964).

First, in certain situations, a treaty may provide for the expedited rendition of fugitives outside the ordinary framework of extradition. Thus, allied soldiers (under Status of Forces Agreements), deserting seamen, and those who commit crimes on board aircraft may be handed over to another country for trial through a sort of "*brevi manu* extradition." *Id.* at 80. Recent provisions for the surrender of fugitives to international criminal tribunals also fall within this category.

Second, exclusion or deportation under the immigration laws can be used to achieve the same results as extradition and even to circumvent deliberately the requirements of the law of extradition. The use of deportation when extradition fails is considered in the first section of the present chapter.

Third, there are cases in which rendition is achieved through unlawful means. Whether particular means for acquiring custody of an offender are unlawful may itself be a controversial question. Luring fugitives, for instance, out of countries where they are safe from extradition, to places where they can be arrested by U.S. law enforcement authorities, or by foreign authorities prepared to surrender them to the U.S., is regarded as a permissible tactic for bringing offenders before the U.S. courts [*see, e.g., United States v. Yunis*, chap. 3, *supra*]. In other countries, it may be regarded as a form of kidnapping, by fraud instead of force, and therefore a violation of the territorial sovereignty of the state of refuge, as well as a violation of the rights of the fugitive under applicable human rights instruments. *See Report of the Committee on Extradition and Human Rights, in* International Law Association, Report of the Sixty-Sixth Congress 142, 162 (1994). Where the means used to obtain custody are determined to be unlawful, there is the further question of whether that determination should operate as a bar to exercising jurisdiction over the fugitive. This question is considered in the second section of the present chapter.

§ 17.02 Deportation

Ruiz Massieu v. Reno

United States District Court for the District of New Jersey
915 F. Supp. 681 (1996)

MARYANNE TRUMP BARRY, DISTRICT JUDGE:

Plaintiff, Mario Ruiz Massieu, seeks a permanent injunction enjoining the deportation proceeding instituted against him pursuant to 8 U.S.C. § 1251(a)(4)(C)(i) and a declaration that the statute, which has not previously been construed in any reported judicial opinion, is unconstitutional. That statute, by its express terms, confers upon a single individual, the Secretary of State, the unfettered and unreviewable discretion to deport any alien lawfully within the United States, not for identified reasons relating to his or conduct in the United States or elsewhere but, rather, because that person's mere presence here would impact in some unexplained way on the foreign policy interests of the United States. Thus, the statute represents a breathtaking departure both from well established legislative precedent which commands deportation based on adjudications of defined impermissible conduct by the alien in the United States, and from well established precedent with respect to extradition which commands extradition based on adjudications of probable cause to believe that the alien has engaged in defined impermissible conduct elsewhere....

Mr. Ruiz Massieu entered this country legally and is not alleged to have committed any act within this country which requires his deportation. Nor, on the state of this record, can it be said that there exists probable cause to believe that Mr. Ruiz Massieu has committed any act outside of this country which warrants his extradition, for the government has failed in four separate proceedings before two Magistrate Judges to establish probable cause. Deportation of Mr. Ruiz Massieu is sought merely because he is here and the Secretary of State and Mexico have decided that he should go back....

The facts of this case read more like a best-selling novel than a typical deportation proceeding. Mario Ruiz Massieu, a citizen of Mexico, is a member of one of Mexico's most influential and politically active families, and, in recent years, has occupied several positions at the upper-most echelons of the Mexican government. For much of the past twenty years, Mr. Ruiz Massieu lived an academic life both as a professor and director of the National University of Mexico. During that time, he authored a number of books on topics such as education, history, law and politics. In 1993, however, Mr. Ruiz Massieu was thrust into the vanguard of Mexican politics as a member of the Institutional Revolutionary Party ("the PRI"), Mexico's only established ruling party. He was appointed Deputy Attorney General in 1993, Under Secretary for the Department of Government in 1994, and Deputy Attorney General, again, in May of 1994.

On September 28, 1994, Mr. Ruiz Massieu's brother, Jose Francisco Ruiz Massieu — Secretary General of the PRI and an outspoken critic of the Mexican political system — was assassinated. Within hours, Mario Ruiz Massieu, as Deputy Attorney General, began an investigation into his brother's murder. In the ensuing weeks, fourteen people were apprehended and indicted as part of a conspiracy uncovered through Mr. Ruiz Massieu's investigatory efforts. Many of the arrested conspirators named Manuel Munoz Rocha, a PRI official, as the architect of the conspiracy. Mr. Munoz Rocha, however, was shielded by official immunity, and could not be interviewed by the Attorney General's office in connection with the case. Mr. Ruiz Massieu requested that President Carlos Salinas de Gortari waive Rocha's immunity, a request that the PRI vigorously opposed. Eventually, the immunity was waived, but not before Mr. Munoz Rocha had disappeared. He was never interviewed or arrested, and remains unaccounted for to this day.

Fifty-seven days after his brother's assassination, Mr. Ruiz Massieu resigned as Deputy Attorney General and withdrew his membership in the PRI. In a dramatic and widely publicized speech on November 23, 1994, Mr. Ruiz Massieu announced that he was resigning from both his office and his party because of the PRI's continuous efforts to frustrate his investigation into his brother's murder. Specifically, he alleged that the PRI was obstructing his search for the persons who might have ordered former Deputy Munoz Rocha to act — persons whom Mr. Ruiz Massieu alleged to be very high-ranking members of the PRI.

In February of 1995, Mr. Ruiz Massieu published a book elaborating on the themes of his resignation address. . . . Immediately, Mexican authorities alleged that Mr. Ruiz Massieu committed the crimes of intimidation, concealment and "against the administration of justice" (a crime analogous to obstruction of justice in this country) in connection with the investigation of his brother's assassination. Contemporaneously, Mr. Ruiz Massieu claimed that he and his family began to receive both death and kidnapping threats. On March 2, 1995, he appeared for an official interrogation before Mexican authorities concerning the allegations of his criminal activity committed while in office.

Later that same day, Mr. Ruiz Massieu and his family lawfully entered the United States as non-immigrant visitors at Houston, Texas, where they have owned a home since October of 1994. After remaining at their Houston home for the night, the family boarded a plane en route to Spain. When the plane touched down at Newark Airport on March 3, 1995, Mr. Ruiz Massieu was arrested by United States Customs officials, pursuant to 31 U.S.C. § 5316, on a charge of reporting only approximately $18,000 of the $44,322 in his possession. The charge was never pursued and was subsequently dismissed at the government's request.

On March 5, 1995, two days after his arrest in Newark, a Mexican court issued an arrest warrant for Mr. Ruiz Massieu charging him with intimidation, concealment, and "against the administration of justice." The following day, at Mexico's request, the United States presented a complaint for Mr. Ruiz Massieu's provisional arrest and sought his extradition to face the charges set forth in the Mexican arrest warrant. On June 9, 1995, a Mexican court consolidated the allegations into a single charge of "against the administration of justice."[3]

On June 13, 1995, the first extradition proceeding began before Magistrate Judge Ronald J. Hedges. After lengthy hearings . . . Magistrate Judge Hedges declined to issue a certificate of extraditability. In so doing, he determined that the government had failed to demonstrate even probable cause to believe that Mr. Ruiz Massieu committed the crimes charged. Significantly, Magistrate Judge Hedges also found that many of the statements submitted by the government were "incredible and unreliable," and might have been altered to remove certain recantations and exculpatory statements. In addition, he found, and the government did not deny, that multiple statements were procured by torture inflicted by the Mexican authorities, including the inculpatory testimony of one of the government's primary affiants.

On June 20, 1995, two days before Magistrate Judge Hedges issued his initial opinion, Mexico filed its second request for extradition based on newly filed charges of embezzlement. The charges focused on the $9,000,000 in the Houston bank account and 2,500,000 pesos allegedly disbursed without adequate documentation while Mr. Ruiz Massieu was in office. In an opinion filed September 25, 1995, Magistrate Judge Hedges again declined to issue a certificate of extraditability on the ground that the government had failed to demonstrate probable cause, or present any evidence whatsoever, that the funds had been illegally obtained or disbursed.

Undeterred, on August 31, 1995, the government refiled its initial request for extradition based on the charge of "against the administration of justice." Although the government produced nine new statements allegedly incriminating Mr. Ruiz Massieu, Magistrate Judge Hedges remained unpersuaded. By letter opinion dated November 13, 1995, the court again ruled that there was no probable cause to believe that Mr. Ruiz Massieu committed the acts alleged, and dismissed the complaint.

On October 10, 1995, the government instituted yet a fourth extradition proceeding by refiling its prior application based on the previously rejected embezzlement charges. This time, the application was heard before Magistrate Judge Stanley R. Chesler. . . . Like Magistrate Judge Hedges before him, Magistrate Judge Chesler issued a lengthy opinion denying the certification of extraditability. Focusing on

3. In the interim, the United States froze and seized, under seal and without notice or explanation, Mr. Ruiz Massieu's Houston bank account containing approximately nine million dollars. On June 15, 1995, the government instituted a civil forfeiture action against the account. [*See United States v. Nine Million Forty One Thousand, Five Hundred Ninety Eight Dollars and Sixty Eight Cents*, 976 F. Supp. 642 (S.D. Tex. 1997), *aff'd*, 163 F.3d 238 (5th Cir. 1998), *cert. denied*, 527 U.S. 1023 (1999).]

the government's paucity of evidence, Magistrate Judge Chesler stated that "the bottom line is that the government's efforts to establish an inference of criminality on the basis of unexplained wealth fails because it does not rise to the level where any nexus between those funds and the funds which Mr. Massieu is alleged to have embezzled has been established." On January 11, 1996, a Mexican court dismissed the embezzlement charges.

With that, the government seemingly accepted defeat as to Mr. Ruiz Massieu's extraditability. It was then, however, that this case took a turn toward the truly Kafkaesque. On December 22, 1995, immediately after Magistrate Judge Chesler issued his opinion, Mr. Ruiz Massieu was taken into custody by the Immigration and Naturalization Service ("the INS") pursuant to a previously unserved and unannounced detainer dated September 29, 1995. In addition, he was served with an INS Order to Show Cause and Notice of Hearing. The notice advised Mr. Ruiz Massieu that he was ordered to show cause as to why he should not be deported because, the Secretary of State has made a determination that, pursuant to Section 241(a)(4)(C) of the Immigration and Nationality [sic] Act, 8 U.S.C. §1251(a)(4)(C), there is reasonable ground to believe your presence or activities in the United States would have potentially serious adverse foreign policy consequences for the United States. No further explanation of the ground for Mr. Ruiz Massieu's alleged deportability was tendered.

Sometime after notice was served on Mr. Ruiz Massieu, the INS produced an October 2, 1995, letter addressed to Attorney General Janet Reno from Secretary of State Warren Christopher. The letter urged the Attorney General to effect Mr. Ruiz Massieu's "expeditious deportation" "to Mexico" based on the Secretary's conclusion that Mr. Ruiz Massieu's presence in the United States will have potentially serious adverse foreign policy consequences for the United States. The letter referenced the "serious allegations" that are pending in Mexico against Mr. Ruiz Massieu and the recent strides that both governments have taken in "our ability to cooperate and confront criminality on both sides of the border." At bottom, the Secretary's request was premised on the proposition that "our inability to return to Mexico Mr. Ruiz Massieu—a case the Mexican Presidency has told us is of the highest importance—would jeopardize our ability to work with Mexico on law enforcement matters. It might also cast a potentially chilling effect on other issues our two governments are addressing."

The relevant deportation statute, §241(a)(4)(C)(i) of the Immigration and Naturalization Act ("INA"), provides simply that "an alien whose presence or activities in the United States the Secretary of State has reasonable ground to believe would have potentially serious adverse foreign policy consequences for the United States is deportable." Because an indication of the Secretary of State's belief is all that the statute by its terms requires, the October 2, 1995 letter, alone, comprised (and remains) the universe of evidence that the INS has offered to support its charge of Mr. Ruiz Massieu's deportability. A master calendar proceeding, the first stage of deportation hearings, was scheduled to begin on January 19, 1996. On January 17, 1996, however,

Mr. Ruiz Massieu filed a complaint in this court requesting that the deportation proceedings be preliminarily and permanently enjoined, and that section 241(a)(4)(C) of the INA be declared unconstitutional.

The complaint contains three core constitutional claims: (1) the deportation proceeding evidences selective enforcement in retaliation for Mr. Ruiz Massieu's exercise of his First Amendment right to criticize the Mexican political system; (2) the deportation proceeding represents a "de facto" extradition and is an attempt to overrule, albeit indirectly, four federal court decisions, in violation of the separation of powers; and (3) section 241(a)(4)(C)(i) is unconstitutionally vague, in violation of the due process clause of the Fifth Amendment....

In terms of due process, plaintiff attacks § 241(a)(4)(C)(i) on two distinct, though related, grounds. The first contention is that the statute is void for vagueness. The second is that, by its terms, the statute denies plaintiff, and any alien deported thereunder, a meaningful opportunity to be heard before being subjected to the severe deprivation of liberty that is deportation. Additionally, the court has sua sponte raised the issue of whether the statute is so devoid of standards that it represents an unconstitutional delegation of legislative power to the executive....

A. Void-for-Vagueness

....

[T]he void-for-vagueness doctrine ... requires that prohibitory statutes define the conduct proscribed with "sufficient definiteness that ordinary people can understand what conduct is prohibited and in a manner that does not encourage arbitrary and discriminatory enforcement." ... It simply cannot be disputed, and indeed the government does not, that [§ 241(a)(4)(C)(i)] provides absolutely no notice to aliens as to what is required of them under the statute. Simply stated, it "contains no standard for determining what a suspect has to do in order to satisfy" its requirements.... While there may be a common understanding, in a definitional sense, of what "foreign policy" is, no one outside the Department of State and, perhaps, the President ever knows what our nation's frequently covert foreign policy is at any given time. Thus, there is no conceivable way that an alien could know, *ex-ante*, how to conform his or her activities to the requirements of the law. Of course, it is even less likely that an alien could know that his or her mere presence here would or could cause adverse foreign policy consequences when our foreign policy is unpublished, ever-changing, and often highly confidential....

Related to the void-for-vagueness doctrine's notice requirement is "the requirement that the legislature establish minimal guidelines to govern law enforcement," so as not to permit "arbitrary and erratic" applications of the law. Here, again, the statute fails to pass constitutional muster. Rather than providing the Secretary of State with a definite standard, [it] grants the Secretary unfettered discretion....

"Foreign policy" cannot serve as the talisman behind which Congress may abdicate its responsibility to pass only sufficiently clear and definite laws when those laws may be enforced against the individual. Although the executive's discretionary authority over foreign affairs is well established, Congress cannot empower the executive to employ that authority against the individual except through constitutional means. See *Valentine v. United States ex rel. Neidecker*, 299 U.S. 5, 9, ("the Constitution creates no executive prerogative to dispose of the liberty of the individual. Proceedings against him must be authorized by law. There is no executive discretion to surrender him to a foreign government, unless that discretion is governed by law"). If the Constitution was adopted to protect individuals against anything, it was the abuses made possible through just this type of unbounded executive authority.

There can be no more graphic illustration of the exercise of unbounded executive authority than that seen in this case. In this case, the Secretary has determined that plaintiff is expendable — for "foreign policy" reasons which the Secretary need neither explicate nor defend — merely because Mexico wants plaintiff back. Had plaintiff overstayed his welcome, had he entered this country illegally, or had he committed a crime while here — all clearly defined grounds for deportation — he would be entitled to a host of protections, not the least of which would be notice of the prohibited conduct and a meaningful opportunity to be heard. Similarly, if it were believed that plaintiff had committed a crime in Mexico, his extradition would, presumably, have again been sought and, again, there would be no problem of vagueness and he would be entitled to substantial protections. Extradition, after all, is the time-tested mechanism used by this country and other civilized countries to send a criminal back, a mechanism that the government has unsuccessfully utilized vis-a-vis plaintiff in four separate court proceedings. Section 241(a)(4)(C)(i) does an end run around and, indeed, subverts the extradition framework, which would never permit the return of an alien merely because he is considered undesirable by his government. . . . [It] authorizes a heretofore unknown scope of executive enforcement power *vis-a-vis* the individual with utterly no standards provided to the Secretary of State or to the legal aliens subject to its provisions. Section 241(a)(4)(C)(i) is void for vagueness.

B. Opportunity to be Heard

For many of the same reasons that § 241(a)(4)(C)(i) is void for vagueness, the statute also deprives aliens such as plaintiff of due process of law by denying them a meaningful opportunity to be heard. . . . [I]n order to determine whether the opportunity afforded to plaintiff under the INA is constitutionally sufficient, this court must apply the now familiar three-part balancing test enunciated by the Supreme Court in *Mathews v. Eldridge*, 424 U.S. 319, 335 (1976). Phrased in terms relevant to the case at bar, this court must consider: (1) the importance to all aliens of not being imprisoned, forced to leave the United States, and sent to the country of our government's choosing; (2) the adequacy of the hearing afforded and the likelihood that increased procedures would diminish the risk of an erroneous deprivation of liberty; and (3) the governmental interest, as well as that of the public, in allowing the Secretary of State to declare an alien deportable in the interests of our foreign policy as well as the increased cost of requiring additional procedures. . . . [Applying this test, the court found that (1) the interest of plaintiff and other aliens in] avoiding the complete deprivation of liberty that results from executive confinement and deportation.... is unquantifiably grave.... [(2)] In light of the "grave nature of deportation," due process requires, at a minimum, that plaintiff be afforded a meaningful opportunity to be heard.... [And (3)] as important as the nation's foreign policy is, this court is aware of no rationale that would justify this extraordinary grant of discretion given the Secretary of State when other equally lofty interests do not warrant a comparable suspension of an alien's constitutional rights.... [Thus] a balancing of the appropriate factors tips well in plaintiff's favor. Absent a meaningful opportunity to be heard, the Secretary of State's unreviewable and concededly "unfettered discretion" to deprive an alien, who lawfully entered this country, of his or her liberty to the extent exemplified by this case is, in this court's view, unconstitutional.

C. Unconstitutional Delegation of Legislative Powers

For many of the same reasons that § 241(a)(4)(C)(i) of the INA is violative of the due process clause, it also is an unconstitutional delegation of legislative power to the executive.... The Constitution grants the power to make laws exclusively to the people's representatives in Congress.... It has long been recognized, however, that some level of legislative delegation is necessary to the efficient administration of the ever-broadening regulatory course charted by Congress. Accordingly, "the most that may be asked under the separation-of-powers doctrine is that Congress lay down the general policy and standards that animate the law, leaving the agency to refine those standards, 'fill in the blanks,' or apply the standards to particular cases." The delegation doctrine, then, functions to ensure that Congress will remain the nation's primary policy maker by requiring it to articulate intelligible standards to guide (1) the exercise of the delegatee's authority, and (2) the judiciary's ability to review the exercise of that authority against a congressionally mandated policy. Section 241(a)(4)(C)(i) fails on both counts.... Here, the government has offered no means of limiting the Secretary's authority under § 241(a)(4)(C)(i) by reference to the text, related statutes, legislative history, or common understandings. Neither can this court conceive of a way to judicially circumscribe the discretion afforded to the Secretary so as to impose a "recognized standard" upon the Secretary's otherwise "totally unrestricted freedom of choice."... More importantly, the Supreme Court's recent nondelegation jurisprudence has emphasized that the adequacy of the standards provided to a delegatee cannot be evaluated in a vacuum, but must be measured in light of the procedures and standards available to ensure meaningful judicial review.... In this way, the Court has brought the focus of the nondelegation doctrine back to its functional core—to safeguard the separation of powers by ensuring that the members of Congress, as the elected lawmaking representatives of the people, remain directly accountable both to their constituents and to the Constitution through the process of judicial review....

With § 241(a)(4)(C)(i), Congress has delegated discretionary authority to the executive that not only is virtually standardless, but is utterly unreviewable by Article I and Article III courts alike. As discussed in Sections A and B, above, the statute completely deprives plaintiff of a meaningful opportunity to be heard and to rebut the allegations of deportability against him. The other side of that same coin, then, is that the judiciary will be prevented from performing its duty to meaningfully review the Secretary's exercise of his discretion.... Section 241(a)(4)(C)(i) ... provides no standards or procedures to allow for judicial review of an agency's discretionary deprivation of an alien's liberty. Accordingly, this court concludes that by leaving deportability determinations to the wholly unguided and unreviewable discretion of the Secretary of State, § 241(a)(4)(C)(i) represents an unconstitutional delegation of legislative power by which Congress eliminated the judiciary's constitutionally required function of review while abdicating its lawmaking responsibilities in favor of standardless executive discretion.

For the reasons stated above, this court now finds that § 241(a)(4)(C)(i) of the INA is unconstitutional. Accordingly, the deportation proceedings instituted against plaintiff, pursuant thereto, will be permanently enjoined.

Notes

(1) The district court's decision in *Ruiz Massieu* was reversed on appeal on the ground that the plaintiff had failed to exhaust his administrative remedies. *See Massieu v. Reno*, 91 F.3d 416 (3d Cir. 1996), *cert. denied*, 527 U.S. 1023 (1999). On May 30, 1997, an immigration judge ruled that Ruiz Massieu was not deportable because the government had produced insufficient evidence to show that his presence in the United States would have potentially serious adverse foreign policy consequences. The INS appealed to the Board of Immigration Appeals. In a 12-2 decision, the board found that the Secretary of State's determination was conclusive and vacated the immigration judge's ruling. *See In re Ruiz-Massieu*, Interim Decision No. 3400 (B.I.A, June 10, 1999). In August 1999, Ruiz Massieu was indicted by a federal grand jury in Houston; the indictment charged that the $9 million he had deposited in Texas banks represented payoffs from narcotics traffickers. On September 15, 1999, two days before he was to appear in Houston for arraignment, Ruiz Massieu committed suicide, by taking an overdose of antidepressants, at the Palisades Park, New Jersey, apartment where he had been living under house arrest for four years. *See* N.Y. Times, Sept. 16, 1999, at A3.

(2) One of the plaintiff's claims in *Ruiz Massieu* was that it is impermissible to use deportation to circumvent the safeguards provided by the law of extradition. The district court did not pass on this claim, since it found the statutory basis for deportation to be unconstitutional. Suppose deportation had been based on a section of the Immigration and Naturalization Act whose constitutionality was not in doubt. Would the fact that it was being used to bypass extradition procedures be a valid reason for enjoining deportation? Consider the following statement by the Board of Immigration Appeals in its Interim Decision in the *Ruiz Massieu* case:

> The respondent argues that the Attorney General should not be allowed to deport him, having failed in her attempt to comply with the Mexican government's attempt to extradite him to Mexico. Extradition proceedings are separate and apart from any immigration proceeding. The standards

> of proof are different. As the Service has pointed out, not all of the charges brought in Mexico were cited as a basis for extradition. Also, the existence of criminal charges is not the only possible basis for a determination that the respondent's presence may have adverse foreign policy consequences. We note that other aliens have been deported after extradition requests were denied by the courts. In *Matter of McMullen*, 17 I. & N. Dec. 542 (B.I.A. 1980), the government petition for extradition was denied.

The respondent was, nevertheless, found deportable. The board stated:

> Decisions resulting from extradition proceedings are not entitled to res judicata effect in later proceedings. Moreover, the res judicata bar goes into effect only where a valid, final judgment has been rendered on the merits, and it is well established that decisions and orders regarding extraditability "embody no judgment on the guilt or innocence of the accused. . . ." The issues involved in a deportation hearing differ from those involved in an extradition case, and resolution of even a common issue in one proceeding is not binding in the other.

In *Matter of Doherty*, 599 F. Supp. 270 (S.D.N.Y. 1984), the respondent was not extradited because the judge, sitting as a magistrate, found that the crimes he committed were political; nevertheless, Doherty was found deportable based on his own concession of deportability. The Attorney General rejected his designation of a country of deportation under section 243(a) of the Act as prejudicial to the interests of the United States. The United States Court of Appeals for the Second Circuit found that section 243(a) gives the Attorney General broad discretion to determine what constitutes prejudice to national interests. *Doherty v. United States Dep't of Justice*, 908 F.2d 1108 (2d Cir. 1990), *rev'd on other grounds, INS v. Doherty*, 502 U.S. 314 (1992).

(3) According to the *Report of the Committee on Extradition and Human Rights*, in International Law Association, Report of the Sixty-Sixth Conference 142, 164 (1994):

> [T]here is no rule which prohibits a state from deporting a suspected criminal to another state, particularly his state of nationality, to stand trial there. This practice is widely condemned as it deprives the deportee of the rights to which he would be entitled if he were extradited. In particular it deprives him of the right to raise the political offence exception. Despite such objections the practice occurs in many countries.

The cases in which the use of deportation to bypass extradition procedures has been judicially condemned typically have involved some kind of further misconduct on the part of the authorities either of the forum state or of the state from which the fugitive was deported or both. In *Regina v. Horseferry Road Magistrates' Court, Ex parte Bennett*, [1994] 1 A. C. 42 (H.L.), the House of Lords held that if, as alleged, the South African and British police had colluded in using deportation as a substitute for extradition, a British court should, in the exercise of its supervisory power, stay the prosecution and order the release of the accused. This holding is limited, however, to cases in which there has been collusion in the decision to deport, and possibly requires some additional illegality, abuse of power, violation of international law, or the domestic law of the foreign state involved. *See Regina v. Staines Magistrates' Court, Ex parte Westfallen*, [1998] 4 All E. R. 210, [1998] 1 W.L.R. 652 (Q.B.). In *Bozano v. France*, 111 Eur. Ct. H. R. (ser. A) (Dec. 18, 1986), where the French courts had refused to extradite a fugitive to Italy, and the French police deported him to Switzerland, which in turn extradited him to Italy, the European Court of Human Rights found a violation of the right to personal liberty guaranteed by Article 5(1) of the European Convention on Human Rights. But, again, the decision turned on the conclusion that the French police probably had violated French law and, in any event, had acted in an arbitrary manner which went beyond what is usual in cases of deportation. The question of whether Italy could conceivably be obligated to reopen the prosecution was not before the court.

§ 17.03 Abduction

United States v. Alvarez-Machain

Supreme Court of the United States
504 U.S. 655 (1992)

Chief Justice Rehnquist delivered the opinion of the Court:

The issue in this case is whether a criminal defendant, abducted to the United States from a nation with which it has an extradition treaty, thereby acquires a defense to the jurisdiction of this country's courts. We hold that he does not, and that he may be tried in federal district court for violations of the criminal law of the United States.

Respondent, Humberto Alvarez-Machain, is a citizen and resident of Mexico. He was indicted for participating in the kidnap and murder of United States Drug Enforcement Administration (DEA) special agent Enrique Camarena-Salazar and a Mexican pilot working with Camarena, Alfredo Zavala-Avelar. The DEA believes that respondent, a medical doctor, participated in the murder by prolonging Agent Camarena's life so that others could further torture and interrogate him. On April 2, 1990, respondent was forcibly kidnaped from his medical office in Guadalajara, Mexico, to be flown by private plane to El Paso, Texas, where he was arrested by DEA officials. The District Court concluded that DEA agents were responsible for respondent's abduction, although they were not personally involved in it. . . .

Respondent moved to dismiss the indictment, claiming that his abduction constituted outrageous governmental conduct, and that the District Court lacked jurisdiction to try him because he was abducted in violation of the extradition treaty between the United States and Mexico. Extradition Treaty, May 4, 1978, [1979] United States-United Mexican States, 31 U.S.T. 5059, T.I.A.S. No. 9656 (Extradition

Treaty or Treaty). The District Court rejected the outrageous governmental conduct claim, but held that it lacked jurisdiction to try respondent because his abduction violated the Extradition Treaty.... The Court of Appeals affirmed the dismissal of the indictment and the repatriation of respondent.... We granted certiorari,... and now reverse.

Although we have never before addressed the precise issue raised in the present case, we have previously considered proceedings in claimed violation of an extradition treaty and proceedings against a defendant brought before a court by means of a forcible abduction. We addressed the former issue in *United States v. Rauscher*, 119 U.S. 407, 7 S. Ct. 234, 30 L. Ed. 425 (1886); more precisely, the issue whether the Webster-Ashburton Treaty of 1842, 8 Stat. 576, which governed extraditions between England and the United States, prohibited the prosecution of defendant Rauscher for a crime other than the crime for which he had been extradited. Whether this prohibition, known as the doctrine of specialty, was an intended part of the treaty had been disputed between the two nations for some time.... Justice Miller delivered the opinion of the Court, which carefully examined the terms and history of the treaty; the practice of nations in regards to extradition treaties; the case law from the States; and the writings of commentators, and reached the following conclusion:

> "[A] person who has been brought within the jurisdiction of the court *by virtue of proceedings under an extradition treaty*, can only be tried for one of the offences described in that treaty, and for the offence with which he is charged in the proceedings for his extradition, until a reasonable time and opportunity have been given him, after his release or trial upon such charge, to return to the country from whose asylum he had been forcibly taken under those proceedings."... (emphasis added).

In addition, Justice Miller's opinion noted that any doubt as to this interpretation was put to rest by two federal statutes which imposed the doctrine of specialty upon extradition treaties to which the United States was a party.... Unlike the case before us today, the defendant in *Rauscher* had been brought to the United States by way of an extradition treaty; there was no issue of a forcible abduction.

In *Ker v. Illinois*, 119 U.S. 436, 7 S. Ct. 225, 30 L. Ed. 421 (1886), also written by Justice Miller and decided the same day as *Rauscher*, we addressed the issue of a defendant brought before the court by way of a forcible abduction. Frederick Ker had been tried and convicted in an Illinois court for larceny; his presence before the court was procured by means of forcible abduction from Peru. A messenger was sent to Lima with the proper warrant to demand Ker by virtue of the extradition treaty between Peru and the United States. The messenger, however, disdained reliance on the treaty processes, and instead forcibly kidnaped Ker and brought him to the United States. We distinguished Ker's case from *Rauscher*, on the basis that Ker was not brought into the United States by virtue of the extradition treaty between the United States and Peru, and rejected Ker's argument that he had a right under the extradition treaty to be returned to this country only in accordance with its terms. We rejected Ker's due process argument more broadly, holding in line with "the highest authorities" that "such forcible abduction is no sufficient reason why the party should not answer when brought within the jurisdiction of the court which has the right to try him for such an offence, and presents no valid objection to his trial in such court." . . .

In *Frisbie v. Collins*, 342 U.S. 519, 72 S. Ct. 509, 96 L. Ed. 541, *rehearing denied*, 343 U.S. 937, 72 S. Ct. 768, 96 L. Ed. 1344 (1952), we applied the rule in *Ker* to a case in which the defendant had been kidnaped in Chicago by Michigan officers and brought to trial in Michigan. We upheld the conviction over objections based on the Due Process Clause and the federal Kidnaping Act and stated:

> "This Court has never departed from the rule announced in *[Ker]* that the power of a court to try a person for crime is not impaired by the fact that he had been brought within the court's jurisdiction by reason of a 'forcible abduction.' No persuasive reasons are now presented to justify overruling this line of cases. They rest on the sound basis that due process of law is satisfied when one present in court is convicted of crime after having been fairly apprized of the charges against him and after a fair trial in accordance with constitutional procedural safeguards. There is nothing in the Constitution that requires a court to permit a guilty person rightfully convicted to escape justice because he was brought to trial against his will." . . .

The only differences between *Ker* and the present case are that *Ker* was decided on the premise that there was no governmental involvement in the abduction, . . . and Peru, from which Ker was abducted, did not object to his prosecution. . . . Respondent finds these differences to be dispositive, ... contending that they show that respondent's prosecution, like the prosecution of *Rauscher*, violates the implied terms of a valid extradition treaty. The Government, on the other hand, argues that *Rauscher* stands as an "exception" to the rule in *Ker* only when an extradition treaty is invoked, and the terms of the treaty provide that its breach will limit the jurisdiction of a court. Therefore, our first inquiry must be whether the abduction of respondent from Mexico violated the Extradition Treaty between the United States and Mexico. If we conclude that the Treaty does not prohibit respondent's abduction, the rule in *Ker* applies, and the court need not inquire as to how respondent came before it.

In construing a treaty, as in construing a statute, we first look to its terms to determine its meaning. . . . The Treaty says nothing about the obligations of the United States and Mexico to refrain from forcible abductions of people from the territory of the other nation, or the consequences under the Treaty if such an abduction occurs. . . . According to respondent, Article 9 embodies the terms of the bargain which the United States struck: If the United States wishes to prosecute a Mexican national, it may request that individual's extradition. Upon a request from the United States, Mexico may either extradite the individual or submit the case to the proper authorities for prosecution in Mexico. In this way, respondent reasons, each nation preserved its right to choose whether its nationals would be tried in its own courts or by the courts of the other nation. This preservation of rights would be frustrated if either nation were free to abduct nationals of the other nation for the purposes of prosecution. More broadly, respondent reasons, as did the Court of Appeals, that all the processes and restrictions on the obligation to extradite established by the Treaty would make no sense if either nation were free to resort to forcible kidnaping to gain the presence of an individual for prosecution in a manner not contemplated by the Treaty. . . .

Article 9 does not purport to specify the only way in which one country may gain custody of a national of the other country for the purposes of prosecution. In the absence of an extradition treaty, nations are under no obligation to surrender those in their country to foreign authorities for prosecution. . . . Extradition treaties exist so as to impose mutual obligations to surrender individuals in certain defined sets of circumstances, following established procedures. . . . The Treaty thus provides a mechanism which would not otherwise exist, requiring, under certain circumstances, the United States and Mexico to extradite individuals to the other country, and establishing the procedures to be followed when the Treaty is invoked.

The history of negotiation and practice under the Treaty also fails to show that abductions outside of the Treaty constitute a violation of the Treaty. As the Solicitor General notes, the Mexican Government was made aware, as early as 1906, of the *Ker* doctrine, and the United States' position that it applied to forcible abductions made outside of the terms of the United States-Mexico Extradition Treaty. Nonetheless, the current version of the Treaty, signed in 1978, does not attempt to establish a rule that would in any way curtail the effect of *Ker*. Moreover, although language which would grant individuals exactly the right sought by respondent had been considered and drafted as early as 1935 by a prominent group of legal scholars sponsored by the faculty of Harvard Law School, no such clause appears in the current Treaty.

Thus, the language of the Treaty, in the context of its history, does not support the proposition that the Treaty prohibits abductions outside of its terms. The remaining question, therefore, is whether the Treaty should be interpreted so as to include an implied term prohibiting prosecution where the defendant's presence is obtained by means other than those established by the Treaty. . . .

Respondent contends that the Treaty must be interpreted against the backdrop of customary international law, and that international abductions are "so clearly prohibited in international law" that there was no reason to include such a clause in the Treaty itself. The international censure of international abductions is further evidenced, according to respondent, by the United Nations Charter and the Charter of the Organization of American States. Respondent does not argue that these sources of international law provide an independent basis for the right respondent asserts not to be tried in the United States, but rather that they should inform the interpretation of the Treaty terms.

The Court of Appeals deemed it essential, in order for the individual defendant to assert a right under the Treaty, that the affected foreign government had registered a protest. . . . Respondent agrees that the right exercised by the individual is derivative of the nation's right under the Treaty, since nations are authorized, notwithstanding the terms of an extradition treaty, to voluntarily render an individual to the other country on terms completely outside of those provided in the treaty. The formal protest, therefore, ensures that the "offended" nation actually objects to the abduction and has not in some way voluntarily rendered the individual for prosecution. Thus the Extradition Treaty only prohibits gaining the defendant's presence by means other than those set forth in the Treaty when the nation from which the defendant was abducted objects.

This argument seems to us inconsistent with the remainder of respondent's argument. The Extradition Treaty has the force of law, and if, as respondent asserts, it is self-executing, it would appear that a court must enforce it on behalf of an individual regardless of the offensiveness of the practice of one nation to the other nation. In *Rauscher*, the Court noted that Great Britain had taken the position in other cases that the Webster-Ashburton Treaty included the doctrine of specialty, but no importance was attached to whether or not Great Britain had protested the prosecution of Rauscher for the crime of cruel and unusual punishment as opposed to murder.

More fundamentally, the difficulty with the support respondent garners from international law is that none of it relates to the practice of nations in relation to extradition treaties. In *Rauscher*, we implied a term in the Webster-Ashburton Treaty because of the practice of nations with regard to extradition treaties. In the instant case, respondent would imply terms in the Extradition Treaty from the practice of nations with regards to international law more generally. Respondent would have us find that the Treaty acts as a prohibition against a violation of the general principle of international law that one government may not "exercise its police power in the territory of another state." . . . There are many actions which could be taken by a nation that would violate this principle, including waging war, but it cannot seriously be contended that an invasion of the United States by Mexico would violate the terms of the Extradition Treaty between the two nations. . . .

Respondent and his *amici* may be correct that respondent's abduction was "shocking," . . . and that it may be in violation of general international law principles. Mexico has protested the abduction of respondent through diplomatic notes, . . . and the decision of whether respondent should be returned to Mexico, as a matter outside of the Treaty, is a matter for the Executive Branch. We conclude, however, that respondent's abduction was not in violation of the Extradition Treaty between the United States and Mexico, and therefore the rule of *Ker v. Illinois* is fully applicable to this case. The fact of respondent's forcible abduction does not therefore prohibit his trial in a court in the United States for violations of the criminal laws of the United States. . . .

The judgment of the Court of Appeals is therefore reversed, and the case is remanded for further proceedings consistent with this opinion. . . .

Justice Stevens, with whom Justice Blackmun and Justice O'Connor join, dissenting.

The Court correctly observes that this case raises a question of first impression.... The case is unique for several reasons. It does not involve an ordinary abduction by a private kidnaper, or bounty hunter, as in *Ker* nor does it involve the apprehension of an American fugitive who committed a crime in one State and sought asylum in another, as in *Frisbie*. Rather, it involves this country's abduction of another country's citizen; it also involves a violation of the territorial integrity of that other country, with which this country has signed an extradition treaty.

A Mexican citizen was kidnaped in Mexico and charged with a crime committed in Mexico; his offense allegedly violated both Mexican and American law. Mexico has formally demanded on at least two separate occasions that he be returned to Mexico and has represented that he will be prosecuted and, if convicted, punished for his offense. It is clear that Mexico's demand must be honored if this official abduction violated the 1978 Extradition Treaty between the United States and Mexico. In my opinion, a fair reading of the treaty in light of our decision in *Rauscher* and applicable principles of international law, leads inexorably to the conclusion that the District Court, ... and the Court of Appeals for the Ninth Circuit, ... correctly construed that instrument.

The extradition treaty with Mexico is a comprehensive document containing 23 articles and an appendix listing the extraditable offenses covered by the agreement. The parties announced their purpose in the preamble: The two governments desire "to cooperate more closely in the fight against crime and, to this end, to mutually render better assistance in matters of extradition." From the preamble, through the description of the parties' obligations with respect to offenses committed within as well as beyond the territory of a requesting party, the delineation of the procedures and evidentiary requirements for extradition, the special provisions for political offenses and capital punishment, and other details, the Treaty appears to have been designed to cover the entire subject of extradition. Thus, Article 22, entitled "Scope of Application," states that the "Treaty shall apply to offenses specified in Article 2 committed before and after this Treaty enters into force," and Article 2 directs that "extradition shall take place, subject to this Treaty, for willful acts which fall within any of [the extraditable offenses listed in] the clauses of the Appendix." Moreover, as noted by the Court, Article 9 expressly provides that neither contracting party is bound to deliver up its own nationals, although it may do so in its discretion, but if it does not do so, it "shall submit the case to its competent authorities for purposes of prosecution."

The Government's claim that the Treaty is not exclusive, but permits forcible governmental kidnaping, would transform these, and other, provisions into little more than verbiage. For example, provisions requiring "sufficient" evidence to grant extradition (Art. 3), withholding extradition for political or military offenses (Art. 5), withholding extradition when the person sought has already been tried (Art. 6), withholding extradition when the statute of limitations for the crime has lapsed (Art. 7), and granting the requested country discretion to refuse to extradite an individual who would face the death penalty in the requesting country (Art. 8), would serve little purpose if the requesting country could simply kidnap the person. As the Court of Appeals for the Ninth Circuit recognized in a related case, "each of these provisions would be utterly frustrated if a kidnapping were held to be a permissible course of governmental conduct." . . . In addition, all of these provisions "only make sense if they are understood as *requiring* each treaty signatory to comply with those procedures whenever it wishes to obtain jurisdiction over an individual who is located in another treaty nation." . . .

It is true, as the Court notes, that there is no express promise by either party to refrain from forcible abductions in the territory of the other nation. . . . Relying on that omission, the Court, in effect, concludes that the Treaty merely creates an optional method of obtaining jurisdiction over alleged offenders, and that the parties silently reserved the right to resort to self-help whenever they deem force more expeditious than legal process. If the United States, for example, thought it more expedient to torture or simply to execute a person rather than to attempt extradition, these options would be equally available because they, too, were not explicitly prohibited by the Treaty. That, however, is a highly improbable interpretation of a consensual agreement, which on its face appears to have been intended to set forth comprehensive and exclusive rules concerning the subject of extradition. In my opinion, "the manifest scope and object of the treaty itself," plainly imply a mutual undertaking to respect the territorial integrity of the other contracting party. That opinion is confirmed by a consideration of the "legal context" in which the Treaty was negotiated. . . .

In *Rauscher*, the Court construed an extradition treaty that was far less comprehensive than the 1978 Treaty with Mexico. . . . After Rauscher had been extradited for murder, he was charged with the lesser offense of inflicting cruel and unusual punishment on a member of the crew of a vessel on the high seas. Although the treaty did not purport to place any limit on the jurisdiction of the demanding state after acquiring custody of the fugitive, this Court held that he could not be tried for any offense other than murder. Thus, the treaty constituted the exclusive means by which the United States could obtain jurisdiction over a defendant within the territorial jurisdiction of Great Britain.

The Court noted that the treaty included several specific provisions, such as the crimes for which one could be extradited, the process by which the extradition was to be carried out, and even the evidence that was to be produced, and concluded that "the fair purpose of the treaty is, that the person shall be delivered up to be tried for that offence and for no other." . . . The Court reasoned that it did not make sense for the treaty to provide such specifics only to have the person "pas[s] into the hands of the country which charges him with the offence, free from all the positive requirements and just implications of the treaty under which the transfer of his person takes place." . . . To interpret the treaty in a contrary way would mean that a country could request extradition of a person for one of the seven crimes covered by the treaty, and then try the person for another crime, such as a political crime, which was clearly not covered by the treaty; this result, the Court concluded, was clearly contrary to the intent of the parties and the purpose of the treaty. . . .

Thus, the Extradition Treaty, as understood in the context of cases that have addressed similar issues, suffices to protect the defendant from prosecution despite the absence of any express language in the Treaty itself purporting to limit this Nation's power to prosecute a defendant over whom it had lawfully acquired jurisdiction.

Although the Court's conclusion in *Rauscher* was supported by a number of judicial precedents, the holdings in these cases were not nearly as uniform as the consensus of international opinion that condemns one nation's violation of the territorial integrity of a friendly neighbor. It is shocking that a party to an extradition treaty might believe that it has secretly reserved the right to make seizures of citizens in the other party's territory.... Thus, a leading treatise explains:

> "A State must not perform acts of sovereignty in the territory of another State....
>
> "It is ... a breach of International Law for a State to send its agents to the territory of another State to apprehend persons accused of having committed a crime. Apart from other satisfaction, the first duty of the offending State is to hand over the person in question to the State in whose territory he was apprehended." 1 OPPENHEIM'S INTERNATIONAL LAW 295, and n.1 (H. Lauterpacht 8th ed. 1955).

Commenting on the precise issue raised by this case, the chief reporter for the American Law Institute's Restatement of Foreign Relations used language reminiscent of Justice Story's characterization of an official seizure in a foreign jurisdiction as "monstrous":

> "When done without consent of the foreign government, abducting a person from a foreign country is a gross violation of international law and gross disrespect for a norm high in the opinion of mankind. It is a blatant violation of the territorial integrity of another state; it eviscerates the extradition system (established by a comprehensive network of treaties involving virtually all states)."

In the *Rauscher* case, the legal background that supported the decision to imply a covenant not to prosecute for an offense different from that for which extradition had been granted was far less clear than the rule against invading the territorial integrity of a treaty partner that supports Mexico's position in this case. If *Rauscher* was correctly decided—and I am convinced that it was—its rationale clearly dictates a comparable result in this case....

A critical flaw pervades the Court's entire opinion. It fails to differentiate between the conduct of private citizens, which does not violate any treaty obligation, and conduct expressly authorized by the Executive Branch of the Government, which unquestionably constitutes a flagrant violation of international law, and in my opinion, also constitutes a breach of our treaty obligations. Thus, at the outset of its opinion, the Court states the issue as "whether a criminal defendant, abducted to the

United States from a nation with which it has an extradition treaty, thereby acquires a defense to the jurisdiction of this country's courts." ... That, of course, is the question decided in *Ker* it is not, however, the question presented for decision today.

The importance of the distinction between a court's exercise of jurisdiction over either a person or property that has been wrongfully seized by a private citizen, or even by a state law enforcement agent, on the one hand, and the attempted exercise of jurisdiction predicated on a seizure by federal officers acting beyond the authority conferred by treaty, on the other hand, is explained by Justice Brandeis in his opinion for the Court in *Cook v. United States*, 288 U.S. 102, 53 S. Ct. 305, 77 L. Ed. 641 (1933). That case involved a construction of a Prohibition Era treaty with Great Britain that authorized American agents to board certain British vessels to ascertain whether they were engaged in importing alcoholic beverages. A British vessel was boarded 11 1/2 miles off the coast of Massachusetts, found to be carrying unmanifested alcoholic beverages, and taken into port. The Collector of Customs assessed a penalty which he attempted to collect by means of libels against both the cargo and the seized vessel.

The Court held that the seizure was not authorized by the treaty because it occurred more than 10 miles off shore. The Government argued that the illegality of the seizure was immaterial because, as in *Ker*, the court's jurisdiction was supported by possession even if the seizure was wrongful. Justice Brandeis acknowledged that the argument would succeed if the seizure had been made by a private party without authority to act for the Government, but that a different rule prevails when the Government itself lacks the power to seize....

The Court's failure to differentiate between private abductions and official invasions of another sovereign's territory also accounts for its misplaced reliance on the 1935 proposal made by the Advisory Committee on Research in International Law.... As the text of that proposal plainly states, it would have rejected the rule of the *Ker* case. The failure to adopt that recommendation does not speak to the issue the Court decides today. The Court's admittedly "shocking" disdain for customary and conventional international law principles ... is thus entirely unsupported by case law and commentary....

As the Court observes at the outset of its opinion, there is reason to believe that respondent participated in an especially brutal murder of an American law enforcement agent. That fact, if true, may explain the Executive's intense interest in punishing respondent in our courts. Such an explanation, however, provides no justification for disregarding the Rule of Law that this Court has a duty to uphold. That the Executive may wish to reinterpret the Treaty to allow for an action that the Treaty in no way authorizes should not influence this Court's interpretation. Indeed, the desire for revenge exerts "a kind of hydraulic pressure ... before which even well settled principles of law will bend," ... but it is precisely at such moments that we should remember and be guided by our duty "to render judgment evenly and dispassionately according to law, as each is given understanding to ascertain and apply it." . . . The way that we perform that duty in a case of this kind sets an example that other tribunals in other countries are sure to emulate.

The significance of this Court's precedents is illustrated by a recent decision of the Court of Appeal of the Republic of South Africa. Based largely on its understanding of the import of this Court's cases — including our decision in *Ker* — that court held that the prosecution of a defendant kidnaped by agents of South Africa in another country must be dismissed. . . . The Court of Appeal of South Africa — indeed, I suspect most courts throughout the civilized world — will be deeply disturbed by the "monstrous" decision the Court announces today. For every nation that has an interest in preserving the Rule of Law is affected, directly or indirectly, by a decision of this character. As Thomas Paine warned, an "avidity to punish is always dangerous to liberty" because it leads a nation "to stretch, to misinterpret, and to misapply even the best of laws." To counter that tendency, he reminds us:

> "He that would make his own liberty secure must guard even his enemy from oppression; for if he violates this duty he establishes a precedent that will reach to himself."

I respectfully dissent.

Notes

(1) In December 1992, Alvarez-Machain was tried and acquitted of the murder. He returned to Mexico. On July 9, 1993, he filed a civil action, which was ultimately unsuccessful, under 42 U.S.C. § 1983 and various other federal statutes. *See Sosa v. Alvarez-Machain* [chap. 1].

(2) On March 30, 1993, President Clinton wrote to the President of Mexico:

> I want to assure you that my administration will not conduct, encourage, or condone illegal transborder abductions in Mexico. I look forward to continuing close cooperation with Mexico in law enforcement matters in the future.

Text supplied by Embassy of Mexico in Washington. The following year, the United States and Mexico negotiated a treaty banning abductions, but it was never ratified by the United States. *See* Treaty to Prohibit Transborder Abductions, Nov. 23, 1994, U.S.-Mex., *reprinted in* MICHAEL ABBELL, EXTRADITION TO AND FROM THE UNITED STATES, at A-303 (2002) (not carried forward into the continuation volume of this work in 2010).

(3) In *United States v. Matta-Ballesteros*, 71 F.3d 754 (9th Cir. 1995), *amended*, 98 F.3d 1100 (9th Cir. 1996), the court found jurisdiction over the defendant despite the fact that he was abducted from Honduras and taken to the United States for trial. The court found that "[t]he treaties between the United States and Honduras contain preservations of rights similar to those which *Alvarez-Machain* held did not sufficiently specify extradition as the only way in which one country may gain custody of a foreign national for purposes of prosecution." In ruling on Matta-Ballesteros'

argument that the circumstances of his abduction warranted dismissal, the court stated:

> The Supreme Court has long held that the manner by which a defendant is brought to trial does not affect the government's ability to try him.... Though we may be deeply concerned by the actions of our government, it is clear in light of recent Supreme Court precedent that the circumstances surrounding Matta-Ballesteros's abduction do not divest this court of jurisdiction in this case.... In the shadow cast by *Alvarez-Machain*, attempts to expand due process rights into the realm of foreign abductions, as the Second Circuit did in *United States v. Toscanino*, 500 F.2d 267 (2d Cir. 1974), have been cut short.
>
> In *Toscanino*, the defendant alleged that United States agents abducted him from Uruguay, pistol-whipped, bound, blindfolded, brutally tortured, and interrogated him for seventeen days, and finally drugged and brought him to the United States by airplane, all with the knowledge of an Assistant United States Attorney.... That court held that if Toscanino's allegations were true, his indictment was subject to dismissal based on the federal court's supervisory powers over the administration of criminal justice first outlined by the Supreme Court in *McNabb v. United States*, 318 U.S. 332, 340–41, 63 S. Ct. 608, 87 L. Ed. 819 (1943). In holding that the supervisory powers of the court could require dismissal, *Toscanino* relied in part on Supreme Court decisions addressing other types of outrageous governmental conduct, ...
>
> This court has held, however, that we have inherent supervisory powers to order dismissal of prosecutions for only three legitimate reasons: (1) to implement a remedy for the violation of a recognized statutory or constitutional right; (2) to preserve judicial integrity by ensuring that a conviction rests on appropriate considerations validly before a jury; and (3) to deter future illegal conduct....
>
> The circumstances surrounding Matta-Ballesteros's abduction, while disturbing to us and conduct we seek in no way to condone, meet none of these criteria. It is particularly troublesome to us that the alleged acts were conducted by United States Marshals, officials who purportedly act in our best interest.... While it may seem unconscionable to some that officials serving the interests of justice themselves become agents of criminal intimidation, like the DEA agents in *Alvarez-Machain*, their purported actions have violated no recognized constitutional or statutory rights. They have likewise engaged in no illegal conduct which this court could attempt to deter in the future by invoking its supervisory powers.
>
> The *only* way we could exercise our supervisory powers in this particular case is if the defendant could demonstrate governmental misconduct "of the most shocking and outrageous kind," so as to warrant dismissal....

> Matta-Ballesteros has not. His alleged treatment, even if taken as true, does not meet this rigorous standard, and the acts alleged were not nearly as egregious as those committed in *Toscanino*. . . .
>
> The district court conducted a limited evidentiary hearing, concluding that Matta-Ballesteros failed to make "'a strong showing of grossly cruel and unusual barbarities inflicted upon him by persons who can be characterized as paid agents of the United States.' . . . Defendant's allegations of mistreatment, even if taken as true, do not constitute such barbarism as to warrant dismissal of the indictment under the caselaw." . . .
>
> During the evidentiary hearing, the court heard testimony from Matta-Ballesteros about the purported torture, and he submitted pictures taken upon his arrival at the federal prison as well as a report on stun guns and the declarations of several eyewitnesses who declared he was shocked with the stun guns. The court also considered testimony or declarations from a psychologist and two physicians who examined Matta-Ballesteros, Dr. Donald Valles and Dr. John Van der Decker, who indicated that the cause of his injuries was inconclusive. Additionally, the court considered the declarations and testimony of Juan Morales and Roberto Escobar, United States Marshals who were present at Matta-Ballesteros's capture in Honduras, and who transported him from the Dominican Republic to Marion. They contradicted his testimony, and alleged that he was not tortured and that no stun gun was used on him.
>
> While we may have a suspicion of Matta-Ballesteros's inhumane treatment, and the evidence reasonably could support a finding that he was tortured, it could also support the conclusion of the district court. Because the district court's account of the evidence is plausible in light of the record viewed in its entirety, we may not reverse it even though we may be convinced that, sitting as the trier of fact, we would have weighed the evidence differently. . . . We are therefore bound by the district court's findings, and hold that its determination regarding the alleged torture was not clearly erroneous. Thus, much as we may want to dismiss this case through an exercise of our supervisory powers, to do so would be unwarranted. The district court did not abuse its discretion in refusing to exercise such powers.

(4) What exactly is the argument in favor of dismissing the charges against a defendant who has been brought within a court's jurisdiction through the use of unlawful force? Is it a matter of a court's supervisory power over law enforcement authorities? Is it a matter of the court keeping its hands clean by refusing to become an accomplice to illegal activities? Is it a matter of vindicating the basic rights of the accused, or of finding an appropriate remedy for a violation of international law involving a breach of the territorial sovereignty of another country? Consider the somewhat similar debate with respect to different possible bases for the rule excluding evidence obtained through an illegal search and seizure in violation of the Fourth Amendment. How would a rule requiring courts to decline jurisdiction

in cases of kidnapping differ in its precise application depending on which of the several possible arguments in support of such a rule were adopted?

United States v. Noriega

United States Court of Appeals for the Eleventh Circuit
117 F.3d 1206 (1997)

KRAVITCH, SENIOR CIRCUIT JUDGE:

Manuel Antonio Noriega appeals: (1) his multiple convictions stemming from his involvement in cocaine trafficking; and (2) the district court's denial of his motion for a new trial based on newly discovered evidence. In attacking his convictions, Noriega asserts that the district court should have dismissed the indictment against him due to his status as a head of state and the manner in which the United States brought him to justice. Noriega also contends that the district court committed two reversible evidentiary errors. Alternatively, he seeks a new trial based on his discovery of: (1) the government's suppression of its pact with a non-witness; and/or (2) certain allegations, lodged after his conviction, that a group associated with the undisclosed, cooperating non-witness bribed a prosecution witness. We affirm Noriega's convictions and the district court's order denying his new trial motion.

. . . .

On February 4, 1988, a federal grand jury for the Southern District of Florida indicted Manuel Antonio Noriega on drug-related charges. At that time, Noriega served as commander of the Panamanian Defense Forces in the Republic of Panama. Shortly thereafter, Panama's president, Eric Arturo Delvalle, formally discharged Noriega from his military post, but Noriega refused to accept the dismissal. Panama's legislature then ousted Delvalle from power. The United States, however, continued to acknowledge Delvalle as the constitutional leader of Panama. Later, after a disputed presidential election in Panama, the United States recognized Guillermo Endara as Panama's legitimate head of state.

On December 15, 1989, Noriega publicly declared that a state of war existed between Panama and the United States. Within days of this announcement by Noriega, President George Bush directed United States armed forces into combat in Panama for the stated purposes of "safeguarding American lives, restoring democracy, preserving the Panama Canal treaties, and seizing Noriega to face federal drug charges in the United States." *United States v. Noriega*, 746 F. Supp. 1506, 1511 (S.D. Fla. 1990). The ensuing military conflagration resulted in significant casualties and property loss among Panamanian civilians. Noriega lost his effective control over Panama during this armed conflict, and he surrendered to United States military officials on January 3, 1990. Noriega then was brought to Miami to face the pending federal charges.

Following extensive pre-trial proceedings and a lengthy trial, a jury found Noriega guilty of eight counts in the indictment and not guilty of the remaining two counts. The district court entered judgments of conviction against Noriega upon the jury's verdict and sentenced him to consecutive imprisonment terms of 20, 15 and five years, respectively. . . .

At trial, the government presented the testimony of numerous witnesses as well as documentary evidence to prove Noriega's guilt. Noriega, through both cross-examination and defense witness testimony, fervently contested the veracity of the witnesses and the significance of the documents offered by the government. Under the defense theory of the case, Noriega's subordinates used his name in their drug-trafficking schemes, but Noriega had no personal connection to the alleged offenses. . . .

From the early 1970s to 1989, Noriega secured progressively greater dominion over state military and civilian institutions in Panama, first as his nation's chief of military intelligence and later as commander of the Panamanian Defense Forces. In the early 1980s, Noriega's position of authority brought him into contact with a group of drug traffickers from the Medellin area of Colombia (the "Medellin Cartel"). Various Medellin Cartel operatives met with Noriega's associates and, later, with Noriega personally, regarding the Medellin Cartel's desire to ship cocaine through Panama to the United States. Eventually, Noriega and the Medellin Cartel reached the first of a series of illicit agreements. Thereafter, from 1982 through 1985, with Noriega's assistance, the Medellin Cartel transported significant quantities of cocaine through Panama to the United States. It also utilized its relationship with Noriega to move ether for cocaine processing and substantial cash proceeds from drug sales from the United States to or through Panama.

Noriega and his associates personally met with Medellin Cartel leaders in Colombia, Panama and Cuba regarding the transhipping arrangement, unofficial asylum for Medellin Cartel members fleeing prosecution and a botched plan to operate a cocaine processing laboratory in the Darien region of Panama. The Medellin Cartel directed large cash payments to Noriega in connection with its drug, ether and cash shipments through Panama. During this period, Noriega opened secret accounts in his name and the names of his family members with the Bank of Credit and Commerce International ("BCCI") in Panama. Noriega's associates made large, unexplained cash deposits into these accounts for him. In 1988, Noriega transferred approximately $20,000,000 of his amassed fortune to banks in Europe. The government ultimately located more than $23,000,000 of funds traceable to Noriega in financial institutions outside of Panama.

Noriega challenges his convictions on five distinct grounds: the first three relate to the district court's decision to exercise jurisdiction over this case and the final two concern evidentiary rulings by the district court. . . .

Noriega first argues that the district court should have dismissed the indictment against him based on head-of-state immunity. He insists that he was entitled to such immunity because he served as the de facto, if not the de jure, leader of Panama. The district court rejected Noriega's head-of-state immunity claim because the United States government never recognized Noriega as Panama's legitimate, constitutional ruler.

The Supreme Court long ago held that "the jurisdiction of courts is a branch of that which is possessed by the nation as an independent sovereign power. The jurisdiction of the nation within its own territory is necessarily exclusive and absolute. It is susceptible of no limitation not imposed by itself." *The Schooner Exchange v. M'Faddon*, 11 U.S. (7 Cranch) 116, 136, 3 L. Ed. 287 (1812). The Court, however, ruled that nations, including the United States, had agreed implicitly to accept certain limitations on their individual territorial jurisdiction based on the "common interest impelling [sovereign nations] to mutual intercourse, and an interchange of good offices with each other. . . ." *Id.* at 137. Chief among the exceptions to jurisdiction was "the exemption of the person of the sovereign from arrest or detention within a foreign territory." . . .

The principles of international comity outlined by the Court in *The Schooner Exchange* led to the development of a general doctrine of foreign sovereign immunity which courts applied most often to protect foreign nations in their corporate form from civil process in the United States. . . . To enforce this foreign sovereign immunity, nations concerned about their exposure to judicial proceedings in the United States:

> followed the accepted course of procedure [and] by appropriate representations, sought recognition by the State Department of [their] claim of immunity, and asked that the [State] Department advise the Attorney General of the claim of immunity and that the Attorney General instruct the United States Attorney for the [relevant district] to file in the district court the appropriate suggestion of immunity. . . .

Ex Parte Republic of Peru, 318 U.S. 578, 581, 63 S. Ct. 793, 87 L. Ed. 1014 (1943) (citations omitted). As this doctrine emerged, the "Court consistently [] deferred to the decisions of the political branches — in particular, those of the Executive Branch — on whether to take jurisdiction over actions against foreign sovereigns and their instrumentalities." . . .

In 1976, Congress passed the Foreign Sovereign Immunities Act ("FSIA"), 28 U.S.C. §§ 1602–1611. The FSIA "contains a comprehensive set of legal standards governing claims of immunity in every civil action against a foreign state or its political subdivisions, agencies, or instrumentalities." . . . It codified the State Department's general criteria for making suggestions of immunity, and transferred the responsibility for case-by-case application of these principles from the Executive Branch to the Judicial Branch. . . . Because the FSIA addresses neither head-of-state immunity, nor foreign sovereign immunity in the criminal context, head-of-state immunity could attach in cases, such as this one, only pursuant to the principles and procedures outlined in *The Schooner Exchange* and its progeny. As a result, this court must look to the Executive Branch for direction on the propriety of Noriega's immunity claim. . . .

Generally, the Executive Branch's position on head-of-state immunity falls into one of three categories: the Executive Branch (1) explicitly suggests immunity; (2) expressly declines to suggest immunity; or (3) offers no guidance. Some courts have held that absent a formal suggestion of immunity, a putative head of state should receive no immunity.... In the analogous pre-FSIA, foreign sovereign immunity context, the former Fifth Circuit accepted a slightly broader judicial role. It ruled that, where the Executive Branch either expressly grants or denies a request to suggest immunity, courts must follow that direction, but that courts should make an independent determination regarding immunity when the Executive Branch neglects to convey clearly its position on a particular immunity request....

....

The Executive Branch has not merely refrained from taking a position on this matter; to the contrary, by pursuing Noriega's capture and this prosecution, the Executive Branch has manifested its clear sentiment that Noriega should be denied head-of-state immunity. Noriega has cited no authority that would empower a court to grant head-of-state immunity under these circumstances. Moreover, given that the record indicates that Noriega never served as the constitutional leader of Panama, that Panama has not sought immunity for Noriega and that the charged acts relate to Noriega's private pursuit of personal enrichment, Noriega likely would not prevail even if this court had to make an independent determination regarding the propriety of immunity in this case.... Accordingly, we find no error by the district court on this point.

Noriega next contends his conviction should be reversed because he alleges he was brought to the United States in violation of the Treaty Providing for the Extradition of Criminals, May 25, 1904, United States of America-Republic of Panama, 34 Stat. 2851 ("U.S.-Panama Extradition Treaty"). The Supreme Court's decision in *United States v. Alvarez-Machain* [*supra*], forecloses this argument. In *Alvarez-Machain*, the Court considered the issue of "whether a criminal defendant, abducted to the United States from a nation with which it has an extradition treaty, thereby acquires a defense to the jurisdiction of this country's courts."... In answer, the Court stated: "We hold that he does not, and that he may be tried in federal district court for violations of the criminal law of the United States."...

In reaching this decision, the Court considered whether the treaty at issue expressly barred abductions. It determined that the treaty's provision that "'neither Contracting Party shall be bound to deliver up its own nationals...' [fails] to specify the only way in which one country may gain custody of a national of the other country for purposes of prosecution."... The Court also rejected the argument that, by entering into an extradition treaty with Mexico, the United States impliedly agreed to seek custody of persons in Mexico only via extradition....

The article of the U.S.-Panama Extradition Treaty upon which Noriega relies for his extradition treaty claim contains almost the same language as the provision of the U.S.-Mexico Extradition Treaty at issue in *Alvarez-Machain*.... Noriega contends that Alvarez-Machain is distinguishable despite the near identity of the relevant clauses because, at the time the United States entered into the U.S.-Panama Extradition Treaty, it knew or should have known that Panama's constitution prohibited the extradition of its nationals. This bald assertion, even if accepted, does not save Noriega's claim. A clause in Panama's constitution regarding the extradition of Panamanians, at most, informs the United States of the hurdles it will face when pursuing such extraditions in Panama; such a provision says nothing about the treaty signatories' rights to opt for self-help (i.e., abduction) over legal process (i.e., extradition).

Under *Alvarez-Machain*, to prevail on an extradition treaty claim, a defendant must demonstrate, by reference to the express language of a treaty and/or the established practice thereunder, that the United States affirmatively agreed not to seize foreign nationals from the territory of its treaty partner. Noriega has not carried this burden, and therefore, his claim fails. . . .

In his pre-trial motion, Noriega also sought the dismissal of the indictment against him on the ground that the manner in which he was brought before the district court (i.e., through a military invasion) was so unconscionable as to constitute a violation of substantive due process. Noriega also argued that to the extent the government's actions did not shock the judicial conscience sufficiently to trigger due process sanctions, the district court should exercise its supervisory power to decline jurisdiction. The district court rejected Noriega's due process argument, and it declared Noriega's alternative supervisory power rationale non-justiciable. On appeal, Noriega offers no substantive argument regarding the due process prong of this claim, but rather discusses only his alternative supervisory power theory. Because, however, the due process and supervisory power issues are intertwined, we discuss them both.

Noriega's due process claim "falls squarely within the [Supreme Court's] *Ker-Frisbie* doctrine, which holds that a defendant cannot defeat personal jurisdiction by asserting the illegality of the procurement of his presence." . . . Noriega has not alleged that the government mistreated him personally, and thus, he cannot come within the purview of the caveat to *Ker-Frisbie* recognized by the Second Circuit in *United States v. Toscanino*, 500 F.2d 267 (2d Cir. 1974), were this court inclined to adopt such an exception. . . . Further, whatever harm Panamanian civilians suffered during the armed conflict that preceded Noriega's arrest cannot support a due process claim in this case. . . .

Noriega's attempt to evade the implications of the *Ker-Frisbie* doctrine by appealing to the judiciary's supervisory power is equally unavailing. Although, "in the exercise of supervisory powers, federal courts may, within limits, formulate procedural rules not specifically required by the Constitution or the Congress," . . . we are aware of no authority that would allow a court to exercise its supervisory power to dismiss an indictment based on harm done by the government to third parties. To the contrary, the Supreme Court has held that "the supervisory power merely permits federal courts to supervise 'the administration of criminal justice' among the parties before the bar." . . . For all the foregoing reasons, Noriega's convictions are

AFFIRMED, and the district court's order denying Noriega's motion for a new trial is AFFIRMED.

Notes

(1) While one often thinks of abductions as occurring silently in the dark of night, some abductions occur in very public ways. In 2021, for example, Belarusian fighter jets intercepted a Ryanair commercial passenger plane flying from Greece to Lithuania while the plane was over Belarusian airspace and forced the plane to land. Once on the ground, authorities removed a journalist from the plane and detained him. The journalist, Roman Protasevich, was the former editor of a dissident media outlet who had left Belarus in 2019. He was returning to Lithuania, where he lived, from a conference with Belarusian dissidents in Athens when he was arrested. The actions of Belarus drew immediate condemnation both because the operation endangered the civilians on the passenger plane and because the operation targeted a dissident journalist. In response, the EU increased already in place sanctions against Belarus, prohibited Belarusian airlines from entering European airspace, and warned European airlines to avoid the country's airspace. *See Belarus plane: What we know and what we don't*, BBC (June 25, 2021), available at https://www.bbc.com/news/world-europe-57239521; Claudia Allen, *Belarus plane arrest—is it a first?*, BBC (May 26, 2021), available at https://www.bbc.com/news/world-europe-57240770 (discussing other examples of individuals arrested while in transit via airplane).

(2) Rendition, or what is sometimes called "extraordinary rendition," has been a subject of concern in the United States. It is a process of removing people from a country without judicial authorization, and taking them to a secret prison or another country for holding or interrogation. In some cases the transfer is done deliberately to take them to a country that will allow for torturing the individual. Extraordinary rendition is beyond the formal extradition process, and in contrast to kidnaping, the person is not being brought to the United States to face charges.

There have been varied reports on the use of extraordinary rendition by the United States. Some United States allies apparently collaborated in such activities. *See* Richard Norton-Taylor & Julian Borger, *Embarrassed Miliband admits two US rendition flights refuelled on British soil*, THE GUARDIAN, Feb. 22, 2008 at 4. One of the most publicized cases in the United States involved a Canadian who graduated from McGill University. While transferring planes in the United States he was detained and taken by an executive jet to Jordan. According to news reports he was tortured there and released one year later without charges being filed against him. *See* Jane Mayer, *Outsourcing Torture*, THE NEW YORKER, Feb. 14, 2005, *available at* http://www.newyorker.com/magazine/2005/02/14/outsourcing-torture; *see also* Bob Herbert, Op-Ed—*No Justice, No Peace*, N.Y. TIMES, Feb. 23, 2006, *available at* http://query.nytimes.com/gst/fullpage.html?res=9903E5DB1E3EF930A15751C0A9609C8B63.

On these renditions, see JORDAN J. PAUST, BEYOND THE LAW: THE BUSH ADMINISTRATION'S UNLAWFUL RESPONSES IN THE "WAR" ON TERROR 34–36 (2007); Leila

Nadya Sadat, *Ghost Prisoners and Black Sites: Extraordinary Rendition Under International Law*, 37 CASE WEST. RES. J. INT'L L. 309 (2006).

The December 13, 2012, decision of the Grand Chamber of the European Court of Human Rights in *Case of El-Masri v. the Former Yugoslav Republic of Macedonia*, *available at* http://hudoc.echr.coe.int/sites/eng/pages/search.aspx?i=001-115621#{%22itemid%22:[%22001-115621%22]} contains extensive discussion of European complicity in "extraordinary renditions." El-Masri, an innocent person, was subjected to rendition when agents of the respondent state handed him over to CIA agents at the Skopje airport. He was transferred, on a special CIA-operated flight, to a CIA-run secret detention facility in Afghanistan, where he was ill-treated for over four months. He was ultimately returned, via Macedonia, to his home in Germany. He was awarded substantial damages for Macedonia's role in the ordeal.

(3) In 2006, the United Nations General Assembly adopted the International Convention for the Protection of all Persons from Enforced Disappearance. G.A. Res. 61/177 (2006), *available at* http://www.ohchr.org/EN/HRBodies/CED/Pages/ConventionCED.aspx (in force Dec. 23, 2010). The Convention, which was co-sponsored by more than 100 Member States and adopted by the Human Rights Council, recognizes the right of persons not to be subjected to enforced disappearance and the right of victims to justice and reparations. The Convention also requires States party to criminalize enforced disappearance, bring those responsible to justice, and implement preventative measures. Examine the below excerpts from the Convention. What type of conduct is covered by the definition of "enforced disappearance?" Is "enforced disappearance" ever permitted?

Article 1

1. No one shall be subjected to enforced disappearance.

2. No exceptional circumstances whatsoever, whether a state of war or a threat of war, internal political instability or any other public emergency, may be invoked as a justification for enforced disappearance.

Article 2

For the purposes of this Convention, "enforced disappearance" is considered to be the arrest, detention, abduction or any other form of deprivation of liberty by agents of the State or by persons or groups of persons acting with the authorization, support or acquiescence of the State, followed by a refusal to acknowledge the deprivation of liberty or by concealment of the fate or whereabouts of the disappeared person, which place such a person outside the protection of the law.

The United States has neither signed nor ratified this Convention. Enforced disappearances may also be prosecuted as crimes against humanity under Article 7 of the Rome Statute of the International Criminal Court (*see* chap. 22), if the jurisdictional threshold for that crime is met.

Chapter 18

Prisoner Transfer and Other Post-Conviction and Foreign Law Issues

§18.01 Prisoner Transfer Treaties

Rosado v. Civiletti

United States Court of Appeals for the Second Circuit
621 F.2d 1179 (1980)

KAUFMAN, CHIEF JUDGE:

... In the case before us, petitioners are held in custody under federal authority. They have urged the district court to discharge its constitutional obligation to hear their claims and release them from custody. They have demonstrated that their convictions, under the laws of the sovereign state of Mexico, manifested a shocking insensitivity to their dignity as human beings and were obtained under a criminal process devoid of even a scintilla of rudimentary fairness and decency. Accordingly, we reaffirm the authority of the federal courts to hear due process claims raised, as they are here, by citizens held prisoner within the territorial jurisdiction of the United States. Nevertheless, we also recognize the laudable efforts of the executive and legislative branches, by both treaty and statute, to ameliorate, to their utmost power, the immense suffering of United States citizens held in Mexican jails. Indeed, because the statutory procedures governing transfers of these prisoners to United States custody are carefully structured to ensure that each of them voluntarily and intelligently agreed to forego his right to challenge the validity of his Mexican conviction, and because we must not ignore the interests of those citizens still imprisoned abroad, we hold that the present petitioners are estopped from receiving the relief they now seek.

I

In 1978, Efran Caban, Raymond Velez, Pedro Rosado, and Felix Melendez filed petitions in the District of Connecticut seeking release from federal incarceration in the Danbury Correctional Facility. The petitioners, all United States citizens, had been arrested in Mexico in November 1975 for narcotics offenses. They were subsequently convicted and sentenced to nine years' imprisonment by the Mexican courts. In December 1977, the petitioners were transferred to United States custody pursuant to a treaty between the United States and Mexico providing for the execution of penal sentences imposed by the courts of one nation in the prisons of the other. Under the terms of the treaty, each transferring prisoner is required to consent to his transfer, and is permitted to contest the legality of any change of custody in the courts of the receiving nation. Thus, the petitioners in this case argued that their consents to transfer had been unlawfully coerced and that their continued detention by United States authorities based upon the convictions in Mexico violated their right to due process of law guaranteed by the Fifth Amendment. . . .

On July 31, 1979, Judge Daly granted the petitions of Caban, Velez, and Rosado, holding, in a thoughtful opinion, that the prisoners' consents to transfer had been unlawfully coerced by the brutal conditions of their confinement in Mexico. Emphasizing what he deemed to be circumstances unique to these petitioners, the district judge observed that the men lived in daily fear of bodily harm, and believed with justification that they would be killed if they remained incarcerated in Mexico. Consequently, he concluded, "petitioners would have signed anything, regardless of the consequences, to get out of Mexico." In view of our duty to make an independent determination of the voluntariness of petitioners' consents to transfer, we shall first explore the history of petitioners' confinement in Mexico and the United States, then proceed to consider the legal principles raised by the Government's appeal in this difficult and perplexing case.

A

. . . .

In substance, the petitioners' testimony establishes that Caban and Freddie DePalm, also a United States citizen, departed New York's Kennedy Airport on November 18, 1975 for a vacation in Acapulco, Mexico. At the airport, the two men had become acquainted with Velez and the three sat together and conversed during the flight to Mexico. When their Aero Mexico airliner made its first scheduled landing in Mexico City, the passengers were informed there would be a one hour delay before proceeding to Acapulco. During the layover, Caban, DePalm, and Velez decided to leave the airport terminal and go to a Holiday Inn nearby. While browsing in the hotel's gift shop, the Americans were approached by six Mexicans in civilian dress, guns drawn, who stated that the Americans were under arrest. No arrest warrants were produced, nor did the Mexicans identify themselves as police officials. Nonetheless, Caban, DePalm, and Velez were each handcuffed and taken to an isolated area of the airport terminal.

In the terminal, Caban watched his captors drag Velez into a room, then heard Velez cry out in pain for close to an hour. Caban himself was taken into a separate room where he was searched, stripped and his legs bound. A watch, jewelry, and $400 in cash were taken from his person, but no drugs or contraband were found in his possession. Caban was then shown a photograph of a man represented to be Ramon Rodriguez and asked whether he knew him. When he denied any knowledge of Rodriguez, water was poured over his naked body and an electric cattle prod applied, first to his mouth, then to his testicles and buttocks. His persistent denial of any acquaintance with the man in the photograph led to repeated torture with the electric prod. Thereafter, Caban's interrogators suspended him from the ceiling by clamping a handcuff to his wrist and attaching it to a hook, causing him to lose consciousness from time to time. He remained in this position throughout the day while his captors continued to beat him, threatening to kill him if he refused to admit an acquaintance with Rodriguez. By the end of the day, the weight of Caban's suspended body against the handcuff caused a bone in his arm to break and tear through his wrist.

That night, Caban, DePalm, and Velez were taken to Los Separos detention center in Mexico City. Caban noticed that Velez was swollen and bruised, and that he was unable to walk unassisted. At Los Separos, the men were placed in small separate cells containing cement slabs for beds and no plumbing. They were held incommunicado for eight days. The food was inedible and the entire cellblock reeked of human excrement. Throughout their stay at Los Separos, interrogators continued to beat and torture the men with an electric prod in an attempt to elicit confessions.

Two days after Caban's arrest in Mexico City, Rosado was arrested in Acapulco upon his arrival on a flight from New York. Though unemployed, Rosado had planned to take a two-day vacation in Acapulco. After passing through customs at the airport, he was confronted by five plainclothes Mexicans bearing pistols and a submachine gun, who asked him to accompany them to a room in the airport. In the room, Rosado saw Melendez, who also had been detained upon his arrival in Acapulco. Rosado was held in the room for two hours while his luggage and personal effects were searched. His ticket, visa, jewelry, and $900 in cash were seized, and he was then driven to a nearby police station along with Melendez.

The following morning, the two Americans were flown to Mexico City along with several other prisoners arrested that day and, like Caban, DePalm, and Velez, ended their journeys at Los Separos. When they arrived, Rosado saw the badly beaten body of a man he later learned to be Caban. Melendez was taken into an interrogation room, and Rosado listened from an adjacent holding area as Melendez screamed in apparent agony. After Melendez was returned to the holding area, Rosado was asked by one Mexican officer whether he was ready to tell the truth. When Rosado's responses failed to satisfy his inquisitor, his hands were handcuffed behind his back, his pants lowered, and an electric prod was applied for several minutes at a time to his testicles and penis. Rosado then watched as Melendez was similarly questioned, with the interrogators alternating between beatings and electric torture.

After seven or eight days of unceasing brutality, each of the prisoners was finally taken to the prosecutor's office at Los Separos. Caban was told to sign a statement acknowledging his acquaintance with Rodriguez, but refused. Instead, he signed a paper disclaiming any knowledge of Rodriguez or his activities. Rosado was given a statement confessing participation in a gang seeking to import cocaine into Mexico, but he too refused to sign, stating that his sole purpose in coming to Mexico was for a vacation. At no time during the prisoners' initial detention and interrogation were they apprised of the charges against them, or permitted to consult with counsel.

Following their visits to the prosecutor, Caban, DePalm, Velez, Rosado, and Melendez were all transferred to Lecumberri Prison, the so-called "Black Castle," where they were crowded into tiny, unheated cells with only two or three beds for ten or twelve prisoners. . . . Shortly after their transfer to Lecumberri, the prisoners were brought to *los hugados*, a courtroom within the prison. There, they were crowded into a small pen separated from the courtroom by a chain link fence. A judge's law secretary briefly informed the men that they had been charged with illegal importation of cocaine, and then sent them back to their cells. Approximately one month later, the prisoners returned to *los hugados* and were formally advised by the law secretary that they had been indicted for illegal importation of cocaine. The men were shown copies of the statements that had previously been read to them by the prosecutor at Los Separos, and asked whether they were true. Both Caban and Rosado disclaimed the reports, insisting that they were false. The law secretary offered to help the prisoners for a fee but was told that they did not have enough money. The entire proceeding lasted no longer than ten minutes.

Two weeks after this "arraignment," the prisoners were brought back to *los hugados*, ostensibly for a *correo constitutional*, that is, an opportunity to confront the witnesses against them. Inside the courtroom, Caban saw the officers who had detained and questioned him at the Mexico City Airport, but none of the officers who had arrested Rosado in Acapulco was present. Once again, the law secretary presided over the proceeding, asking each officer whether he ratified his earlier statement against the defendants. At no time were the prisoners permitted to cross-examine the arresting officers, to read the officers' statements, or to speak to the charges against them. The entire proceeding was over in less than fifteen minutes.

Seven months later, on August 10, 1976, the men returned to *los hugados* and were informed by the law secretary that a judge had considered their cases and had sentenced each man to nine years' imprisonment. At no time did they see the judge who sentenced them, obtain the assistance of counsel, or confront the witnesses against them.

In October 1976, Lecumberri was closed by the Mexican authorities and the appellees were transferred to Oriente Prison, a more modern and sanitary facility. . . . The prisoners remained at Oriente until July 1977, when they were moved to Santa Marta Penitentiary. Initially, the men were placed in "the hole," a windowless, unheated cell in which there was one bed and no toilet. There, the men were held incommunicado for approximately ten days until the prison director informed them that they would be moved to more habitable cells in the dormitory if they promised to pay him $2,000. Although the men knew they did not have sufficient money to pay the director, they promised to pay and were moved to better quarters in the dormitory. Soon, however, the men learned that Santa Marta differed little from Lecumberri. In addition to the dormitory fee, prisoners regularly paid for the basic necessities of life. Those who disobeyed the guards, or were slow in making payments, were subject to brutal beatings by a favored group of inmates known as the "Fourth Guard." At night, those who had angered the Fourth Guard would be taken from their cells, beaten, stabbed, and frequently left for dead. As a result, both Caban and Rosado feared for their lives, since they were certain the Fourth Guard would kill them if they did not soon raise the $2,000 dormitory fee promised to the director.

B

In 1974, public attention was drawn to the outrageous conditions of confinement in Mexico's jails when Congressmen and journalists in the United States began to investigate complaints of American prisoners and their families. . . . Following a case-by-case review of some 514 Americans incarcerated in Mexico, the State Department's Bureau of Security and Consular Affairs reported in January 1976 that the alleged deprivations of basic rights formed a "credible pattern." . . . Finally, in June 1976, Mexico's Foreign Minister proposed a treaty between the two countries permitting the citizens of either nation who had been convicted in the courts of the other country to serve their sentences in the penal institutions of their native land. Negotiations progressed rapidly and a treaty was signed by representatives of both nations in Mexico City on November 25, 1976. Following extensive hearings in the Senate Foreign Relations and Judiciary Committees, the full Senate unanimously approved the treaty by a vote of 90 to 0 on July 21, 1977. (A similar treaty between the United States and Canada was ratified by the Senate two days earlier by a vote of 95 to 0.) Enabling legislation was approved by Congress and signed into law on October 28, 1977, and the treaty became effective on November 30, 1977.

Under the Treaty, a United States citizen convicted of a criminal offense in Mexico may transfer from Mexican to American custody for the balance of his sentence provided certain conditions are met. The offense for which he has been convicted must also be generally punishable in the United States, and can be neither a political nor immigration offense. Moreover, the transferring offender must be both a national of the United States and not a domiciliary of Mexico. Only prisoners with a minimum of six months remaining on their sentence, and for whom no appeal or collateral attack is currently pending in the Mexican courts, are eligible for transfer. Finally, Mexico, the United States, and the transferring prisoner must all give their consent to the change in custody. (To ensure that a prisoner's consent to transfer is given voluntarily and with full knowledge of its conditions, the implementing legislation enacted by Congress provides for a United States magistrate or citizen specifically designated by a judge of the United States to travel to Mexico and to make all necessary inquiries of the offender to determine whether his consent is given voluntarily and knowingly. 18 U.S.C. § 4108. In addition, the offender may receive the advice of counsel prior to the consent verification proceeding, and those who cannot afford counsel must have counsel appointed for them by the verifying officer. *Id.* § 4109.)

The potential benefits to a prisoner transferring under the Treaty are considerable. Not only will he be repatriated to his homeland where the culture and language will be familiar and his family closer at hand, but the Treaty specifically provides that the law of the Receiving State will govern his eligibility for parole, the conditions of his confinement, and any attack he may bring upon the validity of his transfer or the constitutionality of the Treaty and its implementing legislation. In addition, a transferred offender is protected against double jeopardy in the United States on account of the crime for which he was convicted in Mexico, and any prejudice to his civil rights in the United States other than the collateral consequences normally accorded a Mexican conviction by American law. Both the Treaty and implementing legislation specifically provide, however, that the courts of the transferring nation shall have exclusive jurisdiction over proceedings brought by a transferring offender to challenge, modify, or set aside convictions or sentences handed down by its courts. An American citizen seeking transfer to United States custody is required to understand and agree that any action challenging his conviction or sentence must be brought in Mexican, not United States, courts, and any transferred offender who succeeds in establishing the invalidity of his transfer in a United States court may be returned to Mexico to serve the balance of his sentence.

C

Two months after Caban, Velez, and Rosado promised but failed to pay $2,000 to the director of Santa Marta, representatives from the United States Embassy visited the men at the prison and informed them of the possibility of transfer to United States custody pursuant to the Treaty. They were each given booklets prepared by the United States Department of Justice explaining the terms of the Treaty and the consequences of an election to transfer.... After the prisoners expressed an interest in transferring to United States custody, an attorney from the Federal Public Defender's Office in Texas met with each individually and explained in detail the consequences of a transfer under the Treaty. On December 5, 1977, the men appeared separately before a United States magistrate at the prison to verify their consents to transfer. The magistrate questioned each petitioner about his knowledge of the Treaty's provisions, specifically asking each man whether he understood and agreed to abide by the condition requiring challenges to his conviction or sentence to be brought by proceedings instituted in Mexican courts.... In each case, once the magistrate satisfied himself that the applicant's consent to transfer was given knowingly and voluntarily, without threat or coercion, he permitted the petitioner to sign a standard form of consent.

II

In appraising the voluntariness of the petitioners' consents to transfer, Judge Daly relied primarily upon *Schneckloth v. Bustamonte*, 412 U.S. 218, 93 S. Ct. 2041, 36 L. Ed. 2d 854 (1973), in which the Supreme Court upheld the validity of a citizen's consent to a police search of his automobile under the Fourth Amendment. In *Schneckloth*, the Court eschewed any "talismanic definition" of voluntariness, stressing instead that the issue presented a "question of fact to be determined from all the circumstances." In the context of searches and seizures, the Court noted that a balance must be struck between our collective interest in effective law enforcement, and our constitutional insistence upon personal freedom from unwarranted governmental intrusions. Striking that balance in *Schneckloth*, the Court implicitly recognized that its rule would serve to define the degree to which overzealous law enforcement would be deterred, and individual rights vindicated.

In the case at bar, however, we are in no position to deter by our decision the acts complained of by petitioners. The sources of torture, abuse, and coercion to which they point as invalidating their consents emanate not from United States authorities, but Mexican officers, acting within the territorial sovereignty of Mexico, without American direction or involvement. Although the Bill of Rights does apply extraterritorially to protect American citizens against the illegal conduct of United States agents, *Reid v. Covert*, 354 U.S. 1, 77 S. Ct. 1222, 1 L. Ed. 2d 1148 (1957); *United States v. Toscanino*, 500 F.2d 267 (2d Cir. 1974), it does not and cannot protect our citizens from the acts of a foreign sovereign committed within its territory. *Neely v. Henkel*, 180 U.S. 109, 21 S. Ct. 302, 45 L. Ed. 448 (1901); *United States v. Lira*, 515 F.2d 68 (2d Cir.), *cert. denied*, 423 U.S. 847, 96 S. Ct. 87, 46 L. Ed. 2d 69 (1975). For example, in *Lira*, a Chilean national was abducted from his home by Chilean police, beaten, tortured with electric shocks, and then placed on a plane for New York, where he was arrested by federal narcotics agents. In upholding the jurisdiction of the district court to try Lira, we expressly held that relief from acts of torture by foreign agents could be granted only upon a showing of direct United States governmental involvement. Otherwise, we reasoned, the court's holding would serve no deterrent function, and vindicate no constitutionally recognized right. . . .

It is noted that a contrary holding in *Lira* would not only have failed to vindicate any constitutional right of the defendant, but also would have obstructed our national interest in effective law enforcement. Since the United States makes no claim to a valid law enforcement interest with respect to these petitioners, it may be argued that a court should not deny a remedy to one tortured abroad when to do so would serve no countervailing interest.

But the United States does assert two other interests in upholding the validity of these petitioners' consents, both comparably significant. First is the Government's substantial interest in promoting good relations with Mexico by honoring its criminal convictions and recognizing the integrity of its criminal justice system. Since Mexico is a sovereign nation in no sense subject to the judgments of this Court, we could neither deter its officials from committing similar cruelties in the future, nor vindicate the individual interests of those still incarcerated in Mexican prisons, by invalidating these petitioners' consents. At most, we would simply complicate our delicate relations with Mexico. More important, however, is the interest of those Americans who are currently, or may soon find themselves, caught up in Mexico's criminal justice system. If, here, the conduct of Mexican officials on Mexican soil were held to be determinative of the voluntariness of an American prisoner's consent to transfer, those prisoners most desperately in need of transfer to escape torture and extortion, including the petitioners at bar, would never be able to satisfy a magistrate that their consents were voluntarily given.

This anomalous result stems in part from the district court's adoption of a standard of voluntariness designed to govern consensual searches and seizures within the United States. Though we can find no case presenting facts on point to guide us in these extraordinary circumstances, it is readily apparent that a decision whether to permit a police officer to search one's car does not remotely resemble the choice presented to these petitioners under the Treaty. In our view the choice that faces an American imprisoned in Mexico in deciding whether to transfer more closely resembles a decision confronted by nearly every criminal defendant today: whether to plead guilty and accept a set of specified sanctions ranging from probation to a possibly long prison sentence, or to stand trial and face unknown dispositions ranging from possible acquittal to a severe maximum sentence or even death. In the plea bargaining context, as in the case at bar, the choice involves liberty and incarceration on both sides of the equation.

Accordingly, we turn for guidance to the line of cases construing the voluntariness of guilty pleas, beginning with *United States v. Jackson*, 390 U.S. 570, 88 S. Ct. 1209, 20 L. Ed. 2d 138 (1968). In *Jackson*, the Court invalidated a provision of the Federal Kidnapping Act permitting imposition of the death penalty only upon the jury's recommendation, because it concluded the provision unnecessarily induced defendants to waive their constitutional right to a trial by jury. The holding promptly spawned a number of challenges to guilty pleas in general, asserting that the defendant's plea had been involuntarily induced by the risk of receiving a death sentence if he insisted upon his right to a jury trial. In response, the Court quickly made clear that not all guilty pleas were invalid simply because the death penalty could be imposed only after trial by jury. In *Brady v. United States*, 397 U.S. 742, 90 S. Ct. 1463, 25 L. Ed. 2d 747 (1970), the Court explained that the question centers on whether the provision "needlessly penalize[d] the assertion of a constitutional right." If not, the voluntariness of a given plea is to be judged by whether it was a knowing, intelligent act "done with sufficient awareness of the relevant circumstances and likely consequences."

Subsequently, in *North Carolina v. Alford*, 400 U.S. 25, 91 S. Ct. 160, 27 L. Ed. 2d 162 (1970), the Court emphasized that the "voluntariness" of a guilty plea is determined by considering, not whether the defendant's decision reflected a wholly unrestrained will, but rather whether it constituted a deliberate, intelligent choice between available alternatives.... Focusing upon the alternatives open to the defendant when he entered his plea, the Court concluded that the decision to forego a jury trial and thus avoid the risk of a death sentence represented a voluntary and intelligent choice among the available alternatives. "When his plea is viewed in light of the evidence against him, which substantially negated his claim of innocence and which further provided a means by which the judge could test whether the plea was being intelligently entered ... its validity cannot be seriously questioned." Since the evidence of guilt was, for practical purposes, conclusive, the choice between trial by jury and potential death on the one hand, or pleading guilty and certain imprisonment on the other, was not unjustifiably coercive.

Similarly, if the instant petitioners' consents to transfer are viewed in light of the alternatives legitimately available to them, it cannot be seriously doubted that their decisions were voluntarily and intelligently made.... Their choice was ... between continued incarceration under the brutal regime that prevailed in Mexican prisons, or repatriation. In either event, they would retain their right to seek redress from the Mexican courts, but could not challenge their convictions or sentences in United States courts. Though it may well be, as Judge Daly concluded, that anyone in similar circumstances would choose to transfer, the same may also be said for the defendant in *Alford*. In view of the alternatives legitimately available to petitioners, we conclude that their consents to transfer were voluntarily and intelligently made.

III

Regardless of the validity of the petitioners' consents to transfer, it is also claimed that the Treaty and enabling legislation deprive petitioners of their liberty without due process of law in violation of the Fifth Amendment. Though a transferring prisoner's arrest, interrogation, trial, and ultimate conviction all occur in Mexico, at the hands of Mexican authorities, his liberty is restricted by United States authorities once he is placed in American custody. Accordingly, we must determine whether the United States Government may imprison a citizen in execution of a criminal sentence imposed by a foreign tribunal acting within its jurisdiction and, at the same time, deny him access to a United States court to challenge the fundamental fairness of the criminal process that led to his conviction abroad.

A

In dictum too old to question, Chief Justice Marshall declared that "[t]he courts of no country execute the penal laws of another." *The Antelope*, 23 U.S. (10 Wheat.) 66, 123, 6 L. Ed. 268 (1825).... [However,] nothing in the doctrine enunciated by Marshall precludes a sovereign power from extending recognition to another's penal laws where it chooses to do so. Nor does Marshall's dictum suggest any principle limiting the power of sovereign nations to enter into mutual compacts or treaties obligating the signatories to honor and enforce the penal decrees of one another. In the United States, the constitutionality of such measures was decided long ago when the Supreme Court upheld an extradition agreement with foreign nations as a valid exercise of the treaty-making power. Even where the treaty fails to secure to those who are extradited to another country the same constitutional safeguards they would enjoy in an American criminal trial, it does not run afoul of the Constitution. Moreover, criminal convictions imposed by foreign tribunals have served as predicates for enhanced sentencing under state multi-offender statutes.

The instant Treaty does not call upon the United States to enforce Mexico's penal laws or procedures, but only to execute criminal convictions entered in its courts against American citizens who elect to transfer to United States custody. Thus, once a prisoner has consented to transfer, the United States is bound simply to take custody of the offender and, with a few significant exceptions (the principal exception being the reservation to Mexico of jurisdiction over challenges to the prisoners' conviction or sentence) detain him as if he had been convicted in a United States court. The Treaty serves to ameliorate the condition of Americans imprisoned in Mexico by offering them an opportunity for repatriation and, hopefully, better prison conditions and more positive means for rehabilitation. In lessening the number of United States citizens incarcerated in Mexico, the Treaty additionally serves to relieve a worrisome source of tension in Mexican-American relations. In view of these benevolent purposes, we believe the Treaty is a valid exercise of the treaty-making power conferred by Art. II, § 2, cl. 2 of the Constitution.

B

Although we can discern no constitutional impediment to a judgment by the President and Congress that the transfer of convicted criminal defendants is a worthy object of international accord, the execution of foreign penal decrees may not serve as an artifice to circumvent the procedural and substantive guaranties of the Bill of Rights.... It is undisputed that these petitioners have received none of the process constitutionally required for the trial and conviction of criminals in United States courts. Nonetheless, they are incarcerated under federal authority.... Accordingly, we must determine whether Congress can provide for the deprivation of a citizen's liberty through incarceration, while withholding all right of access to United States courts to test the basis for his confinement.

It is an unassailable tenet of our constitutional system that the Government's power to punish citizens may be exercised only in accordance with the due process of law prescribed by the Bill of Rights. Whether the constitutional guarantee of due process further requires that any imposition of punishment carry with it a right of access to a United States court to test the basis for the sanctions imposed is a question never fully resolved. In the case at bar, the Government seeks to deprive the petitioners of their liberty in recognition of a conviction returned by a court beyond the jurisdiction of the United States. Though our research has disclosed no case directly in point, the nature and extent of process to be accorded those committing crimes abroad has been considered in a variety of related contexts.

In *In re Ross*, 140 U.S. 453, 11 S. Ct. 897, 35 L. Ed. 581 (1891), the Supreme Court denied habeas relief to a seaman imprisoned in the United States following his conviction for murder by an American consular court sitting in Japan. Under a treaty with that country, the United States was given jurisdiction over criminal offenses committed by Americans in Japan. The implementing legislation enacted by Congress vested jurisdiction to try all such offenses in consular tribunals. In challenging his conviction in the consular court, Ross argued that he had been denied due process since he had not been indicted or tried by a jury. The court rejected these claims out of hand, holding that the "Constitution can have no operation in another country. When ... the representatives or officers of our government are permitted to exercise authority of any kind in another country, it must be on such conditions as the two countries may agree, the laws of neither one being obligatory upon the other."

The Court had occasion to reconsider *Ross* in *Reid v. Covert, supra*. Covert, the wife of an American serviceman stationed in England, was charged with her husband's killing. Pursuant to a provision of the Uniform Code of Military Justice, all persons accompanying the armed forces abroad were subject to court-martial by a military tribunal for any criminal offense related to the military. Mrs. Covert was tried, convicted, and sentenced to life imprisonment by a military court-martial, then incarcerated in the United States. A district court order granting her release on a writ of habeas corpus was first reversed by the Supreme Court, then affirmed on reconsideration. In withdrawing its earlier decision, a plurality of the Court expressly rejected the reasoning of *Ross*: "[w]hen the Government reaches out to punish a citizen who is abroad, the shield which the Bill of Rights and other parts of the Constitution provide to protect his life and liberty should not be stripped away just because he happens to be in another land." Two concurring justices attempted to distinguish *Ross* by limiting its applicability to instances where historical or political necessities dictate a flexible approach. But a majority agreed that insofar as *Ross* disclaimed any extraterritorial force to the Constitution, it was no longer good law.

Covert was tried and convicted in an American tribunal under a treaty that conferred jurisdiction on United States authorities over crimes committed by American citizens. In the instant case, however, petitioners were convicted in Mexican courts for crimes committed within that country. A somewhat analogous situation was presented in *Hirota v. MacArthur*, 338 U.S. 197, 69 S. Ct. 197, 93 L. Ed. 1902 (1948), where two Japanese citizens held in United States custody in Japan following their conviction for war crimes by an international tribunal sought leave to file original petitions for writs of habeas corpus in the Supreme Court. The Court denied leave, holding that it lacked power or authority to review the convictions.

The following term, the Court again considered petitions filed on behalf of enemy aliens held in custody abroad by United States authorities. *Johnson v. Eisentrager*, 339 U.S. 763, 70 S. Ct. 936, 94 L. Ed. 1255 (1950). While stressing the historic right of access to American courts enjoyed by citizens, the Court found no constitutional right to sue for habeas relief in United States courts where the petitioner was an alien enemy who never resided in the United States, was captured beyond American territory, and was tried, convicted, and imprisoned abroad for offenses committed outside the United States. In contrast to *Eisentrager*, however, the petitioners at bar are United States citizens incarcerated within the territory of the United States.

Another useful point of reference is found in cases where a foreign sovereign seeks to extradite an American citizen for trial abroad. Where extradition is sought pursuant to a valid treaty, the Supreme Court has held that the relator cannot prevent his extradition simply by alleging that the criminal process he will receive fails to accord with constitutional guaranties. Since the Constitution bears no relation to crimes committed beyond the jurisdiction of the United States against the laws of a foreign sovereign, a citizen who "commits a crime in a foreign country cannot complain if required to submit to such modes of trial and to such punishment as the laws of that country may prescribe for its own people, unless a different mode be provided for by treaty stipulations." *Neely v. Henkel, supra*. Thus, where a relator challenges the fairness of foreign process, courts "are bound by the existence of an extradition treaty to assume that the trial will be fair."

In *Neely*, however, minimal safeguards to ensure a fair trial in the foreign tribunal were provided. Moreover, this court has previously indicated that the presumption of fairness routinely accorded the criminal process of a foreign sovereign may require closer scrutiny if a relator persuasively demonstrates that extradition would expose him to procedures or punishment "antipathetic to a federal court's sense of decency." *Gallina v. Fraser*, 278 F.2d 77, 79 (2d Cir.), *cert. denied*, 364 U.S. 851, 81 S. Ct. 97, 5 L. Ed. 2d 74 (1960); *United States ex rel. Bloomfield v. Gengler*, 507 F.2d 925 (2d Cir. 1974). Finally, to the extent that the United States itself acts to detain a relator pending extradition, it is bound to accord him due process. Thus, although the Constitution cannot limit the power of a foreign sovereign to prescribe procedures for the trial and punishment of crimes committed within its territory, it does govern the manner in which the United States may join the effort.

In our view, however, the cases that provide the closest analogy to the instant petitions are those stemming from congressional efforts to limit the immigration of Chinese and Japanese aliens to the United States. . . . In *The Chinese Exclusion Case*, 130 U.S. 581, 9 S. Ct. 623, 32 L. Ed. 1068 (1889), the Supreme Court upheld the power of Congress to provide for the exclusion of Asian aliens solely by means of executive action. Subsequently, the Court held that the power to exclude aliens at the border necessarily included the power to expel those found within the United States without creating any right to judicial review of the administrative action. . . . [However,] in *The Japanese Immigrant Case*, 189 U.S. 86, 23 S. Ct. 611, 47 L. Ed. 721 (1903), the Court. . . . decided that the final authority conferred upon executive officers to pass upon the status of Asian immigrants did not permit arbitrary disregard of the fundamental principles inherent in due process of law. "One of these principles," the Court stated, "is that no person shall be deprived of his liberty without opportunity, at some time, to be heard, before such officers, in respect of the matters upon which that liberty depends." . . . [I]n *Chin Yow v. United States*, 208 U.S. 8, 28 S. Ct. 201, 52 L. Ed. 369 (1908), [the petitioner] claimed that he was a native-born American citizen. . . . [H]is petition for a writ of habeas corpus sought relief from the administrative order denying his entry on the ground that he had been denied a fair opportunity to present his case for citizenship to the executive authorities . . . [W]riting for the majority, [Justice] Holmes stressed the constitutional requirement of a hearing reasonably calculated to produce a correct result. . . . Finally, in *Ng Fung Ho v. White*, 259 U.S. 276, 42 S. Ct. 492, 66 L. Ed. 938 (1922), the Court [decided that] the threat to liberty posed by the exclusion of one claiming to be a citizen was so grave that the determination of citizenship could not be entrusted to executive officers. "Against the danger of such deprivation without the sanction afforded by judicial proceedings, the Fifth Amendment affords protection in its guarantee of due process of law."

The right to a fair procedure reasonably calculated to produce a correct determination of the basis for the imposition of penal sanctions lies at the heart of the due process of law protected by the Fifth Amendment. As *Chin Yow* and *Ng Fung Ho* teach, the United States may not deprive an individual of his liberty unless such a procedure is first accorded. Where one has been denied his right to a fair hearing prior to the imposition of penal sanctions restraining his liberty, habeas corpus provides the appropriate remedy.

In the case at bar, petitioners face not the danger of deprivation, but the reality of liberty already lost. Nonetheless, it is undisputed that at no time did they receive even the barest rudiments of a process calculated to arrive at the truth of the accusations against them. They did not receive the assistance of counsel during the Mexican criminal proceedings against them, nor were they ever accorded an opportunity to appear before the judge who allegedly decided their case. They were not permitted to address the charges against them, or present any evidence at all. No opportunity was given Rosado to confront the witnesses against him, and neither Caban nor Velez was allowed to cross-examine their accusers. Most egregious of all, the law secretary who presided over the proceedings against the petitioners offered the influence of his position to help petitioners for a fee.

Under such circumstances, we believe these petitioners have a right to test the basis for their continued confinement in a United States court. In reaching this conclusion, we by no means imply that each element of due process as known to American criminal law must be present in a foreign criminal proceeding before Congress may give a conviction rendered by a foreign tribunal binding effect. Indeed, we are keenly sensitive to the historical and cultural limitations of our own constitutional heritage, and respect the similarly indigenous underpinnings of the process accorded criminal defendants abroad. We simply hold that a petitioner incarcerated under federal authority pursuant to a foreign conviction cannot be denied all access to a United States court when he presents a persuasive showing that his conviction was obtained without the benefit of any process whatsoever. Having thus determined that petitioners possess a right to challenge the basis for their continued confinement under United States custody, we must proceed to consider the merits of their claim, unless there appears some further reason to withhold relief.

IV

During the petitioners' consent verification proceedings in Mexico, each was specifically asked whether he understood and agreed to abide by the Treaty provision granting Mexico exclusive jurisdiction over all proceedings seeking to challenge, modify, or set aside sentences imposed by its courts. Each indicated that he understood the provision and agreed to abide by the condition. Accordingly, we must decide whether the petitioners are now estopped from challenging their Mexican convictions in United States courts.

In enacting the enabling legislation, Congress went to great lengths to ensure that a transferring prisoner would not only be informed of the Treaty's provisions, but agree to abide by them as well. Section 4108(b)(1) of Title 18 expressly provides that the verifying officer "shall inquire of the offender whether he understands and agrees" that Mexico is given exclusive jurisdiction to hear challenges to his conviction and sentence.

As originally introduced in the Senate, the bill that ultimately became § 4108 simply required that a transferring offender be informed that "by his consent (to transfer) he waives all rights he might have had to institute proceedings in the courts of the United States seeking to challenge. . . . his conviction or sentence." A memorandum prepared for the State Department and submitted to the House subcommittee considering the bill noted, however, that a transferring offender did not possess a right of access to United States courts at the time he executed his consent in Mexico. Accordingly, it cautioned, a consent which purported to waive a right the offender did not possess at the time it was executed might not withstand judicial scrutiny upon the prisoner's transfer to the United States. Instead, it suggested, Congress should employ the doctrine of estoppel and require transferring prisoners to agree not to challenge their Mexican convictions in United States courts.

After witnesses at both House and Senate hearings emphasized the crucial importance of securing a binding, voluntary consent to transfer that would preclude returning prisoners from challenging their Mexican convictions in United States courts, the bill was amended in the Senate Judiciary Committee to require an express agreement by the prisoner to bring any attacks upon his conviction or sentence solely in the Mexican courts. . . .

As we have mentioned, Mexico, the United States, and each offender requesting transfer must give their consent to the change in custody before a prisoner may be transferred. The consents contemplated by the Treaty entail much more than simple expressions of the desire to transfer, and the permission to do so. They also include reciprocal representations by each of the parties upon which the others rely in deciding to give their consent. For example, the United States promises Mexico that it will execute the prisoner's Mexican conviction and provide biannual reports on the status of the offenders who have transferred to the United States. It also promises the prisoner that he will enjoy the benefit of parole in accordance with United States law. Mexico agrees to relinquish custody of an individual found to have committed a criminal offense within its jurisdiction, while promising to hear subsequent challenges to the sentences rendered by its courts. For his part, the transferring prisoner agrees to his change in custody, and further promises to abide by the terms of the Treaty, including the reservation of jurisdiction to Mexico over all challenges to convictions and sentences imposed by its courts.

It requires little imagination to conclude, in light of this background, that if petitioners had refused to agree to abide by the Treaty's conditions, neither Mexico nor the United States would have consented to their transfers. Accordingly, petitioners would have continued to be imprisoned in Mexico, without right of access to American courts. But that fact alone does not persuade us their bargain should be enforced. If, in holding these petitioners to their agreement, we would serve no substantial and legitimate governmental interest which the United States put in jeopardy in reliance upon their promises not to attack their convictions in American courts, we would have difficulty in concluding that their custody should be continued. Unless the Government can satisfy us that it relied to its detriment upon the petitioners' agreement, we see no purpose served in closing our doors to their due process claims. Moreover, in view of our holding that petitioners acquired a right of access to a United States court once they were transferred to American custody, we believe their acceptance of the jurisdictional condition can be sustained only if voluntary and intelligent. We shall consider, therefore, whether the petitioners voluntarily and intelligently agreed to challenge their convictions solely in Mexican courts, and whether the United States advances a sufficiently important interest in holding these prisoners to their bargain.

As with petitioners' consents, we believe *Jackson, supra*, and *Alford, supra*, state the governing principles for determining the voluntariness and intelligence of their agreements. Viewed in the light of the alternatives available to them, we find petitioners' decisions to promise to abide by the Treaty's limitation upon their right to seek relief to have been both informed and intelligent. If, as we have said, they had insisted upon their right, once held in federal custody, to seek review of their Mexican convictions in a United States court, neither the United States nor Mexico would have consented to their transfers. If, however, they agreed to abide by the limitations of the Treaty, petitioners could escape the brutal conditions of Mexican confinement, acquire a hitherto unenjoyed right to parole, and have virtually the same opportunity to challenge their Mexican convictions in Mexico's courts as they previously enjoyed. In addition, petitioners would gain access to United States courts for all claims unrelated to their convictions or sentences.

Although petitioners' decisions to accept the jurisdictional condition to their transfer thus appear to be intelligent choices among the available alternatives, it is less certain that their decisions may be termed "voluntary" within the meaning of *Jackson, supra*. Arguably, the choice between sacrifice of a right to seek judicial redress from a United States court once repatriated, and continued imprisonment in Mexico, "needlessly penalize[d]" the prisoners' constitutional right to a federal forum once they were placed in United States custody. We are satisfied, however, that the congressional decision to require offenders transferring to American custody to agree to abide by the jurisdictional provision was neither needless nor arbitrary. Moreover, we believe the conditional requirement that prisoners agree to challenge their convictions solely in the courts of the transferring nation legitimately serves two important interests that can be vindicated only by holding these prisoners to their agreements.

In assessing the interacting interests of the United States and foreign nations, "we must move with the circumspection appropriate when [a court] is adjudicating issues inevitably entangled in the conduct of our international relations." Since Mexico was unwilling to enter a treaty that provided for review of its criminal judgments by United States courts, American negotiators did not have a completely free hand in structuring the Treaty's terms. Guided throughout by their humane concern to ameliorate the plight of hundreds of United States citizens imprisoned in Mexico, the negotiators obviously extracted a significant number of important concessions. At the same time, however, our negotiators were anxious to improve relations with Mexico and hopefully eliminate what had become an important source of tension between the two nations.

Of paramount importance, however, is the interest of those Americans currently incarcerated in Mexico. Whatever hope the Treaty extends of escaping the harsh realities of confinement abroad will be dashed for hundreds of Americans if we permit these three petitioners to rescind their agreement to limit their attacks upon their convictions to Mexico's courts. We refuse to scuttle the one certain opportunity open to Americans incarcerated abroad to return home, an opportunity, we note, the benefit of which Caban, Velez, and Rosado have already received. In holding these petitioners to their bargain, we by no means condone the shockingly brutal treatment to which they fell prey. Rather, we hold open the door for others similarly victimized to escape their torment.

The judgment of the district court is reversed.

Notes

(1) In addition to the treaties with Mexico and Canada, the United States has entered into bilateral prisoner exchange agreements with Bolivia, Panama, Turkey, Peru, Thailand, France, the Marshall Islands, the Republic of Palau, and Micronesia. It has broadened the scope of its treaty relationships by becoming a party to the 1983 multilateral European Convention on the Transfer of Sentenced Persons [64 parties] and the 1985 Inter-American Convention on Serving Criminal Sentences Abroad [19 parties]. *See* M. Cherif Bassiouni, *United States Policies and Practices on Execution of Foreign Sentences*, *in* 2 International Criminal Law 551, nn.4, 5 (M. Cherif Bassiouni ed., 3d ed. 2008); United States Department of Justice, International Prisoner Transfer Program, *available at* http://www.justice.gov/criminal-oeo/international-prisoner-transfer-program. For general discussion, see Michael Abbell, International Prisoner Transfer (2010).

(2) Other cases upholding the constitutionality of prisoner transfer treaties include *Pfeifer v. U.S. Bureau of Prisons*, 615 F.2d 873 (9th Cir. 1980); *Mitchell v. United States*, 483 F. Supp. 291 (E.D. Wis. 1980). The question of constitutionality was much debated at the time the treaties with Mexico and Canada were concluded. One of the witnesses before the Senate Foreign Relations Committee was Herbert Wechsler, who argued in favor of constitutionality. Compare Judge Kaufman's reasoning in *Rosado* with Professor Wechsler's somewhat less tortured argument:

> First: The purpose and effect of the two treaties is not to impose afflictive sanctions on the offenders who may be transferred with their consent from a foreign country to their home country for service of their sentences but

> rather to alleviate the special hardship incident to confinement or restraint away from home. The assurance of such reciprocal benefits for citizens or nationals of the contracting countries is plainly an appropriate object of the treaty power. . . .
>
> Second: The treaties envisage the use of national power and authority to imprison or restrain as criminals American citizens or nationals who have been convicted abroad of crimes committed abroad within the jurisdiction of a foreign country. . . . It has been suggested that the due process clause of the Fifth Amendment prohibits such imprisonment if the foreign conviction was obtained by procedures lacking those safeguards of the Bill of Rights that the Fourteenth Amendment has been held to impose on state procedures. This seems to me a wholly insupportable conclusion. . . . The Fifth Amendment was no more designed than was the Fourteenth to limit Mexican or Canadian procedures. . . . [N]othing said by Mr. Justice Black in the plurality opinion in *Reid v. Covert* as to the application of the Bill of Rights to trial abroad in American courts or the subjection of the treaty power to the limitations of the Bill of Rights has any application to this problem. The treaty takes away no right that these offenders otherwise would have. Absent the transfer, their convictions and their sentences remain in force and they must serve the sentence in a foreign land. The question that is posed reduces simply, in my view, to this: is it a reasonable exercise of governmental power to imprison or restrain at their election individuals who otherwise would be imprisoned or restrained abroad, and to do so subject to the mitigations that the treaties articulate by making applicable our release procedures and subject also to the safeguards with respect to an informed consent that the legislation would provide. I see no room for argument upon that issue.
>
> Third: If I am right in the analysis I have suggested, no additional complexity is introduced by the provision limiting collateral attack on the conviction or the sentence to the courts of the transferring state. This is not a suspension of the privilege of the writ of habeas corpus. The writ remains available; it is simply a good return that the offender is imprisoned in accordance with the treaty and its implementing legislation. If the treaty and the statute are valid, as I believe they are, the detention does not violate the Constitution, laws or treaties of the United States. The application for the writ must, therefore, be denied.

Penal Treaties with Mexico and Canada: Hearings Before the Senate Comm. on Foreign Relations, 95th Cong. 90, 93–94 (1977).

(3) Article IV(4) of the Treaty with Mexico sets out broad criteria for determining the appropriateness of a transfer: "In deciding upon the transfer of an offender . . . each Party shall bear in mind all factors bearing upon the probability that the transfer will contribute to the social rehabilitation of the offender,

including the nature and severity of his offense and his previous criminal record, if any, his medical condition, the strength of his connections by residence, presence in the territory, family relations and otherwise to the social life of the Transferring State and the Receiving State." Otherwise, no officially published federal regulations set out the guidelines to be used in deciding whether or not to allow a transfer. In *Scalise v. Meese*, 687 F. Supp. 1239 (N.D. Ill. 1988), the district court held that the U.S. implementing legislation imposed a duty on the Attorney General to issue such regulations, which could be enforced through a writ of mandamus, but this decision was reversed by the Seventh Circuit in *Scalise v. Thornburgh*, 891 F.2d 640 (7th Cir. 1989). Similarly, in *Marquez-Ramos v. Reno*, 69 F.3d 477 (10th Cir. 1995), the Tenth Circuit held that the Attorney General's decision to deny a transfer was entirely discretionary and not subject to review through mandamus. In a 2018 decision, the United States Court of Appeals for the D.C. Circuit examined a claim brought under the Administrative Procedure Act by a dual citizen of the United States and Canada claiming that the U.S. government's denial of his request for transfer to Canada was arbitrary and capricious. In affirming the lower court's denial of the APA claim, the appeals court noted that the role of the courts in this area is "narrow." The court stated, "This court has acknowledged that 'a broad grant of discretionary authority is particularly appropriate to prison transfer decisions, depending as they do on a variety of considerations,' both domestic and international. The Attorney General must consider the prisoner's 'best interests' in determining whether to approve a transfer application, but contrary to [petitioner's] view Section 6 [of the prisoner transfer treaty between the U.S. and Canada] does not limit consideration *only* to those interests. Nor does the court's review reach the correctness of the Attorney General's assessment of the factors considered or of the ultimate decision whether to transfer." *Sluss v. United States*, 898 F.3d 1242 (D.C. Cir. 2018).

Within the Department of Justice, decisions involving prisoner transfers have been delegated to the Criminal Division's Office of Enforcement Operations, which has drawn up non-binding guidelines for use in such cases. *See* Maureen T. Walsh & Bruce Zagaris, *The United States-Mexico Treaty on the Execution of Penal Sanctions: The Case for Reevaluating the Treaty and Its Politics in View of the NAFTA and Other Developments*, 2 Sw. J. of L. & Trade Am. 385, 410–12 (1995). Department of Justice statistics for prisoner transfers in 2019 indicate that 28 transfers took place to the United States and 319 from the United States. See material *available at* https://edit.justice.gov/sites/default/files/criminal-oeo/legacy/2014/06/06/Statistics.pdf. Given the numbers of foreigners incarcerated in the federal system alone (about a quarter of the 200 thousand or so federal inmates are foreigners and the state systems are much larger) this suggests that the transfer system is severely underutilized. *See* U.S. Department of Justice, Office of the Inspector- General, *The Department of Justice's Prisoner Transfer Program* (December 2011), *available at* https:://www.oig.justice.gov/reports/2011/e1202.pdf; *see also* U.S. Department of Justice, Office of the Inspector General, *Status Review on the Department's*

International Prisoner Transfer Program (August 2015) (noting that while progress had been made, "more can be done by the Department to improve the effectiveness of the treaty transfer program.").

(4) Under Article V(2) of the Treaty with Mexico, provided the prisoner is not subjected to a longer sentence than that imposed by the transferring state, "the completion of a transferred offender's sentence shall be carried out according to the laws and procedures of the Receiving State, including the application of any provisions for reduction of the term of confinement by parole, conditional release, or otherwise." How has this been affected by adoption of the Federal Sentencing Guidelines? In *Kleeman v. U.S. Parole Commission*, 125 F.3d 725 (9th Cir. 1987), the Ninth Circuit observed:

> In transfer cases, the [U.S. Parole] Commission "is charged with the task of translating a foreign sentence into terms appropriate to domestic penal enforcement." Specifically, the Commission must apply the federal sentencing guidelines to the investigative reports and recommendations of the United States Probation Service to determine a combined term of imprisonment and supervised release for the transferred offender "as though the offender were convicted in the United States district court of a similar offense." 18 U.S.C. § 4106A(b)(1)(A). Regulations provide: "The Commission shall take into account the offense definition under foreign law, the length of the sentence permitted by that law, and the underlying circumstances of the offense behavior, to establish a guideline range that fairly reflects the seriousness of the offense behavior committed in the foreign country." 28 C.F.R. § 2.62(g).

In the *Kleeman* case, the prisoner had been convicted of "simple homicide" (*homicidio simple*) in Baja California, Mexico, and sentenced to ten years' imprisonment. She was granted a transfer to complete service of her sentence in the United States and placed at the Federal Correctional Institution in Dublin, California. The U.S. Probation Office prepared a post-sentence report in anticipation of the transfer hearing which concluded that the most analogous United States offense to the offense of conviction in Mexico was voluntary manslaughter. Accordingly, it listed the applicable guideline range for sentencing as 41 to 51 months. The U.S. Parole Commission's final transfer determination concluded that Kleeman's offense was most similar to second degree murder and set her sentence at 72 months, with 48 months of supervised release. The Ninth Circuit held that:

> the crime of "homicidio simple" of which Kleeman was convicted in Mexico covers certain types of conduct that would be classified as voluntary manslaughter under our law. One convicted of "homicidio simple" may have committed an act that we would treat as murder in the second degree or only as voluntary manslaughter. Because we agree, as a matter of law, that the facts do not establish Kleeman acted with malice, we conclude that the comparable United States offense is voluntary manslaughter.... Therefore, we reverse and remand to the Commission to reclassify Kleeman's offense

as voluntary manslaughter and to determine her term of imprisonment and supervised release accordingly.

(5) "If a Mexican national, who has been convicted of a crime under state law in the United States and has been transferred to Mexico to serve his sentence, escapes from the custody of Mexican authorities and returns to this country, may the Attorney General apprehend him without a warrant and return him to Mexican authorities without extradition proceedings?" *Tavarez v. U.S. Attorney General*, 668 F.2d 805, 806 (5th Cir. 1982). In *Tavarez*, the Fifth Circuit held that formal extradition proceedings are not required, provided the person who is apprehended as an escapee from a foreign prison is given the opportunity to consult with counsel and to raise any issue concerning the legality of his return in a petition for federal habeas corpus.

(6) The United Nations Crime Prevention and Criminal Justice Program has encouraged the negotiation of prisoner transfer treaties and to this end developed a Model Agreement on the Transfer of Foreign Prisoners, *Seventh United Nations Congress on the Prevention of Crime and the Treatment of Offenders*, Milan, 26 August–6 September 1985, Report prepared by the Secretariat, at 53, U.N. Doc. A/CONF.121/22/Rev.1 (1986). The model treaty has, as a particular object, the "social resettlement" of offenders by returning them to where they are more likely to get family support. *See generally* UNITED NATIONS OFFICE ON DRUGS AND CRIME, HANDBOOK ON THE INTERNATIONAL TRANSFER OF SENTENCED PERSONS (2012).

§ 18.02 Recognition of Foreign Criminal Law, Especially Convictions

In *Rosado v. Civiletti*, in the preceding section, Judge Kaufman quotes John Marshall's famous dictum in *The Antelope*, 23 U.S. (10 Wheat.) 66, 123 (1825): "The courts of no country execute the penal laws of another." Contrast the situation obtaining in civil cases, where the U.S. courts, as a matter of comity, routinely enforce foreign judgments. Although not precisely a matter of "executing" foreign penal laws, several modes of international cooperation can result in U.S. courts aiding the efforts of other countries to enforce their own penal laws. These modes of cooperation include mutual assistance [*see* chap. 15] and extradition [*see* chap.16]. European nations have developed the further possibility of transferring criminal proceedings from one country to another. *See* M. Cherif Bassiouni, *Introduction to Transfer of Criminal Proceedings, in* 2 INTERNATIONAL CRIMINAL LAW 515 (M. Cherif Bassiouni ed., 3d ed. 2008).

Apart from prisoner transfers, which appear to represent a genuine exception to Marshall's dictum, there are various other ways in which U.S. law may indirectly give effect to a foreign criminal conviction. *See generally* A. Kenneth Pye, *The Effect of Foreign Criminal Judgments Within the United States*, 32 U.M.K.C. L. REV. 114 (1964), *reprinted in* INTERNATIONAL CRIMINAL LAW 479 (Gerhard O. W. Mueller &

Edward M. Wise eds., 1965). The cases in which questions about the effect of foreign convictions arise can be grouped largely into five categories.

First, the foreign conviction may be pleaded as a bar to a second trial for the same offense in the United States. Since a different sovereign was involved, a second trial would not be barred by the constitutional ban on double jeopardy. But a statute may require that the previous trial or conviction be treated as a bar to re-prosecution. *See id.* at 485–86. For example, California's double jeopardy statute once prohibited trial if the defendant had been tried for the same conduct under the laws of another state or country. California amended this legislation in 2004 so that it now applies only to previous prosecutions under the laws of the United States, or of another state or territory of the United States. The issue of whether this amendment could be applied retroactively was litigated inconclusively. The case involved a 20-year-old murder in Los Angeles for which the accused, a Japanese citizen, was tried and ultimately acquitted in Japan. *See* Tetsuya Morimoto, *Can the Ex Post Facto Clause Save a Japanese Businessman from Extradition to California?*, INT'L ENF. L. REP., May 2008, Laurie L. Levenson, *Ex Post Facto Law*, NAT'L L. J., March 17, 2008 at 15. The proceedings were terminated by the suicide of the accused in October of 2008. *See Japanese Businessman Accused in Murder Case Kills Self*, http://www.cbsnews.com/news/japanese-man-in-murder-plot-found-dead/.

Second, a foreign criminal conviction may provide a basis under the Immigration and Nationality Act for excluding an alien from the United States.

Third, a criminal conviction may be a ground of disqualification, for instance, for a driver's license, or for a license to practice a certain profession or trade, for government employment, for jury service, for public office, or for voting. Insofar as a foreign conviction counts for these purposes, domestic effect is given to the foreign conviction.

Fourth, a witness's record of criminal convictions may be used to attack the competency or credibility of the witness. Insofar as a foreign conviction can be used for this purpose, effect again is given to foreign penal law.

Finally, a foreign conviction may be taken into account for purposes of sentencing—to make the defendant an habitual or multiple offender, or as a factor to be scored under sentencing guidelines. Some repeat offender statutes explicitly authorize, some explicitly prohibit, the use of foreign convictions for these purposes. Others are ambiguous or silent about the use of foreign convictions. *See* Martha Kimes, Note, *The Effect of Foreign Criminal Convictions Under American Repeat Offender Statutes: A Case Against the Use of Foreign Crimes in Determining Habitual Criminal Status*, 35 COLUM. J. TRANSNAT'L L. 503, 506–10 (1997). Not surprisingly, the cases interpreting ambiguous statutes have come out on both sides of the question: some allow and some refuse to allow consideration of a foreign conviction for purposes of sentence enhancement. *See id.* 510–14. A handful of multilateral criminal law treaties contemplate that States may take foreign convictions into account and perhaps even encourage them to do so. *See*, e.g., Single Convention on Narcotic

Drugs, Article 36(2)(iii). A fairly recent example is Article 41 of the United Nations Convention against Corruption [*see* chap. 4]:

> Each State Party may adopt such legislative or other measures as may be necessary to take into consideration, under such terms as and for the purpose that it deems appropriate, any previous conviction in another State of an alleged offender for the purpose of using such information in criminal proceedings relating to an offence established in accordance with the Convention.

By the same token, foreign criminal activity may represent a predicate crime for money laundering. *See, e.g.*, U.N. Convention against Corruption, Article 23 [chap. 4].

In United States law, the significant issue is often one of statutory interpretation Consider the following case.

Small v. United States

Supreme Court of the United States
544 U.S. 385 (2005)

Justice Breyer delivered the opinion of the Court.

The United States Criminal Code makes it "unlawful for any person . . . who has been *convicted in any court*, of a crime punishable by imprisonment for a term exceeding one year . . . to . . . possess . . . any firearm." 18 U.S.C. § 922(g)(1) (emphasis added). The question before us focuses upon the words "convicted in any court." Does this phrase apply only to convictions entered in any *domestic* court or to *foreign* convictions as well? We hold that the phrase encompasses only domestic, not foreign, convictions. . . .

In 1994 petitioner, Gary Small, was convicted in a Japanese court of having tried to smuggle several pistols, a rifle, and ammunition into Japan. Small was sentenced to five years' imprisonment. 183 F. Supp. 2d 755, 757, n.3 (WD Pa. 2002). After his release, Small returned to the United States, where he bought a gun from a Pennsylvania gun dealer. Federal authorities subsequently charged Small under the "unlawful gun possession" statute here at issue. . . . Small pleaded guilty while reserving the right to challenge his conviction on the ground that his earlier conviction, being a foreign conviction, fell outside the scope of the illegal gun possession statute. The Federal District Court rejected Small's argument, as did the Court of Appeals for the Third Circuit. . . . Because the Circuits disagree about the matter, we granted certiorari. Compare *United States v. Atkins*, 872 F.2d 94, 96 (4th Cir. 1989) ("convicted in any court" includes foreign convictions); *United States v. Winson*, 793 F.2d 754, 757–759 (6th Cir. 1986) (same), with *United States v. Gayle*, 342 F.3d 89, 95 (2d Cir. 2003) ("convicted in any court" does not include foreign convictions); *United States v. Concha*, 233 F.3d 1249, 1256 (10th Cir. 2000) (same). . . .

The question before us is whether the statutory reference "convicted in *any* court" includes a conviction entered in a *foreign* court. The word "any" considered alone cannot answer this question. In ordinary life, a speaker who says, "I'll see any film," may or may not mean to include films shown in another city. In law, a legislature that uses the statutory phrase "'any person'" may or may not mean to include "'persons'" outside "the jurisdiction of the state." ... Thus, even though the word "any" demands a broad interpretation, ... we must look beyond that word itself.

In determining the scope of the statutory phrase we find help in the "commonsense notion that Congress generally legislates with domestic concerns in mind." ... This notion has led the Court to adopt the legal presumption that Congress ordinarily intends its statutes to have domestic, not extraterritorial, application.... That presumption would apply, for example, were we to consider whether this statute prohibits unlawful gun possession abroad as well as domestically. And, although the presumption against extraterritorial application does not apply directly to this case, we believe a similar assumption is appropriate when we consider the scope of the phrase "convicted in any court" here.

For one thing, the phrase describes one necessary portion of the "gun possession" activity that is prohibited as a matter of domestic law. For another, considered as a group, foreign convictions differ from domestic convictions in important ways. Past foreign convictions for crimes punishable by more than one year's imprisonment may include a conviction for conduct that domestic laws would permit, for example, for engaging in economic conduct that our society might encourage....

In addition, it is difficult to read the statute as asking judges or prosecutors to refine its definitional distinctions where foreign convictions are at issue. To somehow weed out inappropriate foreign convictions that meet the statutory definition is not consistent with the statute's language; it is not easy for those not versed in foreign laws to accomplish; and it would leave those previously convicted in a foreign court (say of economic crimes) uncertain about their legal obligations. Cf. 1 United States Sentencing Commission, Guidelines Manual § 4A1.2(h) (Nov. 2004) ("Sentences resulting from foreign convictions are not counted" as a "prior sentence" for criminal history purposes).

These considerations, suggesting significant differences between foreign and domestic convictions, do not dictate our ultimate conclusion. Nor do they create a "clear statement" rule, imposing upon Congress a special burden of specificity.... They simply convince us that we should apply an ordinary assumption about the reach of domestically oriented statutes here—an assumption that helps us determine Congress' intent where Congress likely did not consider the matter and where other indicia of intent are in approximate balance.... We consequently assume a congressional intent that the phrase "convicted in any court" applies domestically, not extraterritorially. But, at the same time, we stand ready to revise this assumption should statutory language, context, history, or purpose show the contrary....

We have found no convincing indication to the contrary here. The statute's language does not suggest any intent to reach beyond domestic convictions. Neither does it mention foreign convictions nor is its subject matter special, say, immigration or terrorism, where one could argue that foreign convictions would seem especially relevant. To the contrary, if read to include foreign convictions, the statute's language creates anomalies.

For example, the statute creates an exception that allows gun possession despite a prior conviction for an antitrust or business regulatory crime. . . . In doing so, the exception speaks of "Federal or State" antitrust or regulatory offenses. . . . If the phrase "convicted in any court" generally refers only to domestic convictions, this language causes no problem. But if "convicted in any court" includes foreign convictions, the words "Federal or State" prevent the exception from applying where a *foreign* antitrust or regulatory conviction is at issue. An individual convicted of, say, a Canadian antitrust offense could not lawfully possess a gun, Combines Investigation Act, 2 R. S. C. 1985, ch. C-34, §§ 61(6), (9) (1985), but a similar individual convicted of, say, a New York antitrust offense, could lawfully possess a gun.

For example, the statute specifies that predicate crimes include "a misdemeanor crime of domestic violence." 18 U.S.C. § 922(g)(9). Again, the language specifies that these predicate crimes include only crimes that are "misdemeanors under Federal or State law." § 921(a)(33)(A). If "convicted in any court" refers only to domestic convictions, this language creates no problem. If the phrase also refers to foreign convictions, the language creates an apparently senseless distinction between (covered) domestic relations misdemeanors committed within the United States and (uncovered) domestic relations misdemeanors committed abroad.

For example, the statute provides an enhanced penalty where unlawful gun possession rests upon three predicate convictions for a "serious drug offense." § 924(e)(1) (2000 ed., Supp. II). Again the statute defines the relevant drug crimes through reference to specific federal crimes and with the words "offense under State law." §§ 924(e)(2)(A)(i), (ii) (2000). If "convicted in any court" refers only to domestic convictions, this language creates no problem. But if the phrase also refers to foreign convictions, the language creates an apparently senseless distinction between drug offenses committed within the United States (potentially producing enhanced punishments) and similar offenses committed abroad (not producing enhanced punishments).

For example, the statute provides that offenses that are punishable by a term of imprisonment of up to two years, and characterized under state law as misdemeanors, are not predicate crimes. § 921(a)(20). This exception is presumably based on the determination that such state crimes are not sufficiently serious or dangerous so as to preclude an individual from possessing a firearm. If "convicted in any court" refers only to domestic convictions, this language creates no problem. But if the phrase also refers to foreign convictions, the language creates another apparently senseless distinction between less serious crimes (misdemeanors punishable by more than one year's imprisonment) committed within the United States (not predicate crimes) and similar offenses committed abroad (predicate crimes). These illustrative examples taken together suggest that Congress did not consider whether the generic phrase "convicted in any court" applies to domestic as well as foreign convictions.

The statute's lengthy legislative history confirms the fact that Congress did not consider whether foreign convictions should or should not serve as a predicate to liability under the provision here at issue. Congress did consider a Senate bill containing language that would have restricted predicate offenses to domestic offenses. . . . And the Conference Committee ultimately rejected this version in favor of language that speaks of those "convicted in any court, of a crime punishable by a term of imprisonment exceeding one year." . . . But the history does not suggest that this language change reflected a congressional view on the matter before us. Rather, the enacted version is simpler and it avoids potential difficulties arising out of the fact that States may define the term "felony" differently. And as far as the legislative history is concerned, these latter virtues of the new language fully explain the change. Thus, those who use legislative history to help discern congressional intent will see the history here as silent, hence a neutral factor, that simply confirms the obvious, namely, that Congress did not consider the issue. Others will not be tempted to use or to discuss the history at all. . . .

The statute's purpose *does* offer some support for a reading of the phrase that includes foreign convictions. As the Government points out, Congress sought to "'keep guns out of the hands of those who have demonstrated that they may not be trusted to possess a firearm without becoming a threat to society.'" . . . The force of this argument is weakened significantly, however, by the empirical fact that, according to the Government, since 1968, there have probably been no more than "10 to a dozen" instances in which such a foreign conviction has served as a predicate for a felon-in-possession prosecution. . . . This empirical fact reinforces the likelihood that Congress, at best, paid no attention to the matter.

In sum, we have no reason to believe that Congress considered the added enforcement advantages flowing from inclusion of foreign crimes, weighing them against, say, the potential unfairness of preventing those with inapt foreign convictions from possessing guns. . . . The statute itself and its history offer only congressional silence. Given the reasons for disfavoring an inference of extraterritorial coverage from a statute's total silence and our initial assumption against such coverage, . . . , we conclude that the phrase "convicted in any court" refers only to domestic courts, not to foreign courts. Congress, of course, remains free to change this conclusion through statutory amendment.

For these reasons, the judgment of the Third Circuit is reversed, and the case is remanded for further proceedings consistent with this opinion. . . . It is so ordered.

The Chief Justice took no part in the decision of this case.

Justice Thomas, with whom Justice Scalia and Justice Kennedy join, dissenting.

. . . . In concluding that "any" means not what it says, but rather "a subset of any," the Court distorts the plain meaning of the statute and departs from established principles of statutory construction. I respectfully dissent. . . .

The Japanese Government indicted Small on multiple counts of violating Japan's weapons-control and customs laws. . . . Each offense was punishable by imprisonment for a term exceeding one year.... Small was tried before a three-judge court in Naha, Japan, ... convicted on all counts ... and sentenced to 5 years' imprisonment with credit for 320 days served.... He was paroled on November 22, 1996, and his parole terminated on May 26, 1998.... A week after completing parole for his Japanese convictions, on June 2, 1998, Small purchased a 9-millimeter SWD Cobray pistol from a firearms dealer in Pennsylvania.... Some time later, a search of his residence, business premises, and automobile revealed a .380 caliber Browning pistol and more than 300 rounds of ammunition.... This prosecution ensued....

.... The broad phrase "any court" unambiguously includes all judicial bodies with jurisdiction to impose the requisite conviction—a conviction for a crime punishable by imprisonment for a term of more than a year. Indisputably, Small was convicted in a Japanese court of crimes punishable by a prison term exceeding one year. The clear terms of the statute prohibit him from possessing a gun in the United States....

Of course, the phrase "any court," like all other statutory language, must be read in context.... The context of § 922(g)(1), however, suggests that there is no geographic limit on the scope of "any court." ... Counting foreign convictions, moreover, implicates no special federalism concerns or other clear statement rules that have justified construing "any" narrowly in the past....

Faced with the inescapably broad text, the Court narrows the statute by assuming that the text applies only to domestic convictions ...; criticizing the accuracy of foreign convictions as a proxy for dangerousness ...; finding that the broad, natural reading of the statute "creates anomalies" ...; and suggesting that Congress did not consider whether foreign convictions counted.... None of these arguments is persuasive....

The Court first invents a canon of statutory interpretation—what it terms "an ordinary assumption about the reach of domestically oriented statutes," ... —to cabin the statute's reach. This new "assumption" imposes a clear statement rule on Congress: Absent a clear statement, a statute refers to nothing outside the United States....

The Court's innovation is baseless. The Court derives its assumption from the entirely different, and well-recognized, canon against extraterritorial application of federal statutes: "It is a longstanding principle of American law that legislation of Congress, unless a contrary intent appears, is meant to apply only within the territorial jurisdiction of the United States." *EEOC v. Arabian American Oil Co.*, 499 U.S. 244, 248 (1991) (internal quotation marks omitted). But the majority rightly concedes that the canon against extraterritoriality itself "does not apply directly to this case." ... Though foreign as well as domestic convictions trigger § 922(g)(1)'s prohibition, the statute criminalizes gun possession in this country, not abroad. In prosecuting Small, the Government is enforcing a domestic criminal statute to punish domestic criminal conduct. *Pasquantino v. United States* [§ 3.02], ... (federal wire fraud statute covers a domestic scheme aimed at defrauding a foreign government of tax revenue).

The extraterritoriality cases cited by the Court . . . do not support its new assumption. They restrict federal statutes from applying outside the territorial jurisdiction of the United States. . . . These straightforward applications of the extraterritoriality canon, restricting federal statutes from reaching conduct *beyond U.S. borders*, lend no support to the Court's unprecedented rule restricting a federal statute from reaching conduct *within U.S. borders*.

We have, it is true, recognized that the presumption against extraterritorial application of federal statutes is rooted in part in the "commonsense notion that Congress generally legislates with domestic concerns in mind." . . . But my reading of § 922(g)(1) is entirely true to that notion: Gun possession in this country is surely a "domestic concern." We have also consistently grounded the canon in the risk that extraterritorially applicable U.S. laws could conflict with foreign laws, for example, by subjecting individuals to conflicting obligations. . . . That risk is completely absent in applying § 922(g)(1) to Small's conduct. Quite the opposite, § 922(g)(1) takes foreign law as it finds it. Aside from the extraterritoriality canon, which the Court properly concedes does not apply, I know of no principle of statutory construction justifying the result the Court reaches. Its concession that the canon is inapposite should therefore end this case. . . . The majority's concern with anomalies provides no principled basis for choosing its interpretation of the statute over mine.

The Court never convincingly explains its departure from the natural meaning of § 922(g)(1). Instead, it institutes the troubling rule that "any" does not really mean "any," but may mean "some subset of 'any,'" even if nothing in the context so indicates; it distorts the established canons against extraterritoriality and absurdity; it faults without reason Congress' use of foreign convictions to gauge dangerousness and culpability; and it employs discredited methods of determining congressional intent. I respectfully dissent.

Note

In *United States v. Kole* [chap. 13, *supra*], a prior conviction in the Philippines served as a predicate for treating the defendant as a repeat felony drug offender subject to the 20-year mandatory minimum prescribed in 21 U.S.C. § 960. The federal statute itself barred consideration for this purpose of a prior conviction "obtained in violation of the Constitution of the United States." With respect to foreign convictions, the court declined to interpret the statute as requiring that the prior conviction must have been obtained in full conformity with the Bill of Rights, but rather read it as designed only to exclude a "conviction that was obtained in a manner inconsistent with concepts of fundamental fairness and liberty. . . ." What if the statute had not made a specific exception for convictions "obtained in violation of the Constitution"? Would a U.S. court be entitled to rely, for purposes of sentence enhancement, on a conviction obtained in a manner that contravened "fundamental fairness"? Is this a general limitation on the use of foreign convictions by or in the U.S. courts that applies whether or not it is expressly stipulated by statute? Insofar as this limitation applies, how closely should a court in the United States scrutinize the "fairness" of a foreign system of criminal procedure? What are the criteria to be used in assessing the "fairness" of an alien system? Consider the following case.

United States v. Moskovits

United States District Court for the Eastern District of Pennsylvania
784 F. Supp. 183 (1991)

POLLAK, DISTRICT JUDGE:

In September of 1988, I sentenced Mr. Moskovits to a period of incarceration of seventeen years. Ten years of that sentence was on Count 8 of the indictment, which alleged possession with intent to distribute a cocaine-containing substance which was over 500 grams. Under the statutory scheme, conviction on that count called for a mandatory sentence of five years as a minimum. The mandatory minimum under that statute is increased to ten years, where the person convicted has had a previous felony drug conviction under federal or state or foreign law. . . . The defense was apprised that the government would ask for enhancement on the basis of Mr. Moskovits' conviction in Mexico, in 1983, of the offense of importing narcotic drugs into Mexico. . . .

The central contention made on Mr. Moskovits' behalf, is that the Mexican conviction, which was the basis for enhancement — that is to say my decision that a mandatory minimum sentence of ten years was called for on Count 8 — was an invalid conviction because it was the result of procedures which are not consonant with American constitutional requirements, and hence would not form the basis of sentence enhancement in this United States court. The core of defendant's contention is that the Mexican proceedings were invalid because Mr. Moskovits did not have counsel at crucial phases of the proceeding. . . . I will not undertake to rehearse the full chronology of what happened . . . Suffice it to say, Mr. Moskovits was apprehended at the airport on June 29, 1983, was found by arresting officers to have drugs with him, and was interrogated, made an inculpatory statement, which was signed by Mr. Moskovits. The statement was in Spanish. Mr. Moskovits appended to the margin of the statement on the first page thereof in English the legend, "Under great emotional stress, I admit that this document contains truth."

There were certain preliminary proceedings in July, pursuant to which Mr. Moskovits was held in custody. An attorney, who apparently was not retained, made an appearance on Mr. Moskovits' behalf, but withdrew from the ambiguous representation on August 8. At that time, Mr. Moskovits was advised by the judge that he, Mr. Moskovits, had three days to retain a new attorney, and failing that, a government attorney would be appointed to represent him. The record does not disclose that any such appointment was in fact made.

The record further discloses that Mr. Moskovits next had legal representation on August 22, when Mr. Moskovits' father and Mr. Gilberto Rojo Herrera entered into a retainer agreement. There is disagreement between the government and the defendant as to the nature of that retainer agreement. The position taken by Mr. Moskovits is that the purpose of the retainer was solely to secure a fixed sentence which would enable Mr. Moskovits then to be transferred to United States custody under the Prisoner Exchange Treaty.... It is the government's view that the contract of retainer impose[d] on Mr. Herrera a broader mission.... [going] beyond a petition for a fixed minimum sentence.... I don't find it necessary to resolve the dispute with respect to what the purpose of the retainer agreement was, whether the limited one perceived by the defense, or the broader one perceived by the government.

Suffice it to note that, before Mr. Herrera was retained on August 22, there was the first of the two so-called Careo hearings. At those hearings, Mr. Moskovits appeared without counsel present, and confronted his accusers. The understanding is that the Careo proceeding, which has no clear analogue in American jurisprudence, is an opportunity for such a face-to-face presentation. At the Careo proceeding on August 10, there appears to have been an extended presentation by the arresting officers. Attendant on that [was] the reception of Mr. Moskovits' statement, the one to which I had referred, which was inculpatory and to which he appended the English notation, that it was signed under emotional stress. Mr. Moskovits had the opportunity, which he evidently exercised, to give testimony himself and to explain the inadequacies and inconsistencies of the arresting officer's testimony, and to represent the inappropriateness of their behavior. There was a further Careo hearing on August 29, one week after the retention of Mr. Herrera. Mr. Herrera was not present at the August 29 proceeding either. That proceeding was thought to supplement the August 10 proceeding, and to relate to a so-called missing witness. Again, Mr. Moskovits was there, and clearly represented himself with vigor, but he did not have counsel at his side.

With respect to the nature of Careo hearings, the only evidence supplied to this court is contained in affirmation of one Jose Cruz, a Mexican attorney who has status in New York, not as a member of the bar, but as one admitted to advise on foreign law, that is to say Mexican law. In Mr. Cruz' affirmation, he says:

> I am fully familiar with the Mexican law relating to the so-called "Careo" hearings, and I hereby certify that, in accordance with Article 266 of the "Federal Criminal Procedures Code" of Mexico, the only persons who may appear at such hearings are the parties involved, a judge, and an interpreter, if necessary. The attorney for the defense is not allowed to be present since his or her appearance could influence the demeanor of the parties.
>
> "Careo" hearings are not, in themselves, a trial under Mexican law, but only a phase of the procedure which aids the judge in finding the truth....
>
> After the "Careo" hearing, the judge's impression of the said hearing will be just another piece of evidence but this, by itself, may not direct a resolution of the case in one direction or another, since the "Careo" is not a piece of evidence determinative of the resolution of the case.

The discussion by Mr. Cruz is a very modest one. Perhaps it poses more questions than it answers. It is, however, the only information which has been presented either by the government or by the defense. This was a defense submission. There has been earnest argument about how central the Careo hearings are in Mexican criminal procedure.

With respect to the particulars of the process as it affected Mr. Moskovits — that, of course, is the focus of our interest here today — it appears that after the second Careo hearing, on September 6, there was a ruling by the court — and it does not appear whether this was done in a courtroom proceeding or was simply an order — that recited that the parties were free to submit such further evidence as they thought appropriate, but that no such submissions were made.

On September 15, the first proceeding in which it appears as a matter of record that Mr. Herrera participated in some formal sense, was Mr. Herrera's submission to the court, responsive to a motion for judgment that was filed by the Office of the Attorney General on September 13. . . . [O]n September 20, the court made an extended review of the prior proceedings, and, in particular, considered the material brought forward at the Careo proceedings with respect to Mr. Moskovits' apprehension, statements which Mr. Moskovits had reportedly made, and the contention made by Mr. Herrera on Mr. Moskovits' behalf that Mr. Moskovits should be "absolved," a contention which the court rejected in favor of finding Mr. Moskovits guilty. With respect to sentence, the court concluded that for this defendant, who had no prior criminal record, a seven-year sentence would suffice. And so sentence was imposed. . . . [N]ine days later, a court determined that appeal time had run. Neither the government nor the defense had appealed, and so the seven-year sentence was final and was to be executed.

The record in the Mexican court, as described, calls on us, in my judgment, to return once again to the question already adumbrated, what is the role of the Careo proceeding in Mexican law. As noted, the proceeding was bifurcated. Most of it took place on August 10, a supplementary phase on August 29. Mr. Moskovits did not have an attorney, at either phase, present at the proceeding. . . . What we have then is two days of Careo proceedings, which appear to be the only proceedings at which live testimony was offered, at which there was an opportunity for cross-examination, and on neither of those days was Mr. Moskovits attended by counsel. Evidently, the government also was not represented by counsel in these proceedings.

The government of the United States contends that . . . it would be a mistake to equate the Careo proceedings with those crucial phases of an American criminal proceeding at which evidence is adduced. The better analogy, it is argued, is that these are in the nature of preliminary proceedings akin to a probable cause hearing. Defense, for its part, contends that certain preliminary hearings, having taken place in July in Mr. Moskovits' case, would better carry the legend of probable cause proceedings.

I find more than a little difficulty accepting the view that the Careo proceedings are to be regarded as preliminary proceedings analogous to the probable cause phase in our jurisprudence. If one takes that nomenclature, one then asks, preliminary to what? Where is the central evidentiary proceeding that in our terms would be a trial? The government's view is that such an opportunity for presentation of the defense case, if there would be one, was, at least in this instance, made judicially available on September 6, when the court ruled that the parties had the opportunity to offer evidence as they respectably felt appropriate, and then when no such submissions were made, determined that the record was closed.... [But] the fact is that no submission was made, and so the evidentiary record, on the basis of which the court found guilt and imposed sentence on September 20, was the evidentiary record made at the Careo hearings.

There is nothing before this court to suggest that the procedures utilized in Mr. Moskovits' case departed from Mexican requirements. So I will assume for purposes of discussion that they were in conformity with—at least then—prevailing Mexican requirements. It is the position, of course, of the defense that Mexican requirements are irrelevant because they fail to guarantee the American constitutional norms; irrelevant, that is to say, insofar as the Mexican conviction is relied on in the United States court for sentence enhancement purposes. The government's position is that so long as there was conformity with Mexican requirements and with norms of fundamental fairness, the Mexican conviction and sentence can be relied upon by this court for its sentence enhancement purposes.

Accepting the government's position means that we should test a foreign conviction not by its conformity with every ingredient of what in American terms is fundamental criminal procedure, but we should test a foreign conviction by its conformity with those particular norms of American criminal procedures, jurisprudence constitutionalized, that are the particular domain of absolute rock bottom fundamental fairness.

How does one draw distinctions? In *United States v. Wilson*, 556 F.2d 1177, 1178 (4th Cir.), *cert. denied*, 434 U.S. 986, 98 S. Ct. 614, 54 L. Ed. 2d 481 (1977), the Court of Appeals noted that a German criminal conviction could be relied upon by an American court, notwithstanding the absence of a jury in German criminal procedure. A jury is part of the American constitutional armament. It is guaranteed in federal prosecution by the Bill of Rights, and has been judicially found, via the Fourteenth Amendment, to be an ingredient of the due process which states are required to observe in state criminal proceedings. It would, however, be a form of cultural imperialism for the United States to insist that it would not countenance, for U.S. purposes, recognition of a foreign criminal judgment which came from a legal culture which did not employ the jury. I don't doubt Congress' authority to say that the jury is so important that it wouldn't permit, in looking at foreign criminal judgments for sentence enhancement purposes, reliance on a criminal conviction emanating from Germany or France. But it would seem to me an improbable way to accomplish legitimate American goals of insisting on fairness in American courts. In contradistinction to the jury ingredient, I would find the presence or absence of counsel.

The Supreme Court of the United States found that counsel are required in state criminal proceedings, by virtue of the Constitution of the United States, long before the Supreme Court found that juries were required in state criminal proceedings by the Constitution of the United States. The distinction is not merely a chronological one in the development of the American jurisprudence. The distinction has to do with the basis on which the right to counsel cases lie. The distinction is that without an attorney at one's side, most lay persons are essentially helpless to meet criminal charges. So that what is in form a hearing, is in fact not a hearing when an accused does not have a lawyer. That observation about how the criminal process works is an observation that would not have geographical boundaries, if the Supreme Court were right in its perception about the criminal process in the United States. The determination is one that would seem to me to apply equally well to Mexico or to the United Kingdom or to South Africa or to the Soviet Union or to Zimbabwe.

Accordingly, I think we cannot countenance reliance on a foreign criminal conviction where it can be said, on the basis of the record made, that there was a failure to provide for counsel at crucial stages of the process. That is a conclusion which, in the first instance, I would determine as a matter of statutory implication. I read the statute that Congress passed, which imposes a ten-year minimum via sentence enhancement in reliance on foreign drug convictions, as a statute which implies that the foreign conviction shall be one which meets norms of fundamental fairness as perceived by United States courts. The participation of counsel at crucial stages of the criminal proceeding is one such fundamental norm.

I say I come to that conclusion as a matter of statutory construction because I would attribute to Congress no lower standard. But I would add that if one could suppose the possibility that Congress had not imported such a requirement into the statute, there would be very grave questions as to the constitutionality of that aspect of the sentencing enhancement provision.

In Mr. Moskovits' case, it is plain that he did not have counsel at the August 10 phase of the Careo proceeding. That is to say, he did not have counsel with him, nor was there an attorney either appointed or retained to represent him. The August 10 proceeding was the one at which the bulk of the evidence was reviewed and relied on by the judge on September 20, as adduced. By August 29, the supplementary Careo proceeding, Mr. Moskovits had an attorney representing him, but the attorney was not present at the supplementary Careo proceeding.

If we are to follow Mr. Cruz' analysis of Mexican law — and this record gives me no basis for reliance on anything else — Mr. Herrera could not have been present at the August 29 proceeding, even had he wished to do so. It is the case that Mr. Herrera took no steps that are shown by the record to offer supplementary testimony, that is to say, to pursue the opportunity afforded on September 6th. It is also the case that Mr. Herrera did make a written submission on September 15, and was present in person when judgment was announced on September 20.

I cannot find those belated and marginal activities of counsel sufficient to cure the absence of counsel of August 10, or again on August 29. The requirement which the Supreme Court of our country has found to be a central dimension of American criminal procedure is the presence of counsel at all significant stages of the criminal proceeding. And certainly the Careo proceedings, as they related to Mr. Moskovits' prosecution, can only be characterized as crucial. My understanding is that the Supreme Court calls for the presence of counsel at all significant stages in the American criminal proceeding, and what analysis we can make of the Mexican procedures, as they affected Mr. Moskovits, would show the Careo hearings to have been crucial.

Accordingly, I conclude that the Mexican procedures, resulting in a conviction and sentence of Mr. Moskovits, cannot be regarded as a valid conviction and sentence from the perspective of a United States court.

What is the legal implication of that for this case? The Supreme Court of the United States determined in *United States v. Tucker*, 404 U.S. 443, 92 S. Ct. 589, 30 L. Ed. 2d 592 (1972), that where it was shown that a sentencing judge had relied on criminal convictions, prior criminal convictions, when he was engaged in the sentencing process, and that two of the criminal convictions relied on were invalid for lack of counsel, it was appropriate to remand the case for resentencing. The Supreme Court did not say that the sentencing judge was precluded from considering the tainted criminal proceedings. What the Supreme Court appeared to be saying, through Justice Stewart, and the dissent of Justice Blackmun and Chief Justice Burger, was that if there was ground for supposing that the sentencing judge was operating on the understanding that these were valid convictions, and that had he known they were not valid convictions, he might have arrived at a different sentence, then a remand for resentencing was appropriate.

The *Tucker* case was followed by *United States v. Fleishman*, 684 F.2d 1329, 1346 (9th Cir.), *cert. denied*, 459 U.S. 1044, 103 S. Ct. 464, 74 L. Ed. 2d 614 (1982), in which the Court of Appeals declined to remand for resentencing. In *Fleishman*, the court . . . concluded that resentencing was not called for because the sentencing judge had relied on the uncounseled convictions, not because he thought the convictions *per se* were necessarily valid — the representation that they were uncounseled were made to the judge — but because he thought they reflected prior criminal behavior which he could properly take into account.

That means, in effect, that the question of whether the invalid prior conviction taints the sentence depends on what light the sentencing judge gained from the prior convictions. If it was the conviction *qua* conviction that the sentencing judge looked to, and in that sense relied upon the validity of the conviction under U.S. constitutional norm, then a post-sentence determination that the relied on convictions were invalid would call for resentencing. If, however, the relied on convictions were simply evidentiary of a pattern of antisocial behavior, which to the sentencing judge was relevant to present sentence, then resentencing would not be called for. And so one must look to what the sentencing judge had in mind.

In this case, that inquiry is not a difficult one to make. In this case, the sentencing judge explained on the record that the prior conviction of September 20, 1983, required the sentencing judge to impose a minimum sentence of ten years on Count 8. The sentencing judge, when presented with no reason not to accept that judgment, sentenced accordingly. The sentencing judge was operating under a statutory mandate. He was not exercising his discretion one way or another with respect to whether the Mexican proceedings showed Mr. Moskovits to have been a miscreant a number of years before. Accordingly, since in this case the sentencing judge was relying on the legal verity, the constitutional integrity in American fundamental fairness terms, of the Mexican conviction, the determination made in this 2255 proceeding that the Mexican conviction cannot properly be relied on because it does not comport with fundamental fairness, would appear to require that the sentence imposed be reconsidered. . . .

Accordingly, I will direct that Mr. Moskovits' sentence will be vacated, and we will schedule a new sentencing date.

Notes

(1) Moskovits was resentenced to fifteen years' imprisonment. Subsequently, however, Judge Pollak ordered a new trial on the ground that the defendant also had been denied the effective assistance of counsel at his trial in the U.S. because counsel had not inquired into the validity of the Mexican conviction before advising the defendant that it was likely to be used for impeachment purposes if the defendant testified. *See United States v. Moskovits*, 844 F. Supp. 202 (E.D. Pa. 1993). Moskovits was retried before a different judge. On appeal, his conviction was affirmed, but a sentence to twenty years' imprisonment was vacated on the ground that it impermissibly exceeded the fifteen years imposed by Judge Pollak. *See United States v. Moskovits*, 86 F.3d 1303 (3d Cir. 1996), *cert. denied*, 519 U.S. 1120 (1997).

(2) Who bears the burden of proof as to the fairness of a foreign conviction? Does it depend on the purpose for which the conviction is to be used? Consider the following statement in *People v. Wallach*, 110 Mich. App. 37, 312 N.W.2d 387 (1981), where the Michigan Court of Appeals found it to be error, although harmless error, for the trial court to have ruled that the prosecution could use the defendant's prior Canadian convictions for purposes of impeachment:

> While no previous Michigan case has ruled on whether evidence of foreign convictions can be used for impeachment purposes, a similar problem was considered in *People v. Braithwaite*, 67 Mich. App. 121, 240 N.W.2d 293 (1976). In *Braithwaite*, this Court flatly held that evidence of a conviction under Canadian law would never be a permissible consideration in determining what sentence to impose. The prosecution contends that *Braithwaite* is distinguishable since it deals with sentencing. However, we are not prepared to say that it is more egregious to consider evidence of a foreign conviction for purposes of sentencing than it is to use the same conviction in the trial process. If anything, the latter is more offensive. To the extent that one is concerned about the fundamental fairness of the conviction rendered in the other country, it is certainly preferable to have evidence of that

conviction considered in sentencing as opposed to admitting it during the trial where it can affect the very integrity of any guilty verdict rendered.

We agree with the prosecution, however, that the blanket prohibition of *Braithwaite* should not be followed. The question in any given case should be whether the foreign legal system lacks procedural protections necessary for fundamental fairness. While few, if any, of the other legal systems in the world are as conscientiously dedicated to ensuring that the rights of the accused are as scrupulously honored as the various legal systems in the United States, many of these systems do provide substantial safeguards for the accused, making it inherently unlikely that innocent persons will be convicted of offenses which they did not commit. The problem of the use of evidence of foreign convictions involves a balancing of competing policy interests. On the one hand, we do not want to make use of evidence of convictions obtained in a system which is not fundamentally fair. On the other hand, we do not want miscreants to look upon Michigan as a sanctuary where their criminal activity in foreign countries can have no bearing on issues raised by new illegalities. If evidence of past convictions is relevant to impeach, as similar acts evidence, in sentencing, or otherwise, and the system in which they were rendered sufficiently safeguards the rights of the accused, there exists no compelling reason not to make use of evidence of these convictions, where appropriate.

The prosecution cites us to two federal cases which place the burden on the defendant of establishing that the foreign legal system lacks the procedural protections necessary to guarantee fundamental fairness for the accused. *United States v. Wilson*, 556 F. 2d 1177 (4th Cir.), *cert denied*, 434 U.S. 986 (1977), *United States v. Manafzadeh*, 592 F.2d 81 (2d Cir. 1979). We are urged to follow this same procedure. At this point our views depart from those of the prosecution. In Michigan, the prosecution must sustain the burden of proof on the issue of whether evidence of a prior conviction can be used for impeachment purposes. We see no reason to depart from this standard where admissibility of evidence of a prior conviction also hinges on the fundamental fairness of the foreign legal system. In the case sub judice, no showing was made by the prosecution that the specific legal system in which defendant was convicted is fundamentally fair. Therefore, it was error to allow the use of evidence of the Canadian convictions for impeachment purposes.

(3) Can a court rely on the evidence supporting a questionable foreign conviction without relying on the conviction itself? Consider *United States v. Delmarle*, 99 F.3d 80 (2d Cir. 1996), in which the defendant challenged his sentence for transmitting child pornography, in part on the ground that the district court erroneously had departed upward under the Federal Sentencing Guidelines by taking into account, as part of his criminal history, an *in absentia* Italian conviction for sexual misconduct with minors. In passing on this claim, Judge Kearse observed:

The Guidelines require the sentencing court to calculate a defendant's criminal history principally with reference to his prior sentences as categorized in Guidelines §§ 4A1.1 and 4A1.2. . . . Under Guidelines § 4A1.2(h), a sentence for a foreign conviction is not to be counted.

The Guidelines encourage the sentencing court, however, to consider departing from the criminal history category computed strictly pursuant to §§ 4A1.1 and 4A1.2 "if reliable information indicates that the criminal history category does not adequately reflect the seriousness of the defendant's past criminal conduct or the likelihood that the defendant will commit other crimes." Indeed, § 4A1.2(h) itself notes that a sentence resulting from a foreign conviction "may be considered under § 4A1.3". . . .

In the present case, Delmarle's criminal history category was calculated under §§ 4A1.1 and 4A1.2 without regard to . . . his conviction in Italy for sexual misconduct with three young boys. The resulting criminal history category was I, the lowest category. The district court departed upward by two criminal history category steps pursuant to § 4A1.3 on the ground that category I did not adequately reflect Delmarle's past criminal conduct or the likelihood that he would commit further crimes. Delmarle challenges the departure, contending that . . . the Italian conviction was not entered in accordance with due process. We see no. . . . error in the district court's treatment of the Italian conviction. When the sentencing judge has been apprised of possible constitutional infirmities surrounding a foreign conviction — or even is informed of a conviction that has been vacated for constitutional infirmity — he may nonetheless consider any reliable information concerning the conduct that led to that conviction in order, in an exercise of informed discretion, to determine whether the conduct warrants a departure.

In the present case, Delmarle maintains that the Italian conviction was obtained without due process, having been entered *in absentia* after Delmarle was expelled from Italy by order of the Italian court, and should have been disregarded for that reason. The district court did not rely on the fact of the Italian conviction, however. The events, which occurred while Delmarle was working in Italy as a civilian employee with the United States military, had been investigated by both an Italian agency and the United States Military Police. The court considered the investigative report of the United States Military Police, which was accompanied by extensive documentation. The court found that the investigative records showed that on several occasions, Delmarle had "used his own children as bait to encourage [neighbors'] children to be overnight guests at his home," and that "while they slept in their sleeping bags he molested them." The court found that the information in the report was "reliable and relevant." Delmarle did not point to any specific part of the report or the records that he contended was unreliable; he made only the most conclusory challenge to the reliability of

> "the information on which the [Italian] conviction was based," and argued without elaboration that the underlying evidence was "insufficient." His conclusory argument is insufficient to warrant questioning the district court's assessment that the information was reliable.

(4) How closely should a sentencing judge inquire into the fairness of foreign proceedings? Consider the district court's response to the defendant's challenge to use of a prior German conviction in *United States v. Makki*, 47 F. Supp. 2d 25 (D.D.C. 1999). In *Makki*, the defendant pleaded guilty to charges of possessing and using an altered U.S. passport. The government, on sentencing, requested the court to depart upward under the Federal Sentencing Guidelines and change the defendant's criminal history category from I to IV, in part on the basis of his 1989 German conviction for "attempting to participate in a felony causing an explosion." In ruling on this request, Judge Friedman stated:

> The defendant has no criminal convictions in the United States and therefore has zero criminal history points under the Guidelines. Under a traditional analysis, the defendant therefore would have a Criminal History of I. The government, however, requests that the Court depart from the otherwise applicable Guideline sentencing range to a Criminal History Category of IV pursuant to Section 4A1.3 of the Sentencing Guidelines. Section 4A1.3 allows the Court to depart upward "if reliable information indicates that the criminal history category does not adequately reflect the seriousness of the defendant's past criminal conduct or the likelihood that the defendant will commit other crimes." "Reliable information" includes, among other things, (1) "prior sentence[s] not used in computing the criminal history category (e.g., sentences for foreign or tribal offenses)," and (2) "prior similar adult criminal conduct not resulting in a criminal conviction." The government has the burden of justifying any upward departure by a preponderance of the evidence....
>
> Regarding the "seriousness of the defendant's past criminal conduct," the government asserts that an upward departure is justified because a Criminal History Category of I does not reflect (1) defendant's 1989 conviction in Germany, (2) defendant's false statements on his 1993 visa applications, and (3) defendant's other alleged terrorist activities.... The Court concludes that defendant's criminal conviction in Germany and the misrepresentations made in connection with his 1993 visa applications should be considered as reliable information justifying a departure under Section 4A1.3, but that his alleged membership in the Hizballah and his alleged terrorist activities should not.
>
> A foreign sentence is explicitly contemplated as a grounds for an upward departure under Section 4A1.3. The German Judgment provides a summary of the court proceedings and testimony which led to defendant's conviction for "attempting to participate in a felony of causing an explosion." Among the factual findings the German court made were that defendant

> was conspiring with others to conduct surveillance of American and Israeli sites in Germany in order to identify potential targets for terrorist bombing attacks and that defendant was personally involved in such surveillance. The German court also found that defendant had attempted to send a message to a person in Lebanon stating in code that he had located United States and Israeli targets in Germany and that he would carry out attacks on them if he was provided with weapons and dynamite. The German court rejected his defense that he acted under duress. While defendant argues that the Court should not give full credence to the fairness of criminal proceedings and judgments in all foreign countries, the Court has no reason to view German courts with any skepticism. Defendant was represented by counsel in the German proceedings, was confronted with the witnesses against him and was permitted to testify in his own behalf. The Court will consider defendant's German conviction.

§ 18.03 "Enforcement" of Foreign Law Without a Foreign Conviction?

Occasionally, the courts uphold convictions for violations of U.S. statutory provisions, one of the elements of which involves foreign penal or tax law.

An explicit reference to foreign law as an element of a federal crime was contained in the Lacey Act of 1900, 16 U.S.C. § 3372(a)(2)(A), which makes it an offense, *inter alia*, to deal in various ways in "any fish or wildlife taken, possessed, transported or sold in violation . . . of any foreign law." In *United States v. McNab*, 324 F.3d 1266 (11th Cir. 2003) (as amended May 29, 2003), the prosecution was premised on Honduran law (in the form of a "resolution") prohibiting the transportation of "spiny lobsters." There was considerable factual debate about the meaning and validity of the Honduran law, but the convictions stood.

Circuit Judge Fay dissented in the *McNab* decision, writing:

> Government officials testified on both sides of the issue before the district court. There was no one official voice for the government of Honduras. But, there is now. The Honduran courts have ruled and the Honduran Embassy has filed an *amicus* brief advising us of the Honduran government's position — *Resolution 030-95 is null and void and was so during the critical time charged in the second superceding [sic] indictment.* That is the *only* official government position I am aware of in this record.

McNab, 324 F.3d at 1247. The dissent argued that because the Honduran law did not find the defendant's conduct a violation of its laws, there was no violation of the Lacey Act.

The Lacey legislation was expanded to include illegal dealings in "plants" (defined to cover trees) in § 8204 of the Food, Conservation and Energy Act 2008. In a 2012 *cause célèbre,* the United States settled a case against the Gibson Guitar company over its use of illegal timber from Madagascar in its instruments. *See*, BBC News, *Gibson settles discord on timber, available at* http://www.bbc.com/news/science-environment-19153588. (Read the whole article for more bad puns!)

In some instances, the reference to foreign law is more implicit. Consider *Pasquantino v. United States,* 544 U.S. 349 (2005) [*see* § 3.02]. The conviction for wire fraud there relied, in part, on proof of Canadian tax laws. In *United States v. Lazarenko*, 564 F.3d 1026 (9th Cir. 2009), Lazarenko's convictions for conspiracy and money laundering required proof that his ill-gotten gains were the result of criminal extortion in Ukraine.

Chapter 19

International Human Rights and Criminal Procedure

§ 19.01 General Principles

The Second World War was the great catalyst for international concern with human rights. Before the war, how a state treated its own citizens generally was thought to be beyond the reach of international law. International law was the law governing relations between states. It did not protect individuals as such. After the war, the whole axis of international law began to shift, from an almost exclusive emphasis on states to concern with the rights and welfare of individuals. The Nuremberg Trial [*see* chap. 20] contributed to this shift in perceptions about the nature of international law. The imposition of criminal liability on individuals for breaches of international law confirmed that international law was no longer a body of rules concerned only with states; it dramatized the possibility of an international legal universe in which individual human beings as well as states figure as participants.

There were circumstances in which the law of the pre-war era did protect individuals indirectly. Under international law, as it developed in the nineteenth and early twentieth centuries, a state was bound to accord a certain minimum standard of justice to foreigners whom it had admitted to its territory — although compensation for failure to observe this standard belonged not to the injured individual but to the state of which that individual was a national. There was no guarantee that the home state would push for redress, or "espouse" a claim. Only strong states were in a position to do so. But, at least in principle, it was recognized that aliens were protected by an international standard of fair treatment. Such rules applied, however, only to foreigners. Governments generally were free to treat their own citizens as they liked. What a state did to its own citizens was its own business — a matter of "domestic jurisdiction" — and nothing about which other states were entitled to complain.

Again, there were exceptions. There were efforts through international action to accord certain protections against their own states to distinct classes of people: "humanitarian intervention" to protect religious minorities from atrocious persecution; nineteenth century treaties aimed at the abolition of the slave trade and slavery; the earlier Geneva Conventions affording protections to sick and wounded soldiers and prisoners of war; the early labor treaties, concluded toward the beginning of the twentieth century, on the rights of workers; the system developed under the League of Nations for protecting ethnic minorities in central Europe; and the

League system for examining the record of the colonial powers in certain "mandated territories" which were detached in the First World War from the German and Ottoman Empires. In the 1920s, the International Labor Organization, created alongside the League of Nations in the Treaty of Versailles, invented a supervisory model that was widely followed after 1945. It pioneered the careful examination by experts of reports by States Parties on how they gave effect to their international labor obligations in domestic law and practice. These exceptions, however, remained on the margin of traditional international law.

A revolutionary change occurred at the end of the Second World War. The crucial event was the founding of the United Nations in 1945. The Second World War had been a war to vindicate human rights (in a way that made it different from previous wars, except perhaps the U.S. Civil War — which was a catalyst for similarly significant changes in U.S. constitutional law). References to human rights recur in the U.N. Charter. Article 68 provided for the creation of the U.N. Commission on Human Rights — the only commission specifically named in the Charter. In 2006, the General Assembly replaced the Commission with a Human Rights Council composed of 47 States and responsible for strengthening the global promotion and protection of human rights. A particular feature of the Council's work is its Universal Periodic Review (UPR) under which all Member States have their human rights records reviewed on a regular basis.

It was understood that the first task of the Commission, once it came into being, would be to draft an international bill of rights. At the Commission's first session in February 1947, Eleanor Roosevelt was elected chair, and there was much discussion of the form the international bill should take. Several possibilities were considered: a resolution of the General Assembly, a multilateral treaty, an amendment to the U.N. Charter. A consensus emerged that the process should begin with a declaration of rights adopted by a resolution of the General Assembly. At its second session a year later, the Commission decided that the international bill of rights should have three components: first, a declaration of rights; second, a convention setting out the rights contained in the declaration in more precise language, together with specification of the limitations to which each right was subject; and, third, measures of implementation — machinery for enforcement to be contained in a document apart from the declaration and the convention. Later this scheme was revised again so as to incorporate measures of implementation in the convention, which was both to describe human rights in precise enforceable language and to establish machinery for enforcement. Ultimately, it was decided to have two separate conventions or "covenants": one on civil and political rights, the other on social, economic, and cultural rights, each with its own measures of implementation.

The first component of the international bill of rights, the Universal Declaration of Human Rights, was adopted by the General Assembly in Paris at 3 a.m. on the night of December 10, 1948, by a vote of 48 to 0 with 8 abstentions (the abstentions were from the Soviet bloc, Saudi Arabia and South Africa). The previous day the General Assembly had adopted the Genocide Convention [*see* chap. 23]. The

Universal Declaration of Human Rights contains thirty articles. Article 1 enunciates the basic principle of the Declaration: "All human beings are born free and equal in dignity and rights. They are endowed with reason and conscience and should act towards one another in a spirit of brotherhood." Article 2 sets out the principle of non-discrimination in the enjoyment of human rights. Articles 3–21 are devoted to civil and political rights such as the rights to life, liberty, and property, to freedom from torture or inhumane and degrading treatment, to freedom from arbitrary arrest, detention or exile, to a fair and public hearing by an independent and impartial tribunal, to freedom of thought and religion, to freedom of expression, to peaceful assembly and association, and to take part in the government of one's country. Articles 22–27 deal with economic and social rights: rights to social security, to work, to fair pay and fair conditions of work, to rest and leisure, to an adequate standard of living, to education, and to participate in the cultural life of the community. Articles 29–30 set out certain general limitations on the exercise of human rights requiring, for instance, that they be exercised with respect for the rights and freedoms of others.

In form, the Universal Declaration of Human Rights is simply a General Assembly resolution. Under the U.N. Charter, the General Assembly can only make recommendations. It has no power to make law or to impose binding obligations on states. Eleanor Roosevelt's closing speech in Paris emphasized that the Declaration was not a treaty and imposed no legal obligations, but was rather a statement of principles setting up (as its Preamble says) "a common standard of achievement for all peoples and all nations."

It was recognized at the time that, to be effective, international enforcement of human rights required acceptance of three further principles not stated in the Universal Declaration of Human Rights: (1) that states are under an obligation to respect the rights set out in the Declaration; (2) that observance of human rights being a matter of international obligation, it is within the province of the U.N. to respond to violations of human rights as violations of international law; and (3) that not only governments — which often are reluctant to do so — but also individuals should have a right to complain about human rights violations to the U.N. or to some other agency empowered to do something about them. Since 1948, these principles have been partly but not completely realized: practically every state in the world has voted for subsequent U.N. resolutions that speak of an obligation to observe the provisions of the Universal Declaration. These resolutions treat the Declaration as if it had acquired binding force, as if it were a law which nations are bound to obey. Thus, at least on paper, there appears to be general agreement that the Declaration, contrary to what was thought in 1948, actually does commit states to respect human rights.

The project that began with the Universal Declaration was completed with adoption of the two covenants on human rights — the International Covenant on Civil and Political Rights (ICCPR) and the International Covenant on Economic, Social and Cultural Rights (ICESCR) — in 1966. Both came into effect in 1976. The two covenants have legal force as treaties for the 170 or so states which are parties to them. The U.S. is party to the ICCPR but not the ICESCR.

The Covenant on Economic, Social and Cultural Rights requires states to submit periodic reports on measures adopted in order to comply with the covenant. The Covenant on Civil and Political Rights establishes a Human Rights Committee (not to be confused with the old Commission on Human Rights established under the U.N. Charter). Parties are required to submit reports every five years to this Committee. There also is an optional complaint procedure under which parties to the ICCPR may complain to the Committee about non-compliance by another party. In addition, an Optional Protocol to the Covenant permits aggrieved individuals to submit complaints to the Committee; after receiving a response from the state which has been charged with a violation, the Committee is to "forward its views to the State Party concerned and to the individual." No sanctions are provided for non-compliance with the Committee's expression of its view that the Covenant has been violated. Two-thirds of the parties to the Covenant are also parties to the Optional Protocol, but not the U.S.

In addition to the two covenants, numerous other human rights treaties have been adopted under the auspices of the United Nations. Each imposes obligations with respect to a particular subset of human rights. These additional human rights treaties include several of special importance: the 1965 International Convention on the Elimination of All Forms of Racial Discrimination, the 1979 Convention on the Elimination of All Forms of Discrimination Against Women, the 1984 Torture Convention [*see* chap. 10], the 1989 Convention on the Rights of the Child, the 1990 Convention on the Protection of the Rights of Migrant Workers and their Families and the 2006 Convention on the Rights of Persons with Disabilities. Like the Covenant on Civil and Political Rights, each of these conventions establishes a committee to monitor compliance. Although the International Covenant on Economic, Social and Cultural Rights contemplates that reports about compliance will be transmitted to the U.N. Economic and Social Council (ECOSOC), the Council itself, in 1985, established a special committee to supervise implementation of the Covenant. The committees created under all of these separate treaties are referred to as "treaty bodies" (as opposed to "Charter bodies" like the Human Rights Council and the former Commission on Human Rights, created pursuant to the U.N. Charter).

The Commission on Human Rights was gradually authorized to consider individual complaints when they reflect a consistent pattern of violations of human rights. For the first twenty years of its existence, the Commission was thought to be without any power at all to deal with the numerous complaints regarding human rights violations that, from the beginning, have flooded into the United Nations. Since 1967, several different procedures have evolved by which the organization may respond, at least in part, to such complaints. These include annual public debate focusing on countries in which gross violations of human rights are alleged to have occurred (a procedure that derives from ECOSOC Resolution 1235 (XLII), adopted in 1967); confidential investigation of individual communications that reveal "a consistent pattern of gross and reliably attested violations of human rights" (a procedure that derives from ECOSOC Resolution 1503 (XLVIII), adopted in 1970); and the appointment of "thematic" rapporteurs or working groups to consider violations relating to a specific theme such as torture, disappearances, arbitrary executions, arbitrary detention, violence against women and protection of human rights and fundamental freedoms while countering terrorism. These procedures, sometimes in enhanced form, have devolved from the Commission to the Human Rights Council since its creation in 2006.

Apart from human rights treaties and from declarations about the obligations of states, such as the General Assembly's 1975 Declaration on Torture relied on in the *Filartiga* case [chap. 1, *supra*], the United Nations has produced various standard-setting instruments that purport only to provide guidelines for international action and for national legislation. The U.N. "crime prevention and criminal justice program," for example, which works under the auspices of the United Nations Office of Drugs and Crime (UNODC) in Vienna, has generated a whole compendium of such "standards" in the field of criminal justice. *See* ROGER S. CLARK, THE UNITED NATIONS CRIME PREVENTION AND CRIMINAL JUSTICE PROGRAM: FORMULATION OF STANDARDS AND EFFORTS AT THEIR IMPLEMENTATION (1994). The 1955 U.N. Standard Minimum Rules for the Treatment of Prisoners (updated by the General Assembly in 2015 as "The Nelson Mandela Rules") and the 1985 Declaration of Basic Principles of Justice for Victims of Crime and Abuse of Power are, perhaps, the best known examples. Currently, much of the inspiration for UNODC's work comes from the General Assembly's Sustainable Development Goals (SDGs), adopted in 2015 with a target for achievement by 2030. Proclaimed as a "blueprint to achieve a better and more sustainable future for all," the SDGs include SDG 16 which aims to promote peaceful and inclusive societies for sustainable development, to provide access to justice for all and to build effective, accountable and inclusive institutions at all levels. Among the specific targets for 2030, pursuant to SDG 16, are to reduce corruption and bribery and to significantly reduce illicit financial and arms flows, strengthen the recovery and return of stolen assets and combat all forms of organized crime.

Structural support for the United Nations Human Rights System is provided through the office of the High Commissioner for Human Rights, located in Geneva. The eight officials who have held the position of High Commissioner since its creation in 1993 have developed it into a significant institution representing the conscience of humanity.

Besides the activities of the United Nations in the field of human rights, there are three regional arrangements for human rights protection.

In 1950, the Council of Europe adopted the European Convention on Human Rights. The Council of Europe (a much larger entity than the twenty-seven-member European Union) originally was founded to promote the unity of western European democracies; it now includes forty-seven member states from both Western and Eastern Europe. The European Convention on Human Rights is a comprehensive statement of fundamental rights implemented by the possibility of complaint to the European Court of Human Rights. In the original scheme of the Convention, complaints were screened first by a European Commission on Human Rights. Since 1998, they have gone directly to the Court. For a careful examination of the Convention, *see* WILLIAM A. SCHABAS, THE EUROPEAN CONVENTION ON HUMAN RIGHTS: A COMMENTARY (paperback 2017).

The Organization of American States has two overlapping mechanisms for enforcement of human rights. First, the Inter-American Commission on Human Rights, established in 1960, has competence to hear complaints regarding violations of the American Convention on Human Rights of 1969, which entered into force in 1978. It may decide to refer a complaint to the Inter-American Court of Human Rights if the state involved has accepted the Court's jurisdiction. Second, the Commission is competent to examine complaints regarding a violation of the American Declaration of the Rights and Duties of Man of 1948 by any OAS member, including states which are not parties to the American Convention on Human Rights. Thus, complaints against the United States, which is not a party to the Convention, have nonetheless been entertained by the Commission.

The African Commission of Human and Peoples' Rights was established under the African [Banjul] Charter on Human and Peoples' Rights, June 27, 1981, 21 I.L.M. 59 (1981), which entered into force in 1986.

§ 19.02 Specific Provisions

International Covenant on Civil and Political Rights

General Assembly Resolution 2200A (XXI), Dec. 19, 1966
21 U.N. GAOR Supp. No. 16, at 52, U.N. Doc. A/ 6316 (1966)

Part I

Article 1

1. All peoples have the right of self-determination. By virtue of that right they freely determine their political status and freely pursue their economic, social and cultural development.

2. All peoples may, for their own ends, freely dispose of their natural wealth and resources without prejudice to any obligations arising out of international economic co-operation, based upon the principle of mutual benefit, and international law. In no case may a people be deprived of its own means of subsistence.

3. The States Parties to the present Covenant, including those having responsibility for the administration of Non-Self-Governing and Trust Territories, shall promote the realization of the right of self-determination, and shall respect that right, in conformity with the provisions of the Charter of the United Nations.

Part II

Article 2

1. Each State Party to the present Covenant undertakes to respect and to ensure to all individuals within its territory and subject to its jurisdiction the rights recognized in the present Covenant, without distinction of any kind, such as race, colour, sex, language, religion, political or other opinion, national or social origin, property, birth or other status.

2. Where not already provided for by existing legislative or other measures, each State Party to the present Covenant undertakes to take the necessary steps, in accordance with its constitutional processes and with the provisions of the present Covenant, to adopt such legislative or other measures as may be necessary to give effect to the rights recognized in the present Covenant.

3. Each State Party to the present Covenant undertakes:

(a) To ensure that any person whose rights or freedoms as herein recognized are violated shall have an effective remedy, notwithstanding that the violation has been committed by persons acting in an official capacity;

(b) To ensure that any person claiming such a remedy shall have his right thereto determined by competent judicial, administrative or legislative authorities, or by any other competent authority provided for by the legal system of the State, and to develop the possibilities of judicial remedy;

(c) To ensure that the competent authorities shall enforce such remedies when granted.

Article 3

The States Parties to the present Covenant undertake to ensure the equal right of men and women to the enjoyment of all civil and political rights set forth in the present Covenant.

Article 4

1. In time of public emergency which threatens the life of the nation and the existence of which is officially proclaimed, the States Parties to the present Covenant may take measures derogating from their obligations under the present Covenant to the extent strictly required by the exigencies of the situation, provided that such measures are not inconsistent with their other obligations under international law and do not involve discrimination solely on the ground of race, colour, sex, language, religion or social origin.

2. No derogation from articles 6, 7, 8 (paragraphs 1 and 2), 11, 15, 16 and 18 may be made under this provision.

3. Any State Party to the present Covenant availing itself of the right of derogation shall immediately inform the other States Parties to the present Covenant, through the intermediary of the Secretary-General of the United Nations, of the provisions from which it has derogated and of the reasons by which it was actuated.

A further communication shall be made, through the same intermediary, on the date on which it terminates such derogation.

Article 5

1. Nothing in the present Covenant may be interpreted as implying for any State, group or person any right to engage in any activity or perform any act aimed at the destruction of any of the rights and freedoms recognized herein or at their limitation to a greater extent than is provided for in the present Covenant.

2. There shall be no restriction upon or derogation from any of the fundamental human rights recognized or existing in any State Party to the present Covenant pursuant to law, conventions, regulations or custom on the pretext that the present Covenant does not recognize such rights or that it recognizes them to a lesser extent.

Part III

Article 6

1. Every human being has the inherent right to life. This right shall be protected by law. No one shall be arbitrarily deprived of his life.

2. In countries which have not abolished the death penalty, sentence of death may be imposed only for the most serious crimes in accordance with the law in force at the time of the commission of the crime and not contrary to the provisions of the present Covenant and to the Convention on the Prevention and Punishment of the Crime of Genocide. This penalty can only be carried out pursuant to a final judgement rendered by a competent court.

3. When deprivation of life constitutes the crime of genocide, it is understood that nothing in this article shall authorize any State Party to the present Covenant to derogate in any way from any obligation assumed under the provisions of the Convention on the Prevention and Punishment of the Crime of Genocide.

4. Anyone sentenced to death shall have the right to seek pardon or commutation of the sentence. Amnesty, pardon or commutation of the sentence of death may be granted in all cases.

5. Sentence of death shall not be imposed for crimes committed by persons below eighteen years of age and shall not be carried out on pregnant women.

6. Nothing in this article shall be invoked to delay or to prevent the abolition of capital punishment by any State Party to the present Covenant.

Article 7

No one shall be subjected to torture or to cruel, inhuman or degrading treatment or punishment. In particular, no one shall be subjected without his free consent to medical or scientific experimentation.

Article 8

1. No one shall be held in slavery; slavery and the slave-trade in all their forms shall be prohibited.

2. No one shall be held in servitude.

3. (a) No one shall be required to perform forced or compulsory labour;

(b) Paragraph 3 (a) shall not be held to preclude, in countries where imprisonment with hard labour may be imposed as a punishment for a crime, the performance of hard labour in pursuance of a sentence to such punishment by a competent court;

(c) For the purpose of this paragraph the term "forced or compulsory labour" shall not include:

(i) Any work or service, not referred to in subparagraph (b), normally required of a person who is under detention in consequence of a lawful order of a court, or of a person during conditional release from such detention;

(ii) Any service of a military character and, in countries where conscientious objection is recognized, any national service required by law of conscientious objectors;

(iii) Any service exacted in cases of emergency or calamity threatening the life or well-being of the community;

(iv) Any work or service which forms part of normal civil obligations.

Article 9

1. Everyone has the right to liberty and security of person. No one shall be subjected to arbitrary arrest or detention. No one shall be deprived of his liberty except on such grounds and in accordance with such procedure as are established by law.

2. Anyone who is arrested shall be informed, at the time of arrest, of the reasons for his arrest and shall be promptly informed of any charges against him.

3. Anyone arrested or detained on a criminal charge shall be brought promptly before a judge or other officer authorized by law to exercise judicial power and shall be entitled to trial within a reasonable time or to release. It shall not be the general rule that persons awaiting trial shall be detained in custody, but release may be subject to guarantees to appear for trial, at any other stage of the judicial proceedings, and, should occasion arise, for execution of the judgement.

4. Anyone who is deprived of his liberty by arrest or detention shall be entitled to take proceedings before a court, in order that court may decide without delay on the lawfulness of his detention and order his release if the detention is not lawful.

5. Anyone who has been the victim of unlawful arrest or detention shall have an enforceable right to compensation.

Article 10

1. All persons deprived of their liberty shall be treated with humanity and with respect for the inherent dignity of the human person.

2. (a) Accused persons shall, save in exceptional circumstances, be segregated from convicted persons and shall be subject to separate treatment appropriate to their status as unconvicted persons;

(b) Accused juvenile persons shall be separated from adults and brought as speedily as possible for adjudication.

3. The penitentiary system shall comprise treatment of prisoners the essential aim of which shall be their reformation and social rehabilitation. Juvenile offenders shall be segregated from adults and be accorded treatment appropriate to their age and legal status.

Article 11

No one shall be imprisoned merely on the ground of inability to fulfil a contractual obligation.

Article 12

1. Everyone lawfully within the territory of a State shall, within that territory, have the right to liberty of movement and freedom to choose his residence.

2. Everyone shall be free to leave any country, including his own.

3. The above-mentioned rights shall not be subject to any restrictions except those which are provided by law, are necessary to protect national security, public order (*ordre public*), public health or morals or the rights and freedoms of others, and are consistent with the other rights recognized in the present Covenant.

4. No one shall be arbitrarily deprived of the right to enter his own country.

Article 13

An alien lawfully in the territory of a State Party to the present Covenant may be expelled therefrom only in pursuance of a decision reached in accordance with law and shall, except where compelling reasons of national security otherwise require, be allowed to submit the reasons against his expulsion and to have his case reviewed by, and be represented for the purpose before, the competent authority or a person or persons especially designated by the competent authority.

Article 14

1. All persons shall be equal before the courts and tribunals. In the determination of any criminal charge against him, or of his rights and obligations in a suit at law, everyone shall be entitled to a fair and public hearing by a competent, independent and impartial tribunal established by law. The press and the public may be excluded from all or part of a trial for reasons of morals, public order (*ordre public*) or national security in a democratic society, or when the interest of the private lives of the parties so requires, or to the extent strictly necessary in the opinion of the court in special circumstances where publicity would prejudice the interests of justice; but any judgement rendered in a criminal case or in a suit at law shall be made public except where the interest of juvenile persons otherwise requires or the proceedings concern matrimonial disputes or the guardianship of children.

2. Everyone charged with a criminal offence shall have the right to be presumed innocent until proved guilty according to law.

3. In the determination of any criminal charge against him, everyone shall be entitled to the following minimum guarantees, in full equality:

(a) To be informed promptly and in detail in a language which he understands of the nature and cause of the charge against him;

(b) To have adequate time and facilities for the preparation of his defence and to communicate with counsel of his own choosing;

(c) To be tried without undue delay;

(d) To be tried in his presence, and to defend himself in person or through legal assistance of his own choosing; to be informed, if he does not have legal assistance, of this right; and to have legal assistance assigned to him, in any case where the interests of justice so require, and without payment by him in any such case if he does not have sufficient means to pay for it;

(e) To examine, or have examined, the witnesses against him and to obtain the attendance and examination of witnesses on his behalf under the same conditions as witnesses against him;

(f) To have the free assistance of an interpreter if he cannot understand or speak the language used in court;

(g) Not to be compelled to testify against himself or to confess guilt.

4. In the case of juvenile persons, the procedure shall be such as will take account of their age and the desirability of promoting their rehabilitation.

5. Everyone convicted of a crime shall have the right to his conviction and sentence being reviewed by a higher tribunal according to law.

6. When a person has by a final decision been convicted of a criminal offence and when subsequently his conviction has been reversed or he has been pardoned on the ground that a new or newly discovered fact shows conclusively that there has been a miscarriage of justice, the person who has suffered punishment as a result of such conviction shall be compensated according to law, unless it is proved that the non-disclosure of the unknown fact in time is wholly or partly attributable to him.

7. No one shall be liable to be tried or punished again for an offence for which he has already been finally convicted or acquitted in accordance with the law and penal procedure of each country.

Article 15

1. No one shall be held guilty of any criminal offence on account of any act or omission which did not constitute a criminal offence, under national or international law, at the time when it was committed. Nor shall a heavier penalty be imposed than the one that was applicable at the time when the criminal offence was

committed. If, subsequent to the commission of the offence, provision is made by law for the imposition of the lighter penalty, the offender shall benefit thereby.

2. Nothing in this article shall prejudice the trial and punishment of any person for any act or omission which, at the time when it was committed, was criminal according to the general principles of law recognized by the community of nations.

Article 16

Everyone shall have the right to recognition everywhere as a person before the law.

Article 17

1. No one shall be subjected to arbitrary or unlawful interference with his privacy, family, home or correspondence, nor to unlawful attacks on his honour and reputation.

2. Everyone has the right to the protection of the law against such interference or attacks.

Article 18

1. Everyone shall have the right to freedom of thought, conscience and religion. This right shall include freedom to have or to adopt a religion or belief of his choice, and freedom, either individually or in community with others and in public or private, to manifest his religion or belief in worship, observance, practice and teaching.

2. No one shall be subject to coercion which would impair his freedom to have or to adopt a religion or belief of his choice.

3. Freedom to manifest one's religion or beliefs may be subject only to such limitations as are prescribed by law and are necessary to protect public safety, order, health, or morals or the fundamental rights and freedoms of others.

4. The States Parties to the present Covenant undertake to have respect for the liberty of parents and, when applicable, legal guardians to ensure the religious and moral education of their children in conformity with their own convictions.

Article 19

1. Everyone shall have the right to hold opinions without interference.

2. Everyone shall have the right to freedom of expression; this right shall include freedom to seek, receive and impart information and ideas of all kinds, regardless of frontiers, either orally, in writing or in print, in the form of art, or through any other media of his choice.

3. The exercise of the rights provided for in paragraph 2 of this article carries with it special duties and responsibilities. It may therefore be subject to certain restrictions, but these shall only be such as are provided by law and are necessary:

(a) For respect of the rights or reputations of others;

(b) For the protection of national security or of public order (*ordre public*), or of public health or morals.

Article 20

1. Any propaganda for war shall be prohibited by law.

2. Any advocacy of national, racial or religious hatred that constitutes incitement to discrimination, hostility or violence shall be prohibited by law.

Article 21

The right of peaceful assembly shall be recognized. No restrictions may be placed on the exercise of this right other than those imposed in conformity with the law and which are necessary in a democratic society in the interests of national security or public safety, public order *(ordre public)*, the protection of public health or morals or the protection of the rights and freedoms of others.

Article 22

1. Everyone shall have the right to freedom of association with others, including the right to form and join trade unions for the protection of his interests.

2. No restrictions may be placed on the exercise of this right other than those which are prescribed by law and which are necessary in a democratic society in the interests of national security or public safety, public order (*ordre public*), the protection of public health or morals or the protection of the rights and freedoms of others. This article shall not prevent the imposition of lawful restrictions on members of the armed forces and of the police in their exercise of this right.

3. Nothing in this article shall authorize States Parties to the International Labour Organisation Convention of 1948 concerning Freedom of Association and Protection of the Right to Organize to take legislative measures which would prejudice, or to apply the law in such a manner as to prejudice, the guarantees provided for in that Convention.

Article 23

1. The family is the natural and fundamental group unit of society and is entitled to protection by society and the State.

2. The right of men and women of marriageable age to marry and to found a family shall be recognized.

3. No marriage shall be entered into without the free and full consent of the intending spouses.

4. States Parties to the present Covenant shall take appropriate steps to ensure equality of rights and responsibilities of spouses as to marriage, during marriage and at its dissolution. In the case of dissolution, provision shall be made for the necessary protection of any children.

Article 24

1. Every child shall have, without any discrimination as to race, colour, sex, language, religion, national or social origin, property or birth, the right to such

measures of protection as are required by his status as a minor, on the part of his family, society and the State.

2. Every child shall be registered immediately after birth and shall have a name.

3. Every child has the right to acquire a nationality.

Article 25

Every citizen shall have the right and the opportunity, without any of the distinctions mentioned in article 2 and without unreasonable restrictions:

(a) To take part in the conduct of public affairs, directly or through freely chosen representatives;

(b) To vote and to be elected at genuine periodic elections which shall be by universal and equal suffrage and shall be held by secret ballot, guaranteeing the free expression of the will of the electors;

(c) To have access, on general terms of equality, to public service in his country.

Article 26

All persons are equal before the law and are entitled without any discrimination to the equal protection of the law. In this respect, the law shall prohibit any discrimination and guarantee to all persons equal and effective protection against discrimination on any ground such as race, colour, sex, language, religion, political or other opinion, national or social origin, property, birth or other status.

Article 27

In those States in which ethnic, religious or linguistic minorities exist, persons belonging to such minorities shall not be denied the right, in community with the other members of their group, to enjoy their own culture, to profess and practise their own religion, or to use their own language.

Notes

(1) Part IV of the Covenant (comprising Articles 28–45) establishes the Human Rights Committee. Part V comprises two articles (Articles 46–47) which provide that nothing in the Covenant shall impair either existing powers of U.N. agencies with respect to human rights violations or "the inherent right of all peoples to enjoy and utilize fully and freely their natural wealth and resources." Part VI (comprising Articles 48–53) contains the final clauses dealing with signature, ratification, entry into force, amendment, etc. The Covenant came into force on March 23, 1976.

(2) What are the differences between the procedural guarantees for a criminal defendant contained in the International Covenant on Civil and Political Rights and those contained in the U.S. Bill of Rights and made applicable to the states through the Fourteenth Amendment? Which set of guarantees appears to afford stronger protection to the defendant? To what extent do the differences stem from the fact that, as an instrument meant to apply internationally, the Covenant has to allow for

differences in criminal procedure as between common law and in civil law countries? To what extent are international human rights instruments like the Covenant apt to contribute to a convergence of systems of criminal procedure in countries belonging to these two traditions? For an account of the convergence in criminal procedure in Europe that has come about as a result of the European Convention on Human Rights, *see* Bert Swart & James Young, *The European Convention on Human Rights and Criminal Justice in the Netherlands and the United Kingdom*, *in* Criminal Justice in Europe: A Comparative Study 57 (Christopher Harding, et al., eds., 1995). For particularly useful efforts at synthesis of the criminal procedure material, *see* Amnesty International, Fair Trials Manual (2d ed. 2014); Nigel S. Rodley & Matt Pollard, The Treatment of Prisoners Under International Law (3d ed. 2009); Amal Clooney & Phiilippa Webb, The Right to a Fair Trial In International Law (2020).

(3) The United States became a party to the International Covenant on Civil and Political Rights belatedly in 1992 (though not to the Covenant on Economic, Social and Cultural Rights). Ratification of the ICCPR was subject to five reservations, five understandings, and three declarations. The extent to which the United States qualified its obligations under the Covenant has prompted questions about whether the United States really is a party at all. *See, e.g.*, William A. Schabas, *Invalid Reservations to the ICCPR: Is the United States Still a Party?*, 21 Brooklyn J. Int'l L. 277 (1995). For a more favorable view, *see* David P. Stewart, *United States Ratification of the Covenant on Civil and Political Rights: The Significance of the Reservations, Understandings and Declarations*, 42 DePaul L. Rev. 1183 (1993). Several states objected to some of the reservations as being "incompatible with the object and purpose" of the treaty (echoing the language of the Vienna Convention on the Law of Treaties). The reservations have also come in for considerable criticism when the Human Rights Committee has examined the U.S. reports under the Covenant. The U.S. reservations, understandings, and declarations read as follows:

> Reservations:
>
> (1) That article 20 does not authorize or require legislation or other action by the United States that would restrict the right of free speech and association protected by the Constitution and laws of the United States.
>
> (2) That the United States reserves the right, subject to its Constitutional constraints, to impose capital punishment on any person (other than a pregnant woman) duly convicted under existing or future laws permitting the imposition of capital punishment, including such punishment for crimes committed by persons below eighteen years of age.
>
> (3) That the United States considers itself bound by article 7 to the extent that "cruel, inhuman or degrading treatment or punishment" means the cruel and unusual treatment or punishment prohibited by the Fifth, Eighth, and-or Fourteenth Amendments to the Constitution of the United States.

(4) That because U.S. law generally applies to an offender the penalty in force at the time the offence was committed, the United States does not adhere to the third clause of paragraph 1 of article 15.

(5) That the policy and practice of the United States are generally in compliance with and supportive of the Covenant's provisions regarding treatment of juveniles in the criminal justice system. Nevertheless, the United States reserves the right, in exceptional circumstances, to treat juveniles as adults, notwithstanding paragraphs 2 (b) and 3 of article 10 and paragraph 4 of article 14. The United States further reserves to these provisions with respect to States with respect to individuals who volunteer for military service prior to age 18.

Understandings:

(1) That the Constitution and laws of the United States guarantee all persons equal protection of the law and provide extensive protections against discrimination. The United States understands distinctions based upon race, color, sex, language, religion, political or other opinion, national or social origin, property, birth or any other status — as those terms are used in article 2, paragraph 1 and article 26 — to be permitted when such distinctions are, at minimum, rationally related to a legitimate governmental objective. The United States further understands the prohibition in paragraph 1 of article 4 upon discrimination, in time of public emergency, based "solely" on the status of race, color, sex, language, religion or social origin, not to bar distinctions that may have a disproportionate effect upon persons of a particular status.

(2) That the United States understands the right to compensation referred to in articles 9 (5) and 14 (6) to require the provision of effective and enforceable mechanisms by which a victim of an unlawful arrest or detention or a miscarriage of justice may seek and, where justified, obtain compensation from either the responsible individual or the appropriate governmental entity. Entitlement to compensation may be subject to the reasonable requirements of domestic law.

(3) That the United States understands the reference to "exceptional circumstances" in paragraph 2 (a) of article 10 to permit the imprisonment of an accused person with convicted persons where appropriate in light of an individual's overall dangerousness, and to permit accused persons to waive their right to segregation from convicted persons. The United States further understands that paragraph 3 of article 10 does not diminish the goals of punishment, deterrence, and incapacitation as additional legitimate purposes for a penitentiary system.

(4) That the United States understands that subparagraphs 3 (b) and (d) of article 14 do not require the provision of a criminal defendant's counsel of choice when the defendant is provided with court-appointed counsel on

grounds of indigence, when the defendant is financially able to retain alternative counsel, or when imprisonment is not imposed. The United States further understands that paragraph 3 (e) does not prohibit a requirement that the defendant make a showing that any witness whose attendance he seeks to compel is necessary for his defense. The United States understands the prohibition upon double jeopardy in paragraph 7 to apply only when the judgment of acquittal has been rendered by a court of the same governmental unit, whether the Federal Government or a constituent unit, as is seeking a new trial for the same cause.

(5) That the United States understands that this Covenant shall be implemented by the Federal Government to the extent that it exercises legislative and judicial jurisdiction over the matters covered therein, and otherwise by the state and local governments; to the extent that state and local governments exercise jurisdiction over such matters, the Federal Government shall take measures appropriate to the Federal system to the end that the competent authorities of the state or local governments may take appropriate measures for the fulfillment of the Covenant.

Declarations:

(1) That the United States declares that the provisions of articles 1 through 27 of the Covenant are not self-executing.

(2) That it is the view of the United States that States Party to the Covenant should wherever possible refrain from imposing any restrictions or limitations on the exercise of the rights recognized and protected by the Covenant, even when such restrictions and limitations are permissible under the terms of the Covenant. For the United States, article 5, paragraph 2, which provides that fundamental human rights existing in any State Party may not be diminished on the pretext that the Covenant recognizes them to a lesser extent, has particular relevance to article 19, paragraph 3 which would permit certain restrictions on the freedom of expression. The United States declares that it will continue to adhere to the requirements and constraints of its Constitution in respect to all such restrictions and limitations.

(3) That the United States declares that the right referred to in article 47 ["the inherent right of all peoples to enjoy and utilize fully and freely their natural wealth and resources"] may be exercised only in accordance with international law.

(4) Comparable statements accompany the United States ratification of the 1965 Convention on the Elimination of Racial Discrimination and the 1984 Convention against Torture and Other Cruel, Inhuman or Degrading Treatment or Punishment (both ratified in 1994).

(5) The "not self-executing" declarations mean that it is not possible to rely directly on Covenant provisions in the U.S. courts. International lawyers being

optimists, many of them argue that, nevertheless, the rights in the Covenant may be relied upon to inform interpretation of relevant constitutional, statutory and common law principles, both state and federal. They may also reflect international customary law.

(6) Understanding (5) made at the time of ratification of the Covenant on Civil and Political Rights is some kind of federalism statement. There may be situations in which it could function as a reservation,[1] namely where the U.S. asserts that it is not able to implement a particular obligation in full, either because the Constitution leaves that in the hands of the States, or because the federal authorities have chosen to leave it in the hands of the States. There is some uncertainty how such an approach is to be squared with The Birds Case, *Missouri v. Holland*, 252 U.S. 416 (1920). Justice Holmes's opinion in that case affords the federal legislature sweeping authority under the "treaty" and "necessary and proper" powers to legislate in areas that might otherwise be reserved to the states. There is a pattern of such statements made by the U.S. in ratifying human rights treaties in the past decades and also some examples in international criminal law treaties. These statements have, for the most part, been offered (preemptively?) by the Executive in sending treaties to the Senate for advice and consent. They may represent a trend towards some new kind of federal constraint. For an excellent discussion, *see* Duncan B. Hollis, *Executive Federalism: Forging New Federalist Constraints on the Treaty Power*, 79 S. CAL. L. REV. 1327 (2006).

(7) In its concluding observations on the fourth periodic report of the United States, U.N. Doc. CCPR/C/USA/CO/4, of 23 April 2014, the Human Rights Committee commented, inter alia, on the U.S. position that the Covenant does not apply to individuals under its jurisdiction but outside its territory, racial disparities in the criminal justice system, racial profiling, the death penalty, targeted killings using drones, gun violence, torture, trafficking and forced labor, detention of immigrants, Guantanamo Bay, NSA surveillance and rights of indigenous peoples. On the positive side, it remarked:

> 3. The Committee notes with appreciation the many efforts undertaken by the State party and the progress made in protecting civil and political rights. The Committee welcomes in particular the following legislative and institutional steps taken by the State party:
>
> (a) Full implementation of article 6, paragraph 5, of the Covenant in the aftermath of the Supreme Court's judgment in *Roper v. Simmons*, 543 U.S. 551 (2005) [on non-execution of juveniles], despite the State party's reservation to the contrary;

1. Article 2 (1) (d) of the 1969 Vienna Convention on the Law of Treaties defines a reservation as "a unilateral statement, however phrased or named, made by a State, when signing, ratifying, accepting, approving or acceding to a treaty, whereby it purports to exclude or to modify the legal effect of certain provisions of the treaty in their application to that State."

(b) Recognition by the Supreme Court in *Boumediene v. Bush*, 553 U.S. 723 (2008) of the extraterritorial application of constitutional habeas corpus rights to aliens detained at Guantánamo Bay;

(c) Presidential Executive Orders 13491—Ensuring Lawful Interrogations, 13492—Review and Disposition of Individuals Detained at the Guantánamo Bay Naval Base and Closure of Detention Facilities and 13493—Review of Detention Policy Options, issued on 22 January 2009;

(d) Support for the United Nations Declaration on the Rights of Indigenous Peoples, announced by President Obama on 16 December 2010;

(e) Presidential Executive Order 13567 establishing a periodic review of detainees at the Guantánamo Bay detention facility who have not been charged, convicted or designated for transfer, issued on 7 March 2011.

In April 2019, the Committee issued a "List of issues prior to submission of the fifth periodic report of the United States of America." U.N. Doc. CCR/C/USA/QPR/5 (2019). Many of the questions follow up the matters discussed in relation to the fourth report. The approach (or issue) of a required report is an occasion for commentary and alternative reports from civil society. Several such reports have already appeared from U.S. NGOs. Alas, as this edition goes to print, the governmental report, due in 2020, has not yet emerged.

§ 19.03 The Death Penalty

Soering v. United Kingdom

European Court of Human Rights
161 Eur. Ct. H. R. (ser. A) (1989)

As to the Facts

I. Particular circumstances of the case

11. The applicant, Mr Jens Soering, was born on 1 August 1966 and is a German national. He is currently detained in prison in England pending extradition to the United States of America to face charges of murder in the Commonwealth of Virginia.

12. The homicides in question were committed in Bedford County, Virginia, in March 1985. The victims, William Reginald Haysom (aged 72) and Nancy Astor Haysom (aged 53), were the parents of the applicant's girlfriend, Elizabeth Haysom, who is a Canadian national. Death in each case was the result of multiple and massive stab and slash wounds to the neck, throat and body. At the time the applicant and Elizabeth Haysom, aged 18 and 20 respectively, were students at the University of Virginia. They disappeared together from Virginia in October 1985, but were arrested in England in April 1986 in connection with cheque fraud.

13. The applicant was interviewed in England between 5 and 8 June 1986 by a police investigator from the Sheriff's Department of Bedford County.... [T]he investigator recorded the applicant as having admitted the killings.... The applicant had stated that he was in love with Miss Haysom but that her parents were opposed to the relationship. He and Miss Haysom had therefore planned to kill them. They rented a car in Charlottesville and travelled to Washington where they set up an alibi. The applicant then went to the parents' house, discussed the relationship with them and, when they told him that they would do anything to prevent it, a row developed during which he killed them with a knife. On 13 June 1986 a grand jury of the Circuit Court of Bedford County indicted him on charges of murdering the Haysom parents. The charges alleged capital murder of both of them and the separate non-capital murders of each.

14. On 11 August 1986 the Government of the United States of America requested the applicant's and Miss Haysom's extradition under the terms of the Extradition Treaty of 1972 between the United States and the United Kingdom....

15. On 29 October 1986 the British Embassy in Washington addressed a request to the United States authorities in the following terms:

> Because the death penalty has been abolished in Great Britain, the Embassy has been instructed to seek an assurance, in accordance with the terms of... the Extradition Treaty, that, in the event of Mr Soering being surrendered and being convicted of the crimes for which he has been indicted..., the death penalty, if imposed, will not be carried out.
>
> Should it not be possible on constitutional grounds for the United States Government to give such an assurance, the United Kingdom authorities ask that the United States Government undertake to recommend to the appropriate authorities that the death penalty should not be imposed or, if imposed, should not be executed.

16. On 30 December 1986 the applicant was interviewed in prison by a German prosecutor (*Staatsanwalt*) from Bonn.... On 11 February 1987 the local court in Bonn issued a warrant for the applicant's arrest in respect of the alleged murders. On 11 March the Government of the Federal Republic of Germany requested his extradition to the Federal Republic under the Extradition Treaty of 1872 between the Federal Republic and the United Kingdom....

18. On 8 May 1987 Elizabeth Haysom was surrendered for extradition to the United States. After pleading guilty on 22 August as an accessory to the murder of her parents, she was sentenced on 6 October to 90 years' imprisonment (45 years on each count of murder).

19. On 20 May 1987 the United Kingdom Government informed the Federal Republic of Germany that the United States had earlier "submitted a request, supported by prima facie evidence, for the extradition of Mr Soering." The United Kingdom Government notified the Federal Republic that they had "concluded that, having regard to all the circumstances of the case, the court should continue to

consider in the normal way the United States request." They further indicated that they had sought an assurance from the United States authorities on the question of the death penalty and that "in the event that the court commits Mr Soering, his surrender to the United States authorities would be subject to the receipt of satisfactory assurances on this matter."

20. On 1 June 1987 Mr Updike swore an affidavit in his capacity as Attorney for Bedford County, in which he certified as follows:

> I hereby certify that should Jens Soering be convicted of the offence of capital murder as charged in Bedford County, Virginia . . . a representation will be made in the name of the United Kingdom to the judge at the time of sentencing that it is the wish of the United Kingdom that the death penalty should not be imposed or carried out.

This assurance was transmitted to the United Kingdom Government under cover of a diplomatic note on 8 June. It was repeated in the same terms in a further affidavit from Mr Updike sworn on 16 February 1988 and forwarded to the United Kingdom by diplomatic note on 17 May 1988. In the same note the Federal Government of the United States undertook to ensure that the commitment of the appropriate authorities of the Commonwealth of Virginia to make representations on behalf of the United Kingdom would be honoured.

During the course of the present proceedings the Virginia authorities informed the United Kingdom Government that Mr Updike was not planning to provide any further assurances and intended to seek the death penalty in Mr Soering's case because the evidence, in his determination, supported such action.

21. On 16 June 1987 at the Bow Street Magistrates' Court committal proceedings took place before the Chief Stipendiary Magistrate. The Government of the United States adduced evidence that on the night of 30 March 1985 the applicant killed William and Nancy Haysom at their home in Bedford County, Virginia. In particular, evidence was given of the applicant's own admissions as recorded in the affidavit of the Bedford County police investigator.

On behalf of the applicant psychiatric evidence was adduced from a consultant forensic psychiatrist . . . that he was immature and inexperienced and had lost his personal identity in a symbiotic relationship with his girlfriend—a powerful, persuasive and disturbed young woman. . . . The Chief Magistrate found that the evidence . . . was not relevant to any issue that he had to decide and committed the applicant to await the Secretary of State's order for his return to the United States. . . .

24. . . . . [O]n 3 August 1988 the Secretary of State signed a warrant ordering the applicant's surrender to the United States authorities. However, the applicant has not been transferred to the United States by virtue of the interim measures indicated in the present proceedings firstly by the European Commission and then by the European Court.

25. On 5 August 1988 the applicant was transferred to a prison hospital where he remained until early November 1988 under the special regime applied to suicide-risk

prisoners. According to psychiatric evidence adduced on behalf of the applicant . . . the applicant's dread of extreme physical violence and homosexual abuse from other inmates in death row in Virginia is in particular having a profound psychological effect on him. The psychiatrist's report records a mounting desperation in the applicant, together with objective fears that he may seek to take his own life. . . .

II. Relevant domestic law and practice in the United Kingdom

36. There is no provision in the Extradition Acts relating to the death penalty, but Article IV of the United Kingdom-United States Treaty provides:

> If the offence for which extradition is requested is punishable by death under the relevant law of the requesting Party, but the relevant law of the requested Party does not provide for the death penalty in a similar case, extradition may be refused unless the requesting Party gives assurances satisfactory to the requested Party that the death penalty will not be carried out.

37. In the case of a fugitive requested by the United States who faces a charge carrying the death penalty, it is the Secretary of State's practice, pursuant to Article IV of the United Kingdom-United States Extradition Treaty, to accept an assurance from the prosecuting authorities of the relevant State that a representation will be made to the judge at the time of sentencing that it is the wish of the United Kingdom that the death penalty should be neither imposed no carried out. This practice has been described by Mr David Mellor, then Minister of State at the Home Office, in the following terms:

> The written undertakings about the death penalty that the Secretary of State obtains from the Federal authorities amount to an undertaking that the views of the United Kingdom will be represented to the judge. At the time of sentencing he will be informed that the United Kingdom does not wish the death penalty to be imposed or carried out. That means that the United Kingdom authorities render up a fugitive or are prepared to send a citizen to face an American court on the clear understanding that the death penalty will not be carried out—it has never been carried out in such cases. It would be a fundamental blow to the extradition arrangements between our two countries if the death penalty were carried out on an individual who had been returned under those circumstances. (Hansard, 10 March 1987, col. 955)

There has, however, never been a case in which the effectiveness of such an undertaking has been tested. . . .

III. Relevant domestic law in the Commonwealth of Virginia

42. The sentencing procedure in a capital murder case in Virginia is a separate proceeding from the determination of guilt. Following a determination of guilt of capital murder, the same jury, or judge sitting without a jury, will forthwith proceed to hear evidence regarding punishment. All relevant evidence concerning the offence and the defendant is admissible. Evidence in mitigation is subject to almost no limitation, while evidence of aggravation is restricted by statute. . . .

44. The imposition of the death penalty on a young person who has reached the age of majority—which is 18 years—is not precluded under Virginia law. Age is a fact to be weighed by the jury. . . .

48. Following a moratorium consequent upon a decision of the United States Supreme Court (*Furman v. Georgia*, 92 S. Ct. 2726 (1972)), imposition of the death penalty was resumed in Virginia in 1977, since which date seven persons have been executed. The means of execution used is electrocution.

The Virginia death penalty statutory scheme . . . has been judicially determined to be constitutional. It was considered to prevent the arbitrary or capricious imposition of the death penalty and narrowly to channel the sentencer's discretion. . . . The death penalty under the Virginia capital murder statute has also been held not to constitute cruel and unusual punishment or to deny a defendant due process or equal protection. . . . The Supreme Court of Virginia rejected the submission that death by electrocution would cause "the needless imposition of pain before death and emotional suffering while awaiting execution of sentence." . . .

56. The average time between trial and execution in Virginia, calculated on the basis of the seven executions which have taken place since 1977, is six to eight years. The delays are primarily due to a strategy by convicted prisoners to prolong the appeal proceedings as much as possible. The United States Supreme Court has not as yet considered or ruled on the "death row phenomenon" and in particular whether it falls foul of the prohibition of "cruel and unusual punishment" under the Eighth Amendment to the Constitution of the United States. . . .

61. There are currently 40 people under sentence of death in Virginia. The majority are detained in Mecklenburg Correctional Center, which is a modern maximum-security institution with a total capacity of 335 inmates. . . .

63. The size of a death row inmate's cell is 3m by 2.2m. Prisoners have an opportunity for approximately 7 hours' recreation per week in summer and approximately 6 hours' per week, weather permitting, in winter. The death row area has two recreation yards, both of which are equipped with basketball courts and one of which is equipped with weights and weight benches. Inmates are also permitted to leave their cells on other occasions, such as to receive visits, to visit the law library or to attend the prison infirmary. In addition, death row inmates are given one hour out-of-cell time in the morning in a common area. Each death row inmate is eligible for work assignments, such as cleaning duties. When prisoners move around the prison they are handcuffed, with special shackles around the waist.

When not in their cells, death row inmates are housed in a common area called "the pod." The guards are not within this area and remain in a box outside. In the event of disturbance or inter-inmate assault, the guards are not allowed to intervene until instructed to do so by the ranking officer present.

64. The applicant adduced much evidence of extreme stress, psychological deterioration and risk of homosexual abuse and physical attack undergone by prisoners on

death row, including Mecklenburg Correctional Center. This evidence was strongly contested by the United Kingdom Government on the basis of affidavits sworn by administrators from the Virginia Department of Corrections. . . .

68. A death row prisoner is moved to the death house 15 days before he is due to be executed. The death house is next to the death chamber where the electric chair is situated. Whilst a prisoner is in the death house he is watched 24 hours a day. He is isolated and has no light in his cell. The lights outside are permanently lit. A prisoner who utilises the appeals process can be placed in the death house several times.

69. Relations between the United Kingdom and the United States of America on matters concerning extradition are conducted by and with the Federal and not the State authorities. However, in respect of offences against State laws the Federal authorities have no legally binding power to provide, in an appropriate extradition case, an assurance that the death penalty will not be imposed or carried out. In such cases the power rests with the State. If a State does decide to give a promise in relation to the death penalty, the United States Government has the power to give an assurance to the extraditing Government that the State's promise will be honoured.

According to evidence from the Virginia authorities, Virginia's capital sentencing procedure and notably the provision on post-sentencing reports would allow the sentencing judge to consider the representation to be made on behalf of the United Kingdom Government pursuant to the assurance given by the Attorney for Bedford County. In addition, it would be open to the Governor to take into account the wishes of the United Kingdom Government in any application for clemency. . . .

IV. Relevant law and practice of the Federal Republic of Germany

71. German criminal law applies to acts committed abroad by a German national if the act is liable to punishment at the place where the offence is committed.

72. Murder is. . . . punishable with life imprisonment, the death penalty having been abolished under the Constitution (Article 102 of the Basic Law, 1949).

73. Under the terms of the Juvenile Court Act (1953) as amended, if a young adult — defined as a person who is 18 but not yet 21 years of age at the time of the criminal act — commits an offence, the judge will apply the provisions applicable to a juvenile — defined as a person who is at least 14 but not yet 18 years of age — if, inter alia, "the overall assessment of the offender's personality, having regard also to the circumstances of his environment, reveals that, according to his moral and mental development, he was still equal to a juvenile at the time of committing the offence." The sentence for young adults who come within this section is youth imprisonment of 6 months to 10 years or, under certain conditions, of indeterminate duration. Where, on the other hand, the young adult offender's personal development corresponds to his age, the general criminal law applies but the judge may pass a sentence of 10 to 15 years' imprisonment instead of a life sentence. . . .

As to the Law

80. The applicant alleged that the decision by the Secretary of State for the Home Department to surrender him to the authorities of the United States of America

would, if implemented, give rise to a breach by the United Kingdom of Article 3 of the [European] Convention [on Human Rights], which provides: "No one shall be subjected to torture or to inhuman or degrading treatment or punishment."

A. Applicability of Article 3 in cases of extradition

81. The alleged breach derives from the applicant's exposure to the so-called "death row phenomenon." This phenomenon may be described as consisting in a combination of circumstances to which the applicant would be exposed if, after having been extradited to Virginia to face a capital murder charge, he were sentenced to death.

82. . . . . The applicant . . . submitted that Article 3 not only prohibits the Contracting States from causing inhuman or degrading treatment or punishment to occur within their jurisdiction but also embodies an associated obligation not to put a person in a position where he will or may suffer such treatment or punishment at the hands of other States. For the applicant, at least as far as Article 3 is concerned, an individual may not be surrendered out of the protective zone of the Convention without the certainty that the safeguards which he would enjoy are as effective as the Convention standard.

83. The United Kingdom Government, on the other hand, contended that Article 3 should not be interpreted so as to impose responsibility on a Contracting State for acts which occur outside its jurisdiction. . . . To begin with, they maintained, it would be straining the language of Article 3 intolerably to hold that by surrendering a fugitive criminal the extraditing State has "subjected" him to any treatment or punishment that he will receive following conviction and sentence in the receiving State. Further arguments advanced . . . were that it interferes with international treaty rights; it leads to a conflict with the norms of international judicial process, in that it in effect involves adjudication on the internal affairs of foreign States not Parties to the Convention or to the proceedings before the Convention institutions; it entails grave difficulties of evaluation and proof in requiring the examination of alien systems of law and of conditions in foreign States; the practice of national courts and the international community cannot reasonably be invoked to support it; it causes a serious risk of harm in the Contracting State which is obliged to harbour the protected person, and leaves criminals untried, at large and unpunished.

In the alternative, the United Kingdom Government submitted that the application of Article 3 in extradition cases should be limited to those occasions in which the treatment or punishment abroad is certain, imminent and serious. In their view, the fact that by definition the matters complained of are only anticipated, together with the common and legitimate interest of all States in bringing fugitive criminals to justice, requires a very high degree of risk, proved beyond reasonable doubt, that ill-treatment will actually occur.

85. . . . . [N]o right not to be extradited is as such protected by the Convention. Nevertheless, in so far as a measure of extradition has consequences adversely affecting the enjoyment of a Convention right, it may, assuming that the consequences

are not too remote, attract the obligations of a Contracting State under the relevant Convention guarantee. . . .

86. Article 1 of the Convention, which provides that "the High Contracting Parties shall secure to everyone within their jurisdiction the rights and freedoms defined in Section I," sets a limit, notably territorial, on the reach of the Convention. . . . Further, the Convention does not govern the actions of States not Parties to it, nor does it purport to be a means of requiring the Contracting States to impose Convention standards on other States. Article 1 cannot be read as justifying a general principle to the effect that, notwithstanding its extradition obligations, a Contracting State may not surrender an individual unless satisfied that the conditions awaiting him in the country of destination are in full accord with each of the safeguards of the Convention. . . . in particular. . . .

These considerations cannot, however, absolve the Contracting Parties from responsibility under Article 3 for all and any foreseeable consequences of extradition suffered outside their jurisdiction.

87. In interpreting the Convention regard must be had to its special character as a treaty for the collective enforcement of human rights and fundamental freedoms. Thus, the object and purpose of the Convention as an instrument for the protection of individual human beings require that its provisions be interpreted and applied so as to make its safeguards practical and effective. . . .

88. . . . . The question remains whether the extradition of a fugitive to another State where he would be subjected or be likely to be subjected to torture or to inhuman or degrading treatment or punishment would itself engage the responsibility of a Contracting State under Article 3. That the abhorrence of torture has such implications is recognised in Article 3 of the United Nations Convention Against Torture and Other Cruel, Inhuman or Degrading Treatment or Punishment, which provides that "no State Party shall . . . extradite a person where there are substantial grounds for believing that he would be in danger of being subjected to torture." The fact that a specialised treaty should spell out in detail a specific obligation attaching to the prohibition of torture does not mean that an essentially similar obligation is not already inherent in the general terms of Article 3 of the European Convention. It would hardly be compatible with the underlying values of the Convention, that "common heritage of political traditions, ideals, freedom and the rule of law" to which the Preamble refers, were a Contracting State knowingly to surrender a fugitive to another State where there were substantial grounds for believing that he would be in danger of being subjected to torture, however heinous the crime allegedly committed.

Extradition in such circumstances, while not explicitly referred to in the brief and general wording of Article 3, would plainly be contrary to the spirit and intendment of the Article, and in the Court's view this inherent obligation not to extradite also extends to cases in which the fugitive would be faced in the receiving State by a real risk of exposure to inhuman or degrading treatment or punishment proscribed by that Article.

89. What amounts to "inhuman or degrading treatment or punishment" depends on all the circumstances of the case. Furthermore, inherent in the whole of the Convention is a search for a fair balance between the demands of the general interest of the community and the requirements of the protection of the individual's fundamental rights. As movement about the world becomes easier and crime takes on a larger international dimension, it is increasingly in the interest of all nations that suspected offenders who flee abroad should be brought to justice. Conversely, the establishment of safe havens for fugitives would not only result in danger for the State obliged to harbour the protected person but also tend to undermine the foundation of extradition. These considerations must also be included among the factors to be taken into account in the interpretation and application of the notions of inhuman and degrading treatment or punishment in extradition cases. . . .

91. In sum, the decision by a Contracting State to extradite a fugitive may give rise to an issue under Article 3 and hence engage the responsibility of that State under the Convention, where substantial grounds have been shown for believing that the person concerned, if extradited, faces a real risk of being subjected to torture or to inhuman or degrading treatment or punishment in the requesting country. The establishment of such responsibility inevitably involves an assessment of conditions in the requesting country against the standards of Article 3 of the Convention. Nonetheless, there is no question of adjudicating on or establishing the responsibility of the receiving country, whether under general international law, under the Convention or otherwise. In so far as any liability under the Convention is or may be incurred, it is liability incurred by the extraditing Contracting State by reason of its having taken action which has as a direct consequence the exposure of an individual to proscribed ill-treatment.

B. Application of Article 3 in the particular circumstances of the present case

92. . . . . It therefore has to be determined on the above principles whether the foreseeable consequences of Mr Soering's return to the United States are such as to attract the application of Article 3. This inquiry must concentrate firstly on whether Mr Soering runs a real risk of being sentenced to death in Virginia, since the source of the alleged inhuman and degrading treatment or punishment, namely the "death row phenomenon," lies in the imposition of the death penalty. Only in the event of an affirmative answer to this question need the Court examine whether exposure to the "death row phenomenon" in the circumstances of the applicant's case would involve treatment or punishment incompatible with Article 3.

1. Whether the applicant runs a real risk of a death sentence and hence of exposure to the "death row phenomenon"

98. . . . . [O]bjectively it cannot be said that the undertaking to inform the judge at the sentencing stage of the wishes of the United Kingdom eliminates the risk of the death penalty being imposed. In the independent exercise of his discretion the Commonwealth's Attorney has himself decided to seek and to persist in seeking

the death penalty because the evidence, in his determination, supports such action. If the national authority with responsibility for prosecuting the offence takes such a firm stance, it is hardly open to the Court to hold that there are no substantial grounds for believing that the applicant faces a real risk of being sentenced to death and hence experiencing the "death row phenomenon."

99. The Court's conclusion is therefore that the likelihood of the feared exposure of the applicant to the "death row phenomenon" has been shown to be such as to bring Article 3 into play.

2. Whether in the circumstances the risk of exposure to the "death row phenomenon" would make extradition a breach of Article 3

(a) General considerations

100. As is established in the Court's case-law, ill-treatment, including punishment, must attain a minimum level of severity if it is to fall within the scope of Article 3. The assessment of this minimum is, in the nature of things, relative; it depends on all the circumstances of the case, such as the nature and context of the treatment or punishment, the manner and method of its execution, its duration, its physical or mental effects and, in some instances, the sex, age and state of health of the victim.

Treatment has been held by the Court to be both "inhuman" because it was premeditated, was applied for hours at a stretch and "caused, if not actual bodily injury, at least intense physical and mental suffering", and also "degrading" because it was "such as to arouse in [its] victims feelings of fear, anguish and inferiority capable of humiliating and debasing them and possibly breaking their physical or moral resistance." In order for a punishment or treatment associated with it to be "inhuman" or "degrading." the suffering or humiliation involved must in any event go beyond that inevitable element of suffering or humiliation connected with a given form of legitimate punishment. In this connection, account is to be taken not only of the physical pain experienced but also, where there is a considerable delay before execution of the punishment, of the sentenced person's mental anguish of anticipating the violence he is to have inflicted on him.

101. Capital punishment is permitted under certain conditions by Article 2(1) of the Convention, which reads: "Everyone's right to life shall be protected by law. No one shall be deprived of his life intentionally save in the execution of a sentence of a court following his conviction of a crime for which this penalty is provided by law." In view of this wording, the applicant did not suggest that the death penalty per se violated Article 3. He, like the two Government Parties, agreed with the Commission that the extradition of a person to a country where he risks the death penalty does not in itself raise an issue under either Article 2 or Article 3. On the other hand, Amnesty International in their written comments argued that the evolving standards in Western Europe regarding the existence and use of the death penalty required that the death penalty should now be considered as an inhuman and degrading punishment within the meaning of Article 3.

102. Certainly, "the Convention is a living instrument which . . . must be interpreted in the light of present-day conditions"; and, in assessing whether a given treatment or punishment is to be regarded as inhuman or degrading for the purposes of Article 3, "the Court cannot but be influenced by the developments and commonly accepted standards in the penal policy of the member States of the Council of Europe in this field." De facto the death penalty no longer exists in time of peace in the Contracting States to the Convention. In the few Contracting States which retain the death penalty in law for some peacetime offences, death sentences, if ever imposed, are nowadays not carried out. This "virtual consensus in Western European legal systems that the death penalty is, under current circumstances, no longer consistent with regional standards of justice," to use the words of Amnesty International, is reflected in Protocol No. 6 to the Convention, which provides for the abolition of the death penalty in time of peace. Protocol No. 6 was opened for signature in April 1983, which in the practice of the Council of Europe indicates the absence of objection on the part of any of the Member States of the Organisation; it came into force in March 1985 and to date has been ratified by thirteen Contracting States to the Convention, not however including the United Kingdom.

Whether these marked changes have the effect of bringing the death penalty per se within the prohibition of ill-treatment under Article 3 must be determined on the principles governing the interpretation of the Convention.

103. The Convention is to be read as a whole and Article 3 should therefore be construed in harmony with the provisions of Article 2. On this basis Article 3 evidently cannot have been intended by the drafters of the Convention to include a general prohibition of the death penalty since that would nullify the clear wording of Article 2(1).

Subsequent practice in national penal policy, in the form of a generalised abolition of capital punishment, could be taken as establishing the agreement of the Contracting States to abrogate the exception provided for under Article 2(1) and hence to remove a textual limit on the scope for evolutive interpretation of Article. However, Protocol No. 6, as a subsequent written agreement, shows that the intention of the Contracting Parties as recently as 1983 was to adopt the normal method of amendment of the text in order to introduce a new obligation to abolish capital punishment in time of peace and, what is more, to do so by an optional instrument allowing each State to choose the moment when to undertake such an engagement. In these conditions, notwithstanding the special character of the Convention, Article 3 cannot be interpreted as generally prohibiting the death penalty.

104. That does not mean however that circumstances relating to a death sentence can never give rise to an issue under Article 3. The manner in which it is imposed or executed, the personal circumstances of the condemned person and a disproportionality to the gravity of the crime committed, as well as the conditions of detention awaiting execution, are examples of factors capable of bringing the treatment or punishment received by the condemned person within the proscription under

Article 3. Present-day attitudes in the Contracting States to capital punishment are relevant for the assessment whether the acceptable threshold of suffering or degradation has been exceeded. . . .

(b) The particular circumstances

i. Length of detention prior to execution

106. The period that a condemned prisoner can expect to spend on death row in Virginia before being executed is on average six to eight years. This length of time awaiting death is, as the Commission and the United Kingdom Government noted, in a sense largely of the prisoner's own making in that he takes advantage of all avenues of appeal which are offered to him by Virginia law. . . . Nevertheless, just as some lapse of time between sentence and execution is inevitable if appeal safeguards are to be provided to the condemned person, so it is equally part of human nature that the person will cling to life by exploiting those safeguards to the full. However well-intentioned and even potentially beneficial is the provision of the complex of post-sentence procedures in Virginia, the consequence is that the condemned prisoner has to endure for many years the conditions on death row and the anguish and mounting tension of living in the ever-present shadow of death.

ii. Conditions on death row

107. As to conditions in Mecklenburg Correctional Center, where the applicant could expect to be held if sentenced to death, the Court bases itself on the facts which were uncontested by the United Kingdom Government, without finding it necessary to determine the reliability of the additional evidence adduced by the applicant, notably as to the risk of homosexual abuse and physical attack undergone by prisoners on death row. The stringency of the custodial regime in Mecklenburg [is] . . . described in some detail above. In this connection, the United Kingdom Government drew attention to the necessary requirement of extra security for the safe custody of prisoners condemned to death for murder. Whilst it might thus well be justifiable in principle, the severity of a special regime such as that operated on death row in Mecklenburg is compounded by the fact of inmates being subject to it for a protracted period lasting on average six to eight years.

iii. The applicant's age and mental state

108. At the time of the killings, the applicant was only 18 years old and there is some psychiatric evidence, which was not contested as such, that he "was suffering from [such] an abnormality of mind . . . as substantially impaired his mental responsibility for his acts."

Unlike Article 2 of the Convention, Article 6 of the 1966 International Covenant on Civil and Political Rights and Article 4 of the 1969 American Convention on Human Rights expressly prohibit the death penalty from being imposed on persons aged less than 18 at the time of commission of the offence. Whether or not such a prohibition be inherent in the brief and general language of Article 2 of the European Convention, its explicit enunciation in other, later international instruments, the former of which has been ratified by a large number of States Parties to the European Convention, at the very least indicates that as a general principle the youth of the person concerned is a circumstance which is liable, with others, to put in question the compatibility with Article 3 of measures connected with a death sentence.

It is in line with the Court's case-law . . . to treat disturbed mental health as having the same effect for the application of Article 3.

109. . . . . [T]he applicant's youth at the time of the offence and his then mental state, on the psychiatric evidence as it stands, are therefore to be taken into consideration as contributory factors tending, in his case, to bring the treatment on death row within the terms of Article 3.

iv. Possibility of extradition to the Federal Republic of Germany

110. For the United Kingdom Government . . . , the possibility of extraditing or deporting the applicant to face trial in the Federal Republic of Germany, where the death penalty has been abolished under the Constitution, is not material for the present purposes. Any other approach, the United Kingdom Government submitted, would lead to a "dual standard" affording the protection of the Convention to extraditable persons fortunate enough to have such an alternative destination available but refusing it to others not so fortunate.

This argument is not without weight. Furthermore, the Court cannot overlook either the horrible nature of the murders with which Mr Soering is charged or the legitimate and beneficial role of extradition arrangements in combating crime. . . . However, sending Mr Soering to be tried in his own country would remove the danger of a fugitive criminal going unpunished as well as the risk of intense and protracted suffering on death row. It is therefore a circumstance of relevance for the overall assessment under Article 3 in that it goes to the search for the requisite fair balance of interests and to the proportionality of the contested extradition decision in the particular case.

(c) Conclusion

111. For any prisoner condemned to death, some element of delay between imposition and execution of the sentence and the experience of severe stress in conditions necessary for strict incarceration are inevitable. The democratic character of the Virginia legal system in general and the positive features of Virginia trial, sentencing and appeal procedures in particular are beyond doubt. The Court agrees . . . that the machinery of justice to which the applicant would be subject in the United States is in itself neither arbitrary nor unreasonable, but, rather, respects the rule of law and affords not inconsiderable procedural safeguards to the defendant in a capital trial. Facilities are available on death row for the assistance of inmates, notably through provision of psychological and psychiatric services.

However, in the Court's view, having regard to the very long period of time spent on death row in such extreme conditions, with the ever present and mounting anguish of awaiting execution of the death penalty, and to the personal circumstances of the applicant, especially his age and mental state at the time of the offence, the applicant's extradition to the United States would expose him to a real risk of treatment going beyond the threshold set by Article 3. A further consideration of relevance is that in the particular instance the legitimate purpose of extradition could be achieved by another means which would not involve suffering of such exceptional intensity or duration. Accordingly, the Secretary of State's decision to extradite the applicant to the United States would, if implemented, give rise to a breach of Article 3. . . .

Notes

(1) Soering was ultimately extradited to the United States after the United Kingdom received assurances that he would not be tried in Virginia for a crime carrying the death penalty. He was tried and convicted on June 22, 1990, on two counts of first-degree murder and sentenced to two terms of life imprisonment, *Soering v. Deeds*, 499 S.E.2d 514 (Va. 1998) (denial of habeas corpus). Ms. Haysom was sentenced to 90 years in prison. *See* Nathan Heller, *Blood Ties — Two brilliant college lovers were convicted of a brutal slaying. All these years later, why has this case become a cause?* THE NEW YORKER, Nov. 9, 2015, at 52. In a surprise move, Soering and Haysom were granted parole late in 2019. Soering was deported to Germany and Haysom to Canada, where she is a citizen. Nathan Heller, *A New Chapter in a Double-Murder Case,* THE NEW YORKER, Dec. 21, 2019, *available at* https://www.newyorker.com/culture/culture-desk/a-new-chapter-in-a-double-murder-case. In another stunning development in 2021, Virginia, which had been executing people for over 400 years, abolished the death penalty.

(2) What precisely does *Soering* hold? Is it that *any* provision of a human rights treaty will "trump" a state's obligations under an extradition treaty? Will the obligation under Article 3 of the European Convention not to subject an individual to "torture or inhuman or degrading treatment or punishment" *always* do so? When a state's obligations under two treaties conflict, why should its obligation under a human rights treaty be accorded priority? Insofar as the ban on torture and inhuman or degrading treatment or punishment is supposed to be a norm of customary international law (perhaps even a superior norm of *jus cogens*), would a state be obligated to refuse extradition in circumstances like those in *Soering* even if it were not a party to the European Convention on Human Rights? Could the customary norm be invoked in an extradition hearing in a domestic court as a defense against extradition? *See Report of the Committee on Extradition and Human Rights, in* INTERNATIONAL LAW ASSOCIATION, REPORT OF THE SIXTY-SIXTH CONFERENCE 151–52 (1994). On the relationship between extradition and human rights obligations generally, *see* also John Dugard & Christine Van den Wyngaert, *Reconciling Extradition with Human Rights*, 92 A.J.I.L. 187 (1998); Donald K. Piragoff & Marcia V. J. Kran, *The Impact of Human Rights Principles on Extradition from Canada and the United States: The Role of National Courts,* 3 CRIM. L. F. 225 (1992); Sharon A. Williams, *Human Rights Safeguards and International Cooperation in Extradition: Striking the Balance*, 3 CRIM. L. F. 191 (1992).

(3) Does the death penalty itself violate internationally-guaranteed human rights? On the death penalty in international law generally, *see* WILLIAM A. SCHABAS, THE ABOLITION OF THE DEATH PENALTY IN INTERNATIONAL LAW (3d ed. 2002); ROGER HOOD & CAROLYN HOYLE, THE DEATH PENALTY: A WORLDWIDE PERSPECTIVE (4th ed., 2008); Roger S. Clark, *The Attrition of Capital Punishment Worldwide as the American Law Institute Withdraws Its Model Penal Code Provision Recommending How to Do It*, 21 CRIM. L.F. 511 (2010) (book essay). For data on the status of the death penalty world-wide and on current developments, go to the Amnesty International web-site, https://www.amnesty.org/en/what-we-do/death-penalty/.

In *State v. Makwanyane*, 1995 (3) SALR 391 (CC), the South African Constitutional Court concluded that the death penalty violated the South African constitutional prohibition of cruel, inhuman, or degrading punishment. However, in paragraph 103 of the *Soering* judgment, the European Court concluded that the death penalty *per se* does not violate the European Convention on Human Rights, although it is prohibited by the 1983 Protocol No. 6 to that Convention for states party to the Protocol. (The Russian Federation, alone of the 47 members of the Council of Europe, has not ratified Protocol No. 6, although it has signed it and is exercising a moratorium on the penalty.)

Is a party to Protocol No. 6 bound, apart from the "death row phenomenon," to refuse extradition on a capital charge? In a Dutch case, *The Netherlands v. Short*, 29 I.L.M. 1375 (1990), U.S. military authorities asked the Netherlands to surrender, under the NATO Status of Forces Agreement, an American solider accused of murdering his wife, but refused to give assurances that the death penalty would not be imposed. The Netherlands was a party to Protocol No. 6, so there was a direct conflict between the obligation not to subject individuals to the death penalty and the obligations imposed by the Status of Forces Agreement. The Dutch Supreme Court was not prepared to find that Protocol No. 6 necessarily prevailed over the obligation to surrender the accused. But, balancing the competing interests, did hold that Short's interest in not being surrendered was entitled to priority. He was surrendered when the U.S. authorities agreed not to charge him with a capital crime.

In G.A. Res. 62/149 of December 18, 2007, a majority of the United Nations General Assembly called for a moratorium on the use of the death penalty. European States, especially Italy, had been striving for such a resolution for several years. The resolution drew a Note Verbale dated January 11, 2008 from 58 States (not including the United States which, like the 58, had voted against the resolution) who insisted that "they are in persistent objection to any attempt to impose a moratorium on the use of the death penalty or its abolition in contravention to existing stipulations under international law. . . ." U.N. Doc. A/62/658 (2008). The Assembly reiterated its plea several times subsequently, most recently in G.A. Res. 73/175 (2018). The United Nations, which is on the record in favor of systematic abolition, commissions a report on progress every five years. The most recent quinquennial report, covering the period up to the end of 2018, records that:

> At the end of December 2018, 167 States were deemed abolitionist either in law or in practice and 30 States were classified as retentionist. This compares with 159 abolitionist States and 38 retentionist States at the end of the previous quinquennium (2009–2013). During the survey period 2014–2018, no State that had previously become abolitionist, either in law or in practice, reverted to the use of capital punishment.

Report of the Secretary-General, Capital punishment and the implementation of the safeguards guaranteeing the protection of the rights of those facing the death penalty, U.N. Doc. E/2020/53, para. 6 (2020). It is clear that there is a definite trend towards abolition of the death penalty.

(4) In *Reid v. Covert*, 354 U.S. 1 (1957), the Supreme Court held, in effect, that the Bill of Rights (there, the right to a jury trial) could trump treaty provisions. Might other countries be in the situation where their extradition treaty obligations are shaped by general constitutional provisions concerning due process or specific ones on capital punishment? Bear in mind that all the European states and U.S. partners like Mexico, Canada, Australia and New Zealand are strongly (some would say *stridently*) abolitionist.

In *U.S. v. Burns*, [2001] S.C.R. 283, the defendant resisted extradition from Canada on the basis that the Canadian Government had not sought an absolute assurance that the death penalty would not be applied. The U.S.-Canada Extradition treaty had a similar (non-mandatory) capital punishment provision to that in the U.S.-U.K treaty in *Soering*. The Supreme Court of Canada held that the issue fell to be decided under § 7 of the Canadian Charter of Rights and freedoms that provides: "Everyone has the right to life, liberty and security of the person and the right not to be deprived thereof except in accordance with the principles of fundamental justice." The Court concluded that:

> [T]he Canadian Charter of Rights and Freedoms does not lay down a constitutional prohibition in all cases against extradition unless assurances are given that the death penalty will not be imposed. The Minister is required (as he did here) to balance on a case-by-case basis those factors that favour extradition with assurances against competing factors that favour extradition without assurances. We hold, however, for the reasons which follow, that such assurances are constitutionally required in all but exceptional cases. We further hold that this case does not present the exceptional circumstances that must be shown before the Minister could constitutionally extradite without assurances. By insisting on assurances, Canada would not be acting in disregard of international extradition obligations undertaken by the Canadian government, but rather exercising a treaty right explicitly agreed to by the United States.

In a 1996 Italian case discussed in Andrea Bianchi, *International Decision: Venezia v. Ministero di Grazia e Giustizia*, 91 A.J.I.L. 727 (1997), the Italian Constitutional Court held that it violated the Italian Constitution to vest Italian officials in extradition cases with discretion to rule on the sufficiency of the assurances given by the United States that capital punishment would not be imposed. The constitutional prohibition of the death penalty was absolute and precluded extradition on the basis of such an evaluation. The relevant provision of the Extradition treaty between Italy and the U.S. was a little stronger than the U.K.-U.S. one involved in *Soering*, in that it said that extradition "shall," rather than "may," be refused in the absence of assurances. Nevertheless, the Court held the treaty provision and its empowering legislation unconstitutional.

(5) Does *Soering* hold that the "death row phenomenon" in itself violates Article 3? Or was more, having to do with Soering's age and mental state, required? In *Kindler v. Canada*, U.N.Doc. CCPR/C/48/D/470/1991 (1993), the U.N. Human Rights Committee took the view, in a case involving extradition from Canada to the United States, that "prolonged periods of detention under a severe custodial regime on death row cannot generally be considered to constitute cruel, inhuman or degrading treatment if the convicted person is merely availing himself of appellate remedies." Is this necessarily inconsistent with the European Court's decision in *Soering*? Consider, however, the decision in *Pratt v. Attorney General for Jamaica*, [1994] 2 App. Cas. 1 (P.C. 1993), in which the Judicial Committee of the Privy Council stated that a delay of five years after imposition of a death sentence would amount to inhuman and degrading punishment in violation of an article of the Jamaican Constitution modeled on Article 3 of the European Convention. Responding to the argument that the delay was largely a result of the appellants' deliberate resort to appellate remedies, the Judicial Committee observed:

> It is part of the human condition that a condemned man will take every opportunity to save his life through use of the appellate procedure. If the appellate procedure enables the prisoner to prolong the appellate hearings over a period of years, the fault is to be attributed to the appellate system that permits such delay and not to the prisoner who takes advantage of it.

Other foreign cases on point are reviewed in Justice Breyer's dissent from the denial of certiorari in *Knight v. Florida*, 528 U.S. 990 (1999). Justice Breyer notes, *id.*, at 996–97, that:

> [A]fter *Soering*, the United States Senate insisted on reservations to language imposing similar standards in various human rights treaties, specifying, for example, that the language in question did not "restrict or prohibit the United States from applying the death penalty consistent with the . . . Constitution of the United States, including any constitutional period of confinement prior to the imposition of the death penalty." 136 Cong. Rec. 36192–36199 (1990) (U.S. Senate Resolution of Advice and Consent to Ratification of the Convention Against Torture and Other Cruel, Inhuman or Degrading Treatment or Punishment.)
>
> Nonetheless, the treaty reservations say nothing about whether a particular "period of confinement" is constitutional.

In *Knight v. Florida, supra*, the Supreme Court declined to rule on the "death row phenomenon." It did so once more in *Foster v. Florida*, 537 U.S. 990 (2002) with opinions by Thomas, J., concurring, and Breyer, J., dissenting, and again in *Johnson v. Bredesen*, 558 U.S. 1067 (2009) where Stevens J.'s statement respecting the denial of certiorari was joined by Breyer J. (Johnson spent 29 years on death row in Tennessee before his execution). Justice Breyer has continued his stand seeking reconsideration of the constitutionality of the death penalty. *See, e.g., Glossip v. Gross*, 135 S. Ct. 2726 (2015) (Breyer J. dissenting, with other Justices); *Jordan and Evans v. Mississippi*, 585 U.S. (2018) (Breyer J. dissenting alone from a denial of cert.).

(6) Might the mode of execution used in the requesting state amount to a reason for refusing extradition? In *Ng v. Canada*, U.N. Doc. CCPR/C/49/D/469/1991 (1994), the Human Rights Committee concluded that use of the gas chamber in California had been shown to involve prolonged agony and suffering and therefore violated Article 7 of the International Covenant on Civil and Political Rights. *See also Glossip v. Gross*, 135 S. Ct. 2726 (2015) (5-4 decision upholding denial of preliminary injunction claiming that Oklahoma's execution drug protocol violates the Eighth Amendment).

(7) Recall from § 19.02 that when the United States ratified the Covenant on Civil and Political Rights, it entered a reservation insisting that it retained the right to execute people for crimes committed as juveniles. This reservation was rendered moot in 2005 after the U.S. Supreme Court held that capital punishment for those under the age of 18 at the time of the crime was unconstitutional. *See Roper v. Simmons*, 543 U.S. 551 (2005). In reaching its decision, the majority referred to international developments regarding capital punishment.

§ 19.04 Life Without the Possibility of Parole

While the United States is still debating the propriety of the death penalty, many European, Pacific and Latin American countries have moved on, both domestically and in international forums, to the constitutional and human rights issues of life imprisonment, especially when it means life without the possibility of parole (LWOP). *See*, for a comprehensive study, Dirk Van Zyl Smit & Catherine Appleton, Life Imprisonment: A Global Human Rights Analysis (2019), reviewed by Roger S. Clark in 41 H. Rights Q. 1022 (2019). As an indication of a different attitude to life without parole, in August 2020, New Zealand issued its only such sentence—to a white supremacist who killed 51 people at two mosques. *See* BBC News, *Christchurch Mosque attack: Brenton Tarrant sentenced to life without parole, available at* https://www.bbc.com/news/world-asia-53919624. It is contended that abolishing life without parole does not mean that terrible people will always be released to prey on an unsuspecting public. A life sentence with the possibility of parole can be argued to mean that there is hope, a decision to release may be made in the future—perhaps well into the future—with knowledge of the situation then.

In its 1962 Model Penal Code, the American Law Institute (ALI) was aware of the issue. It was flatly opposed to a penalty that entailed life without the possibility of release. In a massive project amending the 1962 sentencing provisions, the Institute backed off on this absolute position, in the context of alternatives to the death penalty. The relevant commentary reads:

> The Institute's new position has been forged with reluctance. Viewed as an independent policy question, that is, if capital punishment were not part of the nation's legal landscape, the Institute would not endorse penalties of life imprisonment with no chance of release. Natural-life sentences rest on the premise that an offender's blameworthiness cannot change substantially over time—even very long periods of time. The sanction denies the possibility of dramatically altered circumstances, spanning a prisoner's acts of heroism to the pathos of disease or disability that might alter the moral calculus of permanent incarceration. It also assumes that rehabilitation is not possible or will never be detectable in individual cases. Such compound certainties, reaching into a far-distant future, are not supportable....
>
> Despite these concerns, the Institute recognizes the advisability of the penalty of life imprisonment with no chance of release when it is the only alternative to the death penalty. In this circumstance, it is defensible for a legislature to authorize a life prison term that is not subject to later sentence modification under.... The Institute's position on this score should be understood as a concession to the broader landscape that includes capital sentences, not as a freestanding endorsement of natural-life prison sentences. Because of the death penalty's unmatched severity, it exerts a gravitational pull on other sanctions, both in specific cases and in the legislative process.

American Law Institute, Model Penal Code: Sentencing. Proposed Final Draft (April 10, 2017) at 161.

Objections to life imprisonment are now common in extradition practice. The Council of Europe's Protocol amending the European Convention on the Suppression of Terrorism, opened for signature on May 15, 2003, https://rm.coe.int/CoERMPublicCommonSearchServices/DisplayDCTMContent?documentId=090000168008370d, provides, for example, in Article 4(3):

> Nothing in this Convention shall be interpreted either as imposing on the requested State an obligation to extradite if the person subject to the extradition request risks being exposed to the death penalty or, where the law of the requested State does not allow for life imprisonment, to life imprisonment without the possibility of parole, unless under applicable extradition treaties the requested State is under the obligation to extradite if the requesting State gives such assurance as the requested State considers sufficient that the death penalty will not be imposed or, where imposed, will

> not be carried out, of that the person concerned will not be subject to life imprisonment without the possibility of parole.

The earliest example of such a provision seems to have been Article IV of the 1922 United States/Venezuela Extradition Treaty, 49 L.N.T.S. 435. *See also* Rodrigo Lambardini, *Mexico's Supreme Court Clarifies When to Submit Assurances That Life Imprisonment Will Not be Imposed When Requesting Extradition from Mexico,* 20 INT'L ENF. L. REP. 295 (2004).

The trend towards outlawing life without parole gained further support in a decision of the Residual Mechanism for Criminal Tribunals that those subject to life imprisonment should be considered eligible for "early release" after having served more than 30 years of their sentence. *See* Marek Szydło, *Reduction of Life Sentences Imposed by International Criminals after the Galić Decision: Is There Need for Further Improvement?* 13 J. INT'L CRIM. JUST 1099 (2015). The matter is of significant practical import, since the ICTY and the ICTR have issued more than twenty life sentences between them, and their Statutes do not define what is meant by life imprisonment. Should geriatric prisoners be released at some point? The issue will arise eventually with the Rome Statute of the International Criminal Court, Article 77 of which permits "a term of life imprisonment when justified by the extreme gravity of the crime and the individual circumstances of the convicted person." But Article 110 of the Statute insists that even a life sentence must be reviewed after 25 years. "Review" does not mean automatic release, since the Statute and the Court's Rules contain a stringent set of principles that must be applied. Given the absence of any parole system in respect of the relevant tribunals and courts, appropriate decisions will have to be made by the judges.

A subcategory of life without parole cases involves juveniles. In *Roper* v. *Simmons*, 543 U.S. 551 (2005) the Supreme Court held that it is unconstitutional to execute a person for an act committed under the age of eighteen. Treaty law goes further. Article 37 of the 1989 Convention on the Rights of the Child (to which the United States is the only state not a party) provides that "[n]either capital punishment nor life imprisonment without possibility of release shall be imposed for offences committed by persons below eighteen years of age." On December 19, 2007, the United Nations General Assembly adopted G.A. Res. 61/146, on Rights of the child, which included a provision urging States to "abolish by law, as soon as possible, the death penalty and life imprisonment without possibility of release for those under the age of 18 years at the time of the commission of the offence." The United States cast the only negative vote on the resolution. The NGO, Human Rights Watch, reported in January 2008 that there were at least 2,380 people (mostly males) imprisoned in the United States without the possibility of parole for crimes committed while under the age of 18. Only seven were known of in the rest of the World. Human Rights Watch Report, *When I Die, They'll Send Me Home: Youth Sentenced to Life Without Parole in California, available at* http://www.hrw.org/reports/2008/us0108/index.htm. In *Graham v. Florida*, 560 U.S. 48 (2010), a majority of the Supreme Court imposed a categorical ban on sentencing a juvenile to life without parole for a non-homicide crime. In *Miller v. Alabama*, 132 S. Ct. 1733 (2012), however, the court held that mandatory life for murder by a juvenile was contrary to the Eighth Amendment, but that the punishment could be acceptable in some circumstances after careful consideration by judge and jury. Commenting on these developments in its concluding observations on the fourth periodic report of the United States, U.N. Doc. CCPR/C/USA/CO/4 (2014), the Committee on Human Rights insisted, at para. 23:

> While noting with satisfaction the Supreme Court decisions prohibiting sentences of life imprisonment without parole for children convicted of non-homicide offences (*Graham v. Florida*), and barring sentences of mandatory life imprisonment , without parole for children convicted of homicide offences (*Miller v. Alabama*) and the State party's commitment to their retroactive application, the Committee is concerned that a court may still, at its discretion, sentence a defendant to life imprisonment without parole for a homicide committed as a juvenile, and that a mandatory or non-homicide-related sentence of life imprisonment without parole may still be applied to adults. The Committee is also concerned that many states exclude 16 and 17 year olds from juvenile court jurisdictions so that juveniles continue to be tried in adult courts and incarcerated in adult institutions (arts. 7, 9, 10, 14, 15 and 24).

Henry Montgomery, who had been sentenced to life without parole for a murder of a police officer he committed in 1963, aged 17, waited in prison for another four years after *Miller* until the Supreme Court held in his case that indeed *Miller* had retroactive effect. *Montgomery v. Louisiana*, 577 U.S. __, 136 S. Ct. 718 (2016). Some 500 people across the country were released as a result, but not Henry, geriatric and near deaf, who has been a model prisoner. While he was re-sentenced in a manner permitting parole, the Louisiana Parole Board (which requires unanimity in order to grant parole) has not agreed to parole him. In 2019, the Board voted 2-1 for him — not enough. Kriti Mehrota, *Where Is Henry Montgomery Now? Is He Still in Jail?*, The Cinemaholic, Aug. 28, 2020, *available at* https://www.thecinemaholic.com/where-is-henry-montgomery-now-is-he-still-in-jail/. He was finally released in November 2021. In an interesting display of federalism at work, 24 states and the District of Columbia have gone beyond *Miller* and categorically banned life without parole for juveniles. *See* Josh Rovner, *Juvenile Life Without Parole: An Overview*, *available at* https://www.sentencingproject.org/publications/juvenile-life-without-parole (Jan. 25, 2021). (The 2017 version of the Model Penal Code: Sentencing, *supra,* reaches the same result.) The non-governmental Sentencing Project, under whose auspices Rovner was writing, has apparently not been able to ascertain exactly how many people in total were in fact released subsequent to *Miller.* There may well be other Henry Montgomerys. In *Jones v. Mississippi,* 141 S. Ct. 1307 (2021), the majority of the Supreme Court set a very low bar on what substantive principles need to be considered on a re-sentencing.

§ 19.05 The Vienna Convention on Consular Relations

Article 36(1)(b) of the 1963 Vienna Convention on Consular Relations [*see* chap. 14, *supra*] gives foreign nationals the right to request that consular officials of their home state be notified, without delay, whenever they are arrested or detained, so that those officials can interview and arrange appropriate legal representation for them; it also provides that, upon arrest, a foreign national must be informed of these rights, again "without delay." Does failure to follow these rules constitute a reason for suppressing a confession or for reversing the conviction or sentence of the foreign national? Consular officials can help with language difficulties, with obtaining counsel and with obtaining evidence, particularly in death penalty cases, about the defendant's background. The question can arise, of course, in cases, that do not involve the death penalty. *See, e.g., United States v. Lombera-Camorlinga*, 170 F.3d 1241 (9th Cir. 1999), *rev'd en banc*, 206 F.3d 882 (9th Cir. 2000) (39.3 kilos of marijuana; court en banc refuses to suppress post-arrest statements); *United States v. Alvarado-Torres*, 45 F. Supp. 2d 986 (S.D. Calif. 1999) (130.3 pounds of "green, leafy substance;" no suppression of post-arrest statements); *United States v. De La Pava*, 268 F.3d 157 (2nd Cir. 2001) (illegally re-entering U.S after deportation); *United States v. Lawal*, 231 F.3d 1045 (7th Cir. 2000) (heroin). But it has figured most prominently in the highest stakes cases that do involve capital punishment.

In *Breard v. Greene*, 523 U.S. 371 (1998), the petitioner was a Paraguayan national sentenced to death in Virginia. Both he and the government of Paraguay had unsuccessfully challenged his conviction on the ground that he had not been informed of his right to consular access. *See Breard v. Netherland*, 949 F. Supp. 1255 (E.D. Va. 1996), *aff'd sub nom. Breard v. Pruett*, 134 F.3d 615 (4th Cir. 1998); *Republic of Paraguay v. Allen*, 949 F. Supp. 1269 (E.D. Va. 1996), *aff'd*, 134 F.3d 622 (4th Cir. 1998). Paraguay then instituted proceedings against the United States in the International Court of Justice (ICJ). On April 9, 1998, the ICJ issued an order indicating that the United States should try to ensure that Breard was not executed pending a decision on the merits. *Case Concerning the Vienna Convention on Consular Relations (Paraguay v. United States)*, Provisional Measures, 1988 I.C.J. 248 (Order of Apr. 9, 1998). Nonetheless, on April 14, 1998, the U.S. Supreme Court denied certiorari and refused to stay Breard's execution. (The Executive Branch made only half-hearted efforts to give effect to the ICJ's provisional measures.) He was put to death later that evening. Ultimately, the United States issued a formal apology to Paraguay and promised to take steps to ensure that the rights of foreign nationals in the U.S. are respected; and, at Paraguay's request, the proceedings in the I.C.J. were discontinued. 1998 I.C.J. 426 (Order of Nov. 10, 1998). *See Agora: Breard*, 92 A.J.I.L. 666 (1998).

In a similar case, Karl and Walter LaGrand were German nationals sentenced to death in Arizona. The German government issued several diplomatic requests for clemency on the ground that they never had been informed of their right to consular access. Nevertheless, Karl LaGrand was executed on February 24, 1999. Walter

LaGrand's execution was scheduled for March 3. On March 2, 1999, Germany instituted proceedings against the United States before the ICJ, and on March 3, the ICJ issued an order asking the U.S. to ensure that Walter LaGrand was not executed pending a decision on the merits. *Case Concerning the Vienna Convention on Consular Relations (Germany v. United States),* Provisional Measures, 1999 I.C.J. 9 (Order of Mar. 3, 1999). The same day, the U.S. Supreme Court declined to exercise its original jurisdiction in a suit filed by Germany against both the United States and the governor of Arizona. *Federal Republic of Germany v. United States,* 526 U.S. 111 (1999). Walter LaGrand was executed later that evening. Nonetheless, Germany persisted with its case and the ICJ decided it in 2001, *LaGrand Case (Germany v. United States),* 2001 I.C.J. The Court found the United States to be in breach of its obligations under Article 36 of the Consular Convention by not notifying the brothers without delay following their arrest of their rights under the Convention, thereby depriving Germany of the possibility to render assistance in a timely fashion. The Court further held that by not permitting review and reconsideration, in the light of the rights set forth in the Convention, of the convictions and sentences, the United States had breached its obligations to the brothers and to Germany. Moreover, by failing to take all measures at its disposal to ensure that Walter LaGrand was not executed pending the final decision of the Court, the United States breached the obligation incumbent upon it under the Order indicating provisional measures.

Valdez v. Oklahoma

Court of Criminal Appeals of Oklahoma
2002 OK CR 20 (2002)

Johnson, V.P.J.:

Gerardo Valdez, Petitioner, was convicted of First Degree Malice Aforethought Murder and sentenced to death in Grady County District Court. . . . On August 22, 2001, Petitioner, through counsel, filed a Second Application for Post-Conviction Relief. . . .

Certain factual claims are not disputed in this proceeding. The parties agree that the State of Oklahoma did not comply with the requirements of Article 36 of the Vienna Convention on Consular Relations, which requires local authorities to notify a detained foreign national, without delay, of his right to communicate with his consulate. Upon the detainee's request, Article 36 requires the authorities to notify consular officials of the person's incarceration without delay. . . . Because authorities in the State of Oklahoma did not comply with Article 36, the Mexican consulate was not notified of Valdez's arrest, conviction and sentence until April of 2001, when one of Valdez's relatives contacted the Mexican consulate in El Paso, Texas and informed consular officials of Valdez's upcoming execution in Oklahoma.

Once informed, consular officials assisted Valdez at this clemency hearing before the Oklahoma Board of Pardons and Paroles. The Government of Mexico retained experts and experienced attorney(s) to assist Valdez. Through investigation of his background and medical history, it was learned Valdez suffers from severed organic brain damage; was born into extreme poverty; received limited education, and grew up in a family plagued by alcohol abuse and instability. Most significant of these findings, according to counsel for Valdez, is that he experienced head injuries in his youth which greatly contributed to and altered his behavior. . . .

This information was presented to the Oklahoma Pardon and Parole Board at Valdez' clemency hearing, and as a result, the Board recommended that Valdez's death sentence be commuted to life in prison without the possibility of parole. This newly developed information, obtained through the Mexican consulate's efforts and investigation, was then presented to Governor Frank Keating and he denied clemency. While acknowledging the State of Oklahoma had not complied with Article 36 of the Vienna Convention, Governor Keating stated he believed the violation did not have a prejudicial effect on the jury's determination of guilt and sentence. . . .

The State of Oklahoma submits, and we agree, that the legal basis for his claim was available to him from the time of his arrest, and consequently at the time of his first post-conviction application. In fact, other defendants in Oklahoma have raised claims relating to violation of the consular notification provisions of the Vienna Conviction and petitioner has not advanced a reasonable explanation for his failure to previously assert the violation. . . . Therefore, the basis of Petitioner's claim — that his rights were violated when Oklahoma did not notify him of his right to consular notification under the Convention — could have reasonably been formulated prior to the ICJ decision in LaGrand.

Further, LaGrand is not a "new rule of constitutional law that was given retroactive effect by the United States Supreme Court or a court of appellate jurisdiction of this state." 22 O.S. 2001, § 1089(D)(9). Only that portion of LaGrand with pronounced the Convention confers "individual rights" and which addressed our doctrine of procedural default is arguably new "law." . . .

Accordingly, we are not persuaded by Petitioner's claim that rules of procedural default may not be applied to claims arising from a violation of Article 36 of the Vienna Convention. The legal basis for the claim is not new and was available at the time of Petitioner's first Application for Post-conviction Relief regardless of the ICJ's decision in LaGrand. For this Court to decide the ICJ's ruling overrules a binding decision of the United States Supreme Court and affords a judicial remedy to an individual for a violation of the Convention would interfere with the nation's foreign affairs and run afoul of the U.S. Constitution.

For these reasons, this Court cannot reach the merits of Petitioner's subsequent Application for Post-Conviction Relief on the ground that the legal basis for relief was previously unavailable. However, despite the parties' statements the contrary, we believe this Court should review this subsequent Application for Post-Conviction Relief on the ground that it would appear no factual basis of the Petitioner's prior medical problems was ascertained by prior trial or appellate counsel before the filing of Petitioner's prior appeals. . . .

We cannot ignore the significance and importance of the factual evidence discovered with the assistance of the Mexican Consulate. It is evident from the record before this Court that the Government of Mexico would have intervened in the case, assisted with Petitioner's defense, and provided resources to ensure that he received a fair trial and sentencing hearing.

While we have no doubt the evidence discovered with the assistance of the Mexican Consulate could have been discovered earlier, under the unique circumstances of this case, it is plain that the evidence was not discovered due to trial counsel's inexperience and ineffectiveness.... By our ruling today, this Court exercises its power to grant relief when an error complained of has resulted in a miscarriage of justice, or constitutes a substantial violation of a constitutional or statutory right. Accordingly, we hereby GRANT Petitioner's Subsequent Application for Post-Conviction Relief, and REMAND this case to the District Court of Grady County for RESENTENCING.

CHAPEL and STRUBAR, JJ., Concur:

LILE, J., Specially Concurs:

As the United States Supreme Court has noted, in cases such as this, it may be very difficult to establish that a failure to notify defendant of his treaty rights resulted in prejudice. In this case, that difficult burden has been met. Appellant is entitled to a re-sentencing hearing.

LUMPKIN, P.J., Concurs in Part/Dissents in Part:

I concur that the legal basis for Petitioner's claim was available at the time of his first application for post-conviction relief. Not only that, but it was available at trial, on direct appeal, and his petition for habeas corpus relief in the federal courts.... His failure to raise the claim at those times bars future consideration of the issue. Therefore, we do not reach the merits of the claim in this subsequent Application for Post-Conviction Relief.

Because of that fact, I dissent to the review of trial counsel's performance. The issue of ineffective assistance of trial counsel has been previously raised, and rejected....

[Following agreement by the prosecutor, Valdez was sentenced to life imprisonment on 11/16/03. Death Penalty Information Center, http://www.deathpenaltyinfo.org/foreign-nationals-part-iii (visited Feb. 7, 2021).]

Notes

(1) States like Paraguay, Germany and Mexico care enough about even the most unpleasant of their citizens who are arrested abroad to contribute to their defense. Especially in capital cases, where the sentence is the most contested issue, they are able to engage competent counsel and facilitate access to favorable evidence. By early 2003, Mexico, the country with by far the largest number of its nationals in United States incarceration, had over fifty nationals on death rows in nine states, in situations where

it believed there were breaches of the Vienna Convention. There were countless others convicted of non-capital offenses. Mexico therefore entered the fray at the International Court and sought both to protect those nationals from execution and (like Paraguay and Germany) to improve the situation for the future. *See Case Concerning Avena and Other Mexican Nationals (Mexico v. United States of America),* Judgment of 31 March, 2004, 2004 I.C.J. 12. The Court reiterated its basic position in *La Grand*.

Most criminal cases in the United States, like those in the Paraguayan and German cases, take place at the state level. The Vienna Convention is a treaty of the United States and thus binding on the states under the supremacy clause of the Constitution. But how are the treaty rights to be vindicated? Most state courts have broad notions of their own sovereignty and narrow notions of the supremacy clause. Typically, foreign defendants do not raise the issue of lack of consular notice in their state trial because they do not know of their rights (and until recently defense counsel did not for the most part raise this issue). When defendants tried to raise the issue on appeal or on federal habeas corpus, they have usually been deflected by the "procedural default rule" which says that they cannot raise in an appellate court or in collateral proceedings in a federal court what they failed to raise at the trial level. The federal government's efforts to vindicate federal rights do not appear to have been very energetic in *Breard*, but the State Department must be aware of the importance of the Vienna Convention to Americans abroad. In an effort to minimize such incidents within the United States, the State Department made efforts to increase compliance, including issuing and circulating widely, the January 1998 booklet *Consular Notification and Access: Instructions for Federal, State and Local Law Enforcement and Other Officials regarding Foreign Nationals in the United States and the Rights of Consular Officials to Assist Them.* It also developed a small reference card to be carried by individual arresting officers. In *Mexican Nationals*, the International Court said:

> 64. The United States has told the Court that millions of aliens reside, either legally or illegally, on its territory, and moreover that its laws concerning citizenship are generous. The United States has also pointed out that it is a multicultural society, with citizenship being held by persons of diverse appearance, speaking many languages. The Court appreciates that in the United States the language that a person speaks, or his appearance, does not necessarily indicate that he is a foreign national. Nevertheless, and particularly in view of the large numbers of foreign nationals living in the United States, these very circumstances suggest that it would be desirable for enquiry routinely to be made of the individual as to his nationality upon his detention, so that the obligations of the Vienna Convention may be complied with. The United States has informed the Court that some of its law enforcement authorities do routinely ask persons taken into detention whether they are United States citizens. Indeed, were each individual to be told at that time that, should he be a foreign national, he is entitled to ask for his consular post to be contacted, compliance with this requirement under Article 36, paragraph 1 (*b*), would be greatly enhanced. The provision of such information could parallel

> the reading of those rights of which any person taken into custody in connection with a criminal offence must be informed prior to interrogation by virtue of what in the United states is known as the "Miranda rule"; these rights include, inter alia, the right to remain silent, the right to have an attorney present during questioning, and the right to have an attorney appointed at government expense if the person cannot afford one. The court notes that, according to the United States, such a practice in respect of the Vienna Convention rights is already being followed in some local jurisdictions.

(2) Other than apologizing to the state of nationality after the execution, what should be done in cases where proper notification has not been made? In *LaGrand, supra,* 2001 I.C.J. at 516, para. 128(7), the I.C.J. suggested that:

> [S]hould nationals of the Federal Republic of Germany nonetheless be sentenced to severe penalties, without their rights under Article 36, paragraph 1 (b), of the Convention having been respected, the United States of America, by means of its own choosing, shall allow the review and reconsideration of the conviction and sentence by taking account of the violation of the rights set forth in that Convention.

Should the convictions and sentences automatically be vacated? Must the defendant make some showing of prejudice? Or should the burden of proof lie with the prosecution to show that there was no prejudice? The Court returned to such issues in the *Mexican Nationals* case, as follows:

Case Concerning Avena and Other Mexican Nationals (Mexico v. U.S.)

International Court of Justice
2004 I.C.J. 12

130. On this question of "review and reconsideration", the United States takes the position that it has indeed conformed its conduct to the *LaGrand* judgment. In a further elaboration of this point, the United States argues the "[t]he Court said in *LaGrand* that the choice of means for allowing the review and reconsideration it called for 'must be left' to the United States", but that "Mexico would not leave this choice to the United States but have the Court undertake the review instead and decide at once that the breach requires the conviction and sentence to be set aside in each case".

131. In stating in its Judgment in the *LaGrand* case that "the United States of America, *by means of its own choosing*, shall allow the review and reconsideration of the conviction and sentence" (*I.C.J. Reports 2001*, p. 516, para. 128; emphasis added), the Court acknowledged that the concrete modalities for such review and reconsideration should be left primarily to the United States. It should be underlined, however, that this freedom in the choice of means for such review and reconsideration is not without qualification: as the passage of the Judgment quoted above makes

abundantly clear, such review and reconsideration has to be carried out "by taking account of the violation of the rights set forth in the Convention" (*I.C.J. Reports 2001*, p. 514, para. 125), including, in particular, the question of the legal consequences of the violation upon the criminal proceedings that have followed the violation. . . .

134. It is not sufficient for the United States to argue that "[w]hatever label [the Mexican defendant] places on his claim, his right . . . must and will be vindicated if it is raised in *some form* at trial" (emphasis added), and that

> "In that way, even though a failure to label the complaint as a breach of the Vienna Convention may mean that he has technically speaking forfeited his right to raise this issue as a Vienna Convention claim, on appeal that failure would not bar him from independently asserting *a claim that he was prejudiced because he lacked this critical protection needed for a fair trial*." (Emphasis added.)

The crucial point in this situation is that, by the operation of the procedural default rule as it is applied at present, the defendant is effectively barred from raising the issue of the violation of his rights under Article 36 of the Vienna Convention and is limited to seeking the vindication of his rights under the United States Constitution. . . .

138. The Court would emphasize that the "review and reconsideration" prescribed by it in the *LaGrand* case should be effective. Thus is should "tak[e] account of the violation of the rights set forth in [the] Convention" (*I.C.J. Reports 2001*, p. 516, para. 128 (7)) and guarantee that the violation and the possible prejudice caused by that violation will be fully examined and taken into account in the review and reconsideration process. Lastly, review and reconsideration should be both of the sentence and of the conviction.

139. Accordingly, in a situation of the violations of rights under Article 36, paragraph 1, of the Vienna Convention, the defendant raises his claim in this respect not as a case of "harm to a particular right essential to a fair trial"—a concept relevant to the enjoyment of due process rights under the United States Constitution—but as a case involving the infringement of his rights under Article 36, paragraph 1. The rights guaranteed under the Vienna Convention are treaty rights which the United States has undertaken to comply with in relation to the individual concerned, irrespective of the due process rights under United States constitutional law. In this regard, the Court would point out that what is crucial in the review and reconsideration process is the existence of a procedure which guarantees that full weight is given to the violation of the rights set forth in the Vienna Convention, whatever may be the actual outcome of such review and reconsideration. . . .

143. It may be true, as the United States argues, that in a number of cases "clemency in fact results in pardons of convictions as well as commutations of sentences". In that sense and to that extent, it might be argued that the facts demonstrated by the United States testify to a degree of effectiveness of the clemency procedures as a means of relieving defendants on death row from execution. The Court notes,

however, that the clemency process, as currently practiced within the United States criminal justice system, does not appear to meet the requirements described in paragraph 138 above and that it is therefore not sufficient in itself to serve as an appropriate means of "review and reconsideration" as envisaged by the Court in the *LaGrand* case. The Court considers nevertheless that appropriate clemency procedures can supplement judicial review and reconsideration, in particular where the judicial system has failed to take due account of the violation of the rights set forth in the Vienna Convention, as has occurred in the case of the three Mexican nationals referred to in paragraph 114 above. . . .

151. The Court would now re-emphasize a point of importance. In the present case, it has had occasion to examine the obligations of the United States under Article 36 of the Vienna Convention in relations to Mexican nationals sentenced to death in the United States. Its findings as to the duty of review and reconsideration of convictions and sentences have been directed to the circumstance of severe penalties being imposed on foreign nationals who happen to be of Mexican nationality. To avoid any ambiguity, it should be made clear that, while what the Court has stated concerns the Mexican nationals whose cases have been brought before it by Mexico, the Court has been addressing the issues of principle raised in the course of the present proceedings from the viewpoint of the general application of the Vienna Convention, and there can be no question of making an *a contrario* argument in respect of any of the Court's findings in the present Judgment. In other words, the fact that in this case the Court's ruling has concerned only Mexican nationals cannot be taken to imply that the conclusions reached by it in the present Judgment do not apply to other foreign nationals finding themselves in similar situations in the United States.

Notes

(1) Paraguay, Germany and Mexico based jurisdiction in the I.C.J. on the 1963 Optional Protocol to the Vienna Convention on Consular Relations. The U.N. Secretary-General's database of treaty actions records the following:

> On 7 March 2005, the Secretary-General received from the Government of the United States of America, a communication notifying its withdrawal from the Optional Protocol. The communication reads as follows:
>
> > ". . . the Government of the United States of America [refers] to the Optional Protocol to the Vienna Convention on Consular Relations Concerning the Compulsory Settlement of Disputes, done at Vienna April 24, 1963.
> >
> > This letter constitutes notification by the United States of America that it hereby withdraws from the aforesaid Protocol. As a consequence of this withdrawal, the United States will no longer recognize the jurisdiction of the International Court of Justice reflected in that Protocol."

http://treaties.un.org/Pages/ViewDetails.aspx?src=TREATY&mtdsg_no=III-8&chapter=3&lang=en.

(2) President George W. Bush responded to *Avena* in a Memorandum to the Attorney-General as follows:

> I have determined, pursuant to the authority vested in me as President by the Constitution and laws of the United States of America, that the United States will discharge its obligations under the decision of the International Court of Justice, by having State courts give effect to the claim in accordance with general principles of comity in cases filed by the 51 Mexican nationals addressed by that decision.

Medellin v. Texas, 552 U.S. 491, 503 (2008). What did the then-President mean by "comity"? Was he asking Texas to "play nicely" and find some way to save face, or did he believe, as his lawyers later argued, that he had power to insist that Texas deliver? What was clear was that, notwithstanding what the I.C.J. said in paragraph 151 of its decision (*see supra*), he regarded the judgment as applying only to Mexicans, not to citizens of other countries that were in the same situation. Note, moreover, that since the U.S. had now denounced the Optional Protocol to the VCCR, no new cases could be brought by other States (or Mexico, for that matter).

(3) Osvaldo Torres Aguilera was one of the Mexicans named in the I.C.J. proceedings. The I.C.J rendered its Judgment on March 31, 2004. On March 1, 2004, Oklahoma had set an execution date of May 18, 2004. The Court of Criminal Appeals issued a stay on May 13th and ordered an evidentiary hearing on the Vienna Convention and ineffective assistance of counsel issues. Hours later, the Governor commuted the sentence to one of life imprisonment without the possibility of parole. *See* Sean D, Murphy, *Implementation of Avena Decision by Oklahoma Court*, 98 A.J.I.L. 581 (2004). Oklahoma had, to a degree at least, delivered. On the other hand, Texas went ahead and scheduled the execution of Jose Ernesto Medellin. The Supreme Court decided as follows in 2008:

Medellin v. Texas

Supreme Court of the United States
552 U.S. 491 (2008)

CHIEF JUSTICE ROBERTS delivered the opinion of the Court.

The International Court of Justice (ICJ), located in the Hague, is a tribunal established pursuant to the United Nations Charter to adjudicate disputes between member states. In the *Case Concerning Avena and Other Mexican Nationals* (*Mex. v. U.S.*), 2004 I. C. J. 12 (Judgment of Mar. 31) (*Avena*), that tribunal considered a claim brought by Mexico against the United States. The ICJ held that, based on violations of the Vienna Convention, 51 named Mexican nationals were entitled to review and reconsideration of their state-court convictions and sentences in the United States. This was so regardless of any forfeiture of the right to raise Vienna Convention claims because of a failure to comply with generally applicable state rules governing challenges to criminal convictions.

In *Sanchez-Llamas v. Oregon*, 548 U.S. 331 (2006) issued after *Avena* but involving individuals who were not named in the *Avena* judgment—we held that, contrary to the ICJ's determination, the Vienna Convention did not preclude the application of state default rules. After the *Avena* decision, President George W. Bush determined, through a Memorandum to the Attorney General (Feb. 28, 2005) . . . . that the United States would "discharge its international obligations" under *Avena* "by having State courts give effect to the decision."

Petitioner Jose Ernesto Medellin, who had been convicted and sentenced in Texas state court for murder, is one of the 51 Mexican nationals named in the *Avena* decision. Relying on the ICJ's decision and the President's Memorandum, Medellin filed an application for a writ of habeas corpus in state court. The Texas Court of Criminal Appeals dismissed Medellin's application as an abuse of the writ under state law, given Medellin's failure to raise his Vienna Convention claim in a timely manner under state law. We granted certiorari to decide two questions. *First*, is the ICJ's judgment in *Avena* directly enforceable as domestic law in a state court in the United States? *Second*, does the President's Memorandum independently require the States to provide review and reconsideration of the claims of the 51 Mexican nationals named in *Avena* without regard to state procedural default rules? We conclude that neither *Avena* nor the President's Memorandum constitutes directly enforceable federal law that pre-empts state limitations on the filing of successive habeas petitions. We therefore affirm the decision below. . . .

Petitioner Jose Ernesto Medellin, a Mexican national, has lived in the United States since preschool. A member of the "Black and Whites" gang, Medellin was convicted of capital murder and sentenced to death in Texas for the gang rape and brutal murders of two Houston teenagers. . . . Medellin first raised his Vienna Convention claim in his first application for state postconviction relief. The state trial court held that the claim was procedurally defaulted because Medellin had failed to raise it at trial or on direct review. The trial court also rejected the Vienna Convention claim on the merits, finding that Medellin had "fail[ed] to show that any non-notification of the Mexican authorities impacted on the validity of his conviction or punishment." . . .

Medellin first contends that the ICJ's judgment in *Avena* constitutes a "binding" obligation on the state and federal courts of the United States. He argues that "by virtue of the Supremacy Clause, the treaties requiring compliance with the *Avena* judgment are *already* the 'Law of the Land' by which all state and federal courts in this country are 'bound.'" . . . Accordingly, Medellin argues, *Avena* is a binding federal rule of decision that pre-empts contrary state limitations on successive habeas petitions.

No one disputes that the *Avena* decision—a decision that flows from the treaties through which the United States submitted to ICJ jurisdiction with respect to Vienna Convention disputes—constitutes an *international* law obligation on the part of the United States. But not all international law obligations automatically constitute binding federal law enforceable in United States courts. The question we confront here is whether the *Avena* judgment has automatic *domestic* legal effect such that the judgment of its own force applies in state and federal courts.

This Court has long recognized the distinction between treaties that automatically have effect as domestic law, and those that—while they constitute international law commitments—do not by themselves function as binding federal law. The distinction was well explained by Chief Justice Marshall's opinion in *Foster v. Neilson*, 27 U.S. 253 (1829), overruled on other grounds, *United States v. Percheman*, 32 U.S. 51 (1833), which held that a treaty is "equivalent to an act of the legislature," and hence self-executing, when it "operates of itself without the aid of any legislative provision." When, in contrast, "[treaty] stipulations are not self-executing they can only be enforced pursuant to legislation to carry them into effect." *Whitney v. Robertson*, 124 U.S. 190, 194 (1888). In sum, while treaties "may comprise international commitments . . . they are not domestic law unless Congress has either enacted implementing statutes or the treaty itself conveys an intention that it be 'self-executing' and is ratified on these terms." *Igartua-De La Rosa v. United States*, 417 F.3d 145, 150 (CA1 2005) (en banc) (Boudin, C. J.). . . .

Medellin and his *amici* nonetheless contend that the Optional Protocol, United Nations Charter, and ICJ Statute supply the "relevant obligation" to give the *Avena* judgment binding effect in the domestic courts of the United States. . . . Because none of these treaty sources creates binding federal law in the absence of implementing legislation, and because it is uncontested that no such legislation exists, we conclude that the *Avena* judgment is not automatically binding domestic law. . . .

The obligation on the part of signatory nations to comply with ICJ judgments derives not from the Optional Protocol, but rather from Article 94 of the United Nations Charter—the provision that specifically addresses the effect of ICJ decisions. Article 94(1) provides that "[e]ach Member of the United Nations *undertakes to comply* with the decision of the [ICJ] in any case to which it is a party." . . . The Executive Branch contends that the phrase "undertakes to comply" is not "an acknowledgement that an ICJ decision will have immediate legal effect in the courts of U. N. members," but rather "a *commitment* on the part of U. N. Members to take *future* action through their political branches to comply with an ICJ decision." . . .

We agree with this construction of Article 94. The Article is not a directive to domestic courts. It does not provide that the United States "shall" or "must" comply with an ICJ decision, nor indicate that the Senate that ratified the U. N. Charter intended to vest ICJ decisions with immediate legal effect in domestic courts. Instead, "[t]he words of Article 94 . . . call upon governments to take certain action." . . .

In sum, Medellin's view that ICJ decisions are automatically enforceable as domestic law is fatally undermined by the enforcement structure established by Article 94. His construction would eliminate the option of noncompliance contemplated by Article 94(2), undermining the ability of the political branches to determine whether and how to comply with an ICJ judgment. Those sensitive foreign policy decisions would instead be transferred to state and federal courts charged with applying an ICJ judgment directly as domestic law. And those courts would not be empowered to decide whether to comply with the judgment—again, always regarded as an option by the political branches—any more than courts may consider whether to comply with any other species of domestic law. This result would be particularly anomalous in light of the principle that "[t]he conduct of the foreign relations of our Government is committed by the Constitution to the Executive and Legislative—'the political'—Departments." ...

The ICJ Statute, incorporated into the U. N. Charter, provides further evidence that the ICJ's judgment in *Avena* does not automatically constitute federal law judicially enforceable in United States courts.... To begin with, the ICJ's "principal purpose" is said to be to "arbitrate particular disputes between national governments." ... Accordingly, the ICJ can hear disputes only between nations, not individuals.... More important, Article 59 of the statute provides that "[t]he decision of the [ICJ] has *no binding force* except between the parties and in respect of that particular case." ...

Medellin argues that because the *Avena* case involves him, it is clear that he—and the 50 other Mexican nationals named in the *Avena* decision—should be regarded as parties to the *Avena* judgment.... But cases before the ICJ are often precipitated by disputes involving particular persons or entities, disputes that a nation elects to take up as its own....

It is, moreover, well settled that the United States' interpretation of a treaty "is entitled to great weight." ... The Executive Branch has unfailingly adhered to its view that the relevant treaties do not create domestically enforceable federal law.... The pertinent international agreements, therefore, do not provide for implementation of ICJ judgments through direct enforcement in domestic courts, and "where a treaty does not provide a particular remedy, either expressly or implicitly, it is not for the federal courts to impose one on the States through lawmaking of their own." ...

Our conclusion that *Avena* does not by itself constitute binding federal law is confirmed by the "postratification understanding" of signatory nations.... There are currently 47 nations that are parties to the Optional Protocol and 171 nations that are parties to the Vienna Convention. Yet neither Medellin nor his *amici* have identified a single nation that treats ICJ judgments as binding in domestic courts....

In short, and as we observed in *Sanchez-Llamas*, "[n]othing in the structure or purpose of the ICJ suggests that its interpretations were intended to be conclusive on our courts." ... Given that holding, it is difficult to see how that same structure and purpose can establish, as Medellin argues, that *judgments* of the ICJ nonetheless were intended to be conclusive on our courts. A judgment is binding only if there is a rule of law that makes it so. And the question whether ICJ judgments can bind domestic courts depends upon the same analysis undertaken in *Sanchez-Llamas* and set forth above.

Our prior decisions identified by the dissent as holding a number of treaties to be self-executing, . . . stand only for the unremarkable proposition that some international agreements are self-executing and others are not. It is well settled that the "[i]nterpretation of [a treaty] . . . must, of course, begin with the language of the Treaty itself." . . . As a result, we have held treaties to be self-executing when the textual provisions indicate that the President and Senate intended for the agreement to have domestic effect. . . .

Our holding does not call into question the ordinary enforcement of foreign judgments or international arbitral agreements. Indeed, we agree with Medellin that, as a general matter, "an agreement to abide by the result" of an international adjudication—or what he really means, an agreement to give the result of such adjudication domestic legal effect—can be a treaty obligation like any other, so long as the agreement is consistent with the Constitution. . . . The point is that the particular treaty obligations on which Medellin relies do not of their own force create domestic law.

The dissent worries that our decision casts doubt on some 70-odd treaties under which the United States has agreed to submit disputes to the ICJ according to "roughly similar" provisions. . . . Again, under our established precedent, some treaties are self-executing and some are not, depending on the treaty. That the judgment of an international tribunal might not automatically become domestic law hardly means the underlying treaty is "useless." . . . Further, that an ICJ judgment may not be automatically enforceable in domestic courts does not mean the particular underlying treaty is not. Indeed, we have held that a number of the "Friendship, Commerce, and Navigation" Treaties cited by the dissent, ... are self-executing—based on "the language of the[se] Treat[ies]." . . . In addition, Congress is up to the task of implementing non-self-executing treaties, even those involving complex commercial disputes. . . .

Further, Medellin frames his argument as though giving the *Avena* judgment binding effect in domestic courts simply conforms to the proposition that domestic courts generally give effect to foreign judgments. But Medellin does not ask us to enforce a foreign-court judgment settling a typical commercial or property dispute. . . . Rather, Medellin argues that the *Avena* judgment has the effect of enjoining the operation of state law. What is more, on Medellin's view, the judgment would force the State to take action to "review and reconside[r]" his case. The general rule, however, is that judgments of foreign courts awarding injunctive relief, even as to private parties, let alone sovereign States, "are not generally entitled to enforcement." *See* 2 Restatement § 481, Comment *b*, at 595.

In sum, while the ICJ's judgment in *Avena* creates an international law obligation on the part of the United States, it does not of its own force constitute binding federal law that pre-empts state restrictions on the filing of successive habeas petitions. As we noted in *Sanchez-Llamas*, a contrary conclusion would be extraordinary, given that basic rights guaranteed by our own Constitution do not have the effect of displacing state procedural rules. . . . Nothing in the text, background, negotiating and drafting history, or practice among signatory nations suggests that the President or Senate intended the improbable result of giving the judgments of an international tribunal a higher status than that enjoyed by "many of our most fundamental constitutional protections." . . .

Medellin next argues that the ICJ's judgment in *Avena* is binding on state courts by virtue of the President's February 28, 2005 Memorandum. . . . Such considerations, however, do not allow us to set aside first principles. The President's authority to act, as with the exercise of any governmental power, "must stem either from an act of Congress or from the Constitution itself." . . .

Justice Jackson's familiar tripartite scheme provides the accepted framework for evaluating executive action in this area. First, "[w]hen the President acts pursuant to an express or implied authorization of Congress, his authority is at its maximum, for it includes all that he possesses in his own right plus all that Congress can delegate." . . . Second, "[w]hen the President acts in absence of either a congressional grant or denial of authority, he can only rely upon his own independent powers, but there is a zone of twilight in which he and Congress may have concurrent authority, or in which its distribution is uncertain." . . . In this circumstance, Presidential authority can derive support from "congressional inertia, indifference or quiescence." . . . Finally, "[w]hen the President takes measures incompatible with the expressed or implied will of Congress, his power is at its lowest ebb," and the Court can sustain his actions "only by disabling the Congress from acting upon the subject." . . .

The United States marshals two principal arguments in favor of the President's authority "to establish binding rules of decision that preempt contrary state law." . . . The Solicitor General first argues that the relevant treaties give the President the authority to implement the *Avena* judgment and that Congress has acquiesced in the exercise of such authority. The United States also relies upon an "independent" international dispute-resolution power wholly apart from the asserted authority based on the pertinent treaties. Medellin adds the additional argument that the President's Memorandum is a valid exercise of his power to take care that the laws be faithfully executed. . . .

The United States maintains that the President's Memorandum is authorized by the Optional Protocol and the U. N. Charter. . . . That is, because the relevant treaties "create an obligation to comply with *Avena*," they "*implicitly* give the President authority to implement that treaty-based obligation." . . . As a result, the President's Memorandum is well grounded in the first category of the *Youngstown* framework. . . . We disagree.

The President has an array of political and diplomatic means available to enforce international obligations, but unilaterally converting a non-self-executing treaty into a self-executing one is not among them. The responsibility for transforming an international obligation arising from a non-self-executing treaty into domestic law falls to Congress. As this Court has explained, when treaty stipulations are "not self-executing they can only be enforced pursuant to legislation to carry them into effect." ... Moreover, "[u]ntil such act shall be passed, the Court is not at liberty to disregard the existing laws on the subject." ...

The requirement that Congress, rather than the President, implement a non-self-executing treaty derives from the text of the Constitution, which divides the treaty-making power between the President and the Senate. The Constitution vests the President with the authority to "make" a treaty. Art. II, §2. If the Executive determines that a treaty should have domestic effect of its own force, that determination may be implemented "in mak[ing]" the treaty, by ensuring that it contains language plainly providing for domestic enforceability. If the treaty is to be self-executing in this respect, the Senate must consent to the treaty by the requisite two-thirds vote.... consistent with all other constitutional restraints.

Once a treaty is ratified without provisions clearly according it domestic effect, however, whether the treaty will ever have such effect is governed by the fundamental constitutional principle that "'[t]he power to make the necessary laws is in Congress; the power to execute in the President.'" .... Each of the two means described above for giving domestic effect to an international treaty obligation under the Constitution—for making law—requires joint action by the Executive and Legislative Branches: The Senate can ratify a self-executing treaty "ma[de]" by the Executive, or, if the ratified treaty is not self-executing, Congress can enact implementing legislation approved by the President. It should not be surprising that our Constitution does not contemplate vesting such power in the Executive alone. As Madison explained in The Federalist No. 47, under our constitutional system of checks and balances, "[t]he magistrate in whom the whole executive power resides cannot of himself make a law." J. Cooke ed., p. 326 (1961). That would, however, seem an apt description of the asserted executive authority unilaterally to give the effect of domestic law to obligations under a non-self-executing treaty.

The United States nonetheless maintains that the President's Memorandum should be given effect as domestic law because "this case involves a valid Presidential action in the context of Congressional 'acquiescence'." ... Under the *Youngstown* tripartite framework, congressional acquiescence is pertinent when the President's action falls within the second category—that is, when he "acts in absence of either a congressional grant or denial of authority." ... Here, however, as we have explained, the President's effort to accord domestic effect to the *Avena* judgment does not meet that prerequisite.

In any event, even if we were persuaded that congressional acquiescence could support the President's asserted authority to create domestic law pursuant to a non-self-executing treaty, such acquiescence does not exist here. The United States first locates congressional acquiescence in Congress's failure to act following the President's resolution of prior ICJ controversies. A review of the Executive's actions in those prior cases, however, cannot support the claim that Congress acquiesced in this particular exercise of Presidential authority, for none of them remotely involved transforming an international obligation into domestic law and thereby displacing state law....

We thus turn to the United States' claim that—independent of the United States' treaty obligations—the Memorandum is a valid exercise of the President's foreign affairs authority to resolve claims disputes with foreign nations.... The United States relies on a series of cases in which this Court has upheld the authority of the President to settle foreign claims pursuant to an executive agreement....

Rather than relying on the United States' treaty obligations, the President relies on an independent source of authority in ordering Texas to put aside its procedural bar to successive habeas petitions. Nevertheless, we find that our claims-settlement cases do not support the authority that the President asserts in this case.... The claims-settlement cases involve a narrow set of circumstances: the making of executive agreements to settle civil claims between American citizens and foreign governments or foreign nationals....

The President's Memorandum is not supported by a "particularly longstanding practice" of congressional acquiescence,... but rather is what the United States itself has described as "unprecedented action".... Indeed, the Government has not identified a single instance in which the President has attempted (or Congress has acquiesced in) a Presidential directive issued to state courts, much less one that reaches deep into the heart of the State's police powers and compels state courts to reopen final criminal judgments and set aside neutrally applicable state laws....

Medellin argues that the President's Memorandum is a valid exercise of his "Take Care" power.... The United States, however, does not rely upon the President's responsibility to "take Care that the Laws be faithfully executed." U.S. Const., Art. II, § 3. We think this a wise concession. This authority allows the President to execute the laws, not make them. For the reasons we have stated, the *Avena* judgment is not domestic law; accordingly, the President cannot rely on his Take Care powers here.... The judgment of the Texas Court of Criminal Appeals is affirmed.

Justice Stevens, concurring in the judgment.

There is a great deal of wisdom in Justice Breyer's dissent. I agree that the text and history of the Supremacy Clause, as well as this Court's treaty-related cases, do not support a presumption against self-execution.... Moreover, I think this case presents a closer question than the Court's opinion allows. In the end, however, I am persuaded that the relevant treaties do not authorize this Court to enforce the judgment of the International Court of Justice (ICJ) in *Case Concerning Avena and Other Mexican Nationals* (*Mex. v. U.S.*), 2004 I. C. J. 12 (Judgment of Mar. 31) (*Avena*)....

Even though the ICJ's judgment in *Avena* is not "the supreme Law of the Land," U.S. Const., Art. VI, cl. 2, no one disputes that it constitutes an international law obligation on the part of the United States.... By issuing a memorandum declaring that state courts should give effect to the judgment in *Avena*, the President made a commendable attempt to induce the States to discharge the Nation's obligation. I agree with the Texas judges and the majority of this Court that the President's memorandum is not binding law. Nonetheless, the fact that the President cannot legislate unilaterally does not absolve the United States from its promise to take action necessary to comply with the ICJ's judgment.

On the other hand, the costs of refusing to respect the ICJ's judgment are significant. The entire Court and the President agree that breach will jeopardize the United States' "plainly compelling" interests in "ensuring the reciprocal observance of the Vienna Convention, protecting relations with foreign governments, and demonstrating commitment to the role of international law." . . . When the honor of the Nation is balanced against the modest cost of compliance, Texas would do well to recognize that more is at stake than whether judgments of the ICJ, and the principled admonitions of the President of the United States, trump state procedural rules in the absence of implementing legislation.

The Court's judgment, which I join, does not foreclose further appropriate action by the State of Texas.

JUSTICE BREYER, with whom JUSTICE SOUTER and JUSTICE GINSBURG join, dissenting.

. . . .

The critical question here is whether the Supremacy Clause requires Texas to follow, *i.e.*, to enforce, this ICJ judgment. The Court says "no." And it reaches its negative answer by interpreting the labyrinth of treaty provisions as creating a legal obligation that binds the United States internationally, but which, for Supremacy Clause purposes, is not automatically enforceable as domestic law. In the majority's view, the Optional Protocol simply sends the dispute to the ICJ; the ICJ statute says that the ICJ will subsequently reach a judgment; and the U. N. Charter contains no more than a promise to "'undertak[e] to comply'" with that judgment. . . . Such a promise, the majority says, does not as a domestic law matter (in Chief Justice Marshall's words) "operat[e] of itself without the aid of any legislative provision." . . . . Rather, here (and presumably in any other ICJ judgment rendered pursuant to any of the approximately 70 U.S. treaties in force that contain similar provisions for submitting treaty-based disputes to the ICJ for decisions that bind the parties) Congress must enact specific legislation before ICJ judgments entered pursuant to our consent to compulsory ICJ jurisdiction can become domestic law. . . .

In my view, the President has correctly determined that Congress need not enact additional legislation. The majority places too much weight upon treaty language that says little about the matter. The words "undertak[e] to comply," for example, do not tell us whether an ICJ judgment rendered pursuant to the parties' consent to compulsory ICJ jurisdiction does, or does not, automatically become part of our domestic law. To answer that question we must look instead to our own domestic law, in particular, to the many treaty-related cases interpreting the Supremacy Clause. Those cases, including some written by Justices well aware of the Founders' original intent, lead to the conclusion that the ICJ judgment before us is enforceable as a matter of domestic law without further legislation. . . .

[The dissent discusses existing case law.]

. . . .

All of these cases make clear that self-executing treaty provisions are not uncommon or peculiar creatures of our domestic law; that they cover a wide range of subjects; that the Supremacy Clause itself answers the self-execution question by applying many, but not all, treaty provisions directly to the States; and that the Clause answers the self-execution question differently than does the law in many other nations. The cases also provide criteria that help determine *which* provisions automatically so apply — a matter to which I now turn. . . .

The case law provides no simple magic answer to the question whether a particular treaty provision is self-executing. But the case law does make clear that, insofar as today's majority looks for language about "self-execution" in the treaty itself and insofar as it erects "clear statement" presumptions designed to help find an answer, it is misguided. . . .

The many treaty provisions that this Court has found self-executing contain no textual language on the point. . . . These many Supreme Court cases finding treaty provisions to be self-executing cannot be reconciled with the majority's demand for textual clarity. . . . Indeed, the majority does not point to a single ratified United States treaty that contains the kind of "clea[r]" or "plai[n]" textual indication for which the majority searches. . . .

In a word, for present purposes, the absence or presence of language in a treaty about a provision's self-execution proves nothing at all. At best the Court is hunting the snark. At worst it erects legalistic hurdles that can threaten the application of provisions in many existing commercial and other treaties and make it more difficult to negotiate new ones.

The case law also suggests practical, context-specific criteria that this Court has previously used to help determine whether, for Supremacy Clause purposes, a treaty provision is self-executing. . . .

In making this determination, this Court has found the provision's subject matter of particular importance. Does the treaty provision declare peace? Does it promise not to engage in hostilities? If so, it addresses itself to the political branches. . . . Alternatively, does it concern the adjudication of traditional private legal rights such as rights to own property, to conduct a business, or to obtain civil tort recovery? If so, it may well address itself to the Judiciary. Enforcing such rights and setting their boundaries is the bread-and-butter work of the courts. . . .

One might also ask whether the treaty provision confers specific, detailed individual legal rights. Does it set forth definite standards that judges can readily enforce? Other things being equal, where rights are specific and readily enforceable, the treaty provision more likely "addresses" the judiciary. . . . Alternatively, would direct enforcement require the courts to create a new cause of action? Would such enforcement engender constitutional controversy? Would it create constitutionally undesirable conflict with the other branches? In such circumstances, it is not likely that the provision contemplates direct judicial enforcement. . . .

Such questions, drawn from case law stretching back 200 years, do not create a simple test, let alone a magic formula. But they do help to constitute a practical, context-specific judicial approach, seeking to separate run-of-the-mill judicial matters from other matters, sometimes more politically charged, sometimes more clearly the responsibility of other branches, sometimes lacking those attributes that would permit courts to act on their own without more ado. And such an approach is all that we need to find an answer to the legal question now before us. . . .

Applying the approach just described, I would find the relevant treaty provisions self-executing as applied to the ICJ judgment before us (giving that judgment domestic legal effect) for the following reasons, taken together.

First, the language of the relevant treaties strongly supports direct judicial enforceability, at least of judgments of the kind at issue here. . . . . The upshot is that treaty language says that an ICJ decision is legally binding, but it leaves the implementation of that binding legal obligation to the domestic law of each signatory nation. In this Nation, the Supremacy Clause, as long and consistently interpreted, indicates that ICJ decisions rendered pursuant to provisions for binding adjudication must be domestically legally binding and enforceable in domestic courts *at least sometimes.* And for purposes of this argument, that conclusion is all that I need. The remainder of the discussion will explain why, if ICJ judgments *sometimes* bind domestic courts, then they have that effect here.

Second, the Optional Protocol here applies to a dispute about the meaning of a Vienna Convention provision that is itself self-executing and judicially enforceable. The Convention provision is about an individual's "rights," namely, his right upon being arrested to be informed of his separate right to contact his nation's consul. . . . The provision language is precise. The dispute arises at the intersection of an individual right with ordinary rules of criminal procedure; it consequently concerns the kind of matter with which judges are familiar. The provisions contain judicially enforceable standards. . . . And the judgment itself requires a further hearing of a sort that is typically judicial. . . .

Third, logic suggests that a treaty provision providing for "final" and "binding" judgments that "settl[e]" treaty-based disputes is self-executing insofar as the judgment in question concerns the meaning of an underlying treaty provision that is itself self-executing. . . . .

Fourth, the majority's very different approach has seriously negative practical implications. The United States has entered into at least 70 treaties that contain provisions for ICJ dispute settlement similar to the Protocol before us. . . .

Fifth, other factors, related to the particular judgment here at issue, make that judgment well suited to direct judicial enforcement. . . .

Sixth, to find the United States' treaty obligations self-executing as applied to the ICJ judgment (and consequently to find that judgment enforceable) does not threaten constitutional conflict with other branches; it does not require us to engage in nonjudicial activity; and it does not require us to create a new cause of action. The only question before us concerns the application of the ICJ judgment as binding law applicable to the parties in a particular criminal proceeding that Texas law creates independently of the treaty....

Seventh, neither the President nor Congress has expressed concern about direct judicial enforcement of the ICJ decision. To the contrary, the President favors enforcement of this judgment. Thus, insofar as foreign policy impact, the interrelation of treaty provisions, or any other matter within the President's special treaty, military, and foreign affairs responsibilities might prove relevant, such factors *favor,* rather than militate against, enforcement of the judgment before us....

For these seven reasons, I would find that the United States' treaty obligation to comply with the ICJ judgment in *Avena* is enforceable in court in this case without further congressional action beyond Senate ratification of the relevant treaties. The majority reaches a different conclusion because it looks for the wrong thing (explicit textual expression about self-execution) using the wrong standard (clarity) in the wrong place (the treaty language). Hunting for what the text cannot contain, it takes a wrong turn. It threatens to deprive individuals, including businesses, property owners, testamentary beneficiaries, consular officials, and others, of the workable dispute resolution procedures that many treaties, including commercially oriented treaties, provide. In a world where commerce, trade, and travel have become ever more international, that is a step in the wrong direction.

Were the Court for a moment to shift the direction of its legal gaze, looking instead to the Supremacy Clause and to the extensive case law interpreting that Clause as applied to treaties, I believe it would reach a better supported, more felicitous conclusion. That approach, well embedded in Court case law, leads to the conclusion that the ICJ judgment before us is judicially enforceable without further legislative action....

A determination that the ICJ judgment is enforceable does not quite end the matter, for the judgment itself requires us to make one further decision. It directs the United States to provide further judicial review of the 51 cases of Mexican nationals "by means of its own choosing." *Avena,* 2004 I. C. J., at 72, P153(9). As I have explained, I believe the judgment addresses itself to the Judicial Branch. This Court consequently must "choose" the means. And rather than, say, conducting the further review in this Court, or requiring Medellin to seek the review in another federal court, I believe that the proper forum for review would be the Texas-court proceedings that would follow a remand of this case....

The majority's two holdings taken together produce practical anomalies. They unnecessarily complicate the President's foreign affairs task insofar as, for example, they increase the likelihood of Security Council *Avena* enforcement proceedings, of worsening relations with our neighbor Mexico, of precipitating actions by other nations putting at risk American citizens who have the misfortune to be arrested while traveling abroad, or of diminishing our Nation's reputation abroad as a result of our failure to follow the "rule of law" principles that we preach. The holdings also encumber Congress with a task (postratification legislation) that, in respect to many decisions of international tribunals, it may not want and which it may find difficult to execute. . . . At the same time, insofar as today's holdings make it more difficult to enforce the judgments of international tribunals, including technical non-politically-controversial judgments, those holdings weaken that rule of law for which our Constitution stands. . . .

These institutional considerations make it difficult to reconcile the majority's holdings with the workable Constitution that the Founders envisaged. They reinforce the importance, in practice and in principle, of asking Chief Justice Marshall's question: Does a treaty provision address the "Judicial" Branch rather than the "Political Branches" of Government. . . . And they show the wisdom of the well-established precedent that indicates that the answer to the question here is "yes." . . . .

In sum, a strong line of precedent, likely reflecting the views of the Founders, indicates that the treaty provisions before us and the judgment of the International Court of Justice address themselves to the Judicial Branch and consequently are self-executing. In reaching a contrary conclusion, the Court has failed to take proper account of that precedent and, as a result, the Nation may well break its word even though the President seeks to live up to that word and Congress has done nothing to suggest the contrary. . . . For the reasons set forth, I respectfully dissent.

Notes

(1) Congress did not act. Texas executed Medellin on August 5, 2008. *See* Ed Stoddard, *Texas Defies World Court with Execution*, *available at* http://www.reuters.com/article/latestCrisis/idUSN05379236. Texas has executed at least two more of the Mexicans who were the subjects of *Avena*. *See Another Mexican National Executed in Texas in Defiance of* Avena *Decision*, 108 A.J.I.L. 322 (2014).

(2) Many commentators see *Medellin* as departing from previous precedent, and indeed from Article VI of the Constitution, and creating a presumption against self-execution. For a discussion of the issues, *see* John Quigley, *A Tragi-Comedy of Errors Erodes Self-Execution of Treaties:* Medellin v. Texas *and Beyond*, 45 Case W. Res. J. Int'l L. 403 (2012). The Restatement (Fourth) Foreign Relations Law of the United States (2018) stops short of such a presumption. It provides as follows in § 310:

> (2) Courts will evaluate whether the text and context of the provision, along with other treaty materials, are consistent with an understanding by the U.S. treatymakers that the provision would be directly enforceable in courts in the United States. Relevant considerations include:

(a) whether the treaty provision is sufficiently precise or obligatory to be suitable for direct application by the judiciary; and

(b) whether the provision was designed to have immediate effect, as opposed to contemplating additional measures by the political branches.

If the Senate's resolution of advice and consent specifies that a treaty provision is self-executing or non-self-executing, courts will defer to this specification.

(3) Courts will also regard a treaty provision as non-self-executing to the extent that implementing legislation is constitutionally required.

(3) Illinois has created a statute to address consular notification under the Vienna Convention on Consular Relations. The act became effective on January 1, 2016.

Sec. 103-1. Rights on arrest.

(b-5) This subsection is intended to implement and be interpreted consistently with the Vienna Convention on Consular Relations, to which the United States is a party. Article 36 of that Convention guarantees that when foreign nationals are arrested or detained, they must be advised of their right to have their consular officials notified, and if an individual chooses to exercise that right, a law enforcement official is required to notify the consulate. It does not create any new substantive State right or remedy.

(1) In accordance with federal law and the provisions of this Section, the law enforcement official in charge of a custodial facility shall ensure that any individual booked and detained at the facility, within 48 hours of booking or detention, shall be advised that if that individual is a foreign national, he or she has a right to communicate with an official from the consulate of his or her country. This subsection (b-5) does not create any affirmative duty to investigate whether an arrestee or detainee is a foreign national.

(2) If the foreign national requests consular notification or the notification is mandatory by law, the law enforcement official in charge of the custodial facility shall ensure the notice is given to the appropriate officer at the consulate of the foreign national in accordance with the U.S. Department of State Instructions for Consular Notification and Access.

(3) The law enforcement official in charge of the custodial facility where a foreign national is located shall ensure that the foreign national is allowed to communicate with, correspond with, and be visited by, a consular officer of his or her country.

Sec. 109-1. Person arrested.

. . . .

(d) At the initial appearance of a defendant in any criminal proceeding, the court must advise the defendant in open court that any foreign

> national who is arrested or detained has the right to have notice of the arrest or detention given to his or her country's consular representatives and the right to communicate with those consular representatives if the notice has not already been provided. The court must make a written record of so advising the defendant.
>
> (e) If consular notification is not provided to a defendant before his or her first appearance in court, the court shall grant any reasonable request for a continuance of the proceedings to allow contact with the defendant's consulate. Any delay caused by the granting of the request by a defendant shall temporarily suspend for the time of the delay the period within which a person shall be tried as prescribed by subsections (a), (b), or (e) of Section 103-5 of this Code and on the day of the expiration of delay the period shall continue at the point at which it was suspended.

For a detailed discussion of the statute, *see* Cindy Buys, *Illinois Adopts New Law to Better Implement Consular Notification and Access*, The Globe, Oct. 2015, at 3.

The *Avena* case was not the last word from the ICJ on Article 36 of the VCCR. In 2019, it returned to the issue in the *Jadhav* case.

Jadhav Case (India v. Pakistan)

International Court of Justice
2019 I.C.J. 418

[Mr. Jadhav, an Indian citizen, was arrested in Pakistan and accused of involvement in espionage and terrorism. He was sentenced to death by a Pakistani military court. India alleged a breach of his (and India's) rights under Article 36. After rejecting various arguments by Pakistan, notably its claim that there was an exception to Article 36 in the case of espionage, the Court continued to the question of the appropriate remedy.]

133. The Court has already found that Pakistan acted in breach of its obligations under Article 36 of the Vienna Convention, (i) by not informing Mr. Jadhav of his rights under Article 36, para-graph 1 (b); (ii) by not informing India, without delay, of the arrest and detention of Mr. Jadhav; and (iii) by denying access to Mr. Jadhav by consular officers of India, contrary to their right, inter alia, to arrange for his legal representation (see paragraphs 99–119 above).

134. The Court considers that the breaches by Pakistan set out in (i) and (iii) in the paragraph above constitute internationally wrongful acts of a continuing character. Accordingly, the Court is of the view that Pakistan is under an obligation to cease those acts and to comply fully with its obligations under Article 36 of the Vienna Convention. Consequently, Pakistan must inform Mr. Jadhav without further delay of his rights under Article 36, paragraph 1 (b), and allow Indian consular officers to have access to him and to arrange for his legal representation, as provided by Article 36, paragraph 1 (a) and (c).

135. With regard to India's submission that the Court declare that the sentence handed down by Pakistan's military court is violative of international law and the provisions of the Vienna Convention, the Court recalls that its jurisdiction has its basis in Article I of the Optional Protocol. This jurisdiction is limited to the interpretation or application of the Vienna Convention and does not extend to India's claims based on any other rules of international law (see paragraph 36 above). India refers to Article 14 of the International Covenant on Civil and Political Rights to support its requests for remedies. In accordance with the rule reflected in Article 31, paragraph 3(c), of the Vienna Convention on the Law of Treaties, the Covenant may be taken into account, together with the context, for the interpretation of the Vienna Convention on Consular Relations. The Court notes, however, that the remedy to be ordered in this case has the purpose of providing reparation only for the injury caused by the internationally wrongful act of Pakistan that falls within the Court's jurisdiction, namely its breach of obligations under Article 36 of the Vienna Convention on Consular Relations, and not of the Covenant.

136. As regards India's claim based on the Vienna Convention, the Court considers that it is not the conviction and sentence of Mr. Jadhav which are to be regarded as a violation of the provisions of the Vienna Convention. In the Avena case, the Court confirmed that "the case before it concerns Article 36 of the Vienna Convention and not the correctness as such of any conviction or sentencing", and that "it is not the convictions and sentences of the Mexican nationals which are to be regarded as a violation of international law, but solely certain breaches of treaty obligations [on consular access] which preceded them" (Avena and Other Mexican Nationals (Mexico v. United States of America), Judgment, I.C.J. Reports 2004 (I), p. 60, paras. 122–123).

137. With regard to India's contention that it is entitled to restitutio in integrum and its request to annul the decision of the military court and to restrain Pakistan from giving effect to the sentence or conviction, and its further request to direct Pakistan to take steps to annul the decision of the military court, to release Mr. Jadhav and to facilitate his safe passage to India, the Court reiterates that it is not the conviction and sentence of Mr. Jadhav which are to be regarded as a violation of Article 36 of the Vienna Convention. The Court also recalls that "[i]t is not to be presumed . . . that partial or total annulment of conviction or sentence provides the necessary and sole remedy" in cases of violations of Article 36 of the Vienna Convention (ibid., p. 60, para. 123). Thus, the Court finds that these submissions made by India cannot be upheld.

138. The Court reaffirms that "it is a principle of international law . . . that any breach of an engagement involves an obligation to make reparation" and that "reparation must, as far as possible, wipe out all the consequences of the illegal act" (Factory at Chorzów, Merits, Judgment No. 13, 1928, P.C.I.J., Series A, No. 17, pp. 29, 47 (Claim for Indemnity)). The Court considers the appropriate remedy in this case to be effective review and reconsideration of the conviction and sentence of Mr. Jadhav. This is consistent with the approach that the Court has taken in cases of violations of

Article 36 of the Convention (LaGrand (Germany v. United States of America), Judgment, I.C.J. Reports 2001, p. 514, para. 125; Avena and Other Mexican Nationals (Mexico v. United States of America), Judgment, I.C.J. Reports 2004 (I), pp. 65–66, paras. 138–140 and p. 73, para. 153). It is also in line with what the Applicant asks the Court to adjudge and declare in the present case. In the Court's view, India ultimately requests effective remedies for the breaches of the Convention by Pakistan. The Court notes that Pakistan acknowledges that the appropriate remedy in the present case would be effective review and reconsideration of the conviction and sentence.

139. The Court considers that a special emphasis must be placed on the need for the review and reconsideration to be effective. The review and reconsideration of the conviction and sentence of Mr. Jadhav, in order to be effective, must ensure that full weight is given to the effect of the violation of the rights set forth in Article 36, paragraph 1, of the Convention and guarantee that the violation and the possible prejudice caused by the violation are fully examined. It presupposes the existence of a procedure which is suitable for this purpose. The Court observes that it is normally the judicial process which is suited to the task of review and reconsideration (see Avena and Other Mexican Nationals (Mexico v. United States of America), Judgment, I.C.J. Reports 2004 (I), pp. 65–66, paras. 138–140).

140. In the present case, the death sentence imposed on Mr. Jadhav by the Field General Court Martial of Pakistan was confirmed by the Chief of Army Staff on 10 April 2017. The evidence suggests that Mr. Jadhav appealed to the Military Appellate Court under Section 133 (B) of the Pakistan Army Act of 1952, but that the appeal was rejected. With regard to the petition procedure, the evidence suggests that Mr. Jadhav has made a mercy petition to the Chief of Army Staff, and that the mother of Mr. Jadhav has sought to file a petition with the Federal Government of Pakistan under Section 131 and an appeal under Section 133 (B) of the Act. There is no evidence before the Court to indicate the outcome of those petitions or that appeal. . . . .

143. The Court confirms that the clemency process is not sufficient in itself to serve as an appropriate means of review and reconsideration but that "appropriate clemency procedures can supplement judicial review and reconsideration, in particular where the judicial system has failed to take due account of the violation of the rights set forth in the Vienna Convention" (Avena and Other Mexican Nationals (Mexico v. United States of America), Judgment, I.C.J. Reports 2004 (I), p. 66, para. 143). The evidence before the Court suggests that two clemency procedures are available to Mr. Jadhav: a mercy petition to the Chief of Army Staff within 60 days of the decision by the Appellate Court and a mercy petition to the President of Pakistan within 90 days of the decision of the Chief of Army Staff on the mercy petition (see paragraph 29 above). The outcome of the petition submitted by Mr. Jadhav to the Chief of Army Staff (see paragraph 140 above) has not, however, been made known to the Court. No evidence has been submitted to the Court regarding the presidential clemency procedure.

144. In light of these circumstances, the Court considers it imperative to re-emphasize that the review and reconsideration of the conviction and sentence of Mr. Jadhav must be effective. . . .

146. The Court notes that the obligation to provide effective review and reconsideration can be carried out in various ways. The choice of means is left to Pakistan (cf. LaGrand (Germany v. United States of America), Judgment, I.C.J. Reports 2001, p. 514, para. 125). Nevertheless, freedom in the choice of means is not without qualification (Avena and Other Mexican Nationals (Mexico v. United States of America), Judgment, I.C.J. Reports 2004 (I), p. 62, para. 131). The obligation to provide effective review and reconsideration is "an obligation of result" which "must be performed unconditionally" (Request for Interpretation of the Judgment of 31 March 2004 in the Case concerning Avena and Other Mexican Nationals (Mexico v. United States of America) (Mexico v. United States of America), Judgment, I.C.J. Reports 2009, p. 17, para. 44). Consequently, Pakistan shall take all measures to provide for effective review and reconsideration, including, if necessary, by enacting appropriate legislation.

147. To conclude, the Court finds that Pakistan is under an obligation to provide, by means of its own choosing, effective review and reconsideration of the conviction and sentence of Mr. Jadhav, so as to ensure that full weight is given to the effect of the violation of the rights set forth in Article 36 of the Vienna Convention, taking account of paragraphs 139, 145 and 146 of this Judgment.

Chapter 20

The Nuremberg and Tokyo Precedents

§ 20.01 The Nuremberg Trial

Judgment of the International Military Tribunal for the Trial of German Major War Criminals

Nuremberg, Sept. 30 & Oct. 1, 1946 Cmd. 6964

On the 8th August, 1945, the Government of the United Kingdom of Great Britain and Northern Ireland, the Government of the United States of America, the Provisional Government of the French Republic, and the Government of the Union of Soviet Socialist Republics entered into an Agreement establishing this Tribunal for the Trial of War Criminals whose offences have no particular geographical location. . . .

By the Charter annexed to the Agreement, the constitution, jurisdiction and functions of the Tribunal were defined. The Tribunal was invested with power to try and punish persons who had committed crimes against peace, war crimes and crimes against humanity as defined in the Charter. The Charter also provided that at the trial of any individual member of any group or organisation the Tribunal may declare (in connection with any act of which the individual may be convicted) that the group or organisation of which the individual was a member was a criminal organisation. . . .

[I]n accordance with Article 14 of the Charter, an Indictment was lodged against the defendants . . . who had been designated by the Committee of the Chief Prosecutors of the signatory Powers as major war criminals. . . . This Indictment charges the defendants with crimes against peace by the planning, preparation, initiation and waging of wars of aggression, which were also wars in violation of international treaties, agreements and assurances; with war crimes; and with crimes against humanity. The defendants are also charged with participating in the formulation or execution of a common plan or conspiracy to commit all these crimes. The Tribunal was further asked by the Prosecution to declare [certain] named groups or organisations to be criminal within the meaning of the Charter. . . .

The Trial which was conducted in four languages — English, Russian, French and German — began on the 20th November, 1945, and pleas of "Not Guilty" were made by all the defendants except Bormann [who was tried *in absentia*]. The hearing of evidence and the speeches of Counsel concluded on 31st August, 1946. . . .

The Charter Provisions

The individual defendants are indicted under Article 6 of the Charter, which is as follows:

> Article 6. The Tribunal established by the Agreement referred to in Article 1 hereof for the trial and punishment of the major war criminals of the European Axis countries shall have the power to try and punish persons who, acting in the interests of the European Axis countries, whether as individuals or as members of organisations, committed any of the following crimes:
>
> The following acts, or any of them, are crimes, coming within the jurisdiction of the Tribunal for which there shall be individual responsibility:
>
> (a) Crimes against Peace: namely, planning, preparation, initiation or waging of a war of aggression, or a war in violation of international treaties, agreements or assurances, or participation in a common plan or conspiracy for the accomplishment of any of the foregoing:
>
> (b) War Crimes: namely, violations of the laws or customs of war. Such violations shall include, but not be limited to, murder ill-treatment or deportation to slave labour or for any other purpose of civilian population of or in occupied territory, murder or ill-treatment of prisoners of war or persons on the seas, killing of hostages, plunder of public or private property, wanton destruction of cities, towns or villages, or devastation not justified by military necessity:
>
> (c) Crimes against Humanity: namely, murder, extermination, enslavement, deportation, and other inhumane acts committed against any civilian population, before or during the war, or persecutions on political, racial or religious grounds in execution of or in connection with any crime within the jurisdiction of the Tribunal, whether or not in violation of the domestic law of the country where perpetrated.
>
> Leaders, organisers, instigators and accomplices participating in the formulation or execution of a common plan or conspiracy to commit any of the foregoing crimes are responsible for all acts performed by any persons in execution of such plan.

The Common Plan or Conspiracy and Aggressive War

. . . .

Count One of the Indictment charges the defendants with conspiring or having a common plan to commit crimes against peace. Count Two of the Indictment charges the defendants with committing specific crimes against peace by planning, preparing, initiating, and waging wars of aggression against a number of other States. . . .

The charges in the Indictment that the defendants planned and waged aggressive wars are charges of the utmost gravity. War is essentially an evil thing. Its consequences are not confined to the belligerent states alone, but affect the whole world.

To initiate a war of aggression, therefore, is not only an international crime; it is the supreme international crime differing only from other war crimes in that it contains within itself the accumulated evil of the whole.

The first acts of aggression referred to in the Indictment are the seizure of Austria and Czechoslovakia and the first war of aggression charged in the Indictment is the war against Poland begun on the 1st September, 1939.

....

The war against Poland did not come suddenly out of an otherwise clear sky; the evidence has made it plain that this war of aggression, as well as the seizure of Austria and Czechoslovakia, was pre-meditated and carefully prepared, and was not undertaken until the moment was thought opportune for it to be carried through as a definite part of the pre-ordained scheme and plan. For the aggressive designs of the Nazi Government were not accidents arising out of the immediate political situation in Europe and the world; they were a deliberate and essential part of Nazi foreign policy....

The Law of the Charter

The jurisdiction of the Tribunal is defined in the Agreement and Charter, and the crimes coming within the jurisdiction of the Tribunal, for which there shall be individual responsibility, are set out in Article 6. The law of the Charter is decisive, and binding upon the Tribunal.

The making of the Charter was the exercise of the sovereign legislative power by the countries to which the German Reich unconditionally surrendered; and the undoubted right of these countries to legislate for the occupied territories has been recognised by the civilised world. The Charter is not an arbitrary exercise of power on the part of the victorious nations, but in the view of the Tribunal, as will be shown, it is the expression of international law existing at the time of its creation; and to that extent is itself a contribution to international law.

The Signatory Powers created this Tribunal, defined the law it was to administer, and made regulations for the proper conduct of the Trial. In doing so, they have done together what any one of them might have done singly; for it is not to be doubted that any nation has the right thus to set up special courts to administer law. With regard to the constitution of the court, all that the defendants are entitled to ask is to receive a fair trial on the facts and law.

The Charter makes the planning or waging of a war of aggression or a war in violation of international treaties a crime, and it is therefore not strictly necessary to consider whether and to what extent aggressive war was a crime before the execution of the London Agreement. But in view of the great importance of the questions of law involved, the Tribunal has heard full argument from the Prosecution and the Defence, and will express its view on the matter.

It was urged on behalf of the defendants that a fundamental principle of all law—international and domestic—is that there can be no punishment of crime without a pre-existing law. "*Nullum crimen sine lege, nulla poena sine lege.*" It was submitted that *ex post facto* punishment is abhorrent to the law of all civilised nations, that no sovereign power had made aggressive war a crime at the time the alleged criminal acts were committed, that no statute had defined aggressive war, that no penalty had been fixed for its commission, and no court had been created to try and punish offenders.

In the first place, it is to be observed that the maxim *nullum crimen sine lege* is not a limitation of sovereignty, but is in general a principle of justice. To assert that it is unjust to punish those who in defiance of treaties and assurances have attacked neighbouring states without warning is obviously untrue, for in such circumstances the attacker must know that he is doing wrong, and so far from it being unjust to punish him, it would be unjust if his wrong were allowed to go unpunished. Occupying the positions they did in the government of Germany, the defendants, or at least some of them must have known of the treaties signed by Germany, outlawing recourse to war for the settlement of international disputes; they must have known that they were acting in defiance of all international law when in complete deliberation they carried out the designs of invasion and aggression. On this view of the case alone, it would appear that the maxim has no application to the present facts.

This view is strongly reinforced by a consideration of the state of international law in 1939, so far as aggressive war is concerned. The General Treaty for the Renunciation of War of 27th August, 1928, more generally known as the Pact of Paris or the Kellogg-Briand Pact, was binding on sixty-three nations, including Germany, Italy and Japan at the outbreak of war in 1939. . . .

[W]hat was the legal effect of this Pact? The nations who signed the Pact or adhered to it unconditionally condemned recourse to war for the future as an instrument of policy, and expressly renounced it. After the signing of the Pact, any nation resorting to war as an instrument of national policy breaks the Pact. In the opinion of the Tribunal, the solemn renunciation of war as an instrument of national policy necessarily involves the proposition that such a war is illegal in international law; and that those who plan and wage such a war, with its inevitable and terrible consequences, are committing a crime in so doing. War for the solution of international controversies undertaken as an instrument of national policy certainly includes a war of aggression, and such a war is therefore outlawed by the Pact. . . .

But it is argued that the Pact does not expressly enact that such wars are crimes, or set up courts to try those who make such wars. To that extent the same is true with regard to the laws of war contained in the Hague Convention. The Hague Convention of 1907 prohibited resort to certain methods of waging war. These included the inhumane treatment of prisoners, the employment of poisoned weapons, the improper use of flags of truce, and similar matters. Many of these prohibitions had been enforced long before the date of the Convention; but since 1907 they have certainly been crimes, punishable as offences against the laws of war; yet the Hague Convention nowhere designates such practices as criminal, nor is any sentence prescribed, nor any mention made of a court to try and punish offenders. For many years past, however, military tribunals have tried and punished individuals guilty of violating the rules of land warfare laid down by this Convention. In the opinion of the Tribunal, those who wage aggressive war are doing that which is equally illegal, and of much greater moment than a breach of one of the rules of the Hague Convention. In interpreting the words of the Pact, it must be remembered that international law is not the product of an international legislature, and that such international agreements as the Pact have to deal with general principles of law, and not with administrative matters of procedure. The law of war is to be found not only in treaties, but in the customs and practices of states which gradually obtained universal recognition, and from the general principles of justice applied by jurists and practiced by military courts. This law is not static, but by continual adaptation follows the needs of a changing world. Indeed, in many cases treaties do no more than express and define for more accurate reference the principles of law already existing.

The view which the Tribunal takes of the true interpretation of the Pact is supported by the international history which preceded it. In the year 1923 the draft of a Treaty of Mutual Assistance was sponsored by the League of Nations. . . . The preamble to the League of Nations 1924 Protocol for the Pacific Settlement of International Disputes ("Geneva Protocol"), after "recognising the solidarity of the members of the international community," declared that "a war of aggression constitutes a violation of this solidarity and is an international crime." . . . Although the Protocol was never ratified, it was signed by the leading statesmen of the world, representing the vast majority of the civilised states and peoples, and may be regarded as strong evidence of the intention to brand aggressive war as an international crime.

At the meeting of the Assembly of the League of Nations on the 24th September, 1927, all the delegations then present (including the German, the Italian and the Japanese), unanimously adopted a declaration concerning wars of aggression. The preamble to the declaration stated . . . "that a war of aggression . . . is . . . an international crime." The unanimous resolution of the 18th February, 1928, of twenty-one American Republics of the Sixth (Havana) Pan-American Conference, declared that "war of aggression constitutes an international crime against the human species."

All these expressions of opinion, and others that could be cited, so solemnly made, reinforce the construction which the Tribunal placed upon the Pact of Paris, that resort to a war of aggression is not merely illegal, but is criminal. The prohibition of aggressive war demanded by the conscience of the world, finds its expression in the series of pacts and treaties to which the Tribunal has just referred.

It is also important to remember that Article 227 of the Treaty of Versailles provided for the constitution of a special Tribunal, composed of representatives of five of the Allied and Associated Powers which had been belligerents in the first World War opposed to Germany, to try the former German Emperor "for a supreme offence against international morality and the sanctity of treaties." The purpose of this trial was expressed to be "to vindicate the solemn obligations of international undertakings, and the validity of international morality." In Article 228 of the Treaty, the German Government expressly recognised the right of the Allied Powers "to bring before military tribunals persons accused of having committed acts in violation of the laws and customs of war."

It was submitted that international law is concerned with the action of sovereign States, and provides no punishment for individuals; and further, that where the act in question is an act of state, those who carry it out are not personally responsible, but are protected by the doctrine of the sovereignty of the State. In the opinion of the Tribunal, both these submissions must be rejected. That international law imposes duties and liabilities upon individuals as well as upon States has long been recognised. In the recent case of *Ex Parte Quirin,* 317 U.S. 1 (1942), before the Supreme Court of the United States, persons were charged during the war with landing in the United States for purposes of spying and sabotage. The late Justice Stone, speaking for the Court, said: "From the very beginning of its history this Court has applied the law of war as including that part of the law of nations which prescribes for the conduct of war the status, rights and duties of enemy nations as well as enemy individuals." He went on to give a list of cases tried by the Courts, where individual offenders were charged with offences against the laws of nations, and particularly the laws of war. Many other authorities could be quoted, but enough has been said to show that individuals can be punished for violations of international law. Crimes against international law are committed by men, not by abstract entities, and only by punishing individuals who commit such crimes can the provisions of international law be enforced. . . .

The principle of international law, which under certain circumstances, protects the representatives of a state, cannot be applied to acts which are condemned as criminal by international law. The authors of these facts cannot shelter themselves behind their official position in order to be freed from punishment in appropriate proceedings. Article 7 of the Charter expressly declares: "The official position of defendants, whether as Heads of State, or responsible officials in government departments, shall not be considered as freeing them from responsibility, or mitigating punishment."

On the other hand the very essence of the Charter is that individuals have international duties which transcend the national obligations of obedience imposed by the individual State. He who violates the laws of war cannot obtain immunity while acting in pursuance of the authority of the State if the State in authorising action moves outside its competence under international law.

It was also submitted on behalf of most of these defendants that in doing what they did they were acting under the orders of Hitler, and therefore cannot be held responsible for the acts committed by them in carrying out these orders. The Charter specially provides in Article 8: "The fact that the defendant acted pursuant to order of his Government or of a superior shall not free him from responsibility, but may be considered in mitigation of punishment." The provisions of this Article are in conformity with the law of all nations. That a soldier was ordered to kill or torture in violation of the international law of war has never been recognised as a defence to such acts of brutality, though, as the Charter here provides, the order may be urged in mitigation of the punishment. The true test, which is found in varying degrees in the criminal law of most nations, is not the existence of the order, but whether moral choice was in fact possible.

The Law as to the Common Plan or Conspiracy

. . . .

Count One. . . . charges not only the conspiracy to commit aggressive war, but also to commit war crimes and crimes against humanity. But the Charter does not define as a separate crime any conspiracy except the one to commit acts of aggressive war. Article 6 of the Charter provides: "Leaders, organisers, instigators and accomplices participating in the formulation or execution of a common plan or conspiracy to commit any of the foregoing crimes are responsible for all acts performed by any persons in execution of such plan." In the opinion of the Tribunal these words do not add a new and separate crime to those already listed. The words are designed to establish the responsibility of persons participating in a common plan. The Tribunal will therefore disregard the charges in Count One that the defendants conspired to commit war crimes and crimes against humanity, and will consider only the common plan to prepare, initiate and wage aggressive war.

War Crimes and Crimes Against Humanity

The evidence relating to war crimes has been overwhelming, in its volume and its detail. It is impossible for this Judgment adequately to review it, or to record the mass of documentary and oral evidence that has been presented. The truth remains that war crimes were committed on a vast scale, never before seen in the history of war. They were perpetrated in all the countries occupied by Germany, and on the High Seas, and were attended by every conceivable circumstance of cruelty and horror. There can be no doubt that the majority of them arose from the Nazi conception of "total war," with which the aggressive wars were waged. For in this conception of "total war," the moral ideas underlying the conventions which seek to make war more humane are no longer regarded as having force or validity. Everything is made subordinate to the overmastering dictates of war. Rules, regulations, assurances and treaties all alike are of no moment, and so, freed from the restraining influence of international law, the aggressive war is conducted by the Nazi leaders in the most barbaric way. Accordingly, war crimes were committed when and wherever the Fuehrer and his close associates thought them to be advantageous. They were for the most part the result of cold and criminal calculation.

On some occasions, war crimes were deliberately planned long in advance. In the case of the Soviet Union, the plunder of the territories to be occupied, and the ill-treatment of the civilian population, were settled in minute detail before the attack was begun. . . . Similarly, when planning to exploit the inhabitants of the occupied countries for slave labour on the very greatest scale, the German Government conceived it as an integral part of the war economy, and planned and organised this particular war crime down to the last elaborate detail.

Other war crimes, such as the murder of prisoners of war who had escaped and been recaptured, or the murder of Commandos or captured airmen, or the destruction of the Soviet Commissars, were the result of direct orders circulated through the highest official channels. . . .

Prisoners of war were ill-treated and tortured and murdered, not only in defiance of the well-established rules of international law, but in complete disregard of the elementary dictates of humanity. Civilian populations in occupied territories suffered the same fate. Whole populations were deported to Germany for the purposes of slave labour upon defence works, armament production and similar tasks connected with the war effort. Hostages were taken in very large numbers from the civilian populations in all the occupied countries, and were shot as suited the German purposes. Public and private property was systematically plundered and pillaged in order to enlarge the resources of Germany at the expense of the rest of Europe. Cities and towns and villages were wantonly destroyed without military justification or necessity. . . .

Murder and Ill-Treatment of Civilian Population

Article 6(b) of the Charter provides that "ill-treatment . . . of civilian population of or in occupied territory . . . killing of hostages . . . wanton destruction of cities, towns or villages" shall be a war crime. In the main these provisions are merely declaratory of the existing laws of war as expressed by the Hague Convention, Article 46 . . . .

The territories occupied by Germany were administered in violation of the laws of war. The evidence is quite overwhelming of a systematic rule of violence, brutality and terror. . . . One of the most notorious means of terrorising the people in occupied territories was the use of concentration camps. They were first established in Germany at the moment of the seizure of power by the Nazi Government. Their original purpose was to imprison without trial all those persons who were opposed to the Government, or who were in any way obnoxious to German authority. With the aid of a secret police force, this practice was widely extended and in course of time concentration camps became places of organised and systematic murder, where millions of people were destroyed. In the administration of the occupied territories the concentration camps were used to destroy all opposition groups. . . . A certain number of the concentration camps were equipped with gas chambers for the wholesale destruction of the inmates, and with furnaces for the burning of the bodies. Some of them were in fact used for the extermination of Jews as part of the "final solution" of the Jewish problem. . . .

Slave Labour Policy

Article 6 (b) of the Charter provides that the "ill-treatment, or deportation to slave labour or for any other purpose, of civilian population of or in occupied territory" shall be a war crime. The laws relating to forced labour by the inhabitants of occupied territories are found in Article 52 of The Hague Convention, which provides: "Requisition in kind and services shall not be demanded from municipalities or inhabitants except for the needs of the army of occupation. They shall be in proportion to the resources of the country, and of such a nature as not to involve the inhabitants in the obligation of taking part in military operations against their own country."

The policy of the German occupation authorities was in flagrant violation of the terms of this Convention. . . . [T]he German occupation authorities succeed[ed] in forcing many of the inhabitants of the occupied territories to work for the German war effort, and in deporting at least 5,000,000 persons to Germany to serve German industry and agriculture.

Persecution of the Jews

The persecution of the Jews at the hands of the Nazi Government has been proved in the greatest detail before the Tribunal. It is a record of consistent and systematic inhumanity on the greatest scale. The anti-Jewish policy was formulated in [the Nazi] Party Programme. . . . . With the seizure of power, the persecution of the Jews was intensified. A series of discriminatory laws were passed, which limited the offices and professions permitted to Jews; and restrictions were placed on their family life and their rights of citizenship. By the autumn of 1938, the Nazi policy towards the Jews had reached the stage where it was directed towards the complete exclusion of Jews from German life. Pogroms were organised which included the burning and demolishing of synagogues, the looting of Jewish businesses, and the arrest of prominent Jewish business men. A collective fine of one billion marks was imposed on the Jews, the seizure of Jewish assets was authorised, and the movement of Jews was restricted by regulations to certain specified districts and hours. The creation of ghettoes was carried out on an extensive scale, and by an order of the Security Police Jews were compelled to wear a yellow star to be worn on the breast and back.

It was contended for the Prosecution that certain aspects of this anti-Semitic policy were connected with the plans for aggressive war. The violent measures taken against the Jews in November, 1938, were nominally in retaliation for the killing of an official of the German Embassy in Paris. But the decision to seize Austria and Czechoslovakia had been made a year before. The imposition of a fine of one billion marks was made, and the confiscation of the financial holdings of the Jews was decreed, at a time when German armament expenditure had put the German treasury in difficulties, and when the reduction of expenditure on armaments was being considered. . . .

The Nazi persecution of Jews in Germany before the war, severe and repressive as it was, cannot compare, however, with the policy pursued during the war in the occupied territories. Originally the policy was similar to that which had been in force inside Germany. . . . In the summer of 1941, however, plans were made for the "final solution" of the Jewish question in all of Europe. This "final solution "meant the extermination of the Jews, which early in 1939 Hitler had threatened would be one of the consequences of an outbreak of war, and a special section in the Gestapo under Adolf Eichmann, as head of Section B4 of the Gestapo, was formed to carry out the policy. The plan for exterminating the Jews was developed shortly after the attack on the Soviet Union. . . .

Part of the "final solution" was the gathering of Jews from all German occupied Europe in concentration camps. Their physical condition was the test of life or death. All who were fit to work were used as slave labourers in the concentration camps; all who were not fit to work were destroyed in gas chambers and their bodies burnt. Certain concentration camps such as Treblinka and Auschwitz were set aside for this main purpose. . . . Adolf Eichmann, who had been put in charge of this programme by Hitler, has estimated that the policy pursued resulted in the killing of 6,000,000 Jews, of which 4,000,000 were killed in the extermination institutions.

The Law Relating to War Crimes and Crimes Against Humanity

. . . .

The Tribunal is of course bound by the Charter, in the definition which it gives both of war crimes and crimes against humanity. With respect to war crimes, however, as has already been pointed out, the crimes defined by Article 6, section (b), of the Charter were already recognised as war crimes under international law. They were covered by Articles 46, 50, 52, and 56 of the Hague Convention of 1907, and Articles 2, 3, 4, 46 and 51 of the Geneva Convention of 1929. That violations of these provisions constituted crimes for which the guilty individuals were punishable is too well settled to admit of argument.

But it is argued that the Hague Convention does not apply in this case, because of the "general participation" clause in Article 2 of the Hague Convention of 1907. That clause provided: "The provisions contained in the regulations (Rules of Land Warfare) referred to in Article 1 as well as in the present Convention do not apply except between contracting powers, and then only if all the belligerents are parties to the Convention." Several of the belligerents in the recent war were not parties to this Convention.

In the opinion of the Tribunal it is not necessary to decide this question. The rules of land warfare expressed in the Convention undoubtedly represented an advance over existing international law at the time of their adoption. But the Convention expressly stated that it was an attempt "to revise the general laws and customs of war," which it thus recognised to be then existing, but by 1939 these rules laid down in the Convention were recognised by all civilised nations, and were regarded as being declaratory of the laws and customs of war which are referred to in Article 6 (b) of the Charter. . . .

With regard to crimes against humanity, there is no doubt whatever that political opponents were murdered in Germany before the war, and that many of them were kept in concentration camps in circumstances of great horror and cruelty. The policy of terror was certainly carried out on a vast scale, and in many cases was organised and systematic. The policy of persecution, repression and murder of civilians in Germany before the war of 1939, who were likely to be hostile to the Government, was most ruthlessly carried out. The persecution of Jews during the same period is established beyond all doubt. To constitute crimes against humanity, the acts relied on before the outbreak of war must have been in execution of, or in connection with, any crime within the jurisdiction of the Tribunal. The Tribunal is of the opinion that revolting and horrible as many of these crimes were, it has not been satisfactorily proved that they were done in execution of, or in connection with, any such crime. The Tribunal therefore cannot make a general declaration that the acts before 1939 were crimes against humanity within the meaning of the Charter, but from the beginning of the war in 1939 war crimes were committed on a vast scale, which were also crimes against humanity; and insofar as the inhumane acts charged in the Indictment, and committed after the beginning of the war, did not constitute war crimes, they were all committed in execution of, or in connection with, the aggressive war, and therefore constituted crimes against humanity.

The Accused Organisations

Article 9 of the Charter provides:

> At the trial of any individual member of any group or organisation the Tribunal may declare (in connection with any act of which the individual may be convicted) that the group or organisation of which the individual was a member was a criminal organisation.
>
> After receipt of the Indictment the Tribunal shall give such notice as it thinks fit that the prosecution intends to ask the Tribunal to make such declaration and any member of the organisation will be entitled to apply to the Tribunal for leave to be heard by the Tribunal upon the question of the criminal character of the organisation. The Tribunal shall have power to allow or reject the application. If the application is allowed, the Tribunal may direct in what manner the applicants shall be represented and heard.

Article 10 of the Charter makes clear that the declaration of criminality against an accused organisation is final, and cannot be challenged in any subsequent criminal proceeding against a member of that organisation Article 10 is as follows:

In cases where a group or organisation is declared criminal by the Tribunal, the competent national authority of any Signatory shall have the right to bring individuals to trial for membership therein before national, military or occupation courts. In any such case the criminal nature of the group or organisation is considered proved and shall not be questioned.

The effect of the declaration of criminality by the Tribunal is well illustrated by Law Number 10 of the Control Council of Germany passed on the 20th day of December, 1945, which provides:

> Each of the following acts is recognised as a crime:
>
> (d) Membership in categories of a criminal group or organisation declared criminal by the International Military Tribunal. . . .
>
> (3) Any person found guilty of any of the crimes above mentioned may upon conviction be punished as shall be determined by the Tribunal to be just. Such punishment may consist of one or more of the following:

(a) Death.

(b) Imprisonment for life or a term of years, with or without hard labour.

(c) Fine, and imprisonment with or without hard labour, in lieu thereof.

In effect, therefore, a member of an organisation which the Tribunal has declared to be criminal may be subsequently convicted of the crime of membership and be punished for that crime by death. This is not to assume that international or military courts which will try these individuals will not exercise appropriate standards of justice. This is a far-reaching and novel procedure. Its application, unless properly safeguarded, may produce great injustice.

Article 9, it should be noted, uses the words "The Tribunal may declare," so that the Tribunal is vested with discretion as to whether it will declare any organisation criminal. This discretion is a judicial one and does not permit arbitrary action, but should be exercised in accordance with well settled legal principles one of the most important of which is that criminal guilt is personal, and that mass punishments should be avoided. If satisfied of the criminal guilt of any organisation or group this Tribunal should not hesitate to declare it to be criminal because the theory of "group criminality" is new, or because it might be unjustly applied by some subsequent tribunals. On the other hand, the Tribunal should make such declaration of criminality so far as possible in a manner to insure that innocent persons will not be punished.

A criminal organisation is analogous to a criminal conspiracy in that the essence of both is cooperation for criminal purposes. There must be a group bound together and organised for a common purpose. The group must be formed or used in connection with the commission of crimes denounced by the Charter. Since the declaration with respect to the organisations and groups will, as has been pointed out, fix the criminality of its members, that definition should exclude persons who had no knowledge of the criminal purposes or acts of the organisation and those who were drafted by the State for membership, unless they were personally implicated in the commission of acts declared criminal by Article 6 of the Charter as members of the organisation. Membership alone is not enough to come within the scope of these declarations. . . .

Notes

(1) Twenty-four Nazi leaders were indicted before the International Military Tribunal at Nuremberg. One of the twenty-four, Gustav Krupp von Bohlen, was found to be too ill to be tried. One, Robert Ley, committed suicide while in custody. Martin Bormann was tried and sentenced to death *in absentia*. Of the twenty-one who stood trial in person, three (Hjalmar Schacht, Franz von Papen, and Hans Fritzsche) were acquitted. Seven (Rudolf Hess, Walter Funk, Karl Doenitz, Erich Raeder, Baldur von Schirach, Albert Speer, and Constantin von Neurath) were sentenced to prison terms varying from ten years to life. The remaining eleven (Hermann Goering, Joachim von Ribbentrop, Wilhelm Keitel, Ernest Kaltenbrunner, Alfred

Rosenberg, Hans Frank, Wilhelm Frick, Julius Streicher, Fritz Saukel, Alfred Jodl, and Arthur Seyss-Inquart) were sentenced to death. Goering committed suicide before he could be hanged.

The indictment asked for a declaration of criminality against the Leadership Corps of the Nazi Party, the Gestapo, the SS (Black Shirts), its subsidiary the SD, the SA (Brown Shirts), the Reich Cabinet, and the General Staff and High Command of the German Armed Forces. The Leadership Corps, the Gestapo, the SS and SD were declared (with the qualifications set out in the Judgment) to be criminal organizations. The Tribunal declined to make declarations against the SA, Reich Cabinet, and General Staff and High Command.

For some useful studies of the trials from the perspective of United States and Soviet scholars, *see* The Nuremberg Trial and International Law (G. Ginsburgs & V.N. Kudriavtsev, eds., 1990). On the crime of aggression, *see* Roger S. Clark, *Nuremberg and the Crime Against Peace*, 3 Wash. U. Global Stud. L. Rev. 527 (2007). For more recent studies, *see* Beth A. Griech-Polelle, The Nuremberg War Crimes Trial and its Policy Consequences Today (2d revised and extended version 2020); Francine Hirsch, Soviet Judgment at Nuremberg: A New History of the International Military Tribunal after World War 2 (2020).

(2) Following the First World War, a Commission on the Responsibility of the Authors of the War appointed by the Paris Peace Conference recommended establishment of an international tribunal to try both acts which had provoked the war and "violations of the laws and customs of war and the laws of humanity." *See Commission on the Responsibility of the Authors of the War and on Enforcement of Penalties: Report Presented to the Preliminary Peace Conference*, 14 Am. J. Int'l L. 95 (Supp. 1920). The U.S. representatives on the Commission objected to this proposal as being without precedent in international law. The Commission's report did influence the two provisions of the Versailles Treaty mentioned in the Nuremberg Judgment: Article 227, which provided that the Kaiser should be tried "for a supreme offense against international morality and the sanctity of treaties," and Article 228, which provided for the trial before allied tribunals of Germans accused of violating the laws and customs of war. The Kaiser was never put on trial because the Netherlands, where he had taken refuge, was unwilling to give him up; the Allies lost some of their enthusiasm for prosecution; and the German government resisted the surrender of other German nationals. *See* William A. Schabas, The Trial of the Kaiser (2018). As a compromise, a dozen defendants accused of war crimes were prosecuted before the German Supreme Court in Leipzig, but given derisory sentences. *See* Claude Mullins, The Leipzig Trials (1921).

Both the reference to "laws of humanity" in the Paris Commission Report, and the concept of "crimes against humanity," which gained wide currency after its inclusion in the Nuremberg Charter, have intellectual connections to the principle known (after its author) as the "Martens clause" in the preamble to the Fourth Hague Convention of 1907 respecting the Laws and Customs of War on Land. That clause says that, to the extent that certain matters are not specifically dealt with in the Convention, "the inhabitants and the belligerents remain under the protection and the rule of the principles of the law of nations, as they result from the usages established among civilized peoples, from the laws of humanity and the dictates of the public conscience." (The language in the 1899 version of the Convention is a little different, but to the same effect.) In English, at least, the term "crimes against humanity" seems to have been applied occasionally in the nineteenth century to the slave trade and to King Leopold's reign of forced labor (and worse) in The Congo. *See generally* Roger S. Clark, *Crimes Against Humanity and the Rome Statute of the International Criminal Court, in* International Law in Russia and Eastern Europe: Essays in Honor of George Ginsburgs 139 (Roger Clark, Ferdinand Feldbrugge & Stanislaw Pomorski eds., 2001). On 28 May 1915, France, Great Britain and Russia declared that the Turkish massacres of Armenians were "crimes against humanity for which all members of the Turkish Government will be held responsible together with its agents implicated in the massacres." *Id.* at 140–41. There were provisions in the aborted 1920 Treaty of Sèvres between the Allies and Turkey which contemplated trials both for war crimes committed against opposing forces and for internal "massacres" (the term "crimes against humanity" was not used). The point was not pursued in the final peace treaty with Turkey, the 1923 Treaty of Lausanne. For an excellent account of crimes against humanity, see M. Cherif Bassiouni, Crimes Against Humanity in International Law (2nd ed. 1999). Unlike war crimes, that, for the most part, have a treaty foundation, crimes against humanity are not the subject of a separate treaty. Efforts are afoot to remedy this situation. *See* Forging a Convention for Crimes Against Humanity (Leila Sadat ed., 2011). The International Law Commission began to study this issue in 2013. In 2019, it produced a draft Convention which it referred to the General Assembly for further action. *See* Analytical Guide to the work of the Commission, http://legal.un.org/ilc/guide/7_7.shtml.

(3) On which of the "bases of jurisdiction" considered in chapter 2 did the Nuremberg Tribunal exercise jurisdiction over the defendants? What does the Judgment say about this? Does it accord with the statement in the *Demjanjuk* case (in the next section) that the Tribunal's jurisdiction "necessarily derived from the universality principle"? For analysis of the various possibilities, *see* Robert K. Woetzel, The Nuremberg Trials in International Law 58–95 (2d ed. 1962).

(4) In what respects did the law applied by the Tribunal represent a departure from preexisting international law? Did the Tribunal persuasively answer objections based on the principle that there can be no punishment of crime without a preexisting law? Did the Nuremberg Trial comport with the guarantees with respect to criminal proceedings set out in the International Covenant on Civil and Political Rights (*see* chap. 19 *supra*)? Can the trial rationally be justified in terms of its deterrent efficacy? Or does its point lie elsewhere? Was it objectionable as representing "victor's justice"? What were the alternatives in 1946? Consider the following observations in Herbert Wechsler, *The Issues of the Nuremberg Trial*, 62 Pol. Sci. Q. 11, 23–25 (1947):

I have not addressed myself to whether a tribunal of the victors could be impartial, to whether the law of the Charter is *ex post facto* or whether it is "law" at all. These are, indeed, the issues that are currently mooted. But there are elements in the debate that should lead us to be suspicious of the issues as they are drawn in these terms. For, most of those who mount the attack on one or another of these contentions hasten to assure us that their plea is not one of immunity for the defendants; they argue only that they should have been disposed of politically, that is, dispatched out of hand. This is a curious position indeed. A punitive enterprise launched on the basis of general rules, administered in an adversary proceeding under a separation of prosecutive and adjudicative powers is, in the name of law and justice, asserted to be less desirable than an *ex parte* execution list or a drumhead court-martial constituted in the immediate aftermath of the war.... Those who choose to do so may view the Nuremberg proceeding as "political" rather than "legal"—a program calling for the judicial application of principles of liability politically defined. They cannot view it as less civilized an institution than a program of organized violence against prisoners, whether directed from the respective capitals or by military commanders in the field....

No one who examines the record and the judgment ... will question the disinterestedness of the Tribunal; and those who argue that disinterestedness is inherently impossible in this situation may ask themselves why nations that can produce such impartial critics should be intrinsically incapable of producing equally impartial judges. The fact is that the judgment of the Tribunal was mainly a judgment of limitation, its principal operation more significantly that of protecting innocence than that of declaring and punishing guilt....

There is ... too large a disposition among the defenders of Nuremberg to look for stray tags of international pronouncements and reason therefrom that the law of Nuremberg was previously fully laid down. If the Kellogg-Briand Pact or a general conception of international obligation sufficed to authorize England, and would have authorized us, to declare war on Germany in defense of Poland—and in this enterprise to kill countless thousands of German soldiers and civilians—can it be possible that it failed to authorize punitive action against individual Germans judicially determined to be responsible for the Polish attack? To be sure, we would demand a more explicit authorization for punishment in domestic law, for we have adopted for the protection of individuals a prophylactic principle absolutely forbidding retroactivity that we can afford to carry to that extreme. International society, being less stable, can afford less luxury. We admit that in other respects. Why should we deny it here?

(5) On December 11, 1946, the U.N. General Assembly adopted a resolution in which it "reaffirm[ed] the principles of international law recognized by the Charter

of the Nürnberg Tribunal and the judgment of the Tribunal" and directed the International Law Commission (then called the Committee on the Codification of International Law) to "formulate" those principles. G. A. Res. 95 (I), U.N. Doc. A/64/Add.1, at 188 (1946). The International Law Commission produced its distillation of the Nuremberg Principles in 1950. *See Report of the International Law Commission*, 5 U.N. GAOR, Supp. No. 12 (A/1316), at 11–14 (1950). These read as follows:

Principle I

Any person who commits an act which constitutes a crime under international law is responsible therefor and liable to punishment.

Principle II

The fact that internal law does not impose a penalty for an act which constitutes a crime under international law does not relieve the person who committed the act from responsibility under international law.

Principle III

The fact that a person who committed an act which constitutes a crime under international law acted as Head of State or responsible Government official does not relieve him from responsibility under international law.

Principle IV

The fact that a person acted pursuant to order of his Government or of a superior does not relieve him from responsibility under international law, provided a moral choice was in fact possible to him.

Principle V

Any person charged with a crime under international law has the right to a fair trial on the facts and law.

Principle VI

The crimes hereinafter set out are punishable as crimes under international law:

(a) Crimes against peace:

(i) Planning, preparation, initiation or waging of a war of aggression or a war in violation of international treaties, agreements or assurances;

(ii) Participation in a common plan or conspiracy for the accomplishment of any of the acts mentioned under (i).

(b) War crimes: Violations of the laws or customs of war which include, but are not limited to, murder, ill-treatment or deportation to slave-labour or for any other purpose of civilian population of or in occupied territory; murder or ill-treatment of prisoners of war, of persons on the Seas, killing of hostages, plunder of public or private property, wanton destruction of cities, towns, or villages, or devastation not justified by military necessity.

(c) Crimes against humanity: Murder, extermination, enslavement, deportation and other inhuman acts done against any civilian population, or persecutions on political, racial or religious grounds, when such acts are done or such persecutions are carried on in execution of or in connection with any crime against peace or any war crime.

Principle VII

Complicity in the commission of a crime against peace, a war crime, or a crime against humanity as set forth in Principle VI is a crime under international law.

§ 20.02 The Tokyo Trial

The counterpart of the Nuremberg Tribunal in Asia was the International Military Tribunal for the Far East or the "Tokyo Tribunal." It was composed of eleven judges from eleven countries (Australia, Canada, China, France, Great Britain, India, the Netherlands, New Zealand, the Philippines, the U.S.S.R., and the United States) appointed by General MacArthur, the Supreme Allied Commander for the Far East.

Article 5 of its Charter gave the tribunal "the power to try and punish Far Eastern war criminals who as individuals or members of organizations are charged with offenses which include Crimes against Peace." Thus, the tribunal had jurisdiction only over defendants who were charged with crimes against peace, although it might also try them on charges involving conventional war crimes and crimes against humanity. These three crimes were defined in terms similar to, but also different from, those used in the Article 6 of Nuremberg:

a. *Crimes against Peace*: Namely, the planning, preparation, initiation, or waging of a declared or undeclared war of aggression, or a war in violation of international law, treaties, agreements or assurances, or participation in a common plan or conspiracy for the accomplishment of any of the foregoing.

b. *Conventional War Crimes*: Namely, violations of the laws or customs of war.

c. *Crimes against Humanity*: Namely, murder, extermination, enslavement, deportation, and other inhumane acts committed before or during the war, or persecutions on political or racial grounds in execution of or in connection with any crime within the jurisdiction of the Tribunal, whether or not in violation of the domestic law of the country where perpetrated.

Leaders, organizers, instigators and accomplices participating in the formulation or execution of a common plan or conspiracy to commit any of the foregoing crimes are responsible for all acts performed by any person in execution of such plan.

The trial was conducted in English and Japanese. It began on May 3, 1946. It concluded nearly two years later on April 16, 1948. It took the tribunal another seven months to prepare its 1218-page judgment which was rendered on November 4–12, 1948. All twenty-five defendants were found guilty on one or more counts of the indictment, some by a vote of 8-3. (The dissenting judges were Henri Bernard of France, Radhabinod Pal of India, and Bernard V.A. Röling of the Netherlands. Justice Pal, who believed the whole proceedings were misconceived, would have acquitted them all.) Seven defendants were sentenced to death; sixteen to life imprisonment; one to twenty years' and one to seven years' imprisonment. *See* Solis Horwitz, *The Tokyo Trial*, INT'L CONCILIATION No. 465 (1950). The death penalty not being acceptable to the judges from Australia and the USSR, at least one of the decisions to execute had the support of only six judges. *See* Roger S. Clark, *Nuremberg and Tokyo in Contemporary Perspective, in* THE LAW OF WAR CRIMES 171, 179 n.37 (T.L.H. McCormack & G.J. Simpson eds., 1997).

The Tokyo Tribunal never enjoyed the attention and authority of the Nuremberg Tribunal. Even its full judgment remained unpublished until 1977. Justice Pal had, in the meantime, self-published his dissent in India as RADHABINOD PAL, INTERNATIONAL MILITARY TRIBUNAL FOR THE FAR EAST: DISSENTIENT JUDGMENT (1953). On source materials for Tokyo, *see* THE TOKYO WAR CRIMES TRIAL: THE COMPLETE TRANSCRIPTS OF THE PROCEEDINGS OF THE INTERNATIONAL MILITARY TRIBUNAL FOR THE FAR EAST (R. John Pritchard ed., with Sonia Maganua Zaide, 22 vols., 1981). Excellent more recent studies are NEIL BOISTER & ROBERT CRYER, THE TOKYO INTERNATIONAL MILITARY TRIBUNAL: A REAPPRAISAL (2008), and DAVID COHEN & YUMA TOTANI, THE TOKYO WAR CRIMES TRIBUNAL: LAW, HISTORY, AND JURISPRUDENCE (2018).

It will be noticed that, like its Nuremberg model, the Charter for the Far East contained two references to conspiracy, one in paragraph (a) and one in the material at the end of paragraph (c) beginning with "Leaders and organizers. . . ." They correspond roughly to inchoate or preparatory conspiracy (in relation to crimes against peace only) and conspiracy as a form of complicity (applicable to all three crimes). Inchoate conspiracy is a feature of both English and U.S. law, but conspiracy-as-complicity is considered by some to be allowed in federal U.S. law, not accepted in many states, and shunned by the Model Penal Code. Recall that in the Nuremberg indictment, the prosecution sought to plead an inchoate conspiracy with respect to all three offenses but was rebuffed by the Tribunal on the plain language of the Charter. In Tokyo, the prosecution sought to obtain an expansive interpretation by arguing that those responsible for an aggressive war were guilty of multiple war crimes of murder as a result of their participation in the conspiracy. The Tokyo Tribunal declined to go in this direction either. *See* Neil Boister, *The Application of Collective and Comprehensive Criminal Responsibility for Aggression at the Tokyo International Military Tribunal: The Measure of the Crime of Aggression?* 8 J. INT'L CRIM. JUST. 425 (2010). Inchoate conspiracy has a checkered career in International Criminal Law. It turns up, controversially, in *Hamdan v. Rumsfeld* [§ 9.03], and less controversially in the Genocide Convention [§ 23.01[B]]. From the Genocide Convention, it found its way into the Statutes of the Tribunal for Former Yugoslavia and Rwanda, but only in respect of genocide [chap. 21]. Inchoate conspiracy did not find a home in the Rome Statute of the International Criminal Court, although some version of conspiracy-as-complicity is located in Article 25(3)(d) of that Statute [chap. 22].

§ 20.03 Subsequent Trials

Besides the trial before the International Military Tribunal at Nuremberg, a number of other post-war prosecutions in Germany took place under Allied Control Council Law No. 10 (referred to in the Nuremberg Judgment) which authorized the four occupying powers to prosecute German war criminals in their respective zones of occupation. In the American zone, twelve subsequent trials involving 177 individual defendants were held at Nuremberg under this law. *See* Telford Taylor, *Nuremberg Trials: War Crimes and International Law*, INT'L CONCILIATION No. 450 (1949).

The substantive provisions of Control Council Law No. 10 were modeled, more or less, on the Nuremberg Charter. However, in its definition of "crimes against humanity," the Control Council Law did not require a connection to war crimes or crimes against peace. Article II (1)(c) defined "crimes against humanity" as:

> Atrocities and offenses, including but not limited to murder, extermination, enslavement, deportation, imprisonment, torture, rape or other inhumane acts committed against any civilian population, or persecution on political, racial or religious grounds whether or not in violation of the domestic laws of the country where perpetrated.

U.S. tribunals reached conflicting conclusions about whether this actually permitted prosecution for crimes against humanity unrelated to the war. *See* Telford Taylor, *supra*, at 342–44.

A number of individual Allies, including the United States (especially its concentration camp cases), Great Britain and Canada, also held trials in Europe before military commissions, bypassing the Control Council Law No. 10 structure. Professor Ginsburgs has some very tentative figures for Soviet prosecutions (probably in the thousands) in George Ginsburgs, *Moscow and International Legal Cooperation in the Pursuit of War Criminals*, 21 REV. CENT. & E. EUR. L. 1, 12 n.31 (1995); and George Ginsburgs, *Light Shed on the Story of Wehrmacht Generals in Soviet Captivity*, 11 CRIM. L. F. 101 (2000) (reviewing Russian sources).

In Asia, apart from the Tokyo Trial, there also were numerous prosecutions before allied military tribunals. A far greater number of people were charged (and convicted, and executed) than in the Tokyo trial itself—in the thousands. Perhaps the best-known was the trial of General Tomoyuki Yamashita, who was found guilty by a U.S. military commission in the Philippines of failing to take appropriate steps to prevent the troops under his command from committing atrocities against civilians and prisoners of war. *See In re Yamashita*, 327 U.S. 1 (1946). The trial in fact took place before the Tokyo trial. Yamashita was executed. The case generated much argument on both the facts and the law, to the extent that his conviction, on a command responsibility theory, was arguably based on negligence in a situation where he may not have been able to do any better. Other trials were carried out by both the Republic of China and the People's Republic of China, by the Netherlands (in respect of Indonesia), by Australia and the United Kingdom. Fairly soon, the victors began to suffer both prosecution fatigue and incarceration fatigue. For a depressing account of the subsequent British actions, *see* R. John Pritchard, *The Gift of Clemency following British War Crimes Trials in the Far East, 1946–1948*, 7 Crim. L.F. 15 (1996). Several post-1945 trials are discussed in The Hidden Histories of War Crimes Trials (Kevin Jon Heller & Gerry Simpson, eds., 2013). For the 300 Australian trials, *see* Australia's War Crimes Trials 1945–51 (Georgina Fitzpatrick, Tim McCormack & Narrelle Morris eds., 2016). On the numerous British trials in Hong Kong, see Hong Kong's War Crimes Trials (Suzannah Linton ed., 2013). On Indonesia, *see* Fred Borch, Military Trials of War Criminals in the Netherlands East Indies 1946–1949 (2017). On Singapore, *see* Cheah Wui Ling, *Post World War II British 'Hell-ship' Trials in Singapore: Omissions and the Attribution of Responsibility*, 8 J. Int'l Crim. Just. 1035 (2010).

Many of the subsequent domestic trials, as well as Nuremberg and Tokyo, were inspired in part by the often-neglected work of the United Nations War Crimes Commission. Set up in late 1943 by 17 member states of the Allies, the Commission collected evidence of crimes and published a useful series entitled, The Law Reports of Trials of War Criminals, Selected and Prepared by the UNWCC (1949). Its focus was more on national than international prosecution. *See also* History of the United Nations War Crimes Commission and the Development of the Laws of War (1948). For a valuable set of essays on the Commission, see *Symposium: The United Nations War Crimes Commission and the Origins of International Criminal Justice*, 25 Crim. L. Forum. 1 (2014) (Special Issue). An interesting study of the Commission notes how many of the members of the Commission were refugees in London from occupied countries in Europe who had previously worked together at the League of Nations on international criminal law and disarmament issues. They were also familiar with the concept of "crimes against humanity" which became prominent in the Nuremberg Charter and trial. *See* Kerstin von Lingen, *Transnational Epistemic Communities: From the League of Nations to the United Nations War Crimes Commission*, *in* Histories of Transnational Criminal Law 58 (Neil Boister, Sabine Gless & Florian Jeβberger eds., 2021).

There have been many subsequent trials held in civilian courts in Europe and Israel. The most publicized trial was that of Adolph Eichmann in Jerusalem. The classic study is Hannah Arendt, Eichmann in Jerusalem: A Report on the Banality of Evil (1964). Other post-war prosecutions took place before national courts of various countries that had been occupied by Germany during the war and, eventually, before national courts in Germany. The numbers have, of course, dropped off, as memories grow dim and victims and perpetrators alike grow old and die, but efforts continue. Later examples in France of prosecution for crimes committed during the Second World War are the trials of Klaus Barbie in 1987, Paul Touvier in 1994, and Maurice Papon in 1998. *See* Leila Nadya Sadat, *National Prosecutions for International Crimes: The French Experience, in* 3 International Criminal Law (M. Cherif Bassiouni ed., 3d ed., 2008). Professor Sadat has written of a "Nuremberg paradox." In spite of American leadership at Nuremberg, she argues, "French judges seem to have been able to incorporate the Nuremberg principles as a matter of French municipal law in a way that their American counterparts never did. In America, ironically, a nation of lawyers, the Nuremberg principles remain non-justiciable, surviving largely as a symbol of power politics. In France, the Nuremberg principles are, instead, a matter of law." Leila Nadya Sadat, *The Nuremberg Paradox*, 58 Am. J. Comp. L. 151 (2010). Unlike Germany, Japan did not hold any subsequent trials.

With the passage of time, the question became urgent of whether the prosecution of war crimes and crimes against humanity was subject to national statutes of limitations. In 1968, the U.N. General Assembly adopted a Convention on the Non-Applicability of Statutory Limitations to War Crimes and Crimes Against Humanity, Nov. 26, 1968, G. A. Res. 2391 (XXIII), 754 U.N.T.S. 75, which entered into force on November 11, 1970. Its substantive provisions read:

Article I

> No statutory limitation shall apply to the following crimes, irrespective of the date of their commission:
>
> (a) War crimes as they are defined in the Charter of the International Military Tribunal, Nürnberg, of 8 August 1945 and confirmed by resolutions 3 (1) of 13 February 1946 and 95 (I) of 11 December 1946 of the General Assembly of the United Nations, particularly the "grave breaches" enumerated in the Geneva Conventions of 12 August 1949 for the protection of war victims;
>
> (b) Crimes against humanity whether committed in time of war or in time of peace as they are defined in the Charter of the International Military Tribunal, Nürnberg, of 8 August 1945 and confirmed by resolutions 3 (I) of 13 February 1946 and 95 (I) of 11 December 1946 of the General Assembly of the United Nations, eviction by armed attack or occupation and inhuman acts resulting from the policy of apartheid, and the crime of genocide as defined in the 1948 Convention on the Prevention and Punishment of the Crime of Genocide, even if such acts do not constitute a violation of the domestic law of the country in which they were committed.

Article II

If any of the crimes mentioned in article I is committed, the provisions of this Convention shall apply to representatives of the State authority and private individuals who, as principals or accomplices, participate in or who directly incite others to the commission of any of those crimes, or who conspire to commit them, irrespective of the degree of completion, and to representatives of the State authority who tolerate their commission.

Article III

The States Parties to the present Convention undertake to adopt all necessary domestic measures, legislative or otherwise, with a view to making possible the extradition, in accordance with international law, of the persons referred to in article II of this Convention.

Article IV

The States Parties to the present Convention undertake to adopt, in accordance with their respective constitutional processes, any legislative or other measures necessary to ensure that statutory or other limitations shall not apply to the prosecution and punishment of the crimes referred to in articles 1 and 2 of this Convention and that, where they exist, such limitations shall be abolished.

While the principle that there is no statute of limitations for serious crimes under international law is widely accepted, the 1968 Convention had garnered only 56 ratifications and accessions by December 2021, mostly from developing countries and States formed from the former Soviet Union. Many of the Western States objected to equating genocide and apartheid and to the inclusion of "eviction by armed attack or occupation" which they saw as an attack on Israel. Some States had problems with Article II's reference to actors who "tolerate" crimes by others.

Demjanjuk v. Petrovsky

United States Court of Appeals for the Sixth Circuit
776 F.2d 571 (1985)

Lively, Chief Judge:

I

The petitioner, John Demjanjuk, is a native of the Ukraine, one of the republics of the Soviet Union. Demjanjuk was admitted to the United States in 1952 under the Displaced Persons Act of 1948 and became a naturalized United States citizen in 1958. He has resided in the Cleveland, Ohio area since his arrival in this country.

In 1981 the United States District Court for the Northern District of Ohio revoked Demjanjuk's certificate of naturalization and vacated the order admitting him to United States citizenship.... Chief Judge Battisti of the district court entered extensive findings of fact from which he concluded that the certificate and order "were illegally procured and were procured by willful misrepresentation of material facts under 8 U.S.C. § 1451(a)."

The district court found that Demjanjuk was conscripted into the Soviet Army in 1940 and was captured by the Germans in 1942. After short stays in several German POW camps and a probable tour at the Trawniki SS training camp in Poland, Demjanjuk became a guard at the Treblinka concentration camp, also in Poland, late in 1942. In his various applications for immigration to the United States the petitioner misstated his place of residence during the period 1937–1948 and did not reveal that he had worked for the SS at Treblinka or served in a German military unit later in the war. In the denaturalization proceedings Demjanjuk admitted that his statements concerning residence were false and that he had in fact served in a German military unit. He steadfastly denied that he had been at Trawniki or Treblinka, though documentary evidence placed him at Trawniki and five Treblinka survivors and one former German guard at the camp identified Demjanjuk as a Ukrainian guard who was known as "Ivan or Iwan Grozny," that is, "Ivan the Terrible."

Following the denaturalization order the government began deportation proceedings against Demjanjuk. While these proceedings were underway the State of Israel filed with the United States Department of State a request for the extradition of Demjanjuk. . . . Following a hearing the district court entered an order certifying to the Secretary of State that Demjanjuk was subject to extradition at the request of the State of Israel pursuant to a treaty on extradition between the United States and Israel signed December 10, 1962, effective December 5, 1963. . . .

III

The pertinent portions of the treaty (Convention on Extradition) between the United States and Israel (hereafter the Treaty) found in the first three articles and the thirteenth article are set forth:

Article I

> Each Contracting Party agrees, under the conditions and circumstances established by the present Convention, reciprocally to deliver up persons found in its territory who have been charged with or convicted of any of the offenses mentioned in Article II of the present Convention committed within the territorial jurisdiction of the other, or outside thereof under the conditions specified in Article III of the present Convention.

Article II

> Persons shall be delivered up according to the provisions of the present Convention for prosecution when they have been charged with, or to undergo sentence when they have been convicted of, any of the following offenses:
>
> 1. Murder.
> 2. Manslaughter.
> 3. Malicious wounding; inflicting grievous bodily harm. . . .

Article III

When the offense has been committed outside the territorial jurisdiction of the requesting Party, extradition need not be granted unless the laws of the requested Party provide for the punishment of such an offense committed in similar circumstances. . . .

Article XIII

A person extradited under the present Convention shall not be detained, tried or punished in the territory of the requesting Party for any offense other than that for which extradition has been granted nor be extradited by that Party to a third State. . . .

The Israeli warrant on which the extradition request was based was issued pursuant to a request which charged Demjanjuk with having "murdered tens of thousands of Jews and non-Jews" while operating the gas chambers to exterminate prisoners at Treblinka. It further asserts that the acts charged were committed "with the intention of destroying the Jewish people and to commit crimes against humanity." The complaint in the district court equated this charge with the crimes of "murder and malicious wounding [and] inflicting grievous bodily harm," listed in the Treaty. The warrant was issued pursuant to a 1950 Israeli statute, the Nazis and Nazi Collaborators (Punishment) Law. This statute made certain acts, including "crimes against the Jewish people," "crimes against humanity" and "war crimes committed during the Nazi period" punishable under Israeli law. The statute defines these crimes as follows:

"crime against the Jewish people" means any of the following acts, committed with intent to destroy the Jewish people in whole or in part:

1. killing Jews;

2. causing serious bodily or mental harm to Jews;

3. placing Jews in living conditions calculated to bring about their physical destruction;

4. imposing measures intended to prevent births among Jews;

5. forcibly transferring Jewish children to another national or religious group;

6. destroying or desecrating Jewish religious or cultural assets or values;

7. inciting to hatred of Jews;

"crime against humanity" means any of the following acts:

murder, extermination, enslavement, starvation or deportation and other inhumane acts committed against any civilian population, and persecution on national, racial, religious or political grounds;

"war crime" means any of the following acts:

murder, ill-treatment or deportation to forced labour or for any other purpose, of civilian population of or in occupied territory; murder or ill-treatment of prisoners of war or persons on the seas; killing of hostages;

plunder of public or private property; wanton destruction of cities, towns or villages; and devastation not justified by military necessity.[a]

Demjanjuk contends that the district court had no jurisdiction to consider the request for extradition. He. . . . maintains that the crime he is charged with is not included in the listing of offenses in the treaty. It is his position that "murdering thousands of Jews and non-Jews" is not covered by the treaty designation of "murder." . . . We have no difficulty concluding that "murder" includes the mass murder of Jews. This is a logical reading of the treaty language and is the interpretation given the treaty by the Department of State. That interpretation is entitled to considerable deference. . . .

Demjanjuk also argues that the district court had no jurisdiction because there is a requirement of "double criminality" in international extradition cases. . . . We believe the double criminality requirement was met in this case. . . . If the acts upon which the charges of the requesting country are based are also proscribed by a law of the requested nation, the requirement of double criminality is satisfied. Murder is a crime in every state of the United States. The fact that there is no separate offense of mass murder or murder of tens of thousands of Jews in this country is beside the point. The *act* of unlawfully killing one or more persons with the requisite malice is punishable as murder. That is the test. The acts charged are criminal both in Israel and throughout the United States, including Ohio. Demjanjuk's argument that to interpret murder to include murder of Jews would amount to judicial amendment of the Treaty is absurd and offensive.

IV

A separate jurisdictional argument concerns the territorial reach of the statutory law of Israel. Demjanjuk relies on two facts to question the power of the State of Israel to proceed against him. He is not a citizen or resident of Israel and the crimes with which he is charged allegedly were committed in Poland. He also points out that the acts which are the basis of the Israeli arrest warrant allegedly took place in 1942 or 1943, before the State of Israel came into existence. Thus, Demjanjuk maintains that the district court had no jurisdiction because Israel did not charge him with extraditable offenses.

The scope of this nation's international extradition power and the function of the federal courts in the extradition process are set forth in 18 U.S.C. § 3184. . . . Section 3184 clearly provides that the extradition complaint must charge the person sought to be extradited with having committed crimes "within the jurisdiction of any such foreign government," that is, the requesting state. . . . The question is

---

a. Under the relevant Israeli legislation, Nazis and Nazi Collaborators (Punishment) Law, 5710-1950, jurisdiction over crimes against the Jewish people and crimes against humanity encompassed "the period of the Nazi regime" which was said to begin on January 3, 1933, and end on May 8, 1945. War crimes jurisdiction covered "the period of the Second World War," defined as between September 1, 1939, and August 14, 1945. The structure of crimes against the Jewish people was based on the Genocide Convention. The other crimes followed the Nuremberg definitions. — Eds.

whether the murder of Jews in a Nazi extermination camp in Poland during the 1939–1945 war can be considered, for purposes of extradition, crimes within the jurisdiction of the State of Israel.

We look first at the Treaty. Article III provides that when an offense has been committed outside the territorial jurisdiction of the requesting party, "extradition need not be granted unless the laws of the requested party provide for the punishment of such an offense committed in similar circumstances." Demjanjuk maintains that the "need not" language of Article III prohibits extradition in this case because the laws of the United States do not provide punishment for war crimes or crimes against humanity. . . . In our view the treaty language makes two things clear: (1) the parties recognize the right to request extradition for extra territorial crimes, and (2) the requested party has the discretion to deny extradition if its laws do not provide for punishment of offenses committed under similar circumstances. This provision does not affect the authority of a court to certify extraditability; it merely distinguishes between cases where the requested party is required to honor a request and those where it has discretion to deny a request. That the specific offense charged is not a crime in the United States does not necessarily rule out extradition.

The Israeli statute under which Demjanjuk was charged deals with "crimes against the Jewish people," "crimes against humanity" and "war crimes" committed during the Nazi years. It is clear from the language defining the crimes, and other references to acts directed at persecuted persons and committed in places of confinement, that Israel intended to punish under this law those involved in carrying out Hitler's "final solution." This was made explicit in the prosecution of Adolph Eichmann in 1961. *Attorney General v. Eichmann*, 36 I.L.R. 277 (Sup. Ct. Israel 1962). Such a claim of extraterritorial jurisdiction over criminal offenses is not unique to Israel. For example, statutes of the United States provide for punishment in domestic district courts for murder or manslaughter committed within the maritime jurisdiction (18 U.S.C. § 1111) and murder or manslaughter of internationally protected persons wherever they are killed (18 U.S.C. § 1116(c)). We conclude that the reference in 18 U.S.C. § 3184 to crimes committed within the jurisdiction of the requesting government does not refer solely to territorial jurisdiction. Rather, it refers to the authority of a nation to apply its laws to particular conduct. In international law this is referred to as "jurisdiction to prescribe." Restatement § 401(1).

The law of the United States includes international law. *The Paquete Habana*, 175 U.S. 667, 712, 20 S. Ct. 290, 44 L. Ed. 320 (1900). International law recognizes a "universal jurisdiction" over certain offenses. . . . This "universality principle" is based on the assumption that some crimes are so universally condemned that the perpetrators are the enemies of all people. Therefore, any nation which has custody of the perpetrators may punish them according to its law applicable to such offenses. This principle is a departure from the general rule that "the character of an act as lawful or unlawful must be determined wholly by the law of the country where the act is done." *American Banana Co. v. United Fruit Co.*, 213 U.S. 347 (1909).

The wartime allies created the International Military Tribunal which tried major Nazi officials at Nuremberg and courts within the four occupation zones of post-war Germany which tried lesser Nazis. All were tried for committing war crimes, and it is generally agreed that the establishment of these tribunals and their proceedings were based on universal jurisdiction.

Demjanjuk argues that the post-war trials were all based on the military defeat of Germany and that with the disestablishment of the special tribunals there are no courts with jurisdiction over alleged war crimes. This argument overlooks the fact that the post-war tribunals were not military courts, though their presence in Germany was made possible by the military defeat of that country. These tribunals did not operate within the limits of traditional military courts. They claimed and exercised a much broader jurisdiction which necessarily derived from the universality principle. Whatever doubts existed prior to 1945 have been erased by the general recognition since that time that there is a jurisdiction over some types of crimes which extends beyond the territorial limits of any nation.

... Restatement § 443 appears to apply to the present case: "A state's courts may exercise jurisdiction to enforce the state's criminal laws which punish universal crimes (§ 404) or other non-territorial offenses within the state's jurisdiction to prescribe (§§ 402–403)." Israel is seeking to enforce its criminal law for the punishment of Nazis and Nazi collaborators for crimes universally recognized and condemned by the community of nations. The fact that Demjanjuk is charged with committing these acts in Poland does not deprive Israel of authority to bring him to trial.

Further, the fact that the State of Israel was not in existence when Demjanjuk allegedly committed the offenses is no bar to Israel's exercising jurisdiction under the universality principle. When proceeding on that jurisdictional premise, neither the nationality of the accused or the victim(s), nor the location of the crime is significant. The underlying assumption is that the crimes are offenses against the law of nations or against humanity and that the prosecuting nation is acting for all nations. This being so, Israel or any other nation, regardless of its status in 1942 or 1943, may undertake to vindicate the interest of all nations by seeking to punish the perpetrators of such crimes.

We conclude that the jurisdictional challenges to the district court's order must fail. The crime of murder is clearly included in the offenses for which extradition is to be granted under the treaty. Murder is a crime both in Israel and in the United States and is included in the specifications of the Nazis and Nazi Collaborators (Punishment) Law; the requirement of "double criminality" is met; and, the State of Israel has jurisdiction to punish for war crimes and crimes against humanity committed outside of its geographic boundaries. . . .

V

The remaining inquiry relates to how the "principle of specialty" applies to this case. . . .

The district court clearly certified that Demjanjuk was subject to extradition solely on the charge of murder. Though some of the acts which Demjanjuk is charged with may also constitute other offenses listed in the treaty, he may be tried in Israel only on that charge. However, the particular acts of murder for which he may be tried depend upon Israeli law. Israel may try him under the provisions of the Nazis and Nazi Collaborators (Punishment) Law for "crimes against the Jewish people" ("killing Jews," a species of murder), "crimes against humanity" ("murder . . . committed against any civilian population") and "war crimes" ("murder . . . of civilian population of or in occupied territory"). The principle of specialty does not impose any limitation on the particulars of the charge so long as it encompasses only the offense for which extradition was granted. . . .

The judgment of the district court is affirmed.

Notes

(1) Demjanjuk was extradited to Israel in 1986. He was tried and convicted in 1988. The prosecution was based on his identification as the sadistic guard at Treblinka known as Ivan the Terrible. In 1993, the Israeli Supreme Court reversed his conviction, finding that there was reasonable doubt as to whether he was the Treblinka guard. He returned to the United States. The Sixth Circuit vacated the extradition proceedings on the ground that the U.S. government had failed to disclose exculpatory materials in its possession during the earlier litigation. *See Demjanjuk v. Petrovsky*, 10 F.3d 338 (6th Cir. 1993), *cert. denied*, 513 U.S. 914 (1994). Aged 89, he was eventually deported to Germany in May 2009 to stand trial on a charge of accessory to the murder of 29,000 people in the Nazi death camp named Sobibor located in eastern Poland. Nicholas Kulish, *Accused Nazi Arrives in Munich*, N.Y. Times, May 13, 2009. He was tried and convicted for these crimes, and died in 2012 at the age of 91, awaiting the outcome of his appeal against conviction. Robert D. McFadden, *John Demjanjuk, 91, Dogged by Charges of Atrocities as Nazi Camp Guard, Dies*, N.Y. Times, March 17, 2012, *available at* http://www.nytimes.com/2012/03/18/world/europe/john-demjanjuk-nazi-guard-dies-at-91.html?_r=0. For a comprehensive account, *see* Lawrence Douglas, The Right Wrong Man: John Demjanjuk and the Last Great Nazi War Crimes Trial (2016).

(2) Consider how the concept of double criminality applied in *Demjanjuk* differs from double criminality applied by the House of Lords in *Pinochet* [chap. 14, *supra*]. Should the Sixth Circuit also have asked whether the offense for which extradition was sought (a) was one over which the U.S. courts were authorized to exercise extraterritorial jurisdiction, (b) at the time of the offense?

(3) *Demjanjuk* is an instance of conduct during the Second World War being prosecuted before a national court in a country other than the one in which the conduct occurred. An earlier instance was the trial of Adolf Eichmann in Israel in 1961, which is referred to in the *Demjanjuk* opinion. *See Attorney-General v. Eichmann*, 36 I.L.R. 18 (Dist. Ct. Jerusalem 1961), *aff'd*, 36 I.L.R. 277 (Sup. Ct. Israel 1962). Jurisdiction in such cases depends not only on a permissive rule of international law but

also on national legislation. National legislation, where it exists, may have a narrower scope than international law allows. Very often legislation authorizing the exercise of extraterritorial jurisdiction has been enacted to implement obligations under a particular treaty, such as the Torture Convention or the Geneva Conventions of 1949, and is limited to crimes described in the treaty. Some countries have enacted domestic laws that go beyond treaty obligations, but these may cover, for instance, only acts committed abroad by or against nationals. In response to concern with the problem of former Nazi collaborators living in Canada, Canada did enact in 1987 a fairly comprehensive statute providing for the prosecution of war crimes and crimes against humanity committed abroad. *See* Criminal Code, R.S.C. 1985, c. 30, §§ 7 (3.71)–7 (3.77) (Can.); *see also Regina v. Finta*, [1994] 1 S.C.R. 701. British and Australian war crimes statutes, which were prompted by similar concerns, applied, however, only to acts committed during the Second World War. *See* War Crimes Act, 1991, ch. 13, § 1(1) (Eng.); War Crimes Amendment Act, 1989 Austl. Acts No. 3, § 9(1). Likewise, the Israeli statute under which Demjanjuk was charged dealt, as the Sixth Circuit notes, only with crimes committed during the Nazi era (which in this case dated back to 1933 for crimes against the Jewish people and crimes against humanity). The prosecutions in Australia, Canada and Britain were largely unsuccessful. A lonely success is *R. v. Sawoniuk* [2000] 2 Cr. App. R. 220 (Court of Appeal, Criminal Division). Sawoniuk who, as the legislation required for jurisdiction, later became a British resident, was convicted in England for two murders in Belarus committed in 1942.

(4) Demjanjuk's conviction encouraged further German efforts at a reckoning for elderly war criminals. In 2015, Oskar Groening was found guilty by a German court of serving as an accessory to the murder of 300,000 people at Auschwitz. Known as the "bookkeeper of Auschwitz," Groening was responsible for counting the items taken from those arriving at the camp. *See* Paulos Andreadis-Papadimitriou, *Assistance in Mass Murder under Systems of Ill-Treatment: The Case of Oskar Gröning*, 15 J. INT'L CRIM. JUST. 157 (2017) (who has a useful discussion of the causation issues involved). After his conviction, the court sentenced him to four years in prison. In sentencing Groening, who was in his 90s, the court said, "[i]n deciding the penalty, the court in particular considered the plaintiff's age and that he should have a chance to spend some part of his life in freedom after serving his sentence." Laura Smith-Spark & Ben Brumfield, *Former Auschwitz Nazi Officer Oskar Groening Gets 4-Year Sentence*, CNN (July 15, 2015), *available at* http://www.cnn.com/2015/07/15/europe/germany-nazi-death-camp-verdict/. Do you agree with the court's statement? Is four years an appropriate sentence for someone convicted of being an accessory to the murder of 300,000 people? He died in March 2018, hospitalized before he could begin serving his sentence.

In 2015, a 91-year-old woman who worked at Auschwitz as a telegraph operator was charged by German authorities with complicity in the murder of 260,000 Jews. Interestingly, because she was under twenty-one years of age at the time of her alleged conduct, German authorities stated that she would be tried in juvenile court. Due to her health, however, it was unclear if she would ever face trial. *See German Woman Charged Over Nazi Death Camp Allegations*, The Guardian, Sept. 21, 2015, *available at* https://www.theguardian.com/world/2015/sep/21/german-woman-charged-nazi-allegations-auschwitz-death-camp; *see also 96-Year-Old Woman Who Fled Nazi War Crimes Trial is Found*, CNN (Sept. 30, 2021), *available at* https://www.cnn.com/2021/09/30/europe/german-96-year-old-nazi-intl-grm/index.html (discussing charges in German juvenile court of aiding and abetting 11,387 cases of murder against a former stenographer and typist at a concentration camp in Stutthof). As far as known, the trial of the 91-year-old did not continue, as she was unfit to stand trial. If she were convicted, however, what factors should the court consider in determining her sentence?

(5) Consider, finally, the U.S. War Crimes Act of 1996* (codified at 18 U.S.C. § 2441). Does this appear to be a response to the same problem as the Canadian, British, and Australian war crimes statutes? The act reads as follows:

> 18 U.S.C. § 2441. War crimes
>
> (a) Offense. Whoever, whether inside or outside the United States, commits a war crime, in any of the circumstances described in subsection (b), shall be fined under this title or imprisoned for life or any term of years, or both, and if death results to the victim, shall also be subject to the penalty of death.
>
> (b) Circumstances. The circumstances referred to in subsection (a) are that the person committing such war crime or the victim of such war crime is a member of the Armed Forces of the United States or a national of the United States (as defined in section 101 of the Immigration and Nationality Act).
>
> (c) Definition. As used in this section the term "war crime" means any conduct—
>
> > (1) defined as a grave breach in any of the international conventions signed at Geneva 12 August 1949, or any protocol to such convention to which the United States is a party;
> >
> > (2) prohibited by Article 23, 25, 27, or 28 of the Annex to the Hague Convention IV, Respecting the Laws and Customs of War on Land, signed 18 October 1907;
> >
> > (3) which constitutes a grave breach of common Article 3 (as defined in subsection (d)) when committed in the context of and in association with an armed conflict not of an international character; or
> >
> > (4) of a person who, in relation to an armed conflict and contrary to the provisions of the Protocol on Prohibitions or Restrictions on the Use

---

* Subsection (c)(3) was amended and subsection (d) was added by the Military Commissions Act of 2006.—Eds.

of Mines, Booby-Traps and Other Devices as amended at Geneva on 3 May 1996 (Protocol II as amended on 3 May 1996), when the United States is a party to such Protocol, willfully kills or causes serious injury to civilians.

(d) Common Article 3 Violations.—

(1) Prohibited conduct.—In subsection (c)(3), the term "grave breach of common Article 3" means any conduct (such conduct constituting a grave breach of common Article 3 of the international conventions done at Geneva August 12, 1949), as follows:

(A) Torture.—The act of a person who commits, or conspires or attempts to commit, an act specifically intended to inflict severe physical or mental pain or suffering (other than pain or suffering incidental to lawful sanctions) upon another person within his custody or physical control for the purpose of obtaining information or a confession, punishment, intimidation, coercion, or any reason based on discrimination of any kind.

(B) Cruel or inhuman treatment.—The act of a person who commits, or conspires or attempts to commit, an act intended to inflict severe or serious physical or mental pain or suffering (other than pain or suffering incidental to lawful sanctions), including serious physical abuse, upon another within his custody or control.

(C) Performing biological experiments.—The act of a person who subjects, or conspires or attempts to subject, one or more persons within his custody or physical control to biological experiments without a legitimate medical or dental purpose and in so doing endangers the body or health of such person or persons.

(D) Murder.—The act of a person who intentionally kills, or conspires or attempts to kill, or kills whether intentionally or unintentionally in the course of committing any other offense under this subsection, one or more persons taking no active part in the hostilities, including those placed out of combat by sickness, wounds, detention, or any other cause.

(E) Mutilation or maiming.—The act of a person who intentionally injures, or conspires or attempts to injure, or injures whether intentionally or unintentionally in the course of committing any other offense under this subsection, one or more persons taking no active part in the hostilities, including those placed out of combat by sickness, wounds, detention, or any other cause, by disfiguring the person or persons by any mutilation thereof or by permanently disabling any member, limb, or organ of his body, without any legitimate medical or dental purpose.

(F) Intentionally causing serious bodily injury.—The act of a person who intentionally causes, or conspires or attempts to cause, serious bodily injury to one or more persons, including lawful combatants, in violation of the law of war.

(G) Rape.—The act of a person who forcibly or with coercion or threat of force wrongfully invades, or conspires or attempts to invade, the body of a person by penetrating, however slightly, the anal or genital opening of the victim with any part of the body of the accused, or with any foreign object.

(H) Sexual assault or abuse.—The act of a person who forcibly or with coercion or threat of force engages, or conspires or attempts to engage, in sexual contact with one or more persons, or causes, or conspires or attempts to cause, one or more persons to engage in sexual contact.

(I) Taking hostages.—The act of a person who, having knowingly seized or detained one or more persons, threatens to kill, injure, or continue to detain such person or persons with the intent of compelling any nation, person other than the hostage, or group of persons to act or refrain from acting as an explicit or implicit condition for the safety or release of such person or persons.

(2) Definitions.—In the case of an offense under subsection (a) by reason of subsection (c)(3)—

(A) the term "severe mental pain or suffering" shall be applied for purposes of paragraphs (1)(A) and (1)(B) in accordance with the meaning given that term in section 2340 (2) of this title;

(B) the term "serious bodily injury" shall be applied for purposes of paragraph (1)(F) in accordance with the meaning given that term in section 113 (b)(2) of this title;

(C) the term "sexual contact" shall be applied for purposes of paragraph (1)(G) in accordance with the meaning given that term in section 2246 (3) of this title;

(D) the term "serious physical pain or suffering" shall be applied for purposes of paragraph (1)(B) as meaning bodily injury that involves—

(i) a substantial risk of death;

(ii) extreme physical pain;

(iii) a burn or physical disfigurement of a serious nature (other than cuts, abrasions, or bruises); or

(iv) significant loss or impairment of the function of a bodily member, organ, or mental faculty; and

(E) the term "serious mental pain or suffering" shall be applied for purposes of paragraph (1)(B) in accordance with the meaning given the term "severe mental pain or suffering" (as defined in section 2340 (2) of this title), except that—

(i) the term "serious" shall replace the term "severe" where it appears; and

(ii) as to conduct occurring after the date of the enactment of the Military Commissions Act of 2006, the term "serious and non-transitory mental harm (which need not be prolonged)" shall replace the term "prolonged mental harm" where it appears.

(3) Inapplicability of certain provisions with respect to collateral damage or incident of lawful attack.—The intent specified for the conduct stated in subparagraphs (D), (E), and (F) or paragraph (1) precludes the applicability of those subparagraphs to an offense under subsection (a) by reasons of subsection (c)(3) with respect to—

(A) collateral damage; or

(B) death, damage, or injury incident to a lawful attack.

(4) Inapplicability of taking hostages to prisoner exchange.—Paragraph (1)(I) does not apply to an offense under subsection (a) by reason of subsection (c)(3) in the case of a prisoner exchange during wartime.

(5) Definition of grave breaches.—The definitions in this subsection are intended only to define the grave breaches of common Article 3 and not the full scope of United States obligations under that Article.

The United States is a party to Hague Convention IV, to the four Geneva Conventions of 1949 and to the Protocol, as amended in 1996 on Mines, Booby-Traps and Other Devices. It is not a party to either of the 1977 Protocols to the Geneva Conventions, Protocol I, dealing with international armed conflict, or Protocol II dealing with non-international armed conflict. None of the treaties speak of "grave breaches" in relation to Common Article III of the Geneva Conventions. That is a concept found only in the four Conventions of 1949 and in Protocol I of 1977 and applies only in international armed conflict. The material above is an American invention.

Chapter 21

The Ad Hoc and Other Tribunals

§ 21.01 The Ad Hoc Tribunal for the Former Yugoslavia

The Security Council's creation of the Ad Hoc Tribunal for Former Yugoslavia in 1993 represented the revival of the ideas that gave rise to the Nuremberg and Tokyo Trials. It was followed in 1994 by a Tribunal for Rwanda. In each case, the Tribunal was formed with international judges. Subsequently, several other tribunals were created under United Nations auspices that had a mix of local and international judges. They were called "hybrid" tribunals. The more controversial Lockerbie and Iraqi trials, while they were carried out by "domestic" judges, had some of the characteristics of these tribunals. This Chapter, while focusing mainly on the Tribunals for Former Yugoslavia and Rwanda, takes note of the other developments. The Ad Hoc tribunals were created at a time when proposals for a permanent International Criminal Court were again on the international agenda. This Chapter thus foreshadows the arrival on the scene of the International Criminal Court in 2002, which is addressed in Chapter 22.

On October 6, 1992, Security Council Resolution 780 (1992) requested the U.N. Secretary-General to appoint a Commission of Experts to investigate violations of international humanitarian law in the former Yugoslavia. In an interim report in January 1993, the Commission recommended the establishment of an international criminal tribunal to try violators. On February 22, 1993, in Resolution 808 (1993), the Security Council decided to establish such a tribunal and asked the Secretary-General to prepare a report on how to implement its decision. The Secretary-General's report (U.N. Doc. S/25704, May 3, 1993) included a draft statute for an international criminal tribunal. On May 25, 1993, the Security Council adopted Resolution 827 (1993), creating the International Criminal Tribunal for the former Yugoslavia (ICTY), which was to operate under the statute contained in the Secretary-General's report. The Statute and the Rules of Procedure and Evidence adopted by the Tribunal are readily available on the Tribunal's website: http://www.icty.org/.

The Tribunal initially had eleven judges sitting in two Trial Chambers of three judges each and an Appeals Chamber of five judges. The Security Council has from time to time expanded the number of judges, so as to allow for more Trial Chambers. Five of the permanent judges and two of the judges from the International Tribunal for Rwanda (ICTR) constituted the Appeals Chamber, which sat as a panel of five judges. The judges were elected by the U.N. General Assembly from a list of candidates proposed by the Security Council. The Tribunal's Prosecutor was appointed by the Security Council on nomination by the Secretary-General. The Tribunal sat at The Hague. It had jurisdiction over four categories of crime—(1) "grave breaches" of the Geneva Conventions of 1949, (2) "violations of the laws and customs of war," (3) genocide, and (4) "crimes against humanity"—committed in the territory of the former Yugoslavia since January 1, 1991 (and until "a date to be determined by the Security Council upon the restoration of peace"). These four categories of crime comprise the parts of international humanitarian law that the Secretary General's report concluded clearly give rise to individual responsibility as a matter of customary international law. In 2010, the Security Council adopted Resolution 1966 (2010) containing the Statute of the International Residual Mechanism for Criminal Tribunals, a stripped down body to complete the work of the Tribunals for Former Yugoslavia and Rwanda. By the time of the termination of its authority at the end of 2017, the Tribunal had indicted 161 persons, all of whom were ultimately taken into custody. A big disappointment was the death of Slobodan Milošević before his trial could be completed. Nevertheless, by December 2017, 90 had been sentenced, 19 had been acquitted, 13 had been referred to a national jurisdiction, two were in re-trial at the Residual Mechanism and 37 had their indictments withdrawn or were deceased. Fifty-five had served their sentences and six died while serving their sentences. In early 2016, two major verdicts were reached at the ICTY. On March 24, 2016, Radovan Karadzic, the former Bosnian Serb leader, was convicted of genocide, war crimes, and crimes against humanity. He was sentenced to 40 years in prison. *See generally,* the retrospective website of the Tribunal, *available at* https://www.icty.org/.

Prosecutor v. Tadic

International Criminal Tribunal for the former Yugoslavia
Case No. IT-94-1-AR72, Appeals Chamber Decision on the Defense Motion for Interlocutory Appeal on Jurisdiction (Oct. 2, 1995)

I. Introduction

1. The Appeals Chamber ... is seized of an appeal lodged by the Defence against a judgement rendered by Trial Chamber II on 10 August 1995. By that judgement, Appellant's motion challenging the jurisdiction of the International Tribunal was denied....

8. [The grounds of appeal relied on by the Appellant] are offered under the following headings:

a) unlawful establishment of the International Tribunal;

b) unjustified primacy of the International Tribunal over competent domestic courts;

c) lack of subject-matter jurisdiction....

II. Unlawful Establishment of The International Tribunal

Admissibility of Plea Based on the Invalidity of the Establishment of the Tribunal

13. Before the Trial Chamber, the Prosecutor maintained that: (1) the International Tribunal lacks authority to review its establishment by the Security Council; and that in any case (2) the question whether the Security Council in establishing the International Tribunal complied with the United Nations Charter raises "political questions" which are "non-justiciable." The Trial Chamber approved this line of argument. . . .

(1) Does the International Tribunal Have Jurisdiction?

15. To assume that the jurisdiction of the International Tribunal is absolutely limited to what the Security Council "intended" to entrust it with, is to envisage the International Tribunal exclusively as a "subsidiary organ" of the Security Council. . . . t the Security Council not only decided to establish a subsidiary organ . . . it also clearly intended to establish a special kind of "subsidiary organ": a tribunal.

18. [The] power, known as "*la compétence de la compétence*" in French, is part, and indeed a major part, of the incidental or inherent jurisdiction of any judicial or arbitral tribunal, consisting of its "jurisdiction to determine its own jurisdiction." It is a necessary component in the exercise of the judicial function and does not need to be expressly provided for in the constitutive documents of those tribunals. . . .

19. It is true that this power can be limited by an express provision in the arbitration agreement or in the constitutive instruments of standing tribunals. . . . [but since] no such limitative text appears in the Statute of the International Tribunal, the International Tribunal can and indeed has to exercise its "*compétence de la compétence*" and examine the jurisdictional plea of the Defence in order to ascertain its jurisdiction to hear the case on the merits.

(2) Is The Question At Issue Political And As Such Non-Justiciable?

24. The doctrines of "political questions" and "non-justiciable disputes" are remnants of the reservations of "sovereignty," "national honour," etc. in very old arbitration treaties. They have receded from the horizon of contemporary international law, except for the occasional invocation of the "political question" argument before the International Court of Justice in advisory proceedings and, very rarely, in contentious proceedings as well. The Court has consistently rejected this argument as a bar to examining a case. It considered it unfounded in law. As long as the case before it or the request for an advisory opinion turns on a legal question capable of a legal answer, the Court considers that it is duty-bound to exercise jurisdiction over it, regardless of the political background or the other political facets of the issue. . . .

25. The Appeals Chamber does not consider that the International Tribunal is barred from examination of the Defence jurisdictional plea by the so-called "political" or "non-justiciable" nature of the issue it raises.

The Issue of Constitutionality

26. Many arguments have been put forward by Appellant in support of the contention that the establishment of the International Tribunal is invalid under the Charter of the United Nations or that it was not duly established by law.... These arguments raise a series of constitutional issues which all turn on the limits of the power of the Security Council under Chapter VII of the Charter of the United Nations [in] determining what action or measures can be taken under this Chapter, particularly the establishment of an international criminal tribunal....

(1) The Power Of The Security Council To Invoke Chapter VII

28. Article 39 opens Chapter VII of the Charter of the United Nations and determines the conditions of application of this Chapter. It provides: "The Security Council shall determine the existence of any threat to the peace, breach of the peace, or act of aggression and shall make recommendations, or decide what measures shall be taken in accordance with Articles 41 and 42, to maintain or restore international peace and security."...

30. It is not necessary for the purposes of the present decision to examine... the question of the limits of the discretion of the Security Council in determining the existence of a "threat to the peace," for two reasons. The first is that an armed conflict (or a series of armed conflicts) has been taking place in the territory of the former Yugoslavia since long before the decision of the Security Council to establish this International Tribunal. If it is considered an international armed conflict, there is no doubt that it falls within the literal sense of the words "breach of the peace" (between the parties or, at the very least, as a "threat to the peace" of others). But even if it were considered merely as an "internal armed conflict," it would still constitute a "threat to the peace" according to the settled practice of the Security Council and the common understanding of the United Nations membership in general....

The second reason, which is more particular to the case at hand, is that Appellant... no longer contests the Security Council's power to determine whether the situation in the former Yugoslavia constituted a threat to the peace, nor the determination itself.... But he continues to contest the legality and appropriateness of the measures chosen by the Security Council to that end....

(3) The Establishment of the International Tribunal as a Measure under Chapter VII

34. Prima facie, the International Tribunal matches perfectly the description in Article 41 of "measures not involving the use of force."...

35.... Article 41 reads as follows: "The Security Council may decide what measures not involving the use of armed force are to be employed to give effect to its decisions, and it may call upon the Members of the United Nations to apply such measures. These may include complete or partial interruption of economic relations and of rail, sea, air, postal, telegraphic, radio, and other means of communication, and the severance of diplomatic relations."

It is evident that the measures set out in Article 41 are merely illustrative examples which obviously do not exclude other measures. All the Article requires is that they do not involve "the use of force." . . . [N]othing in the Article suggests the limitation of the measures to those implemented by States. . . .

36. . . . . In sum, the establishment of the International Tribunal falls squarely within the powers of the Security Council under Article 41.

37. The argument that the Security Council, not being endowed with judicial powers, cannot establish a subsidiary organ possessed of such powers is untenable: it results from a fundamental misunderstanding of the constitutional set-up of the Charter.

Plainly, the Security Council is not a judicial organ and is not provided with judicial powers . . . The principal function of the Security Council is the maintenance of international peace and security, in the discharge of which the Security Council exercises both decision-making and executive powers.

38. The establishment of the International Tribunal by the Security Council does not signify, however, that the Security Council has delegated to it some of its own functions or the exercise of some of its own powers. Nor does it mean, in reverse, that the Security Council was usurping for itself part of a judicial function which does not belong to it but to other organs of the United Nations according to the Charter. The Security Council has resorted to the establishment of a judicial organ in the form of an international criminal tribunal as an instrument for the exercise of its own principal function of maintenance of peace and security, i.e., as a measure contributing to the restoration and maintenance of peace in the former Yugoslavia. . . .

39. . . . Article 39 leaves the choice of means and their evaluation to the Security Council, which enjoys wide discretionary powers in this regard; and it could not have been otherwise, as such a choice involves political evaluation of highly complex and dynamic situations. It would be a total misconception of what are the criteria of legality and validity in law to test the legality of such measures *ex post facto* by their success or failure to achieve their ends (in the present case, the restoration of peace in the former Yugoslavia, in quest of which the establishment of the International Tribunal is but one of many measures adopted by the Security Council).

40. For the aforementioned reasons, the Appeals Chamber considers that the International Tribunal has been lawfully established as a measure under Chapter VII of the Charter.

(4) Was The Establishment Of The International Tribunal Contrary To The General Principle Whereby Courts Must Be "Established By Law"?

41. Appellant challenges the establishment of the International Tribunal by contending that it has not been established by law. The entitlement of an individual to have a criminal charge against him determined by a tribunal which has been established by law is provided in Article 14, paragraph 1, of the International Covenant on Civil

and Political Rights. It provides: "In the determination of any criminal charge against him, or of his rights and obligations in a suit at law, everyone shall be entitled to a fair and public hearing by a competent, independent and impartial tribunal established by law." Similar provisions can be found in Article 6 (1) of the European Convention on Human Rights. . . . and in Article 8 (1) of the American Convention on Human Rights. . . . In support of this assertion, Appellant emphasises the fundamental nature of the "fair trial" or "due process" guarantees afforded in the International Covenant on Civil and Political Rights, the European Convention on Human Rights and the American Convention on Human Rights. Appellant asserts that they are minimum requirements in international law for the administration of criminal justice.

42. . . . . Appellant has not satisfied this Chamber that the requirements laid down in these three conventions must apply not only in the context of national legal systems but also with respect to proceedings conducted before an international court. . . . [T]he principle that a tribunal must be established by law . . . is a general principle of law imposing an international obligation which only applies to the administration of criminal justice in a municipal setting. It follows from this principle that it is incumbent on all States to organize their system of criminal justice in such a way as to ensure that all individuals are guaranteed the right to have a criminal charge determined by a tribunal established by law. This does not entail however that, by contrast, an international criminal court could be set up at the mere whim of a group of governments. Such a court ought to be rooted in the rule of law and offer all guarantees embodied in the relevant international instruments. Then the court may be said to be "established by law."

43. Indeed, there are three possible interpretations of the term "established by law." First, as Appellant argues, "established by law" could mean established by a legislature. Appellant claims that the International Tribunal is the product of a "mere executive order" and not of a "decision making process under democratic control, necessary to create a judicial organization in a democratic society." Therefore Appellant maintains that the International Tribunal [has] not been "established by law."

The case law applying the words "established by law" in the European Convention on Human Rights has favoured this interpretation of the expression. This case law bears out the view that the relevant provision is intended to ensure that tribunals in a democratic society must not depend on the discretion of the executive; rather they should be regulated by law emanating from Parliament. . . . Or, put another way, the guarantee is intended to ensure that the administration of justice is not a matter of executive discretion, but is regulated by laws made by the legislature.

It is clear that the legislative, executive and judicial division of powers which is largely followed in most municipal systems does not apply to the international setting nor, more specifically, to the setting of an international organization such as the United Nations. Among the principal organs of the United Nations the divisions between judicial, executive and legislative functions are not clear cut. Regarding the judicial function, the International Court of Justice is clearly the "principal judicial organ." There is, however, no legislature, in the technical sense of the term, in the United

Nations system and, more generally, no Parliament in the world community. That is to say, there exists no corporate organ formally empowered to enact laws directly binding on international legal subjects. . . . Consequently the separation of powers element of the requirement that a tribunal be "established by law" finds no application in an international law setting. The aforementioned principle can only impose an obligation on States concerning the functioning of their own national systems.

44. A second possible interpretation is that the words "established by law" refer to establishment of international courts by a body which, though not a Parliament, has a limited power to take binding decisions. In our view, one such body is the Security Council when, acting under Chapter VII of the United Nations Charter, it makes decisions binding by virtue of Article 25 of the Charter.

According to Appellant, however, there must be something more for a tribunal to be "established by law." Appellant takes the position that, given the differences between the United Nations system and national division of powers, discussed above, the conclusion must be that the United Nations system is not capable of creating the International Tribunal unless there is an amendment to the United Nations Charter. We disagree. It does not follow from the fact that the United Nations has no legislature that the Security Council is not empowered to set up this International Tribunal if it is acting pursuant to an authority found within its constitution, the United Nations Charter. As set out above, we are of the view that the Security Council was endowed with the power to create this International Tribunal as a measure under Chapter VII in the light of its determination that there exists a threat to the peace.

In addition, the establishment of the International Tribunal has been repeatedly approved and endorsed by the "representative" organ of the United Nations, the General Assembly: this body not only participated in its setting up, by electing the Judges and approving the budget, but also expressed its satisfaction with, and encouragement of the activities of the International Tribunal in various resolutions.

45. The third possible interpretation of the requirement that the International Tribunal be "established by law" is that its establishment must be in accordance with the rule of law. This appears to be the most sensible and most likely meaning of the term in the context of international law. For a tribunal such as this one to be established according to the rule of law, it must be established in accordance with the proper international standards; it must provide all the guarantees of fairness, justice and even-handedness, in full conformity with internationally recognized human rights instruments. . . . The important consideration in determining whether a tribunal has been "established by law" is not whether it was pre-established or established for a specific purpose or situation; what is important is that it be set up by a competent organ in keeping with the relevant legal procedures, and that it observes the requirements of procedural fairness.

46. An examination of the Statute of the International Tribunal, and of the Rules of Procedure and Evidence adopted pursuant to that Statute leads to the conclusion that it has been established in accordance with the rule of law. The fair trial

guarantees in Article 14 of the International Covenant on Civil and Political Rights have been adopted almost verbatim in Article 21 of the Statute. Other fair trial guarantees appear in the Statute and the Rules of Procedure and Evidence. . . .

47. In conclusion, the Appeals Chamber finds that the International Tribunal has been established in accordance with the appropriate procedures under the United Nations Charter and provides all the necessary safeguards of a fair trial. It is thus "established by law."

III. Unjustified Primacy of The International Tribunal over Competent Domestic Courts

49. The second ground of appeal attacks the primacy of the International Tribunal over national courts [as an infringement on the sovereignty of the states directly affected]. . . .

50. This primacy is established by Article 9 of the Statute of the International Tribunal, which provides:

> **Concurrent jurisdiction**
>
> 1. The International Tribunal and national courts shall have concurrent jurisdiction to prosecute persons for serious violations of international humanitarian law committed in the territory of the former Yugoslavia since 1 January 1991.
>
> 2. *The International Tribunal shall have primacy over national courts.* At any stage of the procedure, the International Tribunal may formally request national courts to defer to the competence of the International Tribunal in accordance with the present Statute and the Rules of Procedure and Evidence of the International Tribunal. (Emphasis added.)

Appellant's submission is material to the issue, inasmuch as Appellant is expected to stand trial before this International Tribunal as a consequence of a request for deferral which the International Tribunal submitted to the Government of the Federal Republic of Germany on 8 November 1994 and which this Government, as it was bound to do, agreed to honour by surrendering Appellant to the International Tribunal. . . .

Appellant's Brief in support of the motion before the Trial Chamber went into further details which he set down under three headings:

(a) domestic jurisdiction;

(b) sovereignty of States;

(c) *jus de non evocando*. . . .

A. Domestic Jurisdiction

54. Appellant argued in first instance that: "From the moment Bosnia-Herzegovina was recognised as an independent state, it had the competence to establish jurisdiction to try crimes that have been committed on its territory." Appellant added that: "As a matter of fact the state of Bosnia-Herzegovina does exercise its jurisdiction,

not only in matters of ordinary criminal law, but also in matters of alleged violations of crimes against humanity, as for example is the case with the prosecution of Mr Karadzic et al."

This first point is not contested and the Prosecutor has conceded as much. But it does not, by itself, settle the question of the primacy of the International Tribunal. . . .

B. Sovereignty Of States

55. . . . . In Appellant's view, no State can assume jurisdiction to prosecute crimes committed on the territory of another State, barring a universal interest "justified by a treaty or customary international law or an *opinio juris* on the issue." Based on this proposition, Appellant argues that the same requirements should underpin the establishment of an international tribunal destined to invade an area essentially within the domestic jurisdiction of States. In the present instance, the principle of State sovereignty would have been violated. The Trial Chamber has rejected this plea, holding among other reasons: "In any event, the accused not being a State lacks the *locus standi* to raise the issue of primacy, which involves a plea that the sovereignty of a State has been violated, a plea only a sovereign State may raise or waive and a right clearly the accused cannot take over from the State."

The Trial Chamber relied on the judgement of the District Court of Jerusalem in *Israel v. Eichmann*: "The right to plead violation of the sovereignty of a State is the exclusive right of that State. Only a sovereign State may raise the plea or waive it, and the accused has no right to take over the rights of that State." Consistently with a long line of cases, a similar principle was upheld more recently in the United States of America in the matter of *United States v. Noriega* [chap. 16, *supra*]: "As a general principle of international law, individuals have no standing to challenge violations of international treaties in the absence of a protest by the sovereign involved."

Authoritative as they may be, those pronouncements do not carry, in the field of international law, the weight which they may bring to bear upon national judiciaries. Dating back to a period when sovereignty stood as a sacrosanct and unassailable attribute of statehood, recently this concept has suffered progressive erosion at the hands of the more liberal forces at work in the democratic societies, particularly in the field of human rights. Whatever the situation in domestic litigation, the traditional doctrine upheld and acted upon by the Trial Chamber is not reconcilable, in this International Tribunal, with the view that an accused, being entitled to a full defence, cannot be deprived of a plea so intimately connected with, and grounded in, international law as a defence based on violation of State sovereignty. To bar an accused from raising such a plea is tantamount to deciding that, in this day and age, an international court could not, in a criminal matter where the liberty of an accused is at stake, examine a plea raising the issue of violation of State sovereignty. Such a startling conclusion would imply a contradiction in terms which this Chamber feels it is its duty to refute and lay to rest.

56. That Appellant be recognised the right to plead State sovereignty does not mean, of course, that his plea must be favourably received. . . .

Appellant can call in aid Article 2, paragraph 7, of the United Nations Charter: "Nothing contained in the present Charter shall authorize the United Nations to intervene in matters which are essentially within the domestic jurisdiction of any State. . . ." However, one should not forget the commanding restriction at the end of the same paragraph: "but this principle shall not prejudice the application of enforcement measures under Chapter VII." Those are precisely the provisions under which the International Tribunal has been established.

Even without these provisions, matters can be taken out of the jurisdiction of a State. In the present case, the Republic of Bosnia and Herzegovina not only has not contested the jurisdiction of the International Tribunal but has actually approved, and collaborated with, the International Tribunal. . . . As to the Federal Republic of Germany, its cooperation with the International Tribunal is public and has been previously noted. The Trial Chamber was therefore fully justified to write, on this particular issue: "It is pertinent to note that the challenge to the primacy of the International Tribunal has been made against the express intent of the two States most closely affected by the indictment against the accused — Bosnia and Herzegovina and the Federal Republic of Germany. The former, on the territory of which the crimes were allegedly committed, and the latter where the accused resided at the time of his arrest, have unconditionally accepted the jurisdiction of the International Tribunal and the accused cannot claim the rights that have been specifically waived by the States concerned. . . ."

57. This is all the more so in view of the nature of the offences alleged against Appellant, offences which, if proven, do not affect the interests of one State alone but shock the conscience of mankind. As early as 1950, in the case of *General Wagener*, the Supreme Military Tribunal of Italy held: "These norms [concerning crimes against laws and customs of war], due to their highly ethical and moral content, have a universal character, not a territorial one." . . . Twelve years later the Supreme Court of Israel in the *Eichmann* case could draw a similar picture: "These crimes constitute acts which damage vital international interests; they impair the foundations and security of the international community; they violate the universal moral values and humanitarian principles that lie hidden in the criminal law systems adopted by civilised nations. . . . They involve the perpetration of an international crime which all the nations of the world are interested in preventing."

58. The public revulsion against similar offences in the 1990s brought about a reaction on the part of the community of nations: hence, among other remedies, the establishment of an international judicial body by an organ of an organization representing the community of nations: the Security Council. This organ is empowered and mandated, by definition, to deal with transboundary matters or matters which, though domestic in nature, may affect "international peace and security." It would be a travesty of law and a betrayal of the universal need for justice, should the concept of State sovereignty be allowed to be raised successfully against human rights. Borders should not be considered as a shield against the reach of the law and as a protection for those who trample underfoot the most elementary rights of humanity. . . .

Indeed, when an international tribunal such as the present one is created, it must be endowed with primacy over national courts. Otherwise, human nature being what it is, there would be a perennial danger of international crimes being characterised as "ordinary crimes" (Statute of the International Tribunal, art. 10, para. 2(a)), or proceedings being "designed to shield the accused," or cases not being diligently prosecuted (Statute of the International Tribunal, art. 10, para. 2(b)). If not effectively countered by the principle of primacy, any one of those stratagems might be used to defeat the very purpose of the creation of an international criminal jurisdiction, to the benefit of the very people whom it has been designed to prosecute. . . .

60. The plea of State sovereignty must therefore be dismissed.

C. Jus De Non Evocando

61. Appellant argues that he has a right to be tried by his national courts under his national laws. No one has questioned that right of Appellant. The problem is elsewhere: is that right exclusive? Does it prevent Appellant from being tried—and having an equally fair trial—before an international tribunal? Appellant contends that such an exclusive right has received universal acceptance: yet one cannot find it expressed either in the Universal Declaration of Human Rights or in the International Covenant on Civil and Political Rights, unless one is prepared to stretch to breaking point the interpretation of their provisions. . . .

62. As a matter of fact—and of law—the principle advocated by Appellant aims at one very specific goal: to avoid the creation of special or extraordinary courts designed to try political offences in times of social unrest without guarantees of a fair trial. This principle is not breached by the transfer of jurisdiction to an international tribunal created by the Security Council acting on behalf of the community of nations. No rights of accused are thereby infringed or threatened; quite to the contrary, they are all specifically spelt out and protected under the Statute of the International Tribunal. No accused can complain. True, he will be removed from his "natural" national forum; but he will be brought before a tribunal at least equally fair, more distanced from the facts of the case and taking a broader view of the matter.

Furthermore, one cannot but rejoice at the thought that, universal jurisdiction being nowadays acknowledged in the case of international crimes, a person suspected of such offences may finally be brought before an international judicial body for a dispassionate consideration of his indictment by impartial, independent and disinterested judges coming, as it happens here, from all continents of the world. . . .

64. For these reasons the Appeals Chamber concludes that Appellant's second ground of appeal, contesting the primacy of the International Tribunal, is ill-founded and must be dismissed.

IV. Lack of Subject-Matter Jurisdiction

65. Appellant's third ground of appeal is the claim that the International Tribunal lacks subject-matter jurisdiction over the crimes alleged. The basis for this

allegation is Appellant's claim that the subject-matter jurisdiction under Articles 2, 3 and 5 of the Statute of the International Tribunal is limited to crimes committed in the context of an international armed conflict. Before the Trial Chamber, Appellant claimed that the alleged crimes, even if proven, were committed in the context of an internal armed conflict. On appeal an additional alternative claim is asserted to the effect that there was no armed conflict at all in the region where the crimes were allegedly committed. . . .

A. Preliminary Issue: The Existence Of An Armed Conflict

66. . . . . Appellant claims that the conflict in the Prijedor region (where the alleged crimes are said to have taken place) was limited to a political assumption of power by the Bosnian Serbs and did not involve armed combat (though movements of tanks are admitted). This argument presents a preliminary issue to which we turn first.

67. International humanitarian law governs the conduct of both internal and international armed conflicts. Appellant correctly points out that for there to be a violation of this body of law, there must be an armed conflict. The definition of "armed conflict" varies depending on whether the hostilities are international or internal but, contrary to Appellant's contention, the temporal and geographical scope of both internal and international armed conflicts extends beyond the exact time and place of hostilities. . . .

70. . . . . [A]n armed conflict exists whenever there is a resort to armed force between States or protracted armed violence between governmental authorities and organized armed groups or between such groups within a State. International humanitarian law applies from the initiation of such armed conflicts and extends beyond the cessation of hostilities until a general conclusion of peace is reached; or, in the case of internal conflicts, a peaceful settlement is achieved. Until that moment, international humanitarian law continues to apply in the whole territory of the warring States or, in the case of internal conflicts, the whole territory under the control of a party, whether or not actual combat takes place there.

Applying the foregoing concept of armed conflicts to this case, we hold that the alleged crimes were committed in the context of an armed conflict. Fighting among the various entities within the former Yugoslavia began in 1991, continued through the summer of 1992 when the alleged crimes are said to have been committed, and persists to this day. Notwithstanding various temporary cease-fire agreements, no general conclusion of peace has brought military operations in the region to a close. These hostilities exceed the intensity requirements applicable to both international and internal armed conflicts. There has been protracted, large-scale violence between the armed forces of different States and between governmental forces and organized insurgent groups. Even if substantial clashes were not occurring in the Prijedor region at the time and place the crimes allegedly were committed — a factual issue on which the Appeals Chamber does not pronounce — international humanitarian law applies. It is sufficient that the alleged crimes were closely related to the hostilities occurring in other parts of the territories controlled by the parties to the conflict. There is no doubt that the allegations at issue here bear the required relationship. The indictment states that in 1992 Bosnian Serbs took control of the Opstina of Prijedor and established a prison camp in Omarska. It further alleges that crimes were committed against civilians inside and outside the Omarska prison camp as part of the Bosnian Serb take-over and consolidation of power in the Prijedor region, which was, in turn, part of the larger Bosnian Serb military campaign to obtain control over Bosnian territory. . . . In light of the foregoing, we conclude that, for the purposes of applying international humanitarian law, the crimes alleged were committed in the context of an armed conflict.

B. Does The Statute Refer Only To International Armed Conflicts?

(1) Literal Interpretation of the Statute

71. On the face of it, some provisions of the Statute are unclear as to whether they apply to offences occurring in international armed conflicts only, or to those perpetrated in internal armed conflicts as well. . . . In order better to ascertain the meaning and scope of these provisions, the Appeals Chamber will therefore consider the object and purpose behind the enactment of the Statute.

(2) Teleological Interpretation of the Statute

72. In adopting resolution 827, the Security Council established the International Tribunal with the stated purpose of bringing to justice persons responsible for serious violations of international humanitarian law in the former Yugoslavia, thereby deterring future violations and contributing to the re-establishment of peace and security in the region. The context in which the Security Council acted indicates that it intended to achieve this purpose without reference to whether the conflicts in the former Yugoslavia were internal or international.

As the members of the Security Council well knew, in 1993, when the Statute was drafted, the conflicts in the former Yugoslavia could have been characterized as both internal and international, or alternatively, as an internal conflict alongside an international one, or as an internal conflict that had become internationalized because of external support, or as an international conflict that had subsequently been replaced by one or more internal conflicts, or some combination thereof. The conflict in the former Yugoslavia had been rendered international by the involvement of the Croatian Army in Bosnia-Herzegovina and by the involvement of the Yugoslav National Army ("JNA") in hostilities in Croatia, as well as in Bosnia-Herzegovina at least until its formal withdrawal on 19 May 1992. To the extent that the conflicts had been limited to clashes between Bosnian Government forces and Bosnian Serb rebel forces in Bosnia-Herzegovina, as well as between the Croatian Government and Croatian Serb rebel forces in Krajina (Croatia), they had been internal (unless direct involvement of the Federal Republic of Yugoslavia (Serbia-Montenegro) could be proven). It is notable that the parties to this case also agree that the conflicts in the former Yugoslavia since 1991 have had both internal and international aspects. . . .

74. . . . . In each of its successive resolutions, the Security Council focused on the practices with which it was concerned, without reference to the nature of the conflict. . . . [It] was clearly preoccupied with bringing to justice those responsible for these specifically condemned acts, regardless of context. . . .

75. The intent of the Security Council to promote a peaceful solution of the conflict without pronouncing upon the question of its international or internal nature is reflected by the Report of the Secretary-General of 3 May 1993 and by statements of Security Council members regarding their interpretation of the Statute. The Report of the Secretary-General explicitly states that the clause of the Statute concerning the temporal jurisdiction of the International Tribunal was "clearly intended to convey the notion that no judgement as to the international or internal character of the conflict was being exercised." . . .

77. . . . . [W]e conclude that the conflicts in the former Yugoslavia have both internal and international aspects, that the members of the Security Council clearly had both aspects of the conflicts in mind when they adopted the Statute of the International Tribunal, and that they intended to empower the International Tribunal to adjudicate violations of humanitarian law that occurred in either context. To the extent possible under existing international law, the Statute should therefore be construed to give effect to that purpose.

78. With the exception of Article 5 dealing with crimes against humanity, none of the statutory provisions makes explicit reference to the type of conflict as an element of the crime; and, as will be shown below, the reference in Article 5 is made to distinguish the nexus required by the Statute from the nexus required by Article 6 of the London Agreement of 8 August 1945 establishing the International Military Tribunal at Nuremberg. Since customary international law no longer requires any nexus between crimes against humanity and armed conflict (see below, paras. 140 and 141), Article 5 was intended to reintroduce this nexus for the purposes of this Tribunal. . . . [A]lthough Article 2 does not explicitly refer to the nature of the conflicts, its reference to the grave breaches provisions suggest that it is limited to international armed conflicts. It would however defeat the Security Council's purpose to read a similar international armed conflict requirement into the remaining jurisdictional provisions of the Statute. Contrary to the drafters' apparent indifference to the nature of the underlying conflicts, such an interpretation would authorize the International Tribunal to prosecute and punish certain conduct in an international armed conflict, while turning a blind eye to the very same conduct in an internal armed conflict. . . .

In light of this understanding of the Security Council's purpose in creating the International Tribunal, we turn below to discussion of Appellant's specific arguments regarding the scope of the jurisdiction of the International Tribunal under Articles 2, 3 and 5 of the Statute.

(3) Logical And Systematic Interpretation of the Statute

Article 2

79. Article 2 of the Statute of the International Tribunal provides:

> The International Tribunal shall have the power to prosecute persons committing or ordering to be committed grave breaches of the Geneva Conventions of 12 August 1949, namely the following acts against persons or property protected under the provisions of the relevant Geneva Convention:
>
> (a) wilful killing;
>
> (b) torture or inhuman treatment, including biological experiments;
>
> (c) wilfully causing great suffering or serious injury to body or health;
>
> (d) extensive destruction and appropriation of property, not justified by military necessity and carried out unlawfully and wantonly;
>
> (e) compelling a prisoner of war or a civilian to serve in the forces of a hostile power;
>
> (f) wilfully depriving a prisoner of war or a civilian of the rights of fair and regular trial;
>
> (g) unlawful deportation or transfer or unlawful confinement of a civilian;
>
> (h) taking civilians as hostages.

By its explicit terms, and as confirmed in the Report of the Secretary-General, this Article of the Statute is based on the Geneva Conventions of 1949 and, more specifically, the provisions of those Conventions relating to "grave breaches" of the Conventions. Each of the four Geneva Conventions of 1949 contains a "grave breaches" provision, specifying particular breaches of the Convention for which the High Contracting Parties have a duty to prosecute those responsible. In other words, for these specific acts, the Conventions create universal mandatory criminal jurisdiction among contracting States. Although the language of the Conventions might appear to be ambiguous and the question is open to some debate, it is widely contended that the grave breaches provisions establish universal mandatory jurisdiction only with respect to those breaches of the Conventions committed in international armed conflicts. . . .

80. . . . . The grave breaches system of the Geneva Conventions establishes a twofold system: there is on the one hand an enumeration of offences that are regarded as so serious as to constitute "grave breaches"; closely bound up with this enumeration a mandatory enforcement mechanism is set up, based on the concept of a duty and a right of all Contracting States to search for and try or extradite persons allegedly responsible for "grave breaches." The international armed conflict element generally attributed to the grave breaches provisions of the Geneva Conventions is merely a function of the system of universal mandatory jurisdiction that those provisions

create. The international armed conflict requirement was a necessary limitation on the grave breaches system in light of the intrusion on State sovereignty that such mandatory universal jurisdiction represents. States parties to the 1949 Geneva Conventions did not want to give other States jurisdiction over serious violations of international humanitarian law committed in their internal armed conflicts—at least not the mandatory universal jurisdiction involved in the grave breaches system. . . .

82. The above interpretation is borne out by what could be considered as part of the preparatory works of the Statute of the International Tribunal, namely the Report of the Secretary-General. There, in introducing and explaining the meaning and purport of Article 2 and having regard to the "grave breaches" system of the Geneva Conventions, reference is made to "international armed conflicts."

83. We find that our interpretation of Article 2 is the only one warranted by the text of the Statute and the relevant provisions of the Geneva Conventions, as well as by a logical construction of their interplay as dictated by Article 2. However, we are aware that this conclusion may appear not to be consonant with recent trends of both State practice and the whole doctrine of human rights—which . . . tend to blur in many respects the traditional dichotomy between international wars and civil strife. . . .

84. [Nevertheless] the Appeals Chamber must conclude that, in the present state of development of the law, Article 2 of the Statute only applies to offences committed within the context of international armed conflicts. . . .

Article 3

86. Article 3 of the Statute declares the International Tribunal competent to adjudicate violations of the laws or customs of war. The provision states:

> The International Tribunal shall have the power to prosecute persons violating the laws or customs of war. Such violations shall include, but not be limited to:
>
> (a) employment of poisonous weapons or other weapons calculated to cause unnecessary suffering;
>
> (b) wanton destruction of cities, towns or villages, or devastation not justified by military necessity;
>
> (c) attack, or bombardment, by whatever means, of undefended towns, villages, dwellings, or buildings;
>
> (d) seizure of, destruction or wilful damage done to institutions dedicated to religion, charity and education, the arts and sciences, historic monuments and works of art and science;
>
> (e) plunder of public or private property.

As explained by the Secretary-General in his Report on the Statute, this provision is based on the 1907 Hague Convention (IV) Respecting the Laws and Customs of War on Land, the Regulations annexed to that Convention, and the Nuremberg

Tribunal's interpretation of those Regulations. Appellant argues that the Hague Regulations were adopted to regulate interstate armed conflict, while the conflict in the former Yugoslavia is *in casu* an internal armed conflict; therefore, to the extent that the jurisdiction of the International Tribunal under Article 3 is based on the Hague Regulations, it lacks jurisdiction under Article 3 to adjudicate alleged violations in the former Yugoslavia. Appellant's argument does not bear close scrutiny, for it is based on an unnecessarily narrow reading of the Statute.

(i) The Interpretation of Article 3

87. A literal interpretation of Article 3 shows that: (i) it refers to a broad category of offences, namely all "violations of the laws or customs of war"; and (ii) the enumeration of some of these violations provided in Article 3 are merely illustrative, not exhaustive.

To identify the content of the class of offences falling under Article 3, attention should be drawn to an important fact. The expression "violations of the laws or customs of war" is a traditional term of art used in the past, when the concepts of "war" and "laws of warfare" still prevailed, before they were largely replaced by two broader notions: (i) that of "armed conflict," essentially introduced by the 1949 Geneva Conventions; and (ii) the correlative notion of "international law of armed conflict," or the more recent and comprehensive notion of "international humanitarian law," which has emerged as a result of the influence of human rights doctrines on the law of armed conflict. As stated above, it is clear from the Report of the Secretary-General that the old-fashioned expression referred to above was used in Article 3 of the Statute primarily to make reference to the 1907 Hague Convention (IV) Respecting the Laws and Customs of War on Land and the Regulations annexed thereto (Report of the Secretary-General, at para. 41). However, as the Report indicates, the Hague Convention, considered *qua* customary law, constitutes an important area of humanitarian international law. In other words, the Secretary-General himself concedes that the traditional laws of warfare are now more correctly termed "international humanitarian law" and that the Hague Regulations constitute an important segment of such law. Furthermore, the Secretary-General has also correctly admitted that the Hague Regulations have a broader scope than the Geneva Conventions, in that they cover not only the protection of victims of armed violence (civilians) or of those who no longer take part in hostilities (prisoners of war), but also the conduct of hostilities; in the words of the Report: "The Hague Regulations cover aspects of international humanitarian law which are also covered by the 1949 Geneva Conventions." These comments suggest that Article 3 is intended to cover both Geneva and Hague law. On the other hand, the Secretary-General's subsequent comments indicate that the violations explicitly listed in Article 3 relate to Hague law not contained in the Geneva Conventions. As pointed out above, this list is, however, merely illustrative: indeed, Article 3, before enumerating the violations provides that they "shall include but not be limited to" the list of offences. Considering this list in the general context of the Secretary-General's discussion of the Hague Regulations and international humanitarian law, we conclude that this list may be construed to include other infringements of international humanitarian law. The only limitation is that such infringements must not be already covered by Article 2 (lest this latter provision should become superfluous). Article 3 may be taken to cover all violations of international humanitarian law other than the "grave breaches" of the four Geneva Conventions falling under Article 2 (or, for that matter, the violations covered by Articles 4 and 5, to the extent that Articles 3, 4 and 5 overlap).

88. That Article 3 does not confine itself to covering violations of Hague law, but is intended also to refer to all violations of international humanitarian law (subject to the limitations just stated), is borne out by the debates in the Security Council that followed the adoption of the resolution establishing the International Tribunal. . . .

89. In light of the above remarks, it can be held that Article 3 is a general clause covering all violations of humanitarian law not falling under Article 2 or covered by Articles 4 or 5, more specifically: (i) violations of the Hague law on international conflicts; (ii) infringements of provisions of the Geneva Conventions other than those classified as "grave breaches" by those Conventions; (iii) violations of common Article 3 and other customary rules on internal conflicts; (iv) violations of agreements binding upon the parties to the conflict, considered *qua* treaty law, i.e., agreements which have not turned into customary international law.

90. The Appeals Chamber would like to add that, in interpreting the meaning and purport of the expressions "violations of the laws or customs of war" or "violations of international humanitarian law," one must take account of the context of the Statute as a whole. A systematic construction of the Statute emphasises the fact that various provisions, in spelling out the purpose and tasks of the International Tribunal or in defining its functions, refer to "serious violations of international humanitarian law." It is therefore appropriate to take the expression "violations of the laws or customs of war" to cover serious violations of international humanitarian law.

91. Article 3 thus confers on the International Tribunal jurisdiction over any serious offence against international humanitarian law not covered by Article 2, 4 or 5. Article 3 is a fundamental provision laying down that any "serious violation of international humanitarian law" must be prosecuted by the International Tribunal. In other words, Article 3 functions as a residual clause designed to ensure that no serious violation of international humanitarian law is taken away from the jurisdiction of the International Tribunal. Article 3 aims to make such jurisdiction watertight and inescapable. . . .

(ii) The Conditions that must be Fulfilled for a Violation of International Humanitarian Law to be Subject to Article 3

94. The Appeals Chamber deems it fitting to specify the conditions to be fulfilled for Article 3 to become applicable. The following requirements must be met for an offence to be subject to prosecution before the International Tribunal under Article 3:

(i) the violation must constitute an infringement of a rule of international humanitarian law;

(ii) the rule must be customary in nature or, if it belongs to treaty law, the required conditions must be met;

(iii) the violation must be "serious," that is to say, it must constitute a breach of a rule protecting important values, and the breach must involve grave consequences for the victim. Thus, for instance, the fact of a combatant simply appropriating a loaf of bread in an occupied village would not amount to a "serious violation of international humanitarian law" although it may be regarded as falling foul of the basic principle laid down in Article 46, paragraph 1, of the Hague Regulations (and the corresponding rule of customary international law) whereby "private property must be respected" by any army occupying an enemy territory;

(iv) the violation of the rule must entail, under customary or conventional law, the individual criminal responsibility of the person breaching the rule.

It follows that it does not matter whether the "serious violation" has occurred within the context of an international or an internal armed conflict, as long as the requirements set out above are met.

[The Judgment goes on to consider at length two of these requirements, namely (i) the existence of customary international rules governing internal strife, and (ii) the question of whether the violation of such rules may entail individual criminal responsibility, "because of the paucity of authoritative judicial pronouncements and legal literature on this matter." It concludes, *inter alia*, that violations of common Article 3 of the 1949 Geneva Conventions can give rise to individual criminal liability under customary international law. A particularly interesting part of the discussion deals with the use of forbidden weapons, notably chemicals, in non-international armed conflict. Reviewing positions taken in respect of Iraq's alleged use of chemical weapons against its Kurdish minority, the Tribunal comments in paragraph 124 that "[i]t is therefore clear that . . . there undisputedly emerged a general consensus in the international community on the principle that use of those weapons is also prohibited in internal armed conflicts."]

(v) Conclusion

137. In the light of the intent of the Security Council and the logical and systematic interpretation of Article 3 as well as customary international law, the Appeals Chamber concludes that, under Article 3, the International Tribunal has jurisdiction over the acts alleged in the indictment, regardless of whether they occurred within an internal or an international armed conflict. Thus, to the extent that Appellant's challenge to jurisdiction under Article 3 is based on the nature of the underlying conflict, the motion must be denied.

Article 5

138. Article 5 of the Statute confers jurisdiction over crimes against humanity. More specifically, the Article provides:

> The International Tribunal shall have the power to prosecute persons responsible for the following crimes when committed in armed conflict, whether international or internal in character, and directed against any civilian population: (a) murder; (b) extermination; (c) enslavement; (d) deportation; (e) imprisonment; (f) torture; (g) rape; (h) persecutions on political, racial and religious grounds; (i) other inhumane acts.

As noted by the Secretary-General in his Report on the Statute, crimes against humanity were first recognized in the trials of war criminals following World War II. The offence was defined in Article 6, paragraph 2(c) of the Nuremberg Charter and subsequently affirmed in the 1948 [sic. 1946] General Assembly Resolution affirming the Nuremberg principles.

139. . . . . [B]oth of these formulations of the crime limited it to those acts committed "in the execution of or in connection with any crime against peace or any war crime." . . .

140. [But] the nexus between crimes against humanity and either crimes against peace or war crimes, required by the Nuremberg Charter, was peculiar to the jurisdiction of the Nuremberg Tribunal. Although the nexus requirement in the Nuremberg Charter was carried over to the 1948 [sic.1946] General Assembly resolution affirming the Nuremberg principles, there is no logical or legal basis for this requirement and it has been abandoned in subsequent State practice with respect to crimes against humanity. Most notably, the nexus requirement was eliminated from the definition of crimes against humanity contained in Article II(1)(c) of Control Council Law No. 10 of 20 December 1945. The obsolescence of the nexus requirement is evidenced by international conventions regarding genocide and apartheid, both of which prohibit particular types of crimes against humanity regardless of any connection to armed conflict. (Convention on the Prevention and Punishment of the Crime of Genocide, 9 December 1948, art. 1, 78 U.N.T.S. 277, (providing that genocide, "whether committed in time of peace or in time of war, is a crime under international law"); International Convention on the Suppression and Punishment of the Crime of Apartheid, 30 November 1973, 1015 U.N.T.S. 243, arts. 1–2.)

141. It is by now a settled rule of customary international law that crimes against humanity do not require a connection to international armed conflict. Indeed. . . . customary international law may not require a connection between crimes against humanity and any conflict at all. Thus, by requiring that crimes against humanity be committed in either internal or international armed conflict, the Security Council may have defined the crime in Article 5 more narrowly than necessary under customary international law. . . .

142. We conclude, therefore, that Article 5 may be invoked as a basis of jurisdiction over crimes committed in either internal or international armed conflicts. In addition, for the reasons stated above (paras. 66–70), we conclude that in this case there was an armed conflict. Therefore, the Appellant's challenge to the jurisdiction of the International Tribunal under Article 5 must be dismissed. . . .

145. For the reasons stated above, the third ground of appeal, based on lack of subject-matter jurisdiction, must be dismissed.

Notes

(1) Tadic was tried on thirty-one counts alleging "grave breaches" of the Geneva Conventions, "violations of the laws and customs of war," and "crimes against humanity." The charges involved murder, torture, and sexual violence committed against Muslims and Croats in northwestern Bosnia during the summer of 1992. On May 7, 1997, he was found guilty on eleven counts involving the brutal mistreatment of prisoners at the Omarska prison camp and of civilians in the nearby village of Kozarac. *See Prosecutor v. Tadic*, Opinion & Judgment, Case No. IT-94-1-T (May 7, 1997). On July 14, 1997, he was sentenced to twenty years' imprisonment, with a recommended minimum term of ten years. The most controversial aspect of the Trial Chamber's judgment was its finding, by a majority of 2-1, that Tadic could not be found guilty of "grave breaches" of the Geneva Conventions, since his victims were no longer "protected persons" under those Conventions after May 19, 1992, when the Yugoslav National Army supposedly withdrew from Bosnia and the conflict therefore ceased to be "international." On appeal by the prosecution, this aspect of the Trial Chamber's judgment was reversed by the Appeals Chamber and the case remanded for resentencing. *See Prosecutor v. Tadic*, Judgment on Appeal against Opinion & Judgment, Case No. IT-94-1-A (July 15, 1999). On November 11, 1999, Tadic was resentenced to a maximum term of twenty-five years' imprisonment. In 2000, the Appeals Chamber reduced his sentence to a maximum term of twenty years. *See Prosecutor v. Tadic*, Judgment on Sentencing Appeals, Case No. IT-94-1-A (Jan. 26, 2000). He was then transferred to Germany to serve the sentence. He received an early release in 2008. (Germany and sixteen other European states agreed to take convicted prisoners to serve sentences.) For an extensive discussion of the case, *see* Michael P. Scharf, Balkan Justice: The Story behind the First International War Crimes Trial since Nuremberg (1997).

(2) Did the Chamber necessarily have to conclude that armed conflict in Bosnia had *both* international and internal aspects? *See* Theodor Meron, *Classification of Armed Conflict in the Former Yugoslavia: Nicaragua's Fallout*, 92 Am. J. Int'l L. 236 (1998), *reprinted in* Theodor Meron, War Crimes Law Comes of Age 286 (1998). This left it to the trial chambers to decide in each case whether the specific conflict in which the accused was engaged was international or non-international in character. For most practical purposes, the categories of "protected persons" in international conflict under the Geneva Conventions, notably "prisoners of war" (Convention III) and "civilian persons" (Convention IV), are coterminous with those covered by Common Article 3, namely "[p]ersons taking no active part in hostilities, including members of the armed forces who have laid down their arms and those placed *hors de combat* by sickness, wounds, detention, or any other cause. . . ." The range of general acts from which they are protected ("violence to life and person . . ." etc.) overlaps the specific protections of the Conventions. Generally, therefore, there is an

appropriate offense with which to charge a perpetrator, whether the conflict is international or non-international. Judging from the Tribunal's sentencing decisions, it does not appear to make any difference to the ultimate disposition whether the conflict was international or non-international, the determining features being what the accused did and his relative significance in the conflict.

(3) The ICTY and ICTR have contributed a large body of jurisprudence on both the substance and procedure of international criminal law, a body too rich to summarize here. *See generally,* ARCHBOLD, INTERNATIONAL CRIMINAL COURTS: PRACTICE, PROCEDURE AND EVIDENCE (Rodney Dixon, Karim A.A. Kahn, Adrian Fulford & John Frederick Archbold eds., 5th ed., 2018); JOHN R. W.D. JONES & STEVEN POWLES, INTERNATIONAL CRIMINAL PRACTICE (3d ed., 2003); GEERT-JAN ALEXANDER KNOOPS, AN INTRODUCTION TO THE LAW OF INTERNATIONAL TRIBUNALS (2014); ANNOTATED LEADING CASES OF INTERNATIONAL TRIBUNALS (André Klip & Göran Sluiter eds., 1999–); SUBSTANTIVE AND PROCEDURAL ASPECTS OF INTERNATIONAL CRIMINAL LAW: THE EXPERIENCE OF INTERNATIONAL AND NATIONAL COURTS (3 vols.) (Gabrielle Kirk McDonald & Olivia Swaak-Goldman eds., 2000); JENNIFER TRAHAN FOR HUMAN RIGHTS WATCH, GENOCIDE, WAR CRIMES AND CRIMES AGAINST HUMANITY: A TOPICAL DIGEST OF THE CASE LAW OF THE INTERNATIONAL CRIMINAL TRIBUNAL FOR THE FORMER YUGOSLAVIA (2006); JENNIFER TRAHAN FOR HUMAN RIGHTS WATCH, GENOCIDE, WAR CRIMES AND CRIMES AGAINST HUMANITY: A DIGEST OF THE CASE LAW OF THE INTERNATIONAL CRIMINAL TRIBUNAL FOR RWANDA (2010); JUDGE RICHARD MAY & MARIEKE WIERDA, INTERNATIONAL CRIMINAL EVIDENCE (2002); WILLIAM SCHABAS, INTERNATIONAL COURTS AND TRIBUNALS (2014). On the impact of the prosecutions, *see* DIANE ORENTLICHER, SOME KIND OF JUSTICE: ICTY'S IMPACT IN BOSNIA AND SERBIA (2d ed. 2019).

§ 21.02 The Ad Hoc Tribunal for Rwanda

Prosecutor v. Akayesu

International Criminal Tribunal for Rwanda
Case No. ICTR-96-4-T, Trial Chamber I
Judgement (Sept. 2, 1998)

1. Introduction

1.1. The International Tribunal

1. This judgment is rendered by Trial Chamber I of the International Tribunal for the prosecution of persons responsible for genocide and other serious violations of international humanitarian law committed in the territory of Rwanda and Rwandan citizens responsible for genocide and other such violations committed in the territory of neighbouring States, between 1 January and 31 December 1994 (the "Tribunal"). The judgment follows the indictment and trial of Jean Paul Akayesu, a Rwandan citizen who was *bourgmestre* of Taba commune, Prefecture of Gitarama, in Rwanda, at the time the crimes alleged in the indictment were perpetrated.

2. The Tribunal was established by the United Nations Security Council by its Resolution 955 of 8 November 1994. After having reviewed various official United Nations reports which indicated that acts of genocide and other systematic, widespread and flagrant violations of international humanitarian law had been committed in Rwanda, the Security Council concluded that the situation in Rwanda in 1994 constituted a threat to international peace and security within the meaning of Chapter VII of the United Nations Charter. Determined to put an end to such crimes and "convinced that . . . the prosecution of persons responsible for such acts and violations . . . would contribute to the process of national reconciliation and to the restoration and maintenance of peace," the Security Council, acting under the said Chapter VII established the Tribunal. . . .

3. The Tribunal is governed by its Statute, annexed to the Security Council Resolution 955, and by its Rules of Procedure and Evidence, adopted by the Judges on 5 July 1995 and amended subsequently. . . . [a]

4. Under the Statute, the Tribunal has the power to prosecute persons responsible for serious violations of international human[itarian] law committed in the territory of Rwanda and Rwandan citizens responsible for genocide and other such violations committed in the territory of neighbouring States, between 1 January and 31 December 1994. According to Articles 2 to 4 of the Statute relating to its *ratione materiae* jurisdiction, the Tribunal has the power to prosecute persons who committed genocide as defined in Article 2 of the Statute, persons responsible for crimes against humanity as defined in Article 3 of the Statute and persons responsible for serious violations of Article 3 Common to the Geneva Conventions of 12 August 1949 on the protection of victims of war, and of Additional Protocol II thereto of 8 June 1977, a crime defined in Article 4 of the Statute. Article 8 of the Statute provides that the Tribunal has concurrent jurisdiction with national courts over which it, however, has primacy.

5. The Statute stipulates that the Prosecutor, who acts as a separate organ of the Tribunal, is responsible for the investigation and prosecution of the perpetrators of such violations. . . . Under the Statute, the Prosecutor of the Tribunal for the former Yugoslavia shall also serve as the Prosecutor of the Tribunal for Rwanda. . . . [b] The Prosecutor of the Tribunal for Rwanda is assisted by a team of investigators, trial attorneys and senior trial attorneys, who are based in Kigali, Rwanda. These officials travel to Arusha [the seat of the Tribunal in Tanzania] whenever they are expected to plead a case before the Tribunal. . . .

---

a. The Tribunal's Statute and Rules of Evidence and Procedure, as well as relevant Security Council resolutions and many other documents are available on the Tribunal's website: http://www.ictr.org.—Eds.

b. Pursuant to Security Council Resolution 1503 (2003), the Security Council provided for a separate Prosecutor for Rwanda. — Eds.

1.4. The Trial

10. On 13 February 1996, the then Prosecutor, Richard Goldstone, submitted an Indictment against Akayesu, which was subsequently amended on 17 June 1997. It contains a total of 15 counts covering genocide, crimes against humanity and violations of Article 3 Common to the 1949 Geneva Conventions and Additional Protocol II of 1977 thereto. More specifically, Akayesu was individually charged with genocide, complicity in genocide, direct and public incitement to commit genocide, extermination, murder, torture, cruel treatment, rape, other inhumane acts and outrages upon personal dignity, which he allegedly committed in Taba commune of which he was the *bourgmestre* at the time of the alleged acts.

[The first part of Akayesu's trial took place between January 9 and May 24, 1997. The prosecution sought to show that, as the official in charge of maintaining law and order in the commune, Akayesu was responsible for the deaths of at least 2000 Tutsi killed in Taba between April 7 and the end of June 1994. A number of these killings were shown to have taken place in his presence and on his orders. The trial was then adjourned to allow the Prosecutor's office to investigate Akayesu's responsibility for rape and other crimes of sexual violence against Tutsi women, evidence of which had emerged during the first phase of the trial. The amended indictment of June 17, 1997, added charges of sexual violence. When trial resumed on October 23, 1997, testimony concerning these charges was presented. The court ordered protective measures for witnesses. No information that could identify the witnesses was given. Letters of the alphabet were used as pseudonyms to refer to protected witnesses. Screens isolated them from the public, although not from the accused or his counsel. The trial concluded on March 26, 1998.]

6. The Law

6.1 Cumulative Charges

461. In the amended Indictment, the accused is charged cumulatively with more than one crime in relation to the same sets of facts. . . .

462. The question which arises at this stage is whether . . . the Chamber . . . may find the accused guilty of all of the crimes charged in relation to those facts or only one. The reason for posing this question is that it might be argued that the accumulation of criminal charges offends against the principle of double jeopardy or a substantive *non bis in idem* principle in criminal law. Thus an accused who is found guilty of both genocide and crimes against humanity in relation to the same set of facts may argue that he has been twice judged for the same offence, which is generally considered impermissible in criminal law.

463. The Chamber notes that this question has been posed, and answered, by the Trial Chamber of the ICTY in the first case before that Tribunal, *The Prosecutor v. Dusko Tadic*. Trial Chamber II, confronted with this issue, stated:

> In any event, since this is a matter that will only be relevant insofar as it might affect penalty, it can best be dealt with if and when matters of penalty

> fall for consideration. What can, however, be said with certainty is that penalty cannot be made to depend upon whether offences arising from the same conduct are alleged cumulatively or in the alternative. What is to be punished by penalty is proven criminal conduct and that will not depend upon technicalities of pleading.

464. In that case, when the matter reached the sentencing stage, the Trial Chamber dealt with the matter of cumulative criminal charges by imposing *concurrent* sentences for each cumulative charge. Thus, for example, in relation to one particular beating, the accused received 7 years' imprisonment for the beating as a crime against humanity, and a 6 year concurrent sentence for the same beating as a violation of the laws or customs of war.

465. The Chamber takes due note of the practice of the ICTY. This practice was also followed in the *Barbie* case, where the French *Cour de Cassation* held that a single event could be qualified both as a crime against humanity and as a war crime.

466. It is clear that the practice of concurrent sentencing ensures that the accused is not twice punished for the same acts. Notwithstanding this absence of prejudice to the accused, it is still necessary to justify the prosecutorial practice of accumulating criminal charges. . . .

468. On the basis of national and international law and jurisprudence, the Chamber concludes that it is acceptable to convict the accused of two offences in relation to the same set of facts in the following circumstances: (1) where the offences have different elements; or (2) where the provisions creating the offences protect different interests; or (3) where it is necessary to record a conviction for both offences in order fully to describe what the accused did. However, the Chamber finds that it is not justifiable to convict an accused of two offences in relation to the same set of facts where (a) one offence is a lesser included offence of the other, for example, murder and grievous bodily harm, robbery and theft, or rape and indecent assault; or (b) where one offence charges accomplice liability and the other offence charges liability as a principal, e.g. genocide and complicity in genocide.

469. Having regard to its Statute, the Chamber believes that the offences under the Statute — genocide, crimes against humanity, and violations of article 3 common to the Geneva Conventions and of Additional Protocol II — have different elements and, moreover, are intended to protect different interests. The crime of genocide exists to protect certain groups from extermination or attempted extermination. The concept of crimes against humanity exists to protect civilian populations from persecution. The idea of violations of article 3 common to the Geneva Conventions and of Additional Protocol II is to protect non-combatants from war crimes in civil war. These crimes have different purposes and are, therefore, never co-extensive. Thus it is legitimate to charge these crimes in relation to the same set of facts. It may, additionally, depending on the case, be necessary to record a conviction for more than one of these offences in order to reflect what crimes an accused committed. If, for example, a general ordered that all prisoners of war

belonging to a particular ethnic group should be killed, with the intent thereby to eliminate the group, this would be both genocide and a violation of common article 3, although not necessarily a crime against humanity. Convictions for genocide and violations of common article 3 would accurately reflect the accused general's course of conduct.

470. Conversely, the Chamber does not consider that any of genocide, crimes against humanity, and violations of article 3 common to the Geneva Conventions and of Additional Protocol II are lesser included forms of each other. The ICTR Statute does not establish a hierarchy of norms, but rather all three offences are presented on an equal footing. While genocide may be considered the gravest crime, there is no justification in the Statute for finding that crimes against humanity or violations of common article 3 and additional protocol II are in all circumstances alternative charges to genocide and thus lesser included offences. As stated, and it is a related point, these offences have different constituent elements. Again, this consideration renders multiple convictions for these offences in relation to the same set of facts permissible.

6.2. Individual criminal responsibility (Article 6 of the Statute)

471. The Accused is charged under Article 6(1) of the Statute of the Tribunal with individual criminal responsibility for the crimes alleged in the Indictment. With regard to Counts 13, 14 and 15 on sexual violence, the Accused is charged additionally, or alternatively, under Article 6(3) of the Statute.... Article 6(1) sets forth the basic principles of individual criminal liability, which are undoubtedly common to most national criminal jurisdictions. Article 6(3), by contrast, constitutes something of an exception to the principles articulated in Article 6(1), as it derives from military law, namely the principle of the liability of a commander for the acts of his subordinates or "command responsibility."

472. Article 6(1) provides that: "A person who planned, instigated, ordered, committed or otherwise aided and abetted in the planning, preparation or execution of a crime referred to in articles 2 to 4 of the present Statute, shall be individually responsible for the crime." Thus, in addition to responsibility as principal perpetrator, the Accused can be held responsible for the criminal acts of others where he plans with them, instigates them, orders them or aids and abets them to commit those acts....

473. Thus, Article 6(1) covers various stages of the commission of a crime, ranging from its initial planning to its execution, through its organization. However, the principle of individual criminal responsibility as provided for in Article 6(1) implies that the planning or preparation of the crime actually leads to its commission. Indeed, the principle of individual criminal responsibility for an attempt to commit a crime obtained only in case of genocide. Conversely, this would mean that with respect to any other form of criminal participation and, in particular, those referred to in Article 6(1), the perpetrator would incur criminal responsibility only if the offence were completed....

479. Therefore, as can be seen, the forms of participation referred to in Article 6(1), cannot render their perpetrator criminally liable where he did not act knowingly, and even where he should have had such knowledge. This greatly differs from Article 6(3) . . . which does not necessarily require that the superior acted knowingly to render him criminally liable; it suffices that he had reason to know that his subordinates were about to commit or had committed a crime and failed to take the necessary or reasonable measures to prevent such acts or punish the perpetrators thereof. In a way, this is liability by omission or abstention. . . .

487. Article 6 (3) stipulates that:

> The fact that any of the acts referred to in Articles 2 to 4 of the present Statute was committed by a subordinate does not relieve his or her superior of criminal responsibility if he or she knew or had reason to know that the subordinate was about to commit such acts or had done so and the superior failed to take the necessary and reasonable measures to prevent such acts or to punish the perpetrators thereof.

488. There are varying views regarding the *mens rea* required for command responsibility. According to one view it derives from a legal rule of strict liability, that is, the superior is criminally responsible for acts committed by his subordinate, without it being necessary to prove the criminal intent of the superior. Another view holds that negligence which is so serious as to be tantamount to consent or criminal intent, is a lesser requirement. . . .

489. The Chamber holds that it is necessary to recall that criminal intent is the moral element required for any crime and that, where the objective is to ascertain the individual criminal responsibility of a person Accused of crimes falling within the jurisdiction of the Chamber, such as genocide, crimes against humanity and violations of Article 3 Common to the Geneva Conventions and of Additional Protocol II thereto, it is certainly proper to ensure that there has been malicious intent, or, at least, ensure that negligence was so serious as to be tantamount to acquiescence or even malicious intent.

490. As to whether the form of individual criminal responsibility referred to Article 6 (3) of the Statute applies to persons in positions of both military and civilian authority, it should be noted that during the Tokyo trials, certain civilian authorities were convicted of war crimes under this principle. Hirota, former Foreign Minister of Japan, was convicted of atrocities — including mass rape — committed in the "rape of Nanking," under a count which charged that he had "recklessly disregarded their legal duty by virtue of their offices to take adequate steps to secure the observance and prevent breaches of the law and customs of war." The Tokyo Tribunal held that:

> Hirota was derelict in his duty in not insisting before the Cabinet that immediate action be taken to put an end to the atrocities, failing any other action open to him to bring about the same result. He was content to rely on assurances which he knew were not being implemented while hundreds of

> murders, violations of women, and other atrocities were being committed daily. His inaction amounted to criminal negligence.

It should, however, be noted that Judge Röling strongly dissented from this finding, and held that Hirota should have been acquitted. Concerning the principle of command responsibility as applied to a civilian leader, Judge Röling stated that:

> Generally speaking, a Tribunal should be very careful in holding civil government officials responsible for the behaviour of the army in the field. Moreover, the Tribunal is here to apply the general principles of law as they exist with relation to the responsibility for omissions. Considerations of both law and policy, of both justice and expediency, indicate that this responsibility should only be recognized in a very restricted sense.

491. The Chamber therefore finds that in the case of civilians, the application of the principle of individual criminal responsibility, enshrined in Article 6 (3), to civilians remains contentious. Against this background, the Chamber holds that it is appropriate to assess on a case by case basis the power of authority actually devolved upon the Accused in order to determine whether or not he had the power to take all necessary and reasonable measures to prevent the commission of the alleged crimes or to punish the perpetrators thereof.

6.3. Genocide (Article 2 of the Statute)

6.3.1. Genocide

492. Article 2 of the Statute stipulates that the Tribunal shall have the power to prosecute persons responsible for genocide, conspiracy to commit genocide, direct and public incitement to commit genocide, attempt to commit genocide and complicity in genocide.

493. In accordance with the said provisions of the Statute, the Prosecutor has charged Akayesu with the crimes legally defined as genocide (count 1), complicity in genocide (count 2) and incitement to commit genocide (count 4).

Crime of Genocide, punishable under Article 2(3)(a) of the Statute

494. The definition of genocide, as given in Article 2 of the Tribunal's Statute, is taken verbatim from Articles 2 and 3 of the Convention on the Prevention and Punishment of the Crime of Genocide [chap. 23, *infra*]. . . .

495. The Genocide Convention is undeniably considered part of customary international law. . . . The Chamber notes that Rwanda acceded, by legislative decree, to the Convention on Genocide on 12 February 1975. Thus, punishment of the crime of genocide did exist in Rwanda in 1994, at the time of the acts alleged in the Indictment, and the perpetrator was liable to be brought before the competent courts of Rwanda to answer for this crime.

497. Contrary to popular belief, the crime of genocide does not imply the actual extermination of [a] group in its entirety, but is understood as such once any one of the acts mentioned in Article 2(2)(a) through 2(2)(e) is committed with the specific intent to destroy "in whole or in part" a national, ethnical, racial or religious group.

498. Genocide is distinct from other crimes inasmuch as it embodies a special intent or *dolus specialis*. Special intent of a crime is the specific intention, required as a constitutive element of the crime, which demands that the perpetrator clearly seeks to produce the act charged. Thus, the special intent in the crime of genocide lies in "the intent to destroy, in whole or in part, a national, ethnical, racial or religious group, as such."

499. Thus, for a crime of genocide to have been committed, it is necessary that one of the acts listed under Article 2(2) of the Statute be committed, that the particular act be committed against a specifically targeted group, it being a national, ethnical, racial or religious group. Consequently, in order to clarify the constitutive elements of the crime of genocide, the Chamber will first state its findings on the acts provided for under Article 2(2)(a) through Article 2(2)(e) of the Statute, the groups protected by the Genocide Convention, and the special intent or *dolus specialis* necessary for genocide to take place.

Killing members of the group (paragraph (a)):

500. With regard to Article 2(2)(a) of the Statute, like in the Genocide Convention, the Chamber notes that the said paragraph states "*meurtre*" in the French version while the English version states "killing." The Trial Chamber is of the opinion that the term "killing" used in the English version is too general, since it could very well include both intentional and unintentional homicides, whereas the term "*meurtre*" used in the French version, is more precise. It is accepted that there is murder when death has been caused with the intention to do so. . . .

Causing serious bodily or mental harm to members of the group (paragraph b):

502. Causing serious bodily or mental harm to members of the group does not necessarily mean that the harm is permanent and irremediable.

503. In the Adolf Eichmann case, who was convicted of crimes against the Jewish people, genocide under another legal definition, the District Court of Jerusalem stated in its judgment of 12 December 1961, that serious bodily or mental harm of members of the group can be caused

> by the enslavement, starvation, deportation and persecution . . . and by their detention in ghettos, transit camps and concentration camps in conditions which were designed to cause their degradation, deprivation of their rights as human beings, and to suppress them and cause them inhumane suffering and torture.

504. For purposes of interpreting Article 2 (2)(b) of the Statute, the Chamber takes serious bodily or mental harm, without limiting itself thereto, to mean acts of torture, be they bodily or mental, inhumane or degrading treatment, persecution.

Deliberately inflicting on the group conditions of life calculated to bring about its physical destruction in whole or in part (paragraph c):

505. The Chamber holds that the expression deliberately inflicting on the group conditions of life calculated to bring about its physical destruction in whole or in

part, should be construed as the methods of destruction by which the perpetrator does not immediately kill the members of the group, but which, ultimately, seek their physical destruction.

506. For purposes of interpreting Article 2(2)(c) of the Statute, the Chamber is of the opinion that the means of deliberate inflicting on the group conditions of life calculated to bring about its physical destruction, in whole or part, include, *inter alia*, subjecting a group of people to a subsistence diet, systematic expulsion from homes and the reduction of essential medical services below minimum requirement.

Imposing measures intended to prevent births within the group (paragraph d):

507. For purposes of interpreting Article 2(2)(d) of the Statute, the Chamber holds that the measures intended to prevent births within the group, should be construed as sexual mutilation, the practice of sterilization, forced birth control, separation of the sexes and prohibition of marriages. In patriarchal societies, where membership of a group is determined by the identity of the father, an example of a measure intended to prevent births within a group is the case where, during rape, a woman of the said group is deliberately impregnated by a man of another group, with the intent to have her give birth to a child who will consequently not belong to its mother's group.

508. Furthermore, the Chamber notes that measures intended to prevent births within the group may be physical, but can also be mental. For instance, rape can be a measure intended to prevent births when the person raped refuses subsequently to procreate, in the same way that members of a group can be led, through threats or trauma, not to procreate.

Forcibly transferring children of the group to another group (paragraph e):

509. With respect to forcibly transferring children of the group to another group, the Chamber is of the opinion that, as in the case of measures intended to prevent births, the objective is not only to sanction a direct act of forcible physical transfer, but also to sanction acts of threats or trauma which would lead to the forcible transfer of children from one group to another.

510. Since the special intent to commit genocide lies in the intent to "destroy, in whole or in part, a national, ethnical, racial or religious group, as such," it is necessary to consider a definition of the group as such. Article 2 of the Statute, just like the Genocide Convention, stipulates four types of victim groups, namely national, ethnical, racial or religious groups.

511. On reading through the *travaux préparatoires* of the Genocide Convention, it appears that the crime of genocide was allegedly perceived as targeting only "stable" groups, constituted in a permanent fashion and membership of which is determined by birth, with the exclusion of the more "mobile" groups which one joins through individual voluntary commitment, such as political and economic groups. Therefore, a common criterion in the four types of groups protected by the Genocide Convention is that membership in such groups would seem to be normally not

challengeable by its members, who belong to it automatically, by birth, in a continuous and often irremediable manner. . . .

516. [T]he Chamber considered whether the groups protected by the Genocide Convention, echoed in Article 2 of the Statute, should be limited to only the four groups expressly mentioned and whether they should not also include any group which is stable and permanent like the said four groups. In other words, the question that arises is whether it would be impossible to punish the physical destruction of a group as such under the Genocide Convention, if the said group, although stable and membership is by birth, does not meet the definition of any one of the four groups expressly protected by the Genocide Convention. In the opinion of the Chamber, it is particularly important to respect the intention of the drafters of the Genocide Convention, which according to the *travaux préparatoires*, was patently to ensure the protection of any stable and permanent group.

520. With regard to the crime of genocide, the offender is culpable only when he has committed one of the offences charged under Article 2(2) of the Statute with the clear intent to destroy, in whole or in part, a particular group. The offender is culpable because he knew or should have known that the act committed would destroy, in whole or in part, a group.

521. In concrete terms, for any of the acts charged under Article 2 (2) of the Statute to be a constitutive element of genocide, the act must have been committed against one or several individuals, because such individual or individuals were members of a specific group, and specifically because they belonged to this group. Thus, the victim is chosen not because of his individual identity, but rather on account of his membership of a national, ethnical, racial or religious group. The victim of the act is therefore a member of a group, chosen as such, which, hence, means that the victim of the crime of genocide is the group itself and not only the individual.

522. The perpetration of the act charged therefore extends beyond its actual commission, for example, the murder of a particular individual, for the realisation of an ulterior motive, which is to destroy, in whole or part, the group of which the individual is just one element.

523. On the issue of determining the offender's specific intent, the Chamber considers that intent is a mental factor which is difficult, even impossible, to determine. This is the reason why, in the absence of a confession from the accused, his intent can be inferred from a certain number of presumptions of fact. The Chamber considers that it is possible to deduce the genocidal intent inherent in a particular act charged from the general context of the perpetration of other culpable acts systematically directed against that same group, whether these acts were committed by the same offender or by others. Other factors, such as the scale of atrocities committed, their general nature, in a region or a country, or furthermore, the fact of deliberately and systematically targeting victims on account of their membership of a particular group, while excluding the members of other groups, can enable the Chamber to infer the genocidal intent of a particular act.

6.3.2. Complicity in Genocide

The Crime of Complicity in Genocide, punishable under Article 2(3)(e) of the Statute

525. Under Article 2(3)(e) of the Statute, the Chamber shall have the power to prosecute persons who have committed complicity in genocide. The Prosecutor has charged Akayesu with such a crime under count 2 of the Indictment. . . .

527. The Chamber notes that complicity is viewed as a form of criminal participation by all criminal law systems, notably, under the Anglo-Saxon system (or Common Law) and the Roman-Continental system (or Civil Law). Since the accomplice to an offence may be defined as someone who associates himself in an offence committed by another, complicity necessarily implies the existence of a principal offence. . . .

530. Consequently, the Chamber is of the opinion that in order for an accused to be found guilty of complicity in genocide, it must, first of all, be proven beyond a reasonable doubt that the crime of genocide has, indeed, been committed.

531. The issue thence is whether a person can be tried for complicity even where the perpetrator of the principal offence himself has not being tried. . . . As far as the Chamber is aware, all criminal systems provide that an accomplice may also be tried, even where the principal perpetrator of the crime has not been identified, or where, for any other reasons, guilt could not be proven. . . .

538. The intent or mental element of complicity implies in general that, at the moment he acted, the accomplice knew of the assistance he was providing in the commission of the principal offence. In other words, the accomplice must have acted knowingly. . . .

540. As far as genocide is concerned, the intent of the accomplice is thus to knowingly aid or abet one or more persons to commit the crime of genocide. Therefore, the Chamber is of the opinion that an accomplice to genocide need not necessarily possess the *dolus specialis* of genocide, namely the specific intent to destroy, in whole or in part, a national, ethnic, racial or religious group, as such.

541. Thus, if for example, an accused knowingly aided or abetted another in the commission of a murder, while being unaware that the principal was committing such a murder, with the intent to destroy, in whole or in part, the group to which the murdered victim belonged, the accused could be prosecuted for complicity in murder, and certainly not for complicity in genocide. However, if the accused knowingly aided and abetted in the commission of such a murder while he knew or had reason to know that the principal was acting with genocidal intent, the accused would be an accomplice to genocide, even though he did not share the murderer's intent to destroy the group.

542. This finding by the Chamber comports with the decisions rendered by the District Court of Jerusalem on 12 December 1961 and the Supreme Court of Israel on 29 May 1962 in the case of Adolf Eichmann. Since Eichmann raised the argument in

his defence that he was a "small cog" in the Nazi machine, both the District Court and the Supreme Court dealt with accomplice liability and found that "even a small cog, even an insignificant operator, is under our criminal law liable to be regarded as an accomplice in the commission of an offence, in which case he will be dealt with as if he were the actual murderer or destroyer."

543. The District Court accepted that Eichmann did not personally devise the "Final Solution" himself, but nevertheless, as the head of those engaged in carrying out the "Final Solution"—"acting in accordance with the directives of his superiors, but [with] wide discretionary powers in planning operations on his own initiative," he incurred individual criminal liability for crimes against the Jewish people, as much as his superiors. Likewise, with respect to his subordinates who actually carried out the executions, "the legal and moral responsibility of he who delivers up the victim to his death is, in our opinion, no smaller, and may be greater, than the responsibility of he who kills the victim with his own hands." The District Court found that participation in the extermination plan with knowledge of the plan rendered the person liable "as an accomplice to the extermination of all . . . victims from 1941 to 1945, irrespective of the extent of his participation." . . .

545. In conclusion, the Chamber is of the opinion that an accused is liable as an accomplice to genocide if he knowingly aided or abetted or instigated one or more persons in the commission of genocide, while knowing that such a person or persons were committing genocide, even though the accused himself did not have the specific intent to destroy, in whole or in part, a national, ethnical, racial or religious group, as such. . . .

6.3.3. Direct and Public Incitement to Commit Genocide

The Crime of Direct and Public Incitement to Commit Genocide, punishable under Article 2(3)(c) of the Statute

549. Under count 4, the Prosecutor charges Akayesu with direct and public incitement to commit genocide, a crime punishable under Article 2(3)(c) of the Statute.

550. Perhaps the most famous conviction for incitement to commit crimes of international dimension was that of Julius Streicher by the Nuremberg Tribunal for the virulently anti-Semitic articles which he had published in his weekly newspaper *Der Stürmer*. The Nuremberg Tribunal found that: "Streicher's incitement to murder and extermination, at the time when Jews in the East were being killed under the most horrible conditions, clearly constitutes persecution on political and racial grounds in connection with War Crimes, as defined by the Charter, and constitutes a Crime against Humanity."

551. At the time the Convention on Genocide was adopted, the delegates agreed to expressly spell out direct and public incitement to commit genocide as a specific crime, in particular, because of its critical role in the planning of a genocide. . . .

554. Under the Statute, direct and public incitement is expressly defined as a specific crime, punishable as such, by virtue of Article 2(3)(c). With respect to such a

crime, the Chamber deems it appropriate to first define the three terms: incitement, direct and public.

555. Incitement is defined in Common law systems as encouraging or persuading another to commit an offence. One line of authority in Common law would also view threats or other forms of pressure as a form of incitement. . . . Civil law systems punish direct and public incitement assuming the form of provocation, which is defined as an act intended to directly provoke another to commit a crime or a misdemeanour through speeches, shouting or threats, or any other means of audio-visual communication. . . .

556. The public element of incitement to commit genocide may be better appreciated in light of two factors: the place where the incitement occurred and whether or not assistance was selective or limited. A line of authority commonly followed in Civil law systems would regard words as being public where they were spoken aloud in a place that were public by definition. According to the International Law Commission, public incitement is characterized by a call for criminal action to a number of individuals in a public place or to members of the general public at large by such means as the mass media, for example, radio or television. It should be noted in this respect that at the time Convention on Genocide was adopted, the delegates specifically agreed to rule out the possibility of including private incitement to commit genocide as a crime, thereby underscoring their commitment to set aside for punishment only the truly public forms of incitement.

557. The "direct" element of incitement implies that the incitement assume a direct form and specifically provoke another to engage in a criminal act, and that more than mere vague or indirect suggestion goes to constitute direct incitement. Under Civil law systems, provocation, the equivalent of incitement, is regarded as being direct where it is aimed at causing a specific offence to be committed. The prosecution must prove a definite causation between the act characterized as incitement, or provocation in this case, and a specific offence. However, the Chamber is of the opinion that the direct element of incitement should be viewed in the light of its cultural and linguistic content. Indeed, a particular speech may be perceived as "direct" in one country, and not so in another, depending on the audience. The Chamber further recalls that incitement may be direct, and nonetheless implicit. Thus, at the time the Convention on Genocide was being drafted, the Polish delegate observed that it was sufficient to play skillfully on mob psychology by casting suspicion on certain groups, by insinuating that they were responsible for economic or other difficulties in order to create an atmosphere favourable to the perpetration of the crime.

558. The Chamber will therefore consider on a case-by-case basis whether, in light of the culture of Rwanda and the specific circumstances of the instant case, acts of incitement can be viewed as direct or not, by focusing mainly on the issue of whether the persons for whom the message was intended immediately grasped the implication thereof.

559. In light of the foregoing, it can be noted in the final analysis that whatever the legal system, direct and public incitement must be defined for the purposes of interpreting Article 2(3)(c), as directly provoking the perpetrator(s) to commit genocide, whether through speeches, shouting or threats uttered in public places or at public gatherings, or through the sale or dissemination, offer for sale or display of written material or printed matter in public places or at public gatherings, or through the public display of placards or posters, or through any other means of audiovisual communication.

560. The *mens rea* required for the crime of direct and public incitement to commit genocide lies in the intent to directly prompt or provoke another to commit genocide. It implies a desire on the part of the perpetrator to create by his actions a particular state of mind necessary to commit such a crime in the minds of the person(s) he is so engaging. That is to say that the person who is inciting to commit genocide must have himself the specific intent to commit genocide, namely, to destroy, in whole or in part, a national, ethnical, racial or religious group, as such.

561. Therefore, the issue before the Chamber is whether the crime of direct and public incitement to commit genocide can be punished even where such incitement was unsuccessful. It appears from the *travaux préparatoires* of the Convention on Genocide that the drafters of the Convention considered stating explicitly that incitement to commit genocide could be punished, whether or not it was successful. In the end, a majority decided against such an approach. Nevertheless, the Chamber is of the opinion that it cannot thereby be inferred that the intent of the drafters was not to punish unsuccessful acts of incitement. In light of the overall *travaux*, the Chamber holds the view that the drafters of the Convention simply decided not to specifically mention that such a form of incitement could be punished.

562. There are under Common law so-called inchoate offences, which are punishable by virtue of the criminal act alone, irrespective of the result thereof, which may or may not have been achieved. The Civil law counterparts of inchoate offences are known as *infractions formelles* (acts constituting an offence *per se* irrespective of their results), as opposed to *infractions matérielles* (strict liability offences). Indeed, as is the case with inchoate offenses, in *infractions formelles*, the method alone is punishable. Put another way, such offenses are "deemed to have been consummated regardless of the result achieved," contrary to *infractions matérielles*. . . . It should be noted, however, that such offences are the exception, the rule being that in theory, an offence can only be punished in relation to the result envisaged by the lawmakers. In the opinion of the Chamber, the fact that such acts are in themselves particularly dangerous because of the high risk they carry for society, even if they fail to produce results, warrants that they be punished as an exceptional measure. The Chamber holds that genocide clearly falls within the category of crimes so serious that direct and public incitement to commit such a crime must be punished as such, even where such incitement failed to produce the result expected by the perpetrator.

6.4. Crimes against Humanity (Article 3 of the Statute)[c]

Crimes against Humanity — Historical development

563. Crimes against humanity were recognized in the Charter and Judgment of the Nuremberg Tribunal, as well as in Law No. 10 of the Control Council for Germany [*see* chap. 20, *supra*] . . . .

565. Crimes against humanity are aimed at any civilian population and are prohibited regardless of whether they are committed in an armed conflict, international or internal in character. In fact, the concept of crimes against humanity had been recognised long before Nuremberg. On 28 May 1915, the Governments of France, Great Britain and Russia made a declaration regarding the massacres of the Armenian population in Turkey, denouncing them as "crimes against humanity and civilisation for which all the members of the Turkish government will be held responsible together with its agents implicated in the massacres." The 1919 Report of the Commission on the Responsibility of the Authors of the War and on Enforcement of Penalties formulated by representatives from several States and presented to the Paris Peace Conference also referred to "offences against . . . the laws of humanity."

566. These World War I notions derived, in part, from the Martens clause of the Hague Convention (IV) of 1907, which referred to "the usages established among civilised peoples, from the laws of humanity, and the dictates of the public conscience." . . .

567. The Chamber notes that, following the Nuremberg and Tokyo trials, the concept of crimes against humanity underwent a gradual evolution in the *Eichmann, Barbie, Touvier and Papon* cases.

568. In the *Eichmann* case, the accused, Otto Adolf Eichmann, was charged with offences under Nazi and Nazi Collaborators (punishment) Law, 5710/1950, for his participation in the implementation of the plan known as "the Final Solution of the Jewish problem." Pursuant to Section I (b) of the said law: "Crime against humanity means any of the following acts: murder, extermination, enslavement, starvation or deportation and other inhumane acts committed against any civilian population, and persecution on national, racial, religious or political grounds." The district court in the Eichmann stated that crimes against humanity differs from genocide in that for the commission of genocide special intent is required. This special intent is not required for crimes against humanity. Eichmann was convicted by the District

---

c. Article 3 ("Crimes Against Humanity") of the Statute of the Rwanda Tribunal provides: "The International Tribunal for Rwanda shall have the power to prosecute persons responsible for the following crimes when committed as part of a widespread or systematic attack against any civilian population on national, political, ethnic, racial or religious grounds: (a) murder; (b) extermination, (c) enslavement; (d) deportation; (e) imprisonment; (f) torture; (g) rape; (h) persecutions on political, racial and religious grounds; (i) other inhumane acts." — Eds.

court and sentenced to death. Eichmann appealed against his conviction and his appeal was dismissed by the supreme court.

569. In the *Barbie* case, the accused, Klaus Barbie, who was the head of the Gestapo in Lyons from November 1942 to August 1944, during the wartime occupation of France, was convicted in 1987 of crimes against humanity for his role in the deportation and extermination of civilians. Barbie appealed in cassation, but the appeal was dismissed. For the purposes of the present Judgment, what is of interest is the definition of crimes against humanity employed by the Court. The French Court of Cassation, in a Judgment rendered on 20 December 1985, stated:

> Crimes against humanity, within the meaning of Article 6(c) of the Charter of the International Military Tribunal annexed to the London Agreement of 8 August 1945, which were not subject to statutory limitation of the right of prosecution, even if they were crimes which could also be classified as war crimes within the meaning of Article 6(b) of the Charter, *were inhumane acts and persecution committed in a systematic manner in the name of a State practising a policy of ideological supremacy, not only against persons by reason of their membership of a racial or religious community, but also against the opponents of that policy, whatever the form of their opposition* (words italicized by the Court). 78 I.L.R. 136, at 137.

570. This was affirmed in a Judgment of the Court of Cassation of 3 June 1988, in which the Court held that:

> The fact that the accused, who had been found guilty of one of the crimes enumerated in Article 6(c) of the Charter of the Nuremberg Tribunal, in perpetrating that crime took part in the execution of a common plan to bring about the deportation or extermination of the civilian population during the war, or persecutions on political, racial or religious grounds, constituted not a distinct offence or an aggravating circumstance but rather *an essential element of the crime against humanity, consisting of the fact that the acts charged were performed in a systematic manner in the name of a State practising by those means a policy of ideological supremacy.*" I.L.R. at 332 & 336 (emphasis added). . . .

571. The definition of crimes against humanity developed in *Barbie* was further developed in the *Touvier* case. In that case, the accused, Paul Touvier, had been a high-ranking officer in the Militia (*Milice*) of Lyons, which operated in "Vichy" France during the German occupation. He was convicted of crimes against humanity for his role in the shooting of seven Jews at Rillieux on 29 June 1994 [sic. 1944] as a reprisal for the assassination by members of the Resistance, on the previous day, of the Minister for Propaganda of the "Vichy" Government.

572. The Court of Appeal applied the definition of crimes against humanity used in *Barbie*, stating that:

> The specific intent necessary to establish a crime against humanity was the intention to take part in the execution of a common plan by committing, in

a systematic manner, inhuman acts or persecutions in the name of a State practising a policy of ideological supremacy.

573. Applying this definition, the Court of Appeal held that Touvier could not be guilty of crimes against humanity since he committed the acts in question in the name of the "Vichy" State, which was not a State practising a policy of ideological supremacy, although it collaborated with Nazi Germany, which clearly did practice such a policy.

574. The Court of Cassation allowed appeal from the decision of the Court of Appeal, on the grounds that the crimes committed by the accused had been committed at the instigation of a Gestapo officer, and to that extent were linked to Nazi Germany, a State practising a policy of ideological supremacy against persons by virtue of their membership of a racial or religious community. Therefore the crimes could be categorised as crimes against humanity. Touvier was eventually convicted of crimes against humanity by the *Cour d'Assises des Yvelines* on 20 April 1994.

575. The definition of crimes against humanity used in *Barbie* was later affirmed by the ICTY in its *Vukovar* Rule 61 Decision of 3 April 1996 (IT-95-13-R61), to support its finding that crimes against humanity applied equally where the victims of the acts were members of a resistance movement as to where the victims were civilians. . . .

Crimes against Humanity in Article 3 of the Statute of the Tribunal

578. The Chamber considers that Article 3 of the Statute confers on the Chamber the jurisdiction to prosecute persons for various inhumane acts which constitute crimes against humanity. This category of crimes may be broadly broken down into four essential elements, namely:

(i) the act must be inhumane in nature and character, causing great suffering, or serious injury to body or to mental or physical health;

(ii) the act must be committed as part of a wide spread or systematic attack;

(iii) the act must be committed against members of the civilian population;

(iv) the act must be committed on one or more discriminatory grounds, namely, national, political, ethnic, racial or religious grounds. . . .

585. Article 3 of the Statute sets out various acts that constitute crimes against humanity, namely: murder; extermination; enslavement; deportation; imprisonment; torture; rape; persecution on political, racial and religious grounds; and; other inhumane acts. Although the category of acts that constitute crimes against humanity are set out in Article 3, this category is not exhaustive. Any act which is inhumane in nature and character may constitute a crime against humanity, provided the other elements are met. This is evident in (i) which caters for all other inhumane acts not stipulated in (a) to (h) of Article 3. . . .

586. The Chamber notes that the accused is indicted for murder, extermination, torture, rape and other acts that constitute inhumane acts. . . .

596. Considering the extent to which rape constitute crimes against humanity, pursuant to Article 3(g) of the Statute, the Chamber must define rape, as there is no commonly accepted definition of this term in international law. While rape has been defined in certain national jurisdictions as non-consensual intercourse, variations on the act of rape may include acts which involve the insertion of objects and/or the use of bodily orifices not considered to be intrinsically sexual.

597. The Chamber considers that rape is a form of aggression and that the central elements of the crime of rape cannot be captured in a mechanical description of objects and body parts. The Convention against Torture and Other Cruel, Inhuman and Degrading Treatment or Punishment does not catalogue specific acts in its definition of torture, focusing rather on the conceptual frame work of state sanctioned violence. This approach is more useful in international law. Like torture, rape is used for such purposes as intimidation, degradation, humiliation, discrimination, punishment, control or destruction of a person. Like torture, rape is a violation of personal dignity, and rape in fact constitutes torture when inflicted by or at the instigation of or with the consent or acquiescence of a public official or other person acting in an official capacity.

598. The Chamber defines rape as a physical invasion of a sexual nature, committed on a person under circumstances which are coercive. Sexual violence, which includes rape, is considered to be any act of a sexual nature which is committed on a person under circumstances which are coercive. This act must be committed (a) as part of a widespread or systematic attack; (b) on a civilian population; (c) on certain catalogued discriminatory grounds, namely: national, ethnic, political, racial, or religious grounds.

6.5. Violations of Common Article 3 and Additional Protocol II (Article 4 of the Statute)

Article 4 of the Statute

599. Pursuant to Article 4 of the Statute, the Chamber "shall have the power to prosecute persons committing or ordering to be committed serious violations of Article 3 common to the four Geneva Conventions of 12 August 1949 for the Protection of War Victims, and of Additional Protocol II thereto of 8 June 1977. These violations shall include, but shall not be limited to: (a) violence to life, health and physical or mental well-being of persons, in particular murder as well as cruel treatment such as torture, mutilation or any form of corporal punishment; (b) collective punishments; (c) taking of hostages; (d) acts of terrorism; (e) outrages upon personal dignity, in particular humiliating and degrading treatment, rape, enforced prostitution and any form of indecent assault; (f pillage; (g) the passing of sentences and the carrying out of executions without previous judgment pronounced by a regularly constituted court, affording all the judicial guarantees which are recognised as indispensable by civilised peoples; (h) threats to commit any of the foregoing acts."

Applicability of Common Article 3 and Additional Protocol II

601. The four 1949 Geneva Conventions and the 1977 Additional Protocol I thereto generally apply to international armed conflicts only, whereas Article 3 common to the Geneva Conventions extends a minimum threshold of humanitarian protection as well to all persons affected by a non-international conflict, a protection which was further developed and enhanced in the 1977 Additional Protocol II. In the field of international humanitarian law, a clear distinction as to the thresholds of application has been made between situations of international armed conflicts, in which the law of armed conflicts is applicable as a whole, situations of non-international (internal) armed conflicts, where Common Article 3 and Additional Protocol II are applicable, and non-international armed conflicts where only Common Article 3 is applicable. Situations of internal disturbances are not covered by international humanitarian law. . . .

604. The Security Council, when delimiting the subject-matter jurisdiction of the ICTR, incorporated violations of international humanitarian law which may be committed in the context of both an international and an internal armed conflict:

> Given the nature of the conflict as non-international in character, the Council has incorporated within the subject-matter jurisdiction of the Tribunal violations of international humanitarian law which may either be committed in both international and internal armed conflicts, such as the crime of genocide and crimes against humanity, or may be committed only in internal armed conflicts, such as violations of article 3 common to the four Geneva Conventions, as more fully elaborated in article 4 of Additional Protocol II.

In that latter respect, the Security Council has elected to take a more expansive approach to the choice of the applicable law than the one underlying the Statute of the Yugoslav Tribunal, and included within the subject-matter jurisdiction of the Rwanda Tribunal international instruments regardless of whether they were considered part of customary international law or whether they have customarily entailed the individual criminal responsibility of the perpetrator of the crime. Article 4 of the Statute, accordingly, includes violations of Additional Protocol II, which, as a whole, has not yet been universally recognized as part of customary international law, for the first time criminalizes common article 3 of the four Geneva Conventions.

605. Although the Security Council elected to take a more expansive approach to the choice of the subject-matter jurisdiction of the Tribunal than that of the ICTY, by incorporating international instruments regardless of whether they were considered part of customary international law or whether they customarily entailed the individual criminal responsibility of the perpetrator of the crime, the Chamber believes, an essential question which should be addressed at this stage is whether Article 4 of the Statute includes norms which did not, at the time the crimes alleged

in the Indictment were committed, form part of existing international customary law. [T]he Chamber recalls the establishment of the ICTY, during which the UN Secretary General asserted that in application of the principle of *nullum crimen sine lege* the International Tribunal should apply rules of International Humanitarian law which are *beyond any doubt part* of customary law. . . .

608. It is today clear that the norms of Common Article 3 have acquired the status of customary law in that most States, by their domestic penal codes, have criminalized acts which if committed during internal armed conflict, would constitute violations of Common Article 3. . . .

609. . . . Additional Protocol II as a whole was not deemed by the Secretary-General to have been universally recognized as part of customary international law. . . . "[M]any provisions of this Protocol [II] can now be regarded as declaratory of existing rules or as having crystallised in emerging rules of customary law," but not all.

610. [However,] it should be recalled that the relevant Article in the context of the ICTR is Article 4(2) (Fundamental Guarantees) of Additional Protocol II. All of the guarantees, as enumerated in Article 4 reaffirm and supplement Common Article 3 and, as discussed above, Common Article 3 being customary in nature, the Chamber is of the opinion that these guarantees did also at the time of the events alleged in the Indictment form part of existing international customary law.

Individual Criminal Responsibility

611. For the purposes of an international criminal Tribunal which is trying individuals, it is not sufficient merely to affirm that Common Article 3 and parts of Article 4 of Additional Protocol II — which comprise the subject-matter jurisdiction of Article 4 of the Statute — form part of international customary law. . . . [I]t must also be shown that an individual committing serious violations of these customary norms incurs, as a matter of custom, individual criminal responsibility thereby. Otherwise, it might be argued that these instruments only state norms applicable to States and Parties to a conflict, and that they do not create crimes for which individuals may be tried.

612. As regards individual criminal responsibility for serious violations of Common Article 3, the ICTY has already affirmed this principle in the *Tadic* case.

613. Basing itself on rulings of the Nuremberg Tribunal, on "elements of international practice which show that States intend to criminalise serious breaches of customary rules and principles on internal conflicts," as well as on national legislation designed to implement the Geneva Conventions, the ICTY Appeals Chamber reached the conclusion: "All of these factors confirm that customary international law imposes criminal liability for serious violations of common Article 3, as supplemented by other general principles and rules on protection of victims of internal armed conflict, and for breaching certain fundamental principles and rules regarding means and methods of combat in civil strife." . . .

615. The Chamber considers this finding of the ICTY Appeals Chamber convincing and dispositive of the issue, both with respect to serious violations of Common Article 3 and of Additional Protocol II. . . .

[On the counts of the indictment charging Akayesu, under Article 4 of the Statute, with violations of Common Article 3 of the Geneva Conventions or of Additional Protocol II, the Trial Chamber found that, while there was an "armed conflict not of an international character" taking place in Rwanda at the time of the events in question, it had not been proved that Akayesu's acts were committed in conjunction with that armed conflict. He therefore could not be found guilty on those counts. He was found guilty under Article 3 on seven counts alleging crimes against humanity (involving murder, extermination, torture, rape, and other inhumane acts). He also was found guilty under Article 2 on two counts alleging genocide and direct and public incitement to commit genocide, but not guilty on a count alleging complicity in genocide, on the ground that the same person cannot be both a principal and an accomplice to the same offense. On October 2, 1998, Akayesu was sentenced to life imprisonment. His appeal was dismissed on June 1, 2001. In *dicta* that did not affect the disposition of the case, the Appeals Chamber stated that, while there must be a nexus between the violations and armed conflict for Common Article 3 and Protocol II to apply, it was not necessary that the accused be a "public agent" or "government representative," although that would often be the case. Along with several others of those convicted by the ICTR, he is serving his sentence in Mali, by agreement between the Tribunal and the Government of Mali.]

Notes

(1) In the three months between April 7 and July 17, 1994, over a half million and perhaps closer to a million Rwandans were killed by their neighbors. Most killers were members of the majority Hutu ethnic group; most victims were minority Tutsi. On July 17, the Tutsi-led Rwandan Patriotic Front achieved military victory and took over the government. *See generally* SAMANTHA POWER, A PROBLEM FROM HELL: AMERICA AND THE AGE OF GENOCIDE, Chapter 10 (2002). In September 1994, the new government asked the U.N. to set up an International Criminal Tribunal on the model of the Yugoslav Tribunal. Ironically, on November 8, 1994, Rwanda, by then a member of the Security Council, cast the sole vote opposing establishment of the ICTR — in part on the ground that, just as Nazi war criminals had been tried in Germany and, if convicted, faced execution, so those guilty of genocide in Rwanda should be tried in Rwanda (rather than Arusha) and also face the death penalty. Rwanda abolished the death penalty in 2007, as West Germany had done in 1949 and East Germany in 1987.

(2) The ICTR was not expected to deal with the bulk of the 120,000 persons arrested for criminal cases arising from the Rwandan genocide. These were assigned to the Rwandan courts, especially the traditional *gacaca* trials which operated until

mid-2012. *See* Madeline H. Morris, *The Trials of Concurrent Jurisdiction: The Case of Rwanda*, 7 Duke J. Comp. & Int'l L. 349 (1997). One of the problems was finding judges. It was reported in 2002 that 72 of the *gacaca* judges had resigned following accusations of their own involvement in the genocide, Judicial Diplomacy 2002, reproduced at http://www.pict-pcti.org/news. Amnesty International's 2009 report records continuing problems with the trials, noting that, "[g]acaca trials were reportedly marred by false accusations and corruption. In addition, defense witnesses were reluctant to come forward because they feared that the authorities would level false accusations against them." *See* http://www.unhcr.org/refworld/topic,4565c2254d,46556ce92,4a1fadc72,0.htm. For a comprehensive retrospective on the courts, *see* Bert Ingelaere, Inside Rwanda's Gacaca Courts: Seeking Justice after Genocide (2017). Of necessity, most of those convicted, other than those involved in planning the genocide, would be released into the community as efforts at reconciliation proceeded. Unless the international community is prepared to invest massive resources into criminal trials (which it is not) what is the alternative to "flawed" justice?

(3) *Akeyesu* was the first international prosecution for genocide. Others followed. The Prime Minister at the relevant time, Jean Kambanda, and other leaders — Cabinet members, senior military personnel, senior administrators, religious leaders, businessmen and even some academics — have either entered guilty pleas or been convicted at trial. There were several life sentences. In all, 93 persons were indicted by the Tribunal and 61 were ultimately sentenced. Fourteen were acquitted, ten referred to national jurisdictions for trial, two indictments were withdrawn before trial, and three accused died prior to or during trial. As the Tribunal wound up its work in 2015, the cases of three remaining fugitives were referred to the Mechanism for International Criminal Tribunals. *See* The ICTR in Brief, *available at* http://www.unictr.org/en/tribunal.

(4) Do the objections raised by the defense in *Tadic* to the jurisdiction of the ICTY have greater (or less) validity when applied to the ICTR? Does it make a difference that the conflict there was more non-international than that in Former Yugoslavia (although there was some spillover to surrounding states)? In *Prosecutor v. Kanyabashi*, Case No. ICTR-96-15-T, Decision on Jurisdiction (Jun. 18, 1997), Trial Chamber II of the Rwanda Tribunal rejected objections to its jurisdiction, referring to the "persuasive authority" of the Appeals Chamber decision on jurisdiction in *Tadic*.

(5) Is the assertion in paragraph 516 of the decision that the intention of the drafters of the Genocide Convention "was patently to ensure the protection of any stable and permanent group" convincing? Can it be reconciled with the plain language of the treaty which refers to four particular groups? Can the preparatory work be used to overcome the language of the treaty? A second Trial Chamber later found that the Tutsi are an ethnic group and did not use the *Akayesu* analysis. *Prosecutor v. Kayishema and Ruzindana*, Case No. ICTR-95-1-T, Judgment, May 21, 1999, para. 94. *See*

generally, WILLIAM A. SCHABAS, GENOCIDE IN INTERNATIONAL LAW: THE CRIME OF CRIMES (2nd ed. 2009).

§ 21.03 The International Residual Mechanism for Criminal Tribunals

The International Residual Mechanism was created to perform some essential functions previously carried out by the Tribunals for Former Yugoslavia and Rwanda. The Security Council resolution creating it, S.C. Res. 1966 of December 22, 2010, spoke of a "small, temporary and efficient structure." It is currently involved in a few residual trials and appeals. It assists domestic jurisdictions in their trials and endeavors to protect witnesses and victims. Perhaps more significantly in the longer term, it has jurisdiction over the conditions of imprisonment of those incarcerated after conviction for crimes in Former Yugoslavia and Rwanda. This includes the power of the President of the Mechanism to make decisions about early release. Given the number of persons involved (about 30 from Rwanda and 20 from Former Yugoslavia) and the length of some sentences, this suggests that "temporary" is wishful thinking. On the Mechanism's jurisdiction and activities, see its website, *available at* https://www.irmct.org/en.

§ 21.04 Hybrid Tribunals

A. Special Court for Sierra Leone

On August 14, 2000, the Security Council adopted Resolution 1315 (2000), in which it asked the Secretary-General "to negotiate an agreement with the Government of Sierra Leone to create an independent special court" to try "crimes against humanity, war crimes and other serious violations of international humanitarian law, as well as crimes under relevant Sierra Leonean law committed within the territory of Sierra Leone." The Special Court has a majority of international judges. The reliance on voluntary contributions has made it vulnerable to international inertia, but it has limped along. There is extensive procedural and substantive caselaw at both the trial and appellate level. *See* the Archives of the Court *available at* http://www.scsldocs.org/, the website of the Residual Special Court which oversees the continuing legal obligations of the Court since its closure in 2013. These obligations include witness protection, supervision of prison sentences, and management of the archives. For a thorough account of the work of the Special Court, *see* CHARLES C. JALLOH, THE LEGAL LEGACY OF THE SPECIAL COURT FOR SIERRA LEONE (2020).

The Court's decision on immunity of a former head of state, Charles Taylor, is especially important. *See Prosecutor v. Taylor,* Case No. SCSL-2003-01-I, May 31, 2004. Another decision worthy of careful attention is *Prosecutor v. Sam Hinga*

Norman, Case No. SCSL-2003-14-AR72(E), Decision on Preliminary Motion based on Lack of Jurisdiction (Child Recruitment), delivered on May 21, 2004. Under Article 4 of its Statute, the Special Court has power to prosecute persons involved, inter alia, in "Conscripting or enlisting children under the age of 15 years into armed forces or groups or using them to participate actively in hostilities." The issue in the Preliminary Motion was whether this was recognized as a crime entailing individual criminal responsibility under customary international law at the time of the acts alleged in the indictments against the accused, which date back to November 1996. The majority was of the view that prior to November 1996 the prohibition on child recruitment had crystallized as customary international law. It found this to be demonstrated by a number of instruments including the Geneva Conventions and their 1977 Protocols, the Convention on the Rights of the Child and the 1990 African Charter on the Rights and Welfare of the Child. Justice Geoffrey Robinson wrote a very powerful dissent. He was in "no doubt that the crime of non-forcible enlistment did not enter international criminal law until the Rome Treaty [for the International Criminal Court] in July 1998." Accordingly, he would have granted a declaration to the effect that the accused must not be prosecuted for any offense of enlistment alleged to have been committed before then. On the child soldier issue in general, see Mary-Jane Fox, *Child Soldiers and International Law: Patchwork Gains and Conceptual Debates*, 7 Hum. Rts. Rev. 27 (2005).

The most dramatic event was the arrest and trial of former Liberian President Charles Taylor who was charged with numerous counts of war crimes and crimes against humanity including acts of terrorism, homicide, rape, the use of child soldiers, enslavement and other abductions and pillage carried out in Sierra Leone. In his case, the last to be tried, the imperatives of security for all concerned trumped the principle of local "ownership" of the trial in Sierra Leone and led to the proceedings being transferred to premises borrowed from the I.C.C. in The Hague. The Appeals Chamber's 2013 decision upholding his conviction is especially interesting for its analysis of criminal responsibility on the basis of an aiding and abetting theory since Taylor did not commit any of the relevant deeds himself. *See Prosecutor v. Taylor*, Appeals Chamber, Special Court for Sierra Leone, Decision of 26 September 2013, SCSL-03-01-A (10766-11114). After his conviction and the failure of his appeal, he was transferred to Great Britain to serve his 50-year sentence.

B. Kosovo and Timor-Leste

Rather different hybrids were created in Kosovo and Timor-Leste by Special Representatives of the U.N. Secretary-General, operating under the authority of the Security Council as part of a peacekeeping effort and transitional international administration. Involving a mix of foreign and local judges, these courts represented an effort to (re-)establish and mentor local judiciaries after a time of strife. There are conflicting views on the success of these ventures. For further discussion, *see* Ellen S. Podgor, Roger S. Clark & Lucian E. Dervan, Understanding International Criminal Law § 17.09 (4th ed. 2022).

C. Cambodian Extraordinary Chambers

During the period 1975 to 1979, the Khmer Rouge regime in Cambodia was responsible for the deaths of somewhere between 1 and 3 million people, about a fifth of the total population. Various negotiations to bring some of those responsible to justice failed until 2003. That year, the current Cambodian authorities and the United Nations reached agreement on trials for surviving senior leaders of the time and those who were most responsible for the crimes and serious violations of Cambodian penal law, international humanitarian law and custom, and international conventions recognized by Cambodia that were committed during the period 17 April 1975 to 6 January 1979.[1] Specific crimes were listed as genocide, crimes against humanity, grave breaches of the Geneva Conventions and certain offenses under Cambodian law. The mechanism that was established is known as the Extraordinary Chambers in the Courts of Cambodia for the Prosecution of Crimes Committed during the Period of Democratic Kampuchea. It is another example of a "hybrid" court, although in this instance, the majority of the judges at both levels are appointed by the Cambodian Government. Funding came from voluntary sources and there have been recurring financial crises. Obstruction by the Cambodian Government has been another recurring theme.

On the establishment of the Chambers in general, *see* Symposium, *Cambodian Extraordinary Chambers—Justice at Long Last?* 4 J. CRIM. JUST 283 (2006). Five surviving, but aging, members of the Khmer Rouge Leadership were placed in custody. The first trial began in March 2009 against Kaing Guek Eav (alias Duch), former chief of the prison camp Tuol Sleng (or "S-21"), where close to 20,000 people were tortured and killed. He was convicted of crimes against humanity and war crimes and the conviction was upheld by the Supreme Court Chamber in 2012. The Supreme Court, increasing the penalty applied at trial, sentenced him to life imprisonment. He died, serving his sentence, in September 2020. Proceedings against two of the others, Ieng Sary and his wife Ieng Thirith, were terminated before verdict. Sary died in 2013. Thirith was found unfit to stand trial as a result of dementia and she too died, in August 2015. The case then proceeded against the last two, Nuon Chea, former Chairman of the Democratic Kampuchea National Assembly and Deputy Secretary of the Communist Party of Kampuchea, and Khieu Samphan, former Head of State of Democratic Kampuchea. ("Democratic Kampuchea" was the name used by the Khmer Rouge for Cambodia.) They were charged with crimes against humanity, war crimes and also genocide against the Muslim Cham and the Vietnamese. Their case was divided into two, and the genocide count was held over. They were both convicted and sentenced to life imprisonment in their first trial. Then in 2018, they were convicted of genocide. Nuon Chea died in August 2019, but

1. Agreement between the United Nations and the Royal Government of Cambodia concerning the Prosecution under Cambodian Law of Crimes Committed during the Period of Democratic Kampuchea, June 6, 2003, *available at* http://www.eccc.gov.kh/sites/default/files/legal-documents/Agreement_between_UN_and_RGC.pdf.

Samphan's appeal in the genocide case was proceeding in 2021. Aged 89, he had become the lone survivor.

The experience of the "killing fields" of Cambodia underscores the requirement for genocide that the killing must be of "another"—the bulk of the killings were by ethnic Khmers of other ethnic Khmers and were thus, in spite of their stunning numbers, not encompassed by the Genocide Convention. Thus, the genocide charges for the small groups of Cham and Vietnamese pale in significance against the crimes against humanity counts. Subsequent charges were brought against four other defendants, Meas Muth, Yin Tith, Im Chaem and Ao An. The cases against all except Meas Muth were discontinued, and Muth's case has been at the Pre-Trial stage since 2018.

In part because of the small number of prosecutions by the court and its relatively large budget, allegations of corruption have clouded the proceedings over the years. In 2009, the UN Assistant-Secretary-General for Legal Affairs submitted a provisional ethics monitoring mechanism to the Cambodian Deputy Prime Minister for consideration. An ethics monitor was eventually appointed.

There is provision in the Rules of the Chamber for participation of victims, a feature of the Rome Statute of the International Criminal Court, but not of the other ad hoc tribunals. Many victims have been participating. In the Duch case, the Trial Chamber awarded as reparations (1) inclusion of the names of admitted Civil Parties and their deceased members in the judgment, and (2) the compilation and publication of all statements of apology and acknowledgement made by Duch.

For extensive documentation, *see Extraordinary Chambers in the Courts of Cambodia*, *available* at https://www.eccc.gov.kh/en/node/39457. For good discussions of the trials, with all their warts, *see* ALEXANDER LABAN HINTON, MAN OR MONSTER? THE TRIAL OF A KHMER ROUGE TORTURER (2016); ALEXANDER LABAN HINTON, THE JUSTICE FACADE: TRIALS OF TRANSITION IN CAMBODIA (2018).

D. Special Tribunal for Lebanon (STL)

On May 30, 2007, the United Nations Security Council adopted Resolution 1757 (2007) approving an agreement between the United Nations and Lebanon for the establishment of a Special Tribunal. *See Symposium on Special Tribunal for Lebanon—A Cripple from Birth?*, 5 J. INT'L CRIM. JUST. 1061 ff. (2007). The subject matter and the time frame for jurisdiction are described thus in the agreement:

Article 1

Establishment of the Special Tribunal

1. There is hereby established a Special Tribunal for Lebanon to prosecute persons responsible for the attack of 14 February 2005 resulting in the death of former Lebanese Prime Minister Rafiq Hariri and in the death or injury of other persons. If the tribunal finds that other attacks that occurred in

> Lebanon between 1 October 2004 and 12 December 2005, or any later date decided by the Parties and with the consent of the Security Council, are connected in accordance with the principles of criminal justice and are of a nature and gravity similar to the attack of 14 February 2005, it shall also have jurisdiction over persons responsible for such attacks. This connection includes but is not limited to a combination of the following elements: criminal intent (motive), the purpose behind the attacks, the nature of the victims targeted, the pattern of the attacks (modus operandi) and the perpetrators.
>
> 2. The Special Tribunal shall function in accordance with the Statute of the Special Tribunal for Lebanon. The Statute is attached to this Agreement and forms an integral part thereof.

The tribunal began functioning on March 1, 2009. While the Tribunal is a hybrid, with a majority of international members on the panels, the substantive law is, unlike that applying in Sierra Leone and Cambodia, entirely domestic Lebanese law. In a controversial interlocutory decision, the Tribunal insisted that, in view of the nature of the tribunal proceedings, Lebanese law had to be interpreted in the light of international customary law and that customary law now contains a criminal prohibition against terrorism.[2] It also issued an important opinion on corporate criminal responsibility in a case involving contempt of the Tribunal. *See* Osama Alkhawaja, *In Defense of the Special Tribunal for Lebanon and the Case for International Corporate Accountability*, 20 Chicago J. Int'l L. 450 (2020).

Like the Nuremberg Tribunal, but unlike most other courts and tribunals, it has power to try persons *in absentia*. In 2011, indictments were confirmed against four individuals related to their alleged involvement in the assassination of Rafik Hariri. The trial in the case began in January 2014. All four defendants were tried *in absentia*, since none of them have been arrested. (Proceedings against another accused were terminated when it became apparent that he was dead.) In August 2020, the Trial Chamber unanimously found Mr. Salim Jamil Ayyash guilty and the other three defendants not guilty. The guilty verdict encompassed five crimes, namely being a co-perpetrator of conspiracy aimed at committing a terrorist act, committing a terrorist act by means of an explosive device, intentional homicide of Mr. Rafik Hariri with premeditation by using explosive materials, intentional homicide of an additional 21 persons with premeditation by using explosive materials, and attempted intentional homicide of 226 persons with premeditation by using explosive materials. The Trial Chamber sentenced Mr. Ayyash on December 11, 2020 to five concurrent sentences of life imprisonment, one for each of the crimes for which he was convicted. *See* the Tribunal's file on the case, *available*

---

2. Interlocutory Decision on the Applicable Law: Terrorism, Conspiracy, Homicide, Perpetration, Cumulative Charging, STL-11-01/1/A/A/R176bis. [*See* Chapter 9.]

at https://www.stl-tsl.org/en/the-cases/stl-11-01. With its funding cut off, the only cases proceeding at the end of 2021 were appeals by the prosecution against the three acquittals.

§ 21.05 Some Creative Variations

A. Lockerbie

See discussion of the "Scottish" trial in the Netherlands in Chapter 9.

B. Iraq

The Iraqi Special Tribunal that tried Saddam Hussein and others of his Government has been described as "an odd creature. . . . an Iraqi-led mechanism designed and supported by foreigners. It is based on international law but relies heavily on Iraqi tradition and procedures." Miranda Sissons, *And Now from the Green Zone . . . Reflections on the Iraq Tribunal's Dujail Trial*, 20 Ethics & Int'l Aff. 505, 505 (2006). Its Statute was originally adopted by the Coalition Provisional Authority in 2003 (Coalition Provisional Authority Order 48, "Delegation of Authority Regarding an Iraqi Special Tribunal", *available at* http://www.loc.gov/law/help/hussein/docs/20031210_CPAORD_48_IST_and_Appendix_A.pdf) and "domesticated" in 2005 (International Center for Transitional Justice Briefing Paper, at 2, n.1 (October 2005), *available at* https://www.ictj.org/sites/default/files/ICTJ_AnnualReport_2004-5.pdf). Under the Statute, the Tribunal has jurisdiction over any Iraqi national or resident accused of the crimes listed in the Statute between July 17, 1968, and May 1, 2003, in Iraq and elsewhere, including crimes committed in connection with Iraq's wars against Iran and Kuwait. The crimes include genocide, crimes against humanity and war crimes (essentially as defined in detail in the Rome Statute of the International Criminal Court). It also includes three crimes under Iraqi law: manipulations of the judiciary; wastage of national resources and squandering of public assets and funds; and "[t]he abuse of position and the pursuit of policies that may lead to the threat of war or the use of the armed forces of Iraq against an Arab country, in accordance with Article 1 of Law Number 7 of 1958, as amended." Statute of the Iraqi Special Tribunal, Art. 14. Iraq is thus one of the fairly small band of countries with a domestic proscription of aggressive war (*See* § 23.01[A] *infra*), yet it is a selective one. Invading Kuwait, an Arab State, was criminal under domestic law; invading Iran, Islamic but not Arab, was not a crime. Potentially the war crimes committed in Iran, like those in Kuwait, could have been charged to the former president. But his execution for crimes committed against his own people rendered this moot. There is an enormous amount of useful information and opinion on the Hussein trial (and other Iraqi trials) on the Case Western Reserve Law School's "Grotian Moment" Blog, *available at* http://law.case.edu/Academics/Academic-Centers/Cox

-International-Law-Center. *See also* Symposium, *Saddam Hussein on Trial: What Went Awry?* 5 J. INT'L CRIM. JUST. 257–300 (2007); Jennifer Trahan, *A Critical Guide to the Iraqi High Tribunal's Anfal Judgment: Genocide Against the Kurds*, 30 MICH. J. INT'L L. 305 (2009).

C. Extraordinary African Chambers in Senegal

See the discussion of the trial of Hissène Habré in Chapter 2, § 2.02[D], *supra*, and in ELLEN S. PODGOR, ROGER S. CLARK & LUCIAN E. DERVAN, UNDERSTANDING INTERNATIONAL LAW (4th ed. 2022), Chap. 17[C].

For some thoughtful assessments of the Ad Hoc tribunals and several of the hybrid ones, see CRITICAL ASSESSMENTS OF INTERNATIONAL CRIMINAL COURTS (Magda Karagiannakis ed., 2009).

§ 21.06 "Mechanisms" Without Trials

In their Joint Separate Opinion in the *Arrest Warrant Case* (D.R. Congo v. Belgium), *supra* § 2.02, Judges Higgins, Kooijmans and Buergenthal commented that "the international consensus that the perpetrators of international crimes should not go unpunished is being advanced by a flexible strategy, in which newly-established international criminal tribunals, treaty obligations and national courts all have their part to play." Given that this "flexible strategy" is not always able to deliver, are there some stopgap measures that might keep the flame alive until a more propitious time arrives? In particular, note that over seventy States have not yet become party to the Rome Statute and that large-power realpolitik limits the ability to refer cases via the Security Council. Moreover, there is no longer any disposition at the United Nations to create new ad hoc or hybrid tribunals. Universal jurisdiction has its challengers. One (desperate) response has been the creation of three fact-finding "Mechanisms," for Syria, Iraq and Myanmar, to record the facts of atrocity crimes in the hope that some national, regional or international jurisdiction will open up in the future. Each was created by a different organ of the United Nations. They are the International, Impartial and Independent Mechanism to Assist in the Investigation and Prosecution of Persons Responsible for the Most Serious Crimes under International Law Committed in the Syrian Arab Republic Since March 2011 (IIIM), created by the General Assembly, G.A. Res. 71/248, Dec. 21, 2016; the United Nations Investigative Team to Promote Accountability for Crimes Committed by Da'esh/ISIL in Iraq (UNITAD), created by the Security Council, S.C. Res. 2379, Sept. 21, 2017; and the Independent Investigative Mechanism for Myanmar (IIMM), created by the Human Rights Council, U.N. Doc. A/HRC/RES/39/2, Sept. 27, 2018. A critical commentator "raises the question whether the creation of such mechanisms . . . represents a retreat for the field of international justice, forced to adapt to a more hostile political landscape that presents more limited opportunities for prosecution." Jennifer Trahan, *International*

Justice and the International Criminal Court at a Critical Juncture, *in* The Future of Global Affairs 123, 123-24 (C. Ankerson & W.P.S. Sidhu eds., 2021). She adds, *id.* at 124: "A key challenge for the international community will be to ensure that in the future such evidence-collection successfully feeds into systematic prosecutions before courts and tribunals that respect due process and refrain from implementing the death penalty."

Chapter 22

The International Criminal Court

§ 22.01 The Rome Statute

The Rome Statute of The International Criminal Court

Adopted by the United Nations Diplomatic Conference of Plenipotentiaries on the Establishment of an International Criminal Court on July 17, 1998 U.N. GAOR, 53d Sess., U.N. Doc. A/ CONF. 183/ 9 (1998)[*]

Preamble

The States Parties to this Statute,

Conscious that all peoples are united by common bonds, their cultures pieced together in a shared heritage, and concerned that this delicate mosaic may be shattered at any time,

Mindful that during this century millions of children, women and men have been victims of unimaginable atrocities that deeply shock the conscience of humanity,

Recognizing that such grave crimes threaten the peace, security and well-being of the world,

Affirming that the most serious crimes of concern to the international community as a whole must not go unpunished and that their effective prosecution must be ensured by taking measures at the national level and by enhancing international cooperation,

Determined to put an end to impunity for the perpetrators of these crimes and thus to contribute to the prevention of such crimes,

Recalling that it is the duty of every State to exercise its criminal jurisdiction over those responsible for international crimes,

Reaffirming the Purposes and Principles of the Charter of the United Nations, and in particular that all States shall refrain from the threat or use of force against the territorial integrity or political independence of any State, or in any other manner inconsistent with the Purposes of the United Nations,

---

* With corrections of November 10, 1998; July 12, 1999; May 8, 2000; January 17, 2001 and January 16, 2002.

Emphasizing in this connection that nothing in this Statute shall be taken as authorizing any State Party to intervene in an armed conflict or in the internal affairs of any State,

Determined to these ends and for the sake of present and future generations, to establish an independent permanent International Criminal Court in relationship with the United Nations system, with jurisdiction over the most serious crimes of concern to the international community as a whole,

Emphasizing that the International Criminal Court established under this Statute shall be complementary to national criminal jurisdictions,

Resolved to guarantee lasting respect for and the enforcement of international justice,

Have agreed as follows:

PART 1. ESTABLISHMENT OF THE COURT

Article 1 — The Court

An International Criminal Court ("the Court") is hereby established. It shall be a permanent institution and shall have the power to exercise its jurisdiction over persons for the most serious crimes of international concern, as referred to in this Statute, and shall be complementary to national criminal jurisdictions. The jurisdiction and functioning of the Court shall be governed by the provisions of this Statute.

Article 2 — Relationship of the Court with the United Nations

The Court shall be brought into relationship with the United Nations through an agreement to be approved by the Assembly of States Parties to this Statute and thereafter concluded by the President of the Court on its behalf.

Article 3 — Seat of the Court

1. The seat of the Court shall be established at The Hague in the Netherlands ("the host State").

2. The Court shall enter into a headquarters agreement with the host State, to be approved by the Assembly of States Parties and thereafter concluded by the President of the Court on its behalf.

3. The Court may sit elsewhere, whenever it considers it desirable, as provided in this Statute.

Article 4 — Legal status and powers of the Court

1. The Court shall have international legal personality. It shall also have such legal capacity as may be necessary for the exercise of its functions and the fulfilment of its purposes.

2. The Court may exercise its functions and powers, as provided in this Statute, on the territory of any State Party and, by special agreement, on the territory of any other State.

PART 2. JURISDICTION, ADMISSIBILITY AND APPLICABLE LAW

Article 5 — Crimes within the jurisdiction of the Court

1. The jurisdiction of the Court shall be limited to the most serious crimes of concern to the international community as a whole. The Court has jurisdiction in accordance with this Statute with respect to the following crimes:

(a) The crime of genocide;

(b) Crimes against humanity;

(c) War crimes;

(d) The crime of aggression.

2. The Court shall exercise jurisdiction over the crime of aggression once a provision is adopted in accordance with articles 121 and 123 defining the crime and setting out the conditions under which the Court shall exercise jurisdiction with respect to this crime. Such a provision shall be consistent with the relevant provisions of the Charter of the United Nations.

Article 6 — Genocide

For the purpose of this Statute, "genocide" means any of the following acts committed with intent to destroy, in whole or in part, a national, ethnical, racial or religious group, as such:

(a) Killing members of the group;

(b) Causing serious bodily or mental harm to members of the group;

(c) Deliberately inflicting on the group conditions of life calculated to bring about its physical destruction in whole or in part;

(d) Imposing measures intended to prevent births within the group;

(e) Forcibly transferring children of the group to another group.

Article 7 — Crimes against humanity

1. For the purpose of this Statute, "crime against humanity" means any of the following acts when committed as part of a widespread or systematic attack directed against any civilian population, with knowledge of the attack:

(a) Murder;

(b) Extermination;

(c) Enslavement;

(d) Deportation or forcible transfer of population;

(e) Imprisonment or other severe deprivation of physical liberty in violation of fundamental rules of international law;

(f) Torture;

(g) Rape, sexual slavery, enforced prostitution, forced pregnancy, enforced sterilization, or any other form of sexual violence of comparable gravity;

(h) Persecution against any identifiable group or collectivity on political, racial, national, ethnic, cultural, religious, gender as defined in paragraph 3, or other grounds that are universally recognized as impermissible under international law, in connection with any act referred to in this paragraph or any crime within the jurisdiction of the Court;

(i) Enforced disappearance of persons;

(j) The crime of apartheid;

(k) Other inhumane acts of a similar character intentionally causing great suffering, or serious injury to body or to mental or physical health.

2. For the purpose of paragraph 1:

(a) "Attack directed against any civilian population" means a course of conduct involving the multiple commission of acts referred to in paragraph 1 against any civilian population, pursuant to or in furtherance of a State or organizational policy to commit such attack;

(b) "Extermination" includes the intentional infliction of conditions of life, *inter alia* the deprivation of access to food and medicine, calculated to bring about the destruction of part of a population;

(c) "Enslavement" means the exercise of any or all of the powers attaching to the right of ownership over a person and includes the exercise of such power in the course of trafficking in persons, in particular women and children;

(d) "Deportation or forcible transfer of population" means forced displacement of the persons concerned by expulsion or other coercive acts from the area in which they are lawfully present, without grounds permitted under international law;

(e) "Torture" means the intentional infliction of severe pain or suffering, whether physical or mental, upon a person in the custody or under the control of the accused; except that torture shall not include pain or suffering arising only from, inherent in or incidental to, lawful sanctions;

(f) "Forced pregnancy" means the unlawful confinement of a woman forcibly made pregnant, with the intent of affecting the ethnic composition of any population or carrying out other grave violations of international law. This definition shall not in any way be interpreted as affecting national laws relating to pregnancy;

(g) "Persecution" means the intentional and severe deprivation of fundamental rights contrary to international law by reason of the identity of the group or collectivity;

(h) "The crime of apartheid" means inhumane acts of a character similar to those referred to in paragraph 1, committed in the context of an institutionalized regime of systematic oppression and domination by one racial group over any other racial group or groups and committed with the intention of maintaining that regime;

(i) "Enforced disappearance of persons" means the arrest, detention or abduction of persons by, or with the authorization, support or acquiescence of, a State or a political organization, followed by a refusal to acknowledge that deprivation of freedom or to give information on the fate or whereabouts of those persons, with the intention of removing them from the protection of the law for a prolonged period of time.

3. For the purpose of this Statute, it is understood that the term "gender" refers to the two sexes, male and female, within the context of society. The term "gender" does not indicate any meaning different from the above.

Article 8 — War crimes

1. The Court shall have jurisdiction in respect of war crimes in particular when committed as part of a plan or policy or as part of a large-scale commission of such crimes.

2. For the purpose of this Statute, "war crimes" means:

(a) Grave breaches of the Geneva Conventions of 12 August 1949, namely, any of the following acts against persons or property protected under the provisions of the relevant Geneva Convention:

(i) Wilful killing;

(ii) Torture or inhuman treatment, including biological experiments;

(iii) Wilfully causing great suffering, or serious injury to body or health;

(iv) Extensive destruction and appropriation of property, not justified by military necessity and carried out unlawfully and wantonly;

(v) Compelling a prisoner of war or other protected person to serve in the forces of a hostile Power;

(vi) Wilfully depriving a prisoner of war or other protected person of the rights of fair and regular trial;

(vii) Unlawful deportation or transfer or unlawful confinement;

(viii) Taking of hostages.

(b) Other serious violations of the laws and customs applicable in international armed conflict, within the established framework of international law, namely, any of the following acts:

(i) Intentionally directing attacks against the civilian population as such or against individual civilians not taking direct part in hostilities;

(ii) Intentionally directing attacks against civilian objects, that is, objects which are not military objectives;

(iii) Intentionally directing attacks against personnel, installations, material, units or vehicles involved in a humanitarian assistance or peacekeeping mission in accordance with the Charter of the United Nations, as long as they are entitled to the protection given to civilians or civilian objects under the international law of armed conflict;

(iv) Intentionally launching an attack in the knowledge that such attack will cause incidental loss of life or injury to civilians or damage to civilian objects or widespread, long-term and severe damage to the natural environment which would be clearly excessive in relation to the concrete and direct overall military advantage anticipated;

(v) Attacking or bombarding, by whatever means, towns, villages, dwellings or buildings which are undefended and which are not military objectives;

(vi) Killing or wounding a combatant who, having laid down his arms or having no longer means of defence, has surrendered at discretion;

(vii) Making improper use of a flag of truce, of the flag or of the military insignia and uniform of the enemy or of the United Nations, as well as of the distinctive emblems of the Geneva Conventions, resulting in death or serious personal injury;

(viii) The transfer, directly or indirectly, by the Occupying Power of parts of its own civilian population into the territory it occupies, or the deportation or transfer of all or parts of the population of the occupied territory within or outside this territory;

(ix) Intentionally directing attacks against buildings dedicated to religion, education, art, science or charitable purposes, historic monuments, hospitals and places where the sick and wounded are collected, provided they are not military objectives;

(x) Subjecting persons who are in the power of an adverse party to physical mutilation or to medical or scientific experiments of any kind which are neither justified by the medical, dental or hospital treatment of the person concerned nor carried out in his or her interest, and which cause death to or seriously endanger the health of such person or persons;

(xi) Killing or wounding treacherously individuals belonging to the hostile nation or army;

(xii) Declaring that no quarter will be given;

(xiii) Destroying or seizing the enemy's property unless such destruction or seizure be imperatively demanded by the necessities of war;

(xiv) Declaring abolished, suspended or inadmissible in a court of law the rights and actions of the nationals of the hostile party;

(xv) Compelling the nationals of the hostile party to take part in the operations of war directed against their own country, even if they were in the belligerent's service before the commencement of the war;

(xvi) Pillaging a town or place, even when taken by assault;

(xvii) Employing poison or poisoned weapons;

(xviii) Employing asphyxiating, poisonous or other gases, and all analogous liquids, materials or devices;

(xix) Employing bullets which expand or flatten easily in the human body, such as bullets with a hard envelope which does not entirely cover the core or is pierced with incisions;

(xx) Employing weapons, projectiles and material and methods of warfare which are of a nature to cause superfluous injury or unnecessary suffering or which are inherently indiscriminate in violation of the international law of armed conflict, provided that such weapons, projectiles and material and methods of warfare are the subject of a comprehensive prohibition and are included in an annex to this Statute, by an amendment in accordance with the relevant provisions set forth in articles 121 and 123;

(xxi) Committing outrages upon personal dignity, in particular humiliating and degrading treatment;

(xxii) Committing rape, sexual slavery, enforced prostitution, forced pregnancy, as defined in article 7, paragraph 2 (f), enforced sterilization, or any other form of sexual violence also constituting a grave breach of the Geneva Conventions;

(xxiii) Utilizing the presence of a civilian or other protected person to render certain points, areas or military forces immune from military operations;

(xxiv) Intentionally directing attacks against buildings, material, medical units and transport, and personnel using the distinctive emblems of the Geneva Conventions in conformity with international law;

(xxv) Intentionally using starvation of civilians as a method of warfare by depriving them of objects indispensable to their survival, including wilfully impeding relief supplies as provided for under the Geneva Conventions;

(xxvi) Conscripting or enlisting children under the age of fifteen years into the national armed forces or using them to participate actively in hostilities.

(c) In the case of an armed conflict not of an international character, serious violations of article 3 common to the four Geneva Conventions of 12 August 1949, namely, any of the following acts committed against persons taking no active part in the hostilities, including members of armed forces who have laid down their arms and those placed hors de combat by sickness, wounds, detention or any other cause:

(i) Violence to life and person, in particular murder of all kinds, mutilation, cruel treatment and torture;

(ii) Committing outrages upon personal dignity, in particular humiliating and degrading treatment;

(iii) Taking of hostages;

(iv) The passing of sentences and the carrying out of executions without previous judgement pronounced by a regularly constituted court, affording all judicial guarantees which are generally recognized as indispensable.

(d) Paragraph 2 (c) applies to armed conflicts not of an international character and thus does not apply to situations of internal disturbances and tensions, such as riots, isolated and sporadic acts of violence or other acts of a similar nature.

(e) Other serious violations of the laws and customs applicable in armed conflicts not of an international character, within the established framework of international law, namely, any of the following acts:

(i) Intentionally directing attacks against the civilian population as such or against individual civilians not taking direct part in hostilities;

(ii) Intentionally directing attacks against buildings, material, medical units and transport, and personnel using the distinctive emblems of the Geneva Conventions in conformity with international law;

(iii) Intentionally directing attacks against personnel, installations, material, units or vehicles involved in a humanitarian assistance or peacekeeping mission in accordance with the Charter of the United Nations, as long as they are entitled to the protection given to civilians or civilian objects under the international law of armed conflict;

(iv) Intentionally directing attacks against buildings dedicated to religion, education, art, science or charitable purposes, historic monuments, hospitals and places where the sick and wounded are collected, provided they are not military objectives;

(v) Pillaging a town or place, even when taken by assault;

(vi) Committing rape, sexual slavery, enforced prostitution, forced pregnancy, as defined in article 7, paragraph 2 (f), enforced sterilization, and any other form of sexual violence also constituting a serious violation of article 3 common to the four Geneva Conventions;

(vii) Conscripting or enlisting children under the age of fifteen years into armed forces or groups or using them to participate actively in hostilities;

(viii) Ordering the displacement of the civilian population for reasons related to the conflict, unless the security of the civilians involved or imperative military reasons so demand;

(ix) Killing or wounding treacherously a combatant adversary;

(x) Declaring that no quarter will be given;

(xi) Subjecting persons who are in the power of another party to the conflict to physical mutilation or to medical or scientific experiments of any kind which are neither justified by the medical, dental or hospital treatment of the person concerned nor carried out in his or her interest, and which cause death to or seriously endanger the health of such person or persons;

(xii) Destroying or seizing the property of an adversary unless such destruction or seizure be imperatively demanded by the necessities of the conflict;

(f) Paragraph 2 (e) applies to armed conflicts not of an international character and thus does not apply to situations of internal disturbances and tensions, such as riots, isolated and sporadic acts of violence or other acts of a similar nature. It applies to armed conflicts that take place in the territory of a State when there is protracted armed conflict between governmental authorities and organized armed groups or between such groups.

3. Nothing in paragraph 2 (c) and (e) shall affect the responsibility of a Government to maintain or re-establish law and order in the State or to defend the unity and territorial integrity of the State, by all legitimate means.

Article 9 — Elements of Crimes

1. Elements of Crimes shall assist the Court in the interpretation and application of articles 6, 7 and 8. They shall be adopted by a two-thirds majority of the members of the Assembly of States Parties.

2. Amendments to the Elements of Crimes may be proposed by:

(a) Any State Party;

(b) The judges acting by an absolute majority;

(c) The Prosecutor.

Such amendments shall be adopted by a two-thirds majority of the members of the Assembly of States Parties.

3. The Elements of Crimes and amendments thereto shall be consistent with this Statute.

Article 10

Nothing in this Part shall be interpreted as limiting or prejudicing in any way existing or developing rules of international law for purposes other than this Statute.

Article 11 — Jurisdiction ratione temporis

1. The Court has jurisdiction only with respect to crimes committed after the entry into force of this Statute.

2. If a State becomes a Party to this Statute after its entry into force, the Court may exercise its jurisdiction only with respect to crimes committed after the entry into force of this Statute for that State, unless that State has made a declaration under article 12, paragraph 3.

Article 12 — Preconditions to the exercise of jurisdiction

1. A State which becomes a Party to this Statute thereby accepts the jurisdiction of the Court with respect to the crimes referred to in article 5.

2. In the case of article 13, paragraph (a) or (c), the Court may exercise its jurisdiction if one or more of the following States are Parties to this Statute or have accepted the jurisdiction of the Court in accordance with paragraph 3:

(a) The State on the territory of which the conduct in question occurred or, if the crime was committed on board a vessel or aircraft, the State of registration of that vessel or aircraft;

(b) The State of which the person accused of the crime is a national.

3. If the acceptance of a State which is not a Party to this Statute is required under paragraph 2, that State may, by declaration lodged with the Registrar, accept the exercise of jurisdiction by the Court with respect to the crime in question. The accepting State shall cooperate with the Court without any delay or exception in accordance with Part 9.

Article 13 — Exercise of jurisdiction

The Court may exercise its jurisdiction with respect to a crime referred to in article 5 in accordance with the provisions of this Statute if:

(a) A situation in which one or more of such crimes appears to have been committed is referred to the Prosecutor by a State Party in accordance with article 14;

(b) A situation in which one or more of such crimes appears to have been committed is referred to the Prosecutor by the Security Council acting under Chapter VII of the Charter of the United Nations; or

(c) The Prosecutor has initiated an investigation in respect of such a crime in accordance with article 15.

Article 14 — Referral of a situation by a State Party

1. A State Party may refer to the Prosecutor a situation in which one or more crimes within the jurisdiction of the Court appear to have been committed requesting the Prosecutor to investigate the situation for the purpose of determining whether one or more specific persons should be charged with the commission of such crimes.

2. As far as possible, a referral shall specify the relevant circumstances and be accompanied by such supporting documentation as is available to the State referring the situation.

Article 15 — Prosecutor

1. The Prosecutor may initiate investigations proprio motu on the basis of information on crimes within the jurisdiction of the Court.

2. The Prosecutor shall analyse the seriousness of the information received. For this purpose, he or she may seek additional information from States, organs of the United Nations, intergovernmental or non-governmental organizations, or other reliable sources that he or she deems appropriate, and may receive written or oral testimony at the seat of the Court.

3. If the Prosecutor concludes that there is a reasonable basis to proceed with an investigation, he or she shall submit to the Pre-Trial Chamber a request for authorization of an investigation, together with any supporting material collected. Victims may make representations to the Pre-Trial Chamber, in accordance with the Rules of Procedure and Evidence.

4. If the Pre-Trial Chamber, upon examination of the request and the supporting material, considers that there is a reasonable basis to proceed with an investigation, and that the case appears to fall within the jurisdiction of the Court, it shall authorize the commencement of the investigation, without prejudice to subsequent determinations by the Court with regard to the jurisdiction and admissibility of a case.

5. The refusal of the Pre-Trial Chamber to authorize the investigation shall not preclude the presentation of a subsequent request by the Prosecutor based on new facts or evidence regarding the same situation.

6. If, after the preliminary examination referred to in paragraphs 1 and 2, the Prosecutor concludes that the information provided does not constitute a reasonable basis for an investigation, he or she shall inform those who provided the information. This shall not preclude the Prosecutor from considering further information submitted to him or her regarding the same situation in the light of new facts or evidence.

Article 16 — Deferral of investigation or prosecution

No investigation or prosecution may be commenced or proceeded with under this Statute for a period of 12 months after the Security Council, in a resolution adopted under Chapter VII of the Charter of the United Nations, has requested the Court to that effect; that request may be renewed by the Council under the same conditions.

Article 17 — Issues of admissibility

1. Having regard to paragraph 10 of the Preamble and article 1, the Court shall determine that a case is inadmissible where:

(a) The case is being investigated or prosecuted by a State which has jurisdiction over it, unless the State is unwilling or unable genuinely to carry out the investigation or prosecution;

(b) The case has been investigated by a State which has jurisdiction over it and the State has decided not to prosecute the person concerned, unless the decision resulted from the unwillingness or inability of the State genuinely to prosecute;

(c) The person concerned has already been tried for conduct which is the subject of the complaint, and a trial by the Court is not permitted under article 20, paragraph 3;

(d) The case is not of sufficient gravity to justify further action by the Court.

2. In order to determine unwillingness in a particular case, the Court shall consider, having regard to the principles of due process recognized by international law, whether one or more of the following exist, as applicable:

(a) The proceedings were or are being undertaken or the national decision was made for the purpose of shielding the person concerned from criminal responsibility for crimes within the jurisdiction of the Court referred to in article 5;

(b) There has been an unjustified delay in the proceedings which in the circumstances is inconsistent with an intent to bring the person concerned to justice;

(c) The proceedings were not or are not being conducted independently or impartially, and they were or are being conducted in a manner which, in the circumstances, is inconsistent with an intent to bring the person concerned to justice.

3. In order to determine inability in a particular case, the Court shall consider whether, due to a total or substantial collapse or unavailability of its national judicial system, the State is unable to obtain the accused or the necessary evidence and testimony or otherwise unable to carry out its proceedings.

Article 18 — Preliminary rulings regarding admissibility

1. When a situation has been referred to the Court pursuant to article 13 (a) and the Prosecutor has determined that there would be a reasonable basis to commence an investigation, or the Prosecutor initiates an investigation pursuant to articles 13 (c) and 15, the Prosecutor shall notify all States Parties and those States which, taking into account the information available, would normally exercise jurisdiction

over the crimes concerned. The Prosecutor may notify such States on a confidential basis and, where the Prosecutor believes it necessary to protect persons, prevent destruction of evidence or prevent the absconding of persons, may limit the scope of the information provided to States.

2. Within one month of receipt of that notification, a State may inform the Court that it is investigating or has investigated its nationals or others within its jurisdiction with respect to criminal acts which may constitute crimes referred to in article 5 and which relate to the information provided in the notification to States. At the request of that State, the Prosecutor shall defer to the State's investigation of those persons unless the Pre-Trial Chamber, on the application of the Prosecutor, decides to authorize the investigation.

3. The Prosecutor's deferral to a State's investigation shall be open to review by the Prosecutor six months after the date of deferral or at any time when there has been a significant change of circumstances based on the State's unwillingness or inability genuinely to carry out the investigation.

4. The State concerned or the Prosecutor may appeal to the Appeals Chamber against a ruling of the Pre-Trial Chamber, in accordance with article 82. The appeal may be heard on an expedited basis.

5. When the Prosecutor has deferred an investigation in accordance with paragraph 2, the Prosecutor may request that the State concerned periodically inform the Prosecutor of the progress of its investigations and any subsequent prosecutions. States Parties shall respond to such requests without undue delay.

6. Pending a ruling by the Pre-Trial Chamber, or at any time when the Prosecutor has deferred an investigation under this article, the Prosecutor may, on an exceptional basis, seek authority from the Pre-Trial Chamber to pursue necessary investigative steps for the purpose of preserving evidence where there is a unique opportunity to obtain important evidence or there is a significant risk that such evidence may not be subsequently available.

7. A State which has challenged a ruling of the Pre-Trial Chamber under this article may challenge the admissibility of a case under article 19 on the grounds of additional significant facts or significant change of circumstances.

Article 19 — Challenges to the jurisdiction of the Court or the admissibility of a case

1. The Court shall satisfy itself that it has jurisdiction in any case brought before it. The Court may, on its own motion, determine the admissibility of a case in accordance with article 17.

2. Challenges to the admissibility of a case on the grounds referred to in article 17 or challenges to the jurisdiction of the Court may be made by:

(a) An accused or a person for whom a warrant of arrest or a summons to appear has been issued under article 58;

(b) A State which has jurisdiction over a case, on the ground that it is investigating or prosecuting the case or has investigated or prosecuted; or

(c) A State from which acceptance of jurisdiction is required under article 12.

3. The Prosecutor may seek a ruling from the Court regarding a question of jurisdiction or admissibility. In proceedings with respect to jurisdiction or admissibility, those who have referred the situation under article 13, as well as victims, may also submit observations to the Court.

4. The admissibility of a case or the jurisdiction of the Court may be challenged only once by any person or State referred to in paragraph 2. The challenge shall take place prior to or at the commencement of the trial. In exceptional circumstances, the Court may grant leave for a challenge to be brought more than once or at a time later than the commencement of the trial. Challenges to the admissibility of a case, at the commencement of a trial, or subsequently with the leave of the Court, may be based only on article 17, paragraph 1 (c).

5. A State referred to in paragraph 2 (b) and (c) shall make a challenge at the earliest opportunity.

6. Prior to the confirmation of the charges, challenges to the admissibility of a case or challenges to the jurisdiction of the Court shall be referred to the Pre-Trial Chamber. After confirmation of the charges, they shall be referred to the Trial Chamber. Decisions with respect to jurisdiction or admissibility may be appealed to the Appeals Chamber in accordance with article 82.

7. If a challenge is made by a State referred to in paragraph 2 (b) or (c), the Prosecutor shall suspend the investigation until such time as the Court makes a determination in accordance with article 17.

8. Pending a ruling by the Court, the Prosecutor may seek authority from the Court:

(a) To pursue necessary investigative steps of the kind referred to in article 18, paragraph 6;

(b) To take a statement or testimony from a witness or complete the collection and examination of evidence which had begun prior to the making of the challenge; and

(c) In cooperation with the relevant States, to prevent the absconding of persons in respect of whom the Prosecutor has already requested a warrant of arrest under article 58.

9. The making of a challenge shall not affect the validity of any act performed by the Prosecutor or any order or warrant issued by the Court prior to the making of the challenge.

10. If the Court has decided that a case is inadmissible under article 17, the Prosecutor may submit a request for a review of the decision when he or she is fully

satisfied that new facts have arisen which negate the basis on which the case had previously been found inadmissible under article 17.

11. If the Prosecutor, having regard to the matters referred to in article 17, defers an investigation, the Prosecutor may request that the relevant State make available to the Prosecutor information on the proceedings. That information shall, at the request of the State concerned, be confidential. If the Prosecutor thereafter decides to proceed with an investigation, he or she shall notify the State to which deferral of the proceedings has taken place.

Article 20 — Ne bis in idem

1. Except as provided in this Statute, no person shall be tried before the Court with respect to conduct which formed the basis of crimes for which the person has been convicted or acquitted by the Court.

2. No person shall be tried by another court for a crime referred to in article 5 for which that person has already been convicted or acquitted by the Court.

3. No person who has been tried by another court for conduct also proscribed under article 6, 7 or 8 shall be tried by the Court with respect to the same conduct unless the proceedings in the other court:

(a) Were for the purpose of shielding the person concerned from criminal responsibility for crimes within the jurisdiction of the Court; or

(b) Otherwise were not conducted independently or impartially in accordance with the norms of due process recognized by international law and were conducted in a manner which, in the circumstances, was inconsistent with an intent to bring the person concerned to justice.

Article 21 — Applicable law

1. The Court shall apply:

(a) In the first place, this Statute, Elements of Crimes and its Rules of Procedure and Evidence;

(b) In the second place, where appropriate, applicable treaties and the principles and rules of international law, including the established principles of the international law of armed conflict;

(c) Failing that, general principles of law derived by the Court from national laws of legal systems of the world including, as appropriate, the national laws of States that would normally exercise jurisdiction over the crime, provided that those principles are not inconsistent with this Statute and with international law and internationally recognized norms and standards.

2. The Court may apply principles and rules of law as interpreted in its previous decisions.

3. The application and interpretation of law pursuant to this article must be consistent with internationally recognized human rights, and be without any adverse

distinction founded on grounds such as gender as defined in article 7, paragraph 3, age, race, colour, language, religion or belief, political or other opinion, national, ethnic or social origin, wealth, birth or other status.

PART 3. GENERAL PRINCIPLES OF CRIMINAL LAW

Article 22 — Nullum crimen sine lege

1. A person shall not be criminally responsible under this Statute unless the conduct in question constitutes, at the time it takes place, a crime within the jurisdiction of the Court.

2. The definition of a crime shall be strictly construed and shall not be extended by analogy. In case of ambiguity, the definition shall be interpreted in favour of the person being investigated, prosecuted or convicted.

3. This article shall not affect the characterization of any conduct as criminal under international law independently of this Statute.

Article 23 — Nulla poena sine lege

A person convicted by the Court may be punished only in accordance with this Statute.

Article 24 — Non-retroactivity ratione personae

1. No person shall be criminally responsible under this Statute for conduct prior to the entry into force of the Statute.

2. In the event of a change in the law applicable to a given case prior to a final judgement, the law more favourable to the person being investigated, prosecuted or convicted shall apply.

Article 25 — Individual criminal responsibility

1. The Court shall have jurisdiction over natural persons pursuant to this Statute.

2. A person who commits a crime within the jurisdiction of the Court shall be individually responsible and liable for punishment in accordance with this Statute.

3. In accordance with this Statute, a person shall be criminally responsible and liable for punishment for a crime within the jurisdiction of the Court if that person:

(a) Commits such a crime, whether as an individual, jointly with another or through another person, regardless of whether that other person is criminally responsible;

(b) Orders, solicits or induces the commission of such a crime which in fact occurs or is attempted;

(c) For the purpose of facilitating the commission of such a crime, aids, abets or otherwise assists in its commission or its attempted commission, including providing the means for its commission;

(d) In any other way contributes to the commission or attempted commission of such a crime by a group of persons acting with a common purpose. Such contribution shall be intentional and shall either:

(i) Be made with the aim of furthering the criminal activity or criminal purpose of the group, where such activity or purpose involves the commission of a crime within the jurisdiction of the Court; or

(ii) Be made in the knowledge of the intention of the group to commit the crime;

(e) In respect of the crime of genocide, directly and publicly incites others to commit genocide;

(f) Attempts to commit such a crime by taking action that commences its execution by means of a substantial step, but the crime does not occur because of circumstances independent of the person's intentions. However, a person who abandons the effort to commit the crime or otherwise prevents the completion of the crime shall not be liable for punishment under this Statute for the attempt to commit that crime if that person completely and voluntarily gave up the criminal purpose.

4. No provision in this Statute relating to individual criminal responsibility shall affect the responsibility of States under international law.

Article 26 — Exclusion of jurisdiction over persons under eighteen

The Court shall have no jurisdiction over any person who was under the age of 18 at the time of the alleged commission of a crime.

Article 27 — Irrelevance of official capacity

1. This Statute shall apply equally to all persons without any distinction based on official capacity. In particular, official capacity as a Head of State or Government, a member of a Government or parliament, an elected representative or a government official shall in no case exempt a person from criminal responsibility under this Statute, nor shall it, in and of itself, constitute a ground for reduction of sentence.

2. Immunities or special procedural rules which may attach to the official capacity of a person, whether under national or international law, shall not bar the Court from exercising its jurisdiction over such a person.

Article 28 — Responsibility of commanders and other superiors

In addition to other grounds of criminal responsibility under this Statute for crimes within the jurisdiction of the Court:

1. A military commander or person effectively acting as a military commander shall be criminally responsible for crimes within the jurisdiction of the Court committed by forces under his or her effective command and control, or effective authority and control as the case may be, as a result of his or her failure to exercise control properly over such forces, where:

(a) That military commander or person either knew or, owing to the circumstances at the time, should have known that the forces were committing or about to commit such crimes; and

(b) That military commander or person failed to take all necessary and reasonable measures within his or her power to prevent or repress their commission or to submit the matter to the competent authorities for investigation and prosecution.

2. With respect to superior and subordinate relationships not described in paragraph 1, a superior shall be criminally responsible for crimes within the jurisdiction of the Court committed by subordinates under his or her effective authority and control, as a result of his or her failure to exercise control properly over such subordinates, where:

(a) The superior either knew, or consciously disregarded information which clearly indicated, that the subordinates were committing or about to commit such crimes;

(b) The crimes concerned activities that were within the effective responsibility and control of the superior; and

(c) The superior failed to take all necessary and reasonable measures within his or her power to prevent or repress their commission or to submit the matter to the competent authorities for investigation and prosecution.

Article 29 — Non-applicability of statute of limitations

The crimes within the jurisdiction of the Court shall not be subject to any statute of limitations.

Article 30 — Mental element

1. Unless otherwise provided, a person shall be criminally responsible and liable for punishment for a crime within the jurisdiction of the Court only if the material elements are committed with intent and knowledge.

2. For the purposes of this article, a person has intent where:

(a) In relation to conduct, that person means to engage in the conduct;

(b) In relation to a consequence, that person means to cause that consequence or is aware that it will occur in the ordinary course of events.

3. For the purposes of this article, "knowledge" means awareness that a circumstance exists or a consequence will occur in the ordinary course of events. "Know" and "knowingly" shall be construed accordingly.

Article 31 — Grounds for excluding criminal responsibility

1. In addition to other grounds for excluding criminal responsibility provided for in this Statute, a person shall not be criminally responsible if, at the time of that person's conduct:

(a) The person suffers from a mental disease or defect that destroys that person's capacity to appreciate the unlawfulness or nature of his or her conduct, or capacity to control his or her conduct to conform to the requirements of law;

(b) The person is in a state of intoxication that destroys that person's capacity to appreciate the unlawfulness or nature of his or her conduct, or capacity to control his or her conduct to conform to the requirements of law, unless the person has become voluntarily intoxicated under such circumstances that the person knew, or disregarded the risk, that, as a result of the intoxication, he or she was likely to engage in conduct constituting a crime within the jurisdiction of the Court;

(c) The person acts reasonably to defend himself or herself or another person or, in the case of war crimes, property which is essential for the survival of the person or another person or property which is essential for accomplishing a military mission, against an imminent and unlawful use of force in a manner proportionate to the degree of danger to the person or the other person or property protected. The fact that the person was involved in a defensive operation conducted by forces shall not in itself constitute a ground for excluding criminal responsibility under this subparagraph;

(d) The conduct which is alleged to constitute a crime within the jurisdiction of the Court has been caused by duress resulting from a threat of imminent death or of continuing or imminent serious bodily harm against that person or another person, and the person acts necessarily and reasonably to avoid this threat, provided that the person does not intend to cause a greater harm than the one sought to be avoided. Such a threat may either be:

(i) Made by other persons; or

(ii) Constituted by other circumstances beyond that person's control.

2. The Court shall determine the applicability of the grounds for excluding criminal responsibility provided for in this Statute to the case before it.

3. At trial, the Court may consider a ground for excluding criminal responsibility other than those referred to in paragraph 1 where such a ground is derived from applicable law as set forth in article 21. The procedures relating to the consideration of such a ground shall be provided for in the Rules of Procedure and Evidence.

Article 32 — Mistake of fact or mistake of law

1. A mistake of fact shall be a ground for excluding criminal responsibility only if it negates the mental element required by the crime.

2. A mistake of law as to whether a particular type of conduct is a crime within the jurisdiction of the Court shall not be a ground for excluding criminal responsibility. A mistake of law may, however, be a ground for excluding criminal responsibility if it negates the mental element required by such a crime, or as provided for in article 33.

Article 33 — Superior orders and prescription of law

1. The fact that a crime within the jurisdiction of the Court has been committed by a person pursuant to an order of a Government or of a superior, whether military or civilian, shall not relieve that person of criminal responsibility unless:

(a) The person was under a legal obligation to obey orders of the Government or the superior in question;

(b) The person did not know that the order was unlawful; and

(c) The order was not manifestly unlawful.

2. For the purposes of this article, orders to commit genocide or crimes against humanity are manifestly unlawful.

PART 4. COMPOSITION AND ADMINISTRATION OF THE COURT

Article 34 — Organs of the Court

The Court shall be composed of the following organs:

(a) The Presidency;

(b) An Appeals Division, a Trial Division and a Pre-Trial Division;

(c) The Office of the Prosecutor;

(d) The Registry.

Article 35 — Service of judges

1. All judges shall be elected as full-time members of the Court and shall be available to serve on that basis from the commencement of their terms of office.

2. The judges composing the Presidency shall serve on a full -time basis as soon as they are elected.

3. The Presidency may, on the basis of the workload of the Court and in consultation with its members, decide from time to time to what extent the remaining judges shall be required to serve on a full-time basis. Any such arrangement shall be without prejudice to the provisions of article 40.

4. The financial arrangements for judges not required to serve on a full-time basis shall be made in accordance with article 49.

Article 36 — Qualifications, nomination and election of judges

1. Subject to the provisions of paragraph 2, there shall be 18 judges of the Court.

2. (a) The Presidency, acting on behalf of the Court, may propose an increase in the number of judges specified in paragraph 1, indicating the reasons why this is considered necessary and appropriate. The Registrar shall promptly circulate any such proposal to all States Parties.

(b) Any such proposal shall then be considered at a meeting of the Assembly of States Parties to be convened in accordance with article 112. The proposal shall be considered adopted if approved at the meeting by a vote of two-thirds of the members of the Assembly of States Parties and shall enter into force at such time as decided by the Assembly of States Parties.

(c) (i) Once a proposal for an increase in the number of judges has been adopted under subparagraph (b), the election of the additional judges shall take place at the next session of the Assembly of States Parties in accordance with paragraphs 3 to 8 inclusive, and article 37, paragraph 2;

(ii) Once a proposal for an increase in the number of judges has been adopted and brought into effect under subparagraphs (b) and (c) (i), it shall be open to the Presidency at any time thereafter, if the workload of the Court justifies it, to propose a reduction in the number of judges, provided that the number of judges shall not be reduced below that specified in paragraph 1. The proposal shall be dealt with in accordance with the procedure laid down in subparagraphs (a) and (b). In the event that the proposal is adopted, the number of judges shall be progressively decreased as the terms of office of serving judges expire, until the necessary number has been reached.

3. (a) The judges shall be chosen from among persons of high moral character, impartiality and integrity who possess the qualifications required in their respective States for appointment to the highest judicial offices.

(b) Every candidate for election to the Court shall:

(i) Have established competence in criminal law and procedure, and the necessary relevant experience, whether as judge, prosecutor, advocate or in other similar capacity, in criminal proceedings; or

(ii) Have established competence in relevant areas of international law such as international humanitarian law and the law of human rights, and extensive experience in a professional legal capacity which is of relevance to the judicial work of the Court;

(c) Every candidate for election to the Court shall have an excellent knowledge of and be fluent in at least one of the working languages of the Court.

4. (a) Nominations of candidates for election to the Court may be made by any State Party to this Statute, and shall be made either:

(i) By the procedure for the nomination of candidates for appointment to the highest judicial offices in the State in question; or

(ii) By the procedure provided for the nomination of candidates for the International Court of Justice in the Statute of that Court.

Nominations shall be accompanied by a statement in the necessary detail specifying how the candidate fulfils the requirements of paragraph 3.

(b) Each State Party may put forward one candidate for any given election who need not necessarily be a national of that State Party but shall in any case be a national of a State Party.

(c) The Assembly of States Parties may decide to establish, if appropriate, an Advisory Committee on nominations. In that event, the Committee's composition and mandate shall be established by the Assembly of States Parties.

5. For the purposes of the election, there shall be two lists of candidates:

List A containing the names of candidates with the qualifications specified in paragraph 3 (b) (i); and

List B containing the names of candidates with the qualifications specified in paragraph 3 (b) (ii).

A candidate with sufficient qualifications for both lists may choose on which list to appear. At the first election to the Court, at least nine judges shall be elected from list A and at least five judges from list B. Subsequent elections shall be so organized as to maintain the equivalent proportion on the Court of judges qualified on the two lists.

6. (a) The judges shall be elected by secret ballot at a meeting of the Assembly of States Parties convened for that purpose under article 112. Subject to paragraph 7, the persons elected to the Court shall be the 18 candidates who obtain the highest number of votes and a two-thirds majority of the States Parties present and voting.

(b) In the event that a sufficient number of judges is not elected on the first ballot, successive ballots shall be held in accordance with the procedures laid down in subparagraph (a) until the remaining places have been filled.

7. No two judges may be nationals of the same State. A person who, for the purposes of membership in the Court, could be regarded as a national of more than one State shall be deemed to be a national of the State in which that person ordinarily exercises civil and political rights.

8. (a) The States Parties shall, in the selection of judges, take into account the need, within the membership of the Court, for:

(i) The representation of the principal legal systems of the world;

(ii) Equitable geographical representation; and

(iii) A fair representation of female and male judges.

(b) States Parties shall also take into account the need to include judges with legal expertise on specific issues, including, but not limited to, violence against women or children.

9. (a) Subject to subparagraph (b), judges shall hold office for a term of nine years and, subject to subparagraph (c) and to article 37, paragraph 2, shall not be eligible for re-election.

(b) At the first election, one third of the judges elected shall be selected by lot to serve for a term of three years; one third of the judges elected shall be selected by lot to serve for a term of six years; and the remainder shall serve for a term of nine years.

(c) A judge who is selected to serve for a term of three years under sub-paragraph (b) shall be eligible for re-election for a full term.

10. Notwithstanding paragraph 9, a judge assigned to a Trial or Appeals Chamber in accordance with article 39 shall continue in office to complete any trial or appeal the hearing of which has already commenced before that Chamber.

Article 37 — Judicial vacancies

1. In the event of a vacancy, an election shall be held in accordance with article 36 to fill the vacancy.

2. A judge elected to fill a vacancy shall serve for the remainder of the predecessor's term and, if that period is three years or less, shall be eligible for re-election for a full term under article 36.

Article 38 — The Presidency

1. The President and the First and Second Vice-Presidents shall be elected by an absolute majority of the judges. They shall each serve for a term of three years or until the end of their respective terms of office as judges, whichever expires earlier. They shall be eligible for re-election once.

2. The First Vice-President shall act in place of the President in the event that the President is unavailable or disqualified. The Second Vice-President shall act in place of the President in the event that both the President and the First Vice-President are unavailable or disqualified.

3. The President, together with the First and Second Vice-Presidents, shall constitute the Presidency, which shall be responsible for:

(a) The proper administration of the Court, with the exception of the Office of the Prosecutor; and

(b) The other functions conferred upon it in accordance with this Statute.

4. In discharging its responsibility under paragraph 3 (a), the Presidency shall coordinate with and seek the concurrence of the Prosecutor on all matters of mutual concern.

Article 39 — Chambers

1. As soon as possible after the election of the judges, the Court shall organize itself into the divisions specified in article 34, paragraph (b). The Appeals Division shall be composed of the President and four other judges, the Trial Division of not less than six judges and the Pre-Trial Division of not less than six judges. The assignment of judges to divisions shall be based on the nature of the functions to be performed by each division and the qualifications and experience of the judges elected to the Court, in such a way that each division shall contain an appropriate combination of expertise in criminal law and procedure and in international law. The Trial and Pre-Trial Divisions shall be composed predominantly of judges with criminal trial experience.

2. (a) The judicial functions of the Court shall be carried out in each division by Chambers.

(b) (i) The Appeals Chamber shall be composed of all the judges of the Appeals Division;

(ii) The functions of the Trial Chamber shall be carried out by three judges of the Trial Division;

(iii) The functions of the Pre-Trial Chamber shall be carried out either by three judges of the Pre-Trial Division or by a single judge of that division in accordance with this Statute and the Rules of Procedure and Evidence;

(c) Nothing in this paragraph shall preclude the simultaneous constitution of more than one Trial Chamber or Pre-Trial Chamber when the efficient management of the Court's workload so requires.

3. (a) Judges assigned to the Trial and Pre-Trial Divisions shall serve in those divisions for a period of three years, and thereafter until the completion of any case the hearing of which has already commenced in the division concerned.

(b) Judges assigned to the Appeals Division shall serve in that division for their entire term of office.

4. Judges assigned to the Appeals Division shall serve only in that division. Nothing in this article shall, however, preclude the temporary attachment of judges from the Trial Division to the Pre-Trial Division or vice versa, if the Presidency considers that the efficient management of the Court's workload so requires, provided that under no circumstances shall a judge who has participated in the pre-trial phase of a case be eligible to sit on the Trial Chamber hearing that case.

Article 40 — Independence of the judges

1. The judges shall be independent in the performance of their functions.

2. Judges shall not engage in any activity which is likely to interfere with their judicial functions or to affect confidence in their independence.

3. Judges required to serve on a full-time basis at the seat of the Court shall not engage in any other occupation of a professional nature.

4. Any question regarding the application of paragraphs 2 and 3 shall be decided by an absolute majority of the judges. Where any such question concerns an individual judge, that judge shall not take part in the decision.

Article 41 — Excusing and disqualification of judges

1. The Presidency may, at the request of a judge, excuse that judge from the exercise of a function under this Statute, in accordance with the Rules of Procedure and Evidence.

2. (a) A judge shall not participate in any case in which his or her impartiality might reasonably be doubted on any ground. A judge shall be

disqualified from a case in accordance with this paragraph if, inter alia, that judge has previously been involved in any capacity in that case before the Court or in a related criminal case at the national level involving the person being investigated or prosecuted. A judge shall also be disqualified on such other grounds as may be provided for in the Rules of Procedure and Evidence.

(b) The Prosecutor or the person being investigated or prosecuted may request the disqualification of a judge under this paragraph.

(c) Any question as to the disqualification of a judge shall be decided by an absolute majority of the judges. The challenged judge shall be entitled to present his or her comments on the matter, but shall not take part in the decision.

Article 42 — The Office of the Prosecutor

1. The Office of the Prosecutor shall act independently as a separate organ of the Court. It shall be responsible for receiving referrals and any substantiated information on crimes within the jurisdiction of the Court, for examining them and for conducting investigations and prosecutions before the Court. A member of the Office shall not seek or act on instructions from any external source.

2. The Office shall be headed by the Prosecutor. The Prosecutor shall have full authority over the management and administration of the Office, including the staff, facilities and other resources thereof. The Prosecutor shall be assisted by one or more Deputy Prosecutors, who shall be entitled to carry out any of the acts required of the Prosecutor under this Statute. The Prosecutor and the Deputy Prosecutors shall be of different nationalities. They shall serve on a full-time basis.

3. The Prosecutor and the Deputy Prosecutors shall be persons of high moral character, be highly competent in and have extensive practical experience in the prosecution or trial of criminal cases. They shall have an excellent knowledge of and be fluent in at least one of the working languages of the Court.

4. The Prosecutor shall be elected by secret ballot by an absolute majority of the members of the Assembly of States Parties. The Deputy Prosecutors shall be elected in the same way from a list of candidates provided by the Prosecutor. The Prosecutor shall nominate three candidates for each position of Deputy Prosecutor to be filled. Unless a shorter term is decided upon at the time of their election, the Prosecutor and the Deputy Prosecutors shall hold office for a term of nine years and shall not be eligible for re-election.

5. Neither the Prosecutor nor a Deputy Prosecutor shall engage in any activity which is likely to interfere with his or her prosecutorial functions or to affect confidence in his or her independence. They shall not engage in any other occupation of a professional nature.

6. The Presidency may excuse the Prosecutor or a Deputy Prosecutor, at his or her request, from acting in a particular case.

7. Neither the Prosecutor nor a Deputy Prosecutor shall participate in any matter in which their impartiality might reasonably be doubted on any ground. They shall be disqualified from a case in accordance with this paragraph if, inter alia, they have previously been involved in any capacity in that case before the Court or in a related criminal case at the national level involving the person being investigated or prosecuted.

8. Any question as to the disqualification of the Prosecutor or a Deputy Prosecutor shall be decided by the Appeals Chamber.

(a) The person being investigated or prosecuted may at any time request the disqualification of the Prosecutor or a Deputy Prosecutor on the grounds set out in this article;

(b) The Prosecutor or the Deputy Prosecutor, as appropriate, shall be entitled to present his or her comments on the matter.

9. The Prosecutor shall appoint advisers with legal expertise on specific issues, including, but not limited to, sexual and gender violence and violence against children.

Article 43 — The Registry

1. The Registry shall be responsible for the non-judicial aspects of the administration and servicing of the Court, without prejudice to the functions and powers of the Prosecutor in accordance with article 42.

2. The Registry shall be headed by the Registrar, who shall be the principal administrative officer of the Court. The Registrar shall exercise his or her functions under the authority of the President of the Court.

3. The Registrar and the Deputy Registrar shall be persons of high moral character, be highly competent and have an excellent knowledge of and be fluent in at least one of the working languages of the Court.

4. The judges shall elect the Registrar by an absolute majority by secret ballot, taking into account any recommendation by the Assembly of States Parties. If the need arises and upon the recommendation of the Registrar, the judges shall elect, in the same manner, a Deputy Registrar.

5. The Registrar shall hold office for a term of five years, shall be eligible for re-election once and shall serve on a full-time basis. The Deputy Registrar shall hold office for a term of five years or such shorter term as may be decided upon by an absolute majority of the judges, and may be elected on the basis that the Deputy Registrar shall be called upon to serve as required.

6. The Registrar shall set up a Victims and Witnesses Unit within the Registry. This Unit shall provide, in consultation with the Office of the Prosecutor, protective measures and security arrangements, counselling and other appropriate assistance for witnesses, victims who appear before the Court and others who are at risk on account of testimony given by such witnesses. The Unit shall include staff with expertise in trauma, including trauma related to crimes of sexual violence.

Article 44 — Staff

1. The Prosecutor and the Registrar shall appoint such qualified staff as may be required to their respective offices. In the case of the Prosecutor, this shall include the appointment of investigators.

2. In the employment of staff, the Prosecutor and the Registrar shall ensure the highest standards of efficiency, competency and integrity, and shall have regard, mutatis mutandis, to the criteria set forth in article 36, paragraph 8.

3. The Registrar, with the agreement of the Presidency and the Prosecutor, shall propose Staff Regulations which include the terms and conditions upon which the staff of the Court shall be appointed, remunerated and dismissed. The Staff Regulations shall be approved by the Assembly of States Parties.

4. The Court may, in exceptional circumstances, employ the expertise of gratis personnel offered by States Parties, intergovernmental organizations or non-governmental organizations to assist with the work of any of the organs of the Court. The Prosecutor may accept any such offer on behalf of the Office of the Prosecutor. Such gratis personnel shall be employed in accordance with guidelines to be established by the Assembly of States Parties.

Article 45 — Solemn undertaking

Before taking up their respective duties under this Statute, the judges, the Prosecutor, the Deputy Prosecutors, the Registrar and the Deputy Registrar shall each make a solemn undertaking in open court to exercise his or her respective functions impartially and conscientiously.

Article 46 — Removal from office

1. A judge, the Prosecutor, a Deputy Prosecutor, the Registrar or the Deputy Registrar shall be removed from office if a decision to this effect is made in accordance with paragraph 2, in cases where that person:

(a) Is found to have committed serious misconduct or a serious breach of his or her duties under this Statute, as provided for in the Rules of Procedure and Evidence; or

(b) Is unable to exercise the functions required by this Statute.

2. A decision as to the removal from office of a judge, the Prosecutor or a Deputy Prosecutor under paragraph 1 shall be made by the Assembly of States Parties, by secret ballot:

(a) In the case of a judge, by a two-thirds majority of the States Parties upon a recommendation adopted by a two-thirds majority of the other judges;

(b) In the case of the Prosecutor, by an absolute majority of the States Parties;

(c) In the case of a Deputy Prosecutor, by an absolute majority of the States Parties upon the recommendation of the Prosecutor.

3. A decision as to the removal from office of the Registrar or Deputy Registrar shall be made by an absolute majority of the judges.

4. A judge, Prosecutor, Deputy Prosecutor, Registrar or Deputy Registrar whose conduct or ability to exercise the functions of the office as required by this Statute is challenged under this article shall have full opportunity to present and receive evidence and to make submissions in accordance with the Rules of Procedure and Evidence. The person in question shall not otherwise participate in the consideration of the matter.

Article 47 — Disciplinary measures

A judge, Prosecutor, Deputy Prosecutor, Registrar or Deputy Registrar who has committed misconduct of a less serious nature than that set out in article 46, paragraph 1, shall be subject to disciplinary measures, in accordance with the Rules of Procedure and Evidence.

Article 48 — Privileges and immunities

1. The Court shall enjoy in the territory of each State Party such privileges and immunities as are necessary for the fulfilment of its purposes.

2. The judges, the Prosecutor, the Deputy Prosecutors and the Registrar shall, when engaged on or with respect to the business of the Court, enjoy the same privileges and immunities as are accorded to heads of diplomatic missions and shall, after the expiry of their terms of office, continue to be accorded immunity from legal process of every kind in respect of words spoken or written and acts performed by them in their official capacity.

3. The Deputy Registrar, the staff of the Office of the Prosecutor and the staff of the Registry shall enjoy the privileges and immunities and facilities necessary for the performance of their functions, in accordance with the agreement on the privileges and immunities of the Court.

4. Counsel, experts, witnesses or any other person required to be present at the seat of the Court shall be accorded such treatment as is necessary for the proper functioning of the Court, in accordance with the agreement on the privileges and immunities of the Court.

5. The privileges and immunities of:

(a) A judge or the Prosecutor may be waived by an absolute majority of the judges;

(b) The Registrar may be waived by the Presidency;

(c) The Deputy Prosecutors and staff of the Office of the Prosecutor may be waived by the Prosecutor;

(d) The Deputy Registrar and staff of the Registry may be waived by the Registrar.

Article 49 — Salaries, allowances and expenses

The judges, the Prosecutor, the Deputy Prosecutors, the Registrar and the Deputy Registrar shall receive such salaries, allowances and expenses as may be decided upon by the Assembly of States Parties. These salaries and allowances shall not be reduced during their terms of office.

Article 50 — Official and working languages

1. The official languages of the Court shall be Arabic, Chinese, English, French, Russian and Spanish. The judgements of the Court, as well as other decisions resolving fundamental issues before the Court, shall be published in the official languages. The Presidency shall, in accordance with the criteria established by the Rules of Procedure and Evidence, determine which decisions may be considered as resolving fundamental issues for the purposes of this paragraph.

2. The working languages of the Court shall be English and French. The Rules of Procedure and Evidence shall determine the cases in which other official languages may be used as working languages.

3. At the request of any party to a proceeding or a State allowed to intervene in a proceeding, the Court shall authorize a language other than English or French to be used by such a party or State, provided that the Court considers such authorization to be adequately justified.

Article 51 — Rules of Procedure and Evidence

1. The Rules of Procedure and Evidence shall enter into force upon adoption by a two — thirds majority of the members of the Assembly of States Parties.

2. Amendments to the Rules of Procedure and Evidence may be proposed by:

(a) Any State Party;

(b) The judges acting by an absolute majority; or

(c) The Prosecutor.

Such amendments shall enter into force upon adoption by a two-thirds majority of the members of the Assembly of States Parties.

3. After the adoption of the Rules of Procedure and Evidence, in urgent cases where the Rules do not provide for a specific situation before the Court, the judges may, by a two — thirds majority, draw up provisional Rules to be applied until adopted, amended or rejected at the next ordinary or special session of the Assembly of States Parties.

4. The Rules of Procedure and Evidence, amendments thereto and any provisional Rule shall be consistent with this Statute. Amendments to the Rules of Procedure and Evidence as well as provisional Rules shall not be applied retroactively to the detriment of the person who is being investigated or prosecuted or who has been convicted.

5. In the event of conflict between the Statute and the Rules of Procedure and Evidence, the Statute shall prevail.

Article 52 — Regulations of the Court

1. The judges shall, in accordance with this Statute and the Rules of Procedure and Evidence, adopt, by an absolute majority, the Regulations of the Court necessary for its routine functioning.

2. The Prosecutor and the Registrar shall be consulted in the elaboration of the Regulations and any amendments thereto.

3. The Regulations and any amendments thereto shall take effect upon adoption unless otherwise decided by the judges. Immediately upon adoption, they shall be circulated to States Parties for comments. If within six months there are no objections from a majority of States Parties, they shall remain in force.

PART 5. INVESTIGATION AND PROSECUTION

Article 53 — Initiation of an investigation

1. The Prosecutor shall, having evaluated the information made available to him or her, initiate an investigation unless he or she determines that there is no reasonable basis to proceed under this Statute. In deciding whether to initiate an investigation, the Prosecutor shall consider whether:

(a) The information available to the Prosecutor provides a reasonable basis to believe that a crime within the jurisdiction of the Court has been or is being committed;

(b) The case is or would be admissible under article 17; and

(c) Taking into account the gravity of the crime and the interests of victims, there are nonetheless substantial reasons to believe that an investigation would not serve the interests of justice.

If the Prosecutor determines that there is no reasonable basis to proceed and his or her determination is based solely on subparagraph (c) above, he or she shall inform the Pre-Trial Chamber.

2. If, upon investigation, the Prosecutor concludes that there is not a sufficient basis for a prosecution because:

(a) There is not a sufficient legal or factual basis to seek a warrant or summons under article 58;

(b) The case is inadmissible under article 17; or

(c) A prosecution is not in the interests of justice, taking into account all the circumstances, including the gravity of the crime, the interests of victims and the age or infirmity of the alleged perpetrator, and his or her role in the alleged crime;

The Prosecutor shall inform the Pre-Trial Chamber and the State making a referral under article 14 or the Security Council in a case under article 13, paragraph (b), of his or her conclusion and the reasons for the conclusion.

3. (a) At the request of the State making a referral under article 14 or the Security Council under article 13, paragraph (b), the Pre-Trial Chamber may review a decision of the Prosecutor under paragraph 1 or 2 not to proceed and may request the Prosecutor to reconsider that decision.

(b) In addition, the Pre-Trial Chamber may, on its own initiative, review a decision of the Prosecutor not to proceed if it is based solely on paragraph 1 (c) or 2 (c). In such a case, the decision of the Prosecutor shall be effective only if confirmed by the Pre-Trial Chamber.

4. The Prosecutor may, at any time, reconsider a decision whether to initiate an investigation or prosecution based on new facts or information.

Article 54 — Duties and powers of the Prosecutor with respect to investigations

1. The Prosecutor shall:

(a) In order to establish the truth, extend the investigation to cover all facts and evidence relevant to an assessment of whether there is criminal responsibility under this Statute, and, in doing so, investigate incriminating and exonerating circumstances equally;

(b) Take appropriate measures to ensure the effective investigation and prosecution of crimes within the jurisdiction of the Court, and in doing so, respect the interests and personal circumstances of victims and witnesses, including age, gender as defined in article 7, paragraph 3, and health, and take into account the nature of the crime, in particular where it involves sexual violence, gender violence or violence against children; and

(c) Fully respect the rights of persons arising under this Statute.

2. The Prosecutor may conduct investigations on the territory of a State:

(a) In accordance with the provisions of Part 9; or

(b) As authorized by the Pre-Trial Chamber under article 57, paragraph 3 (d).

3. The Prosecutor may:

(a) Collect and examine evidence;

(b) Request the presence of and question persons being investigated, victims and witnesses;

(c) Seek the cooperation of any State or intergovernmental organization or arrangement in accordance with its respective competence and/or mandate;

(d) Enter into such arrangements or agreements, not inconsistent with this Statute, as may be necessary to facilitate the cooperation of a State, intergovernmental organization or person;

(e) Agree not to disclose, at any stage of the proceedings, documents or information that the Prosecutor obtains on the condition of confidentiality and solely for the purpose of generating new evidence, unless the provider of the information consents; and Agree not to disclose, at any stage of the proceedings, documents or information that the Prosecutor obtains on the condition of confidentiality and solely for the purpose of generating new evidence, unless the provider of the information consents; and

(f) Take necessary measures, or request that necessary measures be taken, to ensure the confidentiality of information, the protection of any person or the preservation of evidence.

Article 55 — Rights of persons during an investigation

1. In respect of an investigation under this Statute, a person:

(a) Shall not be compelled to incriminate himself or herself or to confess guilt;

(b) Shall not be subjected to any form of coercion, duress or threat, to torture or to any other form of cruel, inhuman or degrading treatment or punishment; and

(c) Shall, if questioned in a language other than a language the person fully understands and speaks, have, free of any cost, the assistance of a competent interpreter and such translations as are necessary to meet the requirements of fairness;

(d) Shall not be subjected to arbitrary arrest or detention; and shall not be deprived of his or her liberty except on such grounds and in accordance with such procedures as are established in the Statute.

2. Where there are grounds to believe that a person has committed a crime within the jurisdiction of the Court and that person is about to be questioned either by the Prosecutor, or by national authorities pursuant to a request made under Part 9 of this Statute, that person shall also have the following rights of which he or she shall be informed prior to being questioned:

(a) To be informed, prior to being questioned, that there are grounds to believe that he or she has committed a crime within the jurisdiction of the Court;

(b) To remain silent, without such silence being a consideration in the determination of guilt or innocence;

(c) To have legal assistance of the person's choosing, or, if the person does not have legal assistance, to have legal assistance assigned to him or her, in any case where the interests of justice so require, and without payment by the person in any such case if the person does not have sufficient means to pay for it;

(d) To be questioned in the presence of counsel unless the person has voluntarily waived his or her right to counsel.

Article 56 — Role of the Pre-Trial Chamber in relation to a unique investigative opportunity

1. (a) Where the Prosecutor considers an investigation to present a unique opportunity to take testimony or a statement from a witness or to examine, collect or test evidence, which may not be available subsequently for the purposes of a trial, the Prosecutor shall so inform the Pre-Trial Chamber.

(b) In that case, the Pre-Trial Chamber may, upon request of the Prosecutor, take such measures as may be necessary to ensure the efficiency and integrity of the proceedings and, in particular, to protect the rights of the defence.

(c) Unless the Pre-Trial Chamber orders otherwise, the Prosecutor shall provide the relevant information to the person who has been arrested or appeared in response to a summons in connection with the investigation referred to in subparagraph (a), in order that he or she may be heard on the matter.

2. The measures referred to in paragraph 1 (b) may include:

(a) Making recommendations or orders regarding procedures to be followed;

(b) Directing that a record be made of the proceedings;

(c) Appointing an expert to assist;

(d) Authorizing counsel for a person who has been arrested, or appeared before the Court in response to a summons, to participate, or where there has not yet been such an arrest or appearance or counsel has not been designated, appointing another counsel to attend and represent the interests of the defence;

(e) Naming one of its members or, if necessary, another available judge of the Pre-Trial or Trial Division to observe and make recommendations or orders regarding the collection and preservation of evidence and the questioning of persons;

(f) Taking such other action as may be necessary to collect or preserve evidence.

3. (a) Where the Prosecutor has not sought measures pursuant to this article but the Pre-Trial Chamber considers that such measures are required to preserve evidence that it deems would be essential for the defence at trial, it shall consult with the Prosecutor as to whether there is good reason for the Prosecutor's failure to request the measures. If upon consultation, the

Pre-Trial Chamber concludes that the Prosecutor's failure to request such measures is unjustified, the Pre-Trial Chamber may take such measures on its own initiative.

(b) A decision of the Pre-Trial Chamber to act on its own initiative under this paragraph may be appealed by the Prosecutor. The appeal shall be heard on an expedited basis.

4. The admissibility of evidence preserved or collected for trial pursuant to this article, or the record thereof, shall be governed at trial by article 69, and given such weight as determined by the Trial Chamber.

Article 57 — Functions and powers of the Pre-Trial Chamber

1. Unless otherwise provided for in this Statute, the Pre-Trial Chamber shall exercise its functions in accordance with the provisions of this article.

2. (a) Orders or rulings of the Pre-Trial Chamber issued under articles 15, 18, 19, 54, paragraph 2, 61, paragraph 7, and 72 must be concurred in by a majority of its judges.

(b) In all other cases, a single judge of the Pre-Trial Chamber may exercise the functions provided for in this Statute, unless otherwise provided for in the Rules of Procedure and Evidence or by a majority of the Pre-Trial Chamber.

3. In addition to its other functions under this Statute, the Pre-Trial Chamber may:

(a) At the request of the Prosecutor, issue such orders and warrants as may be required for the purposes of an investigation;

(b) Upon the request of a person who has been arrested or has appeared pursuant to a summons under article 58, issue such orders, including measures such as those described in article 56, or seek such cooperation pursuant to Part 9 as may be necessary to assist the person in the preparation of his or her defence;

(c) Where necessary, provide for the protection and privacy of victims and witnesses, the preservation of evidence, the protection of persons who have been arrested or appeared in response to a summons, and the protection of national security information;

(d) Authorize the Prosecutor to take specific investigative steps within the territory of a State Party without having secured the cooperation of that State under Part 9 if, whenever possible having regard to the views of the State concerned, the Pre-Trial Chamber has determined in that case that the State is clearly unable to execute a request for cooperation due to the unavailability of any authority or any component of its judicial system competent to execute the request for cooperation under Part 9.

(e) Where a warrant of arrest or a summons has been issued under article 58, and having due regard to the strength of the evidence and the rights of the parties concerned, as provided for in this Statute and the Rules of Procedure and Evidence, seek the cooperation of States pursuant to article 93, paragraph 1 (j), to take protective measures for the purpose of forfeiture in particular for the ultimate benefit of victims.

Article 58 — Issuance by the Pre-Trial Chamber of a warrant of arrest or a summons to appear

1. At any time after the initiation of an investigation, the Pre-Trial Chamber shall, on the application of the Prosecutor, issue a warrant of arrest of a person if, having examined the application and the evidence or other information submitted by the Prosecutor, it is satisfied that:

(a) There are reasonable grounds to believe that the person has committed a crime within the jurisdiction of the Court; and

(b) The arrest of the person appears necessary:

(i) To ensure the person's appearance at trial,

(ii) To ensure that the person does not obstruct or endanger the investigation or the court proceedings, or

(iii) Where applicable, to prevent the person from continuing with the commission of that crime or a related crime which is within the jurisdiction of the Court and which arises out of the same circumstances.

2. The application of the Prosecutor shall contain:

(a) The name of the person and any other relevant identifying information;

(b) A specific reference to the crimes within the jurisdiction of the Court which the person is alleged to have committed;

(c) A concise statement of the facts which are alleged to constitute those crimes;

(d) A summary of the evidence and any other information which establish reasonable grounds to believe that the person committed those crimes; and

(e) The reason why the Prosecutor believes that the arrest of the person is necessary.

3. The warrant of arrest shall contain:

(a) The name of the person and any other relevant identifying information;

(b) A specific reference to the crimes within the jurisdiction of the Court for which the person's arrest is sought; and

(c) A concise statement of the facts which are alleged to constitute those crimes.

4. The warrant of arrest shall remain in effect until otherwise ordered by the Court.

5. On the basis of the warrant of arrest, the Court may request the provisional arrest or the arrest and surrender of the person under Part 9.

6. The Prosecutor may request the Pre-Trial Chamber to amend the warrant of arrest by modifying or adding to the crimes specified therein. The Pre-Trial Chamber shall so amend the warrant if it is satisfied that there are reasonable grounds to believe that the person committed the modified or additional crimes.

7. As an alternative to seeking a warrant of arrest, the Prosecutor may submit an application requesting that the Pre-Trial Chamber issue a summons for the person to appear. If the Pre-Trial Chamber is satisfied that there are reasonable grounds to believe that the person committed the crime alleged and that a summons is sufficient to ensure the person's appearance, it shall issue the summons, with or without conditions restricting liberty (other than detention) if provided for by national law, for the person to appear. The summons shall contain:

(a) The name of the person and any other relevant identifying information;

(b) The specified date on which the person is to appear;

(c) A specific reference to the crimes within the jurisdiction of the Court which the person is alleged to have committed; and

(d) A concise statement of the facts which are alleged to constitute the crime.

The summons shall be served on the person.

Article 59 — Arrest proceedings in the custodial State

1. A State Party which has received a request for provisional arrest or for arrest and surrender shall immediately take steps to arrest the person in question in accordance with its laws and the provisions of Part 9.

2. A person arrested shall be brought promptly before the competent judicial authority in the custodial State which shall determine, in accordance with the law of that State, that:

(a) The warrant applies to that person;

(b) The person has been arrested in accordance with the proper process; and

(c) The person's rights have been respected.

3. The person arrested shall have the right to apply to the competent authority in the custodial State for interim release pending surrender.

4. In reaching a decision on any such application, the competent authority in the custodial State shall consider whether, given the gravity of the alleged crimes, there are urgent and exceptional circumstances to justify interim release and whether

necessary safeguards exist to ensure that the custodial State can fulfil its duty to surrender the person to the Court. It shall not be open to the competent authority of the custodial State to consider whether the warrant of arrest was properly issued in accordance with article 58, paragraph 1 (a) and (b).

5. The Pre-Trial Chamber shall be notified of any request for interim release and shall make recommendations to the competent authority in the custodial State. The competent authority in the custodial State shall give full consideration to such recommendations, including any recommendations on measures to prevent the escape of the person, before rendering its decision.

6. If the person is granted interim release, the Pre-Trial Chamber may request periodic reports on the status of the interim release.

7. Once ordered to be surrendered by the custodial State, the person shall be delivered to the Court as soon as possible.

Article 60 — Initial proceedings before the Court

1. Upon the surrender of the person to the Court, or the person's appearance before the Court voluntarily or pursuant to a summons, the Pre-Trial Chamber shall satisfy itself that the person has been informed of the crimes which he or she is alleged to have committed, and of his or her rights under this Statute, including the right to apply for interim release pending trial.

2. A person subject to a warrant of arrest may apply for interim release pending trial. If the Pre-Trial Chamber is satisfied that the conditions set forth in article 58, paragraph 1, are met, the person shall continue to be detained. If it is not so satisfied, the Pre-Trial Chamber shall release the person, with or without conditions.

3. The Pre-Trial Chamber shall periodically review its ruling on the release or detention of the person, and may do so at any time on the request of the Prosecutor or the person. Upon such review, it may modify its ruling as to detention, release or conditions of release, if it is satisfied that changed circumstances so require.

4. The Pre-Trial Chamber shall ensure that a person is not detained for an unreasonable period prior to trial due to inexcusable delay by the Prosecutor. If such delay occurs, the Court shall consider releasing the person, with or without conditions.

5. If necessary, the Pre-Trial Chamber may issue a warrant of arrest to secure the presence of a person who has been released.

Article 61 — Confirmation of the charges before trial

1. Subject to the provisions of paragraph 2, within a reasonable time after the person's surrender or voluntary appearance before the Court, the Pre-Trial Chamber shall hold a hearing to confirm the charges on which the Prosecutor intends to seek trial. The hearing shall be held in the presence of the Prosecutor and the person charged, as well as his or her counsel.

2. The Pre-Trial Chamber may, upon request of the Prosecutor or on its own motion, hold a hearing in the absence of the person charged to confirm the charges on which the Prosecutor intends to seek trial when the person has:

(a) Waived his or her right to be present; or

(b) Fled or cannot be found and all reasonable steps have been taken to secure his or her appearance before the Court and to inform the person of the charges and that a hearing to confirm those charges will be held.

In that case, the person shall be represented by counsel where the Pre-Trial Chamber determines that it is in the interests of justice.

3. Within a reasonable time before the hearing, the person shall:

(a) Be provided with a copy of the document containing the charges on which the Prosecutor intends to bring the person to trial; and

(b) Be informed of the evidence on which the Prosecutor intends to rely at the hearing.

The Pre-Trial Chamber may issue orders regarding the disclosure of information for the purposes of the hearing.

4. Before the hearing, the Prosecutor may continue the investigation and may amend or withdraw any charges. The person shall be given reasonable notice before the hearing of any amendment to or withdrawal of charges. In case of a withdrawal of charges, the Prosecutor shall notify the Pre-Trial Chamber of the reasons for the withdrawal.

5. At the hearing, the Prosecutor shall support each charge with sufficient evidence to establish substantial grounds to believe that the person committed the crime charged. The Prosecutor may rely on documentary or summary evidence and need not call the witnesses expected to testify at the trial.

6. At the hearing, the person may:

(a) Object to the charges;

(b) Challenge the evidence presented by the Prosecutor; and

(c) Present evidence.

7. The Pre-Trial Chamber shall, on the basis of the hearing, determine whether there is sufficient evidence to establish substantial grounds to believe that the person committed each of the crimes charged. Based on its determination, the Pre-Trial Chamber shall:

(a) Confirm those charges in relation to which it has determined that there is sufficient evidence; and commit the person to a Trial Chamber for trial on the charges as confirmed;

(b) Decline to confirm those charges in relation to which it has determined that there is insufficient evidence;

(c) Adjourn the hearing and request the Prosecutor to consider:

(i) Providing further evidence or conducting further investigation with respect to a particular charge; or

(ii) Amending a charge because the evidence submitted appears to establish a different crime within the jurisdiction of the Court.

8. Where the Pre-Trial Chamber declines to confirm a charge, the Prosecutor shall not be precluded from subsequently requesting its confirmation if the request is supported by additional evidence.

9. After the charges are confirmed and before the trial has begun, the Prosecutor may, with the permission of the Pre-Trial Chamber and after notice to the accused, amend the charges. If the Prosecutor seeks to add additional charges or to substitute more serious charges, a hearing under this article to confirm those charges must be held. After commencement of the trial, the Prosecutor may, with the permission of the Trial Chamber, withdraw the charges.

10. Any warrant previously issued shall cease to have effect with respect to any charges which have not been confirmed by the Pre-Trial Chamber or which have been withdrawn by the Prosecutor.

11. Once the charges have been confirmed in accordance with this article, the Presidency shall constitute a Trial Chamber which, subject to paragraph 8 and to article 64, paragraph 4, shall be responsible for the conduct of subsequent proceedings and may exercise any function of the Pre-Trial Chamber that is relevant and capable of application in those proceedings.

PART 6. THE TRIAL

Article 62 — Place of trial

Unless otherwise decided, the place of the trial shall be the seat of the Court.

Article 63 — Trial in the presence of the accused

1. The accused shall be present during the trial.

2. If the accused, being present before the Court, continues to disrupt the trial, the Trial Chamber may remove the accused and shall make provision for him or her to observe the trial and instruct counsel from outside the courtroom, through the use of communications technology, if required. Such measures shall be taken only in exceptional circumstances after other reasonable alternatives have proved inadequate, and only for such duration as is strictly required.

Article 64 — Functions and powers of the Trial Chamber

1. The functions and powers of the Trial Chamber set out in this article shall be exercised in accordance with this Statute and the Rules of Procedure and Evidence.

2. The Trial Chamber shall ensure that a trial is fair and expeditious and is conducted with full respect for the rights of the accused and due regard for the protection of victims and witnesses.

3. Upon assignment of a case for trial in accordance with this Statute, the Trial Chamber assigned to deal with the case shall:

(a) Confer with the parties and adopt such procedures as are necessary to facilitate the fair and expeditious conduct of the proceedings;

(b) Determine the language or languages to be used at trial; and

(c) Subject to any other relevant provisions of this Statute, provide for disclosure of documents or information not previously disclosed, sufficiently in advance of the commencement of the trial to enable adequate preparation for trial.

4. The Trial Chamber may, if necessary for its effective and fair functioning, refer preliminary issues to the Pre-Trial Chamber or, if necessary, to another available judge of the Pre-Trial Division.

5. Upon notice to the parties, the Trial Chamber may, as appropriate, direct that there be joinder or severance in respect of charges against more than one accused.

6. In performing its functions prior to trial or during the course of a trial, the Trial Chamber may, as necessary:

(a) Exercise any functions of the Pre-Trial Chamber referred to in article 61, paragraph 11;

(b) Require the attendance and testimony of witnesses and production of documents and other evidence by obtaining, if necessary, the assistance of States as provided in this Statute;

(c) Provide for the protection of confidential information;

(d) Order the production of evidence in addition to that already collected prior to the trial or presented during the trial by the parties;

(e) Provide for the protection of the accused, witnesses and victims; and

(f) Rule on any other relevant matters.

7. The trial shall be held in public. The Trial Chamber may, however, determine that special circumstances require that certain proceedings be in closed session for the purposes set forth in article 68, or to protect confidential or sensitive information to be given in evidence.

8. (a) At the commencement of the trial, the Trial Chamber shall have read to the accused the charges previously confirmed by the Pre-Trial Chamber. The Trial Chamber shall satisfy itself that the accused understands the nature of the charges. It shall afford him or her the opportunity to make an admission of guilt in accordance with article 65 or to plead not guilty.

(b) At the trial, the presiding judge may give directions for the conduct of proceedings, including to ensure that they are conducted in a fair and impartial manner. Subject to any directions of the presiding judge, the parties may submit evidence in accordance with the provisions of this Statute.

9. The Trial Chamber shall have, inter alia, the power on application of a party or on its own motion to:

(a) Rule on the admissibility or relevance of evidence; and

(b) Take all necessary steps to maintain order in the course of a hearing.

10. The Trial Chamber shall ensure that a complete record of the trial, which accurately reflects the proceedings, is made and that it is maintained and preserved by the Registrar.

Article 65 — Proceedings on an admission of guilt

1. Where the accused makes an admission of guilt pursuant to article 64, paragraph 8 (a), the Trial Chamber shall determine whether:

(a) The accused understands the nature and consequences of the admission of guilt;

(b) The admission is voluntarily made by the accused after sufficient consultation with defence counsel; and

(c) The admission of guilt is supported by the facts of the case that are contained in:

(i) The charges brought by the Prosecutor and admitted by the accused;

(ii) Any materials presented by the Prosecutor which supplement the charges and which the accused accepts; and

(iii) Any other evidence, such as the testimony of witnesses, presented by the Prosecutor or the accused.

2. Where the Trial Chamber is satisfied that the matters referred to in paragraph 1 are established, it shall consider the admission of guilt, together with any additional evidence presented, as establishing all the essential facts that are required to prove the crime to which the admission of guilt relates, and may convict the accused of that crime.

3. Where the Trial Chamber is not satisfied that the matters referred to in paragraph 1 are established, it shall consider the admission of guilt as not having been made, in which case it shall order that the trial be continued under the ordinary trial procedures provided by this Statute and may remit the case to another Trial Chamber.

4. Where the Trial Chamber is of the opinion that a more complete presentation of the facts of the case is required in the interests of justice, in particular the interests of the victims, the Trial Chamber may:

(a) Request the Prosecutor to present additional evidence, including the testimony of witnesses; or

(b) Order that the trial be continued under the ordinary trial procedures provided by this Statute, in which case it shall consider the admission of guilt as not having been made and may remit the case to another Trial Chamber.

5. Any discussions between the Prosecutor and the defence regarding modification of the charges, the admission of guilt or the penalty to be imposed shall not be binding on the Court.

Article 66 — Presumption of innocence

1. Everyone shall be presumed innocent until proved guilty before the Court in accordance with the applicable law.

2. The onus is on the Prosecutor to prove the guilt of the accused.

3. In order to convict the accused, the Court must be convinced of the guilt of the accused beyond reasonable doubt.

Article 67 — Rights of the accused

1. In the determination of any charge, the accused shall be entitled to a public hearing, having regard to the provisions of this Statute, to a fair hearing conducted impartially, and to the following minimum guarantees, in full equality:

(a) To be informed promptly and in detail of the nature, cause and content of the charge, in a language which the accused fully understands and speaks;

(b) To have adequate time and facilities for the preparation of the defence and to communicate freely with counsel of the accused's choosing in confidence;

(c) To be tried without undue delay;

(d) Subject to article 63, paragraph 2, to be present at the trial, to conduct the defence in person or through legal assistance of the accused's choosing, to be informed, if the accused does not have legal assistance, of this right and to have legal assistance assigned by the Court in any case where the interests of justice so require, and without payment if the accused lacks sufficient means to pay for it;

(e) To examine, or have examined, the witnesses against him or her and to obtain the attendance and examination of witnesses on his or her behalf under the same conditions as witnesses against him or her. The accused shall also be entitled to raise defences and to present other evidence admissible under this Statute;

(f) To have, free of any cost, the assistance of a competent interpreter and such translations as are necessary to meet the requirements of fairness, if any of the proceedings of or documents presented to the Court are not in a language which the accused fully understands and speaks;

(g) Not to be compelled to testify or to confess guilt and to remain silent, without such silence being a consideration in the determination of guilt or innocence;

(h) To make an unsworn oral or written statement in his or her defence; and

(i) Not to have imposed on him or her any reversal of the burden of proof or any onus of rebuttal.

2. In addition to any other disclosure provided for in this Statute, the Prosecutor shall, as soon as practicable, disclose to the defence evidence in the Prosecutor's possession or control which he or she believes shows or tends to show the innocence of the accused, or to mitigate the guilt of the accused, or which may affect the credibility of prosecution evidence. In case of doubt as to the application of this paragraph, the Court shall decide.

Article 68 — Protection of the victims and witnesses and their participation in the proceedings

1. The Court shall take appropriate measures to protect the safety, physical and psychological well-being, dignity and privacy of victims and witnesses. In so doing, the Court shall have regard to all relevant factors, including age, gender as defined in article 2, paragraph 3, and health, and the nature of the crime, in particular, but not limited to, where the crime involves sexual or gender violence or violence against children. The Prosecutor shall take such measures particularly during the investigation and prosecution of such crimes. These measures shall not be prejudicial to or inconsistent with the rights of the accused and a fair and impartial trial.

2. As an exception to the principle of public hearings provided for in article 67, the Chambers of the Court may, to protect victims and witnesses or an accused, conduct any part of the proceedings in camera or allow the presentation of evidence by electronic or other special means. In particular, such measures shall be implemented in the case of a victim of sexual violence or a child who is a victim or a witness, unless otherwise ordered by the Court, having regard to all the circumstances, particularly the views of the victim or witness.

3. Where the personal interests of the victims are affected, the Court shall permit their views and concerns to be presented and considered at stages of the proceedings determined to be appropriate by the Court and in a manner which is not prejudicial to or inconsistent with the rights of the accused and a fair and impartial trial. Such views and concerns may be presented by the legal representatives of the victims where the Court considers it appropriate, in accordance with the Rules of Procedure and Evidence.

4. The Victims and Witnesses Unit may advise the Prosecutor and the Court on appropriate protective measures, security arrangements, counselling and assistance as referred to in article 43, paragraph 6.

5. Where the disclosure of evidence or information pursuant to this Statute may lead to the grave endangerment of the security of a witness or his or her family, the Prosecutor may, for the purposes of any proceedings conducted prior to the commencement of the trial, withhold such evidence or information and instead submit a summary thereof. Such measures shall be exercised in a manner which is not prejudicial to or inconsistent with the rights of the accused and a fair and impartial trial.

6. A State may make an application for necessary measures to be taken in respect of the protection of its servants or agents and the protection of confidential or sensitive information.

Article 69 — Evidence

1. Before testifying, each witness shall, in accordance with the Rules of Procedure and Evidence, give an undertaking as to the truthfulness of the evidence to be given by that witness.

2. The testimony of a witness at trial shall be given in person, except to the extent provided by the measures set forth in article 68 or in the Rules of Procedure and Evidence. The Court may also permit the giving of viva voce (oral) or recorded testimony of a witness by means of video or audio technology, as well as the introduction of documents or written transcripts, subject to this Statute and in accordance with the Rules of Procedure and Evidence. These measures shall not be prejudicial to or inconsistent with the rights of the accused.

3. The parties may submit evidence relevant to the case, in accordance with article 64. The Court shall have the authority to request the submission of all evidence that it considers necessary for the determination of the truth.

4. The Court may rule on the relevance or admissibility of any evidence, taking into account, inter alia, the probative value of the evidence and any prejudice that such evidence may cause to a fair trial or to a fair evaluation of the testimony of a witness, in accordance with the Rules of Procedure and Evidence.

5. The Court shall respect and observe privileges on confidentiality as provided for in the Rules of Procedure and Evidence.

6. The Court shall not require proof of facts of common knowledge but may take judicial notice of them.

7. Evidence obtained by means of a violation of this Statute or internationally recognized human rights shall not be admissible if:

(a) The violation casts substantial doubt on the reliability of the evidence; or

(b) The admission of the evidence would be antithetical to and would seriously damage the integrity of the proceedings.

8. When deciding on the relevance or admissibility of evidence collected by a State, the Court shall not rule on the application of the State's national law.

Article 70 — Offences against the administration of justice

1. The Court shall have jurisdiction over the following offences against its administration of justice when committed intentionally:

(a) Giving false testimony when under an obligation pursuant to article 69, paragraph 1, to tell the truth;

(b) Presenting evidence that the party knows is false or forged;

(c) Corruptly influencing a witness, obstructing or interfering with the attendance or testimony of a witness, retaliating against a witness for giving testimony or destroying, tampering with or interfering with the collection of evidence;

(d) Impeding, intimidating or corruptly influencing an official of the Court for the purpose of forcing or persuading the official not to perform, or to perform improperly, his or her duties;

(e) Retaliating against an official of the Court on account of duties performed by that or another official;

(f) Soliciting or accepting a bribe as an official of the Court in conjunction with his or her official duties.

2. The principles and procedures governing the Court's exercise of jurisdiction over offences under this article shall be those provided for in the Rules of Procedure and Evidence. The conditions for providing international cooperation to the Court with respect to its proceedings under this article shall be governed by the domestic laws of the requested State.

3. In the event of conviction, the Court may impose a term of imprisonment not exceeding five years, or a fine in accordance with the Rules of Procedure and Evidence, or both.

4. (a) Each State Party shall extend its criminal laws penalizing offences against the integrity of its own investigative or judicial process to offences against the administration of justice referred to in this article, committed on its territory, or by one of its nationals;

(b) Upon request by the Court, whenever it deems it proper, the State Party shall submit the case to its competent authorities for the purpose of prosecution. Those authorities shall treat such cases with diligence and devote sufficient resources to enable them to be conducted effectively.

Article 71 — Sanctions for misconduct before the Court

1. The Court may sanction persons present before it who commit misconduct, including disruption of its proceedings or deliberate refusal to comply with its directions, by administrative measures other than imprisonment, such as temporary or permanent removal from the courtroom, a fine or other similar measures provided for in the Rules of Procedure and Evidence.

2. The procedures governing the imposition of the measures set forth in paragraph 1 shall be those provided for in the Rules of Procedure and Evidence.

Article 72 — Protection of national security information

1. This article applies in any case where the disclosure of the information or documents of a State would, in the opinion of that State, prejudice its national security interests. Such cases include those falling within the scope of article 56, paragraphs 2 and 3, article 61, paragraph 3, article 64, paragraph 3, article 67, paragraph 2, article

68, paragraph 6, article 87, paragraph 6 and article 93, as well as cases arising at any other stage of the proceedings where such disclosure may be at issue.

2. This article shall also apply when a person who has been requested to give information or evidence has refused to do so or has referred the matter to the State on the ground that disclosure would prejudice the national security interests of a State and the State concerned confirms that it is of the opinion that disclosure would prejudice its national security interests.

3. Nothing in this article shall prejudice the requirements of confidentiality applicable under article 54, paragraph 3 (e) and (f), or the application of article 73.

4. If a State learns that information or documents of the State are being, or are likely to be, disclosed at any stage of the proceedings, and it is of the opinion that disclosure would prejudice its national security interests, that State shall have the right to intervene in order to obtain resolution of the issue in accordance with this article.

5. If, in the opinion of a State, disclosure of information would prejudice its national security interests, all reasonable steps will be taken by the State, acting in conjunction with the Prosecutor, the Defence or the Pre-Trial Chamber or Trial Chamber, as the case may be, to seek to resolve the matter by cooperative means. Such steps may include:

(a) Modification or clarification of the request;

(b) A determination by the Court regarding the relevance of the information or evidence sought, or a determination as to whether the evidence, though relevant, could be or has been obtained from a source other than the requested State;

(c) Obtaining the information or evidence from a different source or in a different form; or

(d) Agreement on conditions under which the assistance could be provided including, among other things, providing summaries or redactions, limitations on disclosure, use of in camera or ex parte proceedings, or other protective measures permissible under the Statute and the Rules.

6. Once all reasonable steps have been taken to resolve the matter through cooperative means, and if the State considers that there are no means or conditions under which the information or documents could be provided or disclosed without prejudice to its national security interests, it shall so notify the Prosecutor or the Court of the specific reasons for its decision, unless a specific description of the reasons would itself necessarily result in such prejudice to the State's national security interests.

7. Thereafter, if the Court determines that the evidence is relevant and necessary for the establishment of the guilt or innocence of the accused, the Court may undertake the following actions:

(a) Where disclosure of the information or document is sought pursuant to a request for cooperation under Part 9 or the circumstances described in paragraph 2, and the State has invoked the ground for refusal referred to in article 93, paragraph 4:

(i) The Court may, before making any conclusion referred to in subparagraph 7 (a) (ii), request further consultations for the purpose of considering the State's representations, which may include, as appropriate, hearings in camera and ex parte;

(ii) If the Court concludes that, by invoking the ground for refusal under article 93, paragraph 4, in the circumstances of the case, the requested State is not acting in accordance with its obligations under the Statute, the Court may refer the matter in accordance with article 87, paragraph 7, specifying the reasons for its conclusion; and

(iii) The Court may make such inference in the trial of the accused as to the existence or non-existence of a fact, as may be appropriate in the circumstances; or

(b) In all other circumstances:

(i) Order disclosure; or

(ii) To the extent it does not order disclosure, make such inference in the trial of the accused as to the existence or non-existence of a fact, as may be appropriate in the circumstances.

Article 73 — Third-party information or documents

If a State Party is requested by the Court to provide a document or information in its custody, possession or control, which was disclosed to it in confidence by a State, intergovernmental organization or international organization, it shall seek the consent of the originator to disclose that document or information. If the originator is a State Party, it shall either consent to disclosure of the information or document or undertake to resolve the issue of disclosure with the Court, subject to the provisions of article 72. If the originator is not a State Party and refuses consent to disclosure, the requested State shall inform the Court that it is unable to provide the document or information because of a pre-existing obligation of confidentiality to the originator.

Article 74 — Requirements for the decision

1. All the judges of the Trial Chamber shall be present at each stage of the trial and throughout their deliberations. The Presidency may, on a case-by-case basis, designate, as available, one or more alternate judges to be present at each stage of the trial and to replace a member of the Trial Chamber if that member is unable to continue attending.

2. The Trial Chamber's decision shall be based on its evaluation of the evidence and the entire proceedings. The decision shall not exceed the facts and circumstances

described in the charges and any amendments to the charges. The Court may base its decision only on evidence submitted and discussed before it at the trial.

3. The judges shall attempt to achieve unanimity in their decision, failing which the decision shall be taken by a majority of the judges.

4. The deliberations of the Trial Chamber shall remain secret.

5. The decision shall be in writing and shall contain a full and reasoned statement of the Trial Chamber's findings on the evidence and conclusions. The Trial Chamber shall issue one decision. When there is no unanimity, the Trial Chamber's decision shall contain the views of the majority and the minority. The decision or a summary thereof shall be delivered in open court.

Article 75 — Reparations to victims

1. The Court shall establish principles relating to reparations to, or in respect of, victims, including restitution, compensation and rehabilitation. On this basis, in its decision the Court may, either upon request or on its own motion in exceptional circumstances, determine the scope and extent of any damage, loss and injury to, or in respect of, victims and will state the principles on which it is acting.

2. The Court may make an order directly against a convicted person specifying appropriate reparations to, or in respect of, victims, including restitution, compensation and rehabilitation. Where appropriate, the Court may order that the award for reparations be made through the Trust Fund provided for in article 79.

3. Before making an order under this article, the Court may invite and shall take account of representations from or on behalf of the convicted person, victims, other interested persons or interested States.

4. In exercising its power under this article, the Court may, after a person is convicted of a crime within the jurisdiction of the Court, determine whether, in order to give effect to an order which it may make under this article, it is necessary to seek measures under article 93, paragraph 1.

5. A State Party shall give effect to a decision under this article as if the provisions of article 109 were applicable to this article.

6. Nothing in this article shall be interpreted as prejudicing the rights of victims under national or international law.

Article 76 — Sentencing

1. In the event of a conviction, the Trial Chamber shall consider the appropriate sentence to be imposed and shall take into account the evidence presented and submissions made during the trial that are relevant to the sentence.

2. Except where article 65 applies and before the completion of the trial, the Trial Chamber may on its own motion and shall, at the request of the Prosecutor or the accused, hold a further hearing to hear any additional evidence or submissions relevant to the sentence, in accordance with the Rules of Procedure and Evidence.

3. Where paragraph 2 applies, any representations under article 75 shall be heard during the further hearing referred to in paragraph 2 and, if necessary, during any additional hearing.

4. The sentence shall be pronounced in public and, wherever possible, in the presence of the accused.

PART 7. PENALTIES

Article 77 — Applicable penalties

1. Subject to article 110, the Court may impose one of the following penalties on a person convicted of a crime under article 5 of this Statute:

(a) Imprisonment for a specified number of years, which may not exceed a maximum of 30 years; or

(b) A term of life imprisonment when justified by the extreme gravity of the crime and the individual circumstances of the convicted person.

2. In addition to imprisonment, the Court may order:

(a) A fine under the criteria provided for in the Rules of Procedure and Evidence;

(b) A forfeiture of proceeds, property and assets derived directly or indirectly from that crime, without prejudice to the rights of bona fide third parties.

Article 78 — Determination of the sentence

1. In determining the sentence, the Court shall, in accordance with the Rules of Procedure and Evidence, take into account such factors as the gravity of the crime and the individual circumstances of the convicted person.

2. In imposing a sentence of imprisonment, the Court shall deduct the time, if any, previously spent in detention in accordance with an order of the Court. The Court may deduct any time otherwise spent in detention in connection with conduct underlying the crime.

3. When a person has been convicted of more than one crime, the Court shall pronounce a sentence for each crime and a joint sentence specifying the total period of imprisonment. This period shall be no less than the highest individual sentence pronounced and shall not exceed 30 years' imprisonment or a sentence of life imprisonment in conformity with article 77, paragraph 1 (b).

Article 79 — Trust Fund

1. A Trust Fund shall be established by decision of the Assembly of States Parties for the benefit of victims of crimes within the jurisdiction of the Court, and of the families of such victims.

2. The Court may order money and other property collected through fines or forfeiture to be transferred, by order of the Court, to the Trust Fund.

3. The Trust Fund shall be managed according to criteria to be determined by the Assembly of States Parties.

Article 80 — Non-prejudice to national application of penalties and national laws

Nothing in this Part of the Statute affects the application by States of penalties prescribed by their national law, nor the law of States which do not provide for penalties prescribed in this Part.

PART 8. APPEAL AND REVISION

Article 81 — Appeal against decision of acquittal or conviction or against sentence

1. A decision under article 74 may be appealed in accordance with the Rules of Procedure and Evidence as follows:

(a) The Prosecutor may make an appeal on any of the following grounds:

(i) Procedural error,

(ii) Error of fact, or

(iii) Error of law;

(b) The convicted person or the Prosecutor on that person's behalf may make an appeal on any of the following grounds:

(i) Procedural error,

(ii) Error of fact,

(iii) Error of law, or

(iv) Any other ground that affects the fairness or reliability of the proceedings or decision.

2. (a) A sentence may be appealed, in accordance with the Rules of Procedure and Evidence, by the Prosecutor or the convicted person on the ground of disproportion between the crime and the sentence;

(b) If on an appeal against sentence the Court considers that there are grounds on which the conviction might be set aside, wholly or in part, it may invite the Prosecutor and the convicted person to submit grounds under article 81, paragraph 1 (a)or (b), and may render a decision on conviction in accordance with article 83;

(c) The same procedure applies when the Court, on an appeal against conviction only, considers that there are grounds to reduce the sentence under paragraph 2 (a).

3. (a) Unless the Trial Chamber orders otherwise, a convicted person shall remain in custody pending an appeal;

(b) When a convicted person's time in custody exceeds the sentence of imprisonment imposed, that person shall be released, except that if the

Prosecutor is also appealing, the release may be subject to the conditions under subparagraph (c) below;

(c) In case of an acquittal, the accused shall be released immediately, subject to the following:

(i) Under exceptional circumstances, and having regard, inter alia, to the concrete risk of flight, the seriousness of the offence charged and the probability of success on appeal, the Trial Chamber, at the request of the Prosecutor, may maintain the detention of the person pending appeal;

(ii) A decision by the Trial Chamber under subparagraph (c) (i) may be appealed in accordance with the Rules of Procedure and Evidence.

4. Subject to the provisions of paragraph 3 (a) and (b), execution of the decision or sentence shall be suspended during the period allowed for appeal and for the duration of the appeal proceedings.

Article 82 — Appeal against other decisions

1. Either party may appeal any of the following decisions in accordance with the Rules of Procedure and Evidence:

(a) A decision with respect to jurisdiction or admissibility;

(b) A decision granting or denying release of the person being investigated or prosecuted;

(c) A decision of the Pre-Trial Chamber to act on its own initiative under article 56, paragraph 3;

(d) A decision that involves an issue that would significantly affect the fair and expeditious conduct of the proceedings or the outcome of the trial, and for which, in the opinion of the Pre-Trial or Trial Chamber, an immediate resolution by the Appeals Chamber may materially advance the proceedings.

2. A decision of the Pre-Trial Chamber under article 57, paragraph 3 (d), may be appealed against by the State concerned or by the Prosecutor, with the leave of the Pre-Trial Chamber. The appeal shall be heard on an expedited basis.

3. An appeal shall not of itself have suspensive effect unless the Appeals Chamber so orders, upon request, in accordance with the Rules of Procedure and Evidence.

4. A legal representative of the victims, the convicted person or a bona fide owner of property adversely affected by an order under article 73 may appeal against the order for reparations, as provided in the Rules of Procedure and Evidence.

Article 83 — Proceedings on appeal

1. For the purposes of proceedings under article 81 and this article, the Appeals Chamber shall have all the powers of the Trial Chamber.

2. If the Appeals Chamber finds that the proceedings appealed from were unfair in a way that affected the reliability of the decision or sentence, or that the decision

or sentence appealed from was materially affected by error of fact or law or procedural error, it may:

(a) Reverse or amend the decision or sentence; or

(b) Order a new trial before a different Trial Chamber.

For these purposes, the Appeals Chamber may remand a factual issue to the original Trial Chamber for it to determine the issue and to report back accordingly, or may itself call evidence to determine the issue. When the decision or sentence has been appealed only by the person convicted, or the Prosecutor on that person's behalf, it cannot be amended to his or her detriment.

3. If in an appeal against sentence the Appeals Chamber finds that the sentence is disproportionate to the crime, it may vary the sentence in accordance with Part 7.

4. The judgement of the Appeals Chamber shall be taken by a majority of the judges and shall be delivered in open court. The judgement shall state the reasons on which it is based. When there is no unanimity, the judgement of the Appeals Chamber shall contain the views of the majority and the minority, but a judge may deliver a separate or dissenting opinion on a question of law.

5. The Appeals Chamber may deliver its judgement in the absence of the person acquitted or convicted.

Article 84 — Revision of conviction or sentence

1. The convicted person or, after death, spouses, children, parents or one person alive at the time of the accused's death who has been given express written instructions from the accused to bring such a claim, or the Prosecutor on the person's behalf, may apply to the Appeals Chamber to revise the final judgement of conviction or sentence on the grounds that:

(a) New evidence has been discovered that:

(i) Was not available at the time of trial, and such unavailability was not wholly or partially attributable to the party making application; and

(ii) Is sufficiently important that had it been proved at trial it would have been likely to have resulted in a different verdict;

(b) It has been newly discovered that decisive evidence, taken into account at trial and upon which the conviction depends, was false, forged or falsified;

(c) One or more of the judges who participated in conviction or confirmation of the charges has committed, in that case, an act of serious misconduct or serious breach of duty of sufficient gravity to justify the removal of that judge or those judges from office under article 46.

2. The Appeals Chamber shall reject the application if it considers it to be unfounded. If it determines that the application is meritorious, it may, as appropriate:

(a) Reconvene the original Trial Chamber;

(b) Constitute a new Trial Chamber; or

(c) Retain jurisdiction over the matter, with a view to, after hearing the parties in the manner set forth in the Rules of Procedure and Evidence, arriving at a determination on whether the judgement should be revised.

Article 85 — Compensation to an arrested or convicted person

1. Anyone who has been the victim of unlawful arrest or detention shall have an enforceable right to compensation.

2. When a person has by a final decision been convicted of a criminal offence, and when subsequently his or her conviction has been reversed on the ground that a new or newly discovered fact shows conclusively that there has been a miscarriage of justice, the person who has suffered punishment as a result of such conviction shall be compensated according to law, unless it is proved that the non-disclosure of the unknown fact in time is wholly or partly attributable to him or her.

3. In exceptional circumstances, where the Court finds conclusive facts showing that there has been a grave and manifest miscarriage of justice, it may in its discretion award compensation, according to the criteria provided in the Rules of Procedure and Evidence, to a person who has been released from detention following a final decision of acquittal or a termination of the proceedings for that reason.

PART 9. INTERNATIONAL COOPERATION AND JUDICIAL ASSISTANCE

Article 86 — General obligation to cooperate

States Parties shall, in accordance with the provisions of this Statute, cooperate fully with the Court in its investigation and prosecution of crimes within the jurisdiction of the Court.

Article 87 — Requests for cooperation: general provisions

1. (a) The Court shall have the authority to make requests to States Parties for cooperation. The requests shall be transmitted through the diplomatic channel or any other appropriate channel as may be designated by each State Party upon ratification, acceptance, approval or accession.

Subsequent changes to the designation shall be made by each State Party in accordance with the Rules of Procedure and Evidence.

(b) When appropriate, without prejudice to the provisions of subparagraph (a), requests may also be transmitted through the International Criminal Police Organization or any appropriate regional organization.

2. Requests for cooperation and any documents supporting the request shall either be in or be accompanied by a translation into an official language of the requested State or in one of the working languages of the Court, in accordance with the choice made by that State upon ratification, acceptance, approval or accession.

Subsequent changes to this choice shall be made in accordance with the Rules of Procedure and Evidence.

3. The requested State shall keep confidential a request for cooperation and any documents supporting the request, except to the extent that the disclosure is necessary for execution of the request.

4. In relation to any request for assistance presented under Part 9, the Court may take such measures, including measures related to the protection of information, as may be necessary to ensure the safety or physical or psychological well-being of any victims, potential witnesses and their families. The Court may request that any information that is made available under Part 9 shall be provided and handled in a manner that protects the safety and physical or psychological well-being of any victims, potential witnesses and their families.

5. (a) The Court may invite any State not party to this Statute to provide assistance under this Part on the basis of an ad hoc arrangement, an agreement with such State or any other appropriate basis.

(b) Where a State not party to this Statute, which has entered into an ad hoc arrangement or an agreement with the Court, fails to cooperate with requests pursuant to any such arrangement or agreement, the Court may so inform the Assembly of States Parties or, where the Security Council referred the matter to the Court, the Security Council.

6. The Court may ask any intergovernmental organization to provide information or documents. The Court may also ask for other forms of cooperation and assistance which may be agreed upon with such an organization and which are in accordance with its competence or mandate.

7. Where a State Party fails to comply with a request to cooperate by the Court contrary to the provisions of this Statute, thereby preventing the Court from exercising its functions and powers under this Statute, the Court may make a finding to that effect and refer the matter to the Assembly of States Parties or, where the Security Council referred the matter to the Court, to the Security Council.

Article 88 — Availability of procedures under national law

States Parties shall ensure that there are procedures available under their national law for all of the forms of cooperation which are specified under this Part.

Article 89 — Surrender of persons to the Court

1. The Court may transmit a request for the arrest and surrender of a person, together with the material supporting the request outlined in article 91, to any State on the territory of which that person may be found and shall request the cooperation of that State in the arrest and surrender of such a person. States Parties shall, in accordance with the provisions of this Part and the procedure under their national law, comply with requests for arrest and surrender.

2. Where the person sought for surrender brings a challenge before a national court on the basis of the principle of ne bis in idem as provided in article 20, the requested State shall immediately consult with the Court to determine if there has been a relevant ruling on admissibility. If the case is admissible, the requested State

shall proceed with the execution of the request. If an admissibility ruling is pending, the requested State may postpone the execution of the request for surrender of the person until the Court makes a determination on admissibility.

3. (a) A State Party shall authorize, in accordance with its national procedural law, transportation through its territory of a person being surrendered to the Court by another State, except where transit through that State would impede or delay the surrender.

(b) A request by the Court for transit shall be transmitted in accordance with article 87. The request for transit shall contain:

(i) A description of the person being transported;

(ii) A brief statement of the facts of the case and their legal characterization; and

(iii) The warrant for arrest and surrender;

(c) A person being transported shall be detained in custody during the period of transit;

(d) No authorization is required if the person is transported by air and no landing is scheduled on the territory of the transit State;

(e) If an unscheduled landing occurs on the territory of the transit State, that State may require a request for transit from the Court as provided for in subparagraph (b). The transit State shall detain the person being transported until the request for transit is received and the transit is effected; provided that detention for purposes of this subparagraph may not be extended beyond 96 hours from the unscheduled landing unless the request is received within that time.

4. If the person sought is being proceeded against or is serving a sentence in the requested State for a crime different from that for which surrender to the Court is sought, the requested State, after making its decision to grant the request, shall consult with the Court.

Article 90 — Competing requests

1. A State Party which receives a request from the Court for the surrender of a person under article 89 shall, if it also receives a request from any other State for the extradition of the same person for the same conduct which forms the basis of the crime for which the Court seeks the person's surrender, notify the Court and the requesting State of that fact.

2. Where the requesting State is a State Party, the requested State shall give priority to the request from the Court if:

(a) The Court has, pursuant to articles 18 and 19, made a determination that the case in respect of which surrender is sought is admissible and that determination takes into account the investigation or prosecution conducted by the requesting State in respect of its request for extradition; or

(b) The Court makes the determination described in subparagraph (a) pursuant to the requested State's notification under paragraph 1.

3. Where a determination under paragraph 2 (a) has not been made, the requested State may, at its discretion, pending the determination of the Court under paragraph 2 (b), proceed to deal with the request for extradition from the requesting State but shall not extradite the person until the Court has determined that the case is inadmissible. The Court's determination shall be made on an expedited basis.

4. If the requesting State is a State not Party to this Statute the requested State, if it is not under an international obligation to extradite the person to the requesting State, shall give priority to the request for surrender from the Court, if the Court has determined that the case is admissible.

5. Where a case under paragraph 4 has not been determined to be admissible by the Court, the requested State may, at its discretion, proceed to deal with the request for extradition from the requesting State.

6. In cases where paragraph 4 applies except that the requested State is under an existing international obligation to extradite the person to the requesting State not Party to this Statute, the requested State shall determine whether to surrender the person to the Court or extradite the person to the requesting State. In making its decision, the requested State shall consider all the relevant factors, including but not limited to:

(a) The respective dates of the requests;

(b) The interests of the requesting State including, where relevant, whether the crime was committed in its territory and the nationality of the victims and of the person sought; and

(c) The possibility of subsequent surrender between the Court and the requesting State.

7. Where a State Party which receives a request from the Court for the surrender of a person also receives a request from any State for the extradition of the same person for conduct other than that which constitutes the crime for which the Court seeks the person's surrender:

(a) The requested State shall, if it is not under an existing international obligation to extradite the person to the requesting State, give priority to the request from the Court;

(b) The requested State shall, if it is under an existing international obligation to extradite the person to the requesting State, determine whether to surrender the person to the Court or extradite the person to the requesting State. In making its decision, the requested State shall consider all the relevant factors, including but not limited to those set out in paragraph 6, but shall give special consideration to the relative nature and gravity of the conduct in question.

8. Where pursuant to a notification under this article, the Court has determined a case to be inadmissible, and subsequently extradition to the requesting State is refused, the requested State shall notify the Court of this decision.

Article 91 — Contents of request for arrest and surrender

1. A request for arrest and surrender shall be made in writing. In urgent cases, a request may be made by any medium capable of delivering a written record, provided that the request shall be confirmed through the channel provided for in article 87, paragraph 1 (a).

2. In the case of a request for the arrest and surrender of a person for whom a warrant of arrest has been issued by the Pre-Trial Chamber under article 58, the request shall contain or be supported by:

(a) Information describing the person sought, sufficient to identify the person, and information as to that person's probable location;

(b) A copy of the warrant of arrest; and

(c) Such documents, statements or information as may be necessary to meet the requirements for the surrender process in the requested State, except that those requirements should not be more burdensome than those applicable to requests for extradition pursuant to treaties or arrangements between the requested State and other States and should, if possible, be less burdensome, taking into account the distinct nature of the Court.

3. In the case of a request for the arrest and surrender of a person already convicted, the request shall contain or be supported by:

(a) A copy of any warrant of arrest for that person;

(b) A copy of the judgement of conviction;

(c) Information to demonstrate that the person sought is the one referred to in the judgement of conviction; and

(d) If the person sought has been sentenced, a copy of the sentence imposed and, in the case of a sentence for imprisonment, a statement of any time already served and the time remaining to be served.

4. Upon the request of the Court, a State Party shall consult with the Court, either generally or with respect to a specific matter, regarding any requirements under its national law that may apply under paragraph 2 (c). During the consultations, the State Party shall advise the Court of the specific requirements of its national law.

Article 92 — Provisional arrest

1. In urgent cases, the Court may request the provisional arrest of the person sought, pending presentation of the request for surrender and the documents supporting the request as specified in article 91.

2. The request for provisional arrest shall be made by any medium capable of delivering a written record and shall contain:

(a) Information describing the person sought, sufficient to identify the person, and information as to that person's probable location;

(b) A concise statement of the crimes for which the person's arrest is sought and of the facts which are alleged to constitute those crimes, including, where possible, the date and location of the crime;

(c) A statement of the existence of a warrant of arrest or a judgement of conviction against the person sought; and

(d) A statement that a request for surrender of the person sought will follow.

3. A person who is provisionally arrested may be released from custody if the requested State has not received the request for surrender and the documents supporting the request as specified in article 91 within the time limits specified in the Rules of Procedure and Evidence. However, the person may consent to surrender before the expiration of this period if permitted by the law of the requested State. In such a case, the requested State shall proceed to surrender the person to the Court as soon as possible.

4. The fact that the person sought has been released from custody pursuant to paragraph 3 shall not prejudice the subsequent arrest and surrender of that person if the request for surrender and the documents supporting the request are delivered at a later date.

Article 93 — Other forms of cooperation

1. States Parties shall, in accordance with the provisions of this Part and under procedures of national law, comply with requests by the Court to provide the following assistance in relation to investigations or prosecutions:

(a) The identification and whereabouts of persons or the location of items;

(b) The taking of evidence, including testimony under oath, and the production of evidence, including expert opinions and reports necessary to the Court;

(c) The questioning of any person being investigated or prosecuted;

(d) The service of documents, including judicial documents;

(e) Facilitating the voluntary appearance of persons as witnesses or experts before the Court;

(f) The temporary transfer of persons as provided in paragraph 7;

(g) The examination of places or sites, including the exhumation and examination of grave sites;

(h) The execution of searches and seizures;

(i) The provision of records and documents, including official records and documents;

(j) The protection of victims and witnesses and the preservation of evidence;

(k) The identification, tracing and freezing or seizure of proceeds, property and assets and instrumentalities of crimes for the purpose of eventual forfeiture, without prejudice to the rights of bona fide third parties; and

(l) Any other type of assistance which is not prohibited by the law of the requested State, with a view to facilitating the investigation and prosecution of crimes within the jurisdiction of the Court.

2. The Court shall have the authority to provide an assurance to a witness or an expert appearing before the Court that he or she will not be prosecuted, detained or subjected to any restriction of personal freedom by the Court in respect of any act or omission that preceded the departure of that person from the requested State.

3. Where execution of a particular measure of assistance detailed in a request presented under paragraph 1, is prohibited in the requested State on the basis of an existing fundamental legal principle of general application, the requested State shall promptly consult with the Court to try to resolve the matter. In the consultations, consideration should be given to whether the assistance can be rendered in another manner or subject to conditions. If after consultations the matter cannot be resolved, the Court shall modify the request as necessary.

4. In accordance with article 72, a State Party may deny a request for assistance, in whole or in part, only if the request concerns the production of any documents or disclosure of evidence which relates to its national security.

5. Before denying a request for assistance under paragraph 1 (l), the requested State shall consider whether the assistance can be provided subject to specified conditions, or whether the assistance can be provided at a later date or in an alternative manner, provided that if the Court or the Prosecutor accepts the assistance subject to conditions, the Court of the Prosecutor shall abide by them.

6. If a request for assistance is denied, the requested State Party shall promptly inform the Court or the Prosecutor of the reasons for such denial.

7. (a) The Court may request the temporary transfer of a person in custody for purposes of identification or for obtaining testimony or other assistance. The person may be transferred if the following conditions are fulfilled:

(i) The person freely gives his or her informed consent to the transfer; and

(ii) The requested State agrees to the transfer, subject to such conditions as that State and the Court may agree.

(b) The person being transferred shall remain in custody. When the purposes of the transfer have been fulfilled, the Court shall return the person without delay to the requested State.

8. (a) The Court shall ensure the confidentiality of documents and information, except as required for the investigation and proceedings described in the request.

(b) The requested State may, when necessary, transmit documents or information to the Prosecutor on a confidential basis. The Prosecutor may then use them solely for the purpose of generating new evidence;

(c) The requested State may, on its own motion or at the request of the Prosecutor, subsequently consent to the disclosure of such documents or information. They may then be used as evidence pursuant to the provisions of Parts 5 and 6 and in accordance with the Rules of Procedure and Evidence.

9. (a) (i) In the event that a State Party receives competing requests, other than for surrender or extradition, from the Court and from another State pursuant to an international obligation, the State Party shall endeavour, in consultation with the Court and the other State, to meet both requests, if necessary by postponing or attaching conditions to one or the other request.

(ii) Failing that, competing requests shall be resolved in accordance with the principles established in article 90.

(b) Where, however, the request from the Court concerns information, property or persons which are subject to the control of a third State or an international organization by virtue of an international agreement, the requested States shall so inform the Court and the Court shall direct its request to the third State or international organization.

10. (a) The Court may, upon request, cooperate with and provide assistance to a State Party conducting an investigation into or trial in respect of conduct which constitutes a crime within the jurisdiction of the Court or which constitutes a serious crime under the national law of the requesting State.

(b) (i) The assistance provided under subparagraph (a) shall include, inter alia:

(1) The transmission of statements, documents or other types of evidence obtained in the course of an investigation or a trial conducted by the Court; and

(2) The questioning of any person detained by order of the Court;

(ii) In the case of assistance under subparagraph (b) (i) (1):

(1) If the documents or other types of evidence have been obtained with the assistance of a State, such transmission shall require the consent of that State;

(2) If the statements, documents or other types of evidence have been provided by a witness or expert, such transmission shall be subject to the provisions of article 68.

(c) The Court may, under the conditions set out in this paragraph, grant a request for assistance under this paragraph from a State which is not a Party to the Statute.

Article 94 — Postponement of execution of a request in respect of ongoing investigation or prosecution

1. If the immediate execution of a request would interfere with an ongoing investigation or prosecution of a case different from that to which the request relates, the requested State may postpone the execution of the request for a period of time agreed upon with the Court. However, the postponement shall be no longer than is necessary to complete the relevant investigation or prosecution in the requested State. Before making a decision to postpone, the requested State should consider whether the assistance may be immediately provided subject to certain conditions.

2. If a decision to postpone is taken pursuant to paragraph 1, the Prosecutor may, however, seek measures to preserve evidence, pursuant to article 93, paragraph 1 (j).

Article 95 — Postponement of execution of a request in respect of an admissibility challenge

Without prejudice to article 53, paragraph 2, where there is an admissibility challenge under consideration by the Court pursuant to articles 18 or 19, the requested State may postpone the execution of a request under this Part pending a determination by the Court, unless the Court has specifically ordered that the Prosecutor may pursue the collection of such evidence pursuant to articles 18 or 19.

Article 96 — Contents of request for other forms of assistance under article 93

1. A request for other forms of assistance referred to in article 93 shall be made in writing. In urgent cases, a request may be made by any medium capable of delivering a written record, provided that the request shall be confirmed through the channel provided for in article 87, paragraph 1 (a).

2. The request shall, as applicable, contain or be supported by the following:

(a) A concise statement of the purpose of the request and the assistance sought, including the legal basis and the grounds for the request;

(b) As much detailed information as possible about the location or identification of any person or place that must be found or identified in order for the assistance sought to be provided;

(c) A concise statement of the essential facts underlying the request;

(d) The reasons for and details of any procedure or requirement to be followed;

(e) Such information as may be required under the law of the requested State in order to execute the request; and

(f) Any other information relevant in order for the assistance sought to be provided.

3. Upon the request of the Court, a State Party shall consult with the Court, either generally or with respect to a specific matter, regarding any requirements under its national law that may apply under paragraph 2 (e). During the consultations, the State Party shall advise the Court of the specific requirements of its national law.

4. The provisions of this article shall, where applicable, also apply in respect of a request for assistance made to the Court.

Article 97 — Consultations

Where a State Party receives a request under this Part in relation to which it identifies problems which may impede or prevent the execution of the request, that State shall consult with the Court without delay in order to resolve the matter. Such problems may include, inter alia:

(a) Insufficient information to execute the request;

(b) In the case of a request for surrender, the fact that despite best efforts, the person sought cannot be located or that the investigation conducted has determined that the person in the custodial State is clearly not the person named in the warrant; or

(c) The fact that execution of the request in its current form would require the requested State to breach a pre-existing treaty obligation undertaken with respect to another State.

Article 98 — Cooperation with respect to waiver of immunity and consent to surrender

1. The Court may not proceed with a request for surrender or assistance which would require the requested State to act inconsistently with its obligations under international law with respect to the State or diplomatic immunity of a person or property of a third State, unless the Court can first obtain the cooperation of that third State for the waiver of the immunity.

2. The Court may not proceed with a request for surrender which would require the requested State to act inconsistently with its obligations under international agreements pursuant to which the consent of a sending State is required to surrender a person of that State to the Court, unless the Court can first obtain the cooperation of the sending State for the giving of consent for the surrender.

Article 99 — Execution of requests under articles 93 and 96

1. Requests for assistance shall be executed in accordance with the relevant procedure under the law of the requested State and, unless prohibited by such law, in the manner specified in the request, including following any procedure outlined therein or permitting persons specified in the request to be present at and assist in the execution process.

2. In the case of an urgent request, the documents or evidence produced in response shall, at the request of the Court, be sent urgently.

3. Replies from the requested State shall be transmitted in their original language and form.

4. Without prejudice to other articles in this Part, where it is necessary for the successful execution of a request which can be executed without any compulsory measures, including specifically the interview of or taking evidence from a person on a voluntary basis, including doing so without the presence of the authorities of the requested State Party if it is essential for the request to be executed, and the examination without modification of a public site or other public place, the Prosecutor may execute such request directly on the territory of a State as follows:

(a) When the State Party requested is a State on the territory of which the crime is alleged to have been committed, and there has been a determination of admissibility pursuant to articles 18 or 19, the Prosecutor may directly execute such request following all possible consultations with the requested State Party;

(b) In other cases, the Prosecutor may execute such request following consultations with the requested State Party and subject to any reasonable conditions or concerns raised by that State Party. Where the requested State Party identifies problems with the execution of a request pursuant to this subparagraph it shall, without delay, consult with the Court to resolve the matter.

5. Provisions allowing a person heard or examined by the Court under article 72 to invoke restrictions designed to prevent disclosure of confidential information connected with national defence or security shall also apply to the execution of requests for assistance under this article.

Article 100 — Costs

1. The ordinary costs for execution of requests in the territory of the requested State shall be borne by that State, except for the following, which shall be borne by the Court:

(a) Costs associated with the travel and security of witnesses and experts or the transfer under article 93 of persons in custody;

(b) Costs of translation, interpretation and transcription;

(c) Travel and subsistence costs of the judges, the Prosecutor, the Deputy Prosecutors, the Registrar, the Deputy Registrar and staff of any organ of the Court;

(d) Costs of any expert opinion or report requested by the Court;

(e) Costs associated with the transport of a person being surrendered to the Court by a custodial State; and

(f) Following consultations, any extraordinary costs that may result from the execution of a request.

2. The provisions of paragraph 1 shall, as appropriate, apply to requests from States Parties to the Court. In that case, the Court shall bear the ordinary costs of execution.

Article 101 — Rule of speciality

1. A person surrendered to the Court under this Statute shall not be proceeded against, punished or detained for any conduct committed prior to surrender, other than the conduct or course of conduct which forms the basis of the crimes for which that person has been surrendered.

2. The Court may request a waiver of the requirements of paragraph 1 from the State which surrendered the person to the Court and, if necessary, the Court shall provide additional information in accordance with article 91. States Parties shall have the authority to provide a waiver to the Court and should endeavour to do so.

Article 102 — Use of terms

For the purposes of this Statute:

(a) "surrender" means the delivering up of a person by a State to the Court, pursuant to this Statute.

(b) "extradition" means the delivering up of a person by one State to another as provided by treaty, convention or national legislation.

PART 10. ENFORCEMENT

Article 103 — Role of States in enforcement of sentences of imprisonment

1. (a) A sentence of imprisonment shall be served in a State designated by the Court from a list of States which have indicated to the Court their willingness to accept sentenced persons.

(b) At the time of declaring its willingness to accept sentenced persons, a State may attach conditions to its acceptance as agreed by the Court and in accordance with this Part.

(c) A State designated in a particular case shall promptly inform the Court whether it accepts the Court's designation.

2. (a) The State of enforcement shall notify the Court of any circumstances, including the exercise of any conditions agreed under paragraph 1, which could materially affect the terms or extent of the imprisonment. The Court shall be given at least 45 days' notice of any such known or foreseeable circumstances. During this period, the State of enforcement shall take no action that might prejudice its obligations under article 110.

(b) Where the Court cannot agree to the circumstances referred to in subparagraph (a), it shall notify the State of enforcement and proceed in accordance with article 104, paragraph 1.

3. In exercising its discretion to make a designation under paragraph 1, the Court shall take into account the following:

(a) The principle that States Parties should share the responsibility for enforcing sentences of imprisonment, in accordance with principles of equitable distribution, as provided in the Rules of Procedure and Evidence;

(b) The application of widely accepted international treaty standards governing the treatment of prisoners;

(c) The views of the sentenced person; and

(d) The nationality of the sentenced person;

(e) Such other factors regarding the circumstances of the crime or the person sentenced, or the effective enforcement of the sentence, as may be appropriate in designating the State of enforcement.

4. If no State is designated under paragraph 1, the sentence of imprisonment shall be served in a prison facility made available by the host State, in accordance with the conditions set out in the headquarters agreement referred to in article 3, paragraph 2. In such a case, the costs arising out of the enforcement of a sentence of imprisonment shall be borne by the Court.

Article 104 — Change in designation of State of enforcement

1. The Court may, at any time, decide to transfer a sentenced person to a prison of another State.

2. A sentenced person may, at any time, apply to the Court to be transferred from the State of enforcement.

Article 105 — Enforcement of the sentence

1. Subject to conditions which a State may have specified in accordance with article 103, paragraph 1 (b), the sentence of imprisonment shall be binding on the States Parties, which shall in no case modify it.

2. The Court alone shall have the right to decide any application for appeal and revision. The State of enforcement shall not impede the making of any such application by a sentenced person.

Article 106 — Supervision of enforcement of sentences and conditions of imprisonment

1. The enforcement of a sentence of imprisonment shall be subject to the supervision of the Court and shall be consistent with widely accepted international treaty standards governing treatment of prisoners.

2. The conditions of imprisonment shall be governed by the law of the State of enforcement and shall be consistent with widely accepted international treaty standards governing treatment of prisoners; in no case shall such conditions be more or

less favourable than those available to prisoners convicted of similar offences in the State of enforcement.

3. Communications between a sentenced person and the Court shall be unimpeded and confidential.

Article 107 — Transfer of the person upon completion of sentence

1. Following completion of the sentence, a person who is not a national of the State of enforcement may, in accordance with the law of the State of enforcement, be transferred to a State which is obliged to receive him or her, or to another State which agrees to receive him or her, taking into account any wishes of the person to be transferred to that State, unless the State of enforcement authorizes the person to remain in its territory.

2. If no State bears the costs arising out of transferring the person to another State pursuant to paragraph 1, such costs shall be borne by the Court.

3. Subject to the provisions of article 108, the State of enforcement may also, in accordance with its national law, extradite or otherwise surrender the person to the State which has requested the extradition or surrender of the person for purposes of trial or enforcement of a sentence.

Article 108 — Limitation on the prosecution or punishment of other offences

1. A sentenced person in the custody of the State of enforcement shall not be subject to prosecution or punishment or to extradition to a third State for any conduct engaged in prior to that person's delivery to the State of enforcement, unless such prosecution, punishment or extradition has been approved by the Court at the request of the State of enforcement.

2. The Court shall decide the matter after having heard the views of the sentenced person.

3. Paragraph 1 shall cease to apply if the sentenced person remains voluntarily for more than 30 days in the territory of the State of enforcement after having served the full sentence imposed by the Court, or returns to the territory of that State after having left it.

Article 109 — Enforcement of fines and forfeiture measures

1. States Parties shall give effect to fines or forfeitures ordered by the Court under Part 7, without prejudice to the rights of bona fide third parties, and in accordance with the procedure of their national law.

2. If a State Party is unable to give effect to an order for forfeiture, it shall take measures to recover the value of the proceeds, property or assets ordered by the Court to be forfeited, without prejudice to the rights of bona fide third parties.

3. Property, or the proceeds of the sale of real property or, where appropriate, the sale of other property, which is obtained by a State Party as a result of its enforcement of a judgement of the Court shall be transferred to the Court.

Article 110 — Review by the Court concerning reduction of sentence

1. The State of enforcement shall not release the person before expiry of the sentence pronounced by the Court.

2. The Court alone shall have the right to decide any reduction of sentence, and shall rule on the matter after having heard the person.

3. When the person has served two thirds of the sentence, or 25 years in the case of life imprisonment, the Court shall review the sentence to determine whether it should be reduced. Such a review shall not be conducted before that time.

4. In its review under paragraph 3, the Court may reduce the sentence if it finds that one or more of the following factors are present:

(a) The early and continuing willingness of the person to cooperate with the Court in its investigations and prosecutions;

(b) The voluntary assistance of the person in enabling the enforcement of the judgements and orders of the Court in other cases, and in particular providing assistance in locating assets subject to orders of fine, forfeiture or reparation which may be used for the benefit of victims; or

(c) Other factors establishing a clear and significant change of circumstances sufficient to justify the reduction of sentence, as provided in the Rules of Procedure and Evidence.

5. If the Court determines in its initial review under paragraph 3 that it is not appropriate to reduce the sentence, it shall thereafter review the question of reduction of sentence at such intervals and applying such criteria as provided for in the Rules of Procedure and Evidence.

Article 111 — Escape

If a convicted person escapes from custody and flees the State of enforcement, that State may, after consultation with the Court, request the person's surrender from the State in which the person is located pursuant to existing bilateral or multilateral arrangements, or may request that the Court seek the person's surrender, in accordance with Part 9. It may direct that the person be delivered to the State in which he or she was serving the sentence or to another State designated by the Court.

PART 11. ASSEMBLY OF STATES PARTIES

Article 112 — Assembly of States Parties

1. An Assembly of States Parties to this Statute is hereby established. Each State Party shall have one representative in the Assembly who may be accompanied by alternates and advisers. Other States which have signed the Statute or the Final Act may be observers in the Assembly.

2. The Assembly shall:

(a) Consider and adopt, as appropriate, recommendations of the Preparatory Commission;

(b) Provide management oversight to the Presidency, the Prosecutor and the Registrar regarding the administration of the Court;

(c) Consider the reports and activities of the Bureau established under paragraph 3 and take appropriate action in regard thereto;

(d) Consider and decide the budget for the Court;

(e) Decide whether to alter, in accordance with article 36, the number of judges;

(f) Consider pursuant to article 87, paragraphs 5 and 7, any question relating to non-cooperation;

(g) Perform any other function consistent with this Statute or the Rules of Procedure and Evidence.

3. (a) The Assembly shall have a Bureau consisting of a President, two Vice-Presidents and 18 members elected by the Assembly for three-year terms.

(b) The Bureau shall have a representative character, taking into account, in particular, equitable geographical distribution and the adequate representation of the principal legal systems of the world.

(c) The Bureau shall meet as often as necessary, but at least once a year. It shall assist the Assembly in the discharge of its responsibilities.

4. The Assembly may establish such subsidiary bodies as may be necessary, including an independent oversight mechanism for inspection, evaluation and investigation of the Court, in order to enhance its efficiency and economy.

5. The President of the Court, the Prosecutor and the Registrar or their representatives may participate, as appropriate, in meetings of the Assembly and of the Bureau.

6. The Assembly shall meet at the seat of the Court or at the Headquarters of the United Nations once a year and, when circumstances so require, hold special sessions. Except as otherwise specified in this Statute, special sessions shall be convened by the Bureau on its own initiative or at the request of one third of the States Parties.

7. Each State Party shall have one vote. Every effort shall be made to reach decisions by consensus in the Assembly and in the Bureau. If consensus cannot be reached, except as otherwise provided in the Statute:

(a) Decisions on matters of substance must be approved by a two-thirds majority of those present and voting provided that an absolute majority of States Parties constitutes the quorum for voting;

(b) Decisions on matters of procedure shall be taken by a simple majority of States Parties present and voting.

8. A State Party which is in arrears in the payment of its financial contributions towards the costs of the Court shall have no vote in the Assembly and in the Bureau

if the amount of its arrears equals or exceeds the amount of the contributions due from it for the preceding two full years. The Assembly may, nevertheless, permit such a State Party to vote in the Assembly and in the Bureau if it is satisfied that the failure to pay is due to conditions beyond the control of the State Party.

9. The Assembly shall adopt its own rules of procedure.

10. The official and working languages of the Assembly shall be those of the General Assembly of the United Nations.

PART 12. FINANCING

Article 113 — Financial Regulations

Except as otherwise specifically provided, all financial matters related to the Court and the meetings of the Assembly of States Parties, including its Bureau and subsidiary bodies, shall be governed by this Statute and the Financial Regulations and Rules adopted by the Assembly of States Parties.

Article 114 — Payment of expenses

Expenses of the Court and the Assembly of States Parties, including its Bureau and subsidiary bodies, shall be paid from the funds of the Court.

Article 115 — Funds of the Court and of the Assembly of States Parties

The expenses of the Court and the Assembly of States Parties, including its Bureau and subsidiary bodies, as provided for in the budget decided by the Assembly of States Parties, shall be provided by the following sources:

(a) Assessed contributions made by States Parties;

(b) Funds provided by the United Nations, subject to the approval of the General Assembly, in particular in relation to the expenses incurred due to referrals by the Security Council.

Article 116 — Voluntary contributions

Without prejudice to article 115, the Court may receive and utilize, as additional funds, voluntary contributions from Governments, international organizations, individuals, corporations and other entities, in accordance with relevant criteria adopted by the Assembly of States Parties.

Article 117 — Assessment of contributions

The contributions of States Parties shall be assessed in accordance with an agreed scale of assessment, based on the scale adopted by the United Nations for its regular budget and adjusted in accordance with the principles on which that scale is based.

Article 118 — Annual audit

The records, books and accounts of the Court, including its annual financial statements, shall be audited annually by an independent auditor.

PART 13. FINAL CLAUSES

Article 119 — Settlement of disputes

1. Any dispute concerning the judicial functions of the Court shall be settled by the decision of the Court.

2. Any other dispute between two or more States Parties relating to the interpretation or application of this Statute which is not settled through negotiations within three months of their commencement shall be referred to the Assembly of States Parties. The Assembly may itself seek to settle the dispute or make recommendations on further means of settlement of the dispute, including referral to the International Court of Justice in conformity with the Statute of that Court.

Article 120 — Reservations

No reservations may be made to this Statute.

Article 121 — Amendments

1. After the expiry of seven years from the entry into force of this Statute, any State Party may propose amendments thereto. The text of any proposed amendment shall be submitted to the Secretary-General of the United Nations, who shall promptly circulate it to all States Parties.

2. No sooner than three months from the date of notification, the next Assembly of States Parties shall, by a majority of those present and voting, decide whether to take up the proposal. The Assembly may deal with the proposal directly or convene a Review Conference if the issue involved so warrants.

3. The adoption of an amendment at a meeting of the Assembly of States Parties or at a Review Conference on which consensus cannot be reached shall require a two — thirds majority of States Parties.

4. Except as provided in paragraph 5, an amendment shall enter into force for all States Parties one year after instruments of ratification or acceptance have been deposited with the Secretary-General of the United Nations by seven-eighths of them.

5. Any amendment to articles 5, 6, 7 and 8 of this Statute shall enter into force for those States Parties which have accepted the amendment one year after the deposit of their instruments of ratification or acceptance. In respect of a State Party which has not accepted the amendment, the Court shall not exercise its jurisdiction regarding a crime covered by the amendment when committed by that State Party's nationals or on its territory.

6. If an amendment has been accepted by seven-eighths of States Parties in accordance with paragraph 4, any State Party which has not accepted the amendment may withdraw from the Statute with immediate effect, notwithstanding paragraph 1 of article 127, but subject to paragraph 2 of article 127, by giving notice no later than one year after the entry into force of such amendment.

7. The Secretary-General of the United Nations shall circulate to all States Parties any amendment adopted at a meeting of the Assembly of States Parties or at a Review Conference.

Article 122 — Amendments to provisions of an institutional nature

1. Amendments to provisions of the Statute which are of an exclusively institutional nature, namely, article 35, article 36, paragraphs 8 and 9 article 37, article 38, article 39, paragraphs 1 (first two sentences), 2 and 4, article 42, paragraphs 4 to 9, article 43, paragraphs 2 and 3, and articles 44, 46, 47 and 49, may be proposed at any time, notwithstanding article 121, paragraph 1, by any State Party. The text of any proposed amendment shall be submitted to the Secretary-General of the United Nations or such other person designated by the Assembly of States Parties who shall promptly circulate it to all States Parties and to others participating in the Assembly.

2. Amendments under this article on which consensus cannot be reached shall be adopted by the Assembly of States Parties or by a Review Conference, by a two-thirds majority of States Parties. Such amendments shall enter into force for all States Parties six months after their adoption by the Assembly or, as the case may be, by the Conference.

Article 123 — Review of the Statute

1. Seven years after the entry into force of this Statute the Secretary-General of the United Nations shall convene a Review Conference to consider any amendments to this Statute. Such review may include, but is not limited to, the list of crimes contained in article 5. The Conference shall be open to those participating in the Assembly of States Parties and on the same conditions.

2. At any time thereafter, at the request of a State Party and for the purposes set out in paragraph 1, the Secretary-General of the United Nations shall, upon approval by a majority of States Parties, convene a Review Conference.

3. The provisions of article 121, paragraphs 3 to 7, shall apply to the adoption and entry into force of any amendment to the Statute considered at a Review Conference.

Article 124 — Transitional Provision

Notwithstanding article 12 paragraph 1, a State, on becoming a party to this Statute, may declare that, for a period of seven years after the entry into force of this Statute for the State concerned, it does not accept the jurisdiction of the Court with respect to the category of crimes referred to in article 8 when a crime is alleged to have been committed by its nationals or on its territory. A declaration under this article may be withdrawn at any time. The provisions of this article shall be reviewed at the Review Conference convened in accordance with article 123, paragraph 1.

Article 125 — Signature, ratification, acceptance, approval or accession

1. This Statute shall be open for signature by all States in Rome, at the headquarters of the Food and Agriculture Organization of the United Nations, on 17

July 1998. Thereafter, it shall remain open for signature in Rome at the Ministry of Foreign Affairs of Italy until 17 October 1998. After that date, the Statute shall remain open for signature in New York, at United Nations Headquarters, until 31 December 2000.

2. This Statute is subject to ratification, acceptance or approval by signatory States. Instruments of ratification, acceptance or approval shall be deposited with the Secretary-General of the United Nations.

3. This Statute shall be open to accession by all States. Instruments of accession shall be deposited with the Secretary-General of the United Nations.

Article 126 — Entry into force

1. This Statute shall enter into force on the first day of the month after the 60th day following the date of the deposit of the 60th instrument of ratification, acceptance, approval or accession with the Secretary-General of the United Nations.

2. For each State ratifying, accepting, approving or acceding to the Statute after the deposit of the 60th instrument of ratification, acceptance, approval or accession, the Statute shall enter into force on the first day of the month after the 60th day following the deposit by such State of its instrument of ratification, acceptance, approval or accession.

Article 127 — Withdrawal

1. A State Party may, by written notification addressed to the Secretary-General of the United Nations, withdraw from this Statute. The withdrawal shall take effect one year after the date of receipt of the notification, unless the notification specifies a later date.

2. A State shall not be discharged, by reason of its withdrawal, from the obligations arising from this Statute while it was a Party to the Statute, including any financial obligations which may have accrued. Its withdrawal shall not affect any cooperation with the Court in connection with criminal investigations and proceedings in relation to which the withdrawing State had a duty to cooperate and which were commenced prior to the date on which the withdrawal became effective, nor shall it prejudice in any way the continued consideration of any matter which was already under consideration by the Court prior to the date on which the withdrawal became effective.

Article 128 — Authentic texts

The original of this Statute, of which the Arabic, Chinese, English, French, Russian and Spanish texts are equally authentic, shall be deposited with the Secretary -General of the United Nations, who shall send certified copies thereof to all States.

Notes

(1) The Rome Statute was adopted on July 17, 1998, at the conclusion of a five-week diplomatic conference, by a vote of 120 to 7, with 21 abstentions. The vote was taken electronically, but not recorded, so there is no official tally of how particular

states voted. The United States said that it was one of the seven states voting against the Statute. Roger Clark, who was present at the vote, believes that the others were China, India, Iraq, Israel, Vietnam and Qatar. The Rome Conference was preceded by a Preparatory Committee that met in New York on numerous occasions between March 1996 and April 1998. Useful publications on the negotiations up to and including Rome are M. Cherif Bassiouni, The Statute of the International Criminal Court: A Documentary History (1998); and The International Criminal Court: The Making of the Rome Statute, Issues, Negotiations, Results (Roy Lee ed., 1999). For a detailed analysis of the final product and subsequent developments, *see* Rome Statute of the International Criminal Court. Article-by-Article Commentary (Kai Ambos ed., 4th ed. 2021), which also contains an exhaustive multi-language bibliography. *See also* Linda E. Carter, Mark S. Ellis & Charles Chernor Jalloh, The International Criminal Court in an Effective Global Justice System (2016); The Elgar Companion to the International Criminal Court (Margaret M. deGuzman & Valerie Oosterveld eds., 2020).

The Statute came into force on July 1, 2002, having received the necessary 60 ratifications and accessions. The first eighteen judges were elected by the States Parties early in 2003. The first Prosecutor took office on June 16, 2003, the third in June 2021.

139 states signed the Statute and, by September 2021, 125 States, including Palestine (which acceded in January 2015), had become parties, among them 15 that had not signed. Two Parties, Burundi and the Philippines, withdrew in October 2017 and March 2019 respectively, when the Court undertook investigations involving them. Others, notably South Africa and Gambia began to withdraw then withdrew their withdrawals, The United States and Israel both signed the treaty (along with Iran) on the last day it was open for signature, Sunday, December 31, 2000. The United States informed the depositary on May 6, 2002, of its intention not to proceed with ratification [*supra* § 14.05]. Israel made a similar declaration on August 28, 2002. Sudan, which had signed on September 8, 2000, announced on August 26, 2008, that it too had no intention of becoming a party, as did the Russian Federation on November 30, 2016, having signed on September 13, 2000. Current information regarding signatures and ratifications can be found at the United Nations treaty database, https://treaties.un.org/Pages/ParticipationStatus.aspx.

(2) The Rome Conference, in addition to the Statute, adopted several resolutions which are annexed to the "Final Act" of the Conference (U.N. Doc. A/CONF./183/10). One of these (Resolution F) established the Preparatory Commission for the International Criminal Court, composed of representatives of states which signed the Final Act and of others invited to participate. The Preparatory Commission ("PrepCom") was formed to "prepare proposals for practical arrangements for the establishment and coming into operation of the Court," including draft texts of the Court's Rules of Procedure and Evidence, the Elements of Crimes referred to in Article 9 of the Statute, and "proposals for a provision on aggression" (*see* Article 5(2)). The Preparatory Commission completed its work (except for the provision on aggression) in

time to report to the first meeting of the Assembly of States Parties in 2002. Notably, it completed drafts of the Rules of Procedure and Evidence and Elements of Crimes. These documents, approved at the first meeting of the Assembly of States Parties, along with all related instruments are available at the Court's website: http://www.icc-cpi.int. The negotiations to create the Court and the meetings of the Preparatory Commission, as well as the early meetings of the Assembly of States Parties, were undertaken under the auspices of the United Nations. The Court is now a separate international organization with its headquarters in The Hague. It has a "relationship" agreement in place with the United Nations. On the Rules and Elements, *see* THE INTERNATIONAL CRIMINAL COURT: ELEMENTS OF CRIMES AND RULES OF PROCEDURE AND EVIDENCE (Roy Lee ed., 2001); Roger S. Clark, *The Mental Element in International Criminal Law: The Rome Statute of the International Criminal Court and the Elements of Offences,* 12 CRIM. L.F. 291 (2001); KNUT DÖERMANN, ELEMENTS OF WAR CRIMES UNDER THE ROME STATUTE OF THE INTERNATIONAL CRIMINAL COURT: SOURCES AND COMMENTARY (2003). On the provision on aggression, *see* chapter 23. The Court has made significant use of The Elements with little difficulty. *See* Roger S. Clark, *Elements of Crimes in Early Decisions of Pre-Trial Chambers of the International Criminal Court* [2008] NEW ZEALAND Y.B. INT'L L. 209. The essential structure of the Elements was derived from Article 30 of the Statute, which speaks of mental and material elements. Mental elements are intent and knowledge (as defined in Article 30); material (physical) elements are conduct, consequences and circumstances. "Causation," which fits in somewhere in every criminal law structure, is not specifically dealt with either in the Statute or the Elements, but must have a crucial role in some situations. *See* the groundbreaking analysis in Marjolein Cupidodr, *Causation in International Crimes Cases: (Re)Conceptualizing the Causal Linkage*, 32 CRIM. L. FORUM 1 (2021); *see also* Roger S. Clark, *Article 9, in* ROME STATUTE OF THE INTERNATIONAL CRIMINAL COURT. ARTICLE-BY-ARTICLE COMMENTARY 727 (Kai Ambos ed., 4th ed. 2021).

(3) Article 9(1) of the Statute (as amended in 2010 to accommodate the crime of aggression) says that the Elements of Crimes "shall assist the Court in the interpretation and application of articles 6, 7, 8 and 8bis." Article 21(1) says: "The Court shall apply: (a) In the first place, this Statute, Elements of Crimes and its Rules of Procedure and Evidence. . . ." But Article 9(3) insists that the Elements "shall be consistent with this Statute." In light of this language, could the Court properly refuse the "assistance" provided by the Elements of Crimes? Are they binding on it? What weight have they? *See* Roger S. Clark, *Article 9, in* ROME STATUTE OF THE INTERNATIONAL CRIMINAL COURT. ARTICLE-BY-ARTICLE COMMENTARY 727, 755–6 (Kai Ambos ed., 4th ed. 2021).

(4) Should the Statute have given the Court jurisdiction over "international" and "transnational" crimes other than genocide, crimes against humanity, war crimes, and aggression? Consider Resolution E, adopted at the conclusion of the Conference:

> *The United Nations Diplomatic Conference of Plenipotentiaries on the Establishment of an International Criminal Court . . .*

> *Regretting* that no generally acceptable definition of the crimes of terrorism and drug crimes could be agreed upon for the[ir] inclusion, within the jurisdiction of the Court. . . .
>
> Recommends that a Review Conference pursuant to article 123 of the Statute of the International Criminal Court consider the crimes of terrorism and drug crimes with a view to arriving at an acceptable definition and their inclusion in the list of crimes within the jurisdiction of the Court.

No consideration was given to including such crimes in the Statute at the first Review Conference on the Statute in 2010, but the question is still raised from time to time.

Article 121(5) of the Rome Statute discourages the addition of new offenses such as these or any others to the jurisdiction of the Court by effectively limiting their application to nationals of those parties which have accepted the relevant amendment. It provides that:

> Any amendment to articles 5, 6, 7 and 8 of this Statute shall enter into force for those States which have accepted the amendment. . . . In respect of a State Party which has not accepted the amendment, the Court shall not exercise its jurisdiction regarding a crime covered by the amendment when committed by that State Party's nationals or on its territory.

Nevertheless, there is enthusiastic civil society support for the addition of a further crime of "ecocide" in Article 5 and an accompanying definition to be contained in a new Article 8 *ter*. There is some support for this from states such as Vanuatu and Belgium. An Expert Panel convened by the group Stop Ecocide International produced a widely discussed definition in June 2021. *See* Legal Definition of Ecocide, *available at* https://www.stopecocide.earth/legal-definition (containing proposed amendments to the Rome Statute and the Experts' Commentary). The crime would apply in peace and in war and would have different thresholds to war crimes and crimes against humanity. Less enthusiasm is found, e.g., in Kevin Jon Heller, *Skeptical Thoughts on the Proposed Crime of "Ecocide" (That Isn't)*, http://opiniojuris.org/2021/06/23/skeptical-thoughts-on-the-proposed-crime-of-ecocide-that-isnt/.

(5) Except in cases referred by the Security Council, the Court's jurisdiction depends on the consent of the state on whose territory an offense took place or of the state of which the accused is a national (*see* Article 12). The Rome Conference did not adopt a proposal to give the Court jurisdiction whenever a state having custody of the accused is a party to the Statute ("custodial jurisdiction"). Can the jurisdiction conferred by the Statute fairly be described, then, as "universal jurisdiction"? *See* Edward M. Wise, *The International Criminal Court: A Budget of Paradoxes*, 8 Tulane J. Int'l & Comp. Law 261, 270–71 (2000). How far do the limitations imposed on its jurisdiction seriously weaken the potential effectiveness of the ICC?

(6) Article 86 requires the parties to "cooperate fully with the Court in its investigation and prosecution of crimes within the jurisdiction of the Court." What precisely does that obligation entail? Is it true that "the articles that follow are so riddled with exceptions and qualifications" as to suggest the states "are not willing to make

the concessions to international cooperation that are needed to make the Court a success in practice"? Leila Nadya Sadat & S. Richard Carden, *The New International Criminal Court: An Uneasy Revolution*, 88 GEO. L. J. 381, 444 (2000). Is there any way to enforce the obligation imposed by Article 86? Could the Security Council impose sanctions when it has referred a case? Could the Assembly of States Parties do so in other cases? Particularly galling to the Court has been its inability to obtain the arrest of Omar Al Bashir, (now former) President of the Sudan, wanted for genocide and crimes against humanity in Darfur. He has travelled with impunity to several States, both parties and non-parties to the Rome Statute, over the Court's protests. *See* § 14.05. The Security Council, which referred the case to the Court, has not been helpful. Even after he was deposed, Sudan has not delivered him up.

(7) "What are the advantages and disadvantages of the International Criminal Court? Are the disadvantages based upon particular details in the Statute or fundamental conceptual concerns?" Ellen S. Podgor, in *Panel Discussion: Association of American Law Schools Panel on the International Criminal Court*, 36 AM. CRIM. L. REV. 223, 230 (1999).

Consider the controversial answer given by Alfred P. Rubin, *A Critical View of the Proposed International Criminal Court*, 23 FLETCHER F. WORLD AFF. 139 (1999):

> In my opinion, the ICC as outlined in the Statute cannot possibly work as envisaged. This is not because technical problems have been carelessly handled, although there do seem to be some questions, as must be expected in such a work. It is because the ICC is based on a model of international legal order that seems unrealistic. In concentrating on using the positive law to provide a tribunal intended to enforce the "moral law," the framers of the ICC have created an organization that cannot do what is expected of it.

Why did the United States oppose adoption of the Statute in Rome? *See* David J. Scheffer, *The United States and the International Criminal Court*, 93 A.J.I.L. 12 (1999); *see also* Bartram S. Brown, *U.S. Objections to the Statute of the International Criminal Court: A Brief Response*, 31 N.Y.U. J. INT'L L. & POL. 855 (1999); John F. Murphy, *The Quivering Gulliver: U.S. Views on a Permanent International Criminal Court*, 34 INT'L LAW. 45 (2000); Michael P. Scharf, *The Politics Behind U.S. Opposition to the International Criminal Court*, 6 BROWN J. WORLD AFF. 97 (1999); Ron Sievert, *A New Perspective on the International Criminal Court: Why the Right Should Embrace the ICC and How America Can Use It*, 68 U. PITT. L. REV. 77 (2006). On other occasions, the United States has strongly supported the creation of international criminal tribunals. What makes the I.C.C. different?

The stated objections boil down, in large part, to concern that U.S. officials and military personnel, who are involved in peacekeeping and humanitarian interventions throughout the world, will be uniquely vulnerable to prosecution on trumped-up charges of having committed war crimes. (The U.S. is not in fact a significant contributor to U.N. peacekeeping missions which are mostly carried out by nationals of smaller states; and there is debate about the existence of a right of unilateral humanitarian intervention.) United States negotiators therefore proposed in Rome that any prosecution before the Court should be authorized by the U.N. Security Council, in which the United States has a veto; or else that a government's consent be required before one of its nationals can be prosecuted. The Conference was not prepared to adopt a rule allowing a country, once it adhered to the Statute, completely to veto the prosecution of its nationals in a particular case. But a number of provisions in the final text were designed to take account of anxieties voiced by the United States. These include the language of Article 8 limiting the Court's jurisdiction over war crimes to those that are "committed as part of a plan or policy or as part of the large-scale commission of such crimes," thus excluding jurisdiction over random acts of individual soldiers; the provision in Article 15, by which the Prosecutor's decision to investigate a particular case requires the approval of a three-judge pre-trial chamber, which in turn is subject to an interlocutory appeal to the Appeals Chamber; the provision of Article 16 allowing the U.N. Security Council to request that an investigation or prosecution be deferred for a year at a time; and the "complementarity" provisions in Articles 17 and 18, by which a case is inadmissible if it is being dealt with by national authorities, unless there is evidence that those authorities are "unwilling or unable genuinely" to prosecute. Do these compromises represent an adequate response to the objections raised by the United States?

(8) Might U.S. military (and other) personnel be subject to the Court's jurisdiction even though the United States is not a party to the Statute? Evidently, if they commit crimes under the Statute on the territory of a state which is a party or has otherwise consented to the Court's jurisdiction (*see* Article 12). *See* Guilia Pecorella & William A. Schabas, *Article* 12, *in* Rome Statute of the International Criminal Court. Article-by-Article Commentary 805, 817–8 (Kai Ambos ed., 4th ed. 2021). On the effect of the Rome Statute on non-parties generally, see Gennady M. Danilenko, *The Statute of the International Criminal Court and Third States*, 21 Mich. J. Int'l L. 445 (2000). [*See also* § 14.05.] The issue is not whether the treaty "applies" to non-parties. It is whether the territorial state can effectively delegate its undoubted jurisdiction to an international court. The better view is that it can. *See* Dapo Akande, *The Jurisdiction of the International Criminal Court over Nationals of Non-Parties: Legal Basis and Limits*, 1 J Int'l Crim. Just. 618 (2003). As we shall see in the next chapter, the situation may be different in respect of the crime of aggression and certain post-Rome amendments to the war crimes provisions of the Statute. Here, if the relevant amendments are *intra vires* the Statute, jurisdiction is precluded over the nationals of non-States-Parties.

Concern with this possibility led the U.S. delegation to propose during the last days of the Rome Conference that the Court should not have jurisdiction over nationals of a non-party state without that state's consent in cases involving "acts of officials or agents of a state in the course of official duties acknowledged by the state as such." *See* Theodor Meron, *The Court We Want*, Wash. Post, Oct. 13, 1998, at A15. Some observers have suggested that had this been the U.S. opening position, it might have been adopted; but, given all the other compromises made along the way, there was great reluctance to consider it at the end of the Conference. Among the many interesting aspects of this question is the extent to which United States legislation makes criminal the crimes within the jurisdiction of the Court. This is, of course, relevant to the question whether the U.S. (either as a party or as a non-party) can rely upon the principle of complementarity under the Statute in order to pre-empt the jurisdiction of the Court, and generally whether it is fair to exempt U.S. personnel if there is no possibility of U.S. prosecution. *See* the materials in Note (4) to § 14.05, *supra*.

(9) More fundamental objections to the I.C.C. appear to stem from (a) a mistrust of international institutions in general, as posing a threat to "full U.S. sovereignty"; and (b) the view that the U.S. government lacks constitutional authority to participate in a tribunal that will not afford U.S. citizens all of the procedural guarantees contained in the Bill of Rights. How far are these objections valid? On the constitutional issues involved in U.S. participation, *see* Paul D. Marquardt, *Law Without Borders: The Constitutionality of an International Criminal Court*, 33 COLUM. J. TRANSNAT'L L. 73 (1995). In this connection, consider the legislative findings recited in Section 2 of the American Servicemembers' Protection Act of 2002:

> Congress makes the following findings. . . .
>
> (7) Any American prosecuted by the International Criminal Court will, under the Rome Statute, be denied procedural protections to which all Americans are entitled under the Bill of Rights to the United States Constitution, such as the right to trial by jury.
>
> (8) Members of the Armed Forces of the United States should be free from the risk of prosecution by the International Criminal Court, especially when they are stationed or deployed around the world to protect the vital national interests of the United States. The United States Government has an obligation to protect the members of its Armed Forces, to the maximum extent possible, against criminal prosecutions carried out by the International Criminal Court.
>
> (9) In addition to exposing members of the armed forces of the United States to the risk of international criminal prosecution, the Rome Statute creates a risk that the President and other senior elected and appointed officials of the United States Government may be prosecuted by the International Criminal Court. Particularly if the Preparatory Commission agrees on a definition of the Crime of Aggression, senior United States officials may be at risk of criminal prosecution for national security decisions involving such matters as responding to acts of terrorism, preventing the proliferation of weapons of mass destruction, and deterring aggression. No less than members of the Armed Forces, senior officials of the United States Government deserve the full protection of the United States Constitution with respect to official actions taken by them to protect the national interests of the United States. . . .

> (11) It is a fundamental principle of international law that a treaty is binding upon its parties only and that it does not create obligations for nonparties without their consent to be bound. The United States is not a party to the Rome Statute and will not be bound by any of its terms. The United States will not recognize the jurisdiction of the International Criminal Court over United States nationals.

How convincing do you think this is? Does the jury trial argument mean that trials of American service members by court-martial are unconstitutional? Is it unconstitutional to extradite Americans to civil law countries with perfectly fair judicial systems that do not rely on juries?

(10) Some have termed the American Servicemembers' Protection Act of 2002 the "Invade the Hague Act." That designation stems, in part, from the following language in the Act:

> (a) AUTHORITY.—The President is authorized to use all means necessary and appropriate to bring about the release of any person described in subsection (b) who is being detained or imprisoned by, on behalf of, or at the request of the International Criminal Court.
>
> (b) PERSONS AUTHORIZED TO BE FREED.—The authority of subsection (a) shall extend to the following persons:
>
> (1) Covered United States persons.
>
> (2) Covered allied persons.
>
> (3) Individuals detained or imprisoned for official actions taken while the individual was a covered United States person or a covered allied person, and in the case of a covered allied person, upon the request of such government.

See 22 U.S.C. § 7427. Why do you think this language was added to the Act? By what means do you believe the United States would actually seek to gain the release of a covered individual?

(11) Some claim that the United States endeavored to undercut the Court with the American Servicemembers' Protection Act of 2002 (Notes (9) and (10)) and the "Article 98 Agreements" (§ 14.05). Some also claim that there was a further assault during the Trump Administration. An Executive Order issued on June 11, 2020, enabled sanctions on the Court and its officials if it went ahead with investigations in Afghanistan and Palestine. Financial sanctions were subsequently imposed on the then-Prosecutor Fatou Bensouda and one of her senior officials. *See* David Luban, *America the Unaccountable*, The New York Review, at 50, August 20, 2020. Several U.S.-based scholars who feared that their (largely unpaid) advice to the ICC could run afoul of the Executive Order sued to protect their position. The Biden Administration revoked the Order early in April 2021. *See* Beth Van Schaack, *Breaking; Biden Revokes Executive Order Sanctioning Int'l Criminal Court Principals*, Just Security, April 2, 2021. The current Prosecutor appears to have put the U.S, aspects of the Afghanistan case on the back burner.

(12) Recall that in the Nuremberg Case, § 20.01, the International Tribunal skirted the principle that there can be no prosecution without a pre-existing law. Article 22 of the Rome Statute enshrines this principle under the heading "nullem crimen sine lege." In *Prosecutor v. Ali Muhammad Ali-Al-Rahman ("Ali Kushab")*, No. ICC-02/05-01/20 OA8, 1 November 2021, the Appeals Chamber of the Court addressed the application of *nullem crimen sine lege* in the context of a prosecution of an official of Sudan which is not a party to the Statute, the situation having been referred by the Security Council. The Chamber insisted that the matter had to be considered in the light of human rights law, as required by Article 21(3) of the Rome Statute.

> 86. In the context of this Court, this test is satisfied if the State in which the conduct occurred is a Party to the Statute or the accused is a national of a State that is a Party to the Statute, which describes the prohibited conduct clearly and defines the crimes entering into force in July of 2002. However, for conduct that takes place on the territory of a State that is not a Party to the Statute, it is not enough that the crimes charged can be found in the text of the Statute. In interpreting article 22(1) of the Statute in a manner consistent with human rights law, a chamber must look beyond the Statute to the criminal laws applicable to the suspect or accused at the time the conduct took place and satisfy itself that a reasonable person could have expected, at that moment in time, to find him or herself faced with the crimes charged.

The Chamber held, that at least on the facts available at this early stage of the case, a reasonable person in the situation of the defendant could have reasonably expected to be charged with the offences of crimes against humanity and war crimes. The situation, of course, might be different in different circumstances.

(13) In its Report to the United Nations on its activities for 2020–21, U.N. Doc. A/76/293, August 24, 2021, the Court offered this summary of its activities:

> The International Criminal Court made significant progress in its activities during the reporting period despite practical challenges caused by the coronavirus disease (COVID-19) pandemic. Among notable developments, one accused was convicted and sentenced; two first-instance judgments were confirmed on appeal; one trial commenced and the presentation of evidence in another trial continued; charges were confirmed against two accused; two suspects were transferred to the Court; one new investigation was opened; the Prosecutor received one new referral; and four preliminary examinations were concluded. The Court underwent a major change of leadership with the election of six new judges, a new President and a new Prosecutor, and, in addition to its judicial and prosecutorial activities, engaged actively in the review process aimed at strengthening the institution and its overall performance.
>
> In total, since its establishment, the Court has opened 30 cases, involving 46 suspects or accused. Investigations have been opened with regard to 14 situations: Afghanistan, Bangladesh/Myanmar, Burundi, Central African

Republic I and II, Côte d'Ivoire, Darfur (Sudan), Democratic Republic of the Congo, Georgia, Kenya, Libya, Mali, State of Palestine and Uganda.

During the reporting period, Dominic Ongwen was found guilty of 61 counts of crimes against humanity and war crimes committed in northern Uganda between 2002 and 2005 and was sentenced to 25 years' imprisonment. The conviction and sentence are under appeal.

The Appeals Chamber confirmed the conviction and 30-year sentence of Bosco Ntaganda for crimes against humanity and war crimes committed in Ituri, Democratic Republic of the Congo. With regard to the situation in Côte d'Ivoire, the Appeals Chamber upheld the acquittals of Laurent Gbagbo and Charles Blé Goudé.

With regard to Central African Republic II, the trial of Alfred Yekatom and Patrice-Edouard Ngaïssona, alleged senior members of the anti-balaka movement, commenced on 16 February 2021 on charges of crimes against humanity and war crimes. With regard to the same situation, Mahamat Said Abdel Kani, an alleged senior member of the Séléka militia, surrendered and was transferred to the Court's custody pursuant to the warrant of arrest issued in 2019 for alleged crimes against humanity and war crimes.

With regard to the situation in Mali, the trial of Al Hassan Ag Abdoul Aziz Ag Mohamed Ag Mahmoud continued on charges of crimes against humanity and war crimes allegedly committed in 2012 and 2013 in Timbuktu.

With regard to the situation in Darfur, charges of crimes against humanity and war crimes allegedly committed in 2003 and 2004 were confirmed against Ali Muhammad Ali Abd-Al-Rahman, and he was committed to trial. With regard to the situation in Kenya, Paul Gicheru, after having surrendered himself in November 2 020, was committed to trial on charges of offences against the administration of justice consisting in corruptly influencing witnesses of the Court.

With regard to the situation in the State of Palestine, the Prosecutor opened an investigation following a ruling by Pre-Trial Chamber I concerning the Court's territorial jurisdiction. With regard to the situation in the Philippines, the Prosecutor requested judicial authorization to open an investigation; the request is pending.

The Court continued to receive highly valuable cooperation from the United Nations on a wide range of issues on a cost-reimbursable basis, notably in the form of operational assistance in the field. In addition, the cooperation, assistance and support of States parties and other States remained essential to the Court's operations. Court-issued requests for arrest and surrender remain outstanding against 12 individuals:

(a) Democratic Republic of the Congo: Sylvestre Mudacumura, since 2012;

(b) Uganda: Joseph Kony and Vincent Otti, since 2005;

(c) Darfur: Ahmad Harun, since 2007; Omar Al-Bashir, since 2009 and 2010;

Abdel Raheem Muhammad Hussein, since 2012; and Abdallah Banda, since 2014;

(d) Kenya: Walter Barasa, since 2013; Philip Kipkoech Bett, since 2015;

(e) Libya: Saif Al-Islam Gaddafi, since 2011; Al-Tuhamy Mohamed Khaled,

since 2013; and Mahmoud Mustafa Busayf Al-Werfalli, since 2017.

The Court calls on States parties and others to provide the cooperation and assistance necessary for their arrest and surrender to the Court.

The Report noted that the Office of the Prosecutor is in the process of verifying the reported deaths of Sylvestre Mudacumura (in 2019); Al-Tuhamy Mohamed Khaled (in 2021); and Mahmoud Mustafa Busayf Al-Werfalli (in 2021).

(14) One of the individuals against whom the ICC currently has an outstanding arrest warrant is Joseph Kony. Kony is the leader of the Lord's Resistance Army ("LRA") in Uganda. The ICC charged Kony in 2005 with twelve counts of crimes against humanity and twenty-one counts of war crimes. In 2011, President Obama announced that the United States would send troops to Uganda to serve as advisors to Ugandan troops combating the LRA and attempting to capture Kony. In a letter to Congress, President Obama wrote, "For more than two decades, the Lord's Resistance Army (L.R.A.) has murdered, raped and kidnaped tens of thousands of men, women and children in central Africa." In 2014, President Obama sent additional troops and aircraft to Uganda to assist in the search for the fugitive. Interestingly, part of the impetus for sending advisors to Uganda in 2011 may have been the worldwide attention brought to the atrocities committed by Kony and the LRA by a social media movement called "Kony 2012." According to some reports, the commander of U.S. troops in Africa even had a "Kony 2012" poster on his office door for a period. *See* Jeffrey Gettleman, *In vast Jungle, U.S. Troops Aid in Search for Kony*, The New York Times, *available at* http://www.nytimes.com/2012/04/30/world/africa/kony-tracked-by-us-forces-in-central-africa.html (April 29, 2012). The "Kony 2012" video is still available for viewing at http://invisiblechildren.com/kony-2012/. What role can social media movements play related to the work of the ICC? What role should social media movements play? How does one reconcile the fact that the United States is not willing to join the ICC, but is willing to assist militarily in the apprehension of one of the individuals sought by the Court? Is there a certain degree of ambivalence in the U.S. position? Indeed, the U.S. offered a reward of $5 million for assistance in the capture of Kony and other LRA leaders. Eventually, late in 2014, the U.S. was able to capture Dominic Ongwen, a former child soldier, originally kidnapped by the LRA, who rose to its leadership. He was transferred to The Hague and convicted in 2021 of a miscellany of war crimes and crimes against humanity. (The reward does not appear to have been paid.) The search for Kony, who no longer has much of a following, was scaled down in 2017. Ongwen was sentenced in 2021

to 25 years imprisonment, a sentence which treated his experience as an enforced child soldier as mitigating. *See* ICC Press Release, May 6, 2021, *Dominic Ongwen sentenced to 25 years of imprisonment, available at*: https://www.icc-cpi.int/Pages/item.aspx?name=pr1590.

(15) Crimes can be committed using various modalities. To what extent can cyber means be used to commit the Rome Statute offenses, genocide, crimes against humanity, war crimes, and the crime of aggression? *See* The Council of Adviser's Report on the Application of the Rome Statute of the International Criminal Court to Cyberwarfare (Prepared by the Permanent Mission of Liechtenstein to the United Nations, August 2021).

§ 22.02 Prosecutorial Discretion

In a world of limitless crimes and limited resources, a Prosecutor must always have some kind of strategy. Consider the choices facing the Court's third Prosecutor as he took up his task in 2021, as outlined by Janet H. Anderson, *The ICC in Times of Budget Crunch* (December. 13, 2021), *available at* Justiceinfo.net:*

> International Criminal Court (ICC) prosecutor Karim Khan has been joined by two new deputy prosecutors, elected last week during this year's annual meeting of the court. But states did not step up with additional resources, so he will be forced to prune his docket and will be hard pressed to manage expectations from the many constituencies that lobby the court to do more.
>
> The atmosphere during the week-long meeting in the cavern-like setting of the World Forum in the Hague was both upbeat and workmanlike. A new court president, a new chair of the States' meeting and a new prosecutor were all on the top table at the opening session of the Assembly of States Parties (ASP) of the International Criminal Court (ICC). U.S. Sanctions levied over a year ago against the former prosecutor Fatou Bensouda for her attempt to investigate alleged United States war crimes in Afghanistan are not only in the past but had also forced many states to proclaim their allegiance to international criminal justice and support for the court's work. Meanwhile, heavy Covid-19 restrictions meant only a limited number of NGOs monitoring states at this annual jamboree. Candidates for a variety of elections, including positions on the board of the Trust Fund for Victims and for new deputy prosecutors, meanwhile lobbied states delegates in corners, side events were held online, and controversies kept to a minimum.
>
> State members of the ICC looked at the court's request for a 9.5% increase in its annual budget and agreed to less than half the additions, making it

* Reproduced under creative commons license.

only a modest rise to nearly 155 million Euro. "It is notable that it is an increase," says Elizabeth Evenson who monitored proceedings for international NGO Human Rights Watch (HRW), but "it's concerning, it's less than what the Committee on Budget and Finance (CBF) recommended". And the decision comes against the backdrop of pleas from all the court's principals that more cash is needed because of an increase in workloads across the institution, with a doubling of trials predicted for 2022, and a number of changes in the Office of the Prosecutor.

The reality check though — as the [Committee on Budget and Finance] pointed out — is that as of the middle of 2021, the court was owed more than 60 million Euros in back payments from state members and "until States in arrears demonstrate a willingness to substantially reduce outstanding contributions, budgetary increases will be restricted to what is essential only and, in the first instance, internal savings, efficiencies and prioritisation will be used to meet those essential requirements." The considerable size of the accumulated arrears are mainly explained by the economic effects of coronavirus says Alexandrah Bakker, who runs the Lawyering Justice blog for Public International Law & Policy Group (PILPG), a global pro bono law firm, meaning that there's "no easy solution [to the budget crunch]; states are struggling so the court is struggling".

No ghosts no deceit

The new prosecutor Karim Khan had asked states for enough money to flesh out the substantial changes he is making in how his office should investigate and prosecute some of the most serious crimes in the world. At a press conference he justified decisions he's made — for example, to deprioritise the US and Afghan part of a broad investigation into crimes committed there since 2003 — as a result of resource choices, not "timidity" in challenging a superpower. "Ultimately," he said his office "has spread itself too thin" over 11 investigations and 16 preliminary examinations; "there's a degree of realism everybody needs to get".

As part of that approach, he pledged no "ghost teams", without going into details. He indicated that some investigations he inherited are less substantial than he might have expected, as he is conducting his review of all the investigations and preliminary examinations. He said he would not "proceed and give an impression that there is activity [in his office] when there is not, because I think that is not honourable."

"If we keep promising that we can do everything when we've got these resources," he continued, "we're lying, we're deceitful. We're raising expectations and I'm not going to whatever the consequences."

The detail of his decisions to proceed or not with crimes that met the gravity threshold would be backed up by written assessments from his teams assessing the likelihood of successful prosecution. "Is there evidence to give rise to a realistic prospect of conviction?" would be the "yardstick" for action, he said. Cases and the evidence supporting them don't get stronger while the ICC waits to issue an arrest warrant: "The high watermark may well be before somebody is named and you have to make a call then, if the evidence is capable of proving the case beyond reasonable doubt."

Pragmatic approach

The prosecutor's emphasis has been on complementarity — that states themselves have a responsibility to prosecute. He just appointed a new special adviser on mutual legal assistance. But how exactly the court will support states' efforts to reduce the "accountability gap", as Khan terms it, is not yet clear. We can "try to help with our technical expertise as we move forward with investigations. This is something we're doing with Venezuela", he said, referring to a recent agreement he signed with Caracas. "The ideal is the state does it itself. If not, we can try to assist. And a positive complementarity to a degree, realising we're not a development agency," said Khan. He now has to make that happen within the 49.5 million EUR the states have allocated his office.

"He's very honest about the fact that he's trying to be pragmatic," Bakker says. He has been delivering "a difficult message", acknowledges Evenson. But it does not come as surprise, she says: "victims groups have been well aware for many years now that the court doesn't have the resources it needs. And in other ways maybe hasn't had the capacity it needs to meet their very legitimate expectations on the institution. So, I don't think it will come as news. I think the new prosecutor clearly values being very transparent about decision making and saying clearly that some of these decisions are motivated by the need to prioritise in light of limited resources".

Will there be change?

Apart from the budget the ASP as a whole was dealing with the implementation of a damming Independent Expert Report published two years ago with nearly 400 recommendations for change. Evident was an NGO concern about the extent to which states parties should control the implementation process or mainly just monitor how an independent court gets on with it. They heard loud and clear the criticism of civil society.

Was this ASP the new prosecutor's brief 'honeymoon' with states? Nine years ago, Khan's predecessor also enjoyed a bounce of fresh commitments as she took over as ICC prosecutor and states wanted to show their support for her vision. But the hard decisions will remain. Evenson says states are out of touch with what resources are needed for the court's workload: "I'm sceptical that anything's going to change fundamentally about the discourse around the budget needs of international justice". For that HRW is lobbying for a more strategic discussion as suggested in the experts review, to help states parties understand that "there's a real limit to what their demand for prioritisation can bring about; it's already compromising victims access to justice."

Notes

(1) The principle of complementarity, enshrined in the Preamble and Article 1 of the Statute, and made operational by Article 17, is central to the work of the Court. Is this inevitable in a tribunal which is remote from the scene of the crimes and certain to be short of the resources necessary to do perfect justice? Does the prosecutor's policy emphasis hit the right note?

(2) One surprise in the Court's work has been the practice of States (notably Uganda, the Central African Republic and the Democratic Republic of the Congo) in referring situations in their own countries to the Court. Most participants in the discussions leading to Rome and in Rome itself had in mind a model where either *another* State or the Security Council would make the necessary referral. The Security Council was the source of the Darfur and Libya references, but at least three active situations came by "self-referral." The referral of Israel by the State of Palestine means that crimes by Palestine citizens are fair game for the Prosecutor. Does this mean that often States are finding the ICC a convenient way to deal with their opponents? Is this cynical exploitation or a useful addition to the arsenal of a State confronted with a genuine public order challenge? What is the Prosecutor to do in such cases — ignore violations by the Government? Bite the hand that made the referral? *See generally* Claus Kress, *'Self-Referrals' and 'Waivers of Complementarity': Some Considerations of Law and Policy*, 2 J. Int'l Crim. Just. 944 (2004); Paola Gaeta, *Is the Practice of 'Self-Referrals' a Sound Start for the ICC?* 2 J. Int'l Crim. Just. 949 (2004).

(3) The image of the shattered mosaic, with which the preamble to the Rome Statute opens, is meant to invoke the power of restorative justice in the face of "unimaginable atrocities." The preamble also invokes other theories of criminal punishment such as prevention, retribution and vindication of victims. It offers a punitive response to the problem of "impunity" for the perpetrators of "the most serious crimes of concern to the international community as a whole." Is it ironical that among the strongest proponents of the Statute were human rights organizations, not normally associated with penal solutions? How is the prosecutor to deal with conflicting principles of justice? Is the "real" explanation for the Statute, the expressive use of the law? *See* Robert Sloane, *The Expressive Capacity of International Punishment*, Columbia Public Law and Legal Theory Working Papers, No/ 06100 (2006). *See* also Mirjan Damaska, *What Is the Point of International Criminal Justice?* 83 Chicago-Kent L. Rev. 329 (2008). What role is there for other solutions, such as amnesties or truth and reconciliation commissions? Does Article 53 of the Statute permit deference to efforts by states to deal with their painful pasts in such ways? *See* Darryl Robinson, *Serving the Interests of Justice: Amnesties, Truth Commissions and the International Criminal Court*, 14 Europ. J. Int'l L. 481 (2003).

§ 22.03 The First Review Conference on the Court (2010) and the Independent Expert Review (2020)

Any international organization will atrophy unless some efforts are made to "refresh" it from time to time. The annual meetings of the Assembly of States Parties (ASP) and its various standing working groups are obvious places where criticisms or suggestions for growth can be made. Practice can be changed and amendments can be made, within the limits prescribed by the constituent treaty. In addition, the Court has engaged in two quite far-reaching efforts at soul-searching. The first took place at the First Review Conference; the second in the Independent Expert Review established by the ASP in 2019 in ICC-ASP/18/Res.7 (2019).

The First Review Conference on the Court took place in Uganda in 2010. Article 123 of the Statute says that a Review Conference is to be convened seven years after the Statute comes into force to consider "any amendments" to the Statute. In the future, Review Conferences may be called by the Assembly of States Parties whenever a majority of States Parties so agrees. The drafters of Article 123 were well aware that, while Article 109 of the United Nations Charter contemplates a General Conference of the Members to review the Charter, calling such a meeting requires the agreement of the General Assembly and the Security Council. No General Conference to review the Charter has ever occurred. Hence the insistence by some of the Rome negotiators that there be at least one obligatory meeting commanded by the Statute. Although it had been suggested that Review Conferences should occur on a regular seven-year cycle, no other such Conferences have yet been scheduled.

The only subject that the Statute specifically required to be on the agenda of the First Review was Article 124, the "transitional provision." That Article permits States to opt out of the war crimes provisions of Article 8 of the Statute for the first seven years they are parties to the Statute. (Only France and Colombia have availed themselves of this and France withdrew its declaration in August 2008 before the full seven years had elapsed.) Article 124 says that this provision "shall be reviewed" at the first Review Conference. The 2010 Conference decided not to delete Article 124 and to review the situation again at the Assembly of States Parties in 2015. In 2015, the Assembly decided to adopt an amendment to delete Article 124, ICC-ASP/14/Res.2 (November .26, 2015). Pursuant to Article 121(4) of the Statute, the amendment requires, in addition to adoption by the ASP, acceptance by seven-eighths of the parties. To date there are fewer than twenty acceptances.

The most important item on the agenda in 2010 was in fact the draft provision on aggression which had been produced by a Special Working Group of the Assembly of States Parties. A somewhat amended provision was adopted as Resolution RC/Res. 6 on June 11, 2010 (*see* chap. 23). Belgium and others introduced modest proposals concerning forbidden weapons which were adopted, Resolution RC/Res.5 on June 10, 2010.

The Conference also engaged in "stocktaking." A depressing realization was that fewer than half of the States Parties had adopted the necessary empowering legislation to enable them to cooperate with the Court—and to domesticate the crimes set out in the Statute. A State can hardly be able and willing to prosecute domestically unless it has appropriate legislation in place. Actually enacting the necessary legislation is of crucial importance for international and transnational criminal law.

On the Review Conference, *see generally* Roger S. Clark, *Amendments to the Rome Statute of the International Criminal Court Considered at the First Review Conference on the Court, Kampala, 31 May-11 June 2010*, 2 Goettingen J. Int'l. L. 689 (2010).

The Independent Expert Review was different from the Review Conference. The idea was to glean insights from the outside, from a group of experts with experience in international organization. The nine experts chose Justice Richard Goldstone, the former Prosecutor of the ICTY and the ICTR, as chair of the group. In its 348-page report, the group made hundreds of recommendations under three basic clusters of issues, Governance, Judiciary, and Preliminary examinations, investigations and prosecutions. No organs of the Court escaped candid examination of their practices and culture. *See* Independent Expert Review of the International Criminal Court and the Rome Statute System, September 30, 2020, *available at* https://asp.icc-cpi.int/iccdocs/asp_docs/ASP19/IER-Final-Report-ENG.pdf. The following provides a brief extract on the nature of the Court as an institution, and some of the challenges to its operations:

> 26. Inherent in the structure of any international court or tribunal is the dual nature of the institution: the ICC is both a judicial entity (ICC/Court) and an international organization (ICC/IO). As a judicial entity, the Court must benefit from judicial independence. As an international organisation, States Parties reasonably expect to be able to guide and shape the institution. Contradictions can arise between the two attributes of the ICC, and in practice such differences have led to tension between the ICC and the ASP. Whereas the dual nature of the ICC cannot be changed, employing this distinction can improve the clarity of reporting lines and improve cooperation.
>
> 27. The ICC/IO does not carry out judicial activity–it indirectly supports it. It encompasses administrative services customarily found in international organisations (e.g. human resources, budget and finance, procurement, facilities management, general services etc.). It is led by the Registrar as Chief Administrative Officer, similar to a secretary-general. The ICC/IO should function as a unified organization, with a vertical hierarchical structure. States Parties play a key role in the ICC/IO, including by electing its officials, financing its expenses and overseeing its functioning.
>
> 28. The ICC/Court refers to the judicial activity of the ICC. Here, a further distinction is needed between justice and the administration of justice.

Judicial and prosecutorial work (e.g. judgments, deliberations by Judges, the Prosecutor's decisions to initiate or pursue a case, investigations) require absolute independence. Judges and prosecutors must be able to carry out such activity free from any interference. States Parties shall not use their role in the ICC/IO to influence judicial and prosecutorial activity, whether through budget decisions or appointments. Accountability for judicial and prosecutorial work is ensured through the judicial remedies foreseen by the Court's legal framework.

29. The administration of justice, however, does not necessitate the same degree of independence. Confidentiality and independence should not be used as a way of deflecting accountability and preventing oversight. The administration of justice is audited in national systems–the same should be the case for the ICC. Efficiency in the administration of justice can also be monitored through performance indicators.

30. Within the ICC/Court, States Parties' involvement is limited to the legislative function and judicial cooperation.

31. The aforementioned distinctions lead to a three-layered model of governance of the ICC, in line with the provisions of the Rome Statute:

- Layer 1: Judicial and prosecutorial activity;
- Layer 2: Administration of justice;
- Layer 3: Administration of the international organisation.

32. Depending on the type of scope of an activity, it falls under one layer or another. Every layer has a corresponding framework and requires different degrees of independence and accountability.

Id. (footnotes omitted).

Chapter 23

The Substantive Law of International Crimes

§ 23.01 Specific Offenses

A. Aggression

Definition of Aggression

General Assembly Resolution 3314 (XXIX), Dec. 14, 1974
U.N. GAOR, Supp. 31, at 143, U.N.Doc. A/9631 (1974)

The General Assembly,

Basing itself on the fact that one of the fundamental purposes of the United Nations is to maintain international peace and security and to take effective collective measures for the prevention and removal of threats to the peace, and for the suppression of acts of aggression or other breaches of the peace,

Recalling that the Security Council, in accordance with Article 39 of the Charter of the United Nations, shall determine the existence of any threat to the peace, breach of the peace or act of aggression and shall make recommendations, or decide what measures shall be taken in accordance with Articles 41 and 42, to maintain or restore international peace and security,

Recalling also the duty of States under the Charter to settle their international disputes by peaceful means in order not to endanger international peace, security and justice,

Bearing in mind that nothing in this Definition shall be interpreted as in any way affecting the scope of the provisions of the Charter with respect to the functions and powers of the organs of the United Nations,

Considering also that, since aggression is the most serious and dangerous form of the illegal use of force, being fraught, in the conditions created by the existence of all types of weapons of mass destruction, with the possible threat of a world conflict and all its catastrophic consequences, aggression should be defined at the present stage,

Reaffirming the duty of States not to use armed force to deprive peoples of their right to self-determination, freedom and independence, or to disrupt territorial integrity,

Reaffirming also that the territory of a State shall not be violated by being the object, even temporarily, of military occupation or of other measures of force taken by another State in contravention of the Charter, and that it shall not be the object of acquisition by another State resulting from such measures or the threat thereof,

Reaffirming also the provisions of the Declaration on Principles of International Law concerning Friendly Relations and Cooperation among States in accordance with the Charter of the United Nations,

Convinced that the adoption of a definition of aggression ought to have the effect of deterring a potential aggressor, would simplify the determination of acts of aggression and the implementation of measures to suppress them and would also facilitate the protection of the rights and lawful interests of, and the rendering of assistance to, the victim,

Believing that, although the question whether an act of aggression has been committed must be considered in the light of all the circumstances of each particular case, it is nevertheless desirable to formulate basic principles as guidance for such determination,

Adopts the following Definition of Aggression:

Article I

Aggression is the use of armed force by a State against the sovereignty, territorial integrity or political independence of another State, or in any other manner inconsistent with the Charter of the United Nations, as set out in this Definition.

Explanatory note: In this Definition the term "State":

(*a*) Is used without prejudice to questions of recognition or whether a State is a member of the United Nations;

(*b*) Includes the concept of a "group of States" where appropriate.

Article 2

The first use of armed force by a State in contravention of the Charter shall constitute *prima facie* evidence of an act of aggression although the Security Council may, in conformity with the Charter, conclude that a determination that an act of aggression has been committed would not be justified in the light of other relevant circumstances, including the fact that the acts concerned or their consequences are not of sufficient gravity.

Article 3

Any of the following acts, regardless of a declaration of war, shall, subject to and in accordance with the provisions of article 2, qualify as an act of aggression:

(a) The invasion or attack by the armed forces of a State of the territory of another State, or any military occupation, however temporary, resulting from such invasion or attack, or any annexation by the use of force of the territory of another State or part thereof,

(b) Bombardment by the armed forces of a State against the territory of another State or the use of any weapons by a State against the territory of another State;

(c) The blockade of the ports or coasts of a State by the armed forces of another State;

(d) An attack by the armed forces of a State on the land, sea or air forces, or marine and air fleets of another State;

(e) The use of armed forces of one State which are within the territory of another State with the agreement of the receiving State, in contravention of the conditions provided for in the agreement or any extension of their presence in such territory beyond the termination of the agreement;

(f) The action of a State in allowing its territory, which it has placed at the disposal of another State, to be used by that other State for perpetrating an act of aggression against a third State;

(g) The sending by or on behalf of a State of armed bands, groups, irregulars or mercenaries, which carry out acts of armed force against another State of such gravity as to amount to the acts listed above, or its substantial involvement therein.

Article 4

The acts enumerated above are not exhaustive and the Security Council may determine that other acts constitute aggression under the provisions of the Charter.

Article 5

1. No consideration of whatever nature, whether political, economic, military or otherwise, may serve as a justification for aggression.

2. A war of aggression is a crime against international peace. Aggression gives rise to international responsibility.

3. No territorial acquisition or special advantage resulting from aggression is or shall be recognized as lawful.

Article 6

Nothing in this Definition shall be construed as in any way enlarging or diminishing the scope of the Charter, including its provisions concerning cases in which the use of force is lawful.

Article 7

Nothing in this Definition, and in particular article 3, could in any way prejudice the right to self-determination, freedom and independence, as derived from the Charter, of peoples forcibly deprived of that right and referred to in the Declaration on Principles of International Law concerning Friendly Relations and Cooperation among States in accordance with the Charter of the United Nations, particularly peoples under colonial and racist regimes or other forms of alien domination: nor the right of these peoples to struggle to that end and to seek and receive support, in accordance with the principles of the Charter and in conformity with the above-mentioned Declaration.

Article 8

In their interpretation and application the above provisions are interrelated and each provision should be construed in the context of the other provisions.

Notes

(1) The General Assembly adopted Resolution 3314 by consensus, without taking a vote. The explanatory note to Article 1 was meant, in part, to indicate that the term "State" covered divided territories such as Germany, Korea, and China. It also has been considered unacceptable to invade a non-self-governing territory, such as the 1975 invasions of East Timor and Western Sahara based on the claim that they were not states at the relevant time and thus fair game to their neighbors. A non-self-governing territory is a separate legal person that amounts to a state for the purpose of being the subject of aggression. *See* the Declaration of Friendly Principles, G.A. Res. 2625 (XXV); J.J. Smith, *A Four-Fold Evil? The Crime of Aggression and the Case of Western Sahara*, 20 Int'l Crim. L. Rev. 1, 12–14 (2020).

(2) Compare the General Assembly's definition of aggression with the minimalist definition of "crimes against peace" in the Charters of the Nuremberg and Tokyo Tribunals [*see* chap. 20, *supra*]. On the historical problem of defining aggression, and for further references, *see* M. Cherif Bassiouni & Benjamin B. Ferencz, *The Crime Against Peace: From its origins to the I.C.C., in* 1 International Criminal Law 207 (M. Cherif Bassiouni ed., 3d ed. 2008); Benjamin Ferencz, Defining International Aggression: The Search for World Peace (2 Vols., 1975). *See also* material below on defining aggression for the purposes of the ICC.

(3) Over the opposition of the United States and other major powers, Article 5 of the Rome Statute [*see* chap. 22] gives the International Criminal Court jurisdiction over "the crime of aggression," but goes on to provide that the Court can "exercise" jurisdiction over this crime only after an amendment to the Statute is adopted defining the crime and the conditions under which the Court is to exercise jurisdiction over it. Article 5 further stipulates that "[s]uch a provision shall be consistent with the relevant provisions of the Charter of the United Nations." A Special Working Group on the Crime of Aggression (SWGCA), composed of all States that wished to attend (parties and non-parties alike) was created by the Assembly of States Parties of the Court. The Working Group produced its final report early in 2009 and the draft it contained was the basis for the amendments adopted at the Review Conference on the Statute held in Kampala in May-June 2010. (*See infra.*)

(4) The General Assembly's Definition of Aggression is about state responsibility. In devising the definition called for by Article 5 of the Rome Statute, what weight should be given to General Assembly Resolution 3314 (1974)? Does it represent an authoritative statement of international law? Note that, in the *Nicaragua*

case [*Military and Paramilitary Activities in and against Nicaragua (Nicar. v. U.S.)*, Merits, 1986 I.C.J. REP. 14, 103, para. 195 (June 27)], the International Court of Justice indicated that Article 3(g) of the General Assembly's Definition "may be taken to reflect customary international law." But even if the Definition is a statement of existing international law, is it necessarily binding on the Security Council? Consider Article 4 of the definition. Does this make it entirely open-ended?

(5) Recall that Article 39 of the U.N. Charter provides: "The Security Council shall determine the existence of any threat to the peace, breach of the peace, or act of aggression and shall make recommendations, or decide what measures shall be taken . . . to maintain or restore international peace and security." Article 24 of the Charter states that the Security Council has "primary responsibility" for peace and security. "Primary" suggests this is not exclusive. Under the system established by the Charter, is it possible to produce a definition of aggression that does not leave the final decision as to whether aggression occurred to the Security Council? What is to be made of state practice under the Uniting for Peace Resolution, G.A. Res. 377 A (V), 5 U.N. GAOR, Supp. No. 20, at 10, U.N. Doc. A/1775 (1950)? Adopted during the Korean War at the insistence of the Western states, that resolution carves out a role for the General Assembly to make determinations about aggression when the Security Council is paralyzed by the veto. How far, moreover, can the International Court of Justice go in determining questions of the (unlawful) use of force? The Court's decision in *Armed Activities on the Territory of the Congo (Dem. Rep. Congo v. Uganda)*, 2005 I.C.J. 116, suggests that it has broad powers in this respect, even if the majority was reluctant to use the word "aggression." If the Security Council or some other United Nations organ such as the General Assembly or the I.C.J. has the decisive word as to whether aggression occurred, is it possible to devise a definition of aggression for purposes of imposing criminal sanctions on individuals that will not make liability directly depend on the decision of a political body? Can doing so be reconciled with ordinary understandings of how criminal law is supposed to operate? How much traffic will "general part" issues such as mistake (of fact or law) and other grounds for the exclusion of responsibility bear? Why should the I.C.C. not have power to determine for itself the existence of all elements of the offense? Why should a political decision be taken as a "given" for criminal purposes? These were among the many issues canvassed in the Special Working Group on the Crime of Aggression.

(6) Aggression is said to be a "leadership crime." *See* Daniel Nsereko, *Defining the crime of aggression: An important agenda item for the Assembly of States Parties to the Rome Statute of the International Criminal Court*, 2003 ACTA JURIDICA 256, 278–281. How should that be expressed in the drafting? Does it mean that, for the purposes of this crime, some of the general provisions of the Rome Statute, such as Article 25(3)(a)–(d) (complicity in a broad sense) and Article 28 (responsibility of commanders and other superiors) should be replaced by more specific provisions?

(7) Of crucial significance, though, was another disputed issue. Does paragraph 4 or paragraph 5 of Article 121 of the Rome Statute (on amendments) apply to the

aggression provision? Paragraph 4 says that "except as provided in paragraph 5, an amendment shall enter into force for all States Parties one year after instruments of ratification or acceptance have been deposited with the Secretary-General by seven-eighths of them." Paragraph 5 says that "[a]ny amendment to articles 5, 6, 7 and 8 of this Statute shall enter into force for those States Parties which have accepted the amendment one year after the deposit of their instruments of ratification or acceptance." The difference is dramatic. If paragraph 4 applies, nobody is bound by it until acceptance by seven-eighths of the States Parties is achieved. Once that is the case, all parties are bound (subject to a right for dissenters to withdraw entirely from the Statute). If paragraph 5 applies, when the first acceptance of the provisions is deposited and a year passes, the provision applies to the accepting State. So it is with each subsequent accepting State. But the provision would never apply to nationals or the territory of States which do not accept it. Interpreting the relationship between Article 5(2) and 121 is difficult, and the legislative history was largely silent, as these provisions were added at the very end of the Rome Conference. Is the "provision" on aggression an "amendment"? It must be for some purposes, procedural at least. But is it an "amendment" to "article 5"? Arguably it is a "completion" rather than an "amendment." What is the best functional interpretation of the Statute? Aggression is a controversial crime. If everybody is to be bound, will ratification be inhibited? If it is the "supreme international crime" (as the Nuremberg Tribunal suggested [chap. 20]), should it not apply to everybody? Has there been a retreat from Nuremberg? What weight is to be given to the fact that the crime of aggression was *sui generis*, half in and half out of the Rome Statute?

Consider how these issues (and others) are resolved (or left open) in the ICC Amendments adopted in Kampala in 2010 which follow:

Resolution RC/Res. 6

Adopted at the 13th plenary meeting, on 11 June 2010, by consensus

RC/Res.6

The crime of aggression

The Review Conference,

Recalling paragraph 1 of article 12 of the Rome Statute,

Recalling paragraph 2 of article 5 of the Rome Statute,

Recalling also paragraph 7 of resolution F, adopted by the United Nations Diplomatic Conference of Plenipotentiaries on the Establishment of an International Criminal Court on 17 July 1998,

Recalling further resolution ICC-ASP/1/Res.1 on the continuity of work in respect of the crime of aggression, and *expressing its appreciation* to the Special Working Group on the Crime of Aggression for having elaborated proposals on a provision on the crime of aggression,

Taking note of resolution ICC-ASP/8/Res.6, by which the Assembly of States Parties forwarded proposals on a provision on the crime of aggression to the Review Conference for its consideration,

Resolved to activate the Court's jurisdiction over the crime of aggression as early as possible,

1. *Decides* to adopt, in accordance with article 5, paragraph 2, of the Rome Statute of the International Criminal Court (hereinafter: "the Statute") the amendments to the Statute contained in annex I of the present resolution, which are subject to ratification or acceptance and shall enter into force in accordance with article 121, paragraph 5; and *notes* that any State Party may lodge a declaration referred to in article 15 *bis* prior to ratification or acceptance;

2. *Also decides* to adopt the amendments to the Elements of Crimes contained in annex II of the present resolution;

3. *Also decides* to adopt the understandings regarding the interpretation of the above-mentioned amendments contained in annex III of the present resolution;

4. *Further decides* to review the amendments on the crime of aggression seven years after the beginning of the Court's exercise of jurisdiction;

5. *Calls upon* all States Parties to ratify or accept the amendments contained in annex I.

Annex I Amendments to the Rome Statute of the International Criminal Court on the crime of aggression

1. *Article 5, paragraph 2, of the Statute is deleted.*

2. *The following text is inserted after article 8 of the Statute*:

Article 8 *bis*

Crime of aggression

1. For the purpose of this Statute, "crime of aggression" means the planning, preparation, initiation or execution, by a person in a position effectively to exercise control over or to direct the political or military action of a State, of an act of aggression which, by its character, gravity and scale, constitutes a manifest violation of the Charter of the United Nations.

2. For the purpose of paragraph 1, "act of aggression" means the use of armed force by a State against the sovereignty, territorial integrity or political independence of another State, or in any other manner inconsistent with the Charter of the United Nations. Any of the following acts, regardless of a declaration of war, shall, in accordance with United Nations General Assembly resolution 3314 (XXIX) of 14 December 1974, qualify as an act of aggression:

(a) The invasion or attack by the armed forces of a State of the territory of another State, or any military occupation, however temporary, resulting from such invasion or attack, or any annexation by the use of force of the territory of another State or part thereof;

(b) Bombardment by the armed forces of a State against the territory of another State or the use of any weapons by a State against the territory of another State;

(c) The blockade of the ports or coasts of a State by the armed forces of another State;

(d) An attack by the armed forces of a State on the land, sea or air forces, or marine and air fleets of another State;

(e) The use of armed forces of one State which are within the territory of another State with the agreement of the receiving State, in contravention of the conditions provided for in the agreement or any extension of their presence in such territory beyond the termination of the agreement;

(f) The action of a State in allowing its territory, which it has placed at the disposal of another State, to be used by that other State for perpetrating an act of aggression against a third State;

(g) The sending by or on behalf of a State of armed bands, groups, irregulars or mercenaries, which carry out acts of armed force against another State of such gravity as to amount to the acts listed above, or its substantial involvement therein.

3. *The following text is inserted after article 15 of the Statute:*

Article 15 *bis*

Exercise of jurisdiction over the crime of aggression (State referral, *proprio motu*)

1. The Court may exercise jurisdiction over the crime of aggression in accordance with article 13, paragraphs (a) and (c), subject to the provisions of this article.

2. The Court may exercise jurisdiction only with respect to crimes of aggression committed one year after the ratification or acceptance of the amendments by thirty States Parties.

3. The Court shall exercise jurisdiction over the crime of aggression in accordance with this article, subject to a decision to be taken after 1 January 2017 by the same majority of States Parties as is required for the adoption of an amendment to the Statute.

4. The Court may, in accordance with article 12, exercise jurisdiction over a crime of aggression, arising from an act of aggression committed by a State Party, unless that State Party has previously declared that it does not accept such jurisdiction by lodging a declaration with the Registrar. The

withdrawal of such a declaration may be effected at any time and shall be considered by the State Party within three years.

5. In respect of a State that is not a party to this Statute, the Court shall not exercise its jurisdiction over the crime of aggression when committed by that State's nationals or on its territory.

6. Where the Prosecutor concludes that there is a reasonable basis to proceed with an investigation in respect of a crime of aggression, he or she shall first ascertain whether the Security Council has made a determination of an act of aggression committed by the State concerned. The Prosecutor shall notify the Secretary-General of the United Nations of the situation before the Court, including any relevant information and documents.

7. Where the Security Council has made such a determination, the Prosecutor may proceed with the investigation in respect of a crime of aggression.

8. Where no such determination is made within six months after the date of notification, the Prosecutor may proceed with the investigation in respect of a crime of aggression, provided that the Pre-Trial Division has authorized the commencement of the investigation in respect of a crime of aggression in accordance with the procedure contained in article 15, and the Security Council has not decided otherwise in accordance with article 16.

9. A determination of an act of aggression by an organ outside the Court shall be without prejudice to the Court's own findings under this Statute.

10. This article is without prejudice to the provisions relating to the exercise of jurisdiction with respect to other crimes referred to in article 5.

4. The following text is inserted after article 15 bis of the Statute:

Article 15 *ter*

Exercise of jurisdiction over the crime of aggression (Security Council referral)

1. The Court may exercise jurisdiction over the crime of aggression in accordance with article 13, paragraph (b), subject to the provisions of this article.

2. The Court may exercise jurisdiction only with respect to crimes of aggression committed one year after the ratification or acceptance of the amendments by thirty States Parties.

3. The Court shall exercise jurisdiction over the crime of aggression in accordance with this article, subject to a decision to be taken after 1 January 2017 by the same majority of States Parties as is required for the adoption of an amendment to the Statute.

4. A determination of an act of aggression by an organ outside the Court shall be without prejudice to the Court's own findings under this Statute.

> 5. This article is without prejudice to the provisions relating to the exercise of jurisdiction with respect to other crimes referred to in article 5.

5. *The following text is inserted after article 25, paragraph 3, of the Statute:*

> *3 bis.* In respect of the crime of aggression, the provisions of this article shall apply only to persons in a position effectively to exercise control over or to direct the political or military action of a State.

6. *The first sentence of article 9, paragraph 1, of the Statute is replaced by the following sentence:*

> 1. Elements of Crimes shall assist the Court in the interpretation and application of articles 6, 7, 8 and 8 *bis*.

7. *The chapeau of article 20, paragraph 3, of the Statute is replaced by the following paragraph; the rest of the paragraph remains unchanged:*

> 3. No person who has been tried by another court for conduct also proscribed under article 6, 7, 8 or 8 *bis* shall be tried by the Court with respect to the same conduct unless the proceedings in the other court:

Annex II Amendments to the Elements of Crimes

Article 8 *bis*

Crime of aggression

Introduction

> 1. It is understood that any of the acts referred to in article 8 *bis*, paragraph 2, qualify as an act of aggression.
>
> 2. There is no requirement to prove that the perpetrator has made a legal evaluation as to whether the use of armed force was inconsistent with the Charter of the United Nations.
>
> 3. The term "manifest" is an objective qualification.
>
> 4. There is no requirement to prove that the perpetrator has made a legal evaluation as to the "manifest" nature of the violation of the Charter of the United Nations.

Elements

> 1. The perpetrator planned, prepared, initiated or executed an act of aggression.
>
> 2. The perpetrator was a person[1] in a position effectively to exercise control over or to direct the political or military action of the State which committed the act of aggression.

---

1. With respect to an act of aggression, more than one person may be in a position that meets these criteria. [Footnote in original.]

3. The act of aggression — the use of armed force by a State against the sovereignty, territorial integrity or political independence of another State, or in any other manner inconsistent with the Charter of the United Nations — was committed.

4. The perpetrator was aware of the factual circumstances that established that such a use of armed force was inconsistent with the Charter of the United Nations.

5. The act of aggression, by its character, gravity and scale, constituted a manifest violation of the Charter of the United Nations.

6. The perpetrator was aware of the factual circumstances that established such a manifest violation of the Charter of the United Nations.

Annex III

Understandings regarding the amendments to the Rome Statute of the International Criminal Court on the crime of aggression

Referrals by the Security Council

1. It is understood that the Court may exercise jurisdiction on the basis of a Security Council referral in accordance with article 13, paragraph (b), of the Statute only with respect to crimes of aggression committed after a decision in accordance with article 15 *ter*, paragraph 3, is taken, and one year after the ratification or acceptance of the amendments by thirty States Parties, whichever is later.

2. It is understood that the Court shall exercise jurisdiction over the crime of aggression on the basis of a Security Council referral in accordance with article 13, paragraph (b), of the Statute irrespective of whether the State concerned has accepted the Court's jurisdiction in this regard.

Jurisdiction ratione temporis

3. It is understood that in case of article 13, paragraph (a) or (c), the Court may exercise its jurisdiction only with respect to crimes of aggression committed after a decision in accordance with article 15 *bis*, paragraph 3, is taken, and one year after the ratification or acceptance of the amendments by thirty States Parties, whichever is later.

Domestic jurisdiction over the crime of aggression

4. It is understood that the amendments that address the definition of the act of aggression and the crime of aggression do so for the purpose of this Statute only. The amendments shall, in accordance with article 10 of the Rome Statute, not be interpreted as limiting or prejudicing in anyway existing or developing rules of international law for purposes other than this Statute.

5. It is understood that the amendments shall not be interpreted as creating the right or obligation to exercise domestic jurisdiction with respect to an act of aggression committed by another State.

Other understandings

6. It is understood that aggression is the most serious and dangerous form of the illegal use of force; and that a determination whether an act of aggression has been committed requires consideration of all the circumstances of each particular case, including the gravity of the acts concerned and their consequences, in accordance with the Charter of the United Nations.

7. It is understood that in establishing whether an act of aggression constitutes a manifest violation of the Charter of the United Nations, the three components of character, gravity and scale must be sufficient to justify a "manifest" determination. No one component can be significant enough to satisfy the manifest standard by itself.

Note

By late 2017, more than 30 ratifications had been received, and support was building for the activation of the Kampala amendments. *See generally*, The Travaux Préparatoires of the Crime of Aggression (Stefan Barriga & Claus Kreβ eds., 2012); The Crime of Aggression: A Commentary (Claus Kreβ &Stefan Barriga eds., 2017); Roger S. Clark, *Alleged Aggression in Utopia: An International Criminal Law Exam Question for 2020*, in The Ashgate Research Companion to International Criminal Law: Critical Perspectives 63 (William A. Schabas, Yvonne McDermott & Niamh Hayes eds., 2013); Seeking Accountability for the Unlawful Use of Force (Leila Nadya Sadat ed., 2018); Carrie McDougal, The Crime of Aggression under the Rome Statute of the International Criminal Court (2d ed. 2021).

For a negative assessment *see* Harold Hongju Koh & Todd F. Buchwald, *The Crime of Aggression: The United States Perspective*, 109 Am. J. Int'l L. 257 (2015); the authors, leaders of the U.S. observer delegation in Kampala, argue in particular that the definition is insufficiently precise and that this will have a chilling effect in discouraging legitimate uses of force. "It would be truly tragic," they say, *id* at 272, "if this chilling effect discouraged states from stopping preventable genocide, war crimes and crimes against humanity, and thus limited states' responses to *ad hoc* efforts at accountability." Unilateral "humanitarian interventions" and the "responsibility to protect" exercised without the imprimatur of the Security Council are, at best, controversial in current international law. The authors of the Kampala amendments thought they had provided an adequate structure for analyzing such issues in the requirement in Article 8 *bis* (1) that an act of aggression must be a "manifest" violation and in the acceptance in Article 31 (3) of the Rome Statute that there may be customary law "grounds for excluding criminal responsibility."

In December 2017, the Court's Assembly of States Parties adopted the following resolution:

Resolution ICC-ASP/16/Res.5

Adopted at the 13th plenary meeting, on 14 December 2017, by consensus

Activation of the jurisdiction of the Court over the crime of aggression

The Assembly of States Parties,

Recognizing the historic significance of the consensual decision at the Kampala Review Conference to adopt the amendments to the Rome Statute on the crime of aggression, and in this regard recalling resolution RC/Res.6,

Reaffirming the purposes and principles of the Charter of the United Nations,

Recalling its resolve to activate the Court's jurisdiction over the crime of aggression as early as possible, subject to a decision according to paragraphs 3 of article 15 *bis* and article 15 *ter,*

Noting with appreciation the report on the facilitation on the activation of the jurisdiction of the International Criminal Court over the crime of aggression, which summarizes the views of States Parties,

Recalling paragraph 4 of article 15 *bis* and paragraph 5 of article 121,

Recalling also that in paragraph 1 of RC/Res.6 the Review Conference decided to adopt, in accordance with paragraph 2 of article 5 the amendments regarding the crime of aggression, which are subject to ratification or acceptance and shall enter into force in accordance with paragraph 5 of article 121; and noted that any State Party may lodge a declaration referred to in article 15 *bis* prior to ratification or acceptance of the amendments.

1. *Decides* to activate the Court's jurisdiction over the crime of aggression as of 17 July 2018;
2. *Confirms* that, in accordance with the Rome Statute, the amendments to the Statute regarding the crime of aggression adopted at the Kampala Review Conference enter into force for those States Parties which have accepted the amendments one year after the deposit of their instruments of ratification or acceptance and that in the case of a State referral or *proprio motu* investigation the Court shall not exercise its jurisdiction regarding a crime of aggression when committed by a national or on the territory of a State Party that has not ratified or accepted these amendments;
3. *Reaffirms* paragraph 1 of article 40 and paragraph 1 of article 119 of the Rome Statute in relation to the judicial independence of the judges of the Court;
4. *Renews* its call upon all States Parties which have not yet done so to ratify or accept the amendments to the Rome Statute on the crime of aggression.

Notes

(1) By the end of 2021, 41 States were party to the Kampala Amendments, with Italy and Sweden about to join them. To whom do the Kampala Amendments apply? Compare the formula in Article 15 *bis* (4) of Kampala and that in para. 2 of the adopting resolution. Does the opt-out provision in 15 *bis* (4) have any practical import after the 2017 resolution? Are one or both of these resolutions *ultra vires* Article 121 of the Statute?

(2) On the activation, *see* Roger S. Clark, *Exercise of Jurisdiction over the Crime of Aggression (International Criminal Court)*, MAX PLANCK ENCYCLOPEDIA OF INTERNATIONAL PROCEDURAL LAW (2019), *available at* https://opil.ouplaw.com/view/10.1093/law-mpeipro/e3480.013.3480/law-mpeipro-e3480; Claus Kreβ, *On the Activation of ICC Jurisdiction over the Crime of Aggression*, 16 J. INT'L CRIM. JUST. 1 (2018); Meagan S. Wong, *The Activation of the International Criminal Court's Jurisdiction over the Crime of Aggression: International Institutional Law and Dispute Settlement Perspectives,* 22 INT'L COMMUNITY L. REV. 197 (2020). Following the activation resolution, the judges (who have power to make regulations for the operating of the Court) amended those regulations (perhaps not sufficiently) to provide for addressing aggression allegations. *See* Eleni Chatidou, *The Amendments to the Regulations of the Court: Laying the Groundwork for Investigating the Crime of Aggression*, 19 J. INT'L CRIM. JUST. 495 (2019).

(3) On early efforts to domesticate the crime of aggression, *see* Annegret Hartig, *The Early Implementers of the Crime of Aggression*, 17 J. INT'L CRIM. JUST. 485 (2019). Many of them include the leadership requirement. Compare the unusual conviction in Ukraine of lower-level Russian soldiers, discussed in Sergey Sayapin, *A Curious Aggression Trial in Ukraine, Some Reflections on the Alexandrov and Yerofeyev Case*, 16 J. INT'L CRIM. JUSTICE 1093 (2018). (Ukraine signed but has not ratified the Rome Statute, and the legislation under which the prosecution was brought apparently pre-dates the demise of the Soviet Union.)

B. Genocide

Convention on the Prevention and Punishment of the Crime of Genocide

General Assembly Resolution 260 A (III), Dec. 9, 1948
78 U.N.T.S. 277

The Contracting Parties,

Having considered the declaration made by the General Assembly of the United Nations in its resolution 96 (I) dated 11 December 1946 that genocide is a crime under international law, contrary to the spirit and aims of the United Nations and condemned by the civilized world;

Recognizing that at all periods of history genocide has inflicted great losses on humanity; and

Being convinced that, in order to liberate mankind from such an odious scourge, international co-operation is required,

Hereby agree as hereinafter provided:

Article I

The Contracting Parties confirm that genocide, whether committed in time of peace or in time of war, is a crime under international law which they undertake to prevent and to punish.

Article II

In the present Convention, genocide means any of the following acts committed with intent to destroy, in whole or in part, a national, ethnical, racial or religious group, as such:

(a) Killing members of the group;

(b) Causing serious bodily or mental harm to members of the group;

(c) Deliberately inflicting on the group conditions of life calculated to bring about its physical destruction in whole or in part;

(d) Imposing measures intended to prevent births within the group;

(e) Forcibly transferring children of the group to another group.

Article III

The following acts shall be punishable:

(a) Genocide;

(b) Conspiracy to commit genocide;

(c) Direct and public incitement to commit genocide;

(d) Attempt to commit genocide;

(e) Complicity in genocide.

Article IV

Persons committing genocide or any of the other acts enumerated in article III shall be punished, whether they are constitutionally responsible rulers, public officials or private individuals.

Article V

The Contracting Parties undertake to enact, in accordance with their respective Constitutions, the necessary legislation to give effect to the provisions of the present Convention, and, in particular, to provide effective penalties for persons guilty of genocide or any of the other acts enumerated in article III.

Article VI

Persons charged with genocide or any of the other acts enumerated in article III shall be tried by a competent tribunal of the State in the territory of which the act was committed, or by such international penal tribunal as may have jurisdiction with respect to those Contracting Parties which shall have accepted its jurisdiction.

Article VII

Genocide and the other acts enumerated in article III shall not be considered as political crimes for the purpose of extradition.

The Contracting Parties pledge themselves in such cases to grant extradition in accordance with their laws and treaties in force.

Article VIII

Any Contracting Party may call upon the competent organs of the United Nations to take such action under the Charter of the United Nations as they consider appropriate for the prevention and suppression of acts of genocide or any of the other acts enumerated in article III.

Article IX

Disputes between the Contracting Parties relating to the interpretation, application or fulfilment of the present Convention, including those relating to the responsibility of a State for genocide or for any of the other acts enumerated in article III, shall be submitted to the International Court of Justice at the request of any of the parties to the dispute.

Notes

(1) The Genocide Convention contains nineteen articles. Articles 10 to 19 are "final clauses." The Convention came into force on January 12, 1951. It was not ratified by the United States until 1988. The Convention was given effect as part of U.S. law through the Genocide Convention Implementation Act of 1987, Pub. L. 100-106, 102 Stat. 3045, enacted on November 5, 1988. The act is codified at 18 U.S. Code §§ 1091–1093. It reads as follows:

> § 1091. Genocide
>
> (a) Basic offense. Whoever, whether in time of peace or in time of war, in a circumstance described in subsection (d) and with the specific intent to destroy, in whole or in substantial part, a national, ethnic, racial, or religious group as such—
>
> (1) kills members of that group;
>
> (2) causes serious bodily injury to members of that group;
>
> (3) causes the permanent impairment of the mental faculties of members of the group through drugs, torture, or similar techniques;

(4) subjects the group to conditions of life that are intended to cause the physical destruction of the group in whole or in part;

(5) imposes measures intended to prevent births within the group; or

(6) transfers by force children of the group to another group; or attempts to do so, shall be punished as provided in subsection (b).

(b) Punishment for basic offense. The punishment for an offense under subsection (a) is

(1) in the case of an offense under subsection (a) (1), where death results, by death or imprisonment for life and a fine of not more than $1,000,000, or both; and

(2) a fine of not more than $1,000,000 or imprisonment for not more than twenty years, or both, in any other case.

(c) Incitement offense. Whoever in a circumstance described in subsection (d) directly and publicly incites another to violate subsection (a) shall be fined not more than $500,000 or imprisoned not more than five years, or both.

(d) Required Circumstance for Offenses.—The circumstance referred to in subsections (a) and (c) is that—

(1) the offense is committed in whole or in part within the United States;

(2) the alleged offender is a national of the United States (as that term is defined in section 101 of the Immigration and Nationality Act (8 U.S.C. 1101));

(3) the alleged offender is an alien lawfully admitted for permanent residence in the United States (as that term is defined in section 101 of the Immigration and Nationality Act (8 U.S.C. 1101));

(4) the alleged offender is a stateless person whose habitual residence is in the United States; or

(5) after the conduct required for the offense occurs, the alleged offender is brought into, or found in, the United States, even if that conduct occurred outside the United States.[a]

(e) Nonapplicability of certain limitation. Notwithstanding section 3282 of this title, in the case of an offense under subsection (a) (1), an indictment may be found, or information instituted, at any time without limitation.

§ 1092. Exclusive remedies

Nothing in this chapter [18 USC §§ 1091 et seq.] shall be construed as precluding the application of State or local laws to the conduct proscribed by

---

a. The original version of subsection (d) did not include the universal jurisdiction provision now found in (d)(5). The subsection was amended by the Genocide Accountability Act of 2007.—Eds.

this chapter, nor shall anything in this chapter be construed as creating any substantive or procedural right enforceable by law by any party in any proceeding.

§ 1093. Definitions

As used in this chapter [18 USC §§ 1091 et seq.] —

(1) the term "children" means the plural and means individuals who have not attained the age of eighteen years;

(2) the term "ethnic group" means a set of individuals whose identity as such is distinctive in terms of common cultural traditions or heritage;

(3) the term "incites" means urges another to engage imminently in conduct in circumstances under which there is a substantial likelihood of imminently causing such conduct;

(4) the term "members" means the plural;

(5) the term "national group" means a set of individuals whose identity as such is distinctive in terms of nationality or national origins;

(6) the term "racial group" means a set of individuals whose identity as such is distinctive in terms of physical characteristics or biological descent;

(7) the term "religious group" means a set of individuals whose identity as such is distinctive in terms of common religious creed, beliefs, doctrines, practices, or rituals; and

(8) the term "substantial part" means a part of a group of such numerical significance that the destruction or loss of that part would cause the destruction of the group as a viable entity within the nation of which such group is a part.

How does the definition of "genocide" in the U.S. statute differ from that in the Genocide Convention? Note that in ratifying the Convention, the U.S. expressed the interpretive "understanding" that, as used in the Convention, (1) the phrase intent to destroy a group "in whole or in part" means the specific intent to destroy it "in whole or substantial part"; and (2) the term "mental harm" means "permanent impairment of mental facilities through drugs, torture or similar techniques." While several States objected to various United States "reservations" so denominated, no-one objected to this "understanding" which could be seen functionally as a reservation. (On reservations, *see* § 10.01, Note 4, *supra.*)

(2) Does the Convention specifically contemplate the possibility of courts exercising "universal jurisdiction" in cases of genocide? Does that necessarily preclude the exercise of such jurisdiction?

(3) One of the most controversial aspects of the definition of "genocide" in the Convention is its exclusion of political and social groups from the list of those

protected. The term "genocide" was coined by Raphael Lemkin in his book, Axis Rule in Occupied Europe (1944), to describe Nazi efforts to reconstruct social and economic structure, to Aryanize, and to destroy a sense of separate national identity, in German-occupied territories. *See also* Raphael Lemkin, *Genocide as a Crime under International Law*, 41 Am. J. Int'l L. 145 (1947). General Assembly Resolution 96 (I), Dec. 11, 1946, which is referred to in the preamble to the Genocide Convention, declared that "genocide is a crime under international law" and is punishable "whether the crime is committed on religious, racial, political or any other grounds." Two years later, the Convention dropped the possibility that genocide could be committed against a political group. Under the Convention's definition, would the murder of a million or more Cambodians by the Khmer Rouge between 1975 and 1979, as part of an effort to reconstruct the country's social and economic structure, constitute genocide? *See* William A. Schabas, Genocide in International Law: The Crime of Crimes, 138–9 (2nd ed. 2009). Nevertheless, the definition of "genocide" in international instruments has remained remarkably stable since 1948. The definition appears unchanged in Article 6 of the Rome Statute. There was an obvious reluctance to tamper with the canonical statement contained in a widely-ratified agreement. Often in everyday discourse, commentators refer to gross violations of human rights as "genocide" and are then disappointed (and contemptuous of lawyers) when it is explained that the crimes involved are "only" crimes against humanity.

(4) To what extent can the media (print and radio journalists) and political parties contribute to conspiracy to commit genocide, direct and public incitement of genocide and genocide itself? A particularly interesting decision on these issues in the ICTR is *Prosecutor v. Nahimana, Barayagwiza and Ngeze*, Case No. ICTR-99-52-T, Trial Chamber I, Judgement of December 3, 2003 ("The Media Case"). The Tribunal commented, at paragraph 945 of its opinion:

> This case raises important principles concerning the role of the media, which have not been addressed at the level of international criminal justice since Nuremberg. The power of the media to create and destroy fundamental human values comes with great responsibility. Those who control such media are accountable for its consequences.

The Appeals Chamber decision (affirming some grounds for conviction and rejecting others) contains masterful analyses both of the inchoate crime of direct and public incitement to genocide and of the causal connections required between an instigator and the primary perpetrator for the instigator to be responsible for the ultimate result. *See Prosecutor v. Nahimana, Barayagwiza and Ngeze* Case No. ICTR-99-52-A, Judgement of Appeals Chamber, November 28, 2007, discussed in Rickpaul Singh Vander, *The Media Case*, 12 Eyes on the ICC 29 (2017). *See also* Gregory Gordon, Atrocity Speech Law, Foundation, Fragmentation, Fruition (2017) (providing creative ideas on "atrocity speech").

(5) The Genocide Convention is about "prevention and punishment" of the crime. There is a very rich discussion of state obligations under the convention in the 2007

decision of the International Court of Justice in *Application of the Convention on the Prevention and Punishment of the Crime of Genocide (Bosnia and Herzegovina v. Serbia and Montenegro)*, I.C.J. 2007, 43, Judgment of Feb 26, 2007. One important point made by the Court is that a State may be responsible on the basis of the same "acts" that are punishable in the case of an individual under Article III of the Genocide Convention. The Court held that Serbia and Montenegro was not responsible either as a principal or an accomplice for the Bosnian Serb massacre that took place at Srebrenica in July 1995. It was, however, responsible for not making its best efforts to prevent that massacre, the risk of which it should have been aware. It was also internationally responsible for its failure to hand over General Mladic to the ICTY. *See* Roger S. Clark, *State Obligations under the Genocide Convention in Light of the ICJ's Decision in the Case concerning the Application of the Convention on the Prevention and Punishment of the Crime of Genocide,* 61 Rutgers L. Rev. 75 (2008–2009). (Mladic was later handed over and convicted of genocide, war crimes and crimes against humanity. He was sentenced to life imprisonment.) *See also* John Heieck, A Duty to Prevent Genocide: Due Diligence Obligations among the P5 (2018).

(6) A significant issue is what *mens rea* is required of an accomplice or aider and abettor to genocide. Must the aider or abettor both have knowledge of what the principal intends and also share that intent, or is it enough to furnish aid knowing of the other's genocidal intent. The ICTY took the latter position in the case of General Krstic, Commander of the group of the Bosnian Serb army responsible for the massacre in the United Nations "safe area" of Srebrenica. *Prosecutor v. Krstic,* I.C.T.Y., Case No. IT-98-33-A, Appeals Chamber Judgment of April 19, 2004. The Tribunal believed this result was supported by French, German, Swiss, English, Canadian, and Australian law, and by "some jurisdictions in the United States." It is, of course, not the majority rule in the United States, nor the rule espoused in the Model Penal Code § 2.06(3), which requires that the secondary party have the "purpose of promoting or facilitating the commission of the offense." The matter was discussed inconclusively in the 2007 decision of the International Court of Justice in *Application of the Convention on the Prevention and Punishment of the Crime of Genocide (Bosnia and Herzegovina v. Serbia and Montenegro)*, I.C.J. 2007, Judgment of Feb 26, 2007. The Declarations of Judges Keith and Bennouna in that case support the *Krstic* analysis.

(7) *Demjanjuk v. Petrovsky,* excerpted in § 20.03, was decided before the United States ratification of the 1948 Genocide Convention, G.A. Res. 260 A (III), 78 U.N.T.S. 277, became effective in 1988. (Israel ratified it in 1950). Article VII of the Convention provides that "Genocide and the other acts enumerated in article III [the basic definition provision] shall not be considered as political crimes for the purpose of extradition," and that "The Contracting Parties pledge themselves in such cases to grant extradition in accordance with their laws and treaties in force." The first of these provisions must modify (or clarify) any existing bilateral or multilateral extradition treaties between parties to the Genocide Convention by ensuring that

genocide does not come within their definition of a political offense. (The "political" nature of genocide was not discussed in the appellate proceedings in *Demjanjuk* but was apparently rejected by the trial judge in an unreported part of the proceedings.) But what of the second provision? Is it a basis for extradition where there is no existing treaty? Is it just an illusory promise to do what has been agreed upon elsewhere in other obligations? Recall the creative way in which the United States/Israel Extradition Treaty was interpreted to enable Demjanjuk's extradition.

C. Crimes against Humanity

Genocide was not one of the Nuremberg crimes. It was essentially the "persecution" part of crimes against humanity as contained in the Nuremberg Charter [§ 20.01]. Nuremberg crystallized use of the term "crimes against humanity" that had its roots in the nineteenth century where it was applied both to the slave trade and to King Leopold of Belgium's rule in the Congo. *See* Roger S. Clark, *Crimes against Humanity and The Rome Statute of the International Criminal Court*, in International and National Law in Russia and Europe: Essays in Honor of George Ginsburgs 139, 141 (Roger Clark, Ferdinand Feldbrugge & Stanislaw Pomorski eds., 2001). While genocide obtained its own treaty basis in 1948, the broader concept of crimes against humanity did not command definitive treatment until its inclusion in Article 7 of the Rome Statute [chap. 22]. Washington University School of Law started a project in 2009 to bring together a group of experts to draft a multilateral treaty dealing specifically with crimes against humanity. *See* Forging a Convention for Crimes Against Humanity (Leila Nadya Sadat ed., 2011). The International Law Commission decided in 2014 to take up a project to this effect and has produced a draft Convention which awaits action by the General Assembly or a Diplomatic Conference. *See* https://legal.un.org/ilc/guide/7_7.shtml.

Contrast the different definitions of "crimes against humanity" contained in Article 6(c) of the Charter of the Nuremberg Tribunal, in Article 5(c) of the Charter of the Tokyo Tribunal, in Article II(1)(c) of Allied Control Council Law No. 10 [chap. 20, *supra*], in Article 5 of the ICTY Statute, in Article 3 of the ICTR Statute [chap. 21, *supra*], and in Article 7 of the Rome Statute [chap. 22, *supra*]. What precisely are the differences between the various definitions? What accounts for these differences? Assuming (as is generally believed to be the case) that "crimes against humanity" constitute a violation of customary international law, which definition more accurately reflects customary international law? How would one tell? What is the case for requiring, for instance, that "crimes against humanity" must occur during an international armed conflict, or during armed conflict, or be committed on "discriminatory grounds," or be "widespread and systematic"? What is the relationship between "crimes against humanity" under one or another of these definitions and genocide or war crimes? States have, since 1945, been somewhat ambivalent about putting crimes against humanity before an international tribunal. To what extent do differences in the articulation of the offense represent differences in understanding about the substance of the offense? To what extent are they "jurisdictional," that is to say, they represent efforts to narrow the jurisdiction of the particular tribunal? For a comprehensive discussion of the concept of "crimes against humanity," *see* M. CHERIF BASSIOUNI, CRIMES AGAINST HUMANITY IN INTERNATIONAL LAW (2d ed. 1999).

D. War Crimes

The first Hague Peace Conference of 1899 sought to codify the rules governing permissible and impermissible methods for the conduct of war in a series of declarations and conventions. It was followed by a second Hague Peace Conference in 1907. The Regulations attached to Hague Convention IV of 1907 still constitute the basic statement of the rules of land warfare. These are now generally regarded as amounting to rules of customary international law. No conference has been called since to revise or update the laws of war as a whole; but there have been subsequent conventions directed toward specific problems, such as the 1954 Convention for the Protection of Cultural Property in the Event of Armed Conflict, the 1976 Convention on the Prohibition of Military or Any Other Hostile Use of Environmental Modification Techniques, the 1992 Convention on the Prohibition of the Development, Production, Stockpiling and Use of Chemical Weapons and on Their destruction, or the 1997 Convention on the Use, Stockpiling, Production and Transfer of Anti-Personnel Mines and on Their Destruction. For the texts of the various conventions defining what are now considered "war crimes," *see* THE LAWS OF ARMED CONFLICTS: A COLLECTION OF CONVENTIONS, RESOLUTIONS, AND OTHER DOCUMENTS (Dietrich Schindler & Jiri Toman eds., 4th ed. 2004). On the judgments of international tribunals as contributors to the laws of armed conflict, *see* SHANE DARCY, JUDGES, LAW AND WAR. THE JUDICIAL DEVELOPMENT OF INTERNATIONAL HUMANITARIAN LAW (2014).

No provision of the Hague Conventions actually uses the term "war crime" or refers to individual responsibility for breaches of those conventions. It seems to have been assumed that the parties would punish violations under their own municipal law. They were required to do so when violations were committed by their own forces and permitted to do so when violations were committed by the enemy. Punishing violations committed by captured members of enemy forces constituted, in effect, a species of reprisal, which was tolerated on the ground that strong, individualized reprisals are virtually the only means available during the course of hostilities to insure that parties to the conflict continue to observe the rules of war. But, at least since Nuremberg, certain violations of the Hague Conventions have been widely understood as not only conduct that belligerents are required or permitted to punish, but also as conduct that gives rise to individual criminal responsibility under international law.

The Hague Conventions cover methods for the conduct of war. Another part of the law of war is contained in a series of Geneva Conventions, culminating in the four Geneva Conventions of 1949, supplemented by two Additional Protocols in 1977. The four conventions of 1949 respectively set out rules (1) for the Amelioration of the Condition of the Wounded and Sick in Armed Forces in the Field; (2) for the Amelioration of the Condition of the Wounded, Sick and Shipwrecked Members of the Armed Forces at Sea, (3) Relative to the Treatment of Prisoners of War, and (4) Relative to the Protection of Civilians in Time of War (especially in occupied territory). Common provisions in all four conventions single out certain violations as constituting "grave breaches" and require each party "to enact any legislation necessary to provide effective penal sanctions" for such "grave breaches," and "to search for persons alleged to have committed, or to have ordered" them, and to "bring such persons, regardless of their nationality, before its own courts" or, "if it prefers . . . [to] hand such persons over for trial to another High Contracting Party concerned. . . ." These obligations are imposed on states; but, again, the substance of the provisions of the Geneva Convention with respect to "grave breaches"—and perhaps other proscriptions as well—are widely regarded as having been transmuted into rules of customary international law that give rise to individual criminal responsibility. Additional Protocol I of 1977 expands on the rules applicable in international armed conflict and adds new "grave breaches."

Common Article 3, which appears in each of the four Geneva Conventions, applies in cases of "armed conflict not of an international character" which occurs in the territory of one of the parties. It sets out a basic code of humanitarian rules to be followed in such a conflict. 1977 Additional Protocol II likewise applies to non-international armed conflicts and supplements common Article 3. The *Tadic* and *Akayesu* opinions [*see* chap. 21, *supra*] examine the question of how far customary international law imposes individual criminal responsibility for the violation of these rules. Consider the extent to which Article 8 (2) (c) and (d) of the Rome Statute codify the positions taken in *Tadic* and *Akayesu* (at least for parties to the Statute). Consider also Article 8, paragraph (2) (e) of the Statute, dealing with non-international armed conflict. Many of the provisions there were originally found in the Hague Regulations where they applied only to international conflict.

In the Military Commissions Act of 2006, Congress took a different approach from the Rome Statute Article 8 (2) (c) which criminalizes all of Common Article 3. Look again at the distinction drawn in the 2006 amendments to the 1996 War Crimes Act between "grave" and other breaches of Common Article 3. (The War Crimes Act is the last item in chap. 20, *supra*.) Roger S. Clark, *The Military Commissions Act of 2006: An Abject Abdication by Congress*, 6 Rutgers J. L. & Pub. Pol'y 78 (2008), comments (some footnotes omitted):

> Section 6 of the Military Commissions Act, beneath the Orwellian heading "Implementation of Treaty Obligations," revises subsection (c) (3),

retroactively,[3] essentially by re-defining and narrowing the content of common Article 3 for purposes of United States law. This amendment is apparently aimed at avoiding potential criminal responsibility for acts carried out by United States personnel in Abu Ghraib, Guantanamo and elsewhere that might well have been illegal under the 1997 version of the section.

Section 6 contains the remarkable statement that follows:

> (2) PROHIBITION ON GRAVE BREACHES.—The provisions of section 2441 of title 18, United States Code, as added by subsection (b) of this section, fully satisfy the obligation under Article 129 of the Third Geneva Convention for the United States to provide effective penal sanctions for grave breaches which are encompassed in Common Article 3 in the context of an armed conflict not of an international character. No foreign or international source of law shall supply a basis for a rule of decision in the courts of the United States interpreting the prohibitions enumerated in subsection (d) of such section 2241.

The way in which the two disparate thoughts in the first and second sentences of this are run together is bizarre enough, but the content of each sentence is even more so.

As to the first sentence, Article 129 of the Third Convention says nothing about the obligation to "provide effective penal sanctions for grave breaches" in respect of common Article 3. Indeed, common Article 3, itself, does not by its terms rely on a distinction between grave and other breaches. All of the proscribed acts in common Article 3 are equally illegal on the face of the treaty itself.[4] Did nobody in Congress read the relevant treaty material?

The second sentence is no doubt a shot in the war between those who do and those who do not regard international law and comparative law sources as helpful to understanding United States constitutional, statutory or common law. But look what is going on here. We are told that this is an implementation of treaty obligations, but that no international source shall

3. Sec. 6 (2) of the amendment provides that "The amendments made by this subsection, except as specified in subsection (d) (2) (E) of section 2441 of title 18, United States Code, shall take effect as of November 26, 1997, as if enacted immediately after the amendments made by section 583 of Public Law 105-118 (as amended by section 4002 (e) (7) of Public Law 107-273)." [Public Law 105-118, § 583 (1997) added the original material on common Article 3; Public Law 107-273, § 4002 (e) (7) corrected a typographical error referring to § 2401 instead of § 2441 of title 18.] [Footnote in original.]

4. James G. Stewart, *The Military Commissions Act's Inconsistency with the Geneva Conventions: An Overview*, 5 J. INT'L CRIM. JUST. 26, 33 (2007), described "grave breaches of common article 3" as "an unprecedented concept." *But see* Lindsay Moir, *Grave Breaches and Internal Armed Conflicts*, 7 J. INT'L CRIM. JUST 763, 783–74 (2009) (seeing this as a potential example of state practice contributing to new custom that some of the violations contained in the 2006 Act "are not actually (or, at least explicitly) contained within the terms of common Article 3."). Moir notes this and occasional other U.S. and European practice as leaving "whether a new customary law rule has materialized on the issue . . . doubtful." *Id.* at 784. [Footnote in original.]

supply a basis for understanding it! Is there to be no recourse to the treaty itself? To its preparatory work? To the interpretations put forward in such bodies as the Tribunals for Former Yugoslavia and Rwanda? To the interpretations put forward in military manuals of allies like Canada, Australia, Germany or the United Kingdom? To studies by the International Committee of the Red Cross?

By and large, then, the Rome Statute takes an expansive view of the offenses against the laws of armed conflict that are subject to criminal suppression. But on weapons of mass destruction and other forbidden weapons, the politics of the negotiations decreed that a narrow view was taken on what should be within the Court's jurisdiction. *See* Roger S. Clark, *The Rome Statute of the International Criminal Court and Weapons of a Nature to cause Superfluous Injury or Unnecessary Suffering, or which Are Inherently Indiscriminate*, in INTERNATIONAL HUMANITARIAN LAW: CHALLENGES 259 (John Carey, William V. Dunlap & R. John Pritchard eds., 2004). At the Kampala Review Conference, an amendment was adopted to Article 8 (2) (e) of the Statute including the prohibition in non-international armed conflict of the same weapons offenses included in Article 8 (2) (b) dealing with international armed conflict. These are: employing poison or poisoned weapons; employing asphyxiating, poisonous or other gases, and all analogous liquids, materials, or devices; employing bullets which expand or flatten easily in the human body, such as, bullets with a hard envelope which does not entirely cover the core or is pierced with incisions. Resolution RC/Res.5 of June 10, 2010. In doing so, the amendment took a narrow view of the amending provisions in Article 121 of the Statute and excluded from its application non-Parties to the Statute and nationals and the territory of Parties who do not ratify the amendment. The Assembly of States Parties adopted further amendments to Article 8 in 2017 and 2019, similarly limited in their scope of application to those adopted in 2010 (i.e., excluding nationals and the territory of non-States-Parties and of Parties not accepting the amendments). The 2017 amendments (ICC-ASP/16/Res.4 (2017)) proscribe, in both international and non-international armed conflict, the use of microbial and biological agents, weapons that injure by fragments which escape detection by x-rays, and laser weapons designed to cause permanent blindness. The 2019 amendment (ICC-ASP/18/Res.5 (2019)) took the crime of intentionally using starvation of civilians as a method of warfare, which was proscribed only in international armed conflict in 1998, and added it to the proscriptions for non-international conflict. Ratification of these amendments is proceeding glacially.

In 2005 the International Committee of the Red Cross produced a comprehensive study of what it believed is customary international humanitarian law. *See* JEAN-MARIE HENCKAERTS & LOUISE DOSWALD-BECK, CUSTOMARY INTERNATIONAL HUMANITARIAN LAW, 2 Vols (Vol. I, Rules, Vol. II, Pts 1 and 2, Practice) (2005). For a laudatory view of this effort, *see* Theodor Meron, *Revival of Customary Humanitarian Law*, 99 AM. J. INT'L L. 817 (2005). A less enthusiastic response is contained in Letter from John Bellinger III, Legal Adviser, U.S. Dept. of State, and William J. Haynes, General Counsel, U.S. Dept. of Defense to Dr. Jakob Kellenberger, President,

International Committee of the Red Cross, regarding Customary International Law Study, Nov. 3, 2006, 46 I.L.M. 514 (2007). *See also International Committee of the Red Cross: Response of Jean-Marie Henckaerts to Bellinger/Haynes Letter on Customary International Law Study*, July 2007, 46 I.L.M. 959 (2007).

Should there be access to lawyers? Should this access be extended to the battlefield? *See* Laura A. Dickenson, *Military Lawyers on the Battlefield: An Empirical Account of International Law Compliance,* 104 AM. J. INT'L L. 1 (2010) (arguing for the usefulness of such presence).

§ 23.02 The General Part

A system of criminal law does more than proscribe specific offenses (in its "special part"): it also contains principles and rules about what constitutes culpable conduct, about what mental states are required for criminal liability, about when particular results can be attributed to a particular actor, about responsibility for the conduct of others and for inchoate crimes, about general justifications for otherwise wrongful conduct, about excuses that entirely or partially exclude culpability, and about the grading of offenses and sanctions according to different levels and degrees of culpability and harm. The rules pertaining to all of these matters vary as between different national systems. So long as the prosecution of international crimes takes place in national courts, one has to expect that there will be national differences in the general concepts and rules of criminal law applied in such prosecutions. *See* Edward M. Wise, *War Crimes and Criminal Law, in* STUDIES IN COMPARATIVE CRIMINAL LAW 35 (Edward M. Wise & Gerhard O. W. Mueller eds., 1975).

At the same time, in part because the concepts and principles of criminal law have a normative dimension that serves to promote a just as well as effective system of law enforcement, there are, notwithstanding national differences, considerable similarities in basic principles of criminal law throughout the world. It is this measure of commonality that made possible agreement on Part 3 of the Rome Statute [*see* chap. 22, *supra*], which sets out the "General Principles of Criminal Law" to be applied by the International Criminal Court. This is the first time that a treaty formulation has attempted to codify the basic principles of a "general part." *See* Edward M. Wise, *Observations on the Consolidated ICC Text Before the Final Session of the Preparatory Committee* 45 (Association Internationale de Droit Pénal, NOUVELLES ÉTUDES PÉNALES, No. 13 *bis*, Leila Sadat Wexler ed., 1998). For commentary on the Statute's treatment of these general principles, *see* THE ROME STATUTE OF THE INTERNATIONAL CRIMINAL COURT: ARTICLE BY ARTICLE COMMENTARY Articles 22–33 (Kai Ambos ed., 4th ed. 2021); Kai Ambos, *General Principles of Criminal Law in the Rome Statute,* 10 CRIM. L. F. 1 (1999); William A. Schabas, *General Principles of Criminal Law in the International Criminal Court Statute (Part III),* 6 EUR. J. CRIME, CRIM. L. & CRIM. JUST. 400 (1998); Roger S. Clark, *Drafting a General Part to a Penal Code: Some Thoughts Inspired by the Negotiations on the Rome Statute of the*

International Criminal Court and by the Court's First Substantive Law Discussion in the Lubanga Dyilo *Confirmation Proceedings*, 19 CRIM. L. FORUM 519 (2008). Note how the Appeals Chamber of the ICC addressed the general part issues in dealing with its first appeal against conviction, the *Lubanga Dyilo* decision:

Prosecutor v. Thomas Lubanga Dyilo

Appeals Chamber, International Criminal Court No. ICC-01/04-01/06 A 5
Judgment on the Appeal against Conviction, December 14, 2014

D. Alleged errors in the objective and subjective elements of the form of individual criminal responsibility

434. The Appeals Chamber recalls that the Trial Chamber found Mr Lubanga "[g]uilty of the crimes of conscripting and enlisting children under the age of fifteen years into the FPLC and using them to participate actively in hostilities within the meaning of articles 8(2)(e)(vii) and 25(3)(a) of the Statute from early September 2002 to 13 August 2003". The Trial Chamber noted that Mr Lubanga was charged as a co-perpetrator pursuant to the second alternative of article 25 (3) (a) of the Statute ("commits such a crime, [. . .] jointly with another [. . .] person") and stated that it would limit its consideration to this form of liability. The Trial Chamber found that this form of individual criminal liability comprised the following elements, which had to be established by the Prosecutor:

> (i) there was an agreement or common plan between the accused and at least one other co-perpetrator that, once implemented, will result in the commission of the relevant crime in the ordinary course of events;
>
> (ii) the accused provided an essential contribution to the common plan that resulted in the commission of the relevant crime;
>
> (iii) the accused meant to conscript, enlist or use children under the age of 15 to participate actively in hostilities or he was aware that by implementing the common plan these consequences "will occur in the ordinary course of events";
>
> (iv) the accused was aware that he provided an essential contribution to the implementation of the common plan; and
>
> (v) the accused was aware of the factual circumstances that established the existence of an armed conflict and the link between these circumstances and his conduct.

435. In the "Overall Conclusions" section of the Conviction Decision that addresses Mr Lubanga's individual criminal responsibility, the Trial Chamber made several factual findings corresponding to the legal elements set out above. It found that Mr Lubanga and his co-perpetrators (including Floribert Kisembo, Bosco Ntaganda, Chief Kahwa, and commanders Tchaligonza, Bagonza and Kasangaki) "agreed to, and participated in, a common plan to build an army for the purpose of establishing and maintaining political and military control over Ituri". This resulted

"in the ordinary course of events" in the conscription and enlistment of boys and girls under the age of fifteen years, and their use to participate actively in hostilities, including during battles and as soldiers and bodyguards for senior officials, including Mr Lubanga.

436. The Trial Chamber found that Mr Lubanga's contribution was essential to the common plan that resulted in the commission of the crimes. This contribution consisted of his function of being the commander-in-chief of the army and the political leader; his overall coordinating role; the fact that he was informed "on a substantive and continuous basis" of the operations of the UPC/FPLC; that he was involved in planning military operations and had a critical role in providing logistical support; and that he was closely involved in making decisions on recruitment policy and actively supported recruitment initiatives. The Trial Chamber specifically noted the speech Mr Lubanga gave at the Rwampara camp where "he encouraged children, including those under the age of 15 years, to join the army and to provide security for the populace", as well as the fact that Mr Lubanga "personally used children below the age of 15 amongst his bodyguards and he regularly saw guards of other UPC/FPLC members of staff who were below the age of 15".

437. Finally, the Trial Chamber found that Mr Lubanga had the requisite level of intent and knowledge. It held that "Thomas Lubanga was fully aware that children under the age of 15 had been, and continued to be, enlisted and conscripted by the UPC/FPLC and used to participate actively in hostilities during the timeframe of the charges", which "occurred, in the ordinary course of events, as a result of the implementation of the common plan—to ensure that the UPC/FPLC had an army strong enough to achieve its political and military aims".

438. Mr Lubanga alleges several errors in relation to the Trial Chamber's findings regarding his individual criminal responsibility, including three main errors of law in relation to his conviction as a co-perpetrator. Notably, he alleges that the Trial Chamber erred in finding that:

a. "[T]he agreement on a common plan leads to co-perpetration if its implementation embodies a sufficient risk that, in the ordinary course of events, a crime will be committed" (footnote omitted);

b. "'*[A]wareness that a consequence will occur in the ordinary course of events*' means that the participants anticipate, based on their knowledge of how events ordinarily develop, that the consequence will occur in the future. This prognosis involves consideration of the concepts of 'possibility' and 'probability', which are inherent to the notions of 'risk' and 'danger'" (emphasis added, footnote omitted); and

c. "[R]esponsibility under article 25 (3) (a) does not require personal and direct participation in the crime itself and [...] merely exercising, 'jointly with others, control over the crime' [is] sufficient to establish the 'essential contribution' required" (footnote omitted).

439. The Prosecutor argues that Mr Lubanga has not met the burden of substantiating the alleged legal errors. In that regard the Appeals Chamber notes that the Prosecutor's references in footnote 526 of the Response to The Document in Support of the Appeal are misleading because they mainly relate to jurisprudence of the ICTY and the ICTR on alleged *factual* errors. As established above and contrary to the Prosecutor's assertion, an appellant may repeat submissions made before the Trial Chamber. Therefore, the Appeals Chamber finds that Mr Lubanga has sufficiently substantiated the alleged legal errors.

440. The Appeals Chamber notes that Mr Lubanga also raises in relation to each of the above-mentioned alleged legal errors a number of other errors under the heading "factual errors". Some of these allegations are not sufficiently substantiated. Notably, in instances where Mr Lubanga merely repeats factual submissions made at the close of the trial without explaining why the factual findings of the Trial Chamber are unreasonable, the Appeals Chamber has not considered these arguments further. To the extent that the alleged 'factual errors' are sufficiently substantiated, the Appeals Chamber will address them immediately after addressing the relevant alleged legal error.

1. Alleged errors relevant to the common plan

(a) Alleged error in establishing a "risk" requirement

441. In relation to the Trial Chamber's legal findings regarding the common plan, Mr Lubanga argues that the Trial Chamber erred because it applied the "concept of 'sufficient risk' to establish the 'critical element of criminality' of the common plan necessary for co-perpetration". He argues that this is not in line with article 30 (2) of the Statute because it imports the concept of *dolus eventualis*, a concept that, in his opinion, was "not adopted by the drafters of the Statute" (footnote omitted). The Appeals Chamber notes that Mr Lubanga makes the same argument with respect to the Trial Chamber's findings on the mental element, in relation to which the Trial Chamber also referred to the notion of 'risk'. The analysis below equally applies to the error alleged by Mr Lubanga in that regard.

442. The Appeals Chamber recalls that the majority of the Trial Chamber made the following finding as to what has to be proved in relation to the common plan as an element of co-perpetration liability under article 25 (3) (a) of the Statute:

> In the view of the Majority of the Chamber, the prosecution is not required to prove that the plan was specifically directed at committing the crime in question (the conscription, enlistment or use of children), nor does the plan need to have been intrinsically criminal as suggested by the defence. However, it is necessary as a minimum, for the prosecution to establish the common plan included a critical element of criminality, namely that, its implementation embodied *a sufficient risk* that, if events follow the ordinary course, a crime will be committed. [Emphasis added.]

443. After establishing that "committing the crime in question does not need to be the overarching goal of the co-perpetrators", the Trial Chamber explained, with reference to article 30 of the Statute, what it meant by "sufficient risk":

> Hence, in the view of the Majority, the mental requirement that the common plan included the commission of a crime will be satisfied if the co-perpetrators knew that, in the ordinary course of events, implementing the plan will lead to that result. "Knowledge", defined as awareness by the co-perpetrators that a consequence will occur (in the future), necessarily means that the co-perpetrators *are aware of the risk that the consequence, prospectively, will occur.* [Emphasis added, footnotes omitted.]

444. It is this finding that Mr Lubanga challenges. The Prosecutor argues that the Trial Chamber, when referring to the risk criterion, did not import the concept of *dolus eventualis*, but correctly applied article 30 of the Statute. She recalls that the Trial Chamber addressed the mental element and article 30 of the Statute in more detail elsewhere in the Conviction Decision and recalls that the Trial Chamber held in that regard:

> 1012. In the view of the Majority of the Chamber, the "awareness that a consequence will occur in the ordinary course of events" means that the participants anticipate, based on their knowledge of how events ordinarily develop, that the consequence will occur in the future. This prognosis involves consideration of the concepts of "possibility" and "probability", which are inherent to the notions of "risk" and "danger". Risk is defined as "danger, (exposure to) the possibility of loss, injury or other adverse circumstance". The co-perpetrators only "know" the consequences of their conduct once they have occurred. *At the time the co-perpetrators agree on a common plan and throughout its implementation, they must know the existence of a risk that the consequence will occur. As to the degree of risk, and pursuant to the wording of article 30, it must be no less than awareness on the part of the co-perpetrator that the consequence "will occur in the ordinary course of events". A low risk will not be sufficient.*
>
> 1013. The Chamber is of the view that the prosecution must establish, as regards the mental element, that: (i) the accused and at least one other perpetrator meant to conscript, enlist or use children under the age of 15 to participate actively in hostilities or they were aware that in implementing their common plan this consequence "will occur in the ordinary course of events"; and (ii) the accused was aware that he provided an essential contribution to the implementation of the common plan. [Footnotes omitted, emphasis added.]

445. At the outset, the Appeals Chamber considers that, in order to establish that an accused person committed a crime under the jurisdiction of the Court "jointly with another [. . .] person", it has to be established that two or more individuals worked together in the commission of the crime. This requires an agreement

between these perpetrators, which led to the commission of one or more crimes under the jurisdiction of the Court. It is this very agreement–express or implied, previously arranged or materialising extemporaneously — that ties the co-perpetrators together and that justifies the reciprocal imputation of their respective acts. This agreement may take the form of a "common plan".

446. As to the question of whether the common plan must be "designed to further a criminal purpose", the Appeals Chamber considers that it is not required that the common plan between individuals was specifically directed at the commission of a crime. The Appeals Chamber recalls that the Trial Chamber held that it was sufficient or the common plan to involve "a critical element of criminality" and that the Trial Chamber sought to define such an element of criminality by reference to article 30 of the Statute. In the view of the Appeals Chamber, it was as such correct to consider article 30 of the Statute because that provision describes the relevant mental element and may therefore also serve as a yardstick for determining whether two or more individuals agreed to commit a crime. Article 30 of the Statute states:

> 1. Unless otherwise provided, a person shall be criminally responsible and liable for punishment for a crime within the jurisdiction of the Court only if the material elements are committed with intent and knowledge.
>
> 2. For the purposes of this article, a person has intent where:
>
> (a) In relation to conduct, that person means to engage in the conduct;
>
> (b) In relation to a consequence, that *person means to cause that consequence or is aware that it will occur in the ordinary course of events.*
>
> 3. For the purposes of this article, 'knowledge' means *awareness that a circumstance exists or a consequence will occur in the ordinary course of events.* 'Know' and 'knowingly' shall be construed accordingly. [Emphasis Added.]

447. At issue here is the second alternative of both article 30 (2) (b) and (3) of the Statute. The Appeals Chamber notes that these provisions do not refer to the notion of "risk", but employ the term of occurrence of a consequence "in the ordinary course of events". The Appeals Chamber considers that the words "[a consequence] will occur" refer to future events. The verb 'occur' is used with the modal verb 'will', and not with 'may' or 'could'. Therefore, this phrase conveys, as does the French version, certainty about the future occurrence. However, absolute certainty about a future occurrence can never exist; therefore the Appeals Chamber considers that the standard for the foreseeability of events is virtual certainty. That absolute certainty is not required is reinforced by the inclusion in article 30 (2) (b) and (3) of the Statute of the phrase "in the ordinary course of events".

448. The Appeals Chamber recalls that the Trial Chamber held that

> It is necessary, as a minimum, for the prosecution to establish [that] the common plan included a critical element of criminality, namely that its implementation embodied a sufficient risk that, if events follow the ordinary course, a crime will be committed.

449. The Appeals Chamber considers that the term "risk" is usually used in the context of "*dolus eventualis*" or "advertent recklessness", as known in some domestic jurisdictions, a concept that the Trial Chamber specifically excluded from application. The Appeals Chamber considers that it does not help in creating more clarity that the Trial Chamber, in the section on the mental element, explains that this "involves consideration of the concepts of 'possibility' and 'probability', which are inherent to the notions of 'risk' and 'danger'". The Appeals Chamber finds that the use of this phrase is confusing and reference to 'risk' should have been avoided when interpreting article 30 (2) of the Statute.

450. Nevertheless, in the result, the Appeals Chamber does not consider that the Trial Chamber's approach broadened the scope of article 30 (2) and (3) of the Statute, despite the Trial Chamber's use of the term "risk". The Appeals Chamber notes that the Trial Chamber appears to have referred to the term "risk" in this context because the common plan was implemented over a long period of time. Thus, at the time of its conception, the co-perpetrators anticipated future events (as will often be the case when a broad plan is conceived). The Trial Chamber, in defining the requisite level of "risk", specified at paragraph 1012 of the Conviction Decision that this entailed an "awareness on the part of the co-perpetrators that the consequence will occur in the 'ordinary course of events'" and distinguished this from a "low risk". In addition, the Trial Chamber found, in line with article 30 of the Statute, that the Prosecutor needs to establish that, as a consequence of the common plan, the crimes "will occur in the ordinary course of events". Therefore, Appeals Chamber finds that the Trial Chamber, in its legal conclusions, did not deviate from the requirements of article 30 (2) (b) and (3) of the Statute.

451. The Appeals Chamber recalls in this context that, according to the Trial Chamber, Mr Lubanga and the co-perpetrators agreed "to build an effective army in order to ensure the UPC/FPLC's political and military control over Ituri". The Trial Chamber found that, in the circumstances prevailing in Ituri at the time (of which the co-perpetrators were aware), the implementation of this plan led to the recruitment and use to participate actively in hostilities of individuals who were both above and under the age of fifteen years, the latter being a crime falling within the scope of the Statute. Thus, the implementation of the plan, which itself may have included non-criminal goals, in addition to criminal ones, resulted in the commission of crimes under article 8 (2) (e) (vii) of the Statute. Accordingly, the Trial Chamber's requirement of a "critical element of criminality" of the common plan means, in the context of the present case and the specific allegations against Mr Lubanga, that it was virtually certain that the implementation of the common plan led to the commission of the crimes at issue.

452. In conclusion, the Appeals Chamber rejects Mr Lubanga's argument.

Notes

(1) The question of the burden of proof in respect of "defenses" has controversial aspects in both common law and civil law systems. It is fairly generally agreed that

the defense must at least raise such issues. It is sometimes suggested, moreover, that the burden of persuasion as to "affirmative" defenses (an elusive category) may be placed on the accused. Typically, when a burden is placed on the accused, it will be on the lower "balance of probabilities" or "preponderance of the evidence" standard, compared with the prosecution's higher standard, "beyond reasonable doubt." There is little international case-law. JOHN R.W.D. JONES & STEVEN POWLES, INTERNATIONAL CRIMINAL PRACTICE 445–46 (3d ed. 2003) discuss an ICTY trial order that supports placement of the burden of persuasion on the accused (on the balance of probabilities) in respect of diminished or lack of mental capacity. The authors also note Article 67, paragraph (1), sub-paragraph i, of the Rome Statute under which the accused is entitled "[n]ot to have imposed on him or her any reversal of the burden of proof or any onus of rebuttal." They suggest that this provision "has the potential to be of great importance to the defence at the I.C.C." and means that there are no "shifting burdens of proof" in the I.C.C. In *Prosecutor v. Ongwen*, ICC-02/04-01/15, Trial Chamber, Judgment, February 4, 2021, the Court declined to clarify its position, as the defense had requested, during the course of the proceedings. Nevertheless, in its Judgment, it held, in relation to the defenses of mental disease or defect and duress, that

> . . . [t]here is no specific provision in the Statute related to the burden and standard of proof as concerns grounds excluding criminal responsibility under Article 31, and for this reason, the general provisions of the Statute apply. Under Article 66(2) of the Statute, the onus is on the Prosecutor to prove the guilt of the accused, and, under Article 66(3), in order to convict the accused, the Court must be convinced of the guilt of the accused beyond reasonable doubt.

Id., ¶ 2455 (footnote omitted). *See also* ¶ 2588 (discussing duress). Thus, the ultimate burden to negate the defense lies with the prosecution. The *Ongwen* Court denied the applicability of both defenses on the facts, basic elements of each being missing. The Trial Chamber's discussion does not focus on a discussion of authority. (*See also* Article 67(1)(i) of the Rome Statute, which some might think supports it.)

(2) The proper treatment of superior orders has been a matter of great controversy. A part of the controversy goes, however, to words, not substance. It is clear that a crime cannot be justified solely on the ground that the person who committed it was acting under orders. A superior order does not in itself exclude criminal responsibility. In this respect, there is no defense of superior orders *per se*. But the order may form an element of another defense—a defense along the lines of mistake of law in cases in which the accused was entirely unaware of the illegality of the order, or along the lines of duress or compulsion in cases in which the accused's life would have been at risk were the order not obeyed, *i.e.*, where he had no "moral choice" but to follow the order. Insofar as an excuse along one or both of these lines is allowed, it might be said that the law recognizes a defense of superior orders. (Is this an area where the Rome Statute's refusal to distinguish justification and excuse and instead rely, in Article 31, on the generic category "grounds for excluding

criminal responsibility" makes explanation more difficult?) But it also might be said that there is still no special defense: the real ground of exculpation is the broader one that someone who could not reasonably be expected to know that his conduct was illegal, or who could not reasonably be expected to have disobeyed an order, acts without culpability. Whether a defense should be allowed on either of these grounds is controversial as well. But, on one view, it helps to recognize that this — not the question of whether the law permits a defense of superior orders *per se* — is the crucial question. *See Model Draft Statute for the International Criminal Court Based on the Preparatory Committee's Text to the Diplomatic Conference, Rome, June 15-July 17, 1998*, at 58 (Association Internationale de Droit Pénal, Nouvelles Études Pénales No. 13 *ter*, Leila Sadat Wexler ed., 1998). To what extent is Article 33 of the Rome Statute problematic precisely because it fails to recognize this distinction? *See* Kai Ambos, *General Principles of Criminal Law in the Rome Statute*, 10 Crim. L.F. 1, 30–32 (1999). *See also* Otto Triffterer/Stefanie Bock, *Article 33: Superior orders and prescription of law, in* The Rome Statute of the International Criminal Court: Article By Article Commentary 1405 (Kai Ambos ed., 4th ed. 2021).

(3) For extensive discussion of the converse problem of the responsibility of a military or civilian superior for acts of subordinates, *see Prosecutor v. Delalic*, Case No. IT-96-21-T, Judgement (Nov. 16, 1998), paras. 333–63. This is the so-called "Celebici case" noted in chap. 10, *supra*. *See also Prosecutor v. Akayesu* [chap. 21, *supra*], paras. 487–91. In distinguishing between liability under Articles 7 (1) (complicity) and 7 (3) (superior responsibility) of the Statute of the ICTY, the Trial Chamber stated in *Prosecutor v. Kordic and Cerkez*, Case No. IT-95-14/2, Judgement of February 26, 2001, at paras. 367, 369:

> Article 7 (1) is concerned with persons directly responsible for planning, instigating, ordering, committing or aiding and abetting in the planning, preparation or execution of a crime. Thus both the individual who himself carries out the unlawful conduct and his superior who is involved in the conduct, not by physical participation, but for example by ordering or instigating it, are covered by Article 7 (1) . . . . The type of responsibility provided for under Article 7 (3) may be described as "indirect" as it does not stem from a "direct" involvement by the superior in the commission of a crime but rather from his omission to prevent or punish such offence, i.e., of his failure to act in spite of knowledge. . . . Liability under Article 7 (3) is based on an omission as opposed to positive conduct.

Can an accused be charged using both a complicity and a superior responsibility theory? Can that person be convicted on both theories? Sentenced cumulatively on both?

While Article 28 of the Rome Statute makes provision for the responsibility of civilian as well as military superiors, it also distinguishes between the conditions under which the two will be liable for acts of subordinates. Is the distinction drawn in Article 28 the same as that drawn in paragraph 491 of the judgment in *Akayesu* [chap. 21]? Is the liability of military superiors essentially based on a negligence theory? Is liability for civilian leaders based on recklessness? By and large, the Rome Statute avoids responsibility grounded on what U.S. lawyers would call negligence or recklessness. *See* Article 30 of the Rome Statute, which speaks of intent and knowledge. For the most part, the Elements of Crimes follow Article 30's default rule and confine liability to cases where there is either intent or knowledge (or both). Is Article 28 an exception? For a good discussion of Article 28, *see* Shane Darcy, *The Limited Reach of Superior Responsibility*, in FOR THE SAKE OF PRESENT AND FUTURE GENERATIONS: ESSAYS ON INTERNATIONAL LAW, CRIME AND JUSTICE IN HONOUR OF ROGER S. CLARK 374 (Suzannah Linton, Gerry Simpson & William A. Schabas eds., 2015). Although it ultimately resulted in an acquittal, there is analysis of Article 28 in the *Bemba* case, culminating in the discussion in the Appeals Chamber, Judgment on the Appeal of Mr Jean-Pierre Bemba Gombo against Trial Chamber III's "Judgment pursuant to Article 74 of the Statute," ICC-01/05-01/08-3636-Red, June 8, 2018.

(4) *Lubanga Dyilo* was the first prosecution at the Court. The Prosecutor was criticized for not charging offences beyond those involving child soldiers. As it turned out, even proving age was not easy in a country where documentation was not reliable. *See* JIM FREEDMAN, A CONVICTION IN QUESTION: THE FIRST TRIAL AT THE INTERNATIONAL CRIMINAL COURT (2017) (providing what some may consider a critical account of the proceedings).

§ 23.03 Parties to Offenses

Recall that in *Prosecutor v. Furundzija*, Case No. IT-95-17/1-T, Judgement (Dec. 10, 1998), portions of which are reproduced in chap. 10, *supra*, the accused was charged with torture and outrages upon personal dignity including rape, but had not directly committed the acts of sexual violence himself. A long section of the judgment which we have not reproduced (paras. 190–249) deals with the law governing the liability of an accomplice and takes up a number of questions (on which there are divisions between and within legal systems), such as whether an aider and abettor must provide tangible assistance, or whether encouragement or moral support will suffice; whether the accomplice has to be causally responsible for the principal's actions, or need simply in some way facilitate commission of the offense; and whether the accomplice must have the same intent as the principal, or whether knowledge that his action will assist the perpetration of an offense is sufficient. The judgment relies primarily on "international case law." Its discussion of the cases considered relevant is introduced by the statement:

> 194. For a correct appraisal of this case law, it is important to bear in mind, with each of the cases to be examined, the forum in which the case was heard, as well as the law applied, as these factors determine its authoritative value. In addition, one should constantly be mindful of the need for great caution in using national case law for the purpose of determining whether

customary rules of international criminal law have evolved in a particular matter.

A significant development in the international case-law is the evolution of the doctrine that an actor may become liable as an accomplice by acting in a "common purpose" with others engaged in criminal activity. *See* discussion by Appeals Chamber of the ICTY in *Prosecutor v. Tadic*, IT-94-1-A, July 15, 1999, at 80–105. A version of this principle, a variation on the U.S. doctrine that conspirators may be liable for substantive offenses committed by others in the conspiracy, has found its way in terms into some recent treaties, notably the Rome Statute, Article 25 (3) (d) and its model, Article 2 (3) (c) of the 1997 International Convention for the Suppression of Terrorist Bombings, G.A. Res. 52/164, U.N. GAOR, 52nd Sess., Supp. No, 49, at 389, U.N. Doc. A/52/49 (1998). *See generally*, Shane Darcy, Collective Responsibility and International Law, Chapter IV (Conspiracy, Common Plan and Joint Criminal Enterprise Liability) (2007); Marja Lehto, International Responsibility for Terrorist Acts: A Shift Towards More Indirect Forms of Responsibility 216–32 (Joint Criminal Enterprise) (2008). Decisions of the International Criminal Court have perhaps strained to find that the accused is a "principal" in the crime rather than a secondary participant. *See* for example the extract above from the *Lubanga Dyilo* case. This has involved introducing a somewhat different notion of an agreement on a common plan which is not apparent on the face of the language in the Statute. Consider also the following:

Prosecutor v. Thomas Lubanga Dyilo

Appeals Chamber, International Criminal Court No. ICC-01/04-01/06 A 5
Judgment on the Appeal against Conviction, December 14, 2014

2. Alleged errors relevant to the perpetrator's required "contribution"

(a) Alleged error in not requiring "direct" participation

456. Mr Lubanga argues in essence that the Trial Chamber erred in finding that a co-perpetrator does not need to personally and directly participate in the commission of the crime, an interpretation that contravenes, in his view, articles 21 and 22 of the Statute and the principle of legality. Mr Lubanga specifically challenges the finding of the Trial Chamber that the accused can be absent from the scene of the crime, as long as he has the power to decide whether and how the offence will be carried out. In Mr Lubanga's view, this is akin to liability for ordering the commission of a crime or superior responsibility (article 25 (3) (b) and 28 of the Statute, respectively), and therefore cannot establish liability for the commission of a crime under article 25 (3) (a) of the Statute. He argues that, due to this error, the Trial Chamber considered Mr Lubanga's leadership position and his knowledge of the crimes as constituent elements of his "essential contribution". Mr Lubanga avers that this error vitiates the Conviction Decision.

457. The Prosecutor submits that neither article 25 (3) of the Statute and the emerging jurisprudence of the Court, nor the jurisprudence of the ICTY and ICTR require

that the accused person must have committed the crime personally and directly in order to establish "commission" liability. The Prosecutor defends the positions of the Trial and Pre-Trial Chambers, emphasising that "consideration will be given to the actions of all co-perpetrators and not just the Appellant's actions taken alone". The Prosecutor argues that the "control of the crime theory" should not be questioned in the abstract. She recalls that the Trial Chamber assessed not only his leadership role within the UPC/FPLC, but also his "personal involvement as it related to the crimes charged" (footnote omitted). In her submission, both aspects were relevant to the finding that Mr Lubanga's contribution to the common plan was "essential".

458. The Appeals Chamber is not persuaded by Mr Lubanga's arguments under this alleged error. For the reasons that follow, it finds that article 25(3) (a) of the Statute does not establish that co-perpetrators need to carry out the crime personally and directly.

459. Article 25 (2) and (3) of the Statute provides as follows:

[*See* chap. 22 for the text of Article 25.]

460. In the view of the Appeals Chamber, the issue at hand must be resolved by interpreting the phrase "[c]ommits such a crime [. . .] jointly with another [. . .] person", within the limits set by article 22 of the Statute. The Appeals Chamber notes that the text of article 25 (3) (a) of the Statute does not expressly stipulate that a crime is committed jointly with others only if the co-perpetrators directly and personally carry out the incriminated conduct in question.

461. At the outset, the Appeals Chamber notes that article 25 (2) of the Statute, which establishes the principle of individual criminal responsibility, also uses the term "commit" a crime. However, this provision refers generally to individual criminal responsibility for the crimes under the jurisdiction of the Court and therefore cannot assist in defining the term "[c]ommit" in paragraph 3 (a) of the provision. Accordingly, article 25 (2) of the Statute need not be considered any further.

462. What is, however, of relevance to the proper interpretation of the term "[c]ommits such a crime [. . .] jointly with another [. . .] person" is its interplay with other forms of criminal liability set out in article 25 (3) of the Statute. In that regard, the Appeals Chamber observes that, under this provision, an individual can be held criminally responsible for either committing a crime (sub-paragraph a)) or for contributing to the commission of a crime by another person or persons in one of the ways described in sub-paragraphs b) to d). This indicates that the Statute differentiates between two principal forms of liability, namely liability as a perpetrator and liability as an accessory. In the view of the Appeals Chamber, this distinction is not merely terminological; making this distinction is important because, generally speaking and all other things being equal, a person who is found to commit a crime him-or herself bears more blameworthiness than a person who contributes to the crime of another person or persons. Accordingly, it contributes to a proper labelling of the accused person's criminal responsibility.

463. It follows that, in circumstances where a plurality of individuals are involved in the commission of a crime, it becomes necessary to determine on what basis an individual's role is assessed to amount to that of a perpetrator or that of an accessory. In the view of the Appeals Chamber, and as noted above, the starting point for this analysis must be the interaction between the various forms of individual criminal responsibility set out in article 25 (3) of the Statute and their distinctive characteristics.

464. In this regard, the Appeals Chamber notes that article 25 (3) (a) of the Statute provides expressly for three forms of commission liability: a perpetrator may commit a crime "as an individual", "jointly with another [. . .] person", or "through another person".

465. The Appeals Chamber finds that the third form of commission liability assists in the interpretation of the second form of liability, which is at issue in the case at hand. The third form of commission liability is based on the notion that a person can commit a crime 'through another person'. The underlying assumption is that the accused makes use of another person, who actually carries out the incriminated conduct, by virtue of the accused's control over that person, and the latter's conduct is therefore imputed on the former. Accordingly, commission of a crime 'through' another person is a form of criminal responsibility that requires a normative assessment of the relationship between the person actually carrying out the incriminated conduct and the person in the background, as well as of the latter person's relationship to the crime. In that regard, it is noteworthy that article 25 (3) (a) of the Statute provides for commission liability 'through another person 'not only in circumstances where that person is not him-or herself criminally liable and therefore serves as a will-less tool in the hand of the individual in the background. Rather, a person can *commit* a crime also through individuals who are themselves fully criminally responsible for that crime. In such a scenario, the person in the background is considered to bear the same or even more blameworthiness than the person actually executing the incriminated conduct. This indicates more generally that the Statute assumes that a person who did not him-or herself carry out the incriminated conduct can, depending on the circumstances, nevertheless be a perpetrator. The Appeals Chamber notes that such an approach to commission liability is supported by academic commentators and was also applied, for example, by Trial Chamber II in the *Katanga* Trial Judgment. In that Trial Chamber's opinion, it would be contrary to article 25 (3) (a) to adopt an approach according to which only the physical carrying out of elements of the crime would lead to commission liability.

466. The finding that, in order to incur liability as a perpetrator, it is not indispensable that the accused personally carried out the incriminated conduct also has repercussions on co-perpetration liability, which is at issue in the case at hand. In the context of co-perpetration, it follows from the above that it is not required that a person actually carry out directly and personally the incriminated conduct in order to be a co-perpetrator. Rather, in order to determine whether a person is a co-perpetrator, a normative assessment of that person's role is required. In the

paragraphs that follow, the Appeals Chamber will address how this assessment should be carried out.

467. The Appeals Chamber recalls that co-perpetration is not the only form of liability recognised by article 25 (3) of the Statute that involves a plurality of individuals. Accordingly, it becomes necessary to distinguish committing a crime "jointly with others" from other forms of liability, notably those laid down in sub-paragraph b) (ordering, soliciting or inducing a crime), sub-paragraph c) (aiding, abetting or otherwise assisting in the commission of the crime) and sub-paragraph d) (in any other way contributing to the commission of a crime by a group of persons acting with a common purpose). The Trial Chamber noted in this regard that the contribution of a co-perpetrator must be of greater significance than that of individuals held responsible under article 25 (3) (c) and (d) of the Statute. Furthermore, the Trial Chamber recalled that acts that are merely a contribution to the commission of the crime are dependent on "whether the perpetrator acts" and are therefore only accessory to the principal act of "committing the crime". This led the Trial Chamber to conclude that the "notion of principal liability [. . .] requires a greater contribution than accessory liability."

468. The Appeals Chamber notes that, in so concluding, the Trial Chamber chose an objective criterion to distinguish commission liability from accessorial liability, as opposed to, for instance, a distinction based on the accused person's mental relationship to the crime in question. In the view of the Appeals Chamber, it is indeed appropriate to distinguish between liability as a perpetrator and as an accessory primarily based on the objective criterion of the accused person's extent of contribution to the crime. This is because the blameworthiness of the person is directly dependent on the extent to which the person actually contributed to the crime in question.

469. In this context, the Appeals Chamber notes that the Pre-Trial and Trial Chambers have relied on the 'control over the crime' theory in order to distinguish those who are considered to have 'committed' the crimes from those who have contributed to crimes of others. They found that a co-perpetrator is one who makes, within the framework of a common plan, an essential contribution with the resulting power to frustrate the commission of the crime. The essential contribution can be made not only at the execution stage of the crime, but also, depending on the circumstances, at its planning or preparation stage, including when the common plan is conceived. At the core of this approach is the assumption that a co-perpetrator may compensate for his or her lack of contribution at the execution stage of the crime if, by virtue of his or her essential contribution, the person nevertheless had control over the crime. The Appeals Chamber considers that this is a convincing and adequate approach to distinguish co-perpetration from accessorial liability because it assesses the role of the person in question *vis-à-vis* the crime.

470. As regards the argument that this approach was first developed in domestic legal doctrine, which is, as such, not applicable at the Court, the Appeals Chamber

would like to clarify that it is not proposing to apply a particular legal doctrine or theory as a source of law. Rather, it is interpreting and applying article 25 (3) (a) of the Statute. In so doing, the Appeals Chamber considers it appropriate to seek guidance from approaches developed in other jurisdictions in order to reach a coherent and persuasive interpretation of the Court's legal texts. This Court is not administrating justice in a vacuum, but, in applying the law, needs to be aware of and can relate to concepts and ideas found in domestic jurisdictions.

471. In the view of the Appeals Chamber, drawing on ideas developed in domestic jurisdictions and applying a normative approach to co-perpetration does not result in a breach of article 22 of the Statute or the principle of in *dubio pro reo*. In that respect, the Appeals Chamber notes that a normative approach to co-perpetration is well known in international criminal law. Notably, the notion of joint criminal enterprise developed by the *ad hoc* tribunals also uses normative criteria to distinguish co-perpetrators from accessories, although it puts the emphasis on a subjective criterion and not on an objective one.

472. Nevertheless, the Appeals Chamber does not consider that it is legally bound to follow the particular approach of the *ad hoc* tribunals. As set out above, at issue is the interpretation of the terms "commits [. . .] jointly with another". The Appeals Chamber recalls that article 25 (3) of the Statute has a different structure than the relevant provisions of the ICTY and ICTR Statutes and that approaches to the interpretation and application of the latter therefore cannot easily be transposed to the former. The Appeals Chamber finds that the approach adopted by the Trial Chamber better fits the distinction between acts that are considered to be a form of commission and those that are accessory thereto in the context of article 25 (3) of the Statute than the criteria developed by the *ad hoc* tribunals, because the Trial Chamber's approach applies objective criteria to determine whether a person is a perpetrator rather than an accessory and does not rely primarily on subjective criteria.

473. In sum, the Appeals Chamber considers that, in circumstances where a plurality of persons was involved in the commission of crimes under the Statute, the question of whether an accused 'committed' a crime — and therefore not only contributed to the crime committed by someone else — cannot only be answered by reference to how close the accused was to the actual crime and whether he or she directly carried out the incriminated conduct. Rather, what is required is a normative assessment of the role of the accused person in the specific circumstances of the case. The Appeals Chamber considers that the most appropriate tool for conducting such an assessment is an evaluation of whether the accused had control over the crime, by virtue of his or her essential contribution to it and the resulting power to frustrate its commission, even if that essential contribution was not made at the execution stage of the crime. Accordingly, the Appeals Chamber is not convinced by Mr Lubanga's argument that the Trial Chamber erred in its interpretation of article 25 (3) (a) of the Statute and rejects this ground of appeal.

Differing but well-articulated responses to the construction of Article 25(3) of the Rome Statute may be found in James G. Stewart, *The End of "Modes of Liability" for International Crimes*, 25 Leiden J. Int'l L. 165 (2012) and Thomas Weigend, *Perpetrators (Article 25(3) of the ICC Statute)*, in For the Sake of Present and Future Generations: Essays on International Law, Crime and Justice in Honour of Roger S. Clark 356 (Suzannah Linton, Gerry Simpson & William A. Schabas eds., 2015); *see also Symposium, Indirect Perpetration: A Perfect Fit for International Prosecution of Armchair Killers?* 9 J. Int'l Crim. Just. 85 (2011).

§ 23.04 Sentencing and Reparations

Articles 76 and 78 of the Rome Statute on sentencing and Article 75 on reparation to victims (*see* the text in chap. 22) are skeletal at best. They leave the details for future work. Some meat is provided to the sentencing provisions by Rule 145 of the Court's Rules of Procedure and Evidence:

Rule 145 Determination of sentence

1. In its determination of the sentence pursuant to article 78, paragraph 1, the Court shall:

(a) Bear in mind that the totality of any sentence of imprisonment and fine, as the case may be, imposed under article 77 must reflect the culpability of the convicted person;

(b) Balance all the relevant factors, including any mitigating and aggravating factors and consider the circumstances both of the convicted person and of the crime;

(c) In addition to the factors mentioned in article 78, paragraph 1, give consideration, inter alia, to the extent of the damage caused, in particular the harm caused to the victims and their families, the nature of the unlawful behaviour and the means employed to execute the crime; the degree of participation of the convicted person; the degree of intent; the circumstances of manner, time and location; and the age, education, social and economic condition of the convicted person.

2. In addition to the factors mentioned above, the Court shall take into account, as appropriate:

(a) Mitigating circumstances such as:

(i) The circumstances falling short of constituting grounds for exclusion of criminal responsibility, such as substantially diminished mental capacity or duress;

(ii) The convicted person's conduct after the act, including any efforts by the person to compensate the victims and any cooperation with the Court;

(b) As aggravating circumstances:

(i) Any relevant prior criminal convictions for crimes under the jurisdiction of the Court or of a similar nature;

(ii) Abuse of power or official capacity;

(iii) Commission of the crime where the victim is particularly defenceless;

(iv) Commission of the crime with particular cruelty or where there were multiple victims;

(v) Commission of the crime for any motive involving discrimination on any of the grounds referred to in article 21, paragraph 3;

(vi) Other circumstances which, although not enumerated above, by virtue of their nature are similar to those mentioned.

3. Life imprisonment may be imposed when justified by the extreme gravity of the crime and the individual circumstances of the convicted person, as evidenced by the existence of one or more aggravating circumstances.

Notes

(1) The Court's sentencing decisions endeavor to apply Rule 145; they deny that the particular category of participation under Article 25 (3) of which the accused is convicted necessarily plays a determinative role. As the Appeals Chamber put it in *Prosecutor v. Bemba, Kilolo, Manganda, Wandu and Arido*, ICC-10/05/01/13 A6 A7 A8 A9:

> 59. The Appeals Chamber recalls its previous holding that "generally speaking and all other things being equal, a person who is found to commit a crime him- or herself bears more blameworthiness than a person who contributes to the crime of another person or persons". As correctly pointed out by the Prosecutor, this statement does not suggest that, as matter of law, a person who commits a crime within the meaning of article 25 (3) (a) of the Statute is automatically more blameworthy—and thus deserves a higher punishment—than the person who contributes to it. The Appeals Chamber's finding was indeed made only "generally speaking" and under the condition of "all other things being equal". Especially with respect to the distinction between the mode of liability under article 25 (3) (a) of the Statute and that under article 25 (3) (b) of the Statute, the Appeals Chamber is not persuaded that a person who instigates someone to commit a crime is to be generally considered less culpable than the person who acts upon that instigation. Mr Bemba himself concedes as much.

> 60. The Appeals Chamber recognises that a mode of liability describes a certain typical factual situation that is subsumed within the legal elements of the relevant provision, and that the difference between committing a crime and contributing to the crime of others would normally reflect itself in a different degree of participation and/or intent within the meaning of rule 145 (1) (c) of the Rules. This however does not mean that the principal perpetrator of a crime/offence necessarily deserves a higher sentence than the accessory to that crime/offence. Whether this is actually the case ultimately depends upon all the variable circumstances of each individual case. In this regard, the Appeals Chamber observes that the Court's legal framework does not indicate an automatic correlation between the person's form of responsibility for the crime/offence for which he or she has been convicted and the sentence, nor does it provide any form of mandatory mitigation in case of conviction as an accessory to a crime/offence. Rather, as pointed out by the Prosecutor, the sentencing factors enunciated in the Statute and the Rules are fact-specific and ultimately depend on a case-by-case assessment of the individual circumstances of each case. (Footnotes omitted.)

(2) As for reparations, the Rome Statute gives a significant role to victims in the process. *See*, e.g., Article 68 of the Statute. During the drafting of the Statute, many NGO representatives expressed the hope that the funds of convicted persons would be a useful source of reparation for victims. Alas, most accused persons who arrive in the custody of the Court are penurious and in no position to afford a lawyer, let alone disgorge ill-gotten gains to the ICC coffers. Reparation has thus come to date from the Trust Fund for Victims set up under Article 79 of the Rome Statute, funded mostly by voluntary contributions from States.

Mr. Bemba, the main accused in the case mentioned in Note (1), was the first defendant with means (seized on behalf of the Court) that might ultimately be used to fund reparations. He was charged on a command responsibility theory with numerous offenses in the Central African Republic. His conviction in the Trial Chamber was eventually reversed by a 3-2 majority in the Appeals Chamber for what was essentially a failure of proof. Judgment on the Appeal of Mr Jean-Pierre Bemba Gombo against Trial Chamber III's "Judgment pursuant to Article 74 of the Statute," ICC-01/05-01/08-3636-Red, June 8, 2018. The decision was controversial, as the majority gave less deference to the trial decision than had been afforded in prior cases. (Those cases relied on precedent from the ad hoc Tribunals, but the Rome Statute does not have language requiring deference.) The majority's complex joint and separate decisions represent eloquent support for proof beyond reasonable doubt. Meanwhile, Bemba, one of his lawyers and assorted associates were charged with various "offences against the administration of justice" under Article 70 of the Statute. A fine of €300,000 imposed in the Article 70 case was directed to the Trust Fund, in what might be considered by some as a consolation to those disappointed by the failure of the main case.

As to reparations, Article 75 of the Statute says that the Court "shall establish principles relating to reparations to, or in respect of victims, including restitution, compensation and rehabilitation." It was not clear whether the Court was supposed to sit down, declare the law or decide through caselaw. The Court decided on the latter approach and has been trying to explain the principles that may be extrapolated from Article 75 of the Statute case by case. A 2015 Press Release from the Court, http://www.icc-cpi.int/iccdocs/PIDS/publications/Lubanga_QA_03-15_Eng.pdf, captures the essence of these (continuing) efforts:

What Was Decided by the Appeals Chamber in Its Judgment on 3 March 2015?

On 3 March 2015, the Appeals Chamber of the International Criminal Court (ICC) delivered, in open court, its judgment on the appeals against the Trial Chamber's "decision establishing the principles and procedures to be applied to reparations" in the case against Thomas Lubanga Dyilo. The Appeals Chamber amended the Trial Chamber's order for reparations and instructed the Trust Fund for Victims to present a draft implementation plan for collective reparations to the newly constituted Trial Chamber I no later than six months from the issuance of the 3 March 2015 judgment.[b]

The Appeals Chamber established the necessary minimum elements required for a reparations order, and the principles governing the reparations for victims, including the fact that all victims are to be treated fairly and equally as regards reparations, irrespective of whether they participated in the trial proceedings. The Appeals Chamber confirmed the Trial Chamber's finding that reparations programmes should include measures to reintegrate former child soldiers in order to eradicate the victimisation, discrimination and stigmatisation of these young people. It also highlighted that a gender-inclusive approach should guide the design of the principles and procedures to be applied to reparations. The Appeals Chamber found that the Trial Chamber did not err in deciding to award reparations only on a collective basis, and not on an individual basis, and highlighted that the number of victims is an important factor in determining that reparations on a collective basis are more appropriate.

The Appeals Chamber also found that the Trial Chamber erred in not making Mr Lubanga personally liable for the collective reparations due to his current state of indigence. The Appeals Chamber held that reparations orders must establish and inform the convicted person of his personal liability with respect to the reparations awarded, and that if the Trust Fund for Victims advances its resources in

b. For the Trust Fund's Draft Implementation Plan, see www.icc-cpi.int/iccdocs/doc/doc2142455.pdf (November 3, 2015) — Eds.

order to enable the implementation of the order, it will be able to claim the advanced resources from Mr Lubanga at a later date

WHAT ARE THE NEXT STEPS?

The Trust Fund for Victims is to present a draft implementation plan for collective reparations to Trial Chamber I no later than six months from the issuance of the 3 March 2015 appeals judgment.

The parties to the proceedings, as well as the Legal Representatives of the Victims, will be able to present their observations on the draft implementation plan to the judges of Trial Chamber I, who will render a final decision on the plan in due course. This may take some time, and the ICC will keep the public informed about the process.

WHAT IS THE TRUST FUND FOR VICTIMS AND WILL IT HAVE ADEQUATE RESOURCES FOR THESE REPARATIONS?

The establishment of the International Criminal Court on 1 July 2002 also resulted in the creation of the Trust Fund for Victims by the States parties to the Rome Statute. The Fund's mission is to support and implement programmes that address harm resulting from genocide, crimes against humanity and war crimes.

The Trust Fund for Victims is funded by voluntary contributions from States, international organizations and other donors. The money collected allows the Fund to fulfil its two mandates, namely the mandate of general assistance to victims in situations where the ICC is active, and the mandate to contribute to the implementation of orders for reparations to victims in particular cases before the Court. As part of its mandate, in preparing a reparations plan in a particular case, the Fund takes into account the amount it has available. It can, based on a plan adopted by the judges, request further contributions from States and other donors if need be.

The Appeals Chamber also recalled that as part of its first mandate, the Fund may consider providing support to victims of sexual violence in Ituri, although Mr Lubanga has not been accused or convicted of crimes of sexual violence.

(3) Diligent efforts by the Trial Chamber in *Bemba* to work out reparations, including the dispatch of a distinguished panel of experts on a potentially dangerous mission to the Central African Republic, came to naught once the conviction was reversed. This leads to a fundamental question: inevitably in criminal proceedings, what happens when the accused is not convicted? Does this raise false hopes in victims? Given also the lack of vast generosity in the international community, is the Court a proper place to allocate scarce donated resources in the absence of a criminal conviction for some or all of the offenses involved? Note the last sentence of the press release quoted above where there were partial acquittals in important parts of the prosecution's case. Criminal compensation is normally based on

criminal conviction; the Trust Fund has become a hybrid source of compensation, even in the absence of a charge or conviction. Is this appropriate?

(4) The Court's efforts to develop principles for reparation continue as different circumstances arise. An example was the effort of the Trial Chamber and the Appeals Chamber in the *Al Mahdi* case, which involved attacking protected objects — namely a number of mausoleums and the door of a mosque in Timbuktu. *See Prosecutor v. Ahmad Al Faqi Al Mahdi*, Public redacted Judgment on the appeal of the victims against the "Reparations Order," ICC-01/12-01/15-259-Red2, Appeals Chamber, March 8, 2018. How are cultural intangibles to be valuated?

Index

[References are to sections.]

V

W

Y